August 11-14, 2014
Philadelphia, PA, USA

Association for
Computing Machinery

Advancing Computing as a Science & Profession

MobiHoc'14

Proceedings of the 15th ACM International Symposium on
Mobile Ad Hoc Networking and Computing

Sponsored by:
ACM SIGMOBILE

Supported by:
NSF and Temple University

Association for
Computing Machinery

Advancing Computing as a Science & Profession

The Association for Computing Machinery
2 Penn Plaza, Suite 701
New York, New York 10121-0701

ISBN: 978-1-4503-2620-9 (Digital)

ISBN: 978-1-4503-3261-3 (Print)

Additional copies may be ordered prepaid from:

ACM Order Department
PO Box 30777
New York, NY 10087-0777, USA

Phone: 1-800-342-6626 (USA and Canada)
+1-212-626-0500 (Global)
Fax: +1-212-944-1318
E-mail: acmhelp@acm.org
Hours of Operation: 8:30 am – 4:30 pm ET

Printed in the USA

Message from the General Chairs

ACM MobiHoc is the premier international symposium dedicated to addressing the challenges emerging from wireless networking and computing. This year, we have again been fortunate to receive many excellent papers and to have its role continue to grow in the field.

We would like to express our sincere gratitude to everyone whose contributions have made MobiHoc 2014 a conference to be remembered and valued by all attendees. The conference is the result of the hard work of many authors, reviewers, and conference committee members. We are very grateful for everyone's efforts in making this conference a success. Special thanks go to Program Co-Chairs, XiangYang Li and Saswati Sarkar, who put together a very strong technical program. We would also like to thank I-Hong Hou and Srinivas Shakkottai who did an outstanding job in coordinating the six ICDCS workshops. Thanks also go to Marco Gruteser for organizing the poster session, and to Mooi-Choo Chuah, for arranging the demo session. We would like to thank our keynote speakers and panel organizer Ness B. Shroff for their help in making this a thought-provoking and memorable conference.

Numerous other individuals were instrumental in the success of the conference. Special thanks are due to P. R. Kumar, the Steering Committee Chair, for his continuous support and guidance. Shaojie Tang and Yu Wang did a great job organizing the local arrangements and EDAS submissions. A special thanks to Robert Kline for maintaining the conference website. Yingying Chen did an excellent job of coordinating the proceedings publication for the conference, workshop, poster, and demo. Thanks are due to Feng Li for handling student travel grants sponsored by the National Science Foundation, as well as Yunhao Liu, Venkatesha Prasad, Paolo Santi, and Avinash Srinivasan for promoting the conference. Our deepest thanks go to the Registration Chair and Treasurer, Zhen Jiang, for his valuable assistance on numerous occasions, often on short notice. Finally, we thank Temple University for its support and contributing student volunteers, and the National Science Foundation for its student travel grant.

It is with great pride that we host ACM MobiHoc in Philadelphia, the first capital of the United States. We hope that you find our technical program interesting and that you are able to take some time to enjoy the City of Philadelphia.

Jie Wu
Temple University
General Chair

Xiuzhen Cheng
George Washington University
Vice General Chair

Message from the Program Chairs

We are pleased to present the proceedings of the 15th ACM International Symposium on Mobile Ad-Hoc Networking and Computing (ACM MobiHoc 2014), held in Philadelphia, PA, USA, from August 11 to August 14, 2014. This conference continues with the great success of the previous editions. ACM MobiHoc is well recognized as a premier international forum for researchers, practitioners and students for discussions on emerging challenges from mobile networking, computing, and systems. It covers topics ranging from fundamental theory, to technology issues, to applications and system development. To align with the conference vision, the Technical Program Committee has assembled a strong and diverse program, covering a wide range of technical topics, hoping to influence the direction of a broad spectrum of wireless networking research.

This year we received 211 submissions from countries covering all the world regions. Under the guidance of the TPC Co-Chairs, the technical program committee and the reviewers provided outstanding work. Each of the submitted papers, except the early rejected papers due to violation of the rule of anonymity, received, on average, three to four in-depth reviews from Program Committee members, and the process was completed by a TPC review with a recommendation of acceptance/reject/TPC-discussion. The first round review and discussion led by TPC-lead recommended 7 papers for direct acceptance. Based on the TPC recommendation and the review scores, 60 papers were selected for TPC meeting held on May 23, 2014, in Chicago. These papers are randomly grouped into two groups with consideration of balance of paper review scores and avoiding TPC conflict of interests. Extensive discussions of these papers were held among TPC members to advise the TPC Chairs of accepted papers for the program. Only 33 papers were accepted from the TPC meeting. Total 40 papers are included in the final program as regular papers. Due to the large number of submissions, many high quality papers, unfortunately, could not be included in the conference program. Overall, the final program is excellent and diverse, and covers both fundamental issues as well as emerging topics.

The ACM MobiHoc 2014 technical program, in addition to ten technical sessions, consists of three keynote talks, a panel on full-duplex communication chaired by Dr. Ness Shroff, a poster session, a demo session, and a demo pitch session. It is our great pleasure and privilege to invite three world-known researchers, Dr. Farnam Jahanian from NSF, Dr. Joao Barros from University of Porto, and Dr. Roger Wattenhofer from ETH to give three keynote talks on various interesting and timely topics. In addition to the main conference program, seven workshops will be held together with the conference on August 11, 2014.

The success of this conference program would not have been possible without the dedication and hard work of many individuals. First, great thanks to the authors who have submitted papers as well as all of you for attending the conference. We express our sincere appreciation to the conference's General Chair, Dr. Jie Wu from Temple University, and vice General Chair, Dr. Xiuzhen Cheng from George Washington University, and the Steering Committee members, especially, Dr. P.R. Kumar, for their valuable guidance and strong support. We also thank the Program Committee members, and external referees for their diligent work in reviewing and helping to select papers of exceptional quality.

We hope that you will find this program interesting and thought-provoking and that the symposium will provide you with a valuable opportunity to share ideas with other researchers and practitioners from institutions around the world. Enjoy the technical program of ACM MobiHoc 2014!

XiangYang Li & Saswati Sakar
Co-Chairs, Technical Program Committee

Message from the Workshop Chairs

It is our great pleasure to present the MobiHoc 2014 workshops program. On August 11, 2014, seven workshops complement the 15th ACM International Symposium on Mobile Ad-Hoc Networking and Computing at Philadelphia, USA. These workshops are

- MobileHealth: 4th ACM MobiHoc Workshop on Pervasive Wireless Healthcare
- FOMC: The 10th ACM International Workshop on Foundations of Mobile Computing
- The Workshop on Airborne Networks and Communications
- MSCC: The First International Workshop on Mobile Sensing, Computing and Communication
- The Workshop on Interference Alignment
- The Workshop on the Frontiers of Networks: Theory and Algorithms
- WiMobCity: Workshop on Wireless and Mobile Technologies for Smart Cities

The workshops provide focused venues for presenting novel research results on specific topics in a less formal and more interactive setting than the main conference. The topics of the workshops range from foundational theory and algorithms to an applied perspective on hot topics and rapidly advancing technologies. It is hoped that these workshops will bring together researchers from across the world to mingle with each other and take away cross cutting ideas on a variety of areas.

We would like to take this opportunity to thank the workshop organizers, the program committee members of each workshop, as well as the anonymous reviewers, for their diligence and hard work in creating such excellent programs. We sincerely appreciate the support that we received from the MobiHoc 2014 Organizing Committee chaired by Dr. Jie Wu and Dr. Xiuzhen Cheng. We also greatly value the vision and direction provided by the MobiHoc Steering Committee. In particular, we would like to place on record our gratitude to the Steering Committee Chair, Prof. P. R. Kumar, in this regard.

Last, but certainly not least, we thank the workshop authors for their contributions to the workshops, as well as the attendees for their active interest and participation. It is hoped that the workshops will provide inspiration and ideas to foster cutting edge research in the area of wireless communication and networking. We look forward to a successful workshops program!

I-Hong Hou & Srinivas Shakkottai
Workshop Co-Chairs

Table of Contents

SM6: Dynamic Spectrum Access

Session Chair: Yoora Kim *(University of Ulsan)*

Keynote 3

Session Chair: XiangYang Li *(Illinois Institute of Technology)*

SM7: Energy / Offloading

Session Chair: Merkouris Karaliopoulos *(Centre for Research and Technology Hellas)*

SM8: Mobile Networks

Session Chair: Hongyi Wu *(University of Louisianna at Lafayette)*

SM9: Sensor Networks

Session Chair: Jie Gao *(Stony Brook University)*

SM10: System

Session Chair: Ellen Zegura *(Georgia Institute of Technology)*

Demonstrations

Posters

MobiHoc 2014 Organizing Committee

General Chair

Jie Wu, Temple University

Vice General Chair

Xiuzhen Cheng, George Washington University

Program Co-Chairs

XiangYang Li, Illinois Institute of Technology
Saswati Sarkar, University of Pennsylvania

Workshop Co-Chairs

I-Hong Hou, Texas A&M University
Srinivas Shakkottai, Texas A&M University

Panel Chair

Ness B. Shroff, The Ohio State University

Poster Chair

Marco Gruteser, Rutgers University

Demo Chair

Mooi-Choo Chuah, Lehigh University

Local Arrangements and EDAS Co-Chairs

Shaojie Tang, Temple University
Yu Wang, University of North Carolina at Charlotte

Webmaster

Robert Kline, West Chester University

Publication Chair

Yingying Chen, Stevens Institute of Technology

Registration Chair and Treasurer

Zhen Jiang, West Chester University

Publicity Chairs

Yunhao Liu, Tsinghua University, P. R. China
Venkatesha Prasad, Delft University of Technology, Netherlands
Paolo Santi, IIT, CNR, Italy
Avinash Srinivasan, George Mason University

Student Travel Grants Chair

Feng Li, IUPUI

MobiHoc 2014 Steering Committee

P. R. Kumar (Chair), Texas A&M University
Mario Gerla, University of California Los Angeles
Jean-Pierre Hubaux, EPFL
Joseph Macker, Naval Research Lab
Sergio Palazzo, University of Catania
Charles Perkins, WiChorus
Martha Steenstrup, Stow Research L.L.C

MobiHoc 2014 Technical Program Committee

Sem Borst, Alcatel-Lucent, Bell Labs
Gruia Calinescu, Illinois Institute of Technology, USA
Jiming Chen, Zhejiang University, P.R. China
Yingying Chen, Stevens Institute of Technology, USA
Carla-Fabiana Chiasserini, Politecnico di Torino, Italy
Florin Ciucu, University of Warwick, United Kingdom
Do Young Eun, North Carolina State University, USA
Jie Gao, Stony Brook University, USA
Zihui Ge, AT&T Labs - Research, USA
Mario Gerla, University of California at Los Angeles, USA
Marco Gruteser, WINLAB / Rutgers University, USA
I-Hong Hou, Texas A&M University, USA
Wenjun Hu, Microsoft Research Asia, P.R. China
Yih-Chun Hu, University of Illinois at Urbana-Champaign, USA
Jianwei Huang, The Chinese University of Hong Kong, Hong Kong
Bo Ji, AT&T Bell Labs, USA
Koushik Kar, Rensselaer Polytechnic Institute, USA
Sneha Kasera, University of Utah, USA
Vikas Kawadia, BBN Technologies, USA
Li (Erran) Li, Bell Labs, Lucent Technologies
Mo Li, Nanyang Technological University, Singapore
Xiang-Yang Li, Illinois Institute of Technology, USA
Xiaojun Lin, Purdue University, USA
Alex Liu, Michigan State University, USA
Mingyan Liu, University of Michigan, USA
Songwu Lu, University of California at Los Angeles, USA
Jun Luo, Nanyang Technological University, Singapore
Eytan Modiano, MIT, USA
Jayakrishnan Nair, California Institute of Technology, USA
Vishnu Navda, Microsoft Research, India
Panagiotis (Panos) Papadimitratos, KTH, Sweden
Alexandre Proutiere, Microsoft Research, United Kingdom
Lili Qiu, The University of Texas at Austin, USA
Kui Ren, State University of New York at Buffalo, USA
Dan Rubenstein, Columbia University, USA
Ashutosh Sabharwal, Rice University, USA
Paolo Santi, IIT-CNR, Italy
Saswati Sarkar, University of Pennsylvania, USA
Souvik Sen, HP Labs, USA
Sudipta Sengupta, Microsoft Research, USA
Srinivas Shakkottai, Texas A&M University, USA
Bo Sheng, University of Massachusetts Boston, USA
Jinwoo Shin, KAIST, Korea
Evgenia Smirni, College of William and Mary, USA
Thrasyvoulos Spyropoulos, EURECOM, France
Chiu Tan, Temple University, USA
Kun Tan, Microsoft Research Asia, P.R. China
Shaojie Tang, Temple University, Philadelphia
Bhuvan Urgaonkar, Pennsylvania State University, USA
Peng-Jun Wan, Illinois Institute of Technology, USA
Jia Wang, AT&T Labs - Research, USA
Wenye Wang, NC State University, USA
Xinbing Wang, Shanghai Jiaotong University, P.R. China
Yu Wang, University of North Carolina at Charlotte, USA
Carey Williamson, University of Calgary, Canada
Hongyi Wu, University of Louisiana at Lafayette, USA
Mingjun Xiao, University of Science and Technology of China, P.R. China
Guoliang Xue, Arizona State University, USA
Panlong Yang, Institute of Communication Engineering, PLAUST
Zheng Yang, Tsinghua University, P.R. China
Yung Yi, KAIST, Korea
Xinyu Zhang, Univ. of Wisconsin-Madison, USA
Zhi-Li Zhang, University of Minnesota, USA
Xia Zhou, Dartmouth, USA
Gil Zussman, Columbia University, USA

MobiHoc 2014 Sponsor & Supporters

Sponsor:

Supporters:

Opening Keynote

Realizing the Transformative Impact of Computing and Data in a Networked World

Farnam Jahanian
Directorate of Computer and Information Science and Engineering
National Science Foundation
Arlington, VA

Abstract

The computer and information science and engineering disciplines are at the center of an ongoing societal transformation. The explosive growth of scientific and social data, wireless connectivity at broadband speeds for a countless number of mobile endpoints, and seamless access to resources in the "cloud" are transforming the way we work, learn, play, and communicate. Furthermore, the proliferation of mobile devices and new applications is leading to increasing complexity and growth of network traffic.

I will talk about how digitalization, virtualization, and mobility are reshaping our economy, society, and daily lives. I will also talk about these trends catalyze new opportunities for foundational research. I will further explore how advances in computing and communication serve as key drivers of economic competitiveness and how they will be crucial to achieving national priorities.

Bio

Farnam Jahanian serves as the Assistant Director of the National Science Foundation for Computer and Information Science and Engineering (CISE). He leads CISE in its mission to uphold the nation's leadership in scientific discovery and engineering innovation through its support of fundamental research in computer and information science and engineering and of transformative advances in cyberinfrastructure.

Farnam Jahanian is on leave from the University of Michigan, where he holds the Edward S. Davidson Collegiate Professorship and served as Chair for Computer Science and Engineering from 2007 – 2011 and as Director of the Software Systems Laboratory from 1997 – 2000.

Over the last two decades at the University of Michigan, Farnam Jahanian led several large-scale research projects that studied the growth and scalability of the Internet infrastructure, which ultimately transformed how cyber threats are addressed by Internet Service Providers. His research on Internet infrastructure security formed the basis for the successful Internet security services company Arbor Networks, which he co-founded in 2001. Farnam Jahanian served as Chairman of Arbor Networks until its acquisition in 2010. His work on Internet routing stability and convergence has been highly influential within both the network research and the Internet operational communities and was recognized with an ACM SIGCOMM Test of Time Award in 2008.

Farnam Jahanian is the author of over 100 published research papers and has served on dozens of national advisory boards and panels. He has testified before Congress on a broad range of topics, including cybersecurity and Big Data. He has been an active advocate for how basic research can be uniquely central to an innovation ecosystem that drives global competitiveness and addresses national priorities.

In September 2014, Farnam Jahanian will join Carnegie Mellon University as the Vice President for Research. He holds a master's degree and Ph.D. in Computer Science from the University of Texas at Austin. He is a Fellow of the Association for Computing Machinery (ACM), the Institute of Electrical and Electronic Engineers (IEEE), and the American Association for the Advancement of Science (AAAS).

MobiHoc'14, August 11–14, 2014, Philadelphia, PA, USA.
ACM 978-1-4503-2620-9/14/08.
http://dx.doi.org/10.1145/2632951.2633208

Unknown Combinatorial Auction Mechanisms for Heterogeneous Spectrum Redistribution*

Zhenzhe Zheng†, Fan Wu†, Shaojie Tang§, and Guihai Chen†
†Shanghai Key Laboratory of Scalable Computing and Systems, Shanghai Jiao Tong University, China
§Department of Information Systems, University of Texas at Dallas, USA
{zhengzhenzhe,wu-fan}@sjtu.edu.cn, tangshaojie@gmail.com, gchen@cs.sjtu.edu.cn

ABSTRACT

With the growing deployment of wireless communication technologies, radio spectrum is becoming a scarce resource. Auctions are believed to be among the most effective tools to solve or relieve the problem of radio spectrum shortage. However, designing a practical spectrum auction mechanism has to consider five major challenges: strategic behaviors of unknown users, channel heterogeneity, preference diversity, channel spatial reusability, and social welfare maximization. Unfortunately, none of existing work fully considered these five challenges. In this paper, we model the problem of heterogeneous spectrum allocation as a combinatorial auction, and propose AEGIS, which is the first framework of unknown combinatorial Auction mEchanisms for heteroGeneous spectrum redIStribution. AEGIS contains two mechanisms, namely AEGIS-SG and AEGIS-MP. AEGIS-SG is a direct revelation combinatorial spectrum auction mechanism for unknown single-minded users, achieving strategy-proofness and approximately efficient social welfare. We further design an iterative ascending combinatorial auction, namely AEGIS-MP, to adapt to the scenario with unknown multi-minded users. AEGIS-MP is implemented in a set of undominated strategies and has a good approximation ratio. We evaluate AEGIS on two practical datasets: Google Spectrum Database and GoogleWiFi. Evaluation results show that AEGIS achieve much better performance than the state-of-the-art mechanisms.

†F. Wu is the corresponding author.

*This work was supported in part by the State Key Development Program for Basic Research of China (973 project 2014CB340303 and 2012CB316201), in part by China NSF grant 61272443 and 61133006, in part by Shanghai Science and Technology fund 12PJ1404900 and 12ZR1414900, and in part by Program for Changjiang Scholars and Innovative Research Team in University (IRT1158, PCSIRT) China. The opinions, findings, conclusions, and recommendations expressed in this paper are those of the authors and do not necessarily reflect the views of the funding agencies or the government.

MobiHoc'14, August 11–14, 2014, Philadelphia, PA, USA.

http://dx.doi.org/10.1145/2632951.2632964 .

Categories and Subject Descriptors

C.2.1 [**Computer-Communication Networks**]: Network Architecture and Design – *Wireless Communication*

Keywords

Channel Allocation; Combinatorial Auction

1. INTRODUCTION

The fast development of wireless networks and mobile communications is exhausting the limited radio spectrum resource. However, currently, almost all spectrum is statically allocated to large service providers on a long term basis for large geographical regions, which is reflected in the radio regulations published by the International Telecommunication Union (ITU) [11]. Such static spectrum management leads to low utilization in spatial and temporal dimensions. On one hand, many spectrum owners (*i.e.*, primary users) are willing to lease out their idle spectrum and obtain proper profit. On the other hand, new wireless applications (*i.e.*, secondary users), starving for spectrum, would like to pay for using the spectrum. Therefore, an open and market-based framework is highly needed to redistribute the idle spectrum, and thus improve the utilization of spectrum. Spectrum Bridge [25] is an emerging platform that provides services for buying, selling, and leasing idle spectrum.

Due to the fairness and allocation efficiency, auctions are attractive market-based mechanisms to distribute resources. Examples include FCC spectrum license auctions in the Unite States [6], and auctions for UMTS [16] and LTE [18] in Europe. While these auctions target only at large wireless service providers, our focus is secondary spectrum markets of small wireless applications, such as community wireless networks and home wireless networks.

Designing a feasible and practical spectrum auction has its own challenges. The first major challenge comes from the strategic behaviors of rational and selfish wireless users. In practical spectrum auctions, selfish users can not only misreport their valuations, but also their channel demands, to increase their utilities. We call them *unknown users* when both the valuations and channel demands are private information. The model of unknown users does not fall into the family of conventional mechanism design with one-parameter domains [1], and has not been considered in any of the existing work for spectrum auctions.

Another design challenge is to consider both the channel heterogeneity and preference diversity. The channel heterogeneity comes from both spatial heterogeneity and frequency heterogeneity. On one hand, the availability and quality of spectrum vary at different locations. On the other hand, spectrum resided in different frequency bands may have different propagation and penetration characteristics. Due to

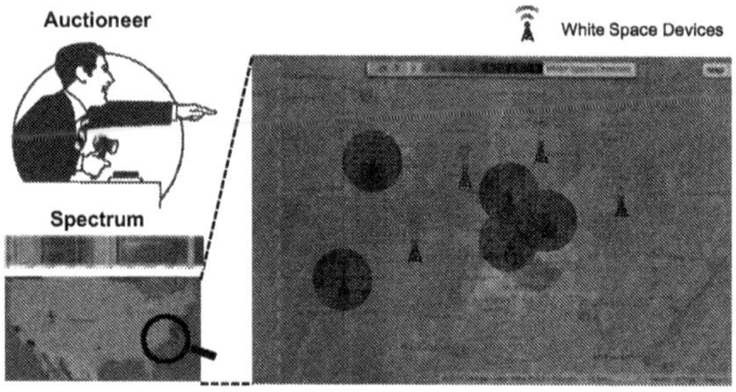

Figure 1: Heterogeneous TV White Space spectrum redistribution based on combinatorial auctions.

the heterogeneity of channels, users may have diverse preferences on different combinations of heterogeneous channels. For instance, a secondary user may be likely to have a valuation for some paired channels to provide LTE-based services, and have another different valuation for unpaired channels to support WiMax services. Therefore, it is necessary to allow users to express different valuations on multiple channel bundles. Considering the channel heterogeneity and preference diversity, it is natural to model the market of heterogeneous spectrum redistribution as a combinatorial auction. However, spectrum is different from traditional goods due to its spatial reusability, by which well-separated users can be allocated on the same spectrum band simultaneously. Thus, traditional combinatorial auction mechanisms cannot be directly applied to spectrum auctions. Figure 1 shows a combinatorial auction mechanism for TV white space spectrum redistribution. The TV white spaces has both spatially and frequency heterogeneity. White space devices at different locations can access to different available white spaces, and have distinct permissive maximum power, adjacent channel interference and noise floor. The frequency of TV broadband ranges from 54MHz to 806Mhz, leading to various frequency characteristics of different white spaces.

The last but not least design challenge is the basic and common objective of auctions: maximizing social welfare, which is defined as the sum of winners' valuations on allocated goods (Please refer to Section 3.2 for the definition). However, finding the optimal social welfare in combinatorial spectrum auctions is normally computationally intractable.

In this paper, we conduct an in-depth study on the problem of dynamic spectrum redistribution, jointly considering the above challenges. We propose a family of unknown combinatorial Auction mEchanisms for heteroGeneous spectrum redIStribution (AEGIS). AEGIS contains two mechanisms, namely AEGIS-SG and AEGIS-MP. Specifically, AEGIS-SG is a direct revelation combinatorial auction for *unknown single minded* users, achieving both strategy-proofness (Please refer to Section 3.3 for the definition) and a good approximation ratio. AEGIS-MP is a novel iterative ascending combinatorial auction for *unknown multiple minded* users. AEGIS-MP achieves approximately efficient social welfare, and is implemented in undominated strategies, which is an important solution concept from game theory (Please refer to Section 3.3 for the definition). To the best of our knowledge, AEGIS is the first combinatorial auction framework considering spectrum redistribution among unknown users.

We summarize our contributions in this paper as follows.

• First, we propose a general combinatorial auction model for the problem of heterogeneous spectrum redistribution, and use the concept of virtual channel to capture the conflict of channel usage among wireless users. This general model is powerful enough to express channel heterogeneity and spatial reusability, as well as preference diversity.

• Second, we begin with considering a simple but classical setting with unknown single minded users, and propose AEGIS-SG, which is a strategy-proof and approximately efficient combinatorial auction mechanism for heterogeneous channel redistribution.

• Third, we further extend this work by considering a more general case, in which users are *unknown multiple minded.* We propose a novel iterative ascending combinatorial auction mechanism, namely AEGIS-MP, which is an algorithmic implementation in undominated strategies, and achieves approximately efficient social welfare.

• Last but not least, we evaluate the performance of AEGIS based on two practical datasets, Google Spectrum Database and GoogleWiFi, and compare AEGIS with the state-of-the-art mechanisms. Our evaluation results show that AEGIS achieves superior performance in terms of social welfare, revenue, user satisfaction ratio, and channel utilization.

The rest of this paper is organized as follows. In Section 2, we review related work. In Section 3, we present the model of combinatorial auction for heterogeneous spectrum redistribution. In Section 4, we propose AEGIS-SG for the case with unknown single minded users. We further consider the case with unknown multiple minded users, and propose AEGIS-MP in Section 5. The evaluation results are presented in Section 6. We conclude the paper in Section 7.

2. RELATED WORK

In recent years, designing auction mechanisms for spectrum redistribution attracts increasing interests [5, 7, 29, 31, 33]. Unfortunately, none of these mechanisms fully consider the above design challenges. Some of the spectrum auction mechanisms (*e.g.*, VERITAS [31] and TRUST [33]) consider channel spatial reusability, but fail in heterogeneous channel scenarios. Recent work CRWDP [5], TAHES [7] and SMASHER [29] consider channel heterogeneity, but CRWDP ignores channel spatial reusability, while TAHES and SMASHER have simple valuation formats. Furthermore, these mechanisms only prevent users from misreporting their valuations to manipulate the auction, and always assume that the channel demands are publicly known to the auctioneer. However, in practice, users can further improve their utilities by cheating on their channel demands. In this work, we design heterogeneous spectrum auction mechanisms, considering both channel spatial reusability and diverse valuation formats. To some extent, our mechanisms are resistant to both valuations and channel demands cheating behaviors.

There are some other related work on spectrum auctions mechanism design, *e.g.*, online spectrum auction [28], revenue generation [15] and spectrum auction with multiple auctioneers [8] Besides auction theory, some other powerful tools, *e.g.*, contract theory [24], queueing theory [13], and randomized algorithm [10], have been applied to different scopes in spectrum markets design.

Another category of related work is combinatorial auction mechanism design. Dobzinski [4] and Papadimitriou *et al.* [23] proved that optimal social welfare and strategy-proofness cannot be achieved simultaneously in general combinatorial auctions. Considering the intractability of combinatorial auctions, a number of strategy-proof auction mechanisms with well bounded approximation ratios are proposed [1, 3, 20]. There are still no positive results (computationally efficient, deterministic and strategy-proof mechanisms with good social welfare approximation) to combinatorial auctions with unknown multi-minded buyers. Our design is based on the iterative wrapper technique for unknown combinatorial auction mechanism [2]. However, none of the above combinatorial auctions considered the spectrum spatial reusability.

3. PRELIMINARIES AND PROBLEM FORMULATION

In this section, we first describe network and auction model for the problem of heterogeneous channel redistribution, and then review related solution concepts used in this paper from game theory. At last, we formulate the channel allocation problem as a classic weighted set packing problem.

3.1 Network Model

We consider a static secondary spectrum market with a primary spectrum holder, called "seller", and some secondary users (*e.g.*, WiFi APs), called "buyers". The primary spectrum holder wants to sell her temporary unused spectrum, and the secondary users would like to lease spectrum to provide wireless services for their customers at certain Quality of Service (QoS). We consider that the trading channels are heterogeneous, and thus buyers have diverse preferences over the different combinations of channels according to their QoS, hardware abilities and the interference conditions of accessible channels. Different from traditional goods, wireless channels can be spatially reused, meaning that conflict-free buyers can be allocated the same channel simultaneously.

We denote the set of m orthogonal and heterogeneous channels for leasing by $\mathbb{C} \triangleq \{c_1, c_2, \ldots, c_m\}$, and the set of buyers by $\mathbb{N} \triangleq \{1, 2, \ldots, n\}$.

Conflict Graph: In spectrum auctions, conflict graphs are usually used to represent the interference among buyers, and can be built by the auctioneer through some measurement methods, *e.g.*, measurement calibrated method [32]. Due to the heterogeneity of channels, each channel may have a distinct conflict graph. Let $\mathcal{G}_k \triangleq (\mathcal{N}_k, \mathcal{E}_k)$ denote the conflict graph on channel c_k, where $\mathcal{N}_k \subseteq \mathbb{N}$ is the set of buyers who can access channel c_k, and each edge $(i, j) \in \mathcal{E}_k$ represents the interference between buyers i and j on channel c_k. We also denote the maximum degree on graph $\mathcal{G}_k$ by Δ_k, and the maximum among all Δ_k's by Δ_{max}, *i.e.*, $\Delta_{max} \triangleq \max_{c_k \in \mathbb{C}}\{\Delta_k\}$.

3.2 Auction Model

We model the process of heterogeneous channels redistribution as combinatorial auctions. We discuss two popular kinds of combinatorial auctions: *direct revelation* combinatorial auction for the case with unknown single-minded buyers, and *iterative ascending* combinatorial auction for the case with unknown multi-minded buyers. Specifically, in the direct revelation combinatorial auction, buyers simultaneously declare their bids and channel demands to a trustworthy auctioneer, and then the auctioneer makes the decision on channel allocation and the charge to each winner. In the iterative ascending combinatorial auction, buyers compete by gradually raising their bids, and the auctioneer maintains a provisional allocation in each iteration. The auction stops when all the remaining active buyers are declared as winners, and winners pay their lastly reported bids. We list some useful notations in our model as follows.

Interested Channel Bundle: Each buyer $i \in \mathbb{N}$ has various private preferences on l_i channel bundles $\hat{\mathbf{S}}_i \triangleq \{\hat{S}_i^1, \hat{S}_i^2, \ldots, \hat{S}_i^{l_i}\}$, in which $\hat{S}_i^j \subseteq \mathbb{C}$ and l_i can be arbitrarily large, even exponential. We call a buyer i, who is interested in l_i channel bundles as l_i*-minded* buyer. We discuss single-minded case ($l_i = 1$ for all $i \in \mathbb{N}$) in Section 4 and multi-minded case ($l_i > 1$ for some $i \in \mathbb{N}$) in Section 5. We denote the interested bundles of all buyers by $\mathbb{S} \triangleq \{\hat{\mathbf{S}}_1, \hat{\mathbf{S}}_2, \cdots, \hat{\mathbf{S}}_n\}$.

Valuation: Each buyer $i \in \mathbb{N}$ has a private valuation v_i^j over each of her interested channel bundle $\hat{S}_i^j \in \hat{\mathbf{S}}_i$. For the other channel bundles not in $\hat{\mathbf{S}}_i$, we adopt the **XOR** operation in combinatorial auctions [21], and formally describe the valuation function of buyer i as

$$V_i(S) \triangleq \begin{cases} \max_{\hat{S}_i^j \in \hat{\mathbf{S}}_i, \hat{S}_i^j \subseteq S} \{v_i^j\}, & \exists\, \hat{S}_i^j \in \hat{\mathbf{S}}_i, \hat{S}_i^j \subseteq S, \\ 0, & \text{otherwise.} \end{cases} \tag{1}$$

We assume that $V_i(\cdot)$ is *normalized* (*i.e.*, $V_i(\varnothing) = 0$) and *monotone* (*i.e.*, $V_i(S) \leq V_i(T)$ for each $S \subseteq T \subseteq \mathbb{C}$). Since the valuation function is derived from the expected quality of wireless service applications, we can assume that the range of the valuation function $V_i(\cdot)$ of buyer i is $[\underline{v}_i, \overline{v}_i]$ and $\underline{v}_i \geq \epsilon$, where ϵ is the minimum monetary unit in auction systems. We denote the maximum value of all $\overline{v}_i$ by $\overline{v}_{max} \triangleq \max_{i \in \mathbb{N}} \overline{v}_i$. We call the valuation function of buyer i is δ_i-close when $\frac{\overline{v}_i}{\underline{v}_i} \leq \delta_i$. This parameter characterizes the diversity of valuation function from one buyer. Let $\delta_{max} \triangleq \max_{i \in \mathbb{N}} \delta_i$. We denote the valuation functions of all buyers by $\vec{\mathcal{V}} \triangleq (V_1(\cdot), V_2(\cdot), \cdots, V_n(\cdot))$.

Bid and Declared Channel Bundle: In the direct revelation combinatorial auction for unknown single-minded case, each buyer $i \in \mathbb{N}$ declares a bid b_i and one channel bundle $\mathbf{S}_i$ to the auctioneer, meaning that she is willing to pay at most b_i, if she is allocated a channel bundle containing $\mathbf{S}_i$. The bid vector of all buyers is represented as $\vec{\mathcal{B}} \triangleq (b_1, b_2, \cdots, b_n)$, and the declared channel bundles of all buyers are denoted by $\vec{\mathcal{S}} \triangleq (\mathbf{S}_1, \mathbf{S}_2, \cdots, \mathbf{S}_n)$. In the iterative ascending combinatorial auction for unknown multi-minded case, active buyer i submits a temporary bid b_i^j and a channel bundle $\mathbf{S}_i^j$ in the jth iteration. The bids of non-active buyers are set to zeros, and their current bundles are the declared bundles when they drop out of the auction. We denote all bids by $\vec{\mathcal{B}}^j \triangleq (b_1^j, b_2^j, \cdots, b_n^j)$ and the declared bundles of buyers by $\vec{\mathcal{S}}^j \triangleq (\mathbf{S}_1^j, \mathbf{S}_2^j, \cdots, \mathbf{S}_n^j)$ in the jth iteration.

Clearing Price and Utility: The auctioneer charges each winner i a clearing price p_i, and let the losers free of any charge. We use vector $\vec{\mathcal{P}} \triangleq (p_1, p_2, \cdots, p_n)$ to represent the clearing prices of all buyers. Each buyer $i \in \mathbb{N}$ has a quasi-linear utility defined as

$$u_i \triangleq V_i(\mathbf{S}_i^*) - p_i, \tag{2}$$

where $\mathbf{S}_i^*$ is the channel bundle allocated to buyer i.

In our model, we consider buyers are *unknown*, *i.e.*, both the valuation functions and interested channel bundles are private information, and unknown to the auctioneer. In such environment, the selfish and rational buyers have more flexibilities to manipulate the results of the auction, and are eager to maximize their own utilities. In contrast to buyers, the overall objective of the auction mechanism is to maximize social welfare, which is defined as follows.

Definition 1 (Social Welfare). *The social welfare in a spectrum auction is the sum of winning buyers' valuations on their allocated bundles of channels, i.e.,*

$$SW \triangleq \sum_{i \in \mathbb{W}^*} V_i(\mathbf{S}_i^*), \tag{3}$$

where $\mathbb{W}^*$ is the set of winners, and $\mathbf{S}_i^*$ is the corresponding allocated channel bundle for winner i.

In this paper, we assume that buyers do not collude with each other, and leave relaxation of this assumption to our future work.

3.3 Economic Properties

We briefly review the solution concepts used in this paper from game theory.

Definition 2 (Dominant Strategy [22]). *A strategy st_i (weakly) dominates another strategy st'_i of player i, if for any other players' strategy profile st_{-i}: $u_i(st_i, st_{-i}) \geq u_i(st'_i, st_{-i})$, and this inequality is strict for at least one instance of st_{-i}.*
A strategy st_i is a dominant strategy for player i if it (weakly) dominates any other strategies of player i.

A strategy st_i is an *undominated strategy* for player i if it is not dominated by any other strategies of player i.

In direct revelation mechanisms, *incentive-compatibility* means that truthfully revealing private information (both the valuations and channel demands in this paper) is a dominant strategy for each player. An accompanying concept is *individual-rationality*, which means that players truthfully participating in the game gain non-negative utilities. The formal definition of *strategy-proof mechanism* is as follows.

Definition 3 (Strategy-Proof Mechanism [19]). *A direct revelation mechanism is strategy-proof when it satisfies both incentive-compatibility and individual-rationality.*

Strategy-proofness is a strong solution concept in mechanism design. However, the requirement of having dominant strategies limits the existence of feasible allocation algorithms in combinatorial auctions for unknown multi-minded buyers [3, 17]. Therefore, we turn our attention to another well-known game theoretic concept: *implementation in undominated strategies*.

Definition 4 (Implementation in Undominated Strategies [2,12]). *A mechanism $\mathcal{M}$ is an implementation of c-approximation in undominated strategies if there exists a non-empty set of undominated strategies D with the following properties.*

- *$\mathcal{M}$ achieves a c-approximation in polynomial time for any combination of undominated strategies from D.* [1]
- *$\mathcal{M}$ is individually rational for players taking undominated strategies from D.*
- *$\mathcal{M}$ has fast undominance recognition property, meaning that a player can efficiently determine if a strategy belongs to D, and if not, compute an undominated strategy in D to dominate it.*

The underlying goal of spectrum auctions is to achieve approximately optimal social welfare in the present of strategic behaviors of buyers. In unknown multi-minded case, we achieve this goal by relaxing the strict strategy-proofness constraint, and allowing the mechanism to leave several strategies in D for the buyers to choose from. We compensate this uncertainly on the game-theoretic side by strengthening the algorithmic analysis, showing that the mechanism can achieve a good approximation for any combination of undominated strategies from D.

3.4 Problem Formulation

We borrow the novel concept of virtual channel [29] to represent the conflict of channel usage among buyers. By using virtual channels, we transform the *channel allocation problem* to a classical *weighted set packing* problem, and formulate it as a binary program. Specifically, a virtual channel $h^k_{i,j}$ indicates that buyers i and j cause interference between each other on channel c_k, when channel c_k is allocated to i and j simultaneously, *i.e.*, virtual channel $h^k_{i,j}$ is corresponding to the edge $(i,j) \in \mathcal{E}_k$ on conflict graph $\mathcal{G}_k$. We now show the process of constructing virtual channels. We first create virtual channel $h^k_{i,j}$ for each edge $(i,j) \in \mathcal{E}_k$ on conflict graph $\mathcal{G}_k$, and then append $h^k_{i,j}$ to the channel bundles containing channel c_k from the buyers i and j. We finally remove the original channels from all channel bundles. Hence, the updated channel bundles only contain virtual channels. From now on, the set $\mathbb{S}$ and vector $\vec{\mathcal{S}}$ ($\vec{\mathcal{S}^j}$) represent the updated interested channel bundles and updated declared channel bundles, respectively. We note that the valuations on updated channel bundles retain the same. Let H_i be the set of virtual channels for the buyer i. All virtual channels are denoted by $\mathbb{H} \triangleq \{H_1, H_2, \cdots, H_n\}$. According to the rule of virtual channel construction, the maximum size of updated interested channel bundle is bounded by $\kappa = m \times \Delta_{max}$.

When virtual channel $h^k_{i,j}$ is added into the channel bundles containing channel c_k from the buyers i and j, at most one of the channel bundles from the buyers i and j can be allocated, ensuring the exclusive allocation of channel c_k for the buyers i and j. If the buyer i obtains all virtual channels $h^k_{i,j}, (i,j) \in \mathcal{E}_k$ on conflict graph $\mathcal{G}_k$, then she is granted channel c_k. We note that the buyer i may not conflict with any other buyers on some channels. For these channels with no interference, we directly allocate them to the buyer i. Consequently, the exclusive allocation of virtual channels implies the feasible channel allocation under conflict graph constraint.

We now transform the channel allocation problem to the weighted κ-set packing problem. The weighted κ-set packing problem can be described as: given a family of weighted sets, each containing at most κ elements drawn from a finite universe, find a maximum weight sub-collection of disjoint sets. In the channel allocation problem, the set of virtual channels $\mathbb{H}$ corresponds to the universe, collection of updated declared channel bundles $\vec{\mathcal{S}}$ ($\vec{\mathcal{S}^j}$) corresponds to the family of weighted sets, and $\kappa = m \times \Delta_{max}$. In the direct revelation combinatorial auction for the single-minded case, the problem of channel allocation can be formulated as an integer programming.

Problem: *Heterogeneous Channel Allocation*
Objective: Maximize $\sum_{i \in \mathbb{N}} (x(i, \mathbf{S}_i) \times b_i)$
Subject to:

$$\sum_{i \in \mathbb{N}} \sum_{\mathbf{S}_i \ni h_k} x(i, \mathbf{S}_i) \leq 1, \quad \forall h_k \in \mathbb{H}, \tag{4}$$

$$x(i, \mathbf{S}_i) \in \{0, 1\}, \quad \forall i \in \mathbb{N}. \tag{5}$$

Here, the variable $x(i, \mathbf{S}_i) = 1$ indicates that channel bundle $\mathbf{S}_i$ is allocated to buyer i; otherwise $x(i, \mathbf{S}_i) = 0$. The first set of constraints represents the exclusive allocation of virtual channels, and the second set of constraints states the binary value of the auctioneer's decision of allocation. In the jth iteration of ascending combinatorial auction, we can formulate the channel allocation problem as a similar integer programming by replacing b_i and $\mathbf{S}_i$ with b^j_i and $\mathbf{S}^j_i$. In the formulation, we use declared information ($\vec{\mathcal{B}}$, $\vec{\mathcal{S}}$, $\vec{\mathcal{B}^j}$ and $\vec{\mathcal{S}^j}$) instead of truly private information ($\mathbb{S}$ and $\vec{\mathcal{V}}$), because the strategy-proof mechanism in Section 4 will guarantee that bidding truthfully is a dominant strategy for each buyer, and the iterative auction mechanism implemented in undominated strategies in Section 5 will ensure that the declared information is close to the truthful information at the end of the auction.

Solving the above integer programming is NP-hard, which makes the general and celebrated VCG mechanism [22] inapplicable. Considering the computational intractability of

[1] In this paper, a mechanism $\mathcal{M}$ achieves c-approximation means that the approximation ratio of $\mathcal{M}$ is $\frac{1}{c}$. The approximation ratio is defined as the ratio between the social welfare achieved by $\mathcal{M}$ and the optimal social welfare.

Algorithm 1: Channel Allocation in AEGIS-SG

Input: A set of buyers $\mathbb{N}$, bid vector $\vec{\mathcal{B}}$, declared channel bundle set $\vec{\mathcal{S}}$.
Output: A pair of sets of winners and allocated channel bundles $(\mathbb{W}^*, \mathbb{S}^*)$.

```
(W*, S*) ← (∅, ∅);
Sort buyers in non-increasing order of their bids:
    Γ1 : b1 ≥ b2 ≥ ··· ≥ bn;
for i = 1 to n do
    if S_i ∩ S* = ∅ then
        (W*, S*) ← (W* ∪ {i}, S* ∪ {S_i});
return (W*, S*);
```

the problem, we present alternative solutions with greedy allocation algorithms to achieve approximately efficient social welfare in following sections.

4. AEGIS-SG

In this section, we begin with a simple but classical setting, in which buyers are unknown single-minded. As shown in section 3.4, finding the optimal auction decision is computationally intractable, even in this restricted case. Therefore, we design AEGIS-SG, which is a direct revelation combinatorial auction mechanism for heterogeneous channel redistribution among unknown single-minded buyers, achieving both strategy-proofness and approximate efficiency.

4.1 Design Details

We first formally define the concept of *unknown single-minded buyers*.

Definition 5 (Unknown Single-Minded Buyer). *Buyer i is an unknown single-minded buyer iff she is only interested in one channel bundle $\hat{\mathbf{S}}_i \subseteq \mathbb{H}$, and has a valuation v_i for any bundle containing $\hat{\mathbf{S}}_i$. Both the valuation v_i and channel demand $\hat{\mathbf{S}}_i$ are private information.*

AEGIS-SG consists of two major components: greedy channel allocation and clearing price calculation. The greedy channel allocation procedure is depicted in Algorithm 1. The algorithm contains two steps:

► Step 1: We sort buyers according to their bids in non-increasing order, and denote the sorted list by Γ_1. We break the tie following any bid-independent rule, *e.g.*, lexicographic order of buyers' IDs or channel numbers.

► Step 2: Following the order in Γ_1, we greedily grant channel bundles, which do not overlap with the previous allocated virtual channels.

The clearing price calculation is based on critical bid.

Definition 6 (Critical Bid). *The critical bid for buyer $i \in \mathbb{N}$ is the minimum bid that the buyer i should declare to win the auction.*

The critical bid of winner $i \in \mathbb{W}^*$ can be calculated by the following steps. Consider the winner i in the sorted list Γ_1, we find the first buyer following i that has been denied but would have been granted a channel bundle when the buyer i is removed from Γ_1, and denote this buyer by $\pi(i)$. We note that such a buyer necessarily conflicts with i. We can formally represent $\pi(i)$ as

$$\pi(i) \triangleq \min\{j | j > i, \mathbf{S}_j \cap \mathbf{S}_i \neq \varnothing \text{ and } \forall k < j, k \neq i, k \text{ is a winner} \Rightarrow \mathbf{S}_k \cap \mathbf{S}_j = \varnothing\}.$$

The critical bid for the winner i is $b_{\pi(i)}$. We show the method of calculating the clearing price for buyer $i \in \mathbb{N}$ by distinguishing two cases.

► If buyer i is a loser or $\pi(i)$ does not exist, she pays zero.

► If there exists a $\pi(i)$, and i is granted $\mathbf{S}_i$, she pays $b_{\pi(i)}$.

4.2 Analysis

In this section, we prove that AEGIS-SG guarantees strategy-proofness in terms of valuations and channel demands, and analyze the approximation ratio of AEGIS-SG. Due to the space limitation, we leave the detailed proofs of these results to our technical report [30].

We first show the monotonicity of channel allocation algorithm, which is essential for a strategy-proof mechanism.

Lemma 1. *AEGIS-SG's channel allocation algorithm is monotonic, i.e., buyer i, who wins by declaring $(\mathbf{S}_i, b_i)$, also wins if she declares $(\mathbf{S}_i', b_i')$, such that, $\mathbf{S}_i' \subseteq \mathbf{S}_i$ and $b_i' \geq b_i$.*

We present the strategy-proofness and approximation ratio of AEGIS-SG.

Theorem 1. *AEGIS-SG is a strategy-proof combinatorial spectrum auction for unknown single-minded buyers.*

Theorem 2. *AEGIS-SG achieves $\mathcal{O}(\kappa)$-approximation.*

5. AEGIS-MP

In this section, we consider a more general scenario, in which buyers are unknown multi-minded. We first give an illustrative example to show that simply extending AEGIS-SG can no longer guarantee strategy-proofness. Furthermore, designing a deterministic, approximately efficient and strategy-proof combinatorial auction mechanism for unknown multi-minded buyers is still an open problem in algorithmic mechanism design, and some negative results are demonstrated [4, 23]. We turn to another well known game theoretic concept, implementation in undominated strategies, and design AEGIS-MP, which is an approximately efficient ascending combinatorial auction for heterogeneous channel redistribution among unknown multi-minded buyers.

We first give the definition of *unknown multi-minded* buyer.

Definition 7 (Unknown Multi-Minded Buyer). *Buyer i is an unknown multi-minded buyer iff she is interested in multiple channel bundles $\hat{\mathbf{S}}_i = \{\hat{S}_i^1, \hat{S}_i^2, \cdots, \hat{S}_i^{l_i}\}, l_i > 1$, and has valuation function $V_i(\cdot)$ defined as Equation (1). The channel demands and valuation function are private information.*

5.1 A Counter Example

In Figure 2, there are three buyers $\{1, 2, 3\}$, and two trading channels $\{c_1, c_2\}$. Since buyers are multi-minded, they

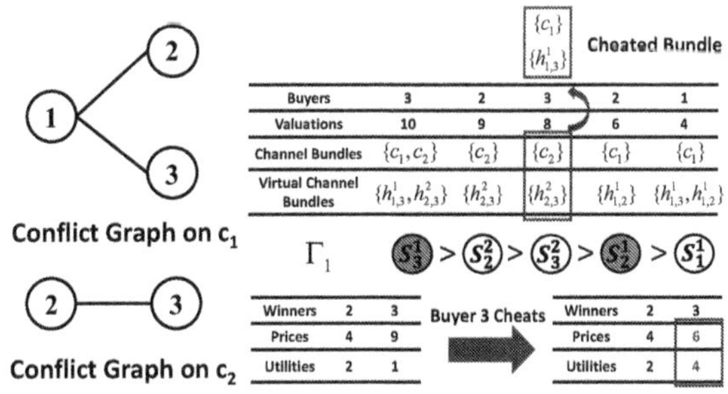

Figure 2: An illustrative example on why extending AEGIS-SG is not strategy-proof in multi-minded scenario. When buyer 3 changes her second interested bundle from $\{c_2\}$ to $\{c_1\}$, she decreases her clearing price from 9 to 6, and obtains higher utility.

may have different valuations on different bundles, *e.g.*, buyer 3 has valuation 10 and 8 over channel bundles $\{c_1, c_2\}$ and $\{c_2\}$, respectively. Based on the conflict graphs and buyers' interested channel bundles, we can construct virtual channel bundles for each buyer. In this example, we assume that buyers truthfully reveal their valuations, and investigate their manipulated strategies on channel demands.

In AEGIS-SG, we sort buyers' declared channel bundles according to the non-increasing order of their bids, and greedily grant channel bundles, ensuring the exclusive allocation of virtual channels. Buyers 2 and 3 are the winners, and obtain channel bundles $\mathbf{S}_2^1 = \{c_2\}$ and $\mathbf{S}_3^1 = \{c_1, c_2\}$, respectively. When bidding truthfully, according to the pricing scheme of AEGIS-SG, buyer 3 should pay 9, which is the bid of buyer 2 on bundle $\mathbf{S}_2^2$, and her utility is $10 - 9 = 1$. However, buyer 3 can cheat by changing her second interested bundle $\mathbf{S}_3^2$ to $\{c_1\}$, and will still be allocated bundle $\mathbf{S}_3^1$ but be charged with 6, increasing her utility to 4. Hence, by declaring untruthful channel demands, buyers can improve their utilities, which leads to the untruthfulness of AEGIS-SG in multi-minded scenario.

5.2 Design Rational

AEGIS-MP is an ascending Japanese auction [14] on top of a greedy channel allocation algorithm. In traditional ascending Japanese auctions, the auctioneer collects temporary bids from active buyers, and maintains a provisional allocation in each iteration. Provisional losers can choose to increase their bids or permanently drop out of the auction. This process is iterated until all remaining active buyers are winners, and their prices are lastly reported bids.

The most challenging part of designing combinatorial auctions for unknown multi-minded buyers is that both the valuations and channel demands are private and unknown to the auctioneer. We overcome this challenge by extending the ascending Japanese auctions to approach the true valuations and channel demands of buyers. Informally, in AEGIS-MP, we also maintain an "active bundle" for each buyer. This active bundle will keep approaching to one of the interested bundles of the buyer during the auction. Another challenge is the impact of manipulative behaviors of selfish buyers, which should be prevented to form a relatively stable market. Since the buyers are rational, they will not take dominated strategies if some undominated strategies can be quickly recognized. By exploiting this rationality of buyers, we carefully design the structure of auctions, such that, at each decision point, buyers can efficiently recognize the undominated strategies and take one of them, leading AEGIS-MP to be implemented in undominated strategies.

5.3 Design Details

We now describe AEGIS-MP in detail. We suppose that GDY_ALG is the approximately efficient greedy-based allocation algorithm, and when given as input vectors of active bundles and temporary bids, it outputs a provisional allocation that is approximate to the optimal solution. In AEGIS-MP, which is shown in Algorithm 2, the vector of bids $\vec{\mathcal{B}}^0$ and active bundles $\vec{\mathcal{S}}^0$ are initialized to $\vec{\epsilon}$ and $(H_1, H_2, \cdots, H_n)$, respectively (Line 2). At the beginning of the jth iteration, the auctioneer knows four parts of information: the previous losers set $\mathbb{L}^j$, the previous winners set $\mathbb{W}^j$, the current active bundle vector $\vec{\mathcal{S}}^j$ and the temporary bid vector of buyers $\vec{\mathcal{B}}^j$. These parameters are handed in as input to GDY_ALG, who, in return, outputs a new set of provisional winners $\mathbb{W}^{j+1}$ and active bundles $\vec{\mathcal{S}}^{j+1}$ (Line 4). The provisional winners retain the same bids, while provisional losers are required to either increase their current bids by multiplying e or permanently drop out of the auction (this is denoted by setting $b_i^{j+1} = 0$) (Lines 5 to 8). Here, parameter e is Euler's Number, and is the best choice over all constants for the optimal approximation ratio. This process is iterated until all remaining active buyers are declared as winners by GDY_ALG. Let the total number of iterations be J, and the set of winners is $\mathbb{W}^J$. Each winner $i \in \mathbb{W}^J$ gets her finally active bundle $\mathbf{S}_i^J \in \vec{\mathcal{S}}^J$, and pays her lastly reported bid $b_i^J \in \vec{\mathcal{B}}^J$. The losers will not be allocated bundles, and are free of any charge (Line 11 to 12).

Algorithm 2: AEGIS-MP: A General Japanese Wrapper Mechanism

Input: A set of buyers $\mathbb{N}$, a set of virtual channels $\mathbb{H}$.
Output: A pair of sets of winners and allocated bundles of channels $(\mathbb{W}^*, \mathbb{S}^*)$. A payment vector $\vec{\mathcal{P}}$.

1 $(\mathbb{W}^*, \mathbb{S}^*) \leftarrow (\varnothing, \varnothing)$; $\vec{\mathcal{P}} \leftarrow \vec{0}$; $j \leftarrow 0$;
2 $\mathbb{W}^0 \leftarrow \varnothing$; $\mathbb{L}^0 \leftarrow \varnothing$; $\vec{\mathcal{S}}^0 \leftarrow (H_1, H_2, \cdots, H_n)$; $\vec{\mathcal{B}}^0 \leftarrow \vec{\epsilon}$;
3 **while** $\mathbb{W}^j \bigcup \mathbb{L}^j \neq \mathbb{N}$ **do**
4     $(\mathbb{W}^{j+1}, \vec{\mathcal{S}}^{j+1}) \leftarrow$ GDY_ALG $\left(\mathbb{N}, \mathbb{L}^j, \mathbb{W}^j, \vec{\mathcal{S}}^j, \vec{\mathcal{B}}^j\right)$;
5     $\vec{\mathcal{B}}^{j+1} \leftarrow \vec{\mathcal{B}}^j$;
6   **foreach** $i \in \mathbb{N} \setminus \left(\mathbb{W}^{j+1} \bigcup \mathbb{L}^j\right)$ **do**
7   i chooses to increase bid: $b_i^{j+1} \leftarrow e \times b_i^{j+1}$ or drop out: $b_i^{j+1} \leftarrow 0$;
8     $\mathbb{L}^{j+1} \leftarrow \left\{i \in \mathbb{N} \middle| b_i^{j+1} = 0\right\}$;
9     $j \leftarrow j + 1$;
10 $J \leftarrow j$;
11 $(\mathbb{W}^*, \mathbb{S}^*) \leftarrow (\mathbb{W}^J, \vec{\mathcal{S}}^J)$;
12 $\vec{\mathcal{P}} \leftarrow \vec{\mathcal{B}}^J$;
13 **return** $(\mathbb{W}^*, \mathbb{S}^*)$, $\vec{\mathcal{P}}$;

We now depict the design of channel allocation algorithm GDY_ALG in details. Algorithm 3 shows the pseudo-code of GDY_ALG procedure. Let $\mathbb{N}^j$ denote the active buyers in the jth iteration. Function $Free(\mathcal{N}, \vec{\mathcal{S}}^j)$ denotes the virtual channels not in $\bigcup_{i \in \mathcal{N}} \mathbf{S}_i^j$. Here, $\mathcal{N} \subseteq \mathbb{N}$ is a subset of buyers, and $\vec{\mathcal{S}}^j$ is a vector of active bundles. GDY_ALG constructs a greedy allocation, $Greedy^{j+1}$, by extending the channel allocation algorithm in AEGIS-SG. Similarly, we sort the active buyers according to their current bids in non-increasing order, and break the tie following any bid-independent rule (Line 2). Following order Γ_2, two steps are performed for the currently considered buyer i.

► **Shrinking Active Bundle:** If the buyer i was previously a provisional loser, then she is given an option to "shrink" her active bundle. If the buyer i chooses to shrink her bundle, the new bundle must satisfy that its valuation is not less than her current bid b_i^j, and it is a subset of the previously reported bundle $\mathbf{S}_i^j$ and disjoints from the bundles of buyers that are already in $Greedy^{j+1}$ (Line 4 to 5).

► **Updating Candidate Winner Sets:** Buyer i is added to the allocation $Greedy^{j+1}$ (or $\mathbb{W}^j$) when her declared bundle $\mathbf{S}_i^{j+1}$ does not intersect the bundles of existing buyers in $Greedy^{j+1}$ (or $\mathbb{W}^j$). This operation ensures that the two allocations $Greedy^{j+1}$ and $\mathbb{W}^j$ are Pareto-efficient[2] with respect to the new active bundles $\vec{\mathcal{S}}^{j+1}$ (Line 6 to 7).

Once all the active buyers have been considered, GDY_ALG outputs the allocation with the maximum value out of the two allocations $Greedy^{j+1}$ and $\mathbb{W}^j$ as the new set of pro-

[2]Pareto-efficiency means that it is impossible to add losers into the winner set without removing at least one winner.

Algorithm 3: GDY_ALG(): Channel Allocation Algorithm

Input: A set of buyers $\mathbb{N}$. A previous losers set $\mathbb{L}^j$ and winners set $\mathbb{W}^j$. A vector of active bundles $\vec{\mathcal{S}}^j$ and a vector of current bid $\vec{\mathcal{B}}^j$ in iteration j.

Output: A provisional winners set $\mathbb{W}^{j+1}$ and a new active bundles $\vec{\mathcal{S}}^{j+1}$ in iteration $(j+1)$.

1 $Greedy^{j+1} \leftarrow \varnothing$; $\vec{\mathcal{S}}^{j+1} \leftarrow \vec{\mathcal{S}}^j$; $\mathbb{N}^j = \mathbb{N} \setminus \mathbb{L}^j$; $n' = |\mathbb{N}^j|$;

2 Sort n' active buyers in non-increasing order of b_i^j: $\Gamma_2 : b_1^j \geq b_2^j \geq \cdots \geq b_{n'}^j$;

3 **foreach** $i = 1$ *to* n' **do**

4   **if** $i \in \mathbb{N} \setminus (\mathbb{L}^j \bigcup \mathbb{W}^j)$ **then**

5   i is allowed to update to any bundle that satisfies $V_i(\mathbf{S}_i^{j+1}) \geq b_i^j$ and $\mathbf{S}_i^{j+1} \subseteq \left(\mathbf{S}_i^j \bigcap Free\left(Greedy^{j+1}, \vec{\mathcal{S}}^{j+1}\right)\right)$;

6   **if** $\mathcal{S}_i^{j+1} \subseteq Free\left(\mathcal{N}, \vec{\mathcal{S}}^{j+1}\right), \mathcal{N} \in \{Greedy^{j+1}, \mathbb{W}^j\}$ **then**

7     $\mathcal{N} \leftarrow \mathcal{N} \bigcup \{i\}$;

8 $\mathbb{W}^{j+1} \leftarrow \arg\max_{\mathcal{N} \in \{Greedy^{j+1}, \mathbb{W}^j\}} \sum_{i \in \mathcal{N}} b_i^j$;

9 **return** $(\mathbb{W}^{j+1}, \vec{\mathcal{S}}^{j+1})$;

visional winners $\mathbb{W}^{j+1}$. It also outputs the updated active bundles $\vec{\mathcal{S}}^{j+1}$ (Line 8 to 9).

We summarize four important properties of GDY_ALG. These properties will be frequently used in next section.

► (**Pareto Efficiency**) For any buyer $i \notin \mathbb{W}^{j+1}$, $\mathbf{S}_i^{j+1} \not\subseteq Free((\mathbb{W}^{j+1}, \vec{\mathcal{S}}^{j+1}))$.

► (**Improvement**) $\sum_{i \in \mathbb{W}^{j+1}} b_i^j \geq \sum_{i \in \mathbb{W}^j} b_i^j$.

► (**Shrinking Sets**) For any buyer $i \in \mathbb{N}$ and any $0 \leq j \leq J-1$, $\mathbf{S}_i^{j+1} \subseteq \mathbf{S}_i^j$.

► (**First Time Shrink**) Let $\mathbb{F}^j \triangleq \{\, i \,||\mathbf{S}_i^j| = |H_i|, |\mathbf{S}_i^{j+1}| < |H_i| \,\}$. For any $i_1, i_2 \in \mathbb{F}^j$, it holds that $\mathbf{S}_{i_1}^{j+1} \bigcap \mathbf{S}_{i_2}^{j+1} = \varnothing$.

5.4 Analysis

In this section, we prove that AEGIS-MP is an implementation in undominated strategies by the following steps. First, we characterize the set of undominated strategies D. Second, we show that AEGIS-MP is individually rational for buyers taking any strategies from D. Third, we demonstrate that AEGIS-MP has fast undominance recognition property. Finally, we analyze the approximation ratio of AEGIS-MP.

We start with defining a type of buyers in AEGIS-MP.

Definition 8 (Drop-out if silent buyers). *Active buyer i is a "drop-out if silent" buyer in the jth iteration if, when she is allowed to shrink her active bundle at Line 5 in GDY_ALG, all the following hold:*

► *(Not a previous winner) $i \in \mathbb{N} \setminus (\mathbb{L}^j \bigcup \mathbb{W}^j)$.*

► *(Drop out if keep silent) $\mathcal{S}_i^{j+1} \not\subseteq Free(Greedy^{j+1}, \vec{\mathcal{S}}^{j+1})$, $\vec{\mathcal{S}}_i^{j+1} \not\subseteq Free(\mathbb{W}^j, \vec{\mathcal{S}}^{j+1})$ and $e \times b_i^j > V_i(\mathcal{S}_i^j)$.*

A buyer can recognize that she is a "drop-out if silent" buyer at Line 5 of GDY_ALG, and if there exists a feasible channel bundle, she will definitely shrink her active bundle. This is because she is guaranteed to drop out of the auction if she keeps silent, and if she shrinks her active bundle, she might win. In terminology of game theory, the strategy that keeping silent is dominated by the strategy of bundle shrinking.

We now characterize strategy set D, and claim that every strategy in D is an undominated strategy.

Definition 9 (Set D). *Let D be the set of all strategies that satisfy the following conditions, for every iteration j:*

► *If buyer i does not drop out, her bid is always less than her valuation on the active bundle, i.e., $\epsilon \leq b_i^j \leq V_i(\mathcal{S}_i^j)$. As $V_i(\mathcal{S}_i^j) \geq \epsilon$, her active bundle $\mathcal{S}_i^j$ must contain some interested bundles.*

► *If buyer i drops out, then $b_i^j > V_i(\mathcal{S}_i^{j+1})/e$.*

► *If buyer i is a "drop-out if silent" buyer (Definition 8), then she will definitely declare some feasible bundle $\mathcal{S}_i^{j+1}$ that satisfies the conditions at Line 5 of GDY_ALG, if such a bundle exists.*

Lemma 2. *Strategy set D is a set of undominated strategies.*

Proof. According to the definition of D, all strategies outside D are dominated strategies, which cannot dominate any strategy in D. We just need to look at any two different strategies of buyer i from the set D (*i.e.*, $st_i, st_i' \in D, st_i \neq st_i'$), and show that neither of them dominates the other. We consider the first point that they differ (*i.e.*, the buyer i has different active bundles). At this point, we can construct the strategies of the other buyers that will cause one strategy to win and the other to lose. Therefore, neither st_i nor st_i' dominates the other, and then both strategies st_i and st_i' are undominated strategies. □

Lemma 3. *AEGIS-MP is individually rational for buyers taking undominated strategies from D.*

Proof. According to the fact that winners pay their lastly reported bids and the first condition of Definition 9, a winner cannot obtain a negative utility when she plays any undominated strategy in D. Obviously, losers' utilities are zeros. Therefore, our claim holds. □

Lemma 4. *AEGIS-MP has fast undominance recognition property, i.e., buyers can efficiently determine if a strategy belongs to D, and if not, compute an undominated strategy in D to dominate it in polynomial time.*

Proof. Clearly, any buyer i can check if her strategy satisfies the conditions of undominated strategies in Definition 9 in polynomial time, and if not, modify her strategy to an undominated strategy that dominates the original one. □

We now analyze the approximation ratio of AEGIS-MP. We first present some notations. Let $\mathrm{OPT}(\mathcal{N}, \vec{\mathcal{S}})$ denote the value of the optimal outcome (in terms of valuation function $\vec{\mathcal{V}}$) for a set of buyers $\mathcal{N} \subseteq \mathbb{N}$ when their channel bundles are $\vec{\mathcal{S}}$. We call $(\mathcal{N}, \vec{\mathcal{S}})$ a valid allocation, if $\mathbf{S}_{i_1} \bigcap \mathbf{S}_{i_2} = \varnothing$ for any $i_1, i_2 \in \mathcal{N}$ and $\mathbf{S}_{i_1}, \mathbf{S}_{i_2} \in \vec{\mathcal{S}}$. Besides the four important properties in the previous section, we present another property, which can be derived from Definition 9.

► (**Value Bound**) For any $i \in \mathbb{N}$, and any $0 \leq j \leq J$, $b_i^j \leq V_i(\mathbf{S}_i^j)$. For buyer i who drops out in the jth iteration, $b_i^j > V_i(\mathbf{S}_i^{j+1})/e$.

Before presenting the main theorem, we give some important lemmas. We first show that the number of iterations in AEGIS-MP is limited.

Lemma 5. *AEGIS-MP stops in at most $J = 2\ln(\overline{v}_{max}/\epsilon) + 1$ steps.*

Proof. We look at a loser i_1 who drops out in the last iteration (the $(J-1)$th iteration). According to the **Pareto Efficiency** property, loser i_1's active bundle must intersect with that of a winner $i_2 \in \mathbb{W}^J$, which implies that $\mathbf{S}_{i_1}^J \bigcap \mathbf{S}_{i_2}^J \neq \varnothing$. Additionally, by the **Shrinking Sets** property, it holds that $\mathbf{S}_{i_1}^j \bigcap \mathbf{S}_{i_2}^j \neq \varnothing$, for any $0 \leq j \leq J-1$. Therefore, we can claim that buyer i_1 and i_2 never win together. Each of them can be a loser, and multiply her bid at most $\ln(\overline{v}_{max}/\epsilon)$ consecutive times. We can get that $J - 1 \leq 2\ln(\overline{v}_{max}/\epsilon)$, and thus the lemma holds. □

We have the following lemma for buyers in AEGIS-MP.

Lemma 6. *For AEGIS-MP, it holds that* $\text{OPT}(\mathbb{L}^J, \vec{\mathcal{S}}^J) < etJ \times \text{OPT}(\mathbb{W}^J, \vec{\mathcal{S}}^J)$*, where* $t = (1+\kappa)$.

Due to the limitation of space, we leave the detailed proof to our technical report [30].

We now present the approximation ratio of AEGIS-MP.

Theorem 3. *AEGIS-MP achieves* $(\delta_{max} + e\delta_{max}tJ^2 + etJ)$*-approximation.*

Proof. Let $\mathbb{O}$ be the set of winners in the optimal allocation, and winners are allocated bundles from $\vec{\mathcal{S}}^O = (\mathbf{S}_1^O, \mathbf{S}_2^O, \cdots, \mathbf{S}_n^O)$. We partition the winners into three categories, and bound the value of them separately.

▷ We denote the winners that also stay in $\mathbb{W}^J$ by $\mathcal{N}_1$. In this case, winners might win other interested channel bundles in the optimal allocation, so we get

$$\text{OPT}(\mathcal{N}_1, \vec{\mathcal{S}}^O) \leq \delta_{max} \times \text{OPT}(\mathbb{W}^J, \vec{\mathcal{S}}^J). \tag{6}$$

▷ We turn to another set of winners $\mathcal{N}_2$, which is the subset of losers in AEGIS-MP, *i.e.*, $\mathcal{N}_2 \subseteq \mathbb{L}^J$. Buyer i belongs to $\mathcal{N}_2$ if and only if she is a winner in the optimal allocation $\mathbb{O}$, and her allocated bundle $\mathbf{S}_i^O$ is not included in $\mathbf{S}_i^J$, which is the bundle that the buyer i declares in AEGIS-MP when she drops out. We have the following claim for winners $\mathcal{N}_2$.

Claim 1: $\text{OPT}(\mathcal{N}_2, \vec{\mathcal{S}}^O) < e\delta_{max}tJ^2 \times \text{OPT}(\mathbb{W}^J, \vec{\mathcal{S}}^J)$.

Proof. Let $\mathbb{F}^j = \left\{ i \in \mathcal{N}_2 \;\middle|\; |\mathbf{S}_i^j| = |H_i|, |\mathbf{S}_i^{j+1}| < |H_i| \right\}$ be the set of buyers from $\mathcal{N}_2$ that first shrink their bundles in the jth iteration, and we have $\mathcal{N}_2 = \bigcup_{j=0}^{J-1} \mathbb{F}^j$. According to the first and third properties of undominated strategy in Definition 9, we can conclude that $\mathbf{S}_i^j$ contains some interested channel bundles for all $i \in \mathbb{N}$ and $0 \leq j \leq J-1$. Therefore, for any $i \in \mathbb{F}^j$, we have

$$V_i(\mathbf{S}_i^O) \leq \delta_{max} \times V_i(\mathbf{S}_i^J), \quad \forall i \in \mathbb{F}^j. \tag{7}$$

According to the **First Time Shrink** property, all bundles $\vec{\mathcal{S}}^{j+1}$ of buyers in $\mathbb{F}^j$ are disjoint. Additionally, by the **Shrinking Sets** property, we have $\mathcal{S}_i^J \subseteq \mathcal{S}_i^{j+1}$, implying bundles $\vec{\mathcal{S}}^J$ of buyers in $\mathbb{F}^j$ are also disjoint. Therefore, $(\mathbb{F}^j, \vec{\mathcal{S}}^J)$ is a valid allocation. Since $\mathbb{F}^j \subseteq \mathcal{N}_2 \subseteq \mathbb{L}^J$, we get

$$\text{OPT}(\mathbb{F}^j, \vec{\mathcal{S}}^J) \leq \text{OPT}(\mathbb{L}^J, \vec{\mathcal{S}}^J). \tag{8}$$

Combining with Inequalities (7)(8), we conclude that

$$\begin{aligned} \text{OPT}(\mathbb{F}^j, \vec{\mathcal{S}}^O) &= \sum_{i \in \mathbb{F}^j} V_i(\mathbf{S}_i^O) \leq \delta_{max} \sum_{i \in \mathbb{F}^j} V_i(\mathbf{S}_i^J) \\ &= \delta_{max}\text{OPT}(\mathbb{F}^j, \vec{\mathcal{S}}^J) \leq \delta_{max}\text{OPT}(\mathbb{L}^J, \vec{\mathcal{S}}^J). \end{aligned} \tag{9}$$

Using Inequality (9) and Lemma 6, we get

$$\text{OPT}(\mathbb{F}^j, \vec{\mathcal{S}}^O) < e\delta_{max}tJ \times \text{OPT}(\mathbb{W}^J, \vec{\mathcal{S}}^J).$$

Finally, we conclude that

$$\text{OPT}(\mathcal{N}_2, \vec{\mathcal{S}}^O) \leq \textstyle\sum_{j=0}^{J-1} \text{OPT}(\mathbb{F}^j, \vec{\mathcal{S}}^O) < e\delta_{max}tJ^2\text{OPT}(\mathbb{W}^J, \vec{\mathcal{S}}^J) \tag{10}$$

□

▷ We denote the winners in $\mathbb{L}^J \backslash \mathcal{N}_2$ by $\mathcal{N}_3$. According to the definition of $\mathcal{N}_2$, the allocated bundles of winners in $\mathcal{N}_3$ are contained in bundles $\vec{\mathcal{S}}^J$, together with Lemma 6, we get

$$\begin{aligned} &\text{OPT}(\mathcal{N}_3, \vec{\mathcal{S}}^O) \leq \text{OPT}(\mathbb{L}^J \backslash \mathcal{N}_2, \vec{\mathcal{S}}^J) \\ \leq\; &\text{OPT}(\mathbb{L}^J, \vec{\mathcal{S}}^J) < (etJ)\text{OPT}(\mathbb{W}^J, \vec{\mathcal{S}}^J). \end{aligned} \tag{11}$$

We now combine these three types of winners together (Inequalities (6)(10)(11)), and conclude that $\text{OPT}(\mathbb{O}, \vec{\mathcal{S}}^O) \leq \text{OPT}(\mathcal{N}_1, \vec{\mathcal{S}}^O) + \text{OPT}(\mathcal{N}_2, \vec{\mathcal{S}}^O) + \text{OPT}(\mathcal{N}_3, \vec{\mathcal{S}}^O) < (\delta_{max} + e\delta_{max}tJ^2 + etJ)\text{OPT}(\mathbb{W}^J, \vec{\mathcal{S}}^J)$. □

From the above analysis, we now can get our main result for AEGIS-MP according to Definition 4.

Theorem 4. *AEGIS-MP is an implementation of an* $\mathcal{O}(\delta_{max}tJ^2)$*-approximation in undominated strategies.*

6. EVALUATION RESULTS

In this section, we show our evaluation results. We implement AEGIS using network simulation, and compare its performance with CRWDP [5] and NSR-MP. CRWDP is an unknown single-minded combinatorial spectrum auction, and NSR-MP is a variant of AEGIS-MP. Neither CRWDP nor NSR-MP considers channel spatial reusability.

6.1 Methodology

We use two complementary datasets, namely Google Spectrum Database [9] and GoogleWiFi [32], to evaluate the performance of our mechanisms. We take Google Spectrum Database as our first dataset. We first extract WiFi nodes in an area (Latitude range: $[40°25'18'', 39°38'29'']$, Longitude range: $[-76°34'40'', -74°52'20'']$) from WiGLE.net [27], and we then query Google Spectrum Database the available TV white spaces and corresponding maximum permissible power for each WiFi node, which is considered as a portable device in the database. Portable devices can work on unused TV channel 21 through 51, except channel 37, 38, 39. To generate conflict graphs, we apply a simple Free Space propagation model [26] to predict the interference range between nodes, and consequently create the conflict graphs.[3] We also evaluate our mechanisms in a practical conflict graph, built from exhaustive signal measurements, in the second data set. The second dataset, GoogleWiFi, records 78 APs in a $7km^2$ residential area of the Google WiFi network in Mountain View, California. It was collected by a research group from UC Santa Barbara in April 2010 [32].

We build a set of auction configurations by sampling WiFi nodes in the first data set, and the number of WiFi nodes varies from 200 to 2000 with increment of 200. For the second data set, we assume the number of leasing channels can be one of three values: 6, 12 and 24. We consider the case of single-minded buyers and the case of multi-minded buyers, who can have up to 10 interested bundles (*i.e.*, $l_i \leq 10$). For each buyer i, her l_i interested channel bundles are randomly generated from her available channel set, and the valuations on bundles are uniformly distributed over $(0, 1]$. The maximum closeness parameter of valuation is set as 5, *i.e.*, $\delta_{max} = 5$. The minimum monetary unit in the auction systems is set as $\epsilon = 10^{-5}$. In AEGIS-MP, since buyers may have multiple undominated strategies at their decision points, we assume that buyers randomly select one of them. All the results of performance are averaged over 200 runs.

Metrics: We evaluate the following five metrics:

► *Social Welfare:* The sum of winning buyers' valuations on their allocated bundles of channels.

► *Revenue:* The sum of payments received from buyers.

► *Satisfaction Ratio:* The fraction of winners over buyers.

► *Channel Utilization:* The number of radios worked on each channel.

► *Channel Eccentricity:* The ratio of allocated channels over actually used channels for one buyer. In AEGIS-MP, for each winner, the final allocated bundle may contain multiple interested bundles and uninterested channels, but the winner only use one interested bundle. Therefore, we use channel eccentricity to measure this channel over-allocation.

[3]Other propagation models, *e.g.*, Egli and Longley-Rice [26], could be used to generate more accurate conflict graphs.

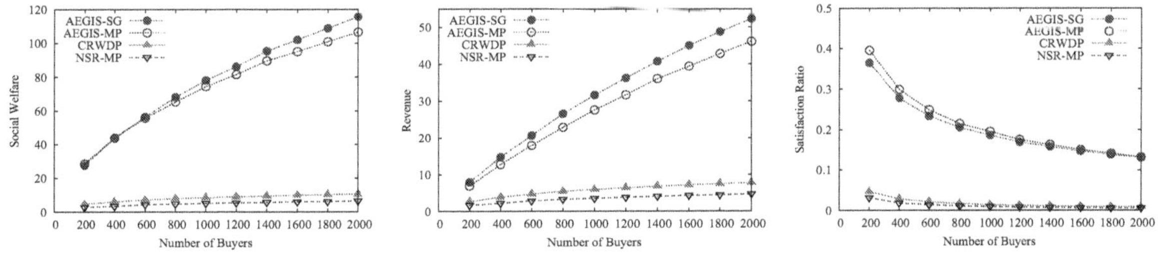

(a) Social Welfare (b) Revenue (c) Satisfaction Ratio

Figure 3: Performance of AEGIS, CRWDP and NSR-MP on Google Spectrum Dataset.

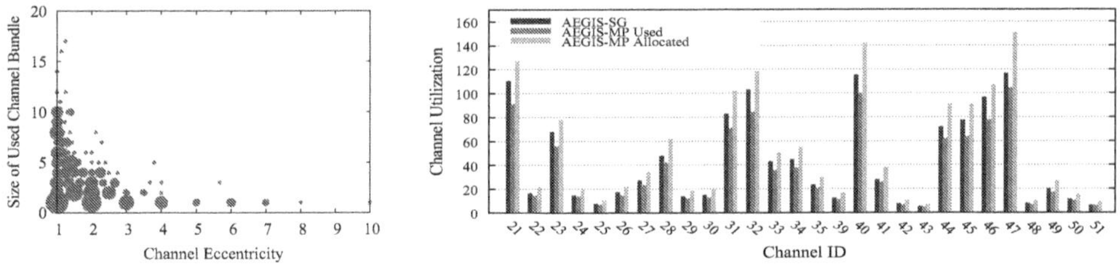

(a) Channel Eccentricity (b) Channel Utilization

Figure 4: Channel eccentricity and channel utilization of AEGIS.

6.2 Performance on Google Spectrum Dataset

By varying the number of buyers, we collect a set of performance data, as illustrated in Figure 3. We can see that AEGIS always outperforms the other two mechanisms, CRWDP and NSR-MP. This result demonstrates that exploiting channel spatial reusability can significantly improve the performance of spectrum auction systems. Figure 3 also shows that when the number of buyers increases, the social welfare and revenue increase, while the satisfaction ratio decreases. On one hand, AEGIS allocates channels more efficiently among more buyers, hence the social welfare and revenue increase. On the other hand, larger number of buyers leads to more intense competition on limited channels, thus decreases the satisfaction ratio. We also observe from Figure 3 that revenue is much lower than social welfare. Similar to previous work [31], we can institute reserve prices for channels to increase revenue, and make a trade-off between revenue and social welfare. How to determine an optimal reserve price is out of the scope of this paper. Intuitively, multi-minded auction mechanisms should perform better than single-minded ones because of the more feasible bundle choices for buyers. However, as shown in Figure 3, AEGIS-MP is slightly worse than AEGIS-SG in terms of social welfare and revenue. As we will discuss later, the channel eccentricity of winners in AEGIS-MP is the main reason for this degradation of system performance.

We now present the evaluation results of channel eccentricity and channel utilization. The channel eccentricity for AEGIS-SG is always equal to 1, because the allocated bundle is exactly buyer's interested bundle. Figure 4(a) shows the channel eccentricity of AEGIS-MP. We randomly select one instance from the 200 simulation instances when the number of buyers is fixed at 2000, and calculate the channel eccentricity for each winner. The placement of a circle in Figure 4(a) indicates one set of winners with the same channel eccentricity and the same size of used channel bundle. The size of a circle is logarithmic to the number of winners. Though some of winners' channel eccentricities are equal to 1, there exist about 67% winners, whose channel eccentricities are larger than 1. On one hand, AEGIS-MP just stimulates buyers to take undominated strategies, such that buyers can still maintain multiple bundles or uninterested channels in their active bundles during the auction. On the other hand, buyers only use the most valuable channel subset among their allocated bundles. Therefore, the size of allocated bundle can be larger than that of actually used bundle in some cases, leading to channel over-allocation.

The channel eccentricity affects the channel utilization of AEGIS-MP. By fixing the number of buyers at 2000 and running 200 simulation instances, we record the average channel utilization for each channel, and plot the results in Figure 4(b). We do not include CRWDP and NSR-MP in this analysis, because they do not consider channel spatial reusability. As shown in the figure, different TV channels have different channel utilization. The reason is that TV white spaces are spatially heterogeneous, *e.g.*, channel 47 can be accessed to almost all buyers, while channel 33 are only available to around 36% buyers. In AEGIS-MP, we distinguish between allocated channels and used channels. We can observe from Figure 4(b) that the allocated number is always larger than the used number for each channel. This is because some winners have channel eccentricity higher than 1. We can also see from Figure 4(b) that the channel utilization of AEGIS-MP is always lower than that of AEGIS-SG. The reason is that the winners with high channel eccentricity in AEGIS-MP disables some possible allocations of their interfering neighbors. From the above analysis, we can get that buyers' manipulated strategies on channel demands indeed impact the performance of spectrum auction systems.

6.3 Performance on GoogleWiFi Dataset

Figure 5 shows the system performance of AEGIS, CRWDP, and NSR-MP on GoogleWiFi dataset when there are 6, 12, 24 channels. Since channels are accessible to all buyers in this setting, we average the channel utilization on all channels on this dataset. Generally, the evaluation re-

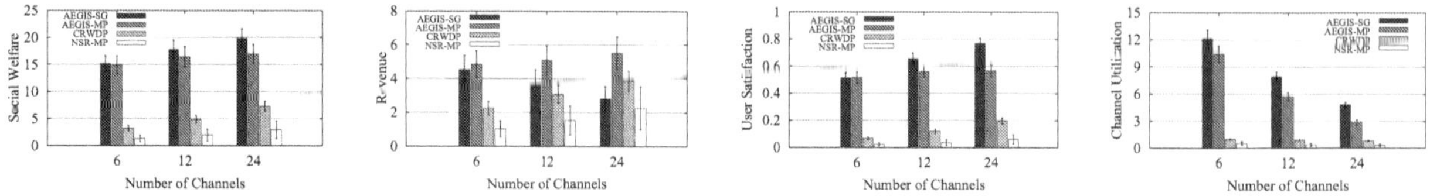

(a) Social Welfare (b) Revenue (c) Satisfaction Ratio (d) Channel Utilization

Figure 5: Performance of AEGIS, CRWDP and NSR-MP on GoogleWiFi Dataset.

sults are similar with those on Google Spectrum Dataset. Again, AEGIS achieves better performance than CRWDP and NSR-MP. Figure 5 also shows that when the number of channels increases, the social welfare and satisfaction ratio increase, and channel utilization decreases. The reason is that fixing the number of buyers, larger supply of channels results in more trades in the auction, and thus increases social welfare and satisfaction ratio. The channel utilization decreases because buyers can be allocated to more channels when the number of channels increases. For revenue, AEGIS-SG decreases with the number of channels, while AEGIS-MP, CRWDP and NSR-MP increase. The clearing price calculation in AEGIS-SG is based on critical bid. When larger number of channels are accessible in the auction, more buyers are allocated channels, reducing the critical bids for winners. Hence, the revenue of AEGIS-SG decreases. Though the clearing price of CRWDP is also calculated based on critical bid, there still exist considerable losers when the number of channels becomes large. Therefore, the critical bids for winners still stay high, so that the revenue continue to grow with the increase of channels. The clearing prices of AEGIS-MP and NSR-MP are the bids of winners at the end of the auctions. Larger supply of channels leads to more winners, and thus revenues in AEGIS-MP and NSR-MP become higher.

7. CONCLUSION

Considering the five challenges for designing a practical spectrum auction mechanism, we have proposed AEGIS, which is the first framework of unknown combinatorial auction mechanisms for heterogeneous spectrum redistribution. For the case with unknown single-minded buyers, we have designed a direct revelation combinatorial auction mechanism, call AEGIS-SG. AEGIS-SG achieves strategy-proofness and approximately efficient social welfare. We have further considered the case with unknown multi-minded buyers, and designed an iterative ascending combinatorial auction, namely AEGIS-MP. AEGIS-MP is implemented in undominated strategies, and has a good approximation ratio. We have implemented AEGIS and evaluated its performance on two practical datasets. Compared with the existing work, AEGIS achieves superior performance, in terms of social welfare, revenue, satisfaction ratio, and channel utilization.

8. REFERENCES

[1] A. Archer and E. Tardos. Truthful mechanisms for one-parameter agents. In *FOCS*, 2001.

[2] M. Babaioff, R. Lavi, and E. Pavlov. Single-value combinatorial auctions and algorithmic implementation in undominated strategies. *Journal of the ACM*, 56(1):4:1–4:32, 2009.

[3] P. Briest, P. Krysta, and B. Vöcking. Approximation techniques for utilitarian mechanism design. In *STOC*, 2005.

[4] S. Dobzinski. An impossibility result for truthful combinatorial auctions with submodular valuations. In *STOC*, 2011.

[5] M. Dong, G. Sun, X. Wang, and Q. Zhang. Combinatorial auction with time-frequency flexibility in cognitive radio networks. In *INFOCOM*, 2012.

[6] Federal Communications Commission (FCC). `http://www.fcc.gov/`.

[7] X. Feng, Y. Chen, J. Zhang, Q. Zhang, and B. Li. TAHES: Truthful double auction for heterogeneous spectrums. In *INFOCOM*, 2012.

[8] L. Gao, Y. Xu, and X. Wang. MAP: Multiauctioneer progressive auction for dynamic spectrum access. *IEEE Transactions on Mobile Computing*, 10(8):1144–1161, 2011.

[9] Google Spectrum Database. `https://www.google.com/get/spectrumdatabase/`.

[10] M. Hoefer and T. Kesselheim. Secondary spectrum auctions for symmetric and submodular bidders. In *EC*, 2012.

[11] Radio Regulations, International Telecommunication Union, Genève, 2012.

[12] M. O. Jackson. Implementation in undominated strategies: A look at bounded mechanisms. *The Review of Economic Studies*, 59(4):757–775, 1992.

[13] K. Jagannathan, I. Menache, G. Zussman, and E. Modiano. Non-cooperative spectrum access: The dedicated vs. free spectrum choice. In *MobiHoc*, 2011.

[14] Japanese Auction. `http://en.wikipedia.org/wiki/Japanese_auction`.

[15] J. Jia, Q. Zhang, Q. Zhang, and M. Liu. Revenue generation for truthful spectrum auction in dynamic spectrum access. In *MobiHoc*, 2009.

[16] P. Klemperer. How (not) to run auctions: The european 3g telecom auctions. *European Economic Review*, 46(4-5):829–845, 2002.

[17] D. Lehmann, L. I. Oćallaghan, and Y. Shoham. Truth revelation in approximately efficient combinatorial auctions. *Journal of the ACM*, 49(5):577–602, 2002.

[18] LTE Spectrum and Network Strategies. `http://www.adlittle.com/downloads/tx_adlreports/ADL_LTE_Spectrum_Network_Strategies.pdf`.

[19] A. Mas-Colell, M. D. Whinston, and J. R. Green. *Microeconomic Theory*. Oxford Press, 1995.

[20] A. Mu'alem and N. Nisan. Truthful approximation mechanisms for restricted combinatorial auctions. *Games and Economic Behavior*, 64(2):612 – 631, 2008.

[21] N. Nisan. Bidding and allocation in combinatorial auctions. In *EC*, 2000.

[22] M. J. Osborne and A. Rubenstein. *A Course in Game Theory*. MIT Press, 1994.

[23] C. Papadimitriou, M. Schapira, and Y. Singer. On the hardness of being truthful. In *FOCS*, 2008.

[24] S.-P. Sheng and M. Liu. Profit incentive in a secondary spectrum market: A contract design approach. In *INFOCOM*, 2013.

[25] Spectrum Bridge. `http://www.spectrumbridge.com/Home.aspx`.

[26] D. Tse and P. Viswanath. *Fundamentals of Wireless Communication*. Cambridge University Press, May 2005.

[27] WiGLE. `https://wigle.net/`.

[28] P. Xu, S. Wang, and X.-Y. Li. SALSA: Strategyproof online spectrum admissions for wireless networks. *IEEE Transactions on Computers*, 59(12):1691 –1702, 2010.

[29] Z. Zheng, F. Wu, and G. Chen. SMASHER: A strategy-proof combinatorial auction mechanism for heterogeneous channel redistribution. In *MobiHoc*, 2013.

[30] Z. Zheng, F. Wu, S. Tang, and G. Chen. Unknown combinatorial auction mechanisms for heterogeneous spectrum redistribution. Technical report, 2014. available at `http://www.cs.sjtu.edu.cn/~fwu/res/Paper/ZWTC14TRAEGIS.pdf`.

[31] X. Zhou, S. Gandhi, S. Suri, and H. Zheng. eBay in the sky: Strategy-proof wireless spectrum auctions. In *MobiCom*, 2008.

[32] X. Zhou, Z. Zhang, G. Wang, X. Yu, B. Y. Zhao, and H. Zheng. Practical conflict graphs for dynamic spectrum distribution. In *SIGMETRICS*, 2013.

[33] X. Zhou and H. Zheng. TRUST: A general framework for truthful double spectrum auctions. In *INFOCOM*, 2009.

Compressive Sensing meets Unreliable Link: Sparsest Random Scheduling for Compressive Data Gathering in Lossy WSNs

Xuangou Wu
Anhui University of Technology
Maanshan, China
University of Science and Technology of China
Hefei, China
wxgou@mail.ustc.edu.cn

Panlong Yang
Institute of Communication Engineering, PLAUST
Nanjing, China
panlongyang@gmail.com

Taeho Jung
Illinois Institute of Technology
Chicago,USA
tjung@hawk.iit.edu

Yan Xiong
University of Science and Technology of China
Hefei, China
yxiong@ustc.edu.cn

Xiao Zheng
Anhui University of Technology
Maanshan,China
zhx@ahut.edu.cn

ABSTRACT

Compressive Sensing (CS) has been recognized as a promising technique to reduce and balance the transmission cost in wireless sensor networks (WSNs). Existing efforts mainly focus on applying CS to reliable WSNs, namely, each wireless link is 100% reliable. However, our experimental results show that traditional compressive data gathering (CDG) could result in arbitrarily bad recovery performance, when the wireless links are lossy. In this paper, we study the impact of packet loss on compressive data gathering and ways to improve its robustness using sparsest random scheduling (SRS). The key idea of our scheme is to treat each sampling value as one CS measurement, which helps us to reduce the impact of packet loss on the recovery accuracy. Our scheme also outperforms the tradition CDG in reliable WSNs in that our scheme has significantly lowered transmission cost. To achieve this, we present a sparsest measurement matrix where each row has only one nonzero element. More importantly, we propose a representation basis to sparsify the gathering data, and prove that our measurement matrix satisfies the restricted isometric property (RIP) with high probability. Extensive experimental results show our scheme can recover the data accurately with packet loss ratio up to 15%, while traditional CDG can hardly recover the data under similar or even better conditions.

MobiHoc'14, August 11–14, 2014, Philadelphia, PA, USA.

http://dx.doi.org/10.1145/2632951.2632969 .

Categories and Subject Descriptors:

C.2.1 [Computer-Communication Networks]: Network Operations, Network monitoring

Keywords

Data gathering, compressive sensing, sparsest random scheduling, restricted isometry property.

1. INTRODUCTION

Wireless sensor networks (WSNs) have been widely used for collectively monitoring and disseminating information about various phenomena of interest [7, 31]. For example, ExScal [1] is an intrusion detection network with more than 1000 sensor nodes. And typically, GreenOrbs [11] and CitySee [15] systems have been built for continuously collecting environmental data including temperature, humidity, illumination, and carbon dioxide etc. Leveraging the spatial-temporal properties in sensory data from real deployments, many Compressive Sensing (CS) based data gathering techniques have been proposed to reduce and balance the in-network data transmission cost (e.g. [13, 16, 17, 25, 26, 29]). As far as we are concerned, all existing works on compressive data gathering (CDG) focus on reliable WSNs, without considering the impact of packet loss on the recovery performance. Unfortunately, our experimental results show that the recovery performance of traditional CDG could be seriously degraded by packet loss, e.g., the recovery accuracy could be arbitrarily bad even with 2% packet loss rate. This problem is especially pronounced in many large scale sensor networks whose packet loss ratio could reach 20% [14]. The prevalence of unreliable links in real-world WSNs [11] has posed a fundamental challenge for maintaining the recovery accuracy under unsatisfactory and lossy conditions.

In general, there are two reasons preventing the traditional CDG from working well in lossy network. (1) There are too many sensors involved for gathering single measurement, when adopting tree-based routing, one packet loss may cause severe decrease on the quality of that measurement; (2) CS theory is originally developed for minimizing the number of measurements, rather than the cost of each measurement, unfortunately, so far we can not find any representation basis for making the measurement matrix sufficiently sparse. To address such deficiencies, we develop a novel CDG scheme that achieves good resilience to packet loss. In our scheme, unlike the traditional CDG, each row of the measurement matrix contains only one nonzero element and each sampling value is considered as one CS measurement. In spite of some existing research in this direction [26][27], our work differs from theirs in that: (1) in sparse random projections [26], each row of measurement matrix requires $O(\log N)$ nonzero elements where N is the network size; (2) single sensor temporal random scheduling data gathering [27] suffers from a lack of a decent theoretical analysis, and this scheme can not work in distributed WSNs. In contrast, we find a suitable representation basis based on Gaussian joint distribution model. More importantly, we are the first to prove that the proposed measurement matrix and representation basis satisfy restricted isometric property (RIP) with high probability, this guarantees that the gathered data can be accurately recovered at the sink. The contributions of this paper are three folds.

(1) We are the first to investigate the impact of packet loss on the performance of traditional CDG in terms of recovery accuracy. We show that the recovery accuracy could be very bad even with 2% packet loss ratio. This motivates us to revisit and enhance existing CDG for achieving better resilience to packet loss.

(2) We propose a novel sparsest random scheduling based CDG scheme (SRS-DG). We present a detailed characterization of its performance through both analytical and numerical results. Our scheme can reduce the impact of packet loss on the recovery accuracy. We also prove that the proposed measurement matrix and representation basis satisfy RIP with high probability.

(3) We empirically demonstrate the effectiveness of our scheme on real data set from CitySee [15]. In particular, we show that the recovery error of our scheme is only 0.1 with packet loss ratio up to 15%. In contrast, traditional CDG can hardly recover the data under similar or even better conditions.

The rest of this paper is organized as follows. In section 2 presents the preliminaries of CS. The motivation and challenges are given in section 3. The detailed design of SRS-DG is presented in Section 4. In section 5, we provide the transmission cost analysis of SRS-DG and its algorithm implementation. Section 6 reports our experimental results. We present a literature review of existing work in section 7 and make a conclusion in Section 8.

2. PRELIMINARIES

CS is a new compression and sampling paradigm compared with traditional Shannon's sampling theorem [2, 4, 10]. CS theory asserts that a relatively small number linear combination of a compressible or sparse signal can contain most of its salient information. Assuming that $\mathbf{s} \in \mathbb{R}^N$ is a k-sparse signal, which is only k nonzero components or $(N-k)$ smallest components can be ignored. Thus, the information can be extracted from $\mathbf{s}$ by $\mathbf{y} = \Phi\mathbf{s}$, where Φ is an $M \times N$ measurement matrix, $\mathbf{y} \in \mathbb{R}^M$ is measurement vector and $M \ll N$. To recover the signal $\mathbf{s}$, two problems need to be answered: (1) How to design Φ such that the salient information can be extracted from any k-sparse signal? (2) How to design recovery algorithm to reconstruct $\mathbf{s}$ from $\mathbf{y}$? To answer the first problem, Φ should satisfy the restricted isometric property (RIP) [6]:

DEFINITION 1 ([6]). *A matrix Φ satisfies the restricted isometry property (RIP) of order k if there exists a $\delta \in (0,1)$ such that*

$$(1-\delta)\|\mathbf{s}\|_2^2 \le \|\Phi\mathbf{s}\|_2^2 \le (1+\delta)\|\mathbf{s}\|_2^2 \quad (1)$$

for all k-sparse vectors $\mathbf{s} \in \mathbb{R}^N$.

Candès, Romberg, and Tao [5] and Donoho [10] have shown many random matrices that satisfy the RIP such as Gaussian identity distribution matrix, ±1 Bernoulli matrix and so on.

To answer the second problem, the signal $\mathbf{s}$ can be recovered via ℓ_1 optimization as

$$\hat{\mathbf{s}} = \arg\min_{\mathbf{s}} \|\mathbf{s}\|_1 \quad s.t. \ \mathbf{y} = \Phi\mathbf{s} \quad (2)$$

If Φ satisfies RIP and $M \ge O(k \cdot log(N/k))$, then $\mathbf{s}$ can be recovered successfully with high probability. If the measurement vector $\mathbf{y}$ contains noise, then the signal $\mathbf{s}$ can be recovered via

$$\hat{\mathbf{s}} = \arg\min_{\mathbf{s}} \|\mathbf{s}\|_1 \quad s.t. \ \|\Phi\mathbf{s} - \mathbf{y}\|_2^2 \le \epsilon \quad (3)$$

where ϵ bounds the noise. There already exist many efficient algorithms to solve the above problems such as basis pursuit [6], orthogonal matching pursuit (OMP) algorithm [24], CoSaMP [20] and so on.

However, the real sensory signals are almost compressible signals instead of sparse signal. Compressible signal can usually be transformed into sparse signal via representation basis transformation. For example, a smooth signal $\mathbf{x} \in \mathbb{R}^N$ can usually be transformed into a sparse signal $\mathbf{s}$ under discrete cosine transformation (DCT) basis or discrete wavelet transformation (DWT) basis. The measurement vector $\mathbf{y}$ can be expressed as

$$\mathbf{y} = \Phi\mathbf{x} = \Phi\Psi\mathbf{s} \quad (4)$$

where Ψ is a $N \times N$ representation basis. If $\Phi\Psi$ satisfies RIP, the sparse signal $\mathbf{s}$ can be recovered accurately with high probability. Then $\mathbf{x}$ can be recovered via $\mathbf{x} = \Psi\mathbf{s}$.

3. MOTIVATION AND CHALLENGES

In this section, we will analyze the recovery performance of traditional CDG in lossy WSNs, and demonstrate that the recovery accuracy is seriously impacted by data packet loss. Based on the experimental results from real deployments, we further investigate the reasons why traditional CDG is not robust to packet loss. Correspondingly, we present the idea of SRS-DG that guarantees good recovery performance even under severe packet loss.

Observation: Our experiments were performed on a real-world data set from CitySee system [19]. CitySee system was deployed in an urban area of Wuxi City, China, which contained thousands of wireless sensor nodes for environmental monitoring. In CitySee system, each sensor sampled once every 10 minutes and sent its sampling value to the sink. We evaluate sensory data recovery performance of traditional CDG under different data packet loss ratios and different number of CS measurements. In our experiment, Gaussian

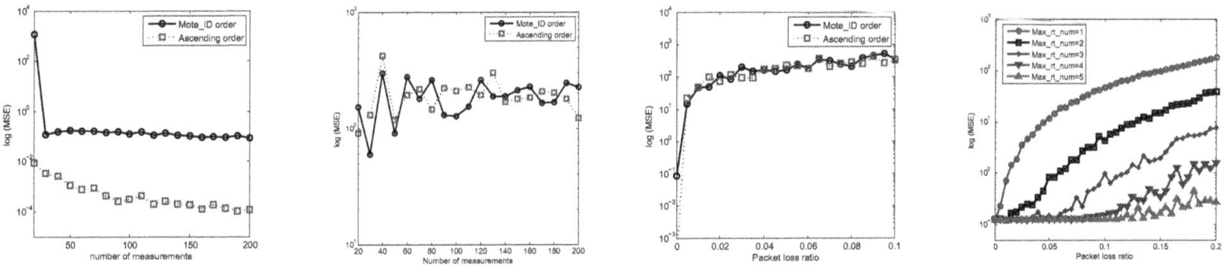

(a) *pl_ratio* = 0 (b) *pl_ratio* = 0.05 (c) $M = 120$ (d) $M = 120$

Figure 1: Recovery error comparisons. (a) No data packet loss. (b) Different number of measurements without retransmission. (c) Different data packet loss ratio without retransmission. (d) Different data packet loss ratio with retransmission.

random matrix and discrete cosine transformation (DCT) are considered as measurement matrix and sparse representation basis, which are denoted by Φ and Ψ_t respectively. The experimental data set is 256 temperature sampling values in the same time interval from 256 sensors. First, we sort the sensory data by Mote_ID order. For better justification, we also evaluate their recovery performance under different orders. Notice that in practice, it is impossible to reorder the sensory data according to their value which is unknown at the beginning. The sparse level under Mote_ID order is around 25, and the sparse level under ascending order is around 5.

Next, we evaluate the recovery performance of the traditional CDG under three different network configurations. (1) Sensor network is reliable without data packet loss. (2) Sensor network is unreliable without allowing lost packet retransmission. (3) Sensor network is unreliable with allowing lost packet retransmission. We build a routing tree containing 256 sensor nodes. Each packet is dropped at random with uniform probability (packet loss ratio) on each link. To simplify the expression, the packet loss ratio and the number of measurements are denoted by *pl_ratio* and M respectively. In our experiment, we use mean square error (MSE) as the recovery error metric. Fig 1 (a) shows the recovery error with no data packet loss. Two types orders sensory data can be recovered accurately, the recovery error of Mote_ID order is decreased within 0.1 (MSE) with at least 30 measurements. And the recovery error of ascending order is even less than 0.01 (MSE) with at least 20 measurements. Fig 1 (b) shows the recovery error under *pl_ratio* = 5% without lost packet retransmission. The recovery error is higher than 60 in the majority of cases. It demonstrates that the sensory data can hardly be recovered under both ascending order and Mote_ID order. Moreover, even we increase the number of measurements, the recovery performance is still poor. Fig 1 (c) displays the recovery error under different packet loss ratios without retransmission. The result shows that the recovery performance could be very bad even with low packet loss ratio (*pl_ratio* < 2%). We next evaluate the recovery performance with retransmissions. Fig 1 (d) depicts the mean recovery error under different *maximum number of retransmissions*, which is denoted by *Max_rt_num*. Unfortunately, limited number of retransmissions does not help much in improving the recovery accuracy. Moreover, retransmission may cause extra communication overhead which is clearly undesirable. This issue is especially pronounced in many large scale sensor

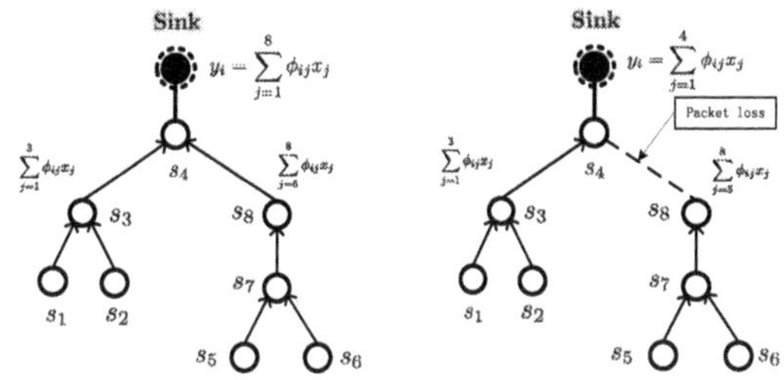

(a) Reliable Network (b) Lossy Network

Figure 2: CS based data gathering in tree routing network.

networks, the average packet loss ratio could still reach 20% with *Max_rt_num* = 30 [14].

Insight: We identify at least two reasons why traditional CDG can not achieve satisfactory recovery performance under lossy WSNs. The first reason is that there are too many sensors involved for gathering single measurement, therefore one packet loss may cause severe drop on the quality of that measurement; The second reason is that CS theory is originally developed for minimizing the number of measurements, rather than the cost of gathering each measurement, unfortunately, so far we can not find any presentation basis for making the measurement matrix sufficient sparse. Although CS theory asserts that it has a strong robustness to noise and data loss [5], distributed sensor networks has many unique features which make traditional CS theory not capable of handling the packet loss. For example, Fig 2 displays the data packet loss under tree based routing. Let s denote the j^t sensor, the corresponding sampling value and projection element are x and ϕ respectively ($j = 1, 2, \cdots, 8$). Fig 2 (b) shows that the data packet of s_8 is lost when it is sent to s_4 during the i^t measurement gathering. Because the i^t measurement is calculated as $y = \sum^{8}_{=1} \phi \ x$, all involved sensory data including x_5, x_6, x_7, and x_8 would be lost. In this case, one packet loss could cause severe drop on the quality of gathered measurements. Because this case could happen to every measurement, simply increasing the number of measurements can not improve the recovery performance.

Challenges: We now investigate how to reduce (or possibly avoid) the consequences of data packet loss on the quality of gathered measurements. Intuitively, if each measurement is represented by only one sampling value, then the received measurements only contains sampling noise. This is because the sink would either gather the entire measurement successfully or lose the entire measurement. Traditional CS theory focuses on minimizing the number of measurements, rather than the number of participation nodes for each measurement. It requires the measurement matrix to satisfy any orthogonal representation basis of compression signal. Although Donoho *et al.* proposed that the partial fourier coefficient can also recover original signal ([5, 10]), it is not suitable for distributed WSNs.

In this paper, we aim to let each sampling value represent one CS measurement. If this goal can be realized, we can reduce both the data transmission cost, and, more importantly, the consequences of packet loss on the data recovery. Then it is possible to develop a novel CDG which can be used even in lossy sensor networks. However, achieving this goal is not trivial, there are two primary challenges: The first challenge is to design appropriate measurement matrix and representation basis, this is critical sparsifying the sensory data and letting each sensory value represent one measurement; The second challenge is to ensure that the sensory data can be accurately recovered under the previous design. To overcome these challenges, we develop a novel CDG scheme SRS-DG in the rest of this paper.

4. SRS-DG DESIGN

In this section, we provide the detailed design and analysis of each sampling values as one CS measurement, namely, the measurement matrix and representation basis design and analyze in SRS-DG. To let each sampling value represent one CS measurement, each row of the measurement matrix should contain only one nonzero element. In order to facilitate the expression, we call this type of measurement matrix as *sparsest measurement matrix*, and the data gathering process as *sparsest random scheduling* for data gathering (SRS-DG). In Section 4.1, we present our sparsest measurement matrix design and its rationale. Accordingly, in Section 4.2, we design a suitable representation basis. We verify that our representation basis can sparsify the spatial correlation sensory data in Section 4.3. We also prove that the sparsest measurement matrix and representation basis satisfy RIP with high probability in Section 4.4, this ensures high recovery accuracy.

Assume that there are N sampling values that need to be gathered, which are denoted by $\mathbf{x} = [x_1, x_2, \cdots, x_N]^T$. During the data gathering, the measurement matrix is denoted by $\Phi = [\phi_1, \phi_2, \cdots, \phi_N]^T$, the i^t CS measurement is calculated as $y = \sum_{=1}^{N} \phi \ x$. If ϕ is nonzero, the j^t sensor node requires to participate in the i^t CS measurement gathering.

4.1 Measurement matrix design and analysis

In this subsection, we present the design of sparsest measurement matrix, where each sampling value represents one CS measurement. We also present the design rationale behind our sparsest measurement matrix.

Measurement matrix design: To balance the resource consumption in WSNs, it is reasonable to define our sparsest measurement matrix Φ as

$$\Phi \ (i,j) = \begin{cases} 1 & j = r \\ 0 & otherwise \end{cases} \quad (5)$$

where $i = 1, 2, \cdots M$, $j = 1, 2, \cdots N$, r represent the independent and identically distributed random indices, and $r < r_{+1}$, $r \in [1, N]$. Based on the definition of Φ , each row of Φ has only one nonzero element. Then, one round of data gathering can be expressed as

$$\mathbf{x_r} = \begin{bmatrix} x_1 \\ x_2 \\ \vdots \\ x_M \end{bmatrix} = \begin{bmatrix} \phi_1 \\ \phi_2 \\ \vdots \\ \phi_M \end{bmatrix} \begin{bmatrix} x_1 \\ x_2 \\ \vdots \\ x_N \end{bmatrix} \quad (6)$$

where $\mathbf{x_r}$ is CS measurement vector, ϕ_i represents the i^t row of Φ . If $\mathbf{x_r}$ is reconstructed by $\mathbf{x}$ based on CS theory, then the decoder can be expressed as

$$\hat{\mathbf{s}} = \arg\min_{\mathbf{s}} \|\mathbf{s}\|_1 \ s.t. \ \|\Phi \ \Psi\mathbf{s} - \mathbf{x_r}\|_2^2 \leq \epsilon \quad (7)$$

where $\mathbf{s} = \Psi^{-1}\mathbf{x}$, Ψ is orthogonal basis of $\mathbf{x}$, ϵ bounds the noise in $\mathbf{x_r}$, $\hat{\mathbf{s}}$ is the recovery signals of $\mathbf{s}$.

Feasibility analysis: The design of sparsest measurement matrix ensures that each sampling value represents one CS measurement, and reduces the impact of packet loss on the recovery performance. The next challenge is to design an appropriate representation basis, by taking into account both the data transmission cost and data recovery quality. In particular, an appropriate representation basis, Ψ, should satisfy the following two conditions: (1) Ψ can sparsify the gathering sensory data; and (2) $\Phi \ \Psi$ satisfies RIP with high probability.

We next demonstrate, from the information extraction aspect, why each row of our measurement matrix contains only one nonzero element. If sensory data $\mathbf{x}$ is sparse under representation basis Ψ, it can be recovered from a small number of CS measurements (i.e., $\mathbf{y} = \Phi\mathbf{x} = \Phi\Psi\mathbf{s}$). The decoding process is to recover the sparse signal $\mathbf{s}$ instead of directly recovering the sensory data $\mathbf{x}$. The sparse signal $\mathbf{s}$ can be recovered because each component of $\mathbf{y}$ contains a part of information of $\mathbf{s}$, namely, each component of $\mathbf{y}$ is a linear combination of $\mathbf{s}$. However, each component of $\mathbf{x}$ is also a linear combination of $\mathbf{s}$. Each component of $\mathbf{x}$ and $\mathbf{y}$ contains the information of the sparse signal $\mathbf{s}$. So, if we design or select a suitable representation basis and make it satisfy RIP with sparsest measurement matrix, the sparse signal $\mathbf{s}$ can be recovered from a part of $\mathbf{x}$.

In what follows, we give the detailed design of our representation basis and illustrate why it satisfies the above two conditions.

4.2 Representation basis design

In [5, 10], Donoho *et al.* have shown that many random matrices satisfy the RIP with any orthonormal representation basis. In addition, they show that if one can find a sparsity representation basis which is similar to a certain random matrix, it is possible to satisfy RIP. Our representation basis is developed based on the correlation of sensory data.

As real-world environmental data usually exhibit strong spatial correlation, Gaussian joint distribution is an effective and reasonable model for further theoretical analysis [9]. Without loss of generality, we define Gaussian kernel function, $\mathcal{K}(x \ , x \ )$, as $\mathcal{K}(x \ , x \ ) = exp\{\frac{-\ _{ij}^{2}}{2\sigma^2}\}$, where $\mathcal{K}(x \ , x \ )$ represents the correlation between x and x , d is the distance between the i^t sensor and the j^t sensor. How much effect between x and x depends on the parameter σ, $\mathcal{K}(x \ , x \ ) = 1$. The parameter σ can be estimated from

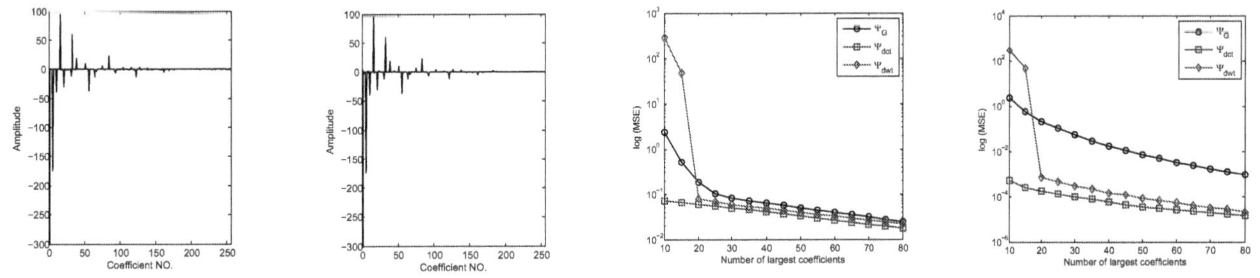

(a) (b) (c) (d)

Figure 3: The transformed signal and recovery error comparisons. (a) Transformed coefficients with Mote_ID order. (b) Transformed coefficients with ascending order. (c) Recovery error comparison with Mote_ID order. (d) Recovery error comparison with Ascending order.

training sensory data by maximum likelihood or Bayesian framework [22]. Based on the above assumptions, the correlation matrix G with N sensor points can be expressed as

$$G = \begin{bmatrix} e^{\frac{-d_{11}^2}{2\sigma^2}} & e^{\frac{-d_{12}^2}{2\sigma^2}} & \cdots & e^{\frac{-d_{1N}^2}{2\sigma^2}} \\ e^{\frac{-d_{21}^2}{2\sigma^2}} & e^{\frac{-d_{22}^2}{2\sigma^2}} & \cdots & e^{\frac{-d_{2N}^2}{2\sigma^2}} \\ \vdots & \vdots & \vdots & \vdots \\ e^{\frac{-d_{N1}^2}{2\sigma^2}} & e^{\frac{-d_{N2}^2}{2\sigma^2}} & \cdots & e^{\frac{-d_{NN}^2}{2\sigma^2}} \end{bmatrix} \quad (8)$$

We map N sensors into 2-dimensional array based on real locations and the distance between neighboring sensors is unitary. Then, G is a Toeplitz matrix which can be diagonalized, namely, G can be expressed as $G = \Psi \Lambda \Psi^{-1}$, where Ψ is orthonormal eigenvector basis, Λ is the diagonal matrix whose diagonal entries are the corresponding eigenvalues of G. We use Ψ as an orthonormal representation basis, then $\mathbf{x}$ can be represented by $\mathbf{x} = \Psi \mathbf{s}$, where $\mathbf{s}$ is transformed signal ($\mathbf{s} = \Psi^{-1}\mathbf{x}$). If $\mathbf{s}$ is sparse and $\Phi \Psi$ satisfy RIP, Ψ would be considered as a representation basis of sparsest random projections.

4.3 Does Ψ sparsify sensory data?

In this section, we experimentally show that Ψ indeed sparsifyies the spatial correlation signal. We also give statistical analysis of Ψ to explain why it can sparsify the spatial correlated sensory data. To evaluate the sparse performance of Ψ , we compare it with DCT basis and DWT basis, which are denoted by Ψ_t and Ψ_{wt} respectively.

Experimental verification: We use the same data set as in Section 3. We still examine two orders: Mote_ID order and ascending order. Ascending order exhibits stronger spatial correlation, and Mote_ID order has weaker spatial correlation.

Fig 3 (a) and (b) show the transformed coefficients under Ψ corresponding to two orders. The transformed coefficients under Ψ are mainly concentrated in a few components, both orders have a good sparse performance. To recover a compressible signal based on CS theory, the number of CS measurement is proportional to the sparsity of the sensory data. For the same spatial correlated signal, different representation basis obtain different sparse level signal. Fig 3 (c) and (d) show the recovery quality under different numbers of largest transformed coefficients corresponding to different orders. The number of largest transformed coefficients can be considered as sparse level of transformed signal. Fig 3 (c) shows that Ψ can sparsify our sensory data, its performance is very close to the one of Ψ_t and

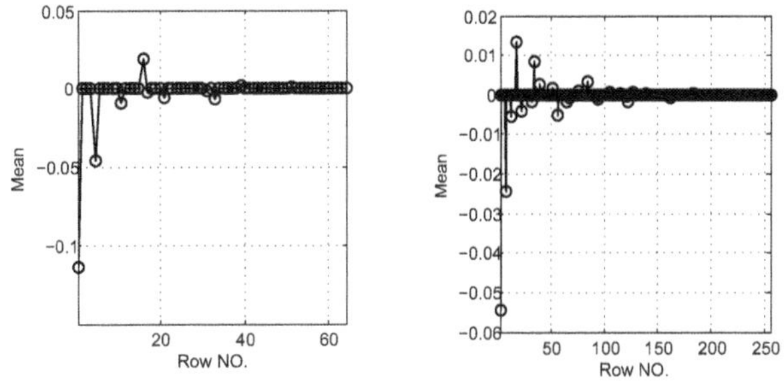

(a) N=64 (b) N=256

Figure 4: The mean of every row of Ψ^{-1} with $\sigma^2 = 1$ and different N.

4-layer 'haar' Ψ_{wt}. Fig 3 (d) illustrates that the recovery performance of Ψ is not as good as Ψ_t and Ψ_{wt}, this is because ascending order is a theoretical ideal case.

Statistical analysis: We also illustrate that Ψ can sparsify the spatial correlation data through analyzing the mean and variance of its row elements. Fig 4 shows the mean of every row of Ψ^{-1} with $\sigma^2 = 1$ and $N = 64$, 256, there are only a few rows whose mean values are nonzero. This also explains that why the transformed signal $\mathbf{s}$, $\mathbf{s} = \Psi^{-1}\mathbf{x}$, is sparse when the spatial correlation signal $\mathbf{x}$ changes smoothly. For the real sensory data, we can learn the optimal value of σ based on the historic sensory data. Based on the above analysis, we show that Ψ can efficiently sparsify the spatial correlated signal.

4.4 Does $\Phi \Psi$ Obey RIP?

In this subsection, we prove that $\Phi \Psi$ satisfy RIP with high probability, this ensures high recovery accuracy. We first present the statistic properties of Ψ . The mean and variance of each row in Ψ with $N = 256$ are shown in Fig 5 (a) and (b) respectively. Both the mean and variance of each row are very stable. Fig 5 (c) illustrates the actual percentage of the mean of each row in the range of $(-0.02, 0.02)$ and N times variance of each row in the range of $(-0.05, 0.05)$. Fig 5 (c) illustrates that both the mean and variance of each row exhibit similar trends with the increasing of N. Based on the law of large numbers, each row of Ψ can be considered as a random sequence generated by a random variable. Ψ is generated by N random variables denoted by $\xi_1, \xi_2, \cdots \xi_N$. These random variables have the same numerical characteristics, namely, $\mathbb{E}(\xi\ ) = 0$, $\mathrm{Var}(\xi\ ) = \mathbb{E}(\xi^2) = 1/N$, $(i = 1, 2, \cdots, N)$.

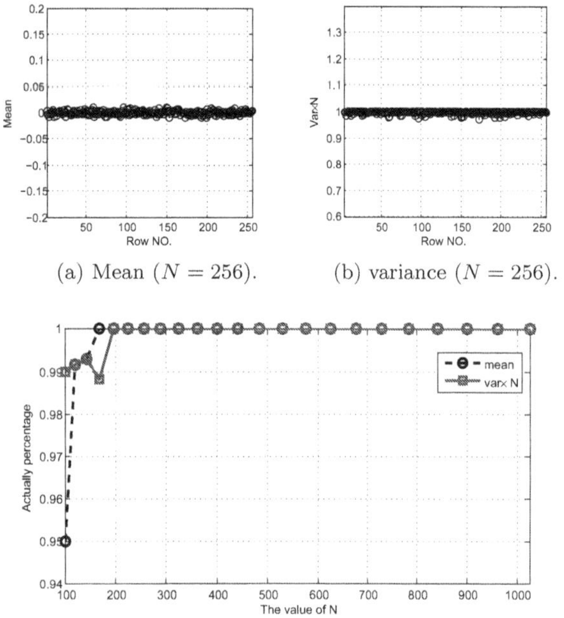

(a) Mean ($N = 256$). (b) variance ($N = 256$).

(c) Actual percentage of mean and variance.

Figure 5: The mean and variance of every row of Ψ with $\sigma^2 = 1$ and different N values.

Let $\Theta = \Phi\ \Psi\ $, since the nonzero elements of each row of Φ are independent of each other, we can assume that each row of Θ is chosen independently at random from Ψ . Meanwhile, Θ is generated by $(i.i.d)$ random variables $\xi_{\ 1}, \xi_{\ 2}, \cdots, \xi_{\ M}$. In the following, we give the definition of *sub-Gaussian* and the related corollary.

DEFINITION 2 (**sub-Gaussian** [3]). *A random variable ξ is called sub-Gaussian if there exists a constant $c > 0$ such that $\forall \lambda \in \mathbb{R}$*

$$\mathbb{E}\left(e^{\lambda \xi}\right) \leq e^{\ 2\lambda^2/2} \tag{9}$$

We say $\xi \sim Sub(c^2)$ iff ξ satisfies the above inequality.

COROLLARY 1. *If the i^t row of Θ is considered as a sequence generated by random variables $\xi_{\ i}$ $(i = 1, 2, ..., M)$, then $\xi_{\ i} \sim Sub(2)$.*

PROOF. Because $\mathbb{E}(\xi_{r_i}) = 0$ and $\mathrm{Var}(\xi_{r_i}) = \mathbb{E}(\xi^2_{r_i}) = 1/N$, then for all $\lambda \in \mathbb{R}$

$$\begin{aligned}\mathbb{E}\left(e^{\lambda \xi_{r_i}}\right) &= \mathbb{E}\left(\sum_{=0}^{\infty} \frac{\lambda\ \xi_{r_i}}{n!}\right) = 1 + \sum_{=2}^{\infty} \frac{\lambda\ \mathbb{E}\left(\xi_{r_i}\right)}{n!} \\ &\leq 1 + \sum_{=2}^{\infty} \frac{\lambda}{n!} \leq e^{|\lambda|} - |\lambda| \leq e^{2\lambda^2/2} \end{aligned} \tag{10}$$

The proof of $e^{|\lambda|} - |\lambda| \leq e^{2\lambda^2/2}$ is given in Appendix. So, $\xi_{r_i} \sim Sub(2)$, $(i = 1, 2, \cdots, N)$. ☐

THEOREM 1 ([8]). *Suppose $\xi_{\mathbf{r}} = [\xi_{\ 1}, \xi_{\ 2}, \cdots, \xi_{\ M}]^T$, where each $\xi_{\ i}$ is i.i.d. $\xi_{\ i} \sim Sub(c^2)$ and $\mathbb{E}\left(\xi^2_{\ i}\right) = \sigma^2$. Then*

$$\mathbb{E}\left(||\xi_{\ i}||_2^2\right) = M\sigma^2 \tag{11}$$

Moreover, $\forall \alpha \in (0,1), \forall \beta \in [c^2/\sigma^2, \beta\ \ ]$, there exists a constant c^* such that $\mathbb{P}\left(||\xi_{\mathbf{r}}||_2^2 \leq \alpha M\sigma^2\right) \leq e^{(-M(1-\alpha)^2/\ ^*)}$ and $\mathbb{P}\left(||\xi_{\mathbf{r}}||_2^2 \geq \beta M\sigma^2\right) \leq e^{(-M(\beta-1)^2/\ ^*)}$.

In the following theorem, we prove that Θ satisfies RIP with probability tending to 1.

THEOREM 2. *Fix $\delta \in (0,1)$ and each row of Θ satisfies $Sub(2)$, if $M = O(k\log(N/k))$, then with high probability, Θ satisfies $(1-\delta) \leq \frac{||\Theta \mathbf{v}||_2^2}{||\mathbf{v}||_2^2} \leq (1+\delta)$ for all N-dimensional k-sparse signal $\mathbf{v}$.*

PROOF. Suppose that the i^t row of Θ is generated by $\xi_{\ i}$. Because each row of Θ is randomly selected based on scheduling sensor, $\xi_{\ 1}, \xi_{\ 2}, \cdots, \xi_{\ M}$ is *i.i.d.* with $\xi_{\ i} \sim Sub(2)$. To simplify the proof, we normalize Θ and $\Theta = \sqrt{N/M}[\theta_1, \theta_2, \cdots, \theta_M]^T$, $\mathbb{E}(\theta\ \ ) = 0$ and $\mathrm{Var}(\theta\ \ ) = \mathbb{E}(\theta^2\ ) = 1/N$. We have

$$\begin{aligned}\mathbb{E}(< \sqrt{\frac{N}{M}}\theta\ , \mathbf{v} >) &= \mathbb{E}(\sqrt{\frac{N}{M}} \sum_{=1}^{N} \theta\ \ v\ \ ) \\ &= \sqrt{\frac{N}{M}} \sum_{=1}^{N} \mathbb{E}(\theta\ \ ) v\ \ = 0 \end{aligned} \tag{12}$$

$$\begin{aligned}\mathrm{Var}(< \sqrt{\frac{N}{M}}\theta\ , \mathbf{v} >) &= \mathrm{Var}(\sqrt{\frac{N}{M}} \sum_{=1}^{N} \theta\ \ v\ \ ) \\ &= \frac{N}{M} \sum_{=1}^{N} \mathrm{Var}(\theta\ \ ) v^2 = \frac{1}{M} \sum_{=1}^{N} v^2 = \frac{||\mathbf{v}||_2^2}{M} \end{aligned} \tag{13}$$

$$\begin{aligned}\mathbb{E}(||\Theta \mathbf{v}||_2^2) &= \mathbb{E}(\sum_{=1}^{M} (< \sqrt{\frac{N}{M}}\theta\ , \mathbf{v} >)^2) \\ &= \sum_{=1}^{M} \mathbb{E}(< \sqrt{\frac{N}{M}}\theta\ , \mathbf{v} >)^2 = \sum_{=1}^{M} \mathrm{Var}(< \sqrt{\frac{N}{M}}\theta\ , \mathbf{v} >) \\ &= \sum_{=1}^{M} \frac{||\mathbf{v}||_2^2}{M} = ||\mathbf{v}||_2^2 \end{aligned} \tag{14}$$

Based on Theorem 1, we set $\alpha = 1 - \delta$ and $\beta = 1 + \delta$, and the following inequality can be obtained $\mathbb{P}\left(\frac{||\Theta \mathbf{v}||_2^2}{||\mathbf{v}||_2^2} \leq 1 - \delta\right) \leq e^{-M\delta^2/\ ^*}$ and $\mathbb{P}\left(\frac{||\Theta \mathbf{v}||_2^2}{||\mathbf{v}||_2^2} \geq 1 + \delta\right) \leq e^{-M\delta^2/\ ^*}$, then we have

$$\mathbb{P}\left(\left|\frac{||\Theta \mathbf{v}||_2^2}{||\mathbf{v}||_2^2} - 1\right| \geq \delta\right) \leq 2e^{-M\delta^2/\ ^*} \tag{15}$$

Since there are $(N,\ k)$ possible k-dimensional subspaces of Θ, based on Sterling's approximation, we have $(N,\ k) \leq (eN/k)\ $, and the probability of k-sparse signal $\mathbf{v}$ which satisfies $\left|\frac{||\Theta \mathbf{v}||_2^2}{||\mathbf{v}||_2^2} - 1\right| \geq \delta$ is

$$(eN/k)\ \ \cdot 2e^{-\frac{M\delta^2}{c^*}} = 2e^{-\frac{M\delta^2}{c^*} + \ \log(\frac{N}{k}) + 1} \tag{16}$$

Therefore, when $M = O(k\log(N/k))$, the probability of Θ satisfies $(1-\delta) \leq \frac{||\Theta \mathbf{v}||_2^2}{||\mathbf{v}||_2^2} \leq (1+\delta)$ for all k-sparse signal $\mathbf{v}$, it trends to 1. ☐

According to the above analysis, we know that Ψ can sparsify spatial correlation signal, and satisfy the RIP with Φ as well.

5. IMPLEMENTATION AND ANALYSIS

In this section, we first give the algorithm implementation of sparsest random scheduling for data gathering (SRS-DG), and then analyze the transmission cost of our scheme.

5.1 Algorithm Implementation

To implement SRS-DG scheme, we first investigate how to select M random scheduling sensors from N sensors to meet Φ . Then we focus on how to adaptively adjust the number of CS measurements based on the recovery error from the previous rounds. For the first task, we develop a probabilistic scheduling strategy which can satisfy the proposed measurement matrix and ensure balanced sensor participation. For the second task, we utilize the recovery error of currently received sampling values to adjust our probabilistic scheduling. We next detailize the implementation of SRS-DG, which contains two components of algorithm implementation. (1) The sink component is responsible for the sensory data recovery and random scheduling probability assignment/adjustment as shown in Algorithm 1. (2) Each sensor component is responsible for sampling and transmitting data to the sink as shown in Algorithm 2.

Sink Component: In Algorithm 1, the inputs are representation basis Ψ , upper bound ϵ_{ub}, lower bound ϵ_{b} on recovery error, and the scheduling probability step length $\triangle p$. In the initializing stage, the scheduling probability is set to 1. The outputs are the recovery sensory data $\hat{\mathbf{x}}$ and sensor scheduling probability p_s. $\hat{\mathbf{x}}$ and $\hat{\mathbf{x}}_{\mathbf{r}}$ are denoted as recovery sparse signal, the whole recovery sensory data, and recovery received sensory data, respectively. During the data gathering, the indices of received sensory data need to be recorded in $\Omega_{\mathbf{r}}$ which has been used for generating Φ . If the recovery error ϵ is greater than ϵ_{ub}, which means there is a lack of CS measurements for recovering the sensory data, we will increase the number of CS measurements. Otherwise, we will decrease the number of CS measurements, namely, the scheduling probability p_s needs to be adjusted when the recovery error is out of the range of $(\epsilon_{b}, \epsilon_{ub})$. Notice that, the scheduling probability should not change frequently since the sparse level of sensory data is relatively stable.

Sensor Component: In Algorithm 2, each sensor obtains a sensing value periodically and decides whether or not to participate in the data gathering. In particular, each sensor will generate a random number $p \in (0, 1)$, if the random number is greater than its scheduling probability, the sensor will send its value to the sink along the shortest routing path. Otherwise, the sensor will not sample and send its value.

5.2 Transmission Cost Analysis

In this subsection, we analyze transmission cost of SRS-DG and compare it with traditional CDG. We compare SRS-DG with three traditional CDG schemes, *dense random projections* for data gathering (DRP-DG) [17], *sparse random projection* for data gathering (SRP-DG) [26] and *hybrid CS* for data gathering (hybrid CS-DG) [18]. For simplicity of analysis, we assume that sensor network contains N sensors, the average hop distance from any sensor to the sink is H. In DRP-DG, each CS measurement gathering require each sensor participation once. In SRP-DG, each row of measurement matrix can only contain $O(\log N)$ nonzero elements, namely, each measurement gathering needs to transmit at least $O(\log N)$ data packets. In hybrid CS-DG

Algorithm 1: Sensory data recovery and scheduling probability assignment.

```
Input  : Ψ , ε_ub ε_b, △p.
Output: x̂, p_s
Φ ← 0;                          /* Initializing measurement matrix */
Ω_r ← {i| if x received };      /* Record received index */
j ← 1;
foreach i ∈ Ω_r do
    Φ (j, i) ← 1;               /* Assign measurement matrix */
    j ← j + 1;
Θ ← Φ * Ψ ;
x̂ = CS_Recovery (x̂ , Θ);       /* Recovery sensory data */
x̂_r ← x̂_{Ω_r};                  /* Extract received recovery sensory data */
ε = MSE(x_r, x̂_r);              /* Recovery error */
p_s ← |Ω_r|/N;                  /* Current scheduling probability */
if ε > ε_ub then
    p_s ← p_s + △p;             /* Increase scheduling probability */
    broadcast p_s to all sensors;
if ε < ε_b then
    p_s ← p_s − △p;             /* Decrease scheduling probability */
    Broadcast p_s to all sensors;
```

Algorithm 2: Random scheduling data gathering for the i^t sensor

```
Input  : p_s
Output: x
p ← rand();                     /* Generate a random probability */
if p ≤ p_s then
    Sampling x ;
    Send x to the sink;
```

, if the number of transmission data packets is larger than CS measurements, the sensor carries out CS compression. Fig 6 shows three types of CS based data gathering schemes under multi-hop tree topology network. In Fig 6, the black sensors represent the participation compression sensor nodes during CS based data gathering and the link labels represent the number of transmission data packets during a round data gathering. Fig 6 illustrates that transmission cost of hybrid CS-DG less than DRP-DG, and transmission cost of our scheme outperforms than hybrid CS-DG and DRP-DG schemes. Considering hybrid CS-DG comes from DRP-DG, we only analyze and compare DRP-DG and SRP-DG with our scheme.

For DRP-DG, each row has $O(N)$ non-zero elements, and each CS measurement gathering requires at least $O(N)$ data packets. Assuming that the sparse level of gathering data is k, the sink needs to gather $O(k \log N)$ measurements to recovery sensory data, then a round data transmission cost, TC_{p}, is

$$TC_{p} = O(N \cdot k \log N) = O(kN \log N) \quad (17)$$

For SRP-DG, the number of nonzero elements is $O(\log N)$ and $O(k^2 \log N)$ measurements are required to recover sensory data. But each nonzero element is random, each CS measurement transmission cost is $O(H \log N)$. The transmission cost of one round, $TC_{s\ p}$, is

$$TC_{s\ p} = O(H \log N \cdot k^2 \log N) = O(k^2 H \log^2 N) \quad (18)$$

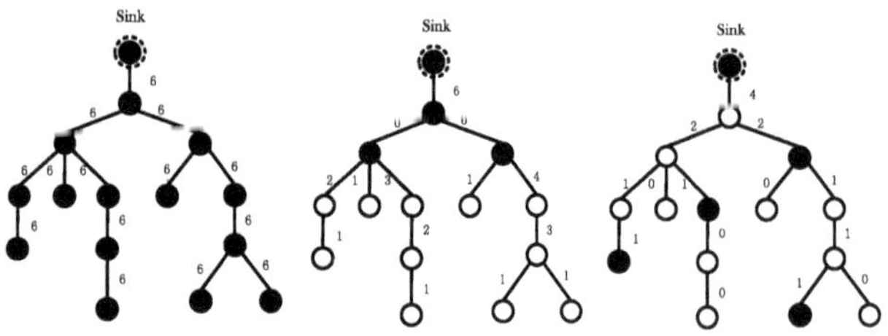

(a) DSP-DG. (b) Hybrid CS-DG. (c) SRS-DG.

Figure 6: Communication cost comparisons with different CDG schemes in multi-hop tree-type topology.

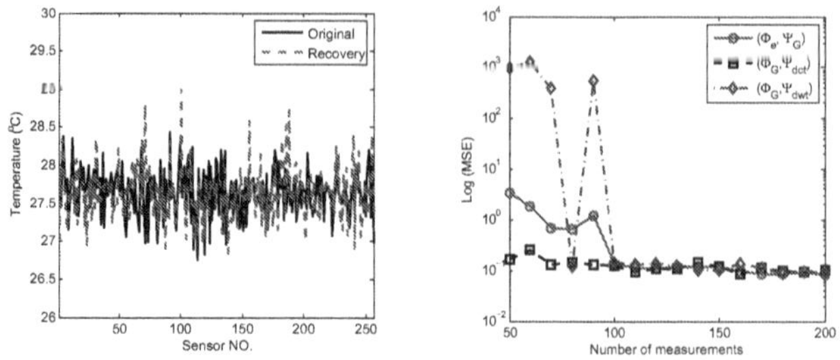

(a) Original and recovery. (b) Recovery errors comparison.

Figure 7: Recovery performance without packet loss.

For SRS-DG, each measurement only has one nonzero entry, and its transmission cost is $O(H)$. Because our proposed sparsest measurement matrix and representation basis satisfy RIP, it suffices to obtain $O(k \log N)$ measurements for achieving accurate data recovery. As a result, the transmission cost of one round SRS-DG, $TC_{s\ s}$, is

$$TC_{s\ s} = O(H \cdot k \log N) = O(kH \log N) \tag{19}$$

So, if $H = O(N)$ such as multi-hop chain topology network, $TC_{s\ s} = TC\ \ _p = O(kN \log N) < O(k^2 N \log^2 N) = TC_{s\ p}$. If $H = O(\log N)$ such as multi-hop tree topology network, $TC_{s\ s} = O(k \log^2 N) < TC\ \ _p = O(kN \log N)$ and $TC_{s\ s} = O(k \log^2 N) < TC_{s\ p} = O(k^2 \log^3 N)$. According to the above transmission cost analysis and comparison, it demonstrates SRS-DC also reduce transmission cost in lossless sensor networks compared with the state of the art traditional CDG schemes.

6. EVALUATION

We conduct extensive experiments using CitySee data set to evaluate the performance of our scheme in both reliable and lossy sensor network. In reliable WSNs with no packet loss, we compare our scheme with some traditional CDG schemes. In lossy WSNs, we evaluate the robustness of our scheme under different packet loss ratios. In particular, we choose random projections as a baseline scheme, it requires fewer measurements and can obtain better recovery performance compared with sparse random projections [5, 17]. In dense random projections, DCT and 4-layer 'haar' wavelet basis (DWT) are considered as different representation bases with recovery algorithm OMP [24].

6.1 Reliable sensor network

As analyzed in Section 5.2, our scheme achieves significantly lower transmission cost than using dense random projections. In our experiment, we evaluate our scheme from the following two aspects:

1. Evaluate recovery quality of gathering data using Φ and Ψ as measurement matrix and representation basis respectively, which compares recovery data with the original data.

2. Compare the recovery errors using $(\Phi\ , \Psi\ )$, $(\Phi\ , \Psi\ _t)$ and $(\Phi\ , \Psi\ _{wt})$ as the pairs of measurement matrix and representation basis, which displays the recovery performance of our scheme compared with dense random projections.

The experimental data set contains 256 temperature sampling values of the CitySee system [15], which are collected from the same monitoring area during the same sampling time interval. Fig 7 (a) shows the original sampling data and the recovery data using 100 CS measurements with our scheme. The mean square error (MSE) of our scheme is 0.1642. Fig 7 (b) depicts recovery error comparisons among $(\Phi\ , \Psi\ )$, $(\Phi\ , \Psi\ _t)$ and $(\Phi\ , \Psi\ _{wt})$. The recovery performance of $(\Phi\ , \Psi\ )$ can be as good as dense random projections when the number of measurements is greater than 90. It shows that our scheme can recover the data accurately without increasing the number of measurements.

6.2 Lossy sensor network

Then we evaluate the robustness of our scheme under different packet loss ratios. In this experiment, we adopt multi-hop tree routing topology. Each packet is dropped at random with uniform probability (packet loss ratio). Firstly, we carry out the experiment without allowing retransmission. Fig 8 (a) shows the recovery errors with different number of measurements under packet loss ratio 10% . We find that the recovery performance of dense random projection could be very bad even when the number of measurements is increased. In contrast, our scheme can always achieve satisfactory recovery accuracy, and the accuracy increases as the number of measurements increases. The MSE of $(\Phi\ , \Psi\ _t)$ and $(\Phi\ , \Psi\ _{wt})$ are greater than 20, while the MSE of our scheme is always less than 0.1. Fig 8 (b) shows the recovery errors with different data packet loss ratios and 160 measurements. It demonstrates that the gathering data of dense random projections cannot be recovered even with 2% data packet loss ratio. The experiment results validate that our scheme is robust to packet loss.

Secondly, we carry out the experiment by allowing retransmission. Although the retransmission strategy is usually used for networks packet loss, it would increase transmission cost and resource consumption. Moreover, many real deployed systems shown that the packet loss ratio could still reach 20% with retransmission strategy [14]. Fig 9 displays the recovery error of different schemes when the max number of retransmissions (denoted by *Max_rt_num*) for each packet is 2. Fig 9 (a) demonstrates that the recovery errors of $(\Phi\ , \Psi\ _t)$ and $(\Phi\ , \Psi\ _{wt})$ are always large with increasing the number of measurement. Fig 9 (a) also demonstrates that when the packet loss ratio is 5%, we can hardly recover the data using dense random projection schemes.

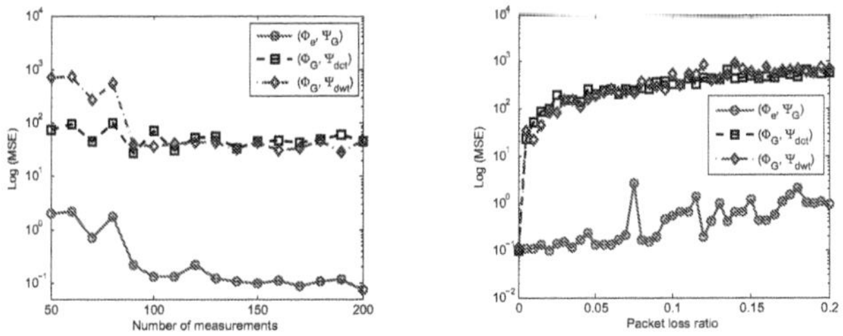

(a) $pl\_ratio = 0.1$ (b) $M = 160$

Figure 8: Recovery performance without retransmission.

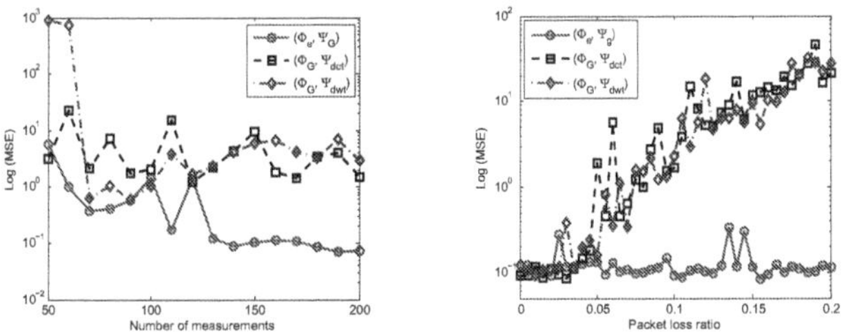

(a) $pl\_ratio = 0.05$ (b) $M = 160$

Figure 9: Recovery performance with retransmission ($Max\_rt\_num = 2$).

7. RELATED WORK

The emergence of CS theory has opened up a new research avenue for in-network compression and sampling. For example, D. Baron *et al.* [23] proposed distributed CS to compress multi-signal exploiting both intra- and inter-signal correlation structures. In [12, 21], Haupt, J. *et al.* applied CS theory to single-hop data gathering in WSNs to obtain efficient compression for network data. In [16], Luo *et al.* applied CS to reduce data transmission cost in large-scale WSNs. In [25, 29, 30], J. Wang *et al.* proposed a dual-layer compressed aggregation and adaptive the number of measurements scheme. These techniques exploited *dense measurement matrix* to gather CS measurements, the transmission cost of each CS measurement is $O(N)$ because each row of measurement matrix has $O(N)$ nonzero elements. To recover k-sparse sensory data, it requires $O(k \log N)$ measurements. In [18], J. Luo *et al.* proposed that applying CS naively may not bring any improvement for WSN data gathering and proposed a hybrid-CS data gathering scheme. In [17], C. Luo *et al.* discovered that $[I, R]$ measurement matrix has also good RIP, I is $M \times M$ identity matrix and R is $M \times (N - M)$ dense random matrix. But each CS measurement matrix transmission cost is still $O(N)$. In [26], W. Wang *et al.* proposed *sparse measurement matrix* can also obtain the salient information of compressible signal, each row of it has $O(\log N)$ nonzero entries, but it requires $O(k^2 \log N)$ CS measurements to recovery k-sparse sensory data. Based on sparse measurement matrix, Lee. S *et al.* [13] proposed low coherence projections for efficient routing data gathering. In [27, 28], X. Wu *et al.* proposed a temporal random sampling data gathering scheme, which only considered one sensor in temporal domain. They didn't consider spatial signal in large-scale WSN data gathering and its representation basis is inflexible. To the best our knowledge, most of existing CS base CDG techniques were discussed in reliable WSNs.

8. CONCLUSION AND FUTURE WORK

In this paper, we discussed a novel sparsest random scheduling scheme for compressive data gathering in lossy sensor networks. Although traditional compressive sensing based data gathering can recovery gathering data accurately, these techniques were not workable in lossy sensor network according to our real experimental results. Our scheme can efficiently avoid recovery performance degraded by link loss, also can reduce transmission cost in reliable networks. We carried out experiment in real CitySee data set, experiment results demonstrated our scheme can recover the sensory data accurately both in reliable and lossy sensor networks. In our scheme, we only consider spatial sparsest random scheduling for compressive data gathering. Future work will extend to spatial-temporal domain to joint optimal sparsest random scheduling for compressive data gathering.

Acknowledgment

This work was supported in part by the National Natural Science Foundation of China (No.61232018, No.61272487, No.61170233, No.61003311).

9. REFERENCES

[1] A. Arora, R. Ramnath, E. Ertin, P. Sinha, S. Bapat, V. Naik, V. Kulathumani, H. Zhang, H. Cao, M. Sridharan, et al. Exscal: Elements of an extreme scale wireless sensor network. In *Embedded and Real-Time Computing Systems and Applications, 2005. Proceedings. 11th IEEE International Conference on*, pages 102–108. IEEE, 2005.

[2] R. Baraniuk. Compressive sensing. *Signal Processing Magazine, IEEE*, 24(4):118–121, 2007.

[3] V. Buldygin and I. Kozachenko. *Metric characterization of random variables and random processes*, volume 188. Amer Mathematical Society, 2000.

[4] E. Candès. Compressive sampling. In *Proceedings oh the International Congress of Mathematicians: Madrid, August 22-30, 2006: invited lectures*, pages 1433–1452, 2006.

[5] E. Candès, J. Romberg, and T. Tao. Robust uncertainty principles: Exact signal reconstruction from highly incomplete frequency information. *Information Theory, IEEE Transactions on*, 52(2):489–509, 2006.

[6] E. Candes and T. Tao. Decoding by linear programming. *Information Theory, IEEE Transactions on*, 51(12):4203–4215, 2005.

[7] C. Chong and S. Kumar. Sensor networks: Evolution, opportunities, and challenges. *Proceedings of the IEEE*, 91(8):1247–1256, 2003.

[8] M. Davenport. *Random observations on random observations: Sparse signal acquisition and processing.* PhD thesis, Texas A&M University, 2010.

[9] A. Deshpande, C. Guestrin, S. R. Madden, J. M. Hellerstein, and W. Hong. Model-driven data acquisition in sensor networks. In *Proceedings of the Thirtieth international conference on Very large data*

bases-Volume 30, pages 588–599. VLDB Endowment, 2004.

[10] D. Donoho. Compressed sensing. *Information Theory, IEEE Transactions on*, 52(4):1289–1306, 2006.

[11] GreenOrbs. http://www.greenorbs.org/all/greenorbs.htm.

[12] J. Haupt, W. Bajwa, M. Rabbat, and R. Nowak. Compressed sensing for networked data. *Signal Processing Magazine, IEEE*, 25(2):92–101, 2008.

[13] S. Lee, S. Pattem, M. Sathiamoorthy, B. Krishnamachari, and A. Ortega. Compressed sensing and routing in multi-hop networks. Technical report, Technical Report, University of Southern California, 2009.

[14] Y. Liu, Y. He, M. Li, J. Wang, K. Liu, L. Mo, W. Dong, Z. Yang, M. Xi, J. Zhao, et al. Does wireless sensor network scale? a measurement study on greenorbs. In *INFOCOM, 2011 Proceedings IEEE*, pages 873–881. IEEE, 2011.

[15] Y. Liu, X. Mao, Y. He, K. Liu, W. Gong, and J. Wang. Citysee: Not only a wireless sensor network. *IEEE NETWORK*, 27(5):42–47, 2013.

[16] C. Luo, F. Wu, J. Sun, and C. Chen. Compressive data gathering for large-scale wireless sensor networks. In *Proceedings of the 15th annual international conference on Mobile computing and networking*, pages 145–156. ACM, 2009.

[17] C. Luo, F. Wu, J. Sun, and C. Chen. Efficient measurement generation and pervasive sparsity for compressive data gathering. *Wireless Communications, IEEE Transactions on*, 9(12):3728–3738, 2010.

[18] J. Luo, L. Xiang, and C. Rosenberg. Does compressed sensing improve the throughput of wireless sensor networks? In *Communications (ICC), 2010 IEEE International Conference on*, pages 1–6. IEEE, 2010.

[19] X. Mao, X. Miao, Y. He, X.-Y. Li, and Y. Liu. Citysee: Urban co_2 monitoring with sensors. In *INFOCOM, 2012 Proceedings IEEE*, pages 1611–1619. IEEE, 2012.

[20] D. Needell and J. Tropp. Cosamp: Iterative signal recovery from incomplete and inaccurate samples. *Applied and Computational Harmonic Analysis*, 26(3):301–321, 2009.

[21] M. Rabbat, J. Haupt, A. Singh, and R. Nowak. Decentralized compression and predistribution via randomized gossiping. In *Proceedings of the 5th international conference on Information processing in sensor networks*, pages 51–59. ACM, 2006.

[22] C. E. Rasmussen. Gaussian processes for machine learning. 2006.

[23] S. Sarvotham, R. Baraniuk, M. Duarte, D. Baron, and M. Wakin. Distributed compressive sensing, 2009.

[24] J. Tropp and A. Gilbert. Signal recovery from random measurements via orthogonal matching pursuit. *Information Theory, IEEE Transactions on*, 53(12):4655–4666, 2007.

[25] J. Wang, S. Tang, B. Yin, and X. Li. Data gathering in wireless sensor networks through intelligent compressive sensing. In *INFOCOM, 2012 Proceedings IEEE*, pages 603 – 611. Ieee, 2012.

[26] W. Wang, M. Garofalakis, and K. Ramchandran. Distributed sparse random projections for refinable approximation. In *Information Processing in Sensor Networks, 2007. IPSN 2007. 6th International Symposium on*, pages 331–339. IEEE, 2007.

[27] X. Wu and M. Liu. In-situ soil moisture sensing: measurement scheduling and estimation using compressive sensing. In *Proceedings of the 11th international conference on Information Processing in Sensor Networks*, pages 1–12. ACM, 2012.

[28] X. Wu, M. Liu, and Y. Wu. In-situ soil moisture sensing: Optimal sensor placement and field estimation. *TOSN*, 8(4):33, 2012.

[29] L. Xiang, J. Luo, C. Deng, A. Vasilakos, and W. Lin. Dual-level compressed aggregation: Recovering fields of physical quantities from incomplete sensory data. *Arxiv preprint arXiv:1107.4873*, 2011.

[30] L. Xiang, J. Luo, and A. Vasilakos. Compressed data aggregation for energy efficient wireless sensor networks. In *Sensor, Mesh and Ad Hoc Communications and Networks (SECON), 2011 8th Annual IEEE Communications Society Conference on*, pages 46–54. IEEE, 2011.

[31] J. Yick, B. Mukherjee, and D. Ghosal. Wireless sensor network survey. *Computer Networks*, 52(12):2292–2330, 2008.

APPENDIX

In Corollary 1, we need to prove $e^{|\lambda|} - |\lambda| \le e^{2\lambda^2/2}$.

PROOF. If $e^{|\lambda|} - |\lambda| \le e^{2\lambda^2/2}$ is corrected, we only need to proof $\ln(e^{|\lambda|} - |\lambda|) \le \lambda^2$, which is equivalent to $\frac{\ln(\ |\lambda| - |\lambda|)}{\lambda^2} \le 1$. Since

$$\frac{\ln(e^{|\lambda|} - |\lambda|)}{\lambda^2} = \frac{\ln(e^{|\lambda|} - |\lambda| - 1 + 1)}{\lambda^2} \le \frac{e^{|\lambda|} - |\lambda| - 1}{\lambda^2}$$

$$= \frac{1}{\lambda^2} \sum_{=2}^{\infty} \frac{(|\lambda|)}{n!} = \sum_{=2}^{\infty} \frac{(|\lambda|) \ ^{-2}}{n!}$$

If $|\lambda| < 1$, then

$$\frac{\ln(e^{|\lambda|} - |\lambda|)}{\lambda^2} \le \sum_{=2}^{\infty} \frac{(|\lambda|) \ ^{-2}}{n!} < \sum_{=2}^{\infty} \frac{1}{n!} = e - 1 - 1 < 1$$

If $|\lambda| \ge 1$, then $\frac{\ln(\ |\lambda| - |\lambda|)}{\lambda^2} \le \frac{|\lambda|}{\lambda^2} \le 1$

So, $e^{|\lambda|} - |\lambda| \le e^{2\lambda^2/2}$ $\square$

A Systematic Study of the Delayed Column Generation Method for Optimizing Wireless Networks

Yu Cheng
Department of Electrical and Computer Engineering
Illinois Institute of Technology
Chicago, IL 60616, USA
cheng@iit.edu

Xianghui Cao
Department of Electrical and Computer Engineering
Illinois Institute of Technology
Chicago, IL 60616, USA
xcao10@iit.edu

Xuemin (Sherman) Shen
Department of Electrical and Computer Engineering
University of Waterloo
Waterloo Ontario N2L 3G1
Canada
xshen@bbcr.uwaterloo.ca

Devu Manikantan Shila
United Technologies Research Center
Hartford, CT 06108 USA
manikad@utrc.utc.com

Hongkun Li
InterDigital
King of Prussia, PA 19406
USA
hongkun.li@interdigital.com

ABSTRACT

The main-thread approach for optimizing the throughput capacity over a multihop wireless network is to apply a multi-commodity flow (MCF) formulation, augmented with a scheduling constraint derived from the conflict graph associated with the network. A fundamental issue with the conflict graph based MCF formulation is that finding all independent sets (ISs) for scheduling is NP-hard in general. If we express the MCF formulation in a matrix format, the constraint matrix will contain a very large number of columns, with each IS being associated with one column. According to the linear programming theorem, such a type of problem can be addressed with the delayed column generation (DCG) method. Unfortunately, applications of the DCG in wireless networks have not received much attention. To the best of knowledge, none of the existing work conducted theoretical studies of the performance of DCG in wireless networks. In this paper, we study the DCG method in the context of a general network flow problem. With a protocol interference model, we rigorously prove that searching an entering column in the DCG operation is equivalent to a maximum weighted independent set (MWIS) problem. A prominent theoretical contribution of this paper is the theorem that: if an MWIS approximation algorithm with the approximation ratio β (< 1) is applied in the DCG method, the maximum flow solved will be at least β of the optimal solution. Furthermore, the DCG method is also applied to the multi-radio multi-channel (MR-MC) networks. With extensive numerical results comparing to the existing methods, we show that the DCG method achieves the most preferred tradeoff between computation complexity and network capacity and maintains good scalability when addressing large-scale networks, particularly in the complex MR-MC context.

MobiHoc'14, August 11–14, 2014, Philadelphia, PA, USA.

http://dx.doi.org/10.1145/2632951.2632978 .

Categories and Subject Descriptors

C.m [**Computer-Communication Networks**]: Miscellaneous

Keywords

Network capacity optimization; delayed column generation; MWIS; approximation ratio; multi-radio multi-channel networks

1. INTRODUCTION

The *network capacity* of fundamental importance to a multihop wireless network is the total throughput traversing the given set of ingress/egress edge nodes. The maximum network capacity is normally coupled with optimal routing and scheduling to form a *network dimensioning* issue [2, 3]. A fundamental issue in the multihop wireless networks is that the neighboring hops along a path, when transmitting over the same spectrum, have to contend for the channel access and can not transmit at the same time. The *conflict graph* is the popular tool to model the interference among different wireless links [4–6]. The main-thread approach for wireless network dimensioning is to apply a *multi-commodity flow* (MCF) formulation, augmented with constraints derived from the conflict graph [2–4, 18].

The conflict-graph constraints are normally based on the concept of independent set [4]: at a moment, the links that can have successful transmissions simultaneously in the network form an independent set over the conflict graph associated with the network. The MCF formulation with the independent set constraints can generate an optimal scheduling (under the assumption of a synchronized slotted system): the maximal independent sets (MISs) take turns in grabbing the channel for data transmission, with the proportion of transmission time for each set determined by the MCF solution. The recent work in [9] develops a generic multi-dimensional conflict graph (MDCG) technique, which enables the conflict graph based MCF formulation for a multi-radio multi-channel (MR-MC) wireless network.

While the conflict graph based MCF formulation is a linear programming problem, finding all ISs to be used is NP-hard in general. A random algorithm for MIS search is proposed in [4] and widely adopted in the literature, which provides a framework while more MISs can be obtained with more rounds of computation. However, in a large scale network (especially for the MR-MC case with the

MDCG involved), the random search method incurs a heavy computation overhead to find a large enough number of MISs for a good approximate MCF solution. The work in [9] develops a heuristic algorithm to search a smaller set of critical MISs, which can considerably reduce the overhead in MIS search compared to the random method. The overhead of searching critical MISs is still significant anyhow in a large-scale network. Moreover, those heuristic MIS search algorithms can not provision a guaranteed capacity region of the MCF solutions.

Regarding the conflict graph based MCF linear programming (LP) problem, if we express all the constraints in a matrix format, the constraint matrix will have a very large number of columns where each IS will be associated with one column.[1] Both searching all the columns and storing the columns for MCF solutions incur high complexity. According to the LP theorem, such a type of problem can be addressed with the delayed column generation (DCG) method [11], where a new column will be iteratively searched online based on the current feasible solution for the most reduced cost till the optimal solution is reached. Unfortunately, applications of the DCG in wireless networks have not received enough attention. We only noticed a couple of studies, which focus on very specific cases. The work in [12] applies the DCG method to study a minimum scheduling problem, with the objective to assign at least one time slot to each node such that the total number of time slots is minimized. In [13, 14], the DCG method is applied to study joint routing, link scheduling and power control in wireless networks. The fundamental issue is that none of the existing studies, to the best of knowledge, conducted theoretical studies of the performance of DCG in wireless networks. In a wireless network with a certain interference model, searching an entering column according to the DCG will be a maximum weighted independent set (MWIS) problem [16] (to be proved rigorously in this paper). Thus, in practice, an approximation algorithm needs to be used to find an entering independent set with a reasonable computation overhead. *A prominent theoretical contribution of this paper is that we prove the following theorem: if an MWIS approximation algorithm with the approximation ratio β (< 1) is applied in the DCG method, the maximum flow solved under such an approximation algorithm will be at least β of the optimal solution.* More specifically, this paper has four-fold contributions.

- We study the DCG method in the context of a general network flow problem, and rigorously prove that searching an entering column in the DCG operation is equivalent to an MWIS problem.

- We conduct theoretical analysis to obtain the lower bound of the network flow, when the MWIS problem involved in the DCG method (which is NP-hard) is addressed with an approximation algorithm. Specifically, if an MWIS approximation algorithm with the approximation ratio β (< 1) is used, the maximum flow solved will be at least β of the optimal solution. Furthermore, we show such a lower bound also applies to the multi-commodity flow problem and the network flow problem with a fairness constraint.

- The DCG method is also applied to the MR-MC network, exploiting the tuple-based network model and multi-dimensional conflict graph technique developed in [9].

- We present extensive numerical results to demonstrate the performance of the DCG method in terms of computation overhead and the achieved network flow capacity, with comparison to that with the random search of MISs [4] and that with the heuristic search of critical MISs [9]. It turns out the DCG method achieves the most preferred tradeoff between computation complexity and network capacity, and maintains good scalability when addressing large-scale MR-MC networks. We also examine the performance of DCG method under different MWIS approximation algorithms.

The remainder of this paper is organized as follows. Section 2 reviews more related work. Section 3 describes the system model. Section 4 conducts a theoretical study of the performance of DCG in solving various network flow problems. In Section 5, the DCG method is applied to MR-MC networks. Section 6 presents extensive numerical results to evaluate the performances of DCG, with comparison to some existing methods. Section 7 gives the concluding remarks.

2. RELATED WORK

The MR-MC wireless networks have received substantial attention in the last few years, especially in the context of wireless mesh networks (WMNs) [1,10,20]. Such a networking model can significantly increase network capacity by simultaneously exploiting multiple non-overlapping channels through different radio interfaces. Compared to the traditional SR-SC networks, MR-MC networking takes place in a multi-dimensional resource space, with dimensions defined by radio interfaces, links, and channels. The central issue of resource allocation in such a multi-dimensional space is to find solutions for a set of coupled problems including *scheduling, channel and radio assignment, and routing* [1, 19], with the objective to optimize the network capacity. The conflict graph tool however did not achieve the similar popularity in MR-MC networks as in SR-SC networks [6, 7], mainly because the link conflict graph is not sufficient for MR-MC networks to describe the extra conflict relations in competing for radio interfaces and channels. The multi-dimensional conflict graph technique developed in [9] fill the gap between optimizing SR-SC and MR-MC networks. Each vertex in the MDCG represents a link-radio-channel (LRC) tuple, a basic resource point in the multi-dimensional resource space. The LRC-tuple based MISs can then be searched over the MDCG to specify the scheduling constraints in the MCF formulation.

Searching all independent sets is however NP-hard in general. While the random search algorithm [4] and the critical MIS search algorithm [9] can reduce the computation overhead in some degree, neither of the two methods can provide performance guarantee of the MCF capacity. With an LP formulation, the independent set induces a large number of columns to the constraint matrix of the MCF problem. The delayed column generation method is expected to be decomposition method addressing such a problem. While the existing studies [12,13] are limited to special scenarios without theoretical analysis, this paper provides a systematic study of the DCG method in the general context of network flow problem. We show that searching an entering column in the DCG method is equivalent to an MWIS problem. The MWIS is a classic problem in combinatorial optimization, which is NP-hard in general and by nature calls for approximation algorithms. For example, [16] studies a simple greedy algorithm which iteratively removes the vertex (and its neighbors) having minimal weighted degree each time from the remaining graph. This method is combined with a linear programming to form an LP-based algorithm [16]. A minimum weighted vertex cover based approximation algorithm is proposed in [17].

[1]Although it is sufficient to just involve maximal independent set (MIS) in the scheduling [4], in this paper, we generally represent the scheduling involving all ISs for the convenience of theoretical analysis.

In this paper, we compare the performances of various embedded MWIS approximation algorithms in our DCG method, and the results show the greedy algorithm is the most efficient one.

3. SYSTEM MODEL

In this section, we mainly present the system model in the SR-SC context. Compared to the MR-MC case, an SR-SC network provides a less entangled environment for theoretically studying the performance of DCG. In Section 5, we do show that the theoretical results obtained in the SR-SC context can be extended to the MR-MC case.

Consider an SR-SC wireless network as a directed graph $G(\mathcal{N}, \mathcal{L})$ with node set $\mathcal{N}$ and physical link set $\mathcal{L}$. A directed link in a graph is also termed as an arc. Let $|\mathcal{N}|$ and $|\mathcal{L}|$ denote the number of nodes and links, respectively. A link $\ell \in \mathcal{L}$ is also denoted by the pair of transmitter and receiver (a, b) for which the capacity is $w_{(a,b)}$. To form a link, nodes a and b should be within each other's *communication range*. We consider the nodes are indexed from 1 to $|\mathcal{N}|$ and links indexed from 1 to $|\mathcal{L}|$.

We adopt the *protocol interference model* defined by an *interference range* [21]. We assume that every node has the same interference range. Two nodes interfere with each other if they are within each other's interference range. Two links conflict with each other if they have interfering nodes. Under such an interference model, a link could have a successful transmission only when both the sender and receiver are free of interference. The interference-free requirement at the sender side ensures that it can receive the acknowledgement returned by the receiver. The interferences among the links can be described by an undirected conflict graph. Each vertex in the conflict graph represents a link in the original network. An edge between two vertices indicates a conflict relationship between the corresponding links in the original network. An independent set over the conflict graph then represents a set of links that can transmit simultaneously in the original network.

We consider a slotted system, where time is divided into slots of unit length. Different ISs share the time for transmission, forming a *scheduling*. Let $\mathcal{I}$ denote an IS over the conflict graph and $\mathcal{M}$ the set of all the ISs. The convex hull of all the ISs, $Co(\mathcal{M})$, defines the network capacity region under scheduling. Let $r_{(a,b)}$ denote a feasible flow allocation over link (a, b) and $\mathbf{r}$ the flow rate vector over all the links. We have $\mathbf{r} \in Co(\mathcal{M})$.

In the sequel, we use boldface letters in lower case and uppercase to denote vectors and matrices, respectively. A vector by default is a column vector. The operator (′) indicates the transpose of a vector or matrix. We use $\mathbf{0}$ and $\mathbf{1}$ to denote the vectors of 0's and 1's, respectively, whose dimensions are clear in the context.

4. DELAYED COLUMN GENERATION

In this section, the theoretical performance of DCG is first studied based on a standard network flow problem with a single flow. We then extend the results to some other important network flow problems, such as maximum flow, multi-commodity flow, and MCF with fairness. Before we present the network flow formulation, let us look at the basic flow conservation constraint and the IS based scheduling constraint.

4.1 Flow Conservation Constraint

Consider a network with a single flow f from the source node $s(f)$ to the destination node $d(f)$. Let $\mathbf{g} = (g_1, g_2, \cdots, g_{|\mathcal{N}|})$ denote the input vector, with $g_i = 0$ for $i \neq s(f)$ and $g_{s(f)} = -g_{d(f)}$. Define the *node-arc incidence matrix* $\mathbf{H}$ as follows: its dimensions are $|\mathcal{N}| \times |\mathcal{L}|$ (each row corresponds to a node and each column corresponds to an arc (i.e., a link)) and its (i, k)th entry h_{ik} is associated with the ith node and the kth link. We let

$$h_{ik} = \begin{cases} 1, & \text{if } i \text{ is the start node of the } k\text{th arc,} \\ -1, & \text{if } i \text{ is the end node of the } k\text{th arc,} \\ 0, & \text{otherwise.} \end{cases}$$

With the node-arc incidence matrix, the flow conservation constraint can be expressed as

$$\mathbf{Hr} = \mathbf{g} \tag{1}$$

Note that the rows of the matrix $\mathbf{H}$ sum to the zero vector and are therefore linearly dependent. In fact, the last flow conservation constraint at node $|\mathcal{N}|$ is a consequence of the flow conservation constraints at the other nodes, and can be omitted without affecting the feasible set. A *truncated node-arc incident matrix* $\tilde{\mathbf{H}}$ can be defined, which consists of the first $|\mathcal{N} - 1|$ rows of the matrix $\mathbf{H}$. Let $\tilde{\mathbf{g}} = (g_1, \cdots, g_{|\mathcal{N}|-1})$. According to [11], the flow conservation constraints without redundancy can be expressed as

$$\tilde{\mathbf{H}}\mathbf{r} = \tilde{\mathbf{g}} \tag{2}$$

We can index the destination node as the last node and truncate it, so $\tilde{\mathbf{g}}$ consists of only zero and positive values. For convenience, we later just use $\mathbf{H}$ and $\mathbf{g}$ to represent the trunked node-arc incidence matrix and the associated input vector.

4.2 Scheduling Constraint

In wireless network, the link capacity under scheduling is constrained by the convex hull of the independent sets. The total flow allocation over link (a, b) should satisfy its capacity constraint.

$$r_{(a,b)} \leq \sum_{m:(a,b)\in\mathcal{I}_m} \alpha_m w_{(a,b)} \tag{3}$$

$$\sum_{m=1}^{|\mathcal{M}|} \alpha_m = 1 \tag{4}$$

where the real number α_m ($0 \leq \alpha_m \leq 1$) represents the proportion of time scheduled to the mth IS.

LEMMA 1. *There exists a scheduling* $(\alpha_1, \cdots, \alpha_u)$, *so that any feasible flow allocation within the capacity region, i.e.,* $\mathbf{r} \in Co(\mathcal{M})$, *has an exact scheduling as*

$$r_{(a,b)} = \sum_{m:(a,b)\in\mathcal{I}_m} \alpha_m w_{(a,b)}, \quad \forall (a,b) \in \mathcal{L} \tag{5}$$

$$\sum_{m=1}^{|\mathcal{M}|} \alpha_m = 1. \tag{6}$$

PROOF. Consider feasible flow allocation within the convex hull. A link (a, b) is termed as *over-scheduled* if

$$r_{(a,b)} < \sum_{m:(a,b)\in\mathcal{I}_m} \alpha_m w_{(a,b)}. \tag{7}$$

We are going to show that the scheduling can be adjusted so that every over-scheduled link becomes exactly scheduled, and the originally exactly scheduled links maintain intact.

Pick an over-scheduled link (a, b) and assume there are n independent sets, with index $(i_1, i_2, \cdots, i_n)$, which have positive time allocation in the scheduling (7). We take the ratio

$$\beta = \frac{r_{(a,b)}}{\sum_{m:(a,b)\in\mathcal{I}_m} \alpha_m w_{(a,b)}} = \frac{r_{(a,b)}}{\sum_{j=1}^{n} \alpha_{i_j} w_{(a,b)}}. \tag{8}$$

Let i' index the independent set that contains the links in $\mathcal{I}_i/(a,b)$, that is, the links of $\mathcal{I}_i$ excluding link (a,b). Then we adjust the scheduling as

$$\tilde{\alpha}_{i_j} = \beta\alpha_{i_j}, \tag{9}$$

$$\tilde{\alpha}_{i'_j} = \alpha_{i'_j} + (1-\beta)\alpha_{i_j} \tag{10}$$

for $j = 1, \cdots, n$. We call the operations in (9) and (10) as a splitting procedure. With a splitting procedure, it can be seen that link (a,b) will become exactly scheduled. The scheduled capacities of other links in $\mathcal{I}_i/(a,b)$ do not change, for which the splitting procedure just redistributes the scheduling time between $\mathcal{I}_i$ and $\mathcal{I}_{i'}$ but maintains the total time allocation. Note that if an independent set includes only the link (a,b), the splitting procedure will lead to a positive time allocation to the empty set, indexed as $i'_j = 0$.

Using the $(\tilde{\alpha}_{i_1}, \tilde{\alpha}_{i'_1}, \cdots, \tilde{\alpha}_{i_n}, \tilde{\alpha}_{i'_n})$ to update the corresponding time allocation in the original scheduling, we get another scheduling denoted as $\tilde{\boldsymbol{\alpha}}$. For $k \notin \{i_1, i'_1, \cdots, i_n, i'_n\}$, we have $\tilde{\alpha}_k = \alpha_k$. Further, we can remove the empty set (if it has positive time allocation) from the scheduling with the normalization operations:

$$\tilde{\alpha}_k = \frac{\tilde{\alpha}_k}{1-\tilde{\alpha}_0}, \quad \text{for } k = 1, \cdots, n.$$

We can then move on to pick another over-scheduled link and apply the splitting procedure to make it exactly scheduled. The scheduling $\tilde{\boldsymbol{\alpha}}$ is then updated according to the splitting. Such a procedure of splitting and schedule updating can be iteratively applied till all over-scheduled links become exactly scheduled. As a result, the final scheduling is still valid. □

The exact scheduling lemma has benefits in two aspects. a) It allows a standard linear programming formulation of the network flow problem over a wireless network, which will facilitate the theoretical analysis of DCG performance. b) It reduces computation complexity in the DCG algorithm. In a non-standard LP problem, extra computation overhead will be required to handle slack variables associated with those inequality constraints [11], if we want to search a new entering column only over the IS columns.

4.3 Delayed Column Generation

Let $\mathbf{u}$ denote a vector of link costs. Consider the standard network flow problem $\mathcal{P}_1$

$$\text{minimize} \quad \mathbf{u}'\mathbf{r} \tag{11}$$

subject to:

$$\mathbf{H}\mathbf{r} = \mathbf{g} \tag{12}$$

$$\mathbf{r} = \mathbf{W}\boldsymbol{\alpha} \tag{13}$$

$$\mathbf{1}'\boldsymbol{\alpha} = 1 \tag{14}$$

$$\mathbf{r} \geq \mathbf{0} \tag{15}$$

$$\boldsymbol{\alpha} \geq \mathbf{0}. \tag{16}$$

where the matrix $\mathbf{W}$ consists of all the independent sets (excluding the empty set), with each column as one different independent set. Consider that there are M non-empty independent sets can be used for the optimization problem. Each independent set $\mathbf{w}_m$ is a vector of $|\mathcal{L}|$ elements, with

$$\mathbf{w}_m(i) = \begin{cases} w_i, & \text{if link } i \text{ is in this set} \\ 0, & \text{otherwise} \end{cases}$$

The matrix $\mathbf{W}$ can be expressed as

$$\mathbf{W} = \begin{bmatrix} | & & | \\ \mathbf{w}_1 & \cdots & \mathbf{w}_M \\ | & & | \end{bmatrix}. \tag{17}$$

In the problem $\mathcal{P}_1$, the decision variables are $\mathbf{r}$ and $\boldsymbol{\alpha}$. The objective function is equivalent to $\mathbf{u}'\mathbf{r} + \mathbf{0}'\boldsymbol{\alpha}$. To get a standard LP problem, we redefine the decision variables as $\mathbf{x} = (\mathbf{r}', \boldsymbol{\alpha}')'$. The cost vector $\mathbf{c} = (\mathbf{u}', \mathbf{0}')'$. Further we rewrite the condition (13) as

$$\mathbf{r} - \mathbf{W}\boldsymbol{\alpha} = \mathbf{0} \tag{18}$$

The problem $\mathcal{P}_1$ can then be reformulated as a standard LP problem $\mathcal{P}_2$

$$\text{minimize} \quad \mathbf{c}'\mathbf{x} \tag{19}$$

subject to:

$$\mathbf{A}\mathbf{x} = \mathbf{b} \tag{20}$$

$$\mathbf{x} \geq \mathbf{0} \tag{21}$$

where

$$\mathbf{A} = \left[\begin{array}{c|c} \mathbf{H}_{(|\mathcal{N}|-1)\times|\mathcal{L}|} & \mathbf{0}_{(|\mathcal{N}|-1)\times M} \\ \hline \mathbf{I}_{|\mathcal{L}|\times|\mathcal{L}|} & -\mathbf{W}_{|\mathcal{L}|\times M} \\ \hline \mathbf{0}_{1\times|\mathcal{L}|} & \mathbf{1}_{1\times M} \end{array}\right] \tag{22}$$

$$\mathbf{b} = (\mathbf{g}'_{1\times(|\mathcal{N}|-1)}, \mathbf{0}'_{1\times|\mathcal{L}|}, 1). \tag{23}$$

Note that the constraint (20) presents in a compact manner the constraints (12), (13), and (14). For the convenience of presentation, we term the columns in $\mathbf{A}$ associated with all the ISs as *right sub-matrix* and the other part as *left sub-matrix*.

The challenge to solve the problem $\mathcal{P}_2$ is that the number of independent sets is in the order of $O(2^{|\mathcal{L}|})$, and it is known that searching all independent sets is an NP-hard problem. Even if all the independent sets can be searched, the number of columns is so large that it is impossible to generate and store the entire matrix $\mathbf{A}$ in memory.

Experience with large problems indicates that, usually, most of the columns never enter the basis, and we can therefore afford not to ever generate those unused columns. The *delayed column generation* method [11] is a sequence of iterations. At the beginning of an iteration, we have a basic feasible solution to the original problem, and an associated basis matrix. We search for a variable with negative reduced cost, possibly by minimizing $\bar{c}_i$ over all i, i.e., solving the problem

$$\text{minimize} \quad \bar{c}_i; \tag{24}$$

if none is found, the algorithm terminates. Suppose that we have found some j such that $\bar{c}_j < 0$. We then form a collection of columns $\mathbf{A}_i$, $i \in \mathcal{Q}$, which contains all of the columns that have been selected before and the new entering one. We then define the *restricted* problem

$$\begin{aligned} \text{minimize} \quad & \sum_{i\in\mathcal{Q}} c_i x_i \\ \text{subject to} \quad & \sum_{i\in\mathcal{Q}} \mathbf{A}_i x_i = \mathbf{b} \\ & \mathbf{x} \geq \mathbf{0} \end{aligned}$$

The solution from the restricted problem is another basic feasible solution to the original problem and serves as the start point for next iteration.

Selecting an initial basic feasible solution. We can select an initial feasible solution by the following algorithm:

Step 1: Randomly select a link, and then search an MIS starting from this link.

Step 2: Randomly select another link from the set of links that have not been included in any of the existing MISs, and then search an MIS starting from the selected link.

Step 3: Repeat Step 2 until all the links are covered.

If n MISs have been selected, we can get a scheduling that assigns $1/n$ of the time to each MIS. Then each link will have the capacity at least w_l/n, with w_l the physical link capacity of link l. In fact, each link capacity under the scheduling could be exactly determined based on how many MISs it is involved in. Given the link capacity under scheduling, a feasible commodity flow can be easily constructed by setting it as the bottleneck capacity of a path between the source and the destination. The set $\mathcal{Q}$ can include all the columns in left sub-matrix and the columns associated with the MISs scheduled. As we already constructed a basic feasible solution over such $\mathcal{Q}$, we know that the restricted problem must have a solution to start the DCG iterations.

THEOREM 1. *The DCG problem to find an entering column can be mapped to an MWIS problem.*

PROOF. Note that when we apply the delayed column generation method, use matrix $\mathbf{B}$ to denote the matrix formed by columns associated with the basic feasible variables $\mathbf{x}_B = \mathbf{B}^{-1}\mathbf{b}$. Define $\mathbf{p}' = \mathbf{c}'_B\mathbf{B}^{-1}$. To find a new column with improved solutions is to find a column

$$\bar{c}_i = c_i - \mathbf{p}'\mathbf{A}_i \leq 0.$$

With delayed column generation, the candidate columns are only in the right sub-matrix of $\mathbf{A}$. For those columns, the associated cost variables are all 0. To pick the one with the largest value of cost reduction, the problem is

$$\text{minimize} \quad -\mathbf{p}'\mathbf{A}_j. \tag{25}$$

Let $\mathbf{w}_j$ be the independent set vector contained in $\mathbf{A}_j$. The minimization problem (25) is then equivalent to

$$\text{minimize} \quad \sum_{i=|\mathcal{N}|}^{|\mathcal{N}|+|\mathcal{L}|-1} p_i\mathbf{w}_j(i-|\mathcal{N}|+1) - p_{|\mathcal{N}|+|\mathcal{L}|}.$$

and further equivalent to

$$\text{maximize} \quad \sum_{i=1}^{|\mathcal{L}|}(-p_{k_i})\mathbf{w}_j(i) \tag{26}$$

by defining $k_i = i + |\mathcal{N}| - 1$. □

Remark: Note that an MWIS algorithm normally considers only non-negative weights. However, in the MWIS problem shown in (26), the weight associated with a link (i.e., $-p_j$) may take either negative or positive values. If some links have negative weights, we can replace the negative weights with a weight of zero and runs the MWIS algorithm. For the MWIS identified, we can exclude those links originally having negative weights from the MWIS and use the remaining set as our solution. It is not difficult to see that such a method indeed gives the MWIS to the original problem with negative weights. The problem that all links have negative weights is a trivial problem, where the solution is just the link with the largest weight. The proof of Theorem 2 in the below will show that the MWIS problem of importance in this paper indeed involves non-negative weights, so we will not have a trivial issue.

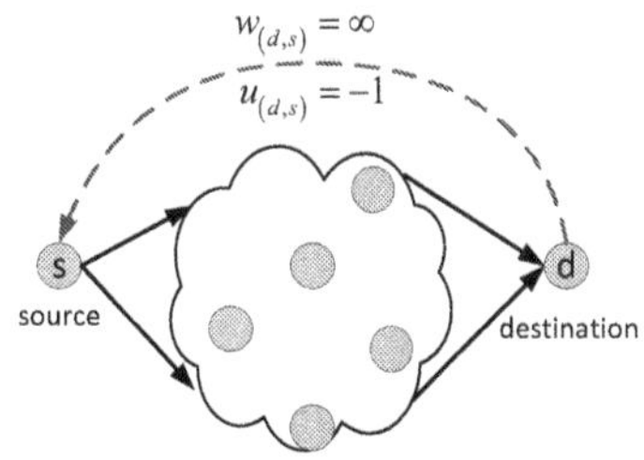

Figure 1: Reformulation of the maximum flow problem as a standard network flow problem.

4.4 DCG in the Maximum Flow Problem

The maximum flow problem can be reformulated as a standard network flow problem as follows. We let the cost of every arc be equal to zero and introduce a new infinite capacity arc (d, s) with cost $u_{(d,s)} = -1$, as shown in Fig. 1. Minimizing $\mathbf{c}'\mathbf{r}$ in the new network is the same as maximizing the flow $x_{(d,s)}$ on the new arc. Since the flow on the arc (d, s) must return from s to d through the original network, maximizing $x_{(d,s)}$ is the same as solving the original maximum flow problem.

In the transformed network, the problem $\mathcal{P}_2$ needs to be updated as follows. The decision variables are now $\mathbf{x} = (r_{(d,s)}, \mathbf{r}', \boldsymbol{\alpha}')$, and the cost vector $\mathbf{c} = (-1, \mathbf{0}_{1\times(|\mathcal{L}|+M)})$. The truncated node-arc incidence matrix $\mathbf{H}$ needs to add one more column (specifically, as the first column) to include the new arc (d, s). The scheduling constraints do not need to be changed. The arc (d, s) is a virtual arc for modeling purpose. It does not interfere with any wireless link. Also the virtual link has an infinite capacity, so does not need an independent set based scheduling. Also, the external input rate is 0 in the reformulated problem, i.e., $\mathbf{g} = \mathbf{0}$. Thus, the problem $\mathcal{P}_2$ is to be updated into the problem $\mathcal{P}_3$, which has

$$\mathbf{A} = \left[\begin{array}{c|c} \mathbf{H}_{(|\mathcal{N}|-1)\times(|\mathcal{L}|+1)} & \mathbf{0}_{(|\mathcal{N}|-1)\times M} \\ \hline \hat{\mathbf{I}}_{|\mathcal{L}|\times(|\mathcal{L}|+1)} & -\mathbf{W}_{|\mathcal{L}|\times M} \\ \hline \mathbf{0}_{1\times(|\mathcal{L}|+1)} & \mathbf{1}_{1\times M} \end{array}\right] \tag{27}$$

$$\mathbf{b} = (\mathbf{0}'_{1\times(|\mathcal{N}|-1+|\mathcal{L}|)}, 1) \tag{28}$$

where

$$\hat{\mathbf{I}}_{|\mathcal{L}|\times(|\mathcal{L}|+1)} = \left[\ \mathbf{0}_{|\mathcal{L}|\times 1} \mid \mathbf{I}_{|\mathcal{L}|\times|\mathcal{L}|}\ \right]. \tag{29}$$

THEOREM 2. *If we apply an approximation algorithm with the approximation ratio β to solve the MWIS problem when search for an entering column, the maximum flow solved under such an approximation algorithm will be at least β of the optimal solution.*

PROOF. Note that we apply the delayed column generation method to the maximum flow problem formulated above. Given a basic feasible solution $\mathbf{x}_B = \mathbf{B}^{-1}\mathbf{b}$, we then have $\mathbf{p}' = \mathbf{c}'_B\mathbf{B}^{-1}$. Further, $\mathbf{p}'\mathbf{b} = \mathbf{c}'_B\mathbf{B}^{-1}\mathbf{b} = \mathbf{c}'_B\mathbf{x}_B = p_{|\mathcal{N}|+|\mathcal{L}|} \leq 0$, where the last step is due to $\mathbf{c} = (-1, \mathbf{0}_{1\times(|\mathcal{L}|+M)})'$ and a feasible solution $\mathbf{x} \geq \mathbf{0}$.

To find a new column with improved solutions is to find a column

$$c_i - \mathbf{p}'\mathbf{A}_i \leq 0$$

With delayed column generation, the candidate columns are only in the right sub-matrix of $\mathbf{A}$. For those columns, the associated cost variables are all 0. To pick the one with the largest value of cost reduction, the problem is to

$$\text{minimize} \quad -\mathbf{p}'\mathbf{A}_j.$$

It is equivalent to

$$\text{minimize} \quad \sum_{i=1}^{|\mathcal{L}|} p_{k_i}\mathbf{w}_j(i) - p_{|\mathcal{N}|+|\mathcal{L}|}$$

and equivalent to

$$\text{maximize} \quad \sum_{i=1}^{|\mathcal{L}|}(-p_{k_i})\mathbf{w}_j(i).$$

When the algorithm stops, we have

$$\mathbf{c}' - \mathbf{p}'\mathbf{A} \geq \mathbf{0}',$$

where $-p_{|\mathcal{N}|+|\mathcal{L}|}$ equals the network flow obtained. That is,

$$\sum_{i=1}^{|\mathcal{L}|} p_{k_i}\mathbf{w}_j(i) - p_{|\mathcal{N}|+|\mathcal{L}|} \geq 0 \quad \forall \text{ independent set}$$

equivalently,

$$\sum_{i=1}^{|\mathcal{L}|}(-p_{k_i})\mathbf{w}_j(i) \leq -p_{|\mathcal{N}|+|\mathcal{L}|} \quad \forall \text{ independent set} \tag{30}$$

Thus,

$$\max_{j\in\mathcal{M}}\left(\sum_{i=1}^{|\mathcal{L}|}(-p_{k_i})\mathbf{w}_j(i)\right) \leq -p_{|\mathcal{N}|+|\mathcal{L}|} \tag{31}$$

When the MWIS problem is solved by an approximation algorithm with an approximation ratio β (<1), let $\tilde{\max}$ denote the maximum value obtained with the algorithm and we can have

$$\beta \max_{j\in\mathcal{M}}\left(\sum_{i=1}^{|\mathcal{L}|}(-p_{k_i})\mathbf{w}_j(i)\right) \leq \tilde{\max_{j\in\mathcal{M}}}\left(\sum_{i=1}^{|\mathcal{L}|}(-p_{k_i})\mathbf{w}_j(i)\right) \tag{32}$$

$$\leq -p_{|\mathcal{N}|+|\mathcal{L}|} \tag{33}$$

That is

$$\max_{j\in\mathcal{M}}\left(\sum_{i=1}^{|\mathcal{L}|}(-p_{k_i})\mathbf{w}_j(i)\right) \leq -\frac{1}{\beta}p_{|\mathcal{N}|+|\mathcal{L}|} \tag{34}$$

The dual problem of $\mathcal{P}_3$ is

$$\begin{aligned} \text{maximize} \quad & \mathbf{p}'\mathbf{b} \\ \text{subject to} \quad & \mathbf{p}'\mathbf{A} \leq \mathbf{c}'. \end{aligned}$$

We now show that the vector $\hat{\mathbf{p}} = (p_1, \cdots, p_{|\mathcal{N}|+|\mathcal{L}|-1}, \frac{1}{\beta}p_{|\mathcal{N}|+|\mathcal{L}|})$ is a feasible solution to the dual problem. The vector $\mathbf{p}$ is associated with the optimal solution of the restricted problem, where all the columns involved are represented as set $\mathcal{Q}$. For a column $i \in \mathcal{Q}$ and associated with the basic variables, we have $c_i - \mathbf{p}'\mathbf{A}_i = 0$; for a column $i \in \mathcal{Q}$ and associated with the non-basic variables, we have $c_i - \mathbf{p}'\mathbf{A}_i \geq 0$ (if not, the solution associated with $\mathbf{p}$ could not be the optimal of the restricted problem). Given a vector $\mathbf{p}$ that stops the DCG algorithm, we can see that replacing the last element $p_{|\mathcal{N}|+|\mathcal{L}|}$ with $\frac{1}{\beta}p_{|\mathcal{N}|+|\mathcal{L}|}$ will not change the value of $\mathbf{p}'\mathbf{A}_i$ for left-submatrix columns, since $\mathbf{A}_i(|\mathcal{N}|+|\mathcal{L}|) = 0$ for those columns. Further the result in (34) ensures that $c_i - \hat{\mathbf{p}}'\mathbf{A}_i \geq 0$ for all the right-submatrix columns. In summary, $c_i - \hat{\mathbf{p}}'\mathbf{A}_i \geq 0$ for all columns of $\mathbf{A}$ and $\hat{\mathbf{p}}$ is a dual feasible solution. Then, by the weak duality, we have

$$\hat{\mathbf{p}}'\mathbf{b} = \frac{1}{\beta}p_{|\mathcal{N}|+|\mathcal{L}|} \leq \mathbf{c}'\mathbf{x}^* \tag{35}$$

That is

$$\text{max flow} = -\mathbf{c}'\mathbf{x}^* \leq -\frac{1}{\beta}p_{|\mathcal{N}|+|\mathcal{L}|} \tag{36}$$

The approximate solution

$$-p_{|\mathcal{N}|+|\mathcal{L}|} \geq \beta \times (\text{max flow}) \tag{37}$$

□

4.5 DCG in the MCF Problem

Consider there are F commodity flows over the network, with source-destination pairs (s_f, d_f) for $f = 1, \cdots, F$, respectively. The multi-commodity flow (MCF) problem is to maximize the summation of all the commodity flows. We can also transform the MCF problem to a standard network flow problem. Specifically, we induce new infinite capacity arcs (d_f, s_f) for $f = 1, \cdots, F$. We set the link costs $u_{(d_f,s_f)} = -1$ for $f = 1, \cdots, F$ and a cost of zero for all the other links.

We now need to determine the link flow allocation for every commodity. Thus we define for commodity flow f the vector

$$\mathbf{x}_f = (r_{(d_f,s_f)}, \mathbf{r}_f') \tag{38}$$

where $\mathbf{r}_f$ indicates the flow allocation vector for commodity f over the original network, i.e., $\mathbf{r}_f$ is the vector of commodity f flow allocation $r^f_{(a,b)}$ for all links $(a,b) \in \mathcal{L}$. The decision variables are

$$\mathbf{x} = (\mathbf{x}_1', \cdots, \mathbf{x}_F', \boldsymbol{\alpha}'). \tag{39}$$

Define the cost vector $\mathbf{c}_f = (-1, \mathbf{0}_{1\times|\mathcal{L}|})$. The cost vector for the transformed network flow problem will be $\mathbf{c} = (\mathbf{c}_1', \mathbf{c}_2', \cdots, \mathbf{c}_F', \mathbf{0}_{1\times M})$.

Each commodity flow allocation $\mathbf{r}_f$ needs to satisfy the flow conservation constraint. For flow f, the truncated node-arc incidence matrix $\mathbf{H}$ needs to add one column (specifically, as the first column) to include the newly induced arc (d_f, s_f); we use $\mathbf{H}^f$ to indicate this updated matrix. Since the induced links are not confined by the scheduling constraint, the matrix $\hat{\mathbf{I}}$ defined in (29) applies to every commodity flow.

Now the problem $\mathcal{P}_2$ is to be updated into the problem $\mathcal{P}_4$, which has

$$\mathbf{A} = \begin{bmatrix} \mathbf{H}^1 & & & & \\ & \mathbf{H}^2 & & & \\ & & \ddots & & \\ & & & \mathbf{H}^F & \\ \hat{\mathbf{I}} & \hat{\mathbf{I}} & \cdots & \hat{\mathbf{I}} & -\mathbf{W}_{|\mathcal{L}|\times M} \\ & & & & \mathbf{1}_{1\times M} \end{bmatrix}$$

$$\mathbf{b} = (\mathbf{0}'_{1\times(F(|\mathcal{N}|-1)+|\mathcal{L}|)}, 1)$$

We define the first $(|\mathcal{L}|+1)F$ columns of matrix $\mathbf{A}$ as left sub-matrix and the leftover M columns as right sub-matrix. It is not difficult to see that the DCG algorithm presented in Section 4.3 and the theoretical analysis regarding the approximated MWIS algorithm in Section 4.4 apply to the problem $\mathcal{P}_4$ too. We thus have the following theorem.

THEOREM 3. *If we apply an approximation algorithm with the approximation ratio β to solve the MWIS problem when search for an entering column, the MCF solved under such an approximation algorithm will be at least β of the optimal solution.*

4.6 DCG in MCF with Fairness Constraint

Ensuring fairness in resource allocation is an important issue. According to [1], an MCF problem with fairness constraint can be formulated as maximizing a factor λ (≤ 1) where at least $\lambda \cdot g_{s_f}$ amount of throughput can be guaranteed for each commodity flow. Here, g_{s_f} is the traffic requirement of commodity flow f. We also transform the problem to a standard network flow problem similarly to the construction in Section 4.5. We induce new infinite capacity arcs (d_f, s_f) and set the link costs $u_{(d_f,s_f)} = -1$ for $f = 1, \cdots, F$, and set a cost of zero for all the other links. With the fairness constraint, we should have

$$r_{(d_f,s_f)} = \lambda g_{s_f} \quad \text{for } f = 1, \cdots, F. \tag{40}$$

We still adopt the vectors $\mathbf{x}_f$ and $\mathbf{x}$ defined in (38) and (39). Let $\mathbf{g}_F = (g_{s_1}, \cdots, g_{s_F})$ denote the vector of traffic requirements of all commodities. Define a $(|\mathcal{L}| + 1) \times 1$ vector $\mathbf{e} = (1, 0, \cdots, 0)$. The constraints in (40) can be expressed in a matrix format as

$$\begin{bmatrix} \mathbf{e}' & & & \\ & \mathbf{e}' & & \\ & & \ddots & \\ & & & \mathbf{e}' \end{bmatrix} \begin{bmatrix} \mathbf{x}_1 \\ \mathbf{x}_2 \\ \vdots \\ \mathbf{x}_F \end{bmatrix} \triangleq \begin{bmatrix} \mathbf{E}_1 & \mathbf{E}_2 & \cdots & \mathbf{E}_F \end{bmatrix} \begin{bmatrix} \mathbf{x}_1 \\ \mathbf{x}_2 \\ \vdots \\ \mathbf{x}_F \end{bmatrix} = \lambda \mathbf{g}_F, \tag{41}$$

where each sub-matrix $\mathbf{E}_f$ is a $F \times (|\mathcal{L}| + 1)$ matrix, with only one non-zero element $\mathbf{E}_f(f, 1) = 1$.

With λ included, the new decision variable is defined as

$$\tilde{\mathbf{x}} = (\lambda, \mathbf{x}_1', \cdots, \mathbf{x}_F', \boldsymbol{\alpha}'), \tag{42}$$

with the corresponding cost vector $\mathbf{c} = (-1, 0, \cdots, 0)$. The problem $\mathcal{P}_2$ can then be updated to problem $\mathcal{P}_5$ with

$$\mathbf{A} = \begin{bmatrix} -\mathbf{g}_F & \mathbf{E}_1 & \mathbf{E}_2 & \cdots & \mathbf{E}_F & \\ & \mathbf{H}^1 & & & & \\ & & \mathbf{H}^2 & & & \\ & & & \ddots & & \\ & & & & \mathbf{H}^F & \\ & \hat{\mathbf{I}} & \hat{\mathbf{I}} & \cdots & \hat{\mathbf{I}} & -\mathbf{W}_{|\mathcal{L}|\times M} \\ & & & & & \mathbf{1}_{1\times M} \end{bmatrix}$$

$$\mathbf{b} = (\mathbf{0}'_{((|\mathcal{N}|-1)(F+1)+|\mathcal{L}|)\times 1}, 1).$$

Again, the DCG algorithm and the theoretical analysis regarding the approximated MWIS algorithm presented in previous cases apply to the problem $\mathcal{P}_5$ too. We thus have the following theorem.

THEOREM 4. *If we apply an approximation algorithm with the approximation ratio β to solve the MWIS problem when search for an entering column, the MCF problem with fairness constraint solved under such an approximation algorithm will be at least β of the optimal solution.*

5. DCG IN MR-MC NETWORKS

The DCG method can be applied to MR-MC networks based on the multi-dimensional conflict graph technique developed in [9]. To facilitate understanding, we here briefly summarize the MDCG technique presented in [9]. We use C to denote the number of available channels and c a specific channel. Although c is used as a link cost in previous sections, there will be no confusions of notation due to the clear context in this section. We use M_a to denote the number of radios available at node a.

An MR-MC network can be interpreted as a multi-dimensional resource space, with *dimensions* defined by links, radios, and channels. The MDCG is to describe the conflict relationships among the resource points, each represented as a link-radio-channel tuple. Specifically, an LRC tuple p is defined in the format:

$$\text{Link-radio-channel tuple:} \quad ((a, b), (y_a, y_b), c). \tag{43}$$

The tuple indicates that link (a, b) operates on channel c, using radios y_a and y_b at nodes a and b, respectively. Note that link (a, b) can be mapped to $M_a \times M_b \times C$ LRC tuples in the MDCG.

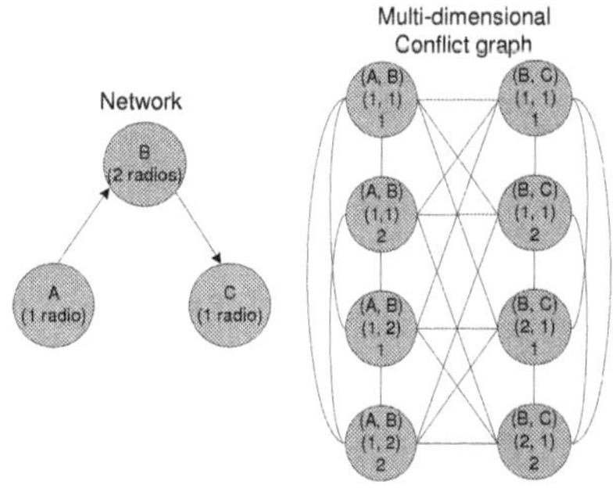

Figure 2: An illustration of MDCG construction [9].

There are two types of conflict relationships among LRC tuples in the MDCG. One is *interference conflict* indicating that co-channel transmissions (geometrically separated) conflict with each other within the interference range. The other is *radio conflict* indicating that multiple transmissions (possibly over different channels) contend for the same radio.

Consider an example of the MDCG. The left side of Fig. 2 shows a small network with directed links and 2 available channels. The right side illustrates the MDCG constructed. With the MDCG, the IS-based scheduling could jointly give the solutions of link scheduling, routing, channel and radio assignment [9].

For a network flow formulation over an MR-MC network, the flow conservation constraint presented in Section 4.1 still applies. The scheduling constraint presented in Section 4.2 needs to be updated according to the MDCG. Let $\mathcal{I}_m^p$ denote the mth independent set over an MDCG and $\mathcal{M}^p$ the set of all of the independent sets over the MDCG. The scheduling constraint is updated as:

$$r_{(a,b)} \leq \sum_{m:(a,b)\in\mathcal{I}_m^p} \alpha_m w_{(a,b)}^{c((a,b),\mathcal{I}_m^p)} \tag{44}$$

$$\sum_{m=1}^{|\mathcal{M}^p|} \alpha_m = 1 \tag{45}$$

where $c((a, b), \mathcal{I}_m^p)$ denotes the operating channel of link (a, b) when it is activated in the IS $\mathcal{I}_m^p$, and $w_{(a,b)}^c$ denotes the channel-dependent capacity of link (a, b) in the multiple-channel context. Note that the scheduling constraint (44) can conveniently exploit the channel diversity to optimally utilize high-quality channels for the maximum network capacity [9].

With the updated scheduling constraints (44) and (45), it can be easily checked that all the analysis and theorems developed in Section 4 remain valid in the MR-MC context. An implementation detail is that each column of the matrix $\mathbf{W}$ now represents a tuple-link based IS over the MDCG. In the implementation, we assume all nodes have the same communication range and interference range over all channels.

6. NUMERICAL RESULTS

In this section, we present numerical results to demonstrate the performance of DCG. For the convenience of comparison with existing methods, we focus on the MCF problem with fairness constraint in an MR-MC network which is considered in [1] and [9]. Our goals are three-fold. 1) We study the efficiency of the DCG algorithm by comparing its performance with three existing algorithms — the joint routing, channel assignment and link scheduling (RCL) algorithm proposed in [1], the random search of ISs [4] over the MDCG (RS-MDCG), and the MDCG based scheduling index ordering (SIO-MDCG) algorithm proposed in [9]. The performance is measured in terms of achieved network capacity λ^*

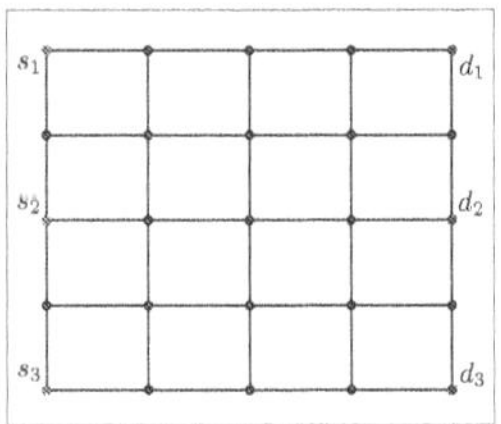

(a) Grid topology

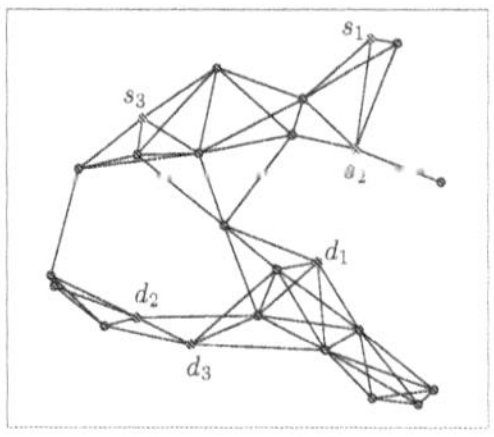

(b) Random topology

Figure 3: Network topologies.

and the total computation time. 2) We then study the scalability of our DCG algorithm versus the number of available channels, the number of radios and the network size. 3) We compare the performance of three MWIS approximation algorithms (i.e., the greedy algorithm in [16], the LP-based algorithm that integrates the greedy algorithm with a relaxed linear programming in [16], and the SRA algorithm in [17]) in affecting the performance of the DCG algorithm in Section 6.3.

In the following, all our results with the DCG algorithm are based on the greedy MWIS algorithm [16], except in Section 6.3 where we explicitly compare the performance of different approximate MWIS algorithms. The DCG algorithm is terminated if the following two events happen: 1) no new entering column is found by the MWIS algorithm; 2) the network capacity improvement in one iteration has held less than 10^{-6} for 100 iterations. The second condition stems from our observation that, after a number of iterations, the algorithm begins continuously finding new entering columns which introduce very limited reduced cost (or have little impact on the capacity). We set the RS-MDCG algorithm stop searching for new MISs when it has already found 2×10^5 MISs.

We develop Matlab programs for each of the above algorithms. We use CPLEX [15] within the Matlab environment to solve all the LPs involved in the above algorithms. In the comparisons, the computation time of each algorithm is measured as the total time including independent set searching (not applicable to the RCL algorithm) and LP optimizations. We run the program on a machine with an 8-core and 3.4GHz CPU and 12GB RAM. Besides, the codes are optimized to further avoid memory leak when solving large-scale LPs. For instance, instead of storing the sparse independent set matrix $\mathbf{W}$, which is very memory expensive, we only store the non-zero elements along with their associated positions in the matrix. Intermediate variables are immediately cleared after last use in order to save memory.

6.1 Performance Comparison

We consider two networks as shown in Fig. 3, each of which has 25 nodes deployed within a 900m $\times$ 900m area. The communication range and interference range of each node are 250m and 500m, respectively. In the grid topology, each node is equipped with 4 radios and there are totally 8 orthogonal channels available to them; in the random topology, 9 orthogonal channels are available and each node has 3 radios. We assume that the channel capacities of all the tuples are the same and are normalized to 1 rate unit. As marked in both figures, there are 3 commodity flows from sources s_1, s_2, s_3 to destinations d_1, d_2, d_3, respectively. Each flow demands a throughput of 3 rate units, i.e., the input to the source nodes $g_i = 3$. As a reference value, an upper bound of λ^* is also calculated by solving an LP relaxation problem proposed in [1]. Note that this upper bound may not be practically feasible. For the RS-MDCG algorithm, in order to achieve comparable capacity, we fix the total number of independent sets to be searched at 2×10^5.

Table 1: Performance comparisons.

Network 1 with 8 channels and each node having 4 radios			
	λ^*	computation time (seconds)	number of independent sets used
Upper bound	1.0	—	—
RCL	0.179	10.6	—
RS-MDCG	0.345	41771.0	2×10^5
SIO-MDCG	0.404	3485.28	31406
DCG	0.435	138.1	1008 (223 iterations)
Network 2 with 9 channels and each node having 3 radios			
	λ^*	computation time (seconds)	number of independent sets used
Upper bound	0.333	—	—
RCL	0.125	23.68	—
RS-MDCG	0.230	46313.22	2×10^5
SIO-MDCG	0.191	2620.25	28718
DCG	0.300	117.32	1118 (285 iterations)

Table 1 summarizes the comparison results. Generally, our algorithm achieves the most preferable tradeoff between network capacity and computation time for both topologies. First, we observe that the DCG algorithm achieves the best capacities with the least computation time among all the three MDCG based algorithms. In fact, both RS-MDCG and SIO-MDCG first find a large amount of maximal independent sets, and then input them into the LP problem $\mathcal{P}_5$ which solves the optimal capacity and scheduling jointly. During searching for independent sets, RS-MDCG just applies random search while the SIO-MDCG does so in a more managed way by taking critical independent sets into account [9]. However, the importance of each independent set to the problem has not been fully explored. Alternatively, the DCG algorithm searches for a new entering independent set in each round which can definitely improve the objective. As the table shows, the DCG algorithm uses only around 1000 ISs (among them 785 and 833 sets are initial ISs) in both networks, respectively. These numbers are significantly smaller than those used by the RS-MDCG and SIO-MDCG algorithms. Second, although the RCL algorithm takes the shortest time, its final capacity is significantly low (less than 50% of the capacity achieved by the DCG algorithm).

6.2 Scalability Evaluation

6.2.1 *The impact of number of channels*

Consider both networks shown in Fig. 3 with the number of available channels ranging from 1 to 10. From the results shown in Fig. 4, we have the following observations. 1) For all the four algorithms, the network capacity basically increases proportionally with the number of available channels. 2) The DCG algorithm always achieves the highest capacity. Moreover, as shown in Fig. 4(b) and 4(d), the computation time of DCG is significantly lower than that of RS-MDCG (its computation time is longer than 6000 seconds and thus omitted from the figures) and of SIO-MDCG. Although the RCL algorithm takes the shortest time, its achieved capacity is significantly lower than all the other three algorithms. 3) The computation time of the SIO-MDCG algorithm is exponential in the number of channels. However, roughly speaking, both the DCG and RCL algorithms run in time polynomial in the number of channels. Such polynomial relationship for the RCL algorithm has been proved in [1]. For the DCG algorithm, we further explore it in Section 6.2.3.

6.2.2 *The impact of number of radios*

Based on the observations above, only the SIO-MDCG algorithm is comparable to our SIO-MDCG algorithm in terms of both

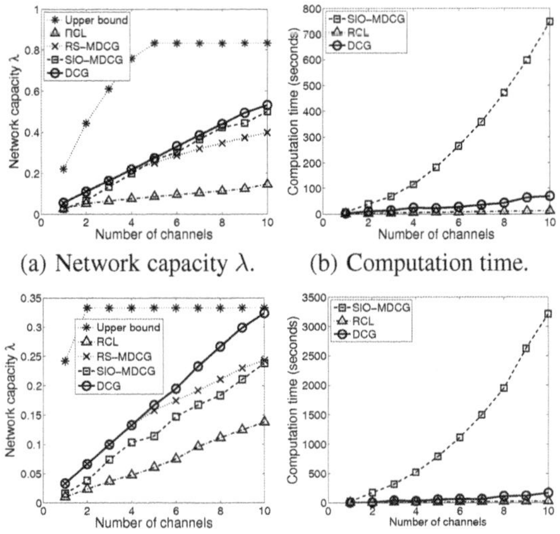

(a) Network capacity λ. (b) Computation time.

(c) Network capacity λ. (d) Computation time.

Figure 4: Impact of multi-channels. (a-b) Grid topology with 4 radios; (c-d) random topology with 3 radios.

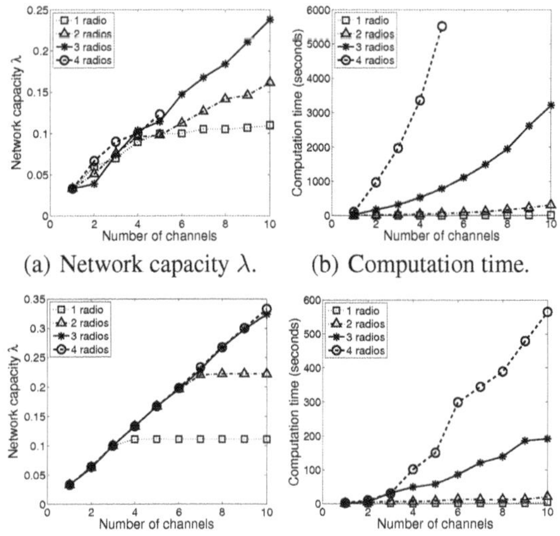

(a) Network capacity λ. (b) Computation time.

(c) Network capacity λ. (d) Computation time.

Figure 5: Impact of multi-radios. (a-b): SIO-MDCG algorithm; (c-d): DCG algorithm.

network capacity and computation complexity. Therefore, we only compare the performance of the DCG and SIO-MDCG algorithms in the following. We consider the random topology with the number of radios varying from 1 to 4. The results for the grid topology are similar and hence are omitted. In addition, in Fig. 5(a) and 5(b), the results for SIO-MDCG with 4 radios and more than 5 channels are omitted because the algorithm's computation time is excessively high while the resultant network capacities are very close to the curve corresponding to 3 radios.

In Fig. 5, we can observe for both algorithms that when there are less than 4 channels available, the number of radios does not have significant impact on the network capacity; in other words, all the four channels can be exploited even with just one radio. The explanation is that in that range, the optimal resource allocation for the highest network capacity is to assign the links within an interference neighborhood each a different channel [20]. When there are still more channels available than the number of links in an interfering neighborhood, which can then be exploited by the extra available channels. In Fig. 5, there are also ranges that the capacity curves become flat, where all the available radios are fully used and can not exploit the extra available channels. Furthermore, the exponential growth of the computation time of the MIO-MDCG algorithm is clearly shown in Fig. 5(b). In contrast, the computation complexity of the DCG algorithm is polynomial in the number of radios as shown in Fig. 5(d).

6.2.3 The impact of network size

In this evaluation, we generate a number of networks with nodes randomly deployed within linearly expanded areas, where the node density maintains the same as that of the random network shown in Fig. 3(b). There are 5 channels available and each node has 3 radios. We consider 3 commodity flows where their sources and destinations are randomly chosen in each of the networks. From the results shown in Fig. 6(a), the network capacities by the two algorithms are almost flat versus the network sizes, but the DCG always performs better than the SIO-MDCG. Such flat shapes are reasonable since the network density is fixed. As the network scale grows, the computation complexity of the SIO-MDCG algorithm climbs much faster than that of the DCG algorithm, as shown in Fig. 6(b).

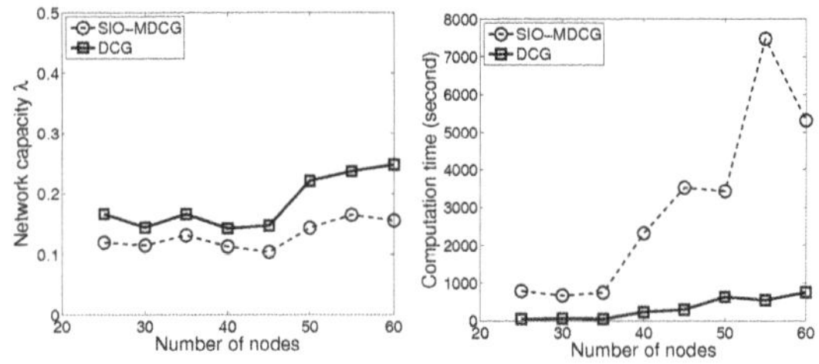

(a) Network capacity λ. (b) Computation time.

Figure 6: Scalability against network size. Random topologies with 3 radios and 5 channels.

Since the tuple-based independent sets have been used in the MR-MC networks, we here more directly demonstrate the algorithm complexity versus the number of tuples. We collect all the data for the DCG algorithm in Fig. 4(b) and 5(d) and re-present them in Fig. 7 as a function of the square of the number of tuples. We can see that the computation time is almost linear to the square of tuple numbers. In fact, fixing the network topology, the number of tuples is proportional to the product of the number of channels (C) and the square of the number of radios ($(\max\{M_a\})^2$). Therefore, these results show that our DCG algorithm is polynomial in time, and the complexity is in the order of $O\left(C^2(\max\{M_a\})^4\right)$.

6.3 Comparison of MWIS Algorithms

With thorough examinations, we find that the major amount of the computation time in DCG is spent by the embedded MWIS algorithm. Therefore, in this part, we study the impact of the MWIS algorithm on DCG by comparing the performance with three MWIS approximation algorithms: the greedy algorithm [16], the LP-based algorithm [16], and the support ratio algorithm (SRA) [17]. We use the random network as shown in Fig. 3(b) with 9 available channels and 3 radios. From Fig. 8, we observe that the simple greedy algorithm converges extremely faster than the other two without sacrificing the network capacity. This is reasonable since both SRA and LP-based algorithms have higher computation complexity than the greedy algorithm. Another observation is that by the three algorithms, the network capacity curves all experience a sharp increasing period.

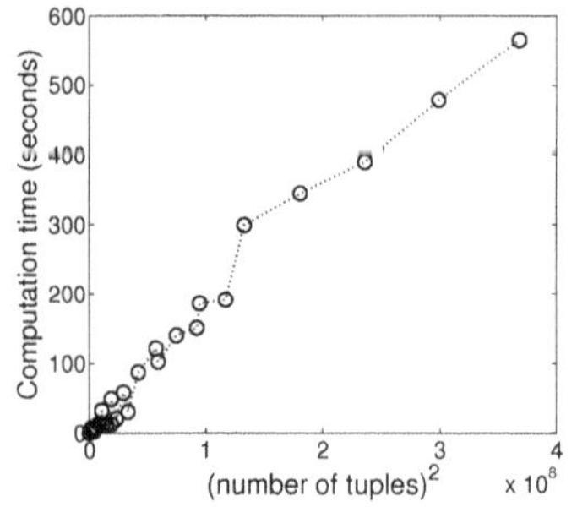

Figure 7: Computation time as a function of square of tuples number.

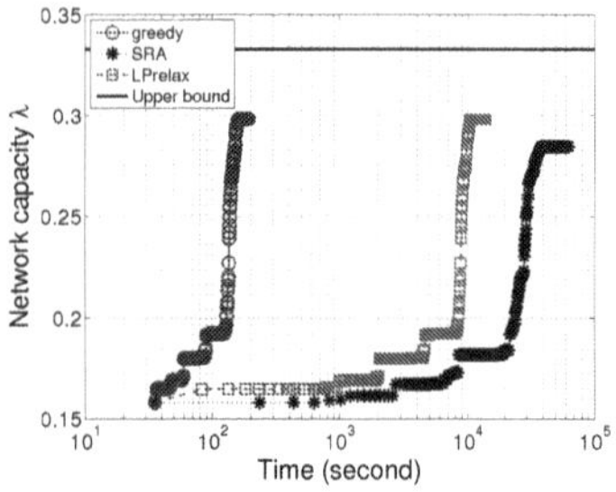

Figure 8: Performance comparison among MWIS algorithms.

7. CONCLUSION

The network capacity of a multi-hop wireless network is fundamentally determined by independent set based scheduling. Searching all ISs over a conflict graph for scheduling is NP-hard in general. In this paper, we systematically study the performance of the delayed column generation method in solving network flow problems augmented with IS-based scheduling, and contribute some original theoretical analysis of the performance of DCG. Extensive numerical results have been presented to demonstrate that the DCG algorithm achieves the most preferred tradeoff between network capacity and computation time among the RCL, RS-MDCG and SIO-MDCG algorithms, and is also scalable versus the number of channels, the number of radios, and the network size. In addition, as for the embedded MWIS algorithm in DCG, it has been shown that the greedy approximation algorithm is a good option for both the performance and the complexity.

8. ACKNOWLEDGMENTS

This work was supported in part by the NSF under grants CNS-1053777 and CNS-1320736.

9. REFERENCES

[1] M. Alicherry, R. Bhatia, and L. Li, "Joint channel assignment and routing for throughput optimization in multi-radio wireless mesh networks," in *Proc. ACM MobiCom*, pp. 58–72, Aug. 2005.

[2] W. Wang, X. Liu, and D. Krishnaswamy, "Robust routing and scheduling in wireless mesh networks", in *Proc. IEEE SECON*, pp. 471–480, 2007

[3] L. Badia, A. Erta, L. Lenzini, and M. Zorzi, "A general interferenceaware framework for joint routing and link scheduling in wireless mesh networks", *IEEE Network*, vol. 22, no. 1, pp. 32–38, Jan./Feb. 2008

[4] K. Jain, J. Padhye, V. Padmanabhan, and L. Qiu, "Impact of interference on multihop wireless network performance", in *Proc. ACM MobiCom*, pp. 66–80, 2003.

[5] W. Li, X. Cheng, T. Jing, Y. Cui, K. Xing, and W. Wang, "Spectrum assignment and sharing for delay minimization in multi-hop multi-flow CRNs, " *IEEE J. Sel. Areas Commun.*, vol. 31, no. 11, pp. 2483–2493, Nov. 2013.

[6] K. N. Ramachandran, E. M. Belding, K. C. Almeroth, and M. M. Buddhikot, "Interference-aware channel assignment in multiradio wireless mesh networks", in *Proc. IEEE INFOCOM*, pp. 1–12, 2006.

[7] J. Tang, S. Misra and G. Xue, "Joint spectrum allocation and scheduling for fair spectrum sharing in cognitive radio wireless networks," *Computer Networks*, vol. 52, no. 11, pp. 2148-2158. 2008.

[8] H. Li, Y. Cheng, X. Tian, and X. Wang, "A generic framework for throughput-optimal control in MR-MC wireless networks," in *Proc. IEEE INFOCOM*, Orlando, Florida, Mar. 25–30, 2012

[9] H. Li, Y. Cheng, C. Zhou, and P. Wan, "Multi-dimensional conflict graph based computing for optimal capacity in MR-MC wireless networks", in *Proc. IEEE ICDCS*, Genoa, Italy, June 21–25, 2010.

[10] I. Ho, P. Lam, P. Chong, and S. Liew, "Harnessing the High Bandwidth of Multi-radio Multi-channel 802.11 n Mesh Networks," *IEEE Trans. Mobile Computing*, vol. 13, no. 2, pp. 448–456, Feb. 2014.

[11] D. Bertsimas and J. N. Tsitsiklis. "Introduction to linear optimization", *Athena Scientific*, 1997.

[12] P. Bjorklund, P. Varbrand, and D. Yuan. "Resource optimization of spatial TDMA in ad hoc radio networks: A column generation approach". In *Proc. IEEE INFOCOM*, 2003.

[13] S. Kompella, J. E. Wieselthier, and A. Ephremides. "Multi-hop routing and scheduling in wireless networks subject to SINR constraints.", *46th IEEE Conference on Decision and Control*, 2007.

[14] J. Luo, C. Rosenberg, A. Girard, "Engineering wireless mesh networks: joint scheduling, routing, power control, and rate adaptation," *IEEE/ACM Trans. Netw.*, vol. 18, no. 5, pp. 1387–1400, Oct. 2010.

[15] IBM ILOG CPLEX Optimizer. `http://www.ilog.com/products/cplex/`.

[16] A. Kako, T. Ono, T. Hirata, and M. M. Halldórsson. "Approximation algorithms for the weighted independent set problem in sparse graphs." *Discrete Applied Mathematics*, vol. 157, no. 4, pp. 617–626, 2009.

[17] S. Balaji, V. Swaminathan, and K. Kannan. "Approximating Maximum Weighted Independent Set Using Vertex Support.", *World Academy of Science, Engineering and Technology*, 35, 2009.

[18] V. S. Anil Kumar, M. V. Marathe, and S. Parthasarathy, "Algorithmic aspects of capacity in wireless neworks," in *Proc. ACM SIGMETRICs*, pp. 133–144, 2005.

[19] X. Lin and S. Rasool, "Distributed and provably-efficient algorithms for joint channel-assignment, scheduling and routing in multi-channel ad hoc wireless networks," *IEEE/ACM Trans. Networking*, vol. 17, no. 6, pp. 1874–1887, Dec. 2009.

[20] P. Kyasanur and N. H. Vaidya, "Capacity of multi-channel wireless networks: Impact of number of channels and interfaces," in *Proc. ACM MobiCom*, Aug. 2005, pp. 43Ű57.

[21] P. Gupta and P. R. Kumar, "The cpacity of wireless networks," *IEEE Trans. Inform. Theory*, vol. 46, no. 2, pp. 388–404, Mar. 2000.

When Backpressure Meets Predictive Scheduling

Longbo Huang*, Shaoquan Zhang♯, Minghua Chen♯, Xin Liu†
*longbohuang@tsinghua.edu.cn, IIIS, Tsinghua University
♯{zsq008, minghua}@ie.cuhk.edu.hk, IE, Chinese University of Hong Kong
†liuxin@microsoft.com, Microsoft Research Asia

ABSTRACT

Motivated by the increasing popularity of learning and predicting human user behavior in communication and computing systems, in this paper, we investigate the fundamental benefit of predictive scheduling, i.e., predicting and pre-serving arrivals, in controlled queueing systems. Based on a lookahead-window prediction model, we first establish a novel queue-equivalence between the predictive queueing system with a *fully-efficient* scheduling scheme and an equivalent queueing system without prediction. This result allows us to analytically demonstrate that predictive scheduling necessarily improves system delay performance and drives it to zero with increasing prediction power. It also enables us to exactly determine the required prediction power for different systems and study its impact on tail delay.

We then propose the `Predictive Backpressure` (`PBP`) algorithm for achieving optimal utility performance in such predictive systems. `PBP` efficiently incorporates prediction into stochastic system control and avoids the great complication due to the exponential state space growth in the prediction window size. We show that `PBP` achieves a utility performance that is within $O(\epsilon)$ of the optimal, for any $\epsilon > 0$, while guaranteeing that the system delay distribution is a *shifted-to-the-left* version of that under the original Backpressure algorithm. Hence, the average delay under `PBP` is strictly better than that under Backpressure, and vanishes with increasing prediction window size. This implies that the resulting utility-delay tradeoff with predictive scheduling can beat the known optimal $[O(\epsilon), O(\log(1/\epsilon))]$ tradeoff for systems without prediction.

1. INTRODUCTION

Due to the rapid development of powerful handheld devices, e.g., smartphones or tablet computers, human users now interact much more easily and frequently with the communication and computing infrastructures, e.g., E-commerce websites, cellular networks, and crowdsourcing platforms. Thus, in order to provide high level quality-of-service, it is important to understand human behavior features and to utilize such information in guiding system control algorithm design. Therefore, various studies have been conducted to learn and predict human behavior patterns, e.g., online social networking [1], online searching behavior [2], and online browsing [3].

In this paper, we take one step further and ask the following important question: *What is the fundamental system benefit of having such user-behavior information?* Our objective is to obtain a theoretical quantification of this gain. To mathematically carry out our investigation, we consider a multi-user single-server queueing system. At every time, user workload arriving at the system will first be queued at corresponding buffer space. Then, the server allocates resources and decides the scheduling for serving the jobs. These operations allow the server to serve certain amount of workload for each user, but also result in a system cost due to resource utilization. Different from most existing work in multi-queue systems, here we assume that the server can *predict and serve future arrivals before they arrive at the system.* Hence, at every time, the server updates his prediction of future arrivals and adapts his control action. The objective is to serve all user workload with minimum cost, and to ensure small job latency for each user.

This is an important problem and can be used to model many practical systems where traffic prediction and preserving can be performed. The first example is scheduling in cellular networks. In this case, the base station handles users' data demand. Instead of waiting for the users to submit their requests, and suffering from a potentially big burst of traffic, which can lead to a large service latency, the base station can "push" the information to the users beforehand, e.g., push the news information at 7am in the morning. The second example scenario is prefetching in computing systems, e.g., [4] [5]. Here, data or instructions are preloaded into memory before they are actually requested. Doing so enables faster access or execution of the commands and enhances system performance. Another example is computing management, e.g., in computers. In this case, each user represents a software application and the server represents a workload management unit. Then, according to the needs of the applications, the managing unit pre-computes some information in case some later applications request them, e.g., branch prediction in computer architecture [6] [7].

There have been many previous works studying multi-queue system scheduling with utility optimization. [8] studies the fundamental tradeoff between energy consumption and packet delay for a single-queue system. [9] extends

MobiHoc'14, August 11–14, 2014, Philadelphia, PA, USA.

http://dx.doi.org/10.1145/2632951.2632983.

the results to a downlink system and designs algorithms to achieve the optimal tradeoff. [10] designs algorithms for minimizing energy consumption of a stochastic network. [11] designs energy optimal scheme for satellites. [12] looks at the problem of quality-of-service guaranteed energy efficient transmission using a calculus approach. [13] studies the tradeoff between energy and robustness for downlink systems. [14] and [15] develop algorithms for achieving the optimal utility-delay tradeoff in multihop networks.

However, we note that all the aforementioned works assume that the system only takes *causal* scheduling actions, i.e., the server will start serving packets only after they enter the system. While this is necessary in many systems, preserving future traffic can actually be done in systems that have highly predictable traffic. While predictive scheduling approaches have been investigated, e.g., [7], not much analytical study has been conducted. Closest to our work are [16], [17], which study the benefit of proactive scheduling, and [18], which studies the impact of future arrival information on queueing delay in $M/M/1$ queues. However, we note that [16] and [17] do not consider the effect of queueing, which very commonly appears in communication and computing systems, whereas [18] does not consider controllable rates and scheduling. Indeed, due to the joint existence of prediction and controlled queueing, the problem considered here is very complicated. Delay problems in stochastic controlled queueing systems are known to be hard. Moreover, arrival prediction advances in a sliding-window pattern over time, i.e., at every time, the system can predict slightly further into the future. Designing control algorithms for such systems often involves dynamic programming (DP). However, since the state space size grows exponentially with the prediction window size, the DP approach may not be computationally practical even for small systems. Even without prediction, the complexity of DP can still be very high due to the large queue state space. Moreover, since the system prediction evolves according to a sliding-window pattern, it is also not possible to apply the frame-based Lyapunov technique as in [19] and [20].

To resolve the above difficulties, we first establish a novel equivalence between the queueing system under prediction and a class of *fully-efficient* scheduling scheme and a queueing system without prediction but with a different initial condition and an equivalent scheduling policy. This connection is made by carrying out a sample-path queueing argument and enables us to analytically quantify the delay gain due to predictive scheduling for general multi-queue single-server systems. Our result shows that for such systems, the packet delay distribution is *shifted-to-the-left* under predictive scheduling. Hence, the average delay necessarily decreases and *approaches zero* as the prediction window size increases. Based on this result, we further propose a low-complexity `Predictive Backpressure` (`PBP`) scheduling policy for utility maximization in such predictive systems. `PBP` retains all desired features of the original Backpressure algorithm [21], e.g., greedy, does not require statistical information of the system dynamics, and has strong theoretical performance guarantee. We prove that the `PBP` algorithm can achieve an average cost that is $O(\epsilon)$ of the minimum cost for any $\epsilon > 0$, while guaranteeing an average delay that is strictly smaller than that under the original Backpressure. Hence, the resulting utility-delay tradeoff with predictive scheduling can beat the known optimal $[O(\epsilon), O(\log(1/\epsilon))]$ tradeoff for systems without prediction. We also demonstrate analytically and numerically with real data trace that when the first-in-first-out (FIFO) queueing discipline is used, `PBP` achieves an average packet delay reduction that is linear in the prediction window size, and that when the last-in-first-out (LIFO) discipline is used, the average packet delay under `PBP` decreases *exponentially* in the window size. These results demonstrate the power of predictive scheduling and provide explicit quantification of the benefits, which also provides useful guidelines for predictive algorithm design.

The rest of the paper is organized as follows. In Section 2, we present our system model and problem formulation. We develop the `Predictive Backpressure` (`PBP`) algorithm in Section 3. The analysis of delay performance under general predictive scheduling and `PBP` is given in Section 4. We extend the results to predictable-only systems in Section 5. Simulation results are presented in Section 6, followed by the conclusions in Section 7.

2. SYSTEM MODEL

We consider a general multi-queue single-server system shown in Fig. 1. In this system, a server serves N queues, one for each user that utilizes the service of the server. [1] This multi-queue system has many applications. For instance, it can be used to model downlink transmission in cellular networks, where the server represents the base station and the users are mobile users. Another example is a task management system of smartphones, where each user represents an application and the server represents the operating system that manages all computing workloads. We assume that the system operates in slotted time, i.e., $t \in \{0, 1, ...\}$.

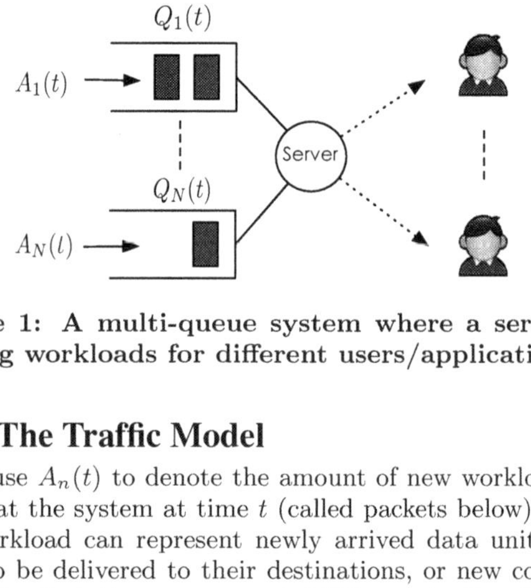

Figure 1: A multi-queue system where a server is serving workloads for different users/applications.

2.1 The Traffic Model

We use $A_n(t)$ to denote the amount of new workload arriving at the system at time t (called packets below). Here the workload can represent newly arrived data units that need to be delivered to their destinations, or new computing tasks that the server must fulfill eventually. We use $\boldsymbol{A}(t) = (A_1(t), ..., A_N(t))$ to denote the vector of arrivals at time t. We assume that $\boldsymbol{A}(t)$ is i.i.d. with $\mathbb{E}\{A_n(t)\} = \lambda_n$. [2] We also assume that for each n, $0 \leq A_n(t) \leq A_{\max}$.

2.2 The Service Rate Model

[1]Though we only consider a multi-queue system here, our results can likely be extended to general multihop queueing systems using the queue-equivalent results in Section 4.

[2]The arrivals can be arbitrarily correlated among different users.

Every time slot, the server allocates power for serving the pending packets. [3] However, due to the potential system dynamics, e.g., channel fading coefficient changes, serving different users at different time may result in different resource consumption and generate different service rates. We model this fact by assuming that the server connects to each user n with a time-varying channel, whose state is denoted by $S_n(t)$. We then denote $\boldsymbol{S}(t) = (S_1(t), ..., S_N(t))$ the system link state. We assume that $\boldsymbol{S}(t)$ is i.i.d. and takes values in $\{s_1, ..., s_K\}$. [4] We use π_{s_i} to denote the probability that $\boldsymbol{S}(t) = s_i$.

The server's power allocation over link n at time t is denoted by $P_n(t)$. We denote the aggregate system power allocation vector by $\boldsymbol{P}(t) = (P_1(t), ..., P_N(t))$. Under a system link state s_i, we assume that the power allocation vector $\boldsymbol{P}(t)$ must be chosen from some feasible power allocation set $\mathcal{P}^{(s_i)}$, which is compact and contains the constraint $0 \leq P_n(t) \leq P_{\max}$. Then, under the given link state $\boldsymbol{S}(t)$ and the power allocation vector $\boldsymbol{P}(t)$, the amount of backlog that can be served for user n is determined by $\mu_n(t) = \mu_n(\boldsymbol{S}(t), \boldsymbol{P}(t))$. We assume that $\mu_n(\boldsymbol{S}(t), \boldsymbol{P}(t))$ is a continuous function of $\boldsymbol{P}(t)$ for all $\boldsymbol{S}(t)$. Also, we assume that there exists $\mu_{\max}$ such that $\mu_n(\boldsymbol{S}(t), \boldsymbol{P}(t)) \leq \mu_{\max}$ for all n, all time t, and under any $\boldsymbol{S}(t)$ and $\boldsymbol{P}(t)$.

2.3 The Predictive Service Model

Different from most previous works, we assume that the server can *predict and serve* future packet arrivals. Specifically, we first parameterize our prediction model by a vector $\boldsymbol{D} = (D_1, ..., D_N)$, where $D_n \geq 1$ is the prediction window size of user n. That is, at each time t, the server has access to the arrival information in the *lookahead window* $\{A_n(t), ..., A_n(t + D_n - 1)\}$, and can allocate rates to serve the future arrivals in the current time slot. [5] Such a lookahead window model approximates practical scenarios and was also used in [18] and [23].

We then use $\{\mu_n^{(d)}(t)\}_{d=0}^{D_n-1}$ to denote the rate allocated to serving the arriving packets in time slot $t + d$ and let $\mu_n^{(-1)}(t)$ denote the rate allocated for serving the packets that are already in the system. Note that we always have $\sum_{d=-1}^{D_n-1} \mu_n^{(d)}(t) \leq \mu_n(t)$. Fig. 2 shows the slot structure and the predictive service model.

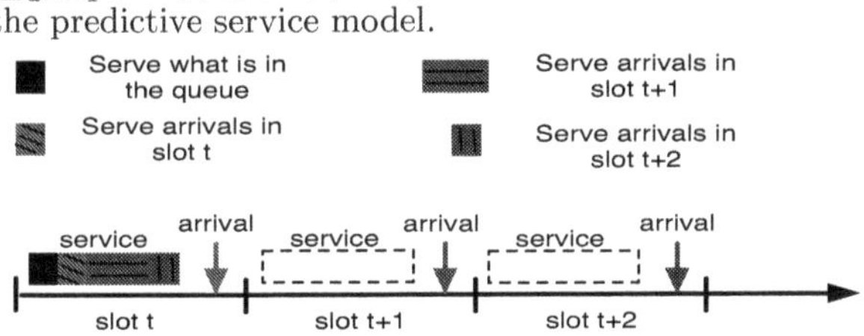

Figure 2: The figure shows what happens in a single time slot in the case of $D_n = 3$. The server predicts and serves the arrivals in timeslots t, $t + 1$ and $t + 2$, respectively.

[3]Our results can be extended to the case where the server consumes multiple types of resources, e.g., power and CPU cycles.

[4]Our results can easily be generalized to the case when both arrivals and channel conditions are Markovian, using the variable-size drift analysis developed in [22].

[5]Since we assume that the arrivals in a time slot can only be served in the next slot, we also consider $A_n(t)$ to be future arrivals.

2.4 Queueing

Denote $Q_n(t)$ the number of packets queued at the server for user n. We assume the following queueing dynamics:

$$Q_n(t+1) = \left[Q_n(t) - \mu_n^{(-1)}(t)\right]^+ + A_n^{(-1)}(t). \tag{1}$$

Here $A_n^{(-1)}(t)$ denotes the number of packets that *actually* enter the queue after going through a series of predictive service phases, i.e., for all $-1 \leq d \leq D_n - 2$,

$$A_n^{(d)}(t) = [A_n^{(d+1)}(t) - \mu_n^{(d+1)}(t - d - 1)]^+, \tag{2}$$

and $A_n^{(D_n-1)}(t) = A_n(t)$. In this paper, we say that the system is *stable* if the following condition holds:

$$Q_{\text{av}} \triangleq \limsup_{t\to\infty} \frac{1}{t} \sum_{\tau=0}^{t-1} \sum_n \mathbb{E}\{Q_n(\tau)\} < \infty. \tag{3}$$

2.5 System Objective

In every time slot, the server spends certain cost due to power expenditure. We denote this cost by $f(\boldsymbol{S}(t), \boldsymbol{P}(t))$. One simple example is $f(S(t), \boldsymbol{P}(t)) = \sum_n P_n(t)$, which denotes the total power consumption. We assume that under any state $\boldsymbol{S}(t)$, there exists a constant $f^{\max}$ such that $f(\boldsymbol{S}(t), \boldsymbol{P}(t)) \leq f^{\max}$. The special case when $f(\boldsymbol{S}(t), \boldsymbol{P}(t))$ is independent of $\boldsymbol{P}(t)$ corresponds to the stability scheduling problem [21].

The system's objective is to find a power allocation and scheduling scheme for minimizing the time average cost, defined as:

$$f_{\text{av}} \triangleq \limsup_{t\to\infty} \frac{1}{t} \sum_{\tau=0}^{t-1} \mathbb{E}\{f(\tau)\}, \tag{4}$$

subject to the constraint that the queues in the system must be stable, i.e., (3) holds. We use $f_{\text{av}}^{\boldsymbol{D}*}$ to denote the minimum average cost under any feasible predictive scheduling algorithm with prediction vector $\boldsymbol{D}$, i.e., those that predict the arrivals for D_n slots and allocates service rates to serving the arrivals within the window $[t, t + D_n - 1]$ for each user n. We then use f_{av}^* to denote the minimum average power consumption incurred under any non-predictive scheduling policy.

2.6 Discussion of the Model

Note that the lookahead-window model is an idealized model which assumes that the system can perfectly predict future arrivals. Because of this, our results can be viewed as upper bounds of the fundamental benefit of predictive scheduling, which provide important criteria for evaluating predictive control algorithms. We also investigate the impact of prediction error in Section 6.

We also note that our model is very different from previous controlled queueing system works, which almost all assume that the system operates in a *causal* manner, i.e., only serves packets after they arrive at the system. Our model is motivated by pre-fetching techniques used in memory management [4], branch prediction in computer architecture [6], as well as recent advancement in data mining for learning user behavior patterns [3].

Our model is most relevant for modeling problems where future workload can be predicted and served before they enter the system. One such application scenario is in mobile networks, where the base station handles users' demand.

Since each user typically requests certain news information at specific times, e.g., 7am in the morning. Instead of waiting for the all the users to submit their requests at the same time, which can lead to a large service latency and high power consumption, one can "push" some information to the users beforehand at times when the link condition is good.

Without such predictive control, the cost minimization problem has been extensively studied and algorithms have been proposed, e.g., [10]. However, very little is known about the fundamental impact of prediction on system performance, let alone finding optimal control policies for such predictive queueing systems. Moreover, due to the existence of prediction windows and the fact that arrival processes are stochastic, the system naturally evolves according to a Markov chain whose state space size grows exponentially in the prediction window size. Thus, this problem is very challenging to solve.

3. PREDICTIVE BACKPRESSURE

In this section, we present our algorithm, which is designed by efficiently incorporating prediction information into the Backpressure technique [21]. Note that since future arrival information is made available in a sliding-window form, prediction couples the current action with future arrivals in every time slot. This prohibits the use of frame-based Lyapunov technique [22], and makes the problem complicated. Fortunately, as we will see, with the development of a novel *queue-equivalence* result, one can incorporate prediction into system control cleanly and significantly reduce the complexity in both algorithm design and analysis.

3.1 Prediction Queues

For our algorithm development and analysis, we now introduce the notion of a prediction queue, which records the number of residual arrivals in every slot in time window $[t, t+D_n-1]$. Specifically, we denote $Q_n^{(d)}(t)$ the number of remaining arrivals currently in future slot $t+d$, i.e., d slots into the future, and denote $Q_n^{(-1)}(t)$ the number of packets already in the system. We see then the queues evolve according to the following dynamics:

1. If $d = D_n - 1$, then:
$$Q_n^{(d)}(t+1) = A_n(t+D_n). \quad (5)$$

2. If $0 \leq d \leq D_n - 2$, then:
$$Q_n^{(d)}(t+1) = \big[Q_n^{(d+1)}(t) - \mu_n^{(d+1)}(t)\big]^+. \quad (6)$$

3. For $Q_n^{(-1)}(t)$, we have:
$$Q_n^{(-1)}(t+1) \quad (7)$$
$$= \Big[Q_n^{(-1)}(t) - \mu_n^{(-1)}(t)\Big]^+ + \big[Q_n^{(0)}(t) - \mu_n^{(0)}(t)\big]^+,$$
with $Q_n^{(-1)}(0) = 0$.

Fig. 3 shows the definition of the prediction queues. One can see that $\{Q_n^{(d)}(t)\}_{d=0}^{D_n-1}$ are not really queues. They simply record the residual arrivals going through the timeline, whereas $Q_n^{(-1)}(t)$ records the true backlog in the system. Notice that $Q_n^{(-1)}(t)$ is exactly the same as $Q_n(t)$ in (1). Since $Q_n^{(-1)}(t)$ is the only actual queue, the system is stable if and only if $Q_n^{(-1)}(t)$ is stable.

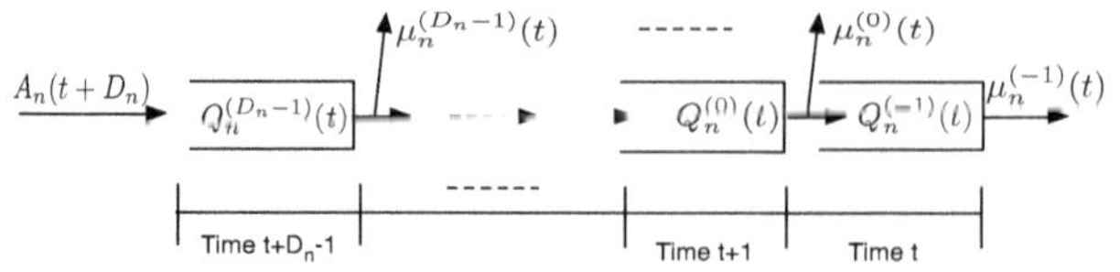

Figure 3: The prediction queues that describe the system evolution.

3.2 Predictive Backpressure

Here we construct our algorithm based on the above prediction queues and Backpressure. Our main idea is to use the sum of all the queues $Q_n^{\text{sum}} \triangleq \sum_{d=-1}^{D_n-1} Q_n^{(d)}(t)$ for decision making.

To describe the algorithm in details, we define the notion of queueing discipline for the predictive system, i.e., how to select packets to serve from queues $\{Q_n^{(d)}(t)\}_{d=-1}^{D_n-1}$. Specifically, we order the packets in $Q_n^{(d)}(t)$ with labels $p_{\sum_{d'<d} Q_n^{d'}(t)+1}$, ..., $p_{\sum_{d'\leq d} Q_n^{d'}(t)}$. Then, all the packets in $\{Q_n^{(d)}(t)\}_{d=-1}^{D_n-1}$ are ordered from p_1 to $p_{Q_n^{\text{sum}}(t)}$. When a particular queueing discipline is applied in the predictive system, we select packets to serve according to the discipline using the order of the packets. For instance, if FIFO is used, then the server will serve the packets $p_1, ..., p_{\min[\mu_n(t), Q_n^{\text{sum}}(t)]}$ from the queues every time. We now also define the notion of a *fully-efficient* predictive scheduling policy.

Definition 1. *A predictive scheduling policy is called* fully-efficient *if for every user n, we have: (i) $\sum_d \mu_n^{(d)}(t) = \mu_n(t)$, and (ii) whenever there exists any $-1 \leq d \leq D_n - 1$ such that $\mu_n^{(d)}(t) > Q_n^{(d)}(t)$, $\mu_n^{d'}(t) \geq Q_n^{d'}(t)$, $\forall d' \neq d$.* $\diamond$

In other words, if a policy is fully-efficient, it will always try to utilize all service opportunities and not allocate more service rate to serve any queue unless all other queues are already fully served. [6] Hence, it will not waste any service opportunity unless there are more. With this definition, we now present our algorithm, in which $V \geq 1$ is a control parameter used to tradeoff utility performance and system delay (See Theorem 5).

`Predictive Backpressure` (PBP): In every time slot, compute $Q_n^{\text{sum}}(t) = \sum_{d=-1}^{D_n-1} Q_n^{(d)}(t)$ for all n. Then, observe the current channel state vector $\boldsymbol{S}(t)$ and perform:

- Choose the power allocation vector $\boldsymbol{P}(t)$ to solve the following problem:

$$\min: \quad Vf(\boldsymbol{S}(t), \boldsymbol{P}(t)) - \sum_n Q_n^{\text{sum}}(t)\mu_n(\boldsymbol{S}(t), \boldsymbol{P}(t)) \quad (8)$$
$$\text{s.t.} \quad \boldsymbol{P}(t) \in \mathcal{P}^{(\boldsymbol{S}(t))}. \quad (9)$$

  Then, allocate the service rates $\{\mu_n^{(d)}(t)\}_{d=-1}^{D_n-1}$ to the queues $\{Q_n^{(d)}(t)\}_{d=-1}^{D_n-1}$ in a fully-efficient manner according to any pre-specified queueing discipline.

- Update the queues according to (5), (6) and (7). $\diamond$

Remark 1. *Notice that the* PBP *algorithm has a very clean format. Indeed,* PBP *can be viewed as weighting the predicted*

[6] It is equivalent to work-conserving in queue scheduling.

future arrivals for different users into current system control. It is worth emphasizing that such a low-complexity algorithm is not possible without the use of prediction queues and the Backpressure technique.

4. PERFORMANCE ANALYSIS

In this section, we first present an important theorem which states that if a predictive scheduling policy is fully-efficient, then the queueing system under the scheme evolves in the exact same way as a non-predictive queueing system with delayed arrivals and a different initial queue state. Using this queue-equivalence result, we obtain an interesting delay distribution shifting theorem. After that, we present our delay analysis for the PBP algorithm.

4.1 Performance of Fully-Efficient Scheduling Policies

We start by presenting the theorem regarding the equivalence between predictive and non-predictive systems.

Theorem 1. *Let $\hat{Q}_n(t)$ be the queue size of a single queue system that (i) has $\hat{Q}_n(0) = \sum_{t=0}^{D_n-1} A_n(t)$, (ii) has arrival $\hat{A}_n(t) = A_n(t+D_n)$, (ii) has service $\hat{\mu}_n(t) = \sum_{d=-1}^{D_n-1} \mu_n^{(d)}(t)$, and (iv) evolves according to:*

$$\hat{Q}_n(t+1) = \Big[\hat{Q}_n(t) - \hat{\mu}_n(t)\Big]^+ + \hat{A}_n(t). \tag{10}$$

Then, if the predictive system uses a fully-efficient predictive scheduling policy (with any queueing discipline) with $Q_n^{(-1)}(0) = 0$ for all n, we have for all t that:

$$Q_n^{sum}(t) = \hat{Q}_n(t), \ \forall\, n. \quad \diamond. \tag{11}$$

PROOF. See Appendix A. □

Theorem 1 provides an important connection between the predictive system and the system without prediction. Using this result, we derive the following theorem, which relates the delay distribution of the predictive system to the equivalent system without prediction.

Theorem 2. *(Delay Distribution Shifting) Denote $\pi_{n,k}^{(D_n)}$ the steady-state probability that a user n packet experiences a delay of k slots under a fully-efficient predictive scheduling policy in the predictive system, and let $\hat{\pi}_{n,k}$ denote the steady-state probability that a user n packet experiences a k-slot delay in $\hat{Q}_n(t)$. Suppose the set of queues $\{Q_n^{(d)}(t)\}_{d=-1}^{D_n-1}$ and $\hat{Q}_n(t)$ use the same queueing discipline. Then, we have for each queue n that:*

$$\pi_{n,0}^{(D_n)} = \sum_{k=0}^{D_n} \hat{\pi}_{n,k} \quad \text{and} \quad \pi_{n,k}^{(D_n)} = \hat{\pi}_{n,k+D_n}, \ k \geq 1. \tag{12}$$

That is, the distribution of the original queue can be viewed as "shifted to the left by D_n slots" under predictive scheduling with D_n-slot prediction. $\diamond$

PROOF. See Appendix B. □

Note that Theorem 2 is important for the general framework of predictive scheduling. It allows us to compare scheduling with prediction with the original queueing system, and enables us to leverage existing results in queueing theory for analyzing predictive systems. To formalize this idea, first notice that if we start with $\hat{Q}_n(0) = 0$ and have $\hat{A}_n(t) = A_n(t)$, then $\hat{Q}_n(t)$ becomes exactly the same as the queueing process in the *original* system *without* prediction. Thus, if the steady-state behavior of $\hat{Q}_n(t)$ does not depend on the initial condition and the shift of the arrival process, e.g., a $G/G/1$ queue [24], then the delay performance of the predictive system can be understood by studying the delay distribution of the original system without prediction.

Corollary 1. *Suppose $\{Q_n^{(d)}(t)\}_{d=-1}^{D_n-1}$ and $\hat{Q}_n(t)$ use the same queueing discipline. For any arrival and service processes under which the delay distribution of $\hat{Q}_n(t)$ does not depend on $\hat{Q}_n(0)$ and the shift in the arrival process, we have:*

$$\pi_{n,0}^{(D_n)} = \sum_{k=0}^{D_n} \pi_{n,k} \quad \text{and} \quad \pi_{n,k}^{(D_n)} = \pi_{n,k+D_n}, \ k \geq 1. \tag{13}$$

Here $\pi_{n,k}$ is the steady-state probability that a user n packet experiences a delay of k slots in the system without prediction. $\diamond$

Note that Corollary 1 applies to general multi-queue single-server systems where the steady-state behavior depends only on the statistical behavior of the arrival and service processes. Note that (13) also quantifies how *tail delay* changes with predictive scheduling. Specifically, we now have in the predictive system that:

$$\Pr\{\text{Delay}_n > K\} = \sum_{k>K} \pi_{n,k+D_n}. \tag{14}$$

This is often exponentially smaller compared to that under the non-predictive system (see the simulation section).

With Theorem 2, we can now quantify how much delay improvement one can obtain via predictive scheduling. This is summarized in the following theorem, in which we use W_{tot} to denote the average delay of the original system without prediction, i.e.,

$$W_{\text{tot}} = \frac{\sum_{n=1}^N \lambda_n \sum_{k\geq 0} k\pi_{n,k}}{\sum_{n=1}^N \lambda_n}. \tag{15}$$

Theorem 3. *Suppose the conditions in Corollary 1 hold. The delay reduction offered by predictive scheduling with prediction window vector $\boldsymbol{D}$, denoted by $R(\boldsymbol{D})$, is given by:*

$$R(\boldsymbol{D}) = \frac{\sum_{n=1}^N \lambda_n \big(\sum_{1\leq k\leq D_n} k\pi_{n,k} + D_n \sum_{k\geq 1} \pi_{n,k+D_n}\big)}{\sum_{n=1}^N \lambda_n}. \tag{16}$$

In particular, if $W_{tot} < \infty$, the average system delay goes to zero as D_n goes to infinity for all queue n, i.e.,

$$\lim_{\boldsymbol{D}\to\infty} R(\boldsymbol{D}) = W_{tot}. \tag{17}$$

Here $\boldsymbol{D} \to \infty$ means $D_n \to \infty$ for all n. $\diamond$

PROOF. See Appendix C. □

Note that Theorems 2 and 3, and Corollary 1 show that *systems with predictive scheduling can be analyzed by studying the original system without prediction.* Also note that the above results hold under *any* queueing discipline. The resulting delay distribution, of course, changes under different disciplines. Hence, the results also provide an efficient way for deciding how much prediction power is needed for different systems under different control policies, e.g., if a system has a delay distribution under which most packets experience a delay of no more than D slots, then using a prediction power of D slots suffices to reap most of the benefit of predictive scheduling, and further investment on improving prediction power can readily be saved.

4.2 Performance of PBP

In this section, we analyze the performance of PBP. We will assume the following *system slack* condition: there exist a set of power vectors and probabilities $\{\boldsymbol{P}_m^{(s_i)}, a_m^{(s_i)}\}$, and a constant $\eta > 0$, such that:

$$\lambda_n - \sum_{s_i} \pi_{s_i} \sum_{m=0}^{\infty} a_m^{(s_i)} \mu_n(s_i, \boldsymbol{P}_m^{(s_i)}) \leq -\eta, \ \forall n. \quad (18)$$

Note that (18) is commonly assumed in stochastic queueing system works and $\eta \geq 0$ is necessary for system stability [21]. The following theorem states that allowing predictive scheduling does not change the optimal average cost.

Theorem 4. *For any vector* $\mathbf{0} \preceq \boldsymbol{D} \prec \infty$*, we have:*

$$f_{av}^{\boldsymbol{D}*} = f_{av}^{*}. \ \diamond \quad (19)$$

PROOF. Omitted due to space limitation. Please see [25] for proof details. □

Theorem 4 is interesting and shows that predictive scheduling does not reduce the minimum cost needed for system stability. Instead, the theorem, together with Theorem 5 below, deliver an important message that predictive scheduling *it improves the system delay given the same utility performance.*

We now have the following theorem, which shows that PBP achieves an average power consumption that is within $O(1/V)$ of the minimum and guarantees an average congestion bound.

Theorem 5. *The* PBP *algorithm achieves the following:*

$$f_{av}^{\text{PBP}} \leq f_{av}^{\boldsymbol{D}*} + \frac{B}{V}, \ Q_{av}^{sum} = Q_{av}^{BP} = \frac{B + Vf^{\max}}{\eta}. \quad (20)$$

Here $B = \frac{N}{2}(\mu_{\max}^2 + A_{\max}^2)$ *is a constant independent of* V*,* Q_{av}^{sum} *denotes the average expected queue size of* $\sum_n Q_n^{sum}(t)$*, and* Q_{av}^{BP} *denotes the average expected queue size of the non-predictive system under Backpressure.* $\diamond$

PROOF. Omitted due to space limitation. Please see [25] for proof details. □

Theorem 5 is similar to the results in previous literature of Backpressure, e.g., [21]. It states that the average size of $\sum_n Q_n^{\text{sum}}(t)$ is the same as $Q_{\text{av}}^{\text{BP}}$ under Backpressure without prediction. Since $Q_n^{\text{sum}}(t)$ is the total size of the actual queue and the prediction queues, we see that the actual queue size is strictly smaller than that under Backpressure. Since the average queue size under PBP is finite, we can apply Theorem 3 to obtain the following immediate corollary.

Corollary 2. *Suppose there exists a steady-state distribution of the queue vector under* PBP*. Then, the average delay under* PBP *goes to zero as* $\boldsymbol{D} \to \infty$*.* $\diamond$

Corollary 2 shows that with predictive scheduling, it is possible to achieve an $O(1/V)$ performance with an average delay that is smaller than $O(\log(V))$. This is fundamentally different from the non-predictive case, in which the best utility-delay tradeoff is $[O(1/V), O(\log(V))]$ [9]. It is also tempting to analyze the exact delay reduction offered by PBP. However, due to the complex queueing dynamics under Backpressure, it is challenging to compute the exact distributions $\pi_{n,k}$ even without prediction. Thus, in the following, we consider a general class of cost-minimization problems, and study the delay reduction due to prediction in this case. For stating the results, we define the following optimization problem:

$$\max: \quad g(\boldsymbol{\gamma}), \quad \text{s.t. } \boldsymbol{\gamma} \succeq \mathbf{0}, \quad (21)$$

where $g(\boldsymbol{\gamma})$ is defined as:

$$g(\boldsymbol{\gamma}) = \sum_{s_i} \pi_{s_i} \inf_{\boldsymbol{P}_m^{(s_i)} \in \mathcal{P}^{(s_i)}} \Big\{ Vf(s_i, \boldsymbol{P}_m^{(s_i)}) \quad (22)$$
$$+ \sum_n \gamma_n [\lambda_n - \mu_n(s_i, \boldsymbol{P}_m^{(s_i)})] \Big\}.$$

We now state our theorem regarding the average backlog reduction due to predictive scheduling. In the theorem, we use $\boldsymbol{\gamma}^*$ to denote an optimal solution of (21).

Theorem 6. *Suppose (i)* $\boldsymbol{\gamma}^* = \Theta(V) > 0$ *is unique, (ii) the* η*-slack condition (18) is satisfied with* $\eta > 0$*, (iii) the dual function* $g(\boldsymbol{\gamma})$ *satisfies:*

$$g(\boldsymbol{\gamma}^*) \geq g(\boldsymbol{\gamma}) + L||\boldsymbol{\gamma}^* - \boldsymbol{\gamma}||, \quad \forall \, \boldsymbol{\gamma} \succeq \mathbf{0}, \quad (23)$$

for some constant $L > 0$ *independent of* V*, (iv) there exists a steady-state distribution of* $\boldsymbol{Q}^{sum}(t)$ *under* PBP*, (v)* $D_n = O(\frac{1}{A_{\max}}[\gamma_n^* - G - K(\log(V))^2 - \mu_{\max}]^+)$ *for all* n*, and (iv) FIFO is used. Then, under* PBP *with a sufficiently large* V*, we have:*

$$Q_{av}^{(-1)} \leq Q_{av}^{BP} - \sum_n D_n \big(\lambda_n - O(\frac{1}{V^{\log(V)}})\big)^+. \ \diamond \quad (24)$$

PROOF. See Appendix D. □

As shown in [15], conditions (i)-(iii) in Theorem 6 are satisfied in many practical network optimization problems, especially when the power allocation sets $\{\mathcal{P}^{(s_i)}\}_{i=1}^M$ are finite. In this case, queue vector $\boldsymbol{Q}(t) = (Q_1(t), ..., Q_N(t))$ mostly stays close to the fixed point $\boldsymbol{\gamma}^*$ [15]. Using Little's theorem, Theorem 6 implies that the system delay is reduced roughly linearly in the prediction window size D_n. Note that the linear reduction in D_n is due to the use of the FIFO discipline and the fact that D_n is constrained. In the case when D_n is larger than $O(\frac{1}{A_{\max}}[\gamma_{Vn}^* - G - K(\log(V))^2 - \mu_{\max}]^+)$, or when LIFO is used, we observe that packet delay decreases *exponentially* in D_n (see Section 6).

5. PREDICTABLE-ONLY ARRIVAL

Here we discuss how PBP can also be applied (with slight modification) to the case when arrivals can only be predicted but not pre-served. The idea is to first pretend that the predictable-only traffic can also be pre-served, and then construct the algorithm and show that pre-serving rarely happens.

`Predictable – Only PBP (POPBP)`: In every time slot, run PBP. In addition, for each queue n, do:

- (Marking) Mark all packets in $\{Q_n^{(d)}(t)\}_{d=0}^{D_n-1}$ served in the current time slot as *mistaken packets.*

- (Dropping) Drop all mistaken packets when they enter $Q_n^{(-1)}(t)$. ◇

Here "run PBP" means carrying out all the steps in PBP including choosing and implementing actions, and updating queue values. Note that $\{Q_n^{(d)}(t)\}_{d=0}^{D_n-1}$ do not exactly correspond to the number of remaining future arrivals, as they are not served under POPBP. Instead, they are equal to the number of future arrivals excluding the mistaken packets.

The performance of POPBP is summarized as follows.

Theorem 7. *Suppose the conditions in Theorem 6 hold. Then, under* POPBP *with a sufficiently large V, we have:*

$$f_{av}^{\text{POPBP}} \leq f_{av}^{\boldsymbol{D}*} + \frac{B}{V}, \tag{25}$$

$$Q_{av}^{(-1)} \leq Q_{av}^{BP} - \sum_n D_n\big(\lambda_n - O(\frac{1}{V^{\log(V)}})\big)^+. \tag{26}$$

Moreover, the average packet dropping rate is $O(\frac{1}{V^{\log(V)}})$. ◇

PROOF. Omitted due to space limitation. Please see [25] for proof details. □

6. SIMULATION

We present simulation results of the PBP algorithm in this section in a 10-user system.

6.1 Parameters and Settings

Real Data Trace: We collected data from 10 different mobile users in a 12-day long period (over five-minute intervals). The data for each user represents the aggregate amount of mobile traffic (over all applications) that is delivered by the base station to the user in that slot. Fig. 4 shows the traffic of a single user and the aggregate traffic of all users in 12 days. In the simulations, we take the traffic data as the workload arriving at the system which needs delivered by the server to different users.

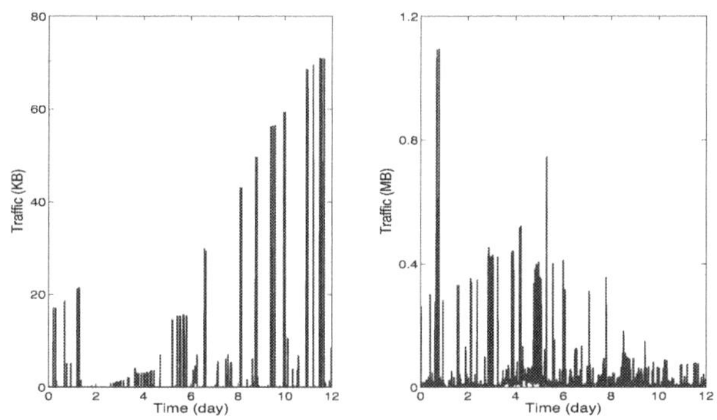

Figure 4: Left: The mobile traffic delivered by the base station to a single user. Right: The aggregate mobile traffic delivered by the base station to 10 different users.

Channel, Power and Prediction: For each user n, we assume that the channel condition $S_n(t)$ takes values $\{1, 2\}$ with equal probabilities, and $P_n(t) \in \mathcal{P}^{(S_n)} \triangleq \{0, 5, 10\}$. We assume that at any time, only one channel receives nonzero power allocation. The service rate is given by $\mu_n(t) = \lfloor 100 \log(1+S_n(t)P_n(t)) \rfloor$ KB/s. The cost function $f(S(t), \boldsymbol{P}(t))$ is set to be $\sum_n P_n(t)$, which denotes the total power consumption. We set $D_n = \rho * 5$ for all n. Then, we simulate the cases $\rho \in \{1, 3, 5, 10\}$ to see the effect of the predictive scheduling. We simulate the algorithm with $V \in \{1, 5, 10, 20, 50, 100\}$.

6.2 Performance of PBP

Fig. 5 shows the performance of PBP with FIFO queueing policy. We see from the left plot that the average power consumption decreases as V increases. The right plot shows the average backlog under PBP. It is not hard to see that the average system backlog scales as $O(V)$. One also sees that as the prediction window sizes increase, the network delay decreases linearly in $\boldsymbol{D}$.

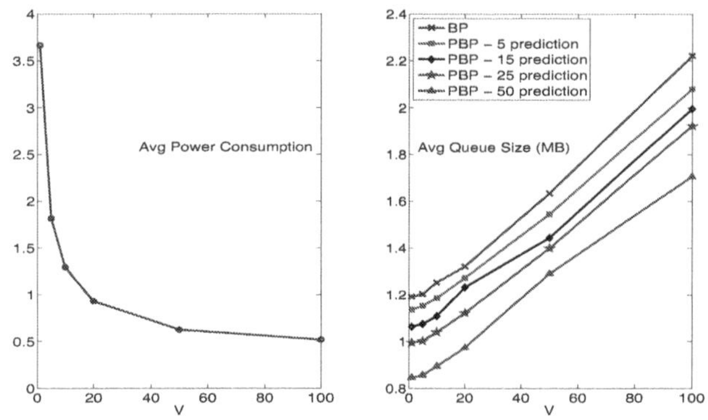

Figure 5: Performance of PBP. Left: Average power consumption under PBP. Right: Average queue size under PBP with different prediction window sizes.

Fig. 6 shows the delay distribution under PBP for the setting with $V = 100$ and $\rho = 1$. We see that the distributions of the latency for queue n are shifted to the left by D_n, as shown in Theorem 2. It can also be verified that Corollary 1 holds.

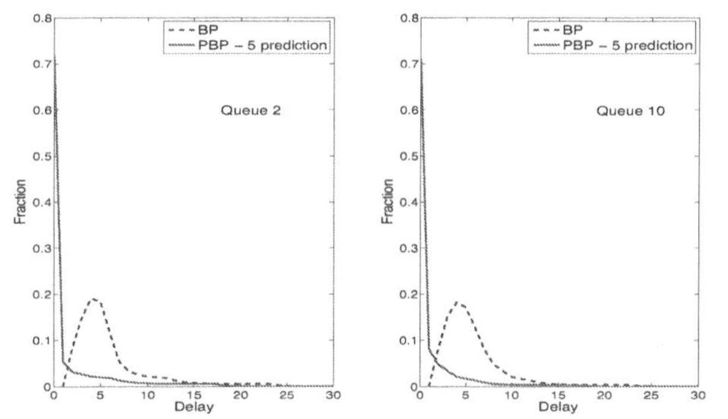

Figure 6: Packet delay distribution under PBP with FIFO scheduling with $V = 100$ and $D_n = 5$ for all n. We see that predictive scheduling effectively shifts the distribution to the left by 5 slots for both queues.

Fig. 7 then shows the delay distribution under PBP and the original Backpressure, under the LIFO discipline. It can be verified that the distribution for the predictive system is also a left-shifted version of the one under Backpressure. We see that large fractions of packets experience zero delay in both queues, i.e., they are served before they arrive at $Q_n^{(-1)}(t)$. This is so because under LIFO Backpressure (no prediction), most packets roughly experience $(\log(V))^2$ delay. Thus, with a moderate size prediction window size, the server can serve most packets before they enter the system. Since we use a log-scale for the x-axis, we do not plot the fraction for packets that have zero delay. Instead, we show the numbers in the plot. We see that, 69% of the packets for queue 2 are served before they enter the system, whereas 73% of the packets are served for queue 10. These results demonstrate the power of predictive scheduling on delay reduction.

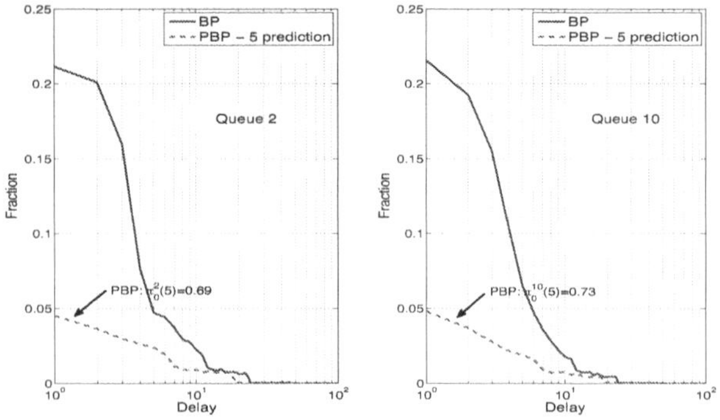

Figure 7: Packet Delay distribution under PBP with LIFO scheduling ($V = 100$ and $D_n = 5$ for all n). We see that a large fraction of the packets now experience zero delay! This is because with a moderate size prediction window, most packets are served before they arrive at $Q_n^{(-1)}(t)$. In the plots, $\pi_0^n(D_n)$ denotes the fraction of packets experience zero delay.

6.3 Impact of Imperfect Prediction

To investigate the impact of imperfect prediction, we consider two types of prediction errors. The first type is failing to predict actual arrivals, i.e., miss detection. When it happens, the arrivals will be out of the system's vision and thus will not appear in prediction queues. Therefore, they cannot be served predictively. The other type is false alarm, which happens when the system mistakenly predicts the existence of non-existing arrivals. Such false arrivals will appear in prediction queues, but will not enter the system. However, the system may incorrectly allocate resources to serve them, resulting in wasted service opportunities.

We model miss detections and false alarms as follows. Each time unit, q fraction of the request arrivals are miss detections, and $\frac{1-p}{p}$ fraction of the rest request arrivals are false alarms ($p \geq 0.5$). Therefore, fraction $\frac{1-q}{p}$ of all predicted requests are actual arrivals, which can be served beforehand. Larger q means more miss detections, and smaller p means more false alarms in the system. For perfect prediction, $q = 0$ and $p = 1$. We simulate three different settings: ($q = 0.5, p = 0.95$), ($q = 0.05, p = 0,75$) and ($q = 0.2, p = 0.85$). The first setting corresponds to the case when the prediction mechanism works very conservatively, which leads to very few false alarms but many miss detections. The second setting corresponds to the case where the prediction mechanism works very aggressively and results in few miss detections but many false alarms. The third setting is in-between.

As discussed above, $Q_n^{(d)}(t)$ ($0 \leq d \leq D_n - 1$) may now contain false alarms besides real arrivals, and the fraction of false alarms is $1 - p$ on average. Thus, the effective queue size of $Q_n^{(d)}(t)$ (the number of real arrivals) is $p \cdot Q_n^{(d)}(t)$. Therefore, in the PBP algorithm, we use $Q_n^{(-1)}(t) + p\sum_{d=0}^{D_n-1} \cdot Q_n^{(d)}(t)$ as the weight in (8) instead of $\sum_{d=-1}^{D_n-1} Q_n^{(d)}(t)$.

Fig. 8 shows the performance of PBP with FIFO queueing policy under imperfect prediction when $D_n = 5$ for all n. We see that PBP still improves the delay performance while at the same time keeping a good power performance. This is because that the chance that PBP serves future arrivals is decreased when V increases. Therefore, the impact of prediction errors on the utility performance of PBP is reduced, showing that PBP is robust against prediction error. Compared to PBP with perfect prediction, prediction errors increase the average backlog of the system and thus the average delay. This is intuitive since miss detections cannot be served beforehand and false alarms waste service opportunities. We also observe that the delay performance of PBP is more sensitive to miss detections. This is because miss detections enter the system directly and may increase the system backlog.

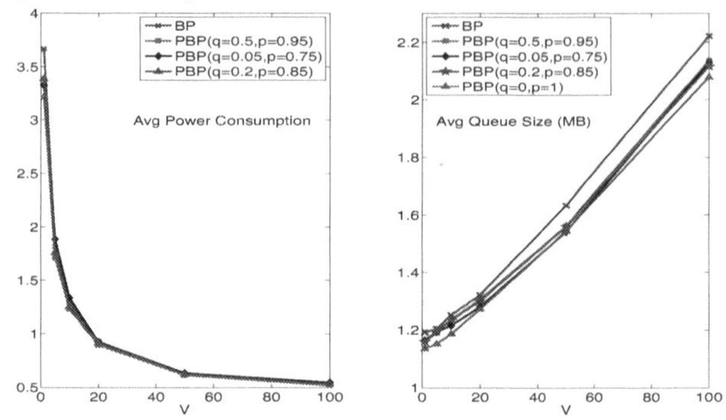

Figure 8: Performance of PBP under imperfect prediction when $D_n = 5$ for all n. Left: Average power consumption under different prediction errors. Right: Average queue size under different prediction errors.

7. CONCLUSION

In this paper, we investigate the fundamental benefit of predictive scheduling in controlled queueing systems. Based on a lookahead prediction window model, we establish a novel queue-equivalence result, which enables exact analysis of queueing systems under predictive scheduling using traditional queueing network control techniques. We then propose the `Predictive Backpressure` (PBP) algorithm, and show that PBP achieves a cost performance that is arbitrarily close to the optimal, while guaranteeing that the average system delay vanishes as the prediction window size increases. Our results can also be used to determine the required prediction power and analyze the tail delay reduction improvement.

8. ACKNOWLEDGEMENT

This work was supported in part by the National Basic Research Program of China Grant 2011CBA00300, 2011CBA00301, the National Natural Science Foundation of China Grant 61033001, 61361136003, 61303195, and the China youth 1000-talent grant. It was also partially supported by the University Grants Committee of the Hong Kong Special Administrative Region, China (Area of Excellence Grant Project No. AoE/E-02/08 and General Research Fund Project No. 411011), and Chancellor's Fellowship and NSF grant CNS114793

Appendix A – Proof of Theorem 1

Here we prove Theorem 1.

PROOF. (Theorem 1) We prove the result by induction with the aid of the following figure showing the evolution of $\hat{Q}_n(t)$.

First, we see that the the result holds for $t = 0$: On one hand, $\hat{Q}_n(0) = \sum_{t=0}^{D_n-1} A_n(t)$. On the other hand, in the

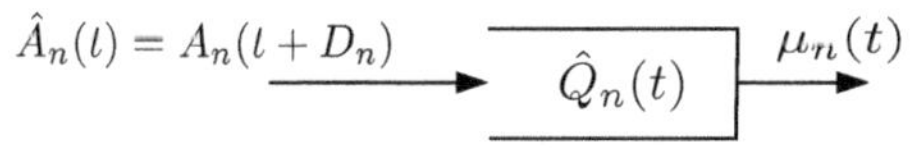

Figure 9: The original queue without prediction and with a delayed arrival process as well as a different initial queue state.

system under predictive scheduling, since $Q_n^{(-1)}(0) = 0$ and $Q_n^{(d)}(0) = A_n(d)$ for $d \in \{0, ..., D_n - 1\}$, we have $Q_n^{\text{sum}}(0) = \sum_{t=0}^{D_n-1} A_n(t)$.

Now suppose the result holds for all $t = 0, ..., k$, we show that it holds for $t = k+1$. Using the queueing dynamic equation (10), we know that in time slot k, $\tilde{\mu}_n(k) = \min[\mu_n(k), \hat{Q}_n(k)]$ packets will be served from $\hat{Q}_n(k)$. Now consider the queues $\{Q_n^{(d)}(k)\}_{d=-1}^{D_n-1}$. Since the scheduling policy is fully-efficient, we must have that the number of packets served from these queues is also $\tilde{\mu}_n(k) = \min[\mu_n(k), \hat{Q}_n(k)]$. To see this, note that if $\tilde{\mu}_n(k) = \mu_n(k)$, there are more packets in the queues than the number of packets that can be served. In this case, we must have $\mu_n^{(d)}(k) \leq Q_n^{(d)}(k)$ for all d. Also, because the policy is fully-efficient, we have $\sum_d \mu_n^{(d)}(k) = \mu_n(k)$. Hence, exactly $\mu_n(k)$ packets will be served from $\{Q_n^{(d)}(k)\}_{d=-1}^{D_n-1}$, resulting in $\hat{Q}_n(k+1) = Q_n^{\text{sum}}(k+1)$. On the other hand, suppose $\tilde{\mu}_n(k) = \hat{Q}_n(k)$. Then, there are enough service opportunities to clear all the awaiting packets. In this case, since the scheduling policy is fully-efficient, exactly $\hat{Q}_n(k)$ packets will be served. Thus, in both cases, we have $\hat{Q}_n(k+1) = Q_n^{\text{sum}}(k+1) = A_n(k + D_n)$. $\square$

Appendix B – Proof of Theorem 2

Here we prove Theorem 2.

Proof. (Theorem 2) From Theorem 1, we see that $Q_n^{\text{sum}}(t) = \hat{Q}_n(t)$ for all time. Hence, if the two queueing systems use the same queueing discipline in choosing what packets to serve, then every packet will experience the exact same delay in both $\hat{Q}_n(t)$ and $\{Q_n^{(d)}(t)\}_{d=-1}^{D_n-1}$.

However, in $Q_n^{\text{sum}}(t)$, a packet will enter the actual system only after spending one unit of time in each of the queues in $\{Q_n^{(d)}(k)\}_{d=0}^{D_n-1}$, which takes exactly D_n slots in total. Thus, any packet experiencing a k-slot delay will experience $[k - D_n]^+$ delay in $Q_n^{(-1)}(t)$. This completes the proof of Theorem 2. $\square$

Appendix C – Proof of Theorem 3

We prove Theorem 3 here.

Proof. (Theorem 3) Using Corollary 1, we see that in the predictive system, the average system backlog size is given by:

$$N_{\text{tot}}^{\text{P}} = \sum_{n=1}^{N} \lambda_n \sum_{k \geq 1} k \pi_{n,k+D_n}. \tag{27}$$

On the other hand, the average system backlog without prediction is given by:

$$N_{\text{tot}} = \sum_{n=1}^{N} \lambda_n \sum_{k \geq 1} k \pi_{n,k}. \tag{28}$$

Using (28) and (27), we conclude that:

$$N_{\text{tot}} - N_{\text{tot}}^{\text{P}} = \sum_{n=1}^{N} \lambda_n \bigg(\sum_{1 \leq k \leq D_n} k \pi_{n,k} + D_n \sum_{k \geq 1} \pi_{n,k+D_n} \bigg). \tag{29}$$

Using Little's theorem and dividing both sides by $\sum_n \lambda_n$, we see that (16) follows.

Now we prove (17). By taking a limit as $\boldsymbol{D} \to \infty$, we first obtain:

$$\lim_{\boldsymbol{D} \to \infty} \sum_n \lambda_n \sum_{1 \leq k \leq D_n} k \pi_{n,k} = N_{\text{tot}}. \tag{30}$$

Then, using the fact that $W_{\text{tot}} < \infty$, we have:

$$\lim_{D_n \to \infty} D_n \sum_{k \geq 1} \pi_{n,k+D_n} = 0, \ \forall\ n. \tag{31}$$

Using the above in (16), we see that (17) follows. $\square$

Appendix D – Proof of Theorem 6

We prove Theorem 6. For our proof, we use the following theorem (which is Theorem 1 in [15]), in which $\boldsymbol{\gamma}^*$ denotes an optimal solution of (21). According to [15], $\boldsymbol{\gamma}^*$ is either $\Theta(V)$ or 0.

Theorem 8. *Suppose (i) $\boldsymbol{\gamma}^*$ is unique, (ii) the η-slack condition (18) is satisfied with $\eta > 0$, (iii) the function $g(\boldsymbol{\gamma})$ satisfies:*

$$g(\boldsymbol{\gamma}^*) \geq g(\boldsymbol{\gamma}) + L||\boldsymbol{\gamma}^* - \boldsymbol{\gamma}||, \quad \forall\, \boldsymbol{\gamma} \succeq \mathbf{0}, \tag{32}$$

for some constant $L > 0$ independent of V. Then, under Backpressure, there exist constants $G, K, c = \Theta(1)$, i.e., all independent of V, such that for any $m \in \mathbb{R}_+$,

$$\mathcal{P}^{(r)}(G, Km) \ \leq \ ce^{-m}, \tag{33}$$

where $\mathcal{P}^{(r)}(G, Km)$ is defined:

$$\mathcal{P}^{(r)}(G, Km) \tag{34}$$
$$\triangleq \limsup_{t \to \infty} \frac{1}{t} \sum_{\tau=0}^{t-1} Pr\{\exists\, n, |Q_n(\tau) - \gamma_n^*| > G + Km\}. \ \diamond$$

Proof. See [15]. $\square$

We are now ready to present the proof of Theorem 6.

Proof. (Theorem 6) We prove the results using Little's theorem. The main idea is to show that the average system queue length is roughly reduced by $\sum_n \lambda_n D_n$. To prove this, we show that the average total service rate allocated to the prediction queues is $O(\frac{1}{V^{\log(V)}})$. Then, the average rate of the packets that go through $\{Q_n^{(d)}(t)\}_{d=0}^{D_n-1}$ will roughly be λ_n, and so the average queue size is reduced by roughly $\sum_n \lambda_n D_n$.

First, using (11) and (33), we see that in steady state,

$$\Pr\big\{|Q_n^{\text{sum}}(t) - \gamma_n^*| > G + Km\big\} \leq ce^{-m}.$$

Using the fact that $Q_n^{\text{sum}}(t) = \sum_{d=-1}^{D_n-1} Q_n^{(d)}(t)$, we have:

$$\Pr\big\{Q_n^{(-1)}(t) < \gamma_n^* - G - Km - \sum_{d=0}^{D_n-1} Q_n^{(d)}(t)\big\} \leq ce^{-m}.$$

Now let $m = (\log(V))^2$. Since $\gamma_n^* = \Theta(V)$, we see that when V is sufficiently large, we have:

$$\gamma_n^* - G - Km - \sum_d Q_n^{(d)}(t)$$

$$= \Theta(V) - G - K(\log(V))^2 - \sum_d Q_n^{(d)}(t)$$

$$\overset{(a)}{\geq} \Theta(V) - G - K(\log(V))^2 - D_n A_{\max}$$

$$\overset{(b)}{\geq} \mu_{\max}. \quad (35)$$

Here (a) follows from the fact that $Q_n^{(d)}(t) \leq A_{\max}$ for all $0 \leq d \leq D_n - 1$, and in (b) we use the fact that V is sufficiently large and $D_n = O(\frac{1}{A_{\max}}[\gamma_n^* - G - K(\log(V))^2 - \mu_{\max}]^+)$ for all n. This shows that the probability for $Q_n^{(-1)}(t)$ to go below $\mu_{\max}$ is at most $ce^{-(\log(V))^2} = \frac{c}{V^{\log(V)}}$.

Using the fact that under the FIFO queueing discipline, a prediction queue $Q_n^{(d)}(t)$ will be served only when $Q_n^{(-1)}(t) < \mu_{\max}$, we conclude that the average service rate allocated to the prediction queues is no more than $\frac{c\mu_{\max}}{V^{\log(V)}}$. Hence, the average traffic rate of the packets that traverse all prediction queues and eventually enter $Q_n^{(-1)}(t)$ is at least $[\lambda_n - \frac{c\mu_{\max}}{V^{\log(V)}}]^+$. Since every packet stays 1 slot in every prediction queue, using Little's theorem, we conclude that the average size of the prediction queues, denoted by $\sum_{d=0}^{D_n-1} \overline{Q}_n^{(d)}$ satisfies $\sum_{d=0}^{D_n-1} \overline{Q}_n^{(d)} \geq (\lambda_n - \frac{c\mu_{\max}}{V^{\log(V)}})^+ D_n$. Hence, (24) follows. □

9. REFERENCES

[1] M. Maia, J. Almeida, and V. Almeida. Identifying user behavior in online social networks. *Proceedings of the 1st Workshop on Social Network Systems, pages 1-6*, 2008.

[2] I. Weber and A. Jaimes. Who uses web search for what? and how? *Web Search and Data Mining (WSDM), pages 21-30*, 2011.

[3] R. Kumar and A. Tomkins. A characterization of online browsing behavior. *Proceedings of the 19th interna- tional conference on World Wide Web, pages 561-570*, 2010.

[4] V. N. Padmanabhan and J. C. Mogul. Using predictive prefetching to improve world wide web latency. *ACM SIGCOMM Computer Communication Review, Volume 26, Issue 3, Pages 22-36*, July 1996.

[5] J. Lee, H. Kim, and R. Vuduc. When prefetching works, when it doesnÕt, and why. *ACM Transactions on Architecture and Code Optimization (TACO), Volume 9, Issue 1*, March 2012.

[6] T. Ball and J. R. Larus. Branch prediction for free. *Proceedings of the Conference on Programming Language Design and Implementation, ACM SIGPLAN Notices, volume 28, pages 300-13*, 1993.

[7] M. U. Farooq, Khubaib, and L. K. John. Store-load-branch (slb) predictor: A compiler assisted branch prediction for data dependent branches. *Proceedings of the 19th IEEE International Symposium on High-Performance Computer Architecture (HPCA)*, February 2013.

[8] R. Berry and R. Gallager. Communication over fading channels with delay constraints. *IEEE Transactions on Information Theory, vol. 48, no. 5, pp. 1135-1149*, May 2002.

[9] M. J. Neely. Optimal energy and delay tradeoffs for multi-user wireless downlinks. *IEEE Transactions on Information Theory vol. 53, no. 9, pp. 3095-3113*, Sept. 2007.

[10] M. J. Neely. Energy optimal control for time-varying wireless networks. *IEEE Transactions on Information Theory 52(7): 2915-2934*, July 2006.

[11] A. C. Fu, E. Modiano, and J. N. Tsitsiklis. Optimal energy allocation and admission control for communications satellites. *IEEE/ACM Transactions on Networking*, vol. 11, no. 3, pp. 488-500, 2003.

[12] M. A. Zafer and E Modiano. A calculus approach to energy-efficient data transmission with quality-of-service constraints. *IEEE/ACM Transactions on Networking, 17(3), 898–911*, 2009.

[13] C. W. Tan, D. P. Palomar, and M. Chiang. Energy-robustness tradeoff in cellular network power control. *IEEE/ACM Transactions on Networking, Vol. 17, No. 3, pp. 912-925*, 2009.

[14] M. J. Neely. Super-fast delay tradeoffs for utility optimal fair scheduling in wireless networks. *IEEE Journal on Selected Areas in Communications (JSAC), Special Issue on Nonlinear Optimization of Communication Systems, vol. 24, no. 8, pp. 1489-1501*, Aug. 2006.

[15] L. Huang and M. J. Neely. Delay reduction via Lagrange multipliers in stochastic network optimization. *IEEE Trans. on Automatic Control, Volume 56, Issue 4, pp. 842-857*, April 2011.

[16] J. Tadrous, A. Eryilmaz, and H. El Gamal. Proactive resource allocation: harnessing the diversity and multicast gains. *IEEE Tansactions on Information Theory*, 2013.

[17] J. Tadrous, A. Eryilmaz, and H. El Gamal. Pricing for demand shaping and proactive download in smart data networks. *The 2nd IEEE International Workshop on Smart Data Pricing (SDP), INFOCOM*, 2013.

[18] J. Spencer, M. Sudan, and K Xu. Queueing with future information. *ArXiv Technical Report arxiv:1211.0618*, 2012.

[19] Y. Yao, L. Huang, A. Sharma, L. Golubchik, and M. J. Neely. Data centers power reduction: A two time scale approach for delay tolerant workloads. *USC CS Technical Report 11-9020*, 2011.

[20] I. Hou and P.R. Kumar. Broadcasting delay-constrained traffic over unreliable wireless links with network coding. *Proceedings of MobiHoc*, 2011.

[21] L. Georgiadis, M. J. Neely, and L. Tassiulas. *Resource Allocation and Cross-Layer Control in Wireless Networks.* Foundations and Trends in Networking Vol. 1, no. 1, pp. 1-144, 2006.

[22] L. Huang and M. J. Neely. Max-weight achieves the exact $[O(1/V), O(V)]$ utility-delay tradeoff under Markov dynamics. *arXiv:1008.0200v1*, 2010.

[23] A. Wierman M. Lin, Z. Liu and L. Andrew. Online algorithms for geographical load balancing. *International Green Computing Conference (IGCC)*, 2012.

[24] R. G. Gallager. *Discrete Stochastic Processes.* Kluwer Academic Publishers, 1996.

[25] L. Huang, S. Zhang, M. Chen, and X. Liu. When Backpressure meets Predictive Scheduling. *arXiv Technical Report*, arXiv:1309.1110v1.

All Your Location are Belong to Us: Breaking Mobile Social Networks for Automated User Location Tracking

Muyuan Li[†‡], Haojin Zhu[†], Zhaoyu Gao[†], Si Chen[‡], Le Yu[†], Shangqian Hu[†], Kui Ren[‡]
[†]Department of Computer Science and Engineering, Shanghai Jiao Tong University
[‡]Department of Computer Science and Engineering, State University of New York at Buffalo
[†]{zhuhaojin, gaozy1987, lewisyu24, hu.shangq}@gmail.com
[‡]{muyuanli, schen23, kuiren}@buffalo.edu

ABSTRACT

Location-based social networks (LBSNs) feature friend discovery by location proximity that has attracted hundreds of millions of users world-wide. While leading LBSN providers claim the well-protection of their users' location privacy, for the first time we show through real world attacks that these claims do not hold. In our identified attacks, a malicious individual with the capability of no more than a regular LBSN user can easily break most LBSNs by manipulating location information fed to LBSN client apps and running them as location oracles.

We further develop an automated user location tracking system and test it on leading LBSNs including Wechat, Skout, and Momo. We demonstrate its effectiveness and efficiency via a 3 week real-world experiment on 30 volunteers and show that we could geo-locate any target with high accuracy and readily recover his/her top 5 locations. Finally, we also develop a framework that explores a grid reference system and location classifications to mitigate the attacks. Our result serves as a critical security reminder of the current LBSNs pertaining to a vast number of users.

1. INTRODUCTION

Mobile social networks have gained tremendous momentum since recent years due to both the wide proliferation of mobile devices such as smartphones and tablets as well as the ubiquitous availability of network services. Millions of users are enabled to access and interact with each other over online social networks via their mobile devices. Moreover, the positioning technologies such as GPS, and wireless localization techniques for mobile devices have made both the generation and sharing of real-time user location updates readily available. This, in turn, leads to the extreme popularity of location-based social networks (LBSNs) such as Facebook Places, Google Plus, PCube, Foursquare, Wechat, Momo, Badoo, Grindr, Blendr, and Tapmee, which boost up to hundreds of millions of users. As one of the most popular LBSNs in China, Wechat achieved more than 300 million registered user accounts in only two years, and is used in over 200 countries [22]. Another LBSN app Momo has 30 million users, 2.2 million of whom use the app on a daily basis [11, 35]. Skout, a very popular dating app in North America, draws 1.5 million new users a month who check into the app an average of nine times a day [2].

MobiHoc'14, August 11–14, 2014, Philadelphia, PA, USA.

http://dx.doi.org/10.1145/2632951.2632953.

In contrast to traditional LBSNs such as Foursquare, which allow users to check-in at locations and share the information with friends within vicinity, the newer ones feature location-based social discovery. Location-based social discovery explicitly enables on-the-spot connection establishments among users based on their physical proximity. Examples of such LBSNs include Google Plus, PCube, Wechat, Momo and Skout. While services like Google Plus and PCube allow their users to control with whom they want to share the location information, popular ones like Wechat, Momo and Skout allow location-based social discovery solely based on users' physical proximity.

Along with the popularity of location-based social discovery is the increasing danger of user privacy breaches due to location information exposure. Recent studies have shown that four spatiotemporal points are sufficient to uniquely identify the individuals in an anonymized mobility data set [12, 21] and little outside or social network information is needed to re-identify a targeted individual or even discover real identities of users [12, 30, 33]. Furthermore, users' location traces can leak much information about the individuals' habits, interests, activities, and relationships as pointed out in [26]. And loss of location privacy can expose users to unwanted advertisement and location-based spams/scams, cause social reputation or economic damage, and make them victims of blackmail or even physical violence.

Recognizing the danger of user location privacy leakage due to the use of mobile device in general, various research efforts have been devoted to location privacy. Most of them focus on developing the general location privacy protection mechanisms for location-based services (LBSs) that allow users to make use of LBSs while limiting the amount of disclosed sensitive information [8, 7, 13, 23, 28, 31, 27, 14]. Existing techniques include anonymous service uses, cloaking based technique [31], mixzone or silent period [13, 27]. Mechanisms are also proposed to enable proximity testing without revealing the mobile users' real location information [34, 24] for privacy preserving distributed social discovery.

User location privacy in real-world LBSN apps, however, has not received enough attention. Current industrial practices are yet to be scrutinized for their (in)adequacy. Most of regular LBSN users have little (if any) idea of the fact that through the attack strategy proposed in our work, the amount of location privacy leak is beyond what the apps tell them. In fact, there are reports that even falsely reassure users that the location privacy protection is adequate and sound [10].

In this paper, we ask and answer two fundamental questions regarding user privacy in the most popular LBSNs protected by the-state-of-art location hiding techniques. First, is it possible to make an involuntary localization of a random LBSN user by exploiting the public available information only? That is, without hacking into the services and using only the client side information that is publicly available through the unmodified app of LBSNs, could we accurately localize a random online user of no priori knowledge? Secondly, could we freely track a particular user within a reasonably short time period? By investigating three most popular LBSN apps (Wechat, Momo and Skout), our answers to these two questions are more than a simple "yes". Our research findings show that: 1) An attacker could perform a range-free, involuntary user localization attack with high localization accuracy; 2) Furthermore, it can successfully establish very accurate user location profile.

We implement an automated user location tracking system for mobile social networks that could track Wechat, Skout and Momo users without any awareness. To demonstrate its effectiveness, we perform a three-week real-world attack towards 30 volunteers from United States, China and Japan. By comparing the collected users' real traces with the inferred traces, it is found that the mean tracking error is 51m for 74 Wechat tests, 25m for 119 Momo tests, and 130m for 156 Skout tests. What's more, the attacker can easily identify users' Top 5 locations. According to the existing works, more than 50% of the individuals could be uniquely identified given top 2 locations [12]. Hence, the newly identified attacks pose a serious threat towards the locations privacy of hundreds of millions of LBSN users.

The rest of paper is organized as follows: Section 2 is the classification of LBSNs. Section 3 describes our attack methodology, which is followed by Section 4 describing the implementation of the attack. Section 5 presents the evaluation results. In Section 6, the mitigation approaches are discussed and Section 7 summarizes the related work. Finally, Section 8 concludes the paper.

2. LBSN: THE STATE-OF-THE-ART

2.1 Classification of LBSNs

With the wide use of mobile devices, and the increasing attention on mobile social networking, location-based social networks (LBSN) focusing on the small local social network derived from a user's geographical location become increasingly popular. In addition to the conventional location-based user check-in apps (e.g., Foursquare), more LBSN apps are exploiting the users' geographical information to achieve distance-based social discovery and location sharing. Based on how real-world LBSNs share the location information among their users in order to allow location-based social discovery, they can be classified into two main categories: I) LBSNs with Exact Location Sharing and II) LBSNs with Indirect Location Sharing. Table 1 is a summary of our surveyed 20 popular real-world LBSNs.

Category I has two subtypes. The Subtype I is *Open Access Location Sharing*. These LBSNs present the exact locations without any restriction. In Banjo, by clicking "Places" tab, the users are allowed to see people of the same city, the exact location of which are explicitly displayed on a map. Subtype II is *User Authorized Location Sharing*. For this type of LBSNs, users have the control to choose with whom they share their exact location information. For example, in Google Plus or PCube, a user decides the set of other users to share location with. In general, we believe users fully aware of potential risks of those kinds of apps.

In Category II, the exact geographic information is obfuscated by a series of location privacy protection techniques. Different from Category I which reveals users' exact locations, Category II LBSNs assure users that their exact location information is never shared by privacy protection techniques. In our investigated apps, LBSN service providers adopt the following location obfuscating techniques.

I. Relative Distance Only: This has been a very common location hiding technique adopted by many popular LBSNs, including Wechat, Skout, and Momo. Users in this case can only see others' geographic distances instead of location coordinates. From the user's point of view, revealing the distances rather than coordinates could hide the exact location but still allow the nearby strangers (or potential friends) to discover the presence of this user.

II. Setting the Minimum Accuracy Limit: Setting a safe localization accuracy limit is a traditional location obfuscation technique [4]. Most of the LBSN apps predefine a certain minimum accuracy limit for geo-localization to further protect the users' exact location. For example, Skout defines localization accuracy to 1 mile, which means that the users will be located with an accuracy no better than 1 mile. Similarly, Wechat and Momo set 100m and 10m as their localization accuracy limits.

III. Setting the Localization Coverage Limits: To prevent malicious users from abusing the geo-localization, an additional functionality, Localization Coverage limit is provided to restrict the users' localization capability to a specific region or under the maximum number of displayed users. For example, Wechat only displays the relative distance of users, the number of which is less than a predefined threshold (e.g., 1000m in Wechat for a high user density region).

In addition to above mentioned location hiding techniques, there are other factors contributing to the localization errors, which will be presented as follows.

2.2 Location Update in LBSNs

In general, the localization accuracy of smartphone relies on which kind of location data sources it uses. The location data sources (location providers) include: GPS, Wi-Fi, and Cell ID (cell tower), that corresponds to localization accuracy of 10m, 80m and 600m [32]. However, in practice, it's up to the app developers themselves to decide which location source to trust and it is always a trade-off between waiting time, precision and energy consumption[16, 3]. To have a better understanding on the updating strategy of LBSN apps, we perform the following accuracy testing experiments.

We mainly perform the accuracy testing on three apps: Wechat, Skout and Momo. We pre-define a reference point both in the physical world (akin a virtual user located in this position) and the virtual machine. We then enlarge the physical distance between our mobile device and the reference point by sending fake locations to the device and record the relative distance displayed on apps. We compare the physical distance and the distance shown in apps and obtain the accuracy testing results, which are depicted in Fig 1.

Since Momo's localization accuracy limit is set to 10m, we choose a test point for every 2m. From Fig 1a, we confirm 10m as the localization accuracy limit with a rounding every 5m. In Skout, the localization accuracy bound is approximately 0.5mile. In the experiment, we evaluate the localization accuracy every 50m. From Fig 1b, it is observed that Skout's minimum coverage is 0.5mile with distance rounding every half a mile and the distance is increased every 1.6km or 1mile. We set the reference point for every 20 meters for Wechat and have observed that the coverage bound can be up to 10km in sparsely populated area and generally 1000m in densely populated places. It is also observed that Wechat has no round-offs in its distance and the boundary is quite clear between every 100m (Fig 1c).

	Distance	Accuracy Limit	Coverage Limit	Number of Users (millions)	Platform or region	SDK	Category
Wechat	Y	100m	1km (Shanghai)	300 millions	iOS/Android/WP	Google	II
Skout	Y	0.5mile	N/A	5 millions	iOS/Android/WP	Google	II
Momo	Y	10m	N/A	30 millions	iOS/Android/WP	Baidu	II
Whoshere	Y	100m	N/A	5 millions in 2012	iOS/Android	Google	II
MiTalk	Y	100m	0.6km (Shanghai)	20 millions	iOS/Android	Baidu	II
Weibo	Y	100m	1600m	500 millions	iOS/Android/WP	Google	II
SayHi	Y	10m	1000km	500 thousands	iOS/Android	Google	I/II
iAround	Y	10m	N/A	10 millions	iOS/Android	Baidu	I/II
Duimian	Y	100m	N/A	500 thousands	iOS/Android	Google	II
Doudou Friend	Y	10m	N/A	1 million	iOS/Android	Amap	II
U+	Y	10m	N/A	10 millions	iOS/Android	Baidu	II
Topface	Y	100m	N/A	50 million	iOS/Android	Google	II
Niupai	Y	10m	N/A	61 thousands	iOS/Android	Google	II
LOVOO	Y	100m	27.8km (Shanghai)		iOS/Android	Google	II
KKtalk	Y	10m	N/A	320 thousands	iOS/Android	Google	II
Meet24	Y	0.5mile	N/A		iOS/Android	Google	II
Anywhered	Y	10m	N/A	750 thousands	Android	Baidu	II
I Part	Y	10m	1000m	8 millions	iOS/Android	Google	II
Path	N	N/A	N/A	10 millions	iOS/Android	Google	I
TweetCaster	N	N/A	N/A	10 millions	iOS/Android/WP	Google	I
Google Plus	N	N/A	N/A	10 millions	iOS/Android/WP	Google	I
eHarmony	N	N/A	N/A	5 millions	iOS/Android	Google	I
SinglesAroundMe	N	N/A	N/A	1 million	iOS/Android	Google	I

Table 1: Summary of Location-based Friend Discovery Apps

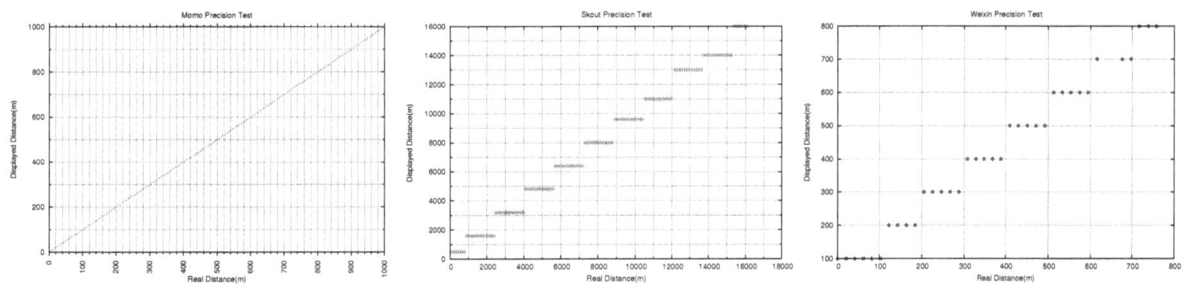

(a) Momo precision test

(b) Skout precision test

(c) Wechat precision test

Figure 1: Updating Strategy Evaluation Results

2.3 User Location Privacy in LBSNs

From above discussions, we can conclude that, in general, the locations reported in LBSN apps honestly reflect mobile users' real locations, though the exact locations are hidden or obfuscated by various location hiding techniques. For example, Momo only adopts the strategy of showing the relative distances (strategy I). Skout only shows the distance and, at the same time, enforces the minimum localization limit (strategy I & II). As a comparison, Wechat adopts all of location hiding strategies I, II, III.

In this paper, we argue that, relying on the above mentioned location privacy hiding techniques may introduce more dangerous location privacy leaking issues. Due to trust on these location hiding/obfuscating techniques, LBSN users are more willing to share the **protected** location information with the potential adversary, which could recover users' exact location or even traces using the methodology proposed in this paper. Without full knowledge of the potential risk, LBSN users may face the serious location privacy leaking issue, while the adversary could gain a significant advantage during the attack process by making involuntary geo-location or even tracking.

3. ATTACK METHODOLOGY

In this section, we introduce our attacker model, as well as the attack methodology in details.

3.1 Attacker Model

In this study, we consider a capability-restricted attacker aiming at geo-locating an LBSN user, who does not need to have a priori social association with him, i.e., an in-app friend. The attacker's capability is restricted in sense that I) It only has the access right no more than a normal user of a given LBSN service, which means that he can only access the publicly available information provided by the LBSN app. II) It is not allowed to hack the LBSN service by interfering its internal operations, that is, we do not consider an attacker that can compromise the LBSN servers and thus can directly access the user location information as a consequence. In summary, our attacker is a very weak one which can't gain any additional information from the LBSN services other than what is entitled to a regular service user. Specifically, the attacker will try to infer a user's location information based only on the relative distance information displayed by the LBSN apps. Note that, to obtain the relative distance, it is even not necessary for the attacker to be friend of the victim. Instead, it will automatically display the relative distance of nearby users in most of considered Category II apps. For

Momo, the attacker can obtain the distance by searching the victim via Momo ID and in Skout, the distance between the victim user and the attacker can always be displayed as long as the attacker has sent a regular message (a greeting for instance) to the victim before. We are concerned that if the LBSN under examination can't resist even such a weak attacker, the user's location privacy is obviously in a great danger as any user can be an attacker.

We further distinguish two different types of attackers, i.e., a Casual Localization Attacker and a Determined Tracking Attacker. A Casual Localization Attacker reviews the profiles of nearby users when logging in to a LBSN app as a regular user, randomly picking up a tracking target and then try to geo-localize the target. A Determined Tracking Attacker may start with a known User ID (UID) as its chosen attacking target and perform the tracking towards a specific victim for a certain duration. The goal of the tracking attacker is revealing users' Top N locations (e.g., his home or office) [33]. Note that, a tracking attacker may start with a target person in mind and exploit certain side-channel information of the target to help obtain the corresponding UID. For example, user photos shared among various social network sites can be used to establish the link for the same user, which in turn can lead to the acquisition of UID in a particular LBSN. Social engineering approaches like this have been widely studied in the literature and is not a focus of this paper [19]. We assume that a determined tracking attacker is able to start with a chosen UID he wants to locate.

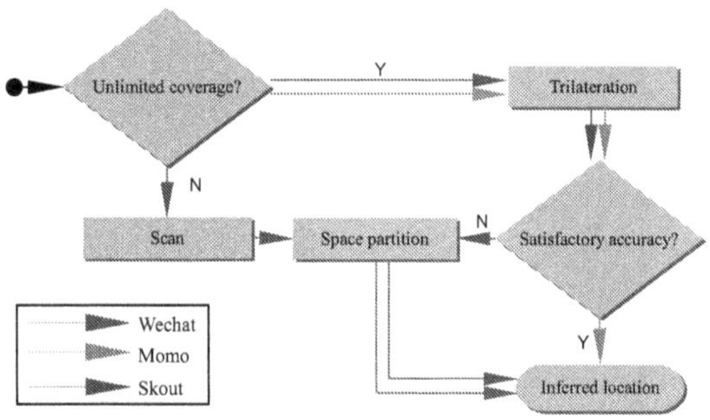

Figure 2: The Attack Flow

3.2 Methodology Overview

The security of the state-of-the-art privacy protection techniques are based on the assumption that the location cannot be faked. Under this assumption, the exact location of the mobile users is hidden/obfuscated by the above mentioned three strategies. Therefore, the intuition behind our attack is that, if the attacker could freely generate the fake anchor points with new locations, LBSN apps will be a distance oracle that always returns the relative distance with these anchor points to the attacker. By exploiting the returned information, the attacker could launch localization algorithms to geo-locate the victim and even break the accuracy limit.

As shown in Fig 2, when the attacker determines a particular victim, it generates three fake anchor locations and obtains the relative distance to the victim. With 3 anchor locations and their corresponding distances, it could trigger the iterative trilateration based localization algorithm and obtain the inferred location. After that, the attacker adopts space partition attack to further improve the accuracy until the distance reaches the predefined accuracy threshold. For those apps with the coverage limit, the attacker can scan the possible locations until the victim is shown in the "nearby list". Then, it takes advantage of space partition attack to make an accurate localization. We introduce each basic algorithm one by one in the following subsections.

3.3 Iterative Trilateration based Localization Algorithm: Skout and Momo

Our localization approach is based on the traditional Trilateration Position Problem. In our long distance tracking, we start from 3 randomly generated positions serving as the first three anchor points. In Section 4.1, we will introduce how to generate the fake locations on Android. The triggered Trilateration algorithm returns the first localization results. To minimize its distance from the target, the least squares solution can be used to solve this problem as suggested in [20]. We iteratively perform trilateration and generate the next reference point from the previous round localization results. We denote P as the list of reference points sorted by the relative distance to the target point from smaller to larger. Without loss of the generality, the first three items of P are represented by p_1, p_2 and p_3. We further define function $dist(a, b)$ to measure the distance between the point a and b, as well as function $Lsp(a, b, c)$ to return the least square estimation of the localization target based on three reference points (a, b, c). We summarize our iterative trilateration localization algorithm in Algorithm 1.

Algorithm 1: The Iterative Trilateration based Localization Algorithm

Data: List $P = \emptyset$, in which the elements are sorted by their distance to targeted node
Result: $p_0 = (x_0, y_0, z_0)$ the location of the target

Put 3 random reference points into P;
$d \leftarrow +\infty$;
while $(d > threshold)$ **do**
  $p_1, p_2, p_3 \leftarrow$ first 3 elements of P;
  $d \leftarrow$ distance between p_1 and target node;
  $t \leftarrow Lsp(p_1, p_2, p_3)$;
  Insert t into P;
end
Output p_1;

3.4 Breaking Minimum Distance Limit via Space Partition Attack: Skout and Wechat

Another best practice measure to protect location privacy is to limit the relative distance to a certain accuracy, (e.g., 800m in Skout or 100m for Wechat). In this section, we propose a space partition attack algorithm to further enhance the localization accuracy and thus breaking the minimum distance limit. The basic idea of space partition attack is similar to space partition algorithm, which is defined as the process of dividing a space (usually a Euclidean space) into two or more non-overlapping regions and thus locating any point in the space to exactly one of the regions. The basic idea of space partition attack is illustrated in Fig 3.

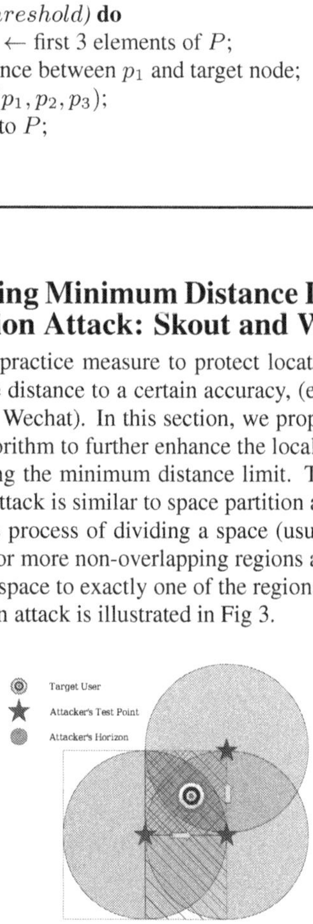

Figure 3: Illustration of Space Partition Attack

For the simplicity of problem presentation, we consider the minimum distance limit as the box rather than the circle. Given the minimum distance limit R, the edge length of the box is set to $2R$. The space partition attack could be illustrated as follows. In each round, the potential area of length r is partitioned into two regions. Then, we will check if it is within one region. If yes, it is derived that the user is in this half. Otherwise, the user is located in the other half. We could repeat this partition for multiple rounds until the expected accuracy is achieved. The whole algorithm is summarized in Algorithm 2.

Algorithm 2: Space Partition Attack Algorithm

Data: An estimated point $p_0 = (c_X, c_Y)$ and its displayed distance from target point T, given in form $dist(p_0, T) \leq R$.
Result: T', the final estimation for T

```
dim = X;
δ_X = R;
δ_Y = R;
while δ_X ≥ threshold or δ_Y ≥ threshold do
    Shift p_0 in dim dimension by R to p';
    if dist(p', T) ≤ R then
        c   =c   + δ   /2;
    end
    else
        c   =c   − δ   /2;
    end
    δ   = δ   /2;
    dim = {X, Y}/dim;
    p_0 = (c_X, c_Y);
end
Output p_0;
```

3.5 Breaking Localization Coverage Bound by Correlating the Social Popularity and Geolocation: Wechat

Some apps such as Wechat set a certain coverage limit. For such kind of apps, a straightforward approach to launch the attack is to scan a certain area, and, at each sub-area, find out if the attacking target appears in the "Nearby" list of this app. In practice, the performance of such a simple scan approach may not be desirable due to the potentially large region in which the target is located. To further improve the performance of the launched attack, we propose a *Social Popularity Index* based approach to speed up the localization process. This approach is motivated by the existing research that human trajectories are regular in space and time, with each individual having a high probability of returning to a few preferred locations according to Zipf's law [29]. In other words, it is more likely for a user to be at the restaurant at 6 pm in the afternoon rather than at office. However, this statement may not hold at 10 am in the morning. The social popularity index is introduced to represent how popular a location is at a particular time slot, and thus can be used to estimate how likely a user is located at this area at this moment. In our implementations, we measure the social popularity index of different locations by collecting their user population information at different time slots. Then, based on the number of users, we could assign a higher priority to those areas with the higher user population.

In addition to the above described methodology, there are still implementation challenges, including: generating the fake locations in smartphone and fetching relative distance readings from Android LBSN apps to make the above methodology to work realistic. More importantly, all of these should be performed in an automated way. We'll introduce the implementation details in the next section.

4. IMPLEMENTATION

Besides the algorithms introduced in previous section, the system implementation involves two other key modules: the location spoofing module and the location reading module. Our system is implemented in Clojure in order to cope with MonkeyRunner to control Android virtual machines and send commands. We also implement a LocationFaker app that receives HTTP request to set the location in Android. To address problems we encounter during location faking and result reading, we tweak parts of the Android framework.

4.1 Generating Fake Locations on Android

To launch the proposed attack, we need to freely generate the anchor location points, which are used to obtain the relative distances of the victim users. To allow fast real-world automated tracking, we set our Android system on real Android X86 images running in VirtualBox. It is important to point out that, since almost all of the LBSN apps cover all of the platforms (please refer to Table 1 for our survey), including iOS/Android/WP, spoofing the android device's locations could allow the attacker to obtain the relative distances with LBSN users on iOS/WP, and thus launch the attack towards the users on all of platforms.

To enable the fast and reliable location retrieval, we implement our location spoofing component, LocationFaker, as a system service to eliminate the possibility that Android system may kill the activities to release resources, which are not supported by existing apps such as Developer Shell and FakeGPS. Further, it has embedded Jetty as a web server to provide stateless http-based interface to set locations and act as a fake location server when we redirect the network traffic. In general, most of the LBSN apps on Android either use built-in Android API (Wechat or Skout) or third-party SDKs (e.g., Momo using Baidu Location SDK), which lead to different spoofing strategies. For built-in Android API, we adopt *fake location provider based location spoofing*. However, according to the official document [6], Baidu Location SDK does not function well on virtual machines. For this case, we achieve location spoofing by using *network redirection*. In the follows, we introduce both approaches in detail.

4.1.1 Location Spoofing with Fake Location Provider

Android apps mostly acquire locations via one or more location providers (e.g., "gps" and "network") from the *location* system service. Since Android allows users to freely add location providers under certain circumstances such as debugging or providing locations from other devices, e.g. Bluetooth, it is possible to add a user-written location provider by enabling "Allow mock location" option in developer options and adopting the API "addTestProvider". It is interesting that we can set the provider's name to "gps" to make it indistinguishable from the real gps, and thus fool the system into believing that they are receiving locations from the real GPS chip. Our fake location provider is running on its thread, feeding location information every $700ms$.

One of the major challenges of spoofing the location on Android is that the provided location should satisfy certain accuracy. Otherwise, the apps will reject it. During our implementation, it is found that Wechat will return error messages if fake provides set fake locations. After checking with Google Map, we discover such fake location provider lacks accuracy information. To address this issue, we decompiled the Android framework with ApkTool and modified the constructor of "android.location.Location" by coercing "mHasAccuracy" to "true" and enforcing "getAccuracy" to always return 70m. This enables apps to retrieve consistently accurate value under different circumstances and the location faking component starts to work as expected.

4.1.2 Location Spoofing with Network Redirection

For those LBSN apps which do not adopt Android built-in APIs for location retrieval, we introduce another approach based on network redirection. In this section, we use Momo as an example to show how it works. Basically, Momo uses Baidu Location SDK to obtain the user location. We start from analyzing the network traffic with Wireshark and Tcpdump. It is observed that the API first posts the coordinates and supplemental information, which is obtained from the device, to http://loc.map.baidu.com/sdk.php. The server returns a plaintext JSON object carrying location information as follows:

```
{"content":{"addr":{"detail":""}, "bldg":"",
 "floor":"", "point":{"y":"","x":""}, "radius":""},
 "result": {"error":,"time":""}}
```

By comparing the failed request against successful one, it is found that the key fields are the x and y coordinates in "point", "radius", the error code and the timestamp. The error code 161 indicates a *successful* query and the y and x carry the computed coordinates of the latitude and longitude. We utilize Iptables in our implementation to build a NAT that redirects all the requests originally sent to Baidu location server back to our embedded Jetty web server running by LocationFaker. LocationFaker will then construct a similar JSON object carrying fake locations to trick Baidu Location SDK to accept the received location as the real location.

4.2 Fetching Location Data Readings

The last component is location-dependent data fetching module, which retrieves the distance readings from APPs based on the fake location setting. The basic strategy is actually running the client and simulating the user's inputs to retrieve distance readings. To simulate user inputs, we adopt the MonkeyRunner library bundled with the Android SDK. With MonkeyRunner scripts provided in Jython, it simulates user inputs in apps to allow us automatically to perform various tests on apps. We integrate the API with our attacking framework to allow user defined inputs. We simulate consecutive operations in forms of touch, drag, scroll, input numbers, shell command and key press to mimic a user's behavior to the apps to trigger a location information update and scroll down the list to read out all items.

To read the distance from the apps, we have modified the TextView widget to dump text to log messages whenever a "setText" method call is made. We then retrieve text from the Adb logcat buffer and reads specific app's output by filtering log level, grepping by PID and tags then matching particular regular expression pattern.

5. REAL-WORLD EVALUATIONS

To evaluate the effectiveness of our strategy, we implement the real-world experiments by recruiting 30 volunteers for the 3 kinds of LBSN apps: Wechat, Skout and Momo. We evaluate the *Localization Accuracy* by comparing the distance between the user's *Real Locations* and *Inferred Locations*, and *Localization Efficiency* by measuring the latency of launching an attack for different apps. In the experiments of real-world tracking, we evaluate the effectiveness by measuring how many top locations could be recovered by using 3-week track.

5.1 Localization Accuracy and Efficiency

To well evaluate the localization accuracy, we set that the attack is triggered as soon as the user reports his real location obtained from location providers (e.g., GPS, Wi-Fi, or cell ID). The attack and real location reporting is set to the synchronous mode because we need to make sure that users' mobility will not impact the localization accuracy. To achieve this, we deploy a web server in which users with HTML5-capable browsers could retrieve their locations directly from location providers of their smart phones, and then submit their real location, user information to the server. The server will immediately put this request into its task queue and each idle node polls and claims a task and schedule an attack, the results of which will be reported to the server and compared with the exact location. Members of our groups regularly submit their locations to the server. We've collected in total of more than 350 location reports and attack results. The testing regions include United States, China and Japan.

5.1.1 Localization Accuracy

The evaluation on localization accuracy is shown in Fig 4. From Fig 4, it is observed that the majority of the results achieve a very high localization accuracy. For Momo, nearly 60% of the attacks can geo-locate a user at the accuracy of less than 20m and only less than 10% of the localization accuracy is more than 60m. In general, it could achieve an average localization accuracy of 25.8m for 119 evaluations. For Skout, though the minimum localization limit is 800m, most of the localization could achieve the accuracy of less than 60m while over 70% of the localization is less than 120m. The average localization accuracy could reach 129.4m for 156 tests, indicating the effectiveness of the Space Partition algorithm. For Wechat with minimum localization limit of 100m, we are able to geo-locate 50% of users in less than 40m. The average accuracy is 51.1m for 74 tests. Note that, different factors contribute to the localization errors such as inconsistent location providers / APIs, various location calculation algorithm / strategy or location cache policy.

5.1.2 Localization Speed

We measure the efficiency with the average execution time of attacks. The results are shown in Fig 5a and Fig 5b, which correspond to the case of randomly setting first 3 anchor points and social popularity enhanced attacking approach.

From Fig 5a, it is shown that over 80% of the attacks for all 3 apps finish within $1200s$. It is important to point out that most of the time is spent on waiting for the app server's response. More specifically, each request for Wechat waits 40s to ensure that the user's location is fetched due to network latency and for Momo, the number increases to 55s while for Skout, it spends on 20s on queuing per query. In the evaluation, Momo has a faster localization speed as the iterative trilateration converges fast and hence requires fewer queries. From Fig 5b, it is shown that, after adding some side information such as social popularity index in Wechat or setting the initialization point in the approximate area (e.g., Shanghai) for Momo or Skout, the localization performance could be enhanced for 1.5 times.

5.2 Real-world Tracking: Tracking Accuracy and Top Location Coverage

In this section, we evaluate the effectiveness in real-world tracking. The basic goal of this experiment is to compare the inferred

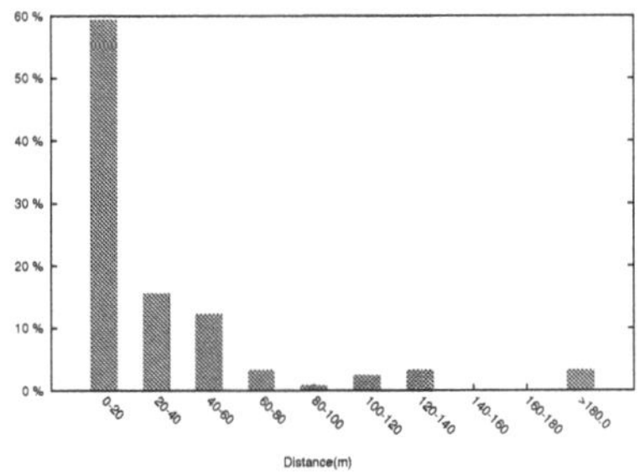

(a) Momo's Localization Accuracy

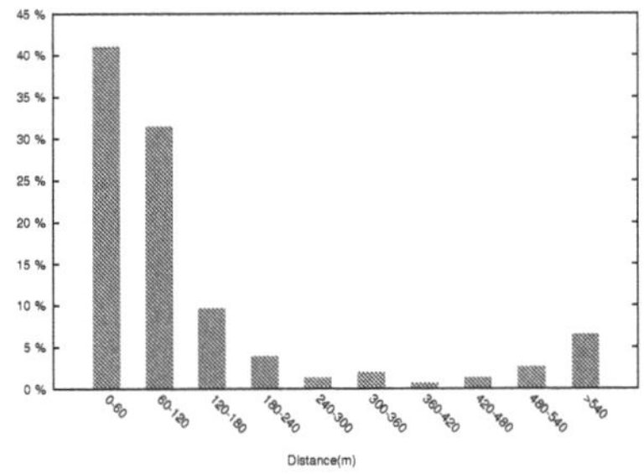

(b) Skout's Localization Accuracy

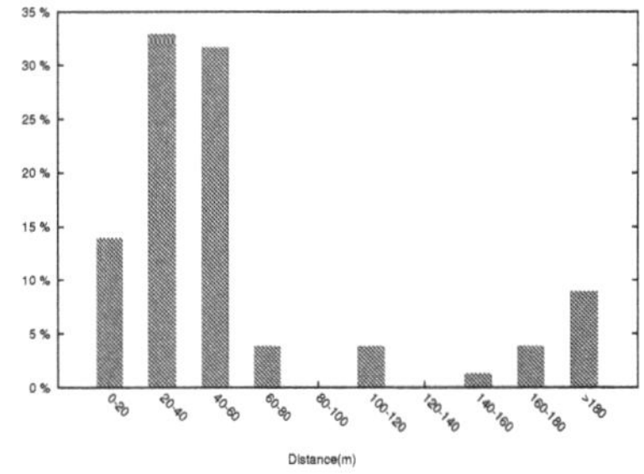

(c) Wechat's Localization Accuracy

Figure 4: Evaluation on Localization Accuracy

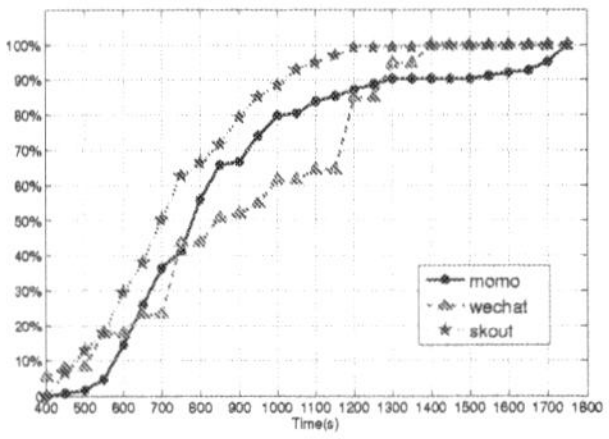

(a) Localization inference time on different apps

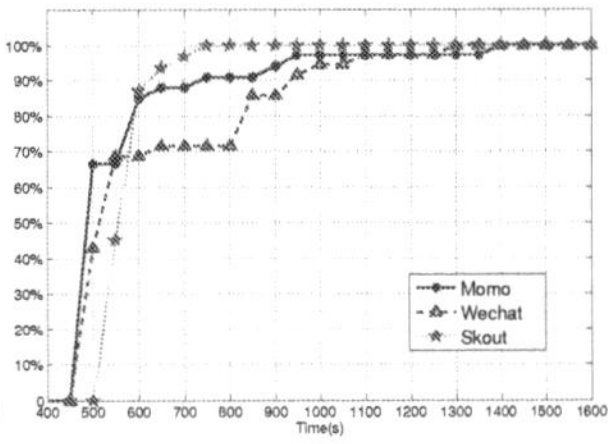

(b) Improved localization inference time on different apps

Figure 5: Localization Efficiency of the Original and Enhanced Scheme

mobility traces of the mobile users with their real mobility trace to measure how much location information the attacker could obtain by tracking the users in a certain duration. In this phase, we recruit 30 volunteers from China, Japan and United States to participate in our three-week real-world experiments. The tracked Skout and Momo volunteers are scattered in all the three countries. For Wechat, due to the coverage limit, we fix a region of the size of 3km$*$5km in Shanghai and 20km$*$20km in Buffalo. In these three weeks, the volunteers use the LBSN apps in the same way as other typical LBSN users. To obtain the ground truth data (or user's real mobility traces), we develop an app based on Baidu Location API to record their locations every half an hour and submit the traces to the server. On the server side, we run 3 Momo tracking instances, 7 Wechat nodes and 3 Skout nodes to track Momo, Wechat and Skout users, respectively. We continuously track them for 3 weeks and collect 3395 inferred points in total.

5.2.1 Tracking Accuracy

In real-world tracking, synchronization of user real trace reporting and our tracking is almost infeasible due to unexpected user usage pattern as well as the randomness of the delay between victim's location updating and our tracking. Therefore, we also evaluate the tracking accuracy in the asynchronous mode. In particular, the user's real-world trace is periodically updated (e.g., 30 mins), and the tracking on users is also periodically launched (40 mins). In this case, we define the *Tracking Accuracy* as the distance of the inferred location and its closest counterpart of the reported user traces (ground truth data) in time domain. Such tracking accuracy provides the upper bound of the localization error.

The evaluation of tracking accuracy is shown in Fig 6. The experiment results demonstrate that the asynchronous tracking can also achieve a very high level of accuracy. As shown in Fig 6a, more than 80% of tracking results on Momo can geo-locate the victims in 40m, more than 90% of tracking results on Skout can break the distance limit of 800m to geo-locate the victims to $0-20$m and $80-100$m, and over half of the tracking on Wechat users can be located to the accuracy of less than 60m.

The factors which may potentially affect the tracking accuracy includes: the location providers (GPS, Wi-Fi, or Cell ID) varied in precision, cache policy defining how long the user's location is buffered at the server side. We've investigated the cache policy of Wechat by comparing the results from China and US, which have different user populations and thus different cache time. The results are indicated in Fig 7. In China, as one of the most popular LBSN apps, Wechat has a huge population of users, which makes the users' locations buffered at the server side for a shorter duration, making user tracking more difficult. It is much easier to track a Wechat user in the US due to smaller number of users and a much longer location cache time.

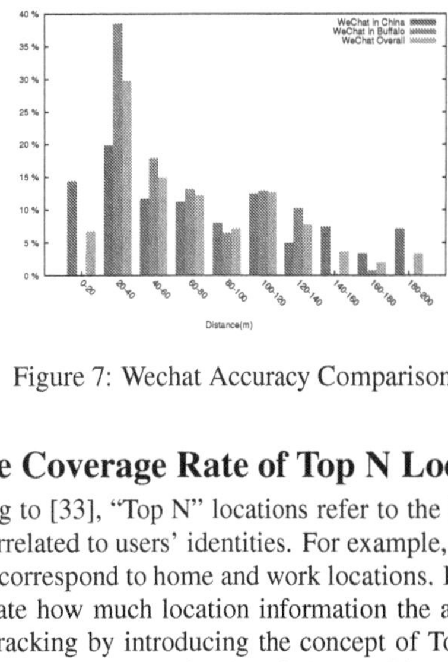

Figure 7: Wechat Accuracy Comparison

5.3 The Coverage Rate of Top N Location

According to [33], "Top N" locations refer to the locations that are most correlated to users' identities. For example, "top 2" locations likely correspond to home and work locations. In the section, we investigate how much location information the attacker could gain from tracking by introducing the concept of Top N location Coverage Rate, which is defined as follows. Given $\mathbb{G}$ as the set of reported traces (ground truth data) and $\mathbb{I}$ as the set of inferred traces, we define $Top_N()$ as the function that returns N most visited locations from a specific trace and thus define Top N Location Coverage rate as

$$TNR = \frac{|Top_N(\mathbb{G}) \cap Top_N(\mathbb{I})|}{N},$$

which refers to the percentage of locations that belongs to both of Top N locations in reported and inferred mobility traces.

Evaluation Results: Without loss of the generality, we set $N=5$ and evaluate the top location coverage rate for three weeks, which

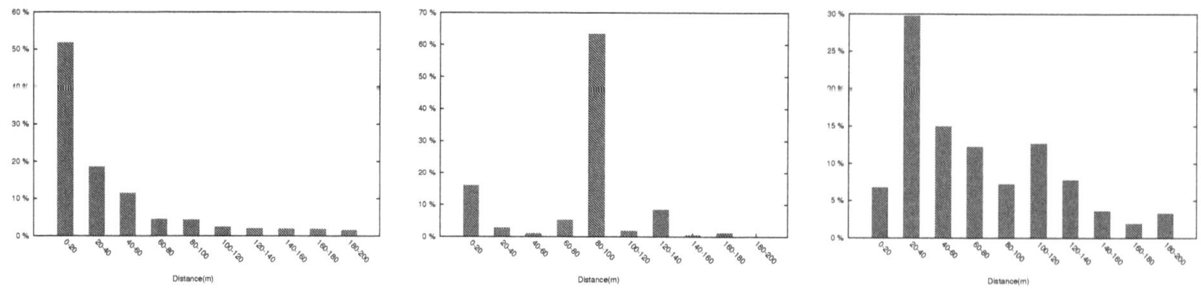

(a) Tracking Accuracy of Momo (b) Tracking Accuracy of Skout (c) Tracking Accuracy of WeChat

Figure 6: Evaluation Results on Tracking Accuracy

top location	one week			two weeks			three weeks		
	Momo	Wechat	Skout	Momo	Wechat	Skout	Momo	Wechat	Skout
1	92.3%	50.0%	20.0%	100.0%	57.1%	60.0%	100.0%	71.4%	60.0%
2	46.1%	21.4%	0.0%	46.1%	21.4%	40.0%	69.2%	21.4%	40.0%
3	30.7%	21.4%	20.0%	46.1%	28.5%	60.0%	38.4%	28.5%	80.0%
4	23.0%	35.7%	20.0%	30.7%	35.7%	40.0%	38.4%	35.7%	40.0%
5	23.0%	21.4%	0.0%	15.3%	21.4%	40.0%	15.3%	14.2%	40.0%

Table 2: Top 5 Location Coverage Result for 3 Weeks

is shown in Table 2. We choose the location match criteria in accordance with each app's accuracy limit, e.g., 100m for Wechat, and the cluster radius of the location region. The cluster radius of location region is the maximum radius for clustering a user's location coordinates in his real trace and it is set to 50m empirically (typical length of a building in the area where experiments are conducted). Thus the location matching precisions for all three apps are 50m (Momo), 100m (Wechat) and 0.5 mile (Skout) in our experiment. From Table 2, it is observed that Momo shows the best coverage rate. After three weeks tracking, we can obtain all the volunteers' top 1 locations and about 70% volunteers' top 2 locations. For Wechat, we could successfully infer 71.4% 21.4%, 28.5% of top $1, 2, 3$ locations after 3 week tracking. For Skout, 60.0%, 40.0%, 80.0% volunteers' top $1, 2, 3$ locations could be successfully recovered. Our evaluation results also show that the temporal factor plays an important role in Top N location recovery. In particular, the Top N location coverage rate will significantly increase along with more tracking days. In general, our attack shows a high Top 5 location coverage rate.

6. A USER-CENTRIC PRIVACY ENHANCEMENT FRAMEWORK

In this section, we aim to propose some suggestions to limit the attacker's capability. Certainly, effective location proof could prevent our attack, but the typical location proof techniques include using the deployed trusted infrastructures (e.g., cell tower or Wi-Fi access points) [25] or using environmental signals as the location tags [24, 34, 9]. However, they either require the presence of trusted infrastructure or are only effective in a small-scale (e.g., less than 100m) due to the spatial diversity of wireless signals. As a result, the existing location proof techniques are only feasible in a small-scale region and less practical in our scenario.

One potential approach of limiting the attacker's capability is that the service provider can compare users' location changes with their mobility patterns or behavior patterns to identify potential anomalous users (e.g, changing the locations too frequently or making too many queries within a short period). For example, from our experiment, it is observed that Wechat has put a limit on the number of queries issued at a certain duration (depending on the workload of the server) and the misbehaving account will be blocked for a specic period, which signicantly slows down attacking process. Our real-world experiments show that, though the attacker may use multiple accounts to speed up the attack, a more stringent limit on the number of queries will increase the difculty of launching the attacks since the attack should be nished between two consequent location updating events of the target.

We notice that Momo and Wechat provide an option to manually remove their locations from the public. However, with no idea about the potential risks brought by LBSN apps, few people do choose this option. This further signifies the importance of making the public more aware of the potential risk, which is one of major motivations of this paper.

Another possible approach for reducing the accuracy of the proposed attack is adding more noises to the location management module of LBSNs to achieve a better privacy protection at the cost of the decrease of users' utility. Here we present a user-centric privacy enhancement framework based on a global grid reference system and location classification to provide the tradeoff of the privacy and the utility.

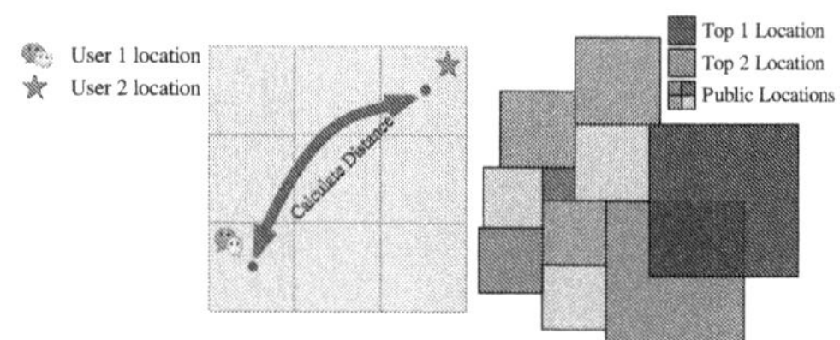

(a) Basic Grid Reference System (b) Classified Grid Reference System

Figure 8: The Grid Reference System

Distance Obfuscation with Grid Reference System: We propose a distance obfuscation technique based on grid reference system, which aims to prevent the attacker from using LBSN as the location oracle to obtain the accurate location information. As shown in Fig 8a, the server maintains a grid reference system, where the location of a mobile user can be expressed as the center of the grid cell that the user is located in. Therefore, the distance of two grid cells expresses the relative distance of two users defined as the minimum path connecting these two cells. The benefit of using grid reference system to express the relative distance of two users is that it obfuscates the real location of mobile users with the center of the cell and the attacker cannot obtain extra information of the target if the generated fake anchors are located at the same cell. It is noted that other advanced obfuscation techniques [5] or differential location privacy [1] could be applied to the proposed global grid reference system to provide the privacy enhancement for LBSNs.

Privacy Definition vs Utility Metrics Similar to other obfuscation techniques, grid reference system will also decrease user utility. Considering the relative distance is the main metric of LBSN, we define the metric of privacy as:

$$\mathbf{Pri} = \mathbf{Dist}(\mathbf{L}_R, \mathbf{L}\ \ ),$$

where $\mathbf{L}_R$ and $\mathbf{L}$ refer to the real and obfuscated location of the mobile user, respectively, and function $\mathbf{Dist}()$ returns the distance of two locations in Grid reference system. By given a specific anchor node at location $\mathbf{L}_A$, we further define the utility metric as

$$\mathbf{UT} = 1 - \frac{|\mathbf{DDist}(\mathbf{L}_R, \mathbf{L}_A) - \mathbf{DDist}(\mathbf{L}\ \ , \mathbf{L}_A)|}{\mathbf{Dist}},$$

where function $\mathbf{DDist}()$ returns the displayed distance in LBSN apps, $\mathbf{Dist}$ represents the maximum distance that the user could tolerate. It is obvious that, when the displayed distance between the real location and anchor point $\mathbf{DDist}(\mathbf{L}_R, \mathbf{L}_A)$ equals displayed distance between the obfuscated location and anchor point $\mathbf{DDist}(\mathbf{L}\ \ , \mathbf{L}_A)$, the utility achieves the maximum value 1. When $\mathbf{DDist}(\mathbf{L}\ \ , \mathbf{L}_A)$ is much larger or smaller than $\mathbf{DDist}(\mathbf{L}_R, \mathbf{L}_A)$ (their gap should not be larger than $\mathbf{Dist}$), the utility is close to 0. By assigning different values to the size of the cells, we could achieve different location privacy protection level as well as different utilities. We evaluate the effectiveness of location privacy protection and its impact on the utility by applying grid reference system to the data set collected from our real world experiments (ground truth data and inferred location data). Fig 9a shows the privacy gain and the utility under different settings of cell size. It is observed that the increase of privacy gain will lead to the decrease of the utility, and vice versa. We will discuss how to achieve the tradeoff of privacy and utility next.

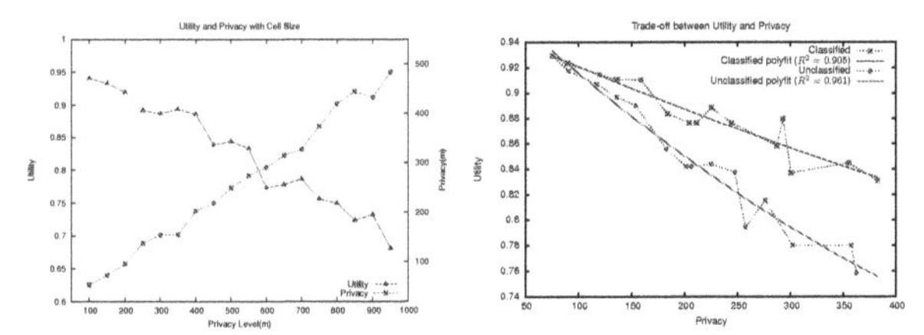

(a) Relationship of Utility/Privacy with Cell Size (b) Comparison of Utility/Privacy Trade-offs

Figure 9: Evaluation on Countermeasure

Achieving Privacy and Utility Trade-off via Classification of Users' Locations: In the previous section, we have shown that the obfuscation techniques decrease the utility. To achieve the tradeoff between the privacy and utility, we introduce a novel user controllable location privacy protection scheme. The proposed scheme is motivated from the observation that the user has different location privacy protection preference for locations. For example, a mobile user cares more about their Top 2 location privacy (e.g., home, work place) but is willing to share locations in public regions (e.g., cafe or bars). Therefore, in a user controllable location privacy protection solution, the mobile users can classify the locations into several categories, which correspond to different privacy protection requirements with different obfuscation parameters. During the subsequent LBSN usage process, users record their location profiles ranked with their visiting frequency and could be dynamically updated along with usage. With such a location profile with different ranking, the most frequently visited locations are given more privacy protection and thus suffer from a lower utility while the less frequently visited locations could enjoy more utility with less privacy protection as indicated in Fig 8b. To implement our idea, we transform the original grid reference system of the uniform cell size to the non-uniform grid reference system, in which top locations cover a larger area while public regions cover a smaller area. Note that the proposed location classification concept could also be applied to other existing obfuscation techniques [5]. To evaluate the proposed solution, we compare the uniform grid reference system with non-uniform grid reference system based on the data set collected from our real-world experiments. In the uniform grid reference system, we tune the cell size from 200m to 1000m, which correspond to the privacy level from 50 to 400. In the non-uniform grid reference system, we fix the cell size of top locations to 1000m to provide highest privacy protection level while tune the cell size of normal location from 200m to 1000m. It is observed that the non-uniform grid reference system based on location classification has a significant advantage in privacy/utility trade-off over the uniform grid reference system as shown in Fig 9b.

7. RELATED WORK

Location Privacy Protection in location-based services is a long-standing topic and has received a lot of attentions in the last decades. The most popular approach to achieve location privacy in LBS is utilizing the obfuscation techniques to coarse the spatial or temporal granularity of the users' real locations [17, 18]. A different approach to hide the users' location is based on mix zones [13]. The third approach is to protect location privacy by adding dummy requests issued by fake location and indistinguishable from real requests [31]. A recent work [28] proposes a game-theoretic framework that enables a designer to find the optimal LPPM for a given location-based service, ensuring a satisfactory service quality for the user. Different from the location privacy issues considered in previous works, providing the relative distance is the key functionality of LBSN apps while the obfuscation will inevitably reduce the utility of LBSNs. Achieving the tradeoff between the location privacy and the utility is of the highest priority. The proposed users' location classification based approach could help to reduce the impact of obfuscation techniques on users' utility, and thus can be a compliment to various obfuscation techniques.

There are many other works on inferring the victim's trajectory and further re-identify other private information [15, 33, 30, 12]. Our work is different from the existing work in that we propose a novel attack approach that allows anyone to perform an involuntary tracking towards any specific target to collect traces for user re-identification.

8. CONCLUSION

LBSN is becoming extremely popular recently. However, most LBSN users are unaware of the location privacy leakage. We target 3 most popular LBSN apps and develop a novel automatic tracking system, which could achieve range-free, accurate, and involuntary tracking towards the target only using the public information. Our real-world attack experiments show that the attack achieves high localization accuracy and the attacker can recover the users' top 5 locations with high possibility. We've discussed various mechanisms to mitigate such threats and analyzed the privacy and utility trade-off. Our study is expected to urge LBSN service providers to revise their location privacy protection techniques and more importantly, serve as a call for more attentions from the public to have the full knowledge of the potential risks brought by LBSN apps. Our mitigation suggestions will provide a guideline for future revisions of these LBSN apps.

9. ACKNOWLEDGEMENT

This work is supported by the National Natural Science Foundation of China (Grant 61272444) and the US National Science Foundation under grant no. CNS-1318948 and CNS-1262275.

10. REFERENCES

[1] M. E. Andrés, N. E. Bordenabe, K. Chatzikokolakis, and C. Palamidessi. Geo-indistinguishability: Differential privacy for location-based systems. In *CCS'13*, 2013.

[2] Apk Apps. Skout 3.4.3 Apk – Meet, Chat, Friend. http://www.apk4.net/applications/social-applications/skout-3-4-3-apk-meet-chat-friend/.

[3] Apple. Location Awareness Programming Guide. http://developer.apple.com/library/ios/#documentation/userexperience/conceptual/LocationAwarenessPG/CoreLocation/CoreLocation.html.

[4] C. A. Ardagna, M. Cremonini, E. Damiani, S. D. C. di Vimercati, and P. Samarati. Location privacy protection through obfuscation-based techniques. In *Data and Applications Security XXI*, pages 47–60. Springer, 2007.

[5] C. A. Ardagna, M. Cremonini, S. De Capitani di Vimercati, and P. Samarati. An obfuscation-based approach for protecting location privacy. *Dependable and Secure Computing, IEEE Transactions on*, 8(1):13–27, 2011.

[6] Baidu. FAQ - Geolocation. http://developer.baidu.com/map/geosdk-android-qa.htm.

[7] A. R. Beresford and F. Stajano. Location privacy in pervasive computing. *Pervasive Computing, IEEE*, 2(1):46–55, 2003.

[8] L. Bindschaedler, M. Jadliwala, I. Bilogrevic, I. Aad, P. Ginzboorg, V. Niemi, and J.-P. Hubaux. Track me if you can: on the effectiveness of context-based identifier changes in deployed mobile networks. In *NDSS'12*, 2012.

[9] J. Brassil, P. Manadhata, and R. Netravali. Traffic signature-based mobile device location authentication. *IEEE Transactions on Mobile Computing*, 2013.

[10] CNET. How Skout attracted millions with its flirty ways. http://news.cnet.com/8301-1035_3-57407367-94/how-skout-attracted-millions-with-its-flirty-ways/.

[11] Craig Smith. How Many People Use the Top Social Media, Apps & Services? http://expandedramblings.com/index.php/resource-how-many-people-use-the-top-social-media/.

[12] Y.-A. de Montjoye, C. A. Hidalgo, M. Verleysen, and V. D. Blondel. Unique in the crowd: The privacy bounds of human mobility. *Scientific reports*, 3, 2013.

[13] J. Freudiger, R. Shokri, and J.-P. Hubaux. On the optimal placement of mix zones. In *Privacy Enhancing Technologies*. Springer, 2009.

[14] B. Gedik and L. Liu. Location privacy in mobile systems: A personalized anonymization model. In *ICDCS'05*. IEEE, 2005.

[15] P. Golle and K. Partridge. On the anonymity of home/work location pairs. In *Pervasive Computing*, pages 390–397. Springer, 2009.

[16] Google. Location Source and Accuracy. http://support.google.com/gmm/bin/ans-wer.py?answer=81873.

[17] M. Gruteser and D. Grunwald. Anonymous usage of location-based services through spatial and temporal cloaking. In *MobiSys'03*. ACM, 2003.

[18] B. Hoh, M. Gruteser, H. Xiong, and A. Alrabady. Preserving privacy in gps traces via uncertainty-aware path cloaking. In *CCS'07*. ACM, 2007.

[19] M. Iasonas, F. George, A. Sotiris, and S. Zanero. All your face are belong to us: Breaking facebook's social authentication. In *ACSAC'12*, 2012.

[20] J. Liu, Y. Zhang, and F. Zhao. Robust distributed node localization with error management. In *MobiHoc'06*. ACM, 2006.

[21] C. Y. Ma, D. K. Yau, N. K. Yip, and N. S. Rao. Privacy vulnerability of published anonymous mobility traces. In *MobiCom'10*. ACM, 2010.

[22] Manila Standard Today. Whats APP? WeChat. http://manilastandardtoday.com/2013/04/06/whats-app/.

[23] J. Meyerowitz and R. Roy Choudhury. Hiding stars with fireworks: location privacy through camouflage. In *MobiCom'09*. ACM, 2009.

[24] A. Narayanan, N. Thiagarajan, M. Lakhani, M. Hamburg, and D. Boneh. Location privacy via private proximity testing. In *NDSS'11*, 2011.

[25] S. Saroiu and A. Wolman. Enabling new mobile applications with location proofs. In *MobiSys'09*. ACM, 2009.

[26] B. Schilit, J. Hong, and M. Gruteser. Wireless location privacy protection. *Computer*, 36(12):135–137, 2003.

[27] R. Shokri, G. Theodorakopoulos, J. Le Boudec, and J. Hubaux. Quantifying location privacy. In *Security and Privacy 2011*. IEEE, 2011.

[28] R. Shokri, G. Theodorakopoulos, C. Troncoso, J.-P. Hubaux, and J.-Y. Le Boudec. Protecting location privacy: Optimal strategy against localization attacks. In *CCS'12*. ACM, 2012.

[29] C. Song, Z. Qu, N. Blumm, and A.-L. Barabási. Limits of predictability in human mobility. *Science*, 327(5968):1018–1021, 2010.

[30] M. Srivatsa and M. Hicks. Deanonymizing mobility traces: Using social network as a side-channel. In *CCS'12*. ACM, 2012.

[31] T. Xu and Y. Cai. Feeling-based location privacy protection for location-based services. In *CCS'09*. ACM, 2009.

[32] P. A. Zandbergen. Accuracy of iphone locations: A comparison of assisted gps, wifi and cellular positioning. *Transactions in GIS*, 13(s1):5–25, 2009.

[33] H. Zang and J. Bolot. Anonymization of location data does not work: A large-scale measurement study. In *MobiCom'11*. ACM, 2011.

[34] Y. Zheng, M. Li, W. Lou, and Y. T. Hou. Sharp: Private proximity test and secure handshake with cheat-proof location tags. In *ESORICS'12*, 2012.

[35] Zhu Feng. Momo Announced Number of Users Exceeded 30 Million, Active 450 Million. http://tech.ifeng.com/mi/detail_2013_03/13/23047454_0.shtml.

Modeling Data Dissemination in Online Social Networks: A Geographical Perspective on Bounding Network Traffic Load

Cheng Wang
Department of Computer Science and Technology
Tongji University
Shanghai, China
chengwang@tongji.edu.cn

Shaojie Tang
Department of Information Systems
University of Texas at Dallas
Richardson, Texas
tangshaojie@gmail.com

Lei Yang
Institute of Trustworthy Networks and Systems
Tsinghua University
Beijing, China
young@tagsys.org

Yi Guo
Department of Computer Science and Engineering
The Hong Kong University of Science and Technology
Kowloon, Hong Kong
guoyithomas@gmail.com

Fan Li
School of Computer Science
Beijing Institute of Technology
Beijing, China
fli@bit.edu.cn

Changjun Jiang
Department of Computer Science and Technology
Tongji University
Shanghai, China
cjjiang@tongji.edu.cn

ABSTRACT

In this paper, we model the data dissemination in online social networks (OSNs) and study the scaling laws of traffic load. We propose a three-layered system model to formulate data dissemination sessions for social applications in OSNs. The layered model consists of the physical network layer, social relationship layer, and application session layer. By analyzing mutual relevances among these three layers, we investigate the geographical distribution feature of dissemination sessions in OSNs. Based on this, we derive the traffic load of OSNs under a realistic assumption that every source sustains a data generating rate of constant order. To the best of our knowledge, this is the first work to address the issue of traffic load scaling for OSNs by modeling the social data dissemination from a layered perspective.

Categories and Subject Descriptors

C.2.1 [**Network Architecture and Design**]: Network communications; Network topology; H.3.4 [**Systems and Software**]: Information networks

General Terms

Performance; Theory

Keywords

Online social networks, data dissemination, traffic load, scaling laws

MobiHoc'14, August 11–14, 2014, Philadelphia, PA, USA.

http://dx.doi.org/10.1145/2632951.2632973.

1. INTRODUCTION

Recent years have witnessed a dramatic growth of user population of online social networks (OSNs). For example, according to the report in March 2013, Facebook has 1.11 billion people using the site each month, which represents a 23 percent growth from a year earlier [3]. OSNs are organized around users [28]. Users publish their profile and any content, build links to other users in whom they are interested. OSN sites act as the basis for maintaining social relationships [18, 28]. In OSNs, the communication pattern based on users' profiles and social relationships is arguably the most important feature [18, 27]. Here, user profiles are usually personal web pages where users can post content, e.g., texts, pictures, music, and videos. For the postings of a user, some of users who follow (are interested in) this user post comments and other content as feedbacks. Thereby, data traffic emerges among OSNs. As OSNs expand rapidly, the traffic load imposed on the underlying communication networks, e.g., the Internet or different types of wireless networks, grows heavier and heavier. Then, how does such traffic load scale as the size of an OSN increases over time? This is the problem we aim to solve in this paper.

For modeling the data traffic pattern and addressing the bounds on network traffic load in OSNs, there are two key factors to consider. The first factor is the architecture of OSNs. In OSNs with the centralized architecture, users' profiles and content are uploaded into servers, and some users request from servers for the information of users of interest [28, 34]. While, in OSNs with the decentralized architecture, users run P2P clients (peers) on their hosts to browse the profiles of friends and post content. Peers form an overlay network for the purpose of collectively sharing and replicating content, serving it on behalf of offline users when needed [27, 36]. Whichever architecture is adopted, a traffic session in the OSN can be essentially modeled as a data dissemination from a source to some specific destinations. The second factor is the architecture of underlying communication network, e.g., wireless, wired, or hybrid networking. This has a significant impact on implementing routing for specific data dissemination sessions. In this paper, we are concerned with the fundamental limits on the traffic load imposed on

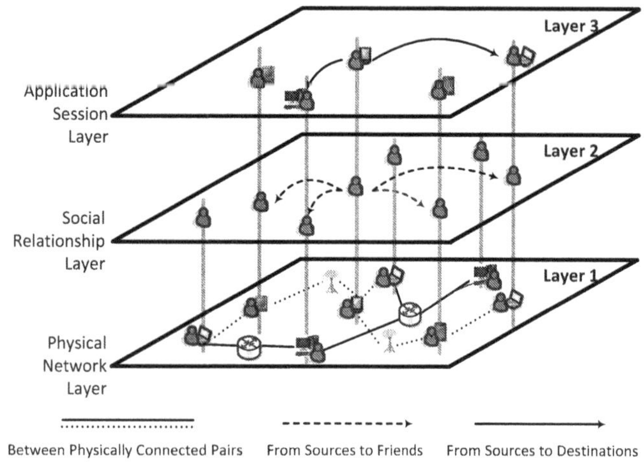

Figure 1: Layered System Model.

the underlying communication networks of OSNs, and mainly pursue the tight lower bounds that can theoretically be achieved over the communication network with the optimal architecture. We address this issue by analyzing the geographic characteristics of data dissemination sessions in OSNs, i.e., the spacial distribution of traffic sessions (the location distribution of sources and destinations).

We propose a three-layered model consisting of the physical network layer (Layer 1), social relationship layer (Layer 2), and application session layer (Layer 3), as illustrated in Fig.1. Then, for the purpose of deriving the spacial distribution of traffic sessions depending on users' geographical distribution, we adopt two steps to clarify the correlation between Layer 3 and Layer 1: Firstly, we start with dredging the correlation between Layer 2 and Layer 1, i.e., the relevance between the formation scheme of users' social relationships and the distribution model of users' geographical locations. We propose an innovative and practical *population-based social formation model* to build the links from Layer 1 to Layer 2, and validate its practicality based on a dataset of the online social network called Brightkite. Secondly, we analyze the correlation between Layer 3 and Layer 2, i.e., the relevance between the traffic pattern for a specific social application and the topology of users' social relationship network, assuming users constantly intend to deliver information to other users with whom they associate (friends or followers). By these two steps, we compute the bound on the aggregate travel distance over which a data packet in a session is transmitted from the source to its destinations. Furthermore, we derive the traffic load of the social network under a realistic assumption that all sources sustain the data generating rates of the constant order.

To emulate the inhomogeneous geographical distribution of users in real-life OSNs, we introduce the shotnoise Cox process [5,29] to model the deployment of users on Layer 1. Under such a model, we present the general density function of social relationship distribution and the general form of traffic load bounds in OSNs, which can serve as the basis for obtaining further an in-depth understanding on scaling laws of traffic load in OSNs (Theorem 1). In particular, we derive the explicit traffic load scaling for the OSNs with a special Layer 1, where users are homogeneously distributed (Theorem 2). The result shows that the traffic load for social-broadcast is monotonically nonincreasing in the range $[\Theta(n), \Theta(n^2)]$ for the clustering exponents of both friendship degree and friendship formation (Section 5.3.3), where n is the number of users in the OSN. It can highlight the differences from results for data dissemination in conventional communication networks. Furthermore, when a specific underlying communication network is introduced, our results on travel distances can also play an important role in analyzing some system performances, e.g., network capacity and latency. To the best of our knowledge, this is the first work to address scaling laws for the traffic load of OSNs by modeling the data dissemination in social networks.

The rest of this paper is organized as follows. We provide the motivation and problem formulation of this work in Section 2, and propose the system model in Section 3. In Section 4, we give the main results on general system model, and derive the representative results for a special model where users are distributed homogeneously on the physical network layer in Section 5. Finally, we draw a conclusion, and make a discussion about the future work in Section 6.

2. PRACTICAL MOTIVATION AND PROBLEM FORMULATION

2.1 Related Work and Our Motivation

Online social networks (OSNs) allow hundreds of millions of the Internet users worldwide to produce and consume content, and provide users with the access to the unprecedented large-scale information repository [15]. They play an important role in the information diffusion by increasing the spread of novel information and diverse viewpoints, and have shown their power in many situations [6,26]. In the research community of OSNs, there are some representative topics that have been extensively studied, such as detecting popular topics [25], modeling information diffusion [30], and identifying influential spreaders [8], and so on. Most existing work mainly focused on the information diffusion scheme over overlay relationship networks of users in social network sites/services (SNSs).

Meanwhile, as SNSs become increasingly popular for information exchange, the traffic generated by social applications rapidly expands [2]. As an argument, according to a report of Shareaholic [4], between November 2012 and November 2013, social media referral traffic from the top five social media sites increased by 111% while search traffic from the top five search engines had decreased by 6%. Thereby, besides the analysis of information diffusion schemes in overlay social networks like in the literature [6,8,25,26,30,37], an in-depth understanding of the impact of increasing traffic generated by OSNs on underlying communication networks, e.g., the Internet, is also necessary for evaluating current OSN systems, optimizing network architectures and the deployment of servers for OSNs, and even designing future OSNs. One of main challenges in addressing this issue is to propose practical modeling and effective analyzing methods for data dissemination of OSNs implemented in underlying communication networks, since OSNs change both information propagation schemes and traffic session patterns in communication networks due to the involvement of overlay social relationships and users' preferences and decisions. Accordingly, in this paper, we aim at modeling data dissemination in OSNs, and analyzing the traffic load for OSNs imposed on the underlying communication networks.

2.2 Formulation of Traffic Load for OSNs

In a communication network, the sum of products of bits and the distances over which they are carried, i.e., the so-called *traffic load*, is a valuable indicator of the network's transport capacity [16, 19]. In this paper, we mainly study the traffic load scaling of data dissemination in OSNs.

Considering an OSN, denoted by $\mathbb{N}$, consisting of n users, denote the set of all users by $\mathcal{U} = \{u_i\}_{i=1}^{n}$; let a subset $\mathcal{S} = \{u_{\mathcal{S},k}\}_{k=1}^{n_s} \subseteq$

$\mathcal{U}$ denote the set of all sources, where $|\mathcal{S}| = n_s$. Before giving the formal definition for the traffic load of the social network $\mathbb{N}$ in Section 2.2.3, we introduce two key conceptions: *data arrival process for users* and *transport distance of messages*.

2.2.1 *Data Arrival Process for Users*

Individual Data Arrival Process: The temporal behavior of messages arriving at a user in an OSN has been addressed by analyzing some real-life OSNs, [7,32]. For example, Perera et al. [32] developed a software architecture that uses a Twitter application program interface (API) to collect the tweets sent to specific users. They indicated that the arrival process of new tweets to a user can be modeled as a Poisson Process. In this work, we just make it as an empirical argument for assuming the data arrival for a user as a data source to follow a Poisson Process. We define a rate vector

$$\mathbf{\Lambda}_{\mathcal{S}} = (\lambda_{\mathcal{S},1}, \lambda_{\mathcal{S},2}, \cdots, \lambda_{\mathcal{S},n_s}),$$

where $\lambda_{\mathcal{S},k}$ is the rate of the Poisson Process at user $u_{\mathcal{S},k}$ (for $k = 1, 2, \cdots, n_s$), and is called *data arrival/generating rate*. Here, we make a reasonable and practical assumption that $\lambda_{\mathcal{S},k} = \Theta(1)$ for $k = 1, 2, \cdots, n_s$.

Data Arrival Rate Distribution: The results of interest in this paper fall within the scope of scaling laws issue. Therefore, although in practise, the individual data arrival/generating process may depend on many factors such as the user's location, it is appropriate to note at this point that the specific distribution of data arrival rate has no impact on the results (in order sense) as long as it holds that $\lambda_{\mathcal{S},k} = \Theta(1)$ for $k = 1, 2, \cdots, n_s$. This is the reason why we do not make an intensive study of the specific distribution of data arrival rates.

2.2.2 *Transport Distance of Messages*

Denote a data dissemination session from a source $u_{\mathcal{S},k}$ by an ordered pair $\mathbb{D}_{\mathcal{S},k} =< u_{\mathcal{S},k}, \mathcal{D}_{\mathcal{S},k} >$, where $\mathcal{D}_{\mathcal{S},k}$ is the set of all destinations of $u_{\mathcal{S},k}$. Define a distance vector

$$\mathbf{D}_{\mathcal{S}} = (d_{\mathcal{S},1}, d_{\mathcal{S},2}, \cdots, d_{\mathcal{S},n_s}),$$

where $d_{\mathcal{S},k}$ represents the *transport distance* over which the message for session $\mathbb{D}_{\mathcal{S},k}$ is successfully transported from the source $u_{\mathcal{S},k}$ to the destinations.

The transport distance depends on the specific architectures of underlying communication networks and routing strategies. While, in this work, we aim to present a general result which is independent of the specific network communication architecture due to the diversity of real-life communication networks. Then, we focus on investigating the achievable lower bound on the transport distance. The lower bound achieved by the optimal communication strategy can serve as a reasonable metric to quantify and bound the transport distances over different underlying communication networks. For a session $\mathbb{D}_{\mathcal{S},k}$, when the underlying communication network is involved, the problem to obtain the optimal transport distance can be reduced to the Euclidean Steiner Tree Problem spanning the set $\{u_{\mathcal{S},k}\} \cup \mathcal{D}_{\mathcal{S},k}$: Given $|\{u_{\mathcal{S},k}\} \cup \mathcal{D}_{\mathcal{S},k}|$ nodes in the plane, the goal is to connect them by lines of minimum total length in such a way that any two nodes may be interconnected by line segments either directly or via other nodes (relay devices in the communication network) and line segments [13].

2.2.3 *Traffic Load for Online Social Networks*

In the OSN $\mathbb{N}$, define the traffic load for a dissemination session, say $\mathbb{D}_{\mathcal{S},k}$, as $\widetilde{\mathbf{L}}_{\mathbb{N},\mathcal{S}}(\mathbb{D}_{\mathcal{S},k}) = \lambda_{\mathcal{S},k} \cdot d_{\mathcal{S},k}$. Furthermore, the total traffic load for data dissemination from all sources in $\mathcal{S}$ can be explicitly defined as

$$\mathbf{L}_{\mathbb{N},\mathcal{S}} = \mathbf{\Lambda}_{\mathcal{S}} * \mathbf{D}_{\mathcal{S}}, \tag{1}$$

where $*$ is an inner product.

Next, we give a basic lemma to derive the traffic load by each session.

LEMMA 1. *Under the assumption that $\lambda_{\mathcal{S},k} = \Theta(1)$ for $k = 1, 2, \cdots, n_s$, it holds that*

$$\widetilde{\mathbf{L}}_{\mathbb{N},\mathcal{S}}(\mathbb{D}_{\mathcal{S},k}) = \Omega\left(|\operatorname{EMST}(\{u_{\mathcal{S},k}\} \cup \mathcal{D}_{\mathcal{S},k})|\right),$$

$$\mathbf{L}_{\mathbb{N},\mathcal{S}} = \Omega\left(\sum\nolimits_{k=1}^{n_s} |\operatorname{EMST}(\{u_{\mathcal{S},k}\} \cup \mathcal{D}_{\mathcal{S},k})|\right),$$

where $\operatorname{EMST}(\cdot)$ *denotes the Euclidean minimum spanning tree over a set.*

PROOF. A minimum spanning tree is a feasible but not usually optimal solution to the Steiner tree problem. The Steiner ratio is the largest possible ratio between the total length of a minimum spanning tree and the total length of a minimum Steiner tree [11]. In the Euclidean Steiner tree problem, the Steiner ratio is conjectured to be $\frac{2}{\sqrt{3}}$. The conjecture is still open [17], although earlier claims of a proof were stated in [11]. Whatever the specific value of the Steiner ratio is, it is definitely a constant. Therefore, when we only care the order of final results in this paper, the value of the Steiner ratio has no impact in order sense. As a result, we can use the total length of the Euclidean spanning tree of session $\mathbb{D}_{\mathcal{S},k}$, i.e., the Euclidean spanning tree over the set $\{u_{\mathcal{S},k}\} \cup \mathcal{D}_{\mathcal{S},k}$, to measure the order of the total length of the optimal transport distance for session $\mathbb{D}_{\mathcal{S},k}$.

Combining with the fact that $\lambda_{\mathcal{S},k} = \Theta(1)$ for all k, we can prove this lemma. □

We remark that the lower bounds in Lemma 1 can be achieved by the optimal underlying communication network architecture and communication strategy.

3. LAYERED SOCIAL NETWORK MODEL

For each session, the geographical distribution of the source and destination(s) plays a key role in generating the traffic load. Then, it is critical to analyze the correlation between the spatial distribution of sessions and geographical distribution of users.

To address this issue, we introduce a three-layer model, consisting of the physical network layer (Layer 1), social relationship layer (Layer 2), and application session layer (Layer 3), as illustrated in Fig.1, for modeling data dissemination in OSNs. The basic procedure of modeling the correlations between the geographical distributions of sessions and users can be described as follows:

1. At first, based on the users' geographical distribution in the physical network layer, we build the relationships among users to form the social relationship layer.

2. Then, based on the formed social relationship layer, we model the geographical distribution of traffic sessions.

3.1 Layer 1: Physical Network Deployment

To embody the uneven population distribution in real-life OSNs, we introduce the cluster random model.

We consider the random network consisting of a random number N (with $\mathbf{E}(N) = n$)[1] users distributed over a square region of area

[1]Throughout the paper, we let $\mathbf{E}[X]$ denote the mean and variance of a random variable X, respectively.

$S := S(n)$. To avoid border effects, we consider wraparound conditions at the network edges. That is, the network area is assumed to be the surface of a two-dimensional Torus, denoted by $\mathcal{O}$. The network physical extension $\sqrt{S}$ is allowed to scale with the average number of nodes, since this is expected to occur in many growing systems.

The so-called clustering random model (CRM) can be denoted by $\mathbb{N}(n, S; \mathbb{C}(m), g(\cdot))$, where the expected number of centers, say m, and the clustering function, say $g(\cdot)$, will be defined later.

To emulate the clustering behavior of users' distribution in real-life OSNs, it is necessary to introduce the shotnoise Cox process (SNCP, [5,29]).

3.1.1 Shotnoise Cox Process

An SNCP can be described by the following construction: First, specify a point process $\mathbb{C}(m)$ of cluster centers, whose positions are denoted by $\mathcal{C} = \{c_j\}_{j=1}^{M}$, where M is a random number with average $\mathbf{E}(M) = m$, and the center points c_j are also called parent points. Then, each center point c_j in turn generates a point process of nodes whose intensity at position X is given by $\rho_j \cdot \kappa(c_j, X)$, where $\rho_j \in (0, \infty)$ and $\kappa(c_j, \cdot)$, called kernel or shot, is a dispersion density function. The nodes generated by each center are referred to as offspring points. The overall node process $\mathbb{P}$ is then given by the superposition of the individual processes generated by the cluster centers. The conditional local intensity at X of the resulting SNCP is

$$\mathbf{d}(X) = \sum_j \rho_j \cdot \kappa(c_j, X),$$

where $\mathbf{d}(X)$ is a random field conditionally over all (ρ_j, c_j). Then, the node process $\mathbb{P}$ forms an inhomogeneous Poisson point process with intensity function $\mathbf{d}(\cdot)$. Let $\mathcal{X} = \{X_i\}_{i=1}^{N}$ denote the collection of nodes positions in a given realization of the SNCP.

Under the above assumptions on the kernel shape, the quantity ρ_j equals the average number of nodes generated by cluster center c_j. We assume that all cluster centers generate on average the same number of nodes, hence it holds that $\rho_j = \rho = \frac{n}{m}$. In this work, we let ρ scale with n as well. That is, clusters are expected to grow in size as the number of nodes increases.

In this paper, we restrict ourselves to kernels $\kappa(c_j, \cdot)$ that are invariant under both translation and rotation. The kernel $\kappa(c_j, X) = \kappa(|X - c_j|)$ depends only on the Euclidean distance $|X - c_j|$ of point X from the cluster center c_j. Moreover, we assume that $\kappa(c_j, \cdot)$ is a summable, non-increasing, bounded and continuous function, and $\int_{\mathcal{O}} \kappa(c_j, X) dX = 1$. Following a common normalizing method, the kernels can be specified by first defining a non-increasing, bounded and continuous *clustering function* $g(s)$ and then normalizing it over the network area $\mathcal{O}$:

$$\kappa(c_j, X) = \frac{g(|X - c_j|)}{\int_{\mathcal{O}} g(|Y - c_j|) dY} \tag{2}$$

3.1.2 Clustering Random Model $\mathbb{N}(n, S; \mathbb{C}(m), g(\cdot))$

We define the *clustering random model* (CRM) by specifying the point process $\mathbb{C}(m)$ of cluster centers.

- When $\mathbb{C}(m)$ is a homogeneous Poisson process (HPP) of intensity $\lambda_c = m/S$ over $\mathcal{O}$, we call such a CRM *Poisson clustering random model.*
- When m are deployed in a regular grid pattern, we call such a CRM *Regular clustering random model.*

For both models, we define $l_c = \sqrt{S/m}$. This quantity represents the length of edges of the square where the expected number of contained cluster centers is equal to 1. We call the case that $l_c = O(1)$ *cluster-dense regime*, and call the case $l_c = \omega(1)$ *cluster-sparse regime*, in which l_c tends to infinity as n increases.

To simplify the description, we assume that the number of nodes is exactly n, and denote the set of nodes by $\mathcal{V} = \{v_k\}_{k=1}^{n}$, which has no impact on our results in order sense.

3.2 Layer 2: Social Relationship Formation

We propose a density-aware social relationship formation model, called *population-based social formation model.* We will clarify the advantages of this model later in Section 3.2.2.

Let $\mathcal{D}(u, r)$ denote the disk centered at a point u with radius r in the deployment region $\mathcal{O}$, and let $N(u, r)$ denote the number of nodes contained in $\mathcal{D}(u, r)$.

3.2.1 Population-based Social Formation Model

For a node $v_k \in \mathcal{V}$, construct its friendship set of q_k, $q_k \geq 1$, nodes/friends, say $\mathcal{F}_k$, by the following procedure:

1. Zipf's Degree Distribution of Social Relations: Assume that the number of friends (or followers) of a particular node $v_k \in \mathcal{V}$, denoted by q_k, follows a Zipf's distribution [24,33], i.e.,

$$\Pr(q_k = l) = \left(\sum_{j=1}^{n-1} j^{-\gamma}\right)^{-1} \cdot l^{-\gamma}. \tag{3}$$

From Eq.(3), we can observe that the degree distribution above depends on the specific network size (the number of users n). We will give a numerical validation based on Brightkite dataset for the Zipf's degree distribution in Appendix B.2.

We notice that the correlations between the users' degree distribution and graphical distribution should not be ignored, although we simplify it in this work. We will address this issue in the future work.

2. Population-Based Formation of Social Relations: Making the position of node v_k as the *reference point*, choose q_k *points* independently on the torus region $\mathcal{O}$ according to a probability distribution with density function:

$$f_{v_k}(X) = \Phi_k(S, \beta) \cdot (\mathbf{E}[N(v_k, |X - v_k|)] + 1)^{-\beta}, \tag{4}$$

where the random variable $X := (x, y)$ denotes the position of a selected point in the deployment region, $|X - v_k|$ denotes the Euclidean distance between point X and node v_k, $\beta \in [0, \infty)$ represents the clustering exponent of friendship formation; the coefficient $\Phi_k(S, \beta) > 0$ depends on β and S (the area of deployment region), satisfying that:

$$\Phi_k(S, \beta) \cdot \int_{\mathcal{O}} (\mathbf{E}[N(v_k, |X - v_k|)] + 1)^{-\beta} dX = 1. \tag{5}$$

3. Nearest-Principle Position of Friends/Followers: Let $\mathcal{A}_k = \{p_{k_i}\}_{i=1}^{q_k}$ denote the set of these q_k points. Let v_{k_i} be the nearest node to p_{k_i}, for $1 \leq i \leq q_k$ (ties are broken randomly). Denote the set of these q_k nodes by $\mathcal{F}_k = \{v_{k_i}\}_{i=1}^{q_k}$. We call point p_{k_i} the *anchor point* of v_{k_i}, and define a set $\mathcal{P}_k := \{v_k\} \cup \mathcal{A}_k$.

Throughout this paper, we use $\mathbb{P}(\delta, \gamma, \beta)$ to denote the population-based social model.

3.2.2 Advantages of Population-Based Social Model

After Kleinberg [20] proposed a distance-based social model relating geographical distance and social friendship, Liben-Nowell et al. [23] introduced the rank-based model, where the probability of befriending a particular person is inversely proportional to the power of the number of closer people. They validated the practicality of rank-based model by analyzing the data of an online social network, the LiveJournal online community. They pointed out that the

Table 1: Notations for Exponents

Notation	Definition
$\delta \in [0, \infty)$	clustering exponent of node distribution
$\gamma \in [0, \infty)$	clustering exponent of friendship degree
$\beta \in [0, \infty)$	clustering exponent of friendship formation

weakness of distance-based models lies in that for a particular user, it underestimates the friendship probability of the distant nodes in the low-density region, when the geographical distribution of users is inhomogeneous in common occurrence.

The rank-based model states that the friendship probability depends on both the geographic distance and node density. Following this observation, by modifying the rank-based model, we propose the distance & density-aware population-based social model. The population-based model is more convenient and systematic for addressing the bounds on aggregate travel distances. Anchor points, defined in Step 3 of Section 3.2.1, are effectively introduced, in order to ensure the independence of length of certain Euclidean spanning trees, thus makes it convenient to bound the total length, e.g., the proof of Lemma 2. However, under the rank-based model where the friendships are directly built over nodes without anchor points, the corresponding independence cannot be guaranteed, which usually brings the difficulty on the theoretical rigor.

We will provide a numerical validation based on Brightkite dataset for the population-based social formation model in Appendix B.3.

3.3 Layer 3: Application Session Construction

After the social layer is formed, social sessions can be defined according to the specific applications: For the *social-unicast/social-multicast*, the source node delivers message to one/multiple selected friend(s).

For the *social-broadcast*, the source node broadcasts message to all its friends, such as tweets in Twitter and posts in Facebook. Accordingly, we can define other session patterns based on the definitions of corresponding non-social sessions, such as *social-anycast* [22] and *social-manycast* [9].

4. MAIN RESULTS FOR GENERAL CLUSTERING RANDOM MODEL

In this paper, we focus on the extended networks [12, 14]) with a constant average node density. Specifically, for the physical network layer under the clustering random model (CRM), denoted by $\mathbb{N}(n, S; \mathbb{C}(m), g(\cdot))$, we let $S = n$ to study the extended model $\mathbb{N}(n, n; \mathbb{C}(m), g(\cdot))$. Furthermore, for the clustering function $g(\cdot)$, we define it as

$$g(s) := \min\left\{1, s^{-\delta}\right\}$$

for the extended model $\mathbb{N}(n, n; \mathbb{C}(m), g(\cdot))$, where $\delta \in [0, \infty)$ is the clustering exponent of node distribution. Note that when $\delta = 0$, the model degenerates into the homogeneous random extended network [12, 14].

To facilitate the reader, we have reported in Table 1 a collection of frequently-used system parameters.

4.1 General Density Function

In the clustering random model $\mathbb{N}(n, n; \mathbb{C}(m), g(\cdot))$, we construct a set of $q + 1$ *points*, denoted by $\mathcal{P} = \{X_i\}_{i=0}^{q}$, by the following procedure:

Step 1. Select arbitrarily a point from $\mathcal{O}$ as the first one in $\mathcal{P}$, denoted by X_0.

Step 2. Making point X_0 as the *reference point* denoted by O', select independently other q points at random according to the probability distribution with density function as described in Eq.(4) (Let $v_k := X_0$).

LEMMA 2. *Making the point X_0 as the reference point O', the distribution of points in $\mathcal{A} := \{X_i\}_{i=1}^{q}$ follows the probability distribution with the density function*

$$f_{X_0}(X) = \frac{\left[\int_{\mathcal{D}(X_0, |X - X_0|)} \mathbf{d}(Y)\, dY + 1\right]^{-\beta}}{\int_{\mathcal{O}} \left[\int_{\mathcal{D}(X_0, |Z - X_0|)} \mathbf{d}(Y)\, dY + 1\right]^{-\beta} dZ} \quad (6)$$

where

$$\mathbf{d}(Y) = \frac{n}{m} \cdot \sum\nolimits_{c_j \in \mathcal{C}} \frac{\min\{1, |Y - c_j|^{-\delta}\}}{\int_{\mathcal{O}} \min\{1, |Z - c_j|^{-\delta}\}\, dZ}.$$

4.2 Traffic Load Distribution

4.2.1 Main Results on Traffic Load

We can use the set $\mathcal{P} = \{X_i\}_{i=0}^{q}$ to represent a social traffic session, where X_0 acts as the source node and $\mathcal{A} := \{X_i\}_{i=1}^{q}$ is the set of all destinations of X_0. Then, we have

THEOREM 1. *For the traffic load by the session with the set $\mathcal{P}$, denoted by $\widetilde{\mathbf{L}}$, it holds that: when $q = \omega(1)$, with high probability $1 - o(1/\hat{N})$, it follows that*

$$\widetilde{\mathbf{L}} = \Omega(\Upsilon), \quad (7)$$

where

$$\Upsilon : \left[\sqrt{q} \cdot \int_{\mathcal{O}} \sqrt{f_{X_0}(X)} dX, \sqrt{q} \cdot \int_{\mathcal{O}} \sqrt{f_{X_0}(X)} dX + \bar{L}\right]^{2}, \quad (8)$$

$f_{X_0}(X)$ is defined in Eq.(6) of Lemma 2, and

$$\bar{L} = \min\left\{L \,\middle|\, \int_{\mathcal{D}(X_0, L)} f_{X_0}(X) dX = \Omega\left(\min\left\{\frac{\log \hat{N}}{q}, 1\right\}\right)\right\} \quad (9)$$

with a given parameter $\hat{N} : (1, n]$ denoting the number of nodes with degree of order $\omega(1)$.

4.2.2 Proof of Theorem 1

Let $\mathrm{EMST}(\mathcal{P})$ and $\mathrm{EMST}(\mathcal{A})$ denote the Euclidean minimum spanning trees of $\mathcal{P} = \{X_i\}_{i=0}^{q}$ and $\mathcal{A} := \{X_i\}_{i=1}^{q}$, respectively.

We first give a lemmas providing the total edge length of Euclidean minimum spanning trees of $\mathcal{P} = \{X_i\}_{i=0}^{q}$, denoted by $|\mathrm{EMST}(\mathcal{P})|$.

LEMMA 3. *When $q = \omega(1)$, it holds that:*
$\triangleright$ *With probability* 1,

$$|\mathrm{EMST}(\mathcal{A})| = \Theta\left(\sqrt{q} \cdot \int_{\mathcal{O}} \sqrt{f_{X_0}(X)} dX\right), \quad (10)$$

where $f_{X_0}(X)$ is defined in Eq.(6) of Lemma 2.

[2]We use the term $f(n) : [\underline{\phi}(n), \overline{\phi}(n)]$ to represent $f(n) = \Omega(\underline{\phi}(n))$ and $f(n) = O(\overline{\phi}(n))$; and use $f(n) : (\underline{\phi}(n), \overline{\phi}(n))$ to represent $f(n) = \omega(\underline{\phi}(n))$ and $f(n) = o(\overline{\phi}(n))$.

$\triangleright$ *With high probability* $1 - o(1/\hat{N})$,

$$|\operatorname{EMST}(\mathcal{P})| : [|\operatorname{EMST}(\mathcal{A})|, |\operatorname{EMST}(\mathcal{A})| + \bar{L}], \quad (11)$$

where $\bar{L}$ *is defined in Eq.(9).*

PROOF. First of all, the cost of an edge (X_i, X_j) is given by

$$\Psi(|X_i - X_j|) = |X_i - X_j|.$$

That is, the exponent σ in Lemma 8 equals 1. In addition, $\Psi(x)$ is a monotonically increasing function.

Let L denote the distance between the center O and reference point. Then, under the center-clustering random model $\mathbb{N}^1(n, S; g(\cdot))$, by Eq.(4) and Eq.(5), the density function is specified into Eq.(13). Then, by Lemma 8, we get that

$$|\operatorname{EMST}(\mathcal{A})| = \Theta\left(\sqrt{q} \cdot \int_{\mathcal{O}} \sqrt{f_{X_0}(X)} dX\right).$$

It is straightforward that

$$|\operatorname{EMST}(\mathcal{P})| = \Omega\left(|\operatorname{EMST}(\mathcal{A})|\right).$$

On the other hand, let $\underline{L}$ denote the smallest distance from the points in $\mathcal{A}$ to point X_0. Then,

$$\left(1 - \int_{\mathcal{D}(X_0, \underline{L})} f_{X_0}(X) dX\right)^q = o(1).$$

That is,

$$\int_{\mathcal{D}(X_0, \underline{L})} f_{X_0}(X) dX = \omega\left(\frac{1}{q}\right).$$

Thus, $\underline{L} \leq \bar{L}$, where $\bar{L}$ is defined in Eq.(9), which completes the proof. Note that we deliberately relax the upper bound of $\underline{L}$ as in Eq.(9) in order to ensure Eq.(11) to hold with uniformly high probability for $\Theta(n)$ Euclidean spanning trees [31]. □

Finally, combining with Lemma 1, we complete the proof.

4.3 Special Results for Single-Center Model

According to the fact that there usually exist a finite number of dense areas in real-life network applications, we mainly focus on the finite-centers clustering random model (FC-CRM), denoted by $\mathbb{N}(n, n; \mathbb{C}(c), g(\cdot))$, where $c > 0$ is a constant.

Since we aim to derive scaling laws of aggregate travel distances, we only care the order of the parameters and performance metrics. Then, it holds that the finite-centers clustering random model is indeed similar to a clustering random model with exactly one center, which is called single-center clustering random model (SC-CRM) here, in terms of scaling behavior. Denote such a SC-CRM by $\mathbb{N}(n, n; \mathbb{C}(1), g(\cdot))$.

We construct a $\mathbb{N}(n, n; \mathbb{C}(1), g(\cdot))$ by the following procedure: First, making a center of $\mathcal{O}$ as the center point, denoted by O. Then, the center point O generates a point process of nodes whose local intensity at position X is given by

$$\mathbf{d}(X) = n \cdot \kappa(O, X) = n \cdot \frac{\min\{1, |Y - O|^{-\delta}\}}{\int_{\mathcal{O}} \min\{1, |Z - O|^{-\delta}\} dZ}. \quad (12)$$

where $\kappa(O, \cdot)$ is the dispersion density function. Then, we get the probability density function as follows.

COROLLARY 1. *Making the point* X_0 *as the reference point* O', *the distribution of points in* $\mathcal{A} := \{X_i\}_{i=1}^q$ *follows the probability with the density function*

$$f_{X_0}(X) = \frac{\left[\int_{\mathcal{D}(X_0, |X - X_0|)} \mathbf{d}(Y)\, dY + 1\right]^{-\beta}}{\int_{\mathcal{O}} \left[\int_{\mathcal{D}(X_0, |Z - X_0|)} \mathbf{d}(Y)\, dY + 1\right]^{-\beta} dZ} \quad (13)$$

where

$$\mathbf{d}(Y) = n \cdot \frac{\min\{1, |Y - O|^{-\delta}\}}{\int_{\mathcal{O}} \min\{1, |Z - O|^{-\delta}\} dZ}.$$

Combining Corollary 1 and Theorem 1, we can obtain the traffic load by a session under the single-center clustering random model.

5. A CASE STUDY: TRAFFIC LOAD FOR OSNS WITH HOMOGENEOUS DISTRIBUTION OF USERS

In this section, in order to obtain an explicit result, we specifically reduce the complexity from three dimensions $(\delta, \gamma, \beta) \in [0, \infty)^3$ to two dimensions $(\gamma, \beta) \in [0, \infty)^2$ by letting $\delta = 0$. In this case of extremely weak clustering behavior, the physical layer degenerates into the homogeneous random network model [12, 16], where $\mathbf{d}(Y) \equiv \Theta(1)$.

From Eq.(3), we get the degree distribution as follows:

$$\Pr(q_k = l) = \begin{cases} \Theta(l^{-\gamma}), & \gamma > 1; \\ \Theta(\frac{1}{\log n} \cdot l^{-1}), & \gamma = 1; \\ \Theta(n^{\gamma - 1} \cdot l^{-\gamma}), & 0 \leq \gamma < 1. \end{cases} \quad (14)$$

We can reasonably assume that all nodes behave as source nodes, i.e., $\mathcal{S} = \mathcal{V}$. Then, the description of social broadcast session $\mathbb{D}_{\mathcal{S},k}$ can be further simplified. That is, the session initiated from node v_k is denoted by $\mathbb{D}_k$.

5.1 Distribution of Anchor Points

For each dissemination session $\mathbb{D}_k$ initiated by the source v_k, we can get the distribution of anchor points directly using Corollary 1.

LEMMA 4. *When the clustering exponent* $\delta = 0$, *for a session* $\mathbb{D}_k$ *under the population-based social model* $\mathbb{P}(\delta = 0, \gamma, \beta)$, *the anchor points of the friends of source* v_k *follows the distribution of density function:*

$$f_{v_k}(X) = \begin{cases} \Theta\left((|X - v_k|^2 + 1)^{-\beta}\right), & \beta > 1; \\ \Theta\left(\left(\log n \cdot (|X - v_k|^2 + 1)\right)^{-1}\right), & \beta = 1; \\ \Theta\left(n^{\beta - 1} \cdot (|X - v_k|^2 + 1)^{-\beta}\right), & 0 \leq \beta < 1. \end{cases}$$

By using Lemma 4, we can get the following result.

LEMMA 5. *For a social-broadcast session* $\mathbb{D}_k$ *under the model* $\mathbb{P}(\delta = 0, \gamma, \beta)$, *it holds that:*

$$\mathbf{E}[|X - v_k|] = \begin{cases} \Theta(1), & \beta > 3/2; \\ \Theta(\log n), & \beta = 3/2; \\ \Theta(n^{\frac{3}{2} - \beta}), & 1 < \beta < 3/2; \\ \Theta(\sqrt{n}/\log n), & \beta = 1; \\ \Theta(\sqrt{n}), & 0 \leq \beta < 1. \end{cases} \quad (15)$$

5.2 Social-Broadcast Sessions

Under the population-based social model, we denote a social-broadcast session $\mathbb{D}_k$ by the set $\{v_k\} \cup \mathcal{F}_k$, where v_k is the source and each element in $\mathcal{F}_k = \{v_{k_i}\}_{i=1}^{q_k}$, say v_{k_i}, is the nearest *node* to the corresponding *anchor point* p_{k_i} in $\mathcal{A}_k = \{p_{k_i}\}_{i=1}^{q_k}$. Recall that $\mathcal{P}_k = \{v_k\} \cup \mathcal{A}_k$, we can get the following Lemma 6 for spanning trees over $\mathbb{D}_k$.

LEMMA 6. *For a social-broadcast session* $\mathbb{D}_k$ *with* $q_k = \omega(1)$ *under the social formation model* $\mathbb{P}(\delta = 0, \gamma, \beta)$, *with probability* 1, *it holds that*

$$|\operatorname{EMST}(\mathcal{A}_k)| = \Theta(L_{\mathcal{P}}(\beta, q_k)),$$

Table 2: $H(\gamma,\beta)$ Depending on Exponents γ and β

γ	$H(\gamma,\beta)$
$\gamma>2$	$\begin{cases}\Theta(n), & \beta>2;\\ \Theta(n\cdot\log n), & \beta=2;\\ \Theta(n^{2-\frac{\beta}{2}}), & 1<\beta<2;\\ \Theta(n^{3/2}/\sqrt{\log n}), & \beta=1;\\ \Theta(n^{3/2}), & 0\le\beta<1.\end{cases}$
$\gamma=2$	$\begin{cases}\Theta(n\cdot\log n), & \beta\ge 2;\\ \Theta(n^{2-\frac{\beta}{2}}), & 1<\beta<2;\\ \Theta(n^{3/2}/\sqrt{\log n}), & \beta=1;\\ \Theta(n^{3/2}), & 0\le\beta<1.\end{cases}$
$3/2<\gamma<2$	$\begin{cases}\Theta(n^{3-\gamma}), & \beta\ge 2\gamma-2;\\ \Theta(n^{2-\frac{\beta}{2}}), & 1<\beta<2\gamma-2;\\ \Theta(n^{3/2}/\sqrt{\log n}), & \beta=1;\\ \Theta(n^{3/2}), & 0\le\beta<1.\end{cases}$
$\gamma=3/2$	$\begin{cases}\Theta(n^{3/2}), & \beta>1;\\ \Theta(n^{3/2}\cdot\sqrt{\log n}), & \beta=1;\\ \Theta(n^{3/2}\cdot\log n), & 0\le\beta<1.\end{cases}$
$1<\gamma<3/2$	$\Theta(n^{3-\gamma})$
$\gamma=1$	$\Theta(n^2/\log n)$
$0\le\gamma<1$	$\Theta(n^2)$

and then

$$|\operatorname{EMST}(\mathcal{P}_k)| = \Omega(L_{\mathcal{P}}(\beta, q_k)),$$

where

$$L_{\mathcal{P}}(\beta,q_k)=\begin{cases}\Theta\left(\sqrt{q_k}\right), & \beta>2;\\ \Theta\left(\sqrt{q_k}\cdot\log n\right), & \beta=2;\\ \Theta\left(\sqrt{q_k}\cdot n^{1-\frac{\beta}{2}}\right), & 1<\beta<2;\\ \Theta\left(\sqrt{q_k}\cdot\sqrt{\frac{n}{\log n}}\right), & \beta=1;\\ \Theta\left(\sqrt{q_k}\cdot\sqrt{n}\right), & 0\le\beta<1.\end{cases} \quad (16)$$

PROOF. From Theorem 3, it follows that with probability 1,

$$|\operatorname{EMST}(\mathcal{A}_k)| = \Theta(L_{\mathcal{P}}(\beta,q_k)) \text{ for } q_k=\omega(1),$$

where $L_{\mathcal{P}}(\beta,q_k)$ is defined in Eq.(16). Combining with the fact that $|\operatorname{EMST}(\mathcal{P}_k)| \ge |\operatorname{EMST}(\mathcal{A}_k)|$, we get the lemma. □

5.3 Main Result on Traffic Load

5.3.1 Lower Bound on Traffic Load

The main result in this section can be described by the following theorem.

THEOREM 2. *Under the social model $\mathbb{P}(\delta=0,\gamma,\beta)$, the traffic load for data dissemination in OSN $\mathbb{N}$, denoted by $\mathbf{L}_{\mathbb{N}}$, is of*

$$\mathbf{L}_{\mathbb{N}} = \Omega\left(H(\gamma,\beta)\right),$$

where $H(\gamma,\beta)$ is defined in Table.2.

5.3.2 Proof of Theorem 2

The bound depends on the bound on $\sum_{k=1}^{n}|\operatorname{EMST}(\mathcal{P}_k)|$. We firstly give a basic lemma for the final proof.

LEMMA 7. *For all social-broadcast sessions $\mathbb{D}_k$ ($k=1,2,\cdots,n$) under the social formation model $\mathbb{P}(\delta=0,\gamma,\beta)$, with high probability, the lower bounds on $\sum_{k=1}^{n}|\operatorname{EMST}(\mathcal{P}_k)|$ hold as described in Table.3.*

PROOF. Let N_l denote the number of sessions with l destinations. First of all, to simplify the proof, we let

$$N_l = n\cdot\Pr(q_k=l) = n\cdot\left(\sum_{j=1}^{n-1} j^{-\gamma}\right)^{-1}\cdot l^{-\gamma},$$

which has no impact on the analysis in order sense according to laws of larger numbers. Based on all $\mathbb{D}_{\mathcal{S},k}$, define two sets

$$\mathcal{K}^1 := \{k|q_k=\Theta(1)\} \text{ and } \mathcal{K}^\infty := \{k|q_k=\omega(1)\}.$$

Then,

$$\sum_{k=1}^{n}|\operatorname{EMST}(\mathcal{P}_k)| = \underline{\Sigma}^1 + \underline{\Sigma}^\infty, \quad (17)$$

where

$$\underline{\Sigma}^1 = \sum_{k\in\mathcal{K}^1}|\operatorname{EMST}(\mathcal{P}_k)|,\ \underline{\Sigma}^\infty = \sum_{k\in\mathcal{K}^\infty}|\operatorname{EMST}(\mathcal{P}_k)|.$$

First, we consider $\underline{\Sigma}^1$. Since for $q_k=\Theta(1)$, it holds that

$$|\operatorname{EMST}(\mathcal{P}_k)| = \Theta(|X-v_k|),$$

then we have

$$\underline{\Sigma}^1 = \sum_{k\in\mathcal{K}^1}|X-v_k|.$$

For $k\in\mathcal{K}^1$, define a sequence of random variables $\xi_k^1 := |X-v_k|/\sqrt{n}$ having finite mean:

$$\mathbf{E}[\xi_k^1] = \mathbf{E}[|X-v_k|]/\sqrt{n},$$

where $\mathbf{E}[|X-v_k|]$ is presented in Lemma 5. Then,

$$\underline{\Sigma}^1 = \Theta\left(\sqrt{n}\cdot\sum_{k\in\mathcal{K}^1}\xi_k^1\right).$$

Thus, by Lemma 9, with probability 1,

$$\sum_{k\in\mathcal{K}^1}\xi_k^1 = \Theta\left(|\mathcal{K}^1|\cdot\mathbf{E}[|X-v_k|/\sqrt{n}]\right),$$

where $|\mathcal{K}^1|$ denotes the cardinality of $\mathcal{K}^1$. Thus, we get that with probability 1,

$$\underline{\Sigma}^1 = \Theta\left(|\mathcal{K}^1|\cdot\mathbf{E}[|X-v_k|]\right). \quad (18)$$

Next, we consider $\underline{\Sigma}^\infty$. For $k\in\mathcal{K}^\infty$, all random variables $|\operatorname{EMST}(\mathcal{P}_k)|$ are *independent*; moreover, from Lemma 6, with probability 1,

$$|\operatorname{EMST}(\mathcal{P}_k)| = \Omega(L_{\mathcal{P}}(\beta,q_k)),$$

where $L_{\mathcal{P}}(\beta,q_k)$ is defined in Eq.(16). Thus, with probability 1,

$$\underline{\Sigma}^\infty \ge \sum_{l:(1,n]} n\cdot\left(\sum_{j=1}^{n-1}j^{-\gamma}\right)^{-1}\cdot l^{-\gamma}\cdot L_{\mathcal{P}}(\beta,l). \quad (19)$$

Finally, combining Eqs.(17), (18) and (19), we complete the proof. □

Then, we begin to prove Lemma 2. Since

$$\sum_{k=1}^{n} q_k = \Theta\left(\sum_{l=1}^{n-1} n\cdot\Pr(q_k=l)\cdot l\right),$$

Table 3: Lower Bounds on $\sum_{k=1}^{n} |\text{EMST}(\mathcal{P}_k)|$

β \ γ	$\gamma > 3/2$	$\gamma = 3/2$	$1 < \gamma < 3/2$	$\gamma = 1$	$0 \leq \gamma < 1$
$\beta > 2$	$\Omega(n)$	$\Omega(n \log n)$	$\Omega(n^{\frac{5}{2}-\gamma})$	$\Omega(n^{3/2}/\log n)$	$\Omega(n^{3/2})$
$\beta = 2$	$\Omega(n \cdot \log n)$	$\Omega(n \cdot (\log n)^2)$	$\Omega(\log n \cdot n^{\frac{5}{2}-\gamma})$	$\Omega(n^{3/2})$	$\Omega(n^{3/2} \cdot \log n)$
$1 < \beta < 2$	$\Omega(n^{2-\frac{\beta}{2}})$	$\Omega(n^{2-\frac{\beta}{2}} \cdot \log n)$	$\Omega(n^{\frac{7}{2}-\gamma-\frac{\beta}{2}})$	$\Omega(n^{(5-\beta)/2}/\log n)$	$\Omega(n^{(5-\beta)/2})$
$\beta = 1$	$\Omega(n^{3/2}/\sqrt{\log n})$	$\Omega(n^{3/2} \cdot \sqrt{\log n})$	$\Omega(n^{3-\gamma}/\sqrt{\log n})$	$\Omega(n^2/(\log n)^{3/2})$	$\Omega(n^2/\sqrt{\log n})$
$0 \leq \beta < 1$	$\Omega(n^{3/2})$	$\Omega(n^{3/2} \cdot \log n)$	$\Omega(n^{3-\gamma})$	$\Omega(n^2/\log n)$	$\Omega(n^2)$

we get that $\sum_{k=1}^{n} q_k = Q(\gamma)$, where

$$Q(\gamma) = \begin{cases} \Theta(n), & \gamma > 2; \\ \Theta(n \log n), & \gamma = 2; \\ \Theta\left(n^{3-\gamma}\right), & 1 < \gamma < 2; \\ \Theta\left(n^2/\log n\right), & \gamma = 1; \\ \Theta\left(n^2\right), & 0 \leq \gamma < 1. \end{cases} \quad (20)$$

Moreover, for all $v_k \in \mathcal{V}$,

$$\mathbf{E}\left[|v_{k_i} - p_{k_i}|\right] = \Theta\left(\int_0^{\sqrt{n}} x \cdot e^{-\pi \cdot x^2} dx\right),$$

that is,

$$\mathbf{E}\left[|v_{k_i} - p_{k_i}|\right] = \Theta(1).$$

Thus, according to Lemma 9, with high probability, it follows that

$$\sum\nolimits_{k=1}^{n} \sum\nolimits_{i=1}^{q_k} |v_{k_i} - p_{k_i}| = \Theta\left(\sum\nolimits_{k=1}^{n} q_k\right). \quad (21)$$

Combining with Lemma 7, we get that: for all social-broadcast sessions $\mathbb{D}_k$, $k = 1, 2, \cdots, n$, under the social model $\mathbb{P}(\delta = 0, \gamma, \beta)$, with high probability,

$$\sum\nolimits_{k=1}^{n} |\text{EMST}(\mathbb{D}_{\mathcal{S},k})| = \Omega(H(\gamma, \beta)),$$

where $H(\gamma, \beta)$ is described in Table.2.

Finally, according to Lemma 1, we can complete the proof of Theorem 2.

5.3.3 *Explanation of Results*

At first, we discuss the impacts of clustering exponents of friendship degree and friendship formation, i.e., γ and β, on the traffic load. The traffic load for social-broadcast is monotonically nonincreasing in the range $[n, n^2]$ for both γ and β. An intuitive explanation can be made as follows: A larger clustering exponent of friendship degree γ can limit the number of friends of each user into a smaller upper bound with high probability, then leads to a lower traffic load; a larger clustering exponent of friendship formation β makes the friends more closer to each user with high probability, then possibly reduces the total transmission distance of each social-broadcast session, finally also leads to a lower traffic load.

Importantly, we notice that this work should be regarded as the first step for investigating the traffic load under the population-based model. Here, we only take into account the case that $\delta = 0$, where the population-based model degenerates to that similar to distance-based model [20,21]. The advantages of population-based model cannot be sufficiently highlighted for such a special model, indeed. It would be a significant future work to clarify the relationships between the general clustering exponent and traffic load in 3-dimensional parameter space, i.e., $(\delta, \gamma, \beta) \in [0, \infty)^3$.

6. CONCLUSION AND FUTURE WORK

We have presented a three-layered architecture to model the data dissemination in online social networks (OSNs), i.e., the physical network layer (Layer 1), social relationship layer (Layer 2), and application session layer (Layer 3). By analyzing mutual relevances among these three layers, we get the geographical distribution characteristics of dissemination sessions in OSNs. Based on this, we presented the density function of general social relationship distribution and the general form of traffic load bounds for OSNs, and derived the tight lower bounds on traffic load of data dissemination in the OSNs.

Much work still remains. Under the profile & social-based information dissemination pattern, a subsequent traffic session from a source is usually triggered by the previous session from another source. While, we have focused exclusively the data arrival model where the correlations of data generating processes at sources have been ignored. Besides this, we have not investigate the correlation between the degree distribution and the geographical distribution of the user in our model. Even for our proposed model, we only provided the explicit result for the model with homogeneous geographical distribution of users. This cannot still highlight sufficiently the characteristics of real-life OSNs and the advantages of the proposed population-based formation model.

Acknowledgements

The research of authors is partially supported by the National Natural Science Foundation of China (NSFC) under Grant No. 61202383, 61370192 and 60903151, the National Basic Research Program of China (973 Program) under Grant No. 2010CB328101, Shanghai Rising-Star Program under Grant No. 14QA1403700, the Program for New Century Excellent Talents in University (NCET) under Grant No. NCET-12-0414, the Natural Science Foundation of Shanghai under Grant No. 12ZR1451200, the Integrated Project for Major Research Plan of the National Natural Science Foundation of China under Grant No. 91218301, the Research Fund for the Doctoral Program of Higher Education of China (RFDP) under Grant No. 20120072120075, the Shanghai Foundation for Development of Science and Technology under Grant No. 11JC1412800, the National Key Technology R&D Program under Grant No. 2012BAH15F03, and the Beijing Natural Science Foundation under Grant No. 4122070.

7. REFERENCES

[1] Brightkite dataset. `http://snap.stanford.edu/data/loc-brightkite.html`.

[2] Cisco visual networking index: Global mobile data traffic forecast update, 2013-2018.

`http://www.cisco.com/c/en/us/solutions/collateral/service-provider/visual-networking-index-vni/white\textunderscorepaper\textunderscorec11-520862.html`.

[3] Number of active user-s at facebook over the years. `http://news.yahoo.com/number-active-users-facebook-over-230449748.html`.

[4] Shareaholic's search traffic vs. social referrals report. `https://blog.shareaholic.com/search-traffic-social-referrals-12-2013/`.

[5] G. Alfano, M. Garetto, and E. Leonardi. Capacity scaling of wireless networks with inhomogeneous node density: Upper bounds. *IEEE Journal on Selected Areas in Communications*, 27(7):1147–1157, 2009.

[6] E. Bakshy, I. Rosenn, C. Marlow, and L. Adamic. The role of social networks in information diffusion. In *Proc. ACM WWW 2012*.

[7] F. Benevenuto, T. Rodrigues, M. Cha, and V. Almeida. Characterizing user behavior in online social networks. In *Proc. ACM IMC 2009*.

[8] J. Borge-Holthoefer, A. Rivero, and Y. Moreno. Locating privileged spreaders on an online social network. *Physical Review E*, 85(6):066123, 2012.

[9] C. Carter, S. Yi, P. Ratanchandani, and R. Kravets. Manycast: exploring the space between anycast and multicast in ad hoc networks. In *Proc. ACM MobiCom 2003*.

[10] E. Cho, S. A. Myers, and J. Leskovec. Friendship and mobility: Friendship and mobility: User movement in location-based social networks. In *Proc. ACM SIGKDD 2011*.

[11] D. Du and F. Hwang. A proof of the Gilbert-Pollak conjecture on the Steiner ratio. *Algorithmica*, 7(1):121–135, 1992.

[12] M. Franceschetti, O. Dousse, D. Tse, and P. Thiran. Closing the gap in the capacity of wireless networks via percolation theory. *IEEE Transactions on Information Theory*, 53(3):1009–1018, 2007.

[13] E. Gilbert and H. Pollak. Steiner minimal trees. *SIAM Journal on Applied Mathematics*, 16(1):1–29, 1968.

[14] G. Grimmett. *Percolation*. Springer, 1999.

[15] A. Guille, H. Hacid, C. Favre, and D. A. Zighed. Information diffusion in online social networks: A survey. *SIGMOD Record*, 42(2):17, 2013.

[16] P. Gupta and P. R. Kumar. The capacity of wireless networks. *IEEE Transactions on Information Theory*, 46(2):388–404, 2000.

[17] A. O. Ivanov and A. A. Tuzhilin. The steiner ratio Gilbert–Pollak conjecture is still open. *Algorithmica*, 62(1-2):630–632, 2012.

[18] L. Jin, Y. Chen, T. Wang, P. Hui, and A. V. Vasilakos. Understanding user behavior in online social networks: A survey. *IEEE Communications Magazine*, 51(9):144–150, 2013.

[19] A. Jovicic, P. Viswanath, and S. R. Kulkarni. Upper bounds to transport capacity of wireless networks. *IEEE Transactions on Information Theory*, 50(11):2555–2565, 2004.

[20] J. Kleinberg. Navigation in a small world. *Nature*, 406(6798):845–845, 2000.

[21] B. Latané, J. Liu, A. Nowak, M. Bonevento, and L. Zheng. Distance matters: Physical space and social impact. *Personality and Social Psychology Bulletin*, 21(8):795–805, 1995.

[22] V. Lenders, M. May, and B. Plattner. Density-based anycast: a robust routing strategy for wireless ad hoc networks. *IEEE/ACM Transactions on Networking*, 16(4):852–863, 2008.

[23] D. Liben-Nowell, J. Novak, R. Kumar, P. Raghavan, and A. Tomkins. Geographic routing in social networks. *PNAS of the United States of America*, 102(33):11623–11628, 2005.

[24] C. Manning and H. Schütze. *Foundations of statistical natural language processing*. MIT press, 1999.

[25] M. Mathioudakis and N. Koudas. Twittermonitor: trend detection over the twitter stream. In *Proc. ACM SIGMOD 2010*.

[26] M.Cataldi, C. L. Di, and C. Schifanella. Emerging topic detection on twitter based on temporal and social terms evaluation. In *Proc. MDMKDD 2010*.

[27] G. Mega, A. Montresor, and G. P. Picco. Efficient dissemination in decentralized social networks. In *Proc. IEEE P2P 2011*.

[28] A. Mislove, M. Marcon, K. Gummadi, P. Druschel, and B. Bhattacharjee. Measurement and analysis of online social networks. In *Proc. ACM IMC 2007*.

[29] J. Møller. Shot noise cox processes. *Advances in Applied Probability*, 35(3):614–640, 2003.

[30] S. A. Myers, C. Zhu, and J. Leskovec. Information diffusion and external influence in networks. In *Proc. ACM SIGKDD 2012*.

[31] M. Penrose. A strong law for the longest edge of the minimal spanning tree. *The Annals of Probability*, 27(1):246–260, 1999.

[32] R. Perera, S. Anand, K. Subbalakshmi, and R. Chandramouli. Twitter analytics: Architecture, tools and analysis. In *Proc. IEEE MILCOM 2010*.

[33] A. Sala, H. Zheng, B. Y. Zhao, S. Gaito, and G. P. Rossi. Brief announcement: revisiting the power-law degree distribution for social graph analysis. In *Proc. ACM PODC 2010*.

[34] F. Schneider, A. Feldmann, B. Krishnamurthy, and W. Willinger. Understanding online social network usage from a network perspective. In *Proc. ACM IMC 2009*.

[35] J. Steele. Growth rates of Euclidean minimal spanning trees with power weighted edges. *The Annals of Probability*, pages 1767–1787, 1988.

[36] J. Sun, X. Zhu, and Y. Fang. A privacy-preserving scheme for online social networks with efficient revocation. In *Proc. IEEE INFOCOM 2010*.

[37] F. Wang, H. Wang, K. Xu, J. Wu, and X. Jia. Characterizing information diffusion in online social networks with linear diffusive model. In *Proc. IEEE ICDCS 2013*.

[38] D. Williams. *Probability with martingales*. Cambridge university press, 1991.

APPENDIX

A. USEFUL LEMMAS

LEMMA 8 (MINIMAL SPANNING TREE [35]). *Let X_i, $1 \leq i < \infty$, denote independent random variables with values in $\mathbb{R}^d$, $d \geq 2$, and let M_n denote the cost of a minimal spanning tree of a complete graph with vertex set $\{X_i\}_{i=1}^n$, where the cost of an* *edge (X_i, X_j) is given by $\Psi(|X_i - X_j|)$. Here, $|X_i - X_j|$ denotes the Euclidean distance between X_i and X_j and Ψ is a monotone function. For bounded random variables and $0 < \sigma < d$, it holds that as $n \to \infty$, with probability 1, one has*

$$M_n \sim c_1(\sigma, d) \cdot n^{\frac{d-\sigma}{d}} \cdot \int_{\mathbb{R}^d} f(X)^{\frac{d-\sigma}{d}} dX,$$

provided $\Psi(x) \sim x^\sigma$, where $f(X)$ is the density of the absolutely continuous part of the distribution of the $\{X_i\}$.

LEMMA 9 (KOLMOGOROV'S STRONG LLN [38]). *Let $\{X_n\}$ be an i.i.d. sequence of random variables having finite mean: for $\forall n$, $\mathbf{E}[X_n] < \infty$. Then, a strong law of large numbers (LLN) applies to the sample mean:*

$$\bar{X}_n \xrightarrow{a.s.} \mathbf{E}[X_n],$$

where $\xrightarrow{a.s.}$ denotes almost sure convergence.

B. A VALIDATION BASED ON BRIGHTKITE DATASET

In this section, we provide the validations of the adopted degree distribution model and the proposed population-based social formation model using Brightkite users' dataset [10].

B.1 Brightkite Dataset

Brightkite was created in 2007. It was once a location-based social networking service provider where users shared their locations by "checking-in" function, [1]. The friendship network was collected using their public API, and consists of 58, 228 nodes and 214, 078 edges. The Brightkite users' dataset in [10] collected a total of 4, 491, 143 checkins of these users over the period from April 2008 to October 2010. It provides each user with the incoming and outgoing friend lists.

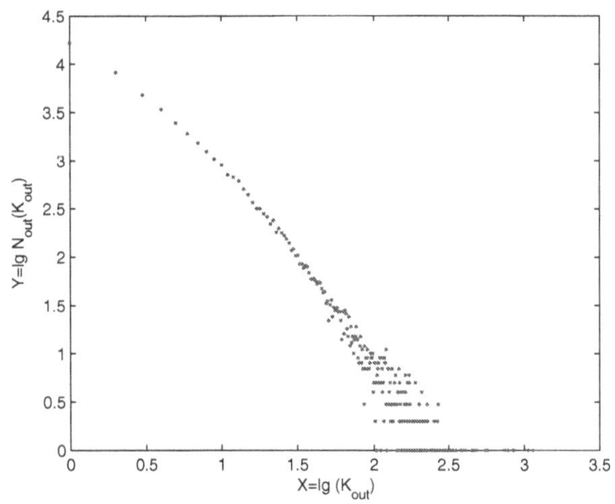

Figure 2: Social Degree Distribution of Brightkite Users.

B.2 Degree Distribution of Brightkite Users

Recall that we assume that the number of friends of a particular node $v_k \in \mathcal{V}$, denoted by q_k, follows a Zipf's distribution [24], i.e.,

$$\Pr(q_k = l) = \left(\sum_{j=1}^{n-1} j^{-\gamma}\right)^{-1} \cdot l^{-\gamma}.$$

We validate the Zipf's degree distribution of social relations by investigating the negative linear correlation between

$$Y := \lg N_{out}(K_{out}) \text{ and } X := \lg K_{out},$$

where K_{out} represents an outgoing degree, and $N_{out}(K_{out})$ denotes the number of the users with the outgoing degree K_{out}.

In the Brightkite dataset [10], the relationship between Y and X is described as Fig.2. It shows that the relationship be approximated to a line segment with negative slope, which basically matches our proposed model.

B.3 Validation of Population-Based Model

Let $d(u, v)$ denote the distance between user u and user v; let $\mathcal{D}(u, v)$ denote the disk centered at u with a radius $d(u, v)$; and let $N(u, v)$ denote the number of nodes in the disk $\mathcal{D}(u, v)$. Furthermore, we define a variable

$$\mathbf{I}(u, v) = \mathbf{1} \cdot \{v \text{ is a friend of } u\}.$$

We validate the power-law degree distribution of social formation by investigating the *negative linear correlation* between Y and X, where $X := \lg N$ with N denoting a number of nodes, and

$$Y := \lg\left(\frac{\sum_{<u,v>\in\mathcal{E}} \mathbf{1} \cdot \{N(u, v) = N\}}{\sum_{u,v\in\mathcal{V}} \mathbf{1} \cdot \{N(u, v) = N\}}\right),$$

with $\mathcal{V}$ and $\mathcal{E}$ denoting the set of all users and the set of all social links, respectively.

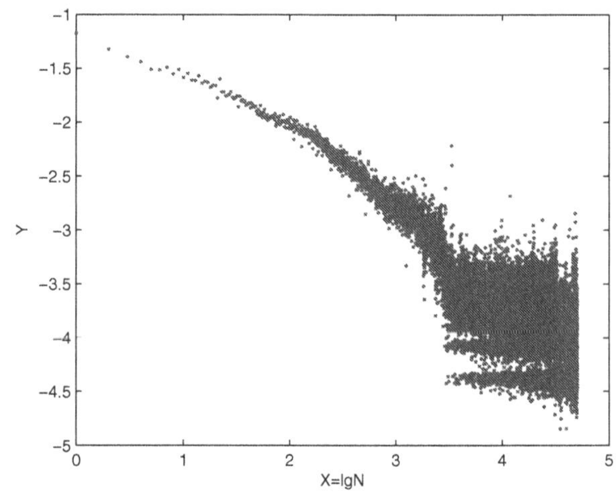

Figure 3: Population-based Social Probability Distribution of Brightkite Users.

In the Brightkite dataset [10], the relationship between Y and X is described as Fig.3. It shows that the relationship tendency is approximated very coarsely to a line segment with negative slope. The experimental result also basically validates our proposed model, although it does not perfectly match. The main reason of mismatch lies in the fact that: (1) The locations of users in the dataset are coarse-grained, and are indeed estimated in the experiments. This reduces the accuracy of experiments. (2) Based on this dataset, more than 90% results fall within the part with $X > 3$. The accumulation of experimental errors here leads to a "bloated" tail in the validation graph.

Load Balanced Short Path Routing in Large-Scale Wireless Networks Using Area-Preserving Maps

Mayank Goswami
MPI, Germany
gmayank@mpi-inf.mpg.de

Chien-Chun Ni
Stony Brook University
chni@cs.sunysb.edu

Xiaomeng Ban
Google Inc.
xban@google.com

Jie Gao
Stony Brook University
jgao@cs.sunysb.edu

Xianfeng Gu
Stony Brook University
gu@cs.sunysb.edu

Vamsi Pingali
Johns Hopkins University
vpingali@math.jhu.edu

ABSTRACT

Load balanced routing in a network, i.e., minimizing the maximum traffic load any node carries for unsplittable flows, is a well known NP-hard problem. Finding practical algorithms remains a long standing challenge. In this paper we propose greedy routing using virtual coordinates that achieves both small path stretch ratio (compared to shortest path) and small load balancing ratio (compared to optimal load balanced routing), in a large scale wireless sensor network deployed densely inside a geometric domain with complex shape. We first provide a greedy routing scheme on a disk with a stretch ratio of at most 2, and under which the maximum load is a factor $4\sqrt{2}$ smaller than the maximum load under shortest path routing. This is the first simple routing scheme with a small stretch that has been proven to outperform shortest path routing in terms of load balancing. Then we transform a network of arbitrary shape to a disk by an area preserving map ϕ. We show that both the path length and the maximum traffic load in the original network only increases by an additional factor of d^2, where d is the maximum length stretch of ϕ. Combined with the result on a disk we again achieve both bounded stretch and bounded load balancing ratio. Our simulation results evaluated the practical performance on both quality measures.

Categories and Subject Descriptors

F.2.2 [**Analysis of Algorithms and Problem Complexity**]: Nonnumerical Algorithms and Problems—*Geometrical problems and computations*; C.2.2 [**Computer-Communication Networks**]: Network protocols—*Routing protocols*

Keywords

Load Balancing; Area-Preserving Maps; Conformal Mapping; Sensor Networks

1. INTRODUCTION

In this paper we study the problem of greedy routing in a large scale wireless sensor networks and focus on the issue of load balancing. While reducing maximum traffic load is a general objective for most networking scenarios, in a battery-powered wireless sensor network this problem becomes more critical. Any subset of nodes used too much faces the risk of running out of battery prematurely; the functionality of the network may dramatically deteriorate even when many nodes still have ample battery life.

The maximum traffic load in a network depends on both the traffic pattern (i.e., the distribution of sources and destinations) and the topology of the network. When all messages are from the same source and/or same destination, the highest traffic is around the common 'sink'. This phenomena is termed the 'energy hole' problem and has been studied extensively in the literature [14]. In this paper we focus on the case of load balancing for general point to point traffic characterized by a general distribution of source destination pairs. This models the scenario when the sensor nodes are tightly embedded in the physical space in which human users reside. Users can query a nearby sensor and issue a message to a particular target sensor retrieving relevant information. This is also a particularly interesting scenario in theory as the topology of the network plays an important role in deciding the max load. Even when traffic pattern is uniform (source and destination chosen uniformly randomly) there can still be overly loaded nodes. In some cases the max load is mainly caused by the network topology (e.g., the nodes in a narrow neck of the network) – and there is little one can do to reduce the max load by different routing algorithms. In some other cases the max load is mainly caused by the routing algorithm (e.g., the overloaded center created by shortest path routing in a circular shaped network). This is what we focus on. We would like to design good routing scheme that achieve or approximate the best max load possible.

We observe that, in order to alleviate load accumulation, we need to spread out traffic, which leads to increased path length. Obviously using short paths is desirable for low delay. In fact, the two objectives, reducing max traffic load and reducing path lengths, have an interesting relationship. On one hand they are in agreement – using paths that are too long will elevate the total traffic load of all nodes, such that the average load (and thus the maximum load) is high by pigeon hole principle. On the other hand, the two objectives are in conflict – if we can only use shortest paths, we have little freedom in choosing paths to spread out traffic. Indeed it has been shown that in a unit disk graph there is a trade-off between the two objectives. One cannot have both load balancing ratio and path stretch bounded by constants simultaneously, without additional constraints on the network topology [10]. This motivates us to investigate what type of network topology can support both good load balancing and short paths simultaneously and how to exploit such structural properties for a practical routing solution.

MobiHoc'14, August 11–14, 2014, Philadelphia, PA, USA.

http://dx.doi.org/10.1145/2632951.2632987 .

Our Approach. We consider networks of wireless nodes uniformly deployed inside a complex geometric domain Ω and consider greedy routing using virtual coordinates. The case of densely deployed sensors inside a geometric domain is an important and natural scenario when sensor networks scale large. The use of greedy routing will make the solution to be practical.

In this paper we assume that the traffic pattern is modeled by a joint distribution Π of the source destination pair. We classify the network topology by the shape of Ω and ask for routing solutions with both good load balancing property and bounded stretch. Nevertheless, load balanced routing even for dense networks inside a simply shape with uniform traffic pattern, without constraints on path stretch, is still very challenging. No good approximations (better than the general case) are known. Existing work mainly focused on simple shapes such as strips, disks or squares; or focused on reducing max load in certain parts of the network such as interior hole boundaries. We are the first to study load balancing of networks inside an irregular domain.

Throughout the paper we use the *path stretch* as the worst case ratio of the routing path length by our algorithm and the shortest path length for the same source destination pair. We use the *load balancing ratio* as the ratio of the maximum traffic load by our algorithm and the maximum traffic load of the *optimal* load balanced routing algorithm (i.e., the minimum of maximum load possible), for the same traffic pattern Π.

The main tool we use is *area-preserving maps*. Under an area-preserving map $\phi : \Omega \to \Omega'$, an ε-area ball is mapped to a piece (not necessarily round) with area ε. The main theoretical result in this paper is the following. Suppose we use a routing algorithm Γ on the original domain Ω with traffic load $\ell_\Gamma(p)$ on node p. Applying the area preserving map ϕ, we obtain a routing algorithm Γ' on the target domain Ω'. We prove that the traffic load $\ell_{\Gamma'}$ at point $\phi(p)$ is bounded by $d \cdot \ell_\Gamma(p)$ from above and $\ell_\Gamma(p)/d$ from below, in which d is the maximum length stretch of the map ϕ.

Applying the above theorem in different directions allows us to prove upper bound on the traffic load in our algorithm, as well as lower bound on the max traffic load in the optimal load balanced routing. Altogether this allows us to transfer a load balanced short path routing algorithm on Ω' to a load balanced short path routing algorithm on Ω. Specifically, if Γ' is has load balancing ratio c and path stretch of λ in domain Ω', we prove that Γ has load balancing ratio $c \cdot d^2$ and path stretch $\lambda \cdot d^2$ in Ω.

We first look at the case of a disk, which is an example of a good network topology. If we send one message between each pair of nodes in a disk shape network using shortest path routing, the maximum traffic load scales in the order of $O(n\sqrt{n})$, which is in fact already asymptotically optimal. We can further improve it by using the Lambert Azimuthal projection (one area-preserving projection) to map a unit disk onto a sphere. By using greedy routing on the spherical coordinates we can reduce the maximum traffic load even further while only using paths of stretch at most 2. Furthermore, we prove that this routing scheme is a factor $4\sqrt{2}$ better than shortest path routing in terms of load balancing, making it the first routing scheme provably better than shortest path routing.

For a network inside a simply connected domain Ω of an arbitrary shape, we take a specific area preserving map ϕ from Ω to a disk and then apply the above mentioned routing algorithm in a disk. Therefore, we can compute virtual coordinate inside the disk for each node x in Ω, with which greedy routing achieves path stretch of $O(d^2(\phi))$ and load balancing ratio of $O(d^2(\phi))$. Here $d(\phi)$ is the maximum length stretch of the mapping ϕ. In particular, $d(\phi)$ gives an effective way of classifying the topology of the network. Any domain that admits an area preserving map ϕ with constant $d(\phi)$ will support greedy routing with constant path stretch and constant load balancing ratio. This provides a qualitative way to measure how the topology of the network affects its load balancing property.

We summarize our contribution below.

1. Establish connection of area-preserving maps to load balanced routing,
2. Provide a distributed, greedy routing scheme on any simply connected domain that has a worst case stretch factor of $O(d^2(\phi))$ and worst-case load balancing ratio of $O(d^2(\phi))$, where d_ϕ is the maximum length stretch of the area-preserving map from the domain to the disk.
3. Provide a routing scheme on the disk that uses routes at most twice the length of the shortest path, and is a factor $4\sqrt{2}$ better in load balancing than shortest path routing.

Note that the average load under the shortest path routing scheme is a lower bound on the maximum load under any routing scheme. Using this quantity, the load balancing ratios of both shortest path routing scheme and our routing scheme can be calculated, and they will differ by a factor $4\sqrt{2}$.

2. RELATED WORK

Load balanced routing on graphs. In the field of networking algorithms, load balanced routing on a graph with given source destination pairs is a long standing problem. One way to formulate this problem is to select routes that minimize congestion (the maximum number of messages that any node/link carries), termed the *unsplittable flow problem*. Solving this problem optimally is NP-hard even in very simple networks (such as grid). The best approximation algorithm has an approximation factor of $O(\log n/ \operatorname{loglog} n)$ [19,20] in a network of n vertices. It is also shown that getting an approximation within factor $\Omega(\operatorname{loglog} n)$ is NP-hard [2]. Another popular way to formulate the problem is to consider node disjoint or edge disjoint paths that deliver the largest number of given source destination pairs. This is again NP-hard [13] and the best approximation factor known is $O(\sqrt{n})$ [6]. It is NP-hard to approximate within a factor of $\Omega(\log^{1/2-\epsilon} n)$ [7]. These approximation algorithms are mostly only of theoretical interest. They require global knowledge and are not suitable for distributed settings.

Load balancing routing on simple shapes. In [9], a greedy routing scheme that achieves both constant stretch factor and constant load balancing ratio is proposed, but only for nodes distributed in a narrow strip. In a general unit disk graph setting, there is a tradeoff between the stretch factor and load balancing ratio [10].

Popa *et al.* [18] studied load balanced routing in a disk. Under uniform traffic pattern, the center is more loaded than nodes near the boundary. By using numerical solvers, they had a numerical approximation of the optimal load balanced routing solution. They also proposed a practical algorithm by using stereographic projection to map the network on a hemisphere. Routing is guided by the spherical distance in a greedy manner. Improved load balancing is shown as the routes are made to 'curve' around the network center. But no theoretical analysis is given.

Mei and Stefa [16] studied load balancing for networks inside a square and propose to use the 'outer space' by creating four copies of the network, wrapped up as a topological torus. The destination has four images and greedy routing is done by using coordinates on the torus towards a randomly selected image of the destination. On the original network, it is as if we are reflecting on the boundaries. The idea is that through mapping on a torus the original boundary or center of the square are essentially removed so they should not present heavy load. By evaluations we found out that the traffic load on the nodes are indeed more even, but unfortunately the traffic at all nodes has been greatly elevated as routing paths through reflections are on average much longer than shortest paths.

Yu *et al.* [23] examined a network inside a simply connected domain and used Ricci flow to generate Thurston's embedding as the skeleton of a convex polytope. The intuition is to map the network on a sphere (or half sphere) as routing on a sphere has no congestion due to perfect symmetry. The choice of a convex polytope is to ensure that greedy routing guarantees delivery [17]. This performs well in simulations but there is no theoretical guarantee on the worst case congestion.

Reducing congestion on centers or hole boundaries. A number of previous works focused on reducing traffic load on hole boundaries. This is because traditional geographical routing [8, 12] tends to send messages to nodes near hole boundaries. In [21], a network of multiple holes is converted to the covering space, such that one maps the network to the interior of each hole, filling it up. Again, since the boundaries are removed, greedy routing, when touching a boundary node, does not follow the boundary but get reflected away from the boundary. Simulation results show that the traffic load on boundaries are greatly reduced. But the average traffic load is increased as routing paths are made longer.

In [5], the focus is to reduce traffic load near the medial axis, which is a generalization of the center of a disk in a domain of general shape and is likely to attract traffic load. The proposed routing algorithm will follow a path parallel to the medial axis or orthogonal to the medial axis, minimizing the intersections with the medial axis. Again no theoretical guarantee is given.

Area preserving maps. Area preserving maps [4] have been used for graphics and visualization applications. This paper is the first to apply area preserving map for improving load balancing in networking.

3. THEORY OF LOAD BALANCING AND AREA-PRESERVING MAPS

3.1 Definitions

In this paper we assume a dense set of wireless nodes distributed inside a simply connected geometric region Ω. We focus on the aspect of load balancing for different routing algorithms. We assume that the scheduling of transmissions and the handling of interference is done by a proper MAC layer protocol. We consider the traffic pattern as modeled by a joint distribution Π on the source destination pair. A routing scheme Γ describes how to find a path between two points inside Ω. For every pair of points (p, q) inside Ω, Γ specifies a path $\gamma_{p,q} \subset \Omega$ that connects p to q. The set Γ is the collection of all such paths.

In the discrete graph setting, the traffic load is taken as the number of messages delivered along each edge/through each node. When node distribution is dense, we would like to use the abstraction of routing in a continuous domain. In the continuous case we follow the definition of load presented in [18], as below.

Definition 1 (Load). *Given a traffic pattern Π and a routing scheme Γ for Ω, for any region $A \subset \Omega$, define the load of A (denoted as $\ell_\Gamma(A)$) under the traffic pattern Π by the following procedure:*

1. *Choose n source-destination pairs $\{(a_i, b_i)\}_{i=1}^n$ from the distribution Π. For all such pairs, find γ_i, the paths as determined by Γ.*
2. *Let $X_n(A)$ be the average length of intersection of the γ_i with A.*
3. *Define $\ell_\Gamma(A) = \lim_{n \to \infty} \frac{X_n(A)}{\text{Area}(A)}$. Here Area$(A)$ denotes the usual Euclidean area of the region A.*

Next, define the load at a point p in the domain by:

1. *Choose a nested sequence of neighborhoods A_n whose intersection is p and which satisfy Area$(A_n) \to 0$ as $n \to \infty$;*
2. *Define $\ell_\Gamma(p) = \lim_{n\to\infty} \ell_\Gamma(A_n)$.*

Clearly the traffic load depends on the specified traffic pattern Π. Throughout the paper we will fix the traffic pattern Π unless specified otherwise. Denote the maximum load over all $p \in \Omega$ under Γ as ℓ_Γ. The optimal load balanced routing problem is to find Γ^* which minimize ℓ_{Γ^*}. We define the *load balancing ratio* of a routing scheme Γ as $\ell_\Gamma/\ell_{\Gamma^*}$. For a particular routing scheme Γ, denote by $|\gamma_{pq}|$ the length of the routing path γ_{pq} from p to q and denote by $|pq|$ the shortest path length. We define the *path stretch* of Γ as

$$\max_{p,q\in\Omega} |\gamma_{pq}|/|pq|.$$

Definition 2 (Area Preserving Map). *Given two domains Ω and Ω' in $\mathbb{R}^n$ with the same area, a map ϕ from Ω to Ω' is area preserving if* $\text{Area}(\phi^{-1}(A)) = \text{Area}(A)$ *for every subregion A of Ω.* Area(A) *is the area of the region A.*

The area-preserving map can be written in axis-parallel coordinates as $\phi : (x, y) \to (u, v)$. The Jacobian matrix $J(\phi)$ is a 2×2 matrix of the partials of u and v with respect to x and y. Now, ϕ is area-preserving, which is equivalent to the determinant of $J(\phi)$ being identically 1 at all points in the domain. Let $\lambda_1(x, y), \lambda_2(x, y)$ denote the two eigenvalues of $J(\phi)$ (not necessarily real). Note that $\lambda_1\lambda_2 = 1$ at every point, and hence $|\lambda_1| = 1/|\lambda_2|$.

Let $d(x, y) = \max(|\lambda_1(x, y)|, |\lambda_2(x, y)|)$ denote the maximum length distortion at point (x, y). When $p = (x, y)$, we will just write $d(p)$. Let

$$d(\phi_{\Omega,\Omega'}) = \sup_{p\in\overline{\Omega}} d(p) \tag{1}$$

$d(\phi)$ is the *maximum length stretch* of the mapping ϕ.

3.2 Bound on Max Load

Given a routing scheme Γ in Ω for the traffic pattern Π, by applying the map $\phi : \Omega \to \Omega'$ we get a routing algorithm Γ', the push-forward of the routing scheme Γ via ϕ in Ω'. Γ' allots the path $\phi(\gamma)$ to the pair (a, b), where γ is the path joining $\phi^{-1}(a)$ and $\phi^{-1}(b)$ as dictated by Γ. In particular, we can consider the traffic load of the routing scheme Γ' under traffic pattern $\Pi' = \phi(\Pi)$. In the following theorem we relate the maximum traffic load of Γ (under traffic pattern Π) and the maximum load of Γ' (under traffic pattern Π').

Theorem 3. *Given a routing scheme Γ on Ω and $\phi : \Omega \to \Omega'$ area-preserving, denote by Γ' the routing scheme on Ω' which allots the path $\phi(\gamma)$ to the pair (a, b), where γ is the path joining $\phi^{-1}(a)$ and $\phi^{-1}(b)$ as dictated by Γ. Then*

$$\frac{1}{d(p)}\ell_\Gamma(p) \le \ell_{\Gamma'}(\phi(p)) \le d(p)\ell_\Gamma(p)\ \forall p \in \Omega \tag{2}$$

PROOF. Fix an $\epsilon > 0$. By continuity of $J_\phi(x, y)$, $\exists\delta > 0$ such that for any p' in the disk of radius δ around p (denoted as $B_\delta(p)$),

$$d(p') < d(p) + \epsilon, \quad \text{and} \quad \frac{1}{d(p')} > \frac{1}{d(p)} - \epsilon \tag{3}$$

Let $B_\delta(p) \supset B_{\delta_1}(p) \supset B_{\delta 2}(p) \supset \cdots$ be a sequence of nested neighborhoods of p such that $\cap_{i=1}^{\infty} B_{\delta_i}(p) = p$. We will calculate the load at $\phi(p)$ using the sequence $\phi(B_{\delta_i}(p))$. Note that $\phi(B_{\delta_i}(p))$ has the same area as $B_{\delta_i}(p)$.

Pick n source destination pairs in Ω' by distribution Π'. Since ϕ is measure preserving, this amounts to picking n pairs in Ω by distribution Π and looking at their images under ϕ. Consider any source destination path γ (joining two points a and b) intersecting $B_{\delta_i}(p)$ in Ω. The fact that ϕ is a homeomorphism implies that $\phi(\gamma)$ intersects the neighborhood $\phi(B_{\delta_i}(p))$ of $\phi(p) \in \Omega'$.

Now let $\gamma_i = \gamma \cap B_{\delta_i}(p)$. As a consequence of Equation 3, the length of $\phi(\gamma_i)$, denoted as $|\phi(\gamma_i)|$ satisfies

$$\left(\frac{1}{d(p)} - \epsilon\right)|\gamma_i| < |\phi(\gamma_i)| < (d(p)+\epsilon)|\gamma_i| \tag{4}$$

as a consequence of which the load of $B_{\delta_i}(p)$ and $\phi(B_{\delta_i}(p))$ (both of which have the same area) satisfy

$$\left(\frac{1}{d(p)} - \epsilon\right)\ell_\Gamma(B_{\delta_i}(p)) < \ell_{\Gamma'}(\phi(B_{\delta_i}(p))) < (d(p)+\epsilon)\ell_\Gamma(B_{\delta_i}(p))$$

Taking limit as $i \to \infty$ gives

$$\left(\frac{1}{d(p)} - \epsilon\right)\ell_\Gamma(p) \le \ell_{\Gamma'}\phi(p) \le (d(p)+\epsilon)\ell_\Gamma(p) \;\; \forall p \in \Omega \tag{5}$$

Since $\epsilon > 0$ chosen above was arbitrary, this proves the theorem. □

By applying the above theorem we can now study maximum load of two algorithms in two domains of different shapes. We provide two theorems doing so, and we omit their straightforward proofs. First we study how the optimal load balanced algorithms in Ω and Ω' relate to each other. Recall that ℓ_Γ denotes the maximum load under Γ.

Theorem 4. *Let Γ^* and Ψ^* be the optimal load balanced routing schemes on domains Ω and Ω' respectively. Let ϕ be an area-preserving map from Ω to Ω' and define $d(\phi_{\Omega,\Omega'})$ as above. Then*

$$\frac{1}{d(\phi_{\Omega,\Omega'})}\ell_{\Gamma^*} \le \ell_{\Psi^*} \le d(\phi_{\Omega,\Omega'})\ell_{\Gamma^*} \tag{6}$$

Remarks on Theorem 4: Here the statement holds for *any* area-preserving homeomorphism between the two domains. Thus, we can find the area preserving map $\phi : \Omega \to \Omega'$ that achieves the minimum length stretch. Clearly the more similar Ω is to Ω' the smaller this length stretch could be.

Besides, the above statement gives non-trivial lower bounds for the best achievable load on any given domain. This has not been accomplished before. It can be intuitively understood that any routing algorithm on domains with narrow bridges/cuts necessarily creates high traffic load at the bridge area – the shape matters. This theorem makes it more precise. Take Ω' as the unit disk. We know that the minimum max load of any routing for uniform traffic pattern has maximum load of at least 0.45 – the average load of a node in the disk when one uses shortest path routing [18]. If the area-preserving mapping ϕ has length distortion at most say δ, then we know that the optimal load on the domain Ω is at least $0.45/\delta$.

The next theorem tells us how to obtain an approximate solution on the original domain Ω by using an approximate (or exact) solution on the target domain Ω'.

Theorem 5. *Let Ψ^c be a factor c approximation of the optimal solution to the* min max *problem on Ω', i.e. $\ell_{\Psi^c} \le c\ell_{\Psi^*}$, where Ψ^* is as in Theorem 4. Let Γ be the routing scheme on Ω that allots the path $\phi^{-1}(\gamma)$ to the source-destination pair (a, b) inside Ω, where γ is the path between $\phi(a)$ and $\phi(b)$ as dictated by Ψ^c. Let Γ^* be the optimal routing scheme on Ω. Then $\ell_\Gamma \le cd^2(\phi_{\Omega,\Omega'})\ell_{\Gamma^*}$.*

3.3 Length stretch bound

It is clear that any other routing scheme on the domain Ω will generate longer paths than shortest path routing. Now we will show that by using area-preserving map ϕ, we also bound the path stretch by a constant factor dependent on $d(\phi)$. Assume that Γ and Ψ are shortest path routing schemes on Ω and Ω' respectively, and let Ψ^c be a routing scheme on the disk such that the path it generates between a source-destination pair (u, v) is at most c times the length of the shortest path between u and v, for all pairs (u, v). We will write this as

$$|\mathcal{R}_{\Psi^c}(u,v)| \le c|R_\Psi(u,v)|$$

here $\mathcal{R}_\Psi(u, v)$ denotes the route between u and v under Ψ and $|.|$ denotes its length. Now let ϕ be an area-preserving map from Ω to Ω', and define $d(\phi_{\Omega,\Omega'})$ as in Equation 1. Let Γ' be the pull-back of Ψ^c via ϕ.

Theorem 6. *Under the above hypothesis,*

$$|\mathcal{R}_{\Gamma'}(a,b)| \le cd^2(\phi_{\Omega,\Omega'})|\mathcal{R}_\Gamma(a,b)| \;\; \forall a,b \in \Omega \tag{7}$$

PROOF. Let Ψ^0 be the push-forward of Γ (the shortest path routing on Ω) via ϕ. From the proof of Theorem 3, one can see that the image of a route $\mathcal{R}$ in Ω (denoted as $\phi(\mathcal{R})$) has length at most $d(\phi_\Omega)$ times that of $\mathcal{R}$. We now have the following string of inequalities:

$$\begin{aligned} |\mathcal{R}_{\Gamma'}(a,b)| &\le d(\phi_\Omega)|\mathcal{R}_{\Psi^c}(\phi(a),\phi(b))| \\ &\le cd(\phi_\Omega)|\mathcal{R}_\Psi(\phi(a),\phi(b))| \\ &\le cd(\phi_\Omega)|\mathcal{R}_{\Gamma^*}(\phi(a),\phi(b))| \\ &\le cd^2(\phi_\Omega)|\mathcal{R}_\Gamma(a,b)| \end{aligned} \tag{8}$$

where the second inequality follows by the hypothesis on Ψ^c, the third by the fact that shortest path routing Ψ will have shorter lengths than Γ^* and the last inequality follows by the same observations as the first (since Γ^* is the image of Γ, the shortest path routing on Ω). □

We will show in the simulation section that in all practical scenarios, the stretch is much smaller than the claimed constant in our proof.

4. LOAD BALANCED SHORT PATH ROUTING IN A DISK

In this section we study load balanced routing for a network inside a disk domain. We will first present the scaling laws of the maximum load for shortest path routing, under uniform traffic pattern, in a disk and on a sphere respectively.

4.1 Scaling Law in Disks, Spheres, Half Spheres

Suppose that we use uniform traffic pattern and deliver one message between each pair of nodes in the network of n nodes. When the network is uniformly distributed in a disk of radius R, the maximum traffic load by shortest path routing occurs in the center [18] and is in the order of $\Theta(n\sqrt{n})$ [11]. Notice that in fact the maximum traffic load is already *asymptotically optimal*. In particular, on average the shortest path between all pairs of nodes has length in the order of $\Theta(R) \approx \sqrt{n}$. Thus the total traffic load on all nodes is

$\Theta(n^2\sqrt{n})$. By pigeon hole principle, the maximum traffic load in the network is at least $\Theta(n\sqrt{n})$. Therefore, shortest path routing in a disk achieves path stretch of 1 and load balancing ratio of $O(1)$.

For a network of n nodes uniformly deployed on a sphere of radius R, the shortest path routing follows the geodediscs on the sphere. Due to perfect symmetry the traffic load is perfectly uniform everywhere on the sphere. Similarly, the total traffic load on all nodes is $\Theta(n^2\sqrt{n})$. Spreading the total traffic load on all nodes uniformly, the traffic load for each node is $\Theta(n\sqrt{n})$. Notice that this is also the optimal load balanced routing algorithm.

For a network of n nodes uniformly deployed inside the bottom half sphere of radius R, shortest path routing using spherical coordinates gives a maximum traffic load of $O(n\sqrt{n})$ as well. To see this, imagine $2n$ nodes uniformly spread inside a whole sphere and issue a message between all pairs of these $2n$ nodes. By the analysis above, the maximum traffic load is $\Theta(n\sqrt{n})$. Now, remove all the messages that involve any node in the top half sphere, the maximum traffic load does not increase and is thus $O(n\sqrt{n})$. The same scaling upper bound applies for other fractional caps of a sphere.

4.2 Improving Load Balancing

The discussion above suggested that for a network with a regular shape, shortest path routing already achieves asymptotically the best load balancing ratio. The improvement margin on reducing maximum load lies in improving the constant factor. This partly explains the limited improvement reported earlier by heuristic algorithms [18]. We will summarize options for greedy routing using virtual coordinates in the case of a disk. This will be used as subroutine for handling networks of general shape in the next section.

Using Lambert azimuthal projection To further reduce the center traffic load, we can map a disk to a sphere by using area-preserving maps and then adopt the spherical coordinates for greedy routing. The intuition is to push paths away from the crowded center. In particular, we use the *Lambert azimuthal equal-area projection.* Denote the (open) disk of radius r centered at the origin in the plane by $\mathbb{D}_r$, and set $\mathbb{D} := \mathbb{D}_1$. The Lambert azimuthal projection, $g : \mathbb{D}_2 \to S^2 \setminus \{(0,0,1)\}$ is the area-preserving map from the disk of radius 2 to the sphere of radius 1 (centered at the origin in $\mathbb{R}^3$) minus its north pole given by:

$$g(x,y) = \left(x\sqrt{1 - \frac{x^2+y^2}{4}}, y\sqrt{1 - \frac{x^2+y^2}{4}}, \frac{x^2+y^2}{2} - 1 \right) \tag{9}$$

One can see that g maps the disk of radius $\sqrt{2}$ to the lower hemisphere, the circle of radius $\sqrt{2}$ to the equator, and the remainder of the bigger disk with radius 2 to the upper hemisphere. Let $\mathcal{S}_H$ denote the lower half sphere, and Γ denote the greedy routing using spherical metric on it. For two nodes $a, b \in \mathcal{D}_{\sqrt{2}}$, we choose the path $g^{-1}(\mathcal{R}_{g(a),g(b)})$, where $\mathcal{R}_{g(a),g(b)}$ is the shortest path between $g(a)$ and $g(b)$ on $\mathcal{S}_H$ using Γ. Denote this routing scheme on $\mathcal{D}_{\sqrt{2}}$ as Ψ. Furthermore, let Δ denote shortest path routing on the disk. We can show that Ψ has maximum load a factor $4\sqrt{2}$ times smaller than the maximum load of Δ, and has path stretch at most two.

Theorem 7. *Let Ψ and Δ be two routing schemes on the disk of radius $\sqrt{2}$ as above. Then $\ell_\Psi = \ell_\Delta/(4\sqrt{2})$.*

PROOF. First, we need to calculate the proportionality constant in Theorem 1 in [18]. Redoing their integration, one finds that the maximum load under Δ is $4\sqrt{2}/\pi^2$.

Now we need to find the load on the south pole (of the unit lower half sphere), under the shortest path routing on the spherical metric. We set up an integral similar to the disk case, using a similar coordinate change. Thus the load on a small disk of radius ϵ at the south pole is found out to be $\frac{I(\epsilon)}{\pi\epsilon^2}$, where $I(\epsilon)$ is the integral mentioned. This integral does not have a closed-form expression.

We then use Taylor series to find out the load at the south pole as

$$\ell_\Psi = \frac{1}{2\pi} \cdot \frac{\partial^2 I}{\partial \epsilon^2} \|_{\epsilon=0}$$

which turns out to be $1/\pi^2$. Comparing with the load of $4\sqrt{2}/\pi^2$ gives us the desired constant. □

Theorem 8. *For any source destination pair (a, b) inside $\mathcal{D}$,*

$$|\mathcal{R}_\Psi(a,b)| \leq 2|\mathcal{R}_\Delta(a,b)|.$$

PROOF. We first find out how much a curve on the disk gets streched when mapped to the lower half sphere via the area-preserving mapping. To do this, we write the Lambert's azimuthal mapping in term of polar coordinates (R, Θ) on the disk and cylindrical coordinates (r, θ, z) on the sphere:

$$(r, \theta, z) = \left(R\sqrt{1 - \frac{R^2}{4}}, \Theta, \frac{R^2}{2} - 1 \right) \tag{10}$$

Given a curve $(R(t), \Theta(t))$ on the disk we find its tangent vector v by differentiating equation 10. Calculating the length of v and normalizing $(R(t), \Theta(t))$ by requiring $\dot{R}^2 + R^2\dot{\Theta}^2 = 1$, we maximize the length keeping in mind that R ranges from 0 to $\sqrt{2}$ and $\dot{R}$ from 0 to 1.

This implies that any curve on the disk when translated to the sphere gets stretched by a factor of at most $\sqrt{2}$. The same statement applies if we interchange the roles of the disk and the sphere. Now consider any two points a and b on the disk, with shortest path $\gamma(a, b)$ of length $\ell(a, b)$. Now $|g(\gamma)| \leq \sqrt{2}\ell(a, b)$ by the above observation on the stretch, and the shortest path $\tilde{\gamma}$ on the lower half sphere from a to b certainly has a length shorter than that of $g(\gamma)$. By the argument for the inverse of the mapping, the pull-back of $\tilde{\gamma}$ on the disk is again stretched by a factor at most $\sqrt{2}$, and this gives us the combined factor of 2 claimed. □

Moreover, it is clear that just by scaling the original network to radius R disk, one can arrange for the map to cover different parts of the sphere. Thus we scale our disk to a radius close to 2 if we want to push routes more towards the boundary and closer to $\sqrt{2}$ if we want them pushed lesser. The former is more aggressive in reducing the center load. In our simulations we provide different values of R for which we apply this map.

Curveball – using stereographic projection Curveball routing uses the same intuition of mapping a disk to a sphere, except that the projection used is the stereographic projection. Stereographic projection preserves angles, not areas. We refer the reader to [18] for details. Again, routing is done greedily using spherical metric on these virtual coordinates. Curveball routing is a heuristic. It can be shown that if the disk is mapped to the bottom halfsphere the length stretch is a constant. But there is no proof on how much the maximum load is reduced compared to that of shortest path routing.

Using approximate optimal An approximate optimal solution to the load balancing problem on the disk was described in [18]. However, since optimal is complicated, one cannot hope to get closed formula for the route from a source to a destination. We refer the reader to Section 3.4 of [18] for details. In our implementation, we weight each edge by its distance r to the center of the disk using the formula $1.8r^3 - 3.1r^2 + 2.3$. We compute the shortest path in the weighted graph and compare the performance with our methods. Notice that this algorithm is not a greedy algorithm and is less practical than the two algorithms above.

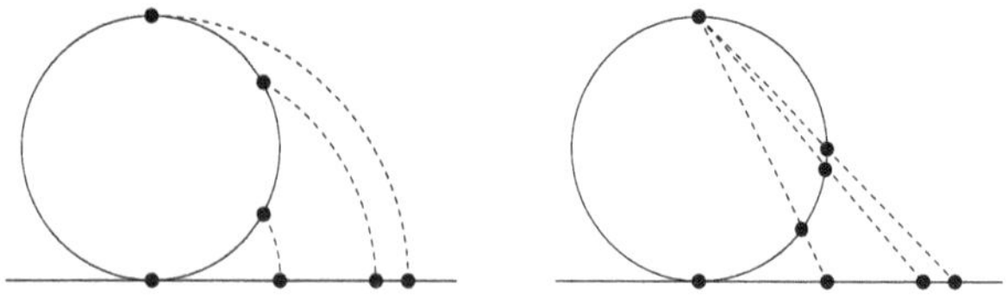

(i) (ii)

Figure 1. A cross sectional view of the sphere and a plane tangent to it at south pole. (i) Area-preserving map: each point on the sphere (except the north pole) is projected to the plane along a circular arc centered at the point of tangency between the sphere and plane. (ii) Stereographic map: a point p on the plane is mapped to the intersection of the line through p and the north pole with the sphere.

5. LOAD BALANCED SHORT PATH ROUTING ON AN ARBITRARY DOMAIN

5.1 Area-Preserving Map to Disk

For an arbitrary domain Ω we again use area-preserving maps. This time we map Ω to a disk such that we can pull back our solution from the previous section. By applying our theory in Section 3 we obtain the following results immediately.

Theorem 9. *For any simply connected domain Ω and an area preserving map ϕ that maps Ω to a disk of the same area, we use Lambert's azimuthal mapping to map the disk to a half sphere and create the virtual coordinates of all nodes in the network as the spherical coordinates on the half sphere. Greedy routing using such spherical virtual coordinates has path stretch of $4d_\phi^2$ and load balancing ratio of d_ϕ^2, where d_ϕ is the maximum length stretch of ϕ.*

We would like to use an example to demonstrate the potential of this approach. Take a look at the L-shape domain with n nodes uniformly spread inside. With a message between every pair of nodes, the nodes near the reflex vertex of the domain have traffic load of $\Theta(n^2)$ by shortest path routing – there are quadratic many nodes whose shortest paths 'bend' at the reflex vertex. See Figure 2. Using the algorithm to be presented below, we can find an area preserving map that maps the L-shape domain to a disk with constant length stretch. Thus we can reduce the maximum load to be $\Theta(n\sqrt{n})$, by only increasing the path stretch by a small constant! In our simulation section (see Figure 7) we report the load reduction and its scaling in network size.

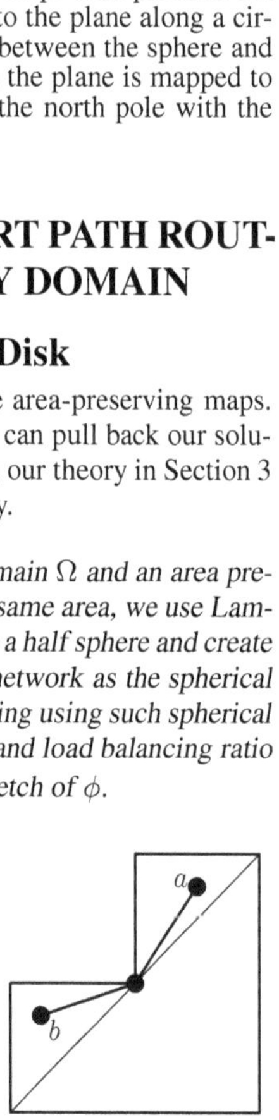

Figure 2. An L-shape domain. The shortest path from the top corner to the left corner will go through the nodes near the reflex vertex. The maximum traffic load near the reflex vertex is about $\Theta(n^2)$.

In the following we will present an distributed algorithm to compute an area preserving map.

5.2 Computing Area Preserving Maps

For some domains (e.g. the square) a closed form for an area-preserving map to the disk is available. Generally, this is not always possible and numerical methods are required. We will present distributed algorithms for computing such a map.

We start with a simply connected domain (with finite area) whose boundary is a piece-wise smooth curve. For our purposes, we can assume that the boundary is a polygon with k vertices. This is reasonable because any smooth boundary can be approximated by polygons. Note that k is often much smaller than the number of sensors, n, inside the domain.

Let Ω denote the interior of such a polygonal region, with $\mathcal{P}$ as the boundary polygon. Our goal is to map Ω to a disk D centered at the origin (of area equal to that of Ω) in an area-preserving way. Consider a real valued function f defined on Ω in such a way that the level sets of f are simple closed curves that fill up Ω. We call f the *contour generating function*. Given f, we will first define an area-preserving mapping from Ω to the disk in terms of f. We will then show how to obtain f for any given Ω in a simple manner.

To describe our bounds, we need to consider the Jacobian of our mapping. Set $u := R\cos\Theta$ and $v := R\sin\Theta$ where R and Θ are the same as in Equation 13, but now we use the conformal mapping g and the contour function f described in the previous section. The new equations for R and Θ now become:

$$\begin{aligned} R(x,y) &= \tilde{f}(x,y) := \sqrt{\text{Area (Int } \{f^{-1}(f(x,y))\})/\pi} \\ \Theta(x,y) &= \frac{1}{\tilde{f}(x,y)} \int_{g^{-1}(f(x,y))}^{x,y} \frac{ds}{(\tilde{f}_x^2 + \tilde{f}_y^2)^{1/2}} \end{aligned} \quad (11)$$

5.2.1 *Area-Preserving map using the contour generating function*

Assume that f has continuous first order partial derivatives everywhere except at $\mathcal{O}$, and not both of the partials are zero at any point. Let $\mathcal{C}$ be the family of contours of f, i.e. $\mathcal{C}$ is a set containing all simple closed curves $\gamma \subset \Omega$, such that there exists a constant c_γ with $f(x,y) = c_\gamma$ for all points $(x,y) \in \gamma$. Let $\mathcal{O}$ be a point interior to all the curves in $\mathcal{C}$, and let $\mathcal{L}$ be a path joining $\mathcal{O}$ to some point on $\mathcal{P}$ such that $\mathcal{L}$ intersects each curve in $\mathcal{C}$ once. See examples of contoured regions in Figure 3(b) and Figure 3(c).

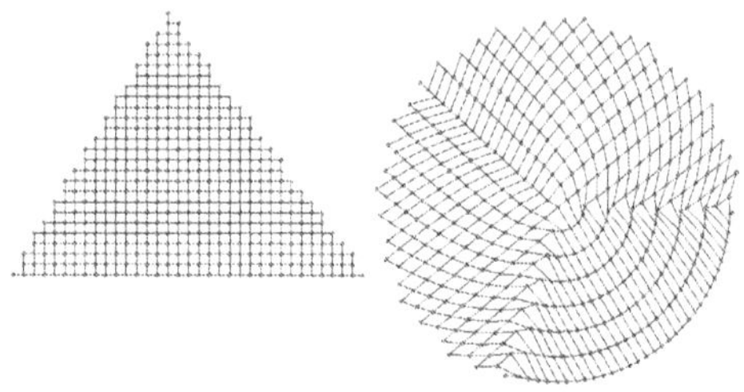

(a) An example of area-preserving map from a triangle to a disk

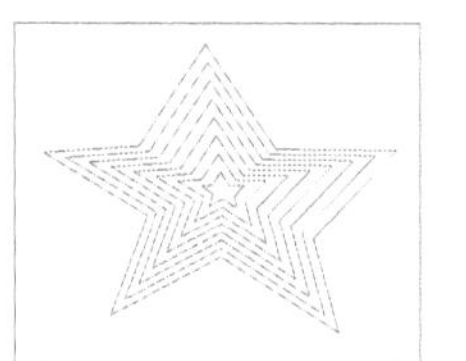

(b) Contoured star-shaped polygon using shrinking boundary method

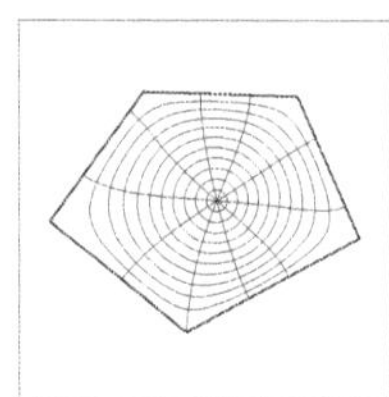

(c) Contoured pentagon using conformal mapping method

Figure 3. Example of area-preserving map and contoured polygons.

The area-preserving mapping $\phi : \Omega \to \mathcal{D}$ we use was first described in [4]. It has the following properties:

1. Every curve $\gamma \in \mathcal{C}$ is mapped to a circle inside $\mathcal{D}$ centered at the origin. Hence the contours are mapped to concentric circles. See Figure 3(a) for an example.

2. The path $\mathcal{L}$ is mapped to any given radius of $\mathcal{D}$.

To construct ϕ, we first modify our f as follows. Define a function $\tilde{f}$ on Ω such that $[\tilde{f}(x,y)]^2$ at any point $(x,y) \in \Omega$ equals $1/\pi$ times the area inside the contour in $\mathcal{C}$ passing through (x,y), i.e.

$$\tilde{f}(x,y) = \sqrt{\text{Area(Int } \gamma_{(x,y)})/\pi}, \tag{12}$$

where $\gamma_{(x,y)} \in \mathcal{C}$ is the contour passing through (x,y). Choose polar coordinates (R,Θ) in $\mathcal{D}$ where Θ is measured from the given radius to which we want to map $\mathcal{L}$. The map $\phi : (x,y) \to (R,\Theta)$ is now given by :

$$R(x,y) = \tilde{f}(x,y) \ , \ \Theta(x,y) = \frac{1}{\tilde{f}(x,y)} \int_{Y(x,y)}^{x,y} \frac{ds}{(\tilde{f}_x^2 + \tilde{f}_y^2)^{1/2}}, \tag{13}$$

where $Y(x,y)$ is the point of intersection of $\mathcal{L}$ with the curve in $\mathcal{C}$ through (x,y), $\tilde{f}_x$ and $\tilde{f}_y$ are the partial derivatives, and the integral is evaluated along the curve of $\mathcal{C}$ from $Y(x,y)$ to (x,y) in the direction for which the interior is on the left.

For the proof that this map is indeed area-preserving, we refer the reader to [4]. Observe that any contour γ passing through (x,y) gets mapped to a circle of radius $\tilde{f}(x,y)$ (see Figure 3(a) for an example), and by the definition of $\tilde{f}$, they have the same area. In general, there are many area-preserving mappings from Ω to $\mathcal{D}$; we choose the above one[1] because of its nice property of mapping contours to circles. Furthermore, we will see later that by choosing $\mathcal{O}$ to be the point with the maximum load, we can achieve good results for load balancing.

Now we describe how to map Ω to $\mathcal{D}$ (the disk of area equal to that of Ω) in a distributed manner. For ease of description we assume first that $\mathcal{D}$ is a unit disk; the method described below can easily be generalized for a larger disk. Recall that the nodes on the same contour (the same value under f) will be mapped to the same circle in $\mathcal{D}$. Thus there are two steps for computing the map. First we need to form the level set of f in a distributed way. Second we will compute the virtual coordinate for each node under the area-preserving map.

There has been previous work on finding contours, one of such robust algorithms in a distributed setting is to use the *cut locus* [22, 24]. In fact, in this setting the level sets are simple – f has only a single minimum inside Ω and no saddles. We discretize the interval $[0,1]$ into $1/\varepsilon$ intervals of width ε each. Here ε depends on the density of the nodes in the network and is in the order of $O(\pi/n)$. We now find one contour cycle γ_i for each interval $[i\varepsilon,(i+1)\varepsilon]$, $0 \leq i \leq n/\pi$. The set of nodes whose values are inside $[i\varepsilon,(i+1)\varepsilon]$, denoted as C_i, naturally occupies an annulus. Note that we will choose ε according to the network density such that C_i is connected. One node, denoted as the root of this contour, r_i floods within C_i. For the purpose of the computations later, we will choose the roots r_i for different levels along a path that maps to a radius under the conformal map g. That is, the nodes whose projection under g on the positive x-axis (or is the closest to the x-axis among neighbors) will be chosen as the roots for the contours. After the flooding from r_i in C_i, the cut locus is defined as a pair of neighboring nodes whose shortest paths to the root are different and far apart. Then connecting the shortest path for the cut pair will give us a closed cycle $\gamma_i = \{z_{ij}\}$ representing the contour at the range $[i\varepsilon,(i+1)\varepsilon]$. The nodes within the band that are not selected to be on the contour cycle will be rounded to the nearest node on the contour cycle and will be handled later. Remark that the flooding is only restricted to the nodes inside the annulus and flooding for different levels does not overlap. Thus the total communication cost is linear in the number of nodes.

At the end of this procedure, we have a closed contour γ_i with a root r_i. Now we can circulate another message along γ_i to calculate the area inside γ_i. Then r_i forms

$$\tilde{f}_i = \sqrt{\text{Area}(\gamma_i)/\pi}$$

and sends this value to all nodes in the contour γ_i. This gives the radius of the circle that γ_i is mapped to. In polar coordinates (R,Θ), R for node z_{ij} lying on contour γ_i is just $\tilde{f}_i$, i.e $R(z_{ij}) = \tilde{f}_i$, $\forall j$. Now we will find the angular coordinate for each node of γ_i by computing a (discrete) integral along γ_i, which approximates the integral in Equation 11.

First we need to calculate the partial derivatives. For every node z_{ij} on the contour γ_i:

1. Locates neighbors x_{ij}^+, x_{ij}^-, y_{ij}^+, and y_{ij}^+, where x_{ij}^+ (y_{ij}^+) is the closest neighbor in the positive direction of the horizontal (vertical) line passing through z_{ij}, x_{ij}^- (y_{ij}^-) is the closest neighbor in the negative direction of the horizontal (vertical) line passing through z_{ij}. Find their values under $\tilde{f}$ through local communications.

2. Computes
$$v_x(z_{ij}) = \frac{\tilde{f}(x_{ij}^+) - \tilde{f}(x_{ij}^-)}{\text{distance}(x_{ij}^+, x_{ij}^-)}, v_y(z_{ij}) = \frac{\tilde{f}(y_{ij}^+) - \tilde{f}(y_{ij}^-)}{\text{distance}(y_{ij}^+, y_{ij}^-)}$$
and $v_{ij} = 1/(\sqrt{(v_x(z_{ij}))^2 + (v_y(z_{ij}))^2})$.

For computing $\Theta(z_{ij})$, we start from the root of the contour $r_i = z_{i0}$, for which $\Theta(r_i) = 0$. Now we just discretize the integral in Equation 11. Let $V_{i0} = 0$. A node z_{ij} gets a value $V_{i(j-1)}$ from node $z_{i(j-1)}$. It then adds the quantity $v_{ij}(\text{distance}(z_{ij}, z_{i(j-1)}))$ to this value and passes it as V_{ij} to node $z_{i(j+1)}$. In other words, the sum

$$V_{ij} = \sum_{k=0}^{j} v_{ij}(\text{distance}(z_{ij}, z_{i(j-1)}))$$

is updated by node z_{ij}. We finally define $\Theta(z_{ij}) = (V_{ij})/(\tilde{f}_i)$. In this way all the nodes on contours find their positions inside the disk in polar coordinates. Setting $u = R\cos\Theta$ and $v = R\sin\Theta$ gets them the cartesian coordinates. Denote this map as $\phi : (x,y) \to (u,v)$.

For nodes that are not on any contour in the above method, a simple "interpolation" function can be used.

5.2.2 *Finding the contour generating function*

The previous section assumed the knowledge of f—the contour generating function. In this section we describe how we generate contours for an arbitrary domain.

For many shapes, the contours can be generated easily just by shrinking the boundary by appropriate factors. For instance, consider the case of star-shaped polygons $\mathcal{P}$; one can find the center of this polygon p (the point from which the entire polygon is "visible") and find the distance of every point x on the boundary to p. Let L_{px} denote the line segment between p and x and ℓ_{px} denote

[1] To the best of our knowledge, the map described in [4] has not been used before for load-balancing purposes.

its length. Define the ith contour γ_i by

$$\gamma_i = \{q_x \in L_{px} : \text{distance}(q_x, p) = \epsilon_i \ell_{px}; x \in \mathcal{P}\}$$

where the $\epsilon_i \in (0, 1)$ are constants. Figure 3(b) shows an example of this. Note that the contours attained in this way are non-differentiable, i.e. they will have corners.

We describe next one elegant and simple method to get a smooth contour generating function for any domain Ω. Let $g : \Omega \to \mathbb{D}$ be the *conformal mapping* from the polygon to the disk. Define $f : \Omega \to [0, 1]$ by $f(x, y) = |g(x, y)|$ where $|g(x, y)|$ denotes the distance of $g(x, y)$ from the origin. It is now clear that $f^{-1}(a)$ for some $a \in [0, 1]$ will be a simple closed curve γ inside Ω. Furthermore, the pre-image of the interval $[0, 1]$ can be seen to be a curve joining $\mathcal{O}$ to $g^{-1}(1)$ which intersects every contour only once. We define $\mathcal{L} := g^{-1}([0, 1])$ and then use the mapping described in the previous section. The second figure in Figure 3(c) illustrates this method for a pentagon. As mentioned, the contours are smoothed out. Care should be taken when deciding on which point inside the polygon is to be mapped to the origin on the unit disk; essentially the point should not be too close to the boundary of the polygon, since then the contours would no longer be uniformly dense.

In a distributed setting, every node z wants to find its image in the unit disk under the conformal mapping $g(z)$. The map g depends only on the polygon $\mathcal{P}$ - boundary of the domain Ω. Another freedom in the Schwarz-Christoffel mapping is that we can choose which node in Ω to be mapped to the origin of disk. For our purposes, we feel it is reasonable to map the node with expected high traffic load (e.g., the centroid of $\mathcal{P}$) under the shortest path routing scheme to the origin. This is because the method that we use to alleviate load in the disk assume the center to be overloaded and then try to route away from it. However, this node should not be very close to the boundary as stated earlier, for so the contours would not be uniformly dense; if this happens, we choose an arbitrary node closer to this node, but is farther from the boundary.

With all this information, a single node (e.g., the base station) computes the parameters of the conformal mapping. Only the information about the parameters in the Schwarz-Christoffel mapping g is relayed to all nodes via flooding. Using the functional form of g, the nodes individually compute their own pre-images and compose with e^{-1} as above to find their coordinates in the disk. Once every sensor node with original coordinate z has found $g(z)$ (its image under the conformal map to the disk), it calculates $f(z)$ which is just the distance of $g(z)$ from the origin. $f(z)$ is the contour generating function. In this method, the information relayed is only $O(k)$, where $k \ll n$ is the number of vertices of the polygon and is much smaller than n, the number of sensors in the domain. The contour function for the shrinking method for star-shaped polygons is just the distance of every node to the center of the star, which can be computed by each node individually by routing to the center node.

5.3 Analysis of the Algorithm

Computational Complexity and Memory Requirements The distributed algorithm provided above is very light-weight in terms of both computational complexity and memory requirements. The parameters of the Schwarz-Christoffel conformal mapping can be computed to ϵ accuracy in $O(k \log \frac{1}{\epsilon})$ computations [3], where k is the number of nodes on the boundary of the domain. Only one node, the base station has to undergo this cost. All the other nodes undergo a subsequent $\Theta(1)$ cost to compute the area-preserving map. Routing on the spherical metric in virtual coordinates also requires $\Theta(1)$ computations per node on the routing path.

The same holds for the memory requirements. The base station has to store the $\Theta(k)$ coordinates of the vertices on the boundary. After the conformal map is computed, all nodes require $\Theta(1)$ memory for storing quantities aiding in the computation of the area-preserving map. Once the virtual corodinates on the disk (and hence on the sphere) are obtained, a node only stores its virtual coordinate and that of its neighbors.

Guaranteeing Delivery For an arbitrary domain, greedy routing can get stuck at a local minima. However, because our coordinates are either in the disk or on the sphere (both convex shapes), for a dense network it is very unlikely that greedy routing gets stuck. Moreover, if the density is not high enough and greedy routing does get stuck, we can still ensure delivery by using the contours. The node at which the packet is stuck can always use the "contour" routes to route along its contour until it finds a node that can continue greedy routing. Although this might change the load function, the effect would not be drastic as 1) Such instances would be rare due to convexity of the target domain in which the virtual coordinates lie and 2) The expected detour would be very small. In the next section, we always compare our newly developed methods to shortest path routing on the original domain Ω because greedy routing can get stuck, in which case packets are not delivered, and our conclusions about the change in load function would be erroneous.

6. SIMULATIONS

All experiments were performed on the $C\#$ Simulator, and for the conformal mapping we use the Schwarz-Christoffel toolbox [1] developed for MATLAB [15]. For the communication network we consider both unit disk graph model and quasi-unit disk graph model. We perform experiments on several networks in domains of different shapes. The first experiment considers a network inside a disk. We place about $1500 - 2000$ nodes on a perturbed grid with an average degree of 7.3. We evaluate different routing schemes on the disk - using the Lambert's azimuthal mapping (and then routing greedily on the spherical coordinates), Curveball Routing [18], the optimal approximation [18] and shortest path routing. For a domain of arbitrary shape, we give it virtual coordinates in the disk using the area-preserving mapping and then implement all the aforementioned routing schemes. We compare them with the shortest path routing on the original domain. We can summarize our observations as follows:

1. For the case of a disk, shortest path routing gives a heavily loaded center. Routing using Lambert's azimuthal mapping gives the best results – lower average and maximum load than those of Curveball routing. The maximum stretch of routing with Lambert's azimuthal mapping is less than 1.9 (compared to the theoretical upper bound of 2 in Theorem 8). Notice that the optimum approximation (presented in [18]) gives even lower average and maximum traffic load in majority of the network, but has a much higher load at the network boundary. See Figure 4.
2. For a domain of arbitrary shape (except the disk), using almost any of the above routing schemes on the disk after applying the area-preserving map gives considerably better results than shortest path routing on the original domain. This improvement occurs for a variety of domains of different shapes. In these experiments, using curveball routing on the disk rather than routing with the Lambert's azimuthal mapping appears to be slightly better for reducing nodes with heavy load.
3. The above statements also hold for a quasi-unit disk graph model with reasonable degree variance and link asymmetry.

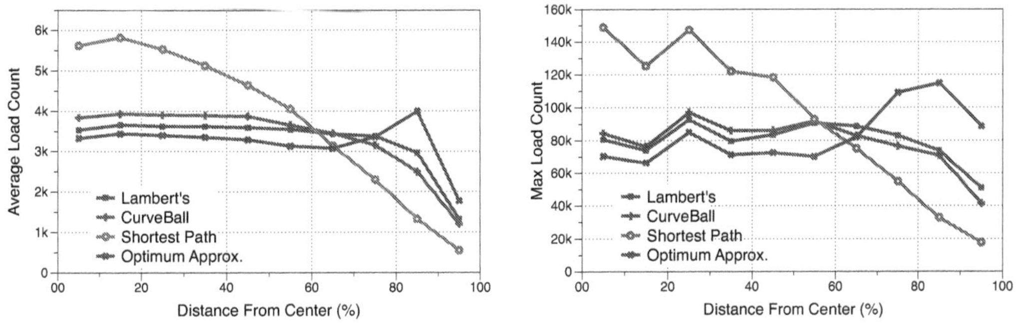

(a) Average load

(b) Maximum load

Figure 4. Histogram of (a) average load and (b) maximum load as a function of distance from the center. The network has 1500 nodes on a perturbed grid.

4. When we decrease the average degree, the difference between our method and shortest path routing begins to diminish, and at average degree around 5 they are very similar. As the network becomes sparse, the choice of paths with bounded stretch becomes fewer. Thus the different routing algorithms converge to roughly the same set of paths.

We provide an example of the area-preserving mapping from a pentagon with 238 nodes and average degree 7.24 to the disk in Figure 5 (a). After getting coordinates on the disk, the comparison of various routing schemes on virtual and original coordinates (in the pentagon) is provided in Figure 5 (b). The maximum load of shortest path routing decreased by about 19% when we use the area-preserving map to the disk and Curveball routing thereafter, and by similar percentages for area-preserving map followed by the azimuthal mapping. Note that this improvement comes only at the cost of maximum 4% increase in the average load (which achieves the minimum by shortest path routing). The optimum approximation in [18] still suffers from abnormally high load at the boundary, but performs similarly otherwise.

Fig. 6 presents the other result of the load balancing performance on a cross shape domain. With Lambert's mapping, the maximum load of the domain is reduced by 18%; while Curveball and optimum approximation achieve even better, up to 30%. This clearly shows that area-preserving mapping to a unit disk drastically reduced the load. Note that for "fat" and convex domains, the reduction in load was even more prominent, which is to be expected.

To demonstrate the scaling law of the maximum traffic load in an irregular shaped domain, we tested the L-shape network for different network size. In particular we try shortest path routing on the original network as well as the Lambert based greedy routing approach after an area preserving map to a disk. We calculate the highest traffic load by both routing algorithm. By our analysis, the first scales in the order of $O(n^2)$ and the second scales in the order of $O(n\sqrt{n})$. See Figure 7.

We also test the routing stretch in domains of different shapes. The maximum routing stretch factor was 1.96.

7. CONCLUSION

A clear open problem is to consider non-simple domains, i.e., domains with holes. We remark that bounded load balancing would become much more challenging as one has to also consider paths of different homotopy types (getting around holes in different ways). In particular, an extreme case of the problem on a multi-connected domain could be load balanced routing on a planar graph, which is known to be NP-hard. New ideas are needed to solve that case and this remains one of the most interesting future directions.

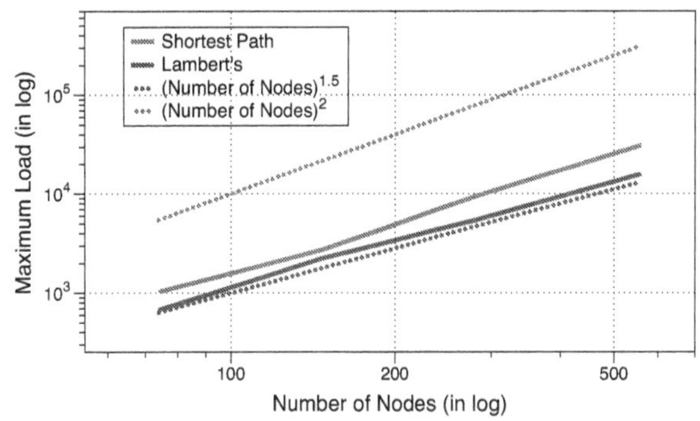

Figure 7. A comparison of maximum load in a L-shaped domain with different routing algorithms. While shortest path have higher maximum load, by Lambert's method, we provide the maximum load closed to $\Theta(n\sqrt{n})$.

We would like to remark that this paper considers load balanced routing by unsplittable flows. Load balanced routing with splittable flows can be reduced to linear programming and thus solved optimally. However, such a solution would be centralized and in some sense less practical. How to incorporate multipath routing using simple, greedy routing solutions will be another interesting direction.

Acknowledgement: Xiaomeng Ban, Jie Gao, Xianfeng David Gu and Chien-Chun Ni acknowledge the support from NSF through CNS-1116881, CNS- 1217823, and DMS-1221339.

8. REFERENCES

[1] *Schwarz-Christoffel toolbox for MATLAB.* http://www.math.udel.edu/~driscoll/SC/.

[2] M. Andrews and L. Zhang. Hardness of the undirected congestion minimization problem. *SIAM Journal on Computing*, 37(1):112–131, 2007.

[3] C. Bishop. Conformal mapping in linear time. *Discrete and Comput. Geometry*, 44(2):330–428, 2010.

[4] A. B. Brown and M. Halperin. On certain area-preserving maps. *Annals of Mathematics*, 36(4):833–837, Oct. 1935.

[5] J. Bruck, J. Gao, and A. Jiang. MAP: Medial axis based geometric routing in sensor networks. *Wireless Networks*, 13(6):835–853, 2007.

[6] C. Chekuri, S. Khanna, and F. B. Shepherd. An $o(\sqrt{n})$-approximation for EDP in undirected graphs and directed acyclic graphs. *Theory of Computing*, 2:137–146, 2006.

[7] J. Chuzhoy and S. Khanna. New hardness results for undirected edge-disjoint paths. Manuscript, 2005.

[8] Q. Fang, J. Gao, and L. Guibas. Locating and bypassing routing holes in sensor networks. In *Mobile Networks and Applications*, volume 11, pages 187–200, 2006.

[9] J. Gao and L. Zhang. Load balanced short path routing in wireless networks. *IEEE Transactions on Parallel and Distributed Systems,*

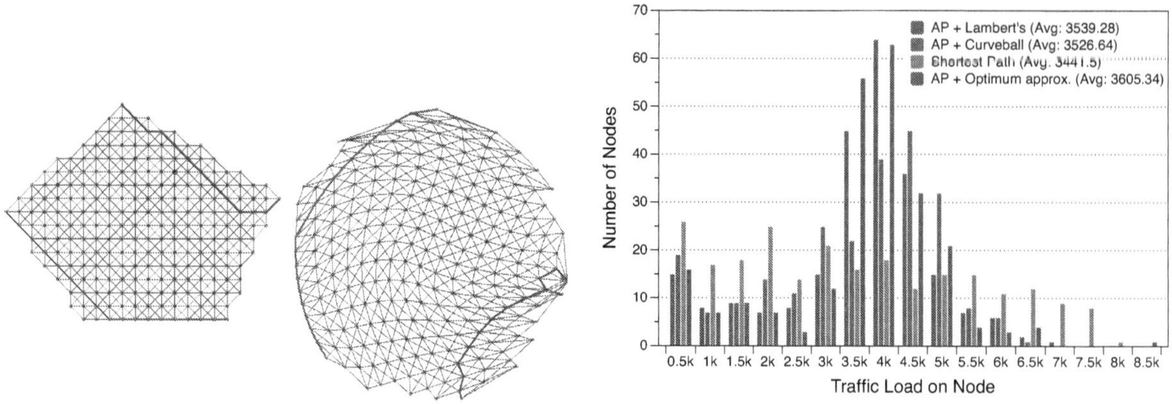

(a) Area preserving map

(b) Load distribution

Figure 5. (a) A pentagon with grid nodes and area-preserving map to disk using contours by conformal mapping method (238 nodes, avg degree 7.24.) (b) A comparison of the routing schemes. The X axis represents the node's traffic load on range of loads, while the Y axis shows number of nodes of the corresponding load range. Note the decrease in maximum load on using area-preserving map followed by either azimuthal or stereographic mapping to sphere compared to shortest path routing.

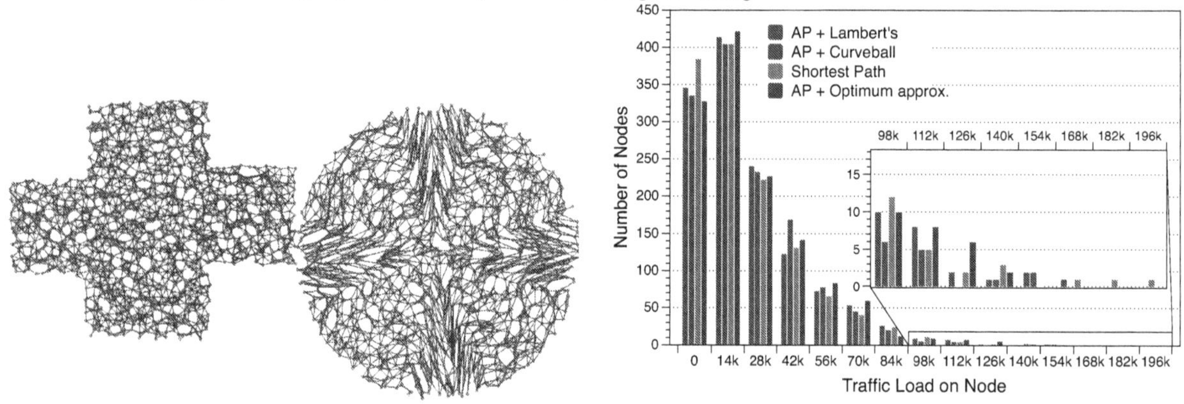

(a) Average load

(b) Maximum load

Figure 6. A network in a cross-shaped domain with 1302 perturbed grid nodes and avg. degree 7.38.

Special Issue on Localized Communications, 17(4):377–388, April 2006.

[10] J. Gao and L. Zhang. Tradeoffs between stretch factor and load balancing ratio in routing on growth restricted graphs. *IEEE Transactions on Parallel and Distributed Computing*, 20(2):171–179, February 2009.

[11] E. A. Jonckheere, M. Lou, F. Bonahon, and Y. Baryshnikov. Euclidean versus hyperbolic congestion in idealized versus experimental networks. *CoRR*, abs/0911.2538, 2009.

[12] B. Karp and H. Kung. GPSR: Greedy perimeter stateless routing for wireless networks. In *Proc. of the ACM/IEEE International Conference on Mobile Computing and Networking (MobiCom)*, pages 243–254, 2000.

[13] R. M. Karp. Reducibility Among Combinatorial Problems. In R. E. Miller and J. W. Thatcher, editors, *Complexity of Computer Computations*, pages 85–103. Plenum Press, 1972.

[14] J. Li and P. Mohapatra. Analytical modeling and mitigation techniques for the energy hole problem in sensor networks. *Pervasive and Mobile Computing*, 3(3):233–254, 2007.

[15] MATLAB. version 7.10.0 (r2010a). *The MathWorks Inc.,Natick, Massachusetts*, 2010.

[16] A. Mei and J. Stefa. Routing in outer space: fair traffic load in multi-hop wireless networks. In *MobiHoc '08: Proceedings of the 9th ACM international symposium on Mobile ad hoc networking and computing*, pages 23–32, New York, NY, USA, 2008. ACM.

[17] C. H. Papadimitriou and D. Ratajczak. On a conjecture related to geometric routing. *Theor. Comput. Sci.*, 344(1):3–14, 2005.

[18] L. Popa, A. Rostamizadeh, R. Karp, C. Papadimitriou, and I. Stoica. Balancing traffic load in wireless networks with curveball routing. In *MobiHoc '07: Proceedings of the 8th ACM international symposium on Mobile ad hoc networking and computing*, pages 170–179, New York, NY, USA, 2007. ACM.

[19] P. Raghavan. Probabilistic construction of deterministic algorithms: approximating packing integer programs. *J. Comp. and System Sciences*, pages 130–143, 1988.

[20] P. Raghavan and C. D. Thompson. Provably good routing in graphs: regular arrays. In *Proceedings of the 17th annual ACM Symposium on Theory of Computing*, pages 79–87, 1985.

[21] R. Sarkar, W. Zeng, J. Gao, and X. D. Gu. Covering space for in-network sensor data storage. In *Proc. of the 9th International Symposium on Information Processing in Sensor Networks (IPSN'10)*, pages 232–243, April 2010.

[22] Y. Wang, J. Gao, and J. S. B. Mitchell. Boundary recognition in sensor networks by topological methods. In *Proc. of the ACM/IEEE International Conference on Mobile Computing and Networking (MobiCom)*, pages 122–133, September 2006.

[23] X. Yu, X. Ban, R. Sarkar, W. Zeng, X. D. Gu, and J. Gao. Spherical representation and polyhedron routing for load balancing in wireless sensor networks. In *Proc. of 30th Annual IEEE Conference on Computer Communications (INFOCOM'11)*, April 2011.

[24] X. Zhu, R. Sarkar, J. Gao, and J. S. B. Mitchell. Light-weight contour tracking in wireless sensor networks. In *Proceedings of the 27th Annual IEEE Conference on Computer Communications (INFOCOM'08)*, pages 960–967, May 2008.

An Overlay Architecture for Throughput Optimal Multipath Routing

Nathaniel M. Jones
MIT Lincoln Laboratory
Lexington, MA

Georgios S. Paschos
MIT, Cambridge, MA &
CERTH-ITI, Greece

Brooke Shrader
MIT Lincoln Laboratory
Lexington, MA

Eytan Modiano
MIT, Cambridge, MA

ABSTRACT

Legacy networks are often designed to operate with simple single-path routing, like shortest-path, which is known to be throughput suboptimal. On the other hand, previously proposed throughput optimal policies (i.e., backpressure) require every device in the network to make dynamic routing decisions. In this work, we study an overlay architecture for dynamic routing such that only a subset of devices (overlay nodes) need to make dynamic routing decisions. We determine the essential collection of nodes that must bifurcate traffic for achieving the maximum multicommodity network throughput. We apply our optimal node placement algorithm to several graphs and the results show that a small fraction of overlay nodes is sufficient for achieving maximum throughput. Finally, we propose a heuristic policy (OBP), which dynamically controls traffic bifurcations at overlay nodes. In all studied simulation scenarios, OBP not only achieves full throughput, but also reduces delay in comparison to the throughput optimal backpressure routing.

Categories and Subject Descriptors

C.2.1 [**Computer-Communication Networks**]: Network Architecture and Design - Packet-Switching Networks

Keywords

overlay; multipath routing; backpressure routing

The Lincoln Laboratory portion of this work was sponsored by the Department of the Air Force under Air Force Contract FA8721-05-C-0002. Opinions, interpretations, conclusions and recommendations are those of the authors and are not necessarily endorsed by the United States Government. This work was also supported by NSF grant CNS-0915988, ONR grant N00014-12-1-0064, and ARO MURI grant W911NF-08-1-0238. The work of G. Paschos was supported in part by the WiNC project of the Action: Supporting Postdoctoral Researchers, funded by national and Community funds (European Social Fund).

MobiHoc'14, August 11–14, 2014, Philadelphia, PA, USA.

ACM 978-1-4503-2620-9/14/08 ...$15.00.
http://dx.doi.org/10.1145/2632951.2632957.

1. INTRODUCTION

We study optimal routing in networks where some legacy nodes are replaced with overlay nodes. While the legacy nodes perform only forwarding on pre-specified paths, the overlay nodes are able to dynamically route packets. *Dynamic backpressure* is known to be an optimal routing policy, but it typically requires a homogeneous network, where all nodes participate in control decisions. Instead, we assume that only a subset of the nodes are controllable; these nodes form a network overlay within the legacy network. The choice of the overlay nodes is shown to determine the *throughput region* of the network.

A first finding is that ring networks require exactly 3 controllable (overlay) nodes to enable the same throughput region as when all nodes are controllable, independent of the total number of nodes in the network. Motivated by this, we develop an algorithm for choosing the minimum number of controllable nodes required to enable the full throughput region. We evaluate our algorithm on several classes of regular and random graphs. In the case of random networks with a power-law degree distribution, which is a common model for the Internet, we find that fewer than 80 out of 1000 nodes are required to be controllable to enable the full throughput region.

Since standard backpressure routing cannot be directly applied to the overlay setting, we develop a heuristic extension to backpressure routing that determines how to route packets between overlay nodes. Simulation results confirm that maximum throughput can be attained with our policy in several scenarios, when only a fraction of legacy nodes are replaced by controllable nodes. Moreover, we observe reduced delay relative to the case where all nodes are controllable and operate under backpressure routing.

1.1 Motivation and Related Work

Backpressure (BP) routing, first proposed in [10], is a throughput optimal routing policy that has been studied for decades. Its strength lies in discovering multipath routes and utilizing them optimally without knowledge of the network parameters, such as arrival rates, link capacities, mobility, fading, etc. Nevertheless, the adoption of this routing policy has not been embraced for general use on the Internet. This is due, in part, to an inability of backpressure routing to coexist with legacy routing protocols. With few exceptions, backpressure routing has been studied in homogeneous networks, where all nodes are dynamically controllable and implement the backpressure policy across

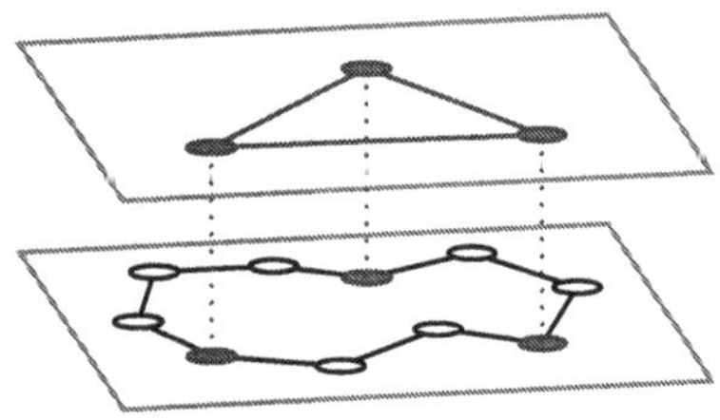

Figure 1: Example of a network overlay. The bottom plane shows the full network graph, while the top plane shows a subset of network nodes and their conceptual overlay connectivity. In this work we study network throughput under the assumption that overlay nodes implement dynamic routing schemes and underlay nodes forward packets using pre-specified paths.

all nodes uniformly. As will be shown, backpressure routing — as proposed in [10] — is suboptimal when applied only to a subset of nodes in the network.

Techniques to provide throughput-optimal multipath routing have been explored in various contexts. The work in [3] considers the problem of setting link weights provided to the Open Shortest Path First (OSPF) routing protocol such that, when coupled with bifurcating traffic equally among shortest paths, the network achieves throughput equal to the optimal multicommodity flow. The authors of [11] use an entropy maximization framework to develop a new throughput-optimal link state routing protocol where each router intelligently bifurcates traffic for each destination among its outgoing links. These techniques all require centralized control, universal adoption by all network nodes, or both; thus none of these techniques could provide incremental deployment of throughput optimal routing to wireless networks. Moreover, these techniques cannot be used in conjunction with throughput optimal dynamic control schemes, such as backpressure.

We would like to enable new network control policies to be deployed in existing networks, alongside legacy nodes that are unaware of the new control policies. There are many reasons to integrate controllable nodes into heterogeneous networks in a gradual manner, not the least of which is the financial cost of replacing all nodes at once. Other reasons include a need to maintain compatibility with current applications and special purpose hardware, a lack of ownership to decommission legacy equipment, and a lack of administrative privilege to modify existing software.

Conceptually, we model controllable nodes as operating in a network overlay on top of a legacy network. Network overlays are frequently used to deploy new communication architectures in legacy networks [8]. To accomplish this, messages from the new technology are encapsulated in the legacy format, allowing the two methods to coexist in the legacy network. Nodes making use of the new communication methods are then connected in a conceptual network overlay that operates on top of the legacy network, as shown in Figure 1.

Several works have considered the use of network overlays to improve routing in the Internet. The work in [1] proposes resilient overlay networks (RON) to find paths around network outages on a faster timescale than BGP. Similarly, [4] proposed a method for choosing placement of overlay nodes to improve path diversity in overlay routes. While both of the preceding works show that their strategies choose high quality single-path routes, we go further and identify multipath routes that offer maximum throughput.

Delay reduction for BP routing has been studied in a variety of scenarios. While multipath routes are required to support the full throughput region, the exploratory phase of BP can lead to large queues when the offered load is low and single-path routes would suffice. In [6], a hybrid policy combining BP with shortest-path routing is proposed, where flows are biased towards shortest-path routes, yet still support the full throughput region. This hybrid policy is extended in [5] to also include digital fountain codes, and shown to achieve good end-to-end delay performance in the presence of random link failures. The work in [12] develops a policy that achieves a similar shortest-path result by minimizing the average hop count used by flows. In a scenario with multiple clusters that are intermittently connected, [9] combines BP with source routing in a network overlay model to separate the queue dynamics of intra-cluster traffic from longer inter-cluster delays. The work in [2] applies shadow queues to allow the use of per-neighbor FIFO queues instead of per-commodity queues, as is typical with differential backlog routing, and finds that this can improve network delay. These prior works assume a homogeneous scenario where all nodes use the same control policy and thus differ fundamentally from our approach.

1.2 Problem Statement and Contributions

Given a graph G with nodes $\mathcal{N}$ supporting shortest-path routes between each pair of nodes, we wish to identify a minimal set of controllable nodes $\mathcal{V} \subseteq \mathcal{N}$ such that if only these nodes are allowed to bifurcate traffic, maximum throughput can be achieved. Given any subset of nodes that are controllable, we also wish to develop an optimal routing policy that operates solely on these nodes.

Ideally, we would like to solve P1,

$$V_1^* = \min_{\mathcal{V} \subseteq \mathcal{N}} |\mathcal{V}| \quad \text{s.t.} \quad \Lambda_G(\mathcal{V}) = \Lambda_G(\mathcal{N}) , \qquad \text{(P1)}$$

where $\Lambda_G(\mathcal{V})$ is the throughput region (i.e., the set of multicommodity arrival rate vectors that can be stably supported by the network) for graph G when only nodes $\mathcal{V}$ are controllable, while $\Lambda_G(\mathcal{N})$ is the throughput region when all nodes are controllable. Note that comparing throughput regions directly can be difficult, so instead we identify a condition that is necessary and sufficient to guarantee the full throughput region, and then we search for the minimal $\mathcal{V}$ that satisfies this condition. Second, we develop a modified BP routing policy and show through simulation that if applied on nodes $\mathcal{V}$, it stabilizes any arrival vector in $\Lambda_G(\mathcal{V})$. Our solutions for the first and second problems are complementary, in the sense that they can be used together to solve the joint problem. However, our node placement algorithm can be used with other policies, and our backpressure policy works under any overlay node placement.

Our contributions are summarized below.

- We formulate the problem of placing the minimum number of overlay (controllable) nodes in a legacy network in order to achieve the full multicommodity throughput region and provide an efficient placement algorithm.
- We apply our placement algorithm to several scenarios of interest including regular and random graphs, show-

ing that in some cases, only a small fraction of overlay nodes is sufficient for maximum throughput.

- We propose a dynamic control policy — OBP — as a modification of BP for use at overlay nodes. We show via simulation that OBP can outperform BP when limited to control at overlay nodes, and that OBP also has better delay performance compared to BP with control at all nodes.

2. MODEL

We model the network as a directed graph $G = (\mathcal{N}, \mathcal{E})$, where $\mathcal{N}$ is the set of nodes in the network and $\mathcal{E}$ is the set of edges. We assume that the underlay network provides a fixed realization for shortest-path routes between all pairs of nodes, and that uncontrollable nodes will forward traffic only along the given shortest-path routes. Further, we assume that only one path is provided between each pair of nodes. Let P_{ab}^{SP} be the shortest path from a to b, and let $\mathcal{P}^{\text{SP}} = (P_{ab}^{\text{SP}})$, for all pairs $a, b \in \mathcal{N}$, be the set of all shortest paths provided by the underlay network. If (i, j) is a link in G, then we assume that the single hop path is available, i.e. $P_{ij}^{\text{SP}} \in \mathcal{P}^{\text{SP}}$. Whenever a packet enters a forwarding node, the node inspects the corresponding routing table and sends the packet towards the pre-specified path. Therefore, the performance of the system depends on the available set of paths $\mathcal{P}^{\text{SP}}$. *Optimal substructure* is assumed for shortest-paths, such that if shortest-path P_{ac}^{SP} from node a to c includes node b, then path P_{ac}^{SP} includes shortest-paths P_{ab}^{SP}, from a to b, and P_{bc}^{SP}, from b to c. This optimal substructure is consistent with shortest-paths in OSPF, a widely used routing protocol based on Dijkstra's shortest-path algorithm [8], where OSPF allows for the use of lowest next-hop router ID as a method for choosing between multiple paths of equal length.

Next, we consider the subset of nodes $\mathcal{V} \subseteq \mathcal{N}$, called *overlay* or *controllable* nodes, which can bifurcate traffic throughput different routes. Intuitively, these nodes can improve throughput performance by generating new paths and enabling multipath routing. The remaining uncontrollable nodes $u \in \mathcal{N} \setminus \mathcal{V}$ provide only shortest-path forwarding in the underlay network, with an exception that any uncontrollable node u can bifurcate all traffic that originates at u; this may occur, for example, in the source applications at uncontrollable nodes, or in a shim-layer between the network-layer and application-layer. Without such an exception, all sources may be required to be controllable nodes.

Controllable nodes can increase the achievable throughput region by admitting new paths to the network as concatenations of existing paths from shortest-path routing. A *2-concatenation* of shortest-paths P_{av}^{SP} and P_{vb}^{SP} is an acyclic path from a to b, P_{ab}, where $v \in \mathcal{V}$ is a controllable node and v is the only node shared between shortest-paths P_{av}^{SP} and P_{vb}^{SP}. Note that a 2-concatenation of acyclic paths will always be acyclic, as we only allow the concatenated paths to share the overlay node v at which concatenation is performed. An *n-concatenation* is then the concatenation of n shortest-paths at $n-1$ controllable nodes, performed as a succession of $(n-1)$ 2-concatenations, and therefore acyclic. Consider the set of paths $\mathcal{P}(\mathcal{V})$, which contains all underlay paths $\mathcal{P}^{\text{SP}}$ as well as all possible n-concatenations of these paths at the controllable nodes $\mathcal{V}$. We will see that this set $\mathcal{P}(\mathcal{V})$ plays a role in the achievability of the throughput region.

3. THROUGHPUT REGION

The *throughput region* $\Lambda_G(\mathcal{V})$ is the set of all arrival rates that can be achieved by any policy implemented at controllable nodes $\mathcal{V}$ on graph G. For the case where all nodes are controllable, i.e., $\mathcal{V} = \mathcal{N}$, the throughput region equals the stability region of graph G. This section characterizes this region for a given set of paths $\mathcal{P}(\mathcal{V})$.

Packets destined for node c are called *commodity* c packets. Let λ_a^c be the rate of exogenous arrivals at node a for commodity c, and let $\boldsymbol{\lambda} = (\lambda_a^c)$ be the multicommodity arrival rate vector for all sources a and commodities c. Let $f_{ij}^{ab,c}$ be the *edge-flow* for commodity c on edge (i, j) along the shortest-path from node a to b. Flow for a path is allowed only on the edges along that path, i.e. $f_{ij}^{ab,c} = 0$ unless $(i, j) \in P_{ab}^{\text{SP}}$. Let $\bar{f}_{ab}^c$ be *path-flow* for commodity c along shortest-path P_{ab}^{SP}, from node a to b. Decision variable $v_i = 1$ if node i is controllable, and $v_i = 0$ otherwise, for all nodes $i \in \mathcal{N}$. The capacity of edge (i, j) is R_{ij}. The controllable throughput region $\Lambda_G(\mathcal{V})$ is then the set of all arrival rate vectors (λ_a^c) such that Eqns. (1-6) can be satisfied.

Flow Conservation:

$$\lambda_v^c = \sum_{b \in \{c, \mathcal{V} \setminus v\}} \bar{f}_{vb}^c - \sum_{d \in \mathcal{V} \setminus v} \bar{f}_{dv}^c \,, \quad \forall\, v \in \mathcal{V}, c \in \mathcal{N} \setminus v \qquad (1)$$

$$\lambda_u^c = \sum_{b \in \{c, \mathcal{V}\}} \bar{f}_{ub}^c \,, \quad \forall\, u \in \mathcal{N} \setminus \mathcal{V}, c \in \mathcal{N} \setminus u \qquad (2)$$

Path Constraint:

$$\bar{f}_{ab}^c = f_{ij}^{ab,c} \,, \quad \forall\, (i,j) \in P_{ab}^{\text{SP}} \,, \forall\, a, b, c \in \mathcal{N} \qquad (3)$$

Overlay Neighbor Constraints:

$$f_{ij}^{ab,c} \le (1 - v_i) R_{ij} \,, \quad \forall\, (i,j) \in P_{ab}^{\text{SP}} \,, a \neq i, \forall c \in \mathcal{N} \qquad (4)$$

$$f_{ij}^{ab,c} \le (1 - v_j) R_{ij} \,, \quad \forall\, (i,j) \in P_{ab}^{\text{SP}} \,, b \neq j, \forall c \in \mathcal{N} \qquad (5)$$

Edge Rate Constraint:

$$\sum_{a,b,c} f_{ij}^{ab,c} \le R_{ij} \,, \quad \forall\, (i,j) \in \mathcal{E} \qquad (6)$$

Eqn. (1) represents flow conservation of commodity c packets at controllable node v. Here, exogenous arrivals at node v equal network departures minus (endogenous) network arrivals at v. Similarly, Eqn. (2) represents flow conservation for exogenous arrivals at uncontrollable nodes. The exogenous arrivals for commodity c at uncontrollable node u are equal to network departures on the shortest-path to destination c plus network departures along shortest-paths to controllable nodes. This is the special case where uncontrollable node u is a source, in that u can dynamically route exogenous arrivals but not endogenous network arrivals. Eqn. (3) is a path constraint for each commodity c along the shortest-path from node a to node b, where the path-flow equals the edge-flow for each edge along path P_{ab}^{SP}. Eqns. (4-5) force edge-flow $f_{ij}^{ab,c} = 0$ if node i or j is a controllable node intermediate to path P_{ab}^{SP}, i.e., for $i \neq a$ and $j \neq b$, as such paths remove routing ability from intermediate controllable nodes. Eqns. (4-5) are necessary to allow for dynamic choice of controllable nodes, and are redundant with Eqn. (6) when nodes i and j both are uncontrollable. Finally, Eqn. (6) is an edge rate constraint for every edge (i, j), such that total flow over an edge is upper bounded by the edge capacity.

If there are no controllable nodes, i.e. $\mathcal{V} = \emptyset$, then Eqn. (2) simplifies to

$$\lambda_a^c = \bar{f}_{ac}^{c}\,, \quad \forall\, a, c \in \mathcal{N}, a \neq c\,, \tag{7}$$

where Eqns. (4-5) can be ignored as they are always redundant with Eqn. (6). The throughput region without controllable nodes, $\Lambda_G^{\mathrm{SP}} \equiv \Lambda_G(\emptyset)$, is thus limited to the set of arrival rate vectors $\boldsymbol{\lambda}$ such that Eqns. (7), (3) and (6) are satisfied. Indeed, these equations specify the shortest-path formulation for the throughput region on graph G, defined as $\Lambda_G^{\mathrm{SP}} \equiv \Lambda_G(\emptyset)$.

If all nodes are controllable, i.e. $\mathcal{V} = \mathcal{N}$, then there are no constraints from underlay paths and all dynamic routing decisions are allowed. Eqns. (1) and (6) simplify to

$$\lambda_a^c = \sum_{b:(a,b)\in\mathcal{E}} \bar{f}_{ab}^c - \sum_{d:(d,a)\in\mathcal{E}} \bar{f}_{da}^c\,, \quad \forall\, a, c \in \mathcal{N}, a \neq c\,, \tag{8}$$

$$\sum_c \bar{f}_{ab}^c \leq R_{ab}\,, \quad \forall\,(a,b) \in \mathcal{E}\,. \tag{9}$$

There are no uncontrollable nodes here, so Eqn. (2) is unused, and Eqns. (3), (4), and (5) are redundant with Eqns. (8) and (9). The full region $\Lambda_G \equiv \Lambda_G(\mathcal{N})$ is then defined as the set of arrival rate vectors $\boldsymbol{\lambda}$ that satisfy Eqns. (8-9). This is the largest region supported by network G.

Any work-conserving policy with shortest-path routing can support the region $\Lambda_G(\emptyset)$, while backpressure routing is known to support the full region $\Lambda_G(\mathcal{N})$. However, how to achieve the heterogeneous region $\Lambda_G(\mathcal{V})$ with a dynamic routing policy is not generally known. For heterogeneous networks, converting an uncontrollable node u into a controllable node v relaxes the constraints for node u from Eqn. (2) into Eqn. (1). Note that when node v becomes controllable, the overlay neighbor constraints from Eqns. (4-5) become active.

Recall that we assume optimal substructure for shortest-paths. We use this structure to find an additional property about the throughput region. Any path P_{ab}^{SP} that passes through a controllable node v can be split into two sub-paths P_{av}^{SP} and P_{vb}^{SP}, where optimal substructure guarantees that both sub-paths are in the set of underlay routes $\mathcal{P}^{\mathrm{SP}}$. Node v can then concatenate these sub-paths to form the original path P_{ab}^{SP}. Therefore, if there exists a flow decomposition of $\boldsymbol{\lambda}$ that uses path P_{ab}^{SP}, then there is also a flow decomposition that uses sub-paths P_{av}^{SP} and P_{vb}^{SP}. Thus, with shortest-path routing, adding controllable nodes can allow the throughput region to grow, but never causes the region to shrink. This implies a subset relationship in the throughput region with shortest-path underlay routing, such that for any overlay node sets $\mathcal{V}_1, \mathcal{V}_2 : \mathcal{V}_1 \subseteq \mathcal{V}_2 \subseteq \mathcal{N}$,

$$\Lambda_G^{\mathrm{SP}} \equiv \Lambda_G(\emptyset) \subseteq \Lambda_G(\mathcal{V}_1) \subseteq \Lambda_G(\mathcal{V}_2) \subseteq \Lambda_G(\mathcal{N}) \equiv \Lambda_G. \tag{10}$$

4. PLACEMENT OF OVERLAY NODES

We would like to place controllable nodes to solve P1, but the constraint $\Lambda_G(\mathcal{V}) = \Lambda_G(\mathcal{N})$ is difficult to evaluate directly. A simple implementation for P1 can use the fact that Λ_G is a convex polytope, choosing the minimum number of controllable nodes to satisfy all points in the throughput region, as

$$V_2^* = \min_{\mathcal{V}\subseteq\mathcal{N}} |\mathcal{V}| \quad \text{s.t.} \quad \boldsymbol{\lambda}^{(i)} \in \Lambda_G(\mathcal{V})\,, \forall \boldsymbol{\lambda}^{(i)} \in \Lambda_G\,, \tag{P2}$$

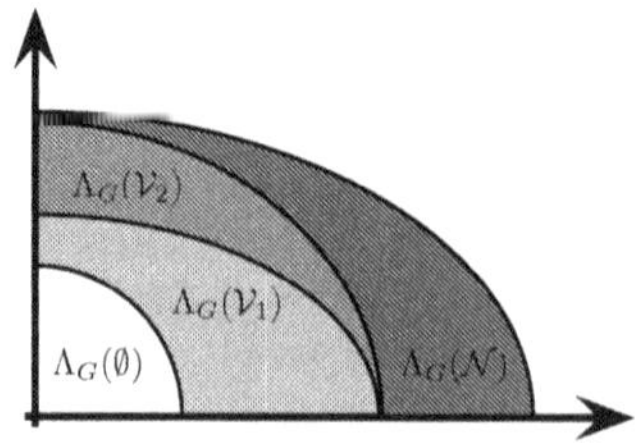

Figure 2: Projection of throughput regions $\Lambda_G(\cdot)$ for sets of overlay nodes $\mathcal{V}_1, \mathcal{V}_2 : \mathcal{V}_1 \subseteq \mathcal{V}_2 \subseteq \mathcal{N}$, indicating subset relationship as described in Eqn. (10).

where $\boldsymbol{\lambda}^{(i)}$ enumerates all extreme points of Λ_G. It is clear that P2 is equivalent to P1, although enumerating all extreme points may be impractical.

Instead of evaluating P2, we propose a surrogate condition that is easier to evaluate while still leading to the same optimal solution. Recall that the set of paths $\mathcal{P}(\mathcal{V})$ includes all underlay paths $\mathcal{P}^{\mathrm{SP}}$ and all n-concatenations (for any n) of these paths at controllable nodes $\mathcal{V}$. Let $\mathcal{P}_G$ be the set of all acyclic paths between all pairs of nodes in G. A first observation is that $\mathcal{P}(\mathcal{N}) = \mathcal{P}_G$. This holds by the assumption that all 1-hop paths are included in the set $\mathcal{P}^{\mathrm{SP}}$, and since all nodes are controllable we can produce any path in G as a concatenation of 1-hop paths. Next, we define an important condition.

Condition C.1 (All-paths) *A set of controllable nodes $\mathcal{V}$ is said to satisfy the* all-paths condition *if $\mathcal{P}(\mathcal{V}) = \mathcal{P}_G$.*

The condition requires the formation of all acyclic paths in a network. Since some of the paths are already given (in our paper $\mathcal{P}^{\mathrm{SP}}$), to satisfy the condition, a set of nodes $\mathcal{V}$ must enable all missing paths $\mathcal{P}_G \setminus \mathcal{P}^{\mathrm{SP}}$ by path concatenations. The following result establishes that this condition is necessary and sufficient for $\Lambda_G(\mathcal{V}) = \Lambda_G$. In other words, to allow for maximum throughput achievability we must choose $\mathcal{V}$ to ensure that the path concatenations on these nodes form all missing paths in the network.

Theorem 1 *Given a placement of controllable nodes $\mathcal{V}$, satisfying the all-paths condition is necessary and sufficient for maximizing the throughput region, i.e.,*

$$\Lambda_G(\mathcal{V}) = \Lambda_G \quad \textit{if and only if} \quad \mathcal{P}(\mathcal{V}) = \mathcal{P}_G.$$

The proof is in the Appendix. Using the all-paths condition C.1, we define P3:

$$V_3^* = \min_{\mathcal{V}\subseteq\mathcal{N}} |\mathcal{V}| \quad \text{s.t.} \quad \text{All-paths condition C.1.} \tag{P3}$$

Corollary 1 *P1 $\iff$ P3, therefore $V_1^* = V_3^*$.*

4.1 Overlay Node Placement Algorithm

We design an algorithm to choose the placement of overlay nodes $\mathcal{V} \subseteq \mathcal{N}$ on a given graph $G = (\mathcal{N}, \mathcal{E})$ such that the choice of overlay nodes is sufficient to satisfy the full throughput region of the network, i.e. $\Lambda_G(\mathcal{V}) = \Lambda_G(\mathcal{N})$. At the end of this section we will show that the proposed algorithm optimally solves P3.

The algorithm consists of three phases: (1) removal of degree-1 nodes; (2) constraint pruning; and (3) overlay node placement. These phases are explained below, while each step is supported by a related claim which will help proving the optimality of the algorithm.

Phase 1: Remove Degree-1 Nodes. An *attached tree* is a tree that is connected to the rest of graph G by only a single edge. An intuitive observation is that the throughput region does not increase by installing controllable nodes on attached trees. Thus, at this preparatory phase, we remove all attached trees by removing degree-1 nodes recursively, as follows. Start with original graph $G = (\mathcal{N}, \mathcal{E})$, and initialize $\mathcal{N}' := \mathcal{N}$ and $\mathcal{E}' := \mathcal{E}$. While there exists any node $n \in \mathcal{N}'$ such that degree$(n) = 1$, set $\mathcal{N}' := \mathcal{N}' \setminus n$ and set $\mathcal{E}' := \mathcal{E}' \setminus e$, where e is the only edge that connects to node n. Repeat until no degree-1 nodes remain. All remaining nodes have a degree of at least 2, thus all attached trees have been removed. The graph that remains is $G' = (\mathcal{N}', \mathcal{E}')$.

Lemma 1 *Suppose that placement $\mathcal{V}$ satisfies the all-paths condition (C.1), and $n \in \mathcal{V}$ lies on an attached tree. Then $\mathcal{V} \setminus n$ also satisfies the all-paths condition.*

PROOF. To prove $\mathcal{P}(\mathcal{V}) = \mathcal{P}(\mathcal{V} \setminus n)$, it is enough to show that for any pair $a, b \in \mathcal{N}$, the acyclic path $P_{ab} \in \mathcal{P}(\mathcal{V})$ can be formed without concatenating paths at n. Note, that if $n \notin P_{ab}$, then the requested is immediately obtained. Thus, we are free to assume that additionally to lying on an attached tree, n is also on the path P_{ab}. We study four cases:

1. Nodes a and b are both on the same attached tree: There is only one path from a to b, and this is the shortest path. Thus, $P_{ab} \in \mathcal{P}^{\text{SP}} = \mathcal{P}(\emptyset) \subseteq \mathcal{P}(\mathcal{V} \setminus n)$.
2. Node a is on a specific attached tree and node b is not on that tree: Assume that overlay nodes $w, v \in \mathcal{V} \cap P_{ab}$ *exist* on path P_{ab} such that w is not on the attached tree of node a and it is the closest overlay node to this tree on path P_{ab} (where distance is defined using hops on the path), while v is the overlay neighbor of w on the tree of a. Observe that values $w = b, n$ and $v = n$ are possible. Unless $w = b$, we have that $P_{wb} \in \mathcal{P}(\mathcal{V} \setminus n)$ since $n \notin P_{wb}$. From the fact $P_{ab} \in \mathcal{P}(\mathcal{V})$ and since v, w are overlay neighbors, we conclude $P_{vw} \in \mathcal{P}^{\text{SP}}$. By optimal substructure, we have that $P_{aw} \in \mathcal{P}^{\text{SP}}$. Concatenating at w we get $P_{ab} \in \mathcal{P}(\mathcal{V} \setminus n)$. For the case $w = b$, we immediately get $P_{vb} \in \mathcal{P}^{\text{SP}}$ and the result follows from optimal substructure. If w does not exist, then $P_{ab} \in \mathcal{P}^{\text{SP}} \subseteq \mathcal{P}(\mathcal{V} \setminus n)$. If v does not exist (this is a special case where b, n must lie on a different attached tree from a) we have $P_{aw} \in \mathcal{P}^{\text{SP}}$ thus we can still concatenate at w. Last if w, v both do not exist, then clearly $P_{ab} \in \mathcal{P}^{\text{SP}}$.
3. Node b is on a specific attached tree and node a is not on that tree: We define again w, v as in the above case. Symmetrically we have $P_{aw} \in \mathcal{P}(\mathcal{V} \setminus n)$ since $n \notin P_{aw}$, $P_{wv} \in \mathcal{P}^{\text{SP}}$ and by optimal substructure $P_{wb} \in \mathcal{P}^{\text{SP}}$. Thus, concatenating at w we obtain $P_{ab} \in \mathcal{P}(\mathcal{V} \setminus n)$. Special cases for w, v are treated in a similar manner.
4. Nodes a and b are both on G': No possible acyclic path from node a to node b can go through attached trees, as entering and exiting an attached tree forms a cycle. Thus, $n \notin P_{ab}$ from which we obtain directly $P_{ab} \in \mathcal{P}(\mathcal{V} \setminus n)$. □

By induction, it suffices to allocate overlay nodes in G' to satisfy the all-paths condition.

Overlay Node Placement Algorithm

Phase 1: Recursively remove all degree-1 nodes $\mathcal{N}_1$ and associated edges $\mathcal{E}_1$ from graph G, until no degree-1 nodes remain. The remaining graph is $G' = \{\mathcal{N}', \mathcal{E}'\}$, where $\mathcal{N}' = \mathcal{N} \setminus \mathcal{N}_1$ and $\mathcal{E}' = \mathcal{E} \setminus \mathcal{E}_1$. This removes all attached trees from G.

Phase 2: Consider the *destination tree* D_n for each node $n \in \mathcal{N}'$, and consider the degree of all nodes $b \in \mathcal{N}' \setminus n$ on tree D_n. If the degree of b on D_n is less than the degree of b on G', then prune destination tree D_n at node b by removing all edges to children of node b on D_n, and remove any nodes and edges that become disconnected from n. The remaining subgraph is the *pruned tree* D'_n.

Phase 3: Solve P4, and place an overlay node at each node n where the solution to P4 has $v_n = 1$.

Figure 3: Summary of node placement algorithm.

Phase 2: Constraint Pruning. In this phase, we define the destination trees which will be used to find the constraints for node placement. Exploiting a necessary condition from Lemma 2 regarding the placement of controllable nodes, we show that proper pruning of these destination trees will identify the set of constraints over which we minimize the allocation of controllable nodes.

By optimal substructure, the union of shortest-paths P^{SP}_{xn} to any destination n from all nodes $x \in \mathcal{N}' \setminus n$ forms destination tree D_n. Define $\{P^{\text{SP}}_{xn}\} \setminus n$ to be the set of nodes on the shortest path from x to n, excluding node n. We have the following.

Lemma 2 *If the degree of node x on tree D_n is less than the degree of x on graph G', and there is no overlay node along the shortest path from x to n (i.e. $\nexists v \in \mathcal{V} : v \in \{P^{SP}_{xn}\} \setminus n$), then the all-paths condition C.1 is not satisfied.*

PROOF. Let (b, x) be an edge in G' but not in D_n, where such an edge exists by the premise of Lemma 2. Consider path p formed from the concatenation of (b, x) and shortest-path P^{SP}_{xn}. We will show that this path cannot be formed if there are no controllable nodes in the shortest path from x to n, and thus the all-paths condition C.1 is not satisfied.

First, observe that since edge (b, x) is not on tree D_n, shortest-path P^{SP}_{bn} does not include this edge. Thus, the path p requires a concatenation of two or more shortest-paths. Such a concatenation must occur at a controllable node on path P^{SP}_{xn}. However, this is impossible since there are no controllable nodes on path P^{SP}_{xn}. Thus, C.1 is not satisfied. □

For Phase 2, we prune destination trees D_n at nodes with degree less in D_n than in G' to obtain *pruned trees* D'_n. By Lemma 2, for the all-paths condition to be satisfied it is necessary to have at least one overlay node on the shortest path to n from every leaf node of pruned tree D'_n. The pruned trees D'_n and this necessary condition from Lemma 2 will be used as constraints in Phase 3.

Phase 3: Overlay Node Placement. Consider the following binary program to place the minimum number of overlay nodes to satisfy Lemma 2 for all nodes on all pruned trees D'_n:

$$V_4^* = \min \sum_n v_n$$
$$\text{s.t.} \quad \sum_{a \in \{P_{bn}^{\text{SP}}\} \setminus n} v_a \geq 1, \ \forall b \in \text{LeafNodes}(D'_n), \ \forall n \quad \text{(P4)}$$
$$v_n \in \{0,1\}, \ \forall n$$

where LeafNodes(D'_n) is the set of all leaf nodes on pruned tree D'_n, and where $\{P_{bn}^{\text{SP}}\} \setminus n$ is defined in Phase 2. Next, we show that the placement determined by the solution of P4 satisfies the all-paths condition.

Lemma 3 *The overlay node placement of P4 satisfies the all-paths condition for graph G'.*

The proof is in the Appendix.

A summary of the algorithm is shown in Figure 3. The following main result establishes the performance of the proposed placement algorithm.

Theorem 2 *Let $\mathcal{V}^*$ be the solution produced by the overlay node placement algorithm. Then, $\mathcal{V}^*$ is an optimal solution to P3. It follows that*

- $\Lambda_G(\mathcal{V}^*) = \Lambda_G$.
- *$\mathcal{V}^*$ is an optimal solution to P1.*

PROOF. By Lemma 2, the constraint of P4 is necessary for the all-paths condition. By Lemmas 1 and 3 it is also sufficient. Thus, we have $P4 \iff P3$. By Theorem 1, the remaining assertions follow. □

Phases 1-2 of the algorithm have complexity $O(N^2)$. P4 solves a vertex cover problem, which is known to be NP-Hard in general. However, note that the constraints of our problem have optimal substructure, which might be exploitable. For our experiments on graphs with 1000 nodes, the solver found most solutions to P4 within 5 seconds, and we only rarely encountered scenarios that required more than a few minutes to solve. Thus, the algorithm is practical.

5. EXPERIMENTS WITH OPTIMAL NODE PLACEMENT

We provide results for various types of network graphs, including specific graph families and random graphs. By Theorem 1, the full throughput region is provided by the placement of our algorithm on all these cases.

5.1 Simple Scenarios

5.1.1 Trees and Forests

Consider trees with single-path underlay routes P_{ab}^{SP} for every pair of nodes a and b. A tree is loop free, and thus each path P_{ab}^{SP} is the unique acyclic path from node a to b. Thus, the all-paths condition is automatically satisfied, and $\Lambda_G(\emptyset) = \Lambda_G(\mathcal{N})$.

It follows that no controllable nodes are required for a forest, which is a disjoint union of trees.

5.1.2 Cycles and Rings

Lemma 4 *Every cycle requires at least 3 controllable nodes to satisfy the all-paths condition.*

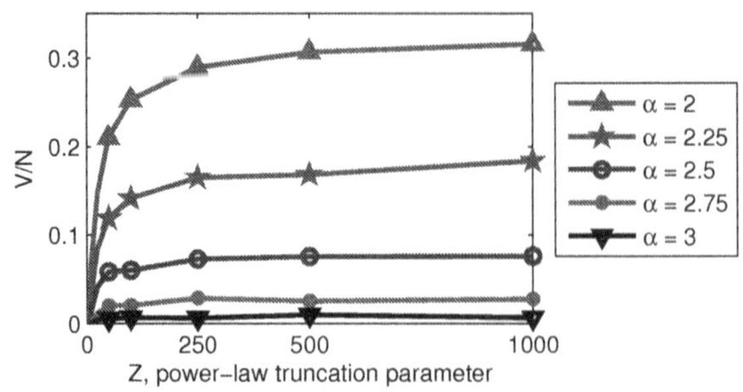

Figure 4: Results of overlay node placement algorithm on random graphs where node degree follows a power-law distribution with exponent α. Graphs generated with configuration model and truncated Zipf distribution.

PROOF. Consider controllable nodes $v, w \in \mathcal{V}$ on a cycle, and without loss of generality assume shortest-path P_{vw}^{SP} is on the cycle. Then path P_{vw}^{SP} allows one direction of flow on the cycle, and at least one additional controllable node is required to allow flow in the counter direction on the cycle. Note that the same problem occurs in scenarios with 0 or 1 controllable node on the cycle, and when path P_{vw}^{SP} is not on the cycle. Thus, at least 3 controllable nodes are required on each cycle in the network. □

Further, the lower bound from Lemma 4 is tight for the case of a ring, where the entire graph is a single cycle.

Lemma 5 *Exactly 3 controllable nodes are required to satisfy the all-paths condition for a ring network with $N \geq 5$ nodes and hop-count as the metric for shortest-path routing.*

The proof is in the Appendix.

5.1.3 Cliques

Consider cliques with single-path underlay routes P_{ab}^{SP} for every pair of nodes a and b. We require all edges (a,b) be included in the underlay routes, however there is an edge between every pair of nodes in a clique. Thus, all underlay routes are single edges, i.e. $P_{ab}^{\text{SP}} = (a,b)$ for all pairs $a, b \in \mathcal{N}$. A Hamiltonian path, traversing all nodes, will require all intermediate nodes to be controllable. Such paths can start and end at any node, therefore the all-paths condition requires all nodes to be controllable for a clique, i.e. $\mathcal{V} = \mathcal{N}$.

5.2 Random Networks

This section considers placement of overlay nodes to support the full throughput region on random graphs. We present here results about power-law graphs, where the degree of nodes is random and roughly follows a power-law distribution. This is recognized as a realistic model for the Internet [7]. We have experimented with several other models for random graphs, which are omitted here due to lack of space.

We construct random networks that have power-law degree distributions using the configuration model and a truncated Zipf distribution [7]. Zipf is a discrete distribution with parameters α and Z, where α is the power-law exponent and Z is a truncation parameter indicating the maximum degree of the distribution. The Zipf PMF is

$$\mathbb{P}(D = d) = \frac{d^{-\alpha}}{\sum_{k=1}^{Z} k^{-\alpha}}, \quad \text{for } d = 1, ..., Z.$$

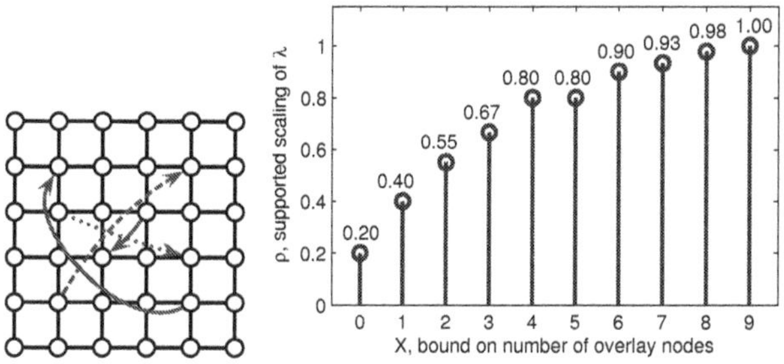

(a) Scenario (b) Node Placement Results

Figure 5: Results of P5 for chosen rate vector on 6×6 grid. (a) Arrival rate vector $\boldsymbol{\lambda}$ includes traffic demands for all all pairs of nodes. Here we consider $\boldsymbol{\lambda}$ with four active traffic demands with symmetric rates, as indicated with arrows. (b) Fraction of $\boldsymbol{\lambda}$ supported when limited to $|\mathcal{V}| \leq X$ controllable nodes.

For a given number of nodes N, the configuration model attaches a number of *stubs* to each node according to the Zipf distribution, where a stub is half of an edge. Pairs of unconnected stubs are then chosen randomly and connected to form edges. Thus, node degree follows a power-law distribution.

Figure 4 shows results from the overlay node placement algorithm for random power-law graphs with $N = 1000$ nodes, averaged over 10 realizations per data point. Values of α between 2 and 3 are considered, with $\alpha = 2.5$ being a frequent estimate for the Internet [7]. For $\alpha = 2.5$, the overlay node placement algorithm finds that less than 8% of nodes need to be controllable for the full throughput region to be achievable.

6. PLACING A LIMITED NUMBER OF OVERLAY NODES

A formulation similar to P2 is useful in scenarios where only a small subset of arrival rate vectors require support, such that the constraints are limited to the specific vectors $\boldsymbol{\lambda}^{(i)}$ of interest. For example, this includes networks with nodes that neither generate nor consume information such as network routers. This approach can also use P2 to minimize the number of controllable nodes required to allow maximum flow between a specific source and destination.

A similar formulation can be used to maximize the achievable flow when the maximum number of controllable nodes is upper bounded by some number X, as shown in P5. This can be useful in scenarios where resource limitations don't allow enough controllable nodes to achieve maximum throughput. As in P2, multiple rate vectors $\boldsymbol{\lambda}^{(i)}$ can be supported with additional constraints $\rho\boldsymbol{\lambda}^{(i)} \in \Lambda_G(\mathcal{V})$.

$$\max_{\mathcal{V}\subseteq\mathcal{N}} \rho \quad \text{s.t.} \quad \rho\boldsymbol{\lambda} \in \Lambda_G(\mathcal{V}), \quad |\mathcal{V}| \leq X. \tag{P5}$$

Figure 5 shows results of P5 on a 6×6 grid for a specific rate vector $\boldsymbol{\lambda}$ with four equal traffic demands. Figure 5b shows that a fraction 80% of throughput is supported in the direction $\boldsymbol{\lambda}$ with only $X = 4$ and diminishing returns from additional overlay nodes, with $X = 9$ required for 100% throughput.

7. BACKPRESSURE OVERLAY POLICY

Subject to the placement of overlay nodes, we study the problem of throughput maximization using dynamic routing decisions at overlay nodes.

7.1 The Control Problem

We are interested in a dynamic policy that is stable for any arrival vector in the region $\Lambda_G(\mathcal{V})$, i.e. achieves maximum throughput. Under policy π, let $\mu_{vn}^c(t,\pi)$ be the service function on the link (v,n) for commodity c packets, where $v \in \mathcal{V}$ and $n \in \mathcal{N}$. The edge rate constraint implies $\sum_c \mu_{vn}^c(t,\pi) \leq R_{vn}$ must be satisfied at every slot. Thus, at each overlay node, the policy chooses the number of packets to be sent to any outgoing neighbor by assigning values to these functions. The uncontrollable nodes $\mathcal{N} \setminus \mathcal{V}$ are assumed to only forward the packets on pre-specified shortest-paths, and are assumed to use a fair scheduler to choose between competing commodities. In our simulations we use the example of proportionally-fair random service on a packet-by-packet basis, such that node a transmits a packet of commodity c with probability $p_a^c = U_a^c / \sum_x U_a^x$, where U_a^x is the queue backlog for commodity x at uncontrollable node a.

Every overlay node $v \in \mathcal{V}$ maintains a queue for each commodity c and we denote its backlog with $Q_v^c(t)$ at slot t. For two overlay neighbors $v, w \in \mathcal{V}$, we define $F_{vw}^c(t)$ the number of commodity c packets that have departed overlay node v but have not yet reached overlay node w. We call these the *packets-in-flight* between overlay nodes v and w for commodity c. While it may be impractical to observe individual queue sizes at uncontrollable nodes, counting F_{vw}^c can be realized by looking at the difference in cumulative count for packets of commodity c sent from v to w versus the cumulative count for these packets received at w. This may be realized using a simple packet acknowledgment scheme for each pair of overlay nodes.

In what follows, we study the problem of controlling this system by observing queue backlogs Q and packets-in-flight F, and choosing service function μ at overlay nodes only.

7.2 Insufficiency of Traditional Backpressure

For an interference-free wired network, the backpressure (BP) routing policy [10] is as follows. For each link (a,b), define the differential backlog $W_{ab}^c(t)$,

$$W_{ab}^c(t) = Q_a^c(t) - Q_b^c(t), \quad \forall\,(a,b) \in \mathcal{E}, \forall\, c \in \mathcal{N},$$

and define commodity $c_{ab}^*(t)$ that maximizes this weight,

$$c_{ab}^*(t) \in \arg\max_{c\in\mathcal{N}} W_{ab}^c\,, \quad \forall\,(a,b) \in \mathcal{E}, \tag{11}$$

with ties broken arbitrarily. Then the BP policy chooses

$$\mu_{ab}^{c_{ab}^*}(t,\text{BP}) = \begin{cases} R_{ab} & \text{if } W_{ab}^{c_{ab}^*} > 0 \\ 0 & \text{otherwise,} \end{cases} \tag{12}$$

where $\mu_{ab}^c(t,\text{BP}) = 0,\ \forall c \neq c_{ab}^*$. In [10], this policy is shown to stabilize any point in the region $\Lambda_G(\mathcal{N})$.

The intuition behind the optimality of BP is that congestion information propagates through the network via queue backlogs. The policy balances neighboring backlogs, such that when node n becomes congested, any upstream neighbors of n also become congested. In our problem, the uncontrollable nodes do not use BP, and thus any congestion

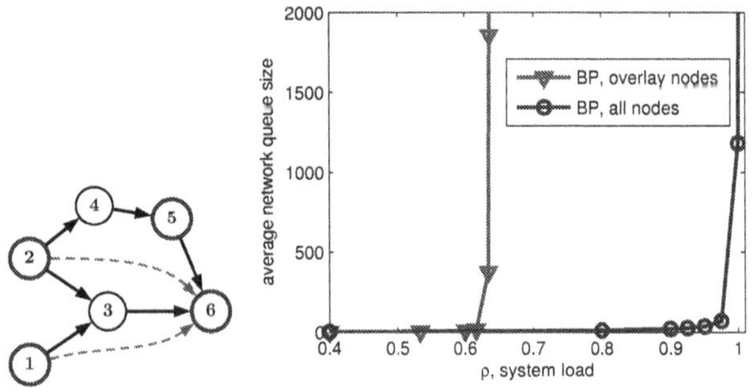

(a) Scenario (b) Simulation Results

Figure 6: Insufficiency of BP in overlay networks. (a) Scenario with contention at uncontrollable node 3. (b) Queue size of BP in overlay vs. BP in underlay.

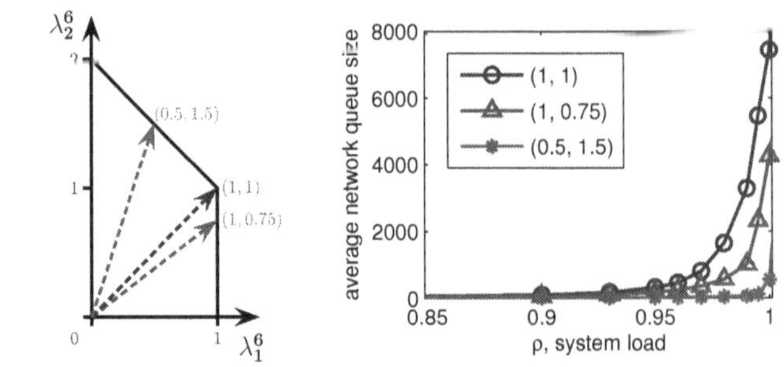

(a) Throughput Region (b) OBP Simulation Results

Figure 7: Evaluation of OBP policy on scenario from Figure 6a. (a) Throughput region of Figure 6a, with select rate vectors indicated. (b) Average queue backlog of OBP, after 1e6 time steps, for rate vectors indicated in (a).

occurring on these nodes is not propagated. This is the primary reason why we do not expect BP to perform well in our system.

Consider the example of Figure 6a, where (controllable) overlay nodes $\mathcal{V} = \{1, 2, 5, 6\}$ are indicated in blue, with directed unit-rate links. It can easily be verified that the all-paths condition C.1 is satisfied for this setting, thus $\Lambda_G(\mathcal{V}) = \Lambda_G(\mathcal{N})$. The dashed red arrows show two traffic demands with symmetric arrival rates λ. With unit-rate links, offered load $\rho = \lambda$, where $\rho < 1$ is required for this network to be stable. We examine two different cases. First, we run BP at all nodes; this achieves maximum throughout and it is stable for all $\rho < 1$. Second, we run BP only at overlay nodes, computing differential backlogs across the overlay edges, e.g. node 2 computes $W^6_{2,5} = Q^6_2 - Q^6_5$ and $W^6_{2,6} = Q^6_2 - Q^6_6$. Simulation results in Figure 6b show that BP at the overlay nodes cannot stabilize $\rho > 2/3$, i.e. it is throughput suboptimal. The intuition is as follows. Note that $Q^6_6 = 0$, since node 6 is a destination. Then, any congestion at uncontrollable node 3 cannot be detected by source node 2, leading to positive traffic flow from source 2 through node 3. This motivates our policy in the following section.

7.3 The Proposed OBP Policy

Let $\overline{\mathcal{E}}$ represent the set of edges in the overlay network. We propose the following policy, both dynamic and distributed, to account for packets-in-flight.

Overlay Backpressure (OBP). Redefine the differential backlog as

$$W^c_{vw}(t) = Q^c_v(t) - Q^c_w(t) - F^c_{vw}(t), \quad \forall (v, w) \in \overline{\mathcal{E}}, \forall c \in \mathcal{N},$$

then determine c^*_{vw} and $\mu^c_{vw}(t, \text{OBP})$ as in Eqns. (11)-(12).

Intuitively, this policy takes into account both the packet accumulation at the neighbor overlay node v, as well as any packets-in-flight on the path P_{vw}, in the form of *negative pressure*. Through simulation we observe the following properties of the algorithm. (i) OBP maximizes throughput in all examined scenarios, including the one of Figure 6a, (ii) OBP outperforms BP applied only at overlay nodes, and (iii) OBP has good delay properties, outperforming BP even when the latter is applied at all nodes.

In Figure 7, we study different arrival vectors for the network of Figure 6a. The simulation results in Figure 7b show that all studied vectors are supported by the OBP policy.

In Figure 8, we study a directed tandem network for the purpose of illustrating the delay properties of OBP. From [2] it is known that for BP on a tandem network, per-node queues grow linearly with distance from the destination, and thus network queue size grows quadratically with the total number of nodes. However, for the OBP policy we observe this linear growth of per-node queues only at controllable nodes, implying smaller total network queues size and improved delay performance when there are few controllable nodes. In this particular example, only the source is controllable, with $n - 1$ legacy nodes, a setting that corresponds to the maximum benefit. Delay is compared between BP and OBP for a fixed offered load in Figure 8b and for a fixed number of nodes in Figure 8c. Although BP is applied at all nodes it is still outperformed by OBP applied only at the source.

Finally, in Figure 9, we show simulation results from three policies: OBP, BP at all nodes, and BP with shortest-path bias (BP+SP) from [6]. Although the latter two are both throughput optimal policies, they yield worse delay than OBP. The reason is threefold: (i) the quadratic network queue size of BP is proportional to the number of controllable nodes used (in this scenario, OBP uses only 5 overlay nodes), (ii) no packets are sent to attached trees in case of OBP, and (iii) under light traffic, packets under BP perform random walks.

While our OBP policy seems to perform well in simulations, we do not believe that it is optimal in general settings. A promising future direction of research is to identify a maximally stable dynamic routing policy for our overlay architecture.

8. CONCLUSIONS

We study optimal routing in legacy networks where only a subset of nodes can make dynamic routing decisions, while the legacy nodes can forward packets only on pre-specified shortest-paths. This model captures evolving heterogeneous networks where intelligence is introduced at a fraction of nodes. We propose a necessary and sufficient condition for the overlay node placement to enable the full multicommodity throughput region. Based on this condition, we devise an algorithm for optimal controllable node placement. We run the algorithm on large random graphs to show that very often a small number of intelligent nodes suffices for full throughput. Finally, we propose a dynamic routing policy to be implemented in a network overlay, that demonstrates superior performance in terms of both throughput and delay.

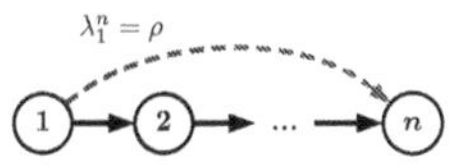

(a) Scenario

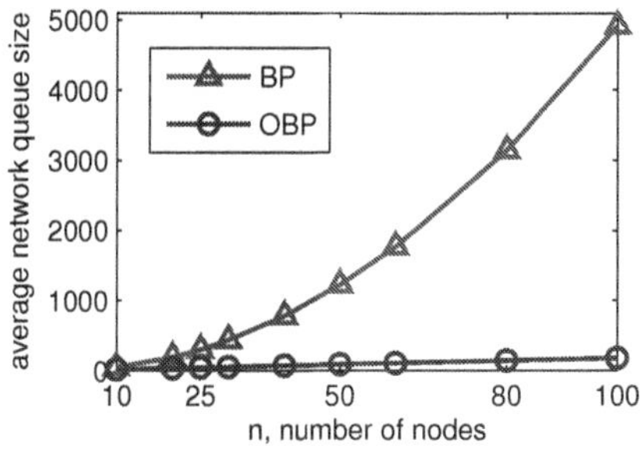

(b) Simulation Results for Fixed $\rho = 0.8$

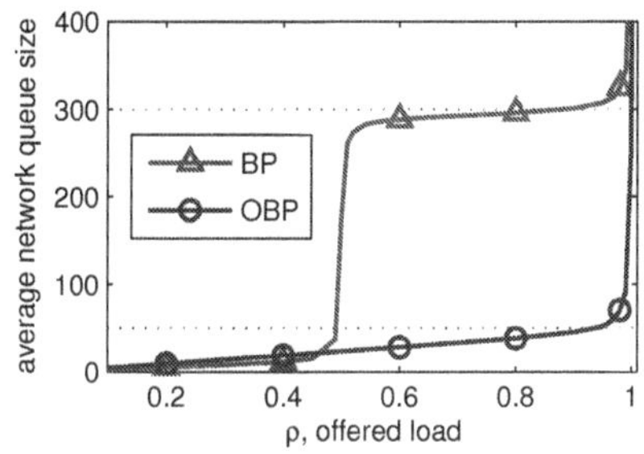

(c) Simulation Results for Fixed $n = 25$

Figure 8: Directed tandem with n nodes. (b) BP versus OBP for offered load $\rho = 0.8$. Quadratic growth for BP. Linear growth for OBP. (c) BP versus OBP for $n = 25$. Quadratic backlog in BP results for $\rho > 0.5$. Dotted horizontal line at $n(n-1)/2$ for BP, and at $2n$ for OBP.

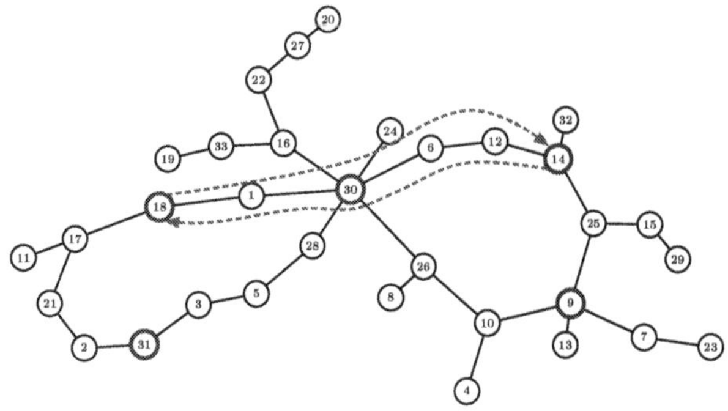

(a) Scenario

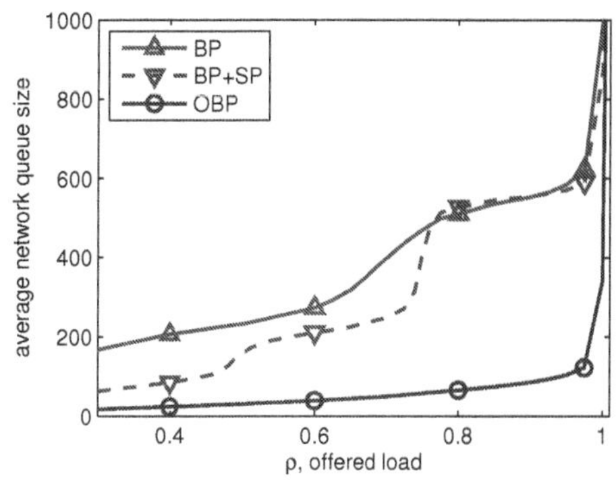

(b) Simulation Results

Figure 9: Comparing OBP with BP on a random graph. (a) Scenario with two symmetric traffic demands. (b) Average queue size for BP, BP+SP, and OBP.

9. REFERENCES

[1] D. Andersen, H. Balakrishnan, F. Kaashoek, and R. Morris. Resilient overlay networks. In *Proc. ACM SOSP*, Oct. 2001.

[2] L. Bui, R. Srikant, and A. Stolyar. Novel architectures and algorithms for delay reduction in back-pressure scheduling and routing. In *Proc. IEEE INFOCOM*, April 2009.

[3] B. Fortz and M. Thorup. Internet traffic engineering by optimizing ospf weights. In *IEEE INFOCOM*, 2000.

[4] J. Han, D. Watson, and F. Jahanian. Topology aware overlay networks. In *Proc. IEEE INFOCOM*, March 2005.

[5] W. Khan, L. B. Le, and E. Modiano. Autonomous routing algorithms for networks with wide-spread failures. In *Proc. IEEE MILCOM*, Oct. 2009.

[6] M. J. Neely, E. Modiano, and C. E. Rohrs. Dynamic power allocation and routing for time varying wireless networks. In *Proc. IEEE INFOCOM*, April 2003.

[7] M. E. J Newman. *Networks: An Introduction.* Oxford University Press, Inc., New York, NY, USA, 2010.

[8] L. L. Peterson and B. S. Davie. *Computer Networks: A Systems Approach.* Morgan Kaufmann Publishers Inc., San Francisco, CA, USA, 4th edition, 2007.

[9] J. Ryu, L. Ying, and S. Shakkottai. Back-pressure routing for intermittently connected networks. In *Proc. IEEE INFOCOM*, March 2010.

[10] L. Tassiulas and A. Ephremides. Stability properties of constrained queueing systems and scheduling policies for maximum throughput in multihop radio networks. *IEEE Trans. Auto. Control*, pages 1936–1948, Dec. 1992.

[11] D. Xu, M. Chiang, and J. Rexford. Link-state routing with hop-by-hop forwarding can achieve optimal traffic engineering. *IEEE/ACM Transactions on Networking*, 19(6):1717–1730, 2011.

[12] L. Ying, S. Shakkottai, and A. Reddy. On combining shortest-path and back-pressure routing over multihop wireless networks. In *Proc. IEEE INFOCOM*, April 2009.

APPENDIX

PROOF OF SUFFICIENCY FOR THEOREM 1. We will show that the all-paths condition is sufficient for supporting any multicommodity vector $\boldsymbol{\lambda} \in \Lambda_G$ while bifurcating traffic only at nodes $\mathcal{V}$. Feasibility of $\boldsymbol{\lambda}$ implies existence of a feasible flow decomposition of $\boldsymbol{\lambda}$. Without loss of generality, choose any one component of $\boldsymbol{\lambda}$ that sends flow from node a to node b with corresponding arrival rate λ_a^b. This arrival rate λ_a^b is supported by flow $f_{ab}^{\boldsymbol{\lambda}}$, where $f_{ab}^{\boldsymbol{\lambda}}$ can be decomposed into subflows $f_{ab}^{\boldsymbol{\lambda}}(p)$ for paths $p \in \mathcal{P}_{ab}$. Since $\mathcal{V}$ satisfies all path condition it follows that all-paths $\mathcal{P}_{ab}$ can be formed as concatenations of available shortest paths on nodes $\mathcal{V}$, and thus the feasible flow decomposition can be constructed with a stationary policy using underlay routes and the given set of controllable overlay nodes. $\square$

PROOF OF NECESSITY FOR THEOREM 1. We will show that given a $\mathcal{V}$ such that there is a path that is not available either as a shortest path or as a concatenation, i.e. the all-paths condition is not satisfied, the full throughput region cannot be achieved. Support of the full throughput region requires support for all arrival rate vectors interior to the rate region allowed by the network. Assume $\Lambda_G(\mathcal{V}) = \Lambda_G$ and some path P^{X}_{ab} is unavailable, both as a shortest-path and as an n-concatenation of shortest-paths at controllable nodes $\mathcal{V}$. Without loss of generality, assume that this unavailable path does not traverse any controllable nodes. Otherwise, split the unavailable path at controllable nodes and choose an unavailable segment induced from the split as path P^{X}_{ab}; such an unavailable segment must exist, otherwise the original path could be formed as an n-concatenation of the induced segments. We will show that there exists a feasible arrival rate vector that requires use of the unavailable path P^{X}_{ab}.

Construct an arrival rate vector $\boldsymbol{\lambda}$ that includes component λ^b_a equal to the maximum flow allowed for path P^{X}_{ab}, plus edge rate R_{ab} if edge (a,b) exists. In vector $\boldsymbol{\lambda}$, also include one-hop traffic demands for all edges $(i,j) \in \mathcal{E} \setminus (a,b)$ by choosing λ^j_i to equal any remaining capacity on edge (i,j). This rate vector $\boldsymbol{\lambda}$ is then feasible by construction.

Let $\mathcal{N}^{\text{X}}_{ab}$ be the set of nodes on path P^{X}_{ab}. For every node j not on path P^{X}_{ab}, i.e., $j \in \mathcal{N} \setminus \mathcal{N}^{\text{X}}_{ab}$, the arrival rate vector $\boldsymbol{\lambda}$ was constructed such that $\sum_i \lambda^j_i = \sum_i R_{ij}$. Applying the edge rate constraints from Equation (6) at node j and taking the sum over all neighbors i, we have $\sum_i \sum_{x,y,c} f^{xy,c}_{ij} \leq \sum_i R_{ij} = \sum_i \lambda^j_i$ for all $j \in \mathcal{N} \setminus \mathcal{N}^{\text{X}}_{ab}$, where the last equality comes from the previous equation. Then flow conservation requires that $f^{xy,c}_{ij} = 0$ for all commodities $c \neq j$. Thus, no feasible flow decomposition of $\boldsymbol{\lambda}$ can route flow for λ^b_a through any nodes in $\mathcal{N} \setminus \mathcal{N}^{\text{X}}_{ab}$. Therefore, it remains to consider only nodes in $\mathcal{N}^{\text{X}}_{ab}$ to support λ^b_a.

If P^{X}_{ab} is the only path from node a to b using nodes from the set $\mathcal{N}^{\text{X}}_{ab}$, then P^{X}_{ab} is clearly necessary to support flow λ^b_a. Otherwise, recall that by assumption there are no controllable nodes intermediate to path P^{X}_{ab}. Then it remains only to consider the case where the shortest-path from node a to b uses a strict subset of nodes in $\mathcal{N}^{\text{X}}_{ab}$, as no controllable nodes are available for path concatenation. Consider edge (i,j) such that nodes i and j are on path P^{X}_{ab}, where edge (i,j) is on P^{SP}_{ab} but not on P^{X}_{ab}. Here, $P^{\text{SP}}_{ij} = (i,j)$ is the only available path from i to j with unused capacity, because no controllable nodes are available. Then, $f^{ij,j}_{ij} = \lambda^j_i = R_{ij}$, and Equation (6) requires $f^{ab,b}_{ij} = 0$. Therefore, there is no unused capacity on path P^{SP}_{ab}, so λ^b_a and λ^j_i cannot be supported simultaneously. There are no other paths to consider from node a to b for a feasible flow decomposition of $\boldsymbol{\lambda}$.

Therefore, $\Lambda_G(\mathcal{V}) \subset \Lambda_G$ if any path is not available. Thus, we have proved the necessity of the all-paths condition for wired networks with shortest-path routing. □

PROOF FOR LEMMA 3. Let $\mathcal{V}$ be a overlay node placement chosen by P4, and consider every acyclic path P_{ab} between all pairs of nodes a and b in graph G'. For all such paths P_{ab}, we will show that either (1) P_{ab} is a shortest-path or (2) P_{ab} can be formed as a concatenation of shortest-paths at overlay nodes $\mathcal{V}$. Thus, $P_{ab} \in \mathcal{P}(\mathcal{V})$ for all-paths P_{ab} on graph G', proving that $\mathcal{P}(\mathcal{V}) = \mathcal{P}_{G'}$, i.e., that the all-paths condition is satisfied.

Define *overlay neighbor tree* D''_n to be the union of shortest path routes to node n from all overlay neighbors of n, i.e. nodes $v \in \mathcal{V}$ such that flow on path P^{SP}_{vn} is allowed by Eqns. (4-5). Because P4 places overlay nodes on the shortest paths from the leaf nodes of D'_n to n, we have the relationship $D''_n \subseteq D'_n \subseteq D_n$. The leaf nodes of D''_n are the closest overlay nodes to n, and we will make use of this construction.

For each path P_{ab}, one of two cases must hold.

(1) The entire path P_{ab} is contained in overlay neighbor tree D''_b. In this case, $P_{ab} = P^{\text{SP}}_{ab}$, so $P_{ab} \in \mathcal{P}(\mathcal{V})$.

(2) There exists an overlay node $v \in D''_b$ such that path P_{ab} is a concatenation of paths P_{av} and P^{SP}_{vb} at v.

Path P^{SP}_{vb} is provided by a shortest-path route, so it only remains to show that path P_{av} is either (1) a shortest-path or (2) can be formed as a concatenation of shortest-paths at overlay nodes $\mathcal{V}$, i.e., $P_{av} \in \mathcal{P}(\mathcal{V})$. To show this, first note that neighbor tree D''_b includes all neighbors of node b, and that v is at least one hop away from b. Then path P^{SP}_{vb} has a positive length, and thus the length of path P_{av} is strictly less than the length of path P_{ab}. We can then iteratively repeat the above two-case argument by letting $b' = v$, and consider sub-path $P_{ab'}$, repeatedly shortening the path until case (1) holds.

Therefore, every path P_{ab} on graph G' is also in the set of paths $\mathcal{P}(\mathcal{V})$. Thus, $\mathcal{P}(\mathcal{V}) = \mathcal{P}_{G'}$, and the all-paths condition is satisfied. □

PROOF FOR LEMMA 5. Lemma 4 establishes the necessity of at least 3 controllable nodes, so it only remains to show that 3 controllable nodes are sufficient to satisfy the all-paths condition.

Starting from any node x, consider nodes y and z that are neighbors, i.e., $(y,z) \in \mathcal{E}$, where shortest-paths P^{SP}_{xy} and P^{SP}_{xz} are disjoint. Without loss of generality assume $|P^{\text{SP}}_{xy}| \leq |P^{\text{SP}}_{xz}|$ where $|p|$ is the length of path p. With hop-count as the shortest-path metric, the length of these disjoint shortest-paths can differ at most by 1. Otherwise, there would exist a contradiction, as the path formed as a concatenation of P^{SP}_{xy} with edge (y,z) would be shorter than shortest-path P^{SP}_{xz}. Then the following inequality holds for any number of nodes $N \geq 5$.

$$|P^{\text{SP}}_{xy}| \geq \left\lfloor \frac{N-1}{2} \right\rfloor \geq \frac{N}{3} \tag{13}$$

Therefore, any node can reach a minimum of $N/3$ nodes in either direction around the ring using shortest-path routing. Conversely, any node can be reached by a minimum of $N/3$ nodes in either direction. Then we can place 3 controllable nodes, v_1, v_2, and v_3, such that shortest-paths $P^{\text{SP}}_{v_iv_j}$ and $P^{\text{SP}}_{v_iv_k}$ are edge-disjoint for all permutations $i,j,k \in \{1,2,3\}$. The overlay edges between these controllable nodes then form a bidirectionally connected ring as shown in Figure 1, making use of all-paths between the controllable nodes. Every uncontrollable u is on the shortest-path between two controllable nodes v_i and v_j; thus, by optimal substructure, paths $P^{\text{SP}}_{uv_i}$ and $P^{\text{SP}}_{uv_j}$ are edge-disjoint paths from u to v_i and v_j, and paths $P^{\text{SP}}_{v_iu}$ and $P^{\text{SP}}_{v_ju}$ are edge-disjoint paths from v_i and v_j to node u. Then every path in the network is either a shortest-path or can be formed as an n-concatenation of shortest paths, and the all-paths condition is satisfied with exactly 3 controllable nodes. □

Just FUN: A Joint Fountain Coding and Network Coding Approach to Loss-Tolerant Information Spreading

Qiuyuan Huang, Kairan Sun, Xin Li, Dapeng Oliver Wu
Dept. of Electrical & Computer Engineering, University of Florida, Gainesville, FL 32611, USA
idfree@ufl.edu, ksun@ufl.edu, shanelee@ufl.edu, wu@ece.ufl.edu

ABSTRACT

To address the problem of information spreading over lossy communication channels, this paper proposes a joint FoUntain coding and Network coding (FUN) approach. Different from the Transmission Control Protocol (TCP), our FUN approach is a mechanism of Forward Error Correction (FEC), which does not use retransmission for recovery of lost packets. The novelty of our FUN approach lies in combining the best features of fountain coding, intra-session network coding, and cross-next-hop network coding. As such, our FUN approach is capable of achieving unprecedented high throughput over lossy channels. Experimental results demonstrate that our FUN approach achieves higher throughput than the existing schemes for multihop wireless networks.

Categories and Subject Descriptors

C.2.1 [**Network Architecture and Design**]: Wireless communication

Keywords

Fountain code; network coding; erasure channel; multihop; multiple sources; loss tolerant; information spreading

1. INTRODUCTION

Information spreading plays a central role in human society. In the information age, how to efficiently and reliably spread information with low delay is critical for numerous activities involving humans and machines, e.g., the spread of tweets in Twitter, the dissemination of data collected by wireless sensor networks, and delivery of Internet TV. This paper is concerned with the problem of information spreading over lossy communication channels (a.k.a., erasure channels) where packets may be lost/discarded due to bit errors or buffer overflow. For wired networks over optical fiber channels, the bit error rate can be as low as 10^{-12}; hence packet loss is mainly due to overflow of the buffers at routers rather than bit errors. For wireless channels, packet loss is mainly due to uncorrectable bit errors[1], which are caused by fading, shadowing, interference, path loss, noise, etc. [13]

To address the packet loss problem, this paper proposes a joint FoUntain coding and Network coding (FUN) approach, which belongs to the category of FEC. Under our FUN coding approach, each source node uses a *fountain code* to encode information packets (which we call as native packets); each intermediate node (or a relay node) uses *intra-session network coding* to re-encode the packets in the same batch of the same session[2] received from the upstream node, and, if possible, uses *cross-next-hop network coding* to re-encode packets destined to different next-hop nodes; a sink node decodes the coded packets on the fly, and is able to reconstruct all the native packets as long as it receives sufficient number of coded packets.

The main contributions of this paper are:

1. We propose an FUN approach, which consists of three coding components, namely, fountain coding, intra-session network coding, and cross-next-hop network coding. The novelty of FUN lies in combining the best features of fountain coding, intra-session network coding, and cross-next-hop network coding. As such, our approach is capable of achieving unprecedented high throughput while allowing uncoordinated multiple source transmission of the same file to the same destination. Hence, FUN is well suited for peer-to-peer content delivery network (CDN), file transfer from distributed storage networks, social networks, social TV, and mobile TV.

2. We develop practical protocols for the proposed FUN approach, which are backward compatible with the existing protocols. Therefore, our protocols can seamlessly work with existing Medium Access Control

[1]At the transmitter, most physical layer schemes encode messages by both an error-detecting code such as cyclic redundancy check (CRC) and an error-correction code. At the receiver, a received packet is first decoded by the error-correction decoder. If the resulting packet has uncorrectable bit errors, it will not pass the check of the error-detecting module. Most physical layer designs, if not all, will drop those packets that have uncorrectable bit errors.

[2]In this paper, a unicast session is identified by a unique source/destination IP address pair while a multicast session is identified by a tuple of the source IP address and all the multicast receiver IP addresses. In our future work, we will consider a session identified by a unique tuple of source/destination IP addresses, source/destination Layer-4 port numbers.

MobiHoc'14, August 11–14, 2014, Philadelphia, PA, USA.

http://dx.doi.org/10.1145/2632951.2632965.

(MAC) protocols, IP, TCP, UDP, HTTP, etc. In addition, the proposed FUN architecture provides a unified framework for existing network coding schemes, our proposed FUN codes, and existing protocols.

To evaluate the performance of FUN, we conduct extensive experiments. Experimental results demonstrate that our approach achieves higher throughput than existing schemes for multihop wireless networks.

The rest of the paper is organized as follows. Section 2 reviews the related work. In Section 3, we present the overview of the FUN architecture. Section 4 describes the FUN coding schemes in detail. In Section 5, we show the experimental results. Section 6 concludes the paper and points out the future directions.

2. RELATED WORK

In this section, we review various FEC mechanisms for erasure channels, i.e., erasure codes, network coding, and joint erasure coding and intra-session network coding.

2.1 Erasure Codes

Erasure codes can be used to recover native packets without feedback and retransmission. Erasure codes include Reed-Solomon codes, LDPC codes, and fountain codes [12]. Compared to erasure codes (including fountain codes), our proposed FUN approach can achieve much higher throughput for communication over multihop wireless networks. The lower bound on the end-to-end packet loss rate under FUN is $\max_{i\in\{1,2,\cdots,N_h\}} p_i$ (where p_i is the packet loss rate of Link i and N_h is the number of hops from the source to the destination) while the end-to-end packet loss rate under an erasure code is $1-\prod_{i=1}^{N_h}(1-p_i)$ [18], which is much larger than $\max_{i\in\{1,2,\cdots,N_h\}} p_i$ for large N_h. For example, for $N_h = 2$ and $p_i = 0.1$ ($i = 1, 2$), the end-to-end packet loss rate under FUN is 0.1 while the end-to-end packet loss rate under an erasure code is 0.19; for $N_h = 10$ and $p_i = 0.1$ ($\forall i$), the end-to-end packet loss rate under FUN is still 0.1 while the end-to-end packet loss rate under an erasure code is 0.65, which is 6.5 times as much as 0.1. The much lower end-to-end packet loss rate achieved by FUN translates to much higher throughput (date rate), compared to erasure codes. In our simulations, we observe that the throughput under FUN is 35 times as large as that under a fountain code (RQ code), for $N_h = 10$ and $p_i = 0.1$ ($\forall i$).

The reason why FUN achieves higher throughput over multihop lossy networks than erasure codes, is because under FUN, each relay node performs network coding and hence coded packets that are lost at each hop are regenerated/re-coded for the next hop. To illustrate how FUN works, here is an analogy: a person carries a leaky tank of water from the source node to the destination; in each hop, the tank leaks p percent of water; at each relay node, the tank gets refilled to its full capacity; finally, the tank only lost p percent of water from the source node to the destination since only the lost water in the last hop is not refilled. In contrast, erasure codes (including fountain codes) are like no refill at any relay node since network coding is not used at any relay node; hence the tank loses $(1-(1-p/100)^{N_h}) \times 100$ percent of water from the source node to the destination. Here, $p/100$ is the percentage, e.g., $p = 10$ gives $p/100 = 10\%$.

2.2 Network Coding

Simply forwarding packets is not an optimal operation at a router from the perspective of maximizing throughput. Network coding was proposed to achieve maximum throughput for multicast communication [2]. Network coding techniques can be classified into two categories: intra-session (where coding is restricted to the same multicast or unicast session) [2, 5, 8] and inter-session (where coding is applied to packets of different sessions) [7, 14, 17]. For wireless communication, cross-next-hop network coding [7,14] and intra-session network coding [10, 18, 19] are usually used. Under cross-next-hop network coding, a relay node applies coding to packets destined to different next-hop nodes. Cross-next-hop network coding is a special type of inter-session network coding.

Cross-next-hop network coding has been heavily studied in the wireless networking area. The major works include [7, 14]. In [7], Katti et al. proposed an opportunistic network coding scheme for unicast flows, called COPE, which can achieve throughput gains from a few percent to several folds depending on the traffic pattern, congestion level, and transport protocol. In [14], Rayanchu el al. developed a loss-aware network coding technique for unicast flows, called CLONE, which improves reliability of network coding by transmitting multiple copies of the same packet, similar to repetition coding [9].

Different from COPE [7], which does not add redundancy to the coded packets, our FUN approach adds redundancy to the received packets at a relay node; specifically, under FUN, a relay node re-codes the received packets, using random linear code [18, 19]. Different from CLONE [14], which uses repetition coding, our FUN approach uses random linear coding, which is more efficient than repetition coding. Our experimental results show that FUN achieves much higher throughput over lossy channels, compared to COPE.

2.3 Joint Erasure Coding and Intra-Session Network Coding

The following Joint Erasure coding and intra-session Network coding (JEN) approach has been used for unicast/multicast communication in [10]: The source node uses *random linear erasure coding* (RLEC) to encode the native packets and add a global encoding vector to the header of each coded packet. A relay node uses *random linear network coding* (RLNC) to re-code the packets it has received, i.e., the relay node generates a coded packet by randomly linearly combining the packets that it has received and stored in its buffer; the relay node also computes the global encoding vector of the re-coded packet, and add the global encoding vector to the header of the re-coded packet. A destination node can decode and recover K native packets as long as it receives enough coded packets that contain K linearly independent global encoding vectors. In practice, under JEN, the data to be transmitted is partitioned into multiple segments [16], or generations [4], or blocks [11], or batches [3], and coding is restricted within the same segment/generation/block/batch. In doing so, the encoding vector is small enough to be put into the header of a coded packet. To combine the best features of JEN and fountain codes, Yang and Yeung proposed BATched Sparse (BATS) codes [18,19]. Our FUN approach combines the best features of fountain coding, intra-session network coding, and cross-next-hop network coding. Different from BATS codes, FUN utilizes cross-next-hop network coding and hence achieves a higher rate.

3. FUN OVERVIEW

In this section, we introduce FUN, a new forwarding architecture for wireless multihop networks. Since a wireless channel is a shared medium, it can be regarded as a broadcast channel, i.e., a transmitted packet can be overheard by all the nodes within the transmission range of the sender of the packet.

We consider a pair of nodes, say Node A and Node B. Assume that there are two unicast flows between the two nodes, i.e., a forward flow from Node A to Node B and a backward flow from Node B to Node A. We propose two coding schemes, i.e., FUN-1 and FUN-2:

- FUN-1 basically combines BATS coding [18] with COPE [7] for two flows. But FUN-1 is not a simple combination of BATS and COPE; a relay node needs to recover BATS-encoded packets of the forward flow before recovering packets of the backward flow.
- FUN-2 combines BATS coding with RLNC for two flows; each relay node needs to add a new encoding vector to the header of a re-coded packet; only the destination node performs decoding.

Under FUN-1, two sub-layers, i.e., Layer 2.1 and Layer 2.2, are inserted between Layer 2 (MAC) and Layer 3 (IP). Layer 2.1 is for cross-next-hop network coding, similar to the functionality of COPE [7]. Layer 2.2 is for BATS coding [18]. At a source node, Layer 2.2 uses a fountain code to encode all native packets from upper layers (similar to the outer code in a BATS code); there is no Layer 2.1 at a source node. At a relay node, Layer 2.1 is used for cross-next-hop network coding and Layer 2.2 is used for intra-session network coding (similar to the inner code in a BATS code); for Layer 2.2, the relay node runs a procedure called *FUN-1-2.2-Proc*, which performs RLNC within the same batch. At a destination node, Layer 2.2 decodes the coded packets received; there is no Layer 2.1 at a destination node.

Under FUN-2, only one sub-layer, i.e., Layer 2.2, is inserted between Layer 2 (MAC) and Layer 3 (IP). At a source node, Layer 2.2 uses a fountain code to encode all native packets from upper layers (similar to the outer code in a BATS code). At a relay node, if Layer 2.2 receives a packet with FUN-2
switch enabled, it will run a procedure called *FUN-2-2.2-Proc* for mixing packets from two flows; otherwise, it will run the procedure *FUN-1-2.2-Proc*, which does not mix packets from two different flows. Note that different from a BATS code, *FUN-2-2.2-Proc* performs re-coding of batches from two different flows. At a destination node, Layer 2.2 decodes the coded packets received.

Different from COPE, FUN-2 is an end-to-end solution, i.e., a re-coded packet is never decoded at a relay node. In contrast, under COPE, a next-hop node, say, Node A, needs to recover the native packet, whose next-hop node is Node A; the recovery process is like decoding; the relay node may not recover the native packet if the relay node does not have enough known packets that are mixed in the XOR-ed packet.

In the current version, both FUN-1 and FUN-2 are restricted to two flows, i.e., forward flow and backward flow between two nodes. The advantage is that there is no need for coordination while a higher coding gain can be achieved. The limitation is that it restricts its use to two flows between two nodes.

Both FUN-1 packet and FUN-2 packet have two headers as shown in Fig. 1. If a re-coded packet is mixed from two flows (i.e., forward and backward flows), it will have a non-empty Header 2; otherwise, there will be no Header 2.

Header 1 and Header 2 have the same structure for FUN-1 and FUN-2. Fig. 2 shows the structure for FUN-1 Header 1 and Header 2. Fig. 3 shows the structure for FUN-2 Header 1 and Header 2. In Figs. 2 and 3, the NC switch consists of two bits and indicates one of the following four schemes is used: 1) FUN-1, 2) FUN-2, 3) RLNC, 4) no network coding. COPE is a special case of FUN-1, where there is no encoding vector in FUN Headers; in other words, if the NC switch equals 00 (in binary format) and there is no encoding vector in FUN Headers, then the packet is a COPE packet. BATS is a special case of FUN-2, where there is no FUN Header 2. The fountain code corresponds to the no-network-coding case with the NC switch equal to 11 (in binary format) and no encoding vectors in FUN header and no Header 2.

In fact, our FUN architecture is extensible to accommodate more than two flows and more than two FUN headers.

4. DESCRIPTION OF FUN CODING

4.1 FUN-1

At a source node, Layer 2.2 uses a RaptorQ (RQ) code [15] to encode all native packets from Layer 3. The RQ code is the most advanced fountain code that is available commercially.

Assume Node A will transmit K native packets to Node B, and Node B will transmit K native packets to Node A[3]. Each packet has T symbols in a finite field $\mathbb{F}_q$, where q is the size of the field. Denote a packet by a column vector in $\mathbb{F}_q^T$. In the rest of the paper, we denote the set of K native packets by the following matrix

$$\mathbf{B} = [b_1, b_2, \cdots, b_K], \tag{1}$$

where b_i is the i-th native packet. With an abuse of notation, when treating packets as elements of a set, we write $b_i \in \mathbf{B}$, $\mathbf{B}' \in \mathbf{B}$, etc.

Next we describe the outer code, inner code, XOR coding, and precoding of FUN-1.

4.1.1 *Outer Code of FUN-1*

The outer code of FUN-1 is the same as the outer code of a BATS code. The outer coding of FUN-1 is performed at a source node at Layer 2.2.

At a source node, each coded batch has M coded packets. The i-th batch $\mathbf{X}_i$ is generated from a subset $\mathbf{B}_i \subset \mathbf{B}$ ($\mathbf{B} \in \mathbb{F}_q^{T\times K}$) by the following operation

$$\mathbf{X}_i = \mathbf{B}_i\mathbf{G}_i \tag{2}$$

where $\mathbf{G}_i \in \mathbb{F}_q^{d_i\times M}$ is called the generator matrix of the i-th batch; $\mathbf{B}_i \in \mathbb{F}_q^{T\times d_i}$; $\mathbf{X}_i \in \mathbb{F}_q^{T\times M}$. Similar to a fountain code, matrix $\mathbf{B}_i$ is randomly formed by two steps: 1) sample a given degree distribution $\Psi = (\Psi_0, \Psi_1, \cdots, \Psi_K)$ and obtain a degree d_i with probability Ψ_{d_i}; 2) uniformly randomly

[3]For simplicity of notation, we let the two flows have the same number K of packets to transmit. Actually, this is not required for the FUN architecture.

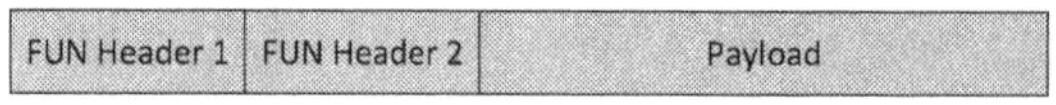

Figure 1: The structure of a FUN-1/FUN-2 packet

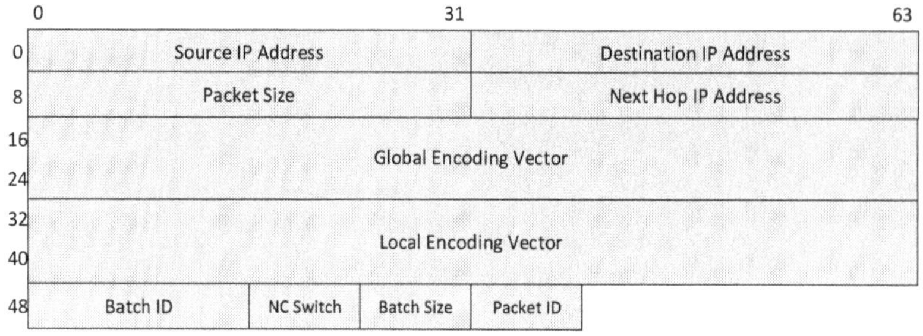

Figure 2: The header structure of a FUN-1 packet

choose d_i packets from $\mathbf{B}$ to form $\mathbf{B}_i$. Matrix $\mathbf{G}_i$ is randomly generated; specifically, all the entries in $\mathbf{G}_i$ are independent, identically distributed with a uniform distribution in $\mathbb{F}_q$. In our implementation, $\mathbf{G}_i$ is generated by a pseudorandom number generator and can be recovered at the destinations using the same pseudorandom number generator with the same seed.

4.1.2 *Inner Code of FUN-1*

At a relay node, Layer 2.2 performs inner coding of FUN-1, which is the same as that for a BATS code. We first consider the first down-stream relay node, say, Node R_1. Assume $\mathbf{X}'_{i,1}$ are the set of packets of the i-th batch correctly received by Node R_1, transmitted by the source. Since there may be lost packets from the source to Node R_1, we have $\mathbf{X}'_{i,1} \subseteq \mathbf{X}_i$. We write

$$\mathbf{X}'_{i,1} = \mathbf{X}_i \mathbf{E}_{i,1} \tag{3}$$

where $\mathbf{E}_{i,1}$ is an erasure matrix, representing the erasure channel between the source and Node R_1. $\mathbf{E}_{i,1}$ is an $M \times M$ diagonal matrix whose entry is one if the corresponding packet in $\mathbf{X}_i$ is correctly received by Node R_1, and is zero otherwise. Hence, matrix $\mathbf{X}'_{i,1} \in \mathbb{F}_q^{T \times M}$ has the same dimensions as $\mathbf{X}_i$. Here, with an abuse of the notation $\mathbf{X}'_{i,1}$, we replace each lost packet in $\mathbf{X}_i$ by a column vector whose entries are all zero, resulting in matrix $\mathbf{X}'_{i,1}$.

At Node R_1, the inner coding of FUN-1 is performed by

$$\mathbf{Y}_{i,1} = \mathbf{X}'_{i,1}\mathbf{H}_{i,1} = \mathbf{X}_i\mathbf{E}_{i,1}\mathbf{H}_{i,1} = \mathbf{B}_i\mathbf{G}_i\mathbf{E}_{i,1}\mathbf{H}_{i,1}, \tag{4}$$

where $\mathbf{H}_{i,1} \in \mathbb{F}^{M \times M}$ is the transfer matrix of an RLNC for the i-th batch at Node R_1. After inner-encoding, each column of the product matrix $\mathbf{E}_{i,1}\mathbf{H}_{i,1}$ is added to the header of the corresponding coded packet as a global encoding vector, which is needed by the destination node for decoding.

At the relay node of the j-th hop, denoted as Node R_j, the following re-coding is performed

$$\begin{aligned} \mathbf{Y}_{i,j} &= \mathbf{X}'_{i,j}\mathbf{H}_{i,j} = \mathbf{Y}_{i,j-1}\mathbf{E}_{i,j}\mathbf{H}_{i,j} \\ &= \mathbf{B}_i\mathbf{G}_i\mathbf{E}_{i,1}\mathbf{H}_{i,1}\cdots\mathbf{E}_{i,j}\mathbf{H}_{i,j}, \end{aligned} \tag{5}$$

where $\mathbf{E}_{i,j}$ is an erasure matrix of the i-th batch for the erasure channel from Node R_{j-1} to Node R_j; $\mathbf{H}_{i,j} \in \mathbb{F}_q^{M \times M}$ is the transfer matrix of an RLNC for the i-th batch at Node R_j. After inner-encoding, each column of the product matrix $\mathbf{E}_{i,1}\mathbf{H}_{i,1}\cdots\mathbf{E}_{i,j}\mathbf{H}_{i,j}$ is used to update the global encoding vector of the corresponding coded packet.

The above inner-coding procedure is implemented in software module *FUN-1-2.2-Proc* mentioned in Section 3.

4.1.3 *XOR Coding of FUN-1*

The XOR coding of FUN-1 is similar to COPE [7]. At Node R_i w.r.t. the forward flow from Node A to Node B, the XOR encoding procedure is shown in Algorithm 1. The XOR decoding procedure is shown in Algorithm 2.

4.1.4 *Precoding of FUN-1*

At a source node, precoding is performed, similar to Raptor codes. The precoding can be achieved by a traditional erasure code such as LDPC and Reed-Solomon code. The precoding of FUN-1 is performed at a source node at Layer 2.2. After precoding, the resulting packets is further encoded by the outer encoder described in Section 4.1.1.

4.2 FUN-2

FUN-2 consists of outer code, inner code, and precoding, which are described as below.

4.2.1 *Outer Code of FUN-2*

The outer code of FUN-2 is the same as the outer code of FUN-1, except the decoding process. In the decoding process, the destination node of the forward flow is also a source node of the backward flow. So this destination node can use its known packets of the backward flow to decode the coded packets of the forward flow. To limit the size of the encoding vector in the packet header, at a relay node, FUN-2 only allows the mixing of two batches from two flows once; i.e., if a packet is already a mixture of two packets from two flows, it will not be re-coded again at a relay node. The FUN-2 outer decoding procedure is shown in Algorithm 3. For simplicity, we denote the two nodes as Node 0 and 1. The equation in Step 17 can be proved as below. Since the inner coding is a mixture of two flows according to Eq. (8), we have

$$\mathbf{Y}_{i,j} = [\mathbf{B}_{i,j}, \mathbf{B}_{k,1-j}][\mathbf{H}_{i,j}, \mathbf{H}_{k,1-j}]^T \tag{6}$$

$$= \mathbf{B}_{i,j}\mathbf{H}_{i,j} + \mathbf{B}_{k,1-j}\mathbf{H}_{k,1-j} \tag{7}$$

Hence, $\mathbf{B}_{i,j}\mathbf{H}_{i,j} = \mathbf{Y}_{i,j} - \mathbf{B}_{k,1-j}\mathbf{H}_{k,1-j}$. Since $\mathbf{B}_{i,j}\mathbf{H}_{i,j}$ are the coded packets of the i-th batch and Destination j, we

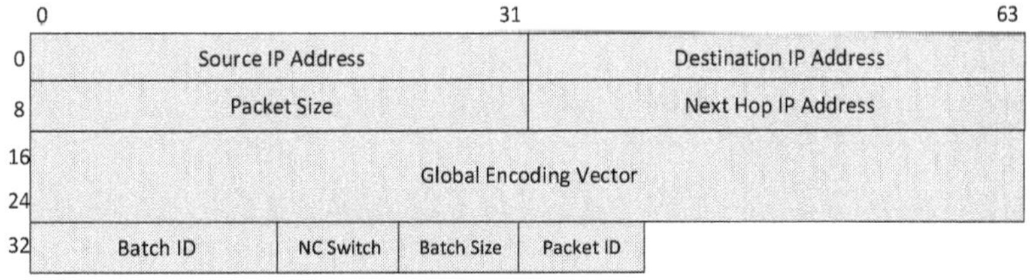

Figure 3: The header structure of a FUN-2 packet

Algorithm 1 XOR encoding of FUN-1

```
while at least one flow (forward or backward flow) is alive do
  if Layer 2.2 output queues for the forward flow and the backward flow both have at least one batch of M re-coded
  packets, say, the i-th batch for the forward flow and the j-th batch for the backward flow then
    for m = 1, ··· , M do
      Pick Packet y_{i,m} at the head of Layer 2.2 output queue for the forward flow;
      Pick packet ȳ_{j,m} at the head of Layer 2.2 output queue for the backward flow;
      p_m = y_{i,m} ⊕ ȳ_{j,m};
      Put the following in the header of packet p_m: 1) packet ID m, 2) the MAC address of the next-hop node of Packet
      y_{i,m}, 3) batch ID i of Packet y_{i,m}, 4) the MAC address of the next-hop node of packet ȳ_{j,m}, 5) batch ID j of packet
      ȳ_{j,m}, 6) local encoding vectors of packets y_{i,m} and ȳ_{j,m};
      Enable the bit FUN_XOR in the header of packet p_m, i.e., FUN_XOR = 1;
      Place packet p_m in Layer 2.1 output queue;
    end for
  else
    if Layer 2.2 output queue of one flow (forward or backward) has at least two batch of M re-coded packets, say, the
    i-th batch being the head-of-line batch then
      for m = 1, ··· , M do
        Pick Packet y_{i,m} at the head of Layer 2.2 output queue of the flow;
        Disable the bit FUN_XOR in the header of packet y_{i,m}, i.e., FUN_XOR = 0;
        Place packet y_{i,m} in Layer 2.1 output queue;
      end for
    end if
  end if
end while
```

assign $\mathbf{B}_{i,j}\mathbf{H}_{i,j}$ to $\mathbf{Y}_{i,j}$. This proves the equation in Step 17.

4.2.2 *Inner Code Encoding of FUN-2*

The inner code of FUN-2 is similar to the inner code of FUN-1 in the sense that both of them use RLNC. The difference is that FUN-2 mixes the packets of two flows while FUN-1 does not. Specifically, under FUN-2, at the relay node of the j-th hop, denoted as Node R_j, the following re-coding is applied to two juxtaposed matrices of received packets:

$$\mathbf{Z}_{i,j} = [\mathbf{Z}_{i,j-1}\mathbf{E}_{i,j}, \mathbf{Z}_{k,j+1}\overline{\mathbf{E}}_{k,j}]\mathbf{H}_{i,j}, \quad (8)$$

where $\mathbf{Z}_{i,j} \in \mathbb{F}_q^{T\times M}$ contains M re-coded packets of the i-th batch, generated by Node R_j; $\overline{\mathbf{E}}_{k,j} \in \mathbb{F}_2^{M\times M}$ is an erasure matrix of the k-th batch for the erasure channel from Node R_{j+1} to Node R_j; $\mathbf{H}_{i,j} \in \mathbb{F}_q^{2M\times M}$ is the transfer matrix of an RLNC for the i-th batch of the forward flow and the k-th batch of the backward flow at Node R_j. The FUN-2 inner-coding procedure is shown in Algorithm 4, where Destination 0 and 1 denote the destination of the forward and backward flow, respectively; Packet $y_{i,m}$ has batch ID i and its position in the batch is m; a buffer being complete means that a buffer is full with M packets OR a newly arriving packet has a batch ID, which is larger than that of the packets in the buffer. After inner-encoding, each column of the matrix $\mathbf{H}_{i,j}$ is added to the global encoding vector of the corresponding coded packet. The inner-coding procedure is implemented in software module *FUN-2-2.2-Proc* mentioned in Section 3.

4.2.3 *Precoding of FUN-2*

The precoding of FUN-2 is the same as the precoding of FUN-1.

5. EXPERIMENTAL RESULTS

5.1 Development of Simulator

We implement our proposed FUN-1 and FUN-2 on QualNet [1]. For comparison, we also implement a BATS code [18], a fountain code (specifically, the RQ code [15]), RLNC [16], and COPE [7] in QualNet. For COPE, we only implement the XOR operation for mixing two flows; and Layer 4 in the COPE scheme is TCP; the reason why we use TCP for COPE is because each scheme needs to achieve perfect recovery of lost packets to make a fair comparison. In the future, we will implement COPE with UDP and hop-by-hop retransmission for packet recovery as in Ref. [7].

For RLNC, a file is segmented into batches, each of which consists of M native packets. Each batch is transmitted in-

Algorithm 2 XOR decoding of FUN-1

while at least one flow (forward or backward flow) is alive **do**
  if the head-of-line packet in Layer 2.1 input queue has $FUN\_XOR = 0$ **then**
    Move this head-of-line packet to Layer 2.2 input queue;
  else
    Move this head-of-line packet to its corresponding queue in the buffer of Layer 2.1 (each queue is uniquely identified by the same set of receiver MAC addresses in the packet header);
    if a queue in the buffer of Layer 2.1 has two batches of received packets (assume the head-of-line XOR-ed batch has batch ID i for the forward flow and batch ID j for the backward flow) **then**
      while the head-of-line packet, say p_m, has its forward-flow batch ID equal i **do**
        Recover the packet of the forward flow by $y_{i,m} = p_m \oplus \bar{y}_{j,m}$, where $\bar{y}_{j,m}$ is a packet in $\overline{\mathbf{Y}}_{j,l-1} = \overline{\mathbf{Y}}_{j,l}\overline{\mathbf{E}}_{j,l-1}\overline{\mathbf{H}}_{j,l-1}$, where l is the index of the current node R_l, $l-1$ is the index of the next-hop node R_{l-1} of the backward flow, $\overline{\mathbf{Y}}_{j,l-1}$ is the matrix whose columns are coded packets, re-coded by Node R_{l-1} for the backward flow, $\overline{\mathbf{E}}_{j,l-1}$ is an erasure matrix for the erasure channel from Node R_l to Node R_{l-1}, $\overline{\mathbf{E}}_{j,l-1}$ can be obtained by Node R_l via the global encoding vector in FUN-1 packet header, $\overline{\mathbf{H}}_{j,l-1}$ is the transfer matrix of an RLNC for the j-th batch at Node R_{l-1} for the backward flow, $\overline{\mathbf{H}}_{j,l-1}$ can be obtained by the local encoding vectors in FUN-1 packet header;
        Recover the packet of the backward flow by $\bar{y}_{i,m} = p_m \oplus y_{j,m}$, where $y_{j,m}$ is a packet in $\mathbf{Y}_{j,l+1} = \mathbf{Y}_{j,l}\mathbf{E}_{j,l+1}\mathbf{H}_{j,l+1}$, where l is the index of the current node R_l, $l+1$ is the index of the next-hop node R_{l+1} of the forward flow, $\mathbf{Y}_{j,l+1}$ is the matrix whose columns are coded packets, re-coded by Node R_{l+1} for the forward flow, $\mathbf{E}_{j,l+1}$ is an erasure matrix for the erasure channel from Node R_l to Node R_{l+1}, $\mathbf{E}_{j,l+1}$ can be obtained by Node R_l via the global encoding vector in FUN-1 packet header, $\mathbf{H}_{j,l+1}$ is the transfer matrix of an RLNC for the j-th batch at Node R_{l+1} for the forward flow, $\mathbf{H}_{j,l+1}$ can be obtained by the local encoding vectors in FUN-1 packet header;
      end while
    end if
  end if
end while

dependently as if it is a single file; there is no coding across two batches. A source node keeps transmitting coded packets of a batch until the source node receives an ACK message from the destination node. A relay node has a buffer of M packets; when a relay node receives a packet from its upstream node, it places the packet in the buffer; if the buffer is full, the newly arriving packet will push out the oldest packet; then the relay node takes all the packets in the buffer as input and generates one RLNC-coded packet, which is then sent out to its downstream node. When a destination node decodes all the native packets in a batch, the destination node transmits an ACK message toward the source node. Upon receiving the ACK message, the source node stops transmitting the coded packets of the current batch, and starts to transmit the coded packets of the next batch.

We use IEEE 802.11b for the physical layer and MAC layer of each wireless node, and use the Ad hoc On-Demand Distance Vector (AODV) protocol for routing. For COPE, we use TCP as the Layer 4 protocol; for FUN-1, FUN-2, BATS, fountain code, and RLNC, we use UDP as the Layer 4 protocol. All the experiments have the following setting: the packet size $T = 1024$ bytes; the batch size $M = 16$ packets.

5.2 Performance Evaluation

We conduct experiments for the following four cases: 1) two hops with no node mobility (fixed topology) under various packet loss rate per hop, 2) various number of hops with no node mobility (fixed topology) under fixed packet loss rate per hop, 3) a large number nodes with node mobility (dynamic topology). There are two flows (forward and backward flows) between each source/destination pair. For each case, we compare the performance of seven schemes, i.e., FUN-1, FUN-2, a BATS code, a fountain code, RLNC, COPE, and TCP.

As we know, the lower the packet sending rate of UDP, the lower throughput. But too high packet sending rate of UDP will incur congestion and packet loss. Hence, in the experiments of FUN-1, FUN-2, BATS, fountain code, and RLNC, which use UDP as their Layer 4 protocol, we tune the packet sending rate of UDP until we find the maximum throughput for each of these five schemes. At the optimal packet sending rate of UDP, we conduct ten experiments for each of these five schemes, and take the average throughput of the ten experiments as the performance measure of each scheme.

For COPE and TCP, we conduct ten experiments for each of these two schemes, and take the average throughput of the ten experiments as the performance measure of COPE and TCP.

5.2.1 *Case 1: Two Hops with No Node Mobility*

The setup of this set of experiments is the following. There are three nodes in the network: a source node, a destination node, and one relay node. The communication path from the source node to the destination node has two hops. All the three nodes are immobile; hence the network topology is fixed.

Denote K the number of native packets to be transmitted by the source. In the experiments, we measure the throughput in Mbits/s under different values of K and different packet loss rate (PLR). The PLR is the same for all the links/hops in the network. Here, the PLR does not include packet loss due to the thermal noise in the physical layer and packet collision, which is out of our direct control; here the PLR is achieved by randomly dropping a correctly received packet at Layer 2 with a probability equal to the given PLR.

Algorithm 3 Outer decoding of FUN-2 at Node j ($j \in \{0, 1\}$)

while not all native packets destined to Node j are decoded **do**
  if the receiving queue of Layer 2.2 is complete **then**
    Pick packets of the same batch from the head of the receiving queue of Layer 2.2;
    if FUN-2 Header 2 is not empty **then**
      if the destination IP address in FUN-2 Header 1 is that of Node j **then**
        Let i equal the batch ID in FUN-2 Header 1 of any picked packet;
        Let k equal the batch ID in FUN-2 Header 2 of any picked packet;
        Let $\mathbf{H}_{k,1-j}$ be a matrix whose columns are the global encoding vectors in FUN-2 Header 2 of all the picked packets;
        Let $\mathbf{B}_{k,1-j}$ be a matrix whose columns are native packets of the k-th batch, sent from Node j to Node $1-j$;
      else
        Let i equal the batch ID in FUN-2 Header 2 of any picked packet;
        Let k equal the batch ID in FUN-2 Header 1 of any picked packet;
        Let $\mathbf{H}_{k,1-j}$ be a matrix whose columns are the global encoding vectors in FUN-2 Header 1 of all the picked packets;
        Let $\mathbf{B}_{k,1-j}$ be a matrix whose columns are native packets of the k-th batch, sent from Node j to Node $1-j$;
      end if
      Let $\mathbf{Y}_{i,j}$ be a matrix whose columns are the payloads of all the picked packets;
      Compute $\mathbf{Y}_{i,j} = \mathbf{Y}_{i,j} - \mathbf{B}_{k,1-j}\mathbf{H}_{k,1-j}$;
    else
      Let i equal the batch ID in FUN-2 Header 1 of any picked packet;
      Let $\mathbf{Y}_{i,j}$ be a matrix whose columns are the payloads of all the picked packets;
    end if
    Do outer decoding in the same way as BATS outer decoding with input packets $\mathbf{Y}_{i,j}$;
  end if
end while

Table 1 shows the total throughput of the two flows (i.e., forward/backward flows) of the seven schemes under Case 1. We have the following observations:

- For both the lossless and lossy situations, FUN-1 and FUN-2 achieve the highest throughput. This is because FUN-1 and FUN-2 combine the best features of fountain coding, intra-session network coding, and cross-next-hop network coding.
- The throughput of FUN-2 is higher than or equal to that of FUN-1. This is because FUN-2 uses RLNC at a relay node and RLNC has a higher coding gain than the XOR operation used in FUN-1.
- For both the lossless and lossy situations, the fountain code achieves a higher throughput than the BATS code. This is because a BATS code only achieves higher throughput than a fountain code when there are more than two hops or the PLR is high (say, 20%).
- For the lossless situation, COPE achieves a higher throughput than the BATS and the fountain code for $K = 1600$ but achieves a lower throughput than the BATS and the fountain code for $K = 6400$ and 16000. This may be due to the fact that BATS codes and fountain codes are erasure channel coding (while COPE is not) and hence, the more native packets to transmit, the higher coding gain.
- For both the lossless and lossy situations, RLNC achieves a lower throughput than the fountain code and the BATS code. This is because a coded packet in RLNC is restricted to one batch of M native packets while a coded packet in the BATS code and the fountain code is a random mixture of all the K native packets; hence each native packet has a less chance of being recovered in RLNC for the same number of coded packets, compared to the BATS code and the fountain code.
- RLNC achieves a lower throughput than COPE in the lossless situation, but achieves a higher throughput than COPE in the lossy situation. This is because RLNC is erasure channel coding: when there is no packet loss, the redundancy induced by RLNC reduces the throughput; when there is packet loss, the reliability induced by RLNC make it achieve a higher throughput.
- TCP achieves the least throughput for the lossless situation. This is because TCP has a slow start and a congestion avoidance phase, which reduces throughput. In contrast, COPE has network coding gain and FUN-1, FUN-2, the BATS code, the fountain code, and RLNC use UDP with optimal packet sending rate.
- For PLR=10%, COPE and TCP time out and could not receive all K number of packets due to high packet loss rate. This is consistent with the fact that TCP performs poorly under environments of high packet loss rates [6].

5.2.2 *Case 2: Various Number of Hops with No Node Mobility*

The setup of this set of experiments is the following. The network consists of a source node, a destination node, and 1 or 2 or 4 relay nodes. All the nodes in the network form a chain topology from the source node to the destination node. The communication path from the source node to the

Table 1: Throughput under Case 1

K	Scheme	Throughput (Mbits/s)	
		PLR = 0	PLR = 10%
1600	FUN-1	0.697	0.652
	FUN-2	0.697	0.668
	BATS	0.484	0.488
	Fountain	0.498	0.508
	RLNC	0.460	0.340
	COPE	0.520	N/A
	TCP	0.375	N/A
6400	FUN-1	0.720	0.665
	FUN-2	0.727	0.669
	BATS	0.517	0.502
	Fountain	0.533	0.513
	RLNC	0.460	0.340
	COPE	0.500	N/A
	TCP	0.378	N/A
16000	FUN-1	0.714	0.637
	FUN-2	0.714	0.655
	BATS	0.521	0.487
	Fountain	0.533	0.493
	RLNC	0.460	0.340
	COPE	0.504	N/A
	TCP	0.379	N/A

destination node has 2 or 3 or 5 hops. All the nodes are immobile; hence the network topology is fixed. For all the experiments in Case 2, we set PLR=10% for each hop/link. Again, the PLR does not include packet loss due to the thermal noise in the physical layer and packet collision.

Table 2 shows the throughput of seven schemes under Case 2. We have the following observations:

- For both the lossless and lossy situations, FUN-1 and FUN-2 achieve similar throughput and their throughput is the highest among the seven schemes.

- When the number of hops is two, the throughput of FUN-2 is not less than than FUN-1. This is because FUN-2 uses RLNC at a relay node and RLNC is better than the XOR operation used in FUN-1.

- When the number of hops is more than two, FUN-1 may achieve a higher throughput than FUN-2. This is because FUN-2 only allows mixing two flows once but FUN-1 allows mixing two flows unlimited number of times. Hence, FUN-1 potentially has a higher coding gain than FUN-2 due to more coding opportunities. However, this is not always true. Since FUN-1 always uses broadcast and FUN-2 has to use unicast when FUN-2 packet has already been mixed from two flows once, FUN-2 unicast packets are more reliably received than FUN-1 broadcast packets under 802.11 MAC. It is known that in the 802.11 unicast mode, packets are immediately acknowledged by their intended next-hop nodes; if no ACK message is received, the 802.11 MAC layer will retransmit the packet a number of times (with exponential backoff) until an ACK message is receiver or a time-out event happens. But a broadcast packet will not be acknowledged and retransmitted under 802.11.

Table 2: Throughput under Case 2

K	Scheme	Throughput (Mbits/s)		
		2 hops	3 hops	5 hops
1600	FUN-1	0.652	0.413	0.045
	FUN-2	0.652	0.364	0.042
	BATS	0.488	0.317	0.036
	Fountain	0.508	0.271	0.005
	RLNC	0.340	0.202	0.024
	COPE	N/A	N/A	N/A
	TCP	N/A	N/A	N/A
6400	FUN-1	0.665	0.376	0.026
	FUN-2	0.669	0.357	0.033
	BATS	0.502	0.327	0.025
	Fountain	0.513	0.220	N/A
	RLNC	0.340	0.202	0.024
	COPE	N/A	N/A	N/A
	TCP	N/A	N/A	N/A

- When the number of hops is two, the fountain code achieves a higher throughput than the BATS code; when the number of hops is more than two, the BATS code achieves a higher throughput than the fountain code.

- COPE and TCP time out and could not receive all K number of packets due to high packet loss rate. Hence, COPE and TCP achieve the least throughput.

- For all the situations in Case 2, RLNC achieves a lower throughput than the BATS code. This is because a coded packet in RLNC is restricted to one batch of M native packets while a coded packet in the BATS code is a random mixture of all the K native packets.

- When the number of hops is 2 and 3, RLNC achieves a lower throughput than the fountain code. This is because a coded packet in RLNC is restricted to one batch of M native packets while a coded packet in the fountain code is a random mixture of all the K native packets. But when the number of hops is 5, RLNC achieves a higher throughput than the fountain code. This is because the more relay nodes, the more opportunities for network coding in RLNC while the fountain code does not have such a benefit.

- For the case of $K = 6400$ and five hops, the fountain code does not receive all the K native packets within 6000 seconds, which we call "timeout". The timeout is because the end-to-end packet loss is too high for five hops.

5.2.3 Case 3: A Large Number of Nodes with Node Mobility

The setup of this set of experiments is the following. There are 400 nodes in the network. All the nodes move under the random waypoint mobility model, i.e., each node selects a random position, moves towards it in a straight line at a constant speed that is randomly selected from a range, and pauses at that destination; each node repeats this process throughout the experiment. Due to node mobility, the communication routes change over time. Hence, the network topology is dynamic.

In this set of experiments, the range of the nodes' speed is from 5 meters/s to 10 meters/s. All the nodes move in a square area of 3000 meters by 3000 meters. We measure the throughput between a specific pair of source/destination nodes. This pair of source/destination nodes do not move and are not in the transmission range of each other. Hence, they need relay nodes to forward packets to the destination. The relay nodes are moving around. The number of hops between the intended source and the intended destination is varying since the relay nodes are moving around.

To make the experiments more realistic, we also generate some background traffic. The background traffic is generated in the following manner: we randomly select 100 pairs of nodes out of the 400 nodes; generate a Constant Bit Rate (CBR) flows between each pair of nodes. Each CBR flow lasts for 30 seconds with a random start time. Since the data rate needs to be constant for CBR, the source generates a packet every T_c second ($T_c \in (0, 1]$); the packet size is 1024 bytes. For example, for $T_c = 1$ second, the data rate is 1024 bytes/s. The number of hops from the source node to the destination node is random, depending on the positions of all the nodes. Since all the nodes are mobile, the network topology is dynamic.

In this set of experiments, the number of native packets to be transmitted by the source under study is 1600 packets, i.e., $K = 1600$. Table 3 shows the throughput of seven schemes under Case 3. We have the following observations:

- FUN-2 achieves the highest throughput and FUN-1 achieves the second highest throughput. This is because the number of hops in Case 3 is usually small (mostly two hops) and hence FUN-2 performs better than FUN-1 as in Case 1.
- COPE achieves the third highest throughput and TCP achieves the fourth highest throughput. Their throughput is higher than the BATS code, the fountain code, and RLNC; this may be because congestion and MAC contention are serious performance-limiting problems in multihop wireless networks and COPE and TCP both have congestion control to avoid congestion/contention with the background traffic while the BATS code, the fountain code, and RLNC do not. We will study how congestion control (e.g., back-pressure) affects the throughput in our future work.
- The fountain code achieves a higher throughput than the BATS code. This is because when a relay node moves out of the transmission range of the source node, the BATS code suffers more than the fountain code. This can be illustrated by an example for the BATS code: a relay node may hold $M/2$ packets of the same batch when it moves out of the transmission range of the source; if this relay node does not come back within the transmission range of the source, the $M/2$ packets will never be forwarded to the destination since they are waiting for the batch to be complete to be allowed to conduct network coding. This waste of $M/2$ packets reduces the throughput of the BATS code. In comparison, the fountain code does not have a batch structure; the relay node always forwards any packet in its buffer without waiting for future packets.
- RLNC achieves a lower throughput than the BATS code as in Case 3.

Table 3: Throughput under Case 3

Scheme	Throughput (Mbits/s)
FUN-1	0.669
FUN-2	0.691
BATS	0.330
Fountain	0.385
RLNC	0.291
COPE	0.493
TCP	0.451

In summary, all the experimental results demonstrate that our FUN approach achieves higher throughput than BATS code, the best fountain code (RQ code), RLNC, COPE, and TCP for multihop wireless networks.

6. CONCLUSION

This paper is concerned with the problem of information spreading over lossy communication channels. To address this problem, a joint FoUntain coding and Network coding (FUN) approach has been proposed. The proposed FUN architecture provides a unified framework for FUN-1, FUN-2, BATS codes, fountain codes, RLNC, COPE, and existing protocols. The novelty of our FUN approach lies in combining the best features of fountain coding, intra-session network coding, and cross-next-hop network coding. As such, our FUN approach is capable of achieving unprecedented high throughput over lossy channels. Experimental results demonstrate that our FUN approach achieves higher throughput than existing schemes for multihop wireless networks.

It is worth mentioned that the computational complexity of FUN-1 and FUN-2 (in terms of number of additions and multiplications per coded packet) is linear w.r.t. the batch size M. Since M is usually small, the delay incurred by FUN-1 and FUN-2 at a terminal node or a relay node is small.

Our future work includes extending intra-session network coding to general intra-session network coding, which applies to both unicast and multicast.

Acknowledgment

This work was supported in part by NSF CNS-1116970. The authors would like to thank Drs. Shenghao Yang and Raymond Yeung for sharing the computer programs of BATS codes and insightful comments. Thanks also go to Dr. Muriel Médard for constructive suggestions and comments.

7. REFERENCES

[1] Qualnet web site. http://web.scalable-networks.com/content/qualnet.

[2] R. Ahlswede, N. Cai, S.-Y. Li, and R. W. Yeung. Network information flow. *IEEE Transactions on Information Theory*, 46(4):1204–1216, 2000.

[3] S. Chachulski, M. Jennings, S. Katti, and D. Katabi. Trading structure for randomness in wireless opportunistic routing. In *Proceedings of ACM SIGCOMM*, 2007.

[4] P. A. Chou, Y. Wu, and K. Jain. Practical network coding. In *Proceedings of 41st Annual Allerton*

Conference on Communication, Control, and Computing, 2003.

[5] T. Ho, R. Koetter, M. Medard, D. R. Karger, and M. Effros. The benefits of coding over routing in a randomized setting. In *Proceedings of IEEE International Symposium on Information Theory (ISIT)*, 2003.

[6] G. Holland and N. Vaidya. Analysis of tcp performance over mobile ad hoc networks. *Wireless Networks*, 8(2/3):275–288, 2002.

[7] S. Katti, H. Rahul, W. Hu, D. Katabi, M. Médard, and J. Crowcroft. Xors in the air: practical wireless network coding. In *ACM SIGCOMM Computer Communication Review*, volume 36, pages 243–254, 2006.

[8] S.-Y. Li, R. W. Yeung, and N. Cai. Linear network coding. *IEEE Transactions on Information Theory*, 49(2):371–381, 2003.

[9] S. Lin and D. J. Costello. *Error control coding.* Pearson Prentice-Hall: Upper Saddle River, NJ, 2nd edition, 2004.

[10] D. S. Lun, M. Médard, R. Koetter, and M. Effros. On coding for reliable communication over packet networks. *Physical Communication*, 1(1):3–20, 2008.

[11] J.-S. Park, M. Gerla, D. S. Lun, Y. Yi, and M. Medard. Codecast: a network-coding-based ad hoc multicast protocol. *IEEE Wireless Communications*, 13(5):76–81, 2006.

[12] J. Qureshi, C. H. Fohy, and J. Cai. Primer and recent developments on fountain codes. *arXiv preprint arXiv:1305.0918*, 2013.

[13] T. S. Rappaport. *Wireless communications: principles and practice.* Prentice-Hall: Upper Saddle River, NJ, 1996.

[14] S. Rayanchu, S. Sen, J. Wu, S. Banerjee, and S. Sengupta. Loss-aware network coding for unicast wireless sessions: design, implementation, and performance evaluation. In *ACM SIGMETRICS Performance Evaluation Review*, volume 36, pages 85–96, 2008.

[15] A. Shokrollahi and M. Luby. Raptor codes. *Foundations and Trends in Communications and Information Theory*, 6(3–4):213–322, 2011.

[16] M. Wang and B. Li. Lava: A reality check of network coding in peer-to-peer live streaming. In *IEEE INFOCOM 2007*, pages 1082–1090.

[17] Y. Wu, P. A. Chou, and S.-Y. Kung. Information exchange in wireless networks with network coding and physical-layer broadcast. Technical report, Microsoft Corporation, Redmond, WA, 2004.

[18] S. Yang and R. W. Yeung. Batched sparse codes. *submitted to IEEE Transactions on Information Theory.*

[19] S. Yang and R. W. Yeung. Coding for a network coded fountain. In *Proceedings of IEEE International Symposium on Information Theory (ISIT)*, pages 2647–2651, 2011.

Algorithm 4 Inner encoding of FUN-2

1: **for** j=0 **to** 1 **do**
2: Initialize two buffers for Destination j, which are denoted by $F_{j,new}$ and $F_{j,old}$;
3: **end for**
4: **while** at least one flow (forward or backward flow) is alive **do**
5: **if** Layer 3 output queue is not empty **then**
6: Pick Packet $y_{i,m}$ at the head of Layer 3 output queue; assume the destination of Packet $y_{i,m}$ is j;
7: **switch** (State of Buffers $F_{j,new}$, $F_{j,old}$, $F_{1-j,old}$)
8: **case** Buffer $F_{j,new}$ is not complete**:**
9: Insert $y_{i,m}$ to the m-th position of Buffer $F_{j,new}$;
10: **if** Buffer $F_{j,new}$ is complete **then**
11: Goto Step 7;
12: **end if**
13: **case** Buffer $F_{j,new}$ is complete **AND** Buffer $F_{j,old}$ is empty **AND** Buffer $F_{1-j,old}$ is empty**:**
14: Move all the packets in $F_{j,new}$ to $F_{j,old}$;
15: **if** the packets in $F_{j,old}$ were mixed before **then**
16: Apply RLNC to all the packets in $F_{j,old}$ and generate M re-coded packets;
17: Move the re-coded packets to the unicast output queue of Layer 2;
18: **end if**
19: **case** Buffer $F_{j,new}$ is complete **AND** Buffer $F_{j,old}$ is empty **AND** Buffer $F_{1-j,old}$ is complete**:**
20: Move all the packets in $F_{j,new}$ to $F_{j,old}$;
21: **if** the packets in $F_{j,old}$ were mixed before **then**
22: Apply RLNC to all the packets in $F_{j,old}$ and generate M re-coded packets;
23: Move the re-coded packets to the unicast output queue of Layer 2;
24: **else**
25: Apply RLNC to all the packets in $F_{j,old}$ and $F_{1-j,old}$ and generate M re-coded packets;
26: Move the re-coded packets to the broadcast output queue of Layer 2;
27: **end if**
28: **case** Buffer $F_{j,new}$ is complete **AND** Buffer $F_{j,old}$ is complete **AND** Buffer $F_{1-j,old}$ is empty**:**
29: Apply RLNC to all the packets in $F_{j,old}$ and generate M re-coded packets;
30: Move the re-coded packets to the unicast output queue of Layer 2;
31: Move all the packets in $F_{j,new}$ to $F_{j,old}$;
32: **if** the packets in $F_{j,old}$ were mixed before **then**
33: Apply RLNC to all the packets in $F_{j,old}$ and generate M re-coded packets;
34: Move the re-coded packets to the unicast output queue of Layer 2;
35: **end if**
36: **end switch**
37: **if** $y_{i,m}$ has not been inserted into $F_{j,new}$ **then**
38: Insert $y_{i,m}$ to the i-th position of $F_{j,new}$;
39: **end if**
40: **end if**
41: **end while**

Minimum-sized Influential Node Set Selection for Social Networks under the Independent Cascade Model

Jing (Selena) He
Department of Computer Science
Kennesaw State University
Kennesaw, GA, 30144
jhe4@kennesaw.edu

Shouling Ji
School of Electrical and Computer Engineering
Georgia Institute of Technology
Atlanta, GA, 30308
sji@gatech.edu

Raheem Beyah
School of Electrical and Computer Engineering
Georgia Institute of Technology
Atlanta, GA, 30308
rbeyah@ece.gatech.edu

Zhipeng Cai
Department of Computer Science
Georgia State University
Atlanta, GA, 30303
zcai@cs.gsu.edu

ABSTRACT

Social networks are important mediums for communication, information dissemination, and influence spreading. Most of existing works focus on understanding the characteristics of social networks or spreading information through the "word of mouth" effect of social networks. However, motivated by applications of alleviating social problems, such as drinking, smoking, addicting to gaming, and influence spreading problems, such as promoting new products, we propose a new optimization problem named the *Minimum-sized Influential Node Set* (MINS) selection problem, which is to identify the minimum-sized set of influential nodes, such that every node in the network could be influenced by these selected nodes no less than a threshold τ. Our contributions are threefold. First, we prove that, under the independent cascade model, MINS is NP-hard. Subsequently, we present a greedy approximation algorithm to address the MINS selection problem. Moreover, the performance ratio of the greedy algorithm is analyzed. Finally, to validate the proposed greedy algorithm, extensive experiments and simulations are conducted both on real world coauthor data sets and random graphs.

Categories and Subject Descriptors

H.4 [**Information Systems Applications**]: Miscellaneous; D.2.8 [**Software Engineering**]: Metrics—*complexity measures, performance measures*

General Terms

Theory

MobiHoc'14, August 11–14, 2014, Philadelphia, PA, USA.

http://dx.doi.org/10.1145/2632951.2632975.

Keywords

Viral Marketing; Influence Spreading; Social Networks; Minimum-sized Influential Node Set; Greedy Algorithm; NP-hard Problem; Performance Ratio

1. INTRODUCTION

A social network (*e.g.*, Facebook and MySpace) is a network made up of a set of nodes (such as individuals or organizations) and the social ties (such as relations and interactions) among these nodes. Ever since social networks appear, they play a fundamental role as a medium for spreading information, ideas, and influences among individuals. With the emergence of social applications (such as MSN, Wikis, Netflix, and Twitter), there have been tremendous interests in exploring social influences from individual-to-individual and individual-to-group interactions [1, 2, 3, 4]. This is because that the social influence is becoming a critical, complex, and subtle force to dominate the dynamics of a social network. As a result, extensive researches have been dedicated to select a set of influential users to spread ideas and information within a group recently. In this paper, motivated by influence spreading applications and alleviating social problems, such as drinking, smoking, and addicting to gaming [5], we aim to find a Minimum-sized Influential Node Set (MINS), which influences every individual in a social network no less than a pre-defined threshold τ.

Constructing an MINS is helpful to alleviate the aforementioned social problems, and it is also helpful for promoting new products in a social network. Consider the following scenario as a motivation example. A small company wants to market a new product in a community. For saving the budget, but to get the maximum profit, the company would like to distribute the product samples to a small number of initial influential users in the community. The company wishes that these initial users would love the product and start to influence their friends in the community. The goal is that every user in the community is influenced by the initially selected users no less than τ eventually. To sum up, the specific problem we investigate in this paper is the following: given a social network, and a threshold τ, how to identify a minimum-sized subset of the individuals in the network such that the subset can result in a influence on every individual in the social network no less than τ.

The proposed MINS selection problem is different from the *influence maximization* problem [6], which tries to find a subset of individuals M, such that, for a preset threshold k, $|M| = k$ and M has the maximum expected number of influenced individuals over other subsets of size k. The problem investigated in this paper is to find a minimum-sized set of influential nodes, so that they have the influence on every node in the network no less than τ. A related work to our research is [7], which is to find a minimum-sized *Positive Influence Dominating Set* (PIDS) D, so that every node has at least half of its neighbors in D. Actually, the authors in [7] studied the MINS selection problem under the *deterministic linear threshold model*, in which the influence from a pair of nodes is represented by a weight and an individual can be positively influenced when the sum of the weights exceeds a pre-determined threshold. To be specific, the authors in [7] assumed that the influence of each social tie is always 1, and an individual can be positively influenced when at least half of its neighbor nodes are in D. Nevertheless, the deterministic linear threshold model cannot fully characterize the social influence between each pair of nodes in a real social network. This is because that, in the physical world, the strength of the social influence between different pairs of nodes may be different and is actually a probabilistic value [1, 2, 3, 4]. Hence, we explore the MINS selection problem under the *independent cascade model* [6], where individuals can influence their neighbors with certain independent probabilities. In this paper, we study MINS under the independent cascade model. We first analyze the NP-hardness of MINS, and then propose a greedy approximation algorithm to solve the problem with performance analysis. Particularly, the main contributions of this paper are summarized as follows.

1) We introduce a new optimization problem, named the Minimum-sized Influential Node Set (MINS) selection problem, which is to identify the minimum-sized set of influential nodes, that could influence every node in the network no less than a pre-defined threshold τ. We further prove that it is a NP-hard problem under the independent cascade model.

2) We define a polymatroid contribution function, which suggests us a greedy approximation algorithm called MINS-GREEDY to address the MINS selection problem. Comprehensive theoretical analysis about its performance ratio is also given in the paper.

3) We also conduct extensive experiments and simulations to validate our proposed algorithm both on real world coauthor data sets and random graphs. The experiment and simulation results show that the proposed greedy algorithm works well to solve the MINS selection problem. More importantly, the solutions obtained by the greedy algorithm is very close to the optimal solutions of MINS in small scale networks.

The rest of this paper is organized as follows: in Section 2, we review some related literatures. In Section 3, we first introduce the network model and then we formally define the MINS selection problem and prove its NP-hardness. The greedy algorithm and the theoretical analysis of the algorithm are presented in Section 4. The experimental results are presented in Section 5 to validate our proposed algorithm. Finally, the paper is concluded in Section 6.

2. RELATED WORK

In this section, we first briefly review the related works of the influence maximization problem, and the PIDS problem. Subsequently, we summarize some related literatures of social influence analysis, followed by some remarks.

2.1 Influence Maximization Problem

Domingos *et al.* [8, 9] were the first to emphasize the node selection problem when propagating information through social networks. They considered the social relations of individuals and proposed a probabilistic information propagation model for the problem, as well as several heuristic solutions. Subsequently, Kempe *et al.* formulated the influence maximization problem and studied the problem under two different models *i.e.*, the linear threshold model and the independent cascade model in [6, 10]. They proposed greedy algorithms and analyzed their performance ratios, which are $1-\frac{1}{e}$ under both models. To address the scalability problem of the algorithms in [6, 10], Leskovec *et al.* [11] presented a "lazy-forward" optimization scheme in selecting initial nodes, which greatly reduces the number of influence spread evaluations. Laterly, Chen *et al.* [12, 13, 14] showed that the problem of computing exact influence in social networks under both the linear threshold model and the independent cascade model is #P-Hard. They also proposed scalable algorithms under both models, which are faster than the greedy algorithms proposed in [6, 10].

On the other hand, Goyal *et al.* [15] studied the influence maximization problem from the data-based perspective. They introduced a new model called *credit distribution*, which directly leverages available propagation traces to learn how influence flows in the network and adopt it to estimate the expected influence spread. They also showed that the influence maximization problem under the credit distribution model is NP-hard, and an approximation algorithm is designed. Dinh *et al.* [16] investigated the cost-effective massive viral marketing problem, taking into the consideration the limited influence propagation. They proposed an efficient algorithm called VirAds to tackle the viral marketing problem on large-scale networks. VirAds guarantees a relative error bound of $O(1)$ from the optimal solutions in power-law networks. Zou *et al.* were the first to add the latency constraint to the influence maximization problem under the linear threshold model, called the *fast information propagation* problem in [17]. They further proved that the fast information propagation problem is NP-hard in [18]. Moreover, two heuristic algorithms are given and their performance ratios are also analyzed. He *et al.* explored the influence maximization problem considering both positive influence and negative influence in [19].

2.2 Positive Influence Dominating Set Problem

Wang *et al.* first proposed the Positive Influence Dominating Set (PIDS) problem under the deterministic linear threshold model in [5], which is to find a set of nodes D such that every node in the network has at least half of its neighbor nodes in D. They proposed a selection algorithm and analyzed its performance on a real online social network data set. Subsequently, Zhu *et al.* proved that PIDS is APX-hard and proposed two greedy algorithms with approximation ratio analysis in [7] and [20], respectively.

2.3 Social Influence Analysis

Saito *et al.* predicted the information diffusion probabilities under the independent cascade model in [1]. They formally defined the likelihood maximization problem and then applied an Expectation-Maximization (EM) algorithm to solve it. Subsequently, Tang *et al.* argued that the effect of the social influence from different angles (topics) may be different. Hence, they introduced Topical Affinity Propagation (TAP) to model topic-related social influence in large social networks in [2]. Later, Tang *et al.* [4] proposed a Dynamic Factor Graph (DFG) model to incorporate the time information to analyze dynamic social influences. Similarly, Goyal *et al.* [3] studied the problem of learning the influence probabilities from historical node actions.

2.4 Remarks

All the above mentioned existing works fall into three categories: one is to understand the properties and characteristics of social networks. Another is to study the influence maximization problem with or without the time constraint. The last is the PIDS problem. Our work different from the influence maximization problem is that we find a minimum-sized set of individuals that guarantees the influence on every node in the network no less than a threshold τ, while the influence maximization problem focuses on choosing a subset of a pre-established size k that maximizes the spread of information. Moreover, our work is also different from the PIDS problem. We study the MINS selection problem under the independent cascade model which is more practical, while PIDS is investigated under the deterministic linear threshold model.

3. PROBLEM DEFINITION AND HARDNESS ANALYSIS

In this section, we first introduce the network model. Subsequently, we formally define the MINS selection problem and make some remarks for the proposed problem. Finally, we analyze the hardness of the MINS selection problem.

3.1 Network Model

We model a social network by an undirected graph $\mathbb{G}(\mathbb{V}, \mathbb{E}, \Lambda(\mathbb{E}))$, where $\mathbb{V}$ is the set of n nodes, denoted by u_i, and $0 \leq i < n$. i is called the node ID of u_i. An undirected edge $(u_i, u_j) \in \mathbb{E}$ represents a social tie between the pair of nodes. $\Lambda(\mathbb{E}) = \{p_{ij} \mid \text{if } (u_i, u_j) \in \mathbb{E}, 0 < p_{ij} \leq 1, \text{else } p_{ij} = 0\}$, where p_{ij} indicates the social influence between nodes u_i and u_j[1]. For simplicity, we assume the links are undirected (bidirectional), which means two linked nodes have the same social influence (*i.e.*, p_{ij} value) on each other. Additionally, we assume every node has an edge to itself. The corresponding p_{ii} value ($0 \leq p_{ii} \leq 1$) represents the social influence to itself.

3.2 Problem Definition

The objective of the MINS selection problem is to identify a subset of influential nodes as the initialized nodes. Such that, all the other nodes in a social network can be influenced by these nodes no less than a threshold τ. For convenient, we call the initial nodes been selected as *active nodes*, otherwise, *inactive nodes*. Therefore, how to define *influence* is critical to solve the MINS selection problem. In the following, we first formally define some terminologies, and then give the definition of the MINS selection problem.

DEFINITION 3.1. *Influential Node Set ($\mathbb{I}$):* For social network $\mathbb{G}(\mathbb{V}, \mathbb{E}, \Lambda(\mathbb{E}))$, the influential node set is a subset $\mathbb{I} \subseteq \mathbb{V}$, such that all the nodes in $\mathbb{I}$ are initially selected to be the active nodes.

DEFINITION 3.2. *Active Neighbor Set ($\mathbb{A}^{\mathbb{I}}(u_i)$):* For social network $\mathbb{G}(\mathbb{V}, \mathbb{E}, \Lambda(\mathbb{E}))$, $\forall u_i \in \mathbb{V}$, the active neighbor set of u_i is defined as:

$$\mathbb{A}^{\mathbb{I}}(u_i) = \{u_i\} \cup \{u_j \mid (u_i, u_j) \in \mathbb{E}, u_j \in \mathbb{I}\}.$$

Followed by Definition 3.2, we know that the set $\mathbb{A}^{\mathbb{I}}(u_i)$ includes all the active neighbor nodes of u_i and u_i itself. Since every node has a self-circled edge to itself as defined in Section 3.1, we define the *self influence* as follows:

DEFINITION 3.3. *Self Influence (p_{ii}):* For social network $\mathbb{G}(\mathbb{V}, \mathbb{E}, \Lambda(\mathbb{E}))$, and $\forall u_i \in \mathbb{V}$, the self influence of u_i is defined as: $p_{ii} = 1$, if $u_i \in \mathbb{I}$; otherwise, $p_{ii} = 0$.

DEFINITION 3.4. *Influence:* For social network $\mathbb{G}(\mathbb{V}, \mathbb{E}, \Lambda(\mathbb{E}))$, a node $u_i \in \mathbb{V}$, and an influential node set $\mathbb{I}$, we define a joint influence probability of $\mathbb{A}^{\mathbb{I}}(u_i)$ on u_i, denoted by $p_{u_i}(\mathbb{A}^{\mathbb{I}}(u_i))$ as

$$p_{u_i}(\mathbb{A}^{\mathbb{I}}(u_i)) = 1 - \prod_{u_j \in \mathbb{A}^{\mathbb{I}}(u_i)} (1 - p_{ij}).$$

If $p_{u_i}(\mathbb{A}^{\mathbb{I}}(u_i)) \geq \tau$, where $0 < \tau < 1$ is a pre-defined threshold, then u_i is said been influenced. Otherwise, u_i is not been influenced.

DEFINITION 3.5. *Minimum-sized Influential Node Set (MINS).* For social network $\mathbb{G}(\mathbb{V}, \mathbb{E}, \Lambda(\mathbb{E}))$, the MINS selection problem is to find a minimum-sized influential node set $\mathbb{I} \subseteq \mathbb{V}$, such that $\forall u_i \in \mathbb{V}$, u_i is influenced, *i.e.*, $p_{u_i}(\mathbb{A}^{\mathbb{I}}(u_i)) = 1 - \prod_{u_j \in \mathbb{A}^{\mathbb{I}}(u_i)} (1 - p_{ij}) \geq \tau$.

In this paper, we study the MINS selection problem. First, we analyze the complexity of the problem, which is NP-hard. Subsequently, we propose a greedy algorithm called MINS-GREEDY to solve the problem with performance analysis.

3.3 Problem Hardness Analysis

In general, given an arbitrary threshold τ, the MINS selection problem is NP-hard. We prove the complexity of the MINS selection problem in a general graph by constructing a polynomial reduction from the Vertex Cover (VC) problem to MINS as shown in the following theorem. We only provide proof sketch of Theorem 1 due to space limitation.

THEOREM 1. The MINS selection problem is NP-hard.

Proof Sketch: We prove the NP-hardness of MINS by constructing a polynomial-time many-one reduction which converts instances of one decision problem, *i.e.*, the decision version of the well known Vertex Cover (VC) problem into instances of a second decision problem, *i.e.*, the decision version of a specific case of the MINS selection problem.

[1]This model is reasonable since many empirical studies have analyzed the social influence probabilities between nodes [1, 2, 3, 4].

The decision version of the VC problem is defined as follows: given a graph $\mathbb{G}(\mathbb{V}, \mathbb{E}, \Lambda(\mathbb{E}))$, where $\Lambda(\mathbb{E}) = \{1 \mid (u_i, u_j) \in \mathbb{E}; u_i, u_j \in \mathbb{V}\}$, and a positive integer d, determine whether $\mathbb{G}$ has a vertex cover[2] of size at most d.

The decision version of a specific case of the MINS selection problem is: given a graph $\mathbb{G}(\mathbb{V}, \mathbb{E}, \Lambda(\mathbb{E}))$, where $\Lambda(\mathbb{E}) = \{p \mid (u_i, u_j) \in \mathbb{E}, 0 < p < \tau, u_i, u_j \in \mathbb{V}\}$[3], a predefined threshold $0 < \tau < 1$, and a positive integer k, determine whether there exists an influential node set $\mathbb{I} \subseteq \mathbb{V}$, such that the size of $\mathbb{I}$ is $|\mathbb{I}| \leq k$, and every node in $\mathbb{G}$ is influenced, *i.e.*,

$$\forall u_i \in \mathbb{V}, p_{u_i}(\mathbb{A}^{\mathbb{I}}(u_i)) = 1 - \prod_{u_j \in \mathbb{A}^{\mathbb{I}}(u_i)} (1 - p_{ij}) \geq \tau.$$

First, for an instance of the VC problem, denoted by graph $\mathbb{G}(\mathbb{V}, \mathbb{E}, \Lambda(\mathbb{E}))$, where $\Lambda(\mathbb{E}) = \{1 \mid (u_i, u_j) \in \mathbb{E}; u_i, u_j \in \mathbb{V}\}$, we construct a new graph $\widehat{\mathbb{G}}$ as follows:

1) We create $|\mathbb{V}| + |\mathbb{E}|$ nodes with $|\mathbb{V}|$ nodes $\{v_{u_1}, v_{u_2}, \cdots, v_{u_{|\mathbb{V}|}}\}$ representing the nodes in $\mathbb{G}$ and $|\mathbb{E}|$ nodes $\{v_{e_1}, v_{e_2}, \cdots, v_{e_{|\mathbb{E}|}}\}$ representing the edges in $\mathbb{G}$.
2) We add an edge with influence weight p between nodes v_{u_i} and v_{e_j} if and only if node u_i is an endpoint of edge e_j.
3) We attach additional $\lceil \log_{1-p}(1-\tau) \rceil$ nodes to each node v_{u_i}, denoted by set $\mathbf{v}^a_{u_i} = \{v^j_{u_i} \mid 1 \leq j \leq \lceil \log_{1-p}(1-\tau) \rceil\}$.
4) We attach additional $\lceil \log_{1-p}(1-\tau) \rceil - 1$ nodes to each node v_{e_j}, denoted by set $\mathbf{v}^a_{e_j} = \{v^j_{e_j} \mid 1 \leq j \leq \lceil \log_{1-p}(1-\tau) \rceil - 1\}$.
5) Then, we have $\widehat{\mathbb{G}} = \{\widehat{\mathbb{V}}, \widehat{\mathbb{E}}\}$, where $\widehat{\mathbb{V}} = \{v_{u_1}, \cdots, v_{u_{|\mathbb{V}|}}\} \cup \{v_{e_1}, \cdots, v_{e_{|\mathbb{E}|}}\} \cup \bigcup_{i=1}^{|\mathbb{V}|} \mathbf{v}^a_{u_i} \cup \bigcup_{i=1}^{|\mathbb{E}|} \mathbf{v}^a_{e_i}$, $\widehat{\mathbb{E}}$ is the set of all the edges associated with the nodes in $\widehat{\mathbb{V}}$, and $\Lambda(\widehat{\mathbb{E}}) = \{p \mid$ for every edge in $\widehat{\mathbb{E}}\}$.

Taking the network shown in Fig. 1(a) as an example to illustrate the construction procedure from $\mathbb{G}$ to $\widehat{\mathbb{G}}$. There are 4 nodes and 6 edges in $\mathbb{G}$. Therefore, we first create $\{v_{u_i}\}_{i=1}^4$ and $\{v_{e_j}\}_{j=1}^6$ nodes in $\widehat{\mathbb{G}}$. And then we add edges with influence weight p between nodes v_{u_i} and v_{e_j} based on the topology shown in $\mathbb{G}$. Subsequently, we add additional nodes $\mathbf{v}^a_{u_i} = \{v^j_{u_i} \mid 1 \leq j \leq \lceil \log_{1-p}(1-\tau) \rceil\}$ to each node v_{u_i}. Similarly, we add additional nodes $\mathbf{v}^a_{e_j} = \{v^j_{e_j} \mid 1 \leq j \leq \lceil \log_{1-p}(1-\tau) \rceil - 1\}$ to each node v_{e_j}. The influence weights on all the additional edges are p. Finally, the new graph $\widehat{\mathbb{G}}$ is constructed as shown in Fig. 1(b).

We will prove that $\mathbb{G}$ has a VC $\mathbb{D}$ of size at most d if and only if $\widehat{\mathbb{G}}$ has an influential node set $\mathbb{I}$ of size at most k by setting $k = |\mathbb{V}| \lceil \log_{1-p}(1-\tau) \rceil + |\mathbb{E}|(\lceil \log_{1-p}(1-\tau) \rceil - 1) + d$.

In conclusion, we proved that a specific case of the MINS selection problem is NP-hard, since the VC problem is NP-hard. Consequently, the general MINS selection problem is also at least NP-hard. □

[2]A vertex cover is defined as a subset of nodes in a graph $\mathbb{G}$ such that each edge of the graph is incident to at least one vertex of the set.

[3]The graph model is a special case of the network model defined in Section 3.1.

Based on Theorem 1, we conclude that MINS cannot be solved in polynomial time unless P = NP. Therefore, we proposed a greedy algorithm to solve the problem in the next section.

4. GREEDY ALGORITHM

Since MINS is NP-hard, we propose a greedy algorithm to solve it. The greedy criterion is that the node influencing the most other nodes will be added into MINS first, which is defined by the following contribution function:

Definition 4.1. *Contribution function ($f(\mathbb{I})$). For a social network represented by graph $\mathbb{G}(\mathbb{V}, \mathbb{E}, \Lambda(\mathbb{E}))$, and an influential node set $\mathbb{I}$, the contribution function of $\mathbb{I}$ to $\mathbb{G}$ is defined as:*

$$f(\mathbb{I}) = -\theta * \log[\prod_{u_i \in \mathbb{V}} \max(\varrho^{\mathbb{I}}_{u_i}, 1 - \tau)],$$

where $\varrho^{\mathbb{I}}_{u_i} = \prod_{u_j \in \mathbb{A}^{\mathbb{I}}(u_i)} (1 - p_{ij})$, $\theta = \max(1/c_1, 1/c_2, 1/c_3)$, $c_1 = -\log(1-\tau)$, $c_2 = \log(\frac{1}{\max_{p_{ij}<1}(1-p_{ij})})$, and

$$c_3 = \log\left(\frac{\min\{\prod_{u_j \in \mathbb{S}}(1-p_{ij}) \mid u_j \in \mathbb{V}, \mathbb{S} \subseteq \mathbb{V}, \prod_{u_j \in \mathbb{S}}(1-p_{ij}) > 1-\tau\}}{1-\tau}\right).$$

For the defined contribution function, it has some important properties as shown in the following lemma. The proof of Lemma 1 is omitted due to space limitation.

Lemma 1. *1) $f(\emptyset) = 0$. 2) $f(\mathbb{I})$ is an increasing function.*

Based on the defined contribution function, we propose a greedy algorithm called MINS-GREEDY as shown in Algorithm 1. MINS-GREEDY starts from an empty influential node set $\mathbb{I}$. Each time, it adds the node having the maximum $f(\cdot)$ value into $\mathbb{I}$. The algorithm terminates when $f(\mathbb{I}) = -\theta * \log[(1-\tau)^{|\mathbb{V}|}]$.

Algorithm 1: MINS-GREEDY Algorithm

Input: A social network represented by graph $\mathbb{G}(\mathbb{V}, \mathbb{E}, \Lambda(\mathbb{E}))$; a pre-defined threshold τ

$\mathbb{I} = \emptyset$;
while $f(\mathbb{I}) < -\theta * \log[(1-\tau)^{|\mathbb{V}|}]$ **do**
  choose $u \in \mathbb{V} \setminus \mathbb{I}$ to maximize $f(\mathbb{I} \bigcup \{u\})$;
  $\mathbb{I} = \mathbb{I} \bigcup \{u\}$;
return $\mathbb{I}$;

To better understand Algorithm 1, we use the social network represented by the graph shown in Fig. 2(a) to illustrate the selection procedure as follows. In the example, $\theta = 4.5$.

1) First round: $\mathbb{I} = \emptyset$.
2) Second round: we first compute $f(\mathbb{I} = \{u_1\}) = 8.64$, $f(\mathbb{I} = \{u_2\}) = 8.64$, $f(\mathbb{I} = \{u_3\}) = 9.63$, $f(\mathbb{I} = \{u_4\}) = 11.21$. Therefore, we have $\mathbb{I} = \{u_4\}$, which has the maximum $f(\mathbb{I})$ value. However, $f(\mathbb{I} = \{u_4\}) = 11.21 < -4.5 * \log(0.2^4) = 12.60$. Consequently, the selection procedure continues.

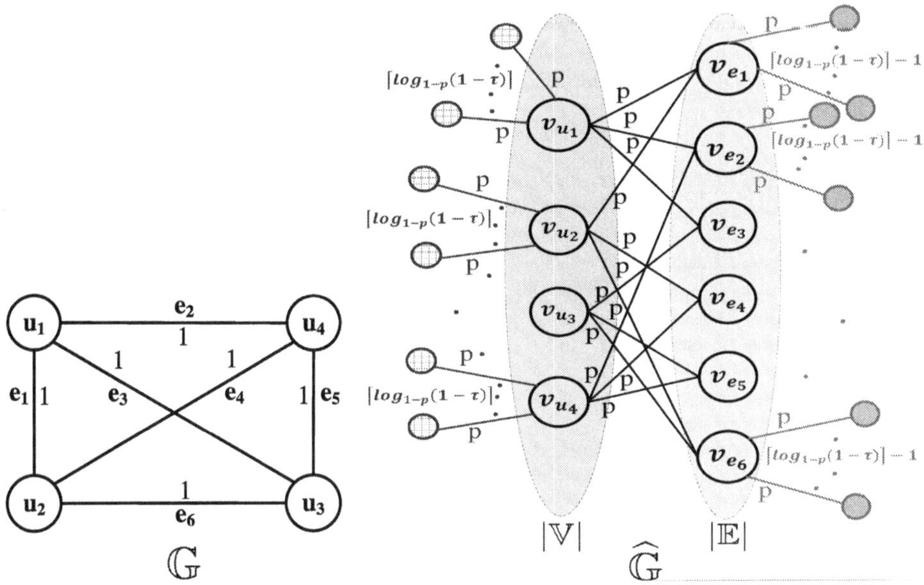

(a) (b)

Figure 1: Illustration of the construction from $\mathbb{G}$ to $\widehat{\mathbb{G}}$.

3) Third round: we first compute $f(\mathbb{I} = \{u_1, u_4\}) = 12.60$, $f(\mathbb{I} = \{u_2, u_4\}) = 12.60$, $f(\mathbb{I} = \{u_3, u_4\}) = 12.60$. Therefore, we have $\mathbb{I} = \{u_1, u_4\}$[4]. Since $f(\mathbb{I} = \{u_1, u_4\}) = -4.5 * \log(0.2^4) = 12.60$, algorithm terminates and outputs set $\mathbb{I} = \{u_1, u_4\}$ as shown in Fig. 2(b), where black nodes represent the selected influential nodes.

It is easy to check that u_2 and u_3 are both influenced. Hence, the constructed $\mathbb{I}$ by running Algorithm 1 is a feasible solution for the MINS selection problem. From this example, we know that the time complexity of Algorithm 1 is $O(n^2)$ in worst case.

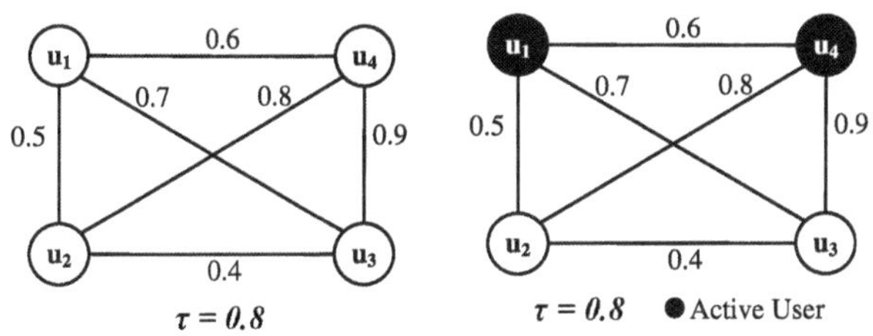

(a) (b)

Figure 2: Illustration of MINS-Greedy algorithm.

Now, we theoretically show the correctness of Algorithm 1 in the following theorem. The proof of Theorem 2 is omitted due to space limitation.

THEOREM 2. Algorithm 1 produces a feasible solution of the MINS selection problem. To be specific, *1)* Algorithm 1 terminates for sure. *2)* $f(\mathbb{I}) = -\lceil \log[(1-\tau)^{|\mathbb{V}|}] * \theta \rceil$ if and only if $\mathbb{I}$ is an influential node set and every node is influenced by nodes in $\mathbb{I}$ no less than τ.

[4]If there is a tie on the $f(\mathbb{I})$ value, we use the node ID to break the tie.

Next, we analyze the performance ratio of the proposed greedy algorithm MINS-GREEDY. As been well known, submodular functions and greedy algorithms have close relationship. Hence, we first introduce some theoretical results about submodular functions and the submodular cover problem. Consider a ground set $\mathbb{V}$ and a real function $f : 2^{\mathbb{V}} \to R$. $f(\cdot)$ is *submodular* if $\forall \mathbb{X} \subseteq \mathbb{Y} \subseteq \mathbb{V}$ and $x \in \mathbb{V} \backslash \mathbb{Y}$, $f(\mathbb{X} \cup \{x\}) - f(\mathbb{X}) \geq f(\mathbb{Y} \cup \{x\}) - f(\mathbb{Y})$. A function $f(\cdot)$ is called a *polymatroid function* if $f(\cdot)$ is submodular and increasing with $f(\emptyset) = 0$. Suppose $f(\cdot)$ is a polymatroid function on $2^{\mathbb{V}}$. A set $\mathbb{X} \subseteq \mathbb{V}$ is said to be a *submodular cover* of $(\mathbb{V}, f(\cdot))$ if $f(\mathbb{X}) = f(\mathbb{V})$. Moreover, consider that $f(\cdot)$ and a cost function $c(\cdot)$ are polymatroid functions on $2^{\mathbb{V}}$. The minimization problem $\min\{c(\mathbb{X}) \mid f(\mathbb{X}) = f(\mathbb{V}), \mathbb{X} \subseteq \mathbb{V})\}$ is called the *Minimum Submodular Cover with Submodular Cost* (MSC/SC) problem, where $c(\mathbb{X})$ is the cost of set $\mathbb{X}$. It is worth to mention that given any influential node set $\mathbb{I} \subseteq \mathbb{V}$, $f(\mathbb{I}) = -\theta * \log((1-\tau)^{|\mathbb{V}|}) = f(\mathbb{V})$. Let the cost function $c(\mathbb{X}) = |\mathbb{X}|$. Then the MINS selection problem can be formulated as: $\min\{c(\mathbb{I}) \mid f(\mathbb{I}) = f(\mathbb{V}), \mathbb{I} \subseteq \mathbb{V})\}$. Since $c(\mathbb{I})$ is linear (*i.e.*, modular), the MINS selection problem is a MSC/SC problem. Then, we have the following theorem [21], which is helpful when analyzing MINS-GREEDY.

THEOREM 3. [21] Suppose $f(\cdot)$ is a polymatroid function on $2^{\mathbb{V}}$, and $f(\mathbb{V}) \geq opt$ where opt is the cost of a minimum submodular cover. For a greedy algorithm, if the selected x in each iteration always satisfied that $\frac{\Delta_x f(\mathbb{X})}{c(x)} \geq 1$, then the greedy solution is a $1 + \rho \ln(\frac{f(\mathbb{V})}{opt})$-approximation, where ρ is the curvature of the submodular cost c, *i.e.*, $\rho = \min_{\mathbb{Y} \subseteq \mathbb{V}} \frac{\sum_{y \in \mathbb{Y}} c(y)}{c(\mathbb{Y})}$. If c is linear (*i.e.*, modular), then $\rho = 1$.

In the following, we will employ Theorem 3 to analyze the performance of MINS-GREEDY. First, we show the submodularity of $\mathbb{I}$ in Lemma 2.

LEMMA 2. $f(\mathbb{I})$ is a submodular function.

PROOF. Based on the definition of a submodular function, it is sufficient to prove that, for arbitrary two influential node sets $\mathbb{S}$ and $\mathbb{T}$, if $\mathbb{S} \subseteq \mathbb{T}$, we have for $\forall u_j \in \mathbb{V} \setminus \mathbb{T}$, $f(\mathbb{S} \cup \{u_j\}) - f(\mathbb{S}) \geq f(\mathbb{T} \cup \{u_j\}) - f(\mathbb{T})$.

Since $\mathbb{S} \subseteq \mathbb{T}$, $\forall u_i \in \mathbb{V}$, we have $\varrho_{u_i}^{\mathbb{S}} \geq \varrho_{u_i}^{\mathbb{T}}$ and $\varrho_{u_i}^{\mathbb{S}\cup\{u_j\}} \geq \varrho_{u_i}^{\mathbb{T}\cup\{u_j\}}$. To prove $f(\mathbb{I})$ is a submodular function, we first prove that when $|\mathbb{T}| - |\mathbb{S}| = 1$, $f(\mathbb{S} \cup \{u_j\}) - f(\mathbb{S}) \geq f(\mathbb{T} \cup \{u_j\}) - f(\mathbb{T})$. Then, we extend it to the general case where $|\mathbb{T}| - |\mathbb{S}| = w > 1$, and the lemma still holds.

First, suppose $\mathbb{S} = \{u_1, u_2, \cdots, u_k\}$, then we have $\mathbb{S} \cup \{u_j\} = \{u_1, u_2, \cdots, u_k, u_j\}$. Let $\mathbb{T} = \{u_1, u_2, \cdots, u_k, u_{k+1}\}$, then we have $\mathbb{T} \cup \{u_j\} = \{u_1, u_2, \cdots, u_k, u_{k+1}, u_j\}$. Let

$$\Delta_{u_j} f(\mathbb{S}, u_i) = -\log(\max(\varrho_{u_i}^{\mathbb{S}\cup\{u_j\}}, 1-\tau)) - (-\log(\max(\varrho_{u_i}^{\mathbb{S}}, 1-\tau))) = \log(\frac{\max(\varrho_{u_i}^{\mathbb{S}}, 1-\tau)}{\max(\varrho_{u_i}^{\mathbb{S}\cup\{u_j\}}, 1-\tau)}),$$

and

$$\Delta_{u_j} f(\mathbb{T}, u_i) = -\log(\max(\varrho_{u_i}^{\mathbb{T}\cup\{u_j\}}, 1-\tau)) - (-\log(\max(\varrho_{u_i}^{\mathbb{T}}, 1-\tau))) = \log(\frac{\max(\varrho_{u_i}^{\mathbb{T}}, 1-\tau)}{\max(\varrho_{u_i}^{\mathbb{T}\cup\{u_j\}}, 1-\tau)}).$$

Furthermore, let

$$\begin{aligned}
\Delta_{u_j} f(\mathbb{S}) &= f(\mathbb{S} \cup \{u_j\}) - f(\mathbb{S}) \\
&= -\theta * \log[\prod_{u_i \in \mathbb{V}} \max(\varrho_{u_i}^{\mathbb{S}\cup\{u_j\}}, 1-\tau)] + \theta * \log[\prod_{u_i \in \mathbb{V}} \max(\varrho_{u_i}^{\mathbb{S}}, 1-\tau)] \\
&= \theta * \sum_{u_i \in \mathbb{V}} [-\log(\max(\varrho_{u_i}^{\mathbb{S}\cup\{u_j\}}, 1-\tau))] + \theta * \sum_{u_i \in \mathbb{V}} [\log(\max(\varrho_{u_i}^{\mathbb{S}}, 1-\tau))] \\
&= \theta * \sum_{u_i \in \mathbb{V}} [\log(\frac{\max(\varrho_{u_i}^{\mathbb{S}}, 1-\tau)}{\max(\varrho_{u_i}^{\mathbb{S}\cup\{u_j\}}, 1-\tau)})] \\
&= \theta * \sum_{u_i \in \mathbb{V}} (\Delta_{u_j} f(\mathbb{S}, u_i)),
\end{aligned}$$

and

$$\Delta_{u_j} f(\mathbb{T}) = f(\mathbb{T} \cup \{u_j\}) - f(\mathbb{T}) = \theta * \sum_{u_i \in \mathbb{V}} (\Delta_{u_j} f(\mathbb{T}, u_i)).$$

To prove that $f(\mathbb{I})$ is a submodular function, we divide all possibilities into the following six cases:

1) For $\forall u_i \in \mathbb{V}$, which is influenced by $\mathbb{S}$, $\mathbb{S} \cup \{u_j\}$, $\mathbb{T}$, and $\mathbb{T} \cup \{u_j\}$, *i.e.*, $1 - \varrho_{u_i}^{\mathbb{S}} \geq \tau$, $1 - \varrho_{u_i}^{\mathbb{S}\cup\{u_j\}} \geq \tau$, $1 - \varrho_{u_i}^{\mathbb{T}} \geq \tau$, and $1 - \varrho_{u_i}^{\mathbb{T}\cup\{u_j\}} \geq \tau$, we have $\Delta_{u_j} f(\mathbb{S}, u_i) = \log(\frac{\max(\varrho_{u_i}^{\mathbb{S}}, 1-\tau)}{\max(\varrho_{u_i}^{\mathbb{S}\cup\{u_j\}}, 1-\tau)}) = \log(\frac{1-\tau}{1-\tau}) = 0$, and $\Delta_{u_j} f(\mathbb{T}, u_i) = \log(\frac{\max(\varrho_{u_i}^{\mathbb{T}}, 1-\tau)}{\max(\varrho_{u_i}^{\mathbb{T}\cup\{u_j\}}, 1-\tau)}) = \log(\frac{1-\tau}{1-\tau}) = 0$. Hence, $\Delta_{u_j} f(\mathbb{S}, u_i) = \Delta_{u_j} f(\mathbb{T}, u_i)$.

2) For $\forall u_i \in \mathbb{V}$, which is influenced by $\mathbb{S} \cup \{u_j\}$, $\mathbb{T}$, and $\mathbb{T} \cup \{u_j\}$, however, not influenced by $\mathbb{S}$, *i.e.*, $1 - \varrho_{u_i}^{\mathbb{S}} < \tau$, $1 - \varrho_{u_i}^{\mathbb{S}\cup\{u_j\}} \geq \tau$, $1 - \varrho_{u_i}^{\mathbb{T}} \geq \tau$, and $1 - \varrho_{u_i}^{\mathbb{T}\cup\{u_j\}} \geq \tau$, we have $\Delta_{u_j} f(\mathbb{S}, u_i) = \log(\frac{\varrho_{u_i}^{\mathbb{S}}}{1-\tau}) > 0$, and $\Delta_{u_j} f(\mathbb{T}, u_i) = \log(\frac{1-\tau}{1-\tau}) = 0$. Hence, $\Delta_{u_j} f(\mathbb{S}, u_i) > \Delta_{u_j} f(\mathbb{T}, u_i)$.

3) For $\forall u_i \in \mathbb{V}$, which is influenced by $\mathbb{S} \cup \{u_j\}$, and $\mathbb{T} \cup \{u_j\}$, however, not influenced by $\mathbb{S}$, and $\mathbb{T}$, *i.e.*, $1 - \varrho_{u_i}^{\mathbb{S}} < \tau$, $1 - \varrho_{u_i}^{\mathbb{S}\cup\{u_j\}} \geq \tau$, $1 - \varrho_{u_i}^{\mathbb{T}} < \tau$, and $1 - \varrho_{u_i}^{\mathbb{T}\cup\{u_j\}} \geq \tau$, we have $\Delta_{u_j} f(\mathbb{S}, u_i) = \log(\frac{\varrho_{u_i}^{\mathbb{S}}}{1-\tau})$, and $\Delta_{u_j} f(\mathbb{T}, u_i) = \log(\frac{\varrho_{u_i}^{\mathbb{T}}}{1-\tau})$. Since $\varrho_{u_i}^{\mathbb{S}} \geq \varrho_{u_i}^{\mathbb{T}} > 1 - \tau$, $\Delta_{u_j} f(\mathbb{S}, u_i) \geq \Delta_{u_j} f(\mathbb{T}, u_i)$.

4) For $\forall u_i \in \mathbb{V}$, which is influenced by $\mathbb{T}$, and $\mathbb{T} \cup \{u_j\}$, however, not influenced by $\mathbb{S}$, and $\mathbb{S} \cup \{u_j\}$, *i.e.*, $1 - \varrho_{u_i}^{\mathbb{S}} < \tau$, $1 - \varrho_{u_i}^{\mathbb{S}\cup\{u_j\}} < \tau$, $1 - \varrho_{u_i}^{\mathbb{T}} \geq \tau$, and $1 - \varrho_{u_i}^{\mathbb{T}\cup\{u_j\}} \geq \tau$, we have $\Delta_{u_j} f(\mathbb{S}, u_i) = \log(\frac{\varrho_{u_i}^{\mathbb{S}}}{\varrho_{u_i}^{\mathbb{S}\cup\{u_j\}}}) = \log(\frac{1}{1-p_{ij}}) > 0$, and $\Delta_{u_j} f(\mathbb{T}, u_i) = \log(\frac{1-\tau}{1-\tau}) = 0$. Hence, $\Delta_{u_j} f(\mathbb{S}, u_i) > \Delta_{u_j} f(\mathbb{T}, u_i)$.

5) For $\forall u_i \in \mathbb{V}$, which is influenced by $\mathbb{T} \cup \{u_j\}$, however, not influenced by $\mathbb{S}$, $\mathbb{S} \cup \{u_j\}$, and $\mathbb{T}$, *i.e.*, $1 - \varrho_{u_i}^{\mathbb{S}} < \tau$, $1 - \varrho_{u_i}^{\mathbb{S}\cup\{u_j\}} < \tau$, $1 - \varrho_{u_i}^{\mathbb{T}} < \tau$, and $1 - \varrho_{u_i}^{\mathbb{T}\cup\{u_j\}} \geq \tau$, we have $\Delta_{u_j} f(\mathbb{S}, u_i) = \log(\frac{\varrho_{u_i}^{\mathbb{S}}}{\varrho_{u_i}^{\mathbb{S}\cup\{u_j\}}})$, and $\Delta_{u_j} f(\mathbb{T}, u_i) = \log(\frac{\varrho_{u_i}^{\mathbb{T}}}{1-\tau})$. Then, we obtain $\Delta_{u_j} f(\mathbb{S}, u_i) - \Delta_{u_j} f(\mathbb{T}, u_i) = \log(\frac{\varrho_{u_i}^{\mathbb{S}}}{\varrho_{u_i}^{\mathbb{S}\cup\{u_j\}}}) - \log(\frac{\varrho_{u_i}^{\mathbb{T}}}{1-\tau}) = \log(\frac{1}{1-p_{ij}} \frac{1-\tau}{\varrho_{u_i}^{\mathbb{T}}}) = \log(\frac{1-\tau}{\varrho_{u_i}^{\mathbb{T}\cup\{u_j\}}})$. Since $\varrho_{u_i}^{\mathbb{T}\cup\{u_j\}} \leq 1-\tau$, we obtain $\Delta_{u_j} f(\mathbb{S}, u_i) - \Delta_{u_j} f(\mathbb{T}, u_i) \geq 0$. Hence $\Delta_{u_j} f(\mathbb{S}, u_i) \geq \Delta_{u_j} f(\mathbb{T}, u_i)$.

6) For $\forall u_i \in \mathbb{V}$, which is not influenced by $\mathbb{S}$, $\mathbb{S} \cup \{u_j\}$, $\mathbb{T}$, or $\mathbb{T} \cup \{u_j\}$, *i.e.*, $1 - \varrho_{u_i}^{\mathbb{S}} < \tau$, $1 - \varrho_{u_i}^{\mathbb{S}\cup\{u_j\}} < \tau$, $1 - \varrho_{u_i}^{\mathbb{T}} < \tau$, and $1 - \varrho_{u_i}^{\mathbb{T}\cup\{u_j\}} < \tau$, we have $\Delta_{u_j} f(\mathbb{S}, u_i) = \log(\frac{\varrho_{u_i}^{\mathbb{S}}}{\varrho_{u_i}^{\mathbb{S}\cup\{u_j\}}}) = \log(\frac{1}{1-p_{ij}})$, and $\Delta_{u_j} f(\mathbb{T}, u_i) = \log(\frac{\varrho_{u_i}^{\mathbb{T}}}{\varrho_{u_i}^{\mathbb{T}\cup\{u_j\}}}) = \log(\frac{1}{1-p_{ij}})$. Hence, $\Delta_{u_j} f(\mathbb{S}, u_i) = \Delta_{u_j} f(\mathbb{T}, u_i)$.

In summary, $\Delta_{u_j} f(\mathbb{S}, u_i) \geq \Delta_{u_j} f(\mathbb{T}, u_i)$ in all the cases. Therefore,

$$\Delta_{u_j} f(\mathbb{S}) = \sum_{u_i \in \mathbb{V}} (\Delta_{u_j} f(\mathbb{S}, u_i)) \geq \sum_{u_i \in \mathbb{V}} (\Delta_{u_j} f(\mathbb{T}, u_i)) = \Delta_{u_j} f(\mathbb{T}).$$

Now, suppose $\mathbb{S} = \{u_1, u_2, \cdots, u_k\}$, and $\mathbb{T} = \{u_1, u_2, \cdots, u_k, u_{k+1}, \cdots, u_{k+w}\}$. We obtain

$$\begin{aligned}
&f(\mathbb{S} \cup \{u_j\}) - f(\mathbb{S}) \geq f(\mathbb{S} \cup \{u_{k+1}, u_j\}) - f(\mathbb{S} \cup \{u_{k+1}\}) \\
&\geq f(\mathbb{S} \cup \{u_{k+1}, u_{k+2}, u_j\}) - f(\mathbb{S} \cup \{u_{k+1}, u_{k+2}\}) \\
&\geq f(\mathbb{S} \cup \{u_{k+1}, u_{k+2}, \cdots, u_w, u_j\}) - f(\mathbb{S} \cup \{u_{k+1}, u_{k+2}, \cdots, u_w\}) \\
&= f(\mathbb{T} \cup \{u_j\}) - f(\mathbb{T})
\end{aligned}$$

Therefore, $f(\mathbb{I})$ is a submodular function. □

Now, we can make the following conclusion.

THEOREM 4. $f(\mathbb{I})$ *is a polymatroid function on* $2^{\mathbb{V}}$.

PROOF. According to Lemma 1 and Lemma 2, $f(\mathbb{I})$ is an increasing, submodular function with $f(\emptyset) = 0$. Hence, we conclude that $f(\mathbb{I})$ is a polymatroid function on $2^{\mathbb{V}}$. □

Before employing Theorem 3 to analyze the performance ratio of MINS-GREEDY, we give the following important lemmas first.

LEMMA 3. In MINS-GREEDY shown in Algorithm 1, if $f(\mathbb{I}) < -\theta * \log[(1-\tau)^{|\mathbb{V}|}]$, then there exists a node $u_k \in \mathbb{V} \setminus \mathbb{I}$ such that $f(\mathbb{I} \cup \{u_k\}) > f(\mathbb{I})$.

PROOF. Let $\mathbb{I}_t$ be the selected influential node set after the t-th iteration. In Algorithm 1, if $f(\mathbb{I}_t) < -\theta * \log[(1-\tau)^{|\mathbb{V}|}]$, the algorithm continues. Therefore, there must exists a node $u_j \in \mathbb{V} \setminus \mathbb{I}$ satisfying $\varrho_{u_j}^{\mathbb{I}_t} > 1-\tau$. Furthermore, let u_k be the node selected to add to $\mathbb{I}_t$ in step 3 of Algorithm 1 during the $(t+1)$-th iteration. Since u_k maximizes the $f(\cdot)$ value based on Algorithm 1, we have

$$\begin{aligned}
f(\mathbb{I}_{t+1}) - f(\mathbb{I}_t) &= f(\mathbb{I}_t \cup \{u_k\}) - f(\mathbb{I}_t) \\
&\geq f(\mathbb{I}_t \cup \{u_j\}) - f(\mathbb{I}_t) \\
= -\theta * \log[\prod_{u_i \in \mathbb{V}} &\max(\varrho_{u_i}^{\mathbb{I}_t \cup \{u_j\}}, 1-\tau)] + \\
&\theta * \log[\prod_{u_i \in \mathbb{V}} \max(\varrho_{u_i}^{\mathbb{I}_t}, 1-\tau)] \\
= \theta * \sum_{u_i \in \mathbb{V}} &-\log(\max(\varrho_{u_i}^{\mathbb{I}_t \cup \{u_j\}}, 1-\tau)) + \\
&\theta * \sum_{u_i \in \mathbb{V}} \log(\max(\varrho_{u_i}^{\mathbb{I}_t}, 1-\tau)) \\
= \theta * \sum_{u_i \in \mathbb{V}} &\log(\frac{\max(\varrho_{u_i}^{\mathbb{I}_t}, 1-\tau)}{\max(\varrho_{u_i}^{\mathbb{I}_t \cup \{u_j\}}, 1-\tau)}) \\
= \theta * [\sum_{u_i \in \mathbb{V} \setminus \{u_j\}} &\log(\frac{\max(\varrho_{u_i}^{\mathbb{I}_t}, 1-\tau)}{\max(\varrho_{u_i}^{\mathbb{I}_t \cup \{u_j\}}, 1-\tau)}) + \\
&\log(\frac{\max(\varrho_{u_j}^{\mathbb{I}_t}, 1-\tau)}{\max(\varrho_{u_j}^{\mathbb{I}_t \cup \{u_j\}}, 1-\tau)})] \\
= \theta * [\sum_{u_i \in \mathbb{V} \setminus \{u_j\}} &\log(\frac{\max(\varrho_{u_i}^{\mathbb{I}_t}, 1-\tau)}{\max(\varrho_{u_i}^{\mathbb{I}_t \cup \{u_j\}}, 1-\tau)}) + \\
&\log(\frac{\varrho_{u_i}^{\mathbb{I}_t}}{1-\tau})] > 0.
\end{aligned}$$

Therefore, we have $f(\mathbb{I}_t \cup \{u_k\}) > f(\mathbb{I}_t)$. □

LEMMA 4. *1)* $f(\mathbb{V}) \geq opt$, where $opt = c(\mathbb{I}_{opt}) = |\mathbb{I}_{opt}|$ is the cost of the optimal solution of the MINS selection problem denoted by $\mathbb{I}_{opt}$. *2)* The selected u_i of each iteration of MINS-GREEDY shown in Algorithm 1 satisfies that $\frac{\Delta_{u_i} f(\mathbb{I})}{c(u_i)} \geq 1$, where $\Delta_{u_i} f(\mathbb{I}) = f(\mathbb{I} \cup \{u_i\}) - f(\mathbb{I})$.

PROOF. For 1), Based on Definition 4.1, we know $\theta \geq 1/(-\log(1-\tau))$. Therefore,

$$f(\mathbb{V}) = -\theta * \log[(1-\tau)^{|\mathbb{V}|}] \geq |\mathbb{V}| \geq |\mathbb{I}_{opt}| = opt.$$

For 2), According to Lemma 3, we know that if $f(\mathbb{I}) < -\theta * \log[(1-\tau)^{|\mathbb{V}|}]$, then there exists a node $u_k \in \mathbb{V} \setminus \mathbb{I}$ such that $f(\mathbb{I} \cup \{u_k\}) > f(\mathbb{I})$. In other words, if Algorithm 1 does not terminate, there must exist a node $u_j \in \mathbb{V}$ satisfying $\varrho_{u_j}^{\mathbb{I}} > 1-\tau$, and

$$\begin{aligned}
\Delta_{u_k} f(\mathbb{I}, u_j) &= -\log(\max(\varrho_{u_j}^{\mathbb{I} \cup \{u_k\}}, 1-\tau)) - \\
&\quad (-\log(\max(\varrho_{u_j}^{\mathbb{I}}, 1-\tau)) \\
&= \log(\frac{\max(\varrho_{u_j}^{\mathbb{I}}, 1-\tau)}{\max(\varrho_{u_j}^{\mathbb{I} \cup \{u_k\}}, 1-\tau)}) > 0.
\end{aligned}$$

Then, we have

$$\begin{aligned}
\Delta_{u_k} f(\mathbb{I}) &= f(\mathbb{I} \cup \{u_k\}) - f(\mathbb{I}) \\
= -\theta * \log[\prod_{u_i \in \mathbb{V}} &\max(\varrho_{u_i}^{\mathbb{I} \cup \{u_k\}}, 1-\tau)] + \\
&\theta * \log[\prod_{u_i \in \mathbb{V}} \max(\varrho_{u_i}^{\mathbb{I}}, 1-\tau)] \\
= \theta * \sum_{u_i \in \mathbb{V}} &[-\log(\max(\varrho_{u_i}^{\mathbb{I} \cup \{u_k\}}, 1-\tau))] + \\
&\theta * \sum_{u_i \in \mathbb{V}} [\log(\max(\varrho_{u_i}^{\mathbb{I}}, 1-\tau))] \\
= \theta * \sum_{u_i \in \mathbb{V}} &[\log(\frac{\max(\varrho_{u_i}^{\mathbb{I}}, 1-\tau)}{\max(\varrho_{u_i}^{\mathbb{I} \cup \{u_k\}}, 1-\tau)})] \\
&= \theta * \sum_{u_i \in \mathbb{V}} (\Delta_{u_k} f(\mathbb{I}, u_i)).
\end{aligned}$$

To prove the lemma, we divide the possibilities into the following two cases:

1) u_j is not influenced by $\mathbb{I} \cup \{u_k\}$. Then,

$$\Delta_{u_k} f(\mathbb{I}, u_j) = \log(\frac{\varrho_{u_j}^{\mathbb{I}}}{\varrho_{u_j}^{\mathbb{I} \cup \{u_k\}}}) = \log(\frac{1}{1-p_{kj}}).$$

Since we know that $\theta \geq \frac{1}{(\log \frac{1}{\max\limits_{p_{ij}<1}(1-p_{ij})})}$. Hence

$$\Delta_{u_k} f(\mathbb{I}) = \theta * \sum_{u_j \in \mathbb{V}} (\Delta_{u_k} f(\mathbb{I}, u_j)) \geq \theta * \log(\frac{1}{1-p_{kj}}) \geq 1.$$

2) u_j is influenced by $\mathbb{I} \cup \{u_k\}$. Then,

$$\Delta_{u_k} f(\mathbb{I}, u_j) = \log(\frac{\varrho_{u_j}^{\mathbb{I}}}{1-\tau}) = \log(\frac{\varrho_{u_j}^{\mathbb{I}}}{1-\tau}).$$

Since $\theta \geq \frac{1}{(\log \frac{\min\{\prod_{u_j \in \mathbb{S}}(1-p_{ij}) \mid u_j \in \mathbb{V}, \mathbb{S} \subseteq \mathbb{V}, \prod_{u_j \in \mathbb{S}}(1-p_{ij}) > 1-\tau\}}{1-\tau})}$, we have

$\Delta_{u_k} f(\mathbb{I}) = \theta * \sum_{u_j \in \mathbb{V}} (\Delta_{u_k} f(\mathbb{I}, u_j)) \geq \theta * \log(\frac{\varrho_{u_j}^{\mathbb{I}}}{1-\tau}) \geq 1.$

In summary, $\frac{\Delta_{u_i} f(\mathbb{I})}{c(u_i)} \geq \frac{\Delta_{u_k} f(\mathbb{I})}{c(u_i)} = \Delta_{u_k} f(\mathbb{I}) \geq 1$. □

Now, we are ready to analyze the performance ratio of Algorithm 1 as follows.

THEOREM 5. The performance ratio of the greedy algorithm shown in Algorithm 1 is $1 + \ln(\frac{-\theta|\mathbb{V}|\log(1-\tau)}{opt})$, where *opt* is the size of the optimal solution of MINS.

PROOF. According to Theorem 4, our proposed contribution function $f(\mathbb{I})$ is a polymatroid function on $2^{\mathbb{V}}$. Moreover, based on Lemma 4, and Theorem 3, MINS-GREEDY produces an approximation solution with a factor of $1 + \ln(\frac{f(\mathbb{V})}{opt}) = 1 + \ln(\frac{-\theta|\mathbb{V}|\log(1-\tau)}{opt})$ from the optimal, where *opt* is the size of the optimal solution of MINS. □

5. PERFORMANCE EVALUATION

Since there are no existing works studying the MINS selection problem under the independent cascade model currently, in the simulations and experiments, the results of MINS-GREEDY (denoted by MINS) are compared with the most related work [7] denoted by PIDS, and the optimal solution of MINS, which are obtained by exhausting searching, denoted by OPTIMAL. To ensure fairness of comparisons, the condition of termination to the algorithm proposed in [7] is changed to find a PIDS, such that every node in the network is influenced no less than the same threshold τ in MINS.

5.1 Simulation Results

5.1.1 Simulation Setting

We build our own simulator to generate random graphs based on the random graph model $G(n,p) = \{G \mid G$ has n nodes and an edge between any pair of nodes is generated with probability $p\}$. For $G = (V,E) \in G(n,p)$, u_i, $u_j \in V$, and $(u_i,u_j) \in E$, the associated social influence $0 < p_{ij} \leq 1$ is randomly generated. For each specific setting, 100 instances are generated. The results are the average values of these 100 instances. In the following, we show the simulation results under different scenarios.

5.1.2 Simulation Results in Random Graphs

The objectives of MINS and PIDS are both to minimize the size of the constructed subsets. In this subsection, we check the size of the solutions of MINS, PIDS and OPTIMAL under different scenarios in random graphs. In this simulation, we consider the following tunable parameters: the network size n, the probability p to create an edge in the random graph model $G(n,p)$, and the user pre-defined influence threshold τ. Since we adopt exhaust searching to find the optimal solution of MINS, it is impractical to test on large scale networks. Hence, we first run a set of simulations on small scale networks of network size changing from 10 to 20, and the results are shown in Fig. 3.

The impacts of n, p, and τ on the size of the solutions of MINS, PIDS, and OPTIMAL are shown in Fig. 3(a), (b), and (c), respectively. From Fig. 3(a), we can see that the sizes of the solutions of all the three algorithms increase when n increases. This is because more nodes need to be influenced when network size increases. Additionally, for a specific network size, PIDS produces a larger sized solution than MINS. This is because MINS tries to find the most influential node of the network (which has the largest $f(\mathbb{I})$ value) in each iteration, while PIDS gives the node with the largest degree the highest priority instead. However, a large degree does not necessarily implies high influence to a social network. Furthermore, we can see that the size of the MINS solution is very close to the optimal result. On average, MINS produces 0.62 more nodes than the optimal solution, while PIDS produces 3.53 more nodes than the optimal solution, which implies that our proposed greedy algorithm MINS-GREEDY can produce a close approximation solution to the optimal solution.

From Fig. 3(b), we can see that the solution sizes of all the three algorithms decrease when p increases. This is because that a large p means more edges in the network, so that one selected influential node may influence more nodes. Again, for a specific p, PIDS produces a larger sized solution than MINS. This is because the objective of PIDS is not aimed to obtain the most influential nodes in the network. MINS again can construct a solution with similar size of the optimal solution. On average, MINS only produces 8.07% more nodes than the optimal solution, while PIDS produces 24.30% more nodes than the optimal solution.

From Fig. 3(c), we can see that the sizes of the solutions of all the algorithms increase when τ increases, since large τ value means that more nodes need to be put into the initial active node set to influence all the other nodes. Furthermore, MINS has similar performance with optimal, and has a better performance than PIDS since the greedy criterion of PIDS is the node with the highest degree first. On average, MINS produces 5.01% more nodes than the optimal solution, while PIDS produces 24.44% more nodes than the optimal solution. This reason is similar as we mentioned before.

Additionally, we run a set of simulations on large scale networks of network size changing from 100 to 1000. The impacts of n, p, and τ on MINS and PIDS are shown in Fig. 4. From Fig. 4(a), we can see that the solution sizes of MINS and PIDS are both increase when n increases. This is because that more influential nodes are required for large social networks. Moreover, MINS can find an influential node set that is much smaller than that of PIDS, since MINS tries to find the most influential node in the network during each iteration. On average, MINS produces an influential node set of size 46.67% less than PIDS.

From Fig. 4(b), we can see that the solution sizes of PIDS and MINS are both decrease when p increases. p increases means the number of edges in the network increases, which further implies that the average number of neighbors of each node increases. Hence, one selected influential node may influence more nodes when p increases. For a specific p, PIDS again produces larger sized solution than MINS. On average, PIDS produces 21.6% more nodes than MINS. Additionally, the decreasing trend of PIDS is fast when p increases. This is because when p is small, the expected degree of all nodes is small. Hence, PIDS may find a solution through many iterations till it find a solution satisfying that every node in the network is influenced by the solution no less than τ. When p is large, larger degree nodes could be added into the solution first, so that PIDS might terminate quicker and followed by an influential node set of small size.

From Fig. 4(c), because of similar reasons as in analyzing Fig. 3(c), we can see that the solution sizes of PIDS and MINS increase when τ increases. Moreover, PIDS outputs more nodes than MINS. On average, PIDS produces 6.15 more nodes than that of MINS.

5.2 Experimental Results

5.2.1 Experimental Setting

We also perform our experiments on a real-world data set: *academic coauthor network*, which is extracted from the academic search system Arnetminer [22]. The coauthor data set consists of 640,134 authors and 1,554,643 coauthor relations [2]. The testing data sets used in this experiment are extracted from the coauthor data set. In this experiment, the network size n, which is the number of authors, is change from 100 to 1100. The social influence of each pair of nodes is calculated using the methodology introduced in [2]. Fig. 5 summarizes the distribution of social influence values among the authors in one testing data set. From Fig. 5, we can see that most of the social influence values fall into the range $0 < p_{ij} < 0.05$, which are very small. Moreover, the largest social influence value in the test data set is close to 0.20. Based on this observation, we let τ change from 0.005 to 0.05 in this experiment. For each specific setting, 100

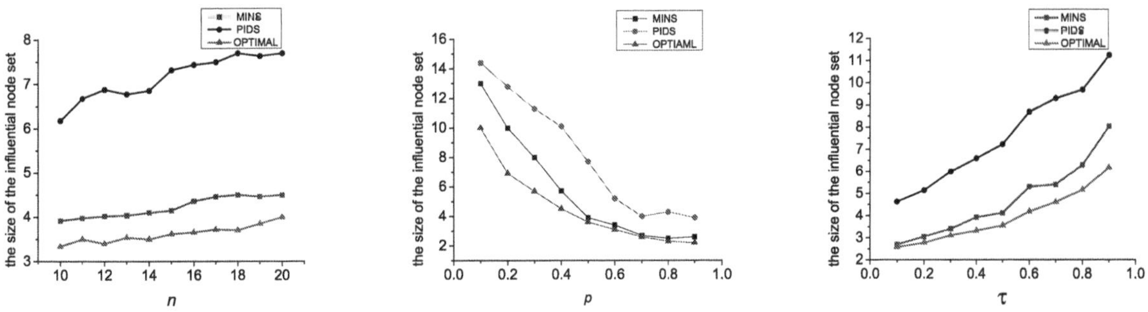

(a) (b) (c)

Figure 3: The size of solutions on small scale networks. The default setting are $n = 15$, $p = 0.5$, and $\tau = 0.5$.

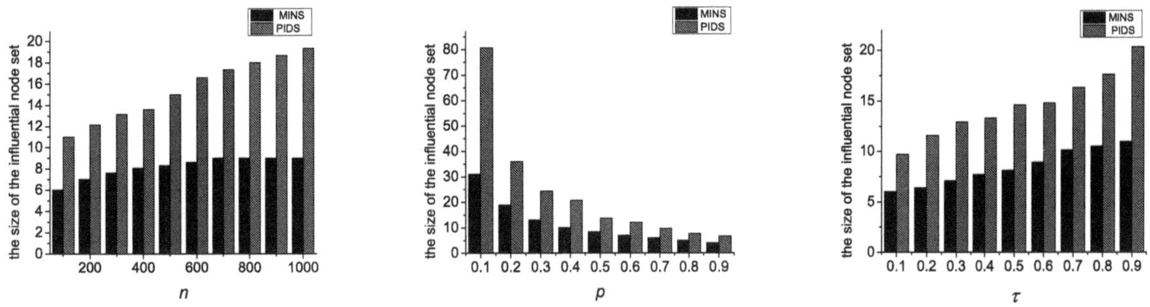

(a) (b) (c)

Figure 4: The size of solutions on large scale networks: The default settings are $n = 500$, $p = 0.5$, and $\tau = 0.5$.

instances are generated. The results are the average values of these 100 instances.

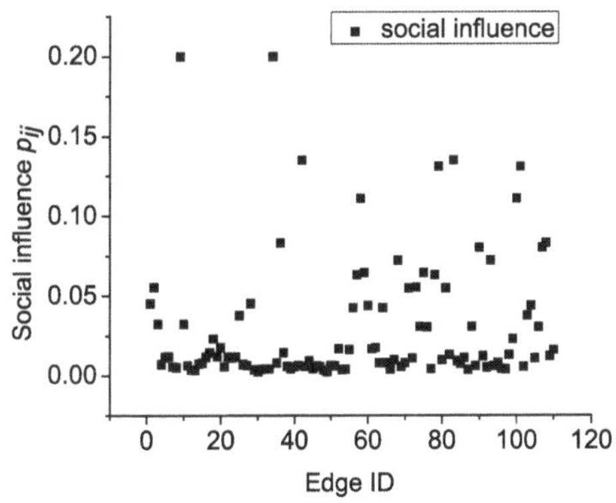

Figure 5: The distribution of social influences of the coauthor data set.

5.2.2 Experiments on Arnetminer Data

For $\tau = 0.008$, the impacts of n on the size of the solutions of MINS and PIDS are shown in Fig. 6(a). From Fig. 6(a), the solution sizes of PIDS and MINS increase when n increases. This is because, when the network becomes large, more influential nodes are requireed to influence the whole network. Furthermore, because of similar reasons analyzed before, MINS produces smaller influence node sets than PIDS. This is consistent with the simulation results. On average, MINS selects 23.49% less influential nodes than that of PIDS.

The impacts of τ on MINS and PIDS are shown in Fig. 6(b). From Fig. 6(b), we can see that the solution sizes of both algorithms increase when τ increases. The reason is obvious, since in order to guarantee the requirement that $\forall u_i \in \mathbb{V}, 1 - \prod_{u_j \in \mathbb{A}^{\mathbb{I}}(u_i)} (1 - p_{ij}) \geq \tau$, more nodes need to be selected as the initial active nodes in both MINS and PIDS. Again, PIDS selects more influence nodes than MINS, since it takes node degree as its greedy criteria instead of node influence. On average, MINS selects 18.45% less influential nodes than PIDS.

We also perform an experiment on a synthesized data set. For the data set used in Section 5.2.1, we randomly generate additional non-redundant p percent of existing edges to the original testing data set. The impacts of p on both algorithms are shown in Fig. 6(c). From Fig. 6(c), we can see that the solution sizes of PIDS and MINS decrease when p increases, since large p value means more edges in the network. In other words, one node may influence more nodes when p increase. Hence, smaller sized initial active node sets may satisfy the requirements both for PIDS and MINS. Again, the size of PIDS's solution is larger than that of MINS's solution, which is also consistent with the simulation results. On average, MINS selects 24.80% less influential nodes than PIDS.

From the results of simulations on the random graphs, and the results of experiments on the real world data sets, we can conclude that the size of the constructed initial active node set of MINS is smaller than it of PIDS. Moreover, the

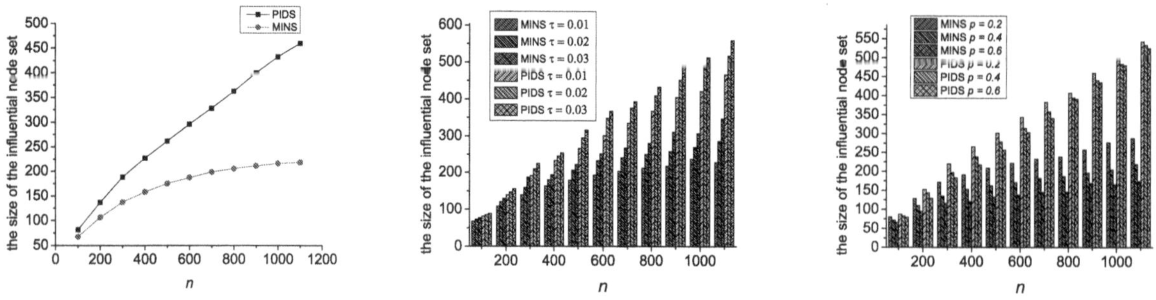

(a) (b) (c)

Figure 6: The size of solutions on real-world data sets.

solution of MINS is very close to the optimal solutions of MINS in small scale networks.

6. CONCLUSION

In this paper, we study the Minimum-sized Influential Node Set (MINS) selection problem which has useful commercial applications in social networks. We show by reduction that MINS is NP-hard under the independent cascade model. Subsequently, a greedy algorithm called MINS-GREEDY is proposed to solve the problem, followed by the theoretical analysis of its performance ratio. Furthermore, we validate our proposed algorithm through simulations on random graphs, and experiments on real world data sets. The simulation results indicate that MINS-GREEDY can construct smaller sized satisfied initial active node sets than the most related work PIDS. Moreover, MINS-GREEDY has very close performance to the optimal solution of MINS in small scale networks.

Acknowledgment

This research is partly supported by the National Science Foundation (NSF) under Grants Nos. CNS-1152001, CNS-1252292, and by the Kennesaw State University College of Science and Mathematics the Interdisciplinary Research Opportunities (IDROP) Program.

7. REFERENCES

[1] K. Saito, R. Nakana, and M. Kimura, *Prediction of Information Diffusion Probabilities for Independent Cadcade Model*, KES'08.

[2] J. Tang, J. Sun, C. Wang, and Z. Yang, *Social Influence Analysis in Large-Scale Networks*, KDD'09.

[3] A. Goyal, F. Bonchi, L. Laskhmanan, *Learning Influence Probabilities in Social Networks*, WSDM'10.

[4] C. Wang, J. Tang, J. Sun, and J. Han, *Dynamic Social Influence Analysis through Time-Dependent Factor Graphs*, ASONAM'11.

[5] F. Wang, E. Camacho, and K. Xu, *Positive Influence Dominating Set in Online Social Networks*, Lecture Notes in Computer Science, 2009.

[6] D. Kempe, J. Kleinberg, and E. Tardos, *Maximizing the Spread of Influence through a Social Network*, KDD'03.

[7] F. Wang, H. Du, E. Camacho, K. Xu, W. Lee, Yan, Shi, and S. Shan, *On Positive Influence Dominating Sets in Social Networks*, TCS, 2011.

[8] P. Domingos, and M. Richardson, *Mining the network value of customers*, KDD'01.

[9] M. Richardson, and P. Domingos, *Mining Knowledge-sharing sites for viral marketing*, KDD'02.

[10] D. Kempe, J. Kleinberg, and E. Tardos, *Influential Nodes in a Diffusion Model for Social Networks*, ICALP'05.

[11] J. Leskovec, A. Krause, C. Guestrin, C. Faloutsos, J. Vanbriesen, and N. Glance, *Cost-effective outbreak detection in networks*, KDD'07.

[12] W. Chen, Y. Yuan, and S. Yang, *Efficient Influence Maximization in Social Networks*, SIGKDD, pp. 199-208, 2010.

[13] W. Chen, Y. Yuan, and L. Zhang, *Scalable Influence Maximization in Social Networks under the Linear Threshold Model*, KDD'10.

[14] W. Chen, C. Wang, and Y. Wang, *Scalable influence maximization for prevalent viral marketing in large-scale social networks*, KDD'10.

[15] A. Goyal, F. Bonchi, and L. Lakshmanan, *A data-based approach to social influence maximization*, VLDB, 5(1):73-84, 2011.

[16] T.N. Dinh, Y. Shen, D.T. Nguyen, and M.T. Thai, *Cost-effective Viral Marketing for Time-critical Campaigns in Large-scale Social Networks*, ToN, Volume:PP, Issue:99, 2013.

[17] F. Zou, Z. Zhang, and W. Wu, *Latency-Bounded Minimum Influential Node Selection in Social Networks*, WASA'09.

[18] F. Zou, J. Willson, Z. Zhang, W. Wu, *Fast Information Propagation in Social Networks*, DMAA, 2010.

[19] J. He, S. Ji, X. Liao, H. M. Haddad, and R. Beyah, *Minimum-sized Positive Influential Node Set Selection for Social Networks: Considering Both Positive and Negative Influences*, IPCCC'13.

[20] X. Zhu, J. Yu, W. Lee, D. Kim, S. Shan, and D. Du, *New Dominating Sets in Social Networks*, JGO, 2010.

[21] P. Wan, D. Du, P. Pardalos, and W. Wu, *Greedy Approcimations for Minimum Submodular Cover with Submodular Cost*, Computer Optimization and Applications, 45:463-474, 2010.

[22] http://arnetminer.org

Not All Content is Created Equal: Effect of Popularity and Availability for Content-Centric Opportunistic Networking

Pavlos Sermpezis
Mobile Communications Department
EURECOM, France
pavlos.sermpezis@eurecom.fr

Thrasyvoulos Spyropoulos
Mobile Communications Department
EURECOM, France
thrasyvoulos.spyropoulos@eurecom.fr

ABSTRACT

Mobile users are envisioned to exploit direct communication opportunities between their portable devices, in order to enrich the set of services they can access through cellular or WiFi networks. Sharing contents of common interest or providing access to resources or services between peers can enhance a mobile node's capabilities, offload the cellular network, and disseminate information to nodes without internet access. Interest patterns, i.e. how many nodes are interested in each content or service (popularity), as well as how many users can provide a content or service (availability) impact the performance and feasibility of envisioned applications. In this paper, we establish an analytical framework to study the effects of these factors on the delay and success probability of a content/service access request through opportunistic communication. We also apply our framework to the data offloading problem and provide insights for its optimization.

Categories and Subject Descriptors

C.2.1 [**Network Architecture and Design**]: Store and forward networks, Wireless communication; C.4 [**Performance of Systems**]: Modeling techniques

Keywords

Performance analysis; Opportunistic networks; Mobile data offloading

1. INTRODUCTION

Opportunistic or Delay Tolerant Networks (DTNs) consist of mobile devices (e.g. smartphones, laptops) that can exchange data using direct communication (e.g. Bluetooth, WiFi Direct) when they are within transmission range. While initially proposed for communication in extreme environments, the proliferation of "smart" mobile devices has led researchers to consider opportunistic networks as a way to support existing infrastructure and/or novel applications, like file sharing [1, 2], crowd sensing [3, 4], collaborative computing [5, 6], offloading of cellular networks [7, 8, 9], etc.

MobiHoc'14, August 11–14, 2014, Philadelphia, PA, USA.

http://dx.doi.org/10.1145/2632951.2632976.

This trend is also shifting the focus from end-to-end to *content-centric* communications. Some content- centric applications for which opportunistic networking has been considered are: (i) *content sharing* [1, 10, 11]: the source(s) of a "content" (e.g. multimedia file, web page) might want to distribute it (e.g. user generated content) or is willing to share it with other nodes (e.g. content downloaded earlier); (ii) *service or resource access* [5, 6]: nodes offer access to resources (e.g. Internet access) or services (e.g. computing resources); (iii) *mobile data offloading* [7, 8, 9]: the cellular network provider, instead of serving separately each node requesting a given "content" (e.g. a popular video, or software update), distributes a few copies of the "content" in some relay nodes (or *holders*) and they can further forward it to any other node that makes a request for it.

The performance of these mechanisms highly depends on *who* is interested, in *what*, and *where* it can be found (i.e. which other nodes have it). While the effect of node mobility has been extensively considered (e.g. [1, 10, 12]) content popularity has been mainly considered from an algorithmic perspective (e.g [9, 11]), and in the context of a specific application. Despite the inherent interest of these studies, some questions remain: Would a given allocation policy work well in a different network setting? Are there interest patterns that would make a scheme generally better than others? Key factors like content popularity and content availability might impact the performance or even decide the feasibility of a given application altogether. In this paper, we try to provide some initial insight into these questions, by contributing along the following key directions:

- We propose a simple analytical framework that is applicable to a range of mobility and content popularity patterns seen in real networks; to our best knowledge, this is the first application-independent effort in this direction (Section 2).

- We provide closed form expressions for important metrics that require few statistics about the aggregate node mobility and content popularity; these results facilitate *online* performance prediction and protocol tuning, compared to approaches requiring detailed per node statistics, as e.g. [9] (Section 3).

- While a detailed application-specific optimization is beyond the scope of this paper, we demonstrate how our analysis can be applied to an example application, mobile data offloading, and can help optimize its performance in a generic setting (Section 4).

Finally, we discuss related work in Section 5, and conclude our paper in Section 6.

2. NETWORK MODEL

2.1 Mobility Model

We consider a network $\mathcal{N}$, where N nodes move in an area, much larger than their transmission range. Data packet exchanges between a pair of nodes can take place only when they are in proximity (*in contact*). Hence, the time points, when the contact events take place, and the nodes involved, determine the dissemination of a message.

We assume that the sequence of the contact events between nodes i and j is given by a random point process with rate λ_{ij} [1]. Analyses of real-world traces suggest that the times between consecutive contacts for a given pair can often be approximated (completely or in the tail) as either exponentially [13, 14] or power-law (e.g. pareto) distributed [15]. Both distributions can be described with a main parameter λ_{ij} (the *contact rate*), and our analysis will be applied to both.

Hence, we can describe the network $\mathcal{N}$ with the contact (or meeting) rates matrix $\mathbf{\Lambda} = \{\lambda_{ij}\}$. Depending on the underlying mobility process, there might be large differences between the different λ_{ij} values in this matrix. Furthermore, it is often quite difficult, in a DTN context, to know $\mathbf{\Lambda}$ exactly, or estimates might be rather noisy. For these reasons, we consider the following simple model for $\mathbf{\Lambda}$:

Assumption 1. *The contact rates λ_{ij} are drawn from an arbitrary distribution with probability density function $f_\lambda(\lambda)$ with known mean μ_λ and variance σ_λ^2 ($CV_\lambda = \frac{\sigma_\lambda}{\mu_\lambda}$).*

By choosing the right function f_λ the above model can capture heterogeneity in the pairwise contact rates, or noise in the estimates. In practice, one would fit the empirical distribution observed in a given measurement trace with an $\hat{f}_\lambda$ and use it in the analysis.

2.2 Content Traffic Model

We assume that each node might be *interested in* one or more "contents". A content of interest might refer to (i) a single piece of data (e.g. a multimedia file, a google map) [7], (ii) all messages/data belonging to a category of interests (e.g. local events, financial news) [2, 16], (iii) updates and feeds (e.g. weather forecast, latest news) [17], etc.

A number of content-sharing applications and mechanisms have been proposed in previous literature, from publish-subscribe mechanisms to "channel"-based sharing and device-to-device offloading, etc., (e.g. [2, 3, 4, 17]). To proceed with our analysis we need to setup a simple model of content/service access that can yet capture different (but of course not all) content-centric applications and approaches.

The main notation we use in our model and analysis is summarized in Table 1.

2.2.1 Content Popularity

We assume that when a node is interested in a content or service, it queries other nodes it *directly* encounters for it. We denote the event that a node $i \in \mathcal{N}$ is *interested in* a content $\mathcal{M}$ (or, equivalently, i requests $\mathcal{M}$) as: $i \rightarrow \mathcal{M}$. We further denote the set of all the contents that nodes are interested in, as: $\mathbf{M} = \{\mathcal{M} : \exists i \in \mathcal{N}, i \rightarrow \mathcal{M}\}$. $|\mathbf{M}| = M$, where $|\cdot|$ denotes the cardinality of a set.

[1]We ignore the contact duration and assume infinite bandwidth; assumptions that are common (e.g. [1, 9]) and orthogonal to the problem we consider here.

Definition 1 (Content Popularity). *We define the popularity of a content $\mathcal{M}$ as the number of nodes $N_p^{(\mathcal{M})}$ that are interested in it*[2]*;*

$$N_p^{(\mathcal{M})} = |\mathcal{C}_p^{(\mathcal{M})}|, \text{ where } \mathcal{C}_p^{(\mathcal{M})} = \{i \in \mathcal{N} : i \rightarrow \mathcal{M}\} \quad (1)$$

We further denote the percentage of contents with a given popularity value n as

$$P_p(n) = \frac{1}{M} \sum_{\mathcal{M} \in M} \mathcal{I}_{N_p^{(\mathcal{M})}=n}, \quad n \in [0, N] \quad (2)$$

where $\mathcal{I}_{N_p^{(\mathcal{M})}=n} = 1$ when $N_p^{(\mathcal{M})} = n$ and 0 otherwise.

In other words, $P_p(n)$ defines a probability distribution over the different contents and associated popularities. In practice, it can be chosen according to common practices (e.g. skewed, pareto) [1, 9, 11], or be fitted to real data, if available.

2.2.2 Content Availability

We assume that a request for a content or service is completed, when (and if) a node that holds (a copy of) the requested content is *directly* encountered. We denote the event that a node i holds (a copy of) a content $\mathcal{M}$ as $i \leftarrow \mathcal{M}$, and we define the availability $N_a^{(\mathcal{M})}$ of a content $\mathcal{M}$ as

Definition 2 (Content Availability). *The availability of a content message $\mathcal{M}$ is defined as the number of nodes $N_a^{(\mathcal{M})}$ that hold a copy of it.*

$$N_a^{(\mathcal{M})} = |\mathcal{C}_a^{(\mathcal{M})}|, \text{ where } \mathcal{C}_a^{(\mathcal{M})} = \{i \in \mathcal{N} : i \leftarrow \mathcal{M}\} \quad (3)$$

The availability of a given content might often (although not always) be correlated with the popularity of that content. A cellular network provider might *allocate* more holders for popular contents [9]. In a content-sharing setting, where some nodes might be more willing than others to maintain and share ("seed") a content after they've downloaded and "consumed" it, popular content will end up being shared by more nodes. We will model such correlations in a *probabilistic* way, as follows.

Definition 3 (Availability vs. Popularity). *The availability of* any *content message $\mathcal{M}$ is related to its popularity through the relation*

$$P\{N_a^{(\mathcal{M})} = m | N_p^{(\mathcal{M})} = n\} = g(m|n) \quad (4)$$

The above conditional probabilities can describe a wide range of cases where availability depends on popularity, and some additional randomness might be present due to factors like: natural churn in the nodes sharing the content, content-dependent differences in the sharing policies applied by nodes, estimation noise, etc. Some special cases of this model include: (i) *uncorrelated availability*, where $g(m|n) \equiv g(m)$; (ii) *deterministic availability*, where:

$$N_a^{(\mathcal{M})} = \rho\left(N_p^{(\mathcal{M})}\right) \Leftrightarrow g(m|n) = \begin{cases} 1, & m = \rho(n) \\ 0, & \text{otherwise} \end{cases}$$

where $\rho(n) : [1, N] \rightarrow [0, N]$ can be an arbitrary function. One such example could be a deterministic approximation of $g(m|n)$ with its average value, namely $\rho(n) = \bar{g}(n) \equiv \sum_m m \cdot g(m|n)$.

3. ANALYSIS OF CONTENT REQUESTS

We will now analyze how different popularity, availability, and mobility patterns (possibly arising from different applications, policies, and network settings) affect key metrics like: (i) the delay to

[2]This could be an average, calculated over some time window.

Table 1: Important Notation

MOBILITY (Section 2.1)		
λ_{ij}	Contact rate between nodes i and j	
$f_\lambda(\lambda)$	Contact rates distribution	
$\mu_\lambda, \sigma_\lambda^2$	Mean value/ variance of contact rates, $CV_\lambda = \frac{\sigma_\lambda}{\mu_\lambda}$	
CONTENT TRAFFIC (Section 2.2)		
$i \to \mathcal{M}$	Node i *is interested / requests* content $\mathcal{M}$	
M	Set of contents in the network, $\|\mathbf{M}\| = M$.	
$N_p^{(\mathcal{M})}$	Popularity of content $\mathcal{M}$	Def. 1
$\mathcal{C}_p^{(\mathcal{M})}$	Set of nodes interested in content $\mathcal{M}$	Def. 1
$P_p(n)$	Probability distribution of content popularity	Eq. (2)
$i \leftarrow \mathcal{M}$	Node i *holds a copy* of content $\mathcal{M}$	
$N_a^{(\mathcal{M})}$	Availability of content $\mathcal{M}$	Def. 2
$\mathcal{C}_a^{(\mathcal{M})}$	Set of nodes that hold a copy of content $\mathcal{M}$	Def. 2
$g(m\|n)$	Availability - Popularity relation	Def. 3
$\rho(n)$	Deterministic case for $g(m\|n)$	
$\overline{g}(n)$	The average value of $g(\cdot\|n)$	
ANALYSIS (Section 3.1)		
$P_p^{req.}(n)$	Popularity distribution of a random request	Lemma 3.1
$P_a^{req.}(n)$	Availability distribution of a random request	Lemma 3.2
T_{ij}	Time of *next* meeting between nodes i and j	
$T_\mathcal{M}$	Content access time	
$X_\mathcal{M}$	Sum of meeting rates of j and nodes $\in \mathcal{C}_a^{(\mathcal{M})}$	Eq. (6)

access a content of interest, (ii) the probability to retrieve a content before a deadline. A key parameter for these metrics is the number of holders for the requested content (availability). The higher this number, the sooner a requesting node will encounter one of them.

While content availability might sometimes be time dependent [11], or the content holders might be chosen based on their mobility properties [9], we first make two additional assumptions that allow us to derive simple, useful expressions. In Section 3.3, we relax both these assumptions.

Assumption 2. *The popularity $N_p^{(\mathcal{M})}$ and availability $N_a^{(\mathcal{M})}$ of a content $\mathcal{M}$ do not change over time.*

Assumption 3. *The set of requesters $\mathcal{C}_p^{(\mathcal{M})}$ and holders $\mathcal{C}_a^{(\mathcal{M})}$ of a content $\mathcal{M}$ are independent of node mobility.*

Assumption 2 is valid (or a good approximation), for example, when the number of holders is chosen by the cellular operator [8, 9] or content provider, and other nodes cannot act as holders or do not have incentives to do so. It is also valid when a given service (e.g. Internet access, or specific sensor) is offered only by a certain number of devices [6], or the "content" refers to a *channel* or *category* and not a particular file [17]. Nevertheless, if a content is disseminating and new nodes are willing to share it [7], then it's availability might change over time.

Assumption 3 is a reasonable approximation when a *mobility oblivious* allocation policy is considered (e.g. [11], or the homogeneous algorithm of [9]) or when there is no knowledge of the interests-mobility correlation, if any. Nevertheless, there exist scenarios where who holds what content might depend on the contact rates with other nodes [10, 9].

3.1 Preliminary Analysis

Assume we observe the network for a long time, during which a large number of requests have been made. Assume further that we pick one such request randomly, which happens to be for content $\mathcal{M}$, and we want to predict its performance. We need to answer the following two questions:

Q.1 What is the popularity of $\mathcal{M}$?

Q.2 How fast does a requesting node meet $\mathcal{M}$'s holders?

Q.1 is needed to predict the availability for $\mathcal{M}$, which according to Assumption 2 does not depend on the exact time of the request. Given the availability of $\mathcal{M}$, Q.2 will estimate the (sum of) contact rates between the requesting node and the holders, according to Assumptions 1 and 3.

Answering **Q.1**

It is easy to see that the popularity of $\mathcal{M}$ should be proportional to $P_p(n)$: the higher the number of different contents with a popularity value n, the higher the chance that $\mathcal{M}$ will be of popularity n. However, the higher the popularity of a content, the more the requests made for it. Hence, a first important observation is that the popularity of the content of such a *random request* is *not* distributed as $P_p(n)$ but is also proportional to the popularity value n.

Consider a stylized example, where only two contents exist in the network, content A with popularity value 10 and content B with popularity value 1. Hence, "half" the contents are of high popularity (10), and "half" of low (1), or in other words $P_p(10) = P_p(1) = \frac{1}{2}$. However, if we observe the network for a long time, 10 times more requests will be made, on average, for content A. Consequently, if we select a request randomly, there is a $10\times$ higher chance that it will be for content A, that is, for the content of popularity 10. Normalizing to have a proper probability distribution gives us the following lemma.

Lemma 3.1. *The probability that a random request is for a content of popularity equal to n is given by*

$$P_p^{req.}(n) = \frac{n}{E_p[n]} \cdot P_p(n)$$

where $E_p[n] = \sum_n n \cdot P_p(n)$ is the average content popularity [3].

Answering **Q.2**

The answer to question Q.2 consists of two separate steps: (i) we calculate the number of holders of $\mathcal{M}$, and then (ii) we calculate how fast the requesting node can meet these holders. Towards answering (i), Lemma 3.2 maps the popularity of the content involved in a random request (derived in Lemma 3.1) to the number of holders for this content. This number is a random variable dependent both on the popularity distribution $P_p(n)$, and on the availability function $g(m|n)$.

Lemma 3.2. *The probability that a random request is for a content of availability equal to m is given by*

$$P_a^{req.}(m) = \frac{E_p[n \cdot g(m|n)]}{E_p[n]}$$

Proof. For a random request for content $\mathcal{M}$, using the property of conditional expectation, we can write [18]:

$$P_a^{req.}(m) = \sum_n P\{N_a^{(\mathcal{M})} = m | N_p^{(\mathcal{M})} = n\} \cdot P_p^{req.}(n)$$

where $P_p^{req.}(n)$ is defined in Lemma 3.1. Substituting, from Def. 3 and Lemma 3.1, the above terms, we successively get

$$P_a^{req.}(m) = \sum_n g(m|n) \cdot \frac{n}{E_p[n]} \cdot P_p(n)$$
$$= \frac{\sum_n g(m|n) \cdot n \cdot P_p(n)}{E_p[n]} = \frac{E_p[n \cdot g(m|n)]}{E_p[n]}$$

which proves the Lemma. □

[3] We use subscript p to denote an expectation over the popularity distribution $P_p(n)$, and n denotes the random popularity values.

Table 2: Performance Metrics when $f_\lambda \sim Gamma$ with μ_λ, CV_λ and $P_p(n) \sim Pareto(n_0, \alpha = 2)$.

$\rho(n) = c \cdot n$	$E[T_{\mathcal{M}}] = \frac{1}{\mu_\lambda \cdot CV_\lambda^2} \left[\frac{c \cdot n_0}{CV_\lambda^2} \cdot \ln\left(\frac{1}{1 - \frac{CV_\lambda^2}{c \cdot n_0}} \right) - 1 \right]$
$\rho(n) = c \cdot \ln(n)$	$P\{T_{\mathcal{M}} \leq TTL\} = 1 - \frac{1}{(1+\ln(\gamma)) \cdot \gamma^{\ln(n_0)}}$ where $\gamma = (1 + \mu_\lambda \cdot CV_\lambda^2 \cdot TTL)^{\frac{c}{CV_\lambda^2}}$

Having computed the statistics for the content availability, we can now calculate how fast the requesting node, say j, meets *any* of the holders i (i.e. nodes $i \in \mathcal{C}_a^{(\mathcal{M})}$). As discussed in Section 2.1, the inter-contact intervals are shown to be either exponentially or pareto distributed:

Exponential Inter-Contact Times. Let T_{ij} denote the inter-contact times between node j and a node $i \in \mathcal{C}_a^{(\mathcal{M})}$, and let T_{ij} be exponentially distributed with rate λ_{ij}. If we denote with $T_{\mathcal{M}}$ the first time until j meets *any* of the nodes $i \in \mathcal{C}_a^{(\mathcal{M})}$ (and, thus, accesses the content), then: $T_{\mathcal{M}} = \min_{i \in \mathcal{C}_a^{(\mathcal{M})}}\{T_{ij}\}$, i.e. $T_{\mathcal{M}}$ is distributed as a minimum of exponential random variables, and it holds that [18]:

$$T_{\mathcal{M}} \sim exp(X_{\mathcal{M}}) \;\Leftrightarrow\; P\{T_{\mathcal{M}} > t\} = e^{-X_{\mathcal{M}} \cdot t} \tag{5}$$

where

$$X_{\mathcal{M}} = \sum_{i \in \mathcal{C}_a^{(\mathcal{M})}} \lambda_{ij} \tag{6}$$

Pareto Inter-Contact Times. Inter-contact times between node j and a node $i \in \mathcal{C}_a^{(\mathcal{M})}$ are pareto distributed with *shape* and *scale* parameters α_{ij} and t_0, respectively:

$$T_{ij} \sim pareto(\alpha_{ij}) \Leftrightarrow P\{T_{ij} > t\} = \left(\tfrac{t_0}{t}\right)^{\alpha_{ij}} \tag{7}$$

Then, it can be shown for $T_{\mathcal{M}} = \min_{i \in \mathcal{C}_a^{(\mathcal{M})}}\{T_{ij}\}$ that

$$T_{\mathcal{M}} \sim pareto(A_{\mathcal{M}}) \Leftrightarrow P\{T_{\mathcal{M}} > t\} = \left(\tfrac{t_0}{t}\right)^{A_{\mathcal{M}}} \tag{8}$$

where $A_{\mathcal{M}} = \sum_{i \in \mathcal{C}_a^{(\mathcal{M})}} \alpha_{ij}$.

Remark: In this case the contact rates will be $\lambda_{ij} = \frac{1}{E[T_{ij}]} = \frac{1}{t_0} \cdot \left(1 - \frac{1}{\alpha_{ij}}\right)$, $\alpha_{ij} > 1$. However, for simplicity, we can use the parameters α_{ij} instead of the rates λ_{ij}, and, correspondingly, a distribution $f_\alpha(\alpha)$, instead of $f_\lambda(\lambda)$.

Clearly, knowing $X_{\mathcal{M}}$ (resp. $A_{\mathcal{M}}$) is needed to proceed with the desired metric derivation. Based on the preceding discussion, $X_{\mathcal{M}}$ (resp. $A_{\mathcal{M}}$) is a random variable that depends on: (i) the number of content holders m (i.e. the cardinality of set $\mathcal{C}_a^{(\mathcal{M})}$ in Eq.(6)), and (ii) the meeting rates with the holders. Applying Assumption 3, it holds that, conditioning on m, $X_{\mathcal{M}}$ (Eq. (6)) is a sum of m i.i.d. random variables $\lambda_{ij} \sim f_\lambda(\lambda)$, i.e

$$X_{\mathcal{M}} \sim f_{m\lambda}(x) = (f_\lambda * f_\lambda \cdots * f_\lambda)_m, \tag{9}$$

where $*$ denotes convolution, and mean value [18]:

$$E[X_{\mathcal{M}} | N_a^{(\mathcal{M})} = m] = E_{m\lambda}[x] = m \cdot \mu_\lambda \tag{10}$$

Similarly, for Pareto intervals $(f_a(\alpha), \mu_\alpha)$:

$$A_{\mathcal{M}} \sim f_{m\alpha}(x) = (f_\alpha * \cdots * f_\alpha)_m, \;\; E_{m\alpha}[x] = m \cdot \mu_\alpha$$

Due to space limitations, the remaining analysis will refer to the case of exponential inter-contact times. The analysis for the Pareto case is similar; when necessary, we might highlight if there are any major differences. We refer the interested reader to [19] for the detailed results of the Pareto case.

3.2 Performance Metrics

We consider two main performance metrics: the *average delay* and *delivery probability*. Based on the analysis of Section 3.1, we derive results under generic content traffic (i.e. $P_p(n)$ and $g(m|n)$) and mobility (i.e. $f_\lambda(\lambda)$) patterns.

3.2.1 Content Access Delay

Result 1. *The expected content access delay can be computed with the expression*

$$E[T_{\mathcal{M}}] = \frac{1}{E_p[n]} \cdot E_p\left[n \cdot \sum_m E_{m\lambda}\left[\frac{1}{x}\right] \cdot g(m|n)\right]$$

Proof. The time $T_{\mathcal{M}}$ a node j needs to access a content $\mathcal{M}$ is exponentially distributed with rate $X_{\mathcal{M}}$. However, $X_{\mathcal{M}}$ is a random variable itself, distributed with $f_{m\lambda}(x)$ (Eq. (9)). Thus, we can write for the expected content access delay:

$$\begin{aligned} E[T_{\mathcal{M}}] &= \sum_m E[T_{\mathcal{M}} | N_a^{(\mathcal{M})} = m] \cdot P_a^{req.}(m) \\ &= \sum_m \int E[T_{\mathcal{M}} | X_{\mathcal{M}} = x, N_a^{(\mathcal{M})} = m] \cdot f_{m\lambda}(x)dx \cdot P_a^{req.}(m) \\ &= \sum_m \int \frac{1}{x} \cdot f_{m\lambda}(x)dx \cdot P_a^{req.}(m) \end{aligned} \tag{11}$$

The last equality follows from the fact that the expectation of an exponential[4] random variable with rate x is $\frac{1}{x}$.

Expressing the integral in Eq. (11) as an expectation over the $f_{m\lambda}(x)$ and substituting $P_a^{req.}(m)$ from Lemma 3.2, gives

$$\begin{aligned} E[T_{\mathcal{M}}] &= \sum_m E_{m\lambda}\left[\frac{1}{x}\right] \cdot \frac{E_p[n \cdot g(m|n)]}{E_p[n]} \\ &= \frac{1}{E_p[n]} \cdot \sum_m E_{m\lambda}\left[\frac{1}{x}\right] \cdot E_p[n \cdot g(m|n)] \end{aligned} \tag{12}$$

Rearranging the expectations and summation in Eq. (12) we get the expression of Result 1. □

If the functions $f_\lambda(\lambda)$, $g(m|n)$ and $P_p(n)$ are known, the expected delay $E[T_{\mathcal{M}}]$ can be computed directly from Result 1, as shown in the following example.

Example Scenario: The contact rates (f_λ) follow a *gamma distribution*, as suggested in [20], with μ_λ and CV_λ. Content popularity $P_p(n)$ is Pareto distributed, as observed in [21], with *scale* and *shape* parameters n_0 and $\alpha = 2$, respectively. Finally, we consider a (deterministic) allocation of holders, $\rho(n) = c \cdot n$ (see Section 2.2.2). Then a closed form expression for $E[T_M]$ is given in the first row of Table 2.

However, in a real implementation, it might not be always possible to know the *exact* distributions of the contact rates (f_λ) and/or the availabilities ($g(m|n)$), needed to compute the expression of Result 1. In the following theorem, we derive an expression for $E[T_M]$ that requires only the *average statistics* (which are much easier to estimate or measure in a real scenario), namely (i) the mean value of the contact rates, μ_λ, and (ii) the average availability for contents of a given popularity, $\overline{g}(n)$.

[4]Considering Pareto intervals, one only needs to change the integral in Eq. (11) as: $\int \frac{x \cdot t_0}{x-1} \cdot f_{m\alpha}(x)dx$.

Theorem 3.3. *A lower bound for the expected content access delay is given by*

$$E[T_{\mathcal{M}}] \geq \frac{1}{\mu_\lambda \cdot E_p[n]} \cdot E_p\left[\frac{n}{\overline{g}(n)}\right]$$

Proof. In Result 1 we can express $E_{m\lambda}\left[\frac{1}{x}\right]$ as $E_{m\lambda}[h(x)]$, where $h(x) = \frac{1}{x}$. Since $h(x)$ is a convex function, applying *Jensen's inequality*, i.e. $h(E[x]) \leq E[h(x)]$, gives

$$E_{m\lambda}\left[\frac{1}{x}\right] \geq \frac{1}{E_{m\lambda}[x]} = \frac{1}{m \cdot \mu_\lambda} \tag{13}$$

where, in the equality, we used Eq. (10).

Substituting Eq. (13) in the expression of Result 1, gives

$$E[T_{\mathcal{M}}] \geq \frac{1}{\mu_\lambda \cdot E_p[n]} \cdot E_p\left[n \cdot \sum_m \frac{1}{m} \cdot g(m|n)\right] \tag{14}$$

The sum in Eq. (14) is the expectation over $g(\cdot|n)$, i.e.

$$\sum_m \frac{1}{m} \cdot g(m|n) = E_g\left[\frac{1}{m}\right] \tag{15}$$

Applying, as before, Jensen's inequality, we get

$$\sum_m \frac{1}{m} \cdot g(m|n) = E_g\left[\frac{1}{m}\right] \geq \frac{1}{E_g[m]} = \frac{1}{\overline{g}(n)} \tag{16}$$

where we used for $E_g[m]$ the notation $\overline{g}(n)$.

Combining Eq. (16) and Eq. (14), the expression of the theorem follows directly. □

3.2.2 *Content Access Probability*

One often needs to also know the probability that a node can access a content by some deadline, i.e. $P\{T_{\mathcal{M}} \leq TTL\}$. E.g, a node might lose its interest in a content (e.g. news) after some time, or in an offloading scenario a node might decide to access a content directly to the base station.

Result 2. *The probability a content to be accessed before a time TTL can be computed with the expression*

$$P\{T_{\mathcal{M}} \leq TTL\} = 1 - \frac{E_p\left[n \cdot \sum_m E_{m\lambda}\left[e^{-x \cdot TTL}\right] g(m|n)\right]}{E_p[n]}$$

Proof. Conditioning on the values of $N_a^{(\mathcal{M})}$ and $X_{\mathcal{M}}$, as in Eq. (11), we can write:

$$P\{T_{\mathcal{M}} \leq TTL\} =$$
$$= \sum_m \int P\{T_{\mathcal{M}} \leq TTL | X_{\mathcal{M}} = x, N_a^{(\mathcal{M})} = m\} \cdot f_{m\lambda}(x)dx \cdot P_a^{req.}(m)$$
$$= 1 - \sum_m \int e^{-x \cdot TTL} \cdot f_{m\lambda}(x)dx \cdot P_a^{req.}(m) \tag{17}$$

where the last equality follows because $T_{\mathcal{M}}$ is exponentially[5] distributed with rate $X_{\mathcal{M}} = x$. After some similar steps as in Theorem 3.3, the final result follows. □

The expression of Result 2 for the example scenario of Section 3.2.1, with a different allocation function $\rho(n) = c \cdot \ln(n)$, is given in the second row of Table 2.

[5]In the Pareto case, the integral in Eq. (17) changes as: $\int \left(\frac{t_0}{TTL}\right)^x \cdot f_{m\alpha}(x)dx$, for $TTL \geq t_0$.

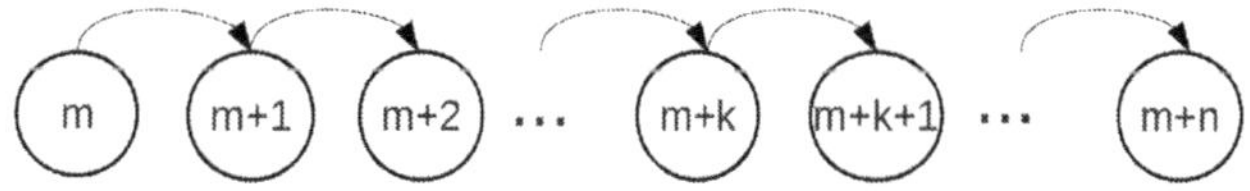

Figure 1: Markov Chain for the dissemination of a content with initial popularity and availability n and m, respectively.

Theorem 3.4. *An upper bound for the probability to access a content by a time TTL is given by*

$$P\{T_{\mathcal{M}} \leq TTL\} \leq 1 - \frac{1}{E_p[n]} \cdot E_p\left[n \cdot e^{-\overline{g}(n) \cdot \mu_\lambda \cdot TTL}\right]$$

Proof. The bound follows easily by observing that $h(x) = e^{-x \cdot TTL}$ is a convex function, and applying *Jensen's inequality* and the methodology of Theorem 3.3. □

3.3 Extensions

In this section, we study how the results of Section 3.2 can be modified, when we remove the Assumptions 2 and 3. Due to space limitations, we state only the main findings; the detailed proofs can be found in [19].

3.3.1 *Popularity / Availability Time Dependence*

Let us assume a scenario where, initially, some nodes hold some *content items* (e.g. data files), in which some other nodes are interested. This can be, for example, a content sharing scenario with contents being, e.g., some google maps. When a node interested in a content item, meets a holder and gets the content, it can hold it in its memory and act as a holder too. Specifically, we describe such scenarios as:

Definition 4.
I. When a requester accesses a content, acts as a holder for it.
II. The initial *content popularity and availability patterns are given by $P_p(n)$ and $g(m|n)$.*

Result 3. *Under time changing availability / popularity (Def. 4), the expected content access delay is approximately given by*

$$E[T_{\mathcal{M}}] = \frac{1}{\mu_\lambda \cdot E_p[n]} \cdot E_p\left[\ln\left(1 + \frac{n}{\overline{g}(n)}\right)\right]$$

Sketch of proof: Let us consider a content $\mathcal{M}$ of initial popularity $N_p^{(\mathcal{M})}(0) = n$ and availability $N_a^{(\mathcal{M})}(0) = m$. When the first requester accesses the content, the number of holders will increase to $m+1$ and the remaining requesters will be $n-1$. Building a Markov Chain as in Fig. 1, where each state denotes the number of holders, it can be shown for the expected delay of moving from state $m+k$ to state $m+k+1$, $k \in [0,1]$, that it holds $E[T_{k,k+1}] \approx \frac{1}{(m+k)\cdot(n-k)\cdot\mu_\lambda}$. Computing the times $E[T_{k,k+1}]$ and averaging over all the contents, gives the expected delay.

The model of Def. 4 can be further extended, e.g. for scenarios where nodes *might* act as holders (with some probability) or holders can also drop some contents. We defer such a study as a part of a future work.

3.3.2 *Mobility Dependent Allocation*

Definition 5 (Mobility Dependent Allocation). *The probability π_{ij} a node i to be a holder for a content in which a node j is interested, is related to their contact rate λ_{ij} such that $\pi_{ij} = \pi(\lambda_{ij})$, where $\pi(\cdot)$ is a function from R^+ to $[0,1]$.*

Result 4. *Under Def. 5, Theorems 3.3 and 3.4 and Result 3 hold if we replace* μ_λ *with* $\mu_\lambda^{(\pi)}$, *where*

$$\mu_\lambda^{(\pi)} = \frac{E_\lambda[\lambda \cdot \pi(\lambda)]}{E_\lambda[\pi(\lambda)]}$$

where $E_\lambda[\cdot]$ *denotes an expectation taken over the contact rates distribution* $f_\lambda(\lambda)$ *(Assumption 1).*

Sketch of proof: Since the requesters-holders contact rates are mobility dependent, the contact rates between them are not distributed with the contact rates distribution $f_\lambda(\lambda)$, but with a modified version of it, i.e. with a distribution:

$$f_\pi(\lambda) = \frac{1}{E_\lambda[\pi(\lambda)]} \cdot \pi(\lambda) \cdot f_\lambda(\lambda)$$

Hence, Eq. (9) and Eq. (10) need to be modified as:

$$X_{\mathcal{M}} \sim f_{m\pi}(x) = (f_\pi * f_\pi \cdots * f_\pi)_m$$

$$E[X_{\mathcal{M}} | N_a^{(\mathcal{M})} = m] = E_{m\pi}[x] = m \cdot \frac{E_\lambda[\lambda \cdot \pi(\lambda)]}{E_\lambda[\pi(\lambda)]} = m \cdot \mu_\lambda^{(\pi)}$$

Example Scenario. The holders of a content $\mathcal{M}$ are selected taking into account their contact rates with the requesters, as following: Each node i (candidate to be a holder) is assigned a weight $w_i = \prod_{j \in \mathcal{C}_p^{(\mathcal{M})}} \lambda_{ij}$. Using such weights, the selection of holders that rarely meet the requesters is avoided. Then, each node is selected to be one of the $N_a^{(\mathcal{M})}$ holders with probability $p_i = \frac{w_i}{\sum_i w_i}$. With respect to Def. 5, it turns out that this mechanism is (approximately) described by $\pi(\lambda) = c \cdot \lambda$. Substituting $\pi(\lambda)$ in Result 4, gives

$$\mu_\lambda^{(\pi)} = \frac{E_\lambda[\lambda \cdot \pi(\lambda)]}{E_\lambda[\pi(\lambda)]} = \frac{E_\lambda[\lambda^2]}{E_\lambda[\lambda]} = \mu_\lambda \cdot (1 + CV_\lambda^2) \quad (18)$$

3.4 Model Validation

As a first validation step, we compare our theoretical predictions to synthetic simulation scenarios conforming to the models of Section 2, in order to consider (a) various mobility and content traffic patterns, and (b) large networks.

Simulation Scenarios: We assign to each pair $\{i, j\}$ a contact rate λ_{ij}, which we draw randomly from a distribution $f_\lambda(\lambda)$, and create a sequence of contact events (Poisson process with rate λ_{ij}). Then, we create M contents and assign to each of them a popularity value ($N_p^{(\mathcal{M})}$), drawn from the distribution $P_p(n)$. According to the given function $g(m|n)$, we assign the availability values ($N_a^{(\mathcal{M})}$). Finally, for each content $\mathcal{M}$, we randomly choose the $N_p^{(\mathcal{M})}$ nodes that are interested in it and its $N_a^{(\mathcal{M})}$ holders.

Mobility / Popularity patterns: In most of the scenarios we present, we use the gamma distribution for the contact rates (i.e. $f_\lambda(\lambda)$), since it has been shown to match well characteristics of real contact patterns [20]. Also, content popularity in mobile social networks has been shown to follow a power-law distribution, e.g. [21]. Therefore, we select $P_p(n)$ to follow Discrete (Bounded) Pareto or Zipf distributions, similarly to the majority of related works [11, 9, 1].

In Fig. 2 we present the simulation results, along with our theoretical predictions, in scenarios of $N = 10000$ nodes with varying mobility and content popularity patterns. The mean contact rate is $\mu_\lambda = 1$ and content popularity follows a Bounded Pareto distribution with shape parameter (i.e. exponent) α and $n \in [50, 1000]$. The availability function is $\rho(n) = 0.2 \cdot n$ (i.e. deterministic). An almost perfect match between simulation results (markers) and

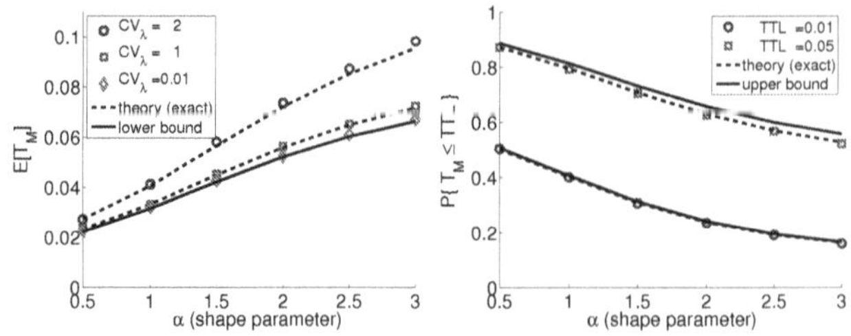

(a) $E[T_{\mathcal{M}}]$ (b) $P\{T_{\mathcal{M}} \leq TTL\}$

Figure 2: (a) $E[T_{\mathcal{M}}]$ and (b) $P\{T_{\mathcal{M}} \leq TTL\}$ in scenarios with varying content popularity (α: shape parameter) and $\rho(n) = 0.2 \cdot n$.

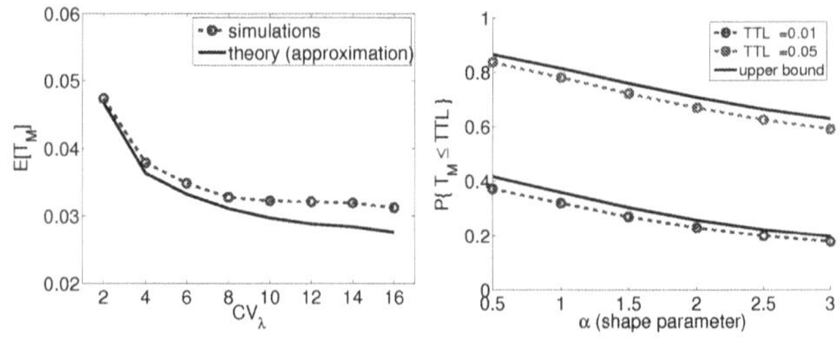

(a) $E[T_{\mathcal{M}}]$ (b) $P\{T_{\mathcal{M}} \leq TTL\}$

Figure 3: (a) $E[T_{\mathcal{M}}]$ in scenarios under Def. 4 and (b) $P\{T_{\mathcal{M}} \leq TTL\}$ in scenarios under Def. 5. $\rho(n) = 0.2 \cdot n$.

the theoretical predictions (dashed lines) of Results 1 and 2 can be observed. In Fig. 2(a), the lower bound (continuous line) of Theorem 3.3 is very tight for low mobility (i.e. small CV_λ) and/or content popularity (i.e. small α) heterogeneity. For the delivery probability $P\{T_{\mathcal{M}} \leq TTL\}$ (Fig. 2(b)), we present the results for two different values of TTL in scenarios with $CV_\lambda = 2$. Here, the upper bound (continuous line) of Theorem 3.4 is very close to the simulation results, despite the very heterogeneous mobility.

In Fig .3(a) we compare Result 3 with simulations on scenarios conforming to Def. 4: $P_p(n)$ is a *Bounded Pareto* distribution with $\alpha = 2$, and $f_\lambda(\lambda) \sim$ *Pareto*. It can be seen that our theoretical prediction (approximation) achieves good accuracy even in these very heterogeneous mobility scenarios.

Results for scenarios with mobility-dependent availability (Def. 5) are presented in Fig. 3(b). $P_p(n)$ is selected as before and $f_\lambda(\lambda) \sim$ *Gamma* with $\mu_\lambda = 1, CV_\lambda = 0.5$. The allocation of holders is made as in the example in Section 3.3.2. The upper bounds of Result 4 are tight in all scenarios, similarly to the case without mobility dependence (Fig. 2(b)).

Finally, we need to mention that we have also performed a large number of other scenarios, with similar conclusions.

4. CASE STUDY: MOBILE DATA OFFLOADING

The results of Section 3 can be used to predict the performance of a given content allocation policy or content-sharing scheme. In this section, we show how these results could be also used to design / optimize policies. We focus on an application that has recently attracted attention, that of *mobile data offloading* using opportunistic networking [7, 8, 9]. Nevertheless, the same methodology applies for a range of other applications where the number of content/service providers must be chosen.

In a mobile data offloading scenario, the cellular network provider distributes content copies only to some of the nodes interested in this content (holders), in order to reduce the cellular traffic (possibly offering some incentives to the holder nodes). The remaining (interested) nodes must then retrieve the content from the designated holders during direct encounters. A tradeoff is involved between the amount of traffic offloaded and the average delay for non-holders. In some cases, an additional *QoS* constraint might exist: if the delay to access a content exceeds a TTL, a requesting node will download it from the infrastructure [7, 8, 9].

Hence, the objective in offloading optimization problems is how the cellular network provider should *choose the set of holders for each content in order to optimize a performance metric*, under a given constraint (e.g. energy or buffer size) and a given popularity distribution $P_p(n)$.

We study cases with and without QoS constraints in Sections 4.1 and 4.2, respectively. For simplicity, we use the expressions of Theorems 3.3 and 3.4 as approximations for $E[T_{\mathcal{M}}]$ and $P\{T_{\mathcal{M}} \leq TTL\}$. Since, these expressions imply that (a) the exact mobility patterns are not known (i.e. only μ_λ is needed) and (b) contents with the same popularity are equivalent, our goal is to select the number of holders for each content with a given popularity. In other words, we try to find the optimal allocation function $g(m|n)$.

4.1 Case 1: no QoS constraints

When no QoS constraints exist, the cellular operator decides the maximum amount of traffic that it wishes to serve directly over the infrastructure. Under this constraint, which can be translated as a constraint on the number of holders for different contents, the objective is to minimize the expected delay $E[T_{\mathcal{M}}]$. The following result, formalizes this optimization problem and provides with the optimal solution for $g(m|n)$.

Result 5. *The minimum expected content access delay, under the constraint of an average number of $c_{\mathcal{M}}$ copies per content, i.e.:*

$$\min\{E[T_{\mathcal{M}}]\} \quad s.t. \quad \sum_{\mathcal{M}} N_a^{(\mathcal{M})} = M \cdot c_{\mathcal{M}} \;,\; N_a^{(\mathcal{M})} \geq 0$$

can be achieved when the allocation function, $g(m|n)$, is deterministic and equal to

$$\rho^*(n) = \frac{c_{\mathcal{M}}}{E_p[\sqrt{n}]} \cdot \sqrt{n}$$

Proof. Using as an approximation for $E[T_{\mathcal{M}}]$ the expression of Theorem 3.3, we can write

$$E[T_{\mathcal{M}}] = \frac{1}{\mu_\lambda \cdot E_p[n]} \cdot E_p\left[\frac{n}{\overline{g}(n)}\right]$$

Jensen's inequality used in Eq. (16), becomes equality when $g(m|n)$ is deterministic. This suggests that among all the functions $g(m|n)$ with the same average value $\overline{g}(n)$, the minimum delay can be achieved in the case: $\rho(n) = \overline{g}(n)$. Thus, the $E[T_{\mathcal{M}}]$ minimization problem becomes equivalent to

$$\min\{E_p\left[\frac{n}{\rho(n)}\right]\} = \sum_n \frac{n}{\rho(n)} \cdot P_p(n) = \sum_n \frac{n}{\rho_n} \cdot P_p(n) \quad (19)$$

where we expressed the expectation as a sum and denoted $\rho_n = \rho(n)$.

Moreover, we can express the content copies constraint as

$$c_{\mathcal{M}} = \frac{\sum_{\mathcal{M}} N_a^{(\mathcal{M})}}{M} = E_p[\rho(n)] = \sum_n \rho_n \cdot P_p(n) \quad (20)$$

Using Eq. (19) and Eq. (20), the optimization problem becomes

$$\min_{\overline{\rho}}\{\sum_n \frac{n}{\rho_n} \cdot P_p(n)\} \quad s.t. \quad \sum_n \rho_n \cdot P_p(n) = c_{\mathcal{M}} \quad (21)$$

where $\overline{\rho}$ denotes the vector with components ρ_n.

The optimization problem of Eq. (21) is *convex* and, thus, it can be solved with the method of Lagrange multipliers [22]. Hence, we need to find the values of $\overline{\rho}$ for which it holds that

$$\nabla\left(\sum_n \frac{n}{\rho_n} \cdot P_p(n)\right) + \nabla\lambda_0\left(\sum_n \rho_n \cdot P_p(n) - c_{\mathcal{M}}\right) = 0$$

where λ_0 is the langrangian multiplier. Here, the constraint $\rho_n \geq 0$ needs also to be taken into account. However, it is proved to be an inactive constraint (the solution satisfies it) and thus we omit it at this step for simplicity. Similarly, we assume a large enough network, i.e. always holds $\rho_n \leq N$.

The differentiation over ρ_n gives

$$\rho_n = \frac{1}{\sqrt{\lambda_0}} \cdot \sqrt{n} \quad (22)$$

Substituting Eq. (22) in the constraint expression $\sum_n \rho_n \cdot P_p(n) = c_{\mathcal{M}}$ (Eq. (21)), we can easily get

$$\sqrt{\lambda_0} = \frac{\sum_n \sqrt{n} \cdot P_p(n)}{c_{\mathcal{M}}} = \frac{E_p[\sqrt{n}]}{c_{\mathcal{M}}} \quad (23)$$

Then, substituting Eq. (23) in Eq. (22), gives

$$\rho(n) = \rho_n = \frac{c_{\mathcal{M}}}{E_p[\sqrt{n}]} \cdot \sqrt{n} \quad (24)$$

Finally, the values of Eq. (24) satisfy the *Karush-Kuhn-Tucker* conditions, which means that the solution of Eq. (24) is a global minimum [22]. □

Result 5 is a generic result, since it holds under *any* content popularity pattern. We also note that an allocation policy of $\rho(n) \propto \sqrt{n}$ has also been shown to achieve optimal results in (conventional) peer-to-peer networks [23]. This is an interesting finding, given the inherent differences between the two settings (e.g. node mobility).

Finally, our result is also consistent in scenarios with *mobility dependent holders allocation*. For example, after choosing the number of copies for a content (Result 5), the selection of holders can be made, taking into account mobility utility metrics, e.g. meeting frequency [10] or node centrality [1].

4.2 Case 2: QoS constraints

In cases where a maximum delay TTL is required, the objective is to minimize the traffic load served by the infrastructure. The metric used in related work, e.g. [9], is the data offloading ratio, $R_{off.}$, which is defined as the percentage of content requests that are served by nodes. Since requests are served by the infrastructure only after the time TTL elapses, it follows that in our framework: $R_{off.} = P\{T_{\mathcal{M}} \leq TTL\}$.

Hence the optimization problem is equivalent to

$$\max P\{T_{\mathcal{M}} \leq TTL\} \;\; s.t. \;\; \sum_{\mathcal{M}} N_a^{(\mathcal{M})} = M \cdot c_{\mathcal{M}},\; N_a^{(\mathcal{M})} \geq 0$$

Using the same notation and arguments as in the Section 4.1 and the expression of Theorem 3.4 as an approximation for $P\{T_{\mathcal{M}} \leq TTL\}$, the above optimization problem becomes:

$$\min_{\rho(n)}\{E_p\left[n \cdot e^{-\rho(n) \cdot \mu_\lambda \cdot TTL}\right]\} \quad s.t. \quad E_p[\rho(n)] = c_{\mathcal{M}} \quad (25)$$

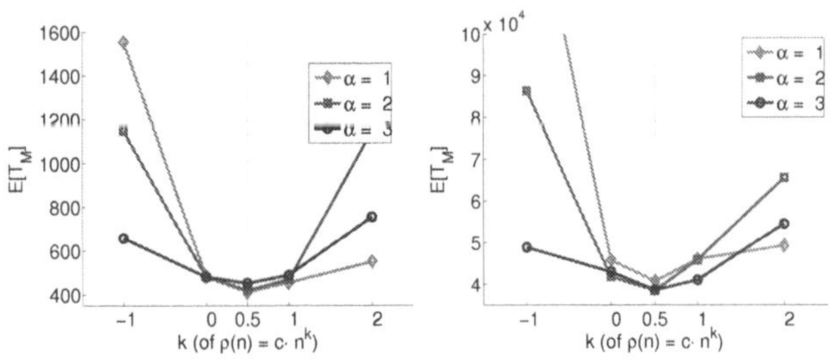

(a) TVCM (b) Cabspotting

Figure 4: Content access delay $E[T_{\mathcal{M}}]$ of different allocation policies $\rho(n) = c_k \cdot n^k$, where $c_k = \frac{c_{\mathcal{M}}}{E_p[n^k]}$.

with $\rho(n) \geq 0$, or, equivalently:

$$\min_{\overline{\rho}} \ \{\sum_n n \cdot e^{-\rho_n \cdot \mu_\lambda \cdot TTL} \cdot P_p(n)\}$$
$$s.t. \ \sum_n \rho_n \cdot P_p(n) = c_{\mathcal{M}} \ , \ \rho_n \geq 0 \quad (26)$$

The optimization problem of Eq. (26) is convex. Although a closed form solution, as in Result 5, cannot be derived[6], it can be solved numerically, using well known methods.

4.3 Performance Evaluation

To investigate whether the policies suggested as optimal by our theory indeed perform better, we conducted simulations on various synthetic scenarios and on traces of real networks, where node mobility patterns usually involve much more complex characteristics than our model (Assumption 1).

The results in the majority of scenarios considered have been encouragingly consistent with our theoretical predictions. Hence, we only present here a small, representative sample, due to space limitations. Specifically, we consider the following traces coming from state-of-the-art mobility models or collected in experiments.

TVCM mobility model [24]: Scenario with 100 nodes divided in 4 communities of unequal size. Nodes move mainly inside their community and leave it for a few short periods.

SLAW mobility model [25]: Network with 200 nodes moving in a square area of $2000m$ (the other parameters are set as in the source code provided in [25]).

Cabspotting trace [26]: GPS coordinates from 536 taxi cabs collected over 30 days in San Francisco. A range of $100m$ is assumed.

Infocom trace [27]: Bluetooth sightings of 98 mobile and static nodes (iMotes) collected in an experiment during Infocom 2006.

4.3.1 Case 1: no QoS constraints

In each scenario, we compare different allocation functions $\rho(n) = c_k \cdot n^k$, where $c_k = \frac{c_{\mathcal{M}}}{E_p[n^k]}$ is a normalization factor such that the constraint $E_p[\rho(n)] = c_{\mathcal{M}}$ is satisfied.

In Fig. 4 we present simulation results in scenarios for the *TVCM* (Fig. 4(a)) and Cabspotting (Fig. 4(b)) traces. Content popularity ($P_p(n)$) follows a *Zipf* distribution with $n \leq 30$ and exponent $\alpha = \{1, 2, 3\}$. The availability constraint is set to $c_{\mathcal{M}} = 10$. It can be seen that the optimal delay $E[T_{\mathcal{M}}]$ is achieved for $k = 0.5$, as Result 5 predicts (despite the fact that we used the expression of the lower bound as an approximation for the expected delay $E[T_{\mathcal{M}}]$).

4.3.2 Case 2: QoS constraints

To evaluate the performance of the allocation function $\rho(n)$ that follows after solving Eq. (26) (i.e. *optimal* allocation), we compare

[6]The difference here is that the constraint $\rho_n \geq 0$ is active.

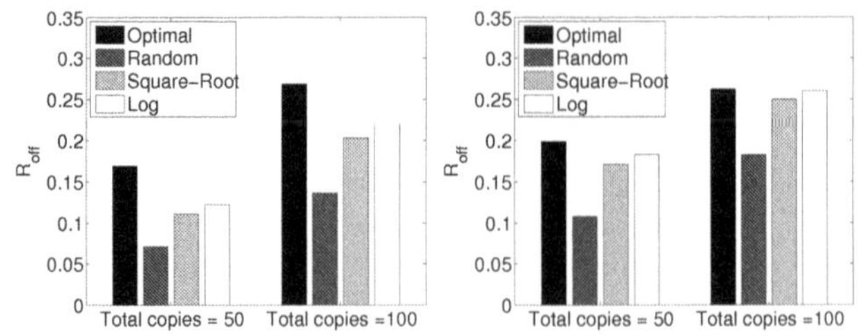

(a) SLAW, $TTL = 530$ (b) Infocom, $TTL = 10000$

Figure 5: Offloading Ratio $R_{off.}$ of different allocation policies $\rho(n)$.

the *offloading ratio* R_{off} it achieves with the offloading ratios of the following policies:

Random: We randomly select a content and give a copy of it to a node. We repeat $M \cdot c_{\mathcal{M}}$ times.

Square Root: We select $\rho(n) \propto \sqrt{n}$ (i.e. the allocation that achieves the minimum expected delay $E[T_M]$).

Log: We select $\rho(n) \propto \log n$.

Random policy has been used in related work as a baseline [9] and *square root* policy is the optimal policy when the metric of interest is the content access delay (Section 4.1). Finally, we observed that the *optimal* policy (Eq. (26)), in the scenarios considered, allocated copies only to the $10\% - 20\%$ highest popularity contents. The *log* policy allocates in a similar manner the copies (e.g. no copies to contents with low popularity).

Simulation results on the *SLAW* and *Infocom* scenarios are presented in Fig. 5(a) and 5(b), respectively. The parameters in these scenarios are: $M = 50$ messages, $P_p \sim Zipf$ with $n \in [1, 30]$ and $\alpha = 1$, total copies $M \cdot c_{\mathcal{M}} = \{50, 100\}$. As it can be seen our *optimal* policy (leftmost bar) achieves the highest offloading ratio $R_{off.}$. The random policy is clearly inferior than the others. Between *square root* and *log* policies, it is the latter that achieves better performance. These results indicate that, to maximize $R_{off.}$, it is better to allocate the available resources only for popular contents, and serve the non-popular exclusively through the infrastructure.

5. RELATED WORK

Content-centric applications were introduced in opportunistic networking under the *publish - subscribe* paradigm [2, 17, 16, 10], for which several data dissemination techniques have been proposed. In [2], authors propose a mechanism that identifies social communities and the nodes-"hubs", and builds an overlay network between them in order to efficiently disseminate data. SocialCast [16] based on information about nodes interests, social relationships and movement predictions, selects the set of holders. Similarly to the above approaches, ContentPlace [10] uses both community detection and nodes social relationships information, to improve the performance of the content distribution.

Under a different setting, [1, 11] study content sharing mechanisms with limited resources (e.g. buffer sizes, number of holders). In [1], authors analytically investigate the data dissemination cost-effectiveness tradeoffs, and propose techniques based on contact patterns (i.e. λ_{ij}) and nodes interests. Similarly, CEDO [11] aims at maximizing the total content delivery rate: by maintaining a utility per content, nodes make appropriate drop and scheduling decisions.

Recently, further novel content-centric application have been proposed, like location-based applications [3, 4] and mobile data offloading [7, 8, 9]. The latter category, due to the rapid increase of mobile data demand, has attracted a lot of attention. In the setting of [7], content copies are initially distributed (through the infrastructure) to a subset of mobile nodes, which then start propagating the contents epidemically. Differently, in [8] the authors consider a limited number of holders, and study how to select the best holders-target-set for each message. In [9], the same problem is considered, and (centralized) optimization algorithms are proposed that take into account more information about the network: namely, size and lifetimes of different contents, and interests, privacy policies and buffer sizes of each node.

In the majority of previous studies, although node interests and content popularity are taken into account, the focus has been on the algorithms and the applications themselves. We believe that our study complements existing work, by providing a common analytical framework for a number of these approaches that can be used both for predicting the performance of proposed schemes, as well as proposing improved ones.

6. CONCLUSION

The increasing number of mobile devices and traffic demand, renders content-centric applications through opportunistic communication very promising. Hence, motivated by the lack of a common analytical framework, we modeled and analyzed the effects of content popularity / availability patterns in the performance of content-centric mechanisms.

As a part of future work we intend to study, in more detail, extensions of our model and to investigate further characteristics of content traffic patterns, like *traffic locality* in location based social networks, and their performance effects.

Acknowledgments

We would like to thank Chadi Barakat, Chiara Boldrini, Jörg Ott, and Andrea Passarella for their feedback while preparing this paper.

7. REFERENCES

[1] W. Gao and G. Cao, "User-centric data dissemination in disruption tolerant networks," in *Proc. IEEE INFOCOM*, 2011.

[2] E. Yoneki, P. Hui, S. Chan, and J. Crowcroft, "A socio-aware overlay for publish/subscribe communication in delay tolerant networks," in *Proc. ACM MSWiM*, 2007.

[3] M. Satyanarayanan, "Mobile computing: The next decade," *SIGMOBILE Mob. Comput. Commun. Rev.*, vol. 15, no. 2, pp. 2–10, 2011.

[4] J. Ott and J. Kangasharju, "Opportunistic content sharing applications," in *Proc. ACM NoM Workshop*, 2012.

[5] M. Conti, S. Giordano, M. May, and A. Passarella, "From opportunistic networks to opportunistic computing," *Communications Magazine, IEEE*, vol. 48, pp. 126–139, sept. 2010.

[6] M. Pitkänen, T. Kärkkäinen, and et al., "SCAMPI: service platform for social aware mobile and pervasive computing," *ACM Comput. Commun. Rev.*, vol. 42, pp. 503–508, 2012.

[7] J. Whitbeck, M. Amorim, Y. Lopez, J. Leguay, and V. Conan, "Relieving the wireless infrastructure: When opportunistic networks meet guaranteed delays," in *Proc. IEEE WoWMoM*, 2011.

[8] B. Han, P. Hui, V. Kumar, M. Marathe, J. Shao, and A. Srinivasan, "Mobile data offloading through opportunistic communications and social participation," *IEEE Trans. on Mob. Comp.,*, vol. 11, no. 5, pp. 821–834, 2012.

[9] Y. Li, M. Qian, D. Jin, P. Hui, Z. Wang, and S. Chen, "Multiple mobile data offloading through disruption tolerant networks," *IEEE Transactions on Mobile Computing*, vol. PrePrints, 2013.

[10] C. Boldrini, M. Conti, and A. Passarella, "Design and performance evaluation of contentplace, a social-aware data dissemination system for opportunistic networks," *Computer Networks*, vol. 54, no. 4, pp. 589–604, 2010.

[11] F. Neves dos Santos, B. Ertl, C. Barakat, T. Spyropoulos, and T. Turletti, "Cedo: Content-centric dissemination algorithm for delay-tolerant networks," in *Proc. ACM MSWiM*, 2013.

[12] A. Picu, T. Spyropoulos, and T. Hossmann, "An analysis of the information spreading delay in heterogeneous mobility dtns," in *Proc. IEEE WoWMoM*, 2012.

[13] W. Gao, Q. Li, B. Zhao, and G. Cao, "Multicasting in delay tolerant networks: a social network perspective," in *Proc. ACM MobiHoc*, 2009.

[14] V. Conan, J. Leguay, and T. Friedman, "Characterizing pairwise inter-contact patterns in delay tolerant networks," in *Proc. ACM Autonomics*, 2007.

[15] A. Chaintreau, P. Hui, J. Crowcroft, C. Diot, R. Gass, and J. Scott, "Impact of human mobility on opportunistic forwarding algorithms," *IEEE Trans. on Mobile Computing*, vol. 6, no. 6, pp. 606–620, 2007.

[16] P. Costa, C. Mascolo, M. Musolesi, and G. Picco, "Socially-aware routing for publish-subscribe in delay-tolerant mobile ad hoc networks," *IEEE JSAC*, vol. 26, no. 5, pp. 748–760, 2008.

[17] V. Lenders, G. Karlsson, and M. May, "Wireless ad hoc podcasting," in *Proc. IEEE SECON*, 2007.

[18] S. M. Ross, *Introduction to Probability Models*. Academic Press, Elsevier, 9 ed., 2007.

[19] P. Sermpezis and T. Spyropoulos, "Effects of content popularity in the performance of content-centric opportunistic networking: Analytical approach and applications," Tech. Rep. RR-14-292, Eurecom, 2014.

[20] A. Passarella and M. Conti, "Analysis of individual pair and aggregate intercontact times in heterogeneous opportunistic networks," *IEEE Trans. on Mobile Computing,*, vol. 12, no. 12, pp. 2483–2495, 2013.

[21] Y. Li, M. Steiner, L. Wang, Z.-L. Zhang, and J. Bao, "Exploring venue popularity in foursquare," in *Proc. IEEE INFOCOM Workshops (NetSciCom)*, 2013.

[22] A. Antoniou and W.-S. Lu, *Practical Optimization: Algorithms and Engineering Applications*. Springer, 2007.

[23] E. Cohen and S. Shenker, "Replication strategies in unstructured peer-to-peer networks," in *Proc. ACM SIGCOMM*, 2002.

[24] W.-J. Hsu, T. Spyropoulos, K. Psounis, and A. Helmy, "Modeling spatial and temporal dependencies of user mobility in wireless mobile networks," *IEEE/ACM Trans. on Networking*, vol. 17, no. 5, pp. 1564–1577, 2009.

[25] K. Lee, S. Hong, S. J. Kim, I. Rhee, and S. Chong, "Slaw: A new mobility model for human walks," in *Proc. IEEE INFOCOM*, 2009.

[26] M. Piorkowski, N. Sarafijanovic-Djukic, and M. Grossglauser, "CRAWDAD data set epfl/mobility (v. 2009-02-24)." http://crawdad.cs.dartmouth.edu/epfl/mobility.

[27] P. Hui, A. Chaintreau, J. Scott, R. Gass, J. Crowcroft, and C. Diot, "Pocket switched networks and human mobility in conference environments," in *Proc. ACM WDTN 2005*.

SmartPhoto: A Resource-Aware Crowdsourcing Approach for Image Sensing with Smartphones

Yi Wang, Wenjie Hu, Yibo Wu and Guohong Cao
Department of Computer Science & Engineering
The Pennsylvania State University
University Park, PA, 16802, USA
{yuw124, wwh5068, yxw185, gcao}@cse.psu.edu

ABSTRACT

Photos obtained via crowdsourcing can be used in many critical applications. Due to the limitations of communication bandwidth, storage and processing capability, it is a challenge to transfer the huge amount of crowdsourced photos. To address this problem, we propose a framework, called *SmartPhoto*, to quantify the quality (utility) of crowdsourced photos based on the accessible geographical and geometrical information (called *metadata*) including the smartphone's orientation, position and all related parameters of the built-in camera. From the metadata, we can infer where and how the photo is taken, and then only transmit the most useful photos. Three optimization problems regarding the tradeoffs between photo utility and resource constraints, namely the Max-Utility problem, the online Max-Utility problem and the Min-Selection problem, are studied. Efficient algorithms are proposed and their performance bounds are theoretically proved. We have implemented SmartPhoto in a testbed using Android based smartphones, and proposed techniques to improve the accuracy of the collected metadata by reducing sensor reading errors and solving object occlusion issues. Results based on real implementations and extensive simulations demonstrate the effectiveness of the proposed algorithms.

Categories and Subject Descriptors

C.2.1 [**Computer-Communication Networks**]: Network Architecture and Design—*Wireless communication*;
C.4 [**Performance of Systems**]: *Modeling techniques*

Keywords

Crowdsourcing; Image sensing; Photo sharing; Camera sensor; Smartphone

1. INTRODUCTION

Equipped with GPS, orientation sensors, mega-pixel cameras and advanced mobile operating systems, smartphones not only change the way people communicate with each other, but also the way they interact with the world. The popularity of online photo sharing services such as Flickr and Instagram indicates that people are willing to take photos and share experiences with others. Thanks to the cost efficiency, timeliness and pervasive nature of these data, numerous opportunities have been created for applications based on photo crowdsourcing, such as grassroots journalism [3], photo tourism [18], and even disaster recovery and emergency management [12].

Consider an example in post-earthquake recovery. First responders survey the damage by taking pictures and then transfer them back to the remote command and control center. As events occur, photos need to be collected and uploaded as quickly as possible. However, there are strict bandwidth constraints, no matter it is based on mobile ad hoc networks, delay tolerant networks, or partly damaged cellular networks. Then, how to make use of the limited bandwidth to upload the most useful photos becomes a challenge.

Another example can be found in our daily life. A map service provider can enhance user experience by showing photos of interesting objects around the world, for example, landmarks like famous buildings. Data can be obtained from visitors taking photos via their smartphones. Once the photos are uploaded and processed, other map users can have virtual tours. Due to the existence of many useful applications, people are sharing billions of photos taken by smartphones. Photos are often geographically correlated and this correlation can be used to enrich traditional map experience. However, the sheer amount of photos poses big challenges for image processing and storage at the server end. Fully understanding the semantic of each photo by traditional resource intensive image recognition techniques would be a luxury if not impossible. Therefore, how to identify the most relevant data and eliminate redundancy becomes an important issue.

The major challenges faced by these applications are as follows. The first is how to characterize the quality (usefulness) of crowdsourced photos in a way that is both meaningful and resource friendly. Most content-based image processing techniques such as [6, 26, 25] may demand too much computational and communication resources at both the user and server ends. On the other hand, existing solutions from description based techniques either categorize photos based on user defined tags, or prioritize them by the GPS location [20]. Obviously, tagging each photo manually is not convenient and may discourage public participation. GPS location itself may not be sufficient to reveal the real point

MobiHoc'14, August 11–14, 2014, Philadelphia, PA, USA.

http://dx.doi.org/10.1145/2632951.2632979.

of interest. Even at the same location, smartphones facing different directions will have different views.

To address these issues, we propose a framework to quantify the quality of crowdsourced photos based on easily accessible geographical and geometrical information, called *metadata*, including the orientation and position of the phone, and the field-of-view (FoV) of the camera. Intuitively, a good photo coverage should have multiple views of the target and cover as many *aspects* as possible. Specifically, given a set of targets and photos, we consider an aspect of a target to be properly covered if it is within a proper range of a photo's viewing direction (defined in Section 2). Then we measure the quality of a photo by *utility*, which indicates how many aspects are covered. The utility is calculated based on the metadata, which can be practically obtained via various embedded sensors in most off-the-shelf smartphones. They are independent of the image content, and hence the computation is very fast and resource friendly compared to traditional content based approaches.

With the above model, we address challenges brought by the resource constraint, which is referred to as the *Max-Utility problem*. Resource constraint of bandwidth, storage and processing capability limits the number of photos that can be uploaded to the server. Given the metadata of the candidate photos, how to find a given number of photos such that the total utility is maximized? Note that this is different from traditional maximization problems on sensor coverage in which a target is covered as long as it is inside the sensing range. Here photos taken at different view points cover different aspects of the target. The total utility depends on how many aspects can be covered and how they are covered, which makes the problem unique and complicated. We also consider online selection/optimization to address the requirements of time critical applications.

Another challenge to be addressed is how to remove the redundancy and find the most representative photos. In general, the amount of candidate photos is significant and redundancy occurs if multiple photos are taken at similar locations and from similar angles. The less number of photos is selected, the less amount of bandwidth, storage and processing capability is needed. In the *Min-Selection problem*, given the coverage requirements of the targets, we want to find the minimum set of photos that satisfy the requirements.

Our contributions are summarized as follows. We propose *SmartPhoto*, a novel framework to evaluate and optimize the selection of crowdsourced photos, based on the collected metadata from the smartphones. We formulate the Max-Utility problem for bandwidth constrained networks, and then extend it into an online optimization problem. We also study the Min-Selection problem for redundancy reduction. Moreover, we propose efficient solutions, and find the performance bounds in terms of approximation or competitive ratios for the proposed algorithms.

We have implemented SmartPhoto in a testbed using Android based smartphones. We make use of multiple embedded sensors in off-the-shelf smartphones, and propose a series of methods to fuse data, correct errors, and filter out false information, to improve the accuracy of the collected metadata. Finally, the performance of the proposed algorithms are evaluated through real implementations and extensive simulations.

The rest of the paper is organized as follows. Section 2 introduces the basic concepts and the model. Section 3 studies the Max-Utility problem and Section 4 studies the Min-Selection problem. Section 5 presents the implementation of the testbed. Performance evaluations are presented in Section 6. Section 7 reviews related work and Section 8 concludes the paper.

2. PRELIMINARIES

Consider a scenario in which a set of predefined targets are to be monitored by a group of people or reporters. They use smartphones to take photos and transfer them back to the processing center. However, due to the limited bandwidth available, only a small number of photos can be transferred. For this reason, reporters first transmit the metadata of the photos, which is extremely light weight compared to the original image. After that, the server runs optimization algorithms to determine what photos to be actually transferred and notifies the reporters to transmit the photos.

We first describe the models used in SmartPhoto to characterize targets and photos. Then the concept of utility is introduced. The idea is based on the observation that a good photo should cover as many aspects of the targets as possible. For an aspect to be properly covered, the target should be in a photo whose viewing direction is not too far away from the direction to which the aspect points. This is similar to the face recognition problem in computer vision: as the angle between the object's facing direction (the aspect) and the camera's viewing direction (the vector from the camera to the object) becomes wider, the detection rate of the recognition algorithm will drop dramatically [4, 14]. The utility defined in this section precisely indicates how many aspects of the target are properly covered.

2.1 Targets and Photos

At the beginning of each event, the application server distributes the information of the interested targets to the public users. The set of targets are denoted by $T = \{T_1, \ldots, T_m\}$. T_i also represents the location of the i-th target if there is no ambiguity. An *aspect* of the target, denoted by $\vec{v}$, is a vector that can be represented by an angle in $[0, 2\pi)$ with 0 degree indicating the one pointing to the right (east on the map). For ease of presentation, this angle is denoted by $arg(\vec{v})$ and is calculated by using arithmetic modulo 2π. For any angle $\alpha \in [0, 2\pi)$, $vec(\alpha)$ represents the corresponding vector.

Given a set of photos: $P = \{P_1, \ldots, P_n\}$, each photo P_j is stored locally and it can be registered to the server with a tuple $(l_j, r_j, \varphi_j, \vec{d_j})$, called the *metadata* of the photo. Here l_j is the location where the photo is taken. To simplify notations, we also use P_j to represent the location if there is no ambiguity. r_j and φ_j are two internal parameters of the camera used to take the photo. r_j is the effective range of the camera, and φ_j is the field-of-view (FOV, represented in angle) of the camera lens. $\vec{d_j}$ is the orientation of the camera when the photo is taken. Note that $\vec{d_j}$ is the normal vector derived from the camera lens and vertical to the image plane. It can be acquired by using various sensors embedded in the smartphone. Details of obtaining these geographical information on the smartphone will be given in Section 5. As shown in Figure 1(a), the metadata defines the effective coverage range of the photo.

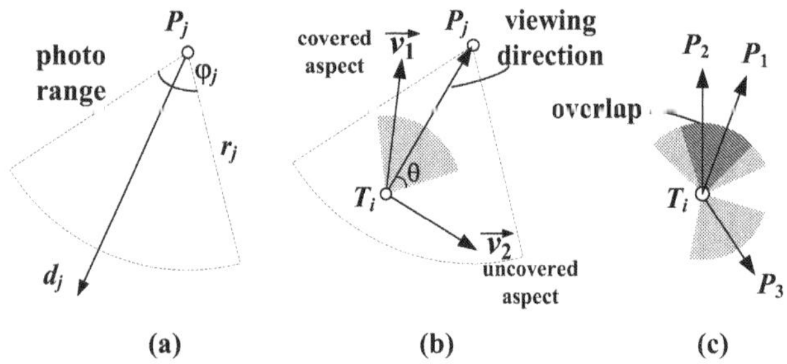

Figure 1: Photo, target and utility.

2.2 Photo Utility

For a target T_i and a photo P_j, T_i is said to be covered by P_j if P_j's range includes T_i. An aspect $\vec{v}$ of T_i is covered if the angle between $\vec{v}$ and $\overrightarrow{T_iP_j}$ is smaller or equal to a predefined angle θ called *effective angle*. Here $\overrightarrow{T_iP_j}$ is the viewing direction of the camera towards the target when the photo is taken[1]. Further, the utility of a photo P_j can be defined based on how many aspects of T_i are covered by this photo.

Definition 1. *[Utility] Given a target T_i and a photo P_j covering the target, the utility of P_j on T_i, denoted by $U_{P_j}(T_i)$, is the portion of aspect that is covered by P_j, i.e., $U_{P_j}(T_i) = \int_0^{2\pi} 1_{P_j}(v)dv$, where $1_{P_j}(v) = 1$ if $\vec{v}$ is covered by P_j, or 0 otherwise.*

Accordingly, the utility of a set of photos $P' = \{P_j : 1 \leq j \leq k\}$ regarding target T_i is the total portion of aspect that is covered by the photos of P', i.e., $U_{P'}(T_i) = \int_0^{2\pi} 1_{P'}(v)dv$, where $1_{P'}(v) = 1$ if $\vec{v}$ is covered by any P_j from P', or 0 otherwise.

Finally, the total utility of the photos regarding all targets $T = \{T_1, \ldots, T_m\}$ is the sum of the utility regarding each target. It is normalized by dividing the total number of targets, i.e., $U_{P'}(T) = \frac{1}{m}\sum_{i=1}^{m} U_{P'}(T_i)$.

For example in Figure 1(b), for target T_i, its aspect $\vec{v_1}$ is covered by photo P_j but aspect $\vec{v_2}$ is not. As a result, if there is only one photo covering the object, the utility is two times the effective angle θ (indicated by the gray area in Figure 1(b)). If there are multiple photos covering the same target, possible overlap (darker area in Figure 1(c)) among photos' coverage needs to be identified and removed. In that case, the overlap can only be counted once towards the total utility, which is reflected by gray area in Figure 1(c).

3. MAX-UTILITY WITH BANDWIDTH CONSTRAINT

In this section, we study the Max-Utility problem and its extension to an online optimization problem.

3.1 Max-Utility Problem

In the scenario described in Section 2, the bandwidth constraint determines the number of photos that can be selected. The problem is defined as follows.

[1]Intuitively, it should be from P_j to T_i, but $\overrightarrow{T_iP_j}$ is used for ease of calculation.

Definition 2. *[Max-Utility Problem] Given a set of m targets with known locations $T = \{T_1, \ldots, T_m\}$ and n photos $P = \{P_1, \ldots, P_n\}$ with known metadata, also given a predefined positive integer $B(\leq n)$, the problem asks for a selection of B photos P' out of the n candidates, such that the total utility of the selected photos $U_{P'}(T)$ is maximized.*

3.1.1 Conversion to Maximum Coverage

Without loss of generalization, we first consider a single target T_i and use the coverage interval $I_i = [0, 2\pi)$ to indicate its aspect to be covered. Let $P = \{P_1, \ldots, P_n\}$ be the set of all photos covering T_i. Then for each P_j, if T_i is covered by P_j, the coverage of P_j on T_i (gray sector in Figure 1(b)) can be represented by a sub-interval of $[0, 2\pi)$, i.e.,

$$S_j \triangleq [x_j, y_j] = [arg(\overrightarrow{T_iP_j}) - \theta, arg(\overrightarrow{T_iP_j}) + \theta] \quad (1)$$

Note that the angles are always calculated by using arithmetic modulo 2π. Here the two end points x_j and y_j are called dividing points, which divides I_i into two parts: one is S_j and the other is $I_i - S_j$. If there are more photos by which T_i is covered, there would be more dividing points.

If there are multiple targets, every target corresponds to a coverage interval $I_i = [0, 2\pi)$ and each I_i is divided into sub-intervals by the corresponding dividing points. Let $U = \{e_1, \ldots, e_w\}$ be a universe set with each element representing a sub-interval and w being the total number of them. The weight of the element is the length of the sub-interval. For each photo P_j, a subset of U can be generated based on what sub-intervals are covered by it. Let S_j denote this subset. Then we have proved the following lemma:

Lemma 1. *A solution to the Max-Utility problem can be obtained by solving the following problem: given a universe set U of (non-negative) weighted elements, an integer B and a collection of subsets $S = \{S_1, \ldots, S_n\}$, find B subsets such that the total weight of the elements covered by the selected subsets is maximized.*

3.1.2 Greedy Selection Algorithm

The general maximum coverage problem is proved to be NP-hard [8]. A greedy algorithm can be used to find a solution. It works as a multi-round selection process. In each round, the weighted contribution (utility) of every unselected photos is calculated. The photo with the most contribution to the total utility is selected. If there are more than one photos with the most contribution, the one with the lowest index is selected. Once a photo is selected, it will be removed from the selection. The elements (sub-intervals) covered by the selected photo will be removed from future consideration. The selection process runs until B photos have been selected or every aspect of all targets has been covered, whichever comes first.

Theorem 1. *Let U_{opt} be the optimal value of the total utility that can be achieved by any B photos from P. Let U_{greedy} be the total utility achieved by the greedy selection algorithm. Then*

$$U_{greedy} \geq [1 - (1 - \frac{1}{B})^B] \cdot U_{opt} > (1 - \frac{1}{e})U_{opt}$$

PROOF. From Lemma 1, a selection of B subsets implies a valid selection of B photos. Moreover, the total utility of the photos is maximized if and only if the corresponding

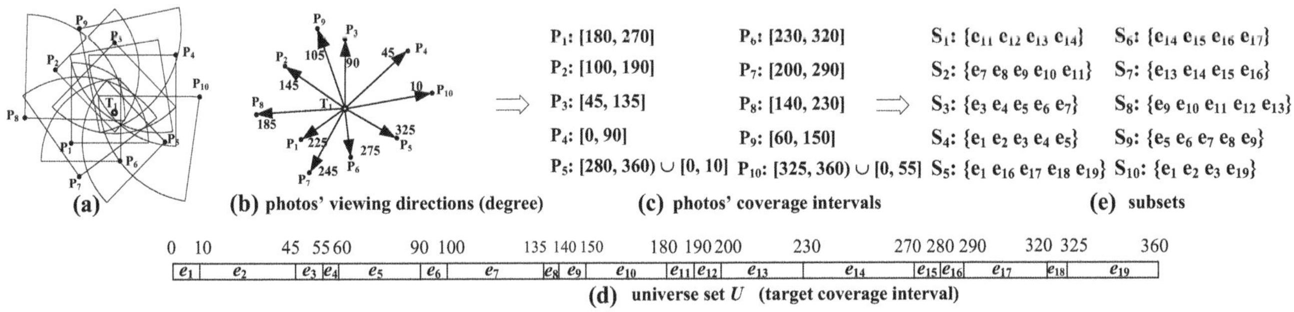

Figure 2: The conversion into a set system.

subsets has the maximum total weight. On the other hand, the subsets selected by the greedy selection can yield a total weight that is at least $(1 - 1/e)$ times the optimal value [8]. Therefore, the total utility of the selected photos is also lower bounded by $(1 - 1/e)$ times the maximum total utility. $\square$

An Example: Figure 2 shows an example of one target and 10 photos. Suppose $\theta = 45, B = 3$. Each photo's position is shown in Figure 2(a). The arrows in Figure 2(b) indicate photos' viewing directions, and the number beside the arrow (e.g., 10 beside $\overrightarrow{T_1P_{10}}$) indicates the angle of the viewing direction of the photo (e.g., P_{10}), which has been defined in Section 2. Based on this, each photo's coverage interval is calculated and shown in Figure 2(c) according to Equation (1). Then target T_1's coverage interval $I_1 = [0, 2\pi)$ is divided into sub-intervals by the endpoints of all photos' coverage intervals (Figure 2(d)). This is the universe set U which is composed of weighted elements from e_1 to e_{19}, and the weight of each element is reflected by its length. Finally, each photo's coverage interval is converted into a subset S_i of elements (Figure 2(e)).

We select 3 photos to maximize the total utility. Initially, each S_i has a weight of $2\theta = 90$, and hence S_1 is selected due to the smallest index. Elements $e_{11}, e_{12}, e_{13}, e_{14}$ are removed from U. Second, the weight of each of S_3, S_4, S_5, S_9 and S_{10} is still 90, but for the others the weights become: S_2 is 80; S_6 is 50; S_7 is 20 and S_8 is 40. Obviously, S_3 is selected. Then elements e_3, e_4, e_5, e_6, e_7 are removed from U. Finally, we consider the remaining subsets. The weights of S_5, S_6, S_7, S_8 are unchanged, but S_2 drops to 45, S_9 drops to 15 and S_{10} drops to 80. Therefore, the last selected photo is S_5. The final selection is S_1, S_3, S_5, corresponding to P_1, P_3, P_5, and the total achieved utility is 270.

3.2 Online Max-Utility Problem

For applications like crisis management, due to the urgency, the server should not wait for the metadata of all photos to come in before it begins the selection. Instead, it should start selecting photos from the beginning based on available metadata, and then gradually improve the photo coverage by continuously and periodically selecting photos when new ones become available.

3.2.1 Problem Statement

Let time be divided into transmission periods. At the beginning of each period, based on the available metadata and the available bandwidth in this period, the server makes decision on what photos to be uploaded in this period, and then notify the users to transfer the photos. Let t_i be the i-th period and B_i be the number of photos that can be uploaded in the i-th period. Then let A_i be the set of available photos (but not being uploaded yet) at the beginning of t_i. Finally, the selected photos to be uploaded in t_i is denoted by C_i. The problem is defined as follows.

Definition 3. *[Online Max-Utility Problem] Given a set of m targets with known locations $T = \{T_1, \ldots, T_m\}$, and the set of available photos A_i at the beginning of each period t_i, and suppose the event happens at period t_0, how does one select the set of photo C_i for each period in an online manner, such that $C_i \subseteq A_i$ and $|C_i| \leq B_i$, and at the end of each period t_i, the total utility of all the selected photos up to t_i, i.e., $U_{C_0 \cup \ldots \cup C_i}(T)$ (defined in Definition 1), is maximized?*

Note that the length of the period is a parameter determined by the application, e.g., how urgent the event is and how often new photos should be collected, etc. The bandwidth constraint B_i can vary from one period to another and not necessary to be constant.

3.2.2 Online Selection Algorithm

In each period, all the photos available up to present are considered. Finding the ones that can maximize the increase of total utility is easy when the number of photos is small, and an enumeration of all possible combinations can always deliver the optimal solution. However, as the process continues and more and more photos are available, computation cost would become prohibitively high.

Our solution is to use the approximation algorithm proposed for the original Max-Utility problem. At the beginning of each period, the server selects photos one by one greedily such that each one maximizes the increase of total utility, until it reaches the number imposed by B_i. Note that the conversion into a weighted set system is the same as before except that the aspects covered by photos selected in previous periods should be excluded. After that, the selected photos will be transferred immediately during the period. The performance of the online selection algorithm is evaluated later in Section 6.2.

4. ACHIEVING BEST UTILITY WITH MIN-SELECTION

In this section, we consider another important scenario: the number of photos is minimized while the total utility is to be above a required level. In many practical applications, the major obstacle is to deal with the sheer amount of raw data (photos) obtained via crowdsourcing. Thus, it is desirable to remove the redundancy and only keep the minimum selections of photos that can satisfy the coverage requirement.

4.1 Problem Statement

Each target T_i is associated with a coverage requirement, represented by a coverage interval $I_i = [a_i, b_i], 0 \leq a_i, b_i < 2\pi$. The requirement is met if any aspect $\vec{v}$ chosen from I_i is covered. The problem is defined as follows.

Definition 4. *[Min-Selection Problem] Given a set of m targets with known locations $T = \{T_1, \ldots, T_m\}$ and n photos $P = \{P_1, \ldots, P_n\}$ with known metadata, also given the coverage requirements for the targets: $I = \{I_1, \ldots, I_m\}$, the problem asks for a minimum selection of photos out of the n candidates, such that the coverage requirement for each target is met.*

Note that in this problem if the requirement can not be met due to the insufficiency of the original set of photos, the best achievable utility will be used as the criteria. Here the best achievable utility on a target is the utility of all photos on it, and the best achievable total utility on all targets is the sum on each targets normalized by the number of targets.

4.2 Min-Selection Algorithm

In the following description, it is assumed that the coverage requirement of each target can be satisfied by the whole set of photos. Then the following theorem shows the main result of our findings.

Theorem 2. *Suppose the target's coverage requirement can be satisfied by all photos in the pool and let N_{opt} be the minimum number of photos to satisfy the requirement. There exists N_{approx} photos that can be found in polynomial time such that each target's requirement can be met by these photos and moreover, $N_{approx} \leq O(\log n) N_{opt}$.*

PROOF. We prove this by constructing the selection using a greedy algorithm.

First, we use a conversion process that is similar to Section 3.1.1. Here each target T_i's coverage requirement I_i is partitioned into sub-intervals by the dividing points, and the dividing points are the end points of the coverage intervals (sub-intervals) of the photos like before. After this preparation, all the sub-intervals are numbered, and can be represented by elements that altogether form an universe set $U = \{e_1, \ldots, e_w\}$, where w is the total number of sub-intervals. Then for each P_j, there is a subset $S_j \subset U$ which is comprised of the elements corresponding to the sub-intervals covered by P_j. Based on this, the problem of finding the minimum photo selection can be converted to the following problem:

Given a universe set U and a collection of subsets of U: $S = \{S_1, \ldots, S_n\}$, and assume $\cup_j^n S_j = U$, how to find a subset S' of S such that $\cup_{S_j \in S'} S_j = U$ and $|S'|$ is minimum?

This is an instance of the Set Cover problem, which has been proved NP-hard [8]. Thus for the Min-Selection problem, we can solve it by an approximation algorithm based on the greedy selection.

Specifically, the algorithm begins by selecting the photo (some S_j) that covers the most number of sub-intervals (elements). Once a photo is selected, it will not be removed. The sub-intervals covered will not be considered in the future. Photos are selected one by one based on how many new sub-intervals can be covered. Each time, the photo covering the most number of new sub-intervals is selected. Ties can be broken arbitrarily, e.g., by giving priority to the one with smaller index. The process stops if all sub-intervals (elements of U) is covered or no more photos can be selected (i.e., either photos are all selected or no more benefit can be achieved).

Once the photos are found, it is obvious all the elements in U is covered which implies the requirement of all targets are satisfied. By using similar argument from Theorem 3.1 in [8], it is easy to see the number of selected photos is upper bounded as shown in the theorem. □

An Example: Again, we use Figure 2 to illustrate the above idea. Consider the problem settings in Figure 2(a) and suppose the required coverage for T_1 is $[0, 360)$. The construction of the universe set and all the subsets are shown in Figure 2(b)-(e). The universe set U consists of 19 elements. The selection works on the subsets S_i.

First, photo S_2 is selected as it covers 5 new elements $\{e_7, e_8, e_9, e_{10}, e_{11}\}$. It has the most elements covered and the smallest index. Then S_5 can be selected as it covers 5, the most number of new elements $\{e_1, e_{16}, e_{17}, e_{18}, e_{19}\}$. In the third round, S_3 can be selected, as it covers 4 new elements $\{e_3, e_4, e_5, e_6\}$. After that, S_1, which covers 3 new elements $\{e_{12}, e_{13}, e_{14}\}$, is selected. Up to now, 17 out of the total 19 elements have been covered. The remaining two are e_2 and e_{15}. To cover e_2, S_4 is selected. Then S_6 is selected to cover e_{15}. The final selection is $S_1, \ldots, S_6$, which correspond to the following 6 photos: $P_1, P_2, P_3, P_4, P_5, P_6$.

The above discussion can be easily applied to the scenario of multiple targets. In that case, each target corresponds to a set U_i of elements (sub-intervals). Elements of all U_i will be considered to determine if a particular S_j can yield the most coverage. The algorithm stops if elements of all U_i are covered or no more progress can be made.

5. TESTBED IMPLEMENTATION

A prototype of SmartPhoto has been implemented in a testbed using Samsung Nexus S running Android 2.3.6, Samsung Galaxy S III running Android 4.0.4, and Google (LG) Nexus 4 running Android 4.2.

In the testbed, the smartphones take photos with the metadata automatically recorded. The metadata is a tuple comprised of a GPS location, a range indicating how far the photo can cover, a field-of-view (FoV) angle of the camera taking the photo and an orientation vector indicating the facing direction of the camera lens. After the photo has been taken, the smartphone uploads the metadata of the photo to a centralized server, which is a PC in our lab running the photo selection algorithm. Then the server notifies the smartphones to upload the selected photos. In this section, we present the technical details on how to obtain the metadata, how to improve the accuracy of orientation measurement, and how to deal with occlusion and out-of-focus issues.

5.1 Metadata Acquisition

One critical issue is how to get the metadata from off-the-shelf smartphones. The location can be directly acquired via the built-in GPS receiver. The camera's field-of-view is accessible via the Android camera API [1]. The range is a little trickier as it depends on the resolution of the lens (and the image sensor), the zooming level (or focal length) and the requirement of the application. Applications requiring a survey of large scale buildings may find the photos useful even if they are taken a hundred meters away by a lower resolution camera, while others may require closer look at the object and hence may exclude photos taken more than a few meters away. In our experiment, as the subjects are buildings on campus, 50 meter is used as a reference range. We find that for our purpose, objects in photos taken within this range are generally recognizable.

Orientation is a key factor that has not yet been fully taken advantage of in previous works. The way used to characterize the orientation in the Android system is to first define a local and a world coordinate system[2], and represent the orientation as a rotation matrix. The rotation matrix is used to transform a local coordinate tuple into a global one. Another way to represent the rotation is to use a three tuple called *azimuth, pitch,* and *roll*, which respectively indicate the phone's rotation around the Z, X and Y axes [13]. The two representations are equivalent and the orientation tuple (i.e., the angles) can be derived from the rotation matrix. In the following description, we use R to denote the rotation matrix.

In Android system, the rotation matrix can be directly obtained based on accelerometer and magnetic field sensor readings. The accelerometer measures the phone's proper acceleration along the three axes in the phone's local coordinate system, including the influence of the gravity. The magnetic field sensor provides the readings measuring the ambient magnetic field along the three axes in the local coordinate system. The coordinates of both the gravity and the ambient magnetic field are known in the world coordinate system. Thus, by combining the above readings and facts, the orientation of the phone can be obtained. Let us call this the "basic" method, and let the result be denoted by R_{basic}.

5.2 Techniques to Improve Accuracy

The rotation matrix R_{basic} is susceptible to noise and errors. It fluctuates quickly due to the vibration of accelerometer's reading. Also, the magnet field sensor's reading is easily affected by nearby magnet objects. Even worse, R_{basic} responses slowly to quick rotation of the phone. Thus, we propose several techniques to improve the accuracy of the orientation.

5.2.1 *Hybrid Method*

Apart from the accelerometer and the magnetic field sensor, gyroscope is now available in most smartphones, and it can also be used to measure the rotation matrix.

Gyroscope measures the angular rotation speeds along all three axes in the phone's local coordinate system. By integrating (multiplying) the angular speed with the time interval between two consecutive sensor readings, we can obtain the rotation vector, which indicates the change of orientation in terms of rotation angles around the three axes. It can also be used to obtain the rotation matrix (denoted by ΔR_{gy}). Given an initial rotation matrix, which can be obtained from

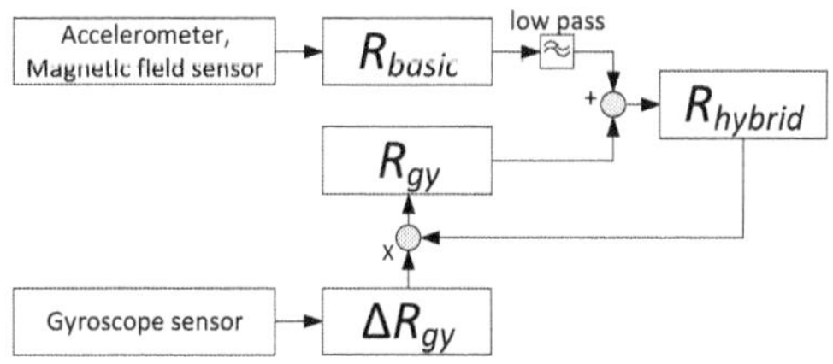

Figure 3: Hybrid method.

R_{basic}, we can get the new rotation matrix, denoted as R_{gy}, by $R_{gy} = R_{gy} \times \Delta R_{gy}$.

However, the cumulative error caused by the integration in R_{gy} can become greater and the result would drift as time goes by. In fact, the orientation derived from R_{gy} alone usually drifts over 10 degrees in about 20 seconds in our lab test.

Thus, we propose a hybrid method which combines the readings from the above sensors to improve the accuracy of orientation, as shown in Figure 3 and explained as below.

First, a simple Infinite Impulse Response (IIR) low pass filter is used on R_{basic} to remove the short term vibration, i.e.,

$$R'_{basic} = R_{basic} + \mu \cdot (R^{prev}_{basic} - R_{basic})$$

where R_{basic} is the current reading and R^{prev}_{basic} is the previous reading from the basic method, and $\mu \in [0, 1]$ is an adjustable parameter balancing the current and previous values. In practice, we find $\mu = 0.3$ is good for our purpose.

Second, we combine R'_{basic} and R_{gy} to take advantage of both values; that is,

$$R_{hybrid} = \nu \times R_{gy} + (1 - \nu) \times R'_{basic}$$

We find $\nu = 0.9$ works well.

Third, R_{hybrid} is the output, and it will also be used as the initial matrix input for the computation of a new R_{gy}.

5.2.2 *Enhancement by Orthonormalization*

We exploit the orthonormal property of the rotation matrix to further improve the accuracy of orientation. In a valid rotation matrix, any pair of columns (or rows) of the rotation matrix are orthogonal, i.e., with unit length and vertical to each other. However, this property may be violated as errors occur. Thus, the rotation matrix R_{hybrid} obtained from the above method can be further calibrated by an orthonormalization process (e.g., the Gram-Schmidt process [24]) to get an enhanced rotation matrix $R_{enhanced}$.

Specifically, consider a 3×3 rotation matrix: $R_{hybrid} = [\alpha_1, \alpha_2, \alpha_3]$, with α_i being a column vector. Let the inner product of the two vectors α and β be $< \alpha, \beta >= \sum_{i=1}^{n} \alpha_i \beta_j$, where $n = 3$ is the dimension.

First, R_{hybrid} is orthogonalized by

$$\begin{aligned} \xi_1 &= \alpha_1 \\ \xi_2 &= \alpha_2 - \frac{< \alpha_2, \xi_1 >}{< \xi_1, \xi_1 >} \xi_1 \\ \xi_3 &= \alpha_3 - \frac{< \alpha_3, \xi_1 >}{< \xi_1, \xi_1 >} \xi_1 - \frac{< \alpha_3, \xi_2 >}{< \xi_2, \xi_2 >} \xi_2 \end{aligned}$$

Second, the above ξ_i's are normalized by

$$\beta_i = \frac{\xi_i}{\sqrt{< \xi_i, \xi_i >}}, i = 1, 2, 3$$

---

[2]In a world coordinate system, Z axis is perpendicular to ground and points to the sky; Y is tangential to the ground and points towards the magnetic north pole; X is the vector product of Y and Z. In the phone's local coordinate system, Z is perpendicular to the phone screen and points outward; the X axis is along the width of the phone and the Y axis is along the length [1, 13].

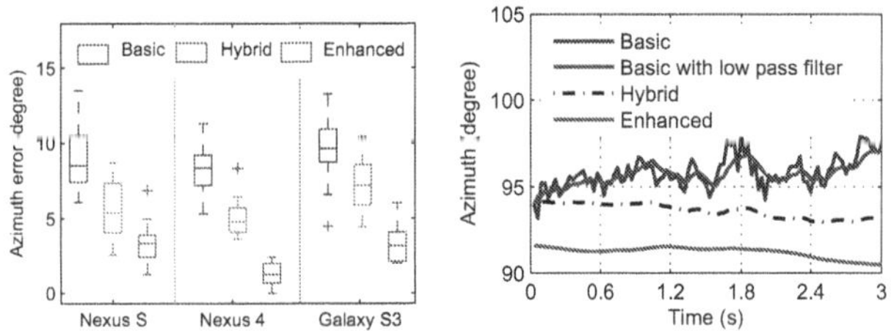

(a) (b)

Figure 4: Orientation errors.

Then, the final rotation matrix is

$$R_{enhanced} = [\beta_1, \beta_2, \beta_3]$$

Comparisons: To verify the effectiveness of the optimization techniques, we measure the orientation using three different methods: the "basic" method, the "hybrid" method, and the "enhanced" method, and compare their results. We place the phone in a horizontal plane, so the orientation is reflected by the azimuth value. Then we rotate the phone 30 degrees and measure its azimuth reading against a commercial compass. Each measurement is repeated 50 times and the statistics are calculated. Figure 4(a) compares the measurement errors (in degree) by these three methods. The short bar in the middle of each box is the median value of the azimuth reading error, and the lower and upper side of the box are the first (25%) and third (75%) quartile, which is denoted by $Q1$ and $Q3$. Then the lower limit is calculated by $Q1-1.5*(Q3-Q1)$ and the upper limit is $Q3+1.5*(Q3-Q1)$. More details about the average error and standard variance of each method are listed in Table 1.

We find that the hybrid method can reduce the average measurement error by 37% compared to the basic method, and the enhanced method can further reduce the measurement error by more than 40% compared to the hybrid method. Also, new phones (e.g., Nexus 4), with more advanced hardware and OS, are more accurate with less variance. For all these phones, with our enhanced method, the average azimuth reading error is under 3.5 degrees, and the error can be reduced to 1.3 degree with the Nexus 4 phone.

Table 1: Average error in azimuth (degree)

	Nexus S	Nexus 4	Galaxy S III
Basic	9.1(±2.0)	8.2(±1.5)	9.6(±2.4)
Hybrid	5.7(±1.9)	5.1(±1.3)	7.3(±1.7)
Enhanced	3.4(±1.4)	1.3(±0.7)	3.4(±1.3)

To understand the effectiveness of these techniques clearly, we show the measurement results of these methods when the phone is turned to 90 degree, and the results are illustrated in Figure 4(b). As can be seen, the basic method oscillates frequently. The hybrid method improves the accuracy compared to the basic method but still carries the reading errors. With orthonormalization, the enhanced method can significantly improve the accuracy of orientation.

5.3 Occlusion and Out-of-focus

After a photo is taken, we assume that the user will visually check if the object appears in the photo, as most people do. However, if the user does not check the photo, and the object is blocked by unexpected obstacles such as a moving vehicle, the photo will not be useful to the server. Even if the user checks the photo and the object is clear, it may be different from what the server is expecting. For example, the server may expect the photo to be about a building, but the user may be looking at a tree in front of the building. Although in the two scenarios, the smartphone may produce the same metadata (e.g., the same facing direction), the content could be very different, and the one focusing on (blocked by) the tree is useless for the server's task. Besides this problem, there are many other occasions that the interested targets are out-of-focus. Uploading these photos will waste lots of bandwidths and storage spaces.

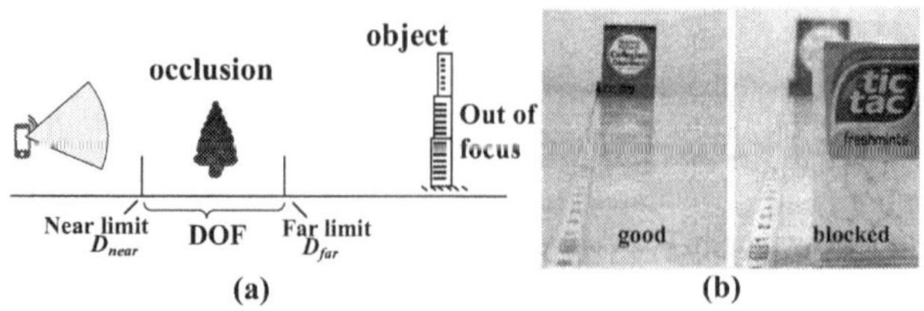

(a) (b)

Figure 5: The use of DOF.

We use a feature called *focus distance*, which is provided by many new smartphones with focusing capability, to solve the problem. The focus distance is the distance between the camera and the object perfectly focused in the photo. Note that the real distance between the camera and our interested target can be calculated by GPS locations. Thus in an ideal case, if the two distances do not match, the target is out-of-focus and the photo should be excluded from consideration.

The measurement of the focus distance is sensible to errors. A slight offset does not necessarily mean the target is out-of-focus. In fact, in photography the distance between the nearest and farthest objects that appear acceptable sharp in a photo is called the Depth-Of-Field (DOF). DOF is determined by four parameters: focal length (f), focus distance (v_o), lens aperture (A), and circle of confusion (CoC). Among these parameters, focal length and lens aperture are built-in and readable from the Android API. CoC (denoted by c) is a predefined number which determines the resolution limit for our application. Focus distance changes from case to case but obtainable from Android API. Therefore, we can calculate the near/far limit of DOF (Figure 5(a)) by the following formulas:

$$D_{near} = \frac{v_o(H-f)}{H+v_o-2f}$$

$$D_{far} = \frac{v_o(H-f)}{H-v_o}$$

where $H = \frac{f^2}{Ac} + f$ is the hyperfocal distance [15].

After a photo is taken, the distance between the target and the camera (phone) is compared with the above two values. If the target falls into the DOF, the photo is considered valid; otherwise, it will be dropped. For example, consider the two photos in Figure 5(b). The dictionary is the interested target. In the left photo, the near and far limit of DOF is 85cm and 105cm respectively. In the right photo, the near and far limit of DOF is 5cm and 10cm respectively. The distance between the camera and the dictionary is 100cm. Based on these parameters, it is clear that the target falls into the DOF in the left photo. From the figure we can see, the dictionary is clear in the left photo but blocked by another object in the right photo. Note that this filtering is done at the user side and the metadata of unqualified photos will not be sent to the server.

Figure 6: Demo results.

Discussions: Photos can be of low quality due to various reasons. Over-exposure or under-exposure causes images to be too bright or too dark; camera movement and shutter speed affect how severe the image is blurred; the quality of lens and digital sensors is also important. These factors are neither included in our coverage model, nor considered by the DOF method. They can be analyzed only by image processing. Thus, before photo selection, some efficient image processing techniques [7] may be applied at the user end to achieve basic quality control, such as detecting photos that are too dark or severely blurred, and thus low quality photos will not be considered in the photo selection. However, existing image processing techniques are computationally expensive, and thus should be carefully adapted considering the resource limitations of mobile devices. Note that our approach is not meant to replace the role played by image recognition algorithms, but to serve as an important complement to improve the utility of the collected photos, especially when there are resource constraints.

6. PERFORMANCE EVALUATIONS

In this section, we first show a real world demo using the smartphone testbed, and then evaluate the performance of the photo selection algorithms by extensive simulations.

6.1 Demo in a Real-World Example

The above testbed is used in a real-world example to demonstrate the effectiveness of the proposed photo selection algorithm. In this demonstration, a landmark (a bell tower) is the target. Photos are taken by using the reprogrammed smartphones around the target with the metadata automatically recorded. The metadata of all photos are later uploaded into a centralized desktop server. There are 30 photos in total. Although most of them are taken around the target, some are not facing the target, and some are blocked by trees or other objects. Also, the distribution is not uniform, due to the reality that people are likely to take pictures of the front (more attractive) side of the building.

After the metadata is retrieved, the Max-Utility problem is solved by choosing 4 photos. The results are shown in Figure 6(a), with the image shown at the top and the positions and orientations of the photos are shown at the bottom. Here the positions and orientations of the original 30 photos are marked as dotted "V" shape, and the selected photos are marked by bold lines. As a comparison, the 4 photos chosen by a random selection algorithm are shown in Figure 6(b). It can be seen obviously that the 4 photos chosen by our algorithm cover the target from 4 different locations well separated from each other, with each one from a totally different angle. The bell towers are viewable from all 4 photos. On the other side, only 2 photos chosen by the random algorithm cover the target. The third photo is facing away from the target, which is because the random selection does not consider the orientation. In the fourth photo (at bottom right), the target is blocked by a **flagpole**, which is bad for random selection. Note that this photo's orientation (in bottom map) does not reveal the real situation. However, based on the DOF information, the target is out of focus. Hence, it is filtered out at the user end and is not considered by our selection.

6.2 Simulation Results

In this section, we evaluate the photo selection algorithms through simulations. The target is randomly distributed in a 100m by 100m square area. Photos are assumed to be taken at random positions, with random orientations from 0 to 2π, in a larger area that is a 200m by 200m square, with the target area in the center.

During the simulation, the random selection algorithm is used for comparison. For a fair comparison, the random selection excludes any photos that have no target covered, but only consider photos that cover at least one target, i.e., relevant photos. Note that a more naive selection could be blindly selecting photos without considering this.

6.2.1 *Results on Max-Utility*

In the first part, we evaluate the performance of our algorithm on addressing the Max-Utility problem. Intuitively, with more bandwidths (larger B), better coverage of the targets (total utility) can be achieved. As shown in Figure 7(a), both our algorithm (denoted by "ours") and the random selection (denoted by "random") achieve more utility (y coordinate) as B (x coordinate) increases. The total utility achieved by all photos (denoted by "best achievable") is also shown to provide an upper bound. The difference between our selection and the random selection is significant and the advantage of our algorithm is obvious especially when B is smaller, i.e., bandwidth is more constrained. Although the performance of both algorithms converges to the best-achievable utility as B becomes larger, the convergence of ours is much faster.

Figure 7(b) shows how the total utility changes as the number of candidate photos increases while other factors including bandwidth ($B = 20$) remain unchanged. The advantage of our algorithm is significant across the range. Considering the bandwidth limitation (only 20 photos can be selected to cover 30 targets), the difference between the utility achieved by ours and the best achievable level is small. Moreover, our algorithm can take advantage of the increasing density of photos, and improve its performance as the number of photos increases.

6.2.2 *Results on Online Max-Utility*

In this part, the algorithm for the online Max-Utility problem is evaluated. We first observe how the total utility

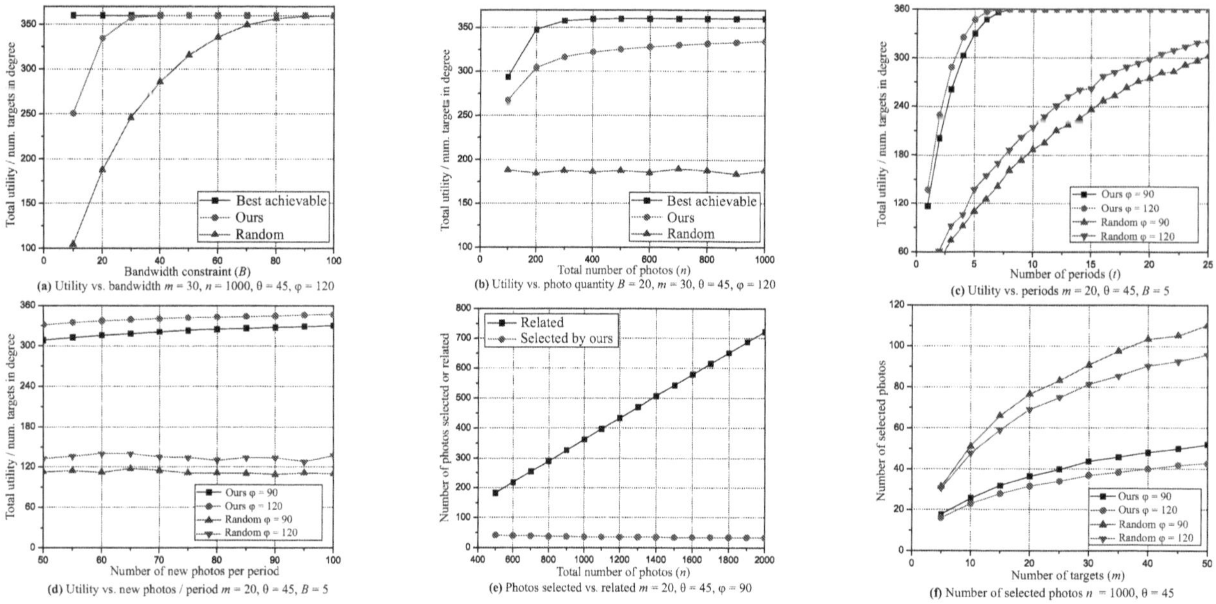

Figure 7: Simulation results: (a)-(b) Max-Utility; (c)-(d) Online Max-Utility; (e)-(f) Min-Selection.

changes as the number of periods increases in Figure 7(c). Here, we use the same target distribution as above, and there are 100 new photos available in every period. Photo parameters are shown in the figure. The normalized total utility at the end of each period is recorded. As can be seen, for both our algorithm and the random algorithm, the total utility increases as the number of periods increases. However, for our algorithm, it quickly approaches to 360. It is actually above 350 after t_7, which means by that time, almost all aspects of the targets are covered by the selected photos. The random algorithm takes much longer (after t_{25}) to reach that level of coverage. Thus, our algorithm is more responsive and effective.

Next, we vary the number of new photos from 50 to 100, with other parameters the same as above except the number of periods which is now fixed to be 5. The total utility of the selected photos after t_5 is shown in Figure 7(d). As the number of available photos increases, the selection algorithm has more choices. As a result, the total utility improves and approaches 360 in our algorithm. In comparison, the performance of the random algorithm is flat (a little fluctuated due to randomness) and very low. Given the same time period, the total utility of our algorithm is much higher than the random algorithm across the range.

6.2.3 Results on Min-Selection Problem

In this part the Min-Selection problem is studied. In reality, the given pool of photos can be very large and the number of relevant photos (i.e., photos covering at least one target) can increase very fast as the total number of randomly taken photos increases. Then, a careful selection of photos can greatly reduce the redundancy. Figure 7(c) shows the effectiveness of our selection algorithm on reducing the redundancy. There are 20 targets on the field, and the camera parameters are shown in the figure. As the total number of photos varies from 500 to 2000, the number of related photos (denoted by "related") increases linearly. However, the number of photos selected by our algorithm (denoted by "selected by ours") to achieve the same coverage does not increase. It actually decreases slightly since our algorithm takes advantage of the increased density of the photos and improves its efficiency.

The algorithms are also evaluated under the situation that the number of targets (m) varies from 5 to 50, while the total number of photos is fixed to be 1000 and all other factors remain the same. As shown in Figure 7(d), the algorithms have to select more photos to cover the increased number of targets. However, the number of photos selected by our algorithm remains very low, and the increasing speed is much slower as the number of targets increases, which is much better than the random algorithm.

7. RELATED WORK

The mass adoption of camera sensors and other position sensors on smartphones makes photo taking and sharing via online social networks much easier and more enjoyable. It creates opportunities for many applications based on camera sensor networks, which have received much attention recently in research [2, 16, 19, 11, 17]. One basic problem is how to characterize the usefulness of the image data and how to optimize the network to achieve better quality of information. However, very little effort has been devoted to this field. One problem studied is called pan and scan [10], which is proposed to maximize the total coverage in a camera sensor networks. For camera sensor placement, various optimization models and heuristics are studied in [9]. However, the coverage model is relatively simple, depending only on the distance between the target and the object, which does not consider the uniqueness of photo coverage.

Our work is inspired by the full-view coverage model which was originally proposed in [22] and later extended in [21, 23]. An object is considered to be full-view covered if no matter which direction the object faces, there is always a sensor whose sensing range includes the object and that sensor's viewing direction is sufficiently close to the object's facing direction. Although our work is based on the full-view coverage model, our model is more general and we study various optimization problems on the tradeoffs between resource constraints and photo coverage.

Another interesting work is PhotoNet [20], which is a picture delivery service that prioritizes the transmission of photos by considering the location, time stamp, and color difference, with the goal of maximizing the "diversity" of the photos. Compared to their model, we consider direction and angle information, and develop techniques to obtain them through off-the-shelf smartphones. These are very important and unique features for photos and enable us to develop much finer optimization models. Moreover, the solutions to our optimization problems are rigorously analyzed.

It is also worth mentioning that there has been much progress in content-based image retrieval techniques (see [6] for a good survey). These techniques have also been used for images obtained from mobile users. One example is to build photo annotated world maps and create 3D models of the objects from 2D photos via online social networks [5]. Some other interesting works have been done for image retrieval/search on smartphones, e.g., [25]. However, most of these works involve power-intensive computation at both user and server end, and some demands human validation to be included into the cycle [25]. These techniques are challenged by the content diversity and the resource constraints.

8. CONCLUSIONS

We proposed a resource-aware framework, called SmartPhoto, to optimize the selection of crowdsourced photos based on the accessible metadata of the smartphone including GPS location, phone orientation, etc. With this model, a remote server can efficiently evaluate and select photos from mobile users under severely constrained resources such as bandwidth, storage, computational power and device energy. Three optimization problems regarding the tradeoffs between photo coverage and resource constraints have been studied. One proposed algorithm is to maximize the total utility subject to the bandwidth constraint. It has been further extended into an online selection algorithm that can periodically select and collect photos to satisfy the requirement of time critical applications. We also provided solutions to minimize the bandwidth usage while satisfying the coverage requirement. The approximation bounds of the algorithms are theoretically proved. We have implemented SmartPhoto in a testbed using Android based smartphones and a desktop as the remote server, and proposed techniques to improve the accuracy of the collected metadata and mitigate the occlusion and out-of-focus issues. Results based on real implementations and extensive simulations validated the effectiveness of the proposed algorithms.

9. ACKNOWLEDGMENT

This work was supported in part by Network Science CTA under grant W911NF-09-2-0053.

10. REFERENCES

[1] SensorManager - Android Developer. http://developer.android.com/reference/android/hardware/SensorManager.html.

[2] I. F. Akyildiz, T. Melodia, and K. R. Chowdhury. A survey on wireless multimedia sensor networks. *Comput. Netw.*, 51(4):921–960, 2007.

[3] N. Alon and J. H. Spencer. *We the Media: Grassroots Journalism by the People, for the People.* O'Reilly Media, Sebastopol, California, 2006.

[4] V. Blanz, P. Grother, P. J. Phillips, and T. Vetter. Face recognition based on frontal views generated from non-frontal images. In *Proc. IEEE Conference on Computer Vision and Pattern Recognition (CVPR)*, pages 454–461, 2005.

[5] D. Crandall and N. Snavely. Modeling people and places with internet photo collections. *Commun. ACM*, 55(6):52–60, June 2012.

[6] R. Datta, D. Joshi, J. Li, and J. Z. Wang. Image retrieval: Ideas, influences, and trends of the new age. *ACM Comput. Surv.*, 40(2):5:1–5:60, May 2008.

[7] S. Gabarda and G. Cristobal. Blind image quality assessment through anisotropy. *Journal of the Optical Society of America A*, 24(12):B42–B51, 2007.

[8] D. S. Hochbaum, editor. *Approximation Algorithms for NP-Hard Problems.* PWS Publishing Company, 1996.

[9] E. Hörster and R. Lienhart. On the optimal placement of multiple visual sensors. In *Proc. ACM International Workshop on Video Surveillance and Sensor Networks (VSSN)*, 2006.

[10] M. P. Johnson and A. Bar-Noy. Pan and scan: Configuring cameras for coverage. In *IEEE INFOCOM*, 2011.

[11] F. Li, J. Barabas, and A. L. Santos. Information processing for live photo mosaic with a group of wireless image sensors. In *Proc. ACM/IEEE Conference on Information Processing in Sensor Networks (IPSN)*, 2010.

[12] S. Liu, L. Palen, J. Sutton, A. Hughes, and S. Vieweg. In search of the bigger picture: The emergent role of on-line photo-sharing in times of disaster. In *Proc. ISCRAM*, 2008.

[13] R. Meier. *Professional Android 2 Application Development, 2nd Ed.* Wiley Publishing, Inc., 2010.

[14] P. J. Phillips, W. T. Scruggs, A. J. O'Toole, P. J. Flynn, K. W. Bowyer, C. L. Schott, and M. Sharpe. FRVT 2006 and ICE 2006 large-scale results. *National Institute of Standards and Technology, Tech. Rep. NISTIR 7408*, 2007.

[15] S. F. Ray. *Applied Photographic Optics.* ocal Press, Oxford, UK, 3 edition, 2002.

[16] B. Rinner and W. Wolf. A bright future for distributed smart cameras. *Proceedings of the IEEE*, 96(10):1562 – 1564, 2008.

[17] Y. Shen, W. Hu, M. Yang, J. Liu, and C. T. Chou. Efficient background subtraction for tracking in embedded camera networks. In *Proc. ACM/IEEE IPSN*, 2012.

[18] N. Snavely, S. M. Seitz, and R. Szeliski. Photo tourism: Exploring photo collections in 3d. In *Proc. ACM SIGGRAPH*, 2006.

[19] S. Soro and W. Heinzelman. A survey of visual sensor networks. *Advances in Multimedia*, 2009:1–22, 2009.

[20] M. Y. S. Uddin, H. Wang, F. Saremi, G.-J. Qi, T. Abdelzaher, and T. Huang. Photonet: A similarity-aware picture delivery service for situation awareness. In *Proc. IEEE Real-Time Systems Symposium (RTSS)*, 2011.

[21] Y. Wang and G. Cao. Barrier coverage in camera sensor networks. In *Proc. ACM Mobihoc*, 2011.

[22] Y. Wang and G. Cao. On full-view coverage in camera sensor networks. In *Proc. IEEE INFOCOM*, 2011.

[23] Y. Wang and G. Cao. Achieving full-view coverage in camera sensor networks. *ACM Transactions on Sensor Networks (ToSN)*, 10(1), 2013.

[24] G. Williams. *Linear Algebra With Applications.* Jones & Bartlett Learning, 2012.

[25] T. Yan, V. Kumar, and D. Ganesan. Crowdsearch: exploiting crowds for accurate real-time image search on mobile phones. In *Proc. ACM MobiSys*, 2010.

[26] C. Zhu, K. Li, Q. Lv, L. Shang, and R. P. Dick. iScope: personalized multi-modality image search for mobile devices. In *Proc. ACM MobiSys*, 2009.

How to Build Vehicular Networks in the Real World

Joao Barros
Universidade do Porto
Porto, Portugal

Abstract

There are now 1 billion vehicles in the world waiting to be connected to the Internet. At the same time, vehicular communication technologies have matured to a point in which massive deployment is both possible and feasible. One option for deployment is to wait for car manufacturers to embed DSRC/WAVE interfaces inside their latest models. However, since only 9% of the world's fleet is new every year, this would result in a time span of up to 20 years until 90% of the vehicles are finally connected. Another option is to rely entirely on cellular communications, such as GPRS, EDGE, 3G and LTE. This cellular only approach is impractical due to the capital expenses required for telecom operators to meet the demands of the impending tsunami of mobile data (expected to grow 1800% until 2016). Clearly, there is need for a low-cost wireless networking solution that can be placed in any vehicle and offers reliable connectivity, improved quality of experience and higher safety for drivers and passengers. This solution, we will argue, is vehicular mesh networking.

Drawing from five years of research and our experience with a large testbed with hundreds of taxis and buses, currently under deployment in Porto, Portugal, we will address how city-scale deployment can be achieved and what kind of connectivity, bandwidth, quality of service and application support can be provided as the density of Internet gateways and the density of connected vehicles grows towards widespread deployment. Some attention will also be given to relevant issues in system design such as channel modeling, mobility patterns, networking protocols and large-scale simulation with manageable complexity. Finally, we will show how a vehicular mesh network can be used as a highly dense urban scanner, producing real-time data on-the-move, which can be leveraged from the cloud to help manage future cities, protect our environment and improve our quality of life.

There are now 1 billion vehicles in the world waiting to be connected to the Internet. At the same time, vehicularcommunication technologies have matured to a point in which massive deployment is both possible and feasible. One option for deployment is to wait for car manufacturers to embed DSRC/WAVE interfaces inside their latest models. However, since only 9% of the world's fleet is new every year, this would result in a time span of up to 20 years until 90% of the vehicles are finally connected. Another option, which is currently the preferred choice, would be to rely entirely on cellular communications, such as GPRS, EDGE, 3G and LTE. However, these solutions are becoming more costly everyday, as telecom operators become increasingly concerned with the capital expenses required to meet the demands of the impending tsunami of mobile data, which is expected to grow 1800% until 2016. Clearly, there is need for a low-cost wireless networking solution that can be placed in any vehicle and offers reliable connectivity, improved quality of experience and higher safety for drivers and passengers. This solution, we will argue, is vehicular mesh networking.

Drawing from five years of research and our experience with a large testbed with hundreds of taxis and buses, currently under deployment in Porto, Portugal, we will address how city-scale deployment can be achieved and what kind of connectivity, bandwidth, quality of service and application support can be provided as the density of Internet gateways and the density of connected vehicles grows towards widespread deployment. Some attention will also be given to relevant issues in system design such as channel modeling, mobility patterns, networking protocols and large-scale simulation with manageable complexity. Finally, we will show how a vehicular mesh network can be used as a highly dense urban scanner, producing real-time data on-the-move, which can be leveraged from the cloud to help manage future cities, protect our environment and improve our quality of life.

Joint work with Susana Sargento, Peter Steenkiste, Michel Ferreira, Ana Aguiar, Muriel Médard and more than twenty colleagues, graduate students and engineers at Universidade do Porto, Universidade de Aveiro, Instituto de Telecomunicações, Carnegie Mellon University, and Veniam'Works, Inc.

ACM Classification:

A.1 General Literature: INTRODUCTORY AND SURVEY; C.2.2 Computer Systems Organization, COMPUTER-COMMUNICATION NETWORKS, Network Protocols: Protocol architecture (OSI model); Routing protocols

Author Keywords: Intelligent transportation systems; Network protocols; Vehicular networks

Bio

João Barros is an Associate Professor of Electrical and Computer Engineering at the University of Porto, Founder and CEO of Veniam'Works and Founding Director of the Institute for Telecommunications (IT) in Porto, Portugal. He was a Fulbright scholar at Cornell University and has held visiting appointments at MIT and Carnegie Mellon. He also teaches at the Porto Business School and co-founded two recent startups, Streambolico and Veniam'Works, commercializing wireless video and vehicular communication technologies, respectively. Between 2009 and 2012, Dr. Barros served as National Director of the Carnegie Mellon Portugal Program, a five-year

MobiHoc'14, August 11–14, 2014, Philadelphia, PA, USA.
ACM 978-1-4503-2620-9/14/08.
http://dx.doi.org/10.1145/2632951.2633209

international partnership funded by the Portuguese Foundation of Science and Technology, with a total budget of 56M Euros.

In recent years, João Barros has been Principal Investigator (PI) and Co-PI of numerous national, European and industry funded projects, co-authoring one book and more than 150 research papers in the fields of networking, information theory and security, with a special focus on smart city technologies, network coding, physical-layer security, sensor networks, and intelligent transportation systems. Dr. Barros has received several awards, including the 2010 IEEE Communications Society Young Researcher Award for the Europe, Middle East and Africa region, the 2011 IEEE ComSoC and Information Theory Society Joint Paper Award, the 2012 BES National Innovation Award, the 2013 Building Global Innovators Grand Prize (ISCTE-IUL and MIT) and a state-wide best teaching award by the Bavarian State Ministry of Sciences, Research and the Arts.

Dr. Barros is frequently invited as an expert speaker by international organizations such as the European Commission, OECD, ITU, EuroDIG and IEEE. He also worked as an independent consultant for various organizations and projects. Dr. Barros is fluent in Portuguese, German, English, French and Spanish. He received his undergraduate education in Electrical and Computer Engineering from the Universidade do Porto (UP), Portugal and Universitaet Karlsruhe, Germany, a performing arts degree in flute from the Music Conservatory of Porto, and the Ph.D. degree in Electrical Engineering and Information Technology from the Technische Universitaet Muenchen (TUM), Germany.

Secrecy Capacity Scaling of Large-Scale Cognitive Networks

Yitao Chen†, Jinbei Zhang†, Xinbing Wang†, Xiaohua Tian†, Weijie Wu‡, Fan Wu‡, Chee Wei Tan§
† Dept. of Electronic Engineering, Shanghai Jiao Tong University, China
‡Dept. of Computer Science and Engineering, Shanghai Jiao Tong University, China
§ Dept. of Computer Science, City University of Hong Kong
{albrecht, abelchina, xwang8, xtian, weijiewu, fwu}@sjtu.edu.cn, cheewtan@cityu.edu.hk

ABSTRACT

Increasingly, more spectrum bands are utilized for unlicensed use in wireless cognitive networks. It is important to study how information-theoretic secrecy capacity is affected in large-scale cognitive networks. We consider two scenarios: (1) non-colluding case, where eavesdroppers decode messages individually. In this case, we propose a new secure protocol model to analyze the transmission opportunities of secondary nodes. We show that the secrecy capacity of the primary network is not affected, while the secondary network can achieve the same performance as a standalone network in the order sense. Since our analysis is general as we only make a few relaxed assumptions on both networks, the conclusions hold when both networks are classic static networks, networks with i.i.d mobility, multicast networks etc. (2) colluding case where eavesdroppers can collude to decode a message. In that case, we show that the lower bound of per-node secrecy capacity of the primary network is $\Omega(\frac{1}{\sqrt{n}}\phi_e^{-\frac{2}{\alpha-1}}(n))$ when the eavesdropper density is $\phi_e(n) = \Omega(\log^2 n)$. Interestingly the existence of secondary nodes increases the secrecy capacity of the primary network.

Categories and Subject Descriptors

C.2.1 [**Computer-Communication Networks**]: Network Architecture and Design—*Wireless Communications*

Keywords

Secrecy Capacity, Cognitive Network, Scaling Law, Colluding Eavesdroppers

1. INTRODUCTION

The fundamental scaling laws in ad hoc networks have been extensively studied since the seminal work of Gupta and Kumar [1]. They showed that for a network with n static nodes randomly located in a unit area, the per-node capacity is lower bounded by $\Omega(1/\sqrt{n \log n})$ and upper bounded by $O(1/\sqrt{n})$. This gap is later closed by Franceschetti *et al.* [2] using percolation theory. Later on, Grossglauser and Tse [3] further found capacity performance can be significantly improved when nodes are mobile. They showed the mobile network can achieve a per-node capacity of $\Theta(1)$ under the 2-hop relay algorithm. However, the significant improvement of capacity is achieved at the expense of a large delay, which is $\Theta(n)$ as proved by Neely *et al.* [4]. Since then, there have been numerous related works, which cover a wide variety of ad hoc networks with different features, such as multicast networks [5], [6] and hierarchically cooperative networks [7].

As the broadcast nature of the wireless medium allows eavesdroppers and attackers to intercept information transmission and can also degrade transmission quality, the security of wireless ad hoc networks has attracted considerable attention recently. In wireless ad hoc networks, the lack of infrastructure makes the key distribution and management required for traditional symmetric-key cryptographic approaches difficult; energy and computational ability limitations at terminals prohibit the use of asymmetric cryptography. As such, most previous works focus on the information-theoretic security, where eavesdroppers are assumed to have infinite computational power. In the analysis of information-theoretic security, the objective is to keep eavesdroppers from getting enough information. Vasudevan *et al.* [8] studied the secrecy-capacity tradeoff in large-scale wireless networks and introduced helpers around transmitters to generate noises to suppress the SINR at eavesdroppers. Koyluoglu *et al.* [9] showed that if the eavesdropper density is $o(1/(\log n)^2)$ in extended networks, then the secrecy rate scales as $1/\sqrt{n}$. Capar *et al.* [10] proposed a new secrecy communication scheme, which can tolerate $o(n/\log n)$ eavesdroppers, without affecting the network throughput. Zhang *et al.* [11] let the receivers generate artificial noises in order to degrade the SINR at eavesdroppers, and studied the impacts of secrecy constraints on the capacity scaling in static networks.

The aforementioned related work mainly focused on the secrecy capacity and delay scaling for a single network. In recent years, the lack of radio resource has led to the development of *cognitive radio* technology. Coexistent with licensed primary users, *cognitive (secondary)* users need to sense their spectral environment to opportunistically access the spectrum without harming the performance of primary

MobiHoc'14, August 11–14, 2014, Philadelphia, PA, USA.

ACM 978-1-4503-2620-9/14/08 ...$15.00.
http://dx.doi.org/10.1145/2632951.2632961 .

users. Jeon *et al.* [12] showed that the static primary network and secondary network can simultaneously achieve the same capacity as stand-alone networks. Yin *et al.* [13] developed similar results for delay-throughput tradeoff. Huang *et al.* [14] characterized the general conditions for cognitive networks to achieve the same throughput and delay scaling as stand-alone networks. Tan *et al.* [16] propose a optimisation algorithm to the spectrum management in multiuser wireless cognitive networks

Degradation in secrecy capacity is mainly caused by those eavesdroppers that are least affected by the artificial noise from receivers [11]. In cognitive networks, secondary users that are least affected by the interference from primary users get transmission opportunities, which can help to suppress the channel qualities of the eavesdroppers. Therefore, we study in depth the secrecy capacity and delay scaling in cognitive networks.

The main contributions of this paper are summarized as follows.

- In the non-colluding case, we propose a new secure protocol model to analyze the transmission opportunities of the secondary network. We give sufficient conditions under which the secondary network can achieve the same order secrecy performance as a standalone network without degrading the secrecy capacity of the primary network.
- In the non-colluding case, our results are derived without requiring specific constraints on the traffic patterns and the mobility models of primary and secondary networks. Thus, we can apply our results to general cognitive networks, such as classic static networks, networks with i.i.d mobility, multicast networks etc.
- In the colluding case, we prove that introducing the secondary nodes into the network increases the secrecy capacity of the primary network. We show that the lower bound of the secrecy capacity is $\Omega(\frac{1}{\sqrt{n}}\phi_e^{-\frac{2}{\alpha-1}}(n))$.

The rest of this paper is organized as follows. In Section 2, we introduce the system model. In Section 3 and 4, we give asymptotic analysis on secrecy capacity in the non-colluding case and colluding case, respectively. Finally, we conclude our paper in Section 5.

2. SYSTEM MODEL

In this paper, we assume that the network area is a square $\mathcal{O}$ with size $\sqrt{n} \times \sqrt{n}$, where n is the number of primary nodes.

2.1 Legitimate Network

We consider the scenario, in which there are two kinds of legitimate nodes, n primary nodes and m secondary nodes, overlapping in the square $\mathcal{O}$. We assume that both primary nodes and the secondary nodes are independently and identically distributed (i.i.d.) in $\mathcal{O}$ according to the uniform distribution. Their positions are denoted by $\{X_i\}_{i=1}^n$ and $\{Y_j\}_{j=1}^m$, respectively. Let $|X_i - Y_j|$ be the distance between two nodes. For two primary nodes forming a transmitter-receiver pair, they share a primary link denoted by $(X_i, X_{Rx(i)})$, where i is the index of the transmitter and $Rx(\cdot)$ is the index of the corresponding receiver. Similarly, we denote a secondary link by $(Y_j, Y_{Rx(j)})$. We denote $\mathcal{L}^p$ as the set of active primary links, $\mathcal{L}^s$ as the set of active secondary links and $\mathcal{L} = \mathcal{L}^p \cup \mathcal{L}^s$. In addition, $\mathcal{T}^p$ ($\mathcal{T}^s$) and $\mathcal{R}^p$ ($\mathcal{R}^s$) are the sets of active primary (secondary) transmitters and receivers, respectively. For active primary link $(X_i, X_{Rx(i)}) \in \mathcal{L}^p$ and active secondary link $(Y_j, Y_{Rx(j)}) \in \mathcal{L}^s$, we denote their transmission ranges as $R_i = |X_i - X_{Rx(i)}|$ and $r_j = |Y_j - Y_{Rx(j)}|$, respectively. We also use the same artificial noise generation scheme as that in [11] to enable the information-theoretic security in the network. We assume that each legitimate node is equipped with three antennas. When a legitimate node acts as a receiver, one antenna is used for message reception, while the other two simultaneously generate artificial noise to suppress the eavesdroppers' channels. The distances between the receiving antenna and the other two respective transmitting antennas satisfy a difference of half the radio wavelength. The interference can thus be eliminated by invoking the techniques of self-interference cancellation. Thereby, each receiver does not experience the artificial noise generated by the node itself.

2.2 Eavesdropper Network

We consider that there are $n\phi_e(n)$ eavesdroppers located in the same network area, where $\phi_e(n)$ is the density of eavesdroppers. Let $\mathcal{E}$ be the set of eavesdroppers and Z_e be the position of each eavesdropper $e \in \mathcal{E}$. We assume that all the eavesdroppers are silent and static, since they can be easily detected if they are active or move drastically. Hence, instead of jamming the signal, the eavesdroppers only overhear messages. We assume that each eavesdropper independently and identically selects a position in the network area $\mathcal{O}$ according to the uniform distribution. We also assume that the eavesdroppers have two overhearing modes, namely independent mode and colluding mode. In the independent mode, each eavesdropper decodes messages independently. In the colluding mode, all the eavesdroppers can communicate and collaborate to decode the messages. Maximum ratio combining is adopted to maximize the sum of SINR that each eavesdropper obtains. Hence, we can regard all the eavesdroppers as one super-eavesdropper. Moreover, since we consider information-theoretic security in this paper, we assume that the eavesdroppers have infinite computation resources. We also assume that both channel state information (CSI) and location information of the eavesdroppers are unknown to the legitimate nodes.

2.3 Communication Model: Physical Model

We describe our communication model in this section. For active primary (secondary) transmitter $i \in \mathcal{T}^p$ ($\mathcal{T}^s$), we use $P_{t,i}^p$ ($P_{t,i}^s$) to denote the transmission power of i, where the subscript t stands for transmitter. For active primary (secondary) receiver $j \in \mathcal{R}^p$ ($\mathcal{R}^s$), we use $P_{r,j}^p$ ($P_{r,j}^s$) to denote the noise generation power of j, where the subscript r stands for receiver. The path loss between node i and node j is denoted by $l(X_i, X_j) = \min\{1, |X_i - X_j|^{-\alpha}\}$. Here, α is the path loss exponent and we assume that $\alpha > 2$, which is a reasonable value range for extended network model. When node i is transmitting messages to node j, the signal to interference and noise ratio (SINR) at the receiver j is given as follows.

For the primary network,

$$\text{SINR}_{ij}^p = \frac{P_{t,i}^p l(X_i, X_j)}{N_0 + I_{pp} + I_{sp}}, \tag{1}$$

where

$$I_{pp} = \sum_{k\in\mathcal{T}^p\setminus\{i\}} P_{t,k}^p l(X_k, X_j) + \sum_{k\in\mathcal{R}^p\setminus\{j\}} P_{r,k}^p l(X_k, X_j),$$

$$I_{sp} = \sum_{k\in\mathcal{T}^s} P_{t,k}^s l(Y_k, X_j) + \sum_{k\in\mathcal{R}^s} P_{r,k}^s l(Y_k, X_j),$$

and N_0 denotes the ambient noise power of the network environment. Note that the transmission power $P_{r,j}^p$ of receiver j causes no interference to itself, since we adopt self-interference cancellation techniques.

Similarly, for the secondary network,

$$\mathrm{SINR}_{ij}^{s} = \frac{P_{t,i}^{s} l(Y_i, Y_j)}{N_0 + I_{ps} + I_{ss}}, \tag{2}$$

where

$$I_{ss} = \sum_{k \in \mathcal{T}^s \setminus \{i\}} P_{t,k}^{s} l(Y_k, Y_j) + \sum_{k \in \mathcal{R}^s \setminus \{j\}} P_{r,k}^{s} l(Y_k, Y_j),$$

$$I_{ps} = \sum_{k \in \mathcal{T}^p} P_{t,k}^{p} l(X_k, Y_j) + \sum_{k \in \mathcal{R}^p} P_{r,k}^{p} l(X_k, Y_j),$$

On the other hand, $P_{r,j}^{p}$ and $P_{r,j}^{s}$ do interfere with the eavesdroppers. When node i is transmitting messages, we give the SINR at eavesdropper e for the primary network as follows (the SINR at e for the secondary network can be easily extended from equation (3)),

$$\mathrm{SINR}_{ie}^{p} = \frac{P_{t,i}^{p} l(X_i, Z_e)}{N_0 + I_{pe} + I_{se}}, \tag{3}$$

where

$$I_{pe} = \sum_{k \in \mathcal{T}^p \setminus \{i\}} P_{t,k}^{p} l(X_k, Z_e) + \sum_{k \in \mathcal{R}^p} P_{r,k}^{p} l(X_k, Z_e),$$

$$I_{se} = \sum_{k \in \mathcal{T}^s} P_{t,k}^{s} l(Y_k, Z_e) + \sum_{k \in \mathcal{R}^s} P_{r,k}^{s} l(Y_k, Z_e).$$

2.4 Performance Metrics

DEFINITION 1. Secrecy Throughput Per Hop*: In the non-colluding case, we define the per hop secure throughput between any active transmitter-receiver pair as*

$$G_f = \log(1 + SINR_{ij}) - \log(1 + \max_{e \in \mathcal{E}} SINR_{ie}).$$

In the non-colluding case, we define the per hop secure throughput as

$$G_f = \log(1 + SINR_{ij}) - \log(1 + \sum_{e \in \mathcal{E}} SINR_{ie})$$

DEFINITION 2. Feasible Throughput*: Per-node throughput $g(n)$ of the primary network is said to be feasible if there exists a spatial and temporal scheme for scheduling transmissions, such that every primary source can send $g(n)$ b/s to its destination on average.*

DEFINITION 3. Asymptotic Per-node Capacity $\lambda_p(n)$ *of the primary network is said to be $\Theta(g(n))$ if there exist two positive constants c and c' such that*

$$\lim_{n \to \infty} Pr\{\lambda_p(n) = cg(n) \text{ is feasible}\} = 1$$

$$\lim_{n \to \infty} Pr\{\lambda_p(n) = c' g(n) \text{ is feasible}\} < 1$$

Similarly, we can define the asymptotic per-node capacity $\lambda_s(m)$ for the secondary network.

3. INDEPENDENT EAVESDROPPERS

In this section, we investigate the secrecy capacity and delay scaling of the cognitive network when eavesdroppers work in the independent mode. Since secondary users occupy extra radio resources, it seems that the secrecy capacity and delay of either primary network or secondary network may be degraded. However, we show that the secondary network can achieve the same secrecy performance as a standalone network in the order sense, while the performance of the primary network is not affected at all.

Table 1: Notations

Notations	Definitions
n	The total number of primary nodes
m	The total number of secondary nodes
$n \cdot \phi_e(n)$	The total number of eavesdroppers
α	The path loss exponent, $\alpha > 2$
X_i	The position of primary node i
Y_j	The position of secondary node j
Z_e	The position of eavesdropper e
$Rx(\cdot)$	The index of corresponding receiver
R_i	The transmission range of primary network link
r_i	The transmission range of secondary network link
$\mathcal{SPR}()$	The feasible family of secure protocol model
$\mathcal{PH}()$	The feasible family of secure physical model
$\mathcal{D}()$	The feasible family of Operation Rule 1
$\mathcal{H}()$	The feasible family of secure hybrid protocol model
P_t^p	The transmission power of primary nodes
P_t^s	The transmission power of secondary nodes
P_r^p	The artificial noise power of primary nodes
P_r^s	The artificial noise power of secondary nodes
$\mathcal{L}^p$	The set of active primary links
$\mathcal{L}^s$	The set of active secondary links
$\mathcal{L}$	$\mathcal{L}^p \cup \mathcal{L}^s$
$\mathcal{T}$	The set of active transmitters at a given time slot
$\mathcal{R}$	The set of active receivers at a given time slot
$\mathcal{E}$	The set of eavesdroppers
$\lvert \cdot \rvert$	The Euclidean length or the number of elements of a set
$l(X_i, X_j)$	The path loss function $\min\{1, \lvert X_i - X_j \rvert^{-\alpha}\}$
$D(x, r)$	The disk with radius r centered at x.
λ	The per-node secure throughput of legitimate node
D	The delay constraint imposed on the packets
G_f	The per hop secure throughput

First, we give the definition of secure transmission in this section.

DEFINITION 4. *We define a transmission from i to j to be successful and secret if the following conditions hold, for primary network,*

$$SINR_{ij}^{p} \geq \gamma_p, \forall e \in \mathcal{E}, SINR_{ie}^{p} \leq \gamma_e$$

for secondary network,

$$SINR_{ij}^{s} \geq \gamma_s, \forall e \in \mathcal{E}, SINR_{ie}^{s} \leq \gamma_e$$

where γ_p, γ_s γ_e are constants and $\gamma_e < \min\{\gamma_p, \gamma_s\}$.

The first condition in the definition ensures that the receiver can decode the message successfully. The second condition guarantees none of eavesdroppers can decode the message. Given Definition 4, there is a subset of links can be active such that all transmissions over active links are successful and secret. We call such a subset of links a *feasible state*, and denote the set of all feasible states as *feasible family*. We use $\mathcal{PH}(\gamma_p, \gamma_s, \gamma_e)$ to denote the feasible family of the physical model.

Next, for tractability of calculation, we give some constraints on the transmission power and artificial noise generation power of the cognitive network.

DEFINITION 5. Power Assignment Scheme*: We say the whole network adopts* power assignment scheme *$\mathcal{A}(b_1, b_2)$, if $P_{t,i}^{p} = P_t^p = P, P_{r,i}^{p} = P_r^p = b_1(1 + R_{\max})^{\alpha} P, P_{t,i}^{s} = P_t^s = b_2 P, P_{r,i}^{s} = P_r^s = b_1 b_2 (1 + r_{\max})^{\alpha} P$, where $R_{\max} = \max\{R_i\}, r_{\max} = \max\{r_j\}$.*

Since the primary nodes and the secondary nodes have different priorities in accessing the radio spectrum, we give them different operation rules to guarantee their transmission opportunities.

OPERATION RULE 1. Decision model for the primary network*:*

$$\frac{P_t^p l(X_i, X_j)}{N_0 + I_{pp}} \geq \gamma_p + \epsilon, \; \frac{P_t^p}{P_r^p}(1 + R_{\max})^{\alpha} \leq \gamma_e \tag{4}$$

The feasible family of the primary decision model is denoted by $\mathcal{D}(\gamma_p + \epsilon, \gamma_e)$.

We do not include any influence of the secondary network in the decision model of the primary network because the primary network needs neither to know the existence of the secondary network nor to adopt to the secondary users. However we put an allowance ϵ in the operation rule to leave some margin to act as buffer against transient interference from the secondary users. The power constraints given by the second equation are used to guarantee secure transmissions.

The objective of the operation rule for the secondary network is that the whole cognitive network complies with the physical model $\mathcal{PH}(\gamma_p, \gamma_s, \gamma_e)$ when the secondary network joins the primary network. The notation $\mathcal{H}$ in the *Operation Rule 2* will be explained later.

OPERATION RULE 2. Decision model for the secondary network: *Let* $\mathcal{L}^p$ *and* $\mathcal{L}^s$ *be the sets of active primary links and active secondary links. If* $\mathcal{L}^p \in \mathcal{D}(\gamma_p + \epsilon, \gamma_e)$ *and* $\mathcal{L}^p \cup \mathcal{L}^s \in \mathcal{H}$, *then* $\mathcal{L}^p \cup \mathcal{L}^s \in \mathcal{PH}(\gamma_p, \gamma_s, \gamma_e)$.

3.1 Secure Protocol Model: To Bound The Interference

We first prove the physical feasibility of our operation scheme. We propose a new secure protocol model to bound the interference.

3.1.1 Hybrid Secure Protocol Model

DEFINITION 6. Secure Protocol Model *for primary network: A transmission from* i *to* j *is feasible if for any* $k \in \mathcal{T}^p \backslash \{i\}$ *and* $l \in \mathcal{R}^p \backslash \{j\}$,

$$1 + |X_k - X_j| \geq C_{tp}(1 + |X_i - X_j|), \quad (5)$$

$$1 + |X_l - X_j| \geq C_{rp}(1 + |X_i - X_j|)^2, \quad (6)$$

where C_{tp} *and* C_{rp} *define the guard zone for transmitters and receivers in the primary network, respectively. The corresponding feasible family is denoted as* $\mathcal{SPR}(C_{tp}, C_{rp})$. *Likewise, we define feasible family* $\mathcal{SPR}$ (C_{ts}, C_{rs}) *for the secondary network.*

We prove that the feasible family in the decision model of the primary network is also feasible in the secure protocol model.

LEMMA 1. *If* $\mathcal{L}^p \in \mathcal{D}(\gamma_p + \epsilon, \gamma_e)$, *there exists constant* C_{tp} *and* C_{rp} *such that* $\mathcal{L}^p \in \mathcal{SPR}(C_{tp}, C_{rp})$.

PROOF. See Appendix A. □

From Lemma 1, we can see that the secure protocol model is much simpler than the secure physical model. We define a new *Hybrid Secure Protocol Model* $\mathcal{H}$ to act as the decision model for the secondary network.

DEFINITION 7. The Hybrid Secure Protocol Model *with feasible family* $\mathcal{H}$: $\forall \mathcal{L} \in \mathcal{H}$, *let* $\mathcal{L}^p \in \mathcal{SPR}(C_{tp}, C_{rp})$, $\mathcal{L}^s \in \mathcal{SPR}(C_{ts}, C_{rs})$. *Furthermore,* $\forall (X_i, X_j) \in \mathcal{L}^p$

$$1 + |Y_k - X_j| \geq C_{tsp}(1 + |X_i - X_j|) \quad \forall k \in \mathcal{T}^s \quad (7)$$

$$1 + |Y_l - X_j| \geq C_{rsp}(1 + |X_i - X_j|)^2 \quad \forall l \in \mathcal{R}^s \quad (8)$$

and $\forall (Y_i, Y_j) \in \mathcal{L}^s$

$$1 + |X_k - Y_j| \geq C_{tps}(1 + |Y_i - Y_j|) \quad \forall k \in \mathcal{T}^p \quad (9)$$

$$1 + |X_l - Y_j| \geq C_{rps}(1 + |Y_i - Y_j|)^2 \quad \forall l \in \mathcal{R}^p \quad (10)$$

where constants $C_{tsp}, C_{rsp}, C_{tps}, C_{rps}$ *define the inter-network guard zone as illustrated in Figure 1.*

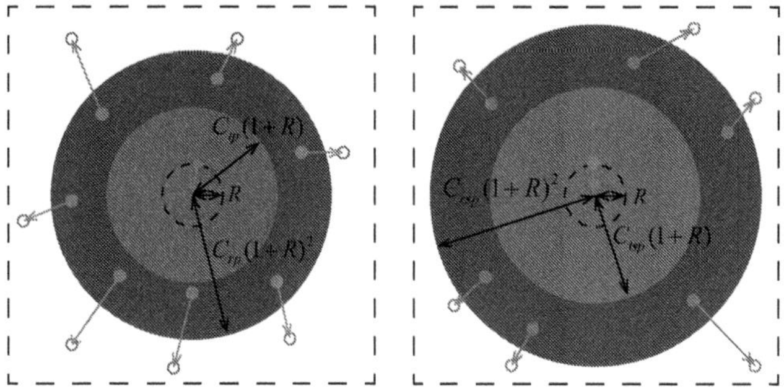

Figure 1: An example of hybrid secure protocol model for a primary transmission pair

3.1.2 Interference at Primary Nodes

We first bound the interference from the secondary network to the primary network. We start this part with a useful property of the hybrid secure protocol model.

LEMMA 2. *Given arbitrary* $Z_i, Z_j, Z_k, Z_l \in \mathcal{O}$, *if* (Z_i, Z_j), (Z_k, Z_l) *are active links (primary or secondary) and* $C_{tx} = 3$, $C_{rx} > 0$ $(x \in \{1, 2\}$ *and* $C_{tx} \in \{C_{tp}, C_{ts}, C_{tps}, C_{tsp}\}$, $C_{rx} \in \{C_{rp}, C_{rs}, C_{rps}, C_{rsp}\})$, *then the* $\frac{C_{r1}}{4}(1 + |Z_i - Z_j|)^2$ *neighborhood of line segment* Z_iZ_j *and the* $\frac{C_{r2}}{4}(1 + |Z_k - Z_l|)^2$ *neighborhood of line segment* Z_kZ_l *are disjoint.*

PROOF. See Appendix B. □

From Lemma 2, we know that C_{rx} dominates the representation of the distances between concurrent transmission pairs. Thus we use C_p, C_s, C_{ps}, C_{sp} to represent $C_{rp}, C_{rs}, C_{rps}, C_{rsp}$ for simplicity from now on. We are ready to give the upper bound of interference at primary receivers from the secondary network in Theorem 1 in the following.

THEOREM 1. *Under the power assignment* $\mathcal{A}(b_1, b_2)$ *and the hybrid secure protocol model, if* $C_{ps} > C_s$, *then for any active primary link* $(X_i, X_{Rx(i)})$, *the interference at* $X_{Rx(i)}$ *from the active links of the secondary network is upper-bounded by* $b_3(P_t^s + P_r^s)(1 + R_i)^{4-2\alpha}(1 + r_{\min})^{-4}$, *where* b_3 *is a constant.*

PROOF. Let $D(X, r)$ be the disk centered at X with radius r. Then, all $D(Y_j, \frac{C_s}{4}(1+r_j)^2), j \in \mathcal{T}^s$ should be mutually disjoint according to Lemma 2. As well, $D(Y_j, \frac{C_{ps}}{4}(1 + r_j)^2), j \in \mathcal{T}^s$ are disjoint with $D(X_{Rx(i)}, \frac{C_{sp}}{4}(1+R_i)^2))$. Because we assume that $C_{ps} > C_s$, then all $D(Y_j, \frac{C_s}{4}(1 + r_j)^2)$ and $D(X_{Rx(i)}, \frac{C_{sp}}{4}(1 + R_i)^2))$ are disjoint.
Then we divide the set $\mathcal{T}^s$ into subsets $\mathcal{T}_k^s$, for $1 \leq k \leq \frac{4\sqrt{2n}}{C_{sp}(1+R_i)^2}$ $\mathcal{T}_k^s = \left\{ j \middle| k\frac{C_{sp}(1+R_i)^2}{4} \leq |Y_j - X_{Rx(i)}| \leq (k + 1)\frac{C_{sp}(1+R_i)^2}{4}, j \in \mathcal{T}^s \right\}$.
The radio resource consumed by each transmitter can be bounded by,

$$\frac{1}{3}\pi[\frac{C_s(1 + r_{\min})^2}{4}]^2 \sum_{l=1}^{k} |\mathcal{T}_l^s| \leq \pi[(k + 1)\frac{C_{sp}(1 + R_i)^2}{4}]^2$$

We denote the interference at $X_{Rx(i)}$ that is caused by transmitters in the secondary network as $I_{sp,t}$, and it can be bounded as follows,

$$
\begin{aligned}
I_{sp,t}(i) &= \sum_{j \in \mathcal{T}^s} \frac{P_{t,j}^s}{(1+|Y_j - X_{Rx(i)}|)^\alpha} \leq \sum_k \frac{P_t^s}{|k\frac{C_{sp}(1+R_i)^2}{4}|^\alpha} |\mathcal{T}_k^s| \\
&\leq \frac{4^\alpha P_t^s}{C_{sp}^\alpha (1+R_i)^{2\alpha}} \sum_k \frac{1}{k^\alpha} (\sum_{l=1}^{k} |T_l^s| - \sum_{l=1}^{k-1} |T_l^s|) \\
&\leq \frac{4^\alpha P_t^s}{C_{sp}^\alpha (1+R_i)^{2\alpha}} \sum_{k=1}^{\infty} [\frac{1}{k^\alpha} - \frac{1}{(k+1)^\alpha}] \sum_{l=1}^{k} |T_l^s| \\
&\leq \frac{4^\alpha P_t^s}{C_{sp}^{\alpha-2} C_s^2 (1+R_i)^{2\alpha-4} (1+r_{\min})^4} \sum_{k=1}^{\infty} \frac{3\alpha(k+1)^2}{k^{\alpha+1}} \\
&= b_3 P_t^s (1+R_i)^{4-2\alpha} (1+r_{\min})^{-4}
\end{aligned}
$$

The interference caused by active receivers can be bounded by similar techniques, $I_{sp,r}(i) = b_3 P_r^s (1+R_i)^{4-2\alpha}(1+r_{\min})^{-4}$. And $I_{sp}(i) = I_{sp,t}(i) + I_{sp,r}(i)$. □

3.1.3 Interference at Secondary Nodes

In this part, we bound the interference at secondary receivers from primary nodes and other secondary nodes in Theorem 2 and Theorem 3, respectively.

THEOREM 2. *Under the power assignment $\mathcal{A}(b_1, b_2)$ and the hybrid secure protocol model, if $C_{sp} > C_p$ for any active link $(Y_i, Y_{Rx(i)})$, the interference at $Y_{Rx(i)}$ from the active primary links is upper-bounded by $b_4(P_t^p + P_r^p)(1+R_{\min})^{-2\alpha}$, where b_4 is a constant.*

THEOREM 3. *Under the power assignment $\mathcal{A}(b_1, b_2)$ and the hybrid secure protocol model, for any active link $(Y_i, Y_{Rx(i)})$, the interference at $Y_{Rx(i)}$ from all other simultaneously active secondary links is upper-bounded by $b_5(P_t^s + P_r^s)(1+r_i)^{4-2\alpha}(1+r_{\min})^{-4}$, where b_5 is a constant.*

The techniques used in the proofs of Theorems 2 and 3 are similar to those in Theorem 1. Thus, we omit the proofs here to avoid redundancy.

3.2 Physical Feasibility of the Hybrid Secure Protocol Model

In this subsection, we show that there exists a power assignment $\mathcal{A}(b_1, b_2)$, making the feasible links under the hybrid secure protocol model also feasible under secure physical model. First, we consider the security of the cognitive network.

LEMMA 3. *Under power assignment $\mathcal{A}(b_1, b_2)$, $\mathcal{L}^p \in \mathcal{D}(\gamma_p + \epsilon, \gamma_e)$ and $\mathcal{L} \in \mathcal{H}$, if $b_1 = 1/\gamma_e$, all active links are secure.*

PROOF. See Appendix C. □

Lemma 3 tells us that in the independent case, the existence of the secondary network neither relaxes nor tightens the condition for secure transmissions in the primary network. Actually the condition $b_1 \geq 1/\gamma_e$ is implicitly contained in the decision model for the primary network.

LEMMA 4. *If $C_{ps} > C_s, \mathcal{L}^p \in \mathcal{D}(\gamma_p + \epsilon, \gamma_e)$ and $\mathcal{L} \in \mathcal{H}$, with the power assignment $\mathcal{A}(1/\gamma_e, b_2)$ such that $b_2 \leq b_3'(1+r_{\min})^4(1+r_{\max})^{-\alpha}(1+R_{\min})^{\alpha-4}$ (b_3' is a constant), all primary links are possible under physical model $\mathcal{PH}(\gamma_p, \gamma_s, \gamma_e)$.*

PROOF. See Appendix D. □

Next, we turn to the secondary network.

LEMMA 5. *Under power assignment $\mathcal{A}(1/\gamma_e, b_2)$ with $b_2 \geq \max\{b_4' \frac{(1+r_{\max})^\alpha (1+R_{\max})^\alpha}{(1+R_{\min})^{2\alpha}}, b_5'(1+r_{\max})^\alpha\}$ (b_4', b_5' are constants), if $\mathcal{L}^p \in \mathcal{D}(\gamma_p + \epsilon, \gamma_e), \mathcal{L} \in \mathcal{H}$ and $C_{sp} > C_p$, all secondary links are feasible under physical model $\mathcal{PH}(\gamma_p, \gamma_s, \gamma_e)$.*

PROOF. See Appendix E. □

Then, we are ready to prove the final result.

THEOREM 4. *If $\alpha > 4$, $(1+r_{\max})^{2\alpha}(1+R_{\max})^\alpha \leq (1+R_{\min})^{3\alpha-4}(1+r_{\min})^4$, there exists a power assignment $\mathcal{A}(b_1, b_2)$, such that if $\mathcal{L}^p \in \mathcal{D}(\gamma_p + \epsilon, \gamma_e)$ and $\mathcal{L} \in \mathcal{H}$, then $\mathcal{L} \in \mathcal{PH}(\gamma_p, \gamma_s, \gamma_e)$.*

PROOF. From Lemma 3, we know $b_1 = \frac{1}{\gamma_e}$ is sufficient to ensure the secure transmissions. If we choose $\alpha > 4$, $(1+r_{\max})^{2\alpha}(1+R_{\max})^\alpha \leq (1+R_{\min})^{3\alpha-4}(1+r_{\min})^4$ and $C_{ps} > C_s, C_{sp} > C_p$, from Lemma 4 and Lemma 5, there exists a range $[b_4'(1+r_{\max})^\alpha(1+R_{\max})^\alpha(1+R_{\min})^{-2\alpha}, b_3'(1+r_{\min})^4(1+r_{\max})^{-\alpha}(1+R_{\min})^{\alpha-4}]$ for b_2. Hence, we prove that there exists a power assignment scheme $\mathcal{A}(b_1, b_2)$ that if $\mathcal{L}^p \in \mathcal{D}(\gamma_p + \epsilon, \gamma_e)$ and $\mathcal{L} \in \mathcal{H}$, $\mathcal{L} \in \mathcal{PH}(\gamma_p, \gamma_s, \gamma_e)$. □

Theorem 4 is explained and discussed as below. First, the condition $\alpha > 4$, resulting from the blend of extended network model and the secure constraints, means a faster attenuation is needed in our model. Second, we represent the result of Theorem 4 in order forms, i.e., $(1+r_{\max})^{2\alpha}(1+r_{\min})^{-4} = O((1+R_{\min})^{3\alpha-4}(1+R_{\max})^{-\alpha})$. Please recall the strict result if you note the order from result is not sufficient to prove Theorem 4 unless proper constants are chosen. We use the order forms to represent our result just for simplicity. In addition, if the transmission ranges of the cognitive network are homogeneous, i.e., $r = r_{\min} = r_{\max}$ and $R = R_{\min} = R_{\max}$, we only need to consider the condition $(1+r) = O((1+R))$.

3.3 Identifying Transmission Opportunities

The previous subsection proves the physical feasibility of our operation scheme. In this section, we construct a scheduling scheme whose configuration complies with our operation scheme to figure out the transmission opportunities of the secondary nodes.

We say a secondary link is *unconstrained*, if it were in a standalone network.

DEFINITION 8. *Given arbitrary $\mathcal{L}_{s.a.}^s \in \mathcal{SPR}(C_s)$ and arbitrary $\mathcal{L}^p \in \mathcal{SPR}(C_p)$, there exists a unique maximal $\mathcal{L}^s \subset \mathcal{L}_{s.a.}^s$ such that $\mathcal{L}^p \cup \mathcal{L}^s \in \mathcal{H}$. We say a link $(Y_i, Y_{Rx(i)}) \in \mathcal{L}_{s.a.}^s$ is* unconstrained *if $(Y_i, Y_{Rx(i)}) \in \mathcal{L}^s$.*

The definition of a TDMA scheme is as follows.

DEFINITION 9. *A TDMA scheduling scheme. First, we tessellate the networks into cells such that each cell is contained in a disk of diameter $\rho(n)$ and we denote cell i as V_i. Second, we assign color to each cell, such that cells with the same color can be active simultaneously and transmit to neighbor cells, where two cells V_i, V_j have the same color if $\inf\{|X - Y| : X \in V_i, Y \in V_j\} \geq 4C_p(4\rho^2(n) + 6\rho(n) + 1)$. Third, we activate different groups of cells with the same constant fraction of time b_6 in a round-robin fashion ($\rho(n) = O(1)$).*

Next, we prove that in the proposed TDMA scheme, the cognitive network complies with our operation scheme. Thus every secondary link could be unconstrained for a constant fraction of time.

LEMMA 6. *Using our TDMA scheduling scheme, if* $1 < C_{ps} < C_p < C_{sp} < 2C_p$, $m > n$, $\alpha > 4$, $R = R_{\max} = R_{\min}$, $r = r_{\max} = r_{\min}$ *and* $(1+r) = O((1+R))$, *every secondary node has* b_6 *fraction of time to be unconstrained.*

PROOF. See Appendix F. □

3.4 Optimal Performance Scaling

In this subsection, we first present our result on secrecy throughput and delay scaling. Then, we apply our result to various situations.

THEOREM 5. *When the cognitive network uses the TDMA scheduling scheme and satisfies the conditions in Lemma 6, and if we assume that the standalone secondary network can achieve per-node secrecy throughput* $\lambda_s^{s.a.}$ *and delay* $D_s^{s.a.}$, *then the secondary network can also achieve per-node secrecy throughput* $\lambda_s^{c.r.} = \Theta(\lambda_s^{s.a.})$ *and delay* $D_s^{c.r.} = \Theta(D_s^{s.a.})$ *in the cognitive network.*

PROOF. If the secondary network is standalone, we denote the throughput rate of link (Y_i, Y_j) by $c_{ij}^{s.a.}$ which is determined by the scheduling scheme. If we assume a slotted time, then a deterministic scheduling scheme is characterized by a sequence $(\mathcal{L}_t^{s.a.})_{t=1}^T, \mathcal{L}_t^{s.a.} \in \mathcal{SPR}(C_s)$,

$$c_{ij}^{s.a.} = \lim_{T\to\infty} \frac{W}{T} \sum_{t=1}^{T} 1((Y_i, Y_j) \in \mathcal{L}_t^{s.a.}(t)),$$

where the function $1(\cdot)$ returns 1, if the variable is true; 0, otherwise. We use a random matrix $[\lambda_{sd}]$ to describe the traffic pattern ($\lambda_{sd} = 1$, if s and d is a source-destination pair, and $\lambda_{sd} = 0$ otherwise). We use f_{sd}^{ij}, the average fraction of traffic from s to d that is routed through link (Y_i, Y_j), to describe the routing scheme. Then, for the per-node secrecy throughput $\lambda_s^{s.a.}$, it holds that

$$\lambda_s^{s.a.} \sum_s \sum_d \lambda_{sd} f_{sd}^{ij} \le c_{ij}^{s.a.} \quad 1 \le i, j \le m.$$

Next, we consider the cognitive network. In that situation, the change is that we only allow the unconstraint secondary links to be active. Denote the corresponding throughput rate of link (Y_i, Y_j) as $c_{ij}^{c.r.}$, and according to Lemma 6, $c_{ij}^{c.r.} = b_6 c_{ij}^{s.a.}$. Letting $\lambda_s^{c.r.} = b_6 \lambda_s^{s.a.} = \Theta(\lambda_s^{s.a.})$, it follows that

$$\lambda_s^{c.r.} \sum_s \sum_d \lambda_{sd} f_{sd}^{ij} \le c_{ij}^{c.r.} \quad 1 \le i, j \le m.$$

Therefore, no edge is overloaded and the secrecy throughput $\lambda_s^{c.r.}$ is feasible.

Next, we consider the delay. In the cognitive network, an extra delay is incurred for the secondary network since at each time a secondary node wants to transmit, it may wait until the link is unconstrained. We can easily figure out that the upper-bound of this waiting time is one round of the TDMA scheduler. Thus the delay $D_s = \frac{1}{b_6} D_s^{s.a.} = \Theta(D_s^{s.a.})$. □

With Theorem 5, we can apply the optimal schemes and results from standalone secure networks to secure cognitive networks. The following corollaries are straightforward from [11]. Other results that use centralized TDMA scheduling scheme can also be derived from our conclusion. We do not list them here due to limited space. Note the degradation factor $\log^{-1} n$ in the secrecy capacity of the secondary network in Corollary 2 is caused by the transmission range of the primary network $R = \Theta(\sqrt{\log n}) \ne O(1)$ and can be eliminated by using percolation theory.

COROLLARY 1. *Assume there are* n *primary nodes,* m *secondary nodes* ($m > n$) *and* $n\phi_e(n)$ *eavesdroppers in the network area with size* $\sqrt{n} \times \sqrt{n}$. *All of them are static and i.i.d according to the uniform distribution. If the traffic pattern is unicast and the eavesdroppers work in the independent mode, the secrecy capacity is* $\lambda_p = \Theta(1/\sqrt{n})$ *for the primary network and* $\Theta(n\lambda_p/m) \le \lambda_s \le \Theta(\sqrt{n}/m)$ *for the secondary network, independent of the density of eavesdroppers.*

COROLLARY 2. *Assume there are* n *primary nodes,* m *secondary nodes* ($m > n$) *and* $n\phi_e(n)$ *eavesdroppers in the network area with size* $\sqrt{n} \times \sqrt{n}$. *All of them are static and i.i.d according to the uniform distribution. For each primary node,* $n_d - 1$ *nodes are randomly chosen as its destinations and for each secondary node,* $m_d - 1$ *nodes are randomly chosen as its destination. If the eavesdroppers work in the independent mode and* $(1 + \sqrt{\frac{n \log m}{m}}) = o((1 + \sqrt{\log n}))$, *the aggregated multicast secrecy capacity is* $\lambda_p = \Theta(\sqrt{\frac{n}{n_d \log n}} \log^{-\frac{\alpha+4}{2}} n)$ *when* $n_d = O(\frac{n}{\log n})$ *for the primary network and is* $\lambda_s = \Theta(\sqrt{\frac{m}{m_d \log m}}(1+\sqrt{\frac{n \log m}{m}})^{-\alpha-4} \log^{-1} n)$ *for the secondary network when* $m_d = O(\frac{m}{\log m})$.

4. COLLUDING EAVESDROPPERS

In this section, we focus on the secrecy capacity scaling problem in the case where eavesdroppers can collude to decode the message.

Before we begin to calculate the secrecy capacity of cognitive networks in the colluding case, we give some explanations to the differences in assumptions between two cases. The first difference is that in colluding case, we assume the network is a Poisson-distributed random network for that mathematical tractability instead of a uniform distributed random network. It is shown in [15] that random networks converge to Poisson scenarios as n goes to infinity, so the two network models are equivalent in asymptotic analysis.

The second difference is that unlike the general analysis of secure cognitive networks in the previous section, in order to calculate the detailed secrecy capacity, we need to specify a routining scheme for wireless transmission. In the colluding case, we use the *Highway System*.

DEFINITION 10. Highway System*: For the primary network, we divide the network into non-overlapping cells with side length* c, *where* c *is a constant. We say a cell is open if there is at least one node in it. Hence, a cell is open with probability* $p = 1 - e^{-c^2}$ *independently based on the Poisson distribution. Denote the number of edges composing the side length of the network area by* $h_p = \frac{\sqrt{n}}{\sqrt{2}c}$ *where* c *is rounded up such that* h_p *is an integer. According to the Theorem 5 in [2], we can choose* c *large enough such that there are w.h.p* $\Omega(h_p)$ *paths crossing the network area from left to right, and these can be grouped into disjoint sets of* $\lceil \delta \log h_p \rceil$ *paths, each group crossing a rectangle of size* $h_p \times (\kappa \log h_p - \epsilon_m)$, *for all* $\kappa > 0$, δ *small enough, and a vanishingly small* ϵ_m *so that the side length of each rectangle is an integer. The same is true for vertical paths. We call these backbone paths the Highway System.*

Based on the *Highway System*, we give our packet routing scheme.

DEFINITION 11. A Routing Scheme*: The scheme consists of three phases. The first phase is used to drain information* *to the highway. The second phase is to transport information on the highways. The third phase is to deliver information from the highway to the destination.*

Next, based on the routing scheme, we compute the lower bound of the primary transmission rate. First, we give a lemma which is useful throughout this section.

LEMMA 7. *If nodes are Poisson-distributed with intensity $\phi(n)$ in the network $\mathcal{O}$, partition the network into disjoint regions with same size $f(n)$, let N_i be the number of nodes in the region i. We have*

$$P\Big(\frac{1}{2}f(n)\phi(n) \leq N_i \leq 2f(n)\phi(n), \forall i\Big) = 1$$

when $f(n)\phi(n) = \omega(\log_{4/e} n)$ and $f(n) = \Omega(1)$.

PROOF. See Appendix G. □

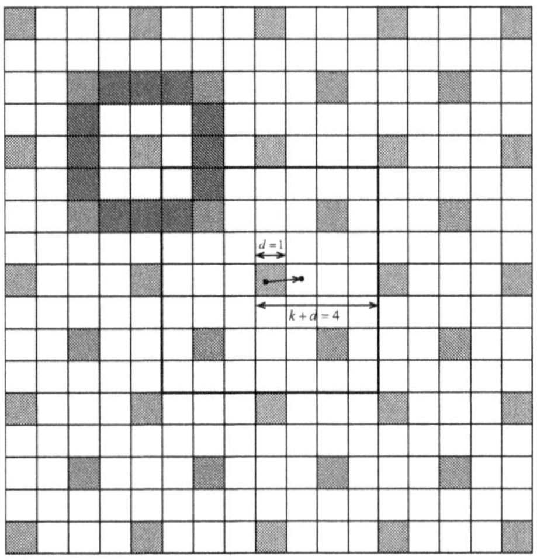

Figure 2: Illustration of network configuration according to the TDMA scheduling scheme. Orange cells contains active primary transmitters. Green cells contains active secondary links.

LEMMA 8. *When a primary node is transmitting to a legitimate receiver that is located d cells apart, the minimum rate that the primary node can receive is lower-bounded by $b_7 P_t^p d^{-\alpha}$, where b_7 is a constant.*

PROOF. See Appendix H. □

Now, we get the per-hop transmission rate of primary nodes in the cognitive network. Recall Definition 1, if we want to know the per-hop secrecy transmission rate, the total SINR of all the eavesdroppers needs to be calculated.

By the definition of SINR_{ie}^p, there are three parts of the interference at each eavesdropper, namely N_0, I_{pe}, I_{se}, where N_0 is constant. In order to bound I_{pe} and I_{se}, we partition the network into disjoint rings with a same size of $f(n)$. The eavesdropper is at the center of all the rings. Let r_i be the external diameter of the ith ring. Since $f(n) = \pi r_1^2 = \pi(r_i^2 - r_{i-1}^2)$ for any $i > 1$, we have $r_i = \sqrt{i} r_1$ for any $i \geq 1$. We know the primary nodes, secondary nodes and eavesdroppers are Poisson-distributed with parameter $\phi_p(n) = 1, \phi_s(n) = \frac{m}{n}$ and $\phi_e(n)$, respectively. Denote the number of secondary nodes and eavesdroppers in the ith ring as N_{si} and N_{ei}, respectively. By Lemma 7, if $f(n) > 1$ and $\phi_s(n)f(n) = \omega(\log_{e/4} n)$, $\phi_e(n)f(n) = \omega(\log_{e/4} n)$, we can conclude $\frac{1}{2}f(n)\phi_s(n) \leq N_{si} \leq 2f(n)\phi_s(n)$ and $\frac{1}{2}f(n)\phi_e(n) < N_{ei} \leq 2f(n)\phi_e(n)$.

LEMMA 9. *The upper bound of the SINR all eavesdroppers get from a given transmission is $\Theta(\frac{k\phi_e(n)P_t^p}{\phi_s(n)P_r^s})$.*

PROOF. See Appendix I. □

THEOREM 6. *Considering the cognitive network where primary nodes, secondary nodes and eavesdroppers are independently Poisson-distributed with parameter $\phi_p(n) = 1, \phi_s(n) = \frac{m}{n}$ and $\phi_e(n)$, respectively, the per-node secrecy capacity for the primary network is,*

$$\lambda_f(n) = \begin{cases} \Omega(\frac{1}{\sqrt{n}}\phi_e^{-\frac{2}{\alpha-1}}(n)) & \phi_e(n) = \Omega(\log^2 n) \\ \Omega(\frac{1}{\sqrt{n}}\log^{-\frac{4}{\alpha-1}} n) & \phi_e(n) = O(\log^2 n) \end{cases} \quad (11)$$

PROOF. Substituting the results of Lemma 8 and Lemma 9 into Definition 1, the secrecy rate $G_f(d)$ that each cell transmits is

$$\begin{aligned} G_f(d) =& \frac{1}{(k+d)^2}(G(d) - G_e) \\ \geq& \frac{1}{(k+d)^2}(b_7 P_t^p d^{-\alpha} - b_8 P_t^p \frac{k\phi_e(n)}{\phi_s(n)P_r^s}). \end{aligned} \quad (12)$$

In order to get positive secrecy rate, let $\phi_s(n)P_r^s = 2\frac{b_8}{b_7}k\phi_e(n)d^\alpha$. According to Lemma 8, $k^\alpha = \Theta(\phi_s(n)P_r^s)$. Therefore, the secrecy transmission rate that each cell can achieve is $\Omega((\phi_e^{\frac{1}{\alpha-1}}(n)d^{\frac{\alpha}{\alpha-1}} + d)^{-2}d^{-\alpha})$. In the following, we compute the secrecy capacity for draining/delivery phase and highway phase, respectively.

Draining/Delivery Phase: According to the highway system, the distance between sources and relay on the highway is never larger than $\kappa \log h_p + \sqrt{2}c$. Thus $d = \Theta(\log n), r_1 = \Theta(\log^2 n)$. We assume $\phi_e(n)f(n) = \Omega(\log^2 n) = \omega(\log n)$, which requires $\phi_e(n) = \Omega(\log^{-2} n)$. If we assume $\phi_e(n) = \Theta(1) = \Omega(\log^{-2} n)$, we have $\phi_e^{\frac{1}{\alpha-1}}(n)\, d^{\frac{\alpha}{\alpha-1}} = \omega(d)$, when $\alpha > 2$. Hence, $G_f(d) = \Omega(\phi_e^{-\frac{2}{\alpha-1}} d^{-(\alpha+\frac{2\alpha}{\alpha-1})}) = \Omega(\phi_e^{-\frac{2}{\alpha-1}}(n) \log^{-(\alpha+\frac{2\alpha}{\alpha-1})} n)$. Since there are at most $\log n$ primary nodes inside a cell, the per-node secrecy capacity is $\Omega(\phi_e^{-\frac{2}{\alpha-1}}(n) \log^{-(\alpha+\frac{3\alpha-1}{\alpha-1})} n)$.

Highway Phases: In the highway phase, the transmission range between T-R pairs is at most $2\sqrt{2}c$. Hence, $d = \Theta(1), r_1 = \Theta(1)$. Similar to the analysis in draining and delivery phase, we have $\phi_e(n) = \Omega(\log^2 n)$ and $G_f(d) = \Omega(\phi_e^{-\frac{2}{\alpha-1}}(n))$. According to the definition of highway system, each source in the ith slice transmit packets to the ith highway in the same rectangle. Since the density of primary nodes is $\phi_p(n) = 1$ and the size of each slice is $w\sqrt{n}$, which satisfies the conditions given by Lemma 7, we deduce that the maximum number of primary nodes inside each slice is no larger than $2w\sqrt{n}$. Hence a node on a highway must relay traffic for at most $2w\sqrt{n}$ nodes. Therefore, the secrecy capacity of the highway phase is $\Omega(\phi_e^{-\frac{2}{\alpha-1}}(n)\frac{1}{\sqrt{n}})$. If $\phi_e(n) = O(\log^2 n)$, the term R_e will be smaller than in the $\phi_e(n) = \Omega(\log^2 n)$ case, when we keep the other parameters the same, and we can obtain per-node secrecy capacity of $\Omega(\frac{1}{\sqrt{n}}\log^{-\frac{4}{\alpha-1}} n)$.

To summarize the above two cases, we find that the bottleneck of the secrecy capacity is in the highway phase and the per-node secrecy capacity is $\Omega(\phi_e^{-\frac{2}{\alpha-1}}(n)\frac{1}{\sqrt{n}})$. □

Last but not least, we compare our results with the results in single networks [11], as illustrated in Figure 3. *Cooperation* in the legend means that legitimate nodes cooperate to generate artificial noise.

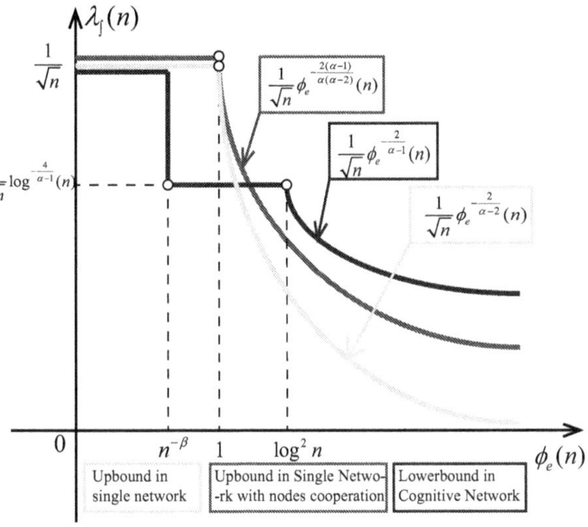

Figure 3: Comparison of our result and the results in single networks

5. CONCLUSION

In this paper, we investigate the impact of introducing secondary users to the network on the secrecy capacity of the primary network. We divide our analysis into two parts according to the two overhearing models of eavesdroppers. In the non-colluding case, we prove that the secondary network can achieve the same performance as standalone networks without adversely affecting the secrecy capacity of the primary network. We also apply our results to various scenarios. In the colluding eavesdroppers case, we calculate the lower bound of the secrecy capacity of the primary network and reveal that the existence of secondary users increases the secrecy capacity of the primary network. Our results may shed insight into the future design of wireless networks, i.e., if we want to enforce the security of primary network, allowing secondary users to co-exist with spectrum sharing is a good security solution. Finally, the secrecy capacity of the secondary network in the colluding case will be studied in a future work.

Acknowledgement

This work is partially supported by NSF China (No. 61325012, 61271219); China Ministry of Education Doctor Program (No. 20130073110025); Shanghai Basic Research Key Project (No.11JC1405100); Shanghai International Cooperation Project: (No. 13510711300); Research Grants Council of Hong Kong Project No. RGC CityU 125212.

6. REFERENCES

[1] P. Gupta and P. R. Kumar, "The Capacity of Wireless Networks," in *IEEE Trans. on Inform. Theory*, vol. 46, no. 2, pp. 388-404, Mar. 2000.

[2] M. Franceschetti, O. Dousse, D. N. Tse and P. Thiran, "Closing the Gap in the Capacity of Wireless Networks via Percolation Theory", in *IEEE Trans. Inform. Theory*, Vol. 53, No. 3, pp. 1009-1018, 2007.

[3] M. Grossglauser and D. N. C. Tse, "Mobility increases the capacity of ad hoc wireless networks," *IEEE/ACM Trans. Netw.*, vol. 10, no. 4, pp. 477-486, Aug. 2002.

[4] M. J. Neely and E. Modiano, "Capacity and Delay Tradeoffs for Ad-Hoc Mobile Networks," *IEEE Trans. Inform. Theory*, vol. 51, no. 6, pp. 1917-1937, 2005.

[5] X.-Y. Li, "Multicast capacity of wireless ad hoc networks," *IEEE/ACM Trans. Netw.*, vol. 17, no. 3, pp. 950-961, 2009.

[6] X.-Y. Li, Y. Liu, S. Li, and S. Tang, "Multicast capacity of wireless ad hoc networks under Gaussian channel model," *IEEE/ACM Trans. Netw.*, vol. 18, no. 4, pp. 1145-1157, Jun. 2010.

[7] A. Ozgur, O. Leveque, and D. N. C. Tse, "Hierarchical cooperation achieves optimal capacity scaling in ad hoc networks," *IEEE Trans. Inf. Theory*, vol. 53, no. 10, pp. 3549-3572, Oct. 2007.

[8] S. Vasudevan, D. Goeckel, and D. Towsley, "Security-capacity trade-off in large wireless networks using keyless secrecy," in *Proc. ACM MobiHoc*, Chicago, IL, USA, Sep. 2010, pp. 21-30.

[9] O. Koyluoglu, E. Koksal and E. Gammel, "On Secrecy Capacity Scaling in Wireless Networks", in *IEEE Trans. Inform. Theory*, vol. 58, no. 5, pp. 3000-3015, 2012.

[10] C. Capar, D. Goeckel, B. Liu, D. Towsley, "Secret communication in large wireless networks without eavesdropper location information," in *Proc. INFOCOM*, pp. 1152-1160, 2012.

[11] J. Zhang, L. Fu, X. Wang, "Asymptotic analysis on secrecy capacity in large-scale wireless networks," to appear in *IEEE/ACM Trans. Netw.*, 2013.

[12] S.-W. Jeon, N. Devroye, M. Vu, S.-Y. Chung, and V. Tarokh, "Cognitive networks achieve throughput scaling of a homogeneous network," *IEEE Trans. Inf. Theory*, vol. 57, no. 8, pp. 5103-5115, Aug. 2011.

[13] C. Yin, L. Gao, and S. Cui, "Scaling laws for overlaid wireless networks: A cognitive radio network versus a primary network," *IEEE/ACM Trans. Netw.*, vol. 18, no. 4, pp. 1317-1329, Aug. 2010.

[14] W. Huang and X. Wang, "Throughput and Delay Scaling of General Cognitive Networks," in *Proceedings of IEEE INFOCOM*, 2011.

[15] M. Penrose, "Random Geometric Graphs", *Oxford Univ. Press*, Oxford, U.K., 2003.

[16] C. W. Tan, S. Friedland and S. H. Low, "Spectrum Management in Multiuser Cognitive Wireless Networks: Optimality and Algorithm", *IEEE Journal on Selected Areas in Communications*, Vol. 29, No. 2, pp. 421-430, 2011.

APPENDIX

Appendix A: Proof to Lemma 1

PROOF. For any active link $(X_i, X_j), (X_k, X_l) \in \mathcal{L}^p$ and $i, k \in \mathcal{T}^p, j, l \in \mathcal{R}^p$, according to the Operation Rule 1,

$$\frac{P_t^p(1+|X_i - X_j|)^{-\alpha}}{P_t^p(1+|X_k - X_j|)^{-\alpha}} \geq \frac{P_t^p l(X_i, X_j)}{N_0 + I_{pp}} \geq \gamma_p + \epsilon.$$

Therefore, $1 + |X_k - X_j| \geq (\gamma_p + \epsilon)^{\frac{1}{\alpha}}(1 + |X_i - X_j|)$ and we can set $C_{tp} \leq (\gamma_p + \epsilon)^{\frac{1}{\alpha}}$. For the second equation of the secure protocol model,

$$\frac{P_t^p(1+|X_i - X_j|)^{-\alpha}}{P_r^p(1+|X_l - X_j|)^{-\alpha}} \geq \frac{P_t^p l(X_i, X_j)}{N_0 + I_{pp}} \geq \gamma_p + \epsilon,$$

$$\frac{P_t^p}{P_r^p}(1+|X_i - X_j|)^{\alpha} \leq \frac{P_t^p}{P_r^p}(1+R_{\max})^{\alpha} \leq \gamma_e.$$

Therefore, $1+|X_l-X_j| \geq (\frac{\gamma_p+\epsilon}{\gamma_e})^{\frac{1}{\alpha}}(1+|X_i-X_j|)^2$ and we can set $C_{rp} \leq (\frac{\gamma_p+\epsilon}{\gamma_e})^{\frac{1}{\alpha}}$. □

Appendix B: Proof to Lemma 2

PROOF. Let P and Q be two arbitrary points on line segment Z_iZ_j and Z_kZ_l, by applying the triangle inequality and the fact Z_i, P, Z_j and Z_k, Q, Z_l are are collinear, respectively, we have

$$\begin{aligned}&|Z_i-Z_j|+|Z_k-Z_l|+2|P-Q|\\=&|Z_i-P|+|P-Q|+|Q-Z_l|\\&+|Z_k-Q|+|P-Q|+|P-Z_j|\\\geq&|Z_i-Z_l|+|Z_k-Z_j|.\end{aligned}$$

Consider the two following cases.

Case 1: $i,k \in \{\mathcal{T}^p, \mathcal{T}^s\}$ and $j,l \in \{\mathcal{R}^p, \mathcal{R}^s\}$, by the definition of hybrid secure protocol model and the above equation, we have,

$$\begin{aligned}&1+|Z_i-Z_j|+1+|Z_k-Z_l|+2|P-Q|\\\geq&1+|Z_i-Z_l|+1+|Z_k-Z_j|\\\geq&C_{t1}(1+|Z_k-Z_l|)+C_{t2}(1+|Z_i-Z_j|)\end{aligned}$$

Simplifying the above equation, we can get $|P-Q| \geq \frac{C_{t1}-1}{2}(1+|Z_k-Z_l|)+\frac{C_{t2}-1}{2}(1+|Z_i-Z_j|)$ which means the first equation of the secure protocol model requires the distance between any two point of a active link is at least $\frac{C_{t1}-1}{2}(1+|Z_k-Z_l|)+\frac{C_{t2}-1}{2}(1+|Z_i-Z_j|)$.

Case 2: $j,k \in \{\mathcal{T}^p, \mathcal{T}^s\}$ and $i,l \in \{\mathcal{R}^p, \mathcal{R}^s\}$, using the conclusion of Case 1 and the second equation of the definition of the secure protocol model, we have,

$$\begin{aligned}&2(1+|Z_i-Z_j|)+2(1+|Z_k-Z_l|)+4|P-Q|\\\geq&2(1+|Z_k-Z_j|)+1+|Z_i-Z_l|+1+|Z_l-Z_i|\\\geq&(C_{t1}-1)(1+|Z_i-Z_j|)+(C_{t2}-1)(1+|Z_k-Z_l|)\\&+1+|Z_i-Z_l|+1+|Z_l-Z_i|\\\geq&C_{r1}(1+|Z_k-Z_l|)^2+C_{r2}(1+|Z_i-Z_j|)^2+(C_{t1}\\&-1)(1+|Z_i-Z_j|)+(C_{t2}-1)(1+|Z_k-Z_l|).\end{aligned}$$

By the condition $C_{tx}=3$, we can conclude $|P-Q| \geq \frac{C_{r1}}{4}(1+|Z_k-Z_l|)^2+\frac{C_{r2}}{4}(1+|Z_i-Z_j|)^2$. □

Appendix C: Proof to Lemma 3

PROOF. For the primary network, by the definition of SINR^p_{ie} and the condition $b_1 = 1/\gamma_e$, $\forall e \in \mathcal{E}$, we have

$$\begin{aligned}\mathrm{SINR}^p_{ie} \leq& \frac{P^p_t(1+|X_i-Z_e|)^{-\alpha}}{P^p_r(1+|X_i-X_{Rx(i)}|+|X_i-Z_e|)^{-\alpha}}\\\leq&\frac{P^p_t}{P^p_r}(1+\frac{R_{\max}}{1+|X_i-Z_e|})^{\alpha} \leq \gamma_e.\end{aligned}$$

Using a similar process, we can prove the security of the secondary links under the condition $b_1 = 1/\gamma_e$. □

Appendix D: Proof to Lemma 4

PROOF. $\mathcal{L}^p \in \mathcal{D}(\gamma_p+\epsilon)$ implies that for any $(X_i, X_{Rx(i)}) \in \mathcal{L}^p$,

$$\frac{P^p_t(1+R_i)^{-\alpha}}{N_0+I_{pp}(i)} \geq \gamma_p+\epsilon. \quad (13)$$

From Theorem 1, we know the upper bound of $I_{sp}(i)$. Combining the upper bound of $I_{sp}(i)$ with the condition $b_2 \leq b'_3(1+r_{\min})^4(1+r_{\max})^{-\alpha}(1+R_{\min})^{\alpha-4}$ and $b'_3 = 2\gamma_e\epsilon/b_3\gamma_p(\gamma_p+\epsilon)$, we have

$$\begin{aligned}&\frac{P^p_t(1+R_i)^{-\alpha}}{I_{sp}(i)}\\\geq&\frac{P^p_t(1+R_i)^{-\alpha}}{b_3(P^s_t+P^s_r)(1+R_i)^{4-2\alpha}(1+r_{\min})^{-4}}\\\geq&\frac{(1+R_i)^{\alpha-4}(1+r_{\max})^{\alpha}}{b_3b'_3[1+b_1(1+r_{\max})^{\alpha}](1+R_{\min})^{\alpha-4}}\\\geq&\frac{2}{b_1b_3b'_3} \geq \frac{\gamma_p(\gamma_p+\epsilon)}{\epsilon}.\end{aligned} \quad (14)$$

Then, from the equation (13) and (14), we have the assertion. □

Appendix E: Proof to Lemma 5

PROOF. From Theorem 2 we know for any $(Y_i, Y_{Rx(i)}) \in \mathcal{H}$, $I_{ps}(i) \leq b_4(P^p_t+P^p_r)(1+R_{\min})^{-2\alpha}$. With $b_2 \geq b'_4(1+r_{\max})^{\alpha}(1+R_{\max})^{\alpha}(1+R_{\min})^{-2\alpha}$ and $b'_4 = 4b_4\gamma_s/\gamma_e$, it follows that

$$\begin{aligned}\frac{P^s_t(1+r_i)^{-\alpha}}{I_{ps}(i)} \geq& \frac{P^s_t(1+r_i)^{-\alpha}}{b_4(P^p_t+P^p_r)(1+R_{\min})^{-2\alpha}}\\\geq&\frac{b_2(1+R_{\min})^{2\alpha}}{b_4[1+b_1(1+R_{\max})^{\alpha}](1+r_i)^{\alpha}}\\\geq&\frac{b'_4(1+r_{\max})^{\alpha}(1+R_{\max})^{\alpha}}{b_4[1+b_1(1+R_{\max})^{\alpha}](1+r_i)^{\alpha}}\\\geq&\frac{b'_4}{2b_1b_4} \geq 2\gamma_s.\end{aligned} \quad (15)$$

Similarly, from Theorem 3, we know $I_{ss}(i) \leq b_5(P^s_t+P^s_r)(1+r_i)^{4-2\alpha}(1+r_{\min})^{-4}$. In the two cases, $I_{ss}(i) \geq N_0$ and $I_{ss}(i) < N_0$, if $b_2 \geq b'_5(1+r_{\max})^{\alpha}$, we can prove

$$\frac{P^s_t(1+r_i)^{-\alpha}}{N_0+I_{ss}(i)} \geq 2\gamma_s. \quad (16)$$

Case 1: If $I_{ss}(i) \geq N_0$, we have,

$$\begin{aligned}\frac{P^s_t(1+r_i)^{-\alpha}}{N_0+I_{ss}(i)} \geq& \frac{P^s_t(1+r_i)^{-\alpha}}{2I_{ss}(i)}\\\geq&\frac{P^s_t(1+r_i)^{\alpha-4}(1+r_{\min})^4}{2b_5(P^s_t+P^s_r)}\\\geq&\frac{(1+r_i)^{\alpha-4}(1+r_{\min})^4}{2b_5[1+b_1(1+r_{\max})^{\alpha}]}\\\geq&\frac{(1+r_{\min})^{\alpha}}{4b_1b_5(1+r_{\max})^{\alpha}} \geq 2\gamma_s\end{aligned}$$

Case2: If $I_{ss}(i) < N_0$, we have

$$\frac{P^s_t(1+r_i)^{-\alpha}}{N_0+I_{ss}(i)} \geq \frac{P^s_t(1+r_i)^{-\alpha}}{2N_0} \geq \gamma_s$$

Combing equation (15) and (16), we have the assertion. □

Appendix F: Proof to Lemma 6

PROOF. For a generic secondary link $(Y_i, Y_{Rx(i)})$. Pick the point X that $|X-Y_i| = 2C_p(4\rho^2(n)+6\rho(n)+1)$ and denote the cell X belongs to is V. We claim whenever V is chosen to be active, the link $(Y_i, Y_{Rx(i)})$ is unconstrained. First, we prove that the primary network will not be interfered by Y_i. For any point P belongs to V, we have $|P-X| <$

$\rho(n)$. For any point Q belongs to a neighbor cell of V, we have $|Q - X| < 2\rho(n)$, then

$$|Y_i - Q| \geq 2C_p(4\rho^2(n) + 6\rho(n) + 1) - 2\rho(n) > C_{sp}(1 + 2\rho(n))^2 \geq C_{sp}(1 + |P - Q|)^2.$$

For other simultaneous active cell V'. Similarly, $X' \in V'$ is $|X' - X| > 4C_p(4\rho^2(n) + 6\rho(n) + 1)$, then $|X' - Y_i| \geq |X' - X| - |X - Y_i| > 2C_p(4\rho^2(n) + 6\rho(n) + 1)$ which means that other simultaneous active cells are also not interfered by Y_i. Second, since $(1 + r) = O((1 + R))$, if $m > n$ and $2C_p > C_{ps}$, $|Q - Y_{Rx(i)}| \geq C_{ps}(1 + |Y_i - Y_{Rx(i)}|)^2$ always holds. Thus we have proved our deployment in the scheduling scheme complies with our operation scheme and complete the proof. □

Appendix G: Proof to Lemma 7

PROOF. N_i is a Poisson variable, and we denote its expectation as $\lambda = f(n)\phi(n)$. Let $N = \max_i\{N_i\}$, $\forall i$. According to the union bounds and Chernoff bounds, we can get

$$P(N \geq 2\lambda) \leq P(\cup_i(N_i \geq 2\lambda)) \leq \sum_i P(N_i \geq 2\lambda)$$

$$\leq \frac{n}{f(n)} e^{-\lambda} (\frac{e\lambda}{2\lambda})^{2\lambda} = \frac{n}{f(n)} (\frac{e}{4})^{f(n)\phi(n)} \to 0,$$

when $f(n)\phi(n) = \omega(\log_{4/e} n)$ and $f(n) = \Omega(1)$.
Similarly, we can show that $\min_i N_i$ is greater than $\frac{1}{2} f(n)\phi(n)$ $w.h.p.$ when conditions hold. □

Appendix H: Proof to Lemma 8

PROOF. First we compute the interference at the receiver. Different from the situation when there is only one kind of nodes, in cognitive network, the primary nodes will get additional noise from active secondary links. We divide the network into disjoint squares of $(k + d) \times (k + d)$, where k and d together define the concurrent range. We use $(k + d)^2$ TDMA scheduling scheme as in Figure 2. Every cell in each sub-square takes a turn to transmit. Consider a given transmitter-receiver pair, the 8 closest primary transmitters and receivers are located in at distance of at least ck and $c(k + d - 1)$ from the receiver. The 16 next closest transmitters and receivers are located in the distance at least $c(2k + d)$ and $c(2k + 2d - 1)$ away from the receiver and so on. The 4 closest cells which contains active secondary links are at least $\sqrt{2}(\frac{k+d}{2} - 1)$, and the 12 next closest cells are at least $\sqrt{2}(\frac{3}{2}(k + d) - 1)$ and so on. By extending the sum of the interferences to the whole plane, this can then be bounded as follows (b'_7, b''_7 are constants):

$$I(d) \leq \sum_{i=1}^{\infty} 8i(P_t^p l(c(i(k + d) - d)) + P_r^p l(c(i(k + d) - 1))) + \sum_{i=1}^{\infty} (8i - 4)\phi_s(n)c^2(P_t^s + P_r^s)l(\sqrt{2}c((k + d)(i - \frac{1}{2}) - 1)) = b'_7(P_t^p + P_r^p)(kc)^{-\alpha} + b''_7(P_t^s + P_r^s)\phi_s(n)(kc)^{-\alpha}.$$

Next, we want to bound the signal received from the transmitter. We observe first that the distance between the transmitter and the receiver is at most $\sqrt{2}c(d + 1)$. Hence, the signal $S(d)$ at the receiver can be bounded by

$$S(d) \geq P_t^p l(\sqrt{2}c(d + 1)) \geq P_t^p(1 + \sqrt{2}c(d + 1))^{-\alpha}.$$

Finally, by combing $S(d)$ and $I(d)$, the lower bound of the rate that a primary transmission pair can achieve can be derived as follows (b'''_7 is a constant):

$$G(d) = \log\left(1 + \frac{S(d)}{N_0 + I(d)}\right) \geq \log\left(1 + \frac{P_t^p(1 + \sqrt{2}c(d + 1))^{-\alpha}}{N_0 + I(d)}\right) \geq b'''_7 P_t^p(1 + \sqrt{2}c(d + 1))^{-\alpha} \geq b_7 P_t^p d^{-\alpha},$$

when choosing $k = \Theta((P_r^s \phi_s(n))^{\frac{1}{\alpha}})$. □

Appendix I: Proof to Lemma 9

PROOF. For a given eavesdropper which is intended to overhear the communication between transmitter u ($u \in \mathcal{T}^p$) and receiver v ($v \in \mathcal{R}^p$), the previous work [11] mainly utilizes the artificial noise generated by the receiver v to suppress the SINR at the eavesdropper. In that case, an active T-R pair mutes other transmissions in the vicinity of size $\Theta(d^4)$, where d is the transmission range. In this paper, we mainly focus on utilizing the artificial noise generated by secondary nodes to suppress the SINR of eavesdroppers. Lemma 8 tells us that in the scheduling configuration as Figure 2, the transmission of secondary nodes does not affect that of the primary nodes. We assume there is also no active secondary transmission pairs in the $\Theta(d^4)$ neighborhood of an active primary transmission pair. Again, we partition the network area into disjoint rings with size $f(n)$ where $r_1 = \Theta(d^2)$ and in this time the transmitter u is at the center of all the rings. And we categorize all eavesdroppers into two sets. The first set contains the eavesdroppers which are in the first ring. The second set contains others. Denote SINR_{eij} as the SINR received by eavesdropper j in the ith ring, and $\mathcal{E}_i$ as the set of eavesdroppers located in the ith ring. Taking the summation of the SINR received by all the eavesdroppers, we have,

$$\text{SINR}_e \leq \sum_{j \in \mathcal{E}_1} \text{SINR}_{e1j} + \sum_{i=2}^{+\infty} \sum_{j \in \mathcal{E}_i} \text{SINR}_{eij}.$$

The SINR of the eavesdroppers in the first set can be bounded,

$$\text{SINR}_{e1j} \leq \frac{P_t^p l(X_u, X_e)}{P_t^p l(X_u, X_v) + \sum_{v' \in \mathcal{R}^s} P_r^s l(X'_v, X_e)},$$

where by Lemma 8, we know the term $\sum_{v' \in \mathcal{R}^s} P_r^s l(X'_v, X_e)$ in the denominator is a constant. The SINR of the eavesdroppers in the second set is,

$$\text{SINR}_{eij} \leq \frac{b'_8 P_t^p r_{i-1}^{-\alpha}}{\frac{1}{2}\phi_s(n)f(n)P_r^s r_1^{-\alpha}} \leq \frac{2b'_8 P_t^p}{\phi_s(n)f(n)P_r^s}(i - 1)^{-\frac{\alpha}{2}}.$$

where $b'_8 = \Theta(k + d) = \Theta(k)$ is the reciprocal of the ratio of active secondary regions and represents the effect of mute regions of other transmitters. So the total SINR can be bounded as,

$$\text{SINR}_e \leq 2f(n)\phi_e(n)\frac{P_t^p l(X_u, X_e)}{P_t^p l(X_u, X_v) + \sum_{v' \in \mathcal{R}^s} P_r^s l(X'_v, X_e)} + \sum_{i=2}^{+\infty} 2f(n)\phi_e(n)\frac{2b'_8 P_t^p}{\phi_s(n)f(n)P_r^s}(i - 1)^{-\frac{\alpha}{2}} = \frac{4b'_8\phi_e(n)P_t^p}{\phi_s(n)P_r^s} \sum_{i=1}^{+\infty} i^{-\frac{\alpha}{2}}.$$

□

Capacity of Wireless Networks with Multiple Types of Multicast Sessions

Xu Zheng† Jianzhong Li† Hong Gao† Zhipeng Cai‡
†School of Computer Science and Technology, Harbin Institute of Technology, Heilongjiang, China
‡Department of Computer Science, Georgia State University, Atlanta, GA, USA
zhengxuhit@gmail.com, {lijzh,honggao}@hit.edu.cn, zcai@gsu.edu

ABSTRACT

A thorough understanding of capacity of wireless networks can help with effective design and efficient employment of wireless networks. Much effort has been spent on investigating capacity of multicast which is a popular communication model and generalization of unicast and broadcast. However, most previous works assume homogeneous traffic patterns, which is not meaningful for practical applications. This paper analyzes the capacity of wireless networks with multiple types of multicast sessions without the assumption of homogeneous traffic patterns. A new network model is proposed accommodating practical traffic patterns and the capacity is analyzed accordingly. A theoretical upper bound is derived, and a feasible transmission scheme with capacity lower bound is presented. Two bounds are asymptotically tight, that is, in the order of $\Theta(\frac{a^2 n_s}{\sum_{i=1}^{n_s} min\{\sqrt{k_i} \cdot R_i \cdot r, R_i^2\}} \cdot W)$, where a is the side length of the deployed region, r is the transmission range, n_s is the number of multicast sessions, and k_i and R_i are parameters of multicast session i. Furthermore, the variation of capacity towards different numbers of and distributions of destinations is illustrated.

Categories and Subject Descriptors

C.2.1 [**Network Architecture and Design**]: Wireless communication

Keywords

Capacity; multicast; heterogeneous traffic; scalability

1. INTRODUCTION

A thorough understanding of the capacity of wireless networks can help with effective design and efficient employment of wireless networks. Therefore, the investigation of the capacity of wireless networks is important and is also a challenging task.

Since the pioneering work [1] appeared, the capacity of wireless networks has been widely studied. These works assume various kinds of network models for different kinds of wireless networks in practice. For example, some of the works study static or mobile pure ad hoc networks [2, 3] while the others focus on hybrid networks [4]. From the view of traffic patterns, all the works can be classified into studies on unicast capacity [5], multicast capacity [2], broadcast capacity [6] and aggregation capacity [7, 8].

Multicast, which is the generalization of unicast and broadcast, has attracted more interests. The estimation of the achievable multicast capacity is required in many applications, such as the ones of sensor networks. Much more works focus on the multicast capacity recently [2][3][4][9][10][11]. Most of the previous studies on multicast capacity assume homogeneous traffic patterns, *i.e.*, the multicast sessions are identical in the number of destinations, and the destinations are randomly distributed in the whole region or within equal sized circles centered at each source node [9]. However, multicast sessions in real applications are often quite different in the number of destinations and the distribution of the destinations. The following are two examples.

Example 1. In a battlefield, military officers often send orders to their soldiers in defence areas via a wireless network. The numbers of the soldiers commended by officers are often various, which goes against the assumption that sessions are identical on the numbers of destinations. Meanwhile, the defence area guarded by each group of soldiers is often a sub-region of the whole battlefield, and the sizes of these sub-regions are usually various. Thus, the second assumption that destinations are randomly distributed in the whole region or equal sized circles is not meaningful.

Example 2. In wireless sensor networks, there may be non-identical multicast sessions at the same time. Some of the multicast sessions may be unicast or broadcast sessions rather than pure multicast sessions. In this case, the homogeneous assumption cannot be guaranteed and the previous results are not applicable.

A theoretical study on wireless networks with multiple types of multicast sessions can enhance the generality of the bounds on network capacity. As far as we know, none of the previous works totally looses the constraints on the identity of the sessions. These constraints can make the derived bounds on capacity more explicable and straightforward, however, it is at the cost of loosing a deeper understanding of the heterogeneity among sessions. This paper focuses on estimating the total traffic load brought by multicast sessions that are quite different from each other, and tries to derive the relationship between the capacity and the variety of sessions. Moreover, this paper aims to point out

MobiHoc'14, August 11–14, 2014, Philadelphia, PA, USA.

http://dx.doi.org/10.1145/2632951.2632985.

some open questions about network capacity that are worth considering.

In this paper, we study the multicast capacity of ad hoc wireless networks without the homogeneous traffic pattern assumption. There may exist multiple types of multicast sessions in a wireless network at the same time, and the sessions have different numbers of destinations and different distributions of destinations. The main contributions are as follows.

- We propose a new wireless network model to support the analysis of the capacity of wireless networks with multiple types of multicast sessions. In this model, the traffic pattern has two features: i) each multicast session in a wireless network can have any number of destinations without the constraint that the numbers must be identical, and ii) the destinations of each source node are uniformly distributed in a circle area centered at the source node with a radius of arbitrary length, rather than that the destinations are uniformly distributed in the whole region covered by the wireless network or within equal sized circles. Compared with the previous work [9], which still has some constraints for the identity of its multicast sessions for simplicity of analysis, our model is more applicable in real applications like the aforementioned two examples. Moreover, the model is a generalization of many previously proposed models.

- The capacity of wireless networks is analyzed towards the proposed model. A theoretical upper bound is derived which is $O(\frac{2a^2 \cdot n_s}{\sum_{i=1}^{n_s} min\{\sqrt{k_i} \cdot R_i \cdot r, R_i{}^2\}} \cdot W)$. In the proof, a new measurement metric, competitive intensity, of a wireless network is proposed. Competitive intensity denotes the number of node pairs or transmission pairs that cannot be scheduled simultaneously. Its bound can help with deriving the capacity bound of a wireless network. Competitive intensity is independent of network models, thus it can be used for the capacity analysis of any kind of wireless network. A feasible transmission scheme for the entire network is also determined with the lower bound of its capacity. The bound is $\Omega(\frac{2a^2 n_s}{3\sum_{i=1}^{n_s} min\{\sqrt{k_i} \cdot R_i \cdot r, R_i^2\}} \cdot W)$, which is asymptotically tight with the theoretical upper bound of the capacity of wireless networks.

- Some observations about the network model and the derived capacity bounds are discussed. First, the variation of the capacity for different numbers of destinations and the distribution area of destinations in multicast sessions is illustrated. Then, it is stated that the previous capacity bounds are the specialization of the capacity bounds derived in this paper when some constraints are added to our network model.

The rest of the paper is organized as follows. Section 2 reviews the related works. Section 3 introduces the network model and some basic definitions. The theoretical upper bound of the capacity of a wireless network is derived in Section 4. Section 5 presents a reachable lower bound on the capacity of a wireless network. In Section 6, some observations about the proposed capacity bounds and network model are discussed. Section 7 concludes the paper.

2. RELATED WORKS

There have been a lot of researches on capacity of wireless networks during the last decade. Gupta and Kumar first proved that the per-flow unicast capacity of random networks is in the order of $\Theta(\frac{W}{\sqrt{n \log n}})$ [1]. They also analyzed the capacity of wireless networks with arbitrary given traffic, that is, $\Theta(\frac{W}{\sqrt{n}})$. This result was then proved under a more general fading channel model in [12]. Later, Franceschetti proposed an optimal scheme to avoid the loss from the randomness using the percolation theory [5], which could achieve the capacity of $\Theta(\frac{W}{\sqrt{n}})$. Broadcast capacity was also studied in previous works. It is shown in [6] that the total broadcast capacity is only $\Theta(W)$. Grossglauser and Tse showed that the unicast capacity could be improved at the cost of larger delay in mobile wireless networks [13]. These works concentrate on either unicast or broadcast, which can be a special case of multicast.

Li studied the multicast capacity of ad hoc networks [2]. In this work, all the multicast sessions have identical number of destination nodes which are uniformly selected in the whole region. The achievable per-flow capacity given in this work is $\Theta(\frac{W}{\sqrt{kn \log n}})$, where k is the number of destination nodes. Shakkottai *et al.* studied the capacity of networks in which there are n^ϵ multicast sessions and each has $n^{1-\epsilon}$ destinations [3]. Their per-flow capacity is $\Theta(\frac{W}{\sqrt{n^\epsilon \log n}})$. Kozart studied the relationship between delay and capacity for multicast sessions [14]. Some other works focus on the multicast capacity of hybrid networks, investigating the effect of the number of base stations on capacity [4] and the traffic balancing between two transmission means [15]. Tang *et al.* focused on the capacity of hybrid networks with limited bandwidth between base stations [10]. All the above works assume that the sessions randomly choose the same number of destinations in the whole region. Our work does not enforce such an assumption.

Peng *et al.* studied the multicast capacity of networks with more general multicast sessions [9]. In their work, the source nodes pick their destinations according to a dispersion density function. These sessions share the same dispersion density function, and most of the sessions have the same numbers of destinations. The percolation theory is used in their work. The achieved capacity is $O(\frac{max\{1, a\delta_o\} W}{\sqrt{n_s}})$, where a is the side length of the whole square region, and δ_0 is the variance of the dispersion density function. Though the network model in [9] allows heterogeneous multicast sessions, one of its main improvements is for the case where the destinations are not uniformly picked from the whole region. The identities of the sessions are still required, which limits the commonality of the network model compared with ours.

Cooperative transmitting was introduced to improve multicast capacity in [11] and [16]. Rahul *et al.* developed a system [17] that could dynamically increase the capacity with user demand. These works take advantage of the extra coding technologies in increasing network capacity, while ours focuses on the network layer.

3. NETWORK MODEL

3.1 Networks

Assume n static wireless communication nodes, denoted as $M = \{m_1, m_2, \ldots, m_n\}$, are uniformly distributed in a region Ω. Ω is a square with side length $a = n^\alpha$, $\alpha \leq 1/2$.

These nodes form a random dense network, which means the node density increases as n grows. All the nodes transmit via the same channel, at a rate of no more than W *bits/s*. Two nodes u and v can transmit directly if $|u-v| \leq r$, where $|u-v|$ is the Euclidean distance between u and v, and r is the transmission range of the sender. For simplicity, all the nodes have the same transmission range r. r is relatively large so that the whole network is connected with high probability, which means any pair of nodes can transmit either directly or in a multi-hop manner.

The protocol model for interference [1] is applied to define conflicts in a network: in each time slot, node i can successfully send a packet to node j if $|i-j| \leq r$ and the Euclidean distance between any other concurrent transmitters and node j is bigger than $(1+\Delta)r$, where Δ is a positive constant number independent of nodes i and j, and it is set to $\Delta \geq 2$ [18] in this paper. Our model also works for $1 \leq \Delta < 2$, which is proved in Section 6.3. Every transmission has a "guard zone" where no nodes can deliver packets simultaneously. This zone is a circle area around the destination with radius $(1+\Delta)r$. The guard zone of a multicast tree is the union of the guard zones of all the nodes in the tree. Two transmissions can occur concurrently if their senders are not within each other's guard zone. In a similar way, two multicast sessions can transmit simultaneously if their involved nodes fall outside of each other's guard zone.

Following are some other assumptions on a network: (1) the wireless channel is multiplexed by TDMA [18] and it is equally divided in a round robin manner when multiple transmissions conflict with each other, (2) the relay nodes only receive, store, and send packets in a multi-hop manner, and (3) the wireless channel is always in a good condition, *i.e.*, there is no packet loss if there is no conflict.

3.2 Traffic Pattern

Let ms_i denote the ith multicast session, $i = 1, 2, \ldots, n_s$, $n_s = \Theta(n^\epsilon)$, and $1/2 < \epsilon \leq 1$. The set of the source nodes is expressed by $S = \{s_1, s_2, \ldots, s_{n_s}\}$. For source node s_i, it randomly picks k_i destination nodes. The k_i destinations are all within a circle area with radius R_i centered at s_i. Each session ms_i independently and randomly determines its k_i and R_i. s_i transmits data to all its destinations via single or multi hops through a multicast tree T_i, which is a Steiner tree connecting the source node and all its destinations with the help of some intermediate nodes. A multicast session must follow the following restrictions: (1) k_i is less than the total number of nodes in its destinations' distributed area for ms_i, and (2) any edge in T_i is not greater than r.

3.3 Capacity

Let $V_s = \{\lambda_1, \lambda_2, \ldots, \lambda_{n_s}\}$ be an instance of the rate vector for all the multicast sessions. Here, λ_i is the transmission rate of source node s_i. Rate vector V_s is called feasible if there is a spatial and temporal scheme for scheduling the transmissions of these multicast sessions so that every source node s_i, $i = 1, 2, \ldots, n_s$, can transmit to all of its destination nodes at a rate of $v_i = \lambda_i$. It is assumed that the buffer at any intermediate node never overflows under this scheme, and thus no data is discarded. For a sufficiently long time T, all the destination nodes can separately receive $T \times \lambda_i$ bits from their corresponding source s_i.

λ_i is called the per-flow throughput capacity of both source node s_i and the multicast session ms_i. The aggregated multicast throughput capacity (capacity for short) of a feasible rate vector V_s is defined as $\Lambda_{n_s}(n) = \sum_{s_i \in S} \lambda_i$. The multicast capacity of random networks is defined as follows.

DEFINITION 1. *(Capacity of Networks)[1]. The total multicast capacity of a network is in the order of $\Theta(f(n))$ bits/s if there is a constant $c > 0$ and $c < c' < +\infty$ such that*

$$\lim_{n\to\infty} Pr(\Lambda_{n_s}(n) = cf(n) \textit{ is feasible}) = 1$$
$$\lim_{n\to\infty} Pr(\Lambda_{n_s}(n) = c'f(n) \textit{ is feasible}) < 1$$

The definition of per-flow capacity of a network is similar.

4. UPPER BOUND FOR MULTICAST CAPACITY

In this section, part 1 analyzes the fundamental constraints that the proposed model must satisfy. Part 2 introduces the competitive intensity in wireless networks and estimates the intensity of a wireless network under the proposed network model. Part 3 derives the theoretical upper bound of the multicast capacity.

4.1 Constraints on Transmission Range and Destinations

Firstly, it is crucial to decide the minimum transmission range ensuring there is no isolated node in a network as n increases to infinity. All multicast sessions finish their transmissions via multicast trees under the new network model. However, when the transmission range r is relatively small, a node may fail to communicate with any other one and the multicast sessions choosing this node as a destination are infeasible. The minimum transmission range is also called the Critical Transmission Range (CTR). As proved in [1], when n nodes are uniformly distributed in a square region with side length a, the CTR is $\sqrt{\frac{\log n+\beta}{\pi n}}a$, where β is a constant. Thus, the actual transmission range must be bigger than CTR. Meanwhile, larger r leads to more conflicts [1], so the transmission range is:

$$\frac{r}{a} = \Theta(\sqrt{\frac{\log n}{\pi n}}) \tag{1}$$

Secondly, k_i and R_i of a multicast session are randomly chosen, and a simple constraint is that k_i must be less than the total number of nodes which fall inside of the circle area with radius R_i. The number of nodes in this circle area is denoted by C_{R_i}. C_{R_i} is independent of k_i because the nodes are uniformly distributed in the region. The following theorem helps quantify the constraint.

THEOREM 1. *When n nodes are uniformly distributed in a square region with side length a, $Pr(C_{R_i} = \Theta(n \cdot \frac{R_i^2}{a^2})) \to 1$ when $n \to \infty$, where $Pr(T) \to 1$ means the occurrence probability of event T approaches to 1.*

PROOF. Since nodes are uniformly distributed, for any node m_i,

$$Pr(m_i \textit{ in circle area with } R_i) = \frac{\pi R_i^2}{a^2},$$

and $Pr(m_i \textit{ in circle area with } R_i)$ is independent of all the nodes. It is obvious that $E(C_{R_i}) = \frac{\pi n R_i^2}{a^2}$, and according to the Chernoff's inequality [19], $Pr(|C_{R_i} - E(C_{R_i})| \geq$

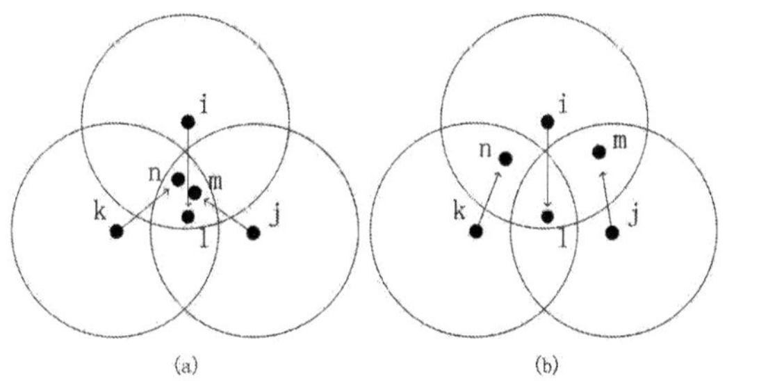

Figure 1: (a) Transmissions (i,l), (k,n), (j,m) conflict with each other. (b) Two transmissions pairs, (i,l), (k,n) and (i,l), (j,m), conflict with each other.

$\frac{E(C_{R_i})}{2}) \le 2e^{-\frac{E(C_{R_i})}{12}}$. When $n \to \infty$, since $a^2 = n^{2\alpha} \le n$, $2e^{-\frac{E(C_{R_i})}{12}} = 2e^{-\frac{\pi n R_i^2}{12a^2}} = 2e^{-\frac{\pi R_i^2 n^{1-2\alpha}}{12}} \to 0$. Thus, $Pr(\frac{E(C_{R_i})}{2} \le C_{R_i} \le \frac{3E(C_{R_i})}{2}) \to 1$ as $n \to \infty$. □

From Theorem 1, we have $k_j = O(\frac{nR_j^2}{a^2})$ for every multicast session ms_j, $j = 1, 2, \ldots, n_s$.

4.2 Competitive Intensity

In a wireless network, all the source-destination pairs communicate via a common wireless channel. Because of the inherent destructive interference [1], two transmission pairs cannot transmit simultaneously if they are sufficiently close to each other. Then we say the two transmissions are competing for the channel with each other. Under the protocol model, a circle area of radius $(1+\Delta)r$ around a destination is called the guard zone. Any other transmitter inside this zone will cause a destructive interference when it delivers packets simultaneously, and the wireless channel has to be equally divided by all these transmitters. This competition, in fact, may be over-estimated, since some of the transmitters in this guard zone can be scheduled at the same time, as shown in Fig.1. In Fig.1(a), transmissions (i,l), (k,n), (j,m) conflict with each other, so node i can be scheduled once in three slots. But in Fig,1(b), transmissions (j,m) and (k,n) can be scheduled at the same time, so node i can actually be scheduled once in two slots. The competitive intensity is thus defined as the number of transmitters that a node or a transmission has to compete with one at a time.

DEFINITION 2. ***Competitive Intensity*** *of node i, denoted as CI_i, is the size of the maximum set of nodes that cannot successfully transmit simultaneously with node i, and also any pair of nodes in the set fails to transmit at the same time.*

Multiple transmissions may choose same nodes as their transmitters, and they are obviously competitors for each other. Then the competitive intensity for a single transmission can be defined similarly.

The competitive intensity is a lower bound of the time intervals that a node or a transmission can be scheduled once. An upper bound of the transmission rate of a node or a transmission can be directly derived. Meanwhile, a multicast session is actually carried out by many pairwise transmissions, so the competitive intensity can help estimate the throughput of a session and then derive a bound on the multicast capacity. The competitive intensity of a single

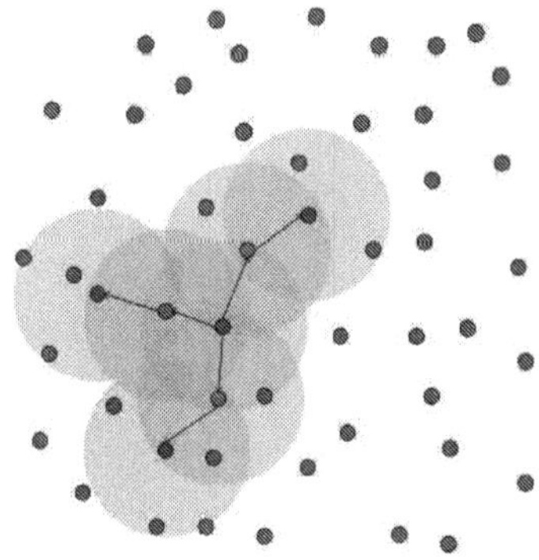

Figure 2: The union of the grey circles is the interference area. Green nodes stand for the intermediate nodes.

transmission under the proposed network model is estimated as follows.

For an arbitrary session ms_i, source node s_i transmits to its destination nodes via a multicast tree T_i. All the nodes in the tree will receive a copy of the data originated by s_i. Meanwhile, all the nodes close to these nodes in the tree will overhear the data. They cannot participate in other sessions at the same time. Here, overhearing means a node is within the range $(1+\Delta)r$ of any interior node in the tree of the current session. (Obviously, an overhearing at a node occurs when it is within the transmission range r of an interior node in the tree). Overhearing increases competitive intensity of these nodes, and leads to smaller transmission rate. In fact, the multicast tree forms an interference area $D(T_i)$, which is the union of the transmission areas of all the nodes in the tree. The nodes in this interference area overhear the data from the nodes in the tree. Fig.2 shows an example of the interference area, which is the union of the grey circles. Evaluating interference areas of all the sessions can help compute how many copies of data a single node will overhear, which is actually a lower bound of competitive intensity.

Consider an arbitrary multicast session ms_i. Its multicast tree T_i is composed of source node s_i, destinations $U = \{d_1, d_2, \ldots, d_{k_i}\}$ and some intermediate nodes. The whole tree falls in a circle region with radius R_i, centered at s_i. Define the total Euclidean length of a tree T's edges as $||T||$. $MST(s_i)$ is the minimum spanning tree connecting s_i and all its destinations. According to a series of theoretical studies [20], it is often believed that $||T_i|| \ge \beta_0 \cdot ||MST(s_i)||$, where β_0 is constant. The following lemma gives a lower bound of $||MST(s_i)||$.

LEMMA 1. *For k_i randomly and uniformly chosen nodes in a circle region with radius R_i centered at node s_i,*

$$||MST(s_i)|| = \beta_1 \cdot c(2) \cdot \sqrt{k_i} \cdot R_i,$$

where β_1 and $c(2)$ are constant.

PROOF. Based on the results in [21],

$$||MST(U)|| = c(2) \cdot \sqrt{k_i} \cdot \sqrt{\pi} R_i \tag{2}$$

$MST(U)$ is the minimum spanning tree connecting all the k_i destinations. When node s_i is added to $MST(U)$, it connects itself to some node in this tree, say d_u. The additional length is no more than R_i. So we have

$$||MST(s_i)|| \leq ||MST(U)|| + R_i.$$

The new spanning tree may not be minimal, and the added node could possibly modify the original edges. But since the destinations are randomly and uniformly picked, when k_i is sufficiently large, the change only affects a small proportion of the tree. Thus,

$$||MST(s_i)|| \geq \beta_2 ||MST(U)||, 0 \leq \beta_2 \leq 1.$$

Combining the above two inequalities, we have

$$||MST(s_i)|| = \beta_1 ||MST(U)||.$$

β_1 is a constant and this can finish the proof when combined with Equation (2). □

For simplicity, let $\beta_3 = \beta_0 \cdot \beta_1 \cdot c(2)$, so $||T_i|| \geq \beta_3 \cdot \sqrt{k_i} \cdot R_i$. The bound of $||T_i||$ can help derive a lower bound on the size of the interference area $D(T_i)$. A similar problem has been considered in [2], which can be extended to the following lemma.

LEMMA 2. *The size of interference area $D(T_i)$, denoted as $|D(T_i)|$, is at least $\beta_4 \cdot \sqrt{k_i} \cdot R_i \cdot r$ with high probability, when $k_i = O(\frac{{R_i}^2}{r^2})$, and $\beta_5 \cdot {R_i}^2$ when $k_i = \theta(\frac{{R_i}^2}{r^2})$. Here, β_4 and β_5 are constant, and r is the common transmission range.*

PROOF. This proof can be derived from Lemma 11 and Lemma 15 in [2]. We only need to change k to k_i and a to R_i.

Firstly, we build a new multicast tree T_i' based on T_i. Various methods [22, 23, 24] can be applied for tree construction. T_i' is a connected dominating set of the nodes in T_i, and it includes source node s_i. It has been proved by Lemma 11 in [2] that the maximum degree d of the nodes in T_i' is no more than 13 and $|D(T_i')| \geq \frac{|T_i'|\pi r^2}{6(d+1)}$, where $|T_i'|$ is the number of the nodes in T_i'.

Based on Lemma 1, $||T_i'|| + k_i \cdot r \geq \beta_0 ||MST(s_i)|| \geq \beta_3 \cdot \sqrt{k_i} \cdot R_i$, and $|T_i'| \geq \frac{||T_i'||}{r}$.

Since the set of the nodes in T_i' is a subset of the set of the nodes in T_i, we have

$$|D(T_i)| \geq |D(T_i')| \geq \frac{|T_i'|\pi r^2}{6(d+1)} \geq \frac{\frac{\beta_3 \cdot \sqrt{k_i} \cdot R_i - k_i \cdot r}{r} \pi r^2}{6(d+1)}.$$

When $k_i = O(\frac{{R_i}^2}{r^2})$,

$$|D(T_i)| \geq \frac{\sqrt{k_i} \cdot \pi r \cdot (\beta_3 R_i - O(R_i))}{6(d+1)} \approx \beta_4 \cdot \sqrt{k_i} \cdot R_i \cdot r,$$

where $\beta_4 = \frac{\pi \cdot \beta_3}{6(d+1)}$, and when $k_i = \theta(\frac{{R_i}^2}{r^2})$, $|D(T_i)| = \Theta(R_i^2)$. □

A limitation is that k_i must be less then C_{R_i}, thus the second assumption of k_i in Lemma 2 is feasible only when $C_{R_i} = \Omega(\frac{{R_i}^2}{r^2})$. $C_{R_i} = \Theta(n \cdot \frac{{R_i}^2}{a^2})$ according to Theorem 1, and since $\frac{r}{a} \geq \sqrt{\frac{\log n}{\pi n}}$, we have $C_{R_i} \geq \frac{{R_i}^2}{r^2}$.

It can be concluded that

$$|D(T_i)| = \begin{cases} \Omega(\sqrt{k_i} \cdot R_i \cdot r) & k_i = O(\frac{{R_i}^2}{r^2}) \\ \Theta({R_i}^2) & k_i = \theta(\frac{{R_i}^2}{r^2}) \end{cases}$$

This bound can be used to estimate the probability that an arbitrary node m_j falls in $D(T_i)$:

$$Pr(m_j \text{ falls in } D(T_i)) = \frac{|D(T_i)|}{a^2} \quad (3)$$

Next lemma estimates the number of sessions whose interference area covers an arbitrary node m_j, denoted as I_j.

LEMMA 3. *For the wireless network and multicast sessions defined in Section 2,*

$$I_j \geq \frac{\sum_{i=1}^{n_s} min\{\sqrt{k_i} \cdot R_i \cdot r, {R_i}^2\}}{2a^2}, \ w.h.p..$$

PROOF. Let $X_i = 1$ when ms_i covers m_j and 0 otherwise, $i = 1, 2, \ldots, n_s$. For a single multicast session ms_i, according to Equation (3),

$$Pr(X_i = 1) = \frac{|D(T_i)|}{a^2}.$$

Since the multicast sessions are generated independently, $I_j = \sum_{i=1}^{n_s} X_i$. So

$$E(I_j) = E(\sum_{i=1}^{n_s} X_i) = \sum_{i=1}^{n_s} E(X_i) = \sum_{i=1}^{n_s} \frac{|D(T_i)|}{a^2}.$$

According to Lemma 2, $|D(T_i)| = min\{\beta_6 \sqrt{k_i} \cdot R_i \cdot r, {R_i}^2\}$, where β_6 is a constant, so

$$E(I_j) = \frac{\sum_{i=1}^{n_s} min\{\sqrt{k_i} \cdot R_i \cdot r, {R_i}^2\}}{a^2}.$$

β_6 is omitted because it only changes $E(I_j)$ by constant times. Then

$$Pr(I_j \leq \frac{E(I_j)}{2}) \leq Pr(|I_j - E(I_j)| \geq \frac{E(I_j)}{2}) \leq 2e^{-\frac{E(I_j)}{12}},$$

which is based on the Chernoff's inequality. Since $E(I_j) \to +\infty$ as the number of nodes goes to infinity, it is clear that $2e^{-\frac{E(I_j)}{12}} \to 0$. So $I_j \geq \frac{E(I_j)}{2}$ with high probability. □

Lemma 3 sets a lower bound on the number of sessions that compete with an arbitrary node m_j. But this may be an over-estimation of the competitive intensity, since some of these sessions can perhaps be scheduled together. Next lemma indicates that these sessions also conflict with each other.

LEMMA 4. *For two multicast sessions ms_i and ms_j, if $D(T_i)$ and $D(T_j)$ both cover a node m, then ms_i and ms_j cannot transmit simultaneously.*

PROOF. If $D(T_i)$ and $D(T_j)$ both cover a node m, obviously there must be nodes m_i and m_j in each session and their Euclidean distance to m is less than r. So the distance between m_i and m_j is less than $2r$. If they are both leaf nodes or non-leaf nodes, then the distance between one node and another's sender or receiver is always less than $3r$. m_i and m_j compete with each other since $\Delta \geq 2$. Otherwise, we assume m_i is a leaf node and m_j is an interior node, then m_j is in m_i's guard zone. ms_i and ms_j cannot transmit simultaneously either. □

Finally, a lower bound on the competitive intensity CI_j can be derived by combining Lemma 3 and Lemma 4:

$$CI_j \geq \frac{\sum_{i=1}^{n_s} min\{\sqrt{k_i} \cdot R_i \cdot r, {R_i}^2\}}{2a^2}$$

4.3 Upper Bound on Capacity

It is crucial to notice that the transmission rate of a multicast tree is no more than that of any node in the tree. Otherwise, the buffers of some nodes may overflow and packets will be dropped. Thus, when the lower bound of the scheduling time interval of a node in the tree is derived, an upper bound of the transmission rate of this multicast session is also obtained. An interval means the time between two assigned slots during which a node transmits for the same session.

A node may be an intermediate node of multiple multicast trees and be assigned multiple slots. The interval of a node is no less than its competitive intensity in a round robin manner. Then the transmission rate is bounded by the reciprocal of its competitive intensity for a single transmission. So the upper bound of the per-flow throughput capacity of a multicast session is given by the following theorem.

THEOREM 2. *For any multicast session ms_i, its per-flow throughput capacity v_i is less than $\frac{2a^2}{\sum_{i=1}^{n_s} min\{\sqrt{k_i}\cdot R_i\cdot r, {R_i}^2\}} \cdot W$ bits/second with high probability.*

PROOF. For multicast tree T_i, take the source node s_i into consideration. Its competitive intensity is at least

$$\frac{\sum_{i=1}^{n_s} min\{\sqrt{k_i}\cdot R_i\cdot r, {R_i}^2\}}{2a^2}$$

with high probability according to Lemma 3 and Lemma 4. Since the channel is equally divided for these sessions, the transmission rate of s_i is no more than $\frac{2a^2}{\sum_{i=1}^{n_s} min\{\sqrt{k_i}\cdot R_i\cdot r, {R_i}^2\}} \cdot W$. This is also an upper bound for session ms_i, then

$$v_i = O(\frac{2a^2}{\sum_{i=1}^{n_s} min\{\sqrt{k_i}\cdot R_i\cdot r, {R_i}^2\}} \cdot W)$$

□

Then the multicast capacity of a random network is bounded by

$$\Lambda_{n_s}(n) = O(\frac{2a^2 \cdot n_s}{\sum_{i=1}^{n_s} min\{\sqrt{k_i} \cdot R_i \cdot r, {R_i}^2\}} \cdot W) \quad (4)$$

5. AN ACHIEVABLE LOWER BOUND

This section provides a feasible transmission scheme for all the multicast sessions, and derives the lower bound of the multicast capacity achieved by this scheme. The basic idea of the scheme has also been used by lots of previous studies on network capacity [1][2][9].

5.1 A Scheme for Multicast

The proposed scheme is based on the idea of a backbone graph [25]. It partitions region Ω into equal-sized square grids $G = \{g_{1,1}, g_{1,2}, \ldots, g_{1,l}, g_{2,1}, \ldots, g_{l,l}\}$, each with side length $\frac{r}{\sqrt{5}}$, $l = \lceil\frac{a}{r/\sqrt{5}}\rceil$. When two grids share a common side, any two nodes in these two grids can communicate directly since their distance is always no bigger than r. In each grid, one node is randomly picked as the leading node. All the leading nodes form a connected graph. In each grid, other nodes can communicate with their leading node in a single hop. The leading nodes actually form a backbone graph for the network. All the sessions route on top of this backbone graph. A transmitter first forwards its packet to its leading node in the grid, then to the receiver's grid via the backbone graph, and finally to its receiver in the last step. The following two principles are proved before we introduce the comprehensive scheme:

1) No grid is empty when n tends to be infinite.

2) Each leading node can be scheduled in constant time intervals by a round robin manner.

LEMMA 5. *For any grid $g_{i,j}$, there is at least one node in the grid with high probability as n approaches to infinity.*

PROOF. For an arbitrary node m_i, $Pr(m_i$ in grid $g_{i,j}) = \frac{r^2}{5a^2}$, so

$$Pr(g_{i,j} \text{ is empty}) = (1 - \tfrac{r^2}{5a^2})^n \le e^{-\frac{nr^2}{5a^2}}.$$

Since $r/a \ge \sqrt{\frac{\log n}{n}}$, when $n \to \infty$,

$$Pr(g_{i,j} \text{ is empty}) \le e^{-\frac{nr^2}{5a^2}} \le e^{-\log n} \to 0.$$

□

Lemma 5 ensures there is almost no empty grid, and the following lemma can support the second principle.

LEMMA 6. *On the backbone graph, every node can transmit once in every P time slots, $P \le 5\pi(3+\Delta)^2$.*

PROOF. If a transmitter u interferes with another node v, the Euclidean distance between u and v is less than $(1+\Delta)r + r$. It means the distance between one receiver and another source could be less than $(1+\Delta)r$. Thus the grid that u falls in is the circle of radius $(1+\Delta)r + r$ centered at v. Then, it is obvious that

$$P \le \frac{\pi((1+\Delta)r+2r)^2}{r^2/5} = 5\pi(3+\Delta)^2.$$

These P leading nodes can be scheduled by a round robin method, and each transmits once in every P time slots. □

The total number of nodes in each of these P grids is in the order of $\Theta(n \cdot \frac{r^2}{a^2}) = \Theta(\log n)$, and the proof is similar to Theorem 1.

The proposed scheme carries out the multicast sessions via multicast trees. The construction of the multicast tree for an arbitrary session ms_i includes three steps:

(1) Repeat steps (2) and (3) for $k = 2, 3, \ldots, k_i$.

(2) In the kth step, partition the circle region into no more than $k_i + 1 - k$ cells. Firstly, the partition is done by $\frac{R_i}{\sqrt{k_i+1-k}} + 1$ vertical lines. The first and last lines tangent to the circle, and others are between them with identical distance $\frac{R_i}{\sqrt{k_i+1-k}}$. Then the process is performed again with a group of horizontal lines.

(3) According to the pigeonhole principle, there is at least a cell containing two or more nodes. Two of the nodes in the same cell are connected by Manhattan Routing and will be considered as an integrated node in the next round. Thus, the number of nodes remained for connection decreases by one at the end of each round until all nodes are connected.

In step (3), when node u expects to transmit to node v, u first horizontally transmits its packet to the leading node of grid $g_{u,v}$. The leading node then vertically forwards the packet to v. Grid $g_{u,v}$ is a grid in the same row with u and same column with v. The routing strategy is called Manhattan Routing, as shown in Fig.3 where the red nodes are the transmitter and receiver, and the green nodes are the leading nodes. A multicast session involves three phases:

Phase 1 The source node in the multicast tree forwards its packets to the leading node of its own grid.

Phase 2 Packets are sent to the grids that contain their receivers via the backbone path of leading nodes. The Manhattan Routing is used in this phase.

Phase 3 Leading nodes deliver packets to their corresponding receivers, and the transmission is finished.

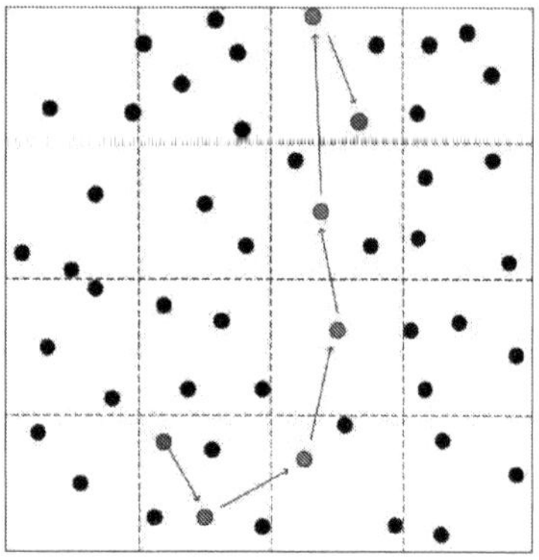

Figure 3: Red nodes are source-destination pair, green nodes are leading nodes, and the side length of a grid is $\frac{r}{\sqrt{5}}$.

It is important to notice that all the destinations connected by a backbone path are actually leaf nodes of the multicast tree, and they do not act as transmitters. Only the source node delivers packets in the first phase.

5.2 Achievable Capacity of the Scheme

We build a feasible multicast tree T_i for a multicast session. This subsection estimates the transmission rate of T_i. For phase 1 and phase 3, it is easy to prove that each node can transmit or receive at the rate of $\Omega(\frac{1}{\log n} \cdot W)$ *bits/second*, since there are $\Theta(\log n)$ nodes in each grid, and a grid can be scheduled once every constant number of time slots. The transmission rate of each multicast session in phase 2 is analyzed below. The proof mainly focuses on estimating the number of sessions that a leading node has to serve. The transmission rate of the leading node is equally partitioned by these sessions.

Lemma 7. *Given a grid g, the probability that a multicast session ms_i will use g is no more than $\beta_7 \frac{\sqrt{k_i} \cdot R_i \cdot r}{a^2}$, where β_7 is a constant, saying ms_i uses g when the leading node of g is an interior node of T_i.*

Proof. First of all, the leading node must fall in the distributed region of ms_i, which happens with probability $\frac{\pi R_i^2}{a^2}$.

According to the proposed scheme, in the kth step, $k = 1, 2, \cdots, k_i$, the probability that grid g is used by Manhattan Routing can be calculated as follow:

$$Pr(X_k = 1) = \frac{1}{k_i+1-k} \cdot p_s(\frac{R_i/\sqrt{k_i+1-k}}{r/\sqrt{5}})$$

Here, $X_k = 1$ means grid g is used in the kth step, and $\frac{1}{k_i+1-k}$ is the probability that the cell in which grid g falls contains more than two destinations. $p_s(\frac{R_i/\sqrt{k_i+1-k}}{r/\sqrt{5}})$ is the probability that grid g is on the transmitting path of the two destinations. L_i stands for the number of columns (rows) of grids in a cell in the ith round. Define $L_i = \frac{R_i/\sqrt{k_i+1-k}}{r/\sqrt{5}}$, then $p_s(L_i) = \frac{m-1}{L_i^2} \cdot \frac{L_i-m+1}{L_i} + \frac{n-1}{L_i^2} \cdot \frac{L_i-n+1}{L_i}$. Let u and v denote the two nodes to be connected in the ith round. The first part of the right side means that u is in the same row with grid g, and node u and v are on different sides of the column that grid g falls in. The second part means v is in the same column with grid g, node u and v are on different sides of grid g's row. Obviously,

$$Ps(L_i) \leq \frac{2}{L_i}$$

p is the probability that grid g is used by the multicast session ms_i when g is inside the distributed region of ms_i. Then for all the k_i steps,

$p \leq \sum_{k=1}^{k_i} Pr(X_k = 1) = \sum_{k=1}^{k_i} \frac{1}{k_i+1-k} \cdot p_s(\frac{R_i/\sqrt{k_i+1-k}}{r/\sqrt{5}}) \leq \frac{4\sqrt{10}}{5} \cdot \sqrt{k_i} \cdot \frac{r}{R_i}$.

Then

$$Pr(ms_i \; use \; g) \leq \frac{\pi R_i^2}{a^2} \cdot \frac{4\sqrt{10}}{5} \cdot \sqrt{k_i} \cdot \frac{r}{R_i} = \beta_7 \frac{\sqrt{k_i} \cdot R_i \cdot r}{a^2} \quad (5)$$

□

Since there are in total n_s independent multicast sessions, Lemma 8 can derive the upper bound of the number of sessions that use a grid g.

Lemma 8. *For any grid g, the number of multicast sessions using g is less than $\frac{3\sum_{i=1}^{n_s} min\{\sqrt{k_i} \cdot R_i \cdot r, R_i^2\}}{2a^2}$ with high probability.*

Proof. Let $Y_i = 1$ when ms_i uses g, and $Y_i = 0$ otherwise, $i = 1, 2, \ldots, n_s$. According to Lemma 7, $Pr(Y_i = 1) \leq \beta_7 \frac{\sqrt{k_i} \cdot R_i \cdot r}{a^2}$. Then

$$E(Y) = E(\sum_{i=1}^{n_s} Y_i) = \sum_{i=1}^{n_s} E(Y_i),$$

also because $Pr(ms_i \; uses \; g) \leq \frac{\pi R_i^2}{a^2} \cdot 1$,

$$E(Y) \leq \frac{\sum_{i=1}^{n_s} min\{\sqrt{k_i} \cdot R_i \cdot r, R_i^2\}}{a^2}.$$

According to the Chernoff's inequality,

$$Pr(Y \geq \frac{3E(Y)}{2}) \leq Pr(|Y - E(Y)| \geq \frac{E(Y)}{2}) \leq 2e^{-E(Y)/12}$$

and then the lemma is proved since $E(Y)$ goes to infinity as n increases. □

Lemma 8 gives an upper bound of the number of sessions that a leading node must serve. According to the previous subsection, a leading node can transmit at a constant rate, and its rate is equally divided by these sessions. Then the per-flow throughput of these multicast sessions can be bounded.

Theorem 3. *For any multicast session ms_i, its per-flow throughput capacity is more than*

$$\frac{2a^2}{3\sum_{i=1}^{n_s} min\{\sqrt{k_i} \cdot R_i \cdot r, R_i^2\}} \cdot W \; bits/second \; w.h.p..$$

Proof. In the proposed scheme, phase 2 is carried out via the backbone path composed of leading nodes. According to Lemma 8, the transmission rate of phase 2 is bigger than $\frac{2a^2}{3\sum_{i=1}^{n_s} min\{\sqrt{k_i} \cdot R_i \cdot r, R_i^2\}} \cdot W$. This is because the wireless channel is equally divided for the sessions. Denote the average value of $\{\sqrt{k_1}R_1, \sqrt{k_2}R_2, \cdots, \sqrt{k_{n_s}}R_{n_s}\}$ as $\overline{\sqrt{k_i}R_i}$.

When $\overline{\sqrt{k_i}R_i} = \Omega(a)$, since $n_s = \Theta(n^\epsilon), 1/2 < \epsilon \leq 1$, the following inequality is true when n goes to infinity:

$$\frac{2a^2}{3\sum_{i=1}^{n_s} min\{\sqrt{k_i \cdot R_i \cdot r}, R_i^2\}} \cdot W \leq \frac{2a^2}{3 \cdot n_s \cdot a \cdot r} \cdot W \leq \frac{W}{\log n},$$

$\Theta(\frac{W}{\log n})$ is an achievable transmission rate of phase 1 and phase 3.

The proof is a little complex when $\overline{\sqrt{k_i}R_i} = O(a)$, where $\overline{\sqrt{k_i}R_i} = \frac{\sum_{i=1}^{n_s}\sqrt{k_i}R_i}{n_s}$. Here is an intuitive description. The detailed proof is omitted due to space limitation. In phase 1 and phase 3, the leading node only serves the sessions whose sources or destinations fall inside its grid, while in phase 2, the leading node also acts as a relay node for other sessions besides receiving the packets towards its own grid. Then the number of packets a leading node sends or receives in phase 2 is larger than that of phase 1 and phase 3.

So the lower bound of the transmission rate for phase 2 is also a lower bound of the per-flow throughput capacity:

$$v_i = \Omega(\frac{2a^2}{3\sum_{i=1}^{n_s} min\{\sqrt{k_i \cdot R_i \cdot r}, R_i^2\}} \cdot W) \quad \square$$

Then a lower bound of multicast capacity is the sum of the achievable throughputs of all the sessions:

$$\Lambda_{n_s}(n) = \Omega(\frac{2a^2 n_s}{3\sum_{i=1}^{n_s} min\{\sqrt{k_i \cdot R_i \cdot r}, R_i^2\}} \cdot W)$$

6. DISCUSSION

In this section, some discussions of the network model and the derived bounds are presented.

6.1 Capacity Variation While R_i And k_i Change

R_i and k_i can decide the size of the interference area of multicast session ms_i based on Lemma 2. A bigger size causes larger traffic load due to the following reasons. More extra nodes serve as the relay nodes and more nodes incur collisions because of falling inside the interference area. Larger traffic load leads to smaller capacity since the channel resource for each session decreases. We are curious about how different R_is and k_is affect the total traffic load of a wireless network in our model, especially the groups of R_is and k_is that make the load sufficiently large or small. The result is shown by the relationship between the capacity and different R_is and k_is.

It is known that unicast and broadcast are two tails of multicast: unicast is the case where each session only contains single or few destinations, and broadcast is the case where the number of destinations of each session is in the same order of the total number of nodes in the network. The unicast capacity of a network is in the order $\Theta(W * \frac{a}{r})$, and the broadcast capacity is in the order $\Theta(W)$. We say that the traffic load of a wireless network is "heavy" when its capacity is in the same order of a broadcast network, and "light" for the unicast-like traffic load.

When R_is and k_is are both non-identical, define the average value of $\{\sqrt{k_1}R_1, \sqrt{k_2}R_2, \ldots, \sqrt{k_{n_s}}R_{n_s}\}$ as $\overline{\sqrt{k_i}R_i}$. Then i) If $\overline{\sqrt{k_i}R_i} = \Omega(\frac{a^2}{r})$, the capacity $\Lambda_{n_s}(n) = \Theta(W)$, which is derived from $\Lambda_{n_s}(n) = \Theta(\frac{a^2 n_s}{\sum_{i=1}^{n_s} min\{\sqrt{k_i \cdot R_i \cdot r}, R_i^2\}} \cdot W)$. The traffic load is heavy in the whole network, because most sessions expect to transmit either to many destinations (*i.e.*, large k_is) or to some destinations quite far away (*i.e.*, large R_is). In this case, the traffic load is like that of a broadcast network. ii) If $\overline{\sqrt{k_i}R_i} = O(a)$, the capacity $\Lambda_{n_s}(n) = \Theta(\frac{a}{r} \cdot W)$. The traffic load is light in the wireless network.

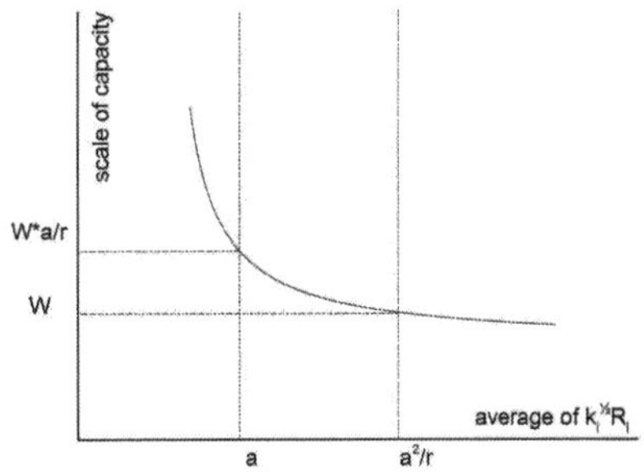

Figure 4: Relationship between $\overline{\sqrt{k_i}R_i}$ and multicast capacity.

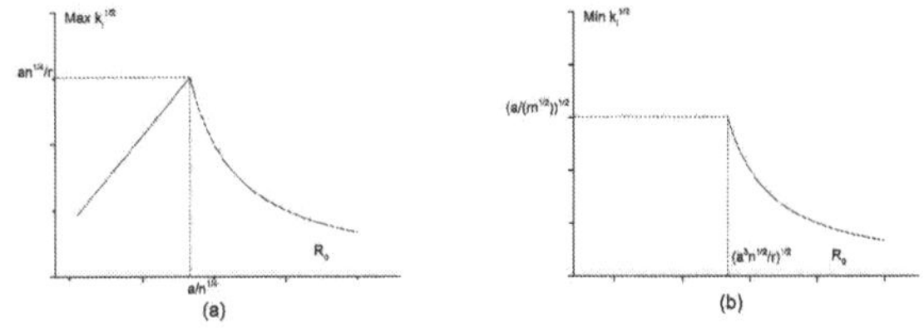

Figure 5: (a) $Max\ \sqrt{k_i}$ keeps traffic load light. (b) $Min\ \sqrt{k_i}$ keeps traffic load heavy.

The interference area of each session is only a small region. There are not many overlaps between these sessions' interference areas even when there are quite many multicast sessions (*i.e.*, $n_s = \Theta(n^\epsilon)$). In this case, the traffic load is like that of an unicast network.

Define the variance of $\{\sqrt{k_1}R_1, \sqrt{k_2}R_2, \ldots, \sqrt{k_{n_s}}R_{n_s}\}$ as $\delta(\sqrt{k} \cdot R)$. The changing of $\delta(\sqrt{k} \cdot R)$ will not affect the capacity, because the multicast capacity is bounded by the total traffic load, and the traffic load is determined by $\overline{\sqrt{k_i}R_i}$ and n_s according to our proofs. The relationship between $\overline{\sqrt{k_i}R_i}$ and $\Lambda_{n_s}(n)$ is shown in Fig.4.

Next, we discuss R_is and k_is separately. The primary question is how k_is (R_is) will affect multicast capacity when R_is (k_is) are set to be identical at some levels.

When R_is are set to be identical, the capacity $\Lambda_{n_s}(n) = \Theta(\frac{a^2 n_s}{\sum_{i=1}^{n_s} R_i \cdot min\{\sqrt{k_i \cdot r}, R_i\}} \cdot W)$, which is a function of $\overline{\sqrt{k_i}}$.

When $R_i = O(\frac{a}{n^{\frac{1}{4}}})$, since $k_i = O(n \cdot \frac{R_i^2}{a^2})$, $\overline{\sqrt{k_i}R_i} = O(\sqrt{n} \cdot \frac{R_i}{a} \cdot R_i) = O(\sqrt{n} \cdot \frac{1}{a} \cdot \frac{a^2}{\sqrt{n}}) = O(a)$. Then the traffic load in the network is always like that of an unicast network. The largest $\overline{\sqrt{k_i}}$ that can ensure that the traffic load is light equals $\frac{a}{R_i}$ if R_i keeps growing. The relationship between R_i and $\overline{\sqrt{k_i}}$ is shown in Fig.5(a).

On the other hand, with identical R_is, when $R_i = O(\sqrt{\frac{a^3}{r \cdot \sqrt{n}}})$, $\overline{\sqrt{k_i}R_i} = O(\sqrt{n} \cdot \frac{R_i}{a} \cdot R_i) = O(\sqrt{n} \cdot \frac{1}{a} \cdot a^2 \cdot \frac{a}{r \cdot \sqrt{n}}) = O(\frac{a^2}{r})$. Then no matter how k_i changes, the total traffic load is never as heavy as that of a broadcast network. The number of overlaps between sessions are relatively small due to the small distribution region of each session. When R_i keeps

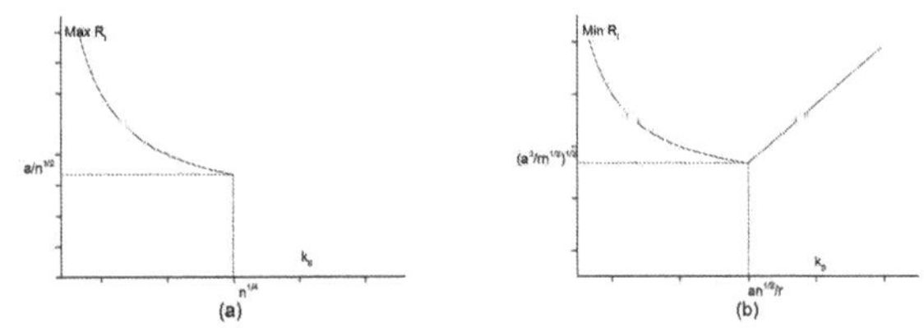

Figure 6: (a) The *max* $\overline{R_i}$ that keeps the traffic load light. (b) The *min* $\overline{R_i}$ that keeps the traffic load heavy.

growing, the smallest $\overline{\sqrt{k_i}}$ that makes the traffic load heavy in the network equals $\frac{a^2}{R_i \cdot r}$, as shown in Fig.5(b).

When $\sqrt{k_i}$s are set to be identical, the analysis is similar. So the result is directly shown here.

1) When $\sqrt{k_i} = O(n^{\frac{1}{4}})$, the biggest $\overline{R_i}$ that can keep the network having light traffic load equals $\frac{a}{\sqrt{k_i}}$. With larger $\sqrt{k_i}$, $\overline{R_i}$ must be large enough to contain these nodes, thus $\overline{\sqrt{k_i} R_i} = \Omega(a)$. The total traffic load is always not in the light tail. The result is shown in Fig.6(a).

2) When $\sqrt{k_i} = O(\sqrt{\frac{a}{r} \cdot \sqrt{n}})$, the smallest R_i that keeps the network's traffic load heavy equals $\frac{a^2}{r \cdot \sqrt{k_i}}$. When $\sqrt{k_i} = \Omega(\sqrt{\frac{a}{r} \cdot \sqrt{n}})$, the traffic load is always like that of a broadcast network, as shown in Fig.6(b).

In the proposed network model, $a = n^{\alpha}, \alpha \leq 1/2$ and $\frac{a}{r} \leq \sqrt{\frac{n}{\log n}}$. Then the following theorem is given to show some bounds of the multicast capacity presented by n. Other results are similar, thus omitted.

THEOREM 4. *For the proposed network model, when* $R_i = O(n^{\frac{1}{4}})$, $\Lambda_{n_s}(n) = \Theta(\sqrt{\frac{n}{\log n}} \cdot W)$, *or when* $k_i = \Omega(\frac{n}{\sqrt{\log n}})$, $\Lambda_{n_s}(n) = \Theta(W)$.

Finally, the multicast capacity of wireless networks under the proposed network model is concluded in Theorem 5.

THEOREM 5. *For the proposed network model,*
1) When $R_i = \Theta(a)$ *and* $k_i = k_0, \forall i = 1, 2, \cdots, n_s$*:*

$$\Lambda_{n_s}(n) = \begin{cases} \Theta(\frac{a}{\sqrt{k_0} \cdot r} \cdot W) & \text{when } \sqrt{k_0} = O(\frac{a}{r}) \\ \Theta(W) & \text{when } \sqrt{k_0} = \omega(\frac{a}{r}) \end{cases}$$

2) When R_i*s and* k_i*s are both independently chosen:*

$$\Lambda_{n_s}(n) = \begin{cases} \Theta(W) & \text{when } \overline{\sqrt{k_i} R_i} = \Omega(\frac{a^2}{r}) \\ \Theta(\frac{a}{r} \cdot W) & \text{when } \overline{\sqrt{k_i} R_i} = O(a) \\ \Theta(\frac{a^2}{\overline{\sqrt{k_i} R_i} \cdot r} \cdot W) & \text{others} \end{cases}$$

3) When R_i*s are identical, and* $R_i = R_0, \forall i = 1, 2, \cdots, n_s$*:*
$\Lambda_{n_s}(n) =$

$$\begin{cases} \Theta(\frac{a}{r} \cdot W) & \text{when } R_0 = O(\frac{a}{n^{\frac{1}{4}}}) \\ \Theta(W) & \text{when } R_0 = \Omega(\sqrt{\frac{a^3}{r \cdot \sqrt{n}}}), \overline{\sqrt{k_i}} = \Omega(\frac{a^2}{R_0 \cdot r}) \\ \Theta(\frac{a^2}{\overline{\sqrt{k_i}} \cdot R_0 \cdot r} \cdot W) & \text{others} \end{cases}$$

4) When k_i*s are identical, and* $k_i = k_0, \forall i = 1, 2, \cdots, n_s$*:*
$\Lambda_{n_s}(n) =$

$$\begin{cases} \Theta(\frac{a}{r} \cdot W) & \text{when } k_0 = O(n^{\frac{1}{2}}), \overline{R_i} = O(\frac{a}{\sqrt{k_0}}) \\ \Theta(W) & \text{when } k_0 = \Omega(\frac{a}{r} \cdot \sqrt{n}) \\ \Theta(\frac{a^2}{\overline{R_i} \cdot \sqrt{k_0} \cdot r} \cdot W) & \text{others} \end{cases}$$

6.2 Generality of the Network Model

The multicast capacity of wireless networks under the proposed network model is in the order of $\Theta(\frac{a^2 n_s}{\sum_{i=1}^{n_s} min\{\sqrt{k_i} \cdot R_i \cdot r, R_i^2\}} \cdot W)$. Firstly, when setting $R_i = \frac{a}{\sqrt{2}}$ and $k_i = k_0$ for all ms_i, all sessions are identical on the number of destinations and randomly pick destinations from the whole region. This is the traffic pattern used by most previous works. The capacity can be changed to $\Lambda_{n_s}(n) = \Theta(\frac{a}{\sqrt{k_0} \cdot r} \cdot W)$ when $k_0 = O(\frac{a^2}{r^2})$ and $\Lambda_{n_s}(n) = \Theta(W)$ when $k_0 = \Omega(\frac{a^2}{r^2})$. It is the same with the result in [2], so our network model is a proper generalization of the previous ones both intuitively and theoretically.

6.3 Applicability of Competitive Intensity

When $1 \leq \Delta \leq 2$, the competitive intensity is still in the order of $\Omega(\frac{\sum_{i=1}^{n_s} min\{\sqrt{k_i} \cdot R_i \cdot r, R_i^2\}}{2a^2})$. Such a Δ is for some indoor applications. The sketch of the proof is given below.

Consider the interference area of a multicast tree T_i,

$$|D(T_i)| = \begin{cases} \Omega(\sqrt{k_i} \cdot R_i \cdot r) & k_i = O(\frac{R_i^2}{r^2}) \\ \Theta(R_i^2) & k_i = \theta(\frac{R_i^2}{r^2}) \end{cases}$$

Let $D'(T_i)$ denote the interference area of T_i's non-leaf nodes. Then $|D'(T_i)| \geq |D(T_i)| - k_i * r^2$ since some destinations may also serve as relay nodes.

(1) When $k_i = O(\frac{R_i^2}{r^2})$, $|D'(T_i)| = \Omega(\sqrt{k_i} \cdot R_i \cdot r - k_i * r^2) = \Omega(\sqrt{k_i} \cdot r(R_i - O(\frac{R_i}{r}) * r)) = \Omega(\sqrt{k_i} \cdot R_i \cdot r)$.

(2) When $k_i = \Omega(\frac{R_i^2}{r^2})$, the union of the circle areas with radium r, centering at each destination, is in the order of $\Theta(R_i^2)$. This is based on the assumption that the destinations are randomly picked. Then there must be a transmitter within or on the edge of each circle area that delivers packets to the destination, and a constant proportion of the circle area is covered by the transmitter. This property holds for all the destinations, thus $|D'(T_i)| = \eta \cdot R_i^2 = \Theta(R_i^2)$, where η is a constant.

Lemma 3 is then proved by replacing $|D(T_i)|$ with $|D'(T_i)|$. All the non-leaf nodes are both transmitters and receivers, thus Lemma 4 holds with $1 \leq \Delta \leq 2$, and the proof is finished.

The proposed network model needs to be extended when the traffic load is heterogeneous around the network. But the competitive intensity is still workable, and the throughput of a single session is no more than the transmission rate of the interior node with the largest competitive intensity.

7. CONCLUSION

This paper studies the capacity of wireless networks with multiple types of multicast sessions. A new network model is proposed ignoring the assumption of traffic patterns being homogeneous. Based on the proposed network model, a theoretical upper bound and a reachable lower bound of the multicast capacity are derived, and two bounds are asymptotically tight. The proposed network model and derived capacity bounds generalize the previous network models and the capacity bounds. Meanwhile, they are more practical and applicable to practical applications.

Acknowledgements

This work is supported in part by National Natural Science Foundation of China under grants No.61190115 and No.61033015; National Science Foundation under grants No. CNS-1152001 and No.CNS-1252292.

8. REFERENCES

[1] P. Gupta and P. R. Kumar, "The capacity of wireless networks," *IEEE Trans. Information Theory*, vol. 46, no. 2, pp. 388–404, 2000.

[2] X.-Y. Li, "Multicast capacity of wireless ad hoc networks," *IEEE/ACM Trans. Networking (TON)*, vol. 17, no. 3, pp. 950–961, 2009.

[3] S. Shakkottai, X. Liu, and R. Srikant, "The multicast capacity of large multihop wireless networks," *IEEE/ACM Trans. Networking (TON)*, vol. 18, no. 6, pp. 1691–1700, 2010.

[4] X. Mao, X.-Y. Li, and S. Tang, "Multicast capacity for hybrid wireless networks," in *In Proc. of the 9th ACM international symposium on Mobile ad hoc networking and computing*, pp. 189–198, ACM, 2008.

[5] M. Franceschetti, O. Dousse, N. David, and P. Thiran, "Closing the gap in the capacity of wireless networks via percolation theory," *IEEE Trans. Information Theory*, vol. 53, no. 3, pp. 1009–1018, 2007.

[6] A. Keshavarz-Haddad, V. Ribeiro, and R. Riedi, "Broadcast capacity in multihop wireless networks," in *In Proc. of the 12th annual international conference on Mobile computing and networking*, pp. 239–250, ACM, 2006.

[7] C. Wang, C. Jiang, Y. Liu, X.-Y. Li, S. Tang, and H. Ma, "Aggregation capacity of wireless sensor networks: extended network case," in *INFOCOM, In Proc.IEEE*, pp. 1701–1709, IEEE, 2011.

[8] S. Ji and Z. Cai, "Distributed data collection in large-scale asynchronous wireless sensor networks under the generalized physical interference model," *IEEE/ACM Trans. Networking*, vol. 21, no. 4, pp. 1270–1283, 2013.

[9] Q. Peng, X. Wang, and H. Tang, "Heterogeneity increases multicast capacity in clustered network," in *INFOCOM, In Proc. IEEE*, pp. 703–711, IEEE, 2011.

[10] S. Tang, X. Mao, T. Jung, J. Han, X.-Y. Li, B. Xu, and C. Ma, "Closing the gap in the multicast capacity of hybrid wireless networks," in *In Proc. of the thirteenth ACM international symposium on Mobile Ad Hoc Networking and Computing*, pp. 135–144, ACM, 2012.

[11] C. Hu, X. Wang, D. Nie, and J. Zhao, "Multicast scaling laws with hierarchical cooperation," in *INFOCOM, IN Proc.IEEE*, pp. 1–9, IEEE, 2010.

[12] L.-L. Xie and P. R. Kumar, "A network information theory for wireless communication: Scaling laws and optimal operation," *IEEE Trans. Information Theory*, vol. 50, no. 5, pp. 748–767, 2004.

[13] M. Grossglauser and D. Tse, "Mobility increases the capacity of ad-hoc wireless networks," in *INFOCOM 2001. Twentieth Annual Joint Conference of the IEEE Computer and Communications Societies. Proc.. IEEE*, vol. 3, pp. 1360–1369, IEEE, 2001.

[14] U. C. Kozat, "On the throughput capacity of opportunistic multicasting with erasure codes," in *INFOCOM 2008. The 27th Conference on Computer Communications. IEEE*, pp. 520–528, IEEE, 2008.

[15] L. K. Law, S. V. Krishnamurthy, and M. Faloutsos, "Capacity of hybrid cellular-ad hoc data networks," in *INFOCOM 2008. The 27th Conference on Computer Communications. IEEE*, pp. 1606–1614, IEEE, 2008.

[16] M. Ji, Z. Wang, H. R. Sadjadpour, and J. Garcia-Luna-Aceves, "The capacity of ad hoc networks with heterogeneous traffic using cooperation," in *INFOCOM, In Proc. IEEE*, pp. 1–9, IEEE, 2010.

[17] H. S. Rahul, S. Kumar, and D. Katabi, "Jmb: scaling wireless capacity with user demands," in *In Proc. of the ACM SIGCOMM 2012 conference on Applications, technologies, architectures, and protocols for computer communication*, pp. 235–246, ACM, 2012.

[18] W. Wang, Y. Wang, X.-Y. Li, W.-Z. Song, and O. Frieder, "Efficient interference-aware TDMA link scheduling for static wireless networks," in *In Proc. of the 12th annual international conference on Mobile computing and networking*, pp. 262–273, ACM, 2006.

[19] M. Mitzenmacher and E. Upfal, *Probability and computing: Randomized algorithms and probabilistic analysis*. Cambridge University Press, 2005.

[20] A. O. Ivanov and A. A. Tuzhilin, "The steiner ratio gilbert–pollak conjecture is still open," *Algorithmica*, vol. 62, no. 1-2, pp. 630–632, 2012.

[21] J. M. Steele, "Growth rates of euclidean minimal spanning trees with power weighted edges," *The Annals of Probability*, pp. 1767–1787, 1988.

[22] J. Blum, M. Ding, A. Thaeler, and X. Cheng, "Connected dominating set in sensor networks and manets," in *Handbook of combinatorial optimization*, pp. 329–369, Springer, 2005.

[23] X. Cheng, X. Huang, D. Li, W. Wu, and D.-Z. Du, "A polynomial-time approximation scheme for the minimum-connected dominating set in ad hoc wireless networks," *Networks*, vol. 42, no. 4, pp. 202–208, 2003.

[24] M. Cardei, M. X. Cheng, X. Cheng, and D.-Z. Du, "Connected domination in multihop ad hoc wireless networks," in *JCIS*, pp. 251–255, 2002.

[25] H. Du, Q. Ye, W. Wu, W. Lee, D. Li, D. Du, and S. Howard, "Constant approximation for virtual backbone construction with guaranteed routing cost in wireless sensor networks," in *INFOCOM, In Proc. IEEE*, pp. 1737–1744, IEEE, 2011.

Capacity Maximization in Wireless MIMO Networks with Receiver-Side Interference Suppression

Peng-Jun Wan
Dept.of Computer Science
Illinois Institute of Technology
Chicago, IL 60616
wan@cs.iit.edu

Boliu Xu
Dept. of Computer Science
Illinois Institute of Technology
Chicago, IL 60616
bxu8@hawk.iit.edu

Ophir Frieder
Dept. of Computer Science
Georgetown University
Washington, DC 20057
ophir@ir.cs.georgetown.edu

Sai Ji
College of Computer And Software
Nanjing University of IST
Nanjing, Jiangsu 210044
jisai@nuist.edu.cn

Baowei Wang
College of Computer And Software
Nanjing University of IST
Nanjing, Jiangsu 210044
wbw.first@163.com

Xiaohua Xu
EECS Department
University of Toledo
Toledo, OH 43606
Xiaohua.Xu@UToledo.edu

ABSTRACT

Multiple-input multiple-output (MIMO) technology provides a means of boosting network capacity without requiring additional spectrum. It has received widespread attention over the past decade from both industry and academic researchers, now forming a key component of nearly all emerging wireless standards. Despite the huge promise and considerable attention, a rigorous algorithm-theoretic framework for maximizing network capacity in multihop wireless MIMO networks is missing in the state of the art. The existing algorithms and protocols for maximizing network capacity in multihop wireless MIMO networks are purely heuristic without any provable performance guarantees. In this paper we conduct a comprehensive algorithm study for maximizing network capacity in multihop wireless MIMO networks with receiver-side interference suppression, including the full characterization of NP-hardness and APX-hardness, the polynomial time approximation schemes, and the practical approximation algorithms with provable performance guarantees.

Categories and Subject Descriptors

C.2.1 [**Computer-Communication Networks**]: Network Architecture and Design—*wireless communication*

Keywords

Capacity, multiple-input multiple-output, stream scheduling

MobiHoc'14, August 11–14, 2014, Philadelphia, PA, USA.

http://dx.doi.org/10.1145/2632951.2632989.

1. INTRODUCTION

In the last decade, there has been rapid technological progress within the wireless industry, targeted at meeting ever-increasing consumer demands for higher speed data transmission and for supporting a plethora of multimedia services and applications. Among various innovations, the multiple-input multiple-output (MIMO) technology has revolutionized the wireless industry, providing a means of boosting network capacity without requiring additional spectrum. With multiple antennas at the transmitter and/or receiver, a MIMO system is capable of increasing the wireless data rate by *spatially multiplexing* multiple data streams over a communication link and allowing links within interference range to be concurrently active by *interference suppression.* The phenomenal impact of MIMO cannot be overstated–it has received widespread attention over the past decade from both industry and academic researchers, now forming a key component of nearly all emerging wireless standards.

Despite the huge promise and considerable attention, a rigorous algorithm-theoretic framework for maximizing network capacity in multihop wireless MIMO networks is still missing in the state of the art even under the simplest protocol interference model. Several MAC protocols for integrating MIMO with the networking stack have been developed in [10, 19, 26] among others. A number of works [3, 4, 16, 15] have studied the selection of a subset of streams with maximum total capacity which can be scheduled in a single time-slot. Among them, the integer linear program formulations of this problems in various setting were given by Blough et al. [3] and Liu et al. [15]. Chu and Wang [4] and Mumey el al. [16] developed polynomial time approximation algorithms for this problem. However, the approximation bounds of these algorithms grow *linearly* with the *product* of maximum number of antennas at individual nodes, maximum number of links incident to a node, and maximum number of links conflicting with individual links.

It remains open whether there is a constant approximation algorithm for this problem. Wang et al. [25] and Mumey et al. [16] have investigated the transmission scheduling of a set of links and their traffic demands in the smallest number of time-slots. In both [25] and [16], purely heuristic algorithms were developed but no theoretic performance analyses of these heuristics were provided. The problem of joint routing and link scheduling for maximizing the throughput (in terms of multiflow) of a given set of end-to-end communication requests has been studied in [2, 6, 7, 14, 20]. Again, only purely heuristic algorithms for this problem have been developed in [2, 6, 7, 14, 20], and none of them has any provable performance guarantees. We remark that if the link scheduling and the stream control are pre-specified, this problem can be reduced to the classic maximum multiflow in wired networks and hence is solvable in polynomial time [5].

In a striking contrast, maximizing network capacity in multihop wireless networks without MIMO capability under the protocol interference model has been much better studied by [8, 13, 22, 23, 24]. On one hand, the MAC layer optimization problems maximum-weighted independent set and the minimum-latency link scheduling and the cross-layer optimization problem maximum (concurrent) multiflow are NP-hard even in very simple setting [22]. On the other hand, all of them admit polynomial-time approximation scheme (PTAS) even in the more general multi-channel multi-radio (MC-MR) setting as long as the number of channels is bounded by a constant [23]. In other words, for any fixed $\varepsilon > 0$, there is a polynomial-time (depending on ε) $(1+\varepsilon)$-approximation algorithm. In addition, a number of faster (polynomial-time) constant-approximation algorithms [24] have been developed in various setting.

The present significant knowledge gap between maximizing network capacity in multihop wireless MIMO networks and maximizing network capacity in multihop wireless networks without MIMO capability motivates us to address the following algorithmic issues:

- While it is expected that maximizing network capacity in multihop wireless MIMO networks is NP-hard, what are the major technical obstacles that have prevented the progress so far?
- Do there exist a PTAS?
- Do there exist polynomial time approximation algorithms with constant approximation bound and practical running time?

In this paper, we address the above three aspects in multihop wireless MIMO networks with receiver-side interference suppression, which is the most practically viable variant of the MIMO technology. Due to the space limitation, we mainly focus on the most fundamental problem of selecting a maximum weighted set of streams which can transmit successfully at the same time under the protocol interference model. For such optimization problem, we fill the present knowledge gap with the following discoveries presented in this paper:

- The problem is NP-hard even when the input streams with positive weight are node-disjoint. The full utilization of the receiver-side interference suppression is the major source of such NP-hardness.
- When the nodes have arbitrary number of antennas, the problem is APX-hard [1] and hence does not admit PTAS unless $P = NP$. Such APX-hardness is due to the half-duplex constraint.
- When the maximum number of antennas at all nodes is bounded by a constant, the problem admits a PTAS.
- When all streams have uniform interference radii or all nodes have the same number of antennas, there exist constant-approximation algorithms with practical polynomial running time.

The remainder of this paper is organized as follows. In Section 2, we give a precise problem description and introduce some basic structural properties. In Section 3, we provide rigorous proofs of the NP-hardness and APX-hardness even in simple settings. In Section 4, we present a PTAS in the setting of constant bounded number of antennas at all nodes. In Section 5, we develop a divide-and-conquer approximation algorithm in the setting of uniform interference radii. In Section 6, we develop a linear programming (LP) based approximation algorithm in the setting of uniform number of antennas at all nodes. Finally, we conclude this paper in Section 7.

2. PRELIMINARIES

Consider an instance of multihop wireless MIMO network on a set V of networking nodes. Each node v has $\tau(v)$ antennas and operates in the half-duplex mode, i.e. it cannot transmit and receive at the same time. Along each node-level directed communication link (u, v), $\min\{\tau(u), \tau(v)\}$ streams can be multiplexed. Let A denote the set of streams of all directed node-level communication links. The directed multigraph (V, A) is referred to as the stream-level communication topology. For each node u and any set B of streams, we use $\delta_B^{out}(u)$ to denote the set of streams in B having u as the sender. Under a protocol interference model, each node-level communication link is associated with an interference range and all its streams inherit the same interference range from it. When a set I of streams in A transmit at the same time, the transmission by a stream $a \in I$ from a sender u to a receiver v succeeds with the receiver-side interference suppression if all the following three constraints are satisfied:

1. **Half-Duplex Constraint**: u is not the receiver of any other stream in I, and v is not the sender of any other stream in I.
2. **Sender Constraint**: u is the sender is at most $\tau(u)$ streams in I. In other words, $\left|\delta_I^{out}(u)\right| \leq \tau(u)$.
3. **Receiver Constraint**: v lies in the interference range of at most $\tau(v)$ streams in I.

A set I of streams is said to be *independent* if all streams in I succeed when they transmit at the same time. Let $\mathcal{I}$ denote the collection of all independent subsets of A. Suppose that each stream $a \in A$ has a non-negative weight $w(a)$. The weight of any subset B of A is defined to be $w(B) = \sum_{a \in B} w(a)$. The problem **Maximum Weighted Independent Set of Streams (MWISS)** seeks an independent set $I \in \mathcal{I}$ with maximum weight.

A set S of streams is said to be *weakly independent* if for each stream $a \in S$ from a sender u to a receiver v, the following two constraints are satisfied:

1. **Sender Constraint**: u is the sender is at most $\tau(u)$ streams in S.
2. **Receiver Constraint**: v lies in the interference range of at most $\tau(v)$ streams in S.

Clearly, weak independence is the relaxation of independence on the **Half-Duplex Constraint**. We present a simple algorithm **ExtractIS** which extracts an independent set I from a weakly independent set S satisfying that $w(I) \geq \frac{1}{4} w(S)$. Let U be the set of end nodes of the streams in S, and $\langle u_1, u_2, \cdots, u_k \rangle$ be an arbitrary ordering of U. Conceptually, the algorithm **ExtractIS** proceeds in two steps

- **Node Partition Step**: U is greedily parititioned into U' and U'' as follows. Initially, $U' = \{u_1\}$ and $U'' = \emptyset$. For $j = 2$ to k, if the set of streams in S between u_j and U' is heavier than the set of streams in S between u_j and U'', u_j is added to U''; otherwise, u_j is added to U'.
- **Stream Partition Step**: The set of streams between U' and U'' is partitioned into two subsets: I_1 consists of the streams from U' to U'', and I_2 consists of the streams from U'' to U'. The heavier one between I_1 and I_2 is output as I, with ties broken arbitrarily.

It is obvious that I is independent. The theorem below asserts that $w(I) \geq \frac{1}{4} w(S)$. Due to the space limitation, its proof is omitted.

THEOREM 2.1. $w(I) \geq \frac{1}{4} w(S)$.

Throughout this paper, we assume that all nodes in V lies in a plane. The Euclidean distance between any pair of nodes u and v in a plane is denoted by $|uv|$. We adopt the following plane-geometric variant of the protocol interference model, which is widely assumed in the literature: The interference range of a stream a from a sender u to a receiver v is the disk centered at u of radius $r(a)$, where $r(a) \geq |uv| / \eta$ for some constant $\eta \in (0,1)$. We denote by

$$\mu = \left\lceil \pi / \arcsin \frac{1-\eta}{2} \right\rceil - 1.$$

Let $\overline{\tau}$ denote the maximum number of antennas at the networking nodes.

LEMMA 2.2. *Suppose that a point o lies in the interference ranges of a weakly independent set I of streams. Then, $|I| \leq \mu \overline{\tau}$.*

The above lemma is an extension of Lemma 8.2 in [22] and the proof is omitted due to lack of space.

We conclude this section with the following property of uniform number of antennas at all nodes.

LEMMA 2.3. *Suppose that all nodes have the same number of antennas. Then any subset B of A satisfying the **Receiver Constraint** also satisfies the **Sender Constraint**.*

PROOF. Let τ be the number of antennas at each node. Consider any node u which is a sender of some stream in B. Let a be a shortest stream in B with u as the sender. Then the receiver of a lies in the interference range of every stream in B with u as the sender (including a itself). By the **Receiver Constraint**, the number of streams in B with u as the sender is at most τ. Hence, the **Sender Constraint** is also satisifed. □

A consequence of the above lemma is that when all nodes have the same number of antennas, a subset of A is weakly independent if and only if it satisfies the **Receiver Constraint**, and is independent if and only if it satisfies the **Receiver Constraint** and the **Half-Duplex Constraint**.

3. NP-HARDNESS AND APX-HARDNESS

In this section, we establish the NP-hardness and APX-hardness of **MWISS** even in very simple settings. For any subset B of A , we use $\mathcal{I}(B)$ to denote the collection of all independent subsets of B. Given a subset B of A, the problem **Maximum Independent Set of Streams (MISS)** seeks an $I \in \mathcal{I}(B)$ with maximum size. Clearly, the problem **MISS** is a special case of **MWISS** in which all stream weights are $\{0,1\}$-valued. As the result, any hardness result of **MISS** extends to **MWISS**. Throughout this section, the hardness of **MISS** are studied in "homogeneous" MIMO networks in which all nodes lie in a plane and have the same number of antennas, and all streams have the same interference radii. By Lemma 2.3, the **Sender Constraint** is redundant for the independence.

In the first and simplest setting of **MISS**, the input set B of streams is *node-disjoint*, in other words, no two streams in B share an endpoint. As the **Half-Duplex Constraint** is trivially satisfied by any subset of B, a subset of B is independent if and only if it satisfies the **Receiver Constraint**. The theorem below asserts that the problem **MISS** remains NP-hard even when restricted to node-disjoint streams, and thus pinpoints the full utilization of the receiver-side interference suppression as a major source of NP-hardness.

THEOREM 3.1. *The problem **MISS** is NP-hard even when restricted to node-disjoint streams with uniform interference radii and when all nodes have uniform and fixed number of antennas.*

Next, we consider a slightly more general setting. A set B of streams is said to be *simple* (respectively, *acyclic*) if the subgraph (V, B) is simple (respectively, acyclic). A pair of streams a and b are said to have *conflict* if the receiver of at least one stream lies in the interference range of the other stream.

THEOREM 3.2. *With uniform but arbitrarily many antennas at each node, the problem **MISS** is NP-hard and APX-hard even when restricted to the sets of simple and acyclic streams which are pairwise conflicting.*

The above theorem implies that unless $P = NP$, the problem **MISS** does not admit PTAS with arbitrary number of antennas at each node. The above theorem also reveals that the **Half-Duplex Constraint** is a major technical obstacle of approximating the problem **MISS**. On the other hand, we will show in the next section that when the number of antennas at each node is bounded by a constant, the problem **MWISS**, and hence **MISS** as well, admits a PTAS. In contrast, in wireless networks without MIMO capability, if all links have pairwise conflict, then the maximum independent set of links is trivially solvable.

The proofs of Theorem 3.1 and Theorem 3.2 are given in the two subsections below respectively.

3.1 Proof of Theorem 3.1

Consider an undirected graph $G = (V, E)$ and a fixed positive integer k. A subset of V is called a *k-restricted independent set* if it induces a subgraph of G with maximum degree less than k. Note that a 1-restricted independent set is simply an independent set of G. The problem maximum k-restricted independent set (**MAX k-RIS**) is that of seeking a largest k-restricted IS of G. For a finite planar point set V and a number $d > 0$, the d-disk graph on V is a simple geometric graph on V in which there is an edge between two nodes if and only if their distance is at most d. In particular, a 1-disk graph is referred to as unit-disk graph (UDG). For any fixed positive integer k, the problem **MAX k-RIS** is NP-hard even restricted to UDGs [9].

The proof of Theorem 3.1 is accomplished by polynomial reduction from **MAX k-RIS** in UDGs to **MISS**. Given a connected UDG $G = (V, E)$ a connected UDG (see Figure 1(a)) and a fixed constant $\eta \in (0, 1)$, we construct a (connected) multihop MIMO wireless network as follows. Let l_1 be the shortest distance between any pair of non-adjacent nodes in G, and set $r = \frac{l_1+2}{3}$ and $r' = \eta r$. Then $1 < r < l_1$. We first construct a set W of at most $(|V| - 1)/\varepsilon$ points such that the r'-disk graph on $V \cup W$ is connected. Compute an Euclidean minimum spanning tree T of G. Since G is connected, all edges of T have length at most one. Initially, W is empty. We subdivide each edge uv in T with $|uv| > r'$ into $\lceil |uv| / r' \rceil$ segments of equal length and adding those $\lceil |uv| / r' \rceil - 1$ endpoints of these segments other than u and v to W (see Figure 1(b)). Since $r > 1$, we have

$$\left\lceil \frac{|uv|}{r'} \right\rceil - 1 \leq \left\lceil \frac{1}{\eta r} \right\rceil - 1 \leq \left\lceil \frac{1}{\eta} \right\rceil - 1 < \frac{1}{\eta}.$$

Thus, $|W| \leq (|V| - 1)/\eta$. In addition, the r'-disk graph on $V \cup W$ is connected.

Now, we construct a duplication V' of V as follows. Let l_2 be the shortest distance between any pair of distinct nodes in $V \cup W$ and set

$$l_3 = \min\left\{\frac{l_1 - 1}{3}, \frac{l_2}{2}\right\}.$$

Then,

$$1 + l_3 \leq r < l_1 - l_3.$$

For each $v \in V$, we put a duplication v' of v straightly below v satisfying that $\|vv'\| = l_3$ (see Figure 1(c)). Then, $v' \notin V \cup W$. Let V' denote the set of duplications v' constructed in this way. Then, $|V'| = |V|$. It is also easy to verify that that for any two distinct u and v nodes in V, $|uv| \leq 1$ if and only if

$$\max\{|uv|, |u'v'|, |uv'|, |u'v|\} \leq r.$$

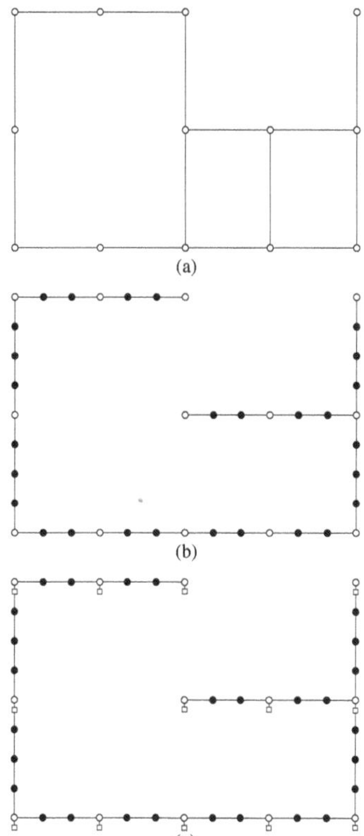

Figure 1: Construction for the reduction: (a) a UDG $G = (V, E)$; (b) Subdivision of edges in an EMST of G; (c) duplication of nodes in V.

Next, we construct a multihop MIMO wireless network on $V \cup W \cup V'$. We equip each node with k antennas. For each pair of nodes apart by at most r', there is a communication link of interference radius r. For each $v \in V$, we pick an arbitrary stream from v' to v and refer it to as a representative stream of v. For each subset U of V, we denote by A_U to set of representive streams of nodes in U. Clearly, A_U is node-node disjoint. Furthermore, U is a k-restricted independent set of G if and only if A_U is an independent set of streams. Thus, a maximum k-restricted independent set of G corresponds to a maximum independent subset of A_V, and vice versa. So, Theorem 3.1 holds.

3.2 Proof of Theorem 3.2

Consider a digraph $D = (V, E)$. A directed cut (or dicut in short) is a set of links in E leaving some vertex subset U (we denote it by $\delta^{out}(U)$). Given a digraph D, the maximum directed cut problem (**MAX DICUT**) is that of finding a dicut $\delta^{out}(U)$ of maximum size. The NP-hardness of **MAX DICUT** follows from the observation that the well-known undirected version of **MAX DICUT** – the maximum cut problem (**MAX CUT**), which is on Karp's original list [11] of 21 NP-complete problems – reduces to **MAX DICUT** by substituting each edge for two oppositely oriented arcs. Even when restricted to directed acyclic graphs (DAGs), the problem **MAX DICUT** is NP-hard and APX-hard [12].

The proof of Theorem 3.2 is accomplished by a polynomial reduction from **MAX DICUT** in DAGs to **MISS**. Given a DAG $D = (V, E)$, we construct a multihop MIMO wireless network on V as follows. We embed V in a disk of unit diameter arbitrarily and equip each node in V with $\tau = |E|$ antennas. For each pair of nodes, there is a communication link of interference radius r for some fixed constant $r \geq 1$. For each $(u, v) \in E$, we pick an arbitrary stream from u to v and refer it to as a representative stream of (u, v). We denote by B the set of representive streams of links in E. Clearly, B is simple and acyclic, and any pair of streams conflict with each other. For any $C \subseteq E$, we denote by B_C the set of representative streams of links in C. Then, C is a dicut of D if and only if B_C is an independent subset of B. Thus a maximum dicut of D corresponds to a maximum independent subset of B, and vice versa. Therefore, Theorem 3.2 holds.

4. PTAS

In this section, we present a PTAS for **MWISS** when the maximum number of antennas $\overline{\tau}$ is bounded by a constant. The PTAS utilizes the shifting strategy combined with dynamic programming in a way similar to the PTAS for maximum weighted independent set of link in MC-MR wireless networks [23].

We first introduce some terms and notations. By scaling, we may assume the interference radii of all streams are at least 1/2. The *level* of a stream is the integer part of the logarithm of its interference diameter. Thus, the interference radius of a stream at level $l \in \mathbb{Z}_+$ is in $[2^{l-1}, 2^l)$. Let L be the largest level of the links in A. All the vertical lines $x = i$ for $i \in \mathbb{Z}$ are called vertical grid lines; all the horizontal lines $y = j$ for $j \in \mathbb{Z}$ are called horizontal grid lines. A vertical grid line $x = i$ is of level $l \in \mathbb{Z}_+$ if $i \bmod 2^l = 0$; similarly, a horizontal grid line $y = j$ is of level l if $j \bmod 2^l = 0$. Clearly, if a grid line is of level l, then it is also level l' for any $0 \leq l' < l$. Let K be an odd integer parameter at least 5. A vertical grid line $x = i$ is k-active for some integer $0 \leq k < K$ if $\left(i - k2^L\right) \bmod K = 0$ (see Figure 2); similarly, a horizontal grid line $y = j$ is k-active if $\left(j - k2^L\right) \bmod K = 0$. It was shown in the proof of Lemma 9 in [21] that each grid line is k-active for exactly one k with $0 \leq k < K$. In addition, each k-active vertical grid line of level l is of the format $x = i'2^l + k2^L$ for some $i' \in \mathbb{Z}$, and each k-active horizontal grid line of level l is of the format $y = j'2^l + k2^L$ for some $j' \in \mathbb{Z}$. For each $0 \leq k < K$ and each $0 \leq l \leq L$, all the k-active grid lines of level l decompose the whole plane into *open* squares of side $K2^l$

$$K2^l\,(i, i+1) \times (j, j+1) + k2^L\,(1, 1)$$

for all $i, j \in \mathbb{Z}$ (see Figure 2). All these squares are called k-active level-l squares.

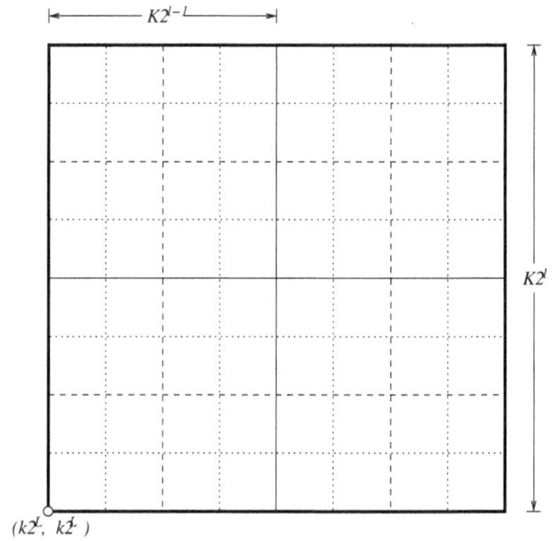

Figure 2: An illustration of k-active grid lines and k-active squares.

A stream a is said to be *covered* by an open square S if its interference range is contained in S. Consider an integer $0 \leq k < K$ and a stream a at level l. It is easy to verify that any k-active square covering a must at level at least $\max\{l - \lfloor \log K \rfloor, 0\}$. The stream a is said to be *k-active* if it is covered by some k-active level-l square, and *k-inactive* otherwise. If a is k-inactive, then the interference range of a intersects some k-active grid line of level l but at most two vertical (respectively, horizontal) grid lines of level l since its diameter is less than 2^{l+1}.

For each $0 \leq k < K$, let A_k (respectively, A'_k) denote the set of k-active (respectively, k-inactive) streams in A. The lemma below is the property underlying the shifting strategy, and its proof is omitted due to the lack of space.

LEMMA 4.1. *Suppose that I_k is a heaviest independent set of A_k for each $0 \leq k < K$, and O is a heaviest independent set of A. Then,*

$$\max_{0 \leq k < K} w(I_k) \geq \left(1 - \frac{4}{K}\right) w(O).$$

In the shifting strategy, a heaviest IS I_k of A_k is computed for each $0 \leq k < K$, and then the heaviest one among those K IS's, which is a $1/(1 - 4/K)$-approximate solution, is returned. Subsequently, we present a polynomial-time dynamic programming algorithm which can compute a heaviest IS of A_k for each $0 \leq k < K$. We introduce the notations adopted in the dynamic programming algorithm.

Fix $0 \leq k < K$. A stream $a \in A_k$ is said to be *minimally covered* by a k-active square S if it is covered by S but not by any k-active square of level less than that of S. Clearly, the minimal covering k-active square of a stream $a \in A_k$ can be computed in polynomial time. Let $\mathcal{S}$ denote the collection of minimal covering k-active squares of streams in A_k. We define a directed forest over $\mathcal{S}$ as follows. For any pair of distinct squares S and S' in $\mathcal{S}$, S is a *parent* of S' (and S' is a *child* of S) if and only if S contains S' and there is no "intermediate" square $S'' \in \mathcal{S}$ such that $S \supset S'' \supset S'$. Each square in $\mathcal{S}$ without any child is referred to as a *sink square*, and each square in $\mathcal{S}$ without parent is referred to as a *root square*. Let $\mathcal{S}_0$ denote the set of root squares in $\mathcal{S}$. In addition, for each square S in $\mathcal{S}$, we use $\mathcal{C}(S)$ to denote the set of child squares of S.

For each $S \in \mathcal{S}$, let A_S (respectively, A_S^*) denote the set of streams in A_k covered (respectively, minimally covered) by S, and let N_S denote the set of streams in $A_k \setminus A_S$ having conflict with at least one stream in A_S. It is obvious that the level of every stream in A_S^* is *at least* the level of S. We further claim that every stream in N_S is minimally covered by some proper ancestor of S and hence its level is *greater than* the level of S. Indeed consider any stream $b \in N_S$ and let S' be the square in $\mathcal{S}$ which minimally covers a. Then S and S' have overlap, and hence one of them is contained in the other. As a is not covered by S, we have $S \subset S'$. So, the claim holds. The claim also implies that N_S is empty if $S \in \mathcal{S}_0$. Clearly, if S is a sink square, then $A_S = A_S^*$; otherwise,

$$A_S = A_S^* \cup \left(\bigcup_{S' \in \mathcal{C}(S)} A_{S'}\right).$$

The next lemma presents constant upper bounds on the sizes of independent sets in $\mathcal{I}(A_S^*)$ and $\mathcal{I}(N_S)$ for any any $S \in \mathcal{S}$. It is a direct consequence of Lemma 2.2, and its proof is omitted due to the lack of space.

LEMMA 4.2. *Consider any $S \in \mathcal{S}$. For any $I \in \mathcal{I}(A_S^*)$ and $J \in \mathcal{I}(N_S)$,*

$$|I| \leq \frac{16K^2}{\pi}\mu\overline{\tau},$$
$$|J| \leq \frac{16K}{\pi}\mu\overline{\tau}.$$

For any $B \subseteq A$ and any $J \in \mathcal{I}$, we denote

$$\mathcal{I}(B \mid J) = \{I \subseteq B : I \cup J \in \mathcal{I}\}$$

For each $S \in \mathcal{S}$ and each $J \in \mathcal{I}(N_S)$, we define

$$f_S(J) := \max_{I \in \mathcal{I}(A_S \mid J)} w(I).$$

Clearly, if S in a sink square then

$$f_S(J) = \max_{I \in \mathcal{I}\left(A_S^* \mid J\right)} w(I);$$

otherwise the following recursive relation holds:

$$f_S(J) = \max_{I \in \mathcal{I}\left(A_S^* \mid J\right)} \left[w(I) + \sum_{S' \in \mathcal{C}(S)} f_{S'}((I \cup J) \cap N_{S'})\right]$$

Furthermore,

$$\sum_{S \in \mathcal{S}_0} f_S(\emptyset) = \max_{I \in \mathcal{I}(A_k)} w(I).$$

The dynamic programming algorithm will build a (dynamic programming) table F_S for each $S \in \mathcal{S}$ which is indexed by the sets in $\mathcal{I}(N_S)$. For each $J \in \mathcal{I}(N_S)$, $F_S(J)$ stores a heaviest set in $\mathcal{I}(A_S \mid J)$. Then, $\bigcup_{S \in \mathcal{S}_0} F_S(\emptyset)$ is a heaviest independent set of A_k and is returned as I_k. By Lemma 4.2, for each $S \in \mathcal{S}$, we can compute $\mathcal{I}(A_S^* \mid J)$ and $\mathcal{I}(N_S)$ in polynomial time. Therefore, the tables F_S for $S \in \mathcal{S}$ can be constructed in the bottom-up manner along the directed forest on $\mathcal{S}$:

- Suppose that S is a leaf square in $\mathcal{S}$. For each $J \in \mathcal{I}(N_S)$, we compute
$$f_S(J) \leftarrow \max_{I \in \mathcal{I}\left(A_S^* \mid J\right)} w(I),$$
$$F_S(J) \leftarrow \arg \max_{I \in \mathcal{I}\left(A_S^* \mid J\right)} w(I).$$
- Suppose that S is a non-leaf square in $\mathcal{S}$. For each $J \in \mathcal{I}(N_S)$, we compute
$$f_S(J) \leftarrow \max_{I \in \mathcal{I}\left(A_S^* \mid J\right)} \left[w(I) + \sum_{S' \in \mathcal{C}(S)} f_{S'}((I \cup J) \cap N_{S'})\right],$$
$$I^* \leftarrow \arg \max_{I \in \mathcal{I}\left(A_S^* \mid J\right)} \left[w(I) + \sum_{S' \in \mathcal{C}(S)} f_{S'}((I \cup J) \cap N_{S'})\right],$$
$$F_S(J) \leftarrow I^* \cup \left(\bigcup_{S' \in \mathcal{C}(S)} F_{S'}((I^* \cup J) \cap N_{S'})\right).$$
- Finally, we output $\bigcup_{S \in \mathcal{S}_0} F_S(\emptyset)$ as I_k.

In summary, we have the following main result.

THEOREM 4.3. *When $\overline{\tau}$ is bounded by a constant, the problem **MWISS** admits a PTAS.*

5. DIVIDE AND CONQUER

Suppose that all streams have uniform interference radii but the nodes may have arbitrary number of antennas. In this setting, a simple spatial divide-and-conquer algorithm for **MWISS** to be described in this section achieves constant approximation bound.

By proper scaling, we assume that all streams have length at most one and (uniform) interference radii $r > 1$. Let A^+ be the set of streams in A with positive weight. The spatial division of A^+ is straightfoward. We tile the plane into regular hexagons of diameter $r - 1$ (see Figure 3(a)). Each hexagon, or cell, is considered to be left-closed and right-open, with only the left-most pair of vertices included (see Figure 3(b)). A stream is said to be associated with a cell if its sender lies in this cell. A cell is said to be non-empty if at least one stream in A^+ is associated with this cell. Those non-empty cells induce a partition of A^+. In Section 5.1, we describe the conquer part of the algorithm, which computes a heaviest weakly independent subset of streams in A^+ associated with each non-empty cell. In Section 5.1, we describe the combination part of the algorithm, which computes a constant-approximate independent set out of those weakly independent sets.

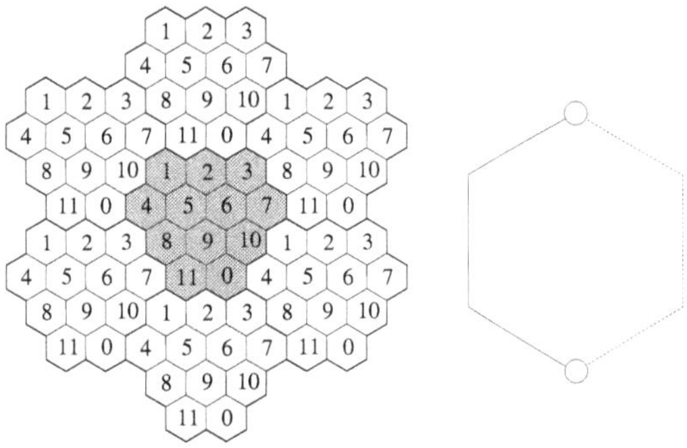

(a) (b)

Figure 3: Tiling of the plane into half-open half closed hexagons of diameter diameter $\rho - 1$.

5.1 Conquer

The conquer part of the algorithm computes a heaviest weakly independent subset of the streams in A^+ associated with each non-empty cell. Consider a particular non-empty cell and let B be the set of streams in A^+ associated with this cell. We present an algorithm which compute a heaviest weakly independent subset S of B.

Our algorithm proceeds in three steps. In the first step, we compute the distinct values of the number of antennas of receivers of the streams in B and sort them in the ascending order. Let $\tau_1, \tau_2, \cdots, \tau_k$ be resulting sorted sequence. In the second step, we compute a subset S_j for each $1 \leq j \leq k$ as follows. Let B_j denote the set of streams in B whose receivers have at least τ_j antennas, and U_j denote the set of senders of the streams in B_j. For each node $u \in U_j$, we only keep the

$$\min\left\{\left|\delta_{B_j}^{out}(u)\right|, \tau(u), \tau_j\right\}$$

heaviest streams in $\delta_{B_j}^{out}(u)$; and let B'_j be the set of these streams kept from B_j. Then, S_j consists of the $\min\left\{\left|B'_j\right|, \tau_j\right\}$ heaviest streams from B'_j, with ties broken arbitrarily. In the third step, the heaviest one among $S_1, S_2, \cdots, S_k$ as S.

Clearly, for each $1 \leq j \leq k$, S_j is a weakly independent subset of B_j. Thus, S is a weakly independent subset of B. The lemma below asserts that S is a heaviest one.

LEMMA 5.1. *S is a heaviest weakly independent subset of B.*

PROOF. For each $1 \leq j \leq k$, define $\mathcal{S}_j$ to be collection of subsets S of B_j satisfying that $|S| \leq \tau_j$ and $\left|\delta_S^{out}(u)\right| \leq \tau(u)$ for each $u \in U_j$. Then, $(B_j, \mathcal{S}_j)$ is a matroid (cf. [18]) on B_j. As S_j is computed by an alternative implementation of the matroid greedy algorithm [18], S_j is a heaviest subset in $\mathcal{S}_j$.

Now, let S^* be a heaviest weakly independent subset of B. Let τ_j be the smallest number of antennas of the receivers in S^*. Then, S^* is a subset of B_j and $S^* \in \mathcal{S}_j$. Thus,

$$w(S^*) \leq w(S_j) \leq w(S).$$

So, the lemma holds. □

5.2 Combination

The combination part of the algorithm makes use of a labelling of the cells satisfying that all cells with the same label are apart from each other at a distance of greater than $r+1$. Figure 3(a) gives one such labelling for $r = 2$. The labelling of the cells can be reduced to the labelling of lattice points. Specifically, we pick an arbitrary non-empty cell and use its center as the origin o. Let e_1 and e_2 be the centers of the straight right cell and the upper right cell respectively. Then, the centers of all the cells are integer combinations of e_1 and e_2. In other words, the centers of all cells form a lattice with e_1 and e_2 as a base. We adopt an oblique coordinate system with e_1 and e_2 as the base vectors, and represent each point $xe_1 + ye_2$ with the oblique coordinates $\left[\begin{smallmatrix} x \\ y \end{smallmatrix}\right]$. It's easy to verify that the squared distance from the origin to a point $\left[\begin{smallmatrix} a \\ b \end{smallmatrix}\right]$ is

$$\frac{3}{4}\left(x^2 + xy + y^2\right)(r-1)^2.$$

A number of the format $x^2 + xy + y^2$ with integers x and y is called *rhombic* number. Rhombic numbers can be characterized in an elegant way by their prime decomposition (see, e.g., [17]).

THEOREM 5.2. *A positive integer greater than one is rhombic if and only if, after removing all square factors, its prime decomposition contains no prime other than 3 and primes of the form $6i + 1$ with $i \in \mathbb{Z}$.*

A representation of a rhombic number λ is a point $\left[\begin{smallmatrix} x \\ y \end{smallmatrix}\right]$ satisfying that $x^2 + xy + y^2 = \lambda$. Among all representations of a rhombic number λ, there is at least one lattice point $x^2 + xy + y^2$ with $x \geq y \geq 0$, which is called a *positive representation* of λ. The rhombic numbers between 7 and 12 are $7, 9, 12$, and their positive representations are

$$\begin{bmatrix} 2 \\ 1 \end{bmatrix}, \begin{bmatrix} 3 \\ 0 \end{bmatrix}, \begin{bmatrix} 2 \\ 2 \end{bmatrix}$$

respectively.

Now, we describe the labelling of all the centers of the cells, which also gives rise to a labelling of the cells. Let λ be the smallest rhombic number at least $\frac{16}{3}\left(\frac{r}{r-1}\right)^2$, which decreases with r. It's easy to verify that for the practical applications with $r \geq 3$, $7 \leq \lambda \leq 12$. We then pick a positive representation $\left[\begin{smallmatrix} x \\ y \end{smallmatrix}\right]$ of λ from the list in the previous paragraph. Let

$$p_1 = \begin{bmatrix} a \\ b \end{bmatrix}, p_2 = \begin{bmatrix} -b \\ a+b \end{bmatrix}.$$

Let P be the half-open half-closed rhombus extended by p_1 and p_2, i.e.,

$$P = \{t_1 p_1 + t_2 p_1 : 0 \leq t_1, t_2 < 1\}.$$

It's well-known that P contains λ lattice points. All these lattice points in P receive distinct labels from the set $\{0, 1, \cdots, \lambda - 1\}$. Repeat the same assignment in other translates of P by the lattice points with p_1 and p_2 as the base. Thus, λ labels are used.

Note that the distance between any pair of lattice points with the same label is at least

$$\sqrt{x^2 + xy + y^2} \cdot \frac{\sqrt{3}}{2}(r-1) = \sqrt{\lambda} \cdot \frac{\sqrt{3}}{2}(r-1) \geq 2r.$$

Thus, for any pair of points in two cells with the same label, their distance is greater than $2r - (r-1) = r+1$. So, any pair of streams with senders in two cells of the same label have no conflict with each other.

Next, we describe the combination algorithm. For each label i between 0 and $\lambda - 1$, let J_i be the union of the heaviest weakly independent subsets of the streams associated with non-empty cells with label i. The heaviest one among them is then chosen as J. Finally, we apply the algorithm **ExtractIS** to extract an IS I from J.

THEOREM 5.3. *The output I is a 4λ-approximte solution.*

PROOF. Let O be an optimal solution. For each label i between 0 and $\lambda - 1$, let O_i be the subsets of the streams in O associated with the non-empty cells with label i. By Lemma 5.1, $w(O_i) \leq w(J_i)$. Hence,

$$w(O) = \sum_{i=0}^{\lambda-1} w(O_i) \leq \sum_{i=0}^{\lambda-1} w(J_i) \leq \lambda w(J) \leq 4\lambda w(I),$$

where the last inequality follows from Theorem 2.1. So, the theorem holds. □

6. LP RELAXATION AND ROUNDING

Suppose that all nodes have the same number of antennas but the streams may have arbitrary interference radii. In this setting, we present a constant-approximation approximation algorithm for **MWISS**. based on the linear programming (LP) approach.

Let τ be the number of antennas at each node, and A^+ be the set of streams in A with positive weight. We will makes use the following fact that for any subset J of A^+, if it satisfies the **Receiver Constraint**, then it also satisfies the **Sender Constraint**. Indeed, consider any node u which is a sender of some stream in J. Let a be a shortest stream with u as the sender. Then the receiver of a lies in the interference range of every stream in J with u as the sender (including a itself). Thus, the number of streams in J with u as the sender is at most τ. A consequence of this fact is that a subset J of A^+ is weakly independent if and only if it satisfies the **Receiver Constraint**.

For any pair of streams a and b in A^+, define $\rho(a,b)$ to be $1/\tau$ if the receiver of b lies within the interference range of a, and to be 0 otherwise. Our LP-based algorithm proceeds in four phases as described below.

Relaxation Phase: Compute an optimal solution x to the following linear program:

$$\begin{array}{lll} (FLP) & \max & \sum_{a \in B} w(a) x(a) \\ & s.t. & \sum_{b \in A^+ \setminus \{a\}} \rho(a,b) x(a) \leq \frac{1}{2}, \forall b \in A^+ \\ & & 0 \leq x(a) \leq 1, \forall a \in A^+. \end{array}$$

Rounding Phase: Initialize

$$B = \{a \in A^+ : 0 < x(a) < 1\}.$$

Repeat the following iteration while B is non-empty: Pick a link $a \in B$ and remove it from B. If

$$\sum_{b \in A^+ \setminus \{a\}} \left(\frac{w(b)}{w(a)} \rho(a,b) + \rho(b,a) \right) x(b) < 1,$$

set $x(a) = 1$; otherwise set $x(a) = 0$. At the end of this phase, x is $\{0,1\}$-valued.

Weakly IS Phase: Initialize

$$J = \{a \in A^+ : x(a) = 1\}.$$

While there exists some $a \in J$ satisfying that

$$\sum_{b \in J \setminus \{a\}} \rho(b,a) \geq 1,$$

remove any such link a from J and reset $x(a)$ to 0. At the end of this phase, J is weakly independent by Lemma 2.3,.

IS Phase: Apply the algorithm **ExtractIS** to extract an independent set I from J.

The theorem below provides an approximation bound of the output I.

THEOREM 6.1. *The output I is a 16μ-approximate solution.*

PROOF. We define a real-valued function f on the set of $x \in [0,1]^{A^+}$ to real numbers by

$$f(x) = \sum_{a \in A^+} w(a) x(a) \left(1 - \sum_{b \in A^+ \setminus \{a\}} \rho(b,a) x(b) \right).$$

Then for each $a \in A^+$, f is a linear function of $x(a)$ with slope

$$\begin{aligned} & w(a) - \sum_{b \in A^+ \setminus \{a\}} (\rho(b,a) w(a) + \rho(a,b) w(b)) x(b) \\ & = w(a) \left(1 - \sum_{b \in A^+ \setminus \{a\}} \left(\frac{w(b)}{w(a)} \rho(a,b) + \rho(b,a) \right) x(b) \right). \end{aligned}$$

Let *opt* be the weight of heaviest independent subset of B. We shall show that at the end of **Relaxation Phase**,

$$f(x) \geq \frac{1}{4\mu} opt,$$

and after each update on x during **Rounding Phase** and **Weakly IS Phase**, $f(x)$ is non-decreasing. As the result, at the end of **Weakly IS Phase**, the weakly IS J satisfies that

$$w(J) = \sum_{a\in A^+} w(a)\,x(a) \geq f(x) \geq \frac{1}{4\mu}opt.$$

By Theorem 2.1, the final output I satisfies that

$$w(I) \geq \frac{1}{4}w(J) \geq \frac{1}{16\mu}opt.$$

Hence the theorem holds.

We first show that at the end of **Relaxation Phase**,

$$f(x) \geq \frac{1}{4\mu}opt.$$

Let O be an optimal solution and define $y \in [0,1]^{A^+}$ by

$$y(a) = \begin{cases} \frac{1}{2\mu}, & \text{if } a \in O; \\ 0, & \text{otherwise.} \end{cases}$$

By Lemma 2.2, for each $b \in A^+$,

$$\begin{aligned} &\sum_{a\in A^+\setminus\{b\}} \rho(a,b)\,y(a) = \frac{1}{2\mu}\sum_{a\in O\setminus\{b\}} \rho(a,b) \\ &= \frac{1}{2\mu}\rho(O\setminus\{b\},b) \leq \frac{1}{2\mu}\mu = \frac{1}{2}. \end{aligned}$$

So, y is a feasible solution to the linear program defined in **Relaxation Phase** and its value is

$$\sum_{a\in A^+} w(a)\,y(a) = \frac{1}{2\mu}\sum_{a\in O} w(a) = \frac{1}{2\mu}opt.$$

Since x is an optimal solution to the same linear program,

$$\sum_{a\in A^+} w(a)\,x(a) \geq \frac{1}{2\mu}opt.$$

Since for each $a \in A^+$,

$$1 - \sum_{b\in A^+\setminus\{a\}} \rho(b,a)\,x(b) \geq 1 - \frac{1}{2} \geq \frac{1}{2},$$

we have

$$\begin{aligned} f(x) &= \sum_{a\in A^+} w(a)\,x(a)\left(1 - \sum_{b\in A^+\setminus\{a\}} \rho(b,a)\,x(b)\right) \\ &\geq \frac{1}{2}\sum_{a\in A^+} w(a)\,x(a) \geq \frac{1}{4\mu}opt. \end{aligned}$$

Next, we show that $f(x)$ is non-decreasing with the iterations during **Rounding Phase**. Consider a particular iteration of **Rounding Phase** and let a be the link picked and them removed from B. If

$$\sum_{b\in A^+\setminus\{a\}} \left(\frac{w(b)}{w(a)}\rho(a,b) + \rho(b,a)\right) x(b) < 1,$$

then the slope of f with respect to $x(a)$ is positive and hence by increasing $x(a)$ to 1, $f(x)$ increases; otherwise, the slope of f with respect to $x(a)$ is non-postive and hence by decreasing $x(a)$ to 0, $f(x)$ either increases or remains unchanged. So, in either case, $f(x)$ is non-decreasing after each iteration during **Rounding Phase**.

Finally, we show that $f(x)$ is non-decreasing with the iterations during **Weakly IS Phase**. Consider a particular iteration of of **Weakly IS Phase** and let a be the link picked and then removed from J. Since

$$\sum_{b\in J\setminus\{a\}} \rho(b,a) \geq 1,$$

we have

$$\begin{aligned} &\sum_{b\in A^+\setminus\{a\}} \left(\frac{w(b)}{w(a)}\rho(a,b) + \rho(b,a)\right) x(b) \\ &= \sum_{b\in J\setminus\{a\}} \left(\frac{w(b)}{w(a)}\rho(a,b) + \rho(b,a)\right) \\ &\geq \sum_{b\in J\setminus\{a\}} \rho(b,a) \geq 1. \end{aligned}$$

So, the slope of f with respect to $x(a)$ is non-positive; and hence by resetting $x(a)$ from 1 to 0, $f(x)$ either increases or remains unchanged. □

7. DISCUSSIONS

In this paper, we have conducted a comprehensive algorithmic study of **MWISS** in multihop wireless MIMO networks with receiver-side interference suppression:

- Both the NP-hardness and APX-hardness were fully characterized.
- In the setting of constant bounded number of antennas at all nodes, a PTAS was developed.
- In the setting of uniform interference radii but arbitrary number of antennas, a practical constant-approximation algorithm based on the divide-and-conquer approach was developed.
- In the setting of uniform number of antennas but arbitrary interference radii, a practical constant-approximation algorithm based on the LP approach was developed.

It remains open whether there exists a practical constant-approximation algorithm in the most general setting of arbitrary interference radii and arbitrary number of antennas.

Following the approach in [22], we can develop approximation-preserving reductions from the following three problems to **MWISS**:

- **Minimum Latency Stream Schedule** (MLSS): Given a set of data traffic demands on individual links, find a shortest stream schedule for this set of traffic demands.
- **Maximum Multiflow** (MMF): Given a set of end-to-end communication requests specified by source-destination pairs, find a stream schedule of length one such that the maximum multiflow subject to the link capacity function determined by this stream schedule is maximized.
- **Maximum Concurrent Multiflow** (MCMF): Given a set of end-to-end communication requests specified by source-destination pairs together with

their demands, find a stream schedule of length one such that the maximum concurrent multiflow subject to the link capacity function determined by this stream schedule is maximized.

Therefore, all of the above three problems can be approximated with the same approximation factor as **MWISS**. The detail will be reported in a separate paper.

ACKNOWLEDGEMENTS: This work was supported in part by the National Science Foundation of USA under grants CNS-1219109 and CNS-1217309.

8. REFERENCES

[1] G. Ausiello, P. Crescenzi, G. Gambosi, V. Kann, A. Marchetti-Spaccamela, and M. Protasi. *Complexity and Approximation: Combinatorial optimization problems and their approximability properties*, Springer-Verlag, 1999.

[2] R. Bhatia and L. Li, Throughput Optimization of Wireless Mesh Networks with MIMO Links, *Proceedings of the IEEE INFOCOM* Mini-conference 2007, pp. 2326–2330.

[3] D. Blough, G. Resta, P. Santi, R. Srinivasan, and L.M. Cortes-Pea, Optimal One-Shot Scheduling for Multihop MIMO Networks, Proceedings of the *IEEE SECON* 2011, pp. 1–9.

[4] S. Chu and X. Wang, Opportunistic and Cooperative Spatial Multiplexing in MIMO Ad Hoc Networks, *Proc. ACM MobiHoc* 2008, pp. 63–72.

[5] S. Chu and X. Wang, MIMO-Aware Routing in Wireless Mesh Networks, *Proceedings of the IEEE INFOCOM* 2010, pp. 1–9.

[6] A. Gkelias, F. Boccardi, C.H. Liu, and K.K. Leung, MIMO routing with QoS provisioning, *Proc. ISWPC* 2008, pages 46–50.

[7] B. Hamdaoui, K. Shin, D. Jiang, Characterization and Analysis of Multi-Hop Wireless MIMO Network Throughput, *Proc. ACM MobiHoc* 2007, pp. 120–129.

[8] B. Han, V. S. A. Kumar, M. V. Marathe, S. Parthasarathy, and A. Srinivasan, Distributed Strategies for Channel Allocation and Scheduling in Software-Defined Radio Networks, *Proc. IEEE INFOCOM* 2009, pp. 1521–1529.

[9] F. Havet, R.J. Kang, J.-S. Sereni, Improper coloring of unit disk graphs, Networks 54(3): 150–164, 2009.

[10] M. Hu and J. Zhang, MIMO Ad Hoc Networks: Medium Access Control, Saturation Throughput and Optimal Hop Distance, *Journal of Communications and Networks*, Special Issue on Mobile Ad Hoc Networks, pages 317–330, Dec. 2004.

[11] R. M. Karp, Reducibility Among Combinatorial Problems. *Complexity of Computer Computations*, R.E. Miller and J.W. Thatcher, Eds., page 85-103. Plenum Press, New York, 1972.

[12] M. Lampis, G. Kaouri, and V. Mitsou, On the Algorithmic Effectiveness of Digraph Decompositions and Complexity Measures. *ISAAC* 2008, Lecture Notes in Computer Science 5369, Springer, pp. 220–231.

[13] X. Lin and S. Rasool, A Distributed Joint Channel-Assignment, Scheduling and Routing Algorithm for Multi-Channel Ad-hoc Wireless Networks, *Proc. IEEE INFOCOM* 2009, pp. 1118-1126.

[14] J. Liu, Y.T. Hou, Y. Shi, and H. Sherali, Cross-Layer Optimization for MIMO-Based Wireless Ad Hoc Networks: Routing, Power Allocation, and Bandwidth Allocation, *IEEE Journal on Selected Areas in Communications* (6):913–926, August 2008.

[15] J. Liu, Y. Shi, and Y.T. Hou, A Tractable and Accurate Cross-Layer Model for Multi-hop MIMO Networks, *Proc. IEEE INFOCOM* 2010, pp. 1–9.

[16] B. Mumey, J. Tang, and T. Hahn, Algorithmic Aspects of Communications in Multihop Wireless Networks with MIMO Links, *Proc. IEEE ICC* 2010, pp. 1–6.

[17] I. Niven, H.S. Zuckerman, and H.L. Montgomery, *An introduction to the theory of numbers* 5th ed., Wiley, 1991.

[18] A. Schrijver, *Combinatorial Optimization: Polyhedra and Efficiency.* Algorithms and Combinatorics, Vol. 24, Springer, Berlin, 2003.

[19] K. Sundaresan, R. Sivakumar, M. Ingram, and T-Y. Chang, Medium Access Control in Ad Hoc Networks with MIMO links: Optimization Considerations and Algorithms, *IEEE Transactions on Mobile Computing*, vol. 3, no. 4, pp. 350-365, 2004.

[20] K. Sundaresan and R. Sivakumar, Routing in ad-hoc networks with MIMO links, *Proc. IEEE ICNP* 2005, pages 85–98.

[21] E.J. van Leeuwen, Better Approximation Schemes for Disk Graphs, *Proc. SWAT 2006*, Lecture Notes in Computer Science 4059, Springer, pp. 316–327.

[22] P.-J. Wan, Multiflows in Multihop Wireless Networks, *ACM MOBIHOC* 2009, pp. 85-94.

[23] P.-J. Wan, Y. Cheng, Z. Wang, and F. Yao, Multiflows in Multi-Channel Multi-Radio Multihop Wireless Networks, *IEEE INFOCOM* 2011.

[24] P.-J. Wan, Z. Wang, L. Wang, Z.G. Wan, and S. Ji, From Least Interference-Cost Paths to Maximum (Concurrent) Multiflow in MC-MR Wireless Networks, *IEEE INFOCOM* 2014.

[25] Y. Wang, D-M. Chiu, J.C.S. Lui, Characterizing the Capacity Gain of Stream Control Scheduling in MIMO Wireless Mesh Networks, *Wireless Communications and Mobile Computing*, vol. 9, no. 6, pp. 819–829, 2009.

[26] M. Zorzi, J. Zeidler, A. Anderson, B. Rao, J. Proakis, A.L. Swindlehurst, M. Jensen, and S. Krishnamurthy, Cross-Layer Issues in MAC Protocol Design for MIMO Ad Hoc Networks, *IEEE Wireless Communication Magzine* (4):62–76, August 2006.

Fully Distributed Algorithms for Blind Rendezvous in Cognitive Radio Networks

Zhaoquan Gu
Institute for Interdisciplinary Information Sciences
Tsinghua University
Beijing, 100084, P.R. China
demin456@gmail.com

Qiang-Sheng Hua
Institute for Interdisciplinary Information Sciences
Tsinghua University
Beijing, 100084, P.R. China
qshua@mail.tsinghua.edu.cn

Weiguo Dai
Institute for Interdisciplinary Information Sciences
Tsinghua University
Beijing, 100084, P.R. China
daiweiguo@yeah.net

ABSTRACT

Rendezvous process is the cornerstone to construct Cognitive Radio Networks (CRNs), through which a secondary user can establish a link for communication with its neighbor on a common channel. Although many blind rendezvous algorithms have been proposed which do not rely on a central controller or a common control channel, all of these works still rely on the global parameters such as the number of licensed channels N and the number of users. This paper aims to design fully distributed blind rendezvous algorithms only based on each user's local information. We first give the Synchronous Check & Hop (SCH) algorithm for two synchronous users where they start the rendezvous process at the same time. The SCH algorithm guarantees rendezvous in $O(\min\{k_a, k_b\}N)$ time slots where k_a, k_b are the corresponding number of sensed channels of these two users. Our main contribution is a fully distributed algorithm called Conversion Based Hopping (CBH), where each user only uses its identifier (ID) and its number of sensed channels. CBH guarantees rendezvous between two asynchronous users in $O((\max\{k_a, k_b\})^2)$ time slots. To our knowledge, this is the first result with rendezvous time independent of the global parameter N. We also derive a lower bound of rendezvous time between two users as $\Omega((k_a - k_g)(k_b - k_g))$ where k_g is the number of their common channels. All of our results also apply to a more general blind rendezvous problem which we call *Oblivious Blind Rendezvous* where each user is free to assign their local labels to the sensed channels. Extensive simulation results compared with the state-of-the-art rendezvous algorithms corroborate our theoretical analyses.

Categories and Subject Descriptors

C.2.1 [**Computer-Communication Networks**]: Network Architecture and Design—*Wireless communication*; C.2.4 [**Computer-Communication Networks**]: Distributed Systems—*Distributed applications*

Keywords

cognitive radio networks; blind rendezvous; distributed algorithm

1. INTRODUCTION

1.1 Blind Rendezvous in Cognitive Radio Networks

Cognitive Radio Network (CRN) is a promising paradigm to solve the spectrum scarcity problem [1], which consists of primary users (PUs) who own the licensed spectrum and secondary users (SUs) who can opportunistically exploit and access the portion of unused licensed spectrum without causing interference to PUs. Unless otherwise specified, 'users' mentioned hereafter in the paper refers to SUs.

Many interesting problems in CRN have been studied, such as neighbor discovery [7, 25], data gathering [5], routing [12], and broadcasting [23]. *Rendezvous* is a fundamental process of these problems where the users attempt to establish a link for communication on a common frequency band (channel) [18]. Some previous works simplify this process by adopting a central controller or a Common Control Channel (CCC), but they incur a bottleneck when an increasing number of users rely on it. Moreover, such centralization is vulnerable to adversary attacks and is not flexible in practical situations. Therefore, many *blind rendezvous* algorithms have been proposed with no centralization [6, 11, 17, 21].

More specifically, all these blind rendezvous algorithms assume the licensed spectrum is divided into N non-overlapping channels with fixed labels $\{1, 2, \ldots, N\}$, and each user can sense the channel not occupied by any nearby PUs as an *available channel*. Time is divided into slots of equal length and each user can access an available channel in each time slot. Rendezvous is achieved only when the users access the same channel in the same time slot. All the extant blind rendezvous algorithms assume they know the global parameter N and the labels of these N channels, some works [6] also assume each user knows the number of users in the network.

Nevertheless, the above assumptions may not be that practical when designing blind rendezvous algorithms. In the first place, all users may not see the same labels for the licensed channels. For example, the 'TV white space' that could be sensed by the users has operating frequencies ranging from $470 - 790$ MHz in Europe [9, 19], but it's located in the VHF (i.e. very high frequency) ($54 - 216$ MHz) and UHF (i.e. ultra high frequency) ($470 - 698$ MHz) bands in the United States [10]. Obviously, the labeling of this space could be different and the same frequency band (channel) may be assigned different labels under different administrations. Secondly, no general standard exists dividing the total licensed spectrum into N channels (for example, IEEE 802.11af only operates frequencies ranging $470 - 710$ MHz [10]), it's impractical for the users to know the N value. Thirdly, all users are physically dispersed in the network and they may join or leave freely, they cannot know the number of users beforehand as no central controller is adopted.

In this paper, we assume the scenario where there is a set of channels within some licensed spectrum that can be sensed by the users, but there is no common labeling that is seen by all users. This is a more general assumption and each user can assign their own labels to its sensed available channels. Without such a common labeling, blind rendezvous becomes much harder since the same frequency band (channel) may have different labels for two users. We call this kind of blind rendezvous as ***oblivious blind rendezvous***. All previous blind rendezvous algorithms are *non-oblivious* where the users see the same labels for the channels and it's a special case of oblivious blind rendezvous. As listed in Table 1, all previous algorithms depend on the global parameters N, M (the largest user ID) and we aim to design ***fully distributed algorithms*** for oblivious blind rendezvous where the users don't know the number of licensed channels (N) and the number of users in the CRN, i.e. only each user's local information can be used. In this paper, this kind of local information is limited to each user's identifier (ID) and the number of available channels each user has.

Oblivious Blind Rendezvous is promising in designing large scale network systems where global information is hard to obtain for the users. However, we face the following challenges in designing fully distributed algorithms for oblivious blind rendezvous. First of all, because each user may have different labels for the channels, traditional methods based on the channels' labels cannot be applied at all. Second, each user doesn't know the number of total licensed channels and the number of users, it's impossible to design global information based algorithms [11]. Third, each user can join the network at any time, and thus algorithms should guarantee the rendezvous for asynchronous users where they may start the rendezvous process at any time. Fourth, the user cannot obtain other users' (even neighbors') information until rendezvous is achieved for communication, thus ***symmetric algorithms*** are preferable, which means all users should execute the same algorithm. In this paper, our proposed algorithms address all these issues.

1.2 Contributions and Paper Organization

In this paper, we design fully distributed algorithms for oblivious blind rendezvous problem between two users and it can be extended smoothly to multiuser multihop scenarios as in [11]. In the first place, we derive a lower bound of oblivious blind rendezvous between two users as $\Omega((k_a - k_g) \cdot (k_b - k_g))$, where k_a, k_b are the number of two users' available channels respectively, and k_g is the number of channels they have in common. Following the lower bound, we introduce a deterministic distributed algorithm called Synchronous Check & Hop (SCH) for two synchronous users, which generates different hopping sequences for the users based on the distinct identifiers. Our main contribution is a fully distributed algorithm called Conversion Based Hopping (CBH) algorithm, which builds on the idea of SCH and guarantees oblivious blind rendezvous between two asynchronous users only based on the user's identifier (ID) and its number of available channels. SCH guarantees rendezvous in $O(\min\{k_a, k_b\}N)$ time slots, and the $MTTR$ value (i.e. Maximum Time to Rendezvous, defined in Section 3) for CBH is bounded by $O((\max\{k_a, k_b\})^2)$ time slots, which is comparable to the lower bound if $k_a = \Theta(k_b)$ and $k_g = o(\max\{k_a, k_b\})$. More importantly, our CBH algorithm is the first result with bounded rendezvous time independent of the global parameter N. Finally, we compare our algorithms with the state-of-the-art rendezvous algorithms through extensive simulations to validate our theoretical analyses. Note that although our algorithms are designed for oblivious blind rendezvous, our results can be applied to traditional non-oblivious blind rendezvous (Table 1) since the latter is a special case of the former problem.

The remainder of the paper is organized as follows. The next section highlights some related work on blind rendezvous. The system model and problem definitions are provided in Section 3. We derive the lower bound of oblivious blind rendezvous between two users in Section 4. The deterministic distributed algorithm for two synchronous users is described in Section 5, and the asynchronous algorithm is proposed in Section 6. Extensive simulations are presented in Section 7 and we conclude the paper in Section 8.

Table 1: MTTR Comparison

Algorithms	Non-Oblivious Blind Rendezvous	Oblivious Blind Rendezvous
Jump-Stay [17]	$3NP^2 + 3P = O(N^3)$	–
Enhanced JS [16]	$4P^2 = O(N^2)$	–
CRSEQ [21]	$P(3P-1) = O(N^2)$	–
DRDS [11]	$3P^2 + 2P = O(N^2)$	–
AHW [6]	$O(N^2 \log M)$	–
MMC [24]	$ETTR = O(N^2)$	$ETTR = O(N^2)$
SCH (this paper)	$O(\min\{k_a, k_b\}N)$	$O(\min\{k_a, k_b\}N)$
CBH (this paper)	$O((\max\{k_a, k_b\})^2)$	$O((\max\{k_a, k_b\})^2)$

Remarks: 1) "–" means the algorithm is not applicable to oblivious blind rendezvous; 2) ETTR means expected time to rendezvous (note: MMC cannot guarantee rendezvous in bounded time); 3) P is the smallest prime number larger than N, $P = O(N)$. 4) k_a and k_b denote the numbers of two users' available channels; 5) SCH in this paper is only suitable for synchronous users.

2. RELATED WORK

2.1 Non-Oblivious Rendezvous Algorithms

Most previous works aiming at non-oblivious rendezvous algorithms can be classified into three categories: centralized algorithms, decentralized algorithms based on Common Control Channel (CCC) and blind rendezvous algorithms.

Centralized algorithms assume a central controller or a CCC exists during the process to simplify the problem [14, 20]. However, the central controller or the CCC could be a bottleneck in practical situations and it's vulnerable to any adversary attacks. Some decentralized algorithms are proposed to establish local CCCs to communicate with the neighbors [13, 15]. Nevertheless, these algorithms incur too much overhead in establishing and maintaining such local CCCs.

Therefore, blind rendezvous algorithms without any CCC have been attracting the attention of many researchers. The main technique used is Channel Hopping (CH), where each user hops among the sensed available channels in different time slot on the basis of certain pre-generated CH sequence, and rendezvous can be achieved once the users hop on the same channel in the same time slot. Several state-of-the-art results are listed in Table 1.

Generated Orthogonal Sequence (GOS) [8] is a pioneering work, which generates an orthogonal sequence of length $N(N+1)$ based on the random permutations of $\{1, 2, \cdots, N\}$. However, GOS is limited to the scenario where all channels are not occupied by PUs and all users can access them. Quorum-based Channel Hopping (QCH) [2,3] works for synchronous users making using of quorum systems, while the enhanced Asynchronous QCH [4] suits for two asynchronous users, but only applicable to two channels.

Jump-Stay (JS) [17], Channel Rendezvous Sequence (CRSEQ) [21], and Disjoint Relaxed Difference Set (DRDS) [11] are three efficient blind rendezvous algorithms. JS generates a sequence of length $O(N^3)$ for each user with *jump*-pattern and *stay*-pattern. Two users are guaranteed to rendezvous in $O(N^3)$ time slots in one of four possible pattern combinations: jump-jump, jump-stay, stay-jump, stay-stay. This result is later improved to $O(N^2)$ as Enhanced JS in [16]. CRSEQ constructs a sequence of $O(N^2)$ numbers on the basis of triangle number (i.e. $T_i = \frac{i(i+1)}{2}$ when $i \in [1, N]$) and modular operations, such that the users repeating the sequence could meet on the same channel quickly. DRDS-based rendezvous algorithm is a new method guaranteeing rendezvous in $O(N^2)$ time slots, by designing a DRDS and transforming the set into a CH sequence. Moreover, a lower bound $\Omega(N^2)$ is also derived in [11] for such blind rendezvous algorithms. Alternate Hop-and-Wait (AHW) [6] generates different sequences for different users with distinct identifiers, such that the users can achieve rendezvous in $O(N^2 \log M)$ time slots where M is the maximum ID value.

2.2 Oblivious Blind Rendezvous Algorithms

Though various algorithms have been proposed for non-oblivious blind rendezvous process in CRN, very few results can be applied to oblivious blind rendezvous problem. Modified Modular Clock (MMC) [24] is the only algorithm which may achieve oblivious blind rendezvous between two users with high probability. MMC constructs a sequence based on $k \leq P \leq 2k$ and some modular operations of a rate value $r < P$, where k is the number of available channels. Nevertheless, MMC cannot guarantee bounded rendezvous. As a step forward, this papers offers fully distributed deterministic algorithms that guarantee oblivious blind rendezvous in bounded time.

3. MODEL AND PROBLEM DEFINITIONS

3.1 System Model

We study a more general blind rendezvous problem in Cognitive Radio Networks (CRNs) called oblivious blind rendezvous with m ($m \geq 2$) users, where each user has a unique identifier (ID) ranging in $[1, M]$ (here M means the maximum value for the users' ID and we assume M is bounded as $M = N^c$, where c could be an arbitrary large constant). The total licensed spectrum is assumed to be divided into N non-overlapping channels as $U = \{u_1, u_2, \cdots, u_N\}$, where u_i represents certain frequency band (e.g. 470 − 478 MHz in TV white space). Each user is equipped with cognitive radios to sense the licensed spectrum and a frequency band (channel) is *available* to a particular user if it's not occupied by any nearby PUs. Because we consider the scenario no central entity exists, all users don't know the label for each frequency band (i.e. they don't know the set U), the number of total licensed channels N, the number of network users m and the maximum ID value M.

After the spectrum sensing, each user can figure out the available frequency bands (channels) and it labels them locally from 1 to k, where k is the number of available channels. For two different users A and B, rewrite the available channel sets as $C_a = \{c_a(1), c_a(2), \ldots, c_a(k_a)\}$ and $C_b = \{c_b(1), c_b(2), \ldots, c_b(k_b)\}$, where k_a, k_b represent the number of available channels for two users, respectively. Each channel $c_a(i) \in C_a$ or $c_b(i) \in C_b$ represents an available frequency band, but $c_a(i)$ and $c_b(i)$ do not necessarily mean the same band (see the example in Fig. 1).

Assume time is divided into slots of equal length $2t$, where t is the time duration for establishing a link for communication if the users access the same channel. According to IEEE 802.22 [22], $t = 10$ ms and thus each time slot has a fixed duration of 20 ms. The idea of setting each time slot to be $2t$ is natural because the network then can be made slot-aligned since $2t$ is sufficient to ensure an overlap of t for link establishment even if the start time of different users is not slot-aligned.

In each time slot, each user can access an available channel and attempt rendezvous with its potential neighbors. *Time to Rendezvous* (*TTR*) denotes the number of time slots cost to achieve rendezvous once all users have begun the process. Since the users are dispersed physically and they may begin the rendezvous process in different time slots, the proposed algorithms should be applicable to both synchronous (i.e. all users start the process at the same time) and asynchronous scenarios. We use *Maximum Time to Rendezvous* (*MTTR*) to evaluate the efficiency of rendezvous algorithms.

3.2 Problem Definition

The *Oblivious Blind Rendezvous Problem* (OBRP) is defined as: Consider a multihop CRN with $m (m \geq 2)$ users where each user has a distinct ID $I \in [1, M]$. Denote the available channel set for user i as $C_i = \{c_i(1), c_i(2), \cdots, c_i(k_i)\}$ where $k_i = |C_i|$. Let $G = \bigcap_i C_i$ and $G \neq \emptyset$. Design a distributed algorithm for the users such that all users are guaranteed to rendezvous on the same channel, regardless of different time when the users begin the process.

The difference between OBRP and non-oblivious blind rendezvous problem is the users don't necessarily see the same labels for the frequency bands. All previous results are designed for non-oblivious blind rendezvous which is a special case of OBRP. Our goal is to design a fully distributed algorithm for OBRP where each user only knows its limited local information: the unique ID and the available frequency bands (channels) (in fact, the available channels set implies only the number of available channels can be used since there is no common labels seen by all users). In this paper, we focus on the rendezvous between two users (OBRP-2) and these algorithms can be extended to multiuser multihop networks as in [11,17].

OBRP-2: Given an available channel set $C \subseteq U$ and the ID $I \in [1, M]$, design the algorithm to access channels over different time slots t : $f_{C,I}(t) \in C$ such that for any two users A and B with $C_a, C_b \subseteq U, C_a \bigcap C_b \neq \emptyset$ and ID $I_a, I_b \in [1, M], I_a \neq I_b$ respectively,

$$\forall \delta, \exists T_\delta, \ s.t. \ f_{C_a,I_a}(T_\delta + \delta) = f_{C_b,I_b}(T_\delta). \tag{1}$$

The TTR value is T_δ when user B starts the rendezvous process δ time slots later than user A. The $MTTR$ value of the algorithm is $MTTR_f = \max_{\forall \delta} T_\delta$ and our goal is to design such algorithms with bounded $MTTR$ to guarantee rendezvous between two users.

User A

Time_a	0	1	2	3	4	5	6	7
Sequence	$c_a(1)$	$c_a(1)$	$c_a(2)$	$c_a(2)$	$c_a(1)$	$c_a(1)$	$c_a(2)$	$c_a(2)$
Channel	u_1	u_1	u_3	u_3	u_1	u_1	u_3	u_3

User B

Time_b	0	1	2	3	4	5	6	7
Sequence	$c_b(1)$	$c_b(2)$	$c_b(3)$	$c_b(4)$	$c_b(1)$	$c_b(2)$	$c_b(3)$	$c_b(4)$
Channel	u_5	u_4	u_2	u_1	u_5	u_4	u_2	u_1

Figure 1: An example of OBRP-2

Fig. 1 is an example for OBRP-2. Assume there are 5 licensed channels as: $U = \{u_1, u_2, u_3, u_4, u_5\}$, of which u_1, u_3 are available channels sensed by user A with ID $I_a = 1$ as $C_a = \{c_a(1), c_a(2)\}$:

$$c_a(1) = u_1, c_a(2) = u_3;$$

while u_1, u_2, u_4, u_5 are sensed available by user B with ID $I_b = 2$ as $C_b = \{c_b(1), c_b(2), c_b(3), c_b(4)\}$:

$$c_b(1) = u_5, c_b(2) = u_4, c_b(3) = u_2, c_b(4) = u_1$$

Consider a simple algorithm: user A repeats accessing the channels by sequence $\{c_a(1), c_a(1), c_a(2), c_a(2)\}$ while user B accesses channels by sequence $\{c_b(1), c_b(2), c_b(3), c_b(4)\}$. When user B starts the process $\delta = 2$ time slots later, rendezvous can be achieved on channel u_1 with $TTR = 4$ when $c_a(1) = c_b(4) = u_1$, as illustrated in Fig. 1.

However, it's easy to check that the above simple algorithm cannot guarantee rendezvous for all scenarios such as $\delta = 0$. Thus we aim to design deterministic distributed algorithm with bounded $MTTR$ value for both synchronous and asynchronous users.

4. LOWER BOUND FOR OBRP-2

Since the users have distinct IDs, different sequences may be generated by different users to access channels, which implies good algorithms could be made with small $MTTR$ value. However, we demonstrate that the $MTTR$ value for any deterministic algorithms could be $\Omega((k_a - k_g) \cdot (k_b - k_g))$ for the worst case situation, where k_a, k_b are the number of available channels for two asynchronous users and k_g is the number of common channels they share.

For any deterministic algorithm $\mathcal{F}$ (i.e. no randomization is involved) to OBRP-2, let a_t, b_t be the channels to access in time slot t when the users run the algorithm with inputs $(I_a, C_a), (I_b, C_b)$, respectively. It's obvious that a_t, b_t depend on the inputs and the previous results as:

$$\begin{aligned} a_t &= \mathcal{F}(a_0, a_1, \cdots, a_{t-1}, I_a, C_a) \\ b_t &= \mathcal{F}(b_0, b_1, \cdots, b_{t-1}, I_b, C_b) \end{aligned}$$

We derive the lower bound as follows:

THEOREM 1. *For any deterministic algorithm $\mathcal{F}$ solving the oblivious blind rendezvous problem between two users with $(I_a, C_a), (I_b, C_b), C_a \bigcap C_b \neq \emptyset, I_a \neq I_b$, there exist mappings $f_a : C_a \mapsto U_a \subseteq U$ and $f_b : C_b \mapsto U_b \subseteq U$ such that the $MTTR$ value is $\Omega((k_a - k_g) \cdot (k_b - k_g))$ where $k_a = |C_a|, k_b = |C_b|, k_g = |C_a \bigcap C_b|$.*

PROOF. Consider the scenario when two users (A and B) start $\mathcal{F}$ at the same time, without loss of generality, let $U_g = \{u_1, u_2, \cdots, u_g\}$ be the common channels they share.

We introduce the Adversary Assignment Graph (AAG) as shown in Fig. 2. There are two rows of nodes in the graph. The number of the upper row is k_a while the other row's number of nodes is k_b, where each row represents the available channels of each user. For each time slot t, connect (a_t, b_t) in the graph if they are not connected before t, where a_t corresponds a node in the upper row and b_t is in the lower row. As shown in Fig. 2, $(c_a(1), c_b(1))$, $(c_a(1), c_b(2))$, $(c_a(2), c_b(3))$, $(c_a(3), c_b(2))$, $\cdots$ are connected and at most one edge is added to the graph in each time slot.

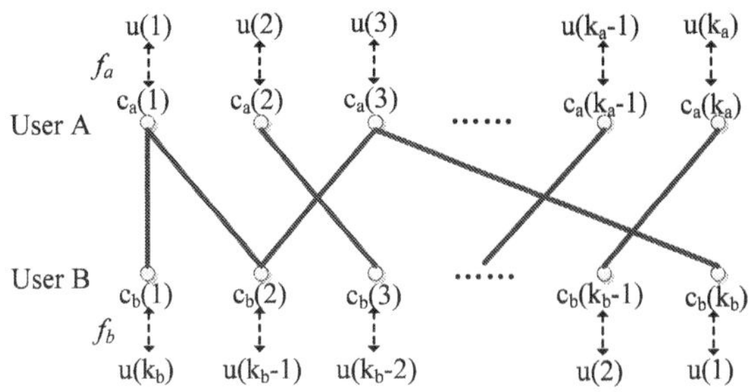

Figure 2: Adversary Assignment Graph

Assume there exists an adversary who can assign any channel $c_a(i) \in C_a$ or $c_b(j) \in C_b$ to any frequency band (channel) $u' \in U$ at any time slot t. As shown in Fig. 2, the adversary maps every channel in C_a as $f_a : c_a(i) \mapsto u(i)$ and C_b as $f_b : c_b(i) \mapsto u(k_b + 1 - i)$. Rendezvous is not achieved if there exists such an assignment that $\forall u' \in U_g$, u' in the upper row is not connected to u' in the lower row. Thus the lower bound of the $MTTR$ value is the smallest t such that for every adversary assignment, there exists $u' \in U_g$ such that (u', u') is connected in the graph.

We demonstrate that rendezvous can't be guaranteed in $t < (k_a - k_g)(k_b - k_g)$ time slots. Denote $A_t = \{a_0, a_1, \cdots, a_t\}$, $B_t = \{b_0, b_1, \cdots, b_t\}$ and construct the AAG described above. Let $\delta_a(i)$ be the degree of node $c_a(i)$ and sort these nodes of the upper row in ascending order as $c_a(1'), c_a(2'), \cdots, c_a(k_a')$ where $\delta_a(1') \leq \delta_a(2') \leq \cdots \leq \delta_a(k_a')$. It can be verified that $\delta_a(i') \leq (k_b - k_g), \forall 1 \leq i \leq k_g$ from the Pigeonhole Principle. Assign these k_g nodes to the universal channels in U_g as:

$$f_a : c_a(i') \mapsto u_i \in U_g, \forall 1 \leq i \leq k_g.$$

When i increases from 1 to k_g, find a node $c_b(\hat{i})$ from the lower row corresponding to node $c_a(i')$ such that $(c_a(i'), c_b(\hat{i}))$ is not connected in the graph. (Since $\delta_a(i') \leq k_b - k_g$, there are at least k_g nodes not connected to node $c_a(i')$, and at most $i - 1 < k_g$ nodes of the lower row are assigned, thus such node exists.) Then assign this node as:

$$f_b : c_b(\hat{i}) \mapsto u_i \in U_g, \forall 1 \leq i \leq k_g.$$

Finally, assign all other nodes to $U \setminus U_g$ as:

$$f_a : c_a(\hat{i}) \mapsto u' \in U'_a, \forall k_g < i \le k_a$$

$$f_a : c_b(\hat{i}) \mapsto u' \in U'_b, \forall k_g < i \le k_b$$

where $c_b(\hat{i})$ represents the nodes haven't been assigned and $U'_a, U'_b \subseteq U \setminus U_g, U'_a \bigcap U'_b = \emptyset$. Thus such adversary assignment exists, which insinuates rendezvous in not achieved. Hence, we conclude that the $MTTR$ value for any deterministic algorithm to OBRP-2 is $\Omega((k_a - k_g) \cdot (k_b - k_g))$. □

5. SYNCHRONOUS OBLIVIOUS BLIND RENDEZVOUS

Oblivious Blind Rendezvous Problem is important and challenging, but most extant works can't guarantee rendezvous even for two synchronous users. In this section, we introduce a deterministic distributed algorithm called Synchronous Check & Hop (SCH) for two synchronous users with bounded $MTTR$ value, which works as a foundation for the fully distributed rendezvous in the next section.

5.1 Algorithm Description

Before we present the SCH algorithm, we introduce a trivial ID conversion algorithm (Alg. 1) with input ID I and the base value b. The output consists of $l+1$ bits where each bit ranges in $[0, b)$. Alg. 1 converts the user's ID to a new number under base b. For example, input $(8, 2)$ corresponds to output $(1, 0, 0, 0)$ which is the common binary representation.

Algorithm 1 ID Conversion (I, b)

```
Input: I, b;
Output: d = {d_0, d_1, ..., d_l};
l := ⌊log_b I⌋, i := l;
while i ≥ 0 do
    d_i := I mod b;
    I := ⌊I/b⌋;
    i := i − 1;
end while
```

In Alg. 2, supposing each user has a unique ID $I \in [1, M]$, available channel set C, and an upper bound estimation of the number of total licensed channels $\widetilde{N} = O(N)$. It consists of two stages: *Synchronous Check Stage* and *Hop Stage*. Synchronous Check Stage generates $CT = p\widetilde{P}$ elements from Lines 9-10, where p is the smallest prime number $p \ge \max\{k, 3\}$, $k = |C|$ and $\widetilde{P}$ is the smallest prime number no less than the estimation $\widetilde{N}$. From Line 10, this stage repeats the sequence $\overrightarrow{z} = \{1, 2, \cdots, p\}$ for $\widetilde{P}$ times, which is then mapped as $\overrightarrow{z'} = \{1, 2, \cdots, k, 1, 2, \cdots, p-k\}$ in Line 16 since only k channels are available. Fig. 3 shows the process of the construction.

Hop Stage generates $HT = p^2(l+2)$ elements from Lines 12-14, where $l = \lfloor log_{p-1} I \rfloor$. It consists of $l+2$ frames and the length of each frame is $FL = p^2$. In the i-th frame, the construction of first p elements can be thought of the user hops in a circle of p nodes with label $\{1, 2, \cdots, p\}$ from $1 \to 1 + D(i) \to (2D(i)) \mod p + 1 \to (3(D(i)) \mod p + 1 \to \cdots$ from Lines 13-14. We call $D(i)$ the *hopping step* as the difference between two consecutive elements. Then the next p elements are constructed the same way by increasing

Algorithm 2 Synchronous Check & Hop Algorithm

```
1: Input: I, C, an estimation Ñ;
2: k := |C|;
3: Find the smallest prime numbers p ≥ max{k, 3}, P̃ ≥ Ñ;
4: l := ⌊log_{p−1} I⌋;
5: Invoke ID Conversion (I, p − 1) and the output is d;
6: D := {d_0 + 1, d_1 + 1, ..., d_l + 1, 0};
7: CT := pP̃, HT = p^2(l + 2), FL = p^2, t := 0;
8: while Not rendezvous and t < CT + HT do
9:     if t < CT then
10:        z = t mod p + 1;
11:    else
12:        x = ⌊(t − CT)/FL⌋, y = (t − CT) mod FL;
13:        y_1 = ⌊y/p⌋, y_2 = y mod p;
14:        z = (y_1 + y_2 · D(x)) mod p + 1;
15:    end if
16:    z' = (z − 1) mod k + 1, access channel c(z') ∈ C;
17:    t = t + 1;
18: end while
```

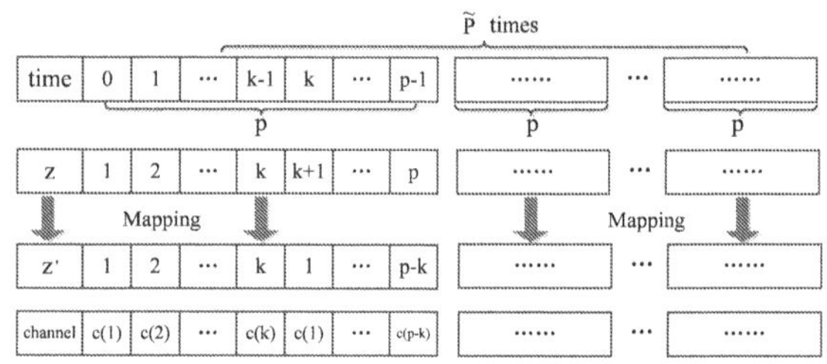

Figure 3: Construction of Synchronous Check Stage

the first element to 2 and holding the same hopping step $D(i)$. Thus the Hop Stage can be constructed iteratively. For example, when $D(i) = 0$,

$$\overrightarrow{z} = \{\underbrace{1, 1, \cdots, 1}_{p}, \underbrace{2, 2, \cdots, 2}_{p}, \cdots, \underbrace{p, p, \cdots, p}_{p}\}$$

and when $D(i) = 1$,

$$\overrightarrow{z} = \{\underbrace{1, 2, \cdots, p}_{p}, \underbrace{2, 3, \cdots, p, 1}_{p}, \cdots, \underbrace{p, 1, 2, \cdots, p-1}_{p}\}$$

5.2 Correctness and Time Complexity

The intuitive idea of constructing the Synchronous Check Stage follows from Lemma 5.1:

LEMMA 5.1. *Consider two vectors* $X = \{x_1, x_2, \cdots, x_m\}$, $Y = \{y_1, y_2, \cdots, y_n\}$, *if* $gcd(m, n) = 1$, *let* $\hat{X} = [\underbrace{XX \cdots X}_{n}]$ *and* $\hat{y} = [\underbrace{YY \cdots Y}_{m}]$, $\forall i \in [1, m], j \in [1, n]$, *there exists* k *such that* $\hat{X}(k) = x_i$ *and* $\hat{Y}(k) = y_j$.

PROOF. From the construction of $\hat{X}$ and $\hat{Y}$, when $k_x = i + m\theta_x, \theta_x \in [0, n)$ and $k_y = j + n\theta_y, \theta_y \in [0, m)$, $\hat{X}(k_x) = x_i$ and $\hat{Y}(k_y) = y_j$. Let $k_x = k_y$, we get:

$$i + m\theta_x = j + n\theta_y \tag{2}$$

Take modular operation on both sides to derive:

$$\begin{cases} i = j + n\theta_y \mod m \\ i + m\theta_x = j \mod n \end{cases}$$

Since $gcd(m,n) = 1$, there exist m^{-1}, n^{-1} such that $m \cdot m^{-1} = 1 \mod n$ and $n \cdot n^{-1} = 1 \mod m$, so $\theta_x = (j-i) \cdot m^{-1} \mod n$ and $\theta_y = (i-j) \cdot n^{-1} \mod m$. Thus such $k = k_x = k_y$ exists that $\hat{X}(k) = x_i$ and $\hat{Y}(k) = y_j$. $\square$

From this lemma, for any two users with (I_a, C_a) and (I_b, C_b), if the corresponding prime numbers in Line 3 of Alg. 2 satisfy $p_a \neq p_b$, which implies $gcd(p_a, p_b) = 1$, then rendezvous is guaranteed in the Synchronous Check Stage.

COROLLARY 1. *For two synchronous users with (I_a, C_a) and (I_b, C_b) running Alg. 2, if $p_a \neq p_b$, they can achieve rendezvous in $T = \min\{CT_a, CT_b\} = \min\{p_a, p_b\}\widetilde{P}$ time slots, where $CT_a = p_a\widetilde{P}, CT_b = p_b\widetilde{P}$ in Line 7.*

When $p_a = p_b$, they may not rendezvous on a common channel in the Synchronous Check Stage. Thus we need Hop Stage to guarantee rendezvous under this particular situation.

LEMMA 5.2. *For two synchronous users with (I_a, C_a) and (I_b, C_b) running Alg. 2, if $p_a = p_b = p$, rendezvous is guaranteed in $T = CT_a + \min\{HT_a, HT_b\} = p\widetilde{P} + (min\{l_a, l_b\} + 2) \cdot p^2$ time slots, where $l_a = \lfloor \log_{p-1} I_a \rfloor, l_b = \lfloor \log_{p-1} I_b \rfloor$.*

PROOF. Denote $HT_a = p_a^2(l_a + 2), HT_b = p_b^2(l_b + 2)$ in Line 7 of Alg. 2. We show that two users with $p_a = p_b$ and $I_a \neq I_b$ can achieve rendezvous in the Hop Stage. Denote the output of ID Conversion of (I_a, p) and (I_b, p) in Alg. 1 as $d_a = \{d_{a,0}, d_{a,1}, \cdots, d_{a,l_a}\}$ and $d_b = \{d_{b,0}, d_{b,1}, \cdots, d_{b,l_b}\}$. Denote D_a, D_b in Line 6 when they run Alg. 2.

CLAIM 5.3. *There exists $\lambda \leq \min\{l_a, l_b\} + 1$ such that $D_a(\lambda) \neq D_b(\lambda)$.*

From the construction of D_a, D_b as Line 6, $D_a(l_a + 1) = D_b(l_b+1) = 0$ and $\forall i \in [0, l_a], \forall j \in [0, l_b], 0 < D_a(i) < p, 0 < D_b(j) < p$. If $l_a \neq l_b$, without loss of generality, suppose $l_a < l_b$, let $\lambda = l_a + 1$, $D_a(\lambda) = 0$ but $D_b(\lambda) = d_{b,l_a} + 1 \geq 1$, thus the claim is proved. When $l_a = l_b$, we can check that there exists $0 \leq \lambda \leq l_a$ such that $d_{a,\lambda} \neq d_{b,\lambda}$ in Alg. 1 since $I_a \neq I_b$, thus $D_a(\lambda) = d_{a,\lambda} + 1 \neq d_{b,\lambda} + 1 = D_b(\lambda)$.

Suppose $C_a \bigcap C_b \neq \emptyset$, for any channel $u' \in C_a \bigcap C_b$, there exists $1 \leq i \leq k_a, 1 \leq j \leq k_b$ such that $c_a(i) = u'$ and $c_b(j) = u'$. Since two users begin the algorithm at the same time with $p_a = p_b = p$, assume they don't rendezvous in the first $T = CT + \lambda \cdot p^2$ time slots, consider the p^2 elements in the λ-th frame of the Hop Stage. For $T < t < T + p^2$, let $y_1 = \lfloor (t - T)/p \rfloor$, $y_2 = (t - T) \mod p$, the goal is to find t such that:

$$\begin{cases} (y_1 + y_2 \cdot D_a(\lambda)) \mod p + 1 = i \\ (y_1 + y_2 \cdot D_b(\lambda)) \mod p + 1 = j \end{cases} \quad (3)$$

Combining the two equations, we derive:

$$y_2 \cdot [D_a(\lambda) - D_b(\lambda)] = i - j \mod p$$

Since $D_a(\lambda) \neq D_b(\lambda)$,the modular reverse $[D_a(\lambda) - D_b(\lambda)]^{-1}$ exists which suits $[D_a(\lambda) - D_b(\lambda)] \cdot [D_a(\lambda) - D_b(\lambda)]^{-1} = 1 \mod p$, thus $y_2 = (i - j) \cdot [D_a(\lambda) - D_b(\lambda)]^{-1} \mod p$. Plug this into Equation (3) to get y_1, thus $t = T + y_1 p + y_2$. Then rendezvous is guaranteed in $CT + (\lambda + 1) \cdot p^2 = p\widetilde{P} + (\min\{l_a, l_b\} + 2) \cdot p^2$ time slots. $\square$

Combining Corollary 1 and Lemma 5.2 to conclude:

THEOREM 2. *For two synchronous users with (I_a, C_a), (I_b, C_b), if $C_a \bigcap C_b \neq \emptyset$, rendezvous can be guaranteed in $T = O(\min\{k_a, k_b\} \cdot N)$ time slots if I_a, I_b are polynomial functions of p_a, p_b, respectively.*

REMARK 5.1. *The smallest prime number $\widetilde{P} \geq \widetilde{N}$ is proved to be $\widetilde{N} \leq \widetilde{P} < 2\widetilde{N}$ from the* Bertrand-Chebyshev Theorem.

6. ASYNCHRONOUS OBLIVIOUS BLIND RENDEZVOUS

In this section, we propose a fully distributed rendezvous algorithm that designs rendezvous sequences only based on the user's identifier (ID) and the number of available channels. It takes advantage of SCH's idea about generating different sequences based on the results of ID conversion. We show the correctness of our proposed algorithm with derived bounded $MTTR$ value for two asynchronous users.

6.1 Conversion Based Hopping Algorithm

Algorithm 3 Conversion Based Hopping Algorithm

1: **Input:** I, C;
2: $k := |C|$;
3: Find the smallest prime numbers $p \geq \max\{k, 3\}$;
4: $l := \lfloor log_{p-1} I \rfloor$;
5: Invoke ID Conversion $(I, p-1)$ and the output is d;
6: **if** $(l + 2) \mod 2 = 0$ **then**
7: $\quad l_p := l + 2$; $D := \{0, d_0 + 1, d_1 + 1, \cdots, d_l + 1\}$
8: **else**
9: $\quad l_p := l + 3$, $D := \{0, 1, d_0 + 1, d_1 + 1, \cdots, d_l + 1\}$
10: **end if**
11: $T := 2l_p \cdot p^2$, $FL := 2l_p \cdot p$, $SL = 2p$;
12: **while** Not rendezvous **do**
13: $\quad t' := t \mod T$;
14: $\quad x := \lfloor t'/FL \rfloor$, $x' = t' \mod FL$;
15: $\quad y_1 := \lfloor x'/SL \rfloor$, $y_2 = x' \mod SL$;
16: $\quad z := x + D(y_1) \cdot y_2 \mod p + 1$;
17: $\quad z' := (z - 1) \mod k + 1$, access channel $c(z') \in C$;
18: $\quad t = t + 1$;
19: **end while**

The Conversion Based Hopping (CBH) Algorithm is described in Alg. 3. With local input (I, C), Alg. 3 finds the smallest prime number $p \geq \max\{k, 3\}$ where $k = |C|$ and invokes ID Conversion $(I, p-1)$ (Alg. 1) to get the results d. This preprocessing is almost the same as Alg. 2. Then it constructs the array D containing l_p elements as Lines 6-10, where l_p is defined to be an even number, which is different from Alg. 2. Following the preprocessing, Alg. 3 generates a sequence of length $T = 2l_p \cdot p^2$ as Lines 13-16. This sequence consists of p frames of equal length $FL = 2l_p \cdot p$, where each frame contains l_p segments of length $SL = 2p$. In Line 17, the sequence is mapped from $[1, p]$ to $[1, k]$ and the corresponding channel is accessed by the user.

The construction of the sequence is illustrated in Fig. 4. It consists of p frames as $\{F_0, F_1, \cdots, F_{p-1}\}$ and each frame has l_p segments as: $\{S_0, S_1, \cdots, S_{l_p-1}\}$. The way to generate S_j of F_i is to construct $2p$ elements, starting with i and the hopping step is $D(j)$, then the k-th element is $(i + kD(j)) \mod p + 1$. The reason each segment contains $2p$ elements is to eliminate the asynchronous situation through doubling

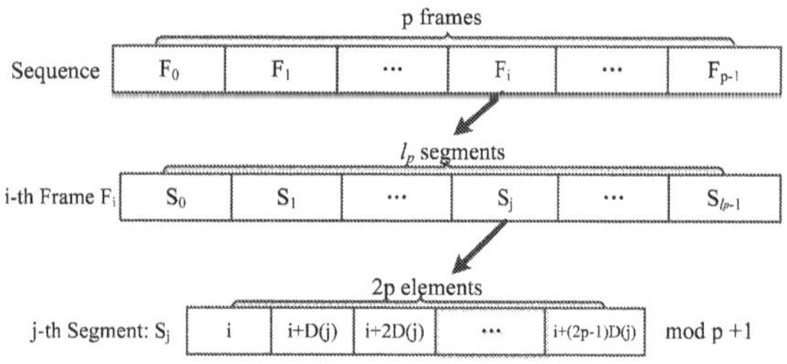

Figure 4: Construction of the sequence in Alg. 3

the length, which is similar with the method transforming time slots into slot-aligned scenarios in Section 3.

There are two intuitive ideas in designing the CBH algorithm. The first one comes from Lemma 5.1 when the corresponding prime numbers of two users in Line 3 satisfy $p_a \neq p_b$, each user repeating its own channels can guarantee rendezvous. When $p_a = p_b$, distinct IDs have different representations through ID conversion, thus accessing the channels with these hopping steps may assure rendezvous. Our proposed CBH algorithm combines these two principles and we'd like to show the correctness in the next part.

6.2 Correctness and MTTR Bound

Assume two asynchronous users (A and B) run Alg. 3 with inputs (I_a, C_a) and (I_b, C_b) where $C_a \bigcap C_b \neq \emptyset, I_a \neq I_b$. Without loss of generality, suppose user B is $\delta \geq 0$ time slots later. Denote $(k_a, p_a, l_a, l_{p_a}, D_a, T_a, FL_a, SL_a, t_a)$ and $(k_b, p_b, l_b, l_{p_b}, D_b, T_b, FL_b, SL_b, t_b)$ be the corresponding variables in Alg. 3. Since $C_a \bigcap C_b \neq \emptyset$, there exists a frequency band (channel) $u' \in C_a \bigcap C_b$ and there exist $1 \leq i \leq k_a$, $1 \leq j \leq k_b$ such that $c_a(i) = u'$ and $c_b(j) = u'$. We show the correctness and derive the $MTTR$ value from the following three cases:

1) $p_a = p_b = p$ and $l_{p_a} = l_{p_b} = l_p$;

2) $p_a = p_b = p$ but $l_{p_a} \neq l_{p_b}$;

3) $p_a \neq p_b$;

Lemma 6.1. *If $p_a = p_b = p$ and $l_{p_a} = l_{p_b} = l_p$, rendezvous between users A and B can be guaranteed in $T = 2l_p \cdot p^2$ time slots.*

Proof. If $0 \leq \delta \mod 2p < p$, there exists $x^* \geq 0, 0 \leq y_1^* < l_p, 0 \leq y_2^* < p$ such that:

$$\delta = x^* \cdot (2pl_p) + y_1^* \cdot (2p) + y_2^* \tag{4}$$

Suppose users A and B can achieve rendezvous on channel u' at time t_a, t_b respectively, and there exists $x(a), x(b) > 0$, $0 \leq y_1(a), y_1(b) < l_p$, $0 \leq y_2(a) < 2p, 0 \leq y_2(b) < p$ such that:

$$t_a = x(a) \cdot (2pl_p) + y_1(a) \cdot (2p) + y_2(a) \tag{5}$$
$$t_b = x(b) \cdot (2pl_p) + y_1(b) \cdot (2p) + y_2(b) \tag{6}$$

From Lines 13-16 of Alg. 3, the corresponding z values could be generated to be i, j, thus:

$$x(a) + D_a(y_1(a)) \cdot y_2(a) \mod p + 1 = i \tag{7}$$
$$x(b) + D_b(y_1(b)) \cdot y_2(b) \mod p + 1 = j \tag{8}$$

Since user B is δ time slots later, i.e. $t_a = t_b + \delta$ and then plug Equations (4-6) to get:

$$[x(a) - x(b) - x^*] \cdot (2pl) + [y_1(a) - y_1(b) - y_1^*] \cdot (2p) + [y_2(a) - y_2(b) - y_2^*] = 0 \tag{9}$$

Since $y_2(b) \in [0, p)$, $y_2(a) - y_2(b) - y_2^* = 0$. Combining this with Equations (7-8) to derive:

$$[D_a(y_1(a)) - D_b(y_1(b))] \cdot y_2(b) + D_a(y_1(a)) \cdot y_2^* = i - x(a) - (j - x(b)) \mod p \tag{10}$$

If we can find $y_1(a), y_1(b)$ satisfying $D(y_1(a)) - D(y_1(b)) \neq 0$ and $y_1(a) - y_1(b) - y_1^* \mod l_p = 0$, Equation (10) can be solved under the constraint Equation (9). Find $y_1(a), y_1(b)$ as follows:

$$\begin{cases} y_1(a) = y_1(b) = k & \text{If } y_1^* = 0 \\ y_1(a) = y_1^*, y_1(b) = 0 & \text{If } 0 < y_1^* \leq l_p - 1 \end{cases} \tag{11}$$

If $y_1^* = 0$, there exist $1 \leq k \leq l_p - 1$ such that $D_a(k) \neq D_b(k)$ from ID conversion. If $0 < y_1^* \leq l_p - 1$, $D_a(y_1(a)) - D_b(y_1(b)) = D_a(y_1^*) > 0$. Thus such $y_1(a), y_1(b)$ exist and $y_1(a) - y_1(b) - y_1^* = 0$.

Since $D_a(y_1(a)) - D_b(y_1(b)) \neq 0$, $y_2(b)$ can be computed from Equation (10) (pluging $x(a) - x(b) = x^*$ from the constraint Equation (9)). Then $x(b) = j - 1 - D_b(y_1(b)) \cdot y_2(b) \mod p$ and thus $x(b) \in [0, p)$. So $TTR = t_b = x(b) \cdot (2pl_p) + y_1(b) \cdot (2p) + y_2(b)$ and it's bounded by $2l_p \cdot p^2$.

For example, users A and B have inputs $I_a = 5, |C_a| = 4$, $I_b = 20, |C_b| = 5$ and $c_a(2) = c_b(4)$ is their only common channel. Thus $p_a = p_b = 5$, $l_a = l_b = 4$ and $D_a = \{0, 1, 2, 2\}$, $D_b = \{0, 2, 2, 0\}$. Let $\delta = 2014$ and it can be rewritten as: $\delta = 50 \cdot 40 + 1 \cdot 10 + 4$, thus $x^* = 50, y_1^* = 1, y_2^* = 4$ from Equation (4). Since $y_1^* = 1$, from Equation (11), $y_1(a) = y_1^* = 1, y_1(b) = 0$ and $x(a) - x(b) = x^* = 50$. From Equation (10), $y_2(b) = 4$ and $x(b) = 3$. Thus $t_b = 3 * 40 + 4 = 124$ and $t_a = t_b + \delta = 2138$. We can check that user A accesses channel $c_a(2)$ and B accesses channel $c_b(4)$ at the same time.

If $p \leq \delta \mod 2p < 2p$, the TTR value is also bounded by $2l_p \cdot p^2$ time slots using the same technique above. Thus the lemma holds. □

Lemma 6.2. *If $p_a = p_b = p$ but $l_{p_a} \neq l_{p_b}$, rendezvous between users A and B can be guaranteed in $T = 2\min\{l_{p_a}, l_{p_b}\} \cdot p^2$ time slots.*

Proof. If $0 \leq \delta \mod 2p < p$, there exists $x^* \geq 0, 0 \leq y_1^* < l_{p_a}, 0 \leq y_2^* < p$ such that:

$$\delta = x^* \cdot (2pl_{p_a}) + y_1^* \cdot (2p) + y_2^*$$

Suppose two users can rendezvous on channel u' at time t_a, t_b respectively, and:

$$t_a = x(a) \cdot (2pl_{p_a}) + y_1(a) \cdot (2p) + y_2(a)$$
$$t_b = x(b) \cdot (2pl_{p_b}) + y_2(b) \cdot (2p) + y_2(b)$$

where $x(a), x(b) > 0, 0 \leq y_1(a) < l_{p_a}, 0 \leq y_1(b) < l_{p_b}, 0 \leq y_2(a) < 2p, 0 \leq y_2(b) < p$. Combining these with $t_a = t_b + \delta$ to derive:

$$[l_{p_a} x(a) - l_{p_b} x(b) - l_{p_a} x^* + y_1(a) - y_1(b) - y_1^*] \cdot 2p + y_2(a) - y_2(b) - y_2^* = 0$$

Similarly, we have:

$$\begin{cases} l_{p_a} \cdot x(a) - l_{p_b} \cdot x(b) - l_{p_a} \cdot x^* + y_1(a) - y_1(b) - y_1^* = 0 \\ y_2(a) - y_2(b) - y_2^* = 0 \end{cases} \quad (12)$$

We also formulate Equations (7-8). If $l_{p_a} > l_{p_b}$, let $y_1(a) = 0$, $y_1(b) = k \neq 0$, $x(a) = (i-1) \mod p$ is derived from Equation (7). Plugging this into Equation (12), $l_{p_b} x(b) = [l_{p_a} x(a) - l_{p_a} x^* - y_1(b) - y_1^*] \mod p$. Since l_{p_b} is an even number, $x(b) \in [0, p)$ can be easily computed. Then from Equation (8), $y_2(b) \in [0, p)$ can be figured out. Thus the TTR value is $t_b = x(b) \cdot (2pl_{p_b}) + y_1(b) \cdot (2p) + y_2(b) \leq 2p^2 l_{p_b}$. If $l_{p_a} < l_{p_b}$, we can bound the $TTR = t_a - \delta = (x(a) - x^*) \cdot (2pl_{p_a}) + (y_1(a) - y_1^*) \cdot (2p) + (y_2(a) - y_2^*) \leq 2p^2 l_{p_a}$. Thus $MTTR \leq 2\min\{l_{p_a}, l_{p_b}\} p^2$.

If $p \leq \delta \mod 2p < 2p$, the TTR value is also bounded by $T = 2\min\{l_{p_a}, l_{p_b}\} \cdot p^2$ time slots using the same technique above. Thus the lemma holds. □

LEMMA 6.3. *If $p_a \neq p_b$, rendezvous between users A and B can be guaranteed in $T = 2l_p \cdot p^2$ time slots, where $p = \max\{p_a, p_b\}$ and l_p is the corresponding value from $\{l_{p_a}, l_{p_b}\}$.*

PROOF. This lemma can be concluded similarly. Suppose $p_a < p_b$, we can derive the following equations:

$$x(a) + D_a(y_1(a)) \cdot y_2(a) \mod p_a + 1 = i$$
$$x(b) + D_b(y_1(b)) \cdot y_2(b) \mod p_b + 1 = j$$

Let $y_1(b) = 0$, then $x(b) = (j-1) \mod p_b$ and $y_2(b) \in [0, 2p_b)$. Suppose $x(a) = i' \mod p_a$ and $y_1(a) \neq 0$, then $y_2(a)$ exists. Since $t_a = t_b + \delta$ and

$$t_a = x(a) \cdot (2p_a l_{p_a}) + y_1(a) \cdot (2p_a) + y_2(a)$$
$$t_b = x(b) \cdot (2p_b l_{p_b}) + y_2(b) \cdot (2p_b) + y_2(b)$$

We can find such $x(a) = i' + v(a)p_a$ satisfying $\delta_b(v_b) + \delta - \delta_a(v_a) \in [2p_a - 2p_b, T_a)$ ($T_a = 2p_a^2 l_{p_a}$ is define above), where $\delta_b(v_b) = (2p_b l_{p_b}) \cdot (j - 1 + v(b)p_b)$ and $\delta_a(v_a) = (2p_a l_{p_a}) \cdot x(a)$. Obviously, $\delta_b(0) \mod T_a \geq 2p_a - 2p_b$, let $v(b) = 0$, $v(a) = \lfloor (\delta_b(0) + \delta)/T_a \rfloor$ and $i' = \lfloor (\delta_b(0) + \delta - v(a)T_a)/FL_a \rfloor)$ ($FL = 2p_a l_{p_a}$), then $y_1(a), y_2(a), y_2(b)$ can be figured out. Thus $TTR = t_b = x(b) \cdot (2p_b l_{p_b}) + y_1(b) \cdot (2p_b) + y_2(b) \leq 2p_b^2 l_{p_b}$. If $p_a > p_b$, $TTR \leq 2p_a^2 l_{p_a}$ can be concluded similarly. Thus the lemma holds. □

Combine Lemmas 6.1-6.3 to conclude:

THEOREM 3. *Two users running Alg. 3 can achieve rendezvous in $MTTR = 2l_p \cdot p^2$ time slots where $p = \max\{p_a, p_b\}$ and l_p is the corresponding value from $\{l_{p_a}, l_{p_b}\}$.*

This theorem reveals that CBH can guarantee oblivious blind rendezvous between two users in short time and it is comparable to the lower bound in Section 4 for most cases. More precisely, $MTTR = 2l_p \cdot p^2 = O(k^2)$ time slots if l_p is a constant, which implies the corresponding ID is a polynomial function of p, where $k = \max\{k_a, k_b\}$. For example, if $k_a > k_b$ (thus $p_a \geq p_b$), and I_a is bounded by $I_a \leq p_a^c$ where c can be an arbitrary large constant, $MTTR = 2l_{p_a} \cdot p_a^2 = O(k_a^2)$. If $k_b = \Theta(k_a)$ and $k_g = o(k_a)$, the $MTTR$ value is comparable with the lower bound in Section 4.

REMARK 6.1. *All these algorithms for OBRP-2 can be applied to OBRP. The intuitive idea is: once every two users achieve rendezvous on some common frequency band, they can exchange their local information and synchronize their labels for the available channels. Therefore, they generate the same sequence afterwards until rendezvous is achieved among all users.*

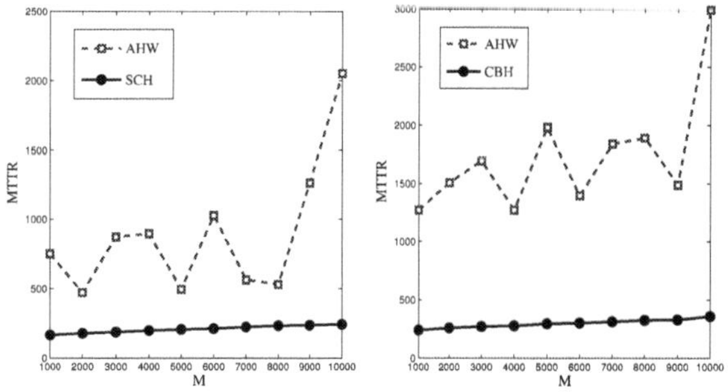

(a) $MTTR$ vs. M (b) $MTTR$ vs. M

Figure 5: $MTTR$ comparison when M increases from 1000 to 10000, $N = 10$, $k_a = k_b = 6$: (a) Synchronous scenario; (b) Asynchronous scenario;

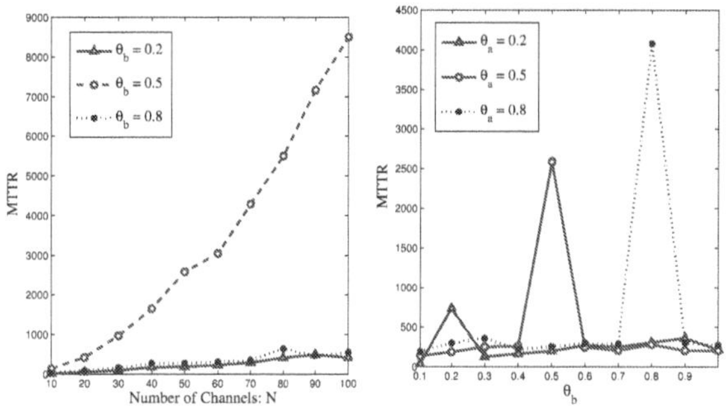

(a) $MTTR$ vs. N (b) $MTTR$ vs. θ_b

Figure 6: $MTTR$ values for SCH algorithm: (a) $\theta_a = 0.5$, $N \in [10, 100]$; (b) $N = 50$, $\theta_b \in [0.1, 1]$;

7. SIMULATION

In this section, we evaluate the performance of our proposed algorithms under various circumstances and compare the results with several state-of-the-art rendezvous algorithms. Three representative algorithms for non-oblivious blind rendezvous are chosen: Jump-Stay (JS) [17], DRDS [11], and AHW [6]. For oblivious blind rendezvous situation, we choose MMC [24] though it cannot guarantee rendezvous in bounded time.

For two users A and B, denote the corresponding identifiers (IDs) and available channel sets are (I_a, C_a) and (I_b, C_b). Denote $k_a = |C_a|, k_b = |C_b|, k_g = |C_a \bigcap C_b|$, define $\theta_a = \frac{k_a}{N}, \theta_b = \frac{k_b}{N}, \theta_g = \frac{k_g}{N}$. In each simulation, I_a, I_b are generated randomly in $[1, M]$ and the starting time of each user is random if they are asynchronous. Based on different circumstances, the available channel sets are also generated randomly. We describe the detailed parameters for the corresponding figures and these results are based on 5000 separate simulation runs.

Since AHW and our proposed algorithms are related to the users' ID, we firstly evaluate the impact of the IDs' maximum value M. Fix $N = 10, k_a = k_b = 6$, as shown in Fig.

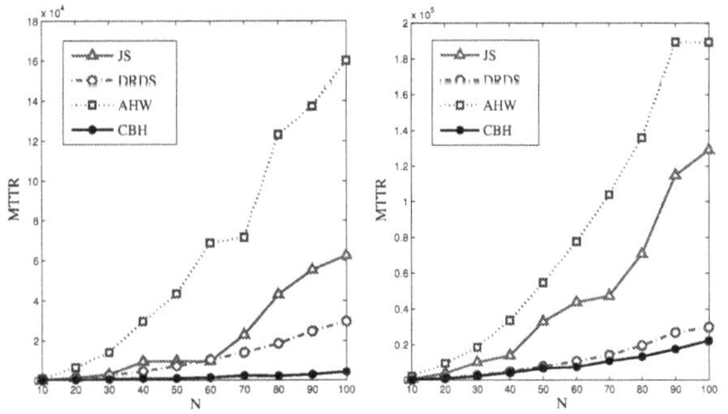

(a) $MTTR$ vs. N (b) $MTTR$ vs. N

Figure 7: $MTTR$ comparison when N increases from 10 to 100, $M = 100$: (a) $\theta_a = \theta_b = 0.2$, $k_g = 1$; (b) $\theta_a = \theta_b = 0.5$, $k_g = 1$;

5(a), both AHW and SCH increase when M increases from 1000 to 10000 for synchronous situation, but SCH is stable and not impacted by the increasing M value largely. For asynchronous scenario, the results in Fig. 5(b) also show that our proposed CBH algorithm performs much better than AHW. In the following scenarios, we set $M = 100$.

In order to evaluate the performance of SCH for two synchronous users, fix $\theta_a = 0.5$ and evaluate the performance when N increases from 10 to 100 for three situations: $\theta_b = 0.2, 0.5, 0.8$, Fig. 6(a) shows that the $MTTR$ value is much larger when $\theta_b = 0.5$. The reason is rendezvous can be guaranteed in the Synchronous Check Stage when $\theta_b = 0.2, 0.8$, but have to achieve rendezvous in the Hop Stage when $\theta_b = \theta_a$. Fix $N = 50$ and $\theta_a = 0.2, 0.5, 0.8$ respectively, when θ_b increases from 0.1 to 1, Fig. 6(b) also shows that the $MTTR$ value is much larger than normal when $\theta_b = \theta_a$.

Although our proposed CBH algorithm is designed for oblivious blind rendezvous, it's also applicable to non-oblivious blind rendezvous and we evaluate the performance in Figs. 7-9.

To begin with, we evaluate the performance compared with JS, DRDS, and AHW for some extreme situations. As shown in Fig. 7(a), fix $\theta_a = \theta_b = 0.2$ and $k_g = 1$ (which means only one common channel exists), when N increases from 10 to 100, it reveals that CBH works best among these algorithms. In Fig. 7(b), CBH also outperforms the others when $\theta_a = \theta_b = 0.5$, $k_g = 1$. JS works badly because it can only guarantee rendezvous in $O(N^3)$ time slots for the worst case, while AHW is influenced by both N and M values.

In Fig. 8(a), $\theta_a = \theta_b = 0.2$, $\theta_g = 0.1$, the results show that CBH works best. In Fig. 8(b), $\theta_a = \theta_b = 0.8$, CBH also outperforms the others, but JS is also comparable to CBH. The reason is that CBH designs rendezvous algorithms based on the number of available channels and the distinct ID, when two users have less available channels, rendezvous can be achieved more quickly. JS algorithm works well when the number of available channels is large [11].

We also evaluate the situations when $k_a \neq k_b$. As shown in Fig. 9, fix $N = 50$ and $\theta_a = 0.2, 0.5$ respectively, when θ_b increases from 0.1 to 1, the results show that CBH has the smallest $MTTR$ value among these algorithms.

For oblivious blind rendezvous algorithm, we also compare the performance with MMC, though it cannot guarantee rendezvous in bounded time for some cases. As shown in

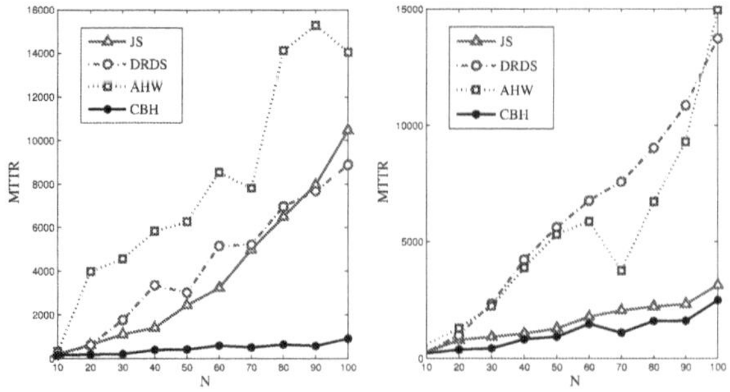

(a) $MTTR$ vs. N (b) $MTTR$ vs. N

Figure 8: $MTTR$ comparison for non-oblivious blind rendezvous when N increases from 10 to 100, $M = 100$: (a) $\theta_a = \theta_b = 0.2, \theta_g = 0.1$; (b) $\theta_a = \theta_b = 0.8$;

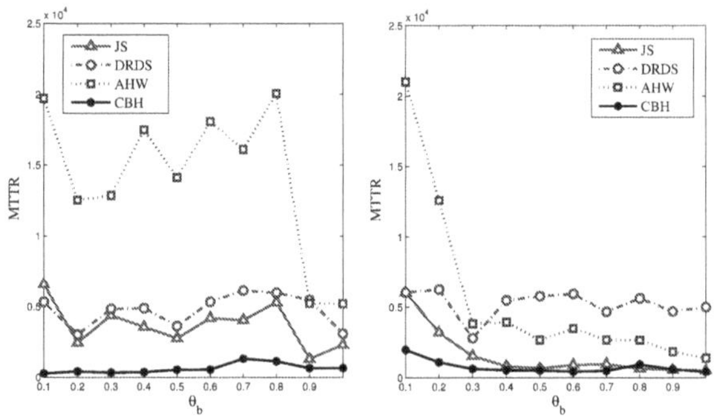

(a) $MTTR$ vs. θ_b (b) $MTTR$ vs. θ_b

Figure 9: $MTTR$ comparison for non-oblivious blind rendezvous when θ_b increases from 0.1 to 1, $M = 100, N = 50$: (a) $\theta_a = 0.2$; (b) $\theta_a = 0.5$;

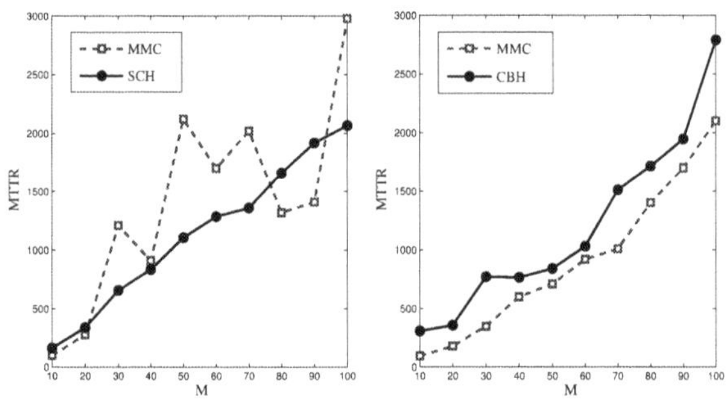

(a) $MTTR$ vs. N (b) $MTTR$ vs. θ_b

Figure 10: $MTTR$ values for oblivious blind rendezvous when N increases from 10 to 100, $M = 100$: (a) $\theta_a = \theta_b = 0.5$; (b) $\theta_a = 0.2, \theta_b = 0.8$;

Fig. 10(a), $\theta_a = \theta_b = 0.5$, CBH is stable when N increases from 10 to 100, while MMC is not stable when $k_a = k_b$. In Fig. 10(b), $\theta_a = 0.2, \theta_b = 0.8$, MMC is slighter better than CBH because the parameters insure that rendezvous can be achieved for MMC. Even though, CBH also works well and the results are comparable to the MMC algorithm.

Accordingly, our proposed SCH algorithm can guarantee two synchronous users in short time when $k_a \neq k_b$ and CBH performs best among the extant non-oblivious blind rendezvous algorithms for most cases. Moreover, CBH is fully distributed based on the users' local information, therefore, it can be used to implement large network system where global information is hard to obtain and maintain.

8. CONCLUSIONS

In this paper, we study the *Oblivious Blind Rendezvous* problem in Cognitive Radio Networks (CRNs), which is more general than the non-oblivious blind rendezvous problems. In the oblivious blind rendezvous problem, all users don't see the same labels for the licensed frequency bands (channels) and thus each user is free to assign its own local label to the sensed channels.

To begin with, we derive a lower bound for oblivious blind rendezvous between two users as $\Omega((k_a - k_g)(k_b - k_g)$, where k_a, k_b are the number of their available channels and k_g is the number of common channels they share. Then, we present a fully distributed algorithm called Conversion Based Hopping (CBH) algorithm, where only the user's identifier (ID) and the number of available channels are used. CBH guarantees rendezvous between two asynchronous users in $O((\max\{k_a, k_b\})^2)$ time slots when the user's ID is a polynomial function of the number of available channels. To our knowledge, this is the first result for blind rendezvous which is independent of the global parameter N. We have also conducted extensive simulations to compare our proposed algorithms with several state-of-the-art rendezvous algorithms, and the results show that our algorithms work much better for most situations

9. ACKNOWLEDGMENTS

This work was supported in part by the National Basic Research Program of China Grant 2011CBA00300, 2011CBA00301, the National Natural Science Foundation of China Grant 61103186, 61033001, 61361136003.

10. REFERENCES

[1] I. Akyildiz, W. Lee, M. Vuran, and S. Mohanty. NeXt Generation//Dynamic Spectrum Access//Cognitive Radio Wireless Networks: A Survey. *Computer Networks*, 50(13): 2127-2159, 2006.

[2] K. Bian, J.-M. Park, and R. Chen. A Quorum-Based Framework for Establishing Control Channels in Dynamic Spectrum Access Networks. In *Mobicom*, 2009.

[3] K. Bian, and J.-M. Park. Asynchronous Channel Hopping for Establishing Rendezvous in Cognitive Radio Networks. In *IEEE INFOCOM*, 2011.

[4] K. Bian, J.-M. Park. Maximizing Rendezvous Diversity in Rendezvous Protocols for Decentralized Cognitive Radio Networks. *IEEE Transactions on Mobile Computing*, 12(7):1294-1307, 2013.

[5] Z. Cai, S. Ji, J. He, and A. G. Bourgeois. Optimal Distributed Data Collection for Asynchronous Cognitive Radio Networks. In *ICDCS*, 2012.

[6] I. Chuang, H.-Y. Wu, K.-R. Lee. and Y.-H. Kuo. Alternate Hop-and-Wait Channel Rendezvous Method for Cognitive Radio Networks. In *INFOCOM*, 2013.

[7] Y. Dai, J. Wu, and C. Xin. Virtual Backbone Construction for Cognitive Radio Networks without Common Control Channel. In *INFOCOM*, 2013.

[8] L. DaSilva, and I. Guerreiro. Sequence-Based Rendezvous for Dynamic Spectrum Access. In *DySPAN*, 2008.

[9] ETSI. EN 301 598 White Space Devices (WSD); Wireless Access Systems Operating in the 470 MHz to 790 MHz Frequency Band. 2012.

[10] A. B. Flores, R. E. Guerra, and E. W. Kightly. IEEE 802.11af: A Standard for TV White Space Spectrum Sharing. *IEEE Communications Magazine*, 2013.

[11] Z. Gu, Q.-S. Hua, Y. Wang, and F. C.M. Lau. Nearly Optimal Asynchronous Blind Rendezvous Algorithm for Cognitive Radio Networks. In *SECON*, 2013.

[12] X. Huang, D. Lu, P. Li, and Y. Fang. Coolest Path: Spectrum Mobility Aware Routing Metrics in Cognitive Ad Hoc Networks. In *ICDCS*, 2011.

[13] J. Jia, Q. Zhang, and X. Shen. HC-MAC: A Hardware-Constrained Cognitive MAC for Efficient Spectrum Management. *IEEE Journal on Selected Areas in Communications*, 26(1):106-117, 2008.

[14] Y. Kondareddy, P. Agrawal, and K. Sivalingam. Cognitive Radio Network Setup without a Common Control Channel. In *MILCOM*, 2008.

[15] L. Lazos, S. Liu, and M. Krunz. Spectrum Opportunity-Based Control Channel Assignment in Cognitive Radio Networks. In *SECON*, 2009.

[16] Z. Lin, H. Liu, X. Chu, and Y.-W. Leung. Enhanced Jump-Stay Rendezvous Algorithm for Cognitive Radio Networks. *IEEE Communications Letters*, to appear.

[17] H. Liu, Z. Lin, X. Chu, and Y.-W. Leung. Jump-Stay Rendezvous Algorithm for Cognitive Radio Networks. *IEEE Transactions on Parallel and Distributed Systems*, 23(10):1867-1881, 2012.

[18] H. Liu, Z. Lin, X. Chu, and Y.-W. Leung. Taxonomy and Challenges of Rendezvous Algorithms in Cognitive Radio Networks. In *ICNC*, 2012.

[19] Ofcom. Regulatory Requirements for White Space Devices in the UHF TV band. http://www.cept.org/Documents/se-43/6161/, 2013.

[20] J. Perez-Romero, O. Salient, R. Agusti, and L. Giupponi. A Novel On-Demand Cognitive Pilot Channel enabling Dynamic Spectrum Allocation. In *DySPAN*, 2007.

[21] J. Shin, D. Yang, and C. Kim. A Channel Rendezvous Scheme for Cognitive Radio Networks. *IEEE Communications Letters*, 14(10):954-956, 2010.

[22] C.R. Stevenson, G. Chouinard, Z. Lei, W. Hu, S.J. Shellhammer, and W. Caldwell. IEEE 802.22: The First Cognitive Radio Wireless Regional Area Network Standard. *IEEE Communications Magazine*, 47(1): 130-138, 2009.

[23] J. Song, J. Xie, and X. Wang. A Novel unified Analytical Model for Broadcast Protocols in Multihop Cognitive Radio Ad Hoc Networks. *IEEE Transaction on Mobile Computing*, 2013.

[24] N.C. Theis, R.W. Thomas, and L.A. DaSilva. Rendezvous for Cognitive Radios. *IEEE Transactions on Mobile Computing*, 10(2):216-227, 2011.

[25] D. Zhang, T. He, F. Ye, R. Ganti, and H. Lei. EQS: Neighbor Discovery and Rendezvous Maintenance with Extended Quorum System for Mobile Sensing Applications. In *ICDCS*, 2012.

A Group-theoretic Framework for Rendezvous in Heterogeneous Cognitive Radio Networks

Lin Chen*, Kaigui Bian*, Lin Chen†, Cong Liu‡, Jung-Min Jerry Park♯, and Xiaoming Li*
*Peking University, Beijing, China. †University Paris-Sud, Orsay, France.
‡Sun Yat-Sen University, China. ♯Virginia Tech, Blacksburg, VA, USA.
*{abratchen, bkg, lxm}@pku.edu.cn, †chen@lri.fr, ‡liucong3@mail.sysu.edu.cn, ♯jungmin@vt.edu

ABSTRACT

In cognitive radio (CR) networks, a pair of CR nodes have to "rendezvous" on a common channel for link establishment. Channel hopping (CH) protocols have been proposed for creating rendezvous over multiple channels to reduce the possibility of rendezvous failures caused by the detection of primary user signals. Rendezvous within a minimal bounded time over multiple channels is a challenging problem in heterogeneous CR networks where two CR nodes may have asynchronous clocks, different sensing capabilities, no common universal channel set, and heterogeneous channel index systems. In this paper, we present a systematic approach using group theory for designing CH protocols that guarantee the maximum number of rendezvous channels and the minimal time-to-rendezvous (TTR) in heterogeneous environments. We derive the minimum upper bound of TTR, and propose two types of rendezvous protocols that are independent of environmental heterogeneity. Analytical and simulation results show that these protocols are resistant to rendezvous failures under various network conditions.

Categories and Subject Descriptors

C.2.2 [**Computer-Communication Networks**]: Network Protocols

Keywords

Cognitive radio, rendezvous, heterogeneous

1. INTRODUCTION

In *cognitive radio* (CR) networks, "rendezvous" is a bootstrapping primitive for two communicating nodes or secondary users (SUs) to find each other on a *rendezvous/control channel* within a bounded time, prior to data communications [12]. However, *rendezvous failure* occurs between two SUs when the rendezvous channel is unavailable due to the detection of primary user (PU) or interference signals.

MobiHoc'14, August 11–14, 2014, Philadelphia, PA, USA.
Copyright 2014 ACM 978-1-4503-2620-9/14/08 ...$15.00.
http://dx.doi.org/10.1145/2632951.2632988.

Two metrics are usually used for evaluating the performance of a rendezvous protocol.

1. Ideally, we want to maximize the number of rendezvous channels—referred to as *rendezvous diversity*—thereby minimizing the risk of rendezvous failures [4];
2. It is also desired to minimize the *time-to-rendezvous (TTR)* for obtaining a small rendezvous delay between two SUs [3, 8, 10, 15].

Since the *common control channel (CCC)* approach is subject to the rendezvous failure problem, *channel hopping (CH) approaches* have been widely used to create multiple rendezvous channels between two SUs [3, 6, 8, 10, 11, 15]. Specifically, each SU starts a channel hopping process according to its own CH sequence and local clock; two SUs' CH sequences are carefully chosen to spread out rendezvous points over multiple pairwise common channels.

There are four primary challenges for designing a CH-based rendezvous protocol that has a small TTR and a high rendezvous diversity in *heterogeneous environments.*

1. *Lack of clock synchronization.* It is difficult to require two independent nodes to have synchronized clocks without any handshake between them. Existing research efforts address this problem by using quorum-based [3, 5], difference set-based [9], modular-based [2, 12, 15], jump-stay [10], and circle-based channel hopping approaches [7].
2. *Different sensing capabilities.* Two CR nodes may have different spectrum sensing capabilities, and thus their perceptions of channel availability or sensible channel sets can be different. Recent studies show that efficient rendezvous can be achieved for two CR nodes without assuming the same sensible channel set [13, 14].
3. *No universal channel set or common channel index system.* Most existing work assumes that all nodes share a known universal channel set, where N frequency channels are mapped to channel indices using a common channel index system. However, a CH-based protocol may fail to guarantee rendezvous when two nodes have no universal channel set or a common way of mapping channel indices to frequency channels. For example, given three channels with center frequencies a, b, c, two nodes using the same CH sequence $\{0, 1, 2\}$ fail to achieve rendezvous when one node maps indices $\{0, 1, 2\}$ to frequencies $\{a, b, c\}$, while the other maps indices $\{0, 1, 2\}$ to $\{b, c, a\}$.

4. *Independence of consecutive integer channel indices.* In many existing works, every node has a set of *consecutive* integer channel indices in a common channel index system which allows the exploitation of arithmetic modular operations for guaranteeing rendezvous in the constructed CH sequences [2, 10, 13, 14]. For instance, it is assumed in [13, 14] that there exists a universal channel set $U = \{c_0, c_1, \ldots, c_{|U|-1}\}$ and that each node i can sense a range of consecutive channels $V_i = \{c_x, c_{x+1}, \ldots, c_{x+|V_i|-1}\}$. However, it is difficult for every node to sense a range of consecutive channels that come from a universal spectrum in practical scenarios.

We would like to point out that it is the holistic combination of the above four challenges that makes the design of rendezvous protocols far from trivial and requires an original study that cannot draw on any existing result which, to the best of our knowledge, addresses only the first and/or the second challenge. Formally, we coin the term *heterogeneous rendezvous* problem in CR networks to denote the following problem: *How can two channel hopping secondary users, given asynchronous local clocks, different sensing capabilities, no universal channel sets, and heterogeneous channel index systems, achieve the maximum "rendezvous diversity" within a minimum upper-bounded TTR?*

In response to the formulated problem, we present a systematic approach based on *group theory* for analyzing and devising CH-based rendezvous protocols that address above challenges altogether. The contributions of this work are summarized as follows.

1. *Establishment of the group-theoretic framework*: We formulate the heterogeneous rendezvous problem from the group-theoretic perspective, and cast the CH-based rendezvous protocol design into the established framework.

2. *Theoretical performance bound of rendezvous protocols*: We derive that the *minimum upper bound for TTR* to achieve the *maximum rendezvous diversity* in heterogeneous environments is N_iN_j, where N_i and N_j are the sizes of two distinct channel sets available to the two nodes i and j.

3. *Design of optimal rendezvous protocols that achieve the derived performance bound*: We first propose rendezvous protocols that achieve maximum rendezvous diversity within a TTR bounded by N_iN_j, given that N_i and N_j are co-prime. By leveraging the *symmetrization* technique, we further propose an advanced rendezvous protocol that achieves maximum rendezvous diversity within a TTR bounded by $O(N_iN_j)$ without assuming co-prime N_i and N_j.

Note that the follow-on tasks after initial rendezvous—such as neighbor discovery handshake [1], channel contention procedure, and data transfer—are outside the scope of this paper.

The rest of this paper is organized as follows. We provide the system model and formulate the problem in Section 2. In Sections 3 and 4, we describe the elementary and advanced CH-based rendezvous protocols respectively. We evaluate the performance of our proposed rendezvous schemes in Section 5, and conclude the paper in Section 6.

2. PROBLEM FORMULATION

2.1 System Model

2.1.1 Heterogeneous network environments

We assume a CR network where every secondary user/node $i \in \Lambda$ is equipped with a CR operating over a number of orthogonal frequency channels that are licensed to primary users, where Λ is the set of user IDs in the network.

Clock drift. We consider a time-slotted communication system. Local clocks of two nodes may differ from each other by a certain amount of *clock drift*. A network node is assumed to be capable of hopping across different channels according to a channel hopping sequence and its local clock.

Different sensible channel sets. We term the set of frequency channels which a secondary user i can sense and operate over its *sensible channel set* or *channel set*, denoted by C_i. $N_i = |C_i| < \infty$ is called its *sensible channel number* or simply *channel number*.

Different channel labeling functions. We do not assume a universal channel set for all nodes whereby their sensible frequency channels are mapped to a set of channel indices in the same way. Hence, each node i has its own channel labeling function to assign each frequency channel in C_i a channel index chosen from its channel label set $\mathbb{Z}_{N_i} = \{0, 1, 2, \ldots, N_i - 1\}$. We call the elements of the label set $\mathbb{Z}_{N_i}$ *channel labels* or *channel indices*. The labeling function λ_i is a 1-1 correspondence between C_i and $\mathbb{Z}_{N_i}$:

$$\lambda_i : C_i \to \mathbb{Z}_{N_i}.$$

Let $\lambda_i^{-1} : \mathbb{Z}_{N_i} \to C_i$ denote the inverse map of λ_i.

Heterogeneous environments. The CR network environment is *heterogeneous* in the sense that

- Tight synchronization is unavailable for different nodes' local clocks.
- C_i is *not necessarily identical* with C_j for two distinct nodes i and j.
- Each node i has its own channel labeling function λ_i, i.e., given the same channel at frequency a, it is possible that $\lambda_i(a) \neq \lambda_j(a)$.

2.1.2 CH sequence

A CH sequence determines the order in which a node visits all available channels. We represent node i's CH sequence u_i with period T as a sequence of channel indices:

$$u_i = \{u_i^0, u_i^1, ..., u_i^t, ..., u_i^{T-1}\},$$

where $u_i^t \in \mathbb{Z}_{N_i}$ denotes the channel index of sequence u_i in the t-th timeslot of a CH period, and $|u_i| = T$.

Given two CH sequences with period T, u_i and u_j, if $\exists t \in [0, T-1]$ s.t.

$$\lambda_i^{-1}(u_i^t) = \lambda_j^{-1}(u_j^t) = a$$

with $a \in C_i \cap C_j$, we say that u_i and u_j *rendezvous* in the t-th timeslot on frequency channel a. The t-th timeslot is called a *rendezvous slot*; frequency channel a is called a *rendezvous channel* between u_i and u_j; u_i^t and u_j^t are called a *pair of rendezvous channel indices*.

Let $\mathcal{C}(u_i, u_j)$ denote the *set of rendezvous channels* between two CH sequences u_i and u_j, and $\mathcal{T}(u_i, u_j)$ denote the *set of rendezvous slots*. Obviously, $\mathcal{C}(u_i, u_j) \subseteq C_i \cap C_j$ and $\mathcal{T}(u_i, u_j) \subseteq [0, T-1]$.

2.1.3 Common period of two CH sequences

Given two CH sequences with different periods, u_i and u_j whose periods are T_i and T_j respectively, we extend them to a CH sequence with period $T = \text{lcm}(T_i, T_j)$[1], such as $u'_i = \prod_{k=1}^{T/T_j} u_i$ and $u'_j = \prod_{k=1}^{T/T_i} u_j$, where $\prod_{k=1}^{K} s_k$ denotes the concatenated sequence $s_1 \parallel s_2 \parallel s_3 \parallel \cdots \parallel s_K$.

$T = \text{lcm}(T_i, T_j)$ is termed the *common period* of u_i and u_j. We define $\mathcal{C}(u_i, u_j) \triangleq \mathcal{C}(u'_i, u'_j) \subseteq C_i \cap C_j$, and $\mathcal{T}(u_i, u_j) \triangleq \mathcal{T}(u'_i, u'_j) \subseteq [0, T-1]$.

2.2 CH Protocol

A CH protocol is a rule of creating a CH sequence for each node and can be represented as a map r

$$\begin{aligned} r : \Lambda \times \mathbb{N} &\rightarrow \bigcup_{T=1}^{\infty} \mathbb{N}^T \\ (i, N_i) &\mapsto r(i, N_i) \end{aligned}$$

where $\mathbb{N}^T$ is the set of natural number sequences with length T and $\bigcup_{T=1}^{\infty} \mathbb{N}^T$ denotes the set of all CH sequences. Node i's CH sequence will be $r(i, N_i)$.

In heterogeneous environments, two nodes may have no knowledge about the clock time, the channel set, and the channel labeling function of each other. A node knows its ID i and the number of sensible channels, i.e., N_i. Our definition of a CH protocol r only relies on a node's ID i and channel number N_i. Note that r is independent of the clock time, the channel set (we are not interested in which channels are available to a node but the total number of available channels) and the channel labeling function, and that node i's CH sequence only relies on its own information and requires no knowledge about other nodes.

2.3 Heterogeneous CH (HCH) System

Given a CH sequence u_i, we use $rotate(u_i, k)$ to denote the *cyclic rotation* of CH sequence u_i by k timeslots, i.e.,

$$rotate(u_i, k) = \{v_i^0, ..., v_i^t, ..., v_i^{T-1}\},$$

where $v_i^t = u_i^{(t+k) \bmod T}$, $t \in [0, T-1]$ and k is an integer. For example, given $u_i = \{0, 1, 2\}$, $rotate(u_i, 2) = \{2, 0, 1\}$.

DEFINITION 1. *A* Heterogeneous CH (HCH) system *for a CR network is a pair $H = (\Lambda, r)$. $\forall i, j \in \Lambda, i \neq j$ and $\forall k, l \in \mathbb{Z}$, H satisfies the following property: if $C_i \cap C_j \neq \varnothing$, then $|\mathcal{T}(rotate(r(i, N_i), k), rotate(r(j, N_j), l))| \geq 1$, where Λ is the set of node IDs in the network, and r is the CH protocol to be designed.*

In Definition 1, the required property states that two nodes' CH sequences should have at least one rendezvous timeslot per common period given any amount of clock drifts k and l, provided that they share at least one common channel. Obviously, it is impossible to rendezvous with no channel in common.

2.4 Group-based Interpretation of Rendezvous

Nodes i and j rendezvous on a frequency channel a in timeslot t, which implies that they simultaneously hop onto the same frequency regardless of their assigned channel indices, $\lambda_i(a) \in \mathbb{Z}_{N_i}$ and $\lambda_j(a) \in \mathbb{Z}_{N_j}$, to a. I.e., frequency a can be mapped to any channel index in $\mathbb{Z}_{N_i}$ and $\mathbb{Z}_{N_j}$. Hence the pair of rendezvous channel indices $(\lambda_i(a), \lambda_j(a))$ can be any element in the group $\mathbb{Z}_{N_i} \oplus \mathbb{Z}_{N_j}$. We intuit that a feasible protocol has to enumerate/generate all elements in $\mathbb{Z}_{N_i} \oplus \mathbb{Z}_{N_j}$. As a result, we transform the concept of rendezvous between two CH sequences to an element in $\mathbb{Z}_{N_i} \oplus \mathbb{Z}_{N_j}$; the maximum rendezvous diversity independent of channel labeling functions corresponds to enumerating/generating all elements in $\mathbb{Z}_{N_i} \oplus \mathbb{Z}_{N_j}$.

Min TTR Bound for Max Rendezvous Diversity. Theorem 1 substantiates the aforementioned intuition, whence additionally we obtain the minimum period, i.e., the minimum TTR bound for the maximum rendezvous diversity ($|C_i \cap C_j|$).

THEOREM 1. *Given CH sequences $r(i, N_i)$ and $r(j, N_j)$, let*

$$u = \prod_{n=1}^{T/|r(j,N_j)|} r(i, N_i); \qquad v = \prod_{n=1}^{T/|r(i,N_i)|} r(j, N_j),$$

where $T = \text{lcm}(|r(i, N_i)|, |r(j, N_j)|)$. The set of channel index pairs in all timeslots equals $\mathbb{Z}_{N_i} \oplus \mathbb{Z}_{N_j}$, i.e. $\forall k, l \in \mathbb{Z}$,

$$\{(rotate(u, k)^t, rotate(v, l)^t | t \in [0, T-1]\} = \mathbb{Z}_{N_i} \oplus \mathbb{Z}_{N_j}.$$

As a corollary, their common period T must be $N_i N_j$ or greater; $r(i, N_i)$ and $r(j, N_j)$ can rendezvous on every channel in $C_i \cap C_j$ within T timeslots.

PROOF. It is obvious that $\{(rotate(u, k)^t, rotate(v, l)^t | t \in [0, T-1]\} \subseteq \mathbb{Z}_{N_i} \oplus \mathbb{Z}_{N_j}$. It suffices to prove $\mathbb{Z}_{N_i} \oplus \mathbb{Z}_{N_j} \subseteq \{(rotate(u, k)^t, rotate(v, l)^t | t \in [0, T-1]\}$.

Suppose $C_i \cap C_j = \{a\}$ and $\exists (n, m) \in \mathbb{Z}_{N_i} \oplus \mathbb{Z}_{N_j}$ but $(n, m) \notin \{(rotate(u, k)^t, rotate(v, l)^t | t \in [0, T-1]\}$. We construct two channel labeling functions $\tilde{\lambda}_i : C_i \rightarrow \mathbb{Z}_{N_i}$ and $\tilde{\lambda}_j : C_j \rightarrow \mathbb{Z}_{N_j}$, such as

$$\tilde{\lambda}_i(x) \triangleq \begin{cases} \lambda_i(x) & \text{if } x \neq a, \lambda_i^{-1}(n) \\ n & \text{if } x = a \\ \lambda_i(a) & \text{if } x = \lambda_i^{-1}(n), \end{cases}$$

$$\tilde{\lambda}_j(x) \triangleq \begin{cases} \lambda_j(x) & \text{if } x \neq a, \lambda_j^{-1}(m) \\ m & \text{if } x = a \\ \lambda_j(a) & \text{if } x = \lambda_j^{-1}(m). \end{cases}$$

We need to prove that i and j cannot rendezvous with channel labeling functions $\tilde{\lambda}_i$ and $\tilde{\lambda}_j$. Suppose $\exists t \in [0, T-1]$ s.t. $\tilde{\lambda}_i^{-1}(rotate(u, k)^t) = \tilde{\lambda}_j^{-1}(rotate(v, l)^t)$. Since $C_i \cap C_j = \{a\}$, $\tilde{\lambda}_i^{-1}(rotate(u, k)^t) = \tilde{\lambda}_j^{-1}(rotate(v, l)^t) = a$, therefore $n = \tilde{\lambda}_i(a) = rotate(u, k)^t$ and $m = \tilde{\lambda}_j(a) = rotate(v, l)^t$. Hence, $(n, m) \in \{(rotate(u, k)^t, rotate(v, l)^t | t \in [0, T-1]\}$, and this is a contradiction.

Hence we conclude that

$$\mathbb{Z}_{N_i} \oplus \mathbb{Z}_{N_j} \subseteq \{(rotate(u, k)^t, rotate(v, l)^t | t \in [0, T-1]\},$$

and that $T \geq |\mathbb{Z}_{N_i} \oplus \mathbb{Z}_{N_j}| = N_i N_j$.

Elements in group $\mathbb{Z}_{N_i} \oplus \mathbb{Z}_{N_j}$ enumerate all possible pairs of rendezvous channel indices, whence the two CH sequences achieve maximum rendezvous diversity. □

2.5 Design Requirements

We identify three design requirements for a CH-based rendezvous protocol to be applicable in heterogeneous environments.

[1] The least common multiple of two integers x and y is usually denoted by $\text{lcm}(x, y)$.

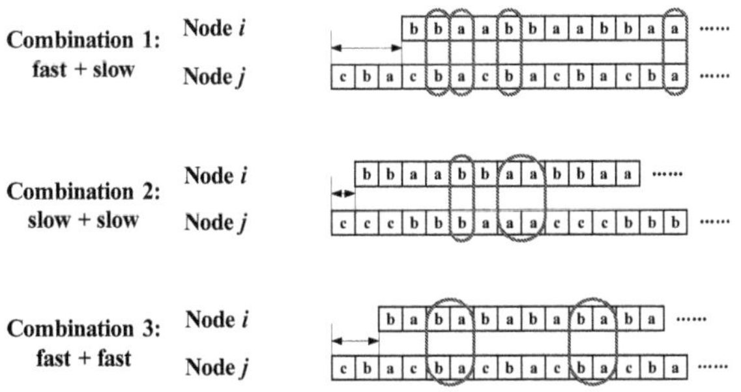

Figure 1: Three combinations of fast and/or slow CH sequences of nodes i and j, with $C_i = \{a, b\}$ and $C_j = \{a, b, c\}$.

1. *Maximum rendezvous diversity.* We have to establish the maximum rendezvous diversity between a pair of rendezvous nodes to minimize the probability of rendezvous failure. As is shown in Theorem 1, it suffices to enumerate all possible pairs of channel indices, i.e., to enumerate all elements in $\mathbb{Z}_{N_i} \oplus \mathbb{Z}_{N_j}$.
2. *Delay bounded by $O(N_iN_j)$.* According to Theorem 1, the common period of two nodes' CH sequences must be at least N_iN_j; therefore we expect that the maximum rendezvous diversity can be achieved within a delay bounded by $O(N_iN_j)$.
3. *Robustness to cyclic rotation.* To be independent of clock synchronization, rendezvous between two CH sequences has to be robust to cyclic rotation.

Fast/slow CH sequences. We define a pair of CH sequences for each node i with $N_i = |C_i|$ sensible channels: (1) a *fast* CH sequence whereby node i changes its current channel every timeslot to traverse all N_i channels in C_i; and (2) a *slow* CH sequence whereby node i changes its current channel every N_i timeslots to traverse all N_i channels in C_i. For example, suppose $N_i = 3$ and $C_i = \{a, b, c\}$, then $\{a, b, c, a, b, c, a, b, c\}$ is a fast CH sequence and $\{a, a, a, b, b, b, c, c, c\}$ is a slow CH sequence. Note that the relative order of a, b and c does not matter, which means that $\{b, a, c, b, a, c, b, a, c\}$ is also a fast CH sequence and $\{c, c, c, a, a, a, b, b, b\}$ is a slow CH sequence as well. Therefore we can use channel labels to represent a CH sequence alternatively. For instance, $\{0, 2, 1, 0, 2, 1, 0, 2, 1\}$ is a fast sequence and $\{2, 2, 2, 0, 0, 0, 1, 1, 1\}$ is a slow sequence, no matter which channel labeling function is used by node i.

There are three possible combinations/pairs of fast and/or slow CH sequences that can be chosen by two nodes (i.e., *fast+slow*, *slow+slow*, and *fast+fast*), as illustrated in Figure 1. Our research findings indicate that the above design requirements can be satisfied when two nodes happen to choose any of these three combinations, then the maximum rendezvous diversity is established within a bounded delay. This conclusion holds despite any amount of cyclic rotation to either CH sequences.

For Combination 1 in Figure 1, one node employs a slow CH sequence while the other employs a fast one. This is the asymmetric CH protocol[2] *ACH* [3,6], where every node knows its pre-assigned role as a sender to use a fast CH sequence, or a receiver to use a slow one. In group theory, using two elements, such as $(1, 0)$ and $(0, 1)$, can easily generate the group $\mathbb{Z}_{N_i} \oplus \mathbb{Z}_{N_j}$. In ACH, the sender node uses the generator $(1, 0)$ to obtain its fast CH sequence while the receiver node uses the generator $(0, 1)$ to obtain its slow CH sequence, which collectively generate the group $\mathbb{Z}_{N_i} \oplus \mathbb{Z}_{N_j}$. The drawback is that two nodes create CH sequences in different/asymmetric ways, which necessitate pre-assigned roles.

For Combination 2 or 3 in Figure 1, both nodes choose a slow (or fast) CH sequence. When N_i and N_j are co-prime, they gaurantee maximum rendezvous diversity with a bounded delay by Chinese Remainder Theorem. We show that such designs with the channel number co-primality constraint meet the above design requirements in Section 3 and term them *elementary HCH systems.* These two designs are called ϵ_1- and ϵ_2-rendezvous in Section 3; ϵ stands for *elementary.*

However, it is impractical to assume that two rendezvous nodes happen to be pre-assigned the sender/receiver role, or meet the co-primality constraint on channel numbers N_i and N_j. In Section 4, we propose an advanced HCH system design, which meets the above design requirements and is independent of all aforementioned assumptions. The advanced design leverages the *symmetrization* technique that enables every node to create a bit string that determines how to interleave its fast and slow CH sequences. Based on Combination 1, this advanced design introduces the notion of *choice sequence* to symmetrize Combination 1 while preserving all its properties.

3. ELEMENTARY HCH SYSTEMS WITH CHANNEL NUMBER CO-PRIMALITY

In this section, we propose two *elementary* HCH systems, termed ϵ_1- and ϵ_2-rendezvous, both of which require co-primality of channels numbers N_i and N_j. We consider generating the group $\mathbb{Z}_{N_i} \oplus \mathbb{Z}_{N_j}$ in a symmetric way—using a single group generator. By Chinese Remainder Theorem, group $\mathbb{Z}_{N_i} \oplus \mathbb{Z}_{N_j}$ is cyclic if and only if N_i and N_j are co-prime; in this case, $\mathbb{Z}_{N_i} \oplus \mathbb{Z}_{N_j} = \mathbb{Z}_{N_iN_j}$.

3.1 CH Sequence Construction

ϵ_1-rendezvous. With N_i and N_j co-prime, $(1, 1)$ is a generator of the cyclic group $\mathbb{Z}_{N_i} \oplus \mathbb{Z}_{N_j}$. For every node $i \in \Lambda$, let $r(i, N_i)^t$ denote the channel index of its CH sequence in timeslot t, which is determined in ϵ_1-rendezvous as follows

$$r(i, N_i)^t = t \bmod N_i,$$

where $t \in [0, N_i - 1]$.

ϵ_2-rendezvous. Similarly, we propose another HCH system that requires N_i and N_j to be co-prime. For every node $i \in \Lambda$, the channel index of its CH sequence in timeslot t is determined in ϵ_2-rendezvous as follows

$$r(i, N_i)^t = \lfloor \frac{t}{N_i} \rfloor \bmod N_i,$$

where $t \in [0, N_i^2 - 1]$.

3.2 Robustness to Heterogeneous Environments

If nodes i and j employ ϵ_1- or ϵ_2-rendezvous, the common periods of their CH sequences are $T = N_iN_j$ and $N_i^2N_j^2$, re-

[2]An *asymmetric* protocol means that two nodes generate their CH sequences in different/asymmetric ways.

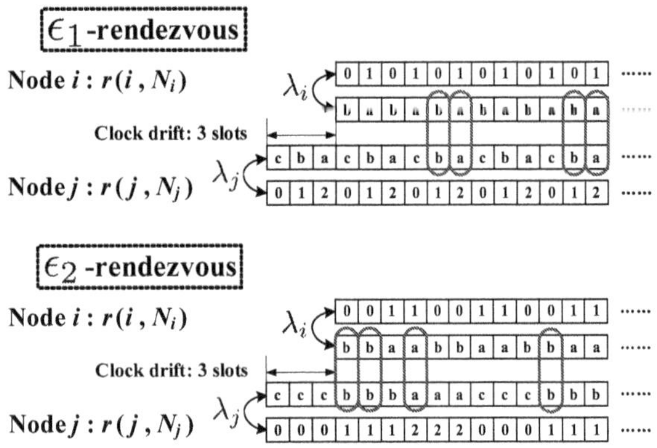

Figure 2: Nodes i and j have different labeling functions: $\lambda_i(b) = 0$, $\lambda_i(a) = 1$; $\lambda_j(c) = 0$, $\lambda_j(b) = 1$, $\lambda_j(a) = 2$. In ϵ_1-rendezvous: node i uses $r(i, 2) = \{0, 1\}$ while node j uses $r(j, 3) = \{0, 1, 2\}$. In ϵ_2-rendezvous: node i uses $r(i, 2) = \{0, 0, 1, 1\}$ while node j uses $r(j, 3) = \{0, 0, 0, 1, 1, 1, 2, 2, 2\}$.

spectively. Figure 2 illustrates examples of elementary HCH systems with $N_i = 2$ and $N_j = 3$. In Figure 2, two nodes rendezvous over all common channels (maximum diversity). The following theorem shows ϵ_1- and ϵ_2-rendezvous protocols' robustness to heterogeneous environments.

THEOREM 2. *For two nodes i and j with N_i and N_j coprime, ϵ_1- and ϵ_2-rendezvous can guarantee maximum rendezvous diversity with a TTR bounded by $N_i N_j$ and $N_i^2 N_j^2$, respectively, despite any possible channel labeling functions and clock drifts.*

PROOF. **ϵ_1-rendezvous.** Suppose node j's clock is k timeslots behind that of node i. Let k' be $k \bmod N_j \in \mathbb{Z}_{N_j}$. Since $r(j, N_j)^t = t \bmod N_j$, we have $rotate(r(j, N_j), k) = r(j, N_j) + k'$, where the addition in the right-hand side means $r(j, N_j)$'s component-wise addition by k' in $\mathbb{Z}_{N_j}$ (For example, $\{0, 1, 2\} + 1 = \{1, 2, 0\}$ in $\mathbb{Z}_3$). Therefore, the sequence

$$\begin{aligned} & \{(r(i, N_i)^t, rotate(r(j, N_j), k)^t)\}_{t \in [0, T-1]} \\ = \quad & \{t \cdot (1, 1)\}_{t \in [0, T-1]} + (0, k'). \end{aligned}$$

By Chinese Remainder Theorem, the group $\mathbb{Z}_{N_i} \oplus \mathbb{Z}_{N_j}$ is cyclic if and only if N_i and N_j are co-prime. Since $(1, 1)$ is a generator of the cyclic group $\mathbb{Z}_{N_i} \oplus \mathbb{Z}_{N_j}$ and t runs from 0 to $T - 1 = N_i N_j - 1$, we have $\{t(1, 1)\}_{t \in [0, T-1]} = \mathbb{Z}_{N_i} \oplus \mathbb{Z}_{N_j}$, thus

$$\begin{aligned} & \{(r(i, \mathbb{Z}_{N_i})^t, rotate(r(j, \mathbb{Z}_{N_j}), k)^t)\}_{t \in [0, T-1]} \\ = \quad & \mathbb{Z}_{N_i} \oplus \mathbb{Z}_{N_j} + (0, k') \\ = \quad & \mathbb{Z}_{N_i} \oplus \mathbb{Z}_{N_j}. \end{aligned}$$

Since λ_i / λ_j is a 1-1 correspondence between the channel set C_i / C_j and the label set $\mathbb{Z}_{N_i} / \mathbb{Z}_{N_j}$, we have

$$\lambda_i^{-1}(\mathbb{Z}_{N_i}) \times \lambda_j^{-1}(\mathbb{Z}_{N_j}) = C_i \times C_j.$$

It follows immediately that it guarantees rendezvous with maximum diversity, irrespective of the clock drift and channel labeling functions.

ϵ_2-rendezvous. In ϵ_2-rendezvous, the common period of nodes i and j is $T = N_i^2 \cdot N_j^2$. Suppose node j's clock is k timeslots behind that of node i. Fix two integers $a \in [0, N_i - 1]$ and $b \in [0, N_j - 1]$ and consider the following simultaneous congruence equations

$$\begin{cases} \lfloor \frac{t}{N_i} \rfloor \equiv a \pmod{N_i} \\ \lfloor \frac{t+k}{N_j} \rfloor \equiv b \pmod{N_j}, \end{cases} \tag{1}$$

where $t \in [0, N_i^2 \cdot N_j^2 - 1]$. Suppose $t = qN_i^2 + r$, where $0 \le r < N_i^2$. We have $\lfloor \frac{t}{N_i} \rfloor = \lfloor \frac{qN_i^2 + r}{N_i} \rfloor = qN_i + \lfloor \frac{r}{N_i} \rfloor$. Thus $\lfloor \frac{r}{N_i} \rfloor \equiv a \pmod{N_i}$. Since $0 \le r < N_i^2$, $0 \le \frac{r}{N_i} < N_i$, $0 \le \lfloor \frac{r}{N_i} \rfloor < N_i$. Note that $a \in [0, N_i - 1]$. We obtain that $\lfloor \frac{r}{N_i} \rfloor = a$ and that $aN_i \le r < (a+1)N_i$. Hence Equation 1 is equivalent to

$$\begin{cases} t \equiv aN_i, \ldots, aN_i + (N_i - 1) \pmod{N_i^2} \\ t \equiv bN_j - k, \ldots, bN_j + (N_j - 1) - k \pmod{N_j^2}. \end{cases} \tag{2}$$

Since N_i and N_j are coprime, by Chinese Remainder Theorem, Equation 2 (and thus Equation 1) has $N_i \cdot N_j$ solutions up to modulo $N_i^2 \cdot N_j^2$. I.e., for each pair $(a, b) \in \mathbb{Z}_{N_i} \oplus \mathbb{Z}_{N_j}$, it appears in the sequence $\{(r(i, N_i)^t, r(j, N_j)^t)\}_{t \in [0, N_i^2 \cdot N_j^2 - 1]}$ for $N_i N_j$ times. It follows immediately that it guarantees rendezvous with maximum diversity, irrespective of the clock drift and channel labeling functions. □

Discussions. Theorem 2 implies that two nodes adopting ϵ_1- or ϵ_2-rendezvous can achieve rendezvous over all common channels in $C_i \cap C_j$ within a bounded time. The average TTR for both elementary HCH systems is the same, i.e., $\frac{N_i N_j}{|C_i \cap C_j|}$. However, the drawback of such elementary protocols is the requirement of channel number co-primality.

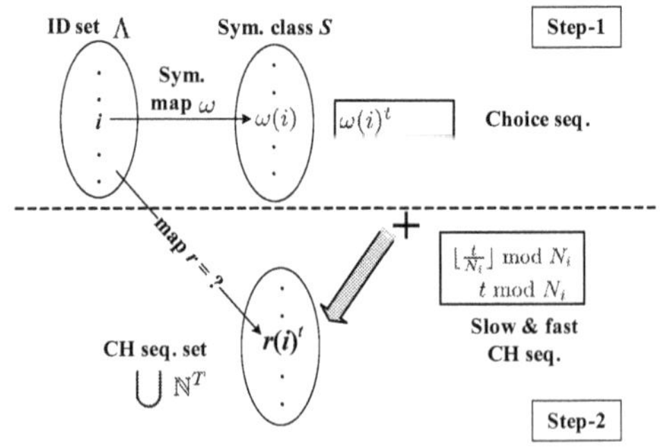

Figure 3: The relationship among ID set, symmetrization map, symmetrization class, and CH sequence, in the advanced HCH system design.

4. ADVANCED HCH SYSTEMS

In this section, we show how to construct the HCH system $H = (\Lambda, r)$ without any assumption on pre-assigned roles, or channel number co-primality. We use a two-step approach and illustrate this procedure in Figure 3.

4.1 A Two-step Approach

The first step is to create a *distinct* equilong bit string for each node i. Let ω be an *injective* map from the ID set Λ to the *bit string* set S that assigns a bit string $\omega(i) \in S$ to each node $i \in \Lambda$. Nodes i and j's bit strings $\omega(i)$ and $\omega(j)$ are said to be *distinct* if they have at least one bit different after any amount of cyclic rotation; in other words, $\omega(i) \neq rotate(\omega(j), k)$, $\forall k \in \mathbb{N}$. If any two bit strings in S are

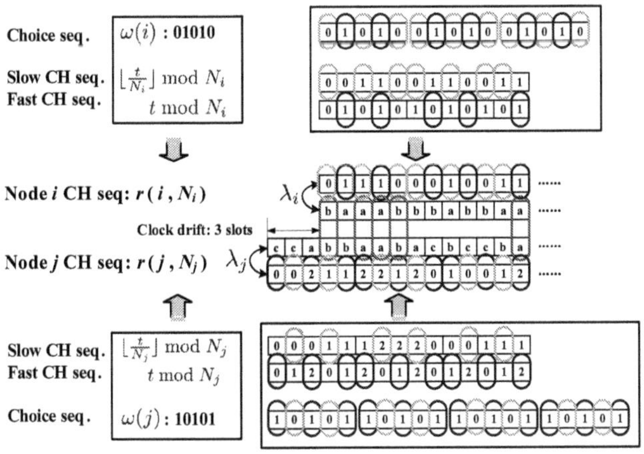

Figure 4: In the advanced HCH design, nodes i and j use $\omega(i) = \{0,1,0,1,0\}$ and $\omega(j) = \{1,0,1,0,1\}$ to construct their CH sequences respectively. For three channels with central frequencies at a, b and c, nodes i and j have different labeling functions: $\lambda_i(b) = 0$, $\lambda_i(a) = 1$; $\lambda_j(c) = 0$, $\lambda_j(b) = 1$, $\lambda_j(a) = 2$.

distinct, we term the *injective* map ω a *symmetrization map* and the bit string set S a *symmetrization class*. Meanwhile, an element (a *bit string*) in S is called a *choice sequence*.

The second step for node i is to use its choice sequence to interleave its slow and fast CH sequences to obtain $r(i, N_i)$—i.e., to choose whether the slow or fast CH sequence should be used in the current timeslot of $r(i, N_i)$. In Figure 4, node i has $N_i = 2$ sensible channels, and it has constructed a slow and a fast CH sequence. The slow CH sequence visits channel ($\lfloor \frac{t}{2} \rfloor$ mod 2) in the t-th timeslot (note that we start from the 0th timeslot)

$$00110011\cdots,$$

and the fast CH sequence visits channel (t mod 2) in the t-th timeslot

$$01010101\cdots.$$

Suppose its choice sequence is $\omega(i) = 01010$. In the t-th slot, node i chooses the channel index in the t-th slot of its corresponding fast (or slow) CH sequence if the t-th bit of its choice sequence is 1 (or 0). For example, since the 0th bit of $\omega(i)$ is 0, node i chooses the channel index of the 0th slot in its slow CH sequence (which is channel index 0). Similarly, since the 1st bit of $\omega(i)$ is 1, node i chooses the channel index of the 1st slot in its fast CH sequence (which is channel index 1).

In the following subsections, we will elaborate on how to construct a choice sequence and CH sequence.

4.2 Existence of Symmetrization Class

Let $\mathbb{F}_2$ denote the Galois field of size 2, and $\mathbb{F}_2^l$ denote the set of all bit strings with length l. $G = \{rotate(\cdot, k) | k \in [0, l-1]\}$ is a cyclic group acting on $\mathbb{F}_2^l$. For $rotate(\cdot, k) \in G$ and $\sigma \in \mathbb{F}_2^l$, the group action $\circ$ is defined by $rotate(\cdot, k) \circ \sigma \triangleq rotate(\sigma, k)$. The orbit of $\sigma \in \mathbb{F}_2^l$ is denoted by $G \circ \sigma$

$$G \circ \sigma \triangleq \{g \circ \sigma | g \in G\} \equiv \{rotate(\sigma, k) | k \in [0, l-1]\}.$$

A subset $S \subseteq \mathbb{F}_2^l$ is said to be an *l-symmetrization class* if it contains distinct bit strings with length l—$\forall \sigma, \tau \in S$, $\sigma \neq \tau$ implies $(G \circ \sigma) \cap (G \circ \tau) = \varnothing$, i.e., $\forall k \in [0, l-1]$, $\sigma \neq rotate(\tau, k)$. Elements in S are called *choice sequences.* For example, when $l = 3$, $S = \{000, 001, 011, 111\}$ is a 3-symmetrization class; however, $S = \{000, 001, 010, 011\}$ is not a 3-symmetrization class because $rotate(001, 1) = 010$.

We define the *rotation Hamming distance* δ_H in $\mathbb{F}_2^l$ such as: for $u, v \in \mathbb{F}_2^l$,

$$\delta_H(u, v) \triangleq \min_{k \in \mathbb{Z}} d_H(u, rotate(v, k)),$$

where d_H is the Hamming distance in $\mathbb{F}_2^l$.

The *degree* of a subset $F \subseteq \mathbb{F}_2^l$, $\delta(F)$, is defined such as $\delta(F) \triangleq \min_{u,v \in F, u \neq v} \delta_H(u, v)$. If $S \subseteq \mathbb{F}_2^l$ is a symmetrization class, $\delta(S) \geq 1$. In other words, any two sequences in S are distinct.

The following lemma shows the existence of an l-symmetrization class for $\forall l \in \mathbb{N}$.

LEMMA 1. *$\forall l \in \mathbb{N}$, there exists an l-symmetrization class. $\forall M \in \mathbb{N}$, there exists $l \in \mathbb{N}$ and an l-symmetrization class S_l such that $|S_l| \geq M$.*

PROOF. Given $l \in \mathbb{N}$, let $\mathbb{F}_2^l/G \triangleq \{G \circ \sigma | \sigma \in \mathbb{F}_2^l\}$ be the set of all orbits in $\mathbb{F}_2^l$ under the action of group G. The number of cycles of group element $g = rotate(\cdot, k) \in G$ as a permutation in $\mathbb{F}_2^l$ is $\gcd(k, l)$. By Polya Enumeration Theorem, $|\mathbb{F}_2^l/G| = \frac{1}{|G|}\sum_{k=0}^{l-1} 2^{\gcd(k,l)} = \frac{1}{l}\sum_{k=0}^{l-1} 2^{\gcd(k,l)} = \frac{1}{l}\sum_{d|l} \varphi(d) 2^{l/d} \geq 2^l/l$. Suppose

$$\mathbb{F}_2^l/G = \{\Sigma_1, \Sigma_2, \ldots, \Sigma_{|\mathbb{F}_2^l/G|}\},$$

and let S_l be$\{\sigma_1, \sigma_2, \ldots, \sigma_{|\mathbb{F}_2^l/G|}\}$ with $\sigma_i \in \Sigma_i$. We conclude that S_l is an l-symmetrization class. Given $M \in \mathbb{N}$, $\exists l \in \mathbb{N}$ s.t. $2^l/l \geq M$, and then S_l is an l-symmetrization class and $|S_l| \geq M$. □

4.3 Construction of Symmetrization Classes And Choice Sequences

Suppose S is a sufficiently large l-symmetrization class for some $l \in \mathbb{N}$, we term

$$\omega : \Lambda \to S$$

a symmetrization map if ω is injective. Intuitively, ω assigns a choice sequence to each node $i \in \Lambda$. Note that any two bit strings in S are distinct. Since ω is injective, for two different nodes i and j, $\omega(i)$ and $\omega(j)$ are distinct bit strings.

Next, we show both centralized and distributed algorithms to construct choice sequences based on a few example symmetrization classes.

A centralized algorithm for optimal (minimum) l-symmetrization class. For $l \in \mathbb{N}$, S_l in the proof of Lemma 1 is called an optimal l-symmetrization class. Given an ID set Λ, we need to find a sufficiently large l such that we can construct a symmetrization map ω from Λ to S_l. To be precise, since $|S_l| = \frac{1}{l}\sum_{d|l} \varphi(d) 2^{l/d} \geq 2^l/l$, we have $|S_l| \geq |\Lambda|$ if $l - \log_2 l \geq \log_2 |\Lambda|$. In this case, there exists an injective map ω from Λ to S_l. S_l is optimal in the sense that it achieves the minimum l to guarantee the existence of a symmetrization map, where the minimum $l \approx g + \log_2 g$ with $g = \lceil \log_2 |\Lambda| \rceil$.

Suppose we have four nodes whose IDs are 00, 01, 10 and 11, respectively. Since $10 = rotate(01, 1)$, we need to assign each of them a distinct bit string. In

$$\mathbb{F}_2^3 = \{000, 001, 010, 011, 100, 101, 110, 111\},$$

for example, elements 001, 010 and 100 are identical under cyclic rotation, so only one of them, say 001, is preserved in the 3-symmetrization class, while the rest of them, 010 and 100, are eliminated. In this manner, we can obtain the optimal 3-symmetrization class $S_3 = \{000, 001, 011, 111\}$, and thus build a symmetrization map $\omega : \mathbb{F}_2^2 \to S_3$ for the four nodes: $\omega(00) = 000$, $\omega(01) = 001$, $\omega(10) = 011$ and $\omega(11) = 111$.

However, the calculation of the optimal symmetrization class requires a centralized controller or that nodes' choice sequences (i.e., bit strings) be pre-assigned. Next, we present two distributed algorithms that allow each node to generate its choice sequence autonomously. Given an ID set Λ, every node can represent its ID to be a $\lceil \log_2 |\Lambda| \rceil$-bit string, i.e. it can construct an injective map

$$\pi : \Lambda \to \mathbb{F}_2^g,$$

where $g = \lceil \log_2 |\Lambda| \rceil$ is the ID length[3].

A distributed algorithm for η_1 symmetrization class. Each node i can generate a $(2g+3)$-bit string using the symmetrization map ω

$$\omega : \Lambda \to \mathbb{F}_2^{2g+3},$$

where

$$\forall i \in \Lambda, \omega(i) \triangleq \pi(i)10^{g+1}1.$$

For any two nodes i and j, their $(2g+3)$-bit strings are distinct. We term $Z \triangleq \{u10^{g+1}1 | u \in \mathbb{F}_2^g\}$ an η_1 symmetrization class. Note that the η_1 symmetrization map can be efficiently computed by each node in one iteration.

For example, suppose node i's ID is a 6-bit string 110110, i.e. $\pi(i) = 110110$ and we have $g = |\pi(i)| = 6$. Then its choice sequence will be

$$\omega(i) = \pi(i)10^{g+1}1 = \pi(i)10^71 = 110110100000001.$$

A distributed algorithm for η_2 symmetrization class. Here we present the η_2 symmetrization class with $l = g + \lceil\sqrt{g}\rceil(2 + \lceil \log_2 g \rceil) + 3$, where $g = \lceil \log_2 \Lambda \rceil$.

Let $\mathbf{b}_h^{(\lceil \log_2 g \rceil)}$ be the $\lceil \log_2 g \rceil$-bit binary representation of natural number h with $h \leq g$. An auxiliary map η_2 is defined on $\bigcup_{h=0}^{g} \{0^h\}$, i.e., the zero strings, such as

$$\eta_2(0^h) = \begin{cases} 0^h & \text{if } h < \lceil\sqrt{g}\rceil; \\ 0^{\lceil\sqrt{g}\rceil}1\mathbf{b}_h^{(\lceil \log_2 g \rceil)} & \text{if } h \geq \lceil\sqrt{g}\rceil. \end{cases}$$

For each node $i \in \Lambda$, suppose

$$\pi(i) = \prod_{k=1}^{K} 1^{o_k}0^{z_k} \triangleq 1^{o_1}0^{z_1}1^{o_2}0^{z_2}\cdots 1^{o_K}0^{z_K},$$

where $\forall k \in [1, K]$, $o_k, z_k \geq 0$ and $\sum_{k=1}^{K}(o_k + z_k) = g$.

Then we define the map $\tilde{\eta_2} : \Lambda \to \bigcup_{n=g}^{\infty} \mathbb{F}_2^n$ such as

$$\forall i \in \Lambda, \tilde{\eta_2}(i) \triangleq \prod_{k=1}^{K} 1^{o_k}\eta_2(0^{z_k}).$$

We compute the ratio of lengths of $\eta_2(0^h)$ to 0^h such as

$$\frac{|\eta_2(0^h)|}{|0^h|} = \frac{\lceil\sqrt{g}\rceil + 1 + \lceil \log_2 g \rceil}{h} \leq \frac{\lceil\sqrt{g}\rceil + 1 + \lceil \log_2 g \rceil}{\lceil\sqrt{g}\rceil},$$

[3]Network nodes' IDs are usually equilong. Map π can be perceived as assigning an ID to each device, so it must be injective. g is the ID length.

and the ratio of lengths of $\tilde{\eta_2}(i)$ to $\pi(i)$ such as

$$\frac{|\tilde{\eta_2}(i)|}{g} = \frac{|\tilde{\eta_2}(i)|}{|\pi(i)|} \leq \frac{\lceil\sqrt{g}\rceil + 1 + \lceil \log_2 g \rceil}{\lceil\sqrt{g}\rceil}.$$

We obtain an upper-bound estimation of the length of $\tilde{\eta_2}(i)$, such as

$$|\tilde{\eta_2}(i)| \leq g \cdot \frac{\lceil\sqrt{g}\rceil + 1 + \lceil \log_2 g \rceil}{\lceil\sqrt{g}\rceil} \leq g + \lceil\sqrt{g}\rceil(1 + \lceil \log_2 g \rceil).$$

On basis of the derived bound for the length of $\tilde{\eta_2}(i)$, we let $l = g + \lceil\sqrt{g}\rceil(2 + \lceil \log_2 g \rceil) + 3$, and construct the symmetrization map $\omega : \Lambda \to \mathbb{F}_2^l$ whereby each node i autonomously generates its choice sequence

$$\omega(i) \triangleq \tilde{\eta_2}(i)10^a1,$$

with $a = l - |\tilde{\eta_2}(i)| - 2 \geq [g + \lceil\sqrt{g}\rceil(2 + \lceil \log_2 g \rceil) + 3] - [g + \lceil\sqrt{g}\rceil(1 + \lceil \log_2 g \rceil)] - 2 = \lceil\sqrt{g}\rceil + 1$.

For any two nodes i and j, their choice sequences are distinct bit strings. We term the set of such bit strings an η_2 symmetrization class.

For instance, suppose node i's ID is an 8-bit string $\pi(i) = 00001001$, with $g = |\pi(i)| = 8$ and $\lceil\sqrt{g}\rceil = 3$. The length of its choice sequence is $l = g + \lceil\sqrt{g}\rceil(2 + \lceil \log_2 g \rceil) + 3 = 8 + 3 \times (2 + 3) + 3 = 26$. $\pi(i)$ can be represented as $\pi(i) = 00001001 = 0^410^21$. Since $4 \geq \lceil\sqrt{g}\rceil = 3$, $\eta_2(0^4) = 0^31100 = 0001100$, where the last three digits 100 is the 3-bit binary representation of 4. Since $2 < \lceil\sqrt{g}\rceil = 3$, $\eta_2(0^2) = 0^2 = 00$. Then we have

$$\tilde{\eta_2}(i) = \eta_2(0^4)1\eta_2(0^2)1 = 00011001001.$$

$|\tilde{\eta_2}(i)| = 11$, then $a = l - |\tilde{\eta_2}(i)| - 2 = 26 - 11 - 2 = 13$. Thus node i's choice sequence is

$$\omega(i) = \tilde{\eta_2}(i)10^{13}1 = 00011001001100000000000001.$$

4.4 Interleaving Slow and Fast CH Sequences

In this subsection, we present the approach to constructing a CH sequence $r(i, N_i)$ for each node i. As aforementioned, node i constructs its choice sequence via a chosen symmetrization map $\omega : \Lambda \to S$.

Initially, we need to make sure that node i's channel number N_i is a prime number and coprime to the length of the choice sequence l, i.e., $\gcd(N_i, l) = 1$. Through a remapping scheme [12, 13], we can increase N_i to the smallest prime number greater than or equal to N_i and co-prime to l, i.e., $N_i \leftarrow \min\{p \in \mathbb{N} |\ \text{prime } p \geq N_i, \gcd(p, l) = 1\}$.

Now we demonstrate how to combine *slow/fast* CH sequences using the choice sequence $\omega(i)$. In timeslot t (t starts from 0), the channel index of its CH sequence, $r(i, N_i)^t$, is calculated in accordance with the choice sequence $\omega(i)$:

- If the (t mod l)-th bit of $\omega(i)$ is 0, then the node visits channel ($\lfloor \frac{t}{N_i} \rfloor$ mod N_i) in timeslot t (i.e., uses the t-th element in the slow sequence). In other words, if $\omega(i)^{t \bmod l} = 0$, let $r(i, N_i)^t = \lfloor \frac{t}{N_i} \rfloor \bmod N_i$;

- If the (t mod l)-th bit of $\omega(i)$ is 1, then the node visits channel (t mod N_i) in timeslot t (i.e., uses the t-th element in the fast sequence). In other words, if $\omega(i)^{t \bmod l} = 1$, let $r(i, N_i)^t = t \bmod N_i$.

The channel index in this advanced HCH system design is jointly determined by the choice sequence, the current time slot t, and N_i, which is independent of which channels are available to node i (i.e., the set C_i), or the way of assigning channel indices.

Robustness to heterogeneous environments. Figure 4 illustrates an example of the advanced HCH system when $N_i = 2$ and $N_j = 3$. The following theorem proves its rendezvous robustness to various network conditions.

THEOREM 3. *For two nodes i and j, the advanced HCH protocol using an l-symmetrization class can guarantee the maximum rendezvous diversity within a TTR bounded by lN_iN_j, irrespective of all possible channel labeling functions and clock drifts.*

PROOF. Given two nodes i and j, suppose node j's is k timeslots behind that of node i. According to node i's clock, group every $l = |\omega(i)| = |\omega(j)|$ timeslots into a frame, i.e., timeslots $0, 1, 2, \ldots, l-1$ form the first frame, timeslots $l, l+1, l+2, \ldots, 2l-1$ form the second frame, etc. Timeslot t is contained in the $\lfloor t/l \rfloor$-th frame.

By the definition of symmetrization class, there exists $c \in [0, l-1]$ such that $\omega(i)^c \neq rotate(\omega(j), k)^c$. Without loss of generality, assume $\omega(i)^c = 0$ and $rotate(\omega(j), k)^c = 1$. Now we focus on timeslots $c + Fl$ with $F = 0, 1, 2, 3, \ldots$. The resulting subsequence of $\{(r(i, N_i)^t, r(j, N_j)^{t+k})\}_{t \geq 0}$ is $\{(r(i, N_i)^{c+Fl}, r(j, N_j)^{c+Fl+k})\}_{F \geq 0}$. By the definition of r, $\{(r(i, N_i)^{c+Fl}, r(j, N_j)^{c+Fl})\}_{F \geq 0}$ equals

$$\{(\lfloor \frac{c + Fl}{N_i} \rfloor \bmod N_i, (c + Fl + k) \bmod N_j)\}_{F \geq 0},$$

Fix two integers $a \in [0, N_i - 1]$ and $b \in [0, N_j - 1]$ and consider the following simultaneous congruence equations with respect to F

$$\begin{cases} \lfloor \frac{c+Fl}{N_i} \rfloor \equiv a \pmod{N_i} \\ c + Fl + k \equiv b \pmod{N_j}, \end{cases} \tag{3}$$

Suppose $c + Fl = qN_i^2 + r$ with $0 \leq r < N_i^2$. We have $\lfloor \frac{c+Fl}{N_i} \rfloor = \lfloor \frac{qN_i^2+r}{N_i} \rfloor = qN_i + \lfloor \frac{r}{N_i} \rfloor$. Thus $\lfloor \frac{r}{N_i} \rfloor \equiv a \pmod{N_i}$. Since $0 \leq r < N_i^2$, $0 \leq \frac{r}{N_i} < N_i$, $0 \leq \lfloor \frac{r}{N_i} \rfloor < N_i$. Note that $a \in [0, N_i - 1]$. We obtain that $\lfloor \frac{r}{N_i} \rfloor = a$ and that $aN_i \leq r < (a + 1)N_i$. Hence Equation 3 is equivalent to

$$\begin{cases} c + Fl \equiv aN_i, \ldots, aN_i + N_i - 1 \pmod{N_i^2} \\ c + Fl + k \equiv b \pmod{N_j}. \end{cases}$$

Since $\gcd(N_i, l) = 1$ and therefore $\gcd(N_i^2, l) = 1$, we have $\exists l^{-1}_{\mathbb{Z}_{N_i^2}} \in \mathbb{Z}$, s.t. $l^{-1}_{\mathbb{Z}_{N_i^2}} l \equiv 1 \pmod{N_i^2}$. Similarly, since $\gcd(N_j, l) = 1$, we have $\exists l^{-1}_{\mathbb{Z}_{N_j}} \in \mathbb{Z}$, s.t. $l^{-1}_{\mathbb{Z}_{N_j}} l \equiv 1 \pmod{N_j}$.

$$\begin{cases} F \equiv l^{-1}_{\mathbb{Z}_{N_i^2}}(aN_i + g - c) \pmod{N_i^2} \qquad g \in [0, N_i - 1] \\ F \equiv l^{-1}_{\mathbb{Z}_{N_j}}(b - c - k) \pmod{N_j}. \end{cases}$$

There are two possible cases to consider.

Case 1: $N_i = N_j$. $\exists g_0 \in [0, N_i - 1]$ s.t. $l^{-1}_{\mathbb{Z}_{N_i^2}}(aN_i + g_0 - c) \equiv l^{-1}_{\mathbb{Z}_{N_j}}(b - c - k) \pmod{N_i}$. Thus $F \equiv l^{-1}_{\mathbb{Z}_{N_i^2}}(aN_i + g_0 - c) \pmod{N_i^2}$.

Case 2: $N_i \neq N_j$. Since N_i and N_j are both primes, we have $\gcd(N_i, N_j) = 1$, and thus $\gcd(N_i^2, N_j) = 1$. By Chinese Remainder Theorem, we obtain that there exists N_i solutions modulo $N_i^2 N_j$.

Table 1: A comparison of CH schemes in heterogeneous environments.

CH protocol	Assumption	Diversity	Avg. TTR
ACH [4]	Sdr/Rvr role; equal/co-prime chan. num.	$\|C_i \cap C_j\|$	$\frac{N_iN_j}{\|C_i \cap C_j\|}$
HH [14] ICH [13]	Univ. set; consec. chan. indices	No max diversity	$O(N_iN_j)$
ϵ_1- or ϵ_2- ele. rdv	Chan. num. co-primality	$\|C_i \cap C_j\|$	$\frac{N_iN_j}{\|C_i \cap C_j\|}$
Adv. rdv		$\|C_i \cap C_j\|$	$\frac{lN_iN_j}{\delta\|C_i \cap C_j\|}$

Table 2: A comparison of different symmetrization classes in the advanced HCH protocol.

Symmetrization class	Degree δ	Choice sequence length l
Optimal	≥ 1	$\approx g + \log_2 g$
η_1	≥ 1	$2g + 3$
η_2	≥ 1	$g + \lceil\sqrt{g}\rceil(2 + \lceil\log_2 g\rceil) + 3$

It follows immediately that it guarantees rendezvous with maximum diversity, despite any amount of clock drift and heterogeneity of channel labeling functions. □

5. PERFORMANCE EVALUATION

5.1 Comparisons of CH-based Rendezvous Protocols in Heterogeneous Environments

A comparison of existing and proposed rendezvous protocols schemes in heterogeneous environments is summarized in Table 1.

Assumptions vs. rendezvous performance. Existing protocols can partially address the rendezvous problem due to dependency on some assumptions. For example, the ACH protocol assumes the pre-assigned role of a node, which limits its application scenarios (e.g., bluetooth pairing). HH and ICH schemes [13,14] assume that each node can sense a set of consecutive channels that come from a universal spectrum; meanwhile, they fail to achieve the maximum rendezvous diversity. The elementary HCH protocols proposed in this paper can achieve the maximum rendezvous diversity $|C_i \cap C_j|$ with an average TTR (ATTR) of $\frac{N_iN_j}{|C_i \cap C_j|}$. However, channel number co-primality is assumed. The advanced HCH protocol is independent of these environmental assumptions, while it can achieve the maximum rendezvous diversity $|C_i \cap C_j|$, with ATTR $\frac{lN_iN_j}{\delta|C_i \cap C_j|}$. Recall that l is the length of the choice sequence and δ is the degree of the symmetrization class. l and δ vary with different symmetrization classes. The advanced HCH protocol incurs a mere performance degradation of a constant factor, l/δ. For a 4-bit ID string, $l/\delta \leq 4 + \log_2 4 = 6$ for the optimal symmetrization class. A comparison of all aforementioned symmetrization classes is summarized in Table 2.

5.2 Simulation Results

In this section, we compare the performance of existing and proposed rendezvous schemes via simulation results.

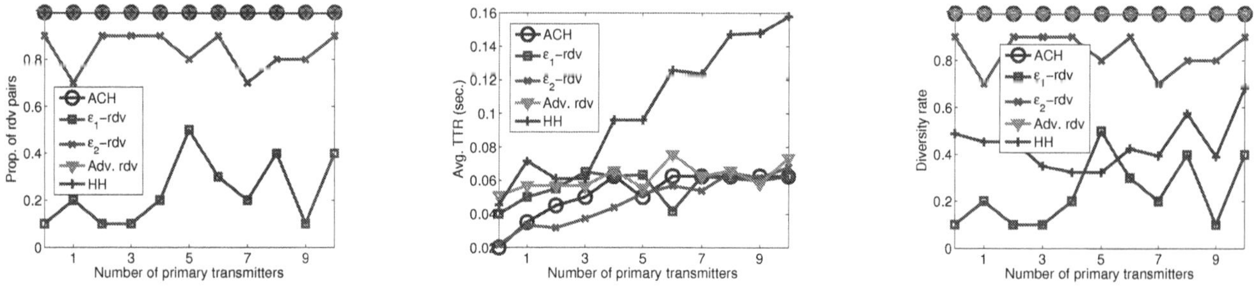

Figure 5: Results in Case 1 with pre-assigned sender/receiver roles, but no channel number co-primality: (a) The proportion of rendezvous pairs; (b) The average rendezvous latency for successful rendezvous pairs; (c) The diversity rate.

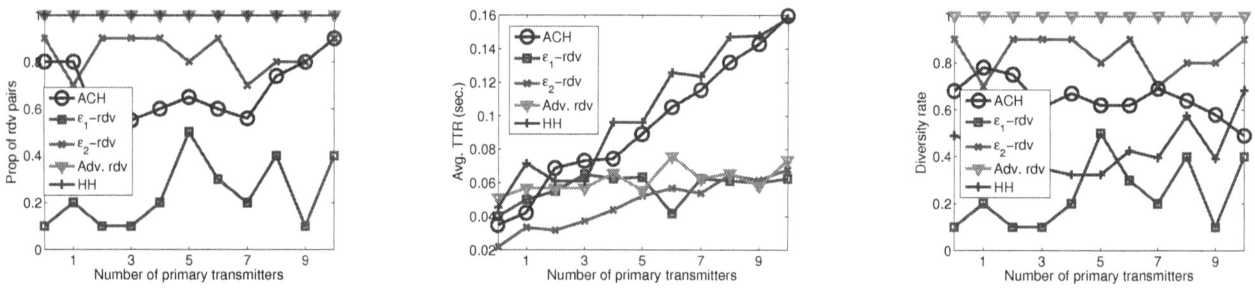

Figure 6: Results in Case 2 with no pre-assigned sender/receiver roles, and no channel number co-primality: (a) The proportion of rendezvous pairs; (b) The average rendezvous latency for successful rendezvous pairs; (c) The diversity rate.

There are a total number of $N = 11$ frequency channels, and 20 pairs of nodes that need to rendezvous via channel hopping. Every node i can only sense and access a number of N_i channels, and its sensible channel set is C_i, where N_i is randomly chosen from $[1, 11]$. The channel labeling function is independently determined by each node. Meanwhile, each node determines its clock time independently, and there is a random clock drift between any two nodes. A node generates its CH sequence using the agreed CH scheme and performs channel hopping in accordance with the CH sequence. The advanced HCH protocol in simulations is based on the η_1 symmetrization class. We simulated $X < N$ primary transmitters operating on X randomly chosen channels. A timeslot has a length of 10 ms. All secondary nodes are within the transmission range of any primary transmitter. A channel is deemed *unavailable* when primary user signals are present on it. Once two nodes hop onto a primary-user free channel in the same timeslot, the rendezvous between them is established.

We employ the following three metrics to evaluate the performance of rendezvous protocols. (1) We define the *proportion of rendezvous pairs* as the percentage of successful rendezvous pairs in all node pairs that attempt to rendezvous; (2) We use the *average time-to-rendezvous* (ATTR) to measure the average rendezvous latency of successful rendezvous pairs; (3) We define the *diversity rate* of two nodes i and j as $\frac{|\mathcal{C}|}{|(C_i \cap C_j) \setminus C_{PU}|}$, where $|\mathcal{C}|$ is the number of rendezvous channels between nodes i and j, and C_{PU} denotes the set of channels on which PUs appear. The diversity rate quantifies a CH scheme's ability to establish rendezvous in diverse possible channels.

5.2.1 *Case 1: pre-assigned sender/receiver roles; no channel number co-primality*

In this case, every node has a pre-assigned role as a sender or a receiver. For any rendezvous node pairs, the sender node, say node i, uses the sender CH sequence $r_s(i, N_i)$; the receiver node, say node j, uses the receiver CH sequence $r_r(j, N_j)$[4]. The co-primality of channel numbers N_i and N_j is not guaranteed. The results are shown in Figure 5.

Proportion of rendezvous pairs. From Figure 5(a), we can see that ACH, ICH and the proposed advanced rendezvous protocol guarantee that every pair of radios successfully rendezvous while ϵ_1- and ϵ_2-rendezvous protocols cannot guarantee that without assuming channel number co-primality.

Average time-to-rendezvous. From Figure 5(b), we can observe that ACH, ϵ_1-/ϵ_2-rendezvous and the advanced rendezvous protocol come very close in terms of ATTR; however, as the number of primary transmitters increases, the average time-to-rendezvous of the ICH scheme increases rapidly due to its limited rendezvous diversity (see Table 1).

[4]In *symmetric* protocols that are independent of pre-assigned roles (e.g., the advanced HCH protocol), $r_s(i, N_i) = r_r(i, N_i) = r(i, N_i)$. Our definition of HCH protocols (Definition 1) focuses on symmetric protocols only because it is unjustifiable to assume pre-assigned roles in practical systems.

Diversity rate. Figure 5(c) shows that ACH and the proposed advanced rendezvous protocol achieve maximum diversity of rendezvous channels; however, ICH, ϵ_1 and ϵ_2 fail to achieve maximum rendezvous diversity. Specifically, ϵ_1-/ϵ_2-rendezvous fails because we do not assume channel number co-primality in this set of simulations.

5.2.2 *Case 2: no pre-assigned sender/receiver roles, and no channel number co-primality*

In this case, every node has no pre-assigned role as a sender/receiver, and node i in ACH randomly selects $r_s(i, N_i)$ or $r_r(i, N_i)$ as its CH sequence. The results in this case are illustrated in Figure 6.

Proportion of rendezvous pairs. Figure 6(a) shows that without assuming pre-assigned sender/receiver roles, ACH cannot guarantee rendezvous for every node pair when both of them select sender (or receiver) sequences simultaneously. When N_i and N_j are not co-prime, ϵ_1- and ϵ_2-rendezvous protocols fail to guarantee rendezvous for all node pairs. In contrast, ICH and the proposed advanced rendezvous protocols can ensure all node pairs to achieve pairwise rendezvous in such a heterogeneous environment.

Average time-to-rendezvous. In Figure 6(b), we measure ATTR for successful rendezvous pairs. Although the ICH scheme leads to a high proportion of rendezvous pairs, we can observe that as the number of primary transmitters increases, the ATTR of ICH increases rapidly. Moreover, in ϵ_1-/ϵ_2- rendezvous protocols, a few node pairs fail to achieve rendezvous (low proportion of rendezvous pairs), but the rendezvous latency for those successful rendezvous pairs is as small as that of the advanced rendezvous protocol.

Diversity rate. In Figure 6(c), two nodes using ACH (no pre-assigned roles are assumed), ϵ_1/ϵ_2-rendezvous (N_i and N_j may not be co-prime), or ICH protocol fail to achieve the maximum rendezvous diversity; therefore the diversity rate is lower than 1 for these protocols. In contrast, the advanced rendezvous protocol is uniquely able to guarantee the maximum rendezvous diversity.

In sum, without assuming pre-assigned sender/receiver roles or channel number co-primality, the proposed advanced rendezvous protocol is uniquely able to guarantee rendezvous between every pair of nodes with the maximum diversity rate and a small average time-to-rendezvous.

6. CONCLUSIONS

This paper presents a systematic approach using group theory for designing optimal CH protocols that guarantee the maximum rendezvous diversity and the minimal TTR in CR networks. We show the minimum upper bound for TTR is N_iN_j, and propose two types of rendezvous protocols that achieve the maximum rendezvous diversity with a latency of $O(N_iN_j)$. Analytical and simulation results show that these protocols are resistant to rendezvous failures in heterogeneous network conditions.

7. ACKNOWLEDGEMENTS

This work was partially supported by National Natural Science Foundation of China under grant number 61201245, Specialized Research Fund for the Doctoral Program of Higher Education (SRFDP) under grant 20120001120128, and by the National Science Foundation through grants CNS-1314598 and IIP-1265886.

8. REFERENCES

[1] C. Arachchige, S. Venkatesan, and N. Mittal. An Asynchronous Neighbor Discovery Algorithm for Cognitive Radio Networks. Proc. of *IEEE DySPAN*, pp. 1–5, 2008.

[2] P. Bahl, R. Chandra, and J. Dunagan. SSCH: Slotted Seeded Channel Hopping for Capacity Improvement in IEEE 802.11 Ad Hoc Wireless Networks. Proc. of *ACM MobiCom*, pp. 216–230, 2004.

[3] K. Bian and J. Park. Asynchronous Channel Hopping for Establishing Rendezvous in Cognitive Radio Networks. Proc. of *IEEE INFOCOM*, Mini-conference, pp. 236–240, 2011.

[4] K. Bian and J. Park. Maximizing Rendezvous Diversity in Rendezvous Protocols for Decentralized Cognitive Radio Networks. *IEEE Trans. on Mobile Computing*, 12(7):1294–1307, July 2013.

[5] K. Bian, J. Park, and R. Chen. A Quorum-based Framework for Establishing Control Channels in Dynamic Spectrum Access Networks. Proc. of *ACM MobiCom*, pp. 25–36, 2009.

[6] K. Bian, J. Park, and R. Chen. Control Channel Establishment in Cognitive Radio Networks using Channel Hopping. *IEEE Journal on Selected Areas of Communications*, 29(4):689–703, April 2011.

[7] G. Chang, W. Teng, H. Chen, and J. Sheu. Novel Channel-Hopping Schemes for Cognitive Radio Networks. *IEEE Transactions on Mobile Computing*, 13(2):407–421, February 2014.

[8] I.-H. Chuang, H.-Y. Wu, K.-R. Lee, and Y. H. Kuo. Alternate Hop-and-Wait Channel Rendezvous Method for Cognitive Radio Networks. Proc. of *IEEE INFOCOM*, pp. 746–754, 2013.

[9] F. Hou, L. Cai, X. S. Shen, and J. Huang. Asynchronous Multichannel MAC Design With Difference-Set-Based Hopping Sequences. *IEEE Transactions on Vehecular Technology*, 60(4):1728–1739, May 2011.

[10] Z. Lin, H. Liu, X. Chu, and Y.-W. Leung. Jump-Stay Based Channel Hopping Algorithm with Guaranteed Rendezvous for Cognitive Radio Networks. Proc. of *IEEE INFOCOM*, pp. 2444–2452, 2011.

[11] Y. Song and J. Xie. A Distributed Broadcast Protocol in Multi-hop Cognitive Radio Ad Hoc Networks without A Common Control Channel. *Proc. IEEE INFOCOM*, pp. 2273–2281, 2012.

[12] N. Theis, R. Thomas and L. DaSilva. Rendezvous for Cognitive Radios. *IEEE Transactions on Mobile Computing*, 10(2):216–227, 2011.

[13] C.-C. Wu, and S.-H. Wu. On Bidging the Gap between Homogeneous and Heterogeneous Rendezvous Schemes for Cognitive Radios. Proc. of *ACM MobiHoc*, pp. 207–216, 2013.

[14] S.-H. Wu, C.-C. Wu, W.-K. Hon, and K. G. Shin. Rendezvous for Heterogeneous Cognitive Radios: Theoretical Foundations. Technical report, 2013.

[15] Y. Zhang, Q. Li, G. Yu, and B. Wang. ETCH: Efficient Channel Hopping for Communication Rendezvous in Dynamic Spectrum Access Networks. Proc. of *IEEE INFOCOM*, 2011.

An Extensible and Flexible Truthful Auction Framework for Heterogeneous Spectrum Markets*

Wei Li, Xiuzhen Cheng
George Washington University
Washington DC, USA
{weili, cheng}@gwu.edu

Rongfang Bie
Beijing Normal University
Beijing, China
rfbie@bnu.edu.cn

Feng Zhao
Guilin University of Electronic Technology, Guilin, China
zhaofeng@guet.edu.cn

ABSTRACT

In this paper, we propose an extensible and flexible truthful auction framework that is individual-rational and self-collusion resistant. By properly setting one simple parameter, this framework can yield efficient auctions (like VCG) and (sub)optimal auctions (like Myerson's Optimal Mechanism (MOM)) with a more computationally-efficient procedure compared to VCG and MOM; by carefully choosing virtual valuation functions for the bidders, it can produce attribute-aware auctions that take the channel diversity into consideration. The framework adopts a novel procedure that can prevent bidder self-collusion resulted from the bid diversity. Theoretical analysis and case studies demonstrate the strength of our auction framework in handling various considerations in a practical heterogeneous spectrum market.

Categories and Subject Descriptors

C.2.1 [**Computer-Communication Networks**]: Network Architecture and Design

Keywords

Truthful auctions; self-collusion resistance; efficient auctions; optimal auctions; heterogeneous spectrum market.

1. INTRODUCTION

Over the past few years a number of auction mechanisms [1, 3–11, 18–22] have been proposed as a powerful market-based spectrum management technique to improve the channel utilization while benefiting both the primary and the secondary users in a spectrum market. The major design goal of these auction schemes focuses on truthfulness to prevent market manipulation, by ensuring that no buyer/seller can obtain a larger utility via cheating on its bid price.

*This research is supported by the National Foundation of the US (CNS-1162057, CNS-1265311), National Natural Science Foundation of China (61171014, 61172055), and the Fundamental Research Funds for the Central Universities.

MobiHoc'14, August 11–14, 2014, Philadelphia, PA, USA.

http://dx.doi.org/10.1145/2632951.2632968.

A number of auction design issues in a heterogeneous spectrum market have been overlooked by the current research. First, a buyer may submit different bid prices for different channels with different attributes (bandwidths, transmission powers, etc), rendering all existing auctions assuming indistinguishable channel properties (homogeneous channels) [1,3,5,7–9,18,20–22] inapplicable; moreover, extending these designs to consider heterogeneous channels is nontrivial. Second, our study (see Section 4) indicates that the well-known MOM [13] and its extensions lose truthfulness when a buyer self-colludes by manipulating its bid prices on different channels; such a self-collusion has never been addressed in literature. Third, existing auction mechanisms proposed for the spectrum market are based on either Vickery-Clarke-Groves (VCG) [16] to maximize the social welfare, or MOM to maximize the expected revenue, or McAfee [12], a greedy double auction mechanism that achieves non-negative budget revenue at the auctioneer at the cost of decreased social welfare and total revenue. Nevertheless, a systematic study to reveal the correlations among VCG, MOM, and McAfee is missing, making it hard to select an appropriate auction mechanism for practical settings. Fourth, attribute-aware auctions have been sporadically studied [4, 6, 10], but no effort has been made to explicitly link the benefit brought by attribute diversity to the auction objectives (maximum social welfare or expected revenue), resulting in the "hardness" of analyzing the effect of auction outputs on networking performance (e.g., throughput).

In this paper, we propose a flexible and extensible truthful auction framework $\mathbf{\Pi}$ that can overcome all the challenges mentioned above. We introduce a parameter λ to capture the tradeoff between marginal revenue and allocation efficiency, based on which VCG and MOM (and McAfee, which is omitted in this paper due to page limit) are unified into a single framework. Motivated by the virtual valuations proposed in MOM to estimate bid uncertainties based on probability distribution functions, we extend the definition of virtual valuations to describe the benefit brought by the allocated channels in an auction and identify the properties these virtual valuation functions must satisfy to be applicable in a spectrum market. Such a new definition is employed in $\mathbf{\Pi}$ to allow the auction objective functions capture the benefit brought by channel diversity. We also define a critical bid vector (*vs.* a single critical bid in existing research) for a potential winning buyer to successfully capture the relationship among its bid prices on different channels, thus achieving self-collusion resistance.

Our auction framework $\mathbf{\Pi}$ is mathematically supported by an optimization problem subject to the economic property constraints and our proposed solution approach is novel. We first consider a simple optimization problem without considering any economic property constraints and prove that a winner in the original problem must win in the simplified problem and a loser in the simplified problem must be a loser in the original problem. Then we define a critical bid vector for each winner in the simplified problem and develop a channel allocation policy and a pricing policy based on the critical bid vectors to compute the winners and their clearing prices for the original problem. Extensive theoretical analysis proves that $\mathbf{\Pi}$ achieves individual-rationality and incentive-compatibility (truthfulness). We also provide a few case study examples to demonstrate the application of $\mathbf{\Pi}$ for various purposes. For instances, by setting $\lambda = 0$ we obtain an efficient auction (like VCG) and by setting $\lambda = 1$ we get an (sub)optimal auction (like MOM); using the preference degree of a buyer over a channel to compute the buyer's virtual bid on that channel we get a bandwidth-aware auction that satisfies all economic properties $\mathbf{\Pi}$ possesses. Note that we have designed a budget-balanced auction ($\lambda \geq 1$) and a McAfee-style greedy auction ($\lambda > 0$) based on $\mathbf{\Pi}$ but due to space limitation they are not included in this paper. Also note that our solution approach provides a more computationally-efficient procedure to get efficient or optimal auctions compared to VCG and MOM. Our framework $\mathbf{\Pi}$ is extensible, which will be further investigated in our future research.

The rest of this paper is organized as follows. Section 2 presents our auction model and economic properties. Classic auction mechanisms and related work are summarized in Section 3. Challenges tackled by our consideration and illustrative examples are described in Section 4. The design and economic property analysis of our proposed auction framework are detailed in Section 5 and 6, respectively. A few case study examples are reported in Section 7, and we conclude this paper in Section 8.

2. AUCTION MODEL AND PROPERTIES

2.1 Auction Model

We consider a heterogeneous spectrum market with m buyers and n sellers, denoted by $\mathcal{M}$ ($|\mathcal{M}| = m$) and $\mathcal{N}$ ($|\mathcal{N}| = n$), respectively. Assume that each buyer (seller) demands (supplies) only one channel and that each channel is allowed to be sold to the buyers that do not interfere with each other. Thus the channel allocation can be modeled as *a bilateral* or *double auction*, which is controlled by an auctioneer. In this paper, we propose an auction framework $\mathbf{\Pi} = (\mathcal{B}, \mathcal{A}, \mathcal{G}, \mathcal{V}^b, \mathcal{V}^s, \mathcal{X}, \mathcal{P}^b, \mathcal{P}^s)$ containing the following eight components:

1. A set of all buyers' bids $\mathcal{B} = \{B_1, B_2, \ldots, B_m\}$, in which $B_i = (b_{i1}, b_{i2}, \ldots, b_{in})$, $1 \leq i \leq m$, represents the bid price vector of buyer i for the n channels. If buyer i does not want to bid channel j, or channel j is not available for buyer i, we set $b_{ij} = Null$.

2. A set of all sellers' bids $\mathcal{A} = \{a_1, a_2, \ldots, a_n\}$, where a_j, $1 \leq j \leq n$, is the ask price of seller j. For simplicity, we use j to represent seller j's channel as each seller has only one channel to sell.

3. A conflicting graph among all buyers $\mathcal{G}(\mathcal{M}, \mathcal{E})$, in which two buyers i and k cannot use the same channel if and only if $e(i,k) \in \mathcal{E}$, where $i, k \in \mathcal{M}$.

4. A virtual valuation function $\mathcal{V}^b$. Each buyer i is associated with a virtual valuation function $\mathcal{V}_i^b : b_{ij} \to \mathbb{R}$, and the virtual bid $\beta_{ij} = \mathcal{V}_i^b(b_{ij})$ indicates the "benefit" that buyer i can obtain from winning channel j.

5. A virtual valuation function $\mathcal{V}^s$. Each seller j is associated with a virtual valuation function $\mathcal{V}_j^s : a_j \to \mathbb{R}$. Accordingly, seller j's virtual bid is $\alpha_j = \mathcal{V}_j^s(a_j)$.

6. An allocation policy $\mathcal{X} : \{\beta_{ij}\}^{m\times n} \times \{\alpha_j\}^{n\times 1} \to \{0,1\}^{m\times n}$, with $x_{ij} = 1$ if and only if channel j is assigned to buyer i.

7. A payment policy $\mathcal{P}^b : \{\beta_{ij}\}^{m\times n} \times \{\alpha_j\}^{n\times 1} \to \mathbb{R}^{m\times n}$ for all buyers, in which p_{ij}^b is the payment charged from buyer i for winning channel j.

8. A payment policy $\mathcal{P}^s : \{\beta_{ij}\}^{m\times n} \times \{\alpha_j\}^{n\times 1} \to \mathbb{R}^{n\times 1}$ for all sellers, in which seller j is paid p_j^s when it successfully sells its channel (channel j) in the auction.

Accordingly, the utility of buyer i can be calculated by

$$\mathcal{U}^b : u_i^b = \sum_{j=1}^{n} x_{ij}(\beta_{ij} - p_{ij}^b), \tag{1}$$

and the utility of seller j is

$$\mathcal{U}^s : u_j^s = y_j(p_j^s - \alpha_j), \tag{2}$$

where

$$y_j = \begin{cases} 0, & \text{if } \sum_{i=1}^{m} x_{ij} = 0; \\ 1, & \text{if } \sum_{i=1}^{m} x_{ij} \geq 1. \end{cases}$$

Note that here we set $y_j = 1$ instead of $\sum_{i=1}^{m} x_{ij}$ when $\sum_{i=1}^{m} x_{ij} \geq 1$, which implies that seller j sells its channel to the auctioneer without caring about how many buyers get the channel via the auction. Such a seller model has been adopted by almost all existing research [4, 7, 10, 11, 18, 19, 21]. We will consider the more practical scenario when sellers bid for each particular area (spatial diversity) in our future research.

As a commonly used criterion to evaluate the performance of an auction mechanism, "social welfare" is defined to be the sum of the valuations of all the allocated resources, i.e.,

$$W = \sum_{i=1}^{m} \sum_{j=1}^{n} x_{ij}\beta_{ij} - \sum_{j=1}^{n} y_j\alpha_j, \tag{3}$$

Remark: Throughout this paper we use a superscript * to represent the auction results in an optimal solution. For example, we use X^* to represent the allocation results when W^* is achieved in an efficient auction.

2.2 Economic Properties

In an auction design, the following economic properties are typically considered:

- **Individual-rationality**, which requires that no winner obtains negative utility, i.e., $u_i^b \geq 0$ if $\sum_{j=1}^{n} x_{ij} = 1$ and $u_j^s \geq 0$ if $y_j = 1$.

- **Incentive-compatibility**, which is also called "truthfulness" or "strategy-proof", indicates that no bidder can improve its received utility via lying about its bid price. Incentive-compatibility ensures that: (i) for each buyer i, $\mathcal{U}^b(B_i^t, \mathcal{B}_{-i}, \mathcal{A}) \geq \mathcal{U}^b(B_i, \mathcal{B}_{-i}, \mathcal{A})$, where B_i^t is the true bid vector of i and $\mathcal{B}_{-i} = \mathcal{B} \setminus B_i$; and (ii) for each seller j, $\mathcal{U}^s(a_j^t, \mathcal{A}_{-j}, \mathcal{B}) \geq \mathcal{U}^s(a_j, \mathcal{A}_{-j}, \mathcal{B})$ with a_j^t being the true ask price of j and $\mathcal{A}_{-j} = \mathcal{A} \setminus \{a_j\}$.
- **Efficiency.** An auction is efficient if it maximizes the social welfare W.
- **Optimality.** An auction is optimal if it maximizes the expected revenue, subject to the individual-rationality and incentive-compatibility constraints.
- **Budget-balance.** In double auctions, budget-balance requires that the total charge collected from all buyers is not less than the total payment to all sellers.

Ideally we should design an auction that achieves all the five properties; but unfortunately the impossibility theory [14] tells us that no incentively-compatible double auction can achieve allocative-efficiency, individual-rationality, and budget-balance at the same time. On the other hand, real-world discussions on how to best structure the FCC spectrum auctions tend to emphasize efficiency [2]. Thus the goal of our study is to design efficient auctions that can guarantee individual-rationality and incentive-compatibility.

3. CLASSIC AUCTIONS AND RELATED RESEARCH

In recent years, truthful spectrum auctions have been extensively studied with an objective of improving channel utilization while preventing market manipulation. Generally speaking, existing auction schemes proposed for the spectrum market can all be regarded as extensions of the three classic auction mechanisms: Vickery-Clarke-Groves (VCG) auction [16], Myerson's Optimal Mechanism (MOM) [13], and McAfee [12]. Therefore in this section we briefly introduce the three classic auction mechanisms and summarize their major extensions in the secondary spectrum market.

3.1 Vickery-Clarke-Groves (VCG)

The VCG auction [16] is an efficient mechanism that ensures individual-rationality and incentive-compatibility. The original unilateral VCG [16] is extended to bilateral (double auction) in [15], which is given by:

- $X^* \in \arg\max_{X \in \{0,1\}^{m \times n}} \sum_{i=1}^{m} \sum_{j=1}^{n} x_{ij} b_{ij} - \sum_{j=1}^{n} y_j a_j$.
- $p_{ij}^b = b_{ij} - (W^* - W_{\mathcal{B}_{-i}}^*)$ and $p_j^s = a_j + (W^* - W_{\mathcal{A}_{-j}}^*)$, where W^* is the maximum social welfare of the auction, and $W_{\mathcal{B}_{-i}}^*$ (correspondingly $W_{\mathcal{A}_{-j}}^*$) is the maximum social welfare when buyer i (correspondingly seller j) is removed from the auction. The prices p_{ij}^b and p_j^s are the so-called "*social opportunity costs*".

Since bilateral VCG is vulnerable to budget-balance [15], unilateral VCG based auctions for spectrum market have been studied in [3, 6, 9, 20, 22]. VERITAS [20] is the first truthful unilateral auction based on VCG pricing policy over traditional auction setting. VCG based online unilateral truthful auctions considering channel reuse at the spatial domain have been addressed in [3].

3.2 Myerson's Optimal Mechanism (MOM)

To maximize the expected revenue in an auction, Myerson proposed a unilateral single item auction mechanism in [13], and a bilateral auction mechanism in [14]. Myerson's double optimal auction mechanism can be set up as follows.

- Set $\beta_{ij} = b_{ij} - \frac{1-F_{ij}^b}{f_{ij}^b}$, with $f_{ij}^b > 0$ being the probability density function of b_{ij} and F_{ij}^b being the cumulative distribution function corresponding to the density f_{ij}^b. Both f_{ij}^b and F_{ij}^b are continuous in $[\underline{b}_{ij}, \bar{b}_{ij}]$.
- Set $\alpha_j = a_j + (\frac{F_j^s}{f_j^s} - 1)$, with $f_j^s > 0$ being the probability density function of a_j and F_j^s being the cumulative distribution function corresponding to the density f_j^s. Both f_j^s and F_j^s are continuous in $[\underline{a}_j, \bar{a}_j]$.
- Accordingly, the expected auction revenue can be expressed as $\mathbf{E}[\sum_{i=1}^{m} \sum_{j=1}^{n} x_{ij}\beta_{ij} - \sum_{j=1}^{n} y_j \alpha_j] = \mathbf{E}[W]$.
- Compute $X^* = \arg\max_{X \in \{0,1\}^{m \times n}} \mathbf{E}[W]$.
- Let $W_{-\beta_{ij}}^* = W^* - \beta_{ij}$ and $W_{+\alpha_j}^* = W^* + \alpha_j$. The critical bids of the winning buyers and sellers are

$$b_{ij}^c = \inf\{z : \mathcal{V}_i^b(z) \geq a_j, \mathcal{V}_i^b(z) + W_{-\beta_{ij}}^* \geq W_{\mathcal{B}_{-i}}^*\},$$

$$a_j^c = \sup\{z : \mathcal{V}_j^s(z) \leq \min_{x_{ij}^*=1} \{x_{ij}^* \beta_{ij}\}, W_{+\alpha_j}^* - \mathcal{V}_j^s(z) \geq W_{\mathcal{A}_{-j}}^*\}$$

- Set $p_{ij}^b = b_{ij}^c$ if $x_{ij}^* = 1$; and 0, otherwise. Similarly, set $p_j^s = a_j^c$ if $y_j^* = 1$; and 0, otherwise.

A double auction scheme based on MOM is studied in DISTRICT-D [18], which is a discriminatory pricing auction that is economically-robust. Under Bayesian setting, [1,5,6, 8] consider truthful unilateral auctions based on MOM. They differ in their approaches to determining the winners and their channels based on algorithms/heuristics with different computational complexity.

Note that in the unilateral scenario, $\alpha_j = 0$ for $1 \leq j \leq n$ and VCG is proved to be optimal [1, 5, 8]. As a result, existing MOM-style unilateral auctions usually compute the critical bids by using the idea of "critical neighbors" based on the VCG allocation policy [1, 5, 8].

3.3 McAfee

McAfee double auctions achieve individual-rationality, incentive-compatibility, and budget-balance at the cost of the auction efficiency reduction [12]. McAfee is applicable only in a homogeneous spectrum market in which $b_{ij} = b_{ih}$ for $1 \leq i \leq m$ and $1 \leq j, h \leq n$; that is, each buyer submits one scalar price as channels are homogeneous in McAfee. Let b_i be the bid price of buyer i.

- Reorder all buyers' bids in a non-increasing order and all sellers' bids in a non-decreasing order. Without loss of generality, assume that $b_1 \geq b_2 \geq \cdots \geq b_m$ and $a_1 \leq a_2 \leq \cdots \leq a_n$.
- Find the largest index k such that $b_k \geq a_k$ and $b_{(k+1)} < a_{(k+1)}$. Then, buyer i (correspondingly, seller j) wins the auction if $i \leq (k-1)$ (correspondingly, $j \leq (k-1)$).

- Charge each winning buyer the price of b_k and pay each winning seller the price of a_k.

To support spatial reuse, [7, 18, 21] first perform a bid-independent buyer grouping based on the interference graph and then apply the McAfee-style winner determination and pricing mechanism for bidder-groups. These auction schemes achieve economic-robustness but lose their truthfulness when extended to heterogeneous bids [4, 11, 19]. A remedy approach is proposed in [19] to remove the channel demand that may cause such kind of intra-collusion for truthfulness guarantee. TAHES [4] and TASG [11] avoid this intra-collusion by performing a buyer-seller matching algorithm, which is independent of the bids of all buyers and sellers, after buyer grouping and before winner determination.

4. CHALLENGES

In this section, we analyze the challenges brought by the channel diversity and channel reuse for truthful auction design. For better elaboration, we employ examples presented in Figs. 1 to 4, in which A, B, C are buyers, and S_1 and S_2 are sellers (selling channel 1 and 2, respectively). The numbers beside the buyers and sellers are their bid values. Two buyers can't share a channel if there exists a solid line between them. The channel allocation is indicated via a red dashed line between a buyer-seller pair. Note that when we apply MOM to the examples, we assume that each buyer (seller) bids the listed price with a probability 1; thus the virtual bid equals the bid price for all examples.

4.1 Impact of Channel Reuse

A unique property of the spectrum market is spectrum reuse – a channel can be sold to multiple buyers as long as they do not interfere with each other when using the channel simultaneously. Channel reuse brings special challenges, as demonstrated by the examples presented in Figs. 1 and 2.

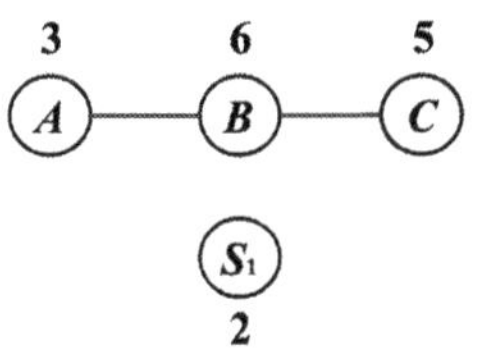

Figure 1: Impact on channel allocation

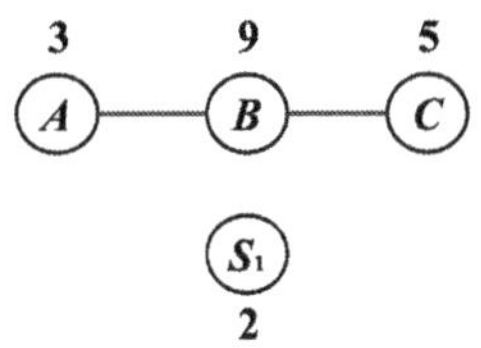

Figure 2: Impact on Pricing

We apply VCG and MOM to the example shown in Fig. 1 and consider the cases with and without channel reuse. The same results for VCG and MOM are obtained: without channel reuse, the sole winning buyer is seller B and $W = 4$; with channel reuse, the winning buyers are A and C and $W = 6$. One can see that with channel reuse, the channel allocation depends on the total bid of the interference-free buyers.

Observation 1. *In the spectrum auctions with channel reuse, resource allocation is dependent on the total bid of the interference-free buyers over a channel.*

For the example shown in Fig. 2, buyer B is the unique winner for both VCG and MOM with and without channel reuse; but the price charged from B is 5 without channel reuse and is 8 with channel reuse for both VCG and MOM. This is attributed to the fact that there is only one critical neighbor for each winning buyer when channel is not reusable while more than one critical neighbors exist if channel reuse is considered. For instance, the unique critical neighbor for buyer B is C without channel reuse, and it has two critical neighbors (both A and C) with channel reuse.

Observation 2. *In the spectrum auctions with channel reuse, a winning buyer may have more than one critical neighbors whose bids may affect its price determination.*

4.2 Truthfulness vs. Self-collusion

The Myerson's optimal auction (MOM) sets the critical bids to be the clearing prices for winning buyers and sellers [13]. Thus, a winning buyer (or seller) will pay (or receive) the smallest (or highest) value that would result in its winning. When each buyer submits a bid vector, however, self-collusion may occur, which can be illustrated via Fig. 3.

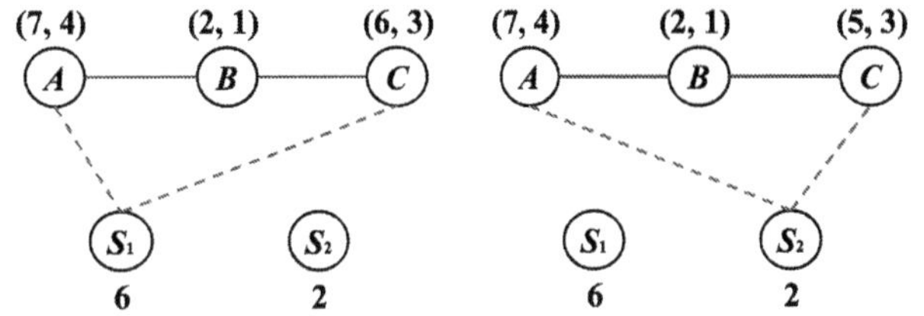

(a) Buyer C submits a true bid vector $(6, 3)$ (b) Buyer C submits a fake bid $(5, 3)$

Figure 3: An example of self-collusion in MOM.

In Fig. 3(a) where buyer C submits its true bid vector $(6, 3)$, the winners are A, C, S_1, and their corresponding payment prices and utilities are 6, 6, 6 and 1, 0, 0, respectively. In Fig. 3(b) where buyer C submits its fake bid vector $(5, 3)$, the winners are A, C, S_2 at the payment prices of 2, 2, 3 and obtaining utilities of 2, 1, 1, respectively. We observe that even though buyer C cannot get a higher utility on S_1's channel when misreporting a fake bid value of 5, it can enhance its utility by winning S_2's channel in the auction. This is attributed to the fact that in MOM, winning different channels may result in different utilities for a particular bidder. Such a "self-collusion" behavior violates truthfulness as it allows a bidder to manipulate its own bid vector for utility increase.

Observation 3. *A buyer can enhance its utility via self-collusion in an auction that allows winning different channels to obtain different utilities.*

4.3 Efficiency vs. Optimality

Many existing works [1, 5, 8] have shown that VCG-style unilateral auctions are also optimal because in these auctions the expected revenue is maximized, the channel allocation is monotonic, and each winner's payment is its critical bid. However, this claim does not hold in a bilateral auction. We take the example in Fig. 4 for demonstration.

The outputs of VCG and MOM are shown in Table 1. In VCG auction, the social welfare is maximum while the total marginal revenue (denoted by Total M-Rev. in Table 1) is only 4. In particular, the received marginal revenue of the allocation between A and S_1 is $2 - 4 = -2 < 0$, implying that VCG double auction is not optimal. On the contrary, all the marginal revenues in MOM are non-negative, but its social welfare is only $7 < 8$, resulting in the inefficiency.

Table 1: Auction results of the example in Fig. 4.

Auction	W or $\mathbf{E}[W]$	Total M-Rev.	Winners' Payment	Winners' Utilities
VCG	8	4	$p^b_{A1}=0, p^b_{B2}=4, p^b_{C1}=2, p^s_1=5, p^s_2=5$	$u^b_A=2, u^b_B=1, u^b_C=5, u^s_1=1, u^s_2=3$
MOM	7	5	$p^b_{A2}=3, p^b_{B1}=4, p^b_{C2}=2, p^s_1=4, p^s_2=5$	$u^b_A=1, u^b_B=0, u^b_C=3, u^s_1=0, u^s_2=3$

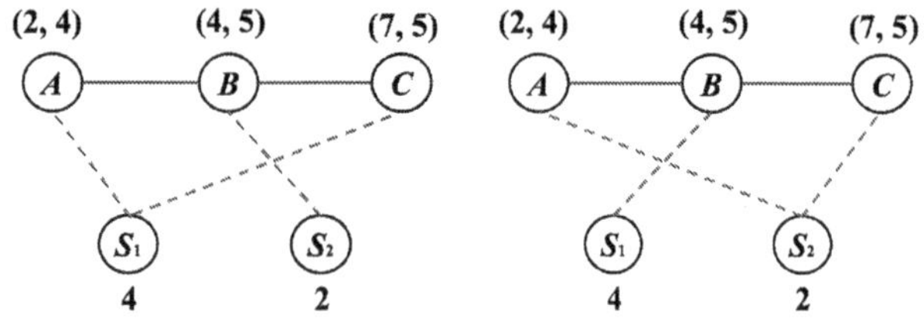

(a) VCG auction (b) MOM auction

Figure 4: A comparison between VCG and MOM.

OBSERVATION 4. *In double auctions, efficiency is not always equivalent to optimality.*

4.4 Summary of Findings

We observe that new challenges arise when considering truthful double auctions in a spectrum market due to channel reuse and channel diversity. First, in order to maximize social welfare, channel allocation should consider the total bid of the interference-free buyers; second, each winning buyer may have more than one critical neighbors whose bids affect its payment; third, the intra-relationship among the bids in a bid vector should be taken into account to achieve truthfulness while avoiding self-collusion; and finally, efficiency and optimality are not always equivalent in a double auction.

5. AUCTION FRAMEWORK DESIGN

In this section, we detail the design of our auction framework $\mathbf{\Pi} = (\mathcal{B}, \mathcal{A}, \mathcal{G}, \mathcal{V}^b, \mathcal{V}^s, \mathcal{X}, \mathcal{P}^b, \mathcal{P}^s)$.

5.1 Problem Formulation

Our spectrum auction is formulated to be the following optimization problem:

$$\max \quad W, \tag{4a}$$
$$\text{s.t.} \quad u^b_i \geq 0, 1 \leq i \leq m, \tag{4b}$$
$$\mathcal{U}^b(B^t_i, \mathcal{B}_{-i}, \mathcal{A}) \geq \mathcal{U}^b(B_i, \mathcal{B}_{-i}, \mathcal{A}), 1 \leq i \leq m, \tag{4c}$$
$$u^s_j \geq 0, 1 \leq j \leq n, \tag{4d}$$
$$\mathcal{U}^s(a^t_j, \mathcal{A}_{-j}, \mathcal{B}) \geq \mathcal{U}^s(a_j, \mathcal{A}_{-j}, \mathcal{B}), 1 \leq j \leq n, \tag{4e}$$
$$x_{ij}(\beta_{ij} - \lambda\alpha_j) \geq 0, 1 \leq i \leq m, 1 \leq j \leq n, \tag{4f}$$
$$\sum_{j=1}^{n} x_{ij} \leq 1, 1 \leq i \leq m, \tag{4g}$$
$$x_{ij} + x_{kj} \leq 1, \forall e(i,k) \in \mathcal{E}, 1 \leq j \leq n, \tag{4h}$$
$$x_{ij} \in \{0, 1\}, 1 \leq i \leq m, 1 \leq j \leq n, \tag{4i}$$
$$p^b_{ij}, p^s_j \in \mathbb{R}, 1 \leq i \leq m, 1 \leq j \leq n. \tag{4j}$$

The constraints (4b) and (4d) enforce individual-rationality; and the constraints (4c) and (4e) ensure incentive-compatibility, i.e., "truthfulness". In the constraint (4f), $\lambda \geq 0$ provides a tradeoff between the marginal revenue, $(\beta_{ij} - \alpha_j)$, and the allocation efficiency. For example, $\lambda = 0$ corresponds to VCG-style auctions and $\lambda = 1$ corresponds to MOM-style auctions, which will be investigated in Section 7. The constraints (4g) and (4h) respectively indicate that each buyer is allocated at most one channel and that two conflicting buyers cannot get the same channel. The ranges of the variables x_{ij}, p^b_{ij}, and p^s_j are determined by (4i) and (4j). Note that we intentionally ignore the virtual valuation functions in the constraints as they do not affect the solution approach; rather, they provide flexibility for our framework to handle general auction settings as discussed in Section 7.

5.2 Independent Virtual Valuation

The concept of "*virtual valuation*" was first proposed by Myerson in [13], which represents the seller's uncertainty about the bid estimates of the buyers for the good. This uncertainty is expressed via a continuous probability distribution of the bid over a finite interval in [13]. Almost all current virtual valuation-based auction mechanisms [1,5,6,8,18] follow this definition, which might raise a strong privacy concern as the buyers' bid intervals and bid probability density functions should be disclosed to the sellers. On the other hand, the bid price is the only factor considered by the objective functions of traditional auctions, which ignores the diversities of supplies and demands in the spectrum market.

Therefore in this paper, we extend the definition of virtual valuation proposed in [13] and employ it to describe the "*benefit estimate*" of the buyers and sellers for the allocated channels in the auction. For example, a buyer could benefit from large channel bandwidth, short transmission power, long transmission time, fair channel allocation, etc., in an auction. With the introduction of this new virtual valuation, we expect that the heterogeneous demands and supplies of the buyers and sellers can be effectively considered. Section 7.1 illustrates how bandwidth diversity is considered via the new definition of virtual validation in an auction.

The independence of virtual valuations implies that a participant's valuation does not impact on others' valuations. In other words, the valuation of a bid price is determined completely by the bidder itself. In order to maintain the consistence between a virtual bid (β_{ij} or α_j) and the corresponding bid price (b_{ij} or a_j), the virtual valuation functions $\mathcal{V}^b_i$ and $\mathcal{V}^s_j$ should be strictly monotonically increasing with respect to b_{ij} and a_j, respectively. Note that b_{ij} and a_j have their lower bounds and upper bounds because the available amount of money spent on a channel is finite. Without loss of generality, we assume that b_{ij} ranges in $[\underline{b}_{ij}, \bar{b}_{ij}]$ and a_j ranges in $[\underline{a}_j, \bar{a}_j]$. Moreover, the channel availability for the buyers and sellers should be correctly reflected by the virtual bids. Thus the virtual valuation functions $\mathcal{V}^b_i$ and $\mathcal{V}^s_j$ should satisfy the following conditions:

- $\mathcal{V}^b_i$ (or $\mathcal{V}^s_j$) is a strictly monotonically increasing function of b_{ij} (or a_j) in $[\underline{b}_{ij}, \bar{b}_{ij}]$ (or $[\underline{a}_j, \bar{a}_j]$).
- $\mathcal{V}^b_i(0) = 0$, $\mathcal{V}^b_i(\mathbb{R}^+) > 0$, $\mathcal{V}^b_i(\mathbb{R}^-) < 0$; $\mathcal{V}^s_j(0) = 0$, $\mathcal{V}^s_j(\mathbb{R}^+) > 0$, $\mathcal{V}^s_j(\mathbb{R}^-) < 0$.

THEOREM 1. *For each buyer i, if the virtual valuation function $\mathcal{V}_i^b$ is strictly monotonically increasing in $[\underline{b}_{ij}, \bar{b}_{ij}]$, then its inverse function $\mathcal{V}_i^{b-1}$ exists and $\mathcal{V}_i^{b-1}$ is also a strictly monotonically increasing function in $[\underline{\beta}_{ij}, \bar{\beta}_{ij}]$, where $\underline{\beta}_{ij} = \mathcal{V}_i^b(\underline{b}_{ij})$ and $\bar{\beta}_{ij} = \mathcal{V}_i^b(\bar{b}_{ij})$.*

PROOF. This claim is resulted from the theorem that for any function, monotonicity is a sufficient condition of the existence of its inverse function. □

With the same argument, we can prove the following theorem for seller j.

THEOREM 2. *For each seller j, if the virtual valuation function $\mathcal{V}_j^s$ is strictly monotonically increasing in $[\underline{a}_j, \bar{a}_j]$, then its inverse function $\mathcal{V}_j^{a-1}$ exists and $\mathcal{V}_j^{a-1}$ is also a strictly monotonically increasing function in $[\underline{\alpha}_j, \bar{\alpha}_j]$,where $\underline{\alpha}_j = \mathcal{V}_j^s(\underline{a}_j)$ and $\bar{\alpha}_j = \mathcal{V}_j^s(\bar{a}_j)$.*

Based on Theorems 1 and 2, the unique bid price b_{ij} (or a_j) can be determined when β_{ij} (or α_j) is given.

5.3 Potential Winner Determination

In this step, we determine the potential winners of the auction without considering the economic properties in problem (4). That is, the potential channel allocation is determined by the following relaxed optimization problem:

$$\max \quad W, \tag{5a}$$

$$\text{s.t.} \quad x_{ij}(\beta_{ij} - \lambda\alpha_j) \geq 0, 1 \leq i \leq m, 1 \leq j \leq n, \tag{5b}$$

$$\sum_{j=1}^{n} x_{ij} \leq 1, 1 \leq i \leq m, \tag{5c}$$

$$x_{ij} + x_{kj} \leq 1, \forall e(i,k) \in \mathcal{E}, 1 \leq j \leq n, \tag{5d}$$

$$x_{ij} \in \{0,1\}, 1 \leq i \leq m, 1 \leq j \leq n. \tag{5e}$$

Let W^{p*} denote the maximum social welfare in (5), $X^{p*} = \arg\max\{W^{p*}\}$, $W^{p*}_{-\beta_{ij}} = W^{p*} - \beta_{ij}$, $W^{p*}_{+\alpha_j} = W^{p*} + \alpha_j$, and $W^{p*}_{\mathcal{B}_{-i}}$ and $W^{p*}_{\mathcal{A}_{-j}}$ are respectively the maximum social welfare corresponding to the bid sets $\mathcal{B}_{-i} \bigcup \mathcal{A}$ and $\mathcal{B} \bigcup \mathcal{A}_{-j}$.

LEMMA 1. *When W^{p*} is achieved, there exists a smallest (or highest) value for buyer i (or seller j) to win in (5).*

PROOF. Suppose buyer i is a winner when W^{p*} is obtained in (5), i.e., $x_{ij}^{p*} = 1$. If buyer i increases its bid from b_{ij} to b'_{ij}, then $\beta'_{ij} > \beta_{ij}$. Thus, in order to obtain the maximum social welfare, we must have $x_{ij}^{p'*} = 1$, receiving an increased maximum social welfare of $W^{p*} + (\beta'_{ij} - \beta_{ij})$. Due to the allocation monotonicity, there must exist a critical bid b_{ij}^c such that $x_{ij}^{p*} = 1$ when $b_{ij} \geq b_{ij}^c$ for buyer i.
With a similar analysis, we can also prove that there exists a critical bid a_j^c for seller j such that $y_j^{p*} = 1$ when $a_j \leq a_j^c$. □

With the same argument, we can obtain the following lemma for the original problem defined in (4).

LEMMA 2. *When W^* is achieved, there exists a smallest (or highest) value for buyer i (or seller j) to win in (4).*

THEOREM 3. *The critical bid of a buyer (or a seller) in (4) is not smaller (or not larger) than that in (5).*

PROOF. By comparing (4) and (5), one can see that the optimal solution space of (4) is a subset of the feasible solution space of (5) and $W^* \leq W^{p*}$. Thus, the critical bid for a buyer (or a seller) in (4) is not smaller (or not larger) than that in (5) since otherwise $W^* > W^{p*}$ would hold according to Lemmas 1 and 2. □

THEOREM 4. *All winners for W^* in (4) can still win the auction for W^{p*} in (5).*

PROOF. From Theorem 3, we conclude that if buyer i (or seller j) wins in (4), it can also win in (5). □

THEOREM 5. *All losers for W^{p*} in (5) are also the losers for W^* in (4).*

PROOF. According to Theorem 3, if a buyer i (or a seller j) loses in (5), it is still a loser in (4). □

Therefore, after obtaining the result X^{p*}, we need to determine whether a winner in (5) is still a winner in (4), which is investigated by considering the economic property constraints in (4) in the following subsections.

5.4 Critical Bids

In this subsection we calculate the critical bids for the potential winners obtained by (5) subject to the economic property constraints in (4). Based on our analysis in Section 4.2, the traditional critical bid definition cannot be directly applied to the case when each buyer has a bid vector, because it does not consider the intra-relationship within the bids of the buyer. To overcome this issue, we propose a new concept termed "critical bid vector" for each buyer. In order to guarantee truthfulness as well as self-collusion resistance, the critical bid vector $B_i^c = (b_{i1}^c, b_{i2}^c, \ldots, b_{in}^c)$ of buyer i should satisfy the following three requirements:

1. When buyer i wins channel j with b_{ij}^c, the corresponding virtual bid $\mathcal{V}_i^b(b_{ij}^c)$ is at least equal to $\lambda\alpha_j$, meeting the constraint (4f).
2. If buyer i can win channel j with b_{ij}^c, the resulted maximum social welfare $\mathcal{V}_i^b(b_{ij}^c) + W^{p*}_{-\beta_{ij}}$ should not be smaller than the optimal output $W^{p*}_{\mathcal{B}_{-i}}$ when buyer i does not join the auction. In other words, $\mathcal{V}_i^b(b_{ij}^c)$ is the lowest virtual bid for buyer i to win channel j in a truthful auction.
3. By submitting B_i^c, buyer i can win any channel, which should generate the same maximum social welfare. That is, allocating any channel to buyer i is indiscriminate in the auction with respect to the maximum social welfare. Therefore, buyer i cannot increase its total received utility by winning different channels with B_i^c, achieving self-collusion resistance.

Based on the above requirements, the critical bid vector $B_i^c = (b_{i1}^c, b_{i2}^c, \ldots, b_{in}^c)$ of buyer i is defined according to (6).
Furthermore, we can calculate the "relative critical bid difference matrix", $\mathbf{\Delta}_i^c$, based on B_i^c, which captures the differences in B_i^c with respect to the virtual bids for buyer i to win any channel at the same maximum social welfare:

$$\mathbf{\Delta}_i^c = \begin{pmatrix} \Delta_i^c(1,1) & \Delta_i^c(1,2) & \ldots & \Delta_i^c(1,n) \\ \Delta_i^c(2,1) & \Delta_i^c(2,2) & \ldots & \Delta_i^c(2,n) \\ \vdots & \vdots & \ddots & \vdots \\ \Delta_i^c(n,1) & \Delta_i^c(n,2) & \ldots & \Delta_i^c(n,n) \end{pmatrix}, \tag{7}$$

$$b_{ij}^c = \inf\{z : \mathcal{V}_i^b(z) \geq \lambda\alpha_j, \mathcal{V}_i^b(z) + W_{-\beta_{ij}}^{p*} \geq W_{\mathcal{B}_{-i}}^{p*}, \mathcal{V}_i^b(z) + W_{-\beta_{ij}}^{p*} = \mathcal{V}_i^b(b_{ih}^c) + W_{-\beta_{ih}}^{p*}, 1 \leq h < n, h \neq j\} \tag{6}$$

where $\Delta_i^c(j,h) = \mathcal{V}_i^b(b_{ij}^c) - \mathcal{V}_i^b(b_{ih}^c)$ for $1 \leq j, h \leq n$.

Similarly, we define the "critical bid" a_j^c for seller j in (8):

$$a_j^c = \sup\{z : \lambda\mathcal{V}_j^s(z) \leq \min_{x_{ij}^{p*}=1} \{x_{ij}^{p*}\beta_{ij}\}, W_{+\alpha_j}^{p*} - \mathcal{V}_j^s(z) \geq W_{\mathcal{A}_{-j}}^{p*}\}. \tag{8}$$

5.5 Resource Allocation

Based on $\{\mathcal{V}_i^b\}$, $\{B_i\}$, $\{B_i^c\}$, and $\{\Delta_i^c\}$, the intra-relationship within a bid vector can be taken into consideration by the resource allocation policy $\mathcal{X}$, which is described as follows.

1. If $\sum_{j=1}^{n} x_{ij}^{p*} = 0$, we set $x_{ij} = 0$ for all $1 \leq j \leq n$.
2. For every potential winning buyer i in (5), compute the set of *profitable channels*,

   $$\Phi_i = \{j : b_{ij} \geq b_{ij}^c, \beta_{ij} - \beta_{ih} \geq \Delta_i^c(j,h), 1 \leq h \leq n\}.$$

   Channel j is said to be profitable for buyer i if the following two conditions are simultaneously satisfied: (i) $b_{ij} \geq b_{ij}^c$, indicating that buyer i can help enhance the social welfare if it wins channel j; and (ii) $\beta_{ij} - \beta_{ih} \geq \Delta_i^c(j,h)$ for $\forall h \in \{1, 2, \cdots, n\}$, implying that winning channel j can generate a higher social welfare than winning other channels. The number of profitable channels $|\Phi_i|$ for the potential winning buyer i ranges in $[0, n]$.
3. For all potential winning buyers, if $x_{ij}^{p*} = 1$ and $j \in \Phi_i$, set $x_{ij} = 1$; if $x_{ij}^{p*} = 1$ while $j \notin \Phi_i$, set $x_{ij} = 0$.

LEMMA 3. *In our allocation policy $\mathcal{X}$, if $x_{ij} = 1$ then $b_{ij} \geq b_{ij}^c$; if $x_{ij} = 0$ then $b_{ij} \leq b_{ij}^c$.*

PROOF. When $x_{ij} = 1$, we have $x_{ij}^{p*} = 1$ and $j \in \Phi_i$; thus $b_{ij} \geq b_{ij}^c$.

When $x_{ij} = 0$, we need to consider two cases: (i) $x_{ij}^{p*} = 0$; and (ii) $x_{ij}^{p*} = 1, j \notin \Phi_i$. In case (i), we know that allocating channel j to buyer i cannot improve the social welfare according to (6), thus $b_{ij} \leq b_{ij}^c$. In case (ii), since $x_{ih}^{p*} = 0$ for $\forall h \neq j$, $x_{ij}^{p*} = 1$, and $j \notin \Phi_i$, we have $b_{ih} \leq b_{ih}^c$ and $b_{ij} < b_{ij}^c$ according to the construction of Φ_i. ☐

LEMMA 4. *In the allocation policy $\mathcal{X}$, if $y_j = 1$, then $a_j \leq a_j^c$; otherwise, $a_j \geq a_j^c$.*

PROOF. On one hand, when seller j wins the auction, there must exist at least one buyer i such that $x_{ij} = 1$. That is, for buyer i, purchasing channel j can generate a social welfare that is not smaller than buying other channels, which is consistent with (8). Thus we have $a_j \leq a_j^c$.

On the other hand, if seller j loses the auction, we have two cases: (i) there exists at least one other seller $h \neq j$ such that the social welfare resulted from assigning channel h is not lower than that when allocating channel j; and (ii) no buyer can afford the price of channel j. Both cases imply $a_j \geq a_j^c$ according to (8). ☐

Remark: Note that there might be multiple sellers whose bids are equal to their critical bids; that is, there may exist more than one optimal solution in the auction with respect to these sellers.

5.6 Pricing Schemes

After channel allocation, we compute the winners' payments according to the following policy.

- **Payments of Winning Buyers:**
  For each buyer i,

  $$\mathcal{P}^b : p_{ij}^b = \begin{cases} 0, & \text{if } x_{ij} = 0; \\ \mathcal{V}_i^b(b_{ij}^c), & \text{if } x_{ij} = 1. \end{cases} \tag{9}$$

- **Payments of Winning Sellers:**
  For each seller j,

  $$\mathcal{P}^s : p_j^s = \begin{cases} 0, & \text{if } y_j = 0; \\ \mathcal{V}_j^s(a_j^c), & \text{if } y_j = 1. \end{cases} \tag{10}$$

The example presented in Fig. 3 is used to illustrate our auction framework $\mathbf{\Pi}$ when $\lambda = 1$ and the results are reported in Table 2. We observe that MOM cannot prevent a buyer's self-collusion because its critical bid does not consider the intra-relationship among the buyer's bids and thus potential profit can be obtained via winning different channels. In contrast, our auction $\mathbf{\Pi}$ prevents self-collusion because a buyer will receive the same utility if it can win different channels (see the computation of Φ_i); thus no potential profit can be gained via lying about its own bids.

6. ECONOMIC PROPERTY ANALYSIS

In this section, we prove that our proposed auction framework $\mathbf{\Pi} = (\mathcal{B}, \mathcal{A}, \mathcal{G}, \mathcal{V}^b, \mathcal{V}^s, \mathcal{X}, \mathcal{P}^b, \mathcal{P}^s)$ presented in Section 5 is individually-rational, incentively-compatible, and self-collusion resistant.

THEOREM 6. *The proposed auction $\mathbf{\Pi}$ is individually-rational for all winners.*

PROOF. For each winning buyer i, $p_{ij}^b = \mathcal{V}_i^b(b_{ij}^c) \leq \mathcal{V}_i^b(b_{ij}) = \beta_{ij}$, thus $u_i^b = \sum_{j=1}^{n} x_{ij}(\beta_{ij} - p_{ij}^b) \geq 0$.

For each winning seller j, since $p_j^s = \mathcal{V}_j^s(a_j^c) \geq \mathcal{V}_j^s(a_j) = \alpha_j$, we have $u_j^s = y_j(p_j^s - \alpha_j) \geq 0$.

Therefore, $\mathbf{\Pi}$ is individually-rational for all winners. ☐

LEMMA 5. *For each buyer i, if $j, h \in \Phi_i$, then $\beta_{ij} - \mathcal{V}_i^b(b_{ij}^c) = \beta_{ih} - \mathcal{V}_i^b(b_{ih}^c)$, i.e., winning channel j or h receives equal utility.*

PROOF. Since $j, h \in \Phi_i$, we have (i) $b_{ij} \geq b_{ij}^c$ and $\beta_{ij} - \beta_{ih} \geq \Delta_i^c(j,h) = \mathcal{V}_i^b(b_{ij}^c) - \mathcal{V}_i^b(b_{ih}^c)$; and (ii) $b_{ih} \geq b_{ih}^c$ and $\beta_{ih} - \beta_{ij} \geq \Delta_i^c(h,j) = \mathcal{V}_i^b(b_{ih}^c) - \mathcal{V}_i^b(b_{ij}^c)$. Thus, we conclude that $\beta_{ij} - \beta_{ih} = \Delta_i^c(j,h)$, $\beta_{ih} - \beta_{ij} = \Delta_i^c(h,j)$, and $\beta_{ij} - \mathcal{V}_i^b(b_{ij}^c) = \beta_{ih} - \mathcal{V}_i^b(b_{ih}^c)$. ☐

THEOREM 7. *The proposed allocation policy $\mathcal{X}$ is monotonic to all buyers. That is, if buyer i wins channel j with a bid vector $(b_{i1}, \ldots, b_{i(j-1)}, b_{ij}, b_{i(j+1)}, \ldots, b_{in})$, it can still win channel j by bidding with $(b_{i1}, \ldots, b_{i(j-1)}, b'_{ij}, b_{i(j+1)}, \ldots, b_{in})$, where $b'_{ij} > b_{ij}$.*

Table 2: An illustration of $\mathbf{\Pi}$ when $\lambda = 1$ for the example in Fig. 3.

Auction Mechanism	Winners' Critical Bids	Winners' Payments	Winners' Utilities	Self-collusion
MOM in Fig. 3(a)	$B_A^c = (6,2), B_C^c = (6,2), a_1^c = 6$	$p_{A1}^b = 6, p_{C1}^b = 6, p_1^s = 6$	$u_A^b = 1, u_C^b = 0, u_1^s = 0$	
MOM in Fig. 3(b)	$B_A^c = (6,2), B_C^c = (6,2), a_2^c = 3$	$p_{A2}^b = 2, p_{C2}^b = 2, p_2^s = 3$	$u_A^b = 2, u_C^b = 1, u_2^s = 1$	Yes
$\mathbf{\Pi}$ in Fig. 3(a)	$B_A^c = (6,5), B_C^c = (6,5), a_1^c = 6$	$p_{A1}^b = 6, p_{C1}^b = 6, p_1^s = 6$	$u_A^b = 1, u_C^b = 0, u_1^s = 0$	
$\mathbf{\Pi}$ in Fig. 3(b)	$B_A^c = (8,2), a_2^c = 3$	$p_{A2}^b = 2, p_2^s = 3$	$u_A^b = 2, u_2^s = 1$	No

PROOF. If $x_{ij} = 1$, then $x_{ij}^{p*} = 1$ and $j \in \Phi_i$. After increasing b_{ij} to b'_{ij}, $\beta'_{ij} > \beta_{ij}$ and $x_{ij}^{p'*} = 1$ for $W^{p'*}$ in (5). Additionally, since $b_{ij} \geq b_{ij}^c$ and $\beta_{ij} - \beta_{ih} \geq \Delta_i^c(j,h)$, we have $b'_{ij} > b_{ij}^c$ and $\beta'_{ij} - \beta_{ih} > \Delta_i^c(j,h)$. According to Lemma 5, there is only one profitable channel for buyer i, i.e., $\Phi_i = \{j\}$. Thus, $x'_{ij} = 1$. □

THEOREM 8. *The proposed auction* $\mathbf{\Pi}$ *can guarantee incentive-compatibility and self-collusion resistance for all buyers.*

PROOF. With a true bid vector B_i^t and a fake bid vector $B_i \neq B_i^t$, buyer i's received utility can be analyzed as follows:

(i) If buyer i loses the auction with both B_i and B_i^t, it receives a zero-utility with or without cheating.

(ii) If buyer i loses the auction with B_i while winning with B_i^t, then $u_i^b = 0 \leq \sum_{j=1}^{n} x_{ij}[\mathcal{V}_i^b(b_{ij}^t) - p_{ij}^b]$.

(iii) If buyer i wins channel j with B_i while losing the auction with B_i^t, from Lemma 3 and Theorem 7, we have $b_{ij} \geq b_{ij}^c \geq b_{ij}^t$. As a result, the received utility is $u_i^b = \mathcal{V}_i^b(b_{ij}^t) - \mathcal{V}_i^b(b_{ij}^c) \leq 0$.

(iv) If buyer i wins the same channel j with both B_i and B_i^t, then $u_i^b = \mathcal{V}_i^b(b_{ij}^t) - \mathcal{V}_i^b(b_{ij}^c) \geq 0$.

(v) Buyer i wins channel j with B_i and wins channel h with B_i^t. Suppose Φ_i and Φ_i^t are the profitable channel sets corresponding to $B_i \bigcup \mathcal{B}_{-i} \bigcup \mathcal{A}$ and $B_i^t \bigcup \mathcal{B}_{-i} \bigcup \mathcal{A}$, respectively. Accordingly, $j \in \Phi_i$ and $h \in \Phi_i^t$. If $j \in \Phi_i^t$, then $u_i^b = \mathcal{V}_i^b(b_{ij}^t) - \mathcal{V}_i^b(b_{ij}^c) = \mathcal{V}_i^b(b_{ih}^t) - \mathcal{V}_i^b(b_{ih}^c) \geq 0$ according to Lemma 5. If $j \notin \Phi_i^t$, we have $\mathcal{V}_i^b(b_{ij}^t) - \mathcal{V}_i^b(b_{ih}^t) \leq \Delta_i^c(j,h)$, indicating that $u_i^b = \mathcal{V}_i^b(b_{ij}^t) - \mathcal{V}_i^b(b_{ij}^c) \leq \mathcal{V}_i^b(b_{ih}^t) - \mathcal{V}_i^b(b_{ih}^c)$.

Notice that cases (i) to (v) consider both cheating and self-collusion when $B_i \neq B_i^t$. Thus we conclude that our auction framework $\mathbf{\Pi}$ is truthful and self-collusion resistant for all buyers. □

THEOREM 9. *The allocation policy* $\mathcal{X}$ *in* $\mathbf{\Pi}$ *is monotonic for all sellers. That is, if seller* j *wins the auction with* a_j, *then it can also win by asking* a'_j *with* $a'_j < a_j$.

PROOF. If $y_j = 1$, there is at least one buyer i such that $x_{ij}^{p*} = 1$, $j \in \Phi_i$, and $x_{ij} = 1$. When seller j submits a lower bid $a'_j < a_j$, we get $\alpha'_j < \alpha_j$ and $x_{ij}^{p'*} = 1$ for $W^{p'*}$ in (5). Moreover, since $\alpha'_j < \alpha_j$, we have $b_{ij}^{c'} \leq b_{ij}^c \leq b_{ij}$ and $j \in \Phi'_i$. Therefore, $x'_{ij} = 1$ and $y'_j = 1$. □

THEOREM 10. *The proposed auction* $\mathbf{\Pi}$ *achieves incentive-compatibility for all sellers.*

PROOF. When seller j untruthfully reports a bid a_j with $a_j \neq a_j^t$, the following cases should be considered:

(i) $a_j < a_j^t$. If seller j wins the auction with a_j^t, it can also win with a_j and receive the same utility $u_j^s = p_j^s - \mathcal{V}_j^s(a_j^t) \geq 0$. If seller j wins with a_j while losing with a_j^t, we have $a_j \leq a_j^c \leq a_j^t$ and $u_j^s = p_j^s - \mathcal{V}_j^s(a_j^t) \leq 0$. Finally, if seller j loses the auction with both a_j and a_j^t, the received utility is $u_j^s = 0$.

(ii) $a_j > a_j^t$. If seller j wins (or loses) the auction with both a_j and a_j^t, then $u_j^s = p_j^s - \mathcal{V}_j^s(a_j^t) \geq 0$ (or $u_j^s = 0$). If seller j wins with a_j^t while losing with a_j, we have $u_j^s = 0 \leq p_j^s - \mathcal{V}_j^s(a_j^t)$.

Therefore, from (i) and (ii), one can conclude that cheating on a_j cannot enhance the utility of seller j. □

THEOREM 11. *Let* W *be the output of* $\mathbf{\Pi}$. $W = W^*$ *when* $W_{\mathcal{B}_{-i}}^{p*} - W_{-\beta_{ij}}^{p*} \geq \lambda\alpha_j$ *for all winners in (5).*

PROOF. From Theorems 6, 8, and 10, one can see that the output of $\mathbf{\Pi}$ is a feasible solution to the problem (4), i.e., $W \leq W^*$. On the other hand, $W^* \leq W^{p*}$.

If $W_{\mathcal{B}_{-i}}^{p*} - W_{-\beta_{ij}}^{p*} \geq \lambda\alpha_j$ for $1 \leq i \leq m, 1 \leq j \leq n$, the calculations of b_{ij}^c and a_j^c are respectively equivalent to the following expressions:

$$b_{ij}^c = \mathcal{V}_i^{b-1}(W_{\mathcal{B}_{-i}}^{p*} - W_{-\beta_{ij}}^{p*}), a_j^c = \mathcal{V}_j^{a-1}(W_{+\alpha_j}^{p*} - W_{\mathcal{A}_{-j}}^{p*}).$$

Thus, for the winning buyer i with $x_{ij}^{p*} = 1$ in (5), we have $b_{ij} \geq b_{ij}^c$ and $b_{ih} \leq b_{ih}^c$ where $h \neq j$, implying that $j \in \Phi_i$. According to the allocation policy $\mathcal{X}$, we have $X = X^{p*}$ and $W = W^{p*}$. Therefore, $W = W^* = W^{p*}$.

Particularly, when $\lambda = 0$, $b_{ij}^c = \mathcal{V}_i^{b-1}(W_{\mathcal{B}_{-i}}^{p*} - W_{-\beta_{ij}}^{p*})$ and $a_j^c = \mathcal{V}_j^{a-1}(W_{+\alpha_j}^{p*} - W_{\mathcal{A}_{-j}}^{p*})$ always hold; therefore $W = W^* = W^{p*}$. □

Remark: Theorem 8 indicates that truthfulness together with self-collusion resistance are guaranteed in our auction framework $\mathbf{\Pi}$ by ensuring that every buyer i obtains a constant utility when winning the auction if this buyer has multiple winning choices with B_i^t. As a result, when $W_{\mathcal{B}_{-i}}^{p*} - W_{-\beta_{ij}}^{p*} < \lambda\alpha_j$, some solutions with higher values of W may be excluded because of the constraints $\mathcal{V}_i^b(b_{ij}^c) \geq \lambda\alpha_j$ and $\mathcal{V}_i^b(b_{ij}^c) + W_{-\beta_{ij}}^{p*} = \mathcal{V}_i^b(b_{ih}^c) + W_{-\beta_{ih}}^{p*}$, leading to $W \leq W^*$.

7. CASE STUDY EXAMPLES

In our auction framework $\mathbf{\Pi}$, the two virtual valuation functions $\mathcal{V}_i^b$ and $\mathcal{V}_j^s$, and the parameter λ can enable us to flexibly design auctions satisfying different requirements. A few examples are presented in the following subsections.

7.1 Bandwidth-Aware Auction

In a heterogeneous spectrum market, channel bandwidth is a key factor that should be considered in an auction design. For example, seller j supplies a channel with an available bandwidth r_j^s, and buyer i requires a channel with a bandwidth at least r_i^b. To satisfy the diverse bandwidth requirements of the buyers, we introduce *preference degree* θ_{ij} to quantify the preference of buyer i over channel j based on the Sigmoid function that can be used to assess the satisfaction degree of the obtained service [17].

$$\theta_{ij} = \begin{cases} 0, \text{ if } r_i^b > r_j^s; \\ \frac{1}{1+e^{-(r_j^s - r_i^b)}}, \text{o.w.} \end{cases} \tag{11}$$

The value of $\theta_{ij} \in \{0\} \bigcup [0.5, 1)$ quantifies the buyer i's preference level over channel j with respect to channel bandwidth. Let $\alpha_j = a_j$ and $\beta_{ij} = \theta_{ij} b_{ij}$ for $1 \leq i \leq m, 1 \leq j \leq n$. The virtual bid β_{ij} reflects the "willingness degree" of paying full price when buyer i purchases channel j, i.e., a buyer would like to pay more for channels with higher preference degrees. After obtaining α_j and β_{ij}, we can apply our auction framework proposed in Section 5 directly to compute the winners and their clearing prices.

THEOREM 12. *The proposed bandwidth-aware auction is individually-rational, incentively-compatible (value-truthful), and self-collusion resistant.*

PROOF. The theorem holds directly from Theorems 6, 8, and 10. □

In addition, bandwidth-truthfulness should be ensured in an bandwidth-aware auction. Note that bandwidth-truthfulness is defined for buyers (SUs) only, as sellers (PUs) have no incentive to lie about their available channel bandwidths since such information is generally public [10].

Definition 1. An auction is bandwidth-truthful if no buyer can enhance its utility by reporting untruthful bandwidths $r_i^b \neq r_i^{bt}$, where r_i^{bt} is the true bandwidth.

THEOREM 13. *The proposed bandwidth-aware auction is bandwidth-truthful for all buyers.*

PROOF. We first claim that no buyer has the incentive to report a bandwidth that is smaller than its minimum required value in its bid. Therefore, the buyer may lie about its bandwidth requirement by bidding $r_i^b > r_i^{bt}$.

From (11), if buyer i bids $r_i^b > r_i^{bt}$, we have $\theta_{ij} \leq \theta_{ij}^t$ and $\beta_{ij} = \theta_{ij} b_{ij}^t \leq \theta_{ij}^t b_{ij}^t = \beta_{ij}^t$ for $1 \leq j \leq n$, in which θ_{ij}^t is the true preference degree and β_{ij}^t is the true virtual bid of buyer i. Moreover, as $\theta_{ij} \leq \theta_{ij}^t$, buyer i will get a non-decreased critical bid $b_{ij}^c \geq b_{ij}^{ct}$ for all channels, with b_{ij}^{ct} being the true critical bid. Therefore, buyer i cannot obtain a higher utility according to Theorem 8. □

Remark: Besides channel bandwidth, other channel attributes such as the available starting/ending time and duration, transmission power, center frequency, available location, etc., should also be considered. In our future research, we will employ our flexible auction framework to investigate the various demand and supply diversities by designing appropriate virtual valuation functions to tackle the practical challenges of heterogeneous spectrum markets.

7.2 Efficient Auction ($\Pi_{\lambda=0}$)

We can construct an efficient double auction $\mathbf{\Pi}_{\lambda=0}$ according to our auction framework $\mathbf{\Pi}$ proposed in Section 5 by setting $\lambda = 0$, $\beta_{ij} = b_{ij}$, and $\alpha_j = a_j$ for $1 \leq i \leq m$, $1 \leq j \leq n$.

THEOREM 14. *When $\lambda = 0$, $\beta_{ij} = b_{ij}$, and $\alpha_j = a_j$ for $1 \leq i \leq m$, $1 \leq j \leq n$, the proposed auction $\mathbf{\Pi}$ is efficient, individually-rational, incentively-compatible, and self-collusion resistant.*

PROOF. According to Theorems 6, 8, 10, and 11, $\mathbf{\Pi}$ can achieve efficiency, individual-rationality, incentive-compatibility, and self-collusion resistance simultaneously when $\lambda = 0$.

Moreover, when $\lambda = 0$, the critical bid of buyer i for channel j (see (6)), which is also the payment for buyer i to

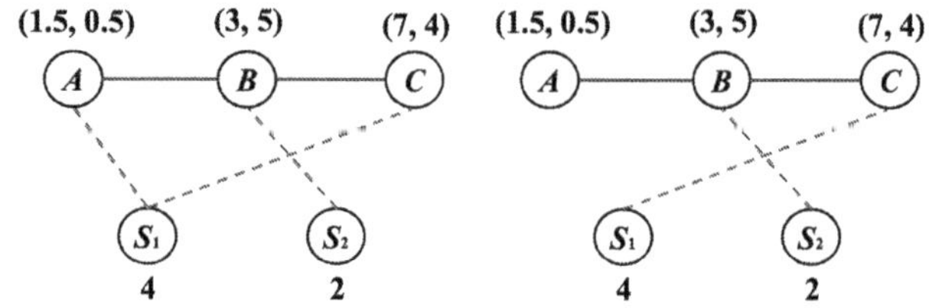

(a) VCG and $\Pi_{\lambda=0}$ (b) MOM and $\Pi_{\lambda=1}$

Figure 5: A spectrum market with 3 buyers and 2 channels. The auction results are shown in Table 3.

purchase channel j in $\mathbf{\Pi}$, can be simplified as $b_{ij}^c = W_{\mathcal{B}_{-i}}^* - W_{-b_{ij}}^* = b_{ij} - (W^* - W_{\mathcal{B}_{-i}}^*)$, which is exactly the social opportunity cost in VCG. On the other hand, the critical bid for seller j (see (8)), which is also the payment to seller j, can be rewritten to $a_j^c = W_{+a_j}^* - W_{\mathcal{A}_{-j}}^* = a_j + (W^* - W_{\mathcal{A}_{-i}}^*)$, which is exactly the social opportunity cost of seller j. Thus when $\lambda = 0$, $\mathbf{\Pi}$ is a VCG-style efficient double auction. □

Remark: From Theorems 11 and 14, one can see that VCG-style (double) auctions [15, 16] are self-collusion resistant for the buyers.

7.3 Suboptimal Auction ($\Pi_{\lambda=1}$)

Based on our framework $\mathbf{\Pi}$, we can construct a suboptimal auction $\mathbf{\Pi}_{\lambda=1}$ by setting $\lambda = 1$ and adopting the virtual valuation functions ($\mathcal{V}^b$ and $\mathcal{V}^s$) introduced in MOM [13].

THEOREM 15. *When $\lambda = 1$, the proposed auction $\mathbf{\Pi}$ is optimal if $W_{\mathcal{B}_{-i}}^{\mathcal{P}*} - W_{-\beta_{ij}}^{\mathcal{P}*} \geq \alpha_j$ for all winners in (5).*

PROOF. From Theorems 6, 8, and 10, one can conclude that $\mathbf{\Pi}$ is individually-rational, incentively-compatible, and self-collusion resistant when $\lambda = 1$.

According to Theorem 11, the auction mechanism $\mathbf{\Pi}$ can obtain the optimal solution when $\lambda = 1$ and $W_{\mathcal{B}_{-i}}^{\mathcal{P}*} - W_{-\beta_{ij}}^{\mathcal{P}*} \geq \alpha_j$ for all winners in (5). □

Remark: A carful analysis on the two cases proposed in Subsection 7.2 for $\lambda = 0$ and Subsection 7.3 for $\lambda = 1$ reveals that (i) a buyer's virtual bid may be smaller than its matched seller's virtual bid leading to a negative marginal revenue in the efficient auction; and (ii) the non-negative revenue in the optimal auction is ensured at the price of social welfare loss. When $0 \leq \lambda \leq 1$, the marginal revenue turns negative if $\alpha_j > \beta_{ij} \geq \lambda \alpha_j$. As λ gradually increases, the optimal solution space is shrunk, resulting in a smaller optimal social welfare W^* and a larger received marginal revenue $\beta_{ij} - \alpha_j$. Obviously, there exists a tradeoff between efficiency and optimality in our proposed auction framework when $0 \leq \lambda \leq 1$.

7.4 Comparison and Discussions

We employ an example shown in Fig. 5 to demonstrate the differences among VCG, $\Pi_{\lambda=0}$, MOM, and $\Pi_{\lambda=1}$. The results are reported in Table 3. We obtain the following observations:

- Both VCG and $\Pi_{\lambda=0}$ obtain the maximum social welfare but some sellers may receive negative marginal revenues. For example in Fig. 5, $W = 7.5$ while $b_{A1} - a_1 = 1.5 - 4 = -2.5 < 0$, resulting in a smaller total

Table 3: Auction results for the example in Fig. 5.

Auction	W or $\mathbf{E}[W]$	Total M-Rve.	Winners' Payments	Winners' Utilities
VCG	7.5	3.5	$p^b_{A1} = 0, p^b_{B2} = 2, p^b_{C1} = 2.5, p^s_1 = 8.5, p^s_2 = 5$	$u^b_A = 1.5, u^b_B = 3, u^b_C = 4.5, u^s_1 = 4.5, u^s_2 = 3$
$\Pi_{\lambda=0}$	7.5	3.5	$p^b_{A1} = 0, p^b_{B2} = 2, p^b_{C1} = 2.5, p^s_1 = 8.5, p^s_2 = 5$	$u^b_A = 1.5, u^b_B = 3, u^b_C = 4.5, u^s_1 = 4.5, u^s_2 = 3$
MOM	6	6	$p^b_{B2} = 2, p^b_{C1} = 4, p^s_1 = 7, p^s_2 = 5$	$u^b_B = 3, u^b_C = 3, u^s_1 = 3, u^s_2 = 3$
$\Pi_{\lambda=1}$	6	6	$p^b_{B2} = 2, p^b_{C1} = 4, p^s_1 = 7, p^s_2 = 5$	$u^b_B = 3, u^b_C = 3, u^s_1 = 3, u^s_2 = 3$

marginal revenue (denoted by Total M-Rve. in Table 3) of 3.5 compared to MOM and $\Pi_{\lambda=1}$.

- MOM and $\Pi_{\lambda=1}$ receive a higher total marginal revenue at the cost of maximum social welfare reduction. For instance in Fig. 5, the total marginal revenue of MOM and $\Pi_{\lambda=1}$ is $6 > 3.5$, but their social welfare is only $6 < 7.5$. Moreover, since $W^{p*}_{\mathcal{B}_{-B}} - W^{p*}_{-\beta_{B2}} = 2 = \alpha_2$ and $W^{p*}_{\mathcal{B}_{-C}} - W^{p*}_{-\beta_{C1}} = 4 = \alpha_1$, $\Pi_{\lambda=1}$ is optimal, which is consistent with Theorems 11 and 15.

The above illustrative example effectively confirms the flexibility and strength of our proposed auction framework $\mathbf{\Pi}$, which can achieve different economic properties via carefully selecting the value of λ. On the other hand, the virtual valuation functions provide the flexibility and capability for us to design auctions that can take into consideration the various spectrum attributes and its spatial and temporal diversities. In fact, we have successfully designed a McAfee-style greedy auction ($\lambda > 0$) and a budget-balanced auction ($\lambda \geq 1$) based on our framework $\mathbf{\Pi}$; but unfortunately these designs can't be included in this paper due to the page limitation.

8. CONCLUSION

In this paper we propose an extensible auction framework $\mathbf{\Pi}$ targeting the unique challenges of heterogeneous spectrum market. This novel framework is proved to be individually-rational, incentively-compatible, and self-collusion resistant. The case study examples demonstrate the strength of $\mathbf{\Pi}$ to flexibly achieve different auction design objectives under different conditions and parameter settings.

9. REFERENCES

[1] M. Al-Ayyoub and H. Gupta. Truthful spectrum auctions with approximate revenue. In *IEEE INFOCOM*, pages 2813–2821, 2011.

[2] L. M. Ausubel and P. Cramton. The optimality of being efficient: designing auctions. Technical Report WPS1985, Department of Economics, University of Maryland, June 1999.

[3] L. Deek, X. Zhou, K. Almeroth, and H. Zheng. To preempt or not: Tackling bid and time-based cheating in online spectrum auctions. In *IEEE INFOCOM*, pages 2219 – 2227, 2011.

[4] X. Feng, Y. Chen, J. Zhang, Q. Zhang, and B. Li. Tahes: Truthful double auction for heterogeneous spectrums. *IEEE Transactions on Wireless Communications*, 11(11):4038–4047, 2012.

[5] A. Gopinathan, Z. Li, and C. Wu. Strategyproof auctions for balancing social welfare and fairness in secondary spectrum markets. In *IEEE INFOCOM*, pages 3020–3028, 2011.

[6] H. Huang, Y. e Sun, X.-Y. Li, Z. Chen, W. Yang, and H. Xu. Near-optimal truthful spectrum auction mechanisms with spatial and temporal reuse in wireless networks. In *ACM MobiHoc*, pages 237–240, 2013.

[7] Q. Huang, Y. Tao, and F. Wu. Spring: A strategy-proof and privacy preserving spectrum auction mechanism. In *IEEE INFOCOM*, pages 851–859, 2013.

[8] J. Jia, Q. Zhang, Q. Zhang, and M. Liu. Revenue generation for truthful spectrum auction in dynamic spectrum access. In *ACM MobiHoc*, pages 3–12, 2009.

[9] M. Li, P. Li, M. Pan, and J. Sun. Economic-robust transmission opportunity auction in multi-hop wireless networks. In *IEEE INFOCOM*, pages 1890–1898, 2013.

[10] W. Li, S. Wang, and X. Cheng. Truthful multi-attribute auction with discriminatory pricing in cognitive radio networks. In *ACM MobiCom Workshop on CRAB*, pages 21–30, 2013.

[11] P. Lin, X. Feng, Q. Zhang, and M. Hamdi. Groupon in the air: A three-stage auction framework for spectrum group-buying. In *IEEE INFOCOM*, pages 2061–2069, 2013.

[12] R. P. McAfee. A dominant strategy double auction. *Journal of Economic Theory*, 56(2):434–450, 1992.

[13] R. B. Myerson. Optimal auction design. *Mathematics Operations Research*, 6(1):58–73, 1981.

[14] R. B. Myerson and M. A. Satterthwaite. Efficient mechanisms for bilateral trading. *Journal of Economic Theory*, 29(2):265–281, 1983.

[15] D. C. Parkes, J. Kalagnanam, and M. Eso. Achieving budget-balance with vickrey-based payment schemes in exchanges. In *International Joint Conference on Artificial Intelligence*, pages 1161–1168, 2001.

[16] W. Vickrey. Counterspeculation, auctions, and competitive sealed tenders. *The Journal of Finance*, 16(1):8–37, 1961.

[17] D. H. von Seggern. *CRC Standard Curves and Surfaces with Mathematica*. Chapman & Hall/CRC, 2006.

[18] W. Wang, B. Liang, and B. Li. Designing truthful spectrum double auctions with local markets. *IEEE Transactions on Mobile Computing*, 13(1):75–88, 2014.

[19] F. Wu and N. Vaidya. Small: A strategy-proof mechanism for radio spectrum allocation. In *IEEE INFOCOM Mini-Conference*, pages 76–80, 2011.

[20] X. Zhou, S. Gandhi, S. Suri, and H. Zheng. eBay in the sky: Strategy-proof wireless spectrum auctions. In *ACM MobiCom*, pages 2–13, 2008.

[21] X. Zhou and H. Zheng. Trust: A general framework for truthful double spectrum auctions. In *IEEE INFOCOM*, pages 999–1007, 2009.

[22] Y. Zhu, B. Li, and Z. Li. Truthful spectrum auction design for secondary networks. In *IEEE INFOCOM*, pages 873–881, 2012.

Differentially Private Spectrum Auction With Approximate Revenue Maximization

Ruihao Zhu[§] Zhijing Li[‡] Fan Wu[‡] Kang G. Shin[§] Guihai Chen[‡]

§Department of Electrical Engineering and Computer Science, University of Michigan, Ann Arbor, MI 48109, USA
‡Shanghai Key Laboratory of Scalable Computing and Systems, Shanghai Jiao Tong University, Shanghai, China
Email: {rhzhu,kgshin}@umich.edu; {lizhijing,fwu,gchen}@cs.sjtu.edu.cn

ABSTRACT

Dynamic spectrum redistribution—under which spectrum owners lease out under-utilized spectrum to users for financial gain—is an effective way to improve spectrum utilization. Auction is a natural way to incentivize spectrum owners to share their idle resources. In recent years, a number of strategy-proof auction mechanisms have been proposed to stimulate bidders to truthfully reveal their valuations. However, it has been shown that truthfulness is not a necessary condition for revenue maximization. Furthermore, in most existing spectrum auction mechanisms, bidders may infer the valuations—which are private information—of the other bidders from the auction outcome. In this paper, we propose a **D**ifferentially privat**E** spectrum auction mechanism with **A**pproximate **R**evenue maximization (**DEAR**). We theoretically prove that DEAR achieves approximate truthfulness, privacy preservation, and approximate revenue maximization. Our extensive evaluations show that DEAR achieves good performance in terms of both revenue and privacy preservation.

Categories and Subject Descriptors

C.2.1 [**Computer-Communication Networks**]: Wireless Communication

General Terms

Algorithm, Differential Privacy, Economics

Keywords

Spectrum Auction, Mechanism Design, Privacy

1. INTRODUCTION

Radio spectrum is a critical yet scarce resource in this age of fast growing wireless technology. However, the traditional static, expensive, and inefficient spectrum allocation has hampered the growth of the wireless networks and its applications. Under this type of allocation, the utilization of radio spectrum is low in spatial and temporal dimensions [1]. Thus, a new trend is to make spectrum access dynamic [2]. With dynamic spectrum access (DSA), new wireless applications may take advantage of (instantaneous) spectrum usage opportunities left over by primary spectrum users. Open markets, such as Spectrum Bridge [3], have already emerged to improve spectrum utilization by providing services of selling, buying, and leasing idle spectrum chunks.

Auctions are the best-known market-based allocation mechanisms due to their perceived fairness and efficiency in resource allocation. One important objective of an auction mechanism is to generate a maximum revenue (*i.e.*, total payments collected from the bidders) [8]. Revenue maximization is not only the sellers' goal in the auctions, but also the basic motivation for spectrum owners to sell or lease out under-utilized spectrum.

In recent years, a number of strategy-proof spectrum auction mechanisms (*e.g.*, [10, 11, 12]) with approximate revenue maximization have been proposed, but under a strong assumption that the auctioneer knows the probability distribution of bidders' valuations. However, none of these mechanisms consider privacy preservation. In existing studies, a strategy-proof spectrum auction mechanism motivates each bidder to report her true valuation, which is commonly termed as *type* in the literature. However, once the true valuations of the bidders are reported as bids, one (other than the auctioneer) may infer the private valuation of a bidder based on the outcomes of the auction. In most of the dynamic spectrum auctions, the permissions of using the wireless channels are granted to the bidders for a certain period of time, and the bidders would soon compete again for the usage of the channels. This makes the inference of the bidders' types even easier. For example, n bidders participate in an auction for a set of channels and winners are granted the permissions to use the spectrum within a certain period of time. After the period of time expires, the auctioneer holds another round of the auction for the same set of channels, and the same group of bidders except for one, who leaves the auction, participate in the second round. In both rounds, the participants bid truthfully in order to maximize their utilities, given the strategy-proofness of the auction mechanism. However, the difference between the two auction outcomes may probably expose the type of the bidder who only participates in the first round of the auction to the others. The true types of bidders are critical commercial secrets of the bidders, because they can reflect the potential revenues of the wireless service providers gained through use of the

MobiHoc'14, August 11–14, 2014, Philadelphia, PA, USA.

http://dx.doi.org/10.1145/2632951.2632974 .

spectrum. Therefore, it is important to achieve bid-privacy preservation in spectrum auctions.

Besides, truthfulness, which means revealing truthful information is the dominant strategy for every bidder, is a too strong assumption, since it prevents the mechanism from having very desirable properties [25, 34]. A number of studies (*e.g.*, [20, 25]) emphasized that proper relaxations on truthfulness can help achieve a good approximation to the revenue and the social welfare in auction mechanisms.

To tackle the problem of privacy preservation, we consider the concept of differential privacy [21], which is a paradigm for private data analysis developed in recent years. Differential privacy aims to reveal information about the population as a whole, while protecting the privacy of each individual. A differentially private mechanism was first investigated by McSherry and Talwar [22]. However, spectrum is different from traditional goods, due to its spatial reusability. Two spectrum users cannot share the same channel simultaneously if their services interfere with each other. Therefore, existing differentially private mechanisms cannot be directly applied to spectrum auctions, in which a slight change of a bidder's bid may change the outcome dramatically.

In this paper, we aim at designing a differentially private spectrum auction mechanism with approximate revenue without prior information on the distribution of the bidders' valuations. We present a Differentially privatE spectrum auction mechanism with Approxiamte Revenue (DEAR). In DEAR, the auctioneer will first partition all bidders into groups and subgroups, and then randomly select the payment and allocation which generates approximate revenue with high probability while protecting the privacy.

Our contributions in this paper are summarized as follows.

- Existing differentially private auction mechanisms cannot be directly applied to spectrum allocations, and hence DEAR is the first to bridge differentially private mechanism design and dynamic spectrum redistribution. It protects bidders' privacy without heavy-weighted cryptographic tools.
- We proposed a polynomial-time spectrum auction mechanism with approximate truthfulness achieving 2ϵ differential privacy and yielding an expected revenue of at least $OPT/7 - 3ln(e + \epsilon OPT|\mathbb{P}|)/\epsilon$ in a prior-free setting, where OPT is the optimal revenue, $\mathbb{P}$ is the set of possible bids and $\epsilon > 0$ is a small constant.
- DEAR is further extended for the case of multi-channel bids with budget constraints, still guaranteeing 2ϵ differential privacy and providing an expected revenue of at least $OPT/7 - 3c \cdot ln(e + \epsilon OPT|\mathbb{P}|)/\epsilon$, where c is the number of channels.
- We implement DEAR and extensively evaluated its performance. Our evaluation results show that DEAR generates more revenue than the other mechanisms, while protecting bid-privacy.

The rest of this paper is organized as follows. Section 2 briefly reviews related work, while Section 3 covers technical preliminaries. Section 4 presents the detailed design of DEAR for the single channel request case. Section 5 extends DEAR to support multi-request bidders with budget constraints. Section 6 presents our evaluation results of the proposed mechanism. Finally, we conclude the paper in Section 7.

2. RELATED WORK

In recent years, dynamic spectrum allocation has been suggested as a viable solution to efficiently utilize and share the available spectrum [1, 4, 7]. In this architecture, the spectrum is allocated dynamically in spatial and temporal domains. Periodically, the spectrum owners allocate channels to the bidders under interference constraints with the financial goal.

In traditional economic theory, revenue-maximizing auctions are designed under the assumption that the auctioneer knows the probability distribution of the bidders' valuations; by applying Vickrey-Clarke-Groves (VCG) mechanism using *virtual valuation* of bidders [13], the resulting auctions can be both strategy-proof and revenue-maximizing (*e.g.*, [10, 11]).

Without prior information of the distribution of bidders' valuations, Gandhi *et al.* [8] used a linear programming approach to model interference constraints. This work does not consider strategic user behavior, and assumes truthful bids for free. Strategic behavior is considered by Sengupta and Chatterjee, who proposed a knapsack-based auction for dynamic spectrum allocation to optimize the revenue [9]. However, they did not address the problem of interference in spectrum. Considering the spectrum interference constraints, Gopinathan and Li [24] proposed a strategy-proof and revenue maximization spectrum auction mechanism, providing a guarantee on expected revenue. However, none of these mechanisms provides any guarantee on privacy preservation.

The design of privacy-preserving mechanisms has been studied extensively. In [32, 33], the authors presented auction protocols that prune the auctioneers' ability to falsify the auction outcome and reveal confidential information by introducing a new third party. In [15, 16, 17, 18], the authors employed various cryptography techniques to achieve security in various auction schemes. But these cryptography tools will incur high computation and overheads. Huang *et al.* [14] proposed a strategy-proof and privacy-preserving mechanism called *SPRING*, to achieve k-anonymity in spectrum auctions. Later, Huang *et al.* [36] proposed PPS, which is a privacy-preserving and strategy-proof mechanism for approximate social welfare maximization in spectrum auctions. However, none of these mechanisms considered the problem without prior knowledge of revenue maximization.

Recently, differential privacy was first introduced by Dwork [21]. Then, McSherry and Talwar [22] elegantly integrated differential privacy with mechanism designs, and pointed out that differential privacy implies approximate truthfulness as well as resilience to collusion. In particular, they studied the problem of revenue maximization in digital auctions and attribute auctions. They also suggested use of the exponential mechanism, which can achieve differential privacy, to solve mechanism design problems with different objective functions like revenue. Later studies gave further results on mechanism design via differential privacy, e.g., in [38]. Huang and Kannan examined the properties of the exponential mechanism, which can be thought of as a noisy version of VCG. They showed that, with appropriate payments, this mechanism is truthful, individually rational, approximately efficient, and differentially private.

3. PRELIMINARIES

In this section, we first present the auction model, and then briefly review important solution concepts drawn from differential privacy and mechanism design.

3.1 Auction Model

We consider a collusion-free spectrum auction with an *auctioneer* (seller) and a group of *bidders* (buyers). The auctioneer has a set $\mathbb{C} = \{1, 2, \dots, c\}$ of orthogonal channels. Unlike the allocation of traditional goods, wireless channels can be spatially reused, meaning that multiple well-separated bidders can work on the same channel simultaneously, if they do not interfere with each other. Also, a set $\mathbb{N} = \{1, 2, \dots, n\}$ of bidders compete for the use of channels. Each bidder $i \in \mathbb{N}$ requests a single channel (in Section 4) or multiple channels within its budget (in Section 5). For the case of multi-channel requests, we assume that the bidders do not have preference over different channels.

Each bidder has valuation v_i for a channel. The valuation, which is known as *type* in the literature, is private to the bidder for since can reflect the potential revenue the bidder gains, the valuation of each bidder may need to be kept private. Let $\vec{v} = (v_1, v_2, \dots, v_n)$ denote the profile of the bidders' private valuations. Without loss of generality, we can normalize the bidders' valuations to the interval of $(0, 1]$.

The bidders' bids for the channels are based on their valuations in the auction, and each bidder has a bid b_i per channel. Let $\vec{b} = (b_1, b_2, \dots, b_n)$ denote the profile of the bidders' bids, which are also in the range of $(0, 1]$. The bidders may lie about their valuations, and thus for each bidder i, b_i may not be equal to v_i. The auctioneer also initializes a set of prices $\mathbb{P} = \{\rho_1, \rho_2, \dots, \rho_h\}$, including all the different possible valuation/bid values in $(0, 1]$.

In the auction, the bidders are located in a geographical region. For every bidder, there is a region called *interference area* around her. We say bidders i and j interfere with each other if their interference areas overlap. We assume that a bidder's interference area is a unit-radius disk [11] (*i.e.*, the interference range is 2). The interference among bidders can be model as a *conflict graph* $\mathcal{G} = \{\mathbb{N}, \mathbb{E}\}$, in which the vertices are the bidders, and a pair of bidders is connected if and only if their interference areas overlap.

The auctioneer wishes to allocate channels, such that every pair of the winning bidders do not interfere with each other, and set prices to maximize the total revenue. So, the outcome of an auction includes an allocation profile and a charging profile, which is based on some criteria over the bidding profile $\vec{b}$. Let $\vec{x} = (x_1, x_2, \dots, x_n)$ denote the allocation profile, where x_i is the number of channels bidder i could get. Let p_i denote the payment for bidder i, and $\vec{p} = (p_1, p_2, \dots, p_n)$ denote the charging profile.

In the auction, each bidder i is considered selfish and rational [29, 30], and always tries to maximize her own utility u_i:

$$u_i = v_i x_i - p_i.$$

The revenue of an auction mechanism is the sum of the payments $\Sigma_i p_i$ collected from the bidders. Clearly, if the bidders bid untruthfully, the lower bids (than their actual valuations) may indirectly lower the revenue. However, truthfulness is shown to be too strong as a solution, which will impact the allocation scheme and may lower the revenue. So, we want to enforce approximate truthfulness. Specifically, we aim at maximizing the revenue without any prior information, while enforcing approximate truthfulness and protecting bidders' privacy.

3.2 Related Solution Concept

We now review some of the important and closely related solution concepts from mechanism design and differential privacy.

(1) γ-truthful

We first introduce *Dominant Strategy* [30], a strong solution concept from mechanism design.

DEFINITION 1. *(Dominant Strategy [30]) Strategy s_i is a player i's dominant strategy in a game, if for any strategy $s_i' \neq s_i$ and any other players' strategy profile s_{-i},*

$$u_i(s_i, s_{-i}) \geq u_i(s_i', s_{-i}).$$

The concept of dominant strategy is based on truthfulness. Truthfulness in an auction means that revealing truthful information is a dominant strategy for every bidder. However, exact truthfulness sometimes turns out to be too strict as a solution, so we consider approximate truthfulness, or γ-truthfulness [23].

DEFINITION 2. *(γ-truthful [23]) Let s_i denote the strategy when player i behaves truthfully. A mechanism is said to be γ-truthful if for every player i, for any strategy $s_i' \neq s_i$ and any other players' strategy profile s_{-i},*

$$E[u_i(s_i, s_{-i})] \geq E[u_i(s_i', s_{-i})] - \gamma,$$

where $\gamma > 0$ is a small constant.

(2) Differential Privacy

Differential privacy has been studied extensively in the community of theoretical computer science. It guarantees that the probability distributions of possible outcomes are nearly identical, when the (input) data profiles are nearly identical. Formally,

DEFINITION 3. *(Differential Privacy[21]) A mechanism $\mathcal{M}$ gives ϵ differential privacy if for any two data profiles D_1 and D_2 differing in a single element, and all $S \subseteq Range(\mathcal{M})$,*

$$\boldsymbol{Pr}[\mathcal{M}(D_1) \in S] \leq exp(\epsilon) \times \boldsymbol{Pr}[\mathcal{M}(D_2) \in S],$$

where $\epsilon > 0$ is a small constant.

When integrating differential privacy with an auction mechanism, two neighboring profiles are the bid profiles $\vec{b} = (b_1, b_2, \dots, b_n)$ and $\vec{b'}$ which differs from $\vec{b}$ in one bid (added, removed or changed).

A differentially private mechanism $\mathcal{M}$ can address the concern of personal input leakage. In an auction, any change in a bidder's bid won't bring significant changes to the outcome, and thus, the others cannot infer information of this particular bidder just from the outcomes.

(3) Exponential Mechanism

A powerful tool in the literature of differential privacy is the exponential mechanism proposed by McSherry and Talwar [22].

The exponential mechanism is a general technique for constructing differentially private algorithms over an arbitrary range P of outcomes and any objective function $F(\vec{b}, p)$ that maps a pair consisting of a data profile $\vec{b}$ and a feasible outcome $p \in P$ to a real-valued score.

In our setting, $\vec{b}$ is the declared valuation (bid) profile, p is every winning bidder's payment per channel. In basic DEAR, the objective function $F(\vec{b}, p)$ is the revenue function; and in extended DEAR, the objective function is the revenue function divided by the number of channels. In a spectrum auction, once the graph of bidders' location is given, the allocation scheme $\vec{x}$ is only depends on parameter $\vec{b}$ and p. Thus, we can denote the revenue function as $Q(\vec{b}, p)$, and $Q(\vec{b}, p) = p\Sigma_i x_i(\vec{b}, p)$.

Given a range P, a data profile $\vec{b}$, an objective function F, and a small constant ϵ, the exponential mechanism $Exp(P, \vec{b}, F, \epsilon)$ chooses an outcome p from the range P with probability

$$\mathbf{Pr}[Exp(P, \vec{b}, F, \epsilon) = p] \propto exp\left(\epsilon F\left(\vec{b}, p\right)\right),$$

THEOREM 1. *The exponential mechanism gives $2\epsilon\Delta$ differential privacy [22].*

Here, Δ is the Lipschitz constant of the objective function F, *i.e.*, for any two data profiles $\vec{b}$ and $\vec{b}'$ differing in a single element, and for any outcome p, the score $F(\vec{b}, p)$ and $F(\vec{b}', p)$ differs by at most Δ.

Theorem 1 highlights that the exponential mechanism will be the most useful when Δ is small. In DEAR, a small Δ ensures that a single change in the bid of a bidder has a small effect on the outcome.

4. DEAR

We now present DEAR, a differentially private spectrum auction mechanism with approximate revenue maximization.

4.1 Design Rationale

DEAR integrates the exponential mechanism with spectrum auction to achieve both approximate revenue maximization and differential privacy. Basically, DEAR is a single price auction, in which all the winning bidders will be charged with a uniform price. The main idea of DEAR is to randomly select a price from a set of prices with a carefully designed probability distribution. For each price, there are a corresponding allocation and a generated revenue. The probability of a price to be chosen is set to be proportional to its corresponding revenue. Thus, approximate revenue maximization and differential privacy can be achieved. We briefly illustrate the design challenges and our ideas in meeting them.

(1) Payment Selection

In a non-informative-prior setting, the auctioneer has no information on the distribution of bidders' valuations. The obstacle in such a setting is to design a mechanism that can select the optimal/sub-optimal price to charge bidders. Setting p either too high or too low may reduce the revenue. Moreover, we want the payment selection to guarantee approximate truthfulness, which should force bidders in the auction to have limited incentive to lie. To achieve these objectives, we integrate the exponential mechanism with spectrum auction to determine the price. DEAR sets the probability of each price to be chosen to be proportional to its corresponding generated revenue. Therefore, DEAR could choose the price that generates a high revenue with high probability, while protecting privacy.

(2) Spectrum Allocation

For each price ρ in the set of prices, the auctioneer wants to allocate channels to as many bidders as possible in order to maximize her revenue. Unlike traditional goods, spectrum is reusable among bidders subject to the spatial interference constraints. It has been shown that it's NP-complete [35] to find the optimal spectrum allocation. DEAR partitions the bidders into groups according to their geographic locations. For each price ρ, DEAR allocates channels to groups that can generate the highest revenue.

4.2 Design Details

Following the guidelines in Section 4.1, we now describe the detailed design of DEAR. It performs the auction in three steps. It first partitions the bidders into groups and subgroups. Then, it initializes the set of prices, and calculates the probability distribution over the set. Finally, it randomly selects a price from the set of prices as the payment with the carefully designed probability distribution and allocates the channels to the winners.

Step 1: Grouping of Bidders

Before running the spectrum auction, DEAR first divides the set of bidders $\mathbb{N}$ into groups and subgroups.

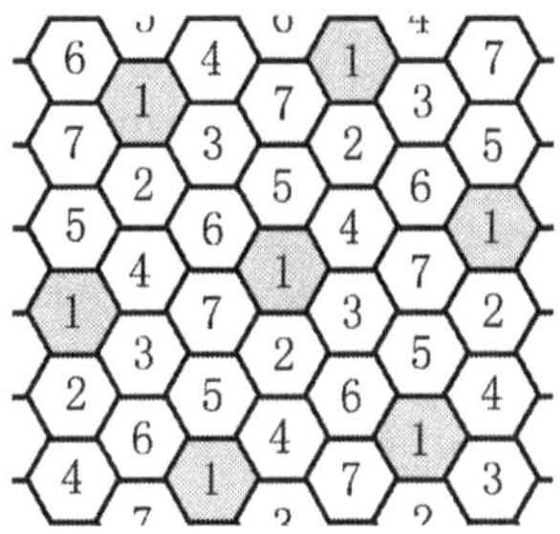

Figure 1: Hexagons uniformly-colored using 7 colors. No adjacent hexagons are in the same color.

Since the bidders are located in a geographic region, DEAR basically divides the entire region into small hexagons with unit side-length [11], and then uniformly colors the hexagons with seven colors, as illustrated in Fig. 1.

Let g_i denote the group that contains all the subgroups in color i, and g_i^j denote the j'th subgroup of g_i which contains the bidders located in the same hexagonal region. Like in Fig. 1, g_1 contains all the bidders located in the yellow region, and $g_1^j(j = 1, \ldots, |g_1|)$ contains bidders located in each separate yellow hexagon.

Since there are seven colors, we denote the set of groups as:

$$\mathbb{G} = \{g_1, g_2, \ldots, g_7\},$$

and denote the set of subgroups in group $g_k, k \in \{1, 2, \ldots, 7\}$ as:

$$g_k = \left\{g_k^1, g_k^2, \ldots, g_k^{|g_k|}\right\}.$$

In such a grouping, we have the following two properties.

Property 1 Any pair of bidders from the same subgroup cannot be allocated on the same channel due to the interference constraint.

Property 2 Any pair of bidders from different subgroups in the same group can share the same channel.

Any pair of bidders from the same subgroup are in the same hexagon with unit side-length (*i.e.*, half of the interference range), so the distance between them is no more than 2. Since every bidder's interference area is an unit-radius disk, then any two bidders' interference areas intersect with each other, so no two bidders from the same subgroup could share a common channel. Thus, Property 1 holds.

Property 2 can be obtained from the observation that since each bidder's interference area is a unit-radius disk, the distance between any pair of bidders from two different subgroups but in the same group is at least $(\frac{\sqrt{3}}{2})^2 + (\frac{5}{2})^2 = \sqrt{7}$. $\sqrt{7} > 2$, which means that the distance between the two bidders is far enough for these bidders to be out of interfere with each other. Thus, they can share the same channel.

These two properties tell us that: (A) For each subgroup g_k^i, the number of winning bidders in it is at most $\min(|g_k^i|, c)$; (B) Winning bidders from different subgroups in the same group can be combined to obtain the whole set of winners.

Step 2: Calculation of Probability Distribution

For each price $\rho_j \in \mathbb{P}$, DEAR removes the bidders with bids less than ρ_j in every subgroup. This changes $g_k^i \in g_k$ to $g_k^{i\prime}$, and changes $g_k \in \mathbb{G}$ to $g_k{}'$, and we denote this step as

$$\mathbb{G}' = Remove(\mathbb{N}, \mathbb{G}, \rho_j),$$

where *Remove*() is the removing function that returns the set of groups containing bidders with bids at least ρ_j.

For the remaining bidders in subgroup $g_k^{i\prime} \in g_k{}'$, DEAR randomly selects $min(|g_k^{i\prime}|, c)$ bidders as candidates. Obviously, this method of candidate selection is not related to bidders' bids. We denote this step as

$$W_k^i(\rho_j) = Select(g_k^{i\prime}, min(|g_k^{i\prime}|, c)),$$

where *Select*() is the candidate selection function.

For each group $g_k{}' \in \mathbb{G}'$, DEAR combines the candidates from all its subgroups to form the set of candidates $W_k(\rho_j)$ in group $g_k{}'$ at price ρ_j:

$$W_k(\rho_j) = \bigcup_{i=1}^{|g_k{}'|} W_k^i(\rho_j).$$

DEAR picks up the group with most candidates from the seven groups, let $W(\rho_j)$ be the group with the most candidates when the price is ρ_j:

$$k_0 = \underset{k}{\text{argmax}}|W_k(\rho_j)|, \quad (1)$$

$$W(\rho_j) = W_{k_0}(\rho_j) \quad (2)$$

The tentative price for the candidates in $W(\rho_j)$ is set to ρ_j. Thus, the revenue when setting the price to ρ_j is:

$$Q(\vec{b}, \rho_j) = \rho_j|W(\rho_j)|. \quad (3)$$

DEAR calculates the corresponding revenue when setting the price to all possible values in $\mathbb{P}$. Then, DEAR sets the probability of price $\rho_j \in \mathbb{P}$ to be chosen proportional to its corresponding revenue, *i.e.*,

$$Pr(\rho_j) = \frac{exp(\epsilon Q(\vec{b}, \rho_j))}{\Sigma_{\rho_i \in \mathbb{P}} exp(\epsilon Q(\vec{b}, \rho_i))}.$$

Algorithm 1 Calculation of Probability over Prices

Input: A set of bidders $\mathbb{N}$, a set of channels $\mathbb{C}$, a bid profile $\vec{b}$, a set of prices $\mathbb{P}$ and a set of groups $\mathbb{G}$.
Output: A probability vector of possible prices $\vec{Pr}$.

for all $\rho_j \in \mathbb{P}$ **do**
  $G' \leftarrow Remove(\mathbb{N}, \mathbb{G}, \rho_j)$.
  for all $g_k{}' \in \mathbb{G}'$ **do**
    $W_k(\rho_j) \leftarrow \varnothing$.
    for all $g_k^{i\prime} \in g_k{}'$ **do**
      $W_k^i(\rho_j) \leftarrow Select(g_k^{i\prime}, min(|g_k^{i\prime}|, c))$.
      $W_k(\rho_j) \leftarrow W_k(\rho_j) \cup W_k^i(\rho_j)$.
    end for
  end for
  $k_0 \leftarrow \underset{k}{\text{argmax}}|W_k(\rho_j)|$.
  $W(\rho_j) \leftarrow W_{k_0}(\rho_j)$
  $Q(\vec{b}, \rho_j) \leftarrow \rho_j|W(\rho_j)|$.
end for
for all $\rho_j \in \mathbb{P}$ **do**
  $Pr(\rho_j) \leftarrow \frac{exp(\epsilon Q(\vec{b}, \rho_j))}{\Sigma_{\rho_i \in \mathbb{P}} exp(\epsilon Q(\vec{b}, \rho_i))}$.
end for
Return $\vec{Pr}$;

Algorithm 1 shows the pseudo-code of the probability calculation over the prices in set $\mathbb{P}$.

Step 3: Price Selection and Channel Allocation

After calculating the probabilities of all the prices in set $\mathbb{P}$ to be chosen as payment, we get the probability vector $\vec{Pr} = (Pr(\rho_1), Pr(\rho_2), \ldots, Pr(\rho_{|\mathbb{P}|}))$. DEAR randomly selects a price $p \in \mathbb{P}$ as the auction payment per channel according to the probability vector. Then, the corresponding candidates $W(p)$ are the winners and will be allocated channels.

4.3 Analysis

We now analyze the privacy, approximate truthfulness, and revenue of DEAR.

First, we show that the carefully designed grouping can limit the Lipschitz constant Δ of the objective function Q. This way, DEAR can guarantee good differential privacy.

THEOREM 2. *DEAR achieves* 2ϵ *differential privacy.*

PROOF. We consider two bid profiles $\vec{b}$ and $\vec{b'}$ differing in only one bid. Let M denote the outcome function, which corresponds to the per-channel charge determined by the auctioneer in DEAR. We denote the probability of price $p \in \mathbb{P}$ to be chosen when the bid profile is $\vec{b}$ and $\vec{b'}$ as $Pr(\mathcal{M}(\vec{b}) = \rho)$ and $Pr(\mathcal{M}(\vec{b'}) = \rho)$, respectively. We define $\Delta Q \geq 0$, which is the Lipschitz constant of the objective function Q, to be the largest possible difference in Q, when applied to two bid profiles that differ only in one bid, for all p. Then,

$$\frac{Pr(\mathcal{M}(\vec{b}) = \rho)}{Pr(\mathcal{M}(\vec{b'}) = \rho)}$$

$$= \frac{exp(\epsilon Q(\vec{b}, \rho))/\Sigma_{\rho_i \in \mathbb{P}} exp(\epsilon Q(\vec{b}, \rho_i))}{exp(\epsilon Q(\vec{b'}, \rho))/\Sigma_{\rho_i \in \mathbb{P}} exp(\epsilon Q(\vec{b'}, \rho_i))}$$

$$= \frac{exp(\epsilon Q(\vec{b}, \rho))}{exp(\epsilon Q(\vec{b'}, \rho))} \times \frac{\Sigma_{\rho_i \in \mathbb{P}} exp(\epsilon Q(\vec{b'}, \rho_i))}{\Sigma_{\rho_i \in \mathbb{P}} exp(\epsilon Q(\vec{b}, \rho_i))}$$

$$\leq \frac{exp(\epsilon Q(\vec{b'}, \rho) + \epsilon \Delta Q)}{exp(\epsilon Q(\vec{b'}, \rho))} \times \frac{\Sigma_{\rho_i \in \mathbb{P}} exp(\epsilon Q(\vec{b'}, \rho_i))}{\Sigma_{\rho_i \in \mathbb{P}} exp(\epsilon Q(\vec{b}, \rho_i))}$$
$$\leq exp(\epsilon \Delta Q) \times \frac{\Sigma_{\rho_i \in \mathbb{P}} exp(\epsilon Q(\vec{b}, \rho_i) + \epsilon \Delta Q)}{\Sigma_{\rho_i \in \mathbb{P}} exp(\epsilon Q(\vec{b}, \rho_i))}$$
$$= exp(\epsilon \Delta Q) \times exp(\epsilon \Delta Q)$$
$$= exp(2\epsilon \Delta Q) \tag{4}$$

Since in DEAR, for any $\rho \in \mathbb{P}$, any bidder $i \in \mathbb{N}$ can change the revenue function $Q(\vec{b}, \rho)$ by at most

$$\Delta Q = px_i(\vec{b}, \rho) \leq \rho \leq 1. \tag{5}$$

From (1) and (2), we get

$$Pr(\mathcal{M}(\vec{b}) = p) \leq exp(2\epsilon) Pr(\mathcal{M}(\vec{b'}) = p). \tag{6}$$

Therefore, DEAR achieves 2ϵ differential privacy. □

Next, we show the approximate truthfulness of DEAR.

THEOREM 3. *DEAR is 4ϵ-truthful.*

PROOF. Let $E[u_i(b_i, b_{-i})]$ denote the expected utility of bidder i, when she bids b_i. M is the outcome function and ϵ is very small (satisfying $exp(2\epsilon) < 1 + 4\epsilon$).

Suppose bidder i bids $b_i \neq v_i$. We distinguish the following two cases:

- **Case 1:** We consider the scenario where i bids lower than her true value, $b_i \leq v_i$.

  For all $\rho \in \mathbb{P}$, if $b_i < \rho$, the bidder will be removed and then $x_i(b_i, b_{-i}, \rho)v_i - \rho = 0$; if $b_i \geq \rho$, the bidder is still in the subgroup, and $x_i(b_i, b_{-i}, \rho) = x_i(v_i, b_{-i}, \rho)$ for the candidate selection function *Select*() is not related to the bid. In Theorem 2, we proved that DEAR achieves 2ϵ differential privacy. Obviously, the utility of each bidder with a single demand is less than 1, so we have:

$$E[u_i(b_i, b_{-i}, v_i, \mathbb{P})]$$
$$= \Sigma_{\rho \in \mathbb{P}} Pr[M(b_i, b_{-i}) = \rho] \times (x_i(b_i, b_{-i}, p)v_i - \rho)$$
$$\leq \Sigma_{\rho \in \mathbb{P}} exp(2\epsilon) Pr[M(v_i, b_{-i}) = \rho]$$
$$\times (x_i(v_i, b_{-i}, \rho)v_i - \rho)$$
$$= exp(2\epsilon) E[u_i(v_i, b_{-i}, v_i, \mathbb{P})]$$
$$\leq (1 + 4\epsilon) E[u_i(v_i, b_{-i}, v_i, \mathbb{P})]$$
$$\leq E[u_i(v_i, b_{-i}, v_i, \mathbb{P})] + 4\epsilon \tag{7}$$

- **Case 2:** We consider the scenario where $b_i > v_i$.

  For all $\rho \in \mathbb{P}$, if $v_i \geq \rho$, then $b_i > \rho$ and bidder i will still be in the subgroup. Since the selection function *Select*() is not related to the bid, $x_i(b_i, b_{-i}, \rho) = x_i(v_i, b_{-i}, \rho)$. For all $\rho \in \mathbb{P}$ satisfying $v_i < \rho$, if $b_i < \rho$, then bidder i will be removed and the utility is 0; else if $b_i \geq \rho$, bidder i will still be in the subgroup. If she loses, her utility is 0; if she wins, her utility

$$u_i(b_i, b_{-i}, v_i, \rho) = v_i - \rho < 0.$$

  Thus, for all $\rho \in \mathbb{P}$ satisfying $v_i < \rho$, misreporting leads the utility to non-positive. Then,

$$E[u_i(b_i, b_{-i}, v_i, \mathbb{P})]$$
$$= \Sigma_{\rho \in \mathbb{P}} Pr[M(b_i, b_{-i}) = \rho] \times (x_i(b_i, b_{-i}, \rho)v_i - \rho)$$
$$\leq \Sigma_{(\rho \in \mathbb{P}) \wedge (\rho \leq v_i)} Pr[M(b_i, b_{-i}) = \rho]$$
$$\times (x_i(b_i, b_{-i}, \rho)v_i - \rho)$$
$$\leq \Sigma_{(\rho \in \mathbb{P}) \wedge (\rho \leq v_i)} Pr[M(v_i, b_{-i}) = \rho]$$
$$\times (x_i(v_i, b_{-i}, \rho)v_i - \rho)$$
$$\leq E[u_i(v_i, b_{-i}, v_i, \mathbb{P})] \tag{8}$$

Thus, the theorem follows. □

THEOREM 4. *DEAR has an expected revenue of at least $OPT/7 - 3ln(e + \epsilon OPT|\mathbb{P}|)/\epsilon$, where $|\mathbb{P}|$ is the number of different bids from $\mathbb{P}$, which is the set of price.*

To prove this theorem, we first give the following lemmas. Let $OPT^* = max_\rho Q(\vec{b}, p) = max_\rho \rho |W_1(\rho)'|$, let OPT denote the optimal single price revenue for the spectrum auction.

LEMMA 1. *OPT^* is within a factor of 7 of OPT,* i.e., *$OPT/7 \leq OPT^* \leq OPT$.*

PROOF. Suppose the revenue of the spectrum auction reaches OPT when the charged price to each winner is ρ'. Then, for price ρ', DEAR chooses the group with the most candidates (also with the highest revenue) from the seven groups. Since OPT is upper-bounded by the sum of the optimal revenue of each of the seven groups. Thus, $OPT/7 \leq OPT^* \leq OPT$. □

LEMMA 2. *Letting $S_t = \left\{\rho : Q(\vec{b}, \rho) > OPT^* - t\right\}$. For those t satisfying $t \geq ln(|\mathbb{P}|OPT^*/(t|S_t|))/\epsilon$, the expected revenue generated by our mechanism $E[REV(\mathcal{M})] \geq OPT^* - 3t$.*

PROOF. Let $\overline{S_{2t}} = \left\{\rho : Q(\vec{b}, \rho) \leq OPT^* - 2t\right\}$, we first prove that $Pr(\rho \in \overline{S_{2t}})$ is at most $\frac{|P| exp(-\epsilon t)}{|S_t|}$.

The probability $Pr(\rho \in \overline{S_{2t}})$ is no more than $Pr(\rho \in \overline{S_{2t}})/Pr(\rho \in S_t)$, as the new denominator is at most one. Then, we can write:

$$\frac{Pr(\rho \in \overline{S_{2t}})}{Pr(\rho \in S_t)}$$
$$= \frac{\Sigma_{\rho \in \overline{S_{2t}}} exp(\epsilon Q(\vec{b}, \rho))/\Sigma_{\rho_i \in \mathbb{P}} exp(\epsilon Q(\vec{b}, \rho_i))}{\Sigma_{\rho \in S_t} exp(\epsilon Q(\vec{b}, \rho))/\Sigma_{\rho_i \in \mathbb{P}} exp(\epsilon Q(\vec{b}, \rho_i))}$$
$$= \frac{\Sigma_{\rho \in \overline{S_{2t}}} exp(\epsilon Q(\vec{b}, \rho))}{\Sigma_{\rho \in S_t} exp(\epsilon Q(\vec{b}, \rho))}$$
$$< \frac{exp(\epsilon(OPT^* - 2t))|\overline{S_{2t}}|}{exp(\epsilon(OPT^* - t))|S_t|}$$
$$= exp(-\epsilon t)\frac{|\overline{S_{2t}}|}{|S_t|}$$
$$\leq \frac{|\mathbb{P}| exp(-\epsilon t)}{|S_t|}. \tag{9}$$

Then, DEAR selects price $\rho \in \mathbb{P}$ that achieves revenue at least $OPT^* - 2t$ with probability of at least $1 - \frac{|\mathbb{P}| exp(-\epsilon t)}{|S_t|}$. By using the assumption on t, we make this probability at least $1 - \frac{t}{OPT^*}$. Multiplying them, we get:

$$E[REV(\mathcal{M})] \geq (1 - \frac{t}{OPT^*})(OPT^* - 2t)$$
$$> OPT^* - 3t. \tag{10}$$

□

Next, we use the above lemmas to prove Theorem 4.

PROOF. Let $t = ln(e + \epsilon OPT^*|\mathbb{P}|)/\epsilon$, notice that $t \geq 1/\epsilon$, then we have,

$$\begin{aligned} ln(OPT^*|\mathbb{P}|/(t|S_t|))/\epsilon &< ln(OPT^*|\mathbb{P}|/t)/\epsilon \\ &< ln(e + OPT^*|\mathbb{P}|/t)/\epsilon \\ &< ln(e + \epsilon OPT^*|\mathbb{P}|)/\epsilon \end{aligned} \quad (11)$$

We apply Lemma 2 using t $= ln(e + \epsilon OPT^*|\mathbb{P}|)/\epsilon$ and by Lemma 1, we have:

$$\begin{aligned} E[REV(\mathcal{M})] &\geq OPT^* - 3t \\ &\geq \frac{1}{7}OPT - \frac{3}{\epsilon}ln(e + \epsilon OPT^*|\mathbb{P}|) \\ &\geq \frac{1}{7}OPT - \frac{3}{\epsilon}ln(e + \epsilon OPT|\mathbb{P}|). \end{aligned} \quad (12)$$

This completes the proof. □

5. EXTENSION TO MULTI-DEMAND BIDDERS WITH BUDGET CONSTRAINTS

In the previous section, we proposed a differentially private spectrum auction mechanism with approximate revenue maximization, in which each bidder bids for a single channel. Here we extend it to adapt to a more practical scenario in which a bidder can bid for multiple channels with a budget constraint. This extension also achieves privacy preservation, approximate truthfulness and approximate revenue maximization.

Different from the existing spectrum auction with bidders having multiple requests, we consider the budget of each bidder instead of the demand number. The budget of a bidder is the maximum upper bound on her ability to pay; this is a very common constraint. Also, budget constraints are studied extensively in the theoretical computer science community and are a central feature of many real auctions.

In the extended mechanism, we allow bidders to bid for multiple channels by submitting their budgets. Let $\mathbb{B} = (B_1, B_2, \ldots, B_n)$ denote the budget profile of the bidders. We assume that each bidder has an identical valuation on different channels. In the auction, each bidder $i \in \mathbb{N}$ submits not only her per-channel bid $b_i \in (0, 1]$, but also the budget $B_i \in [0, c]$ to the auctioneer. Here, c is the number of channels.

5.1 Virtual Bidder

In the extended DEAR, bidders with adequate budgets may get more than one channels. Here, we introduce the concept of virtual bidder to turn the extended problem into the basic problem.

For price $\rho \in \mathbb{P}$, bidder i with a bid greater than ρ could get at most $\lfloor B_i/\rho \rfloor$ different channels. Thus, DEAR creates $\lfloor B_i/\rho \rfloor$ replicas called *virtual bidders* for bidder i. Each virtual bidder can be allocated at most one channel. DEAR places these virtual bidders in the same subgroup with bidder i. Therefore, any two virtual bidders of a bidder should be allocated different channels. Then, DEAR sets the bids of all the virtual bidders to ρ.

Let's consider an illustrative example of virtual bidder.

Suppose there are 20 channels in the auction, bidder $i \in g_k^j$ is willing to buy spectrum at the price of 0.4 per channel, and she has a budget of 0.9. Assume a price from the price set is $\rho = 0.3$. Given p, bidder i could buy at most $\lfloor 0.9/0.3 \rfloor$ $= 3$ different channels and will be charged at 0.3 per channel. So, DEAR creates 3 virtual bidders i^1, i^2 and i^3instead of the original bidder i in subgroup g_k^j, and then set the bids of these virtual bidders to 0.3, as shows in Fig. 2.

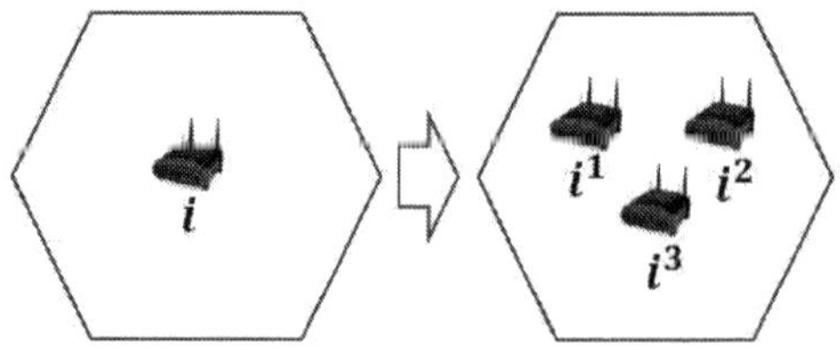

Figure 2: An illustrative example.

5.2 Extended DEAR

The procedures of bidder grouping and random selection and allocation are nearly the same as those in DEAR. Due to space limitation, we will focus on the differences in the step of probability calculation.

Step 1: Bidder Grouping

Please refer to subsection 4.2 for details.

Step 2: Calculation of Probability Distribution

For each price $\rho_j \in \mathbb{P}$, DEAR first removes the bidders with bids less than ρ_j in every subgroup. This changes each subgroup $g_k^i \in g_k$ to $g_k^{i\,\prime}$, changes each group $g_k \in \mathbb{G}$ to $g_k{}'$, and changes $\mathbb{G}$ to $\mathbb{G}'$. Then, for the remaining bidders in each subgroup $g_k^{i\,\prime} \in g_k'$, DEAR creates virtual bidders for each bidder $l \in g_k^{i\,\prime}$ according to her budget and the price ρ_j. Let $\hat{g_k^i}{}'$ denote the set of virtual bidders in subgroup $g_k^{i\,\prime}$.

DEAR randomly selects $min(|\hat{g_k^i}{}'|, c)$ virtual bidders as virtual candidates, represented by $\hat{W_k^i(\rho_j)}$. This method of virtual candidate selection is not related to biddersa̧ŕ bids.

For each group $g_k' \in \mathbb{G}'$, DEAR combines the virtual candidates from all its subgroups to form the set of virtual candidates $\hat{W_k(\rho_j)}$ in group g_k' at price ρ_j:

$$\hat{W_k(\rho_j)} = \bigcup_{i=1}^{|g_k'|} \hat{W_k^i(\rho_j)}.$$

DEAR picks up the group with most virtual candidates from the seven groups, let $\hat{W(\rho_j)}$ be the group with the most virtual candidates when the setting price is ρ_j.

The tentative price for the virtual candidates in $\hat{W(\rho_j)}$ is set to ρ_j. Thus, the revenue when setting the price to ρ_j is:

$$Q(\vec{b}, \rho_j) = \rho_j |\hat{W(\rho_j)}|.$$

DEAR calculates the corresponding revenue when setting the price to all possible values in $\mathbb{P}$. Then, DEAR sets the probability of price $\rho_j \in \mathbb{P}$ to be chosen proportional to its corresponding revenue divided by the number of channels, *i.e.*,

$$Pr(\rho_j) = \frac{exp(\epsilon Q(\vec{b}, \rho_j)/c)}{\Sigma_{\rho_i \in \mathbb{P}} exp(\epsilon Q(\vec{b}, \rho_i)/c)}.$$

Step 3: Price Selection and Channel Allocation

DEAR selects the price and virtual winners according to subsection 4.2. Winners will be the bidders of the winning virtual bidders, and the number of channels each winner gets is equal to the number of her virtual winners.

For the extended DEAR, we get the following theorem.

THEOREM 5. *The extended DEAR is individually rational, and every bidder pays within her budget.*

PROOF. Suppose DEAR selects $p \in \mathbb{P}$ as the payment and allocates channels to the corresponding winning bidders. If the bid of bidder $i \in \mathbb{N}$ is less than p, then she will be charged nothing. Otherwise, bidder $i \in \mathbb{N}$ will get at most $\lfloor B_i/\rho \rfloor$ channels and will pay at most $\rho\lfloor B_i/\rho \rfloor \leq B_i$. Thus, every bidder pays within her budget. The mechanism achieves individual rationality. □

THEOREM 6. *The extended DEAR gives 2ϵ differential privacy, an expected revenue at least $OPT/7 - 3c \cdot ln(e + \epsilon OPT|\mathbb{P}|)/\epsilon$, where $|\mathbb{P}|$ is the number of different bids of $\mathbb{P}$, and the extended DEAR is $4\epsilon(max_{i\in\mathbb{N}}E[u_i])$-truthful.*

PROOF. Here, the objective function is $Q(\vec{b}, \rho)/c$.

As for any $\rho \in \mathbb{P}$, any bidder $i \in \mathbb{N}$ can change the revenue function $Q(\vec{b}, \rho)$ by at most

$$p\lfloor B_i/\rho \rfloor \leq B_i \leq c.$$

Thus, $\Delta(Q/c)$ could be at most 1. Similar to the proof of Theorem 2, the extended mechanism gives 2ϵ differential privacy.

The proof of approximate truthfulness and revenue analysis is similar to the proof of Theorem 3 and Theorem 4 respectively. □

6. EVALUATION

We have implemented DEAR and extensively evaluated its performance. On one hand, our evaluation results show that DEAR can generate a relatively high revenue despite randomness. On the other hand, the evaluation results show that DEAR achieves good differential privacy.

6.1 Methodology

When evaluating the revenue of DEAR, we compare DEAR with a greedy and truthful spectrum auction mechanism (denoted by "GREEDY") proposed in [10] and another truthful spectrum auction mechanism (denoted by "TSAWAP") in [11]. For the extended DEAR, since there exists no other privacy-preserving spectrum auction mechanism for bidders with budget constraints, we evaluate its performance under various settings without comparison with others.

We vary the number of bidders from 100 to 1500 with a step of 100, and set the number of channels to be 15, 20, and 30. The bidders are randomly deployed in a square area of 5000m×5000m. Each bidder has an interference range of 425m [37]. Any pair of bidders who lie within each other's interference range are in conflict, and thus cannot be allocated on the same channel simultaneously. We assume that each bidder's bid is uniformly distributed over (0,1] with a precision of 2 decimal places. In the case of extended DEAR, we further assume that each bidder has a budget B_i randomly chosen from $[b_i,c]$, c is the number of channels. We set the privacy constant ϵ to 0.1 and 0.5.[1] All the results are averaged over 1000 runs.

We use two performance metrics to evaluate DEAR, including revenue and privacy. The revenue is referred to as the sum of charges to the bidders. A mechanism guarantees good privacy if the outcome of probability distribution over prices has a as small as possible change when any bidder unilaterally reports a different bid. We definite the notion of *Privacy Leakage* according to the definition of differential privacy to quantitatively measure the privacy guarantee of DEAR.

DEFINITION 4 (PRIVACY LEAKAGE). *Given a mechanism $\mathcal{M}$, suppose $\vec{a}$ and $\vec{a'}$ are probability distributions over a price set $\mathbb{P}$ for bidding profiles $\vec{b}$ and $\vec{b}'$, which only differ in a single bid, respectively. The privacy leakage between the two bidding profiles is the maximum of absolute differences between the logarithmic probabilities of the two distributions,* i.e.,

$$\max_{i\in\{1,2,\ldots,|\mathbb{P}|\}} |\ln a_i - \ln a'_i|. \quad (13)$$

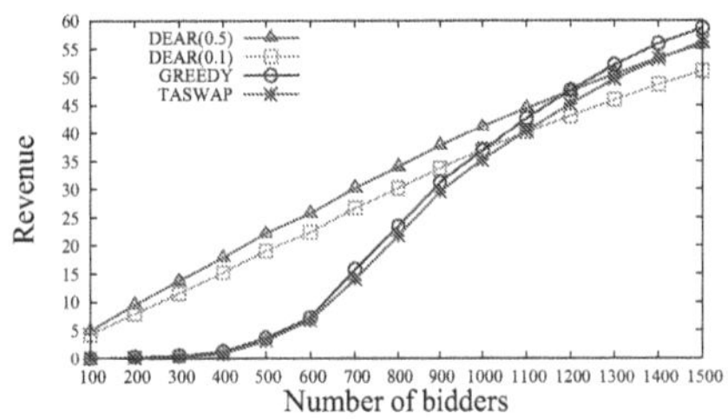

(a) 15 Channels

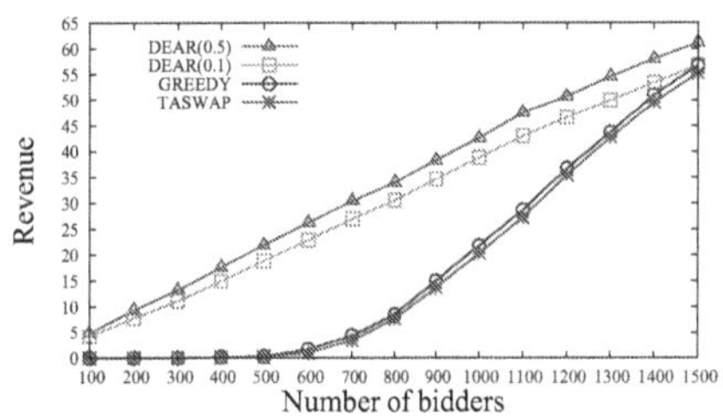

(b) 20 Channels

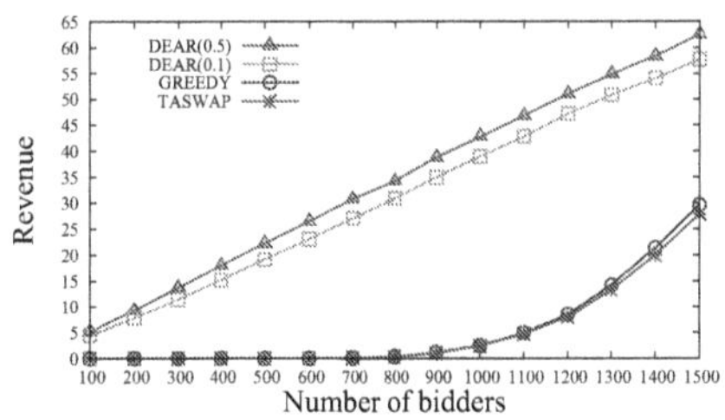

(c) 30 Channels

Figure 3: Revenue comparison among GREEDY, TSAWAP and DEAR.

[1]The range of each bidder's valuation/bid, budget, and the value of ϵ can be chosen differently from those used here. However, the results of using different setups are similar to the results shown in this paper. Therefore, we only show the results for the above setup.

6.2 Revenue

We first evaluate DEAR and extended DEAR's performances in terms of revenue.

Fig. 3(a) shows the comparison results of DEAR with GREEDY and TSAWAP, when the number of channels is 15. From these results, we can see that DEAR outperforms GREEDY and TSWAP in nearly all the cases in terms of revenue. The only exceptions are when the number of bidders is greater than 1200 (for $\epsilon = 0.5$), and when the number of bidders is greater than 1000 (for $\epsilon = 0.1$), GREEDY and TSWAP can generate slightly more revenues than DEAR. This is because both GREEDY and TSAWAP rely on the existence of critical neighbors to generate revenue, and when the number of bidders grows, GREEDY and TSAWAP can find critical neighbors with higher and higher bids.

Figs. 3(b) and 3(c) show the comparison results of DEAR with GREEDY and TSAWAP, when the number of channels are 20 and 30, respectively. From these results, we can see that DEAR outperforms GREEDY and TSWAP significantly in all the cases in terms of revenue. This is because DEAR does not rely on the existence of critical neighbor to generate revenue, and when the number of channels grows, some winning bidders may not have any critical neighbor.

These results imply that DEAR is suitable for secondary spectrum markets with relatively sparse bidders.

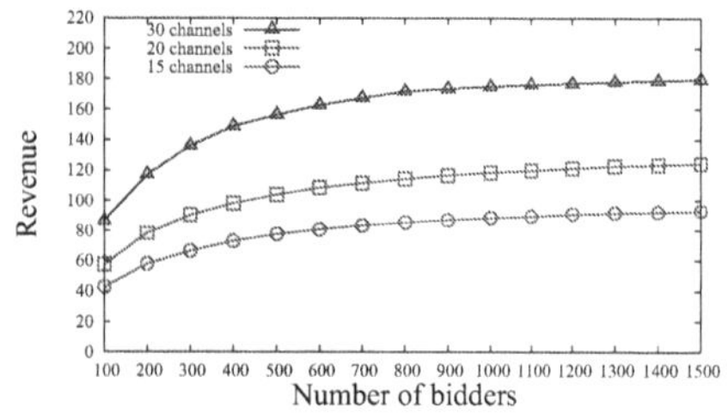

(a) Revenue (with $\epsilon = 0.1$)

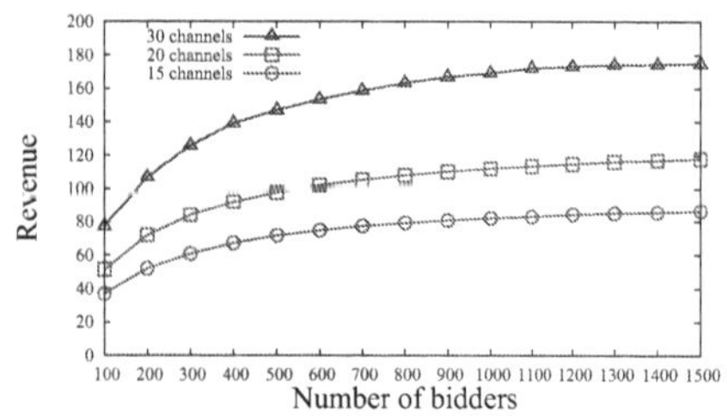

(b) Revenue (with $\epsilon = 0.5$)

Figure 4: Revenue generated by extended DEAR

Fig. 4 shows the revenue generated by extended DEAR, when bidders bid for multiple channels with budget limits. We observe that, the larger the number of channels is, the higher the revenue is. When the number of channels is fixed, the growth rate of revenue becomes slower as the number of bidders increases. This is because the number of winning bidder in each subgroup is bounded by the number of channels, and thus, the generated revenue converges.

6.3 Privacy

We finally evaluate DEAR and extended DEAR in terms of privacy. We set the number of channels to 20, and vary the number of bidders from 100 to 1500. Fig. 5 shows the privacy leakage of DEAR and extended DEAR.

Fig. 5(a) shows the privacy leakage of DEAR. The results show that when $\epsilon = 0.1$, DEAR's privacy leakage is always less than 0.018, and when $\epsilon = 0.5$ DEAR's privacy leakage is always less than 0.085. From the evaluation results, we see that in both cases the privacy performance of DEAR are far better than 0.2−differential privacy and 1−differential privacy, respectively. This implies that it is nearly impossible for any agent to learn the bid information of the others. Thus, DEAR can guarantee good privacy performance.

Fig. 5(b) shows the privacy leakage of extended DEAR. Similar to DEAR, the results show that in both cases of $\epsilon = 0.1$ and 0.5, the privacy leakages of extended DEAR are small, and the privacy performance of DEAR are far better than 0.2−differential privacy and 1−differential privacy, respectively. Besides, we can see that when the number of bidders increases, the privacy leakage of extended DEAR decreases. This is because extended DEAR allows each bidder to bid for multiple channels, and thus the impact of a single bid change is limited.

These results show that (extended) DEAR achieves good differential privacy.

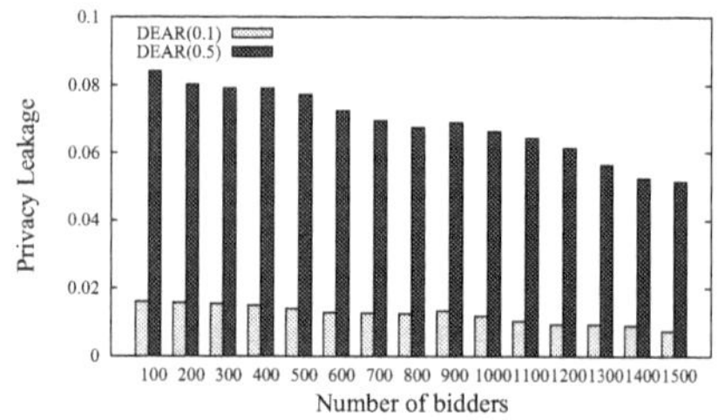

(a) DEAR

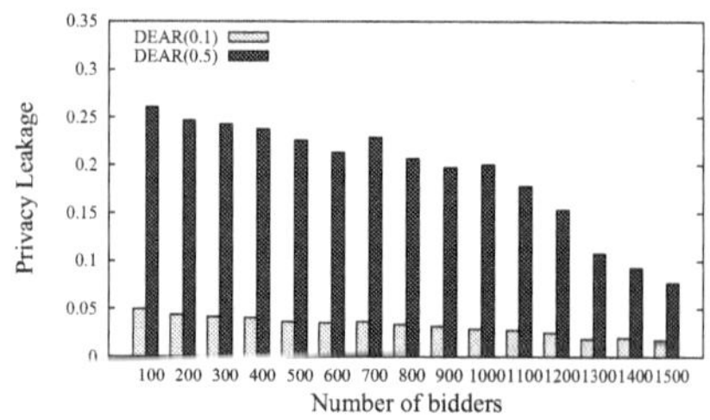

(b) Extended DEAR

Figure 5: Privacy performance.

7. CONCLUSION

In this paper, we have presented the first differentially private spectrum auction mechanism, called DEAR, with approximate revenue maximization. DEAR performs well with both single- and multi-channel requests when bidders have budget constraints. For both cases, we have theoretically proven the properties in revenue and privacy. We have also implemented DEAR and extensively evaluated its performance. Our mechanisms are shown to be able to generate relatively high and stable revenue, while protecting the bid-privacy.

8. ACKNOWLEDGEMENT

The UM authors were supported in part by the US NSF under Grant No. CNS-1114837. The SJTU authors of this paper were supported in part by the State Key Development Program for Basic Research of China (973 project 2014CB340303 and 2012CB316201), China NSF grant 61272443 and 61133006, Shanghai Science and Technology fund 12PJ1404900 and 12ZR1414900, and Program for Changjiang Scholars and Innovative Research Team in University (IRT1158, PCSIRT) China. The opinions, findings, conclusions, and recommendations expressed in this paper are those of the authors and do not necessarily reflect the views of the funding agencies.

9. REFERENCES

[1] I. F. Akyildiz, W. Y. Lee, M. C. Vuran, and S. Mohanty, "NeXt generation/dynamic spectrum access/cognitive radio wireless networks: A survey," *Computer Networks*, vol. 50, no. 13, pp. 2027-2159, 2006.

[2] Spectrum Policy Task Force, "Spectrum policy task force report," *Federal Communications Commission ET docket*, 02-135, 2002.

[3] Spectrum Bridge, Inc., http://www.spectrumbridge.com

[4] Z. Ji and K. Liu, "Dynamic spectrum sharing: A game theoretical overview," *IEEE Communications Magazine*, vol. 45, no. 5, pp. 88-94, 2007.

[5] X. Zhou and H. Zheng, "TRUST: A general framework for truthful double spectrum auctions," in *INFOCOM'09*, 2009.

[6] F. Wu and N. Vaidya, "SMALL: A strategy-proof mechanism for radio spectrum allocation," in *INFOCOM'11*, 2011.

[7] J. Peha, "Approaches to spectrum sharing," *IEEE Communications Magazine*, vol. 43, no. 2, pp. 10-12, 2005.

[8] S. Gandhi, C. Buragohain, L. Cao, H. Zheng, and S. Suri, "A general framework for wireless spectrum auctions," in *DySPAN'07*, 2007.

[9] S. Sengupta, and M. Chatterjee, "An economic framework for dynamic spectrum access and service pricing," *IEEE/ACM Transactions on Networking*, vol. 17, no. 4, pp. 1200-1213, 2009.

[10] J. Jia, Q. Zhang, Q. Zhang, and M. Liu, "Revenue generation for truthful spectrum auction in dynamic spectrum access," in *MobiHoc'09*, 2009.

[11] M. Al-Ayyoub and H. Gupta, "Truthful spectrum auctions with approximate revenue," in *INFOCOM'11*, 2011.

[12] A P. Subramanian, M. Al-Ayyoub, H. Gupta, et al. "Near-optimal dynamic spectrum allocation in cellular networks," in *DySPAN'08*, 2008.

[13] R. Myerson, "Optimal auction design," *Mathematics of operations research*, vol. 6, no. 1, pp. 58-73, 1981.

[14] Q. Huang, Y. Tao, and F. Wu, "SPRING: A strategy-proof and privacy preserving spectrum auction mechanism," in *INFOCOM'13*, 2013.

[15] M. Jakobsson and A. Juels, "Mix and match: Secure function evaluation via ciphertexts," in *ASIACRYPT'00*, 2000.

[16] K. Sako, "An auction protocol which hides bids of losers," in *PKC'00*, 2000.

[17] K. Peng, C. Boyd, E. Dawson, and K. Viswanathan, "Robust, privacy protecting and publicly verifiable sealed-bid auction," in *ICICS'02*, 2002.

[18] Y. F. Chung, K. H. Huang, H. H. Lee, F. Lai, and T. S. Chen, "Bidder-anonymous english auction scheme with privacy and public verifiability," *Journal of Systems and Software*, vol. 81, no. 1, pp. 113-119, 2008.

[19] A. Archer and E. Tardos, "Frugal path mechanisms," in *TALG'07*, 2007

[20] J. Feigenbaum, and S. Shenker, "Distributed algorithmic mechanism design: Recent results and future directions," September, in *DialM'02*, 2002.

[21] C. Dwork, "Differential privacy," in *ICALP'06*, 2006

[22] F. McSherry and K. Talwar, "Mechanism design via differential privacy," in *FOCS'07*, 2007.

[23] A. Gupta, K. Ligett, F. McSherry, A. Roth and K. Talwar. "Differentially private combinatorial optimization," in *SODA'10*, 2010.

[24] A. Gopinathan and Z. Li, "A prior-free revenue maximizing auction for secondary spectrum access," in *INFOCOM'11*, 2011.

[25] A. Kothari, DC. Parkes, and S. Suri, "Approximately-strategyproof and tractable multiunit auctions," *Decision Support Systems*, vol. 39, no. 1, pp. 105-121, 2005.

[26] A. Mu'Alem, and N. Nisan, "Truthful approximation mechanisms for restricted combinatorial auctions," *Games and Economic Behavior*, vol. 64, no. 1, pp. 612-631, 2008.

[27] K. Nissim, R. Smorodinsky and M. Tennenholtz, "Approximately optimal mechanism design via differential privacy," in *ITCS'12*, 2012.

[28] C. Dwork, "Differential privacy: A survey of results," in *TAMC'08*, 2008.

[29] V. Krishna, "Auction theory," Academic Press, 2002.

[30] N. Nisan, "Algorithmic game theory," Cambridge University Press, 2007.

[31] L. Sweeney, "k-anonymity: A model for protecting privacy," *International Journal on Uncertainty, Fuzziness and Knowledge based Systems*, vol. 10, no. 5, pp. 557-570, 2002.

[32] M. Naor, B. Pinkas, and R. Sumner, "Privacy preserving auctions and mechanism design," in *EC'99*, 1999.

[33] H. Lipmaa, N. Asokan, V. Niemi, "Secure Vickrey auctions without threshold trust," in *FC'03*, 2003.

[34] J. Schummer, "Almost-dominant strategy implementation: exchange economies," *Games and Economic Behavior*, vol. 48, no. 1, pp. 154-170, 2004.

[35] K. Jain, J. Padhye, V. N. Padmanabhan, and L. Qiu, "Impact of interference on multi-hop wireless network performance," in *MobiCom'03*, 2003.

[36] H. Huang, X. Li, Y. Sun, H. Xu, and L. Huang, "PPS: Privacy-Preserving Strategyproof Social-Efficient Spectrum Auction Mechanisms," in *http://arxiv.org/pdf/1307.7792v1.pdf*, 2013.

[37] F. Wu and N. Vaidya, "A Strategy-Proof Radio Spectrum Auction Mechanism in Noncooperative Wireless Networks," in *IEEE Transaction on Mobile Computing*, vol. 12, no. 5, pp. 885-894, 2013.

[38] Z. Huang and S. Kannan, "The exponential mechanism for social welfare: Private, truthful, and nearly optimal," in *FOCS'12*, 2012.

Bounded Rationality Can Increase Parking Search Efficiency

Merkourios Karaliopoulos
Center for Research and Technology - Hellas
Information Technologies Institute
78 Filikis Etaireias Str., 38334 Volos, Greece
mkaraliopoulos@iti.gr

Konstantinos Katsikopoulos
Center for Adaptive Behavior and Cognition
Max Planck Institute for Human Development
Lentzeallee 94, 14195 Berlin, Germany
katsikop@mpib-berlin.mpg.de

Lambros Lambrinos
Department of Communication and Internet Studies
Cyprus University of Technology
30 Arch. Kyprianou Str., 3036 Lemesos, Cyprus
lambros.lambrinos@cut.ac.cy

ABSTRACT

The search for parking space in busy urban districts is one of those routine human activities that can benefit from the widespread adoption of pervasive sensing and radio communication technologies. Proposed parking assistance solutions combine sensors, either as fixed infrastructure or onboard vehicles, wireless networking technologies and mobile social applications running over smartphones to collect, share and present to drivers real-time information about parking availability and demand. One question that arises is how does (and should) the driver actually use such information to take parking decisions, *e.g.*, whether to search for on-street parking space or drive to a parking lot and, in the latter case, which one. The paper is, hence, a performance analysis study that seeks to capture the highly behavioral and heuristic dimension of drivers' decisions and its impact on the efficiency of the parking search process. To this end we model drivers as agents of *bounded rationality* and consider *lexicographic heuristics*, an instance of the fast and frugal heuristics developed in behavioral sciences such as psychology and biology, as the mechanisms for their decisions.

We analyze the performance of the search process under these heuristics and compare it against the predictions of normative game-theoretic models assuming fully rational strategically acting agents. We derive conditions under which the simpler heuristic decision-making rules outperform the complex norms and show their satisfaction under a broad range of scenarios concerning the fees charged for the parking resources and their distances from drivers' destinations. The practical implications of these results for parking assistance solutions are identified and thoroughly discussed.

MobiHoc'14, August 11–14, 2014, Philadelphia, PA, USA.

ACM 978-1-4503-2620-9/14/08 ...$15.00.
http://dx.doi.org/10.1145/2632951.2632955.

1. INTRODUCTION

The increasing integration of advanced sensing and wireless technologies with urban infrastructures transforms dramatically the way citizens access and interact with them. At the same time, smartphones and other smart mobile devices turn their owners to potential mobile sensing platforms and engage them actively in the generation and distribution of various kinds of information. The two trends combined fuel the concept of smart city, whereby fundamental daily activities and operations are carried out more efficiently in favor of individual citizens and the society as a whole.

The parking space forms an instance of urban resource that is daily accessed and shared by multiple drivers. Often scarce in places such as shopping areas and business districts, it has to be properly managed to avoid congestion effects and the unfavorable consequences of cruising for parking, *e.g.*, waste of time and fuel and environmental burden [1]. Parking assistance systems seek to address the parking problem by expanding the reach of pervasive computing within the city roads and turning them to smart spaces. Combining sensors at the parking spots or onboard vehicles and radio communication technologies, often including the vehicular network [2], they collect and distribute information about parking demand and supply to the vehicular nodes. More recent approaches to the assisted parking search, such as [3] or [4], add a social media layer over the vehicular network. The drivers can use a mobile social application running on their smartphones to share their knowledge about parking space with other application users and even handover parking spots to save the overheads of parking search.

Despite the amount of work on the proposal and design of parking assistance systems, surprisingly little attention has attracted their actual performance. Directly relevant to the performance issue is the amount of information that *can* or *should be* used when selecting parking resource, *e.g.*, on-street or parking lot(s), or searching for an on-street parking spot. The major assumption is that these decisions involve, in one way or another, humans. The drivers are those who actually make decisions when the parking assistance system only provides information about parking resources without making recommendations. But even when they are assisted by on-board mounted software agents, the human factor is present either through some offline profile description or, again, through direct participation in online decision-making.

The paper, thus, focuses on the decision-making task and the management of supplied information by the drivers. It seeks to answer how *efficient* is the parking search process when drivers employ *plausible* heuristics to choose between different parking resources. The efficiency of parking search is assessed by how much drivers end up paying to get a parking spot, including the overhead costs due to needless cruising. For the decision-making process, we consider two major approaches. The first one views drivers as fully rational entities who process all information at hand and act strategically so as to maximize their return. The second approach is inspired by the significant body of work in behavioral sciences such as psychology and biology on a family of heuristics called *fast* and *frugal* heuristics. These heuristics are generally simple, seek to *describe* the actual cognitive tasks involved in the decision and approach humans as boundedly rational *satisficers* rather than optimizers: namely, when faced with a choice problem, they seek for a good enough alternative rather than the best one and they do so without necessarily processing all information available to them.

It has been repeatedly shown that fast and frugal heuristics describe well human choices in various settings [5][6]. Less intuitively, they have been shown to perform comparably and sometimes better than more complex choice selection models such as linear regression or classification and regression trees. In our work, we essentially propose and analyze some of the most popular heuristics in the context of two representative instances of the parking resource selection problem. In the first one, drivers have to chose between the scarce but cheap on-street parking spots and the more expensive yet abundant parking lot(s) space. The second instance features two distinct parking lots, located at different distances from the drivers' common destination, adding distance as a second decision criterion beyond cost.

Methodologically, we follow the same steps in both problem instances: first, we formulate and analyze the games that emerge under strategic fully rational decision-making, then we analyze the performance of the parking search application under the heuristics and finally we compare them. For the single-attribute problem instance we derive analytically the conditions that let heuristics result in higher efficiency. Our results suggest that in most realistic scenarios the use of decision heuristics results in more efficient parking search process than when the drivers (or the parking assistance software agents) act strategically in line with the game-theoretic prescriptions.

To the best of our knowledge, this is the first study importing tools and modeling approaches from the field of cognitive psychology to a problem that has been treated for years by transportation engineers and, more recently, also by computer scientists. Section 2 summarizes the problem setting, results that are known about it and background on the cognitive heuristics. Sections 3-4 then contain the paper's main contributions. Section 3 devises and analyzes the priority heuristic for choosing between the cheap but scarce on-street parking and the spacious yet more expensive parking lot(s). It also compares its outcomes with those of the game-theoretic model in [7]. Section 4 considers the problem version with two types of parking lots. It formulates and analyzes the game emerging under the assumption of strategic decision-makers, devises the decision heuristic drawing on data from surveys and compares the two models under different parameter sets. We discuss the implications of our work for actual parking assistance systems in Section 5.

2. BACKGROUND

A typical dilemma faced by drivers when approaching their destinations in busy urban areas is: Should they invest time and effort in searching for cheaper on-street parking space or should they drive straight ahead towards one of the more expensive parking lots? The first option involves the risk of failing to find a vacant spot and eventually paying an excess cost due to cruising in terms of fuel consumption and time wastage.

2.1 The parking spot selection game

In [7], this dilemma is formulated as a resource selection problem. On-street parking space and parking lot(s) are two discrete types of parking resources with per time unit costs c_1 and c_2, respectively, with $c_1 < c_2$. An additional excess cost c_{exc} becomes relevant when vehicles end up in a parking lot after failing to seize an on-street parking spot. The vehicular nodes are viewed as fully rational agents that determine their strategies taking full advantage of the available information to them. The outcome of their actions and the respective payoffs depend on the decisions of all nodes so that their interaction is formulated as a game, the *parking spot selection game*:

DEFINITION 1. *The* Parking Spot Selection Game *is a tuple* $\Gamma_1(N) = (\mathcal{N}, \mathcal{R}, (A_i)_{i \in \mathcal{N}}, (w_j), j \in \{1, 2\})$, *where:*

- $\mathcal{N} = \{1, ..., N\}$, $N > 1$ *is the set of drivers searching for parking space,*
- $\mathcal{R} = \mathcal{R}_1 \cup \mathcal{R}_2$ *is the set of parking spots;* $\mathcal{R}_1$ *is the set of on-street spots, with* $R = |\mathcal{R}_1| \geq 1$; $\mathcal{R}_2$ *is the set of spots in the parking lot(s), with* $|\mathcal{R}_2| \geq N$,
- $A_i = \{1, 2\}$ *is the action set for each driver* $i \in \mathcal{N}$, *action "1" denoting search for on-street parking space and "2" driving directly to a parking lot,*
- $w_1(\cdot)$ *and* $w_2(\cdot)$ *are the cost functions of the two actions, respectively.*

where

$$w_1(n) = min(1, R/n)c_1 + max(0, 1 - R/n)(c_2 + c_{exc}) \quad (1)$$

and $w_2(n) = c_2$, $n \in [1, N]$.

It is shown in [7] that at the Nash Equilibrium (NE) states of the game, whether pure or mixed, the vehicular nodes tend to over-compete for the scarce on-street parking space. Namely, the vehicles, N_{cmp}^{NE}, that choose to compete for on-street parking outnumber its supply, R, so that some of them end up in a parking lot only after incurring the excess cruising cost, c_{exc}. More formally, the game $\Gamma_1(N)$ has:

- a single pure strategy NE, $N_{cmp}^{NE} = N$, or equivalently a single symmetric mixed NE with $p_{cmp}^{NE} = 1$, if $N \leq N_0$
- $\binom{N}{\lfloor N_0 \rfloor}$ pure NE with $N_{cmp}^{NE} = \lfloor N_0 \rfloor$, if $N > N_0$ and N_0 is not an integer,

- $\binom{N}{N_0}$ pure NE with $N_{cmp}^{NE} = N_0$ and $\binom{N}{N_0-1}$ pure NE with $N_{cmp}^{NE} = N_0 - 1$, if $N > N_0$ and N_0 is an integer,
- one symmetric mixed NE with $p_{cmp}^{NE} = N_0/N$, if $N > N_0$

where

$$N_0 = \frac{c_2 + c_{exc} - c_1}{c_{exc}} R \tag{2}$$

In either case, and given that $N_{cmp}^{NE} = N \cdot p_{cmp}^{NE}$, the aggregate cost (fees+excess cost) paid by the drivers equals

$$C_{agg}^{NE} = min(R, N)c_1 + max(0, N_{cmp}^{NE} - R)(c_2 + c_{exc}) + (N - N_{cmp}^{NE})c_2$$

2.2 Fast and frugal decision heuristics

The NE is a solution concept with strong implications for the properties of decision-makers: they are agents with perfect processing capacity to analyze the available information and assess the alternatives presented to them. Most importantly, they can also analyze the possible strategies of other agents and identify the equilibrium choice, from which they have no reason to unilaterally deviate.

In this paper we are interested instead in a breed of heuristics developed in behavioral sciences such as psychology and biology, called fast and frugal heuristics [8]. Fast and frugal heuristics are models for making decisions, that: (i) rely heavily on core human capacities (such as memory recognition and recall); (ii) do not necessarily use all available information, and process the information they use by simple computations (such as using only one piece of information); (iii) are easy to understand, apply, and explain.

An important family of fast and frugal heuristics are the *lexicographic* heuristics, whereby the user inspects the attributes in a specified order and makes a decision based on the first attribute that allows for a decision to be made, without consulting other attributes. For example, consider the *priority heuristic* for choices among risky gambles [9]. Let us say we want to choose one of X = $(x_{min}, p; x_{max}, 1-p)$ and Y = $(y_{min}, q; y_{max}, 1-q)$, where for X the numerical outcome x_{min} is obtained with probability p and x_{max} is obtained with 1 - p and $0 < x_{min} < x_{max}$ (and analogously for Y).

If $|x_{min} - y_{min}| > thr_1 \cdot max\{x_{max}, y_{max}\}$, no other attributes are inspected and the gamble with the higher value on its minimum outcome is chosen. Otherwise, if $|p - q| > thr_2$[1], a decision is made in favor of the gamble with the lower probability of minimum outcome without considering attributes beyond the second. In the opposite case, the gamble with the higher maximum outcome is chosen (and if the maximum outcomes are equal, a choice is made randomly).

Such lexicographic heuristics describe well people's choices of consumer goods such as microwaves and apartments [5]. And, Katsikopoulos and Gigerenzer [6] have analytically shown that the priority heuristic predicts a host of major empirical phenomena in risky choice such as violations of the common consequence and common ratio axioms as well as the fourfold pattern of risk attitudes [10]. Another model of bounded rationality for a risky choice between two gambles, similar to the priority heuristic, was developed by Rubinstein in [11]. Both models attempt to model the underlying psychological processes and do not transform values or probabilities. But, unlike the priority heuristic, Rubinstein's model does not employ limited search and is not lexicographic.

[1]The value 0.1 is used for both thresholds thr_1 and thr_2 in [9] as a global constant across all humans.

Another example of a lexicographic heuristic describing people's *multi-attribute* choices under certainty is deterministic elimination by aspects (DEBA) [12]. In DEBA, the decision maker first orders the attributes according to the magnitude of their importance weights $(x_1, x_2, ...)$. She then inspects the value of all alternatives on the first attribute x_1. If all alternatives score equally on x_1, this attribute is eliminated. If exactly one alternative outperforms the rest on x_1, this alternative is chosen. Otherwise, all alternatives with a value on x_1 less than the maximum are eliminated and the process is repeated for the second attribute x_2. The process continues this way until an alternative is chosen. If more than one alternatives are left after all attributes are inspected, then one of them is chosen randomly.

The performance of lexicographic heuristics, in terms of accuracy or utility maximization, has been studied, via computer simulations and mathematical analysis in datasets from business, medicine and psychology. Overall, three major stylized facts have emerged [13]. First, there are small differences in performance between heuristics and more complex benchmarks such as linear regression, neural networks, classification and regression trees or naive Bayes. Second, simple heuristics often have higher performance in out-of-sample prediction. Third, each one of heuristics or benchmarks outperforms the other under certain conditions.

In what follows, an implementation of the priority heuristic guides the drivers' decisions between the two parking resources, when those consider only the fees charged for them. In section 4, we let decisions take account of both fees and distances of the resources from the drivers' destinations.

3. THE PRIORITY HEURISTIC FOR SELECTING PARKING RESOURCE

3.1 Description of the heuristic

We devise an implementation of the priority heuristic for the parking choice problem drawing on its generic description in Section 2. Since the problem setting involves losses (costs) rather than gains, the heuristic prescribes that drivers consider first the minimum cost related to each parking alternative; then the probabilities that these costs emerge out of their choices; and, finally, if no decision is made by that time, the maximum costs they may incur when choosing the one or the other alternative. More specifically, invoking the notation in Section 2.2, the on-street parking space can be viewed as the risky gamble $X = (-c_1, min(1, R/N); -(c_2 + c_{exc}), 1 - min(1, R/N))$, whereas the option of parking lot as the fixed-outcome gamble $Y = -c_2$ with probability 1. Then,

- (step 1) drivers decide to search for on-street parking space if the minimum possible costs of the two alternatives, c_1 and c_2 respectively, differ by more than a percentage thr_c of the worst-case cost they may incur as a result of their selection (*i.e.*, $c_2 + c_{exc}$).
- (step 2) In the opposite case, *i.e.*, $u = \frac{c_2 - c_1}{c_2 + c_{exc}} \leq thr_c$, they postpone their decision until after considering the probabilities of minimum costs: if their difference exceeds a threshold thr_p, they head for a parking lot.
- (step 3) Otherwise, when $1 - min(1, R/N) < thr_p$ so that neither the second criterion helps them reach a decision, they compare the maximum possible costs, $c_2 + c_{exc}$ and c_2, and decide in favor of the parking lot.

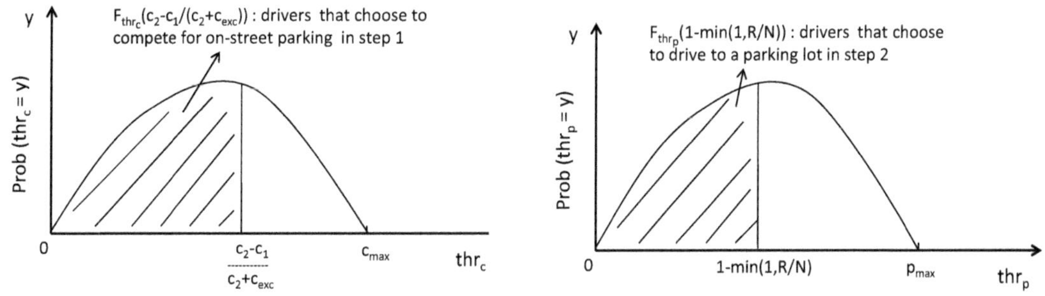

a. Parking fees/cost

b. Parking demand

Figure 1: Probability distributions for the sensitivity of drivers to the minimum parking cost (left) and the respective probabilities (right).

Table 1: Conditions for more efficient parking resource selection under the priority heuristic.

A *vs.* B	Corresponding r_{dc} range	
$A > B$	$r_{dc} < B$	(C1)
	$r_{dc} \geq A$	(C2)
	$max(B, \frac{N \cdot F_{thr_c}(\frac{c_2-c_1}{c_2+c_{exc}})-R}{R}) \leq r_{dc} < A$	(C3)
$A < B$	$r_{dc} \geq B$	(C4)
	$r_{dc} < A$	(C5)
	$A \leq r_{dc} < min(B, \frac{N-R}{N \cdot F_{thr_c}(\frac{c_2-c_1}{c_2+c_{exc}})-R})$	(C6)
$A = \frac{N-R}{R}$, $B = (1+\frac{c_2}{c_{exc}}) \cdot F^{-1}_{thr_c}(R/N)$		

As mentioned in Section 2.2, the original generic description of the priority heuristic in [9] recommends a single driver-agnostic constant (*i.e.*, 0.1) for both threshold parameters, thr_c and thr_p. We argue instead that these values vary across drivers reflecting differences in their financial status, the reason of their trip (business or leisure) and their individual preferences. This heterogeneity of drivers is modeled statistically through two probability distribution functions, f_{thr_c} and f_{thr_p} respectively. If F_{thr_c} and F_{thr_p} are the respective cumulative distribution functions, the number of drivers competing for on-street parking spots equals (ref. Fig. 1)

$$N^{PH}_{cmp} = N \cdot F_{thr_c}(\frac{c_2-c_1}{c_2+c_{exc}}) \quad (3)$$

whereas the drivers selecting the parking lot alternative are

$$N^{PH}_{PL} = N \cdot \Big(1 - F_{thr_c}(\frac{c_2-c_1}{c_2+c_{exc}})\Big) \quad (4)$$

Note that the partitioning of drivers into the two groups is independent of the distribution f_{thr_p}. Drivers who do not decide to compete for on-street parking space in step 1 will end up in a parking lot either in step 2 or in the last step. What f_{thr_p} determines is the portion of drivers deciding in favor of a parking lot in step 2 rather than in the last step.

3.2 Comparison with the game model $\Gamma_1(N)$

It is then convenient to analyze the efficiency of the parking search process under the game and the priority heuristic models as a function of the *decision certainty ratio* $r_{dc} = (c_2 - c_1)/c_{exc}$. This ratio grows as the parking fee difference increases or the cruising cost, *e.g.*, the risk related to competing for on-street parking, declines. It, thus, reflects the overall attractiveness of the on-street parking alternative. Theorem 1 summarizes the comparison of the two decision-making models.

THEOREM 1. *The parking search process when drivers' choices are driven by the priority heuristic is more efficient than when they act as fully rational strategic agents under the conditions listed in Table 1.*

PROOF. As already mentioned in Section 2.1, whenever $N > R$, the number of competing drivers induced by the strategic game exceeds the on-street parking capacity, *i.e.*, $N^{NE}_{cmp} > R$. On the contrary, under the priority heuristic, this number may generally be greater or smaller than R. We consider these two cases separately.

$N^{PH}_{cmp} < R$: This implies that

$$r_{dc} < (1 + \frac{c_2}{c_{exc}}) \cdot F^{-1}_{thr_c}(R/N) \quad (5)$$

and the difference in the aggregate cost induced by the two decision-making models is

$$\begin{aligned} \Delta C_{agg} &= C^{PH}_{agg} - C^{NE}_{agg} \\ &= (R - N^{PH}_{cmp})(c_2 - c_1) - (N^{NE}_{cmp} - R)c_{exc} \quad (6) \end{aligned}$$

If $N^{NE}_{cmp} = N_0 < N$, *i.e.*, $r_{dc} < N/R - 1$, then

$$\Delta C_{agg} = -N^{PH}_{cmp}(c_2 - c_1) < 0 \quad (7)$$

without additional conditions.

On the other hand, if $N^{NE}_{cmp} = N$, *i.e.*,

$$r_{dc} \geq N/R - 1 \quad (8)$$

$$\Delta C_{agg} = R(c_2 - c_1 + c_{exc}) - N(F_{thr_c}(\frac{c_2-c_1}{c_2+c_{exc}})(c_2-c_1) + c_{exc})$$

is negative when $r_{dc} < (N-R)/(N \cdot F_{thr_c}(\frac{c_2-c_1}{c_2+c_{exc}}) - R)$ so that, in combination with (8), r_{dc} must satisfy

$$\frac{N-R}{R} \leq r_{dc} < \frac{N-R}{N \cdot F_{thr_c}(\frac{c_2-c_1}{c_2+c_{exc}}) - R} \quad (9)$$

This interval of values is non-empty only when

$$r_{dc} < F^{-1}_{thr_c}(\frac{2R}{N})(1 + \frac{c_2}{c_{exc}}) \quad (10)$$

Constraint 10 is inactive since, for $N^{PH}_{cmp} < R$, it is dominated by constraint (5).

$N^{PH}_{cmp} \geq R$: Now $r_{dc} \geq (1 + \frac{c_2}{c_{exc}}) \cdot F^{-1}_{thr_c}(R/N)$ and the aggregate cost under both decision-making models can be written as function of N_{cmp} as

$$C_{agg} = R \cdot (c_1 - c_2 - c_{exc}) + N \cdot c_2 + N_{cmp} \cdot c_{exc} \quad (11)$$

so that

$$\Delta C_{agg} = (N^{PH}_{cmp} - N^{NE}_{cmp})c_{exc} \quad (12)$$

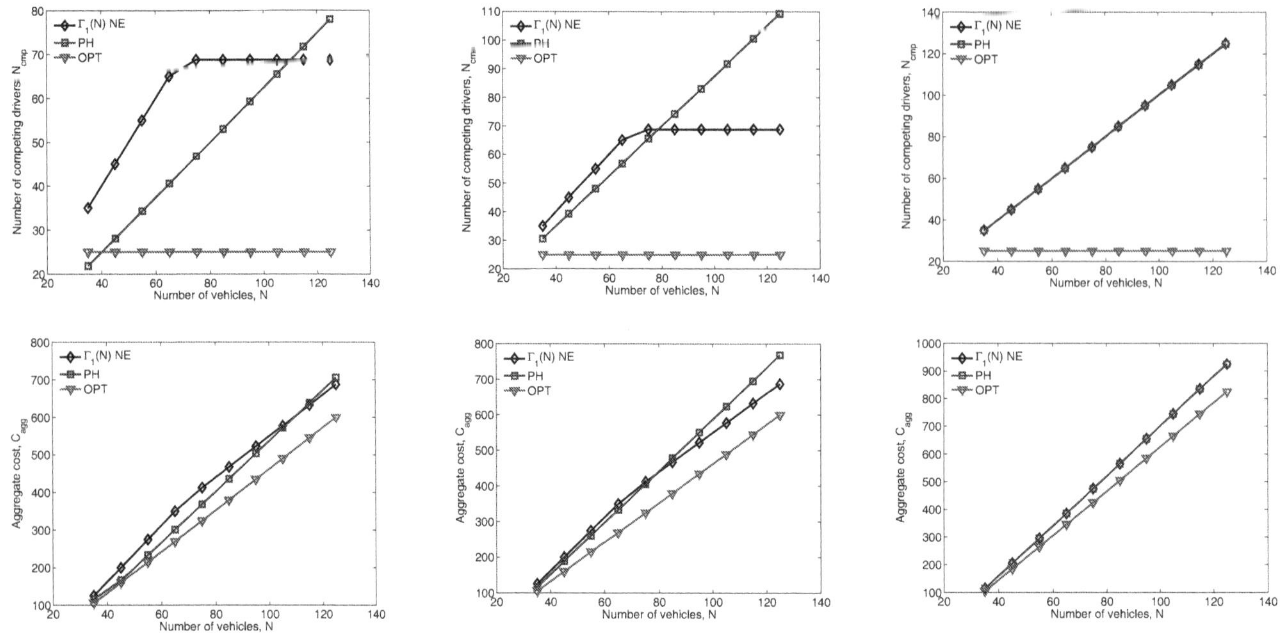

a. $c_1 = 2, c_2 = 5.5, c_{exc} = 2, c_{max} = 0.8$ b. $c_1 = 2, c_2 = 5.5, c_{exc} = 2, c_{max} = 0.6$ c. $c_1 = 1, c_2 = 8, c_{exc} = 1, c_{max} = 0.8$

Figure 2: Number of drivers competing for on-street parking and aggregate cost as a function of the parking demand: R=25.

and it suffices to compare the numbers of drivers that end up competing for on-street parking space under the two models.

When $N_{cmp}^{NE} = N$, *i.e.*, $r_{dc} > N/R - 1$

$$\Delta C_{agg} = N \cdot (F_{thr_c}(\frac{r_{dc}}{1 + c_2/c_{exc}}) - 1) < 0 \quad (13)$$

without additional conditions. Otherwise, when $r_{dc} \leq N/R - 1$, it must also hold

$$r_{dc} > \frac{N \cdot F_{thr_c}(\frac{r_{dc}}{1+c_2/c_{exc}})}{R} - 1 \quad (14)$$

Combining (5)-(14) we get Table 1. □

COROLLARY 1. *The parking search process when drivers' choices are driven by the priority heuristic is coherently more efficient than when they act as fully rational strategic agents as long as either:*

$$\frac{N \cdot F_{thr_c}(\frac{c_2 - c_1}{c_2 + c_{exc}}) - R}{R} < (1 + \frac{c_2}{c_{exc}}) \cdot F_{thr_c}^{-1}(R/N) < \frac{N - R}{R}$$

or

$$\frac{N - R}{R} < (1 + \frac{c_2}{c_{exc}}) \cdot F_{thr_c}^{-1}(R/N) < \frac{N - R}{N \cdot F_{thr_c}(\frac{c_2 - c_1}{c_2 + c_{exc}}) - R}$$

PROOF. By inspection of Table 1 (2nd column, lines 3 and 6), these conditions enforce negative ΔC_{agg} throughout the range of possible r_{dc} values. □

What are plausible choices for the distribution $f_{thr_c}(x)$? One such choice would be a parabolic function of the type $f_{thr_c}(x) = \alpha x^2 + \beta x + \gamma$ over $[0, c_{max}]$ implying that more drivers risk competing at medium values of the u ratio rather than at very low or high fee differences. HEnce, imposing $\int_0^{c_{max}} f_{thr_c}(x) = 1$ and $f_{thr_c}(0) = f_{thr_c}(c_{max}) = 0$, we get

$$f_{thr_c}(x) = \begin{cases} \frac{6x}{c_{max}^2}(1 - \frac{x}{c_{max}}) & \text{if } x \in [0, c_{max}] \\ 0 & \text{otherwise} \end{cases}$$

3.3 Numerical results

We validate the analysis of Section 3.2 and demonstrate the operational dynamics of the parking search process under the two decision-making models for different values for the fees charged c_1, c_2, the cruising cost c_{exc}, and the driver's sensitivity to their difference (c_{max}).

In Fig. 2a ($r_{dc} = 1.75$) the game model prescribes that $min(N_0 = 68.75, N)$ vehicles should be competing for on-street parking space. The priority heuristic, on the other hand, requires that a fixed 62% of the population should do so, resulting in under-utilization of on-street parking space for $N < 40$. The aggregate cost remains consistently lower under the heuristic even for demand/supply ratios N/R exceeding four and up to $N \leq 110$, where the condition (C3) of Table 1 is violated (for N=110, A=3.6, B=0.95, $N \cdot F_{thr_c}(\frac{c_2 - c_1}{c_2 + c_{exc}}) - R)/R = 1.7447$).

As drivers become more sensitive to the charged fee differences (Fig. 2b, c_{max}=0.6), the priority heuristic directs more of them to compete for on-street parking space. The aggregate paid cost exceeds that at the NE of the strategic game faster but not before the demand/supply ratio N/R exceeds 3 (for N=80, A=2.4, B=0.837, $N \cdot F_{thr_c}(\frac{c_2 - c_1}{c_2 + c_{exc}}) - R)/R$ = 1.796). The predictions of the two decision-making models are identical when the fee difference $c_2 - c_1$ a) makes the parking lot prohibitive for all drivers deciding heuristically; b) renders the expected cost of competition for on-street parking (1) smaller than the parking lot fee for any (realistic) value of parking demand. This is the case in Fig. 2c.

4. TWO PARKING LOTS AND THE DISTANCE-COST TRADEOFF

The assumption underlying $\Gamma_1(N)$ is that the parking lots do not differentiate with respect to their location and fees. Equivalently, all parking lots are located within ap-

Table 2: Pure NE of $\Gamma_2(N)$ for different values of N

Range of N	NE states (N_1^{NE}, N_2^{NE})	Number of realizations	Conditions
$[1, N_{12}]$	$(N, 0)$	1	-
$(N_{12}, N_{12}+R_2]$	$(\lfloor N_{12}\rfloor, N-\lfloor N_{12}\rfloor)$	$\binom{N}{\lfloor N_{12}\rfloor}$	$N_{12} \notin \mathbb{N}^*$
	$(N_{12}, N-N_{12})$	$\binom{N}{N_{12}}$	$N_{12} \in \mathbb{N}^*$
	$(N_{12}-1, N-N_{12}+1)$	$\binom{N}{N_{12}-1}$	$N_{12} \in \mathbb{N}^*$
$(N_{12}+R_2, N_{13}+N_{23}]$	$(\lfloor \frac{N_{13}}{N_{13}+N_{23}}N\rfloor, \lceil \frac{N_{23}}{N_{13}+N_{23}}N\rceil)$	$\binom{N}{\lfloor \frac{N_{13}}{N_{13}+N_{23}}N\rfloor}$	$\frac{N_{13}}{N_{13}+N_{23}}N \notin \mathbb{N}^*$
	or $(\lceil \frac{N_{13}}{N_{13}+N_{23}}N\rceil, \lfloor \frac{N_{23}}{N_{13}+N_{23}}N\rfloor)$	$\binom{N}{\lceil \frac{N_{13}}{N_{13}+N_{23}}N\rceil}$	$\frac{N_{13}}{N_{13}+N_{23}}N \notin \mathbb{N}^*$
	$(\frac{N_{13}}{N_{13}+N_{23}}N, \frac{N_{23}}{N_{13}+N_{23}}N)$	$\binom{N}{\frac{N_{13}}{N_{13}+N_{23}}N}$	$\frac{N_{13}}{N_{13}+N_{23}}N \in \mathbb{N}^*$
$(N_{13}+N_{23}, \infty)$	$(\lfloor N_{13}\rfloor, \lfloor N_{23}\rfloor)$	$\frac{N!}{\lfloor N_{13}\rfloor!\lfloor N_{23}\rfloor!(N-\sum_{j=1}^{2}\lfloor N_{j3}\rfloor)!}$	$N_{13}, N_{23} \notin \mathbb{N}^*$
	(N_{13}, N_{23})	$\frac{N!}{N_{13}!N_{23}!(N-N_{13}-N_{23})!}$	$N_{13}, N_{23} \in \mathbb{N}^*$
	$(N_{13}-1, N_{23}-1)$	$\frac{N!}{(N_{13}-1)!(N_{23}-1)!(N-\sum_{j=1}^{2}N_{j3}-2)!}$	$N_{13}, N_{23} \in \mathbb{N}^*$
	$(N_{13}-1, N_{23})$	$\frac{N!}{(N_{13}-1)!N_{23}!(N-\sum_{j=1}^{2}N_{j3}-1)!}$	$N_{13}, N_{23} \in \mathbb{N}^*$
	$(N_{13}, N_{23}-1)$	$\frac{N!}{N_{13}!(N_{23}-1)!(N-\sum_{j=1}^{2}N_{j3}-1)!}$	$N_{13}, N_{23} \in \mathbb{N}^*$

proximately the same area (*e.g.*, business district) and they charge the same fee for their parking space so that drivers do not have strong preference for the one or the other.

In this section, we relax these two assumptions, introducing differentiation with respect to both charged fees and distances from travel destination. We consider two parking lots as alternatives to on-street parking. The first one is co-located with the drivers' common travel destination (distance $r_1 = 0$) and charges a fee c_3 per time unit. The second parking lot is further away at distance $r_2 > 0$ and charges a fee c_2, with $c_1 < c_2 < c_3$. On a more technical note, these assumptions turn the original single-attribute choice problem with essentially two alternatives into a two-attribute (cost, distance) choice problem with three alternatives. As before, we first formulate a game model for it, which becomes relevant under the highly normative assumption that that the vehicular nodes decide and act strategically and fully rationally. We then tailor the simpler DEBA heuristic (ref. Section 2) to the problem and compare the solutions it induces against the NE of the game model.

4.1 Strategic fully rational decision-making

The game model that captures the strategic interactions of drivers under full rationality stands in direct analogy with $\Gamma_1(N)$, as defined in Section 2.1.

DEFINITION 2. *The* Extended Parking Spot Selection Game *is a tuple* $\Gamma_2(N) = (\mathcal{N}, \mathcal{R}, (A_i)_{i\in\mathcal{N}}, (w_j), j \in \{1,2,3\})$, *where:*

- $\mathcal{N} = \{1, ..., N\}$, $N > 1$ *is the set of drivers searching for parking space,*
- $\mathcal{R} = \mathcal{R}_1 \cup \mathcal{R}_2 \cup \mathcal{R}_3$ *is the set of parking spots;* $\mathcal{R}_1$ *is the set of on-street spots, with* $R = |\mathcal{R}_1| \geq 1$; $\mathcal{R}_2$ *is the set of spots in the more distant yet cheaper parking lot, with* $|\mathcal{R}_2| = R_2 > 1$ *and* $R_1 + R_2 < N$; *and* $\mathcal{R}_3$ *is the set of parking spots in the spacious but expensive lot that lies next to the travel destination, with* $|\mathcal{R}_3| = R_3 > N$.
- $A_i = \{1, 2, 3\}$ *is the action set for each driver* $i \in \mathcal{N}$, *action "1" denoting search for on-street parking space, "2" driving directly to the cheaper and "3" to the more expensive parking lot.*
- $w_j(\cdot, \cdot)$, $j = 1, 2, 3$ *are the cost functions of the three actions, respectively.*

With respect to the original game $\Gamma_1(N)$, cost functions have now to account for the non-monetary cost related to the distance of the three alternatives and the effort related to driving and walking from/to them. If $f_r(\cdot)$ is a function that monetizes this cost, it holds that $f_r(r_2) > f_r(r_1) > f_r(r_3) = 0$. Then $w_1(n_1, n_2)$ is given by $(15)^2$,

$$w_2(n_1, n_2) = min(1, \frac{R_2}{n_2})(c_2 + f_r(r_2)) + \lceil 1 - R_2/n_2\rceil^+(c_3 + c_{exc})$$

[2]The assumption in (15) is that drivers that fail to seize an on-street parking spot will first seek for parking space in the distant cheaper lot and only if this does not work out for them, they will resort to the expensive lot with guaranteed parking space.

$$w_1(n_1,n_2) = min(1, \frac{R_1}{n_1})(c_1+f_r(r_1)) + \lceil 1-\frac{R_1}{n_1}\rceil^+ \Big(\frac{\lceil R_2-n_2\rceil^+ \cdot (c_2+c_{exc}+f_r(r_2))}{\lceil n_1-R_1\rceil^+ + \lceil n_2-R_2\rceil^+} + (1-\frac{\lceil R_2-n_2\rceil^+}{\lceil n_1-R_1\rceil^+ + \lceil n_2-R_2\rceil^+})(c_3+c_{exc})\Big) \quad (15)$$

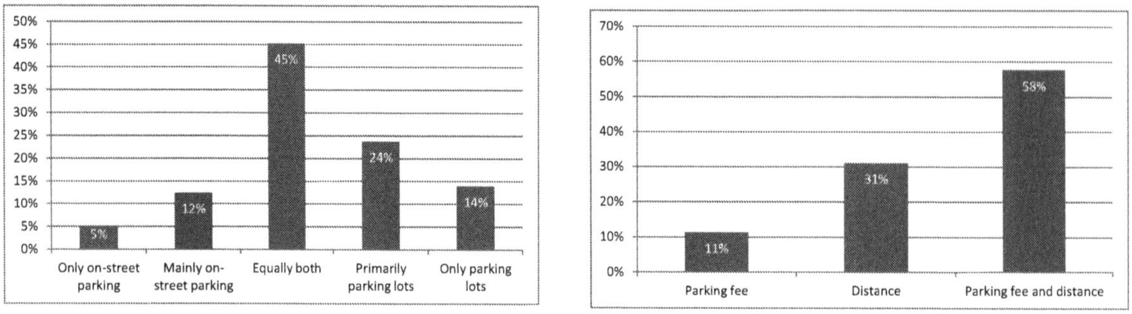

a. Parking resource used

b. Criteria for selecting parking lot

Figure 3: Survey outcomes regarding the parking preferences of 1200 drivers in Nicosia, Cyprus.

and $w_3(n_1,n_2) = c_3$, where $\lceil x\rceil^+ = max(x,0)$ and (n_1,n_2) describes the state of the system, *i.e.*, the numbers of vehicular nodes that decide to compete for on-street parking capacity and drive towards the cheaper distant parking lot, respectively[3].

In principle, $f_r(\cdot)$ is driver-specific; extra driving and walking effort is not equally annoying to all drivers. Yet for computational tractability purposes, we restrict ourselves to symmetric users, assuming that $f_r(\cdot)$ has similar semantics for all users. Defining:

$$N_{12} = \frac{c_2+f_r(r_2)+c_{exc}-(c_1+f_r(r_1))}{c_{exc}}R_1$$
$$N_{13} = \frac{c_3+c_{exc}-(c_1+f_r(r_1))}{c_{exc}}R_1 \quad \text{and}$$
$$N_{23} = \frac{c_3+c_{exc}-(c_2+f_r(r_2))}{c_{exc}}R_2 \quad (16)$$

we can show that

THEOREM 2. *The game $\Gamma_2(N)$ has the pure NE listed in Table 2.*

PROOF. The proof is given in the Appendix A. □

PROPOSITION 1. *For any value of $N > R_1$, the NE of the game $\Gamma_2(N)$ induce over-competition for the on-street parking capacity.*

PROOF. The proof is given in the Appendix B. □

4.2 Heuristic decision-making

The game-theoretic model for the drivers' decisions among the three alternatives has normative rather than descriptive value. Besides acquiring and exhaustively processing information about the demand and supply of parking resources, vehicular nodes also need to "monetize" the cost related to the distance of parking resources from the drivers' destination. As a more realistic decision model, we introduce a heuristic that essentially modulates the generic DEBA heuristic in [12] with application-specific data obtained via a paper survey. The survey was carried out in Nicosia, Cyprus, during the summer months of 2012 with the participation of around 1200 drivers replying to more than twenty questions about their parking habits and preferences.

[3]Apparently a state $\{n_1,n_2\}$ implies that the remaining $N - n_1 - n_2$ vehicular nodes select the more expensive parking lot.

The replies of drivers about the parking resource type they make use of and their selection criteria are summarized in Figure 3. They reveal two distinct stages at their decision-making process as well as high heterogeneity regarding their decision criteria. First, the population of drivers is partitioned into five groups reflecting their preferences about the type of parking resource (on-street parking *vs.* parking lot) and the frequency of their usage. Then, drivers using parking lots either exclusively or occasionally, are further divided into three groups, depending on the criteria (cost and/or distance from destination) directing their decisions.

Technically speaking, let $i \in [1,5]$ and $j \in [1,3]$ index the groups of drivers emerging at the first and second stage, respectively, in left-to-right order as they appear in Fig. 3. For example, $i=2$ denotes the group of drivers that primarily seek on-street parking and $j=1$ the parking lot users who consider only the charged fees when selecting a lot. If p_i and q_j are the percentage volumes of the respective groups, the expected number of drivers who search for on-street parking space is:

$$N_1^H = N \cdot (p_1 + \alpha p_2 + 0.5p_3 + (1-\alpha)p_4) \quad (17)$$

where $0.5 < \alpha \leq 1$ is the quantitative interpretation of "primarily" in the responses of drivers. The plausible assumption in (17) is that all on-street parking spots are subject to the same charging policy throughout the area of interest and their distance from the drivers' common destination does not vary considerably.

Likewise, the expected number of users that will end up in a parking lot is

$$N_{PL}^H = N_2^H + N_3^H = N \cdot (p_5 + \alpha p_4 + 0.5p_3 + (1-\alpha)p_2) \quad (18)$$

The way these N_{PL}^H users further decide between the two parking lots is dictated by the right plot in Fig. 3. The cheaper but remote (expensive yet destination-adjacent) parking lot is chosen by the $N_{PL}^H \cdot q_1(q_2)$ drivers plus part of the $N_{PL}^H \cdot q_3$ drivers who account for both criteria in their decisions. We argue that these drivers essentially consider the two criteria sequentially: first, the distance, then the parking fees. If the distance of (walking time from) the remote lot is prohibitive (*e.g.*, beyond a driver-specific threshold thr_w), they drive to the destination-adjacent parking lot. Otherwise, they consider the difference in the fees charged

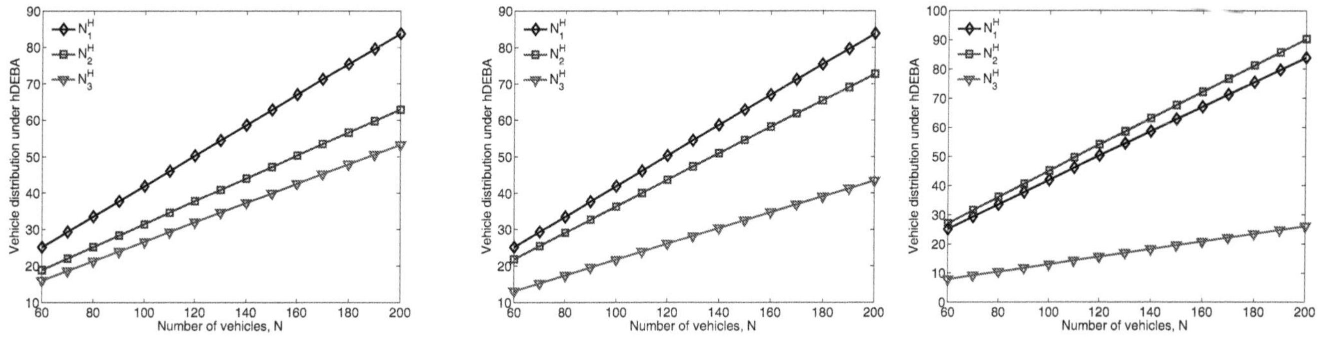

a. $c_1 = 1.5, c_2 = 5, c_3 = 8, c_{exc} = 2, w_2 = 6$ b. $c_1 = 1.5, c_2 = 5, c_3 = 8, c_{exc} = 2, w_2 = 4$ c. $c_1 = 1.5, c_2 = 5, c_3 = 10, c_{exc} = 2, w_2 = 6$

Figure 4: Distribution of vehicles to the three parking resources when decisions use the hDEBA heuristic: R_1=25, R_2=40, $w_{min} = 3$, $w_{max} = 12$, $c_{max} = 5$.

by the two lots, $c_3 - c_2$. If this is "small" enough, (*e.g.*, below a driver-specific threshold thr_c), they pay the higher fee of the nearby lot to save the additional driving and walking overhead; otherwise, they drive to the remote parking lot.

As in section 3, we capture the heterogeneous sensitivity of drivers to the parking lot distance and fees statistically through negative parabolic distributions of the type $f(x) = \alpha x^2 + \beta x + \gamma$. We let thr_w vary in $[w_{min}, w_{max}]$ and enforcing $f(w_{min}) = f(w_{max}) = 0$ we get $\alpha = -6/(w_{max} - w_{min})^3$, $\beta = -\alpha \cdot (w_{min} + w_{max})$ and $\gamma = \alpha \cdot w_{min} w_{max}$.

The fee difference threshold, on the other hand, is let vary in $[0, c_{max}]$ according to

$$f_{thr_c}(x) = \frac{6x}{c_{max}^2}(1 - \frac{x}{c_{max}}) \tag{19}$$

For given distance (*i.e.*, expected walking time) w_2 of the distant parking lot, the number of drivers that select it is

$$N_2^H = N_{PL}^H \cdot \Big(q_1 + q_3(1 - F_{thr_w}(w_2)) \cdot F_{thr_c}(c_3 - c_2)\Big)$$

whereas

$$N_3^H = N_{PL}^H \cdot \Big(q_2 + q_3 \cdot (F_{thr_w}(w_2) + (1 - F_{thr_w}(w_2)) \cdot (1 - F_{thr_c}(c_3 - c_2))\Big)$$

will drive to the nearer and more expensive parking lot. The way the actual distance of the remote parking lot and the fee difference partition the drivers' population into the three parking resources is shown in Fig. 4. As expected, more parking lot users are directed to the cheaper remote one with parallel reduction of the expensive lot users as w_2 decreases and the fee c_3 of the expensive lot increases.

It is worth remarking that the proposed heuristic is essentially a driver heterogeneity-aware adaptation of the original DEBA heuristic; we, thus, call it hDEBA. The practice in lexicographic multi-attribute selection is to encode the three parking resource alternatives as vectors of three attributes (a_1, a_2, a_3) in order of decreasing importance weight (priority). The attribute with the highest priority corresponds to the parking resource type and is binary. An expected number of N_1^H drivers *implicitly* set $a_1 = 1$ if the type is "on-street parking" and $a_1 = 0$ if it is "parking lot"; the opposite holds for the remaining N_{PL}^H drivers. The second attribute corresponds to the distance from the destination and is turned to a binary one through the driver-specific threshold thr_w. Finally, the third attribute is the fee of the parking resource, which is conceptually set to zero or one by each driver depending on the relation of $c_3 - c_2$ to her threshold thr_c. Note that $thr_w \to 0$ for the $N_{PL}^H q_2$ drivers that decide exclusively on the basis of the distance attribute and $thr_w \to \infty$, $thr_c \to 0$ for the $N_{PL}^H \cdot q_1$ drivers who only consider the charged fees.

4.3 Strategic *vs.* heuristic predictions

However the decision is made, the aggregate cost that drivers will have to pay is a function of their partitioning to the three groups $\{N_1, N_2, N_3\}$. Its most general expression is given by (20).

The analytical comparison of the two decision-making models along the lines of Theorem 1 is not straightforward. Instead, we plot in Fig. 5 the partitions of the vehicles' population and compare the aggregate cost generated by the NE of the $\Gamma_2(N)$ game and the operation of the hDEBA heuristic for typical parameter values. In all four scenarios, and many more that are not shown here due to space constraints, the trend is similar: the number of vehicles that select the on-street parking space is consistently higher under strategic decision-making than under hDEBA, whereas the situation is reversed for the vehicle population that selects the cheaper distant parking lot, at least for low and moderate demand/supply ratios. The excess cruising cost due to the first group of vehicles is higher than the excess cost paid by vehicles that do not manage to get a parking space in the distant parking lot and perforce end up in the expensive parking lot. As a result, the aggregate cost under hDEBA turns out to be smaller than that induced by the NE of $\Gamma_2(N)$ and sometimes even very close to the minimum possible (OPT).

5. DISCUSSION-CONCLUSIONS

We have carried out a performance analysis study that acknowledges the role of cognitive heuristics in drivers' decision-making and assesses their impact on the efficiency of the parking search process. These heuristics cater for humans' bounded rationality and present a radical departure from the normative model of strategic decision-maker who systematically aims at maximizing (minimizing) its gains (losses). Two parking search scenarios have been considered and treated as instances of multi-attribute choice problems with two (three) alternatives, respectively. The proposed lexicographic heuristics draw on research in the field of cognitive psychology and we show analytically that their use reduces the aggregate cost paid for satisfying the parking demand when compared to the prescriptions of game-theoretic models as-

$$
\begin{aligned}
C_{agg} &= min(R_1, N_1)(c_1 + f_r(r_1)) + min(max(N_1 - R_1, 0), max(N_2 - R_2, 0))(c_2 + c_{exc} + f_r(r_2)) \\
&+ max(N_1 - R_1 - max(R_2 - N_2, 0), 0)(c_3 + c_{exc}) + min(R_2, N_2)(c_2 + f_r(r_2)) + max(N_2 - R_2, 0)(c_3 + c_{exc}) + N_3 c_3
\end{aligned} \quad (20)
$$

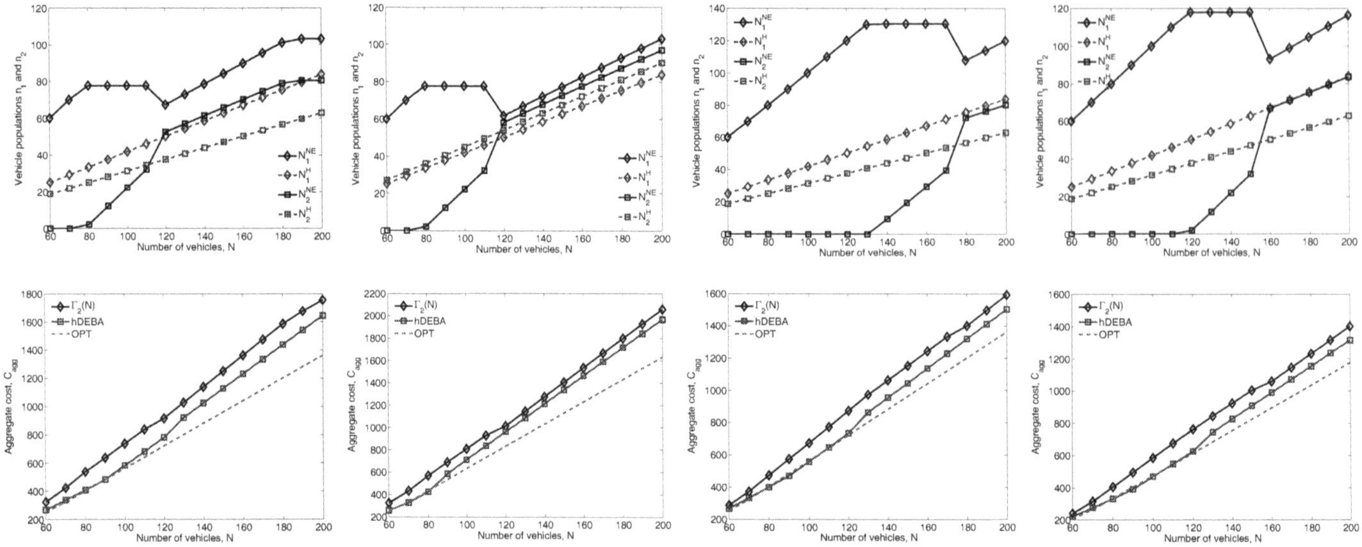

a. {1.5,5,8,2,6} b. {1.5,5,10,2,6} c. {1.5,5,8,1,6} d. {1,4,7,1,6}

Figure 5: Distribution of vehicles to the three parking resources and respective aggregate cost for different parameter sets $\{c_1, c_2, c_3, c_{exc}, w_2\}$: R_1=25, R_2=40, $w_{min} = 3$, $w_{max} = 12$, $c_{max} = 5$.

suming fully rational decision-makers, over a broad selection of scenarios' settings.

The main implications of this work concern the software agents running over the devices that are mounted onboard the vehicles. One configuration possibility for them is to try to mimic the fully rational strategic agents. In that case, the parking assistance system infrastructure needs to provide them with detailed information about the available parking resources, the fees they charge and estimates of the parking demand. They then compute the NE of the respective game and make the respective recommendations to the driver. A simpler configuration alternative would allow for some driver personalization, possibly upon first use by her. The driver could enter very simple profile information such as whether she prefers parking lots over on-street space, what is the acceptable fee difference between the two and how far from her destination she is willing to park. The software could then just try to make recommendations that respect its owner's preferences. According to the results of the paper, in the majority of the scenarios, the second option will result in a socially more efficient parking selection process.

One of the main advantages of the heuristic decision-making models is that they directly describe how a decision is reached. Fig. 6 implies that these models may be also much more informative with respect to the sensitivity of the parking search efficiency to parameters such as, in this case, the difference in fees charged by the different parking resources. The expected number of competing vehicles is significantly more responsive to this difference under the priority heuristic model than it is under the game model $\Gamma_1(N)$.

Finally, on the methodological front, the steps taken in this paper for the performance analysis of the parking search process, *i.e.*, (a)game formulation and analysis for establishing a reference; b) adaptation and analysis of a cognitive (lexicographic) heuristic to the problem; (c) comparison of the prescriptions of the two models, could serve as a template for the analysis of many more problems. They are essentially applicable to various networking operations, whereby decisions are taken by multiple end users and jointly determine the outcome of the operation. The radio access network selection (*e.g.*, WiFi *vs.* cellular) is one such case.

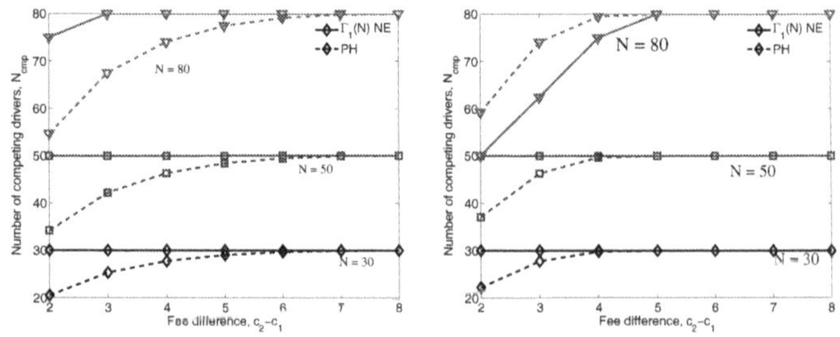

a. $c_1 = 1, c_{exc} = 1, c_{max} = 0.8$ b. $c_1 = 1.5, c_{exc} = 2, c_{max} = 0.6$

Figure 6: Sensitivity of competing vehicles to the difference of parking resource fees: priority heuristic *vs.* game $\Gamma_1(N)$, R=25.

On the other hand, there is an open question as to whether drivers do *actually* practice such heuristics when searching for parking space. There is compelling evidence that lexicographic heuristics are employed by humans in a wide range of very different selection tasks and can justify several well-reported empirical phenomena that result from their choices [5][6]. Yet, the ultimate validation of the heuristics' relevance calls for large-scale experimentation in real or semi-real (*i.e.*, emulator) conditions. Such experimentation is currently an open challenge for various research communities including psychologists and transportation engineers.

$$
\begin{aligned}
N_{cmp}^{NE} &\geq \frac{N_{13}\cdot(N_{12}+R_2)}{N_{13}+N_{23}} = \frac{\Big(c_3+c_{exc}-\big(c_1+f_r(r_1)\big)\Big)R_1\cdot\Big(\frac{c_2+f_r(r_2)+c_{exc}-\left(c_1+f_r(r_1)\right)}{c_{exc}}R_1+R_2\Big)}{\Big(c_3+c_{exc}-\big(c_1+f_r(r_1)\big)\Big)R_1+\Big(c_3+c_{exc}-\big(c_2+f_r(r_2)\big)\Big)R_2} \\
&> R_1\frac{\Big(c_3+c_{exc}-\big(c_1+f_r(r_1)\big)\Big)R_1+\Big(c_3+c_{exc}-\big(c_1+f_r(r_1)\big)\Big)R_2}{\Big(c_3+c_{exc}-\big(c_1+f_r(r_1)\big)\Big)R_1+\Big(c_3+c_{exc}-\big(c_2+f_r(r_2)\big)\Big)R_2} \quad \textit{since } N_{12}/R_1>1 \\
&> R_1\frac{\Big(c_3+c_{exc}-\big(c_1+f_r(r_1)\big)\Big)R_1+\Big(c_3+c_{exc}-\big(c_2+f_r(r_2)\big)\Big)R_2}{\Big(c_3+c_{exc}-\big(c_1+f_r(r_1)\big)\Big)R_1+\Big(c_3+c_{exc}-\big(c_2+f_r(r_2)\big)\Big)R_2} = R_1 \quad \textit{since } c_2+f_r(r_2)>c_1+f_r(r_1) \qquad (21)
\end{aligned}
$$

6. ACKNOWLEDGMENTS

M. Karaliopoulos acknowledges the support of ERC08-RECITAL project, co-financed by Greece and the European Social Fund through the Operational Program "Education and Lifelong Learning"- NCRF 2007-2013.

7. REFERENCES

[1] D. Shoup, "Cruising for parking," *Transport Policy*, vol. 13, no. 3, 2006.

[2] M. Caliskan, D. Graupner, and M. Mauve, "Decentralized discovery of free parking places," in *Proc. 3rd VANET (in conjunction with ACM MobiCom)*, Los Angeles, CA, USA, 2006.

[3] http://www.parkingcarma.com.

[4] ParkShark: parking system for New York City, available online in http://www.parkshark.mobi/www/.

[5] J. K. Ford, N. Schmitt, S. L. Schechtmann, B. M. Hults, and M. L. Doherty, "Process tracing methods: Contributions, problems and neglected research questions," *Organizational Behavior and Human Decision Processes*, pp. 42, 75–117, 1989.

[6] K. V. Katsikopoulos and G. Gigerentzer, "One-reason decision-making: Modeling violations of expected utility theory," *Journal of Risk and Uncertainty*, vol. 37, no. 1, pp. 35–56, 2008.

[7] E. Kokolaki, M. Karaliopoulos, and I. Stavrakakis, "Leveraging information in parking assistance systems," *Vehicular Technology, IEEE Transactions on*, vol. 62, no. 9, pp. 4309–4317, 2013.

[8] G. Gigerenzer, R. Hertwig, and T. E. Pachur, *Heuristics: The Foundations of Adaptive Behavior.* New York: Oxford University Press, 2011.

[9] E. Brandstatter, G. Gigerenzer, and R. Hertwig, "The priority heuristic: making choices withour trade-offs," *Psychological Review*, vol. 113, no. 2, pp. 409–432, 2006.

[10] D. Kahneman, *Thinking, Fast and Slow.* Farrar, Straus and Giroux, 2011.

[11] A. Rubinstein, *Modeling bounded rationality.* Cambridge, MA, USA: MIT Press, 1998.

[12] R. M. Hogarth and N. Karelaia, "Simple models for multiattribute choice with many alternatives: When it does and does not pay to face tradeoffs with binary attributes?" *Management Science*, vol. 51, no. 12, pp. 1860–1872, 2005.

[13] K. V. Katsikopoulos, "Psychological heuristics for making inferences: Definition, performance, and the emerging theory and practice," *Decision Analysis*, vol. 8, no. 1, pp. 10–29, 2011.

APPENDIX

A. PROOF OF THEOREM 2

We provide a sketch of the proof avoiding notation formalities that burden its comprehensibility. As long as the drivers are fewer than the on-street parking spots R_1, the NE prescribes that all of them should direct thereto. The same holds for all N values up to N_{12}, where the expected cost of choosing to search for curbside parking reaches that of the second choice (head for the distant parking lot)

$$\frac{R_1}{N_{12}}(c_1+f_r(r_1))+(1-\frac{R_1}{N_{12}})(c_2+f_r(r_2)+c_{exc})=c_2+f_r(r_2)$$

Any additional up to R_2 drivers beyond the N_{12} ones should then head for the distant cheaper parking lot. Therefore, as N varies in $[N_{12}, N_{12}+R_2]$ the *individual* driver cost at the equilibrium remains constant and equals $c_2+f_r(r_2)$.

When N exceeds $N_{12}+R_2$, the expected *individual* cost of the first choice (on-street parking search) experiences a sudden increase since upon failure to seize an on-street spot, a driver can only drive to the expensive parking lot; the cheaper one is no longer an option. Hence, the split of (n_1, n_2) in the NE for $N = N_{12}+R_2+1$ features $n_1 < N_{12}$ and $n_2 > R_2$. The NE states (n_1, n_2) should satisfy

$$\frac{R_1}{n_1}(c_1+f_r(r_1))+(1-\frac{R_1}{n_1})(c_3+c_{exc})=\frac{R_2}{n_2}(c_2+f_r(r_2))+(1-\frac{R_2}{n_2})(c_3+c_{exc})$$

Since $n_1+n_2=N$, it comes out that $n_1=\frac{N_{13}}{N_{13}+N_{23}}N$ and $n_2=\frac{N_{23}}{N_{13}+N_{23}}N$. NE states with $n_3>0$ emerge only when the expected costs of the first and the second choice equal the cost (fees) of the expensive parking lot. This occurs for $n_1=N_{13}$ and $n_2=N_{23}$ values satisfying

$$\frac{R_1}{N_{13}}(c_1+f_r(r_1))+(1-\frac{R_1}{N_{13}})(c_3+c_{exc})=c_3, \text{ and} \qquad (22)$$

$$\frac{R_2}{N_{23}}(c_2+f_r(r_2))+(1-\frac{R_2}{N_{23}})(c_3+c_{exc})=c_3 \qquad (23)$$

respectively. At the NE, any amount of drivers beyond $N_{13}+N_{23}$ select the expensive parking lot so that the individual driver's cost is steady at c_3. Table 2 provides the full set of NE that emerge considering explicitly whether the aforementioned equilibria values are integers or not. Their validity check is straightforward.

B. PROOF OF PROPOSITION 1

The number of vehicles N_{cmp}^{NE} that compete for on-street parking capacity for $R_1 \leq N < N_{12}$ is $N \geq R_1$. For N in $(N_{12}, N_{12}+R_2]$, the respective number is (16)

$$N_{cmp}^{NE}=N_{12}=(1+\frac{(c_2-c_1)+(f_r(r_2)-f_r(r_1))}{c_{exc}})R_1>R_1$$

Likewise, for $N > N_{13}+N_{23}$ the equilibrium value is

$$N_{cmp}^{NE}=N_{13}=(1+\frac{c_3-c_1-f_r(r_1)}{c_{exc}})R_1>R_1$$

Finally, the inequalities (21) assert that the equilibrium number $N\cdot N_{13}/(N_{13}+N_{23})$ of competing vehicles also exceeds R_1 when N lies in $[N_{12}+R_2, N_{13}+N_{23}]$.

Optimal Determination of Source-destination Connectivity in Random Graphs

Luoyi Fu, Xinbing Wang
Dept. of Electronic Engineering
Shanghai Jiao Tong University
Shanghai, China
{yiluofu,xwang8}@sjtu.edu.cn

P. R. Kumar
Dept. of Electrical and Computer Engineering
Texas A&M University
College Station, Texas
prk@tamu.edu

ABSTRACT

This paper investigates the problem of optimally determining source-destination connectivity in random graphs. We consider the classic Erdos-Renyi (ER) random graph with n nodes, where an edge independently exists between any two nodes with probability p. The problem examined is that of determining whether a given pair of nodes, a source S and a destination D, are connected by a path. Assuming that at each step one edge can be tested to see if it exists or not, we determine an optimal policy that minimizes the total expected number of steps.

The optimal policy has several interesting features. In order to establish connectivity of S and D, a policy needs to check all edges on some path to see if they all exist, but to establish disconnectivity it has to check all edges on some cut to see if none of them exists. The optimal policy has the following form. At each step it examines the condensation multigraph formed by contracting each known connected component to a single node, and then checks an edge that is simultaneously on a shortest S-D path as well as in a minimum S-D cut. Among such edges, it chooses that which leads to the most opportunities for connection. Interestingly, the optimal strategy does not depend on p or n, even though the entire graph itself undergoes a sharp transition from disconnectivity to connectivity around $p = \ln n/n$. The policy is efficiently implementable, requiring no more than $30\log_2 n$ operations to determine which edge to test next.

The result also extends to some more general graphs.

Categories and Subject Descriptors

C.2.1 [**Computer-Communication Networks**]: [Computer-Communication Networks]

General Terms

Connectivity, Random Networks, Random Graphs

MobiHoc'14, August 11-14, 2014, Philadelphia, PA, USA.
Copyright 2014 ACM 978-1-4503-2620-9/14/08:.$15.00.
http://dx.doi.org/10.1145/2632951.2632990.

Keywords

Connectivity; Random graphs; Optimization

1. INTRODUCTION

Connectivity of random graphs has long been a topic of intensive study. A widely studied model, known as the $G(n,p)$ model, was proposed by Gilbert [1] in 1959. It refers to a graph with n nodes, with an edge existing independently between any pair of nodes with probability p. Erdos and Renyi [2, 3] showed that this graph is connected with probability approaching one as $n \to \infty$, if $p(n)$, the probability p as a function of n, satisfies $p(n) > \frac{(1+\epsilon)\ln n}{n}$, and contains isolated nodes with probability approaching one as $n \to \infty$, if $p(n) < \frac{(1-\epsilon)\ln n}{n}$. We will refer to the $G(n,p)$ model as the ER graph, in conformity with common usage. In a wireless networking context, Gilbert [4], and, more recently, Penrose [5] and Gupta and Kumar [6], have studied geometric random graphs where nodes have random uniform i.i.d. locations in a unit disk, and showed that if the radio transmission range of each node is $r(n) = \sqrt{\frac{\ln n + c(n)}{n\pi^2}}$, then the whole network is connected with probability approaching one as $n \to \infty$, if and only if $c(n) \to +\infty$. Ever since, there has been much research effort directed towards studying asymptotic connectivity of randomly distributed wireless networks [7–15].

In this paper we consider ER Graphs. The above works all focus on the connectivity of the entire network in the asymptotic regime where the number of nodes goes to infinity. The focus here is different in the following three ways: (i) It is non-asymptotic, (ii) it is specific to the specific realization of the random network that is being studied, and, (iii) instead of studying the whole network's connectivity, the issue is the connectivity between a specified source S and destination D. We examine the fundamental problem of designing a policy that determines the connectivity of S and D in minimum expected number of steps, where at each step one edge can be chosen and tested to see if it exists. The algorithm we present concludes either with the discovery of a route or the discovery of a cut between S and D. It is designed to reach a conclusion regarding one or the other in the shortest expected time in ER graphs. It should be noted that quickest discovery of a route is very different from discovering the shortest path route, which is a very well understood problem.

We start by considering the classic ER random graph, with a designated source S and destination D. The independence of edge occurrences and their equal probabilities turn out to give ER graphs a great advantage in terms of solvability over other more complicated graph structures. Subsequently, we consider some slightly more general graphs in Section 5, where there is some additional deterministic structure known a priori about the presence or absence of certain edges.

The question of whether S and D are connected can be resolved if one can either display an S-D path, or an S-D cut. However, we do not know a priori whether the graph is connected or not, thereby making it difficult to know what to do – try to find a path or try to find a cut. The optimal policy has to be dynamic, based on the presence or absence of previously tested edges. This inherent tension in the problem of determining connectivity makes the problem somewhat challenging. Another difficulty is that we do not know the optimal solution for general graphs where some edges are known to exist, some known not to exist, and others existing i.i.d. with probability p, which is what one generally has after some steps of testing. Thus the proof of optimality is not based on dynamic programming-like arguments. Yet another aspect of interest is that the random graph exhibits a phase transition depending on the value of p. For $p > \frac{(1+\epsilon)\ln n}{n}$, the entire graph itself, and not just the particular S-D pair, is connected with high probability for large n, while for $p < \frac{(1-\epsilon)\ln n}{n}$, it is disconnected with high probability. Thus, one may possibly expect that the optimal strategy will depend on the value of p. Very interestingly, however, the optimal policy does not depend on p or n at all!

The main result is the optimality of the following simple testing strategy: At each stage, form the condensation multigraph by contracting each known connected component to a single node. It is a multigraph since the edges between nodes are inherited by the components to which they are contracted. In the set of edges that lie both on a shortest S-D path as well on the minimal S-D cut, test an edge that leads to the most opportunities for connectivity. The policy also has minimal complexity; it requires no more than $30\log_2 n$ operations to determine which edge to test next.

The policy is illustrated for a four-node ER graph in Figure 1. Figure 2 shows the number of steps, averaged over 100 simulations, that the optimal policy takes to establish S-D disconnectivity/connectivity in an ER graph with 1000 nodes, as a function of p. Determining S-D connectivity at around its phase transition can involve many steps. In between disconnectivity at very low p (say 10^{-5}) that takes about 999 steps to establish, and connectivity at very high p (around $p = 1$) that can be established in 1 step, the value of p passes through a phase transition around $p = 0.002$ (slightly smaller than the value of $p = \ln n/n \approx 0.006$ under the phase transition to connectivity of the entire network), where it takes a very large number of steps (about 15000) to determine if S and D are connected or not.

The proof of optimality of the policy follows from the proofs of optimality of the following three rules, which, when combined together give rise to the policy equivalently described above in terms of the condensation multigraph: Rule 1) The testing starts with a tactic that can lead to early termination by finding an S-D path: it first tests the edges, i.e., one-hop paths, connecting the component containing S and the component containing D. Rule 2) If there are no such edges, then it switches to checking for S-D disconnectivity by testing the edges on the S-D cut that contains the minimum number of untested edges. Rule 3) Among the edges in that cut, test the edge that leads to most opportunities for connection. These three rules optimally resolve the tension between checking for paths and cuts.

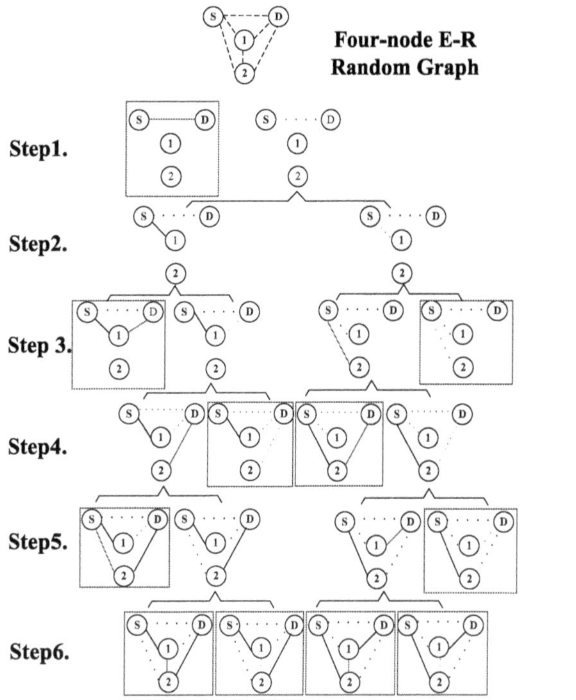

Figure 1: Illustration of the evolution of the optimal policy on a four-node ER random graph. The line in red shows the edge selected for testing at each step. A full line indicates that the edge was found to exist after testing, while a dotted line indicates that the edge was found to not exist after testing.

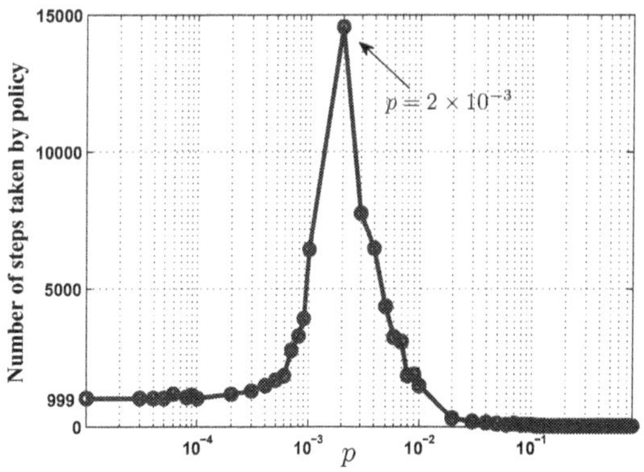

Figure 2: Number of steps needed to determine S-D disconnectivity/connectivity in a 1000 node ER Graph, as a function of p.

Related Works: We note that there is no other work, to the best of our knowledge, that addresses connectivity between a designated source and destination in random graphs. Rather, as noted earlier, it is asymptotic connectivity of the whole graph that has been intensively studied. Inspired by Erdos and Renyi [2,3], there have been many works [16–21] dedicated to investigating connectivity of the entire network when the number of nodes is sufficiently large.

Our work also has ties to wireless networks where connectivity is determined by distance. Gilbert [4] initiated the study of random graphs when nodes are randomly distributed on a plane. Penrose [5] and Gupta and Kumar [6] have determined the critical range for establishing overall connectivity with probability approaching one as n goes to infinity. This range results in each node connecting to $\log n$ neighbors on average. Xue and Kumar [8], and, subsequently, [9] and [10], further considered the number of nearest neighbors that nodes need to connect to, in order to ensure the network connectivity. The condition of full connectivity was relaxed by Dousse et. al. [11], which analyzed the scenario where the sink is connected (in a multihop fashion) to a set of nodes that span the entire network. The impact of node degree, density and network dimension on connectivity is also investigated [7], [12]. Due to the emergence of ad hoc networks, mesh networks and sensor networks, there has also been research interest in analysis of k-connectivity [13], [14], [15].

2. MODEL AND DEFINITIONS

Consider an ER Random Graph with n nodes. An edge exists between any pair of nodes with equal probability p, independently of others. At each step, one can test a potential (i.e., untested) edge of the graph to see if it indeed exists. Two specific nodes are identified, labeled S and D. Our objective is to construct a sequential testing strategy terminating in the minimal expected number of steps, to determine if S and D are connected or not. Termination occurs with

- Connectivity, when it has verified the existence of all edges on some S-D path, or
- Disconnectivity, when it has verified the absence of all edges on some S-D cut.

We employ three terms, *known edge*, *known non-edge* and *potential edge* (also sometimes called an "untested edge."). A known edge is one that has already been tested and found to exist. Similarly, a known non-edge is one that has already been tested but found to not exist. Finally, a potential edge is an edge that is yet to be tested, which upon testing may turn out to exist or not exist. In Table 1, we list other definitions used.

3. POLICY FOR CHECKING S-D CONNECTIVITY IN ER RANDOM GRAPHS

We now present a policy $\pi^* = \{\pi_0^*, \pi_1^*, \ldots, \pi_N^*\}$, which we call the alternating policy, for checking S-D connectivity in an ER random graph. We label the nodes other than the designated S and D as $1, 2, \ldots, n-2$. Each π_t^* maps $\mathcal{G}_t$ (defined in Table 1) to one of the remaining potential edges. It specifies which potential edge should be tested at time t. Note that $N = n(n-1)/2$ is the upper bound on the number of edges in the graph, and thus the step by which the policy must necessarily have terminated.

The policy π^* has been defined in a brief manner in terms of the condensation multigraph in Section 1. Now we define it in a detailed manner in terms of three rules more suitable for illustration and proof.

Table 1: Notations

Notation	Definition
e_t	The edge tested at step t.
$\mathcal{G}_t$	The graph state known at step t. It is a list of (i) those potential edges that have been tested and found to exist, i.e., "known edges," (ii) those potential edges that were tested and found to not exist, called "non-edges," and (iii) the remaining potential edges that have not yet been tested. Abbreviated to $\mathcal{G}$ if there is no confusion (similarly for the notation below).
$C_{S,t}$ (or $C_{D,t}$, or $C_{i,t}$)	The connected component containing the source (or destination, or the i-th component not containing the source or destination), in the graph comprised of the known edges at step t.
$\mathcal{M}_{\mathcal{G}}$	A *minimum cut* for a graph state $\mathcal{G}$, defined as a set which contains the minimum number of potential edges at time t, which if they were found to not exist, would lead to the conclusion that C_S and C_D are not connected by a path. Note that a minimum cut may be non-unique.

3.1 The Alternating Policy π^*

Rule 1: The policy tests a potential edge between C_S and C_D as long as there exists one such direct, one-hop, potential edge between them. Clearly, if such a direct edge is found to exist, then the policy terminates with the finding that S and D are connected.

Rule 2: If there are no potential edges connecting C_S and C_D as specified in Rule 1, then choose an edge from the list $\mathcal{L}$ defined as follows.

First list all the paths, comprised of known or potential edges, connecting C_S to C_D with the minimum number of potential edges. One such path is illustrated in Figure 3(a). Such a path must necessarily have potential edges only *between* connected components. If the path traverses only one component, say C_1, on its path from C_S to C_D, then it must have exactly two potential edges on it, one connecting C_S to C_1, and another connecting C_1 to C_D, as shown in Figure 3(a). The remaining portion of the path must only consist of known edges *within* connected components C_S, C_1 or C_D. The same rule holds on the remaining potential *shortest* paths, each traversing through only one component, say C_i $(2 \leq i \leq r)$, on its path from C_S to C_D.

Fix a minimum cut $\mathcal{M}_{\mathcal{G}}$ for the graph state $\mathcal{G}$ at that time. Figure 3(a) shows two cuts, one separating C_S from $C_1 \cup C_2 \cup \ldots C_r$, and another separating C_D from $C_1 \cup C_2 \cup \ldots C_r$. (Suppose that, as in the case illustrated, the former is a Minimum Cut, and the latter contains more edges. In the sequel we will show that shortest paths are of length at most two, and minimum cuts will be precisely of this form, as long as the policy keeps testing the edges in the prescribed way.)

Among all the potential edges that are on the aforementioned shortest paths, list only those potential edges that are also in the chosen minimum set $\mathcal{M}_{\mathcal{G}}$. Define this as the list $\mathcal{L}$. Such a list is shown in Figure 3(b).

For convenience of definition of Rule 3 below, we also list the set of components $\{C_1, C_2, \ldots, C_r\}$ $(0 \leq r \leq n-2)$ to which the edges belonging to this list $\mathcal{L}$ are connecting. Let us call this set of components as $\mathcal{C}$, i.e., $\mathcal{C} := \{C_1, C_2, ..., C_r\}$. Figure 3(b) illustrates this set $\mathcal{C}$ of components too.

Rule 3: In Rule 3 we further sharpen Rule 2 by specifying which particular edge in $\mathcal{L}$ should be tested.

Rule 2 when followed will lead to the following structural property, as we prove in the sequel. All edges in $\mathcal{L}$ are either between C_S and $U_{i=1}^{r} C_i$, or all edges are between C_D and $U_{i=1}^{r} C_i$. (Certainly this is true at the outset for the ER graph, and if an edge is chosen from $\mathcal{L}$, as in Rule 2, then it retains that property). Suppose all edges in $\mathcal{L}$ connect to C_S, i.e., have one endpoint in C_S. Then, for each C_i, let n_i be the number of direct potential edges between C_i and C_D. Sort the components in $\mathcal{C}$ based on n_i in decreasing order.

Suppose that n_1 is the largest. Test any edge in $\mathcal{L}$ that connects C_S to C_1. This is illustrated in Figure 3(c).

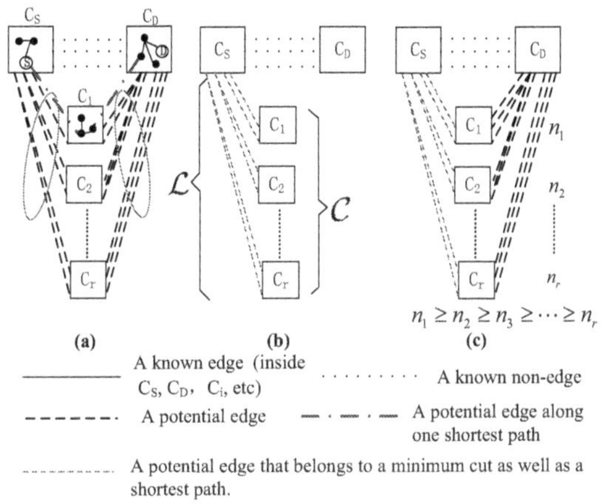

Figure 3: The illustration of Rules 2 and 3.

4. THE PROOF OF OPTIMALITY OF THE ALTERNATING POLICY π^*

We now commence the proof of optimality of the Alternating Policy π^*. It uses a carefully chosen stochastic coupling in several places. We will consider the graph shown in Figure 3(c); the general case proceeds similarly. The edges meeting Rules 2 and 3 are the potential edges between C_S and C_1. Note that compared to the other C_i's, C_1 has the greatest chance of subsequently having an edge connected to C_D, if an edge is found between C_1 and C_S.

4.1 Proof of Optimality of Rules 1 and 2

The optimality of Rule 1 follows from the following:

LEMMA 1. *Suppose that there are direct potential edges between C_S and C_D. Then for any policy A that tests an edge other than such a direct potential edge, there is a policy $\widetilde{\mathcal{A}}$ that does test a direct potential edge and has a lower expected cost than A.*

PROOF. See Appendix A. □

Next, *assuming* that Rule 1 is always followed, we prove the optimality of Rule 2. The following lemma establishes a preliminary property.

LEMMA 2. *When the policy follows both Rules 1 and 2, all the edges in the minimum cut at any step will be between $\cup_{i=1}^{r} C_i$ and C_S, or they will all be between $\cup_{i=1}^{r} C_i$ and C_D.*

PROOF. A minimum set partitions the connected components into two classes, with one class containing C_S and another class containing C_D. An equivalent claim of the lemma is that at any step t, all the components other than C_S or C_D will lie in one class. Suppose that not all the components lie in the same class. Then, in order to determine the S-D disconnectivity, the edges between components, in particular those that traverse two classes, say C_i and C_j will need to be tested, in addition to those between C_S and the components in C_i, and those between C_D and the components in C_j. Therefore, extra steps are wasted on testing the edges between components. However, those edges will never need to be tested when a cut is chosen to make all the components lie within one class. □

Therefore, to prove Rule 2 in our scenario we only need to prove Lemma 3 stated as follows.

LEMMA 3. *When there are no direct edges between C_S and C_D, listing all the potential shortest paths and sampling the edges in the minimum set on them will lead to smaller expected cost than sampling any other edge first.*

PROOF. See Appendix B. □

4.2 Proof of Optimality of Rule 3

Proving Rule 3 is equivalent to proving that in choosing between any two components from the set $\{C_1, , \ldots, C_r\}$ at step t, the expected cost will be smaller if we first pick the component with a larger number of direct edges to the other side. Without loss of generality, let us suppose that there are only two components, C_1 and C_2. Based on Lemma 2, all the edges in the minimum cut $\mathscr{M}_{\mathcal{G}_t}$ are always on the same side. Let k_{11} and k_{21} be the number of edges from $\mathscr{M}_{\mathcal{G}_t}$ that connect to C_1 and C_2, respectively, as shown in Figure 4(a). Similarly, let k_{12} and k_{22} be the number of direct edges C_1 and C_2 have to C_D. Assuming that $k_{12} \geq k_{22}$ in Figure 4, we have the following lemma regarding Rule 3.

LEMMA 4. *Among all the potential edges that C_1 and C_2 connect to in $\mathscr{M}_{\mathcal{G}_t}$, it incurs smaller expected cost to first test the ones that C_1 is connected to.*

PROOF. We prove this by induction on the number of potential edges, in the graph of the type that results at each step from following Rules 1 and 2. Based on Lemma 2, such type of graph contains singleton components with the edges in the minimum cut all being between C_S and singletons, or all being between C_D and singletons. Clearly, Rules 1, 2 and 3 are all true for the graph with 2 potential edges. Assume that Rule 3 is true for graphs with k potential edges. We now consider the case where the graph has $k+1$ edges. Similar to the proof of Rule 1, we introduce two policies $\widetilde{\mathcal{A}}$ and $\mathcal{A}$, both of which always follow Rules 1 and 2. $\widetilde{\mathcal{A}}$ first tests an edge connecting C_S to C_1, as prescribed by Rule 3. If it finds an edge, then by Rule 1 it subsequently tests edges from C_1 to C_D. If not, according to Rule 2, the same cut continues to be minimum, and by induction, since the number of potential edges is reduced by one after the first test, it continues to test the remaining edges between C_1 and C_S. In contrast, the policy $\mathcal{A}$ violates Rule 3 on the first

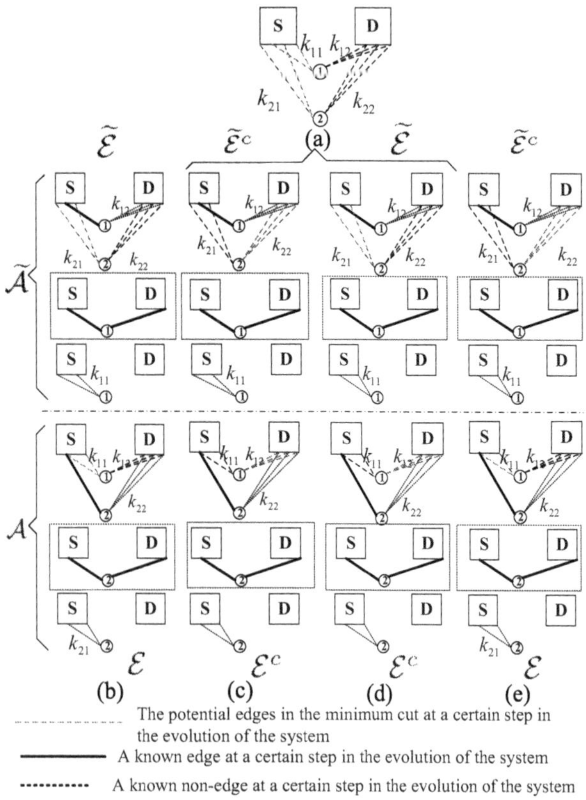

Figure 4: The illustration of the four cases ($\widetilde{\mathcal{E}}$,$\mathcal{E}$), ($\widetilde{\mathcal{E}}^c$,$\mathcal{E}^c$), ($\widetilde{\mathcal{E}}$,$\mathcal{E}^c$) and ($\widetilde{\mathcal{E}}^c$,$\mathcal{E}$).

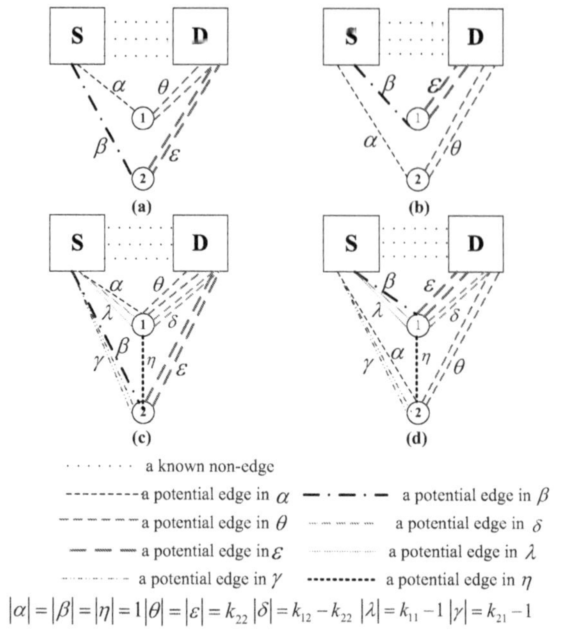

Figure 5: The stochastic coupling of the edges under policy $\widetilde{\mathcal{A}}$ (shown in (a)) and policy $\mathcal{A}$ (shown in (b)).

test by testing an edge connecting to C_2, and then follows the optimal policy for the graph with k edges. We have four possible cases, which are listed as follows:

$\widetilde{\mathcal{E}}$: $\widetilde{\mathcal{A}}$ finds an edge between C_S and C_1, and subsequently no edges between C_1 and C_D, and then the minimum cut turns out to be on the same side as C_S; or $\widetilde{\mathcal{A}}$ finds an edge between C_S and C_1 and subsequently an edge between C_1 and C_D; or $\widetilde{\mathcal{A}}$ finds no edges between C_S and C_1.

$\widetilde{\mathcal{E}}^c$ $\widetilde{\mathcal{A}}$: finds an edge between C_S and C_1, and subsequently no edges between C_1 and C_D, and the minimum cut therefore subsequently switches to the side of C_D.

$\mathcal{E}$: $\mathcal{A}$ finds an edge between C_S and C_2, and subsequently no edges between C_2 and C_D, and then the minimum cut turns out to be on the same side as C_S; or $\mathcal{A}$ finds an edge between C_S and C_2 and subsequently an edge between C_2 and C_D; or $\mathcal{A}$ finds no edges between C_S and C_2.

$\mathcal{E}^c$: $\mathcal{A}$ finds an edge between C_S and C_2, and subsequently no edges between C_2 and C_D, and the minimum cut therefore subsequently switches to the side of C_D.

The four cases, i.e., ($\widetilde{\mathcal{E}}$,$\mathcal{E}$), ($\widetilde{\mathcal{E}}^c$,$\mathcal{E}^c$), ($\widetilde{\mathcal{E}}$,$\mathcal{E}^c$) and ($\widetilde{\mathcal{E}}^c$,$\mathcal{E}$) are illustrated in Figures 4(b), (c), (d) and (e), respectively. Consider Figure 4(b), which is the case ($\widetilde{\mathcal{E}}$,$\mathcal{E}$). We will prove using a stochastic coupling argument that testing C_1 first leads to smaller expected cost. We couple the edges labeled with the same symbol (e.g., β) tested under $\widetilde{\mathcal{A}}$ and $\mathcal{A}$, as shown in Figures 5 (a), (b), (c) and (d). Note in particular that, edges in α and β under policy $\widetilde{\mathcal{A}}$ are switched under policy $\mathcal{A}$, and edges in θ and ε under policy $\widetilde{\mathcal{A}}$ are also switched under policy $\mathcal{A}$, as shown in Figures 5 (a) and (b). The edges in δ, λ, γ and η under policy $\widetilde{\mathcal{A}}$ are the same as those in δ, λ, γ and η under policy $\mathcal{A}$, as shown in Figures 5 (c) and (d). The edges with different labels are defined in Table 2. Since testing each potential edge has two possible outcomes depending on whether it exists or not, the corresponding sample paths generated under $\widetilde{\mathcal{A}}$ and $\mathcal{A}$ are illustrated in Figures 6 (a) and (b), respectively. The nodes in the figures represent the tested edges, while the outcome of each tested edge is indicated by a label, 1 if it exists, or 0 otherwise. Let $P_{D,i}$ ($i = 1, 2, \ldots$) be the ith path where C_S and C_D are found to be disconnected under $\widetilde{\mathcal{A}}$ ($\mathcal{A}$), and let $P_{C,i}$ be ($i = 1, 2, \ldots$) the ith path where C_S and C_D are found to be connected under $\widetilde{\mathcal{A}}$ ($\mathcal{A}$). Note that the paths with the same label have the same probability. As an example, consider paths labeled as $P_{D,4}$ in both Figures 6 (a) and (b). We can see that the outcome 0 from node α in Figure 6(a) has the same probability as the outcome 0 from nodes β in Figure 6(b). The outcome 1 from node β in Figure 6(a) has the same probability as the outcome 1 from node α in Figure 6(b). Nodes α and β have the same number of edges, and the outcomes of the edges from nodes θ, δ, ε and λ are the same in both figures. Another example is the paths labeled with $P_{C,2}$ in both figures. It can be seen that the outcome 1 from node θ in Figure 6(a) has the same probability as the outcome 1 from node ε in Figure 6(b). Nodes θ and ε have the same number of edges, and the outcomes of the edges emanating from nodes α and λ are the same in both figures. Similar relationships hold for the remaining paths with the same labels in Figures 4 (a) and (b), and we therefore omit their explanations. As for the paths $\widetilde{P}_{D,1}$ and $\widetilde{P}_{D,2}$ in Figure 6(a) and paths $\widehat{P}_{D,1}$ and $\widehat{P}_{D,2}$ in Figure 6(b), it is trivially true that any terminating time belonging to the range $[k_{12}+2, 1+k_{11}+k_{12}]$

under the paths $\widetilde{P}_{D,1}$ and $\widetilde{P}_{D,2}$ can also be found under the paths $\widehat{P}_{D,1}$ and $\widehat{P}_{D,2}$. Therefore, the only paths that have different probabilities are shown in the form of bold lines under both $\widetilde{\mathcal{A}}$ and $\mathcal{A}$ (specifically, path $\alpha\theta^c\delta$ under $\widetilde{\mathcal{A}}$, and paths $\alpha\theta^c\beta\delta$, $\alpha\theta^c\beta^c\lambda\delta$ and $\alpha^c\lambda^c\beta\varepsilon^c\delta$ under A.). Obviously, $\alpha\theta^c\delta$ dominates the paths $\alpha\theta^c\beta\delta$, $\alpha\theta^c\beta^c\lambda\delta$ and $\alpha^c\lambda^c\beta\varepsilon^c\delta$, which indicates that testing C_1 first will lead to smaller expected cost. This completes the proof of the case in Figure 4(b).

Table 2: Definitions of the edges for coupling $\widetilde{\mathcal{A}}$ and $\mathcal{A}$

Notation	Definition
α	The first potential edge that policy $\widetilde{\mathcal{A}}$ ($\mathcal{A}$) tests.
β	The first potential edge that policy $\widetilde{\mathcal{A}}$ ($\mathcal{A}$) tests between C_S and C_2 (C_1).
θ	The first k_{22} potential edges that policy $\widetilde{\mathcal{A}}$ ($\mathcal{A}$) tests after an edge is found between C_1 (C_2) and C_S. Recall that $k_{12} \geq k_{22}$.
ε	k_{22} potential edges to be tested by policy $\widetilde{\mathcal{A}}$ ($\mathcal{A}$) after β is found to exist.
δ	The $k_{12} - k_{22}$ remaining potential edges yet to be tested by policy $\widetilde{\mathcal{A}}$ ($\mathcal{A}$) between C_D and C_1, after no edges are found to exist in θ (ε).
λ	The $k_{11} - 1$ remaining potential edges yet to be tested by policy $\widetilde{\mathcal{A}}$ ($\mathcal{A}$) between C_S and C_1, after the first edge between C_S and C_1 is found to not exist.
γ	The $k_{21} - 1$ remaining potential edges between C_S and C_2.
η	The potential edge between C_1 and C_2.

Next we turn to the case ($\widetilde{\mathcal{E}}^c$,$\mathcal{E}^c$) shown in Figure 4(c). The paths generated under $\widetilde{\mathcal{A}}$ and $\mathcal{A}$ using coupling are illustrated in Figures 7 (a) and (b), respectively. Again, the paths with the same label have the same probability, and they can be checked as in the aforementioned case ($\widetilde{\mathcal{E}}$,$\mathcal{E}$). As for the paths $\widetilde{P}_{D,1}$ and $\widetilde{P}_{D,2}$ in Figure 7(a) and paths $\widehat{P}_{D,1}$ and $\widehat{P}_{D,2}$ in Figure 7(b), it is trivially true that any terminating time belonging to the range $[k_{12} + k_{21} + k_{22} + 2, k_{11} + k_{12} + k_{21} + k_{22} + 1]$ under the paths $\widetilde{P}_{D,1}$ and $\widetilde{P}_{D,2}$ can also be found under the paths $\widehat{P}_{D,1}$ and $\widehat{P}_{D,2}$. The same conclusion also holds for the paths $\widetilde{P}_{C,1}$ and $\widetilde{P}_{C,2}$ in Figure 7(a), and paths $\widehat{P}_{C,1}$ and $\widehat{P}_{C,2}$ in Figure 7(b). Hence, we highlight the paths that will terminate in different time with bold lines under both $\widetilde{\mathcal{A}}$ and $\mathcal{A}$ (specifically path $\alpha\theta^c\delta$ under $\widetilde{\mathcal{A}}$ and paths $\alpha\theta^c\delta\beta$, $\alpha\theta^c\delta\beta^c\lambda$ and $\alpha^c\lambda^c\beta\varepsilon^c\delta$ under $\mathcal{A}$.). Obviously, $\alpha\theta^c\delta$ terminates earlier than $\alpha\theta^c\delta\beta$, $\alpha\theta^c\delta\beta^c\lambda$ as well as $\alpha^c\lambda^c\beta\varepsilon^c\delta$, which indicates that testing C_1 first will lead to smaller expected cost. This completes the proof of the case in Figure 4(c).

Now we proceed to prove cases ($\widetilde{\mathcal{E}}$,$\mathcal{E}^c$) and ($\widetilde{\mathcal{E}}^c$,$\mathcal{E}$), shown in Figures 4(d) and 4(e), respectively. We first consider case ($\widetilde{\mathcal{E}}$,$\mathcal{E}^c$). This case implies that the minimum cut turns out to be on the same side of C_S, after an edge is found between C_1 and C_S but no edges are found between C_1 and C_D by $\widetilde{\mathcal{A}}$. Due to Rule 2, it leads to smaller expected cost for $\widetilde{\mathcal{A}}$ to subsequently test the edges between C_2 and C_S rather than those between C_2 and C_D. This means the expected cost of case ($\widetilde{\mathcal{E}}$,$\mathcal{E}^c$) is smaller than that of case ($\widetilde{\mathcal{E}}^c$,$\mathcal{E}^c$). Moreover, we have already proved that the expected cost is smaller

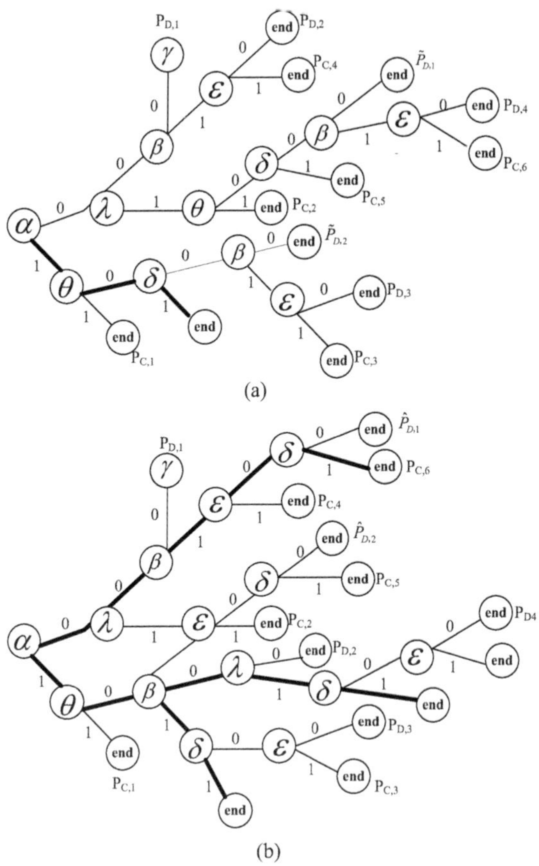

Figure 6: Paths generated by the coupling of $\widetilde{\mathcal{A}}$ (a) and $\mathcal{A}$ (b) for the case shown in Figure 4(b).

under policy $\widetilde{\mathcal{A}}$ in case ($\widetilde{\mathcal{E}}^c$,$\mathcal{E}^c$). By transitivity, we conclude that $\widetilde{\mathcal{A}}$ leads to smaller cost than $\mathcal{A}$ does in case ($\widetilde{\mathcal{E}}$,$\mathcal{E}^c$). Now consider the last case, ($\widetilde{\mathcal{E}}^c$,$\mathcal{E}$). This case implies that the minimum cut switches to the side of C_D, after an edge is found between C_1 and C_S but no edges are found between C_1 and C_D by $\widetilde{\mathcal{A}}$. According to Rule 2, it incurs smaller expected cost if $\widetilde{\mathcal{A}}$ subsequently tests the edges between C_2 and C_D rather than those between C_2 and C_S. Since we have already proved that the cost is smaller under policy $\widetilde{\mathcal{A}}$ in case ($\widetilde{\mathcal{E}}$,$\mathcal{E}$), it follows that by transitivity that $\widetilde{\mathcal{A}}$ leads to smaller expected cost than $\mathcal{A}$ in case ($\widetilde{\mathcal{E}}^c$,$\mathcal{E}$). □

The low complexity of the policy, of no more than 30 $\log_2 n$ operations per step, follows from the fact that except for C_S and C_D, all other components are singletons, and moreover are only of three kinds, either having a known non-edge to S, or a known non-edge to D, or neither. Hence all computations involving these components are extremely simple.

5. EXTENSION TO GENERAL GRAPHS

In this section, we indicate extensions of the optimality results, without proofs, to certain more general classes of random graphs.

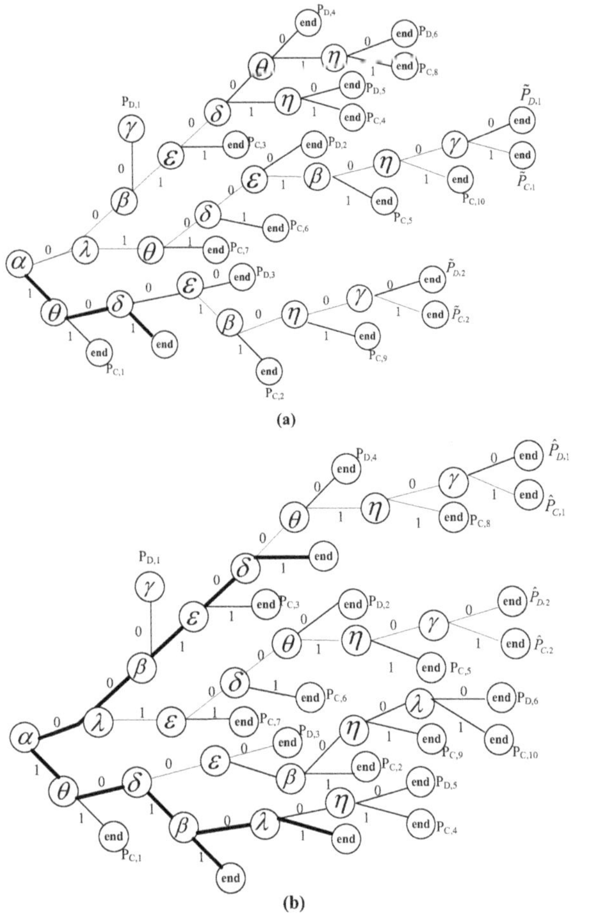

Figure 7: Paths generated by the coupling of $\widetilde{\mathcal{A}}$ (a) and $\mathcal{A}$ (b) for the case shown in Figure 4(c).

5.1 (1,p) Random Graphs

By a (1,p) random graph, we mean a graph that initially contains two types of edges, "1" edges and "p" edges. The former are edges that are known to exist, i.e., exist with probability one, while the latter are potential edges that independently exist with probability p. The Alternating Policy remains optimal under the condition that the size of each component, excluding C_S and C_D, is the same.

5.2 (1,0,p) Random Graphs

By a (1,0,p) random graph, we mean a graph that also initially contains "0" edges. A "0" edge is simply an edge that we already know to not exist. Unfortunately, determining the optimal policy for all types of (1,0,p) random graphs appears to be intractable. The Alternating Policy remains optimal for certain types of (1,0,p) graph patterns – series graphs, parallel graphs, SP graphs, PS graphs, series of parallel of series (SPS) graphs and parallel of series of parallel (PSP) graphs.

5.2.1 Optimal policy for Series of Parallel (SP) Graphs

An SP graph consists of several parallel graphs arranged in series, as shown in Figure 8. It consists of n parallel graphs labeled $\mathcal{P}_1, \mathcal{P}_2, \ldots, \mathcal{P}_n$, with m_i potential edges (i.e., existing independently with equal probability p) in the ith parallel graph.

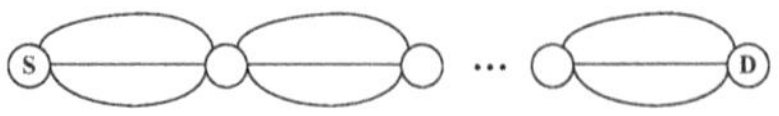

Figure 8: A series of parallel (SP) graph.

THEOREM 1. *The optimal policy is to test the parallel subgraph with the fewest number of potential edges.*

5.2.2 Optimal Policy for Parallel of Series (PS) Graphs

A PS graph consists of a series graphs arranged in parallel, as shown in Figure 9. It consists of n series graphs labeled $\mathcal{S}_1, \mathcal{S}_2, \ldots, \mathcal{S}_n$, with m_i potential edges in the ith series graph.

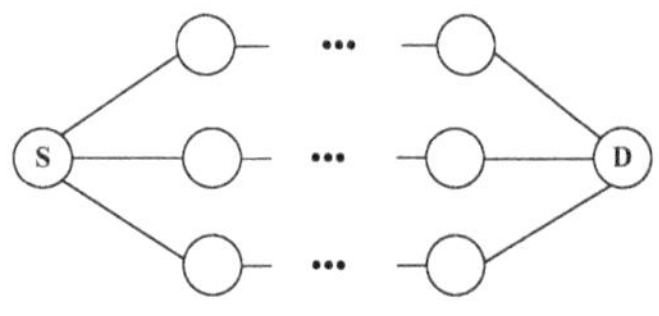

Figure 9: A parallel of series (PS) graph.

THEOREM 2. *The optimal policy is to test any edge on the series subgraph that contains the fewest number of potential edges.*

5.2.3 The Optimal Policy for SPS Graphs

An SPS graph consists of several PS graphs arranged in series, as shown in Figure 10. It consists of n PS graphs labeled $\mathcal{PS}_1, \mathcal{PS}_2, \ldots, \mathcal{PS}_n$, with m_i potential edges in the ith ($1 \le i \le n$) PS graph.

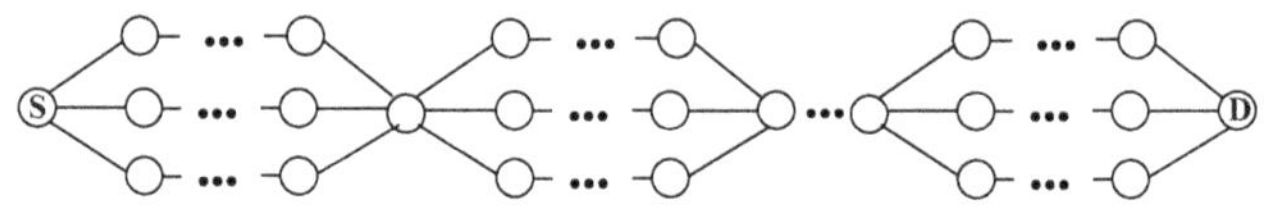

Figure 10: A series of parallel of series (SPS) graph.

THEOREM 3. *The optimal policy is to test any edge in that series graph which has the fewest number of edges in the PS graph that contains the minimum number of series graphs.*

5.2.4 The Optimal Policy for PSP Graphs

A PSP graph consists of several SP graphs arranged in parallel, as shown in Figure 11. It consists of n SP graphs labeled as $\mathcal{SP}_1, \mathcal{SP}_2, \ldots, \mathcal{SP}_n$, with m_i potential edges in the ith ($1 \le i \le n$) SP graph.

THEOREM 4. *The optimal policy is to test any edge in that parallel graph which contains the fewest number of edges in the SP graph that contains the minimum number of parallel graphs.*

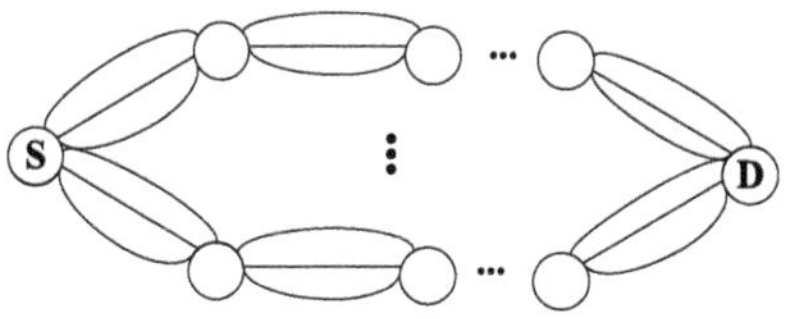

Figure 11: A parallel of series of parallel (PSP) graph.

6. CONCLUSION

We have studied the problem of optimally determining S-D connectivity of random graphs. We have considered the class of classic ER Random Graphs with a finite number n of nodes, for any value of n. Assuming that each testing of an edge has the same unit cost, we have determined a policy for establishing whether the designated source and destination are connected with minimum expected cost. Interestingly, though ER graphs exhibit a sharp transition between disconnectivity of the entire graph and connectivity of the entire graph around $p = \ln n/n$, the optimal policy turns out to not depend on the specific value of p, or even of which side of the phase transition p lies. The policy simply contracts each known connected component to a single super node at each step, and in that condensation multigraph it simply tests an edge that is both on the shortest path containing the super nodes containing S and D, as well as on a minimum S-D cut, giving higher priority to sampling the edges that will lead to more opportunities for S-D connectivity. The policy is also extendable to certain types of more generalized graph structures consisting of additional deterministic structure.

Acknowledgement

This paper is partially based on work supported by NSF under Contract Nos. CNS-1302182 and CCF-0939370, and AFOSR under Contract No. FA-9550-13-1-0008, and NSF China (No. 61325012, 61271219), and National Key Project (2012ZX03002009-004).

7. REFERENCES

[1] E. N. Gilbert. Random graphs. *Annals of Mathematical Statistics*, 30(4):1141–1144, 1959.

[2] P. Erdos and A. Renyi. On random graphs. I. *Publicationes Mathematicae 6*, pages 290–297, 1959.

[3] P. Erdos and A. Renyi. On the evolution of random graphs. *the Mathematical Institute of the Hungarian Academy of Sciences 5*, 17-61, 1960.

[4] E. N. Gilbert. Random plane networks. *J. SIAM*, 9:533–543, Dec. 1961.

[5] M. D. Penrose. The longest edge of the random minimal spanning tree. *The Annals of Probability*, 7:340–361, 1997.

[6] P. Gupta and P. R. Kumar. Critical power for asymptotic connectivity in wireless networks. *Stochastic Analysis, Control, Optimization and Applications: A Volume in Honor of W.H. Fleming, W.M. McEneaney, G. Yin, and Q. Zhang*, pages 547–566, 1998.

[7] C. Bettstetter. On the minimum node degree and connectivity of a wireless multihop network. *Proc. of ACM MobiHoc*, 2002.

[8] F. Xue and P. R. Kumar. The number of neighbors needed for connectivity of wireless networks. *Wireless Networks*, 10:169–181, Mar. 2004.

[9] F. Xue and P. R. Kumar. On the theta-coverage and connectivity of large random networks. *Joint Special Issue of IEEE Trans. on Inform. Theory and IEEE/ACM Trans.s on Netw. and Inform. Theory*, 52:2289–2399, June 2006.

[10] P. Balister, B. Bollobas, A. Sarkar, and M. Walters. Connectivity of random k-nearest-neighbour graphs. *Advances in Applied Probability*, 37:1–24.

[11] O. Dousse, P. Mannersalo, and P. Thiran. Latency of wireless sensor networks with uncoordinated power saving mechanisms. *Proc. of ACM MobiHoc'04*, May 2004.

[12] H. M. Ammari and S. K. Das. Asymptotic critical transmission radius for k-connectivity in wireless ad hoc networks. *IEEE Trans. Para. and Dis. System*, 20:872–885, 2009.

[13] P. J. Wan and C. W. Yi. Critical density for coverage and connectivity in three-dimensional wireless sensor networks using continuum percolation. *IEEE/ACM Transactions on Networks and Information Theory*, 56:2867–2874, May 2010.

[14] X. L. Bai, C. Zhang, D. Xuan, and W. J. Jia. Full-coverage and k-connectivity ($k = 14, 6$) three dimensional networks. *Proc. of IEEE INFOCOM*, July 2009.

[15] X. Wang, X. Lin, Q. Wang, and W. Luan. Mobility increases the connectivity of wireless networks. *IEEE/ACM Trans. on Netw.*, 21:440–454, Apr. 2012.

[16] P. Erdos, E. M. Palmer, and R. W. Robinson. Local connectivity of a random graph. *J. of Graph Theory*, 7(4):411–417, 1983.

[17] B. Bollobas, S. Janson, and O. Riordan. The phase transition in inhomogeneous random graphs. *J. Random Structures and Algorithms*, 31(1):3–122, 2007.

[18] G. Han and A. M. Makowski. One-dimensional geometric random graphs with nonvanishing densities: Part I: A strong zero-one law for connectivity. *J. IEEE. Trans. on Inform. Theory*, 55(12):5832–5839, 2009.

[19] M. D. Penrose. On k-connectivity for a geometric random graph. *Random Structure and Algorithms*, 15(2):145–164, Sept. 1999.

[20] C. Hirsch, D. Neuhauser, and V. Schmidt. Connectivity of random geometric graphs related to minimal spanning forests. *Advances in Applied Probability*, 45:1–36, 2013.

[21] L. Devroye and N. Fraiman. Connectivity of inhomogeneous random graphs. *J. Random Structures and Algorithms*, 2013.

Appendix

Appendix A: Proof of Lemma 1

The proof uses stochastic coupling. We need to consider a general hybrid graph that may be the state at some intermediate time. Such a graph will contain C_S, C_D, and some other components with different sizes, as well as some edges that we already know to not exist. Consider such an initial graph state, and consider any policy $\mathcal{A}$ which does not first test a potential direct edge (denoted by d) between C_S and C_D at step 0. (We note that all direct potential edges are identical.). Let $U_i(\omega)$ denote the choice made by $\mathcal{A}$ at a subsequent step i, with ω representing the sample path, with an outcome of sampling being either 1 (edge existing) or 0 (not existing). Denote by $T(\omega)$ the termination time of $\mathcal{A}$, and by $n_d(\omega)$ the first time that A tests d, i.e., $n_d(\omega) = \inf\{t \geq 1 : U(t) = d\}$. Since $\mathcal{A}$ may never get to check d, we say that $n_d(\omega) = +\infty$ if $U_1(\omega) \neq d, U_2(\omega) \neq d, \ldots, U_{T(\omega)}(\omega) \neq d$.

The sequence of edges tested under $\mathcal{A}$ till it terminates can be divided into three cases, as follows:

- Case 1: $\{U_1(\omega), U_2(\omega), \ldots, U_{T(\omega)}(\omega)\}$ where $U_i(\omega) \neq d$, $i = 1, \ldots, T(\omega)$. In this case, we have $T(\omega) < n_d(\omega) = +\infty$.
- Case 2: $\{U_1(\omega), U_2(\omega), \ldots, U_{n_d(\omega)-1}(\omega), U_{n_d(\omega)}(\omega) = d\}$. Obviously, in this case we have $T(\omega) = n_d(\omega)$.
- Case 3: $\{U_1(\omega), U_2(\omega), \ldots, U_{n_d(\omega)-1}(\omega), U_{n_d(\omega)}(\omega) = d, U_{n_d(\omega)+1}(\omega), \ldots, U_{T(\omega)}(\omega)\}$ where we have $T(\omega) > n_d(\omega)$.

Now we construct a family of policies $\{\mathcal{A}^i\}$, where $\mathcal{A}^i$ follows $\mathcal{A}$, except that if $\mathcal{A}$ has not tested d by step i, then $\mathcal{A}^i$ does test d at step i, and subsequently continues to test the same edges tested by $\mathcal{A}$ except delayed by one step, and catches up with $\mathcal{A}$ when $\mathcal{A}$ tests d. We note that each $\mathcal{A}^i$ is a feasible policy, i.e., it only uses information that $\mathcal{A}^i$ will provide (even though it is supposed to emulate $\mathcal{A}$ after step i). In particular, let us consider $\mathcal{A}^1$, where the d is tested at the first step, and which subsequently follows $\mathcal{A}$ (delayed by one step below). Correspondingly, we denote T^i as the termination time of $\mathcal{A}^i$. The sequence of resulting edges tested by $\mathcal{A}^1$ till it terminates has three possible cases.

- Case 1: $\{d\}$ if $T^1 = n_d(\omega)$ or $\{T^1 < n(\omega), e_d = 1\}$.
- Case 2: $\{d, U_1(\omega), U_2(\omega), \ldots, U_{T^1}(\omega)\}$ if $T^1 < n_d(\omega)$ and $e_d = 0$.
- Case 3: $\{d, U_1(\omega), U_2(\omega), \ldots, U_{n_d(\omega)-1}(\omega),$ $U_{n_d(\omega)}(\omega), U_{n_d(\omega)+1}(\omega), \ldots, U_{T^1}(\omega)\}$ if $T^1 > n_d(\omega)$ and $e_d = 0$.

Based on this, T^1 can be expressed as

$$\begin{aligned}|T^1| =& \mathbf{1}\left(T^1 = n_d(\omega)\right) + \mathbf{1}\left(T^1 < n_d(\omega), e_d = 1\right) \\ &+ \mathbf{1}\left(T^1 < n_d(\omega), e_d = 0\right)\left[|T^1| + 1\right] \\ &+ \mathbf{1}\left(T^1 > n_d(\omega), e_d = 0\right)|T^1|.\end{aligned}$$

Based on this, we have

$$\begin{aligned}T^1 - T^i =& \mathbf{1}\left(T^i = n_d(\omega)\right)[1 - T^i] \\ &+ \mathbf{1}\left(T^i < n_d(\omega), d = 1\right)[1 - T^i] \\ &+ \mathbf{1}\left(T^i < n_d(\omega), d = 0\right) 1.\end{aligned}$$

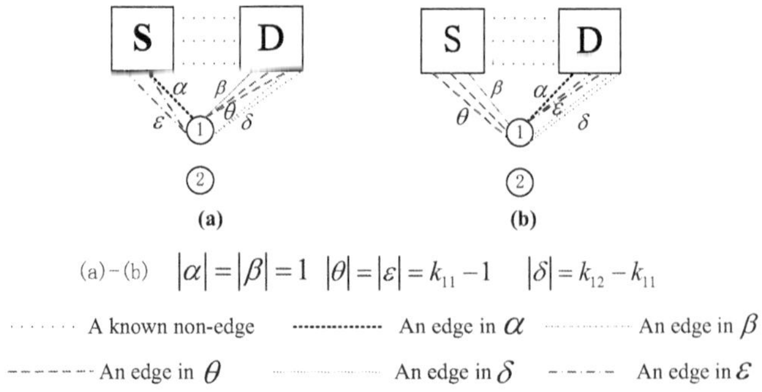

Figure 12: The edges coupled under policies $\widetilde{\mathcal{A}}$ (a) and $\mathcal{A}$ (b).

Now we consider the policy $\mathcal{A}^2$, and define T^2 similarly. Then we have

$$\begin{aligned}\mathbb{E}[T^1 - T^2] &= \mathbb{E}[\mathbf{1}\left(T^2 = 2\right)(1-2) + \mathbf{1}\left(T^2 < 2, e_d = 1\right)(1-1) \\ &\quad + \mathbf{1}\left(T^2 < 2, e_d = 0\right)|T|] \\ &= \mathbb{E}\left[\mathbf{1}(T^2 = 2)(-1) + \mathbf{1}(T^2 = 1, e_d = 0)\right] \\ &= -p + 0 = -p.\end{aligned}$$

Hence $\mathcal{A}^1$ has lower cost than $\mathcal{A}^2$. Similarly, we can prove that each $\mathcal{A}^i$ has lower cost than $\mathcal{A}^{i+1}$. Noting that $\mathcal{A}^N = \mathcal{A}$, we thus conclude that $\mathcal{A}^1$ has lower cost than $\mathcal{A}$, proving the lemma. □

Appendix B: Proof of Lemma 3

We prove by induction on the number of steps. Clearly, by Lemma 1, the conclusion holds at step 1. Suppose it is true till a certain step t. From Lemma 2, it follows that all the edges in the minimum cut at step t are either all between C_S and $\cup_{i=1}^r C_i$, or they are all between C_D and $\cup_{i=1}^r C_i$. Furthermore, since all those edges are also along all the potential shortest paths, they also belong to the set $\mathcal{L}$. Without loss of generality, suppose that all the edges in $\mathcal{L}$ at step t are between C_S and $\cup_{i=1}^r C_i$. Now we consider step $t+1$.

We introduce two policies $\widetilde{\mathcal{A}}$ and $\mathcal{A}$, where $\widetilde{\mathcal{A}}$ always follows Rule 2. Specially, at step $t+1$, $\widetilde{\mathcal{A}}$ will test the edges in $\mathscr{M}_{\mathcal{G}_t}$, starting from an edge between some component, say C_1, and C_S. If an edge is found between C_1 and C_S, then, due to Rule 1, $\widetilde{\mathcal{A}}$ subsequently tests all the edges between C_1 and C_D. If not, then the same cut continues to be the minimum cut, and $\widetilde{\mathcal{A}}$ continues to test the remaining edges between C_1 and C_S. In contrast, $\mathcal{A}$ violates Rule 2 at step $t+1$ by testing an edge between C_1 and then follows $\widetilde{\mathcal{A}}$.

We prove that testing the edges between C_1 and C_S leads to smaller expected cost, by again employing a stochastic coupling. Note that the number of edges between C_1 and C_S can be either larger or smaller than the number of the edges between C_1 and C_D. We only consider the former case; the latter is proved similarly. We couple the edges tested under $\widetilde{\mathcal{A}}$ and $\mathcal{A}$, as shown in Figures 12. Table 3 lists the permutations of the nodes labels involved in the coupling. The paths generated under both $\widetilde{\mathcal{A}}$ and $\mathcal{A}$ for the cases in Figures 12(a) and (b) are shown in Figure 13. The nodes in the figures represent the edges tested while the outcomes of the tested edges are indicated using lines with 1 (or 0)

Table 3: Definitions of the edges coupled under $\widetilde{\mathcal{A}}$ and $\mathcal{A}$

Notation	Definition
α	The first potential edge that policy $\widetilde{\mathcal{A}}$ ($\mathcal{A}$) tests.
β	The first potential edge that policy $\widetilde{\mathcal{A}}$ ($\mathcal{A}$) tests between C_1 and C_D (C_S).
θ	The $k_{11}-1$ potential edges that policy $\widetilde{\mathcal{A}}$ ($\mathcal{A}$) tests between C_1 and C_D (C_S) after β is found not to exist between C_1 and C_D (C_S).
δ	The remaining $k_{12}-k_{11}$ ($k_{11}-k_{12}$) potential edges to be tested by policy $\widetilde{\mathcal{A}}$ ($\mathcal{A}$) between C_D and C_1.
ε	The remaining $k_{11}-1$ potential edges between C_1 and C_S to be tested by policy $\widetilde{\mathcal{A}}$ and the $k_{11}-1$ potential edges between C_1 and C_D to be tested by policy $\mathcal{A}$.

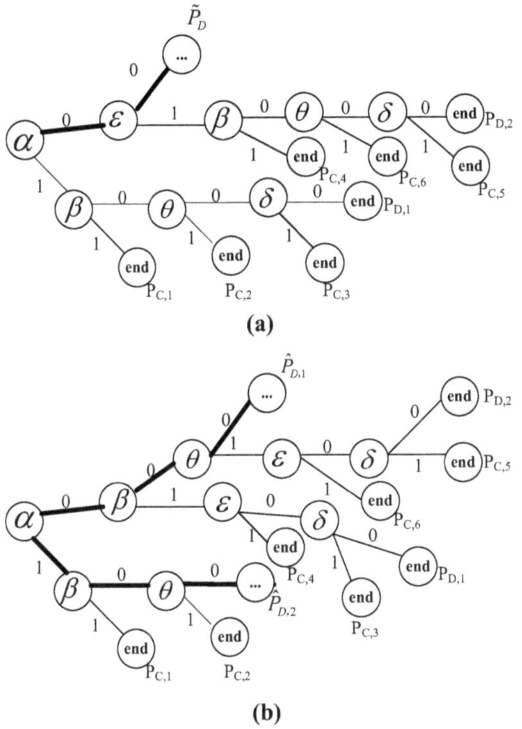

Figure 13: Paths generated by the coupling on $\widetilde{\mathcal{A}}$ (a) and $\mathcal{A}$ (b) for the case shown in Figures 12 (a)-(b).

meaning that the edges turn out to exist (or not exist). The paths that terminate at the same time are marked with the same labels under $\widetilde{\mathcal{A}}$ and $\mathcal{A}$. The two paths highlighted in bold lines in Figure 13(b), i.e., $\hat{P}_{D,1}$ and $\hat{P}_{D,2}$, represent the graph states where none of the edges between C_1 and C_S exist while one edge between C_1 and C_D is found to exist in $\hat{P}_{D,2}$ and not to exist in $\hat{P}_{D,1}$ under policy $\mathcal{A}$. The path in bold line in Figure 13(a) represents the graph state where none of the edges between C_1 and C_S exist under policy $\widetilde{\mathcal{A}}$, with the circle containing dots being the possible edges that $\widetilde{\mathcal{A}}$ will subsequently test. Notice that if the circle represents an edge between C_1 and C_D, i.e., if $\widetilde{\mathcal{A}}$ chooses to test an edge between C_1 and C_D, then both Figures 13(a) and (b) will have the same termination probability. However, the expected cost will be smaller if $\widetilde{\mathcal{A}}$ tests any edge between C_S (C_D) and one of the remaining components. Similarly, we can prove that the expected cost can be even smaller if the edge tested belongs to the remaining edges in $\mathcal{L}$. The proof is completed by checking all the components. □

Supporting Mobile Users in Database-Driven Opportunistic Spectrum Access*

Bo Gao
Department of Electrical and Computer Engineering
Virginia Tech
Blacksburg, Virginia, USA
bgao@vt.edu

Jung-Min "Jerry" Park
Department of Electrical and Computer Engineering
Virginia Tech
Blacksburg, Virginia, USA
jungmin@vt.edu

Yaling Yang
Department of Electrical and Computer Engineering
Virginia Tech
Blacksburg, Virginia, USA
yyang8@vt.edu

ABSTRACT

In database-driven opportunistic spectrum access, location information of secondary users plays an important role. In a database query-and-update procedure, a secondary user reports to the geolocation database of its location information, so that the updated knowledgebase facilitates location-aided incumbent protection and network coexistence. However, such database-driven spectrum sharing becomes very challenging when the secondary users are mobile. In this paper, we propose a probabilistic coexistence framework that supports mobile users by incorporating the solutions to solve two core problems: (i) white space allocation (WSA) at the database and (ii) location update control (LUC) at the users. We frame the two problems such that they interact through dynamic control of the users' location uncertainty levels. For WSA, we derive a centralized real-time solution to mitigate mutual interference among secondary users and protect primary users against harmful interference. For LUC, we design a local two-level strategy to enable both movement-driven and interference-driven control of location uncertainty. This strategy makes an appropriate trade-off between the effectiveness of interference mitigation and the cost of database queries. To evaluate our algorithms, we have carried out both theoretical model-driven and real-world trace-driven simulation experiments. Our simulation results show that the proposed framework can determine and adapt the database query intervals of mobile users to achieve near-optimal interference mitigation with minimal location updates.

Categories and Subject Descriptors

C.2.1 [**Computer-Communication Networks**]: Network Architecture and Design

Keywords

Opportunistic spectrum access; geolocation database; spectrum sharing; mobility management

*This work was partially sponsored by the National Science Foundation through grants CNS-1054697, CNS-1228903, CNS-1314598, and IIP-1265886.

MobiHoc'14, August 11–14, 2014, Philadelphia, PA, USA.

http://dx.doi.org/10.1145/2632951.2632984.

1. INTRODUCTION

In opportunistic spectrum access (OSA), primary users (a.k.a. incumbent users) and secondary users are usually co-located and share the same swaths of spectrum. Incumbent protection (i.e., primary-secondary spectrum sharing) then becomes the major concern, and can be addressed by spectrum sensing techniques and/or geolocation database services. Protecting incumbent users while effectively identifying white spaces is challenging when spectrum sharing relies solely on sensing-only cognitive radios (CRs) [1, 2]. Here, the "white space" refers to fallow spectrum that secondary users can use under the constraint that they do not cause harmful interference to primary users. For this reason, database-driven white space networks [3, 4, 5] have found favor with the spectrum regulators and the wireless industry. Henceforth, we assume a database-driven spectrum sharing system that is consistent with the Spectrum Access System (SAS) for spectrum sharing in the 3.5 GHz band [6, 7], which has recently been proposed by the Federal Communications Commission (FCC). A geolocation database has access to the operating characteristics of incumbent users, such as service types, channel reservations, and protection requirements. In database-driven OSA, a registered secondary user (or its home base station) exchanges information with the geolocation database through a database query-and-update procedure. On the one hand, the user queries the database by its location information and retrieves local white space availability. On the other hand, the user updates the database with its operating information, including its location, so that the updated knowledgebase can facilitate location-aided incumbent protection and network coexistence (i.e., secondary-secondary spectrum sharing) [6, 7, 8, 9].

The above database-driven spectrum sharing system can work well with static secondary networks. However, when the secondary users are *mobile*, the problem of incumbent protection becomes very challenging [4, 10]. Furthermore, the problem of network coexistence, i.e., spatial spectrum reuse and mutual interference mitigation among mobile secondary users, is even more difficult, and has not been addressed in the existing work. When supporting mobile users, each user can query and update the database at a fixed interval, and the *database query interval* (or location update interval) is a key operational parameter that impacts the performance of the spectrum sharing system [7]. On the one hand, during these intervals, the database may have to rely on past location information to ensure incumbent protection and mitigate mutual interference. This leads to considerable loss of white space opportunities [4] and increased likelihood of suboptimal resource allocations. On the other hand, it can be unacceptable to blindly reduce the intervals because of limited database processing capacity, significant communication overhead rise, and needless network resource waste. This causes the database to become a bottleneck in processing spectrum sharing information. The goal of this paper is to study the strategies for determining and adapting the database query intervals to strike an appropriate trade-off between interference-aware spectrum sharing and cost-effective database access. To the best of our knowledge, this paper is the first work addressing this problem.

We focus on two major problems for supporting secondary user mobility: (i) *white space allocation* (WSA) and (ii) *location update control* (LUC). The database performs WSA and centrally allocates white spaces for secondary users based on their probabilistic *location uncertainty* levels to mitigate co-channel interference among them and ensure no interference with primary users. Each mobile user performs LUC and locally adjusts its location uncertainty level by adapting its database query interval, so that an appropriate trade-off between interference mitigation effectiveness and database query cost can be achieved. The two problems are solved alternately through dynamic control of location uncertainty.

Formulating a solution approach that jointly solves these two problems is challenging. First, the location uncertainty level of a user has to be quantified to model WSA and LUC. Second, the LUC design for each user has to locally adapt database query interval to the time-varying spectrum environment without global knowledge. Third, the WSA design for the database has to promptly adjust resource allocation in response to the dynamic changes in spectrum availability, location uncertainty, and mutual interference probability.

In this paper, we make the following contributions:

- We propose a probabilistic coexistence framework, which incorporates WSA at the database and LUC at the users. This framework jointly addresses the issues of spectrum sharing and database access in database-driven OSA.
- For WSA, we derive a centralized real-time solution that minimizes the probability of mutual interference among secondary users and guarantees full protection of primary users. For LUC, we design a local two-level strategy that minimizes the weighted sum of mutual interference probability and database query frequency (i.e., inverse of the interval). This strategy combines movement-driven and interference-driven control of location uncertainty.
- We evaluate the algorithms for WSA and LUC in two types of simulation experiments. In the first experiment, we have simulated WiFi-like secondary networks using a theoretical mobility model. In the second experiment, we have simulated cellular-like secondary networks using a real-world mobility trace dataset. Our results suggest that the proposed framework determines and adapts the database query intervals of mobile users to realize near-optimal interference mitigation with minimal location updates.
- We provide discussions on system design guidelines and real-world deployment issues in database-driven OSA.

The rest of this paper is organized as follows. Related work is discussed in section 2. System overview is described in section 3. The problems of WSA and LUC are formulated and solved in sections 4 and 5, respectively. Simulation results are shown in section 6. Implementation discussions are presented in section 7, and conclusion is drawn in section 8.

2. RELATED WORK

Recently, the FCC issued a NPRM for enabling small cell use in the 3.5 GHz band [6, 7]. In the proposed framework, spectrum sharing can be achieved among three tiers of users, including tier-1 incumbent access users, tier-2 priority access users, and tier-3 general authorized access users. The tier-1 and tier-2 users are protected in certain exclusion zones, while tier-3 users have to opportunistically access the band. All the users register with the SAS that incorporates a geolocation database and various interference mitigation techniques. The SAS needs to i) specify appropriate operations across the tiers of users based on location-specific data on spectrum occupancy; ii) resolve interference issues promptly; and iii) coordinate the registered users, if necessary, based on user-generated data on spectrum sharing. The SAS is able to collect location information of registered secondary users and achieve location-aided spectrum sharing.

The research on supporting secondary user mobility in OSA is still in its infancy. The problem of protecting primary users from being interfered with by mobile secondary users has been studied in [4, 10]. In [4], the authors propose a service called SenseLess, which is a database-driven white space network. To enable mobile users without loss of white space opportunities, the database query interval of a user traveling at 60 miles/hour is suggested to be shorter than 30 seconds. However, such a high database query frequency may not always be necessary. When the database manages resource allocation, a certain loss of white spaces is acceptable as long as the remaining white spaces can be enough to offer what the user has requested. For a practical database query strategy, one should consider the trade-off between interference mitigation effectiveness and database query cost. Furthermore, the authors oversimplify the way of setting a database query interval—i.e., they propose that the database query interval of a user is inversely proportional to the speed of the user. For a cost-effective database query strategy, however, one should consider the behaviors of all the primary users and coexisting secondary users in the vicinity to determine the interval. In [10], the authors propose enabling mobile users in a sensing-only CR network. To protect primary users under the location uncertainty of a secondary user, a guard distance is controlled to enlarge each primary exclusion zone for an extra protection. In database-driven spectrum sharing, however, it would be more challenging to achieve the coexistence of mobile secondary users due to the need for dynamic control of both interfering and interfered users' location uncertainty levels.

In CR networks without the issue of location uncertainty, the problems of joint resource allocation have been studied in [11, 12, 13, 14, 15]. In our problem, however, we try to find out how certain a location estimate should be to jointly optimize spectrum sharing and database access.

3. SYSTEM OVERVIEW

In this section, we introduce our coexistence framework and explain basic assumptions and system model.

3.1 Basic Assumptions

We assume a spectrum sharing system similar to that in the 3.5 GHz band [6, 7]. A set of primary users $\mathcal{P}$ and a set of secondary users $\mathcal{S}$ are co-located and share the same set of channels $\mathcal{K}$. The primary users are protected from any harmful interference in certain pre-defined exclusion zones, while the secondary users have to tolerate harmful interference from others. All the users register with a central database server similar to the SAS in the 3.5 GHz band, which operates a geolocation database with the database query-and-update functionality and performs WSA for the registered users. In this work, the terms "central database server" and "database" will be used interchangeably. The

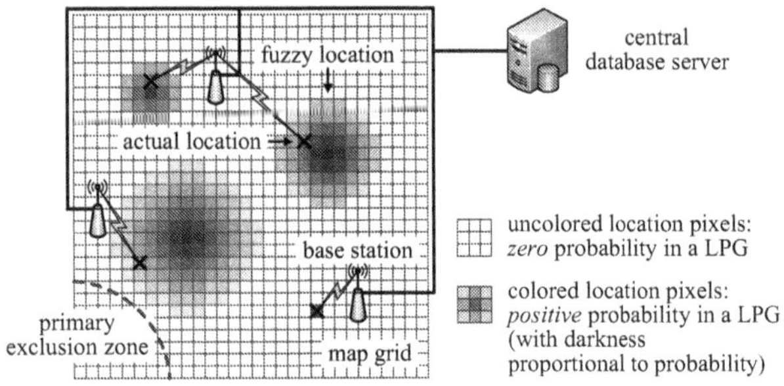

Figure 1: A database-driven spectrum sharing scenario.

base stations offer the interfaces between the registered users and the database. Each user $s \in \mathcal{S}$ can be mobile, and performs LUC for itself. At a certain interval, it updates the database with its current operating information, including its location, and queries the database for location-specific resource allocation. We assume that the users do not share location information among each other for privacy protection and overhead reduction. We assume a time-slot-based system. At the beginning of each time slot, location updates are submitted from the users according to the decisions for LUC in the previous time slot. Using the location updates, the database makes a decision for WSA and notifies the users of changed resource allocation when necessary through their home base stations. Note that even if a user does not query the database, the database still computes resource allocation based on its estimation of the user's location. In this work, a database query is equivalent to a location update. A user accesses the database at most once in each time slot.

3.2 Location Probability Grid

The issues of incumbent protection and spectrum reuse in database-driven spectrum sharing rely on the location information of secondary users. When the users are mobile, their locations can become uncertain and thus affect resource allocation decisions. Hence, a database-driven system needs to quantify the location uncertainty level of a user between successive location update events so that the decisions for WSA and LUC can be adjusted accordingly. In this work, we utilize *location probability grids* (LPGs) to achieve this. In the current designs of geolocation databases, spectrum availability is computed for each location pixel in a pre-defined map grid $\mathcal{L}$ (e.g., a map grid with the granularity of 50m×50m pixel). Hence, as illustrated in Figure 1, we can define a LPG for each mobile user as the probability distribution of the user's location estimate over the map grid $\mathcal{L}$. For each user $s \in \mathcal{S}$, its LPG is defined by $\mathcal{Q}_s(t) \triangleq \{q_{s,l}(t) \text{ for } l \in \mathcal{L}\}$, where each $q_{s,l}(t)$ is the probability that user s is at location pixel l in time slot t. The LPG of each user defines the fuzziness of its location estimate at the database, which is a function of the elapsed time since the latest location update. The *fuzzy location* (or called movement contour) of user s is defined by $\mathcal{L}_s(t) \triangleq \{l \,|\, q_{s,l}(t) > 0 \text{ for } l \in \mathcal{L}\}$, which includes all the possible locations of the user in time slot t. Let $\ell_s(t)$ denote the *actual location* of user s in time slot t, which may not be known by the database. The database has to perform WSA based on the knowledge of LPGs. Each user needs to perform LUC to update its LPG when necessary and make its fuzzy location capture its actual location.

3.3 A Coexistence Framework

Intuitively, there exists a trade-off between interference mitigation effectiveness and database query cost. On the one hand, frequent database access decreases the fuzziness of location estimates and keeps the system deterministic, so that the database can precisely allocate white spaces without losing spectrum opportunities or creating mutual interference. But frequent database access may not always be necessary. For example, when a user occupies a channel exclusively or the user is far away from other co-channel users, fuzzy location of the user is acceptable due to low likelihood of mutual interference. Moreover, too frequent database access may cause delay in server response time or introduce other types of cost such as battery power drain. On the other hand, infrequent database access increases the fuzziness of location estimates, so that large user movement contours may lead to overconservative resource allocation and thus low spectrum utilization. Hence, an optimal database query frequency needs to be found to address the trade-off.

The above trade-off issue involves two problems: (i) WSA, i.e., spectrum sharing controlled by the database; and (ii) LUC, i.e., database access controlled by the mobile users. For WSA, the database first generates LPGs based on the current and past location updates, and then minimizes the probability of mutual interference among secondary users while guaranteeing full protection of primary users based on the updated LPGs. For LUC, the users determine whether to submit location updates next to minimize the weighted sum of mutual interference probability and database query frequency based on the local measurements of user movement and co-channel interference. The problems are solved alternately through the control of LPGs. In the next two sections, the two problems are addressed separately.

4. WHITE SPACE ALLOCATION

In this section, we formulate the problem of WSA and provide a centralized real-time solution.

4.1 Problem Formulation

In each time slot t, the central database server updates its estimation of all the registered users' LPGs based on their current and past location updates. Using the updated LPGs, the database performs WSA to minimize the probability of mutual interference among secondary users under the constraint that the users do not cause harmful interference to primary users. The database achieves this by coordinating the channel assignments and transmit power levels of secondary users. The decision for WSA can be broadcasted to the users through their home base stations.

For WSA that mitigates mutual interference, we need to first create a model of likely interference among secondary users with fuzzy locations. For each user $s \in \mathcal{S}$ and each channel $k \in \mathcal{K}$, define $X_{s,k}(t)$ as a binary channel allocation indicator such that $X_{s,k}(t) = 1$ (0) represents user s is (is not) allocated to channel k in time slot t. Due to spatial spectrum reuse, denote the set of coexisting users that share the same channel k in time slot t by $\mathcal{S}_k(t) \triangleq \{s \,|\, X_{s,k}(t) = 1 \text{ for } s \in \mathcal{S}\} = \{s_1, ..., s_{M_k}\}$. A possible location distribution of the co-channel users is $(l_1, ..., l_{M_k}) \in \mathcal{L}^{M_k}$. Given $\mathcal{Q}_{s_m}(t)$ for all $s_m \in \mathcal{S}_k(t)$, the probability that a particular location distribution $(l_1, ..., l_{M_k})$ happens is $\prod_{m=1}^{M_k} q_{s_m,l_m}(t)$. Thus, the database computes the probability of interference experienced at each user s_m on channel k in time slot t by

$$I_{s_m,k}(t) \triangleq \sum_{(l_1,...,l_{M_k}) \in \mathcal{L}^{M_k}} J_{s_m|l_1,...,l_{M_k}}(t) \prod_{m=1}^{M_k} q_{s_m,l_m}(t), \quad (1)$$

where $J_{s_m|l_1,...,l_{M_k}}(t)$ is a binary interference indicator such that $J_{s_m|l_1,...,l_{M_k}}(t) = 1$ (0) represents certain intolerable interference is (is not) experienced at user s_m for location distribution $(l_1, ..., l_{M_k})$. Given a certain $(l_1, ..., l_{M_k})$, the database can utilize a radio wave propagation model to compute the signal-to-interference-plus-noise ratio (SINR) at the receiver of link s_m, denoted by $R_{s_m|l_1,...,l_{M_k}}(t)$. Here, link s_m refers to the link in which user s_m can be either a transmitter (in the uplink) or a receiver (in the downlink). We consider basic path loss model as an example, and other models can also be applied in our framework. Let

$$R_{s_m|l_1,...,l_{M_k}}(t) = \frac{Y_{s_m,k}(t) H_{l_m,l_m}(t)}{\sum_{\substack{m'=1 \\ m' \neq m}}^{M_k} Y_{s_{m'},k}(t) H_{l_{m'},l_m}(t) + Z_0}, \quad (2)$$

where $Y_{s_m,k}(t)$ is transmit power from link s_m on channel k, $H_{l_m,l_m}(t)$ is transmission gain in link s_m, $H_{l_{m'},l_m}(t)$ is interference gain from link $s_{m'}$ to link s_m, and Z_0 is noise power. Assume a threshold $\check{R}_{s_m}$ such that harmful interference to link s_m occurs if $R_{s_m|l_1,...,l_{M_k}}(t) < \check{R}_{s_m}$. Let

$$J_{s_m|l_1,...,l_{M_k}}(t) = \mathbf{1}\left(R_{s_m|l_1,...,l_{M_k}}(t) < \check{R}_{s_m}\right), \quad (3)$$

where $\mathbf{1}()$ is an indicator function that is equal to 1 (0) if its condition is true (false). Combining (1), (2), and (3), $I_{s,k}(t)$ is a function of $\mathcal{Q}_s(t)$, $X_{s,k}(t)$, $Y_{s,k}(t)$ for $s \in \mathcal{S}$.

Having formulated $I_{s,k}(t)$ under location uncertainty, we can now formulate the problem of WSA. Given $\mathcal{Q}_s(t)$ for all $s \in \mathcal{S}$, the database needs to find $X_{s,k}(t)$ and $Y_{s,k}(t)$ for $s \in \mathcal{S}$, $k \in \mathcal{K}$ to minimize the global objective function

$$I(t) \triangleq \frac{1}{|\mathcal{S}|} \sum_{s \in \mathcal{S}} I_s(t), \quad (4)$$

where $I_s(t)$ is the average value of $I_{s,k}(t)$ over $K_s(t) \triangleq \sum_{k \in \mathcal{K}} X_{s,k}(t)$ channels taken by user s at a time, namely

$$I_s(t) = \frac{1}{K_s(t)} \sum_{k \in \mathcal{K}} X_{s,k}(t) I_{s,k}(t). \quad (5)$$

There are three constraints for WSA. The first constraint ensures the protection of primary users. In database-driven white space networks, primary users are protected in predefined exclusion zones. Hence, all the possible locations of secondary users under location fuzziness must be outside the exclusion zones of co-channel primary users. Suppose each channel k is occupied by a set of primary users $\mathcal{P}_k(t)$ and a set of secondary users $\mathcal{S}_k(t)$. The union of the exclusion zones of primary users in $\mathcal{P}_k(t)$ is defined by $\tilde{X}_{k,l}(t)$, which is a binary channel occupancy indicator such that $\tilde{X}_{k,l}(t) = 1$ (0) represents channel k is not (is) available for secondary users at location pixel l in time slot t. The fuzzy location of each secondary user s is characterized by $\mathcal{L}_s(t)$. Hence, the constraint for incumbent protection is defined as

$$q_{s,l}(t)[1 - (X_{s,k}(t) + \tilde{X}_{k,l}(t))] \geq 0 \quad \text{for } s \in \mathcal{S}, k \in \mathcal{K}, l \in \mathcal{L}. \quad (6)$$

The second constraint avoids secondary user starvation by ensuring a minimum number of channels, $\check{K}_s$, to be taken by each user s, which is expressed as

$$K_s(t) \geq \check{K}_s \text{ for } s \in \mathcal{S}. \quad (7)$$

The third constraint limits the maximum transmit power, $\hat{Y}_s$, of each user s, which is expressed as

$$Y_{s,k}(t) \leq X_{s,k}(t) \hat{Y}_s \text{ for } s \in \mathcal{S}, k \in \mathcal{K}. \quad (8)$$

In summary, the problem of WSA solved at the central database server in time slot t can be written as follows.

Algorithm 1 for WSA at the database in time slot t

1: **compute** $\mathcal{Q}_s(t)$ for $s \in \mathcal{S}$ according to past location update history submitted from user s
2: **for** each generation **do**
3: **clone** a number of best feasible solutions from previous generation as offsprings
4: **select** enough pairs of good feasible solutions from previous generation as parents
5: **for** each pair of parents **do**
6: **reproduce** a pair of offsprings via crossover, which randomly swaps some rows in matrices $[X_{s,k}(t)]_{|\mathcal{S}|\times|\mathcal{K}|}$ for parent 1 and $[X'_{s,k}(t)]_{|\mathcal{S}|\times|\mathcal{K}|}$ for parent 2 (same crossover is applied for $[Y_{s,k}(t)]_{|\mathcal{S}|\times|\mathcal{K}|}$ and $[Y'_{s,k}(t)]_{|\mathcal{S}|\times|\mathcal{K}|}$)
7: **mutate** each offspring according to a probability, where a row in matrix $[X_{s,k}(t)]_{|\mathcal{S}|\times|\mathcal{K}|}$ is randomly reordered without loss of feasibility (same mutation is applied for $[Y_{s,k}(t)]_{|\mathcal{S}|\times|\mathcal{K}|}$)
8: **end for**
9: **break** when runtime reaches a threshold
10: **end for**

Problem 1	(White Space Allocation)
Given:	$\mathcal{Q}_s(t)$ for $s \in \mathcal{S}$;
Find:	$X_{s,k}(t), Y_{s,k}(t)$ for $s \in \mathcal{S}, k \in \mathcal{K}$;
Minimize:	$I(t)$;
Subject to:	(6), (7), (8).

Because each $\mathcal{Q}_s(t)$ for computing $I(t)$ follows a general probability distribution, Problem 1 is a mixed-integer nonlinear program (MINLP), which is NP-hard in general. Furthermore, since the database needs to solve Problem 1 in every time slot, it cannot afford the time to find the real optimal solution. Therefore, we extend the genetic algorithm in [11] to derive a fast heuristic solution to Problem 1.

4.2 A Genetic Algorithm

Due to the complexity of Problem 1 and the requirement of fast database response, we apply a variant of genetic algorithm [11] to derive a solution for WSA iteratively in real time. In Algorithm 1, line 1 updates LPGs for computing the objective value, and line 3 and lines 4-8 implement the two stages of cloning and breeding in a genetic algorithm, respectively. In each step of a generation, the candidate solutions are guaranteed to be feasible to Problem 1. A heuristic solution with the best objective value can be obtained when Algorithm 1 terminates. In section 6, we will evaluate the optimality gap of the solution given by Algorithm 1.

5. LOCATION UPDATE CONTROL

In this section, we formulate the problem of LUC and design a local strategy with no need for global knowledge.

5.1 Problem Formulation

In time slot t, each mobile user $s \in \mathcal{S}$ performs LUC to adjust $\mathcal{Q}_s(t+1)$ for the next WSA by determining whether it wants to submit a location update in the next time slot $t+1$. For user s, define $A_s(t)$ as a binary database query indicator such that $A_s(t) = 1$ (0) represents user s submits (does not submit) a location update to the database in time slot t. In general, $\mathcal{Q}_s(t)$ can be generated by a movement prediction model based on the sequence of $A_s(t')$ for $t' = t, t-1, ...$ and the past location update history in the database.

For LUC that addresses cost-effective database access, we first define the weighted average database query cost (i.e., database query frequency) of mobile users in time slot t by

$$C(t) \triangleq \frac{\theta}{|\mathcal{S}|} \sum_{s \in \mathcal{S}} A_s(t), \quad (9)$$

where θ is a positive weight factor, and can be set to reflect various overhead associated with processing query requests at both servers and devices. It may reflect cost factors such as computing power [4], energy consumption, control communication overhead, server response delay, and resource reallocation frequency. Expression (9) makes the cost function scale proportional to the frequency of database queries.

Having modeled $C(t)$, we can now formulate the problem of LUC, assuming global knowledge of $\mathcal{Q}_s(t)$, $X_{s,k}(t)$, $Y_{s,k}(t)$ for $s \in \mathcal{S}$, $k \in \mathcal{K}$ and future knowledge of $X_{s,k}(t+1)$, $Y_{s,k}(t+1)$ for $s \in \mathcal{S}$, $k \in \mathcal{K}$ at this time. In time slot t, given the solutions to Problem 1 obtained from time slot t and predicted from time slot $t+1$, the mobile users need to find $A_s(t+1)$ for $s \in \mathcal{S}$ to minimize the objective function

$$G(t+1) \triangleq \delta I(t+1) + (1-\delta)C(t+1), \quad (10)$$

where $I(t+1)$ is the objective function of Problem 1, and $\delta \in [0,1]$ is a weight factor that can be set on demand.

In addition to the constraints (6), (7), and (8), there is one more constraint for LUC, which ensures that the estimated $\mathcal{L}_s(t)$ can always capture the actual $\ell_s(t)$. We have

$$\ell_s(t) \in \mathcal{L}_s(t) \text{ for } s \in \mathcal{S}. \quad (11)$$

This constraint (11) is needed to guarantee the effectiveness of incumbent protection and interference mitigation in Problem 1. If any $\ell_s(t) \notin \mathcal{L}_s(t)$ occurs, even though constraint (6) makes sure that $\mathcal{L}_s(t)$ does not overlap with any primary exclusion zone, it is likely that $\ell_s(t)$ moves into an exclusion zone, resulting in harmful interference from user s to primary users. Without constraint (11), it is also possible that the value of $I(t)$ computed using $\mathcal{L}_s(t)$ cannot accurately reflect the actual interference from or to user s located at $\ell_s(t)$.

In summary, the problem of LUC solved at the mobile users in time slot t can be written as follows.

Problem 2 (Location Update Control)
Given: $A_s(t')$ for $t' = t, t-1, \ldots, s \in \mathcal{S}$;
$X_{s,k}(t), Y_{s,k}(t)$ for $s \in \mathcal{S}, k \in \mathcal{K}$;
$X_{s,k}(t+1), Y_{s,k}(t+1)$ for $s \in \mathcal{S}, k \in \mathcal{K}$;
Find: $A_s(t+1)$ for $s \in \mathcal{S}$;
Minimize: $G(t+1)$;
Subject to: (6), (7), (8), (11).

If Problem 2 is solved centrally at the database, constraint (11) cannot be guaranteed. Because user s does not have to continuously query and update the database in every time slot, the database cannot always keep track of $\ell_s(t)$. It is possible that a rapid change in a user's speed or direction makes the estimated movement contour become inaccurate and lose track of the user. This constraint, however, can be easily satisfied at a user. Each user s knows $\ell_s(t)$ (e.g., via GPS) and its past location update history. The user can locally compute $\mathcal{Q}_s(t)$ ($\mathcal{L}_s(t)$) using the same movement prediction model as used at the database [16] and compare it with $\ell_s(t)$ to see whether constraint (11) holds. In the rest of this section, we will derive a local heuristic solution to Problem 2 through a local strategy for setting each $A_s(t+1)$.

5.2 A Local Two-Level Strategy

Solving Problem 2 locally at mobile users is challenging. Each user s cannot have the future knowledge of $\mathcal{Q}_{s'}(t+1)$ for $s' \neq s$ and $X_{s,k}(t+1)$, $Y_{s,k}(t+1)$ for $s \in \mathcal{S}$. As a heuristic, we can assume a short-term prediction based on the correlation between time slot t and time slot $t+1$ [17] and the fact that the local decision of a user has limited impact on the global decision for all the users. We have

$$X_{s,k}(t+1) = X_{s,k}(t), \quad Y_{s,k}(t+1) = Y_{s,k}(t) \text{ for } s \in \mathcal{S}, k \in \mathcal{K}. \quad (12)$$

Then, each user s only needs to set its own $A_s(t+1)$ as a part of a solution to Problem 2. However, user s cannot have the global knowledge of $\mathcal{Q}_{s'}(t)$, $X_{s',k}(t)$, $Y_{s',k}(t)$ for $s' \neq s$. Keeping track of such information locally at each user demands real-time message exchanges among all the users at all time. This is prohibitively expensive and very impractical. Thus, we need to propose a local strategy for each user s to find the proper setting of $A_s(t+1)$ that solves Problem 2 only based on local measurements.

The basic idea for our heuristic local strategy is based on locally evaluating the impact of a location update on the minimization of mutual interference $I(t+1)$ in (10). Local measurements of user movement and co-channel interference can be used to set $A_s(t+1)$ through a two-level strategy. On the first level, a *movement*-driven strategy (MDS) identifies the "must-update" and "no-update" instances with regard to the constraints of Problem 2. A location update is necessary if skipping it will violate constraint (11) or harm spectrum utilization greatly due to white space loss caused by constraint (6). A location update is avoidable if skipping it will not negatively affect interference mitigation and constraint satisfaction. For the instances when MDS is not sufficient to tell the impact of a location update, on the second level, an *interference*-driven strategy (IDS) further identifies the "no-update" instances from these uncertain instances with regard to the objective function of Problem 2. A location update is unnecessary in this step if doing it will not improve interference mitigation. In the rest of this section, we will first illustrate the designs of the two strategies, and then combine them as a local heuristic algorithm for LUC.

5.2.1 *Movement-Driven Strategy*

The MDS for LUC locally identifies the "must-update" and "no-update" instances with regard to the constraints of Problem 2. These instances are identified according to two design needs. First, constraint (11) should always hold. Second, constraint (6) should not lead to inefficient spectrum utilization. To explain our design formally, we will show how we mathematically quantify the location accuracy and location fuzziness of $\mathcal{Q}_s(t)$ for each user $s \in \mathcal{S}$ and how to use these two values in meeting the two needs.

We define the *location accuracy* of $\mathcal{Q}_s(t)$ by $q_s(t) \triangleq q_{s,\ell_s}(t)$, which is the probability of locating $\ell_s(t)$ by $\mathcal{Q}_s(t)$. The first need is addressed by the following two propositions.

Proposition 1 For each user $s \in \mathcal{S}$, constraint (11), i.e., $\ell_s(t) \in \mathcal{L}_s(t)$, is locally guaranteed if $q_s(t) > 0$ holds.
Proof Please refer to the definition of $\mathcal{L}_s(t)$. □

In robot navigation research, a LPG is often created by using Bayes filters, which probabilistically estimate the location of an object from noisy observations. In our problem, however, each mobile user exactly reports its location information. Hence, we only need to implement one prediction step of general Bayes filters without sequential localization error correction. We integrate grid-based localization [18] and sampling-based localization [19, 20] to generate LPGs.

Specifically, the database can utilize the sequence of $A_s(t')$ for $t' = t, t-1, \ldots$ and the past location update history to generate $\mathcal{Q}_s(t)$. Suppose that the latest location update from user s happens in time slot t_0, i.e., $A_s(t_0) = 1$ and $A_s(t') = 0$ for $t' = t, t-1, ..., t_0+1$. Define $\tilde{t}_s(t) = t - t_0$ as the elapsed time since the last location update. The past location update history can include the reported location $\tilde{l}_s$ and velocity vector $\tilde{\mathbf{v}}_s$ in time slot t_0. In each prediction step for locating user s using a technique of sampling-based Monte Carlo localization, all the samples for location estimation are placed at $\tilde{l}_s$ initially. Then, each sample is shifted according to its randomly generated succeeding location

$$\dot{L}_s(t) \triangleq \tilde{l}_s + (\tilde{\mathbf{v}}_s + \tilde{\mathbf{w}}_s)\,\tilde{t}_s(t), \quad (13)$$

where $\dot{L}_s(t)$ is a random variable generated by the movement prediction model representing an estimate of $\ell_s(t)$, and $\tilde{\mathbf{w}}_s$ is a vector of random variables characterizing the uncertainty in generating $\mathcal{Q}_s(t)$. The $\mathcal{Q}_s(t)$ is essentially the probability distribution of $\dot{L}_s(t)$ over $\mathcal{L}$. Using (13), we have

$$q_s(t) = Pr\{\tilde{l}_s + (\tilde{\mathbf{v}}_s + \tilde{\mathbf{w}}_s)\,\tilde{t}_s(t) = \ell_s(t)\}. \quad (14)$$

The probability distribution of $\tilde{\mathbf{w}}_s$ varies with the applied movement prediction model and the knowledge of underlying terrain data. As an example, we assume $\tilde{\mathbf{w}}_s$ follows a bivariate normal distribution with parameters $(\mu_x = 0, \mu_y = 0, \sigma_x^2, \sigma_y^2, \rho)$ in the two-dimensional map grid with no terrain knowledge. Then, we have the following common results.

Proposition 2 For bivariate normal $\tilde{\mathbf{w}}_s$, $q_s(t)$ is upper bounded by a monotonically decreasing function of $\tilde{t}_s(t)$, i.e.,

$$\tilde{q}_s(t) = Pr\{\tilde{l}_s + (\tilde{\mathbf{v}}_s + \tilde{\mathbf{w}}_s)\,\tilde{t}_s(t) = E[\dot{L}_s(t)]\},$$

where $E[\dot{L}_s(t)] = \tilde{l}_s + \tilde{\mathbf{v}}_s\tilde{t}_s(t)$. As $\ell_s(t)$ deviates from $E[\dot{L}_s(t)]$, $q_s(t)$ is a monotonically decreasing function of $\tilde{t}_s(t)$.

Proof Let $\tilde{\mathbf{w}}_s = (W_x, W_y)$ and define a vector of random variables $(L_x, L_y) = \tilde{t}_s(W_x, W_y) + (\tilde{l}_x, \tilde{l}_y)$, where $(\tilde{l}_x, \tilde{l}_y) = \tilde{l}_s + \tilde{\mathbf{v}}_s\tilde{t}_s$ can be viewed as a constant vector. Based on the probability density function (PDF) of (W_x, W_y) and the properties for linear transformations of bivariate random variables, the joint PDF of (L_x, L_y) can be derived as

$$f_{L_x,L_y}(l_x, l_y) = \frac{1}{2\pi\sigma_x\sigma_y\sqrt{1-\rho^2}}\frac{1}{\tilde{t}_s^2}\times \quad (15)$$
$$\exp\left(-\frac{\left(\frac{l_x-\tilde{l}_x}{\sigma_x}\right)^2 + \left(\frac{l_y-\tilde{l}_y}{\sigma_y}\right)^2 - 2\rho\left(\frac{l_x-\tilde{l}_x}{\sigma_x}\right)\left(\frac{l_y-\tilde{l}_y}{\sigma_y}\right)}{2(1-\rho^2)}\frac{1}{\tilde{t}_s^2}\right).$$

Hence, $q_s(t)$ is the double integral of $f_{L_x,L_y}(l_x, l_y)$ over the small area of location pixel $\ell_s(t)$, and is a function of $\tilde{t}_s(t)$ for $\tilde{t}_s(t) > 0$. Because the size of $\ell_s(t)$ is fixed, $q_s(t)$ is only determined by $f_{L_x,L_y}(l_x, l_y)$. For $\rho \in (-1, 1)$, we know that $\frac{\left(\frac{l_x-\tilde{l}_x}{\sigma_x}\right)^2 + \left(\frac{l_y-\tilde{l}_y}{\sigma_y}\right)^2 - 2\rho\left(\frac{l_x-\tilde{l}_x}{\sigma_x}\right)\left(\frac{l_y-\tilde{l}_y}{\sigma_y}\right)}{2(1-\rho^2)} \geq 0$. Hence,

$$f_{L_x,L_y}(l_x, l_y) \leq \frac{1}{2\pi\sigma_x\sigma_y\sqrt{1-\rho^2}}\frac{1}{\tilde{t}_s^2}. \quad (16)$$

The equality in (16) holds when $(l_x, l_y) = (\tilde{l}_x, \tilde{l}_y)$. In this perfect case, $\ell_s(t)$ can always be captured by $E[\dot{L}_s(t)]$, which is on the top of the bell-shaped joint density $f_{L_x,L_y}(l_x, l_y)$. In this case, $q_s(t)$ reaches its upper bound $\tilde{q}_s(t)$, which is the double integral of $f_{L_x,L_y}(l_x, l_y)$ over $\ell_s(t) = E[\dot{L}_s(t)]$. Since $\tilde{q}_s(t)$ is determined by $f_{L_x,L_y}(l_x, l_y) = \frac{1}{2\pi\sigma_x\sigma_y\sqrt{1-\rho^2}}\frac{1}{\tilde{t}_s^2}$, $\tilde{q}_s(t)$ is a monotonically decreasing function of $\tilde{t}_s(t)$.

As $\ell_s(t)$ deviates from $E[\dot{L}_s(t)]$, $d_{\ell_s,\tilde{l}_s}(t) < d_{\ell_s,\tilde{l}_s}(t+1)$, where $d_{\ell_s,\tilde{l}_s}(t)$ is the distance between $\ell_s(t)$ and $E[\dot{L}_s(t)]$. It is easy to show $q_s(t) > q_s(t+1)$ through (15). □

Even though $q_s(t)$ may have local fluctuations when $\tilde{t}_s(t)$ increases due to likely irregular trajectory of user s, it is bounded by the monotonically decreasing upper bound and it is common that $\ell_s(t)$ deviates from $E[\dot{L}_s(t)]$ without localization correction. Its general trend is decreasing with time. Hence, setting $A_s(t+1) = 0$ will mostly lead to a further decrease in $q_s(t)$. To ensure $q_s(t+1) > 0$, user s needs to track the drop in $q_s(t)$ and set $A_s(t+1) = 1$ when $q_s(t)$ is too low. This addresses the first need for constraint (11).

We define the *location fuzziness* of $\mathcal{Q}_s(t)$ by $|\mathcal{L}_s(t)|$, which is the covered pixel area of $\mathcal{L}_s(t)$. The second need can be addressed by the following proposition.

Proposition 3 For bivariate normal $\tilde{\mathbf{w}}_s$, $|\mathcal{L}_s(t)|$ is a monotonically increasing function of $\tilde{t}_s(t)$.

Proof The size of $|\mathcal{L}_s(t)|$ depends on the covariance matrix of $(L_x, L_y) = \tilde{t}_s(W_x, W_y) + (\tilde{l}_x, \tilde{l}_y)$, which is

$$\begin{bmatrix} (\tilde{t}_s\sigma_x)^2 & \rho(\tilde{t}_s\sigma_x)(\tilde{t}_s\sigma_y) \\ \rho(\tilde{t}_s\sigma_x)(\tilde{t}_s\sigma_y) & (\tilde{t}_s\sigma_y)^2 \end{bmatrix},$$

where both $\tilde{t}_s\sigma_x$ and $\tilde{t}_s\sigma_y$ grow with $\tilde{t}_s(t)$. Hence, for a fixed ρ, $|\mathcal{L}_s(t)|$ enlarges as $\tilde{t}_s(t)$ increases. □

Hence, setting $A_s(t+1) = 0$ will lead to a further increase in $|\mathcal{L}_s(t)|$, which indicates that $\mathcal{L}_s(t+1)$ is a fuzzier estimate of $\ell_s(t+1)$ compared with $\mathcal{L}_s(t)$ as an estimate of $\ell_s(t)$. To avoid significant loss of white space opportunities and high chance of inaccurate resource allocations, user s needs to set $A_s(t+1) = 1$ when necessary. This addresses the second need for not being affected by constraint (6) too much.

If $\tilde{\mathbf{w}}_s$ follows a general probability distribution, different movement prediction models can achieve different levels of location estimation deviation, but the properties of lower location accuracy and greater location fuzziness are usually true as the elapsed time increases.

Local MDS The MDS works as follows. Each user s can track $q_s(t)$ and set $A_s(t+1)$ using two thresholds: α_1 and α_2 ($\alpha_1 \geq \alpha_2$). There are three possible cases:

a. When $q_s(t) \geq \alpha_1$, user s assumes "no-update" case and sets $A_s(t+1) = 0$.

b. When $\alpha_2 < q_s(t) < \alpha_1$, user s assumes uncertain case and needs to consider using IDS for further investigation.

c. When $q_s(t) \leq \alpha_2$, user s assumes "must-update" case and sets $A_s(t+1) = 1$.

For case a, a relatively small $|\mathcal{L}_s(t)|$ ensures that $\mathcal{L}_s(t)$ nicely captures $\ell_s(t)$ and thus constraints (11) and (6) are easy to satisfy. If user s sets $A_s(t+1) = 1$, it is very likely that this action has little impact on the resource allocation decision under the slightly reduced location uncertainty. For case c, a relatively large $|\mathcal{L}_s(t)|$ tends to cause significant loss of white space opportunities due to constraint (6) and high chance of inaccurate interference estimation. If user s sets $A_s(t+1) = 0$, it is very likely that the database makes a suboptimal resource allocation decision under the increased location uncertainty. More importantly, if $q_s(t)$ is very low, $q_s(t+1) = 0$ is possible and thus violates constraint (11). For case b, IDS is needed as an additional step to set $A_s(t+1)$.

5.2.2 *Interference-Driven Strategy*

The IDS for LUC further locally identifies the "no-update" instances among the uncertain instances from MDS (in case b) with regard to the objective function of Problem 2. To decide whether $A_s(t+1)$ should be 0 or 1, user s needs to predict which action will lead to a smaller objective value. Ideally, user s can take the following process. First, user s solves Problem 1 for time slot $t+1$ to obtain the values of

$I(t+1)$ for both $A_s(t+1)=0$ and $A_s(t+1)=1$ cases. Next, user s compares the values of $G(t+1)$ for the two cases. Whichever objective value that comes the smallest corresponds to the optimal setting of $A_s(t+1)$ for Problem 2. However, this process requires user s to have perfect global knowledge, which is impractical to obtain. Thus, we need to derive a heuristic strategy to set $A_s(t+1)$, which can approximate this process but only requires local knowledge.

Based on (9) and (10), we know that the key in the design of IDS is to find a local way to determine whether

$$I(t+1)|_{A_s(t+1)=0} - I(t+1)|_{A_s(t+1)=1} > \frac{(1-\delta)\theta}{\delta|\mathcal{S}|}. \quad (17)$$

If (17) is likely to be true (false), set $A_s(t+1)=1$ (0).

Global IDS To find a way to judge (17), we consider that user s using a channel $k \in \mathcal{K}$ has a set of co-channel neighbors $s' \in \mathcal{S}_k(t)$, $s' \neq s$. As an example, we discuss IDS with global knowledge based on the co-channel interference in the uplink from user s to others s'. Define $d_{s'}(t)$ as the protection radius from the receiver of each interfered link s', and define $d_{s,s'}(t)$ as the distance between the transmitter of the interfering link s and the receiver of each interfered link s'. Define $\omega_1 \in [0,1)$ and $\omega_2 \in (1,\infty)$. With proper ω_1 and ω_2, there are three possible relative location cases:

1. When $d_{s,s'}(t) \le \omega_1 d_{s'}(t)$ for any $s' \in \mathcal{S}_k(t)$, $s' \neq s$, user s assumes "no-update" case and sets $A_s(t+1)=0$.
2. When $\omega_1 d_{s'}(t) < d_{s,s'}(t) < \omega_2 d_{s'}(t)$ for any $s' \in \mathcal{S}_k(t)$, $s' \neq s$, user s sets $A_s(t+1)=1$.
3. When $d_{s,s'}(t) \ge \omega_2 d_{s'}(t)$ for all $s' \in \mathcal{S}_k(t)$, $s' \neq s$, user s assumes "no-update" case and sets $A_s(t+1)=0$.

For case 1, user s is deep inside the protection area of a link s'. Because MDS guarantees that $\ell_s(t) \in \mathcal{L}_s(t)$ and $|\mathcal{L}_s(t)|$ is not too large in case b, there should be a relatively full overlap between $\mathcal{L}_s(t)$ and the protection area of link s'. Thus, even setting $A_s(t+1)=0$, Problem 1 is likely to judge that links s and s' have a high probability of mutual interference and make a resource allocation decision as same as that in the case of setting $A_s(t+1)=1$ (so that the mutual interference probability is 1). Because the decisions for WSA in both update and no-update cases should be the same, (17) is likely to be false. For case 3, user s is far outside the protection area of any link $s' \in \mathcal{S}_k(t)$. The movement contour of user s is likely to be mostly outside the protection area of any link s'. Thus, even setting $A_s(t+1)=0$, Problem 1 is likely to judge that links s and s' have a low probability of mutual interference and make a resource allocation decision as same as that in the case of setting $A_s(t+1)=1$ (so that the mutual interference probability is 0). Because the decisions for WSA in both update and no-update cases should be the same, (17) is likely to be false. For case 2, user s is near the boundary of the protection area of a link s'. The movement contour of user s is partly inside and partly outside the protection area of link s'. If user s sets $A_s(t+1)=1$, Problem 1 can precisely know whether there is mutual interference between links s and s'. If there exists mutual interference, the database will try to reallocate channels to links s and s' to eliminate the interference. If there exists no mutual interference, the database is likely to keep the interference to be zero. In both cases, the solution to Problem 1 usually makes the probability of mutual interference between links s and s' be zero. If user s sets $A_s(t+1)=0$, Problem 1 can only use the movement contour to obtain a positive value of mutual interference probability. The left-hand side of (17) is usually large, so (17) is likely to be true.

Unfortunately, user s cannot precisely know which case it belongs to without perfect knowledge of other co-channel users' location information, which is impractical to obtain. However, user s can estimate which relative location case it is likely in based on its local measurement of $R_{s,k}(t)$, the SINR that user s has observed on channel k in time slot t.

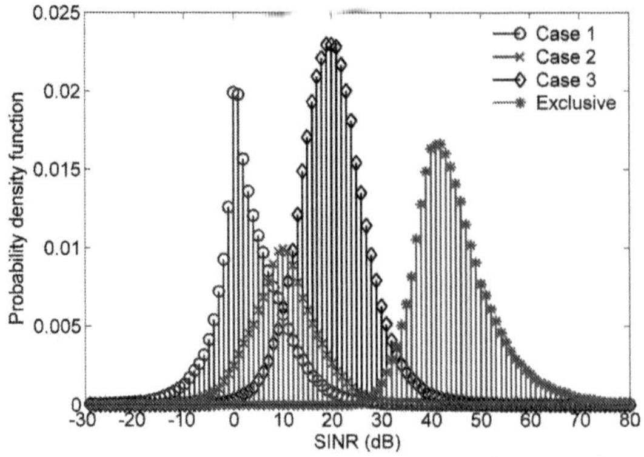

Figure 2: PDFs of $R_{s,k}(t)$ ($\omega_1 = \frac{2}{3}$, $\omega_2 = \frac{4}{3}$).

Proposition 4 The relative location cases and the local measurement of $R_{s,k}(t)$ are correlated in a stochastic sense.

For example, we use numerical results to create Figure 2, which shows the PDFs of $R_{s,k}(t)$ observed in different relative location cases. The exclusive case refers to the situation where there is no any other user sharing the channel with user s. Obviously, a location update is not needed in the exclusive case. The PDFs of the other three cases are averaged when the number of co-channel users ranges from 2 to 7. The details of the 7-cell system will be presented in section 6. We observe that when the locally measured $R_{s,k}(t)$ is either low enough or high enough, the false judgement rates for the "no-update" cases (except for case 2) are relatively low due to their distinct peaks in the PDFs. Then, user s can usually identify the "no-update" instances properly.

Local IDS The IDS works as follows. Each user s that takes a channel k can measure $R_{s,k}(t)$ and set $A_s(t+1)$ using two thresholds: β_1 and β_2 ($\beta_1 \le \beta_2$). There are three possible cases mapping with the relative location cases:

1' When $R_{s,k}(t) \le \beta_1$, user s assumes "no-update" case and sets $A_s(t+1)=0$.

2' When $\beta_1 < R_{s,k}(t) < \beta_2$, user s sets $A_s(t+1)=1$.

3' When $R_{s,k}(t) \ge \beta_2$, user s assumes "no-update" case and sets $A_s(t+1)=0$.

For case 1', user s is most likely in case 1. For case 3', user s is very likely in either case 3 or the exclusive case. For case 2', user s can be in case 1, 2, or 3. Using a safe strategy that cares more about interference mitigation effectiveness than database query cost, user s assumes the worst case 2.

5.2.3 Combining MDS and IDS

The local two-level strategy for LUC that combines MDS and IDS is summarized in Algorithm 2. Two sets of thresholds, i.e., movement-related α_1 and α_2, and interference-related β_1 and β_2, are used to identify the cases where a location update is unnecessary (in cases a, 1', 3') or necessary (in cases c, 2'). Running Algorithm 2 at mobile users gives a heuristic solution to Problem 2. After the thresholds have been determined, the complexity of Algorithm 2 mainly comes from computing $\mathcal{Q}_s(t)$ through one prediction step of a Bayes filter, which is not very expensive. In sections 6 and 7, we will discuss how these thresholds can be set.

6. PERFORMANCE EVALUATION

In this section, we evaluate the proposed algorithms using the results from two simulation experiments. First, we have

Algorithm 2 for LUC at user $s \in \mathcal{S}$ in time slot t

```
if A_s(t) == 1 (0) then
  query (do not query) the database
end if
access white space spectrum according to X_{s,k}(t),
  Y_{s,k}(t) for k ∈ K assigned by the database
compute Q_s(t) as in Algorithm 1, and measure q_s(t)
if case a (c) then
  set A_s(t+1) = 0 (1)
else
  set A_s(t+1) = 0
  measure R_{s,k}(t) for all k with X_{s,k}(t) == 1
  if case 2' for any k then
    set A_s(t+1) = 1
  end if
end if
```

simulated WiFi-like secondary networks using a theoretical mobility model. Second, we have simulated cellular-like secondary networks using a real-world mobility trace dataset.

6.1 Model-Driven Simulation

In the first experiment, we study a 7-cell spectrum sharing system, in which the seven base stations for secondary networks are placed at the center and six vertices of a regular hexagon with the edge length of 1500 m. Total m channels are shared by m primary users and $2m$ secondary users. Each primary user occupies a different channel in its exclusion zone with the radius of 1500 m, and its duty cycle is λ. The primary users are uniformly distributed. Each secondary user is randomly associated with a base station, and let $\check{K}_s = 1$, $\hat{Y}_s = 100$ mW, $\check{R}_s = 10$ dB. The random movement of each user is defined by a semi-Markov smooth mobility model [21]. The target direction in the model is restricted back when the user is more than 1500 m away from its home base station, and the average target speed is on the order of human walking speed. The granularity of the map grid is 50m×50m, and the duration of a time slot is 120 s. In this example, the cells largely overlap with each other, and user mobility relative to the size of map grid is high enough to generate dynamic inter-cell interference. We explain the settings of α_1, α_2 in MDS and β_1, β_2 in IDS to adapt the database query intervals. The average objective function is recorded as $\bar{G} = \delta\bar{I} + (1-\delta)\bar{C}$, where $\bar{I}$ is the average fraction of time for unsuccessful reception in each link and $\bar{C}$ is the average value of $C(t)$ over time with $\theta = 1$.

First, we show the impact of α_1 and α_2 on $\bar{G}$. In Figure 3, fixing $\alpha_2 = 0.01$, $\beta_1 = 5$ dB, $\beta_2 = 14$ dB, we increase α_1 from α_2 to 1. This increases the probability of case 2' in IDS and thus increases $\bar{C}$. In Figure 4, fixing $\alpha_1 = \alpha_2$, we increase α_2 from 0 to 1. This increases the probability of case c in MDS and thus increases $\bar{C}$. To balance between $\bar{I}$ and $\bar{C}$, larger α_1 and larger α_2 are chosen for larger δ to keep higher location accuracy and smaller location fuzziness. Larger $\alpha_1 - \alpha_2$ is used to give more preference to IDS.

Second, we show the impact of β_1 and β_2 on $\bar{G}$. According to Figure 2, too small β_1 or too large β_2 can create a lot of unnecessary location updates due to falsely treating case 1 or 3 as case 2'. On the contrary, too large β_1 or too small β_2 can omit a lot of necessary location updates due to falsely treating case 2 as case 1' or 3'. The values of β_1 and β_2 should be chosen with regard to the false judgement rates for the relative location cases. In Figure 5, fixing $\alpha_1 = 0.7$, $\alpha_2 = 0.01$, we increase $\beta_2 - \beta_1$ from 0 (decreasing β_1 from 9.5 dB and increasing β_2 from 9.5 dB). This increases

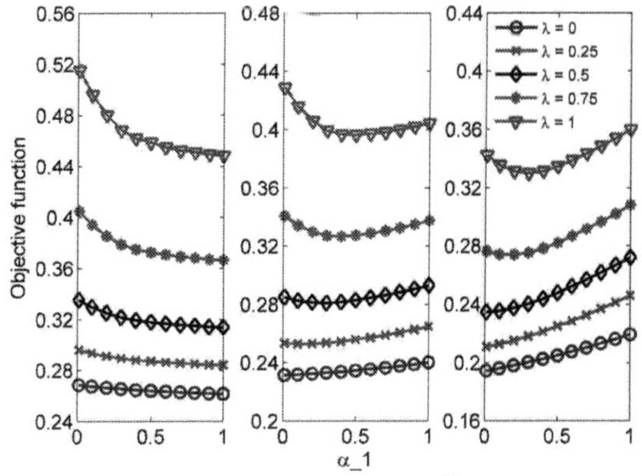

Figure 3: Impact of α_1 on $\bar{G}$ ($m = 28$): (a) $\delta = 1$ (left); (b) $\delta = 0.8$ (middle); (c) $\delta = 0.6$ (right).

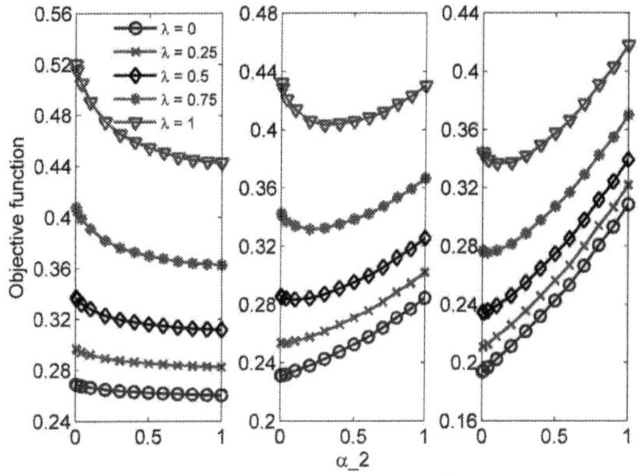

Figure 4: Impact of α_2 on $\bar{G}$ ($m = 28$): (a) $\delta = 1$ (left); (b) $\delta = 0.8$ (middle); (c) $\delta = 0.6$ (right).

the probability of case 2' in IDS and thus increases $\bar{C}$. To balance between $\bar{I}$ and $\bar{C}$, smaller β_1 and larger β_2 are chosen for larger δ to reduce the false judgements that cause missing necessary location updates, while larger β_1 and smaller β_2 are chosen for smaller δ to reduce the false judgements that cause unnecessary location updates.

Third, we compare the value of $1-\bar{I}$ given by our heuristic mechanism with the value given by an impractical optimal mechanism. Here, our mechanism is called movement-driven and interference-driven database query strategy (MIDQ). We also consider two alternative heuristic mechanisms: a pure movement-driven database query strategy (MDQ) (by fixing $\alpha_1 = \alpha_2$) and a periodic database query strategy (PDQ) (as used in [4]). The optimal mechanism assumes perfect global knowledge, so that all the users' actual locations are known (without location update cost) and an optimal resource allocation is performed accordingly. The ratio of $1-\bar{I}$ from a heuristic solution to that from the optimal solution is depicted in Figure 6. It can be seen that the ratio grows with increasing database query frequency. For MIDQ, $\bar{C}$ is increased by first increasing α_1 ($\alpha_2 = 0.01$, $\beta_1 = 5$ dB, $\beta_2 = 14$ dB) from 0.01 to 1 and then increasing $\beta_2 - \beta_1$. For MDQ, $\bar{C}$ is increased by increasing $\alpha_1 = \alpha_2$ from 0.01 to 1. Compared with MDQ and PDQ, the proposed MIDQ achieves better reduction of mutual interference with the same level of database query frequency (cost). With a high enough database query frequency, MIDQ can achieve almost the same interference level as the optimal mechanism.

6.2 Trace-Driven Simulation

In the second experiment, we have utilized a real-world mobility trace dataset that contains the GPS coordinates of

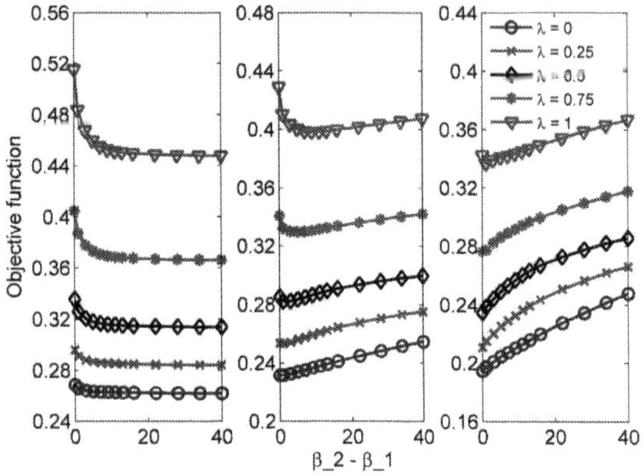

Figure 5: Impact of β_1 and β_2 on $\bar{G}$ ($m = 28$): (a) $\delta = 1$ (left); (b) $\delta = 0.8$ (middle); (c) $\delta = 0.6$ (right).

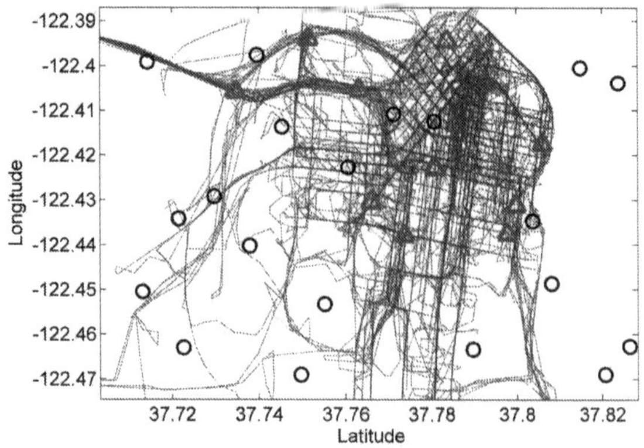

Figure 7: A trace-driven simulation scenario in San Francisco (lines: taxi movement trajectories; triangles: secondary base stations; circles: primary exclusion zone centres).

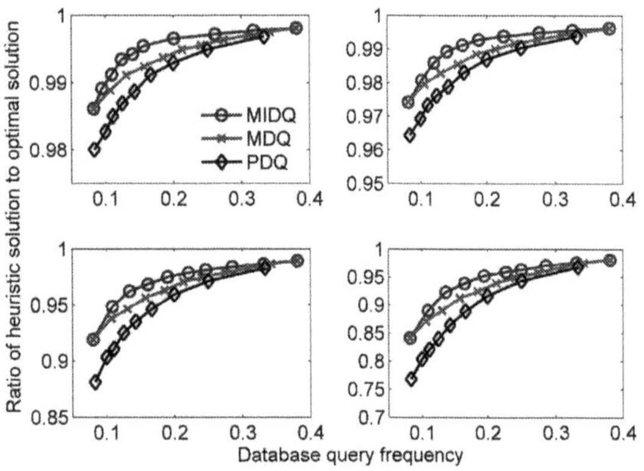

Figure 6: Optimality gap of heuristic WSA and LUC ($m = 28$): (a) $\lambda = 0$ (top-left); (b) $\lambda = 0.25$ (top-right); (c) $\lambda = 0.75$ (bottom-left); (d) $\lambda = 1$ (bottom-right).

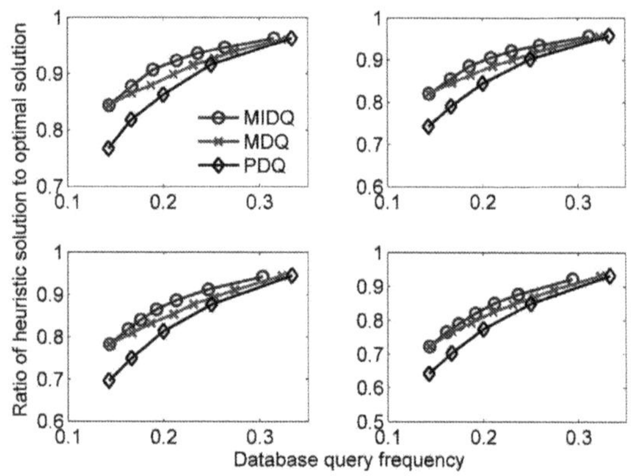

Figure 8: Optimality gap of heuristic WSA and LUC (traces): (a) $\lambda = 0$ (top-left); (b) $\lambda = 0.25$ (top-right); (c) $\lambda = 0.75$ (bottom-left); (d) $\lambda = 1$ (bottom-right).

real taxis collected in the San Francisco Bay Area [22]. In this experiment, a taxi represents a mobile secondary user. However, we need to deploy the base stations for secondary networks, since the dataset does not include any location information of cellular base stations or WiFi access points. We use a similar method as used in [23]. The possible locations of the base stations to be deployed are the location points that have been traveled by the taxis in the dataset, and the points are along roads and around buildings. Each point is assigned with a selection probability, which is the frequency at which the location point has been visited by the taxis. In this way, more base stations are deployed in more heavily traveled areas. Total m channels are shared by m primary users and $2m$ secondary users. As shown in Figure 7, the traces of 48 taxis are selected, and 12 base stations are deployed. We assume that each taxi is associated with the nearest base station, i.e., inter-cell handover is enabled. The exclusion zones of the primary users with a radius of 3000 m are uniformly distributed in the simulation area. The granularity of the map grid is 100m×100m, and the duration of a time slot is 60 s. Similar to Figure 6, the ratio of the heuristic solution to the optimal solution is shown in Figure 8. From the results, we can see that the proposed MIDQ still outperforms MDQ and PDQ. The overall performance of the heuristic mechanisms degrades in this experiment compared with that in the first experiment. Besides the impact of incumbents, this should be caused by the high-speed vehicular mobility that leads to less accurate movement prediction and the dynamic user-cell association that leads to less accurate local interference estimation.

7. DISCUSSIONS

In this section, we discuss system design guidelines and real-world deployment issues in database-driven OSA.

1 The database query interval of each mobile user should be adapted according to both internal factors (e.g., user mobility, database processing capacity, and location privacy) and external factors (e.g., incumbent protection, and network coexistence) to achieve a proper balance between spectrum sharing and database access. In general, a higher frequency of database queries is necessary if i) user movement pattern is more dynamic; ii) interference mitigation effectiveness is of higher priority than database query cost; iii) location information is less sensitive at the database; iv) the duty cycle of primary users is larger, i.e., less channels are available for certain users; v) mutual interference is more likely to occur, i.e., more users share certain channels.

2 In a probabilistic coexistence framework as proposed in this work, the database can set the system parameters offline (e.g., via statistical analysis) or online (e.g., via a stochastic decision process). For example, the thresholds α_1 and α_2 can be empirically set according to the maximum and minimum desired levels of location accuracy or location fuzziness, respectively, for a certain movement prediction model. The thresholds β_1 and β_2 can be dynamically adjusted according to the changes in the spectrum environment (e.g., primary user activity, secondary user density and mobility, and resource reallocation) and the results from past decisions (e.g., the rate at which erroneous decisions have been made in determining the appropriate case for a user). To reduce complexity, the thresholds can also be empirically set according to the PDFs as in Figure 2. One can learn the amount of false judgement for each case given a particular setting of β_1 and β_2, and thus make an educated choice. The offline and online decisions can be combined to mediate a trade-off between performance and complexity.

3 For the estimation of user movement pattern at the database, the applied localization method or movement prediction model determines how the location uncertainty level of a user changes with time. In general, a more advanced localization technique (e.g., a method that integrates GPS, maps, and user behaviors) achieves a slower drop in location accuracy and a slower rise in location fuzziness, and requires less location updates for localization error correction.

4 For the estimation of harmful interference to primary users and mutual interference among secondary users at the database, the applied radio wave propagation model affects the effectiveness of spectrum availability prediction and resource allocation. In general, a more sophisticated signal propagation model (e.g., Longley-Rice with terrain data [4]) achieves better incumbent protection and higher spectrum utilization, and even further improves local decisions at the users for mutual interference mitigation.

5 It is hard to quantify the cost of database queries in database-driven spectrum sharing. However, one of major bottlenecks in such a system is the capacity of the central database server. In a fine-grained system, each single user performs LUC, and the central server manages spectrum sharing information and performs WSA at the user-level granularity. The computational complexity of resource allocation is affected by the number of registered users and the spatial granularity of map grid, and the resource allocation has to meet the timely requirement if a time slot is very short. Hence, when designing a database-driven spectrum sharing system, the maximum number of registered users that can be served by each server needs to be considered. Alternatively, each base station can manage the users in its cell as a whole. In such a coarse-grained system, each base station performs LUC, and the central server offers the services at the cell-level granularity. In this approach, each base station further performs WSA at the user-level granularity. In general, the fine-grained system is recommended when database processing capacity is not a problem, while the coarse-grained system is preferred when server response delay or resource reallocation frequency is too high.

8. CONCLUSION

In this paper, we have addressed two major problems for supporting mobile users in database-driven OSA: WSA and LUC. In the proposed coexistence framework, WSA is performed centrally, while LUC is performed locally. We have used a LPG to quantify the location uncertainty level of each user. The problems of WSA and LUC have been jointly solved through dynamic control of LPGs. The local strategy for adapting database query intervals combines practical MDS and IDS to reduce database query cost without negatively impacting interference mitigation effectiveness. Our model-driven and trace-driven simulation results have shown that the intervals can be adapted to yield near-optimal interference mitigation with minimal location updates.

References

[1] S. Haykin. Cognitive radio: Brain-empowered wireless communications. *IEEE J. Sel. Area. Comm.*, 23(2), Feb. 2005.

[2] I. F. Akyildiz, W.-Y. Lee, M. C. Vuran, and S. Mohanty. Next generation/dynamic spectrum access/cognitive radio wireless networks: A survey. *Elsevier Comp. Netw.*, 50(13), Sep. 2006.

[3] D. Gurney, G. Buchwald, L. Ecklund, S. Kuffner, and J. Grosspietsch. Geo-location database techniques for incumbent protection in the tv white space. In *Proc. IEEE DySPAN'08*, Oct. 2008.

[4] R. Murty, R. Chandra, T. Moscibroda, and P. Bahl. Senseless: A database-driven white spaces network. *IEEE Trans. Mobi. Comp.*, 11(2), Feb. 2012.

[5] M. Barrie, S. Delaere, G. Sukareviciene, J. Gesquiere, and I. Moerman. Geolocation database beyond tv white spaces? matching applications with database requirements. In *Proc. IEEE DySPAN'12*, Oct. 2012.

[6] FCC. Enabling innovative small cell use in 3.5 ghz band nprm & order. GN Docket No. 12-354, FCC 12-148, Dec. 2012.

[7] FCC. Wireless telecommunications bureau and office of engineering and technology call for technical papers on the proposed spectrum access system for the 3.5 ghz band. GN Docket No. 12-354, DA 13-2213, Nov. 2013.

[8] C. Ghosh, S. Roy, and D. Cavalcanti. Coexistence challenges for heterogeneous cognitive wireless networks in tv white spaces. *IEEE Wirel. Comm.*, 18(4), Aug. 2011.

[9] B. Gao, J.-M. Park, Y. Yang, and S. Roy. A taxonomy of coexistence mechanisms for heterogeneous cognitive radio networks operating in tv white spaces. *IEEE Wirel. Comm.*, 19(4), Aug. 2012.

[10] A. W. Min, K.-H. Kim, J. P. Singh, and K. G. Shin. Opportunistic spectrum access for mobile cognitive radios. In *Proc. IEEE INFOCOM'11*, Apr. 2011.

[11] H. Kim and K. G. Shin. Asymmetry-aware real-time distributed joint resource allocation in ieee 802.22 wrans. In *Proc. IEEE INFOCOM'10*, Mar. 2010.

[12] Q. Ni and C. C. Zarakovitis. Nash bargaining game theoretic scheduling for joint channel and power allocation in cognitive radio systems. *IEEE J. Sel. Area. Comm.*, 30(1), Jan. 2012.

[13] B. Gao, J.-M. Park, and Y. Yang. Uplink soft frequency reuse for self-coexistence of cognitive radio networks operating in white-space spectrum. In *Proc. IEEE INFOCOM'12*, Mar. 2012.

[14] Y. Tachwali, B. F. Lo, I. F. Akyildiz, and R. Agustí. Multiuser resource allocation optimization using bandwidth-power product in cognitive radio networks. *IEEE J. Sel. Area. Comm.*, 31(3), Mar. 2013.

[15] B. Gao, Y. Yang, and J.-M. Park. A credit-token-based spectrum etiquette framework for coexistence of heterogeneous cognitive radio networks. In *Proc. IEEE INFOCOM'14*, Apr. 2014.

[16] Y. Xu, J. Winter, and W.-C. Lee. Dual prediction-based reporting for object tracking sensor networks. In *Proc. ACM MobiQuitous'04*, Aug. 2004.

[17] Q. Xu, S. Mehrotra, Z. M. Mao, and J. Li. Proteus: Network performance forecast for real-time, interactive mobile applications. In *Proc. ACM MobiSys'13*, Jun. 2013.

[18] W. Burgard, D. Fox, D. Hennig, and T. Schmidt. Estimating the absolute position of a mobile robot using position probability grids. In *Proc. AAAI'96*, Aug. 1996.

[19] F. Dellaert, D. Fox, W. Burgard, and S. Thrun. Monte carlo localization for mobile robots. In *Proc. IEEE ICRA'99*, May 1999.

[20] M. S. Arulampalam, S. Maskell, N. Gordon, and T. Clapp. A tutorial on particle filters for online nonlinear/non-gaussian bayesian tracking. *IEEE Trans. Sign. Proc.*, 50(2), Feb. 2002.

[21] M. Zhao and W. Wang. A novel semi-markov smooth mobility model for mobile ad hoc networks. In *Proc. IEEE GLOBECOM'06*, Nov. 2006.

[22] M. Piorkowski, N. Sarafijanovic-Djukic, and M. Grossglauser. CRAWDAD data set epfl/mobility (v. 2009-02-24). online: http://crawdad.org/epfl/mobility/, Feb. 2009.

[23] S. Dimatteo, P. Hui, B. Han, and V. O.K. Li. Cellular traffic offloading through wifi networks. In *Proc. IEEE MASS'11*, Oct. 2011.

Belief Propagation for Spatial Spectrum Access Games

Yi-Kai Wang
State Key Laboratory of Novel Software Technology, Nanjing University, 210046, China
yikai.wang@hotmail.com

Yitong Yin
State Key Laboratory of Novel Software Technology, Nanjing University, 210046, China
yinyt@nju.edu.cn

Sheng Zhong
State Key Laboratory of Novel Software Technology, Nanjing University, 210046, China
zhongsheng@nju.edu.cn

ABSTRACT

Consider a wireless network in which selfish users compete with each other for usage of spectrum. We view this competition as a spatial spectrum access game. There are two fundamental questions regarding this game: how to converge to the optimal Nash equilibrium, and how to converge fast. To answer these two questions, we apply a technique called Belief Propagation to design algorithms for users in this game, which can guarantee fast convergence to an optimal or nearly optimal pure strategy Nash equilibrium. Specifically, when the interference graph is an undirected tree or a directed acyclic graph, our algorithms can find the optimal Nash equilibrium in linear time. For general undirected interference graph, our algorithm converges fast as long as the game is potential (which is the case for many typical scenarios). For some other typical spatial spectrum access games, our algorithms can provide a good approximation to the optimal Nash equilibrium.

Categories and Subject Descriptors

C.2.1 [**Network Architecture and Design**]: Wireless Communication

Keywords

Wireless Network; Distributed Algorithm; Game Theory; Belief Propagation

1. INTRODUCTION

With the rapid development of mobile computing technology, the number of computing nodes in a network grows explosively while the number of available channels is an invariable natural resource limited by physical laws. Consider a multi-hop wireless network, e.g., a wireless ad-hoc network or a vehicular network. Since the nodes of the network usually belong to different users, these users will compete with each other for the usage of channels.

Naturally, we can view the above competition among users as a game, which is called *spatial spectrum access game* [5]. The players of this game are the selfish users, while the utilities of these users correspond to the network performance they experience. In principle, this spatial spectrum access game will converge to a Nash equilibrium eventually. Once the Nash equilibrium is reached, each user has no incentive to further change her own strategy, and thus a stable state of the entire network is achieved.

While this picture of converging to Nash equilibrium (stable state of network) looks nice, there are still two fundamental questions. First, a spatial spectrum access game can have multiple Nash equilibria, with completely different utitlities for users. How can users choose their strategies such that they have the best possible utilities in the finally reached Nash equilibrium? Second, the convergence to a Nash equilibrium can be a slow process. What strategies should users choose such that the entire network enter the stable state as quickly as possible? Our goal in this paper is to answer these two questions. That is, we would like to design distributed algorithms that converge *fast* to an *optimal* or near-optimal pure strategy Nash equilibrium in spatial spectrum access games.

In order to achieve this goal, we adopt the model of graphical game, in which the underlying graph is the interference graph, which captures the interference relations among users. We focus on the pure strategy Nash equilibrium (PSNE) because the probabilistic behavior of users can be hard-coded into the space of pure strategies. Our first step is to reduce the task of finding an optimal PSNE of a graphical game to the *maximum a posteriori* (MAP) estimation in a graphical model. We then use a modified version of *max-product belief propagation* (BP) algorithm to find the optimal PSNE. The BP algorithm has the following virtues:

1. BP is simple and easy to implement. We only need a single control channel for message passing.

2. BP is flexible so that the utility function of each user can be locally defined and needs not to be known by other users, satisfying privacy requirement. The final outcome of the PSNE reflects the utilities of all users.

3. The max-product BP is a greedy algorithm maximizing the utility of each user in every round, which is consistent with the selfishness of users. Moreover, each user only has local information. None of them could have enough information to be cheating.

Our Results In a general model (which can be used for, e.g., FDMA, TDMA, CDMA and CSMA/CA), we show the spatial spectrum access games on undirected interference graphs are potential games, guaranteeing the convergence to PSNE. We give a general reduction from the problem of finding optimal PSNE of graphical games to the MAP estimation in graphical model. The algorithmic results we obtain include:

MobiHoc'14, August 11–14, 2014, Philadelphia, PA, USA.
Copyright 2014 ACM 978-1-4503-2620-9/14/08 ...$15.00.
http://dx.doi.org/10.1145/2632951.2632952 .

1. When the interference graph is an undirected tree or a directed acyclic graph, max-product belief propagation converges to the optimal PSNE of graphical games in linear time.

2. For any undirected interference graph, the BP-guided local dynamics converges to a PSNE as long as the game is potential, and experiments show that the convergence is fast for the considered protocols.

3. For some typical spatial spectrum access games, including the weighted q-state independent set, weighted q-coloring where $q > \Delta$, where q is the number of channels and Δ is the maximum degree of the interference graph, there is a *polynomial-time approximation scheme* (PTAS) for finding the optimal solution on planar graphs.

4. For k-outerplanar graphs where k is any fixed constant, there is a linear-time dynamic programming algorithm for finding the optimal PSNE for any spatial spectrum access games.

Related Work Mechanism design for spatial spectrum access has been studied extensively for different protocols [8, 13, 18]. This problem was modeled as various combinatorial problem such as independent set [19, 28], coloring [15, 23, 30] and matching [19, 28]. Designing spectrum sharing mechanism in the context of game theory has been studied in [5, 10, 13, 15, 22]. Static game was used to analyze channel assignment for single collision domain in [10]. Channel assignment for multi-collision domain by game theory was studied in [13, 22, 5]. Graphical game was first applied to address spatial spectrum access on undirected interference graphs in [22]. Then in [3] the model was generalized to directed interference graphs on which the graphical congestion game with linear latency function was studied. In [5], the concept of spatial spectrum access games was proposed and the convergence of real network protocols was answered for the first time. All the previous works on spatial spectrum access games focused on searching for a PSNE rather than finding the optimal PSNE for spatial spectrum access.

The graphical game was first studied in [20]. The connection between graphical models and graphical games was first discussed in [7], which was used to deciding the existence of PSNE on graphs with bounded treewidth.

Belief propagation is rediscovered many times in the history and has been widely used in artificial intelligence, information theory, statistical physics and many other related fields. In [26], they were developed for exact probabilistic inference in acyclic Bayesian networks. Much earlier in [11], they were used for decoding low-density parity-check (LDPC) codes. Recently, max-product and min-sum belief propagation were used to design various message-passing algorithms for combinatorial optimization problems, such as min-cost flow [12], maximum weight matching [2], maximum weight independent set [27]. All these optimization problems are special cases of optimization for PSNE of graphical games.

2. SYSTEM MODEL

We consider a wireless network with n heterogeneous users $V = \{1, \ldots, n\}$ and q orthogonal channels $Q = \{1, \ldots, q\}$. Each user is a transmitter with multiple radios and can access multiple channels simultaneously. In a fading environment, each user v_i has a limited interference range whose diameter is denoted by r_i. The distance between user v_i and user v_j is denoted by d_{ij}. The interference relations among all users are described by an interference graph $G = (V, E)$, with each vertex $v \in V$ representing a user in the network, and a directed edge going from u to v if and only if $r_u > d_{uv}$. For each user v, we use $N_{in}(v) = \{u : (u, v) \in E\}$ and $N_{out}(v) = \{u : (v, u) \in E\}$ to denote the set of in-neighbors and out-neighbors of v respectively, and $d_{in}(v) = |N_{in}(v)|$ and $d_{out} = |N_{out}(v)|$ the in-degree and out-degree of v respectively. If for any two users $u, v \in V$, when u can interfere with v, v can also interfere with u, the interference graph becomes an undirected graph. The directed edges (u, v) and (v, u) can be replaced by a single undirected edge $\{u, v\}$ and $N_{in}(v) = N_{out}(v) = N(v)$ for all $v \in V$. For each user i, let f_i denote her utility function, which maps the channel assignment to payoff. The median access problem is modeled as a graphical game on interference graph with these utility functions, where the notion of graphical game is to be formally defined later. We consider the utility functions realized by the MAC protocols extensively used in practice, including the contention-based protocol CSMA/CA, and the contention-free protocols FDMA, TDMA and CDMA.

1. For FDMA, TDMA and CDMA, a channel is divided equally into frequency bands, time slots or orthogonal codes. A strategy of user $i \in V$ is a boolean vector $s_i = (s_{i,1}, \ldots, s_{i,q})$ where $s_{i,j}$ indicates whether user i is using channel j. And $\sum_{j=1}^{q} s_{i,j} \leq \delta_i$ where δ_i is the number of radios of user i. The utility function f_i is defined as in [10, 13]:
$$f_i = \sum_{j \in Q} \theta_j \frac{s_{i,j}}{s_{i,j} + \sum_{k \in N_{in}(i)} s_{k,j}},$$
where θ_j is the rate of channel j, which is assumed to be shared equally by the users.

2. For the CSMA/CA protocol, strategies of each user $i \in V$ are samely defined as above. When a channel j is sensed busy, user i makes a delay of time $\tau_{i,j}$ uniformly generated from $[0, \lambda_j]$. The utility function f_i is defined as in [5]:
$$\begin{aligned} f_i &= \sum_{j \in Q} s_{i,j} \int_0^{\lambda_j} \frac{\theta_j}{\lambda_j} \prod_{k \in N_{in}(i)} \left(\Pr[\tau_{k,j} > \tau_{i,j}]\right)^{s_{k,j}} \mathrm{d}\tau_{i,j} \\ &= \sum_{j \in Q} s_{i,j} \int_0^{\lambda_j} \frac{\theta_j}{\lambda_j} \left(\frac{\lambda_j - x}{\lambda_j}\right)^{p_j} \mathrm{d}x, \end{aligned}$$
where $p_j = \sum_{k \in N_{in}(i)} s_{k,j}$ and θ_j is the rate of channel j.

For time-varying channels, θ_j may be the expectation value of a stationary stochastic process.

Note that for all the considered protocols, we do not need to consider the case that two radios of the same user compete the usage of the same channel simultaneously.

In interference graphs, a directed cycle of length 2 is formed by two directed edges $(u, v), (v, u) \in E$ between the same pair of vertices. And we have the following simple proposition.

PROPOSITION 1. *In any directed interference graph, if there is no directed cycle of length 2, then there is no directed cycle of length greater than 2.*

PROOF. If $(u, v) \in E$ and $(v, u) \notin E$, then we have $r_u > d_{uv}$ and $r_v < d_{uv}$, and hence $r_u > r_v$. Let G be an interference graph with no directed cycle of length 2. If there is a directed cycle $L = (u_1, u_2, \ldots, u_\ell, u_1)$ with $\ell > 2$ in G, then we have $r_{u_1} > r_{u_2} > \ldots > r_{u_\ell} > r_{u_1}$, which leads to a contradiction. □

By this proposition, in our model the interference graph as shown in Figure 1 will never appear. Therefore, it is safe to characterize all directed acyclic interference graphs by the following definition.

DEFINITION 2. *An acyclic interference graph is a directed interference graph with no cycle of length 2.*

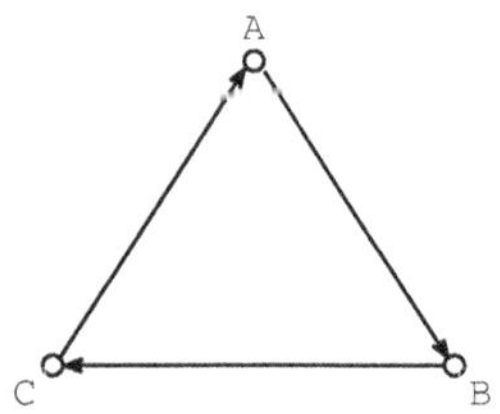

Figure 1: An Impossible Directed Interference Graph

3. PRELIMINARIES

3.1 Graphical games

The classic graphical game [20] is defined on undirected graphs. Here we consider the more general setting of directed graphs [3, 5].

DEFINITION 3. *(Graphical Game) A graphical game is a pair* (G, F) *where* $G = (V, E)$ *is a directed or undirected graph over* $V = \{1, \ldots, n\}$, *and* $F = \{f_i : i \in V\}$ *is a set of local payoff functions. Each node* $i \in V$ *represents a player whose in-neighborhood is defined as* $N_{in}(i) = \{j : (j, i) \in E\}$ *and strategy set is defined as* S_i. *For any joint action* $s = (s_1, \ldots, s_n) \in S = S_1 \times \ldots \times S_n$, *the payoff of i is given by* $f_i(s_i, s_{N_{in}(i)})$ *where* $s_{N_{in}(i)}$ *is the strategy profile of its neighbors.*

Note that f_i can be written as $f_i(s_i, s_{N_{in}(i)})$ as long as we consider only symmetric functions.

DEFINITION 4. *The pure strategy Nash equilibrium (PSNE) of a graphical game* (G, F) *is defined as a strategy profile* $s = (s_1, \ldots, s_n)$ *that for each* s_i *where* $i \in V$, $s_i = \text{argmax}_{y \in S_i} f_i(y, s_{N_{in}(i)})$.

DEFINITION 5. *A graphical game is called an ordinal potential game if there exist a potential function* $\Phi : S \rightarrow \mathbb{R}^+$ *such that when player i changes its strategy* s_i *to* s'_i, $\text{sgn}(\Phi(s) - \Phi(s')) = \text{sgn}(f_i(s) - f_i(s'))$ *where* $s = (s_1, \ldots, s_i, \ldots, s_n)$ *and* $s' = (s_1, \ldots, s'_i, \ldots, s_n)$.

DEFINITION 6. *A graphical game is called an exact potential game if there exist a potential function* $\Phi : S \rightarrow \mathbb{R}^+$ *such that when player i changes its strategy* s_i *to* s'_i, $\Phi(s) - \Phi(s') = f_i(s) - f_i(s')$ *where* $s = (s_1, \ldots, s_i, \ldots, s_n)$ *and* $s' = (s_1, \ldots, s'_i, \ldots, s_n)$.

DEFINITION 7. *A graphical game is called a weighted potential game if there exist a potential function* $\Phi : S \rightarrow \mathbb{R}^+$ *such that when player i changes its strategy* s_i *to* s'_i, $\Phi(s) - \Phi(s') = w_i(f_i(s) - f_i(s'))$ *where* $s = (s_1, \ldots, s_i, \ldots, s_n)$ *and* $s' = (s_1, \ldots, s'_i, \ldots, s_n)$.

It is well-known that if a game is potential it must possess a PSNE [24]. The PSNE can be achieved by the local improvement of strategies as long as the potential function exists [29]. When the potential function is maximal or minimal, the strategy profile is a PSNE. This is known as the *finite improvement property* (FIP).

3.2 Factor graphs

A factor graph [21] is one type of graphical model $\mathcal{G} = (X, \mathcal{F}, \mathcal{E})$, which is a bipartite graph where $X = \{X_1, \ldots, X_k\}$ is the set of variable nodes, with each X_i being a random variable whose joint distribution to be specified later, and $\mathcal{F} = \{F_1, \ldots, F_\ell\}$ is the set of function nodes, and $\mathcal{E} = \{\{X_i, F_j\} : i \in [k], j \in [\ell]\}$ is the set of edges adjoining variable nodes and function nodes. The bipartite graph $\mathcal{G}$ represents a function $g(x_1, \ldots, x_n) = \prod_{j=1}^{m} F_j(x_{\partial j})$ where $x_{\partial j}$ denotes the restriction of $\boldsymbol{x} = (x_1, x_2, \ldots, x_n)$ on the neighborhood $\partial j = \{i : \{X_i, F_j\} \in \mathcal{E}\}$ of j in $\mathcal{G}$. We assume that F_j depends only on those variables x_i with $i \in \partial j$ so that g is well-defined. This gives rise to a natural probability distribution, in which the joint probability of any $\boldsymbol{x} \in X_1 \times \ldots \times X_n$ is defined as

$$P(\boldsymbol{x}) = \frac{1}{Z} \prod_{j=1}^{m} F_j(x_{\partial j})$$

where the normalizing factor $Z = \sum_{\boldsymbol{x}} \prod_{j=1}^{m} F_j(x_{\partial j})$ is called the *partition function.*

A compelling reason for adopting factor graph is because of its simplicity and flexibility for analysis. When the environmental constraints change, the factor graph can be easily modified to adapt to the new environment by changing function nodes. For instance, in cognitive radio networks, secondary users cannot use a channel which is being used by a primary user. Thus once an idle channel c is occupied by a primary user, all the function nodes associated with variable nodes corresponding to a secondary user interfering with the primary user can be changed to new function nodes by each combining with a new function node whose constraint function is a Boolean indicator function indicating that $x_i \neq c$ for all involved variables.

3.3 The reduction

Given a graphical game $(G, \mathcal{F})$ where $G = (V, E)$, a strategy profile $s = (s_1, \ldots, s_n)$ is a PSNE if and only if for all $i \in V$, s_i is the best response for $s_{N_{in}(i)}$. Hence a graphical game $(G, \mathcal{F})$ can be represented by a factor graph $\mathcal{G} = (V, F, \mathcal{E})$ in such a way that for each player $i \in V$, we have a variable node in the factor graph which takes the strategy s_i of play i as value, and for each player $i \in V$, we also have a function node F_i adjacent to the variable nodes corresponding to players in $N_{in}(i)$, including player i itself. The function F_i is defined as

$$F_i = \begin{cases} \exp(f_i) & \text{if } s_i = \text{argmax}_{y \in S_i} f_i(y, s_{N_{in}(i)}), \\ 0 & \text{otherwise.} \end{cases} \quad (1)$$

Then searching the optimal pure strategy Nash equilibrium with maximum total payoff is equivalent to finding an assignment of variables with maximum product value in the factor graph, as follows:

$$\max \sum_{i=1}^{n} f_i = \max \left(\exp \left(\sum_{i=1}^{n} f_i \right) \right) \Leftrightarrow \max \prod_{i=1}^{n} F_i.$$

If the utility f_i is interpreted as "cost" and each player strives to minimize her cost, then F_i can be set as the dual version of max-product, that is

$$F_i = \begin{cases} \exp(-f_i) & \text{if } s_i = \text{argmax}_{y \in S_i} f_i(y, s_{N_{in}(i)}), \\ 0 & \text{otherwise.} \end{cases}$$

Then searching the optimal pure strategy Nash equilibrium with minimum total payoff is still equivalent to

$$\min \sum_{i=1}^{n} f_i = \max \left(\exp \left(- \sum_{i=1}^{n} f_i \right) \right) \Leftrightarrow \max \prod_{i=1}^{n} F_i.$$

Hence both utility maximization and cost minimization in graphical games can be reduced to computing the *maximum a posteriori* (MAP) value in corresponding factor graphs.

Sometimes we need to make a tradeoff between utility maximization and fairness. In this case, the constraint function F_i can

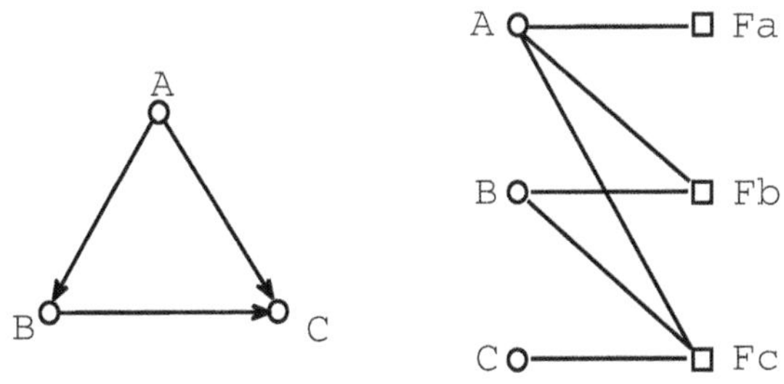

Figure 2: Factor Graph for Directed Acyclic Graph

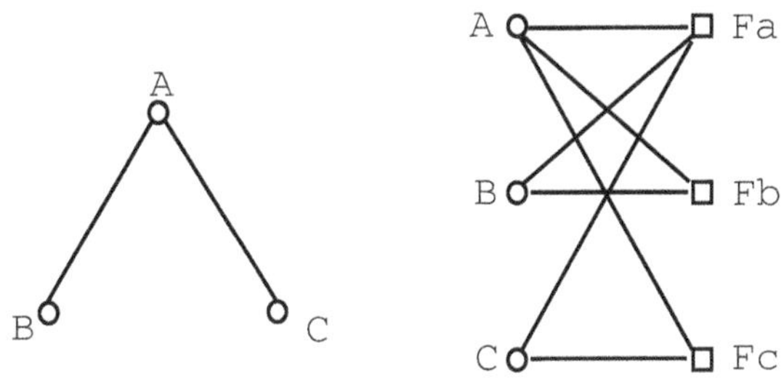

Figure 3: Factor Graph for Undirected Tree

be simply set as

$$F_i = \begin{cases} f_i = \exp(\log f_i) & \text{if } s_i = \text{argmax}_{y \in S_i} f_i(y, s_{N_{in}(i)}), \\ 0 & \text{otherwise.} \end{cases}$$

By the inequality of arithmetic and geometric means, $n\left(\prod_{i=1}^{n} f_i\right)^{1/n}$ provides a lower bound for $\sum_{i=1}^{n} f_i$ and the equality holds if and only if $f_1 = \ldots = f_n$, which means the maximization of $\prod_{i=1}^{n} F_i$ (equivalently, $\prod_{i=1}^{n} f_i$) provides a tradeoff between utility maximization and fairness. We call this algorithm *"fairness propagation"*. However, this algorithm can only be used in a limited amount of cases where the maximization of $\prod_{i=1}^{n} F_i$ can be exactly and efficiently computed. In other cases the performance of this algorithm cannot be well measured.

3.4 Belief Propagation

A tutorial of classic BP and max-product BP can be found in [21]. By our reduction, the factor graph translated from a directed acyclic interference graph may not always be a tree. An example is shown in Figure 2. In addition, even for the undirected interference graph which is a tree, the resulting factor graph may not be a tree either, as shown in Figure 3.

We modify the standard max-product BP algorithm to deal with this complication. Let $\mu^{(t)}_{a\to i}$ denote the message sent from function node a to variable node i in t-th iteration and $x_{\partial a}$ denote the joint configuration of the neighbors (variable nodes) of a when the strategy s_j is fixed to be x_j for every player j. If a is F_i, then

$$\mu^{(t)}_{a\to i}(x_i) = \max_{x_{\partial a \setminus i}} \left\{ F_a(x_{\partial a}) \prod_{j \in \partial a \setminus i} \mu^{(t)}_{j\to a}(x_j) \right\}.$$

Otherwise, $\mu^{(t)}_{a\to i}(x_i) = 1$. Let $\mu^{(t)}_{i\to a}$ denote the message sent from variable node i to function node a in t-th iteration. Then

$$\mu^{(t+1)}_{i\to a}(x_i) = \prod_{b \in \partial i \setminus a} \mu^{(t)}_{b\to i}(x_i) = \mu^{(t)}_{F_i\to i}(x_i).$$

Each message is a key-value map where the key is x_i and the value is $\mu_{i\to a}(x_i)$ or $\mu_{a\to i}(x_i)$. From now on, when mentioning BP or max-product BP equations, we refer to this modified version.

Observe that if in the graphical game PSNE does not exist, then in the factor graph the messages $\mu_{F_i\to i}(x_i) = 0$ for all $x_i \in s_i$. Therefore, the fixed point representing the nonexistence of PSNE is

$$\mu_{i\to a}(x_i) = \begin{cases} 1 & \text{if } a \text{ is } F_i, \\ 0 & \text{otherwise,} \end{cases} \quad \mu_{a\to i}(x_i) = \begin{cases} 0 & \text{if } a \text{ is } F_i, \\ 1 & \text{otherwise.} \end{cases}$$

The belief propagation algorithm on factor graphs can be easily translated back to distributed algorithm on interference graphs in the following way. Since for every graphical game, the corresponding factor graph has the same number of variable node and function node, the function node F_i can be treated as the decision making process of player i. Therefore the messages exchanged between i and F_i will not appear in the network. The messages exchanged from variable node i and F_i to variable node j and F_j are the messages exchanged between player i and player j. By this translation, we have the distributed algorithm in the network.

4. THE EXISTENCE OF PSNE

We show that in undirected interference graphs, for the spatial spectrum access games using considered protocols, Nash equilibrium always exists, by showing that the games are potential.

LEMMA 8. *All spatial spectrum access games on undirected graphs using FDMA, TDMA and CDMA are potential games.*

PROOF. We transform throughput maximization to delay minimization where the delay of user i using channel j is defined as $s_{i,j} + \sum_{k \in N(i)} s_{k,j}$ if $s_{i,j} = 1$, which is a linear function of the number of neighbors of user i using channel j. When the delay function is linear, by the main result of [3], the spatial spectrum games using FDMA, TDMA and CDMA are potential games. □

When the utility function is $f'_i = \log f_i$, it is proved in [5] that spatial spectrum access games on undirected interference graph using CSMA/CA are ordinal potential games.

LEMMA 9. *All spatial spectrum access games on undirected graphs using CSMA/CA are potential games.*

PROOF. A PSNE for f'_i is also a PSNE for f_i since $\log f_i(s_1, \ldots, s_i, \ldots, s_n) \geq \log f_i(s_1, \ldots, s'_i, \ldots, s_n)$ for $\forall i \in V$ implies $f_i(s_1, \ldots, s_i, \ldots, s_n) \geq f_i(s_1, \ldots, s'_i, \ldots, s_n)$ for $\forall i \in V$. □

Since a potential game always has PSNE [24], we have the following theorem.

THEOREM 10. *For spatial spectrum access games on undirected graphs using FDMA, TDMA, CDMA, and CSMA/CA protocols, PSNE always exists.*

When the interference graph is directed, for $(i, j) \notin E$ and $(j, i) \in E$, we have $\frac{\partial^2 f_i}{\partial s_i \partial s_j} \neq 0$ and $\frac{\partial^2 f_j}{\partial s_i \partial s_j} = 0$, thus the ratio between them is $\pm\infty$. By Theorem 4.5 in [24], the potential function does not exist. This shows an evidence that for directed interference graphs, PSNE of spatial spectrum access game may not always exist.

We can use a similar local message-passing algorithm called *survey propagation* [4] to decide whether a PSNE exists. As in Section 3.3, the graphical game is translated into a *constraint satisfaction problem* (CSP), with constraints set as

$$F_i = \begin{cases} 1 & \text{if } s_i = \text{argmax}_{y \in S_i} f_i(y, s_{N_{in}(i)}), \\ 0 & \text{otherwise.} \end{cases} \tag{2}$$

Then the PSNE exists if and only if there exists a truth assignment for the CSP.

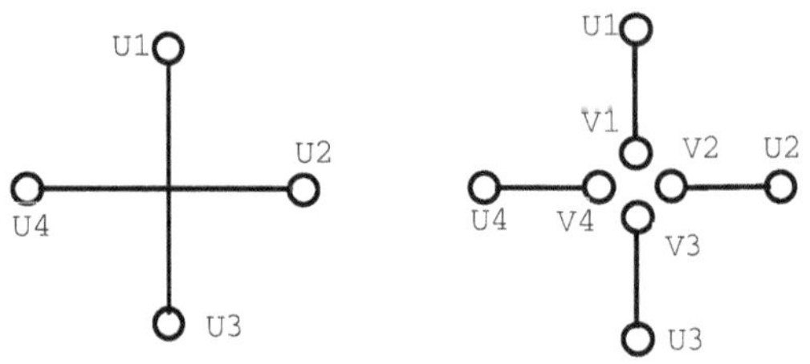

Figure 4: Reduction by Crossing Replacement

5. COMPUTATIONAL COMPLEXITY

In this section, we explore the computational complexity of graphical games to see how hard the problem is in general. It is known that deciding the existence of PSNE for graphical games is NP-complete [14]. The following theorem says the problem remains hard even on planar graphs.

THEOREM 11. *Deciding the existence of PSNE for graphical games on planar graphs is NP-complete.*

PROOF. This can be proved by a reduction from computing PSNE for graphical games $(G, \mathcal{F})$ on general graphs to computing PSNE for graphical games $(G', \mathcal{F}')$ on planar graphs, which is constructed by simply replacing each crossing with 4 new additional player whose payoff is always 0 and whose strategy will not affect other players' payoff, as shown in Figure 4. The strategies of additional player satisfy $s_{V_1} = s_{U_3}$, $s_{V_2} = s_{U_4}$, $s_{V_3} = s_{U_1}$ and $s_{V_4} = s_{U_2}$, then $(G, \mathcal{F})$ has a PSNE only if $(G', \mathcal{F}')$ has a PSNE. This completes the reduction. □

Since graphical congestion game [3] is a spacial case of graphical game, by the PLS-completeness result for classic congestion games [9], which are graphical congestion games on complete graph, we have the following theorem.

THEOREM 12. *Computing PSNE for graphical games is PLS-complete.*

On the other hand, the decision problem becomes trivial on directed acyclic graphs.

THEOREM 13 (CHEN *et al.* [5]). *There always exists a PSNE for graphical games on directed acyclic graphs.*

The PSNE of graphical games on directed acyclic graphs can be found in $O(|V| + |E|)$ time by topological sorting.

Observing that load balancing is a special case of graphical congestion game, by the NP-completeness of load balancing, the following theorem holds.

THEOREM 14. *Given a graphical game defined on an undirected graph and an integer $k > 0$, determining whether there exists a PSNE with cost at most k is NP-complete.*

The following theorem can be proved by the same reduction used in the proof of Theorem 11.

THEOREM 15. *Given a graphical game defined on an undirected* planar *graph and an integer $k > 0$, determining whether there exists a PSNE with cost at most k is NP-complete.*

Indeed, graphical game is a general model which covers many combinatorial optimization problems. When the utility function is properly set, as in Equation (3), the maximum independent set (MIS) problem can be coded as finding optimal PSNE in a special class of graphical games. Another observation is that the maximum weight q-coloring with $q > \Delta$ can also be reduced to optimizing PSNE of graphical games. It is known that MIS is MAX SNP-complete [25] and NP-hard to approximate within polynomial factor in polynomial time [16], which leads to the following inapproximability results.

THEOREM 16. *Computing optimal PSNE of graphical games is MAX SNP-complete.*

THEOREM 17. *For any $\epsilon > 0$, there does not exist any $n^{\epsilon-1}$-approximation algorithm for computing optimal PSNE of graphical games unless P = NP.*

PROOF. Both theorems can be proved by reducing maximum independent set to finding optimal PSNE in graphical games. We can set f_i as

$$f_i = \begin{cases} 1 & \text{if } s_{i,j} = 1 \text{ and } \forall j \in N(i),\ s_j = 0, \\ 0 & \text{if } s_{i,j} = 0 \text{ and } \exists j \in N(i),\ s_j = 1, \\ -1 & \text{if } s_{i,j} = 1 \text{ and } \exists j \in N(i),\ s_j = 1. \end{cases} \tag{3}$$

Then each PSNE is a maximal independent set and the optimal PSNE is a maximum independent set. Then by the inapproximability of maximum independent set, the theorem follows. □

6. ALGORITHM FOR ACYCLIC GRAPHS

In [20], an algorithm called "TreeNash" was proposed to compute a PSNE on undirected trees. Now we show that when the graphical game is defined on directed acyclic graphs or undirected trees, our modified max-product BP converge very fast to the fixed point $s = (s_1, \ldots, s_n)$ maximizing the total payoff $\sum_{i=1}^n f_i$. Indeed, on these graphs, the max-product BP is equivalent to a parallel dynamic programming.

THEOREM 18. *For a graphical game on an undirected tree, suppose t^* is the diameter of the tree,*

1. *The max-product BP equations converge to a fixed point after $t > t^*$ iterations. That is, for any edge (i, a) in the factor graph and any $t > t^*$, $\mu^{(t)}_{i\to a} = \mu^{(t^*)}_{i\to a}$ and $\mu^{(t)}_{a\to i} = \mu^{(t^*)}_{a\to i}$.*
2. *The convergent fixed point is an optimal PSNE: for any player i and any $t > t^*$, $\mu^{(t)}_i(x_i) = \prod_{a\in\partial i} \mu^{(t-1)}_{a\to i}(x_i) = \max_{s:s_i=x_i} \prod_i F_i = \max_{s:s_i=x_i} \exp(\sum_i f_i)$.*

PROOF. We set the function associated to the function nodes as in Equation (1). Initially, for each player i, the message $\mu^{(1)}_{i\to a}(x_i) = 1$ if $s_i = x_i$. Otherwise $\mu^{(1)}_{i\to a}(x_i) = 0$. The proof is by induction on the depth of the tree. The base step of the induction is for the case of single-node graph whose factor graph contains one variable node and one function node connected by a single edge. We define the message from empty set is 1. In the first round, the message from F_i to i is

$$\mu^{(1)}_{F_i\to i}(x_i) = \begin{cases} F_i(x_i) & \text{if } x_i \text{ is the best strategy,} \\ 0 & \text{otherwise.} \end{cases}$$

It is easy to see that the messages have converged and $F_i(x_i) = \max(\exp(\sum_i f_i))$ is the maximum total utility of the graphical game on the single-node tree. Then $\mu^{(t)}_{i\to F_i}(x_i) = 1$ and $\mu^{(t)}_{F_i\to i}(x_i) = \mu^{(1)}_{F_i\to i}(x_i)$ for any $t > 1$. Hence the messages have converged.

Suppose it holds for tree with depth τ, then we show that it also holds for tree with depth $\tau+1$. Consider the tree rooted at i of depth is $\tau+1$, whose the subtree is of depth at most τ. Then after at most τ rounds, $\mu_{j\to F_i}(x_j)$ where $j\in\partial F_i\backslash i$ is the maximum total utility for subtree T_j rooted at j whose configuration is x_j. Then we have

$$\mu^{(\tau)}_{F_i\to i}(x_i) = \max_{\partial F_i\backslash i}\left\{F_i(x_{\partial F_i})\prod_{j\in\partial F_i\backslash i}\mu^{(\tau)}_{j\to F_i}(x_j)\right\}.$$

We can see that $\mu_i^{(\tau+1)}(x_i) = \prod_{a\in\partial i}\mu^{(\tau)}_{a\to i}(x_i) = \mu^{(\tau)}_{F_i\to i}(x_i)$ is the maximum total utility of graphical game when s_i is fixed to x_i. This complete the induction. □

THEOREM 19. *For a graphical game on a directed acyclic interference graph, suppose t^* is the length of the longest path from any of the node whose in-degree is 0 to any of the node whose out-degree is 0. Such nodes always exist since the interference graph is acyclic.*

1. *The max-product BP equations converge to a fixed point after $t>t^*$ iterations. That is, for any edge (i,a) in the factor graph and any $t>t^*$, $\mu^{(t)}_{i\to a} = \mu^{(t^*)}_{i\to a}$ and $\mu^{(t)}_{a\to i} = \mu^{(t^*)}_{a\to i}$.*
2. *The convergent fixed point is an optimal PSNE: for any player i and any $t>t^*$, $\mu_i^{(t)}(x_i) = \prod_{a\in\partial i}\mu^{(t-1)}_{a\to i}(x_i) = \max_{s:s_i=x_i}\prod_i F_i = \max_{s:s_i=x_i}\exp\left(\sum_i f_i\right)$.*

PROOF. This theorem is proved by a structural induction on the depth of the directed interference graph. The depth of node i is defined as the maximum length of shortest paths from any node whose in-degree is 0. The depths of the nodes with in-degree 0 are set as 0.

It is easy to see that the function nodes of variable nodes with depth larger than 0 will only sends "1" messages to the variable nodes with depth 0, which will not affect their computation of messages after round 0. Hence in round 0 the messages of nodes with depth 0 has converged. Similarly, the function nodes of variable nodes with depth larger than $t+1$ will only sends "1" messages to the variable nodes with depth t. Hence if in round t the messages of nodes with depth t converge, then the messages of nodes with depth $t+1$ will converge in round $t+1$. The computation details are similar to theorem 18. This completes the induction. □

7. ALGORITHM FOR CYCLIC GRAPHS

We study the convergence rate of our max-product BP algorithm to PSNE on cyclic undirected graphs. We start by showing an impossibility result.

THEOREM 20. *Synchronous max-product BP does not always converge for spatial spectrum access games on cyclic graphs.*

PROOF. We set the function associated to the function nodes as in Equation (2), with the initial condition $\mu^{(1)}_{i\to a}(x_i)=1$ if $s_i=x_i$ and $\mu^{(1)}_{i\to a}(x_i)=0$ if otherwise. Let $\mu^{(t)}_{i\to a}(x_i)$ and $\mu^{(t)}_{a\to i}(x_i)$ denote the messages sent from i to a and from a to i in the t-th iteration respectively. Then for $i\in V$, we have

$$\mu^{(1)}_{F_i\to i}(x_i) = \begin{cases}1, & \text{if } x \text{ is the best response of } s_{N(i)},\\ 0, & \text{otherwise.}\end{cases}$$

Hence it holds that

$$\mu^{(2)}_{i\to a}(x_i) = \begin{cases}1, & \text{if } a \text{ is } F_i,\\ \mu^{(1)}_{F_i\to i}(x_i), & \text{otherwise.}\end{cases}$$

We defined $s^{(t)} = \{s_1^{(t)},\dots,s_n^{(t)}\}$ where $s_i^{(t)} = x_i$ such that $\mu^{(2)}_{i\to a}(x_i)=1$ for $a\neq F_i$. Then for $i\in V$, we have

$$\mu^{(t)}_{F_i\to i}(x_i) = \begin{cases}1, & \text{if } x_i \text{ is the best response of } s^{(t)}_{N(i)},\\ 0, & \text{otherwise.}\end{cases}$$

Suppose the interference graph is an undirected complete graph of n vertices and $Q=\{1,2,3\}$. The rates of the channels satisfy $\theta_1=\theta_3>\theta_2$. All users initialize their strategies by randomly choosing channel from $Q'=\{1,2\}$. Then for $t\in\mathbb{N}^+$,

$$\mu^{(2t-1)}_{F_i\to i}(x_i) = \begin{cases}1, & \text{if } x_i=3\\ 0, & \text{otherwise,}\end{cases}\quad \mu^{(2t)}_{F_i\to i}(x_i) = \begin{cases}1, & \text{if } x_i=1\\ 0, & \text{otherwise.}\end{cases}$$

Then the BP process falls into a infinite loop and never converge. □

We can avoid this issue by introducing the concept of *BP-guided local dynamics* where the strategy update is guided by the *asynchronous max-product BP* equations:

$$\mu^{(t+1)}_{i\to a}(x_i) = \mu^{(t)}_{F_i\to i}(x_i),$$
$$\mu^{(t)}_{F_i\to i}(x_i) = \max_{\partial F_i\backslash i}\left\{F_i(x_{\partial F_i})\prod_{j\in\partial F_i\backslash i}\mu^{(\tau_j)}_{j\to F_i}(x_j)\right\}$$

where $\mu^{(\tau_j)}_{j\to F_i}(x_j)$ is the τ_j-th and the latest message sent from j to F_i. By setting F_i as in Equation (2), $\mu^{(1)}_{i\to a}(x_i)=1$ if $s_i=x_i$ and $\mu^{(1)}_{i\to a}(x_i)=0$ if otherwise, then $\mu^{(t)}_{F_i\to i}(x_i)=1$ if x_i is the best response for $s_{N_{in}(i)}$. If the best response x_i computed by $\mu^{(t)}_{F_i\to i}(x_i)$ is not the current s_i, then user i modify its strategy to $s_i=x_i$.

For BP-guided local dynamics, the convergence time is measured by the number of strategy modification of all the users instead of the number of rounds. We further require that no two updates of strategies involving interfering users can occur simultaneously, then the following holds.

THEOREM 21. *The BP-guided local dynamics converges to a PSNE for spatial spectrum access games on undirected graphs if the game is potential.*

PROOF. For potential games, the utility improvement of each user will also improve the value of potential function. When the potential function is maximal, the strategy profile $s=(s_1,\dots,s_n)$ is a PSNE after convergence. And by the finite improvement property, this algorithm will terminate in finite steps. □

By Theorem 12, computing a PSNE for graphical games is PLS-complete. Therefore, instead of exact PSNE we study the convergence rate to approximate PSNE, called ϵ-PSNE, defined in [6].

DEFINITION 22. *(ϵ-PSNE) A state $s=(s_1,\dots,s_n)$ is an ϵ-PSNE if no player can improve its payoff by a factor greater than $\epsilon\in[0,1)$. If f_i is interpreted as cost, then $f_i(s_1,\dots,s_i',\dots,s_n)\geq(1-\epsilon)f_i(s_1,\dots,s_i,\dots,s_n)$ for all $s_i'\in S_i$. If f_i is interpreted as utility, then $f_i(s_1,\dots,s_i',\dots,s_n)\leq(1+\epsilon)f_i(s_1,\dots,s_i,\dots,s_n)$ for all $s_i'\in S_i$.*

To reach an ϵ-PSNE, a user will change its strategy if and only if it can improve its utility by a factor at least ϵ, which is called ϵ-move [6]. To study the rate of convergence to a ϵ-PSNE, we transform the utility maximization problem into its dual version, the cost minimization. The cost is defined as $C_i=\sum_{j\in s_i}C_{i,j}=\sum_{j\in s_i}1/f_{i,j}$ where $f_{i,j}$ is the utility of user i using channel j, which can be naturally defined for all our considered protocols. Note that $f_{i,j}$ is a function of the number of neighbors using channel j, we define α as the lower bound of a constant which satisfies $f_{i,j}(x)\leq\alpha\cdot f_{i,j}(x+1)$ for $x\in[n-1]$. Then $C_{i,j}(x+1)\leq\alpha\cdot C_{i,j}(x)$, satisfying the *$\alpha$-bounded jump* condition [6]. By this transformation, the spatial spectrum access games using FDMA, TDMA and CDMA becomes exact potential games, and hence possess a potential function Φ [3].

We show the convergence rates of BP-guided local dynamics which are assumed to satisfy the following conditions.

1. **Condition 1:** The player with maximum cost can make an ϵ-move.

2. **Condition 2:** If the player v with maximum cost cannot make an ϵ-move, at least one of its neighbors $u \in N(v)$ has cost greater than any player $u' \in N(u)\backslash v$ and can make an ϵ-move.

Let Δ denote the maximum degree of the interference graph and Φ denote the potential function of spatial spectrum access games. The upper bounds of convergence time for the dynamics satisfying conditions 1 and 2 are given by the following theorems.

THEOREM 23. *If a spatial spectrum access game possesses an exact potential function Φ and the dynamics satisfies the condition 1, then the convergence time is $O(n\epsilon^{-1} \log \Phi_{\max})$.*

PROOF. Since $\Phi(s) \leq \sum_i C_i(s)$ for any strategy profile s, then each time the player with maximum cost makes a ϵ-move, it decreases the potential function at least a factor $\frac{\epsilon}{n}$. Hence $(1-\frac{\epsilon}{n})^t\Phi_{\max} < \Phi_{\min}$, then $t = O(n\epsilon^{-1} \log \Phi_{\max})$. □

THEOREM 24. *If a spatial spectrum access game possesses an exact potential function Φ and the dynamics satisfies the condition 2, then the convergence time is $O(n\alpha^{\Delta}\epsilon^{-1} \log \Phi_{\max})$.*

PROOF. Suppose i is the user with maximum cost. For $(i, j) \in E$, let $s = (s_1, \ldots, s_i, \ldots, s_j, \ldots, s_n)$ and $s' = (s_1, \ldots, s'_i, \ldots, s_j, \ldots, s_n)$, $s'' = (s_1, \ldots, s_i, \ldots, s'_j, \ldots, s_n)$. If user j moves from s_j to s'_j, then $C_j(s'') \leq (1 - \epsilon)C_j(s)$. Since user i did not move to s'_i, then $(1-\epsilon)C_i(s) \leq C_i(s')$. For each channel $e \in s'_i$, $C_{i,e}(s') \leq \alpha^{\Delta}C_{j,e}(s'')$, then $C_i(s') \leq \alpha^{\Delta}C_j(s'')$. Hence it holds that $(1 - \epsilon)C_i(s) \leq C_i(s') \leq \alpha^{\Delta}C_j(s'') \leq \alpha^{\Delta}(1 - \epsilon)C_j(s)$. The ϵ-move made by player j will decrease the potential function by a constant at least $\frac{\epsilon}{n\alpha^{\Delta}}$. Hence $(1 - \frac{\epsilon}{n\alpha^{\Delta}})^t\Phi_{\max} < \Phi_{\min}$, then $t = O(n\alpha^{\Delta}\epsilon^{-1} \log \Phi_{\max})$. □

If the condition 1 and 2 to is loosed such that they are satisfied at least once respectively during T strategy updates, then the convergence time becomes $O(nT\epsilon^{-1} \log \Phi_{\max})$ and $O(nT\alpha^{\Delta}\epsilon^{-1} \log \Phi_{\max})$. This technique can be easily generalized to weighted potential games.

8. ALGORITHM FOR PLANAR GRAPHS

We give approximation algorithms for computing optimal PSNE in some typical spatial spectrum access games on planar graphs in the sense of *polynomial time approximation scheme*. This is useful because the interference graphs of wireless mesh networks are often planar.

DEFINITION 25. *A polynomial time approximation scheme (PTAS) for an optimization problem is an polynomial time algorithm $A(I, \epsilon)$ which takes an instance I of the problem and a parameter ϵ and always return a solution with accuracy $(1 - \epsilon)$ for maximization and $(1 + \epsilon)$ for minimization.*

We consider the spatial spectrum access games induced by independent sets or colorings studied in [19, 28, 15, 23, 30]. When transmission time is long and users can be blocked to avoid collisions, then the optimization of spatial spectrum access can be modeled as a q-state maximum weight independent set (q-MWIS) problem where the set of state is denote as $\{0, \ldots, q-1\}$. A user is in state $j \in [1, q-1]$ means the user is using channel j, and state 0 means the user is idle or blocked. The model of independent set for scheduling and congestion control in wireless networks has been widely studied [19, 28].

If the system requires high quality of service (QoS) which blocking user is not allowed, then the game can be modeled as a maximum weight q-coloring (q-MWC) problem as in [15, 23, 30], where the set of colors is $\{1, \ldots, q\}$. A user is of color j means the user is using channel j. Since deciding the existence of a proper coloring is nontrivial for $q \leq \Delta$ where Δ is the maximum degree of the graph, we only consider the case where $q > \Delta$. Both q-MWIS and q-MWC can be formulated as computing optimal PSNE of spatial spectrum access games. We have the following algorithmic result generalized from the PTAS for maximum independent set problem on planar graphs in [1].

THEOREM 26. *There exist PTAS for computing (q-state) maximum weight independent set and maximum weight q-coloring with $q > \Delta$ on planar graphs.*

Given a planar embedding of planar graph G, the level-1 vertices are the vertices on exterior face, and a vertex is a level-k if it is on the exterior face by deleting all the vertices of level $< k$. A planar graph is k-outerplanar if for some embedding it has no vertex of level $> k$.

THEOREM 27. *The optimal PSNE of graphical games can be exactly computed in $O(q^{O(k)} \cdot n)$ time for k-outerplanar graphs.*

The algorithm in this theorem is a dynamic programming algorithm, which can either be generalized from the dynamic programming in [1] for computing MIS on k-outerplanar graphs, or specialized from the dynamic programming in [31] for counting CSPs on graphs of bounded treewidth $O(k)$ (which cover k-outerplanar graphs). In particular, for q-MWIS and q-MWC, this exact algorithm can be combined into a PTAS on planar graphs using the same routine designed in [1] for maximum independent sets. This gives us the PTAS in Theorem 26. We omit detailed proofs here.

The next theorem shows that in general we may not expect to always have good approximation of PSNE as in the cases of q-MWIS and q-MWC.

THEOREM 28. *There is no PTAS for computing optimal PSNE for graphical games on planar graphs unless P = NP.*

PROOF. If the PTAS exists, then there is an algorithm can approximate the total payoff of PSNE within accuracy $(1 - \epsilon)$ for any $\epsilon > 0$, which implies a polynomial time algorithm for deciding the existence of PSNE on planar graphs, which is NP-hard by Theorem 11. □

The following heuristics can be considered to cope with the above inapproximability result. Given a spatial spectrum access game on planar graph G, we can use the linear-time algorithm in [17] to generate a planar embedding. Fix a constant k. Applying the dynamic programming algorithm in Theorem 27, we can find an optimal PSNE for the k-outerplanar components separated by the level-ℓ vertices for all $\ell \mod (k+1) = 0$, and then randomly assign channels for the level ℓ vertices. Since the game is potential, we can then apply the asynchronous max-product BP to converge to a PSNE. The heuristic part is that we wish the randomly assigned channels would not distort too much from a globally optimal PSNE.

9. EVALUATIONS

We evaluate the performance of BP-guided local dynamics for spatial spectrum access games. We consider the case where the size of the network is $1000m \times 1000m$ and $q = 5$. The rates of channels is in the range from 10Mbit/s to 60Mbit/s. Each user has a interference range 50m. The locations of n users are uniformly distributed in the network. For each case, we generate a random interference graph and evaluate the performance for 11 rounds to test the robustness. Since the utility functions of FDMA, TDMA and CDMA has the same form, we only evaluate the performance of FDMA for the contention-free protocols, and the CSMA/CA for the contention-based protocol.

We first evaluate the performance of random dynamics on undirected interference graphs, which is BP-guided local dynamics where the order of users updating their strategies is random. We consider four cases where the number of users $n = 100, 200, 500, 1000$. For each case compare the total utility of users between random access and PSNE, as shown in Figure 5 and Figure 6. The corresponding convergence time which is measured by the number of total strategy updates is shown in Figure 7 and Figure 8. Since the PSNE may not exist on directed interference graphs, we only evaluate the performance for cases where n is relatively small. The performance is similar to those of undirected interference graphs as long as the dynamics can converge.

We can see that for all the communication protocols considered in this paper the BP-guided local dynamics can improve the total utility of users by more than 60%. And this improvement is very stable which does not decrease when the number of users increases from 100 to 1000. Moreover, the evaluation shows that the average number of strategy updates of each user is about 0.7-0.8, which is less than 1. This shows the BP-guided local dynamics can converge very fast to a PSNE of spatial spectrum access games. Thus the cost of spectrum mobility is very small.

We then consider the cases where the orders of users updating their strategies are not random. We consider six types of dynamics. The first three has been considered in [6] to study the convergence properties of congestion games where the orders are determined by global priorities, listed as follows:

1. Largest cost dynamics (LCD): the players with largest delay (minimum throughput) has priority to move, that is, $f_i(s) \leq f_j(s)$ for all $j \in V$.
2. Largest gain dynamics (LGD): the players with largest absolute improvement has priority to move, that is, $f_i(s') - f_i(s) \geq f_j(s'') - f_j(s)$ for all $j \in V$, where s' is the strategy profile after user i updates its strategy and s'' is the strategy profile after user j updates its strategy.
3. Largest ratio dynamics (LRD): the players with largest relative improvement has priority to move, that is, $\frac{f_i(s')-f_i(s)}{f_i(s)} \geq \frac{f_j(s'')-f_j(s)}{f_j(s)}$ for all $j \in V$, where s' is the strategy profile after user i updates its strategy and s'' is the strategy profile after user j updates its strategy.

The next three types of dynamics is similar to the above three, except the orders of strategy updates are determined by local priorities, listed as follows:

1. Local Largest cost dynamics (LLCD): the players with largest delay (minimum throughput) has priority to move, that is, $f_i(s) \leq f_j(s)$ for all $j \in N(i)$.
2. Local Largest gain dynamics (LLGD): the players with largest absolute improvement has priority to move, that is, $f_i(s') - f_i(s) \geq f_j(s'') - f_j(s)$ for all $j \in N(i)$, where s' is the strategy profile after user i updates its strategy and s'' is the strategy profile after user j updates its strategy.
3. Local Largest ratio dynamics (LLRD): the players with largest relative improvement has priority to move, that is, $\frac{f_i(s')-f_i(s)}{f_i(s)} \geq \frac{f_j(s'')-f_j(s)}{f_j(s)}$ for all $j \in N(i)$, where s' is the strategy profile after user i updates its strategy and s'' is the strategy profile after user j updates its strategy.

It is easy to see that all the users who have local priorities to move form an independent set of the interference graph. We do not require them to move simultaneously. From the evaluation we can see that for all the communication protocols considered in this paper, the performances of LGD (LLGD) and LRD (LLRD) are almost the same, which is similar to random dynamics that can improve the network performance by more than 60%, as shown in Figure 9. When n is small, the performance of LCD (LLCD) is very close to LGD (LLGD) and LRD (LLRD). However, as n increases, the performance of LCD (LLCD) decreases compared to LGD (LLGD) and LRD (LLRD). When $n = 1000$, for all the considered protocols, the LCD can only improve the network performance by 25%. The LLCD is better, when $n = 1000$ it can improve the network performance by about 50%, as shown in Figure 10.

Due to the space limit, we omit the evaluation of convergence time of these dynamics. Actually, the convergence time of LGD (LLGD) and LRD (LLRD) is almost the same for all the communication protocols considered in this paper, which is similar to their performances. For LCD (LLCD), although its performance is poorer, the convergence is faster. An empirical conclusion is, when the improvement is larger, the convergence time is longer. This provides a method to make a tradeoff between the performance and convergence.

10. CONCLUSION

We translate the problem of finding optimal pure strategy Nash equilibrium (PSNE) in spatial spectrum access games for channel assignment in wireless networks into estimating maximum a posteriori (MAP) assignment in factor graphs, and then propose to use a modified version of max-product belief propagation to solve the problem. Our algorithms are guaranteed to converge in linear time to an optimal PSNE if the interference graph is an undirected tree or directed acyclic interference graph, and converge fast to a near-optimal PSNE when the interference graph is undirected. Moreover, the optimization problem can be exactly solved on k-outerplanar graphs and for some typical special cases it has polynomial time approximation scheme on planar graphs. There are some interesting problems remaining open such as the approximability of finding the optimal PSNE for spatial spectrum access games on planar graphs or families of graphs arising from wireless networks.

Acknowledgement

Y. Wang and Y. Yin were supported by NSFC grants 61272081 and 61321491, S. Zhong was supported by RPGE, NSFC-61321491 and NSFC-61300235.

11. REFERENCES

[1] B. S. Baker. Approximation algorithms for np-complete problems on planar graphs. *Journal of the ACM (JACM)*, 41(1):153–180, 1994.

[2] M. Bayati, D. Shah, and M. Sharma. Max-product for maximum weight matching: Convergence, correctness, and lp duality. *IEEE Transactions on Information Theory*, 54(3):1241–1251, 2008.

[3] V. Bilò, A. Fanelli, M. Flammini, and L. Moscardelli. Graphical congestion games. *Algorithmica*, 61(2):274–297, 2011.

[4] A. Braunstein, M. Mézard, and R. Zecchina. Survey propagation: An algorithm for satisfiability. *Random Structures & Algorithms*, 27(2):201–226, 2005.

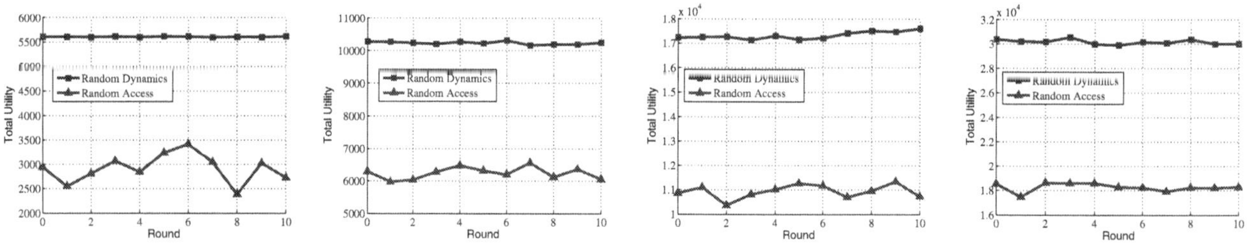

Figure 5: Performance evaluation for FDMA when $n = 100, 200, 500, 1000$

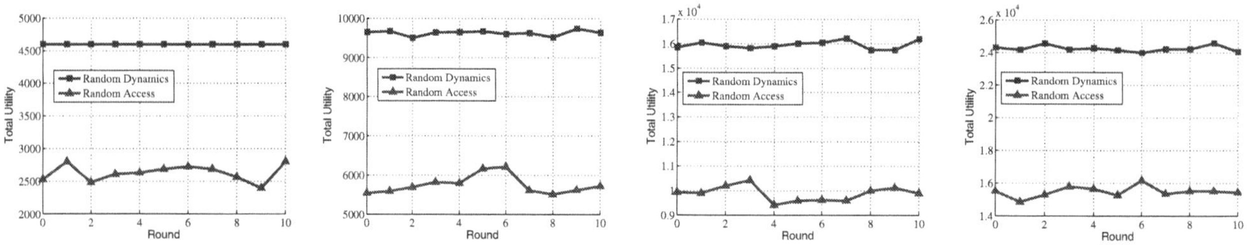

Figure 6: Performance evaluation for CSMA/CA when $n = 100, 200, 500, 1000$

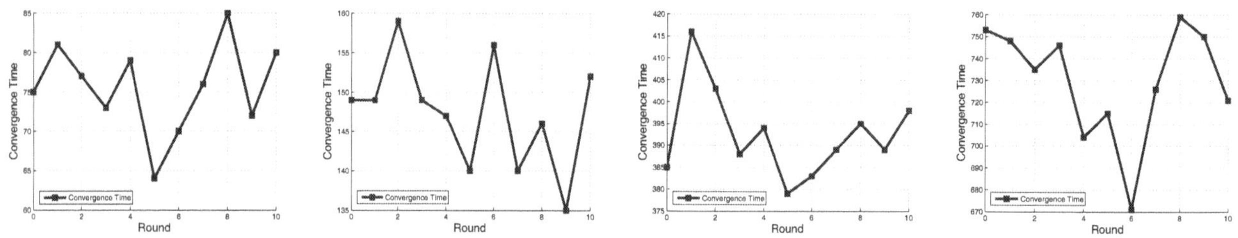

Figure 7: Convergence time for FDMA when $n = 100, 200, 500, 1000$

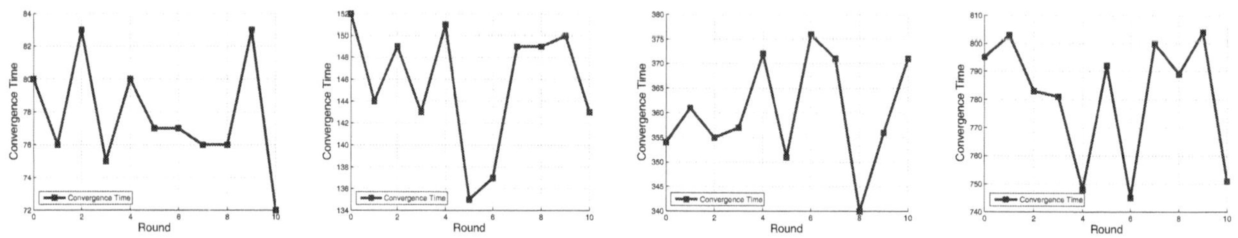

Figure 8: Convergence time for CSMA/CA when $n = 100, 200, 500, 1000$

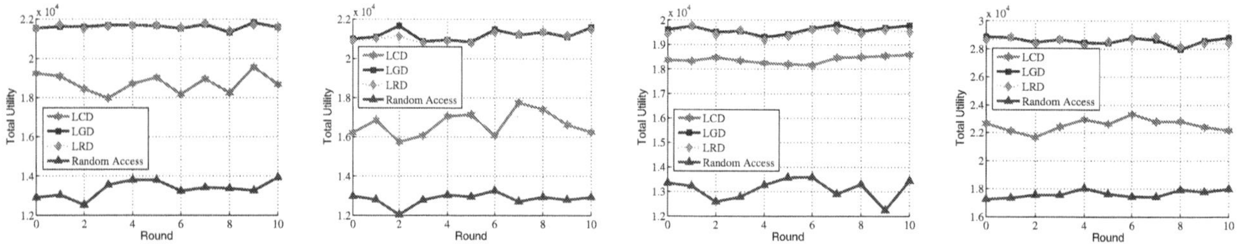

Figure 9: Performance evaluation of global-priority dynamics for FDMA and CSMA/CA when $n = 500, 1000$

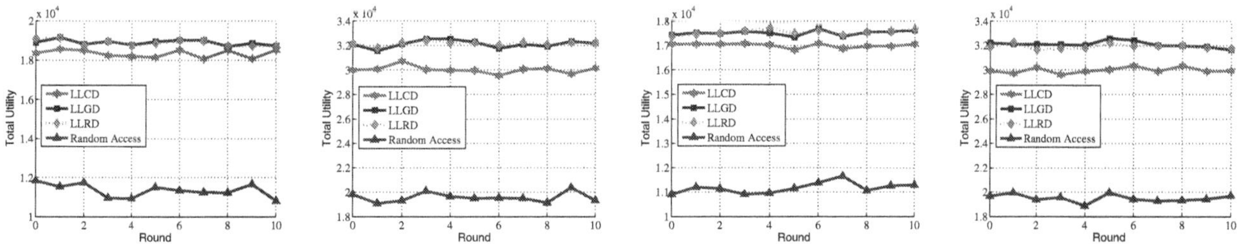

Figure 10: Performance evaluation of local-priority dynamics for FDMA and CSMA/CA when n = 500, 1000

[5] X. Chen and J. Huang. Spatial spectrum access game: Nash equilibria and distributed learning. In *Proceedings of the thirteenth ACM international symposium on Mobile Ad Hoc Networking and Computing (MobiHoc)*, pages 205–214, 2012.

[6] S. Chien and A. Sinclair. Convergence to approximate nash equilibria in congestion games. In *Proceedings of the eighteenth annual ACM-SIAM symposium on Discrete algorithms*, pages 169–178, 2007.

[7] C. Daskalakis and C. H. Papadimitriou. Computing pure nash equilibria in graphical games via markov random fields. In *Proceedings of the 7th ACM conference on Electronic commerce (EC)*, pages 91–99, 2006.

[8] S. C. Ergen and P. Varaiya. Tdma scheduling algorithms for wireless sensor networks. *Wireless Networks*, 16(4):985–997, 2010.

[9] A. Fabrikant, C. Papadimitriou, and K. Talwar. The complexity of pure nash equilibria. In *Proceedings of the thirty-sixth annual ACM symposium on Theory of computing (STOC)*, pages 604–612, 2004.

[10] M. Felegyhazi, M. Cagalj, S. S. Bidokhti, and J.-P. Hubaux. Non-cooperative multi-radio channel allocation in wireless networks. In *Proceedings of the 26th IEEE International Conference on Computer Communications (INFOCOM)*, pages 1442–1450, 2007.

[11] R. Gallager. Low-density parity-check codes. *IRE Transactions on Information Theory*, 8(1):21–28, 1962.

[12] D. Gamarnik, D. Shah, and Y. Wei. Belief propagation for min-cost network flow: Convergence and correctness. *Operations Research*, 60(2):410–428, 2012.

[13] L. Gao and X. Wang. A game approach for multi-channel allocation in multi-hop wireless networks. In *Proceedings of the 9th ACM international symposium on Mobile ad hoc networking and computing (MobiHoc)*, pages 303–312, 2008.

[14] G. Gottlob, G. Greco, and F. Scarcello. Pure nash equilibria: Hard and easy games. In *Proceedings of the 9th conference on Theoretical aspects of rationality and knowledge (TARK)*, pages 215–230, 2003.

[15] M. M. Halldórsson, J. Y. Halpern, L. E. Li, and V. S. Mirrokni. On spectrum sharing games. In *Proceedings of the twenty-third annual ACM symposium on Principles of distributed computing (PODC)*, pages 107–114, 2004.

[16] J. Hastad. Clique is hard to approximate within $n^{1-\epsilon}$. In *Proceedings of the 37th Annual Symposium on Foundations of Computer Science (FOCS)*, pages 627–636, 1996.

[17] J. Hopcroft and R. Tarjan. Efficient planarity testing. *Journal of the ACM (JACM)*, 21(4):549–568, 1974.

[18] L. Jiang and J. Walrand. A distributed csma algorithm for throughput and utility maximization in wireless networks. *IEEE/ACM Transactions on Networking (TON)*, 18(3):960–972, 2010.

[19] C. Joo, X. Lin, J. Ryu, and N. B. Shroff. Distributed greedy approximation to maximum weighted independent set for scheduling with fading channels. In *Proceedings of the fourteenth ACM international symposium on Mobile ad hoc networking and computing (MobiHoc)*, pages 89–98, 2013.

[20] M. Kearns, M. L. Littman, and S. Singh. Graphical models for game theory. In *Proceedings of the Seventeenth conference on Uncertainty in artificial intelligence*, pages 253–260. Morgan Kaufmann Publishers Inc., 2001.

[21] F. R. Kschischang, B. J. Frey, and H.-A. Loeliger. Factor graphs and the sum-product algorithm. *IEEE Transactions on Information Theory*, 47(2):498–519, 2001.

[22] H. Li and Z. Han. Competitive spectrum access in cognitive radio networks: Graphical game and learning. In *Wireless Communications and Networking Conference (WCNC), 2010 IEEE*, pages 1–6, 2010.

[23] A. Mishra, S. Banerjee, and W. Arbaugh. Weighted coloring based channel assignment for wlans. *ACM SIGMOBILE Mobile Computing and Communications Review*, 9(3):19–31, 2005.

[24] D. Monderer and L. S. Shapley. Potential games. *Games and economic behavior*, 14(1):124–143, 1996.

[25] C. H. Papadimitriou and M. Yannakakis. Optimization, approximation, and complexity classes. *Journal of computer and system sciences*, 43(3):425–440, 1991.

[26] J. Pearl. *Probabilistic reasoning in intelligent systems: networks of plausible inference*. Morgan Kaufmann, 1988.

[27] S. Sanghavi, D. Shah, and A. S. Willsky. Message passing for maximum weight independent set. *IEEE Transactions on Information Theory*, 55(11):4822–4834, 2009.

[28] G. Sharma, R. R. Mazumdar, and N. B. Shroff. On the complexity of scheduling in wireless networks. In *Proceedings of the 12th annual international conference on Mobile computing and networking (MobiCom)*, pages 227–238, 2006.

[29] C. Tekin, M. Liu, R. Southwell, J. Huang, and S. H. A. Ahmad. Atomic congestion games on graphs and their applications in networking. *IEEE/ACM Transactions on Networking*, 20(5):1541–1552, 2012.

[30] W. Wang and X. Liu. List-coloring based channel allocation for open-spectrum wireless networks. In *IEEE Vehicular Technology Conference*, volume 62, page 690, 2005.

[31] Y. Yin and C. Zhang. Approximate counting via correlation decay on planar graphs. In *SODA*, pages 47–66. SIAM, 2013.

Truthful Prioritization for Dynamic Bandwidth Sharing

Victor Shnayder and David C. Parkes
Harvard University
{shnayder,parkes}@eecs.harvard.edu

Vikas Kawadia
Raytheon BBN Technologies
vkawadia@bbn.com

Jeremy Hoon
Facebook
jhoon@fb.com

ABSTRACT

We design a protocol for dynamic prioritization of data on shared routers such as untethered 3G/4G devices. The mechanism prioritizes bandwidth in favor of users with the highest value, and is incentive compatible, so that users can simply report their true values for network access. A revenue pooling mechanism also aligns incentives for sellers, so that they will choose to use prioritization methods that retain the incentive properties on the buy-side. In this way, the design allows for an open architecture. In addition to revenue pooling, the technical contribution is to identify a class of stochastic demand models and a prioritization scheme that provides allocation monotonicity. Simulation results confirm efficiency gains from dynamic prioritization relative to prior methods, as well as the effectiveness of revenue pooling.

Categories and Subject Descriptors

C.2 [**Computer Communication Networks**]: Miscellaneous;

Keywords

Mechanism design; bandwidth sharing.

1. INTRODUCTION

Many mobile broadband data users overpay for data plans, buying a data plan with sufficient monthly quota for their maximum needs even though the average consumption is only about 15% of the monthly quota [1]. Analysis of cell phone data has also shown *quota dynamics* [2] in users, i.e., sensitivity to quota balance and time to the end of the quota period. One way to address these inefficiencies is to allow surplus bandwidth to be shared. In this paper we propose an auction-based protocol for such bandwidth-sharing. Sellers have wireless broadband (3G/4G) devices with a WiFi like WLAN radio, and can share network access through tethering apps that allow them to act as routers. Buyers have WiFi devices and pay sellers to relay their data.

Rather than finding optimal static allocations to users, our focus is on dynamic prioritization of access to bandwidth. Dynamic prioritization is more efficient because it can handle temporal heterogeneity in user demand. We design an auction protocol to prioritize network access in favor of those with highest value. In ensuring simplicity for users, we seek an incentive compatible design, so that truthful reporting of value and straightforward use of the shared bandwidth (no delaying of traffic, no padding of traffic) is optimal for a user. Incentive compatibility is also useful in avoiding "churn" and system overhead that can occur if users can benefit by adapting reported values given reports of others. Similar arguments have been made in the context of sponsored search markets [7].

Our positive results are stated for users with linear (per-byte) valuation functions. Give this, incentive compatibility requires that the cumulative quantity of network resources consumed by a user is non-decreasing in bid value, a property referred to as *monotonicity*. Our main technical contribution is to establish conditions on user demand models for which a strict priority-queue approach to resource access control satisfies monotonicity. An important property satisfied by the demand models is that a user's cumulative consumption of network bandwidth over a user session weakly increases as a function of her total consumption up to any intermediate time. An additional technical challenge that we address is to ensure that users cannot benefit through delayed use of allocated network resources, or by introducing fake traffic to increase demand.

Payments are computed by adopting an approach due to Babaioff, Kleinberg, and Slivkins [4] (BKS). This involves adding an additional, random perturbation to bids.[1] In a typical auction setting, the auctioneer knows how an allocation of resources would have changed given different bids. This counterfactual information is essential to standard payment schemes but unavailable here. It would require knowledge of how much bandwidth a user would consume under a different priority, but this requires knowledge that the network infrastructure does not have about a user's demand model. The only information available for the purpose of determining payments is the actual realization of consumption based on the actual assignment of priority. The introduction of random perturbation by the BKS scheme avoids the need for this counterfactual information.

We also extend our design so that it embraces open network architectures. In particular, we are robust to router devices that can install alternative routing software, for example to change prioritization schemes, or otherwise tamper with methods to compute payments. Thus, we seek to align incentives on the sell side as well as the buy side of the market. Our solution adopts lightweight cryptography and revenue pooling across sellers, and has the effect of aligning the interests of sellers with adopting routing policies that

MobiHoc'14, August 11–14, 2014, Philadelphia, PA, USA.

ACM 978-1-4503-2620-9/14/08 ...$15.00.
http://dx.doi.org/10.1145/2632951.2632956.

[1] A side effect is that the scheme does not reduce to fair share in the case of n identical buyers. Rather, the scheme randomly perturbs each bid before ranking them for the purpose of determining network prioritization.

maximize total buyer value. This is sufficient for monotonicity of user allocations, which is in turn sufficient for buyer truthfulness. Revenue pooling makes the market design appear simultaneously as a first-price market for sellers and a second-price market for buyers. For sellers, this means they prefer to maximize the (bid) value of the allocation. For buyers, this retains the second-price-like BKS scheme, and thus incentive compatibility.

A simulation study confirms that the mechanism achieves arbitrarily close approximations to full allocative efficiency for simple demand models (allocating the shared resource to those who value it the most), shows that reserve prices can increase efficiency of non-prioritized routing methods, demonstrates a scenario where sellers have practical efficiency-improving deviations, and examines the distributional effects of revenue pooling. We have also prototyped our scheme using the traffic control module in the Linux kernel.

1.1 Related work

Sen et al. [18] provide an exhaustive survey of the large literature on smart data pricing. We focus on describing work related to the specific techniques that we use.

Babaioff et al. [5] and Devanur et al. [6] show that the unavailability of counterfactuals impedes the design of truthful mechanisms in the context of multi-armed bandit problems. We employ the BKS scheme in a new application domain. The effect is that the payment scheme that we adopt accounts for varying user demand, providing an unbiased estimate of the cost imposed on other buyers by the prioritization associated with a buyer's device. In contrast, an earlier scheme due to Varian and Mackie-Mason (VMM) [23] adopts a myopic, per-packet viewpoint on the cost imposed on other users and is not incentive compatible when buyers have adaptive demand patterns. Other approaches from dynamic mechanism design are unsuitable, either because they rely on counterfactual information [10] or rely on a probabilistic demand model [16]. VMM's work inspired other approaches, such as the progressive second-price auction [11], and some follow-on work [12]. As with VMM, they also do not achieve incentive alignment in dynamic settings.

Godfrey et al. [8] study incentive compatibility of congestion control mechanisms in networks. Our technical analysis of the separation between bidders is similar to the separation between flows in this earlier model, but the domain of study and main results are otherwise incomparable. In a different domain, Shneidman and Parkes [22] study the problem of faithful network protocols for BGP routing, where the algorithms adopted by network users must themselves form part of an equilibrium. In this sense, our revenue pooling scheme attains faithfulness with respect seller routing algorithms.

Also related is a large literature on the use of cryptographic solutions to provide trustworthy auctions; e.g. [15]. However, these solutions incur too much overhead in the context of dynamic bandwidth prioritization. Porter and Shoham [17] provide an analysis of how the presence of cheating provides a second-price auction with first-price semantics. Our revenue pooling scheme, used for aligning trust does the opposite: we give a second-price auction first-price semantics from the perspective of the auctioneer (or seller, in our model), thereby mitigating incentives for manipulation; the scheme borrows ideas from a random-sampling approach used in a very different domain, that of the design of revenue-optimal digital good auctions [9].

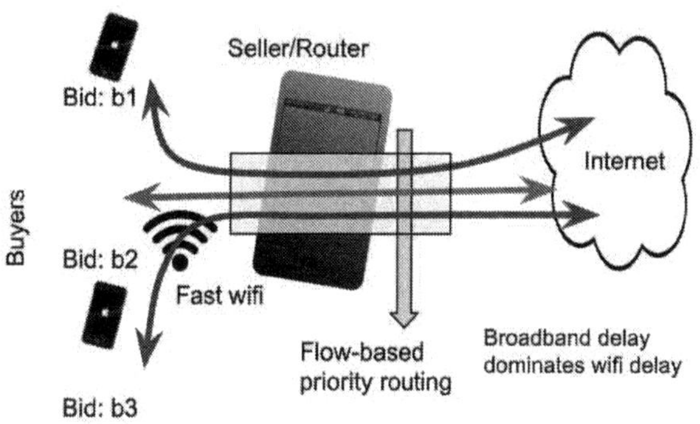

Figure 1: Illustration of our model.

2. MODEL

In this section we describe our model, also shown in Fig. 1.

Time and value: Time is modeled in discrete epochs. Each buyer (agent) i has an allocation period $[\alpha_i, \beta_i]$, with $\alpha_i \geq 0$ and $\beta_i \geq \alpha_i$. This is the period of time over which the buyer associates value with receiving bandwidth. Each buyer has constant value $v_i \geq 0$ per byte (a linear valuation), and bids once before sending data.

Routing: We adopt a flow model of traffic, with a single flow modeling both upstream and downstream traffic for each buyer. The router's link to the Internet is assumed to have fixed capacity $c > 0$. Each buyer has bid $b_i \geq 0$, and receives a *priority* based on this reported value.

We consider three schemes for network prioritization:

1. First-in First-out (FIFO) routes data in a first-in, first-out order as it arrives at the router. Since we do not model the queue of a router directly, we model FIFO as a within-epoch allocation proportional to within-epoch demand.

2. Fair queueing (FQ) allocates bandwidth to all buyers evenly, dividing any unused capacity recursively: in each period, each of the n buyers is guaranteed to be able to consume c/n. Any unused capacity is divided evenly among buyers with further demand, and this repeats until everyone is satisfied or capacity is exhausted.

3. Strict Priority Queueing (SPQ) first allocates capacity to the buyer with the highest bid in each epoch, up to c or the demand of the buyer. Then, capacity is allocated to the buyer with the second highest bid, and so forth, as long as capacity is available. Ties are broken at random.

Let $c_{i,t}$ denote the network capacity available to buyer i in epoch t (this depends on her bid, as well as the bid and network usage of others.)

Transport: We assume that the local network between router and buyers is much faster than the router's link to the Internet and neglect delays there.

Demand: Let $x_{i,t}$ (bytes) denote the cumulative amount of traffic (upload or download) associated with buyer i up to and including time t. This may be smaller than the total capacity available to buyer i up to and including time t because it depends on the buyer's demand.

Let $D_i(t, x)$ (bytes) denote the demand of buyer i during epoch t, where x is the cumulative amount of traffic (upload or download) used so far; i.e., $x = x_{i,t-1}$. Equivalently, this represents the maximum amount of network capacity that buyer i wants to consume during the epoch. $D_i(t, x)$ is a random variable, and we adopt $d_i(t, x)$ to denote a specific realization. We consider demand models D_i that satisfy the following condition:

DEFINITION 1. *A demand model $D_i(t, x)$ is* natural *if all realizations $d_i(t, x)$ satisfy for all t, for all $x \geq x'$ and all $c \geq 0$:*

$$x + \min(c, d_i(t, x)) \geq x' + \min(c, d_i(t, x')).$$

A demand model is natural when getting more capacity earlier might increase demand in the future, and should not decrease future demand below the total amount given lower capacity. In presenting some examples of demand models that are natural in this sense, we focus on deterministic examples. Randomized models can be created through random perturbations to the parameters of the example, and also through randomization over the different kinds of models.

Constant demand: A buyer i who simply wants to send at some constant rate: $d_i(t, x) = k$.

Time-varying demand: A buyer i with an arbitrary time-dependent generation process $g(t)$ that generates data that must be sent immediately to be useful: $d_i(t, x) = g(t)$.

Buffered demand: A buyer i with an arbitrary time-dependent generation process $g(t)$ that generates data, and wants to send as much of that as possible, buffering demand until it is allocated: $d_i(t, x) = \sum_{p \leq t} g(p) - x$.

Impatient buyer: A buyer i who sends until time p, and then goes away if some minimum amount of service m has not been met:

$$d_i(t, x) = \begin{cases} k \text{ if } t \leq p \\ k \text{ if } t > p \text{ and } x > m \\ 0 \text{ else} \end{cases}$$

This can be generalized to multiple thresholds, reduction to a lower, but non-zero rate, etc.

Increasing demand (in rate) A buyer that has $d_i(t, x) = g(x/t)$, with g weakly increasing.

Increasing demand (in total) A buyer that has $d_i(t, x) = g(x)$, with g weakly increasing.

This impatient buyer model illustrates that the requirement of "natural" demand functions allow those users to be modeled whose future value for network access falls if they don't receive enough bandwidth.

These demand models capture many realistic types of demand, but some demand functions do not fit our model. In particular, we do not allow demand to depend on recent usage, precluding models like "if I have not been able to use the network in the last 30 seconds, give up".

3. PRIORITIZATION AND PAYMENTS

Having introduced the basic elements of our model, we now describe some variations on payment schemes.

3.1 Fixed price

A baseline comparison is provided by a fixed price payment scheme. This can be used together with the FIFO and FQ routing policies, where only the users who bid above the fixed price are considered by the prioritization schemes.

3.2 VMM mechanism

The VMM mechanism provides a second comparison point. This mechanism uses the SPQ routing policy. For payments, the original paper by Varian and Mackie-Mason used a per-packet model, and charged the owner of each forwarded packet the *immediate externality* imposed by the packet. This is the value of the highest value packet that was dropped while the forwarded packet was in the router's queue.

Since we do not model the router queue directly, we adapt the idea behind the payment mechanism to our flow-based model by charging the immediate externality imposed by a buyer's flow in each period, computed using the standard Vickrey-Clarke-Groves (VCG) mechanism, charging $V_{-i} - V^*_{-i}$ for each buyer i in each period, where V_{-i} is the total (reported) value to all the other buyers in the (counterfactual) optimal allocation when i is removed, and V^*_{-i} is the total (reported) value to all the other buyers in the real optimal allocation with i included.

VMM is a natural mechanism, and has inspired a lot of work on bandwidth pricing. However, the VMM approach is not incentive compatible in a setting with variable demand. Consider the following:

Example 1. *Suppose that the router link capacity is 1 packet per second, and there is one buyer with value \$3 per packet who wants to send one packet every second and a second buyer with value \$2 per packet who wants to send a single packet, and keeps trying until she succeeds. Truthful bidding by buyer 1 will result in the second buyer's packet being dropped every period, and a charge of \$2 for each packet, representing the per-epoch externality on buyer 2. On the other hand, a bid of less than \$2 would "flush" the packet of buyer 2 and then allow buyer 1 to send for the remaining epochs with payment \$0. The tradeoff is to reduce the amount of data forwarded by 1 packet in return for a significant reduction in total payment.*

3.3 The BKS Mechanism

In the example above, VMM over-estimates the externality because it does not have access to the information that buyer 2 only has a single packet to send. This information is not available, since we assume that demand models are not described by users or known by the prioritization scheme.

In this domain, the BKS mechanism adopts the SPQ routing policy. Payments are determined following a self-sampling approach, where a randomized perturbation to bids obviates the need for counterfactual information. The idea is to obtain an estimate of the network resources that a user would have consumed at some lower bid as a side-effect of the randomization. We adapt the scheme to also allow the seller to employ a *reserve price* $r \geq 0$, which is the minimal per-byte price a seller will accept.[2] The scheme is parameterized by $\mu \in (0, 1)$, which governs the probability of introducing a random perturbation into bids.

The scheme is most easily explained in terms of an *allocation rule* $\mathcal{A}$. For us, this encapsulates the combined effect

[2]To support the reserve price, we use the *h-canonical self-resampling procedure* described by BKS, with $h(z, b) = r + z(b - r)$, which has distribution function $F_h(a, b) = (a - r)/(b - r)$. In Section 3.4, the BKS paper claims that $F_h = F_0$ for all h, where F_0 is the distribution function for the canonical resampling procedure, but F_0 doesn't satisfy their condition on F_h: $h(F_h(a, b), b) = a$ for all $a, b \in I, a < b$. $F_h(a, b) = (a - r)/(b - r)$ does satisfy this condition.

of realized demand (including possible strategic effects by users delaying demand or creating fake demand), the routing policy, the total capacity constraint on the router, and user bids. Taken together, these elements define the total amount of traffic consumed by each user (equivalently, the realized allocation).

The allocation $\mathcal{A}(\tilde{b}, d)$ generated by the rule is *ex ante* uncertain—it depends on realized demand $d = (d_1, \ldots, d_n)$, where d_i denotes the realized demand by i in each epoch, and is applied to randomly perturbed bids $\tilde{b}$. The BKS payment scheme works as follows:

DEFINITION 2 (BKS). Given an allocation rule $\mathcal{A}$ and a parameter $\mu \in (0, 1)$, the BKS procedure in our setting is:

1. Upon arrival, each bidder i submits a bid $b_i \geq r$.
2. The mechanism computes transformed bids $\tilde{b}_i$ $\forall$ i:
   (a) With probability $1 - \mu$, $\tilde{b}_i = b_i$
   (b) Else, compute a reduced bid: pick $\gamma \in [0, 1]$ uniformly at random, and set $\tilde{b}_i = r + (b_i - r) \cdot \gamma^{1/(1-\mu)}$
3. For all epochs, the router uses the allocation rule $\mathcal{A}(d, \tilde{b})$ applied to the transformed bids $\tilde{b}$ of the active users and given realized demand $d = (d_1, \ldots, d_n)$.
4. Given the amount of network data, $x_i \geq 0$, associated with each user i, (as realized by the allocation rule $\mathcal{A}$ applied to transformed bids), collect payment from user i as:
   (a) Collect $b_i x_i$.
   (b) If $\tilde{b}_i < b_i$, give a *rebate* $R_i = \frac{1}{\mu}(x_i(b_i - r))$. Otherwise, $R_i = 0$.

Bids are perturbed, used for prioritized routing, the total number of bytes associated with a user is observed, and payments are made through a randomized adjustment via the rebate in step 4. Each user's rebate can be determined at the end of her allocation period, allowing the user's payment to be computed while other users are still active.

DEFINITION 3. A mechanism is *truthful-in-expectation* if a risk-neutral buyer maximizes expected utility by bidding truthfully, whatever the bids of others, where the expectation is taken with respect to random coin flips of the mechanism.

Let $\mathcal{A}_i(b', d)$ denote the allocation to buyer i given some bid vector b' and demand vector d. (We write b' to denote a generic bid vector and avoid confusion with the b submitted as input to BKS.) An allocation rule is *ex post monotone* if $\mathcal{A}_i(b'', d) \geq \mathcal{A}_i(b', d)$, for all bid vectors b', all demand vectors d, and all $b'' = (b'_1, \ldots, b''_i, \ldots, b'_n)$ such that $b''_i > b'_i$. This is *ex post* in the sense that whatever the bids and whatever the demand, a buyer's total traffic consumption weakly increases with her bid. We use the following result:

THEOREM 3.1. *Applying the* BKS *procedure with probability of perturbation μ to an allocation rule that is* ex post *monotone results in a truthful-in-expectation mechanism.*

The proof in [4] shows that the scheme obtains an unbiased sample of an integral that defines the payment rule in the canonical approach of incentive-compatible mechanism design [13]. The allocation is the same as in the original allocation rule with probability at least $1 - n\mu$, where n is the number of buyers.

Example 2. *Let's revisit the earlier example of manipulation in the* VMM *scheme. Under* BKS*, when the first buyer's bid is not resampled, she pays \$3 per packet, and has some total allocation k. When her bid is resampled, the first buyer will have allocation k or $k-1$, depending on whether the resampled bid was below \$2. This will result in a large rebate, and in expectation, the first buyer's total payment will be essentially \$2, with the exact value depending on μ.*

4. BUYER INCENTIVES

To establish truthfulness of the BKS mechanism in our setting we need to show that SPQ combined with natural demand models implies that the allocation rule is *ex post* monotone. We first show that SPQ provides an isolation property on buyers, and then analyze the monotonicity of our allocation rule.

LEMMA 4.1 (ISOLATION). *For any t, capacity $c_{i,t}$ under* SPQ *is independent of how capacity is used by buyer i in time $< t$, and weakly increases with bid b_i.*

PROOF. Consider n buyers, and order them by bids $b_1 \geq b_2 \geq \ldots \geq b_n$ with ties broken at random. Let's first consider the claim that capacity $c_{i,t}$ in epoch t is independent of how the capacity is used by buyer i in earlier epochs. Proceed by strong induction. For buyer 1, then this is immediate since the buyer always gets to use full the capacity of the channel. For buyer $i > 1$, given the induction hypothesis for buyers $< i$, buyer i cannot affect demand or allocation to higher priority buyers and is not affected by the use of the capacity by lower priority buyers. The result is that buyer i gets all capacity that is unused by the higher priority buyers. The capacity $c_{i,t}$ is weakly increasing with bid value because of SPQ routing. In particular, if buyer $i > 1$ gets a higher priority $i' < i$ then her capacity in period t will be the capacity unused by all buyers $i'' < i'$, whereas previously its capacity was that unused by all buyers $i'' < i$. □

Given this lemma, we can now focus on an arbitrary buyer i, and simplify notation by omitting the subscript i. In particular, we use d_t to denote the realized demand of the buyer in period t (keeping the dependence on total network capacity used so far silent), and c_t to denote the buyer's realized capacity. Both d_t and c_t are realizations of a random process (the latter due to its dependence on the demand models of other buyers.) We first establish monotonicity and truthfulness properties of the mechanism under the assumption that the buyer is greedy in her use of the channel.

DEFINITION 4. *Given realized capacity c_t and demand d_t in epoch t, a buyer using the* greedy *policy sends* $\min(c_t, d_t)$ *to the router in epoch t.*

The greedy policy stipulates that the buyer makes her demand d_t available to the router (up to capacity c_t), and neither pads the demand with fake traffic nor hides demand by introducing a delay.

LEMMA 4.2 (MONOTONICITY). *If buyer i's demand model is natural, then fixing bids of other buyers and realized demand, buyer i's allocation up to and including any epoch t under the greedy policy is* ex post *monotone in bid value b_i.*

PROOF. The proof uses the following lemma.

LEMMA 4.3. *For any t, when the demand function is natural, then fixing bid values and realized demand, following the greedy policy in every period up to and including t maximizes the total amount of network capacity used by the buyer, x_t, up to and including period t.*

PROOF. We proceed by induction on t. By fixing bid values and fixing realized demand we have isolation. The base case is simple: if $t = 1$ then using less than $\min(c_1, d_1)$ for any c_1, d_1 does not maximize x_1.

Consider $t > 1$. Suppose for contradiction that there is some natural demand function d and realization of capacity c such that using $\min(c_p, d_p)$ in every epoch $p \leq t$ does not maximize x_t. Let f be a sequence of usage amounts that does maximize x_t.

If $f_t < \min(c_t, d_t)$, setting $f_t = \min(c_t, d_t)$ increases the allocation in epoch t and thus the total amount consumed, contradicting the fact that f maximizes x_t.

If $f_t = \min(c_t, d_t)$, then there exists some $p < t$ such that $f_p < \min(c_p, d_p)$. Let x_{t-1} be the total amount used up to and including epoch $t-1$ under f. Consider a sequence f' of usage amounts that is greedy for all epochs $\leq t$, and let x'_{t-1} be the total used up to and including $t-1$ under f'. By the induction hypothesis, f' maximizes the amount used up to and including $t-1$, so $x'_{t-1} \geq x_{t-1}$. Because the demand function d is natural,

$$x'_t = x'_{t-1} + d(t, x'_{t-1}) \geq x_{t-1} + d(t, x_{t-1}) = x_t,$$

so f' is indeed a maximizing sequence, establishing a contradiction. □

Using this lemma, we obtain Lemma 4.2. Suppose otherwise. Then it would be the case that following the greedy policy and using the capacity c_p in every epoch $p \leq t$ leads to a smaller allocation by epoch t than using the greedy policy and using the capacity c'_p where $c'_p \leq c_p$ for all $p \leq t$ (and c_t is the capacity under a higher bid $b_i > b'_i$, with this relationship between c'_t and c_t following from Lemma 4.1). But this is a contradiction with Lemma 4.3.

LEMMA 4.4. *If the buyer is restricted to the greedy policy then the* BKS *mechanism is truthful and the dominant strategy is to submit a truthful bid $b_i = v_i$.*

PROOF. Follows directly from Lemma 4.2 and the properties of BKS in Theorem 3.1. □

But we are also want to show that users cannot benefit by delaying network usage, or padding traffic with fake packets.

THEOREM 4.5. *The dominant strategy of a user in the* BKS *mechanism is to bid its true value and follow the greedy policy.*

PROOF. We first consider padding with fake traffic in some epochs. In particular, consider the final epoch t in which the buyer does this, and for it to matter assume $d_t < c_t$. Fix any bid value b_i (perhaps untruthful). We establish that this weakly increases the buyer's expected payment without providing additional value (since it is fake traffic.) The expected payment in BKS is equal (through the self-sampling approach) to the Myerson payment, and thus by the Myerson [13] rule, we require

$$b_i x'_i(b_i) - \int_0^{b_i} w x'_i(w) dw \geq b_i x_i(b_i) - \int_0^{b_i} w x_i(w) dw,$$

where $x'_i(w)$ is the total allocation given bid w with the padding in epoch t and $x_i(w)$ is the total allocation given bid w without padding in epoch t. This inequality holds since $x'_i(b_i) - x_i(b_i) \geq x'_i(w) - x_i(w)$ for all $w \leq b_i$, since for lower values the buyer may at some point receive a lower priority at t and thus be able to send less incremental traffic through padding, from which we have,

$$b_i(x'_i(b_i) - x_i(b_i)) \geq \int_0^{b_i} w \left(x'_i(w) - x_i(w)\right) dw.$$

Second, consider holding back demand in some epochs such that not all the capacity is utilized. Now that padding of demand has been precluded, it follows from monotonicity with respect to bid value, and the truthfulness of BKS, that it is a weakly dominant strategy for a user to bid her true per-byte value. Moreover, since the expected payment in BKS is equal to the payments in the Myerson auction, then $v_i x^* z^* \geq v_i x' z'$ for all alternate allocations $x' \leq x^*$ obtained through demand reduction, where x^* is the allocation achieved under the greedy policy, and z^* and z' the expected payment in BKS at allocation x^* and x' respectively. From this, it follows immediately that the buyer cannot benefit by holding back demand. □

On this basis, we conclude that the BKS mechanism has the "truthful in expectation" property in that it supports both truthful bidding and also straightforward revelation of demand (and use of the capacity made available through SPQ applied to perturbed bids).

5. SELL-SIDE INCENTIVES

We have assumed so far that the seller and router device can be trusted; e.g., to follow SPQ and BKS pricing. However, a self-interested seller can do better by deviating from the scheme as currently described. This is a concern because it would also lead buy-side incentives to unravel. For example, consider the following profitable seller manipulations, and the failure of simple fixes:

(1) The simplest profitable manipulation for sellers is to simply never give rebates, justifying this by claiming that the randomized bid resampling in BKS just happened to work out that way. A natural fix to this is to insist that the seller send the signed bids to a trusted central server for resampling. The central server would now know whether a buyer should pay her bid or get a rebate for a particular allocation, and since the server handles the accounting, it could appropriately credit or debit the buyer's account when it learned the final allocation.

(2) If the seller cannot tamper with the bid resampling process, it can still manipulate by reducing the allocation to resampled bidders, since they will be getting rebates and giving them service will reduce the seller's revenue. A partial fix to this is to note that to implement SPQ, the seller only needs to know the priority order of bidders, and not their bids, so bids can be encrypted when sent to the central server, which would report just the order to the router, keeping the seller ignorant of the bids.

(3) Unfortunately, the seller can still infer enough from the order to manipulate, even in a single allocation period. We omit the math here, but it can be shown that the expected revenue from the lowest priority user is negative, so the seller would have an incentive to reduce the user's allocation.

To preclude such manipulations, we propose a combination of lightweight cryptographic methods and incentive engineering. In particular, we take advantage of the presence of *multiple* sellers in envisioned applications. Precisely, we need enough sellers that share the same reserve price.

The approach, ALIGN-TRUST, extends the BKS scheme described so far, using a trusted central server for accounting and validation, logically inserting it between the buyer and seller. Buyers pay the center directly, and the center pools the revenue across sellers in a particular way, making payments to sellers that address incentive concerns.

We do not assume that the central server can observe or enforce anything about the sellers' routing policy. We merely rely on it to verify the cryptographic signatures on buyer bids to ensure that sellers cannot tamper with bids, to keep track of account balances for buyers and sellers, and to verify that bid perturbation is done correctly. We explain the approach in the next section.

5.1 The Align-Trust mechanism

One way to think about the problem with seller incentives in BKS is that prioritizing in favor of buyers with resampled bids has negative value to sellers. (Recall that a bid is only resampled with some probability μ.) We fix this by first paying sellers the perturbed bid value for data, rather than the rebate-adjusted, perturbed bid amount. From the seller's perspective, this makes the auction have "first price" semantics, and aligns incentives.

Because the BKS mechanism also pays rebates to buyers, just paying the sellers based on perturbed bid amounts would leave the center with a deficit. Instead, we compensate by taxing the sellers a percentage of their revenue. We ensure that sellers can only reduce their individual tax rate by improving efficiency, so sellers maximize revenue by routing to maximize efficiency (i.e., total value) with respect to the resampled bids, which we establish is sufficient to retain incentives on the buy-side of the market.

For the purpose of ALIGN-TRUST, we assume time is divided into *accounting periods*, perhaps a month long in practice. These periods encapsulate many BKS style auctions, as various sellers provide bandwidth to buyers.

Recall that BKS allows a seller to adopt a reserve price to increase revenue. To align trust on the sell-side, we insist that each seller selects a reserve price from a small set of reserve prices. Based on this, we can now consider the *pool* of sellers that select the same reserve price. We apply the following system-wide payment mechanism for the auctions involving these sellers:

DEFINITION 5 (ALIGN-TRUST). *Consider an accounting period, and a set of sellers M with the same reserve price. Let $\Gamma(s)$ be the set of buyers served by seller s during the accounting period.*

1. *Charge each buyer the* BKS *payment $b_i x_i - R_i$ for each completed auction. Credit each seller $s \in M$ the* first-price *revenue at the perturbed bids, without including the rebates: $\sum_{i\in\Gamma(s)} x_i \tilde{b}_i$.*

2. *Randomly split the sellers in M into two disjoint sets S_1, S_2 of equal size. Let*
$$C_1 = \sum_{s\in S_1} \sum_{i\in\Gamma(s)} x_i(\tilde{b}_i - r)$$
denote the total credit above reserve price to sellers in S_1. Let
$$T_1 = \sum_{s\in S_1} \sum_{i\in\Gamma(s)} (b_i - r)x_i - R_i$$
denote the total above-reserve payments from buyers associated with S_1. Define C_2 and T_2 similarly for sellers in S_2. Because the payments from buyers include the BKS *rebates, and the credits to sellers are at the first-price resampled bids $\tilde{b}$, this leaves the center with a* deficit *$\delta = C - T$ for each set.*

3. *To make up the deficit, the center will tax the sellers. Define the* tax rate *for each set as: $tax_1 = \frac{\delta_2}{C_1}$, $tax_2 = \frac{\delta_1}{C_2}$. Collect $tax_1 C_1$ from sellers in S_1, charging tax rate tax_1 uniformly across all sellers. Collect $tax_2 C_2$ from sellers in S_2, charging tax rate tax_2 uniformly across all sellers.*

This construction has several nice properties. First of all, as long as sellers continue to use SPQ it has no effect on buyer incentives, because ALIGN-TRUST is identical to BKS from the buyer's point of view. In addition, we have:

LEMMA 5.1. *The total payment in* ALIGN-TRUST *is exactly balanced.*

PROOF. The reserve price payments effectively go directly from buyers to sellers. The total above-reserve payment to the system is $T_1 - C_1 + T_2 - C_2 + tax_1 C_1 + tax_2 C_2 = 0$ □

A tax rate is admissible if it is no greater than one. This will be true with high probability when no seller accounts for a large fraction of rebates. This is formalized in the full version of the paper by characterizing a reasonable (*admissibility*) condition on supply and using Hoeffding's inequality [21]. We assume this admissibility condition for the theoretical results that we state in the sequel.

In addition, from a seller's viewpoint, ALIGN-TRUST transforms the mechanism into a first-price auction (with respect to perturbed bids) with a tax collected on revenue, where the seller cannot usefully manipulate his tax rate:

LEMMA 5.2. *If the tax rate for a seller is weakly less than one, the seller's strict preference is to allocate in order to maximize the total value given perturbed bids.*

PROOF. Consider a seller s in S_1. The tax rate for s is $\frac{\delta_2}{C_1}$. δ_2 depends only on sellers in S_2, and C_1 is the sum of the revenues of other sellers in S_1, which s cannot affect, and the total revenue for s. Increasing revenue lowers the tax rate facing s, so as long as the tax rate is less than 1, this is doubly good for s.[3] □

5.2 Seller Incentives

Under ALIGN-TRUST, seller incentives are aligned with using a routing policy that maximizes total pre-tax revenue $\sum_i \tilde{b}_i x_i$. This follows from Lemma 5.2. In this section, we examine the effect that this has on whether sellers want to follow SPQ, and on the effect of potential deviations on buy-side incentives.

First, we characterize situations where sellers cannot profit by deviating from SPQ. Second, we look at situations when

[3]In practice, it would make sense to cap the tax rate at 1, putting the risk on the center instead of the sellers.

the seller may profit from using a different routing policy, and show that such deviations improve efficiency with respect to perturbed bids and preserve incentive alignment with truthful bidding for buyers. The crucial property that we need to retain under seller deviations is that of monotonicity, or a relaxed form of expected monotonicity.

5.2.1 Demand models where SPQ is optimal

We first consider cases where the seller's selfish preference is to follow SPQ. The intuition is that deviating results in an immediate drop in revenue from sending lower priority traffic ahead of higher priority traffic, so in order for this to increase revenue, the seller has to expect to make up the lost revenue later. If this is not possible under a given demand model then SPQis optimal for the seller. In the following, we consider *ex post efficiency*, which requires that an allocation rule maximizes total realized value whatever the bids and whatever the realized demand. The following lemma follows from Lemma 5.2, given admissibility.

LEMMA 5.3. *If* SPQ *is* ex post *efficient (with respect to perturbed bids), the seller cannot increase his revenue by deviating from* SPQ.

We now specialize the natural demand models to understand when SPQ will be ex post efficient. A sufficient property is that the demand model be memoryless, so that it does not depend on the routing policy, with demand invariant to the total allocation made so far: $d_i(t, x) = d_i(t, y)$ for all x, y and for all realizations of a user's random demand model. SPQ is greedy in regard to bid, and if there is no impact on future demand from a deviation from myopic value maximization in the current period then SPQ will maximize realized value, so applying Lemma 5.3 gives the following:

THEOREM 5.4. *If the user demand models are memoryless, then the seller maximizes revenue by using* SPQ, *and the* BKS *mechanism combined with* ALIGN-TRUST *retains truthfulness-in-expectation for buyers despite seller self-interest.*

5.2.2 Other Demand Models

The seller can benefit by deviating from SPQ for some natural demand models. For example, consider the model of an impatient buyer, as in the example in Section 2. Such a buyer will stop transmitting if it does not get some minimum amount of traffic by some time. If the seller knows this, it can sometimes increase revenue by increasing the buyer's priority, increasing her allocation over the minimum, and ensuring continuing transmission and continuing revenue.

We first consider the extreme case in which the seller can form a perfect prediction of the future demand and bid values. Let Δ denote a set of routing policies considered by the seller, and let $x_i(\rho)$ be the total allocation to i under routing policy ρ, given the realized demand of all buyers.

LEMMA 5.5. *If the seller implements the optimal routing policy in Δ, maximizing*

$$\underset{\rho \in \Delta}{\operatorname{argmax}} \sum_i \tilde{b}_i x_i(\rho),$$

with respect to perturbed bids $\tilde{b}$, then the implied allocation rule is ex post *monotone and the resulting mechanism is truthful-in-expectation for buyers.*

The proof is available in the full version of the paper [21].

This illustrates the basic way in which the use of ALIGN-TRUST aligns incentives for sellers so that they act in a way that retains buy-side truthfulness.

Rather than ex post monotone, a weaker property of *monotone-in-expectation* requires the expected total amount of bandwidth used by a buyer to be weakly increasing with bid value. The expectation is taken with respect to a probabilistic model of demand and bid values and also considering the random perturbation of bids in BKS.

The dominant-strategy equilibrium property for buyers no longer holds for this seller deviation, because the optimality of the seller's policy holds only in expectation, given distributional assumptions about other buyers. In its place, we adopt the standard notion of *Bayes-Nash incentive compatibility*, which in our case requires that truthful bidding and following the greedy policy maximizes a buyer's expected utility, given that other buyers do the same.

THEOREM 5.6. *If the seller implements a routing policy that is optimal in expectation, solving*

$$\underset{\rho \in \Delta}{\operatorname{argmax}} \sum_i E\left[\tilde{b}_i x_{i,\geq t}(\rho)\right],$$

forward from any time t, where $x_{i,\geq t}(\rho)$ is the total additional allocation (bytes) to i between t and the departure time of i, given perturbed bids $\tilde{b}$, then the resulting mechanism is Bayes-Nash incentive compatible.

The proof is available in the full version of the paper [21].

Example 3. *An example to illustrate this idea: imagine a case where the seller knows that a buyer is impatient, with constant demand 10 in each round for the first 60 rounds, leaving after that if they do not get a minimum amount m, drawn uniformly from $[300, 450]$. There is no uncertainty about this buyer's demand, and the seller computes his best estimates of the other buyers' future demand. Using these estimates, the seller can compute the probability that this buyer will reach each amount between 300 and 450 under* SPQ *routing. Then it can consider switching the routing order in some rounds to increase the buyer's allocation, and consider how much that increases the likelihood of the buyer making it to her (unknown) m and the likely future gains from that, versus the immediate revenue reduction such a deviation requires. The intuition for why this is still monotone should be clear— if the buyer's traffic is worth more, there is a smaller revenue reduction from increasing her priority, and a larger potential future payoff, so the seller would be more likely to increase the buyer's allocation.*

Buyers do not need to know whether the seller is using SPQ or an expected-efficiency maximizing policy, since BKS remains monotone, and thus incentives are aligned with truthful bidding either way. The buyer only needs to believe that the seller is not irrationally reducing his expected revenue by changing priorities away from SPQ. Another useful property is that these results hold for any set of routing policies Δ considered by the router— as long as the router always chooses the best policy (in expectation) from a fixed set, we still get monotonicity, and thus buyer truthfulness.

6. SIMULATION RESULTS

We now present simulations that explore the quantitative difference between mechanisms, and illustrate the effects

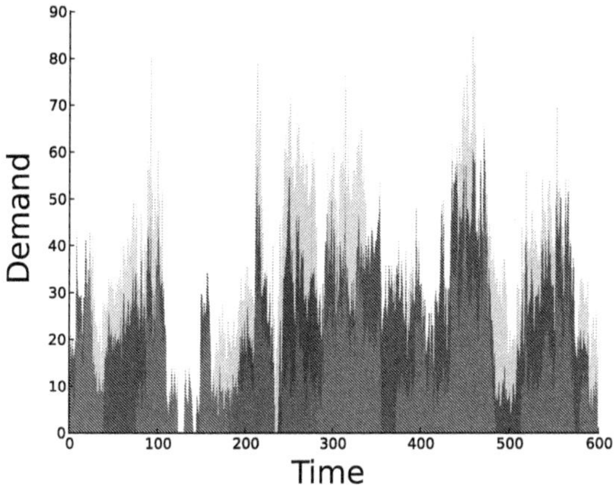

Figure 2: Sample demand realization for 3 buyers with our trace-inspired model for 600 simulated secs. Each color is a buyer's demand.

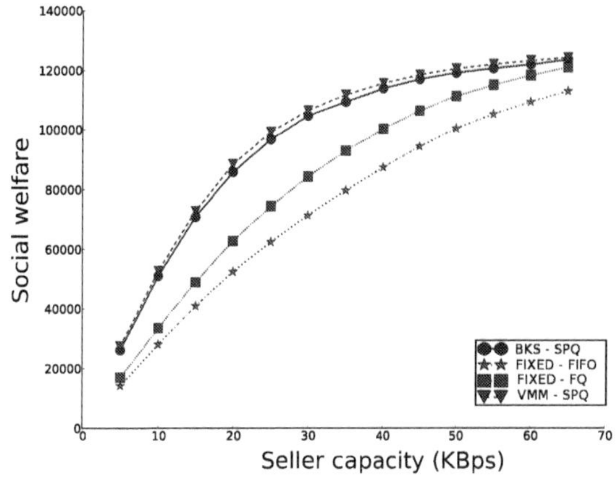

Figure 3: Efficiency of routing policies with truthful bidding. The VMM allocation is optimal in this setting, so the drop to BKS is the efficiency loss due to bid resampling necessary to obtain truthfulness. SPQ routing for VMM and BKS is much more efficient than the non-prioritized routing policies.

predicted by our theoretical analysis. We confirm that BKS achieves arbitrarily close approximations to allocative efficiency for simple demand models, show that reserve prices can increase efficiency of non-prioritized routing methods, demonstrate a scenario where sellers have practical efficiency-improving deviations, and examine the distributional effects of revenue pooling.

6.1 Our simulator

We adopt a custom flow-level simulator, closely matching our theoretical model. Each epoch is one second, and we run simulations for 10 minutes, or 600 epochs. Demand and capacity are specified in KBps. The simulator supports arbitrary user demand models. We use a stochastic demand model motivated by patterns observed in real networks, somewhat simplifying the trace-based model described in [14]. A user's demand is composed of *flows* with total demand equal to the sum of the demands of the flows active at any time, flow arrival times are a Poisson process, flow duration is sampled from a lognormal distribution, and each flow has Poisson demand.

We use the following parameters: flow durations have both mean and standard deviation 30 seconds, average flow inter-arrival times are 30 seconds, and each flow has average rate of either 10 or 30 KBps, as specified. This results in average demand equal to the average flow rate.

Fig. 2 shows an example demand trace of three such buyers, each with demand 10 KBps. The pattern is bursty both at short timescales, reflecting the Poisson demand of each flow, and at longer timescales, reflecting the random flow arrival process.

The simulator supports the SPQ, FQ, and FIFO routing policies described in Section 2. Unless otherwise specified, we simulate VMM with SPQ routing, BKS with SPQ routing with priorities based on resampled bids, and fixed price with FQ and FIFO routing. The BKS resampling frequency μ is 0.2, chosen as a compromise between reducing the magnitude of rebates and not sacrificing efficiency. The results are not very sensitive to the choice of μ. We show the expected allocation over 1000 allocations for BKS.

We simulate truthful bidding for both BKS and VMM, even though VMM is not a truthful mechanism. For memoryless demand models, this means that VMM results in the optimal allocation, acting as a benchmark for the truthful mechanisms.

6.2 Efficiency

From our analysis, we know that SPQ is efficient for memoryless demand models, but may not be efficient for other demand models. Here, we look at both cases, and look at the magnitude of this effect in some scenarios. We also examine the drop in efficiency due to bid resampling in BKS.

Fig. 3 shows the social welfare (sum of buyer and seller utilities) for a scenario with three buyers. The first two have per-KB values 10 and 4, and average demand 10 KBps each, simulating a high value and a medium value user. The last buyer has a per-KB value of only 1, but has a higher average demand–30 KBps. All buyers use the stochastic demand model described above, and we compare four different mechanisms–BKS and VMM, both with SPQ routing and truthful bids, and FQ and FIFO, with a fixed price of 1. (We study the effect of changing this fixed price in the next experiment). As the seller capacity increases, the social welfare increases for all the mechanisms, until all the demand is satisfied. The demand models in this simulation are memoryless, so SPQ routing for VMM is optimal given that we insist on truthful bidding.

The small difference between the performance of VMM and BKS is the efficiency cost of the sampling necessary for the truthfulness provided by BKS. SPQ routing for BKS is much more efficient than either of the non-prioritized fixed price policies. The difference between FQ and FIFO is also interesting–with FIFO, the allocation is proportional to demand, so the low value, high-demand buyer gets three-fifth of the channel on average, reducing efficiency.

Fig. 4 shows the effect of reserve price on efficiency, in the same scenario, with seller capacity fixed at 25 KBps. Raising the reserve price slightly to avoid allocating to the lowest value buyer improves efficiency for FIFO and FQ. Since VMM and BKS naturally prioritize high value data, raising the reserve price removes opportunities to send low priority data when there is spare capacity, reducing efficiency.

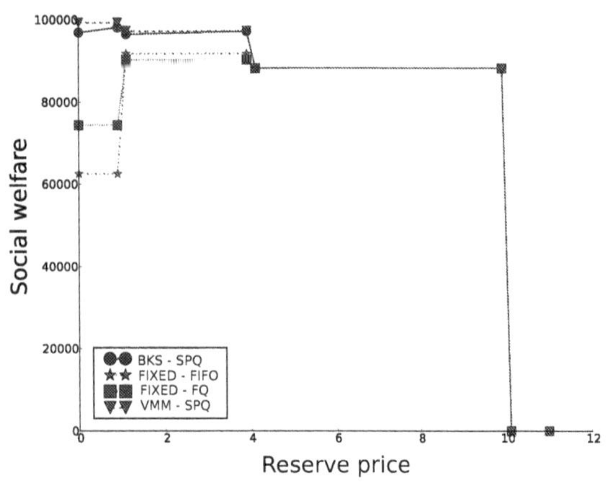

Figure 4: Efficiency of routing policies as reserve prices varies. Seller capacity is 25 KBps. Increasing the reserve price improves the efficiency of FQ and FIFO.

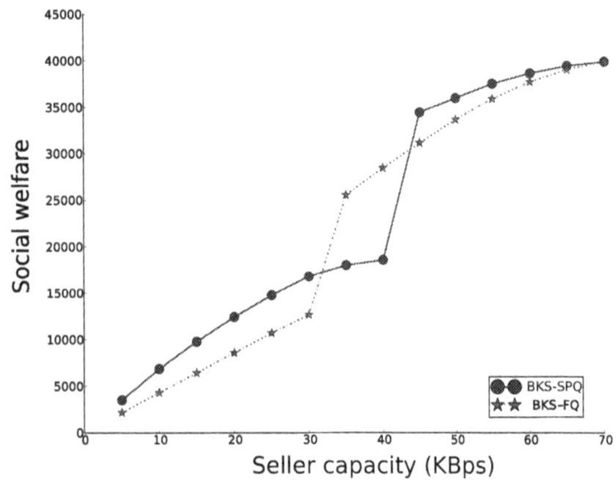

Figure 5: Efficiency for SPQ and FQ when high value buyers leave early, and a low value buyer is impatient. Deviating to FQ from SPQ is profitable for a range of seller capacities.

We now look at a case where a seller can profit by deviating from SPQ. The scenario is similar to the one above: three buyers, with per-KB values 10, 4, and 1, and average demands 10, 10, and 30 KBps. However, now the high and medium value buyers depart after 90 seconds, and the low value buyer is impatient, leaving after 60 seconds if her allocation is less than 500KB, and otherwise continuing to send for the full 600 seconds. If the seller fails to allocate at least 500KB to the third buyer in the first minute, she misses out on forwarding extra traffic later, once the two higher value bidders are gone. Fig. 5 shows the efficiency of BKS with SPQ and FQ routing. For some intermediate capacities, the value-ignorant FQ routing policy is better, because it results in the low priority buyer continuing to send. Of course, if the seller knew the impatience threshold, it could use a better hybrid strategy, allocating just enough to buyer 3 to ensure she stays, and then allocating optimally to others.

6.3 Revenue pooling

Next, we study the effects of revenue pooling in ALIGNTRUST, first looking at a simplified case where all sellers

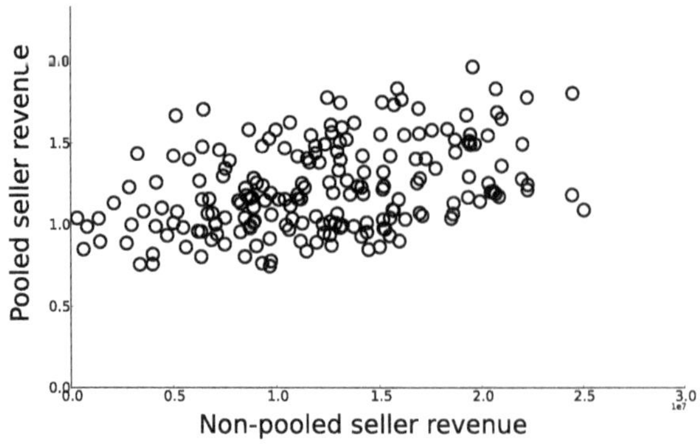

Figure 6: Effect of revenue pooling when sellers are similar.

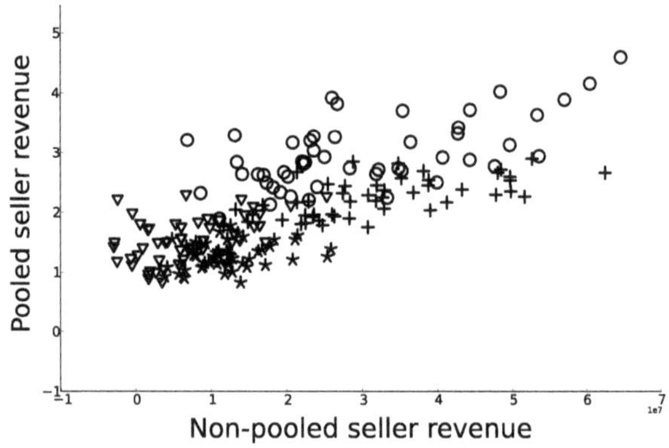

Figure 7: Effect of revenue pooling when sellers are different.

have the same buyer distribution, and then a more complex case where there are several seller distributions. We confirm our theoretical results, showing that the center will not have to run a deficit, and also show that pooling reduces the variance of seller revenue. Fig. 6 shows the pooled revenue vs unpooled revenue for 200 sellers from a single distribution, with seller capacity 40, buyers with per-KB values 2 and 3 and demand 10 KBps, a buyer with value 5 and demand 30 KBps, and no reserve price. In addition to the primary goal of making BKS faithful for sellers, pooling drastically reduces the variance in seller revenue, with non-trivial pooled revenue for all sellers. This also shows that the tax rate for both pools is lower than 1, as predicted by the theory.

Fig. 7 shows the pooled revenue vs unpooled revenue for 200 sellers from four different settings: seller capacities 40 or 60, and buyers with total demand 50 or 70, with higher buyer value when demand is 70. These are indicated by different markers. Note the dramatic reduction in variance of pooled seller revenue for each seller category: without revenue pooling, some sellers have negative revenue while others have very high revenue. Pooling reduces this variance, while preserving the relative ordering between seller types–sellers with higher non-pooled revenue have higher expected pooled revenue.

7. SYSTEM IMPLEMENTATION ISSUES

Our scheme has three main components: a protocol for buyers to send bids to the sellers, a priority queueing facility for sellers to allocate bandwidth to buyer flows according to BKS, and a central server for revenue pooling and accounting. We have prototyped the first two components.

An app on the buyer's side sends bids (along with duration of validity of the bid) to a service on the seller device. The seller device resamples the bids and uses them for allocating bandwidth, using the standard traffic control (`tc`) facilities in the Linux kernel (also used by Android). Specifically, upon receiving bids or updates to bids, the seller device sets (`tc`) filters to classify flows into one of a fixed number of priority classes based on their resampled bids, which enables the kernel to enqueue packets in the appropriate priority queue. Thus, we get efficient strict priority queuing without any kernel modifications, with the caveat that we can only use a small fixed number of queues. This implies that we need to round down the resampled bids to the nearest priority level. However, this modification preserves truthfulness since the modified allocation function is still (weakly) monotone in bids. Payments are made according to the unrounded resampled bids.

8. CONCLUSION

We have introduced an approach to prioritized bandwidth access in a dynamic environment. The method succeeds in aligning incentives on both the buy-side and the sell-side of the market for a variety of stochastic demand models. While auctions can introduce an extra burden on users over charging a flat fee, they can provide for efficient allocation and the complexity can be hidden through automated bidding agents [19, 20].

There are many areas for future work. Natural extensions to the theory include expanding to more expressive demand models, and considering valuation models other than linear per byte such as value per rate and multi-dimensional valuations. The BKS scheme has been extended to handle the appropriate generalization of monotonicity through a self-sampling approach [3], and the challenge would be design dynamic prioritization schemes that satisfy this cyclic monotonicity property for stochastic demand models.

We make several assumptions that are useful in analysis and developing engineering insights, even if they might not quite hold in reality. Detailed packet level simulations would be useful to study situations where our assumptions such as natural demand models and linear per-byte valuations do not hold. Analyzing real demand to determine the extent to which it confirms to our models is also future work. Finally, developing our dynamic prioritization system prototype further by designing appropriate user interfaces for eliciting buyer values, integrating with applications to allow setting traffic values, and evaluating performance metrics such as computational overhead also remains to be done.

Acknowledgments: Research was sponsored by the Army Research Laboratory and was accomplished under Cooperative Agreement Number W911NF-09-2-0053 (the ARL Network Science CTA). The views and conclusions contained in this document are those of the authors and should not be interpreted as representing the official policies, either expressed or implied, of the Army Research Laboratory or the U.S. Government. The U.S. Government is authorized to reproduce and distribute reprints for Government purposes notwithstanding any copyright notation here on.

9. REFERENCES

[1] Cisco Visual Networking Index: Mobile Forecast.

[2] M. Andrews, G. Bruns, M. K. Dogru, and H. Lee. Understanding quota dynamics in wireless networks. Technical report, Bell Labs, 2013.

[3] M. Babaioff, R. Kleinberg, and A. Slivkins. Multi-parameter mechanisms with implicit payment computation. In *ACM Conf. on Electronic Commerce(EC)*, 2013.

[4] M. Babaioff, R. D. Kleinberg, and A. Slivkins. Truthful mechanisms with implicit payment computation. In *ACM EC*, 2010.

[5] M. Babaioff, Y. Sharma, and A. Slivkins. Characterizing truthful multi-armed bandit mechanisms: extended abstract. In *ACM EC*, 2009.

[6] N. R. Devanur and S. M. Kakade. The price of truthfulness for pay-per-click auctions. In *ACM EC*, pages 99–106, 2009.

[7] B. Edelman and M. Ostrovsky. Strategic bidder behavior in sponsored search auctions. *Decision Support Systems*, 43(1):192–198, 2007.

[8] P. Godfrey, M. Schapira, A. Zohar, and S. Shenker. Incentive compatibility and dynamics of congestion control. *ACM SIGMETRICS*, June 2010.

[9] A. V. Goldberg and J. D. Hartline. Competitive auctions for multiple digital goods. In *European Symposium on Algorithms*, 2001.

[10] M. Hajiaghayi, R. Kleinberg, M. Mahdian, and D. C. Parkes. Online auctions with re-usable goods. In *ACM EC*, 2005.

[11] A. Lazar and N. Semret. The progressive second price auction mechanism for network resource sharing. *8th International Symposium on Dynamic Games, Maastricht, The Netherlands*, 1998.

[12] P. Maillé et al. The progressive second price mechanism in a stochastic environment. *Publication interne-IRISA*, 2003.

[13] R. B. Myerson. Optimal auction design. *Mathematics of Operations Research*, 6:58–73, 1981.

[14] M. Papadopouli and H. Shen. Characterizing the duration and association patterns of wireless access in a campus. *European Wireless Conference*, 2005.

[15] D. C. Parkes, M. O. Rabin, S. M. Shieber, and C. Thorpe. Practical secrecy-preserving, verifiably correct and trustworthy auctions. *Electronic Commerce Research and Applications*, 2007.

[16] D. C. Parkes and S. Singh. An MDP-Based approach to Online Mechanism Design. In *NIPS*, 2003.

[17] R. Porter and Y. Shoham. On cheating in sealed-bid auctions. *Decis. Support Syst.*, 39(1):41–54, Mar. 2005.

[18] S. Sen, C. Joe-Wong, S. Ha, and M. Chiang. A survey of smart data pricing: Past proposals, current plans, and future trends. *ACM Comput. Surv.*, Nov. 2013.

[19] S. Seuken, K. Jain, D. Tan, and M. Czerwinski. Hidden Markets: UI Design for a P2P Backup Application. In *CHI*, 2010.

[20] S. Seuken, D. C. Parkes, E. Horvitz, K. Jain, M. Czerwinski, and D. Tan. Market User Interface Design. In *ACM Conf. on Electronic Commerce*, 2012.

[21] V. Shnayder, D. Parkes, V. Kawadia, and J. Hoon. Truthful prioritization schemes for spectrum sharing. Technical report, 2014.

[22] J. Shneidman and D. Parkes. Specification faithfulness in networks with rational nodes. *ACM PODC*, 2004.

[23] H. Varian and J. Mackie-Mason. Pricing the Internet. *Public Access to the Internet*, 1994.

Ad Hoc Networks: Pushing Mobile and Wireless Communication Since 1970

Roger Wattenhofer
ETH Zurich, Switzerland

Abstract

Researchers in ad hoc networks are used to study some of the prevalent technical difficulties in networking: Without a fixed infrastructure, challenges such as mobility or wireless communication must be investigated in their purest form. As a consequence one learns a great deal about the fundamentals of networking. In my talk I will present a few exciting research questions that I learned when studying ad hoc networks: I will discuss how mobility leads to distributed complexity, why clock synchronization is unexpectedly difficult, and what difference it makes to assume a more accurate wireless model. Along my talk I will present several open questions.

ACM Classification:
C.2 [Computer-Communication Networks]

Author Keywords: Mobile Networks, Wireless Communication, Distributed Complexity, Clock Synchronization, Signal-to-interference-plus-noise-ratio

Bio

Roger Wattenhofer is a full professor at the Information Technology and Electrical Engineering Department, ETH

Zurich, Switzerland. He received his doctorate in Computer Science in 1998 from ETH Zurich. From 1999 to 2001 he was in the USA, first at Brown University in Providence, RI, then at Microsoft Research in Redmond, WA. He then returned to ETH Zurich, originally as an assistant professor at the Computer Science Department.

Roger Wattenhofer's research interests are a variety of algorithmic and systems aspects in computer science and information technology, currently in particular wireless networks, wide area networks, mobile systems, social networks, and physical algorithms. He publishes in different communities: distributed computing (e.g., PODC, SPAA, DISC), networking (e.g., SIGCOMM, MobiCom, SenSys), or theory (e.g., STOC, FOCS, SODA, ICALP). He has served as a PC chair on more than a dozen international conferences, including MobiHoc in 2005. More information can be found at www.disco.ethz.ch

MobiHoc'14, August 11–14, 2014, Philadelphia, PA, USA.
ACM 978-1-4503-2620-9/14/08.
http://dx.doi.org/10.1145/2632951.2633210

ESync: An Energy Synchronized Charging Protocol for Rechargeable Wireless Sensor Networks

Liang He
Singapore University of Technology and Design
he_liang@sutd.edu.sg

Lingkun Fu*
Zhejiang University, China
lkfu@iipc.zju.edu.cn

Likun Zheng
University of California, Irvine
likunz@uci.edu

Yu Gu
Singapore University of Technology and Design
jasongu@sutd.edu.sg

Peng Cheng, Jiming Chen
Zhejiang University, China
{jmchen}@iipc.zju.edu.cn

Jianping Pan
University of Victoria, Canada
pan@uvic.ca

ABSTRACT

Different from energy harvesting which generates dynamic energy supplies, the mobile charger is able to provide stable and reliable energy supply for sensor nodes, and thus enables sustainable system operations. While previous mobile charging protocols either focus on the charger travel distance or the charging delay of sensor nodes, in this work we propose a novel *Energy Synchronized Charging* (ESync) protocol, which simultaneously reduces both of them. Observing the limitation of the *Traveling Salesman Problem* (TSP)-based solutions when nodes energy consumptions are diverse, we construct a set of nested TSP tours based on their energy consumptions, and only nodes with low remaining energy are involved in each charging round. Furthermore, we propose the concept of energy synchronization to synchronize the charging requests sequence of nodes with their sequence on the TSP tours. Experiment and simulation demonstrate ESync can reduce charger travel distance and nodes charging delay by about 30% and 40% respectively.

1. INTRODUCTION

To address the energy constraints of sensor nodes [1–6], the concepts and implementations of adopting mobile chargers to replenish nodes energy supply in rechargeable sensor networks have attracted a lot of attentions in the research community recently [7–12]. Different from traditional energy harvesting sensor networks [13–17], where the harvested energy is dynamic in both the spatial and temporal dimensions, the mobility-assisted energy replenishment provides a stable and reliable energy supply for sensor nodes and thus enables truly sustainable operations of sensor networks [18–20].

Due to the limited mobility of the charger, the scheduling of charging tasks for sensor nodes in the network plays a critical role in achieving a high charging efficiency. The *Traveling Salesman Problem* (TSP)-based charging protocols are a family of classic solutions to the mobile charging problem [10, 18, 21], with which in general, the mobile charger *periodically* carries out the charging process following a *pre-optimized* tour. As a result, the charging of nodes can be accomplished with a short charger travel distance and thus a short time duration.

However, the limitation of TSP-based solutions is that when nodes energy consumptions are diverse, it may lead to the unnecessary visits of energy-sufficient nodes. This not only increases the charger travel distance when performing the charging tasks of sensor nodes, but also prolongs the waiting time before the energy-hungry nodes can be charged. To address this issue, in this paper, we investigate the on-demand mobile charging scenario where nodes are charged only when necessary. Specifically, sensor nodes send out charging requests to the mobile charger when their energy levels are low, and the charger replenishes their energy supply according to those received requests. We aim to design a novel mobile charging protocol that is able to leverage on the advantages of existing designs while minimizing the impact of their limitations.

The most significant feature in our design is *synchronizing the energy supply of sensor nodes based on a set of nested TSP tours*. Upon achieving such energy synchronization, we can realize the ideal mobile charging paradigm that the charger can simply travel according to the TSP tours to reduce its travel distance, and whenever a sensor node runs short of energy, the charger will *happen to* be traveling towards it. Our major intellectual contributions in this paper are three-fold:

- To the best of our knowledge, our work is the first to jointly improve the charging process for both sensor nodes and the mobile charger, while existing designs only adopt either one of them as the design objective.
- At the macro-level of the mobile charging process, to leverage the advantage of the TSP-based solutions while minimizing the impact of their limitations when node energy consumptions are highly diverse, we construct a set of nested TSP tours based on the energy consumption rates of sensor nodes. Then for each round of the charging process, a novel tour selection algorithm is designed to only involve the energy-hungry nodes into the charging schedule during that round.
- At the micro-level focusing on the charging schedule during individual rounds, observing that nodes charging requests

*The first two authors contributed equally to this work.

MobiHoc'14, August 11–14, 2014, Philadelphia, PA, USA.

http://dx.doi.org/10.1145/2632951.2632970.

sequence may significantly affect the charging performance, we propose the concept of *energy synchronization* among nodes to proactively match nodes charging requests sequence to the selected TSP tour in each charging round, which is achieved by carefully selecting the node to be charged next and controlling the amount of energy charged to individual nodes. As a result, both the charger travel distance and the charging delay of sensor nodes are reduced.

- We evaluate the performance of *ESync* through both experiment and simulations, and the results demonstrate that *ESync* can reduce the charger travel distance and charging latency by 30% and 40% respectively.

The paper is organized as follows. Section 2 briefly reviews the literature. We introduce the problem statement in Section 3. Our design on the nested TSP tours is presented in Section 4, and the design on the energy synchronization among nodes is introduced in Section 5. Section 6 and Section 7 present the evaluation results obtained through both experiment and simulations, and we conclude in Section 8.

2. RELATED WORK

The mobility-assisted energy replenishment provides stable and reliable energy supply for sensor nodes, and has attracted increasing attentions from the research community recently [7–10, 18–21]. The mobile charging process can be evaluated from the perspective of the charger and sensor nodes respectively. For the charger, the optimization objective is to minimize its travel distance when performing the charging tasks [9, 20]. The most intuitive approach is to periodically charge nodes along an optimal TSP tour constructed based on network deployment [10]. The idea is extended to the case of charging multiple nodes simultaneously in [18].

Several other designs tackle the mobile charging problem from the perspective of individual sensor nodes [7, 8, 22]. A scheme jointly exploring the routing and charging of individual nodes is proposed in [7], which proactively guides the routing activities in the network and delivers energy to where it is needed. A greedy charging algorithm that always charges the node with the shortest remaining lifetime to its full capacity is proposed in [8], and is further improved by incorporating the remaining energy levels of other nodes when determining which node to charge next and how much energy to charge to. Another way to greedily performing the charging tasks is to always select the nearest requesting node to charge, i.e., the Nearest-Job-Next discipline. The performance of Nearest-Job-Next is analytically evaluated in [23, 24]. Although asymptotically promising, the worst-case performance of Nearest-Job-Next is difficult to guarantee.

With the concept of energy synchronization among nodes based on a set of nested TSP tours, we propose a novel mobile charging protocol that leverages on the advantages of both the existing designs while minimizing the impact of their drawbacks. Our design reduces the charger travel distance by scheduling based on the nested TSP tours, and reduces the charging delay of sensor nodes with the concept of energy synchronization within each round of selected tours.

3. PRELIMINARIES

3.1 Problem Statement

With the advancement of the energy transferring technologies, the time to replenish the energy supply of sensor nodes has been dramatically reduced [20,25]. Zhu et al. have implemented an energy sharing system with capacitor-array powered sensor nodes [17], in which the energy supply in the network is transferred from energy-sufficient nodes to energy-hungry nodes. From the empirical results reported in [16], the time to charge a 10 F capacitor from empty to a voltage of 2.5 V is in the order of 10 s normally. This greatly shortened charging time indicates that adopting mobile chargers to replenish nodes energy supply is a promising direction for stable and sustainable network operations.

In this work, we investigate the on-demand mobile charging problem in rechargeable sensor networks, where a mobile energy charger travels within the deployment field, and replenishes the energy supply of nodes via short-distance or direct-contact charging technologies such as *inductive charging* [26]. The mobile charger is controllable in both its travel trajectory and the amount of energy charged to individual sensor nodes.

When the remaining energy levels of sensor nodes are low, the nodes initiate charging requests to the mobile charger either by the communications (potentially in multiple hops) between themselves and the charger [27,28] or with the assistance of a sink [7,8] [1]. Our objective is to design an efficient mobile charging protocol for the charger to effectively serve the received charging requests. Here by *serving* a charging request, we mean the charger travels to the requesting sensor node and replenishes its energy supply to the desired level. The mobile charging process can be evaluated from two aspects.

• **Charging Delay** For the requesting sensor nodes, the charging process is evaluated based on their *charging delay*, defined as the time since they send out their charging requests to the time their energy is replenished by the charger. A shorter charging delay implies a higher charging efficiency.

• **Charger Travel Distance** For the mobile charger, the charging efficiency is evaluated in terms of its *travel distance* to carry out the charging tasks of nodes. A shorter travel distance indicates a higher charging efficiency.

Most existing works choose only one of the two aspects above as the design objective. For example, reducing the charging latency of sensor nodes is emphasized in [7,8,22], while the charging process is optimized by shortening the charger travel distance in [10,18]. To the best of our knowledge, our work is the first attempt to jointly tackle these two objectives.

3.2 State-of-the-Art and Limitations

The TSP-based solutions are a classic family of the designs on the mobile charging problem [10,18,21]. In general, with the TSP-based solutions, the mobile charger *periodically* travels along a pre-optimized TSP tour to replenish the energy supply of nodes in each round of the charging process, and thus the charger travel distance in replenishing the energy of all nodes is minimized. However, to take advantage of the pre-optimized TSP tour in the on-demand mobile charging scenario, there are two facts that would significantly degrade the charging performance.

3.2.1 Diversity in Nodes Energy Consumption

The efficiency of the TSP-based solutions degrades when nodes energy consumption rates are highly diverse, which is unfortunate-

[1]A remaining energy level threshold can be adopted for sensor nodes to initiate their charging requests. For the ease of description, we assume a threshold of 0% in this paper. Furthermore, as both the time for the charger to travel to the requesting node and the time to replenish nodes energy supply are normally much longer than the communication delay, we assume a negligible time to deliver charging requests from nodes to the charger, similar to [29].

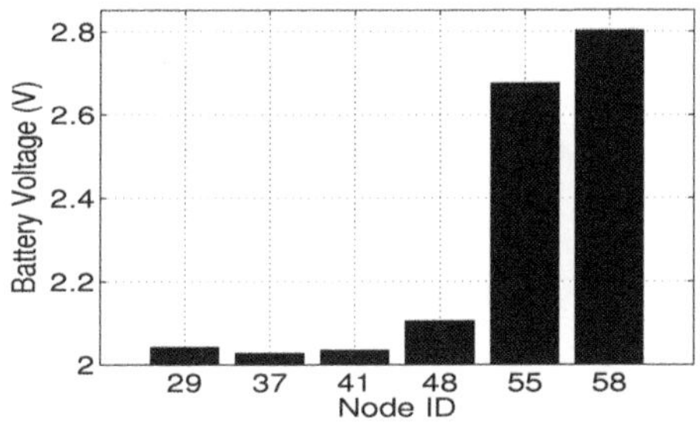

Figure 1: Diverse nodes remaining energy (original data is provided by [30]).

ly true in most cases for multihop sensor networks [29]. The high energy consumption diversity may cause highly diverse nodes remaining energy levels, and as a result, traveling along the pre-optimized tour leads to the unnecessary visits of energy-sufficient nodes. This not only increases the charger travel distance but also prolongs the charging delay of energy-hungry nodes.

To clearly demonstrate the potentially unnecessary visits of energy-rich nodes, Figure 1 presents the voltage readings of six sensors at a specific time in a data trace provided by Intel Berkeley Research Lab, which is collected with the granularity of 1 second between February 28th and April 5th, 2004 [30]. We can observe the obvious voltage diversity among the nodes. In this case, if the charger carries out the charging process based on the TSP tour constructed according to these six nodes, it would arrive at node-55 and node-58 only to find out that they have little demand for energy replenishment.

3.2.2 *Sequence of Nodes Charging Requests*

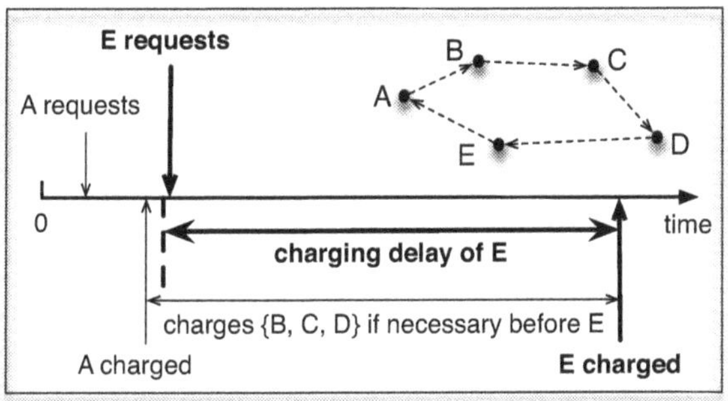

Figure 2: Requests sequence affects the charging performance significantly: the charging delay of E is long if E requests charging when the charger has already passed it in the current charging round.

Furthermore, in the on-demand charging scenario, even if nodes have similar energy consumptions, indicating they may all need to be charged in a given round, their charging requests sequence plays a critical role in determining the performance of the periodic charging process, which must be considered if we want to utilize the advantage of the TSP-based solutions in minimizing the charger travel distance. Figure 2 demonstrates an example on how the charging requests sequence affects the charging performance. Consider the network shown in the upper-right corner of the figure, where the charger periodically carries out the charging tasks according to the optimal TSP tour shown with the dashed lines. If node E requests charging when the charger has just charged A, meaning the charger has already passed E in this round, the charger would first charge

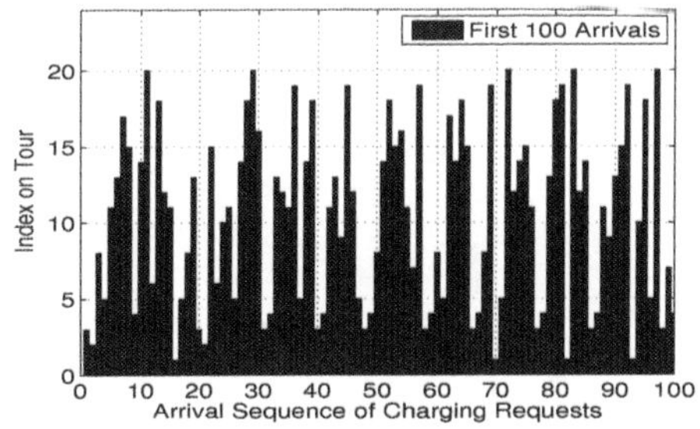

Figure 3: Requests sequence mismatches nodes sequence along the tour.

node B, C, and D if necessary. In this way, the energy of E will not be replenished until the charger reaches it in the next round, which leads to a large charging delay of E.

The fundamental reason for E's long charging delay in the above example is that the charging requests sequence mismatches with the node sequence on the optimal TSP tour. To examine whether the mismatching between the two sequences exists in practice, we simulate a small environment monitoring sensor network consisting of 20 sensor nodes with similar energy consumptions. We construct a near-optimal TSP tour based on the nodes deployment with the open source TSP solver *Concorde* [31], and index nodes according to their sequence along the tour. We record the charging requests sequence of nodes, and the first 100 requests are shown in Fig. 3. We can see the indexes of requesting nodes are quite random with regard to the nodes requesting sequence, which would lead to the undesired case shown in Fig. 2.

It is possible to avoid the undesired case shown in Fig. 2 by removing the periodic property from the charging process, e.g., performing charging tasks according to the classic Nearest-Job-Next discipline [23]. However, removing the periodic property may lead to the *zig-zag* travel of the charger and cause unfairness issue among sensor nodes. Our evaluation results show that our design outperforms Nearest-Job-Next by about 30%-40%, as will be explained in Section 6 and Section 7.

3.3 Design Overview

In this paper, focusing on the scenario where the energy consumption rates are diverse among sensor nodes, we propose the *Energy Synchronized Charging* (*ESync*) protocol, which addresses the above two limitations by first *constructing a set of nested TSP tours* and then *synchronizing nodes energy according to the tours*. The motivation of the nested TSP tours is to only involve nodes with low remaining energy levels in each charging round to reduce the charger travel distance. The motivation for the energy synchronization among nodes is to proactively adjust nodes charging requests sequence to synchronize it with the TSP tour selected in each round, and thus reduce the charging delay of sensor nodes.

4. CONSTRUCTION OF NESTED TOURS

The limitation of the TSP-based solutions with diverse node energy consumptions inspires us to cluster nodes according to their energy consumption rates, and then based on these clusters, we construct multiple TSP tours in a *nested* manner. We further present a corresponding tour selection algorithm to guide the charging process in each round.

4.1 Nodes Clustering

Before introducing the design of our clustering algorithm, we first use a simplified example as shown in Fig. 4 to present our

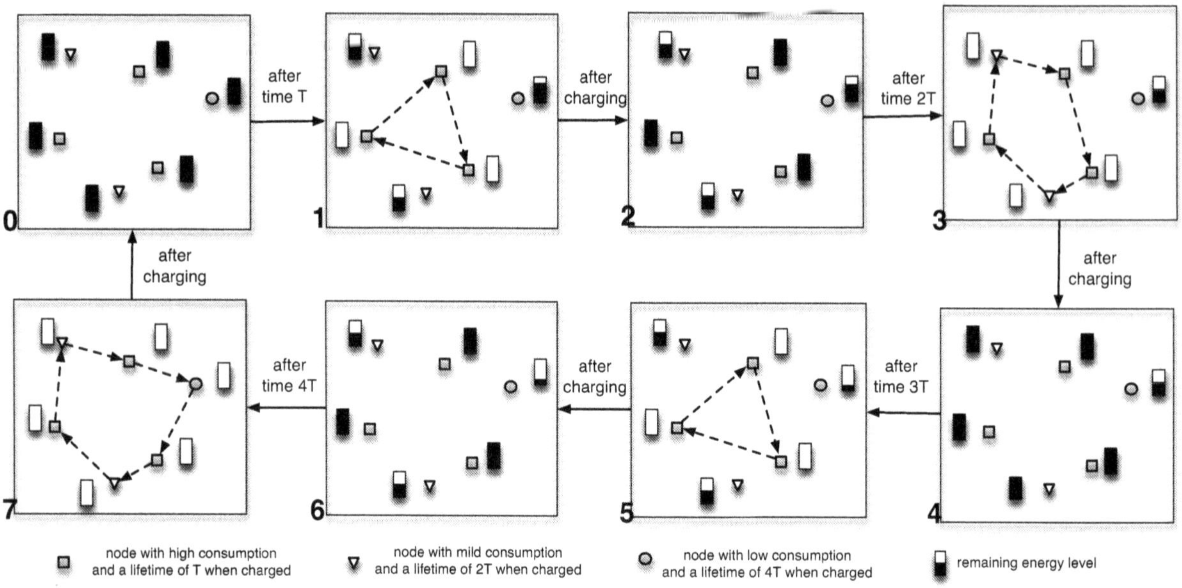

Figure 4: Clustering nodes according to their energy consumption rates, and then a set of nested TSP tours is constructed. One of these TSP tours is selected to guide the charging tasks in each charging round.

idea. The energy consumption rates of nodes represented by the squares are twice of the triangle nodes and four times of the circle nodes. Denote the lifetime of square nodes when fully charged by T. Consequently, the triangle and circle nodes have a $2T$ and $4T$ lifetime when fully charged, respectively [2].

If we take these three categories of nodes as three clusters, then when the square nodes deplete their energy after an operation time of T, the charger only needs to charge the square cluster as both the triangle and circle nodes still have sufficient energy supply (Fig. 4(1)). The nodes remaining energy levels after the charging of the square nodes are shown in Fig. 4(2) [3]. After another operation time of T, both the square and triangle nodes deplete their energy, and this time the charger needs to charge the two corresponding clusters as shown in Fig. 4(3). When an operation time of $4T$ is passed, the charger needs to replenish the energy supply of all nodes, as shown in Fig. 4(7), and the process repeats afterwards.

In this example, the nodes clusters can accurately separate the energy-hungry nodes from the energy-rich nodes in each charging round, and thus the charger only needs to consider the nodes clusters, instead of individual nodes, to carry out the charging process. The fundamental property leads to this effect is that nodes in the same cluster have similar energy consumptions. Based on this observation, we propose a novel *power-α* clustering algorithm to group nodes according to their energy consumptions.

Assume all nodes are initially fully charged, we begin our design from the time that at least one charging request has been received from each node. This ensures the charger has certain knowledge on the energy consumption conditions of all nodes, based on which the estimation on their energy consumption rates is feasible [32].

[2]To highlight the motivation of our design, the nodes energy consumption rates in this example are intentionally set to be diverse. However, our design is also applicable to scenarios where nodes have similar energy consumptions.

[3]The time to finish the charging of these nodes is assumed to be negligible for the ease of demonstration, which is further investigated in Section 7.

The charger can adopt any existing charging protocols before this time [7, 23, 24].

Denote $r_{\max}$ and $r_{\min}$ as the maximal and minimal nodes energy consumption rate, respectively. We construct a total number of m intervals and

$$m = \lceil \log_\alpha(\frac{r_{\max}}{r_{\min}}) \rceil^+, \quad (1)$$

where $\lceil x \rceil^+$ returns the first integer that is larger than x [4], and α is an integer design parameter that is larger than 1. With the ascending order of energy consumption rates, these m intervals are: $[r_{\min}, \frac{r_{\max}}{\alpha^{m-1}}]$, $(\frac{r_{\max}}{\alpha^{m-1}}, \frac{r_{\max}}{\alpha^{m-2}}]$, $\cdots$, $(\frac{r_{\max}}{\alpha^2}, \frac{r_{\max}}{\alpha^1}]$, $(\frac{r_{\max}}{\alpha^1}, r_{\max}]$. Note that the length of each interval increases exponentially with α. For each node s, it is clustered into the i-th cluster if its energy consumption rate $r(s)$ falls into the i-th interval. For example, if $r_{max} = 6$, $r_{min} = 1$, and $\alpha = 2$, then $m = \lceil \log_2 \frac{6}{1} \rceil^+ = 3$ intervals are constructed. The three intervals are $[1, 1.5]$, $(1.5, 3]$, and $(3, 6]$, respectively. For clarity, we refer to the interval with the highest consumption rate (i.e., $(3, 6]$) as the 1-st interval and the corresponding cluster as the 1-st cluster. Similarly, the interval $(1.5, 3]$ and $[1, 1.5]$ are referred to as the 2-nd and 3-rd intervals, and the corresponding clusters as the 2-nd and 3-rd clusters, respectively.

With this clustering approach, the ratio between the maximal and the minimal energy consumption rates of nodes in the same cluster is upper bounded by α. Clearly, α plays a critical role in determining the charging performance. We will elaborate the optimal setting of α in Section 4.4, and our evaluation results in Section 7 indicate that an α of 2 leads to the best performance in most cases.

Note that in event-driven sensor network applications such as target tracking, the energy consumption rates of individual sensor nodes may vary over time. In this case, we need to dynamically adjust the clustering of nodes (and the constructed TSP tours as will be introduced below) to guarantee the energy similarity of nodes in the same cluster. An important observation on these event-driven

[4]Note its difference with the traditional operator $\lceil x \rceil$ when x is an integer.

applications is that although the energy consumptions for individual nodes may not be constant, their activities demonstrate certain periodicity and predicability [33], which can be used to dynamically adjust the clustering of sensor nodes.

4.2 Nested Tour Construction

The next step is to construct TSP tours according to the m clusters in a nested manner. We construct m TSP tours based on the first i clusters ($i = 1, 2, \cdots, m$), and denote these tours as $\{T^1_{tsp}, T^2_{tsp}, \cdots, T^m_{tsp}\}$. Because the tours are constructed in a nested manner, their length satisfies the following relationship

$$|T^1_{tsp}| \leq |T^2_{tsp}| \leq |T^3_{tsp}| \leq \cdots \leq |T^m_{tsp}|. \quad (2)$$

In the example shown in Fig. 4, three nested TSP tours are constructed based on these three nodes clusters. The shortest tour T^1_{tsp} is shown in Fig. 4(1), the second shortest tour T^2_{tsp} is shown in Fig. 4(3), and the longest tour T^3_{tsp} is shown in Fig. 4(7).

4.3 Tour Selection for Each Round

With the nested TSP tours, the mobile charger periodically carries out the charging tasks by selecting one of these nested tours in each round, and charges the nodes involved in the tour if necessary. Thus, the next question we need to decide is which tour the mobile charger should select for a given round of the on-demand charging process.

4.3.1 Key Observation

Again, before introducing our design on the tour selection algorithm, we first use the example shown in Fig. 4 to present our basic idea. With the *Power-α* clustering algorithm and the tour construction method introduced above, we obtain three node clusters (i.e., square, triangle, and circle) and three nested TSP tours (i.e., T^1_{tsp}, T^2_{tsp}, and T^3_{tsp} as in Fig. 4(1), Fig. 4(3), and Fig. 4(7)). For the mobile charger, it is desirable to select the shortest TSP tour containing all the energy depleted nodes in each charging round. In the 1-st round of the charging process, only the square nodes deplete their energy supply, and thus the charger would prefer to select the shortest tour containing the square nodes, i.e., T^1_{tsp}, as the tour to guide the charging process (Fig. 4(1)). Similarly, in the 2-nd round, the charger would prefer to select the shortest tour containing the square and triangle nodes, i.e., T^2_{tsp}, to follow (Fig. 4(3)). T^1_{tsp} is selected again in the 3-rd round since now only the square nodes are out of energy supply (Fig. 4(5)). Then in the 4-th round, all nodes deplete their energy supply, and the TSP tour containing all of them is selected (Fig. 4(7)). From this example, we can see the tour selection algorithm is expected to identify the shortest TSP tour containing all the energy-hungry nodes in each charging round, and the following observation inspires us the solution.

For any given α and m, every $j \in \{0, 1, \cdots, \alpha^{m-1}\}$ can be represented in the form of

$$j = \sum_{i=0}^{m-1} c^j_i \cdot \alpha^i, \quad (3)$$

where $c^j_i \in \{0, 1, \cdots, \alpha - 1\}$. To clearly demonstrate the relationship between the selected tour in j-th round and j's sum expression in (3), let us define an ordered set $\mathcal{C}_j = <c^j_0, c^j_1, \cdots, c^j_{m-1}>$. For the ease of description, further define $\mathcal{C}_0 = <0, 0, \cdots, 0>$ and $|\mathcal{C}_0| = m - 1$. Then with $\alpha = 2$ and $m = 3$, the sum expressions and the corresponding $\mathcal{C}_j$ for the first four rounds of the mobile charging process are shown in Fig. 5.

We can see that in the 1-st round, the only element in $\mathcal{C}_1$ that is larger than the corresponding element in $\mathcal{C}_0$ is the 1-st element,

$$\begin{aligned}
0 &= 0\times 2^0 + 0\times 2^1 + 0\times 2^2 &\rightarrow\ & \mathcal{C}_0 = <0, 0, 0>,\\
1 &= 1\times 2^0 + 0\times 2^1 + 0\times 2^2 &\rightarrow\ & \mathcal{C}_1 = <1, 0, 0>,\\
2 &= 0\times 2^0 + 1\times 2^1 + 0\times 2^2 &\rightarrow\ & \mathcal{C}_2 = <0, 1, 0>,\\
3 &= 1\times 2^0 + 1\times 2^1 + 0\times 2^2 &\rightarrow\ & \mathcal{C}_3 = <1, 1, 0>,\\
4 &= 0\times 2^0 + 0\times 2^1 + 1\times 2^2 &\rightarrow\ & \mathcal{C}_4 = <0, 0, 1>.
\end{aligned}$$

Figure 5: Tour selection based on the sum expression in (3).

and from the example in Fig. 4, we know the 1-st tour (i.e., T^1_{tsp}) is desirable to be selected in the 1-st round. For the second round, the 2-nd element in $\mathcal{C}_2$ is larger than the 2-nd element in $\mathcal{C}_1$, and on the other hand, the second tour T^2_{tsp} is desirable to be selected in the 2-nd round. This agreement holds for the 3-rd and 4-th rounds as well. For the 3-rd round, the 1-st element in $\mathcal{C}_3$ is larger than that in $\mathcal{C}_2$, and the desirable tour is T^1_{tsp}. For the 4-th round, the 3-rd element in $\mathcal{C}_4$ is larger than that in $\mathcal{C}_3$, and the desirable tour is T^3_{tsp}.

This relationship between the tour selected in the j-th round and j's sum expression inspires us the design of the tour selection algorithm.

4.3.2 Tour Selection Algorithm Design

For a given round index $j \in \{1, 2, \cdots, \alpha^{m-1}\}$, we first identify the corresponding $\mathcal{C}_j$. Then we compare it with $\mathcal{C}_{j-1}$, and find the k ($k = 0, 1, \cdots, m-1$) such that c^j_k is larger than c^{j-1}_k. It can be proved that one and only one such k can be found for every round index j, which is not included here due to the space limit. As a result, the charger takes the $(k + 1)$-th tour in the j-th round. The sequence of the adopted tours repeats every α^{m-1} rounds.

We can see that with the proposed tour construction and selection algorithms, for each round of the charging process, the charger always selects the shortest TSP tour that contains all the sensor nodes with low remaining energy levels. As a result, the charger travel distance during the charging process is reduced.

4.4 Determining the Optimal Power Factor

We have introduced how to construct the nested TSP tours and which tour to select for each charging round with a given power factor α. Next we explain how to identify the optimal setting of α. The optimal α is jointly determined by nodes energy consumption rates and their locations. This means identifying the optimal α before network deployment is challenging. However, once at least one charging request has been received from each node, both the estimated energy consumption rates and nodes locations can be made available to the charger, e.g., by piggybacking these information in the charging requests, based on which the optimal α can be identified.

For the ease of description, we extend our previous notation on T^i_{tsp} by denoting the i-th TSP tour obtained with a specific α as $T^i_{\text{tsp}(\alpha)}$. Denote m_α as the number of clusters obtained with power factor α. With the proposed tour selection algorithm, the sequence of adopted tours will repeat every $\alpha^{m_\alpha - 1}$ rounds. The worst-case charger travel distance during these rounds Y_α is

$$Y_\alpha = |T^{m_\alpha}_{\text{tsp}(\alpha)}| + \sum_{i=1}^{m_\alpha - 1} \alpha^{m_\alpha - i - 1} |T^i_{\text{tsp}(\alpha)}|,$$

and thus an upper bound Z_α of the asymptotic average travel distance for each round is

$$Z_\alpha = Y_\alpha / (\alpha^{m_\alpha - 1}).$$

Then the mobile charger can adopt the α with the minimum Z_α to carry out the charging tasks

$$\hat{\alpha} = \{\alpha : \min\{Z_\alpha\}\}$$

Note that when $\alpha > \frac{r_{\max}}{r_{\min}}$, only one cluster containing all the nodes will be formed, and *ESync* regresses to the simple case where only the TSP tour containing all nodes is involved in the charging process. Thus the charger only needs to check the potential value of α in $[2, \frac{r_{\max}}{r_{\min}}]$ to determine its optimal setting.

4.5 Time Complexity

We needs a time of $\mathcal{O}(m_\alpha C_{\text{tsp}})$ to accomplish the node clustering and tour construction with a specific α, where C_{tsp} is the time complexity to obtain the near-optimal TSP tour. As mentioned earlier, the charger needs to check at most $(\frac{r_{\max}}{r_{\min}} - 1)$ possible values of α to determine the optimal setting. As a summary, the computation complexity in constructing the nested TSP tours is $\mathcal{O}(C_{\text{tsp}} \frac{r_{\max}}{r_{\min}} \log \frac{r_{\max}}{r_{\min}})$. The charger needs a time of $\mathcal{O}(\log_\alpha \frac{r_{\max}}{r_{\min}})$ to select the tour in each round.

5. ENERGY SYNCHRONIZATION AMONG NODES

With the nested TSP tours and the tour selection method, only energy-hungry nodes are involved in each charging round. In this section, we further improve the charging process by synchronizing the energy supply of nodes to proactively adjust their charging requests sequence. As a result, the charging requests sequence of nodes is synchronized with their sequence on the TSP tours. Specifically, if the charging requests from two neighboring nodes are sent out according to their sequence on the selected TSP tour, we say these two nodes are *energy synchronized* in the charging process. This energy synchronization among nodes is achieved by carefully controlling the amount of energy charged to individual nodes.

In generally, the mobile charger needs to address two questions to carry out the charging process in each round: which node to charge next, and then how much energy to charge to the node.

5.1 Which Node to Charge Next

In our design, the node to be charged next is determined according to the selected TSP tour in each round. Specifically, after completing the charging of the current node, the mobile charger selects the requesting node that is closest to its current location along the TSP tour as the next node to charge.

Although our method demonstrates greedy feature, which may cause the unfairness issue among sensor nodes. Because we only applies the greedy feature based on the TSP tour, the potential unfairness issue is significantly alleviated.

5.2 How Much to Charge

To achieve the energy synchronization among nodes, the charger does not always fully charge individual nodes, and next we explain how to determine the amount of energy charged to the selected node. In our design, we determine the amount of energy charged to individual nodes with the objective of synchronizing their energy supplies. Thus given the selected charging node, we first need to identify the node to which to synchronize its energy, i.e., its *synchronization target*.

Assume the mobile charger is currently working in the j-th round following tour $T_{tsp}^{f(j)}$, where $f(j)$ is the tour index returned by the tour selection algorithm. To find the synchronization target of a given node s in this round, which belongs to the i-th cluster, we first identify the round j' in which s is involved the next time by

$$j' = j + \alpha^{i-1} \quad (i = 1, 2, \cdots, m). \tag{4}$$

The adopted tour in the j'-th round, $T_{tsp}^{f(j')}$, can be calculated by the tour selection algorithm. Then we find the previous node of s along $T_{tsp}^{f(j')}$ as the synchronization target of s in the j-th round, which is denoted as u for the ease of description. This is because the desired effect we want to achieve is when s requests energy replenishment the next time, the mobile charger has just accomplished the charging of u in the j'-th round, meaning the energy of s is synchronized with u in the j'-th round.

Two pieces of information are needed to calculate the amount of charged energy to achieve the energy synchronization between s and u: the energy consumption rates of s and u, and the time duration until u is charged in the j'-th round.

The nodes energy consumption rates can be estimated based on the history of charging requests. As an example, the energy consumption rate of a specific node can be estimated based on its operation time with a single full charging [32]. We emphasize that the perfect estimation is extremely challenging. Our design does not require the perfect estimation of nodes energy consumption rates, and we will further discuss and investigate the charging performance under varying estimation errors in Section 7. Through our extensive simulation, we observe that our design can tolerate up to 30% estimation errors, which can be easily guaranteed by the state-of-the-art power monitoring solutions [34, 35].

Next we explore the time duration until u is charged in the j'-th round. The number of rounds that u is involved between the j-th and j'-th round can be calculated in a similar manner as (4), and denote it as q. The total amount of energy charged to u in these q rounds is at most qE, and thus the time from now till u requests charging in the j'-th round is at most $\frac{qE+e_r(u)}{r(u)}$, where $e_r(u)$ is the current remaining energy of u and $r(u)$ is its energy consumption rate.

As a result, the amount of energy charged to s is calculated according to

$$e(s) = r(s)\left(\frac{qE + e_r(u)}{r(u)} + t_c\right) - e_r(s), \tag{5}$$

where t_c is the worst-case charging time to fully replenish nodes energy supply (i.e., the longest possible time to charge u in the j'-th round), and thus $(\frac{qE+e_r(u)}{r(u)} + t_c)$ is the time before the charger arrives to charge s the next time. Note that $e(s) \in [0, E - e_r(s)]$.

Determining the amount of charged energy according to (5) indicates that the charger would not always fully charge individual nodes. However, this occasionally partially charging of nodes facilities the energy synchronization among nodes, and thus the overall charging performance outperforms that when the charger always fully charge nodes. Specifically, from our evaluation results in Section 7, we observe a 30% and 40% reduction in the charger travel distance and the charging delay of sensor nodes, respectively.

During the charging process in each round, the charger needs a time of $\mathcal{O}(n)$ to determine the next node to charge, and another time of $\mathcal{O}(\log_\alpha \frac{r_{\max}}{r_{\min}})$ is needed to determine the amount of charged energy.

5.3 Charger Energy Replenishment

Although usually the mobile charger has a much larger energy capacity than sensor nodes, the energy replenishment of the charger itself also needs to be considered in practical implementations, especially when the deployment field or the number of deployed nodes is large. *ESync* can seamlessly incorporate the energy replen-

Table 1: Average energy consumption rates.

Node	#1	#2	#3	#4	#5	#6	#7	#8	#9
r_i	4	2	4	2	1	4	1	4	2

Table 2: Scale-down a realistic network for the experiment

	Envisioned Network	Experiment
Network Area	$1,000 \times 1,000\ m^2$	$3 \times 3\ m^2$
Nodes Lifetime	10–40 hours	100–400 s
Fully Charge Time	20 min	3.33 s

ishment of the charger into the charging process. Assume there is an energy tank from which the charger energy can be replenished. Whenever the energy level of the charger is low, we treat it as a *virtual charging request* initiated by the energy tank. The energy tank can be included into the nested tours construction based on the charger's operation time with a single charge, just as a usual sensor node. As a result, the charger's energy replenishment can be handled in the same way as the sensor nodes.

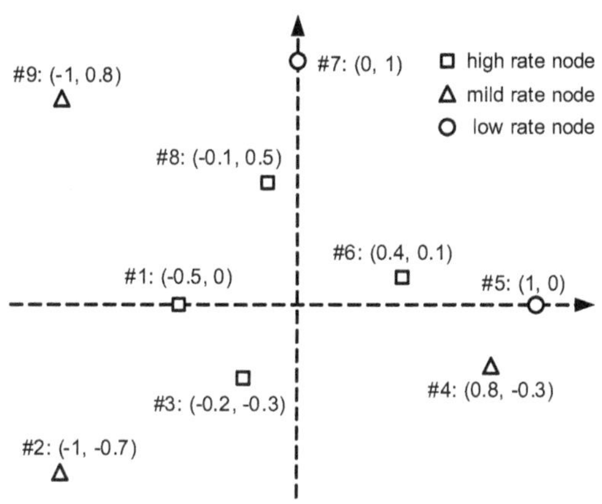

Figure 6: Nodes locations.

6. EXPERIMENT EVALUATION

We evaluate the performance of *ESync* through both experiments and simulations. The experiment results are presented in this section, and the insights obtained through large-scale simulations will be introduced in the next section.

In our experiment, we randomly deploy 9 sensor nodes in an open field of $3\times3\ m^2$, and a LEGO Mindstorms NXT robot with an average travel speed of $0.1\ m$ per second is adopted as the mobile charger. The locations of these nodes are shown in Fig. 6.

Figure 8 shows the relationship between battery voltage and the charging time obtained with our empirical measurements. The battery can be rapidly charged in the early charging stage, during which the battery voltage and the charging time demonstrate clear linear relationship (as shown in the box in Fig. 8). However, as the battery approaches its full voltage, the charging speed significantly slows down. Similar charging curves are reported in the data sheets of off-the-shelf battery products [36]. Based on this observation, we implement a simple linear charging model to emulate the charging of nodes. Specifically, the time to accomplish the charging of a specific node s is calculated by $\frac{e(s)}{E}t_c$ where $e(s)$ is the amount of energy charged to s, E is the full energy capacity of nodes, and t_c is the time to fully charge an energy depleted node. This simplified charging model is sufficient for our evaluation purpose, especially when not all the nodes are fully charged in our energy synchronized charging design (which avoids the non-linear portion of the charging curve). Specifically, we emulate a scenario where $E = 100$ units and the charging rate of the charger is 30 units per second, indicating the worst-case charging time $t_c = \frac{100}{30} \approx 3.3$ s. The average energy consumption rates of nodes are shown in Table 1.

The rationale behind these settings is because of our limited testbed size (i.e., $3 \times 3\ m^2$ as stated above), we need to scale-down a realistic network in both the spatial and temporal dimensions. Specifically, we envision a network area of $1,000 \times 1,000\ m^2$ where the average nodes lifetime is about $10 - 40$ hours upon fully charged. The charger needs a charging time of about 20 minutes to fully charge an energy-depleted node, as with the commercial fast charger for AA batteries commonly adopted on sensor nodes. Then we map the considered network area to our experiment field, and scale-down other settings accordingly, as shown in Table 2.

These 9 sensor nodes are organized into 3 clusters based on their energy consumption rates (i.e., $\{1,3,6,8\}$, $\{2,4,9\}$, and $\{5,7\}$), and 3 nested TSP tours are constructed accordingly, as highlighted in Fig. 7. Sensor nodes send out charging requests to the charger when their energy supply is depleted, and the charger carries out these charging tasks according to *ESync*.

We evaluate the performance of *ESync* and compare it with two classic baselines: TSP [24] and Nearest-Job-Next [23], upon which most existing designs are based [10, 18]. For TSP, the charger travels and charges nodes following the TSP tour, and its travel is independent of whether the charging request from the node has been received. For Nearest-Job-Next, the charger always selects the geographically nearest requesting node as the next node to charge. Both these two baselines adopt the full charging of nodes throughout the charging process.

To capture the fact that nodes energy consumption rates are usually dynamic in practice, we introduce an estimation error parameter ϵ to generate the actual energy consumption of nodes in each second. Specifically, the energy consumption of node-i in each second is randomly generated in

$$[(1-\epsilon)r_i, (1+\epsilon)r_i], \tag{6}$$

where r_i is the average energy consumption rate of node-i as shown in Table 1. [5]

A mobile charging process of 15 minutes is performed in each experiment, and the requests charging delay and charger travel distance during these charging processes are recorded for evaluation. To better visualize the mobile charging process, Figure 9 shows the recorded charger travel trajectory during a particular experiment. Note that the charger trajectory is not straight lines due to the kinetic constraints.

The charger travel distance and requests charging delay resultant with ϵ varing from 0–30% are shown in Fig. 10 and Fig. 11, respectively. We can see the charger travel distance resultant by *ESync* is about 30% and 20% shorter than those obtained by TSP and Nearest-Job-Next, and the request charging delay is reduced by about 50%. Furthermore, we can see that although the performance of *ESync* degrades with a larger estimation error on nodes energy consumption rates, it still noticeably outperforms both TSP and N-JN even with an ϵ as large as 30%, indicating a good tolerance of *ESync* on the energy consumption variance of sensor nodes.

To clearly illustrate the evolution of nodes remaining energy during a mobile charging process of 15 minutes, we show the energy level of node-1, node-2, and node-5 in Fig. 12, one for each of the

[5]However, we assume a perfect estimation on nodes energy consumption rates for TSP and Nearest-Job-Next.

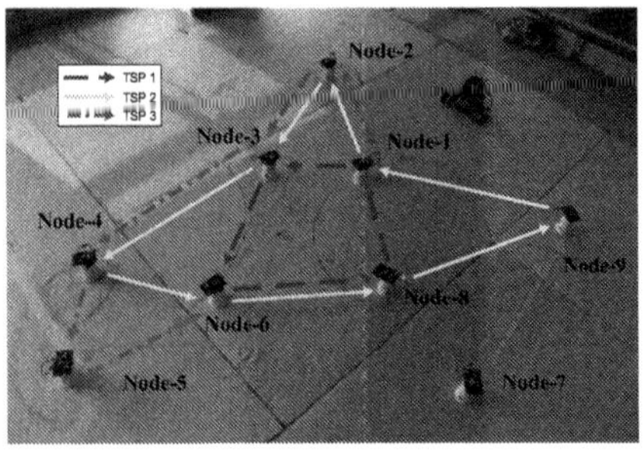

Figure 7: Overview of the experiment settings.

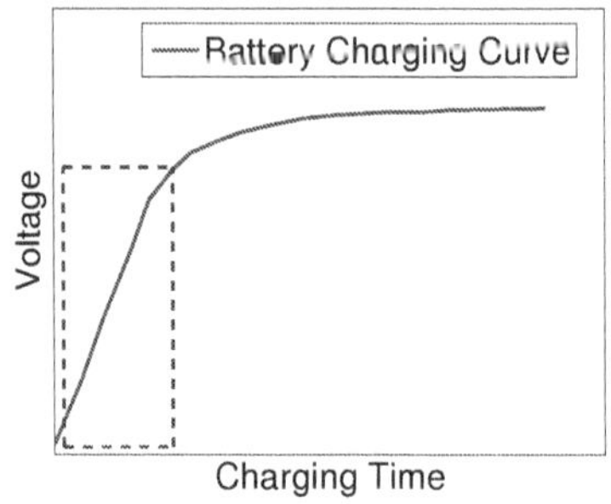

Figure 8: Typical battery charging curve over time.

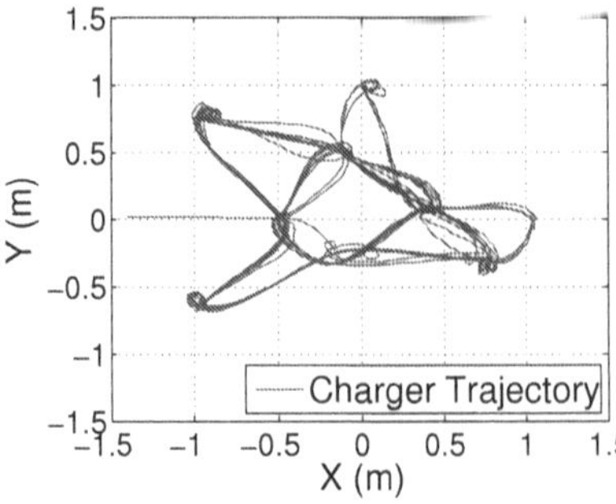

Figure 9: Charger trajectory during the mobile charging process.

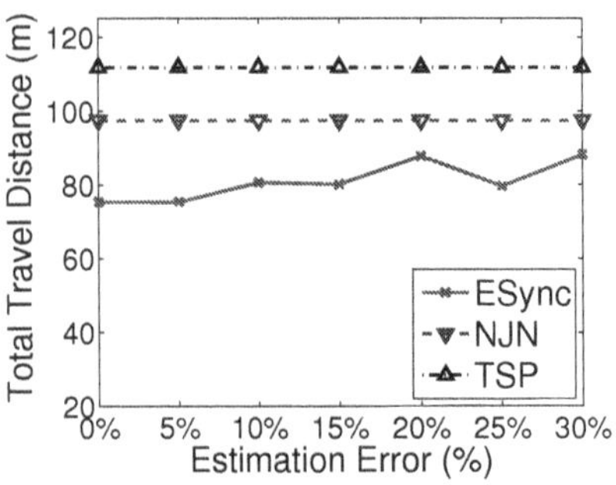

Figure 10: Charger travel distance with estimation error ϵ.

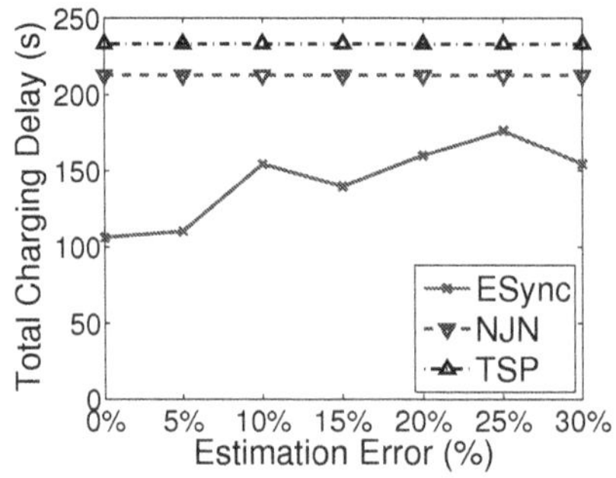

Figure 11: Charging delay with estimation error ϵ.

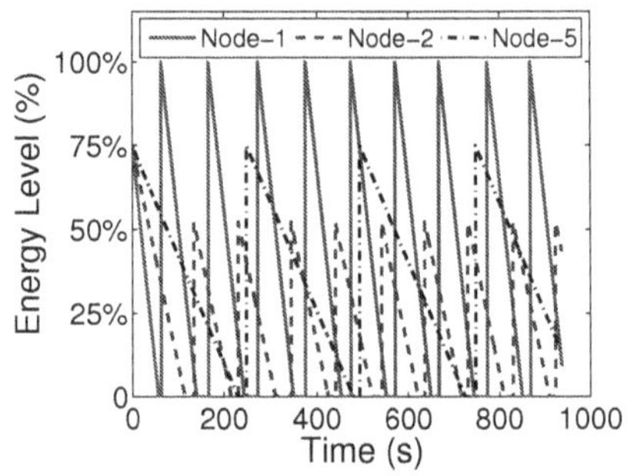

Figure 12: Nodes energy during experiment.

three nodes clusters. We can see node-1 is always charged to its full capacity because it has the highest energy consumption rates (and thus the shortest lifetime) in the network, while node-2 and node-5 are only partially charged. Furthermore, the frequencies for the three nodes to be charged decrease with the order of node-1, node-2, and node-5. This is because node-1 is involved in all three nested TSP tours while node-5 is only involved in the 3rd tour, as shown in Fig. 7.

7. SIMULATION EVALUATION

In this section, we evaluate the performance of *ESync* through extensive simulations.

7.1 Simulation Setup

We simulate an environment monitoring sensor network with 20–200 randomly deployed nodes. The sensing field size varies from $60\ m \times 60\ m$ to $160\ m \times 160\ m$, and a sink is located at the field center. The nodes energy capacity is $1,000\ mAH$. The energy consumption rate for the sensing tasks is $0.75\ mA \times 2\ V = 1.5\ mW$, which is typical for a light sensor [37]. The communication energy costs of sensor nodes are set based on the data sheet of MICA2 node: with transmitting and receiving current draw of $25\ mA$ and $8\ mA$ respectively, the corresponding energy consumption rates are $25mA \times 2\ V = 50mW$ and $8mA \times 2\ V = 16mW$ with a typical voltage of $2\ V$. After nodes deployment, a routing structure is constructed based on the TinyOS standard CTP [38]. Then the environment information, after captured by individual nodes, is transmitted to the sink through multi-hop communications. Sensor nodes send out charging requests to the charger when their remaining energy approaches zero. The charger travel speed is $1\ m/s$ unless otherwise specified [29]. We simulate a network operation period of $500,000\ s$, and record the total distance the mobile charger traveled and the total charging delay of sensor nodes. We adopt *Concorde* [31], an open source TSP solver with verified efficiency, to obtain the near-optimal TSP tours in our simulation. The mobile charging process is simulated with Matlab.

7.2 Visualizing the Effect of Energy Synchronization

Before evaluating the performance of *ESync*, we first run *ESync* on the same setting as in Fig. 3 to visualize the effect of energy synchronization when only a single TSP tour is constructed. With a simulated time of $500,000\ s$, during which a total number of 948 charging requests are served, the last 100 requests in the simulation are shown in Fig. 13. We can see although the realization of energy synchronization is not perfect due to the dynamics in the charging process, the requests sequence greatly matches the TSP tour, and thus our design is validated. Furthermore, we observe that the effect of energy synchronization begins to show as early as from the 200-th to 300-th requests, indicating a short time to achieve the energy synchronization.

7.3 Performance Evaluation

7.3.1 Impact of Network Scale

To investigate the scalability of *ESync*, we evaluate its performance with different network scales w.r.t. the number of deployed sensor nodes. The resultant charger travel distance and charging delay of sensor nodes are shown in Fig. 14(a) and Fig. 14(b) respectively, where the number of nodes varies from 20 to 200. Note that due to the large gap among the results returned by the three charging protocols, the y-axis in the figures is in *log-scale*. We can see *ESync* achieves the best performance for all the network scales investigated. For example, the charger travel distance (charging

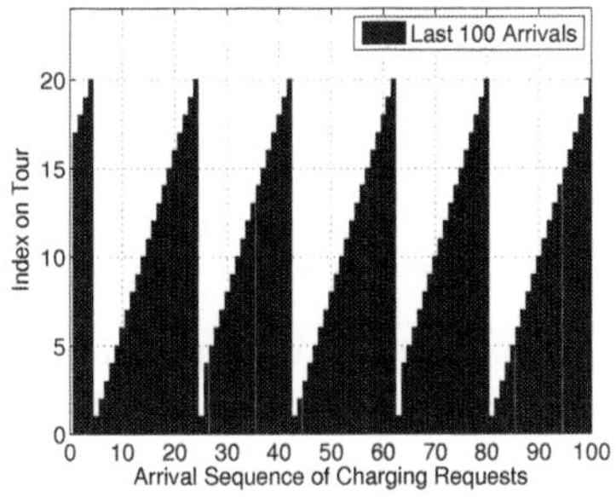

Figure 13: Effect of energy synch.

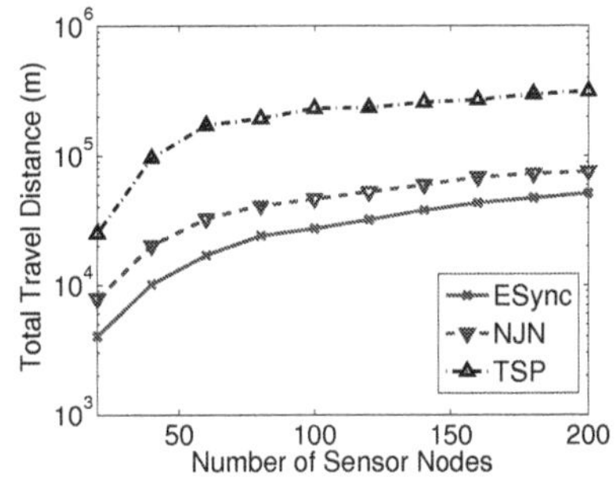

(a) Total travel distance

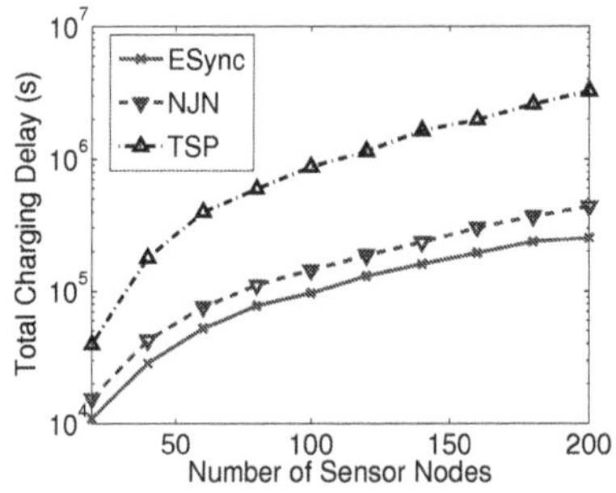

(b) Total charging delay

Figure 14: Impact of nodes number n.

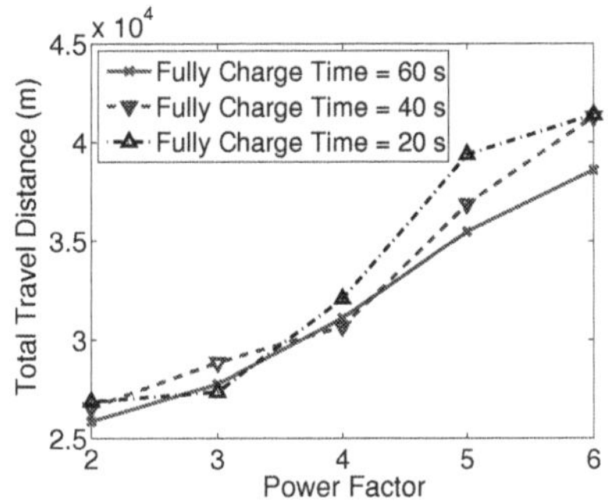

(a) Total travel distance

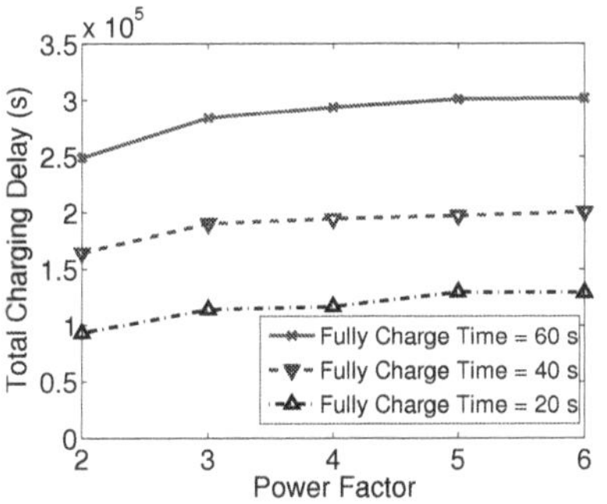

(b) Total charging delay

Figure 15: Impact of power factor α.

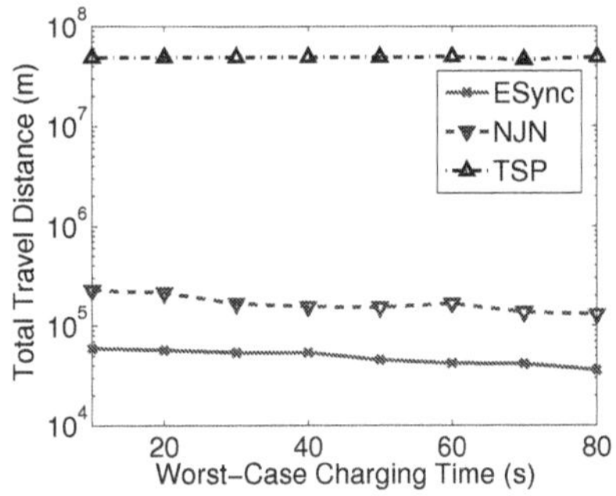

(a) Total travel distance

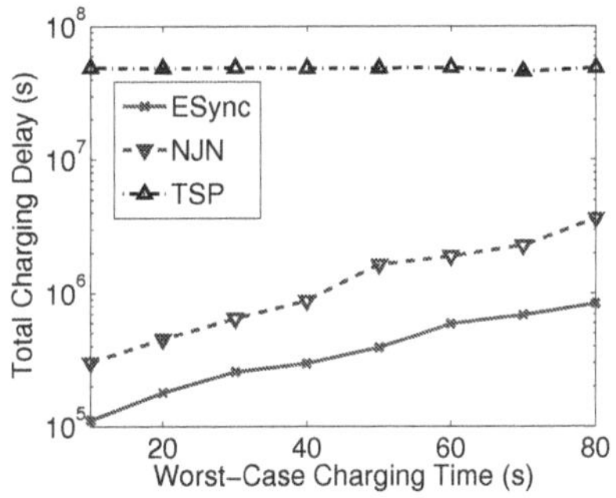

(b) Total charging delay

Figure 16: With random consumptions.

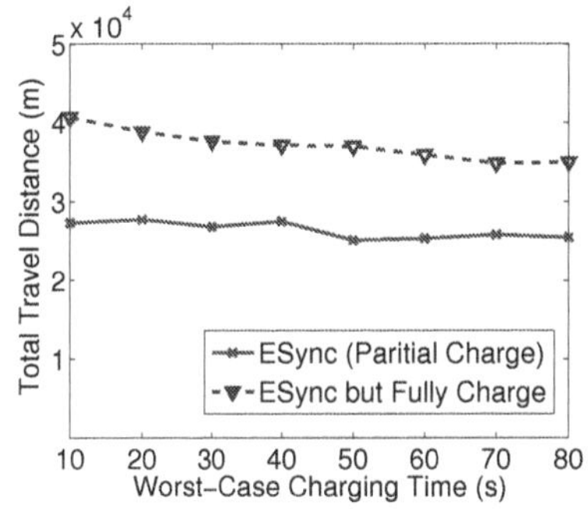

(a) Total travel distance

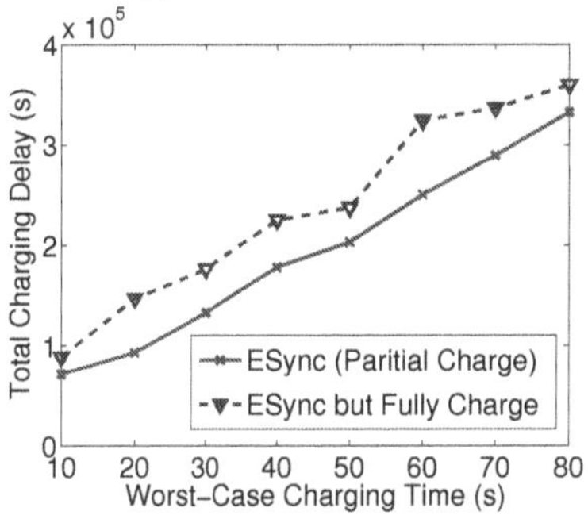

(b) Total charging delay

Figure 17: Advantage of partial charging.

delay of nodes) resultant with *ESync* is about 58.78% (67.11%) of that returned by Nearest-Job-Next when 100 nodes are deployed. When compared with TSP, the two ratios are further reduced to 11.73% and 11.03% respectively. The charging performance degrades as the network scale increases. Thus multiple chargers may be needed in large-scale networks. We will further investigate the collaborative mobile charging process in our future work.

7.3.2 Impact of Power Factor

From our simulation results, we observe that a power factor of 2 is adopted for most of the time. To further investigate the impact of α, we fix the network scale at 100 nodes in a 100 $m \times 100$ m field, and explore *ESync* with α varying from 2 to 6. The results are shown in Fig. 15(a) and Fig. 15(b). A clear increasing trend of the travel distance and the charging delay can be observed as α becomes larger, which agrees with our observation, and thus validates our method in determining the optimal α.

7.3.3 Energy Spatial Randomness

It is intuitive that for multi-hop sensor networks where the sink is located at the center, *ESync* achieves promising performance because nodes near the sink have higher energy consumption rates. To investigate whether *ESync* performs well in networks without this spatial-correlated energy consumption pattern, we modify the simulation by randomly generating nodes energy consumption rates, and the results returned by *ESync*, Nearest-Job-Next, and TSP are shown in Fig. 16(a) and Fig. 16(b). We can see that even when nodes energy consumptions are irrelevant with their spatial locations, *ESync* still outperforms Nearest-Job-Next and TSP significantly. The advantages of *ESync* over different network scenarios verify its versatility.

7.3.4 Ratio of Partial Charging

To facilitate the energy synchronization, sometimes nodes may be only partially charged. To investigate whether this occasionally partially charging of nodes degrades the overall charging performance when compared with always fully charging nodes, we modify *ESync* by making the charger always charge sensor nodes to their full capacity, and compare the resultant charging performance with that obtained by the proposed *ESync*. The results are shown in Fig. 17(a) and Fig. 17(b). We can see that although only a small ratio of the requesting nodes are partially charged, they can significantly improve the charging performance when compared with always fully charging. Specifically, the charger travel distance and the charging delay of nodes are reduced by around 25% and 20%, respectively.

8. CONCLUSIONS

In this paper, we have proposed *ESync*, a novel mobile charging protocol for rechargeable sensor networks. Observing the inefficiency of the classic TSP-based mobile charging solutions, we have proposed a *power-*α clustering algorithm to cluster nodes based on their energy consumption rates and then a set of nested optimal TSP tours is constructed accordingly. A tour selection algorithm has been presented accordingly. As a result, only energy-hungry nodes are involved in the selected TSP tour in each charging round, and thus the charger travel distance is reduced. Furthermore, we proactively adjust the requests sequence of sensor nodes to synchronize it with the selected TSP tour in each charging round, which reduces the charging delay of sensor nodes. The efficiency of *ESync* is verified through both experiments and simulations.

Acknowledgment: This research was supported in part by iTrust IGDSi1305013, SUTD-ZJU/RES/03/2011, Singapore-MIT International Design Center IDG31000101, NSFC 61222305, NSERC Canada, ZJNSF LY14F030016, and National Program for Special Support of Top-Notch Young Professionals.

9. REFERENCES

[1] D. Chu, N. D. Lane, T. Lai, C. Pang, X. Meng, Q. Guo, F. Li, and F. Zhao, "Balancing energy, latency and accuracy for mobile sensor data classification," in *SenSys'11*, 2011.

[2] T. Park, J. Lee, I. Hwang, C. Yoo, L. Nachman, and J. Song, "E-gesture: A collaborative architecture for energy-efficient gesture recognition with hand-worn sensor and mobile devices," in *SenSys'11*, 2011.

[3] Y. Wang, R. Tan, G. Xing, X. Tan, J. Wang, and R. Zhou, "Spatiotemporal aquatic field reconstruction using robotic sensor swarm," in *RTSS'12*, 2012.

[4] X. Wang, S. Han, Y. Wu, and X. Wang, "Coverage and energy consumption control in mobile heterogeneous wireless sensor networks," *IEEE Transactions on Automatic Control*, vol. 58, no. 4, pp. 975–988, 2013.

[5] X. Mao, S. Tang, X. Xu, X.-Y. Li, and H. Ma, "Energy-efficient opportunistic routing in wireless sensor networks," *Parallel and Distributed Systems, IEEE Transactions on*, vol. 22, no. 11, pp. 1934–1942, 2011.

[6] K. Han, L. Xiang, J. Luo, and Y. Liu, "Minimum-Energy Connected Coverage in Wireless Sensor Networks with Omni-Directional and Directional Features," in *Proc. of the 13th ACM/SIGMOBILE Symposium on Mobile Ad Hoc Networking & Computing (MobiHoc'12)*, 2012, p. 85ą94.

[7] Z. Li, Y. Peng, W. Zhang, and D. Qiao, "J-roc: a joint routing and charging scheme to prolong sensor network lifetime," in *ICNP'11*, 2011.

[8] Y. Peng, Z. Li, W. Zhang, and D. Qiao, "Prolonging sensor network lifetime through wireless charging," in *RTSS'10*, 2010.

[9] S. Zhang, J. Wu, and S. Lu, "Collaborative mobile charging," *IEEE Transactions on Computers*, to appear.

[10] Y. Shi, L. Xie, Y. T. Hou, and H. D. Sherali, "On renewable sensor networks with wireless energy transfer," in *INFOCOM'11*, 2011.

[11] L. Fu, P. Cheng, Y. Gu, J. Chen, and T. He, "Minimizing Charging Delay in Wireless Rechargeable Sensor Networks," in *INFOCOM'13*, 2013.

[12] L. He, Y. Gu, and T. He, "Poster abstract: Energy synchronized charging in sensor networks," in *SenSys'12*, 2012.

[13] C. Park and P. Chou, "Ambimax: autonomous energy harvesting platform for multi-supply wireless sensor nodes," in *SECON'06*, 2006.

[14] M. Gorlatova, P. Kinget, I. K. and D. Rubenstein, X. Wang, and G. Zussman, "Challenge: ultra-low-power energy-harvesting active networked tags (EnHANTs)," in *MOBICOM'09*, 2009.

[15] A. Kansal, J. Hsu, S. Zahedi, and M. Srivastava, "Power management in energy harvesting sensor networks," *ACM TECS*, vol. 6, no. 4, 2007.

[16] T. Zhu, Z. Zhong, Y. Gu, T. He, and Z.-L. Zhang, "Leakage-aware energy synchronization for wireless sensor networks," in *MOBISYS'09*, 2009.

[17] T. Zhu, Y. Gu, T. He, and Z. Zhang, "eShare: a capacitor-driven energy storage and sharing network for long-term operation," in *SenSys'10*, 2010.

[18] L. Xie, Y. Shi, Y. T. Hou, W. Lou, H. D. Serali, and S. F. Midkiff, "On renewable sensor networks with wireless energy transfer: The multi-node case," in *SECON'12*, 2012.

[19] B. Tong, Z. Li, G. Wang, and W. Zhang, "How wireless power charging technology affects sensor network deployment and routing," in *ICDCS'10*, 2010.

[20] M. Zhao, J. Li, and Y. Yang, "Joint mobile energy replenishment and data gathering in wireless rechargeable sensor networks," in *ITC'11*, 2011.

[21] L. Xie, Y. Shi, Y. T. Hou, W. Lou, and H. D. Serali, "On traveling path and related problems for a mobile station in a rechargeable sensor network," in *MobiHoc'13*, 2013.

[22] J. Li, C. Wang, F. Ye, and Y. Yang, "Netwrap: An NDN based real time wireless recharging framework for wireless sensor networks," in *Mobile Ad-Hoc and Sensor Systems (MASS), 2013 IEEE 10th International Conference on*, 2013, pp. 173–181.

[23] E. Altman and H. Levy, "Queueing in space," *Advances in Applied Probability*, vol. 26, no. 4, pp. pp. 1095–1116, 1994.

[24] J. Bertsimas and G. V. Ryzins, "A stochastic and dynamic vehicle routing problem in the Euclidean plane," *Operations Research*, vol. 39, 1991.

[25] "Supercapacitors," http://batteryuniversity.com.

[26] B. P. Wells, "Series resonant inductive charging circuit," in *U. S. Patent 6 972 543*, 2005.

[27] X. Liu, H. Zhao, X. Yang, X. Li, and N. Wang, "Trailing mobile sinks: a proactive data reporting protocol for wireless sensor networks," in *MASS'10*, 2010.

[28] V. Kulathumani, A. Arora, M. Sridharan, and M. Demirbas, "Trail: a distance-sensitive sensor network service for distributed object tracking," *ACM Trans. on Sens. Net.*, vol. 5, no. 2, 2009.

[29] G. Xing, T. Wang, W. Jia, and M. Li, "Rendezvous design algorithms for wireless sensor networks with a mobile base station," in *MOBIHOC'08*, 2008.

[30] "Intel Berkeley Research Lab Data," http://www.select.cs.cmu.edu/data/labapp3/index.html.

[31] "Concorde TSP Solder," http://www.tsp.gatech.edu/concorde.html.

[32] Y. Wang, M. C. Vuran, and S. Goddard, "Stochastic analysis of energy consumption in wireless sensor networks," in *SECON'10*, 2010.

[33] H. Sabbineni and K. Chakrabarty, "Data collection in event-driven wireless sensor networks with mobile sinks," *International Journal of Distributed Sensor Networks*, vol. 2010, 2010.

[34] X. Jiang, P. Dutta, D. Culler, and I. Stoica, "Micro power meter for energy monitoring of wireless sensor networks at scale," in *IPSN'07*, 2007.

[35] V. Shnayder, M. Hempstead, B. R. Chen, G. W. Allen, and M. Welsh, "Simulating the power consumption of large-scale sensor network applications," in *SenSys'04*, 2004.

[36] "NCR18650," http://www.panasonic.com.

[37] "Elixir II," https://play.google.com/store/apps/.

[38] O. Gnawali, R. Fonseca, K. Jamieson, D. Moss, and P. Levis, "Collection Tree Protocol," in *SenSys'09*, November 2009.

Energy Efficient Multipath TCP for Mobile Devices

Qiuyu Peng
Dept. of EE, Caltech

Minghua Chen
Dept. of IE, CUHK

Anwar Walid
Bell Lab, Alcatel Lucent

Steven H. Low
Dept. of CMS & EE, Caltech

ABSTRACT

Most mobile devices today come with multiple access interfaces, *e.g.*, 4G and WiFi. Multipath TCP (MP-TCP) can greatly improve network performance by exploiting the connection diversity of multiple access interfaces, at the expense of higher energy consumption. In this paper, we design MP-TCP algorithms for mobile devices by jointly considering the performance and energy consumption. We consider two main types of mobile applications: realtime applications that have a fixed duration and file transfer applications that have a fixed data size. For each type of applications, we propose a two-timescale algorithm with theoretical guarantee on the performance. We present simulation results that show that our algorithms can reduce energy consumption by up to 22% without sacrificing throughput compared to a baseline MP-TCP algorithm.

Categories and Subject Descriptors

C.2.5 [**Computer-Communication Networks**]: Local and Wide-Area Networks

Keywords

Multipath TCP; Energy Efficiency; Mobile Devices

1. INTRODUCTION

Even though most mobile devices today are equipped with multiple access interfaces such as 4G, 3G and WiFi, they only use one interface at any time. One access interface however may not be able to support the bandwidth requirement of emerging applications such as high definition video. It is therefore advantageous to enable concurrent use of the multiple interfaces.

Multipath TCP (MP-TCP), which is being standardized by the IETF [5], is a TCP extension that allows a TCP connection to stripe traffic over multiple interfaces. Various benefits of deploying MP-TCP on mobile devices have been reported in the literature. In [19], Wischik, *et al* show that the throughput can be improved by using WiFi and 3G network together. In [17], Raiciu, *et al* show that MP-TCP enables smooth handovers between WiFi and 3G. Thus, MP-TCP is promising in providing more reliable and faster connections for mobile devices by leveraging connection diversities under dynamic environments.

One major concern of using MP-TCP in mobile devices is the higher energy required for maintaining multiple active interfaces [16]. A major portion of the energy for mobile devices is spent on communication [13, 15]. Thus, designing algorithms that can efficiently use multiple interfaces will greatly improve the battery lifespan. In [16, 17], energy saving mechanisms have been proposed to reduce energy consumption for mobile devices when MP-TCP is enabled. They periodically probe all paths and shift all traffic to the most energy efficient path and mute the other paths. It limits the throughput performance to that achieved using only one path. In addition, since energy cost is the only criterion for path selection, the throughput performance would be degraded significantly if the energy efficient path turns out to be the most congested path.

Our goal is to design MP-TCP algorithms that intelligently tradeoff throughput performance and energy consumption for mobile devices. We consider applications that need bulk data transport, *e.g.* video streaming and file transfer.

Real-time applications[1]: The duration T of a data transfer is usually fixed for this type of applications such as video streaming. The energy consumption is $P\times T$, where P is the instantaneous power. Since T is usually determined by external factors and can be regarded as a constant, the energy consumption is proportional to the instantaneous power P.

File transfer applications: The size B of a data transfer is usually fixed for this type of applications such as file download. The energy consumption is $P \times B/x$, where x is the throughput. Since B is usually determined by external factors and can be regarded as a constant, the energy consumption is proportional to P/x, termed "energy per bit".

Due to the difference in requirement of the real-time and file transfer applications, we need to design algorithms separately for each of them. We will see that sometimes the

[1]The issue of whether TCP is appropriate for these applications is beyond the scope of the paper; however, it has been reported that more than 50% of commercial streaming traffic is carried over HTTP/TCP [2], and popular applications such as Skype and Windows Media Services use TCP to pass through NATs and firewalls that block UDP traffic. Multipath live streaming over traditional TCP was studied in [18].

MobiHoc'14, August 11–14, 2014, Philadelphia, PA, USA.

http://dx.doi.org/10.1145/2632951.2632971 .

most energy efficient path for file transfer applications is 4G while for real-time applications is WiFi.

Contributions: The contributions of this paper are three-fold.

▷ We formulate a global optimization problem for real-time application that considers both throughput and energy consumption, whose tradeoff can be controlled by properly setting certain design parameters. The problem is hard to solve because the power consumption is not a continuous function of rate, *i.e.*, there is sunk cost of maintaining an active access interface. To solve the problem in a distributed manner, we propose a heuristic to decompose it into two subproblems: *path selection* and *congestion control*. For *path selection*, each source individually select a subset of paths to use to optimize certain objective based on its local information. We show that it is NP hard and propose an algorithm to solve it approximately with bounded suboptimality gap. For *congestion control*, we propose an algorithm that adapts the rates on the chosen paths based on both network congestion and energy consumption.

▷ We formulate a global optimization problem for file transfer application that considers both throughput and energy consumption, whose tradeoff can be controlled by properly setting certain design parameters. The problem has the additional difficulty of being non-convex even if the power consumption is linear in rate. We also decompose the problem into two subproblem: *path selection* and *congestion control*. Fortunately, we solve the *path selection* problem, which is mixed integer with nonconvex objective function, optimally under mild conditions. However, the non-convexity could lead to unstable *congestion control* algorithms and we stabilize it through a regulation term.

▷ We evaluate the algorithms for both real-time and file transfer applications through simulations. Our simulations show that the proposed algorithms indeed save energy and guarantee users' performance. In particular, the algorithms can reduce energy consumption by as much as 22% without sacrificing throughput compared to a baseline MP-TCP algorithm.

While path selection and congestion control problems have been studied in the literature before, our algorithms are unique in jointly optimizing the throughput and energy consumption whereas previous solutions focus only on throughput. Moreover, to incorporate energy consumption in the formulation, we need to deal with the additional non-convexity.

The rest of the paper is organized as follows. In Section 2, we describe our network model and present a model of power consumption for mobile devices. The path selection and congestion control algorithms for both types of applications are proposed in Sections 3 and 4, respectively. We illustrate the effectiveness of the algorithms through simulations in Section 5 and conclude the paper in Section 6. The proof of the theorems are relegated to the Appendix. The proof of the lemmas are skipped due to space limitation.

2. SYSTEM MODEL

In this section, we describe our network model, background of MP-TCP and the power consumption model for mobile devices. Unless otherwise specified, a boldface letter is used to denote a vector, whose dimension is clear from the context. $\|\mathbf{x}\|_n := (\sum x_i^n)^{1/n}$ defines the L^n-norm of a vector $\mathbf{x}$.

2.1 Network model and Multipath TCP

Consider a network that consists of a set $\mathcal{L} = \{1, \ldots, L\}$ of links. The network is shared by a set $\mathcal{S} = \{1, \ldots, S\}$ of sources. Available to source $s \in \mathcal{S}$ is a fixed collection of routes (paths) r. A path r consists of a set of links l. We abuse notation and use s both to denote a source and the set of paths r available to it, depending on the context. Likewise, r is used both to denote a path and the set of links l in the path. Let $\mathcal{R} := \{r \mid r \in s, s \in \mathcal{S}\}$ be the collection of all routes in the network. Let $H \in \{0,1\}^{|\mathcal{L}| \times |\mathcal{R}|}$ be the routing matrix: $H_{lr} = 1$ if link l is in route r (denoted by '$l \in r$'), and 0 otherwise.

For each path r, Let $x_r(t)$ be its sending rate at time t and τ_r denote its round trip time (RTT). For each link l, let $p_l(t)$ denote its congestion price at time t and c_l denote its bandwidth. Let $q_r(t) := \sum_{l \in \mathcal{L}} H_{lr} p_l(t)$ be the aggregate price on route r and $y_l(t) := \sum_{r \in \mathcal{R}} H_{lr} x_r(t)$ be the aggregate traffic on link l. We associate two state variables $(x_r(t), q_r(t))$ for each route $r \in s$. Let $\mathbf{x}_s(t) := (x_r(t), r \in s)$ and $\mathbf{q}_s(t) := (q_r(t), r \in s)$. Then $(\mathbf{x}_s(t), \mathbf{q}_s(t))$ represents the corresponding state variables for each source $s \in \mathcal{S}$.

Congestion control is a distributed algorithm that adapts $\mathbf{x}(t)$ and $\mathbf{p}(t)$ in a closed loop. In [14], all the congestion control algorithms (including both single-path and multi-path TCP) are modeled by

$$\dot{x}_r = k_r(\mathbf{x}_s)\left[\phi_r(\mathbf{x}_s) - q_r\right]^+_{x_r} \qquad r \in s \quad s \in \mathcal{S} \tag{1}$$

$$\dot{p}_l = \gamma_l \left[y_l - c_l\right]^+_{p_l} \qquad l \in \mathcal{L}, \tag{2}$$

where $[a]_b^+ = a$ if $b > 0$ and $\max\{0, a\}$ if $b \leq 0$. We omit the time t in the expression for simplicity. (1) models how sending rate is adapted in the congestion avoidance phase by TCP on each path and (2) models how the congestion price is updated on each link by AQM.

TCP (MP-TCP) adapts the size of its congestion window to control the sending rate, the corresponding parameters $(k_r(\mathbf{x}_s), \phi_r(\mathbf{x}_s))$ uniquely determine the window adaptation as described in [14, section 2.2]. Here $k_r(\mathbf{x}_s) \geq 0$ is a positive gain that determines the dynamic property and $\phi_r(\mathbf{x}_s)$ determines the equilibrium property.

The AQM is specified by γ_l, where $\gamma_l > 0$ is a positive gain that determines the dynamic property. This is a simplified model for the random early detection(RED) algorithm that assumes the loss probability is proportional to the backlog.

2.2 Utility Maximization

For single-path TCP, where the rate x_s is a scalar, under very mild conditions, one can show that the TCP/AQM algorithms (1)-(2) solve a network utility maximization problem below [8, 10, 11]:

$$\max \sum_{s \in \mathcal{S}} U_s(x_s) \quad \text{s.t.} \quad y_l \leq c_l \text{ for } l \in \mathcal{L} \tag{3}$$

where $U_s(x_s)$, which is called the utility of source s and satisfies C1 below, represents user's satisfaction at rate x_s, and $y_l \leq c_l$ represents the constraint on each link l that its input traffic y_l is no more than available bandwidth c_l.

C1: For $s \in \mathcal{S}$, $U_s(x_s)$ is twice continuously differentiable and strictly concave increasing in $(0, \infty)$.

Table 1: Comparison of 4G, 3G and WiFi. [7]

	4G	3G	WiFi
Median Upload Speed (Mbps)	5.64	0.72	0.94
Median Download Speed (Mbps)	12.74	1.10	4.12
Download b_r (mW/Mbps)	52.0	122.1	137
Upload b_r (mW/Mbps)	438.4	869	238.2
θ_r (mW)	1288	817.9	132.9

The utility function of most single-path TCP algorithms take the form of α-fairness function [12] as defined in (4).

$$U_s(x; \alpha) = \frac{\gamma}{1-\alpha} x^{1-\alpha}, \tag{4}$$

where $\alpha, \gamma \geq 0$ are constants. For instance, the utility function of the well known TCP NewReno is

$$U_s(x) = -\frac{2}{\tau^2 x}, \tag{5}$$

where τ is the round trip time. It corresponds to $(\alpha, \gamma) = (2, 2\tau^{-2})$ in (4). When multiple paths are available, a natural generalization of (3) is

$$\max \sum_{s \in \mathcal{S}} U_s(\mathbf{1}^T \mathbf{x}_s) \quad \text{s.t.} \quad y_l \leq c_l \text{ for } l \in \mathcal{L} \tag{6}$$

where $\mathbf{1}$ is the all one vector and $\mathbf{1}^T\mathbf{x}_s$ represents the aggregate throughput of source s over all its paths. In (6), each source s only cares about its aggregate throughput $\mathbf{1}^T\mathbf{x}_s$ without considering its energy consumption. In the following, we amend (6) to include energy consumption in the objective. We first investigate the power consumption characteristics of mobiles.

2.3 Power consumption for mobile devices

The wireless interfaces on most mobile devices are 4G, 3G and WiFi. In [7], Huang, *et al* found that the the power consumption $P_r(x_r)$ on path r depends on the throughput x_r according as

$$P_r(x_r) = b_r x_r + \theta_r 1_{\{x_r > 0\}}, \tag{7}$$

where $\theta_r > 0$ models the sunk power cost of being active and $b_r > 0$ models the power consumed per unit throughput. Note that $P_r(x_r)$ is not continuous at $x_r = 0$, making the design of energy efficient algorithm a challenge. The model (7) captures power consumption for most telecommunication standards such as 4G, 3G and WiFi. Some representative parameter values from [7] are summarized in Table 1.

3. REAL-TIME APPLICATIONS

For realtime applications, *e.g.* video streaming, the amount of time T for communication is controlled by users. The energy spent on communication for this type of applications is $T(\sum_{r \in s} P_r(x_r))$. Thus, optimizing energy consumption is equivalent to optimizing power consumption $\sum_{r \in s} P_r(x_r)$. For this type of applications, we add an additional penalty term to represent energy consumption in (6) and the problem becomes

$$\max \sum_{s \in \mathcal{S}} \left(U_s(\mathbf{1}^T \mathbf{x}_s) - \alpha_s \sum_{r \in s} P_r(x_r) \right) \tag{8a}$$

$$\text{s.t.} \quad y_l \leq c_l \text{ for } l \in \mathcal{L} \tag{8b}$$

We assume for each source $s \in \mathcal{S}$, $U_s(\mathbf{1}^T\mathbf{x}_s)$ satisfies C1 and can be interpreted as users' level of satisfaction for the throughput. $\sum_{r \in s} P_r(x_r)$ represents the power consumption. The parameters $\alpha_s \geq 0$ control the tradeoff between users' satisfaction and power consumption.

Solving (8) is hard because $P_r(x_r)$ is discontinuous at $x_r = 0$ as described in (7). In Lemma 3.2 below, we will show that the problem is NP hard even if there is only one source in the network. To tackle the problem efficiently, we propose to solve the problem in two steps as follows:

1. *Path Selection*: The source first decides a subset of paths $s^* \subseteq s$ to use based on available local information, *e.g.* power characteristics, bandwidth available on each path $r \in s$.
2. *Congestion Control*: Once the set of paths s^* is fixed, the source s turns on the interfaces of these paths and adapts sending rates to network congestion level and energy consumption.

Paths should be re-selected from time to time to adapt to changes in power characteristics or available bandwidths, but these conditions usually change at a much slower timescale than congestion level does. Normally we can periodically probe each path as [17] and rerun path selection after that. However, we should avoid doing it too frequently due to the high energy switching cost for turning interfaces on and off. Next, we will formally define each subproblem and solve it.

3.1 Path Selection

In this step, each source s selects a subset $s^* \subseteq s$ of paths based on local information, *e.g.* the available bandwidth c_r of the access link, allocated by the base stations (4G/3G) or the hotspots (WiFi), and the parameters (b_r, θ_r) in (7) for each path $r \in s$. Then the source s seeks to solve the following problem:

Path Selection Problem-I(PSP-I):

$$\max \quad U_s(\mathbf{1}^T \mathbf{x}_s) - \alpha_s \sum_{r \in s} P_r(x_r) \tag{9a}$$

$$\text{s.t.} \quad x_r \leq c_r \text{ for } r \in s \tag{9b}$$

Let the optimal solution to PSP-I be $\mathbf{x}_s^*$. The paths selected by s are then $s^* = \{r \mid x_r^* > 0, r \in s\}$. Comparing PSP-I with the global optimization problem (8), PSP-I ignores the bandwidth constraints except at the access links. Thus PSP-I provides an upper bound on the throughput. It is a good estimate of the global optimization problem (8) if the access links are bottleneck, which usually holds for most telecommunication standards such as 4G, 3G and WiFi.

Remark: Various path selection problems are formulated in the literature. In [9], Key, *et al* study the performance of both randomized and game theoretic approach to select a fixed number of paths from a pool of available paths. In [3], the markov approximation approach is proposed for choosing peers in P2P system. Unlike PSP-I, neither of them considers the sunk cost but limits the number of peers one can select to implicitly reduce the sunk cost.

Table 2: Candidate for PSP-I with $|s| = 2$

x_1	x_2
$\min\{c_1, (U'_s)^{-1}(\alpha_s b_1)\}$	0
0	$\min\{c_2, (U'_s)^{-1}(\alpha_s b_2)\}$
c_1	$\min\{\max\{(U'_s)^{-1}(\alpha_s b_2) - c_1, 0\}, c_2\}$

We now characterize an optimal solution to PSP-I in Lemma 3.1.

Lemma 3.1. *Suppose C1 holds and $b_i \le b_j$ for $1 \le i < j \le |s|$ without loss of generality. Then the path s^* being chosen is given as*

$$s^* = \arg\max_{s' \subseteq s} \left\{ U_s(\sum_{r \in s'} x_r(s')) - \alpha_s \sum_{r \in s'} P_r(x_r(s')) \right\},$$

where for each subset $s' := \{k_1, \ldots, k_{|s'|}\}$ of s,

$$x_{k_i}(s') := \left[(U'_s)^{-1}(\alpha_s b_{k_i}) - \sum_{j=1}^{i} c_{k_j} \right]_0^{c_{k_i}}$$

and $[a]_b^c := \max\{b, \min\{a, c\}\}$.

Based on Lemma 3.1, we need to compare the objective value of each subset of s to obtain the optimal solution to PSP-I. Solving PSP-I is in general NP hard because the knapsack problem, which is a well known NP complete problem, can be reduced to PSP-I as shown in Lemma 3.2 below.

Lemma 3.2. *Suppose C1 holds. Then PSP-I is NP hard.*

However, there are only two interfaces (4G and WiFi) for most mobiles and we only need to check each combination in Table 2 according to Lemma 3.1.

When there are many WiFi hotspots around, the number of available paths $|s|$ can be larger [4]. Thus PSP-I is hard to be solved efficiently according to Lemma 3.2. We now propose an efficient heuristic for solving PSP-I that has linear complexity and a bounded suboptimality gap.

First consider the case where $\theta_r = 0$ for all $r \in s$ (recall that θ_r is the sunk power cost of using path r), then PSP-I degenerates to a convex program:

$$\max \quad U_s(\mathbf{1}^T \mathbf{x}_s) - \alpha_s \sum_{r \in s} b_r x_r \tag{10a}$$

$$\text{s.t.} \quad x_r \le c_r \text{ for } r \in s \tag{10b}$$

The KKT conditions imply that the source s uses path i if and only if all the links j with $b_j < b_i$ have been fully used. Assume without loss of generality $b_j \le b_i$ for $j < i$. We initialize $x_r = 0$ for all $r \in s$.Then we select path 1 and calculate the maximum of $U_s(x_1) - \alpha_s b_1 x_1$ for $x_1 \in [0, c_1]$. We stop if its solution $x_1 < c_1$, which means the objective is maximized merely by path 1. Otherwise if $x_1 = c_1$, which means the first path is fully utilized, we add path 2 and calculate maximum of $U_s(c_1 + x_2) - \alpha_s(b_1 c_1 + b_2 x_2)$ for $x_2 \in [0, c_2]$. Likewise, we stop if its solution $x_2 < c_2$ and add path 3 if $x_2 = c_2$. The paths will be added sequentially until $x_k < c_k$ for some $k < |s|$ or $k = |s|$. Then the corresponding $\mathbf{x}_s$ is an optimal solution to (10) and the paths we use are $\{1, \ldots, k\}$.

Motivated by the above procedure to solve (10), we design an algorithm to solve PSP-I when $\theta_r \neq 0$, in a similar manner. For $r \in s$, let $b'_r := b_r + \theta_r / c_r$, which is the power consumption per unit throughput on path r when the throughput $x_r = c_r$. Without loss of generality, assume $b'_i \le b'_j$ for $1 \le i < j \le |s|$. Then we mimic what we do to solve (10): add path in increasing order of b'_i and stop if the newly added path is not fully utilized, as stated in Algorithm 1.

Algorithm 1: Path Selection Algorithm for PSP-I
Input: $U_s(x)$, α_s and (b_r, θ_r, c_r) for $r \in s$.
Output: Subset $s^* \subseteq s$.
1. Calculate $\tilde{x}_k$ and O_k as below:
$$\tilde{x}_k = \left[(U'_s)^{-1}(\alpha_s b_k) - \sum_{1 \le i < k} c_i \right]_0^{c_k} \tag{11}$$
$$O_k = U_s(\tilde{x}_k + \sum_{1 \le i < k} c_i) - \alpha_s(\sum_{1 \le i < k} (b_i c_i + \theta_i) + \theta_k + b_k \tilde{x}_k)$$
2. Let $k^* = \arg\max\{O_k, k \le |s|\}$ and $s^* \leftarrow \{1, \cdots, k^*\}$

Algorithm 1 is not guaranteed to find a global optimal solution to PSP-I since b'_r may not be the real power consumption per unit throughput. Next, we bound the gap between the optimal value of PSP-I O^* and the objective value of Algorithm 1 $\hat{O}$. Denote

$$\hat{x}_k := \left[(U'_s)^{-1}(\alpha_s b'_k) - \sum_{1 \le i < k} c_i \right]_0^{c_k} \tag{12}$$

$\hat{k} := \max\{k \mid \sum_{i=1}^{k-1} c_i \le (U'_s)^{-1}(\alpha_s b'_k)\}$ and $\hat{c} := \sum_{i=1}^{\hat{k}-1} c_i$.

Theorem 3.1. *Suppose C1 holds. Then*

$$O^* - \hat{O} \le \min \left\{ \frac{1}{2} \hat{x}_{\hat{k}} (U'_s(\hat{c}) - \alpha_s b'_{\hat{k}}), \alpha_s \theta_{\hat{k}} (1 - \frac{\hat{x}_{\hat{k}}}{c_{\hat{k}}}) \right\}$$

Theorem 3.1 implies that the gap is upper bounded by $\alpha_s \theta_{\hat{k}}$, *i.e.* the algorithm works better when θ_k are smaller and the gap is closed if there are no sunk costs.

3.2 Congestion Control

Once the source fixes the paths $s^* \subseteq s$ it uses, it turns on the access interfaces of the corresponding paths and adapts the rate on those paths to network congestion and energy consumption. Similar to the design of congestion control for regular MP-TCP in [14], we need to design $(k_r(\mathbf{x}_s), \phi_r(\mathbf{x}_s))$ in (1)-(2) and then we convert it to window based algorithm following a standard procedure derived in [14].

The power consumption is determined by the equilibrium properties (steady state throughput), which is not affected by $k_r(\mathbf{x}_s)$, so we will use the same $k_r(\mathbf{x}_s)$ as proposed in [14]:

$$k_r(\mathbf{x}_s) = \frac{1}{2} x_r (x_r + \|\mathbf{x}_s\|_\infty). \tag{13}$$

Interested readers can refer to [14, section 4.2] for more details. Next, we need to design $\phi_r(\mathbf{x}_s)$ such that (1)-(2) solves (8). Note that the discontinuity in (8) disappears since the paths for each source are fixed in the path selection step, a standard primal dual decomposition shows that by setting

$$\phi_r(\mathbf{x}_s) = U'_s(\mathbf{1}^T \mathbf{x}_s) - \alpha_s b_r,$$

for $r \in s^*$, (1)-(2) is guaranteed to converge to an optimal solution of (8). This algorithm however is not responsive in a dynamic network because the Hessian of $U_s(\mathbf{1}^T\mathbf{x}_s)$ is only negative semidefinite [1]. To obtain a more responsive algorithm, we multiply a regulation term $f_r(\mathbf{x}_s)$ in front of $U_s'(\mathbf{1}^T\mathbf{x}_s)$ as done in [14] such that

$$\phi_r(\mathbf{x}_s) = f_r(\mathbf{x}_s)U_s'(\mathbf{1}^T\mathbf{x}_s) - \alpha_s b_r.$$

A proper $f_r(\mathbf{x}_s)$ ensures that the Jacobian of $\Phi_s(\mathbf{x}_s) := (\phi_r(\mathbf{x}_s), r \in s)$ is strictly negative definite. We use the same $f_r(\mathbf{x}_s)$ as proposed in [14]:

$$f_r(\mathbf{x}_s) = \beta\frac{\|\mathbf{x}_s\|_\infty}{x_r} + 1 - \beta, \tag{14}$$

where $\beta \in [0,1]$ and larger β yields a more responsive algorithm. However, it is shown in [14] that a more responsive MP-TCP algorithm is less friendly[2] to single-path TCP. The parameter β controls the tradeoff between responsiveness and friendliness and a larger β yields a more responsive but less friendly algorithm. Here we use $\beta = 0.2$ as suggested in [14] and stability of the system (1)-(2) can be proved in a similar manner as [14].

Remark: To the best of our knowledge, all existing MP-TCP algorithms can be modeled by multiplying a regulation term $f_r(\mathbf{x}_s)$ in front of a marginal utility $U_s'(\mathbf{1}^T\mathbf{x}_s)$, *e.g.* [6,14,19]. This improves the responsiveness compared to an algorithm without a regulation term, but effectively modifies the utility function in (8). Indeed, for some $f_r(\mathbf{x}_s)$, the resulting algorithm does not maximize any (modified) utility functions [14].

In summary, the congestion control algorithm for realtime application is given as sequel.

Congestion Control for Realtime Application:
$$k_r(\mathbf{x}_s) := \frac{1}{2}x_r(x_r + \|\mathbf{x}_s\|_\infty).$$ $$\phi_r(\mathbf{x}_s) := f_r(\mathbf{x}_s)U_s'(\mathbf{1}^T\mathbf{x}_s) - \alpha_s b_r.$$
where $f_r(\mathbf{x}_s)$ is defined in (14).

4. FILE TRANSFER APPLICATIONS

In this section, we design an energy efficient MP-TCP algorithm for file transfer applications. Similar to real-time applications, there are two steps in the algorithms: path selection and congestion control. Each source decides a subset of paths to use in the path selection step and adapts rates on the chosen paths to network congestion and energy consumption.

Unlike realtime application, the size of a data transfer B is fixed for file transfer application. Then the total energy consumed for source s is $(\sum_{r\in s} P_r(x_r))\frac{B}{\mathbf{1}^T\mathbf{x}_s}$ per transfer. Since the data size B is controlled by the users and can be regarded as a constant, optimizing energy consumption is equivalent to optimize energy per bit $\frac{\sum_{r\in s} P_r(x_r)}{\mathbf{1}^T\mathbf{x}_s}$. For this type of applications, we amend (6) and seek to solve the following optimization problem

$$\max \sum_{s\in\mathcal{S}}\left(U_s(\mathbf{1}^T\mathbf{x}_s) - \alpha_s\frac{1}{\mathbf{1}^T\mathbf{x}_s}\sum_{r\in s} P_r(x_r)\right) \tag{15a}$$

$$\text{s.t.} \quad y_l \le c_l \text{ for } l \in \mathcal{L} \tag{15b}$$

Similar to (8), the problem (15) considers users' satisfaction through the utility function $U_s(\mathbf{1}^T\mathbf{x}_s)$ and the energy consumption through the energy per bit $\frac{\sum_{r\in s} P_r(x_r)}{\mathbf{1}^T\mathbf{x}_s}$. Solving (15) is hard not only because of the discontinuity of $P_r(x_r)$ at $x_r = 0$, but also the nonconvexity of the fractional $\frac{\sum_{r\in s} P_r(x_r)}{\mathbf{1}^T\mathbf{x}_s}$. Similar to what we do in section 3, we will also decompose the problem into two steps: path selection and congestion control.

4.1 Path Selection

In this step, each source selects a subset of paths $s^* \subseteq s$ to use based on prior local information, *e.g.* the available bandwidth c_r and the power throughput characteristic b_r, θ_r for each path r of source s. Then the source s seeks to solve the following problem:

Path Selection Problem-II (PSP-II):

$$\max \quad U_s(\mathbf{1}^T\mathbf{x}_s) - \alpha_s\frac{1}{\mathbf{1}^T\mathbf{x}_s}\sum_{r\in s} P_r(x_r) \tag{16a}$$

$$\text{s.t.} \quad x_r \le c_r \text{ for } r \in s \tag{16b}$$

Compared with PSP-I, PSP-II is nonconvex even if the sunk cost $\theta_r = 0$ in $P_r(x_r)$. Fortunately, we will show below that under a mild condition C2, which covers most existing TCP algorithms, on the utility functions $U_s(x)$, Algorithm 2 solves PSP-II exactly. Again, let $b_r' := b_r + \theta_r/c_r$ and assume $b_i' \le b_j'$ for $1 \le i < j \le |s|$ without loss of generality.

Algorithm 2: Path Selection Algorithm-II
Input: $U_s(x)$, α_s and (b_r, θ_r, c_r) for $r \in s$.
Output: Subset $s^* \subseteq s$.
1. Calculate $$O_k = U_s(\sum_{i=1}^k c_i) - \alpha_s\frac{\sum_{i=1}^k b_i'c_i}{\sum_{i=1}^k c_i}$$
2. Let $k^* = \arg\max_{1\le k\le\|s\|}\{O_k\}$ and $s^* \leftarrow \{1,\ldots,k^*\}$.

C2 : $x^2U_s'(x)$ is a nondecreasing function of x.

Theorem 4.1. *Suppose C1 and C2 hold. Then Algorithm 2 obtains an optimal solution to PSP-II.*

Suppose the utility function takes the α-fairness form in (4), then

$$x^2U_s'(x;\alpha) = \gamma x^{2-\alpha},$$

which means α-fairness function satisfies C2 when $\alpha \in [0,2]$. Thus, PSP-II can be solved exactly by Algorithm 2 for TCP algorithms with α-fairness utility functions provided $\alpha \in [0,2]$. For most existing TCP protocols, their $\alpha \in [0,2]$, *e.g.* TCP Vegas/FAST ($\alpha = 1$) and TCP NewReno ($\alpha = 2$).

Here we need to point out that for Algorithm 1, the sequence $\{O_k, 1 \le k \le |s|\}$ is unimodal and hence the algorithm can stop once the sequence O_k becomes nonincreasing at some k. However, this property does not hold for

[2]Friendliness performance is a metric describing how much MP-TCP flows overtake single-path TCP flows at bottleneck links.

Algorithm 2 due to the non-convexity of the objective function. Thus, we need to check every element in the sequence $\{O_k, 1 \leq k \leq |s|\}$

4.2 Congestion Control

Similar to the design of realtime applications, we need to specify $(k_r(\mathbf{x}_s), \phi_r(\mathbf{x}_s))$ in (1). For $k_r(\mathbf{x}_s)$, we use the same one as realtime application (13) because it does not affect the equilibrium properties (throughput). For $\phi_r(\mathbf{x}_s)$, even though the discontinuity disappears once paths $s^* \subseteq s$ are fixed, a standard primal dual algorithm (1)-(2) with

$$\phi_r(\mathbf{x}_s) = U_s'(\mathbf{1}^T\mathbf{x}_s) - \alpha_s \frac{\partial E_s(\mathbf{x}_s)}{\partial x_r} \tag{17}$$

where $E_s(\mathbf{x}_s) := \frac{\sum_{r\in s} P_r(x_r)}{\mathbf{1}^T\mathbf{x}_s}$, may not be stable since the Jacobian of $\Phi_s(\mathbf{x}_s) := (\phi_r(\mathbf{x}_s), r \in s)$ is indefinite. Similar to the scenario of real time application in section 3, we multiply a regulation term $f_r(\mathbf{x}_s)$ in front of $U_s'(\mathbf{1}^T\mathbf{x}_s)$ such that

$$\phi_r(\mathbf{x}_s) = f_r(\mathbf{x}_s)U_s'(\mathbf{1}^T\mathbf{x}_s) - \alpha_s \frac{\partial E_s(\mathbf{x}_s)}{\partial x_r} \tag{18}$$

The regulation term $f_r(\mathbf{x}_s)$ is merely used to make the algorithm more responsive in section 3. Here, it guarantees a stable algorithm by compensating the indefiniteness of the Jacobian, as the following theorem shows. For convenience, we will only prove the result for the utility function of TCP NewReno defined in (5). Stability can be proved in a similar manner for other utility functions.

Theorem 4.2. *Suppose the round trip time τ of each path is the same. For $\phi_r(\mathbf{x}_s)$ in (18), $f_r(\mathbf{x}_s)$ in (14), and $U_s(x)$ in (5), the system (1)-(2) is stable if*

$$\|\mathbf{x}_s\|_\infty \leq \frac{\beta}{2\alpha_s\tau^2} \frac{9/|s^*| - 1}{\max_{r\in s^*} b_r - \min_{r\in s^*} b_r}, \tag{19}$$

Only the selected paths in s^* needs to satisfy (19). When the tradeoff parameter α_s increases, the size of s^* becomes small, which means $\max_{r\in s^*} b_r - \min_{r\in s^*} b_r$ also decreases and the bound becomes looser. The bound in (19) is satisfied for most practical scenario. For instance, the bound reduces to $\|\mathbf{x}_s\|_\infty \leq 0.02\frac{\beta}{\alpha_s\tau^2}$ for smartphones with both 4G and WiFi interface using the median value of b_r in Table 1. In our simulations, $\alpha_s\tau^2$ is typically in $(10^{-5}, 10^{-3})$. If $\beta = 1$, (19) becomes $\|\mathbf{x}_s\|_\infty \leq$ 2000Mbps for $\alpha_s\tau^2 = 10^{-5}$ and $\|\mathbf{x}_s\|_\infty \leq$ 20Mbps for $\alpha_s\tau^2 = 10^{-3}$, which seems realistic. In addition, the algorithm is alway stable in our preliminary simulations even if the round trip time is different. Thus, the bound develop in Theorem 4.2 is conservative.

In summary, the congestion control algorithm for file transfer application is given as sequel.

Congestion Control for File Transfer Application:
$k_r(\mathbf{x}_s) := \frac{1}{2}x_r(x_r + \|\mathbf{x}_s\|_\infty).$ $\phi_r(\mathbf{x}_s) := f_r(\mathbf{x}_s)U_s'(\mathbf{1}^T\mathbf{x}_s) - \alpha_s \frac{\partial E_s(\mathbf{x}_s)}{\partial x_r}.$ where $f_r(\mathbf{x}_s)$ is defined in (14) and $E_s(\mathbf{x}_s) := \frac{\sum_{r\in s} P_r(x_r)}{\mathbf{1}^T\mathbf{x}_s}$.

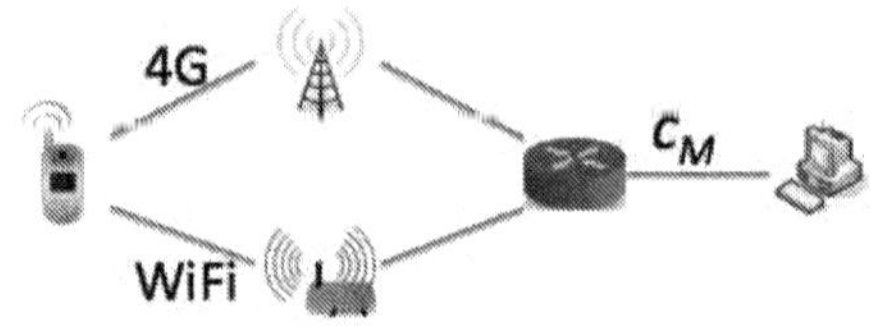

Figure 1: Smartphone with both 4G and WiFi access

5. DISCUSSIONS

In this section, we discuss how to setup the parameters of the algorithms and their impacts on the performance. In particular, we find that the algorithms can save up to 22% of the energy consumption without sacrificing the throughput. We also discuss the cases when there are multiple long term TCP flows from the same device. Unless otherwise specified, we use Table 1 for parameter values: For WiFi network, (c_r, b_r, θ_r) =(4.12 Mbps,238.2 mW/Mbps,132.9 mW); for 4G network, (c_r, b_r, θ_r)=(12.74 Mbps,52 mW/Mbps,1288 mW). As to estimation of these physical parameters, it is beyond the scope of the paper. In general, we can estimate these parameters through probing the network periodically. Interested readers may refer to [13, 15–17] for details.

5.1 Parameters setting and energy saving performance

Most of the existing MP-TCP algorithms [6, 14, 19] use TCP-NewReno as a benchmark single path TCP as specified by the IETF working group [5]. Thus, all of their associated utility functions take the form of (5). To achieve balanced performance between friendliness and responsiveness, a regulation term $f_r(\mathbf{x}_s)$ is multiplied in front of the marginal utility function $U_s'(\mathbf{1}^T\mathbf{x}_s)$, such that $\phi_r(\mathbf{x}_s) = f_r(\mathbf{x}_s)U_s'(\mathbf{1}^T\mathbf{x}_s)$ in (1). Different algorithms correspond to different regulation term $f_r(\mathbf{x}_s)$, which controls the tradeoffs between friendliness and responsiveness.

For the proposed algorithms in section 3 and 4, we also let the utility function $U_s(\mathbf{1}^T\mathbf{x}_s)$ take the form of (5) since TCP-NewReno is the benchmark. The regulation term takes the form of (14). Then the only parameter left unset is α_s, which controls the tradeoff between users' satisfaction and energy consumption. In normal operations, the users can tune α_s based on their own preference: they can save energy by increasing α_s but maybe suffer throughput reduction. Fortunately, sometimes the proposed algorithms can still save energy consumption without affecting the throughput compared to regular MP-TCP. Next, we will study the impact of the value of α_s on throughput and energy consumption through simulations.

Almost all smartphones have both 4G and WiFi access as shown in Fig. 1. In the first set of simulations, we assume the bottleneck is in the network by setting c_M = 10Mbps, while the bandwidth of the WiFi and 4G access are 4.12 Mbps and 12.74 Mbps as described in Table 1. Under such scenario, we test the algorithms for both video streaming, which represents realtime application and file download, which represents file transfer application. The simulation results are plotted in Fig. 2. For video streaming, we plot the aggregate throughput and power consumption $\sum_{r\in s} P_r(x_r)$ under different values of α_s. For file download, we plot the aggregate throughput and the energy per bit $\frac{\sum_{r\in s} P_r(x_r)}{\mathbf{1}^T\mathbf{x}_s}$ under different values of α_s. For comparison, we plot the en-

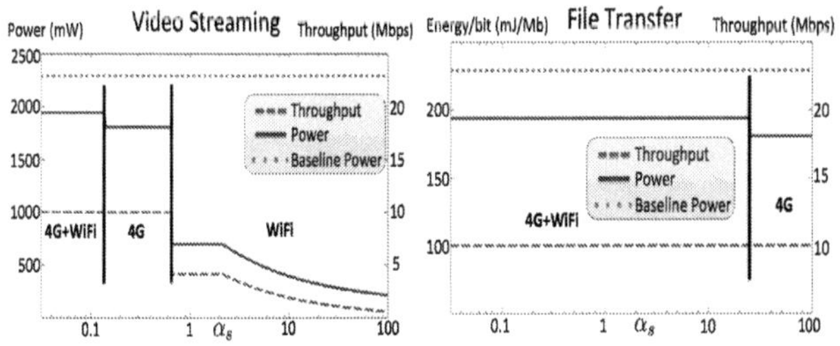

Figure 2: Energy, throughput vs α_s for c_M = 10Mbps. The pink dotted line represents the energy consumption of regular MP-TCP.

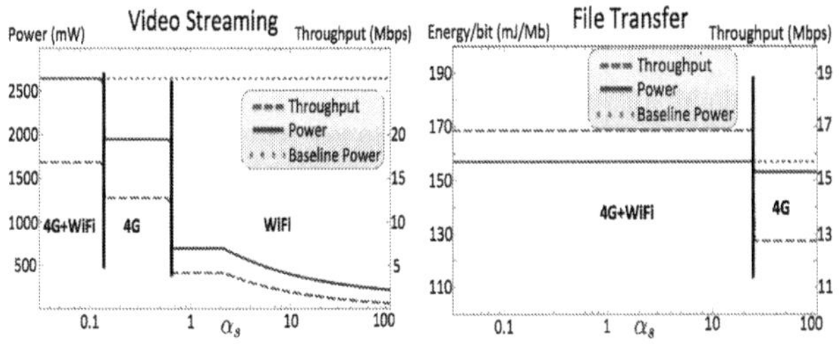

Figure 3: Energy, throughput vs α_s for large c_M. The pink dotted line represents the energy consumption of regular MP-TCP.

ergy consumed by running baseline regular MP-TCP, whose throughput is always c_M.

For video streaming, the smartphone uses both 4G and WiFi when α_s is small, it switches to 4G as α_s increases and eventually switch to WiFi network. The baseline MP-TCP consumes 2291mW power while the proposed algorithm consumes less power for any $\alpha_s > 0$. In particular, the proposed algorithm only consumes 1808mW when $\alpha_s \in [0.11, 0.65]$ while the throughput is the same as running regular MP-TCP. Thus, the proposed algorithm saves 22% energy without affecting the throughput. When $\alpha_s \geq 0.65$, both power and throughput decreases as α_s increases and there is tradeoff between throughput and energy consumption. For file download, the smartphone still uses both 4G and WiFi when α_s is small. Similar to video streaming, the proposed algorithm also saves 22% energy without affecting the throughput when $\alpha_s \geq 24$. However, the smartphone always uses 4G interface and operates at rate 10Mbps however large α_s is. Thus, the most energy efficient path depends on the applications and sometimes may not be the same.

We also simulate the case when the bottleneck is at the access link, assuming the bandwidth c_M is very large. The results are shown in Fig. 3 and are similar to our first set of simulations where c_M =10Mbps. The proposed algorithms still save energy compared to regular MP-TCP for any α_s. However, it cannot save energy without affecting throughput as our first set of simulations, *i.e.* we need to sacrifice more throughput if we want to save more energy.

Based on the above simulations, the path selection algorithms for realtime and file transfer applications end up at different paths for large α_s, *i.e.* the most energy efficient path is different for these two applications in the simulation scenario. Actually, we can explain the phenomena using the following two lemmas, which characterize the most energy efficient path for both types of applications. For source

Table 3: Comparisons of Algorithm 1 and Algorithm 2.

	Throughput of video call	Completion time of file transfer	Total energy consumed
Regular MPTCP (4G+WiFi)	8.42 Mbps	119 s	794 J
Algorithm 1(WiFi)	0.40 Mbps	369 s	213 J
Algorithm 2(4G)	0.64 Mbps	82.7 s	161.4 J

s, let $S_1 = \arg\min\{b_r \mid r \in \arg\min\{\theta_k \mid k \in s\}\}$ and $S_2 = \arg\min\{b'_r \mid r \in s\}$.

Lemma 5.1. *Suppose C1 holds. Let* $\mathbf{x}^*_s(\alpha_s)$ *be the optimal solution to PSP-I given* α_s. *Then there exists an* $\bar{\alpha}_s > 0$ *such that when* $\alpha_s \geq \bar{\alpha}_s$, *there is only one nonzero element in* $\mathbf{x}^*_s(\alpha_s)$, *which can be any element* $r_1 \in S_1$. *In addition,* $\lim_{\alpha_s \to \infty} x^*_{r_1}(\alpha_s) = 0$.

Lemma 5.1 describes the optimal path being selected for α_s large enough. It says that the most energy efficient path is the one with minimal θ_r for realtime applications, and the throughput approaches 0 as α_s increases.

Lemma 5.2. *Suppose C1 and C2 hold. Let* $\mathbf{x}^*_s(\alpha_s)$ *be the optimal solution to PSP-II given* α_s. *Then there exists a* $\bar{\alpha}_s > 0$ *such that when* $\alpha_s \geq \bar{\alpha}_s$

$$x^*_r(\alpha_s) = \begin{cases} 0 & r \in s \setminus S_2 \\ c_r & r \in S_2 \end{cases}$$

Lemma 5.2 describes the limiting behavior of file transfer when α_s is large enough. Different from realtime application, its most energy efficient path is the one with minimal b'_r for α_s large enough and it occupies all the available bandwidth on paths with minimal b'_r.

5.2 Multiple TCP connections from a single device

In the above analysis, we assume there is only one long termed TCP connection initiated from a single device. Sometimes there will be multiple concurrent long termed TCP connections initiated from a single device, *e.g.* there are two concurrent file downloads. In this case, we need to jointly optimize across all the TCP connections from one device because the total power power consumption is not separable for each connection, *i.e.* they are coupled through the 0-1 sunk cost in (7). However, we can run the same congestion control algorithms as described in section 3 and 4 since the sunk cost becomes a constant once the paths are selected. Thus, we only need to modify the path selection algorithms.

When all the TCP connections carry traffic of the same type of applications (either real time or file transfer application), the proposed path selection algorithms are ready to be generalized. Suppose all the TCP connections carry realtime traffic. Each TCP connection can access the same set of interfaces and will share the bandwidth equally, thus PSP-I (9) can be generalized as sequel.

$$\max \quad NU_s(\mathbf{1}^T\mathbf{x}_s) - \alpha_s \sum_{r \in s} P_r(x_r) \tag{20a}$$

$$\text{s.t.} \quad x_r \leq \frac{c_r}{N} \quad r \in s \tag{20b}$$

where N is the number of TCP connections. The problem (20) can be solved using Algorithm 1 by replacing $U_s(\mathbf{1}^T\mathbf{x}_s)$

with $NU_s(\mathbf{1}^T\mathbf{x}_s)$. Algorithm 2 can be modified in a similar manner when all the TCP connections are file transfer applications.

When there are TCP connections of both types of applications, the path selection algorithm is not ready to generalize. However, we can still run Algorithm 1 (or Algorithm 2) assuming all of them are realtime (or file transfer) applications. The simulation results say that Algorithm 2 selects better paths most of the time. For instance, there are two concurrent TCP connections: one video call of duration 5 mins and one file transfer of size 125Mb, from a smartphone with both 4G and WiFi interfaces as in Fig. 1. For small α_s, both paths will be selected and there is no difference between Algorithm 1 or Algorithm 2. For large α_s, WiFi path is optimal for realtime application while 4G path is optimal for file transfer application. Then we run the congestion control algorithms on those paths individually. The simulation results are shown in Table 3. By using 4G path selected by Algorithm 2, we can save more energy and have larger throughput than the WiFi path selected by Algorithm 1.

6. CONCLUSION

In this paper, we design MP-TCP algorithms by jointly considering both throughput and energy consumption for mobile devices. We consider two types of applications: realtime applications, such as video streaming, and file transfer applications, such as file download/upload. We develop energy efficient MP-TCP algorithms for both of them with theoretical performance guarantee. Our preliminary simulation results show that the algorithms can indeed shift traffic to energy efficient path. More specifically, we can reduce energy consumption up to 22% without affecting throughput as compared to baseline MP-TCP algorithm.

7. REFERENCES

[1] S. P. Boyd and L. Vandenberghe. *Convex optimization.* Cambridge university press, 2004.

[2] E. Brosh, S. A. Baset, V. Misra, D. Rubenstein, and H. Schulzrinne. The delay-friendliness of tcp for real-time traffic. *IEEE/ACM Transactions on Networking*, 18(5):1478–1491, 2010.

[3] M. Chen, S. C. Liew, Z. Shao, and C. Kai. Markov approximation for combinatorial network optimization. In *Proceedings of IEEE INFOCOM*, pages 1–9, 2010.

[4] Y.-C. Chen, E. M. Nahum, R. J. Gibbens, and D. Towsley. Measuring cellular networks: Characterizing 3g, 4g, and path diversity. Technical report, UMass Amherst Technical Report: UM-CS-2012-022.

[5] A. Ford, C. Raiciu, M. Handley, S. Barre, and J. Iyengar. Architectural guidelines for multipath tcp development. *RFC6182 (March 2011), www. ietf. ort/rfc/6182*, 2011.

[6] M. Honda, Y. Nishida, L. Eggert, P. Sarolahti, and H. Tokuda. Multipath congestion control for shared bottleneck. In *Proc. PFLDNeT workshop*, 2009.

[7] J. Huang, F. Qian, A. Gerber, Z. M. Mao, S. Sen, and O. Spatscheck. A close examination of performance and power characteristics of 4g lte networks. In *Proceedings of ACM MobiSys*, pages 225–238, 2012.

[8] F. P. Kelly, A. K. Maulloo, and D. K. Tan. Rate control for communication networks: shadow prices, proportional fairness and stability. *Journal of the Operational Research society*, 49(3):237–252, 1998.

[9] P. Key, L. Massoulié, and P. Towsley. Path selection and multipath congestion control. In *Proceedings of IEEE INFOCOM 2007*, pages 143–151, 2007.

[10] S. H. Low. A duality model of tcp and queue management algorithms. *IEEE/ACM Transactions on Networking (TON)*, 11(4):525–536, 2003.

[11] S. H. Low and D. E. Lapsley. Optimization flow control-i: basic algorithm and convergence. *IEEE/ACM Transactions on Networking (TON)*, 7(6):861–874, 1999.

[12] J. Mo and J. Walrand. Fair end-to-end window-based congestion control. *IEEE/ACM Transactions on Networking (ToN)*, 8(5):556–567, 2000.

[13] A. Pathak, Y. C. Hu, and M. Zhang. Where is the energy spent inside my app?: fine grained energy accounting on smartphones with eprof. In *Proceedings of ACM european conference on Computer Systems*, pages 29–42, 2012.

[14] Q. Peng, A. Walid, J. Hwang, and S. H. Low. Multipath tcp: Analysis design and implementation. *arXiv preprint arXiv:1308.3119*, 2013.

[15] G. P. Perrucci, F. H. Fitzek, and J. Widmer. Survey on energy consumption entities on the smartphone platform. In *IEEE Vehicular Technology Conference (VTC Spring)*, pages 1–6, 2011.

[16] C. Pluntke, L. Eggert, and N. Kiukkonen. Saving mobile device energy with multipath tcp. In *Proceedings of the international workshop on ACM MobiArch*, pages 1–6, 2011.

[17] C. Raiciu, D. Niculescu, M. Bagnulo, and M. J. Handley. Opportunistic mobility with multipath tcp. In *Proceedings of the international workshop on ACM MobiArch*, pages 7–12, 2011.

[18] B. Wang, W. Wei, Z. Guo, and D. Towsley. Multipath live streaming via tcp: scheme, performance and benefits. *ACM Transactions on TOMCCAP*, 5(3):25, 2009.

[19] D. Wischik, C. Raiciu, A. Greenhalgh, and M. Handley. Design, implementation and evaluation of congestion control for multipath tcp. In *Proceedings of USENIX conference on Networked systems design and implementation*, pages 8–8, 2011.

8. ACKNOWLEDGEMENTS

This work was supported by Bell Labs, Alcatel-Lucent, National Basic Research Program of China (Project No. 2013CB336700) and the University Grants Committee of the Hong Kong Special Administrative Region, China (Theme-based Research Scheme Project No. T23-407/13-N).

APPENDIX

A. PROOF OF THEOREMS

A.1 Proof of Theorem 3.1

To characterize the sub-optimality gap of Algorithm 1, we introduce the following optimization problem, which can be regarded as a convex relaxation of PSP-I.

Relaxation of Path Selection Problem-I(RPSP-I):

$$\max \quad U_s(\mathbf{1}^T\mathbf{x}_s) - \alpha_s \sum_{r\in s} b'_r x_r \tag{21a}$$

$$\text{s.t.} \quad x_r \le c_r \text{ for } r \in s \tag{21b}$$

RPSP-I is a convex problem obtained by relaxing the non-continuous $P_r(x_r)$ to $b'_r x_r$. It is hard to evaluate the optimal solution to PSP-I due to its nonconvexity, but we can obtain an upper bound of its optimal value through RPSP-I. Then we study the gap between this upper bound and the objective value given by Algorithm 1.

Lemma A.1. *RPSP-I provides an upper bound for PSP-I. Moreover, the solution of RPSP-I $\mathbf{x}_s^*$ is optimal to PSP-I if and only if x_r^* is either 0 or c_r for all $r \in s$.*

Proof. For every feasible $\mathbf{x}_s$, the objective value of RPSP-I is no less than PSP-I, which follows from

$$b'_r x_r \le b_r x_r + \theta_r 1_{\{x_r>0\}} = P_r(x_r) \tag{22}$$

for any $r \in s$. Since equality can be obtained if and only if x_r is either 0 or c_r in (22), the relaxation provides an exact solution to PSP-I if and only if the solution to RPSP-I x_r^* is either 0 or c_r for each $r \in s$. □

Next, we provide a close form solution to RPSP-I in Lemma A.2.

Lemma A.2. *Suppose C1 holds. Then $\hat{\mathbf{x}}_s$ (defined in (12)) is an optimal solution to RPSP-I. Moreover,*

$$\hat{x}_i = \begin{cases} c_i & i < \hat{k} \\ (U_s')^{-1}(\alpha_s b_{\hat{k}}') - \sum_{i=1}^{\hat{k}-1} c_i & i = \hat{k} \\ 0 & i > \hat{k} \end{cases} \tag{23}$$

and $\hat{k} := \max\{k \mid \sum_{i=1}^{k-1} c_i \le (U_s')^{-1}(\alpha_s b_k')\}$

PROOF. The Lagrangian of RPSP-I can be written as

$$\begin{aligned} L(\mathbf{x}, \mu) &= U_s(\sum_{i=1}^{|s|} x_i) - \alpha_s \sum_{i=1}^{|s|} b_i' x_i - \sum_{i=1}^{|s|} \mu_i (x_i - c_i) \\ &= U_s(\sum_{i=1}^{|s|} x_i) - \sum_{i=1}^{|s|} (\alpha_s b_i' + \mu_i) x_r + \sum_{i=1}^{|s|} \mu_i c_i, \end{aligned}$$

where $\mu_i \ge 0$ is the dual variable corresponding to each constraint $x_i \le c_i$. By C1, $U_s(x)$ is strictly concave and differentiable , the KKT conditions imply that, at optimality

$$\left[U_s'(\sum_{i=1}^{|s|} x_i) - (\alpha_s b_k' + \mu_k) \right]_{x_k}^{+} = 0 \tag{24}$$

$$[c_k - x_k]_{\mu_k}^{+} = 0 \tag{25}$$

since RPSP-I is a convex problem. Now we will show $\hat{x}_k$ together with some $\hat{\mu}_k$ satisfy (24) and (25), meaning that $\hat{x}_k$ is indeed an optimal solution. Denote

$$L_k := (U_s')^{-1}(\alpha_s b_k') - \sum_{1 \le i < k} c_i,$$

which is a monotone decreasing sequence and $L_{i+1} - L_i \le -c_i$. By definition of $\hat{k}$, $0 \le L_{\hat{k}} \le c_{\hat{k}}$ and

$$\begin{aligned} L_k &\ge \sum_{i=k}^{\hat{k}-1} c_i \ge c_k \text{ for } k < \hat{k} \\ L_k &\le L_{\hat{k}} - \sum_{i=\hat{k}}^{k} c_i < 0 \text{ for } k > \hat{k}, \end{aligned}$$

from which we can obtain (23). In addition, define

$$\hat{\mu}_k := \left[U_s'(\sum_{i=1}^{k} \hat{x}_i) - \alpha_s \sum_{i=1}^{k} b_i' \right]_0^{+}$$

and clearly that $\hat{x}_k$ together with $\hat{\mu}_k$ satisfy (24) and (25), which means $\hat{x}_k$ is the optimal solution to RPSP-I. □

By Lemma A.1, the optimal solution of PSP-I O^* is upper bounded by the optimal value of RPSP-I. By Lemma A.2, $\hat{\mathbf{x}}_s$ is the optimal solution to RPSP-I, thus

$$\begin{aligned} O^* &\le U_s(\mathbf{1}^T \hat{\mathbf{x}}_s) - \alpha_s \sum_{r \in s} b_r' \hat{x}_r \\ &= U_s(\sum_{i=1}^{\hat{k}-1} c_i + \hat{x}_{\hat{k}}) - \alpha_s \left(\sum_{i=1}^{\hat{k}-1} b_i' c_i + b_{\hat{k}}' \hat{x}_{\hat{k}} \right), \end{aligned} \tag{26}$$

Using the upper bound of O^* in (26), we have

$$\begin{aligned} &O^* - O_{\hat{k}} \\ =&\alpha_s \theta_{\hat{k}} - \alpha_s (b_{\hat{k}}' - b_{\hat{k}}) \hat{x}_{\hat{k}} - \int_{\hat{c}+\hat{x}_{\hat{k}}}^{\hat{c}+\tilde{x}_{\hat{k}}} (U_s'(y) - \alpha_s b_{\hat{k}}) dy \\ \le&\alpha_s \theta_{\hat{k}} - \alpha_s (b_{\hat{k}}' - b_{\hat{k}}) \hat{x}_{\hat{k}} \\ =&\alpha_s \theta_{\hat{k}} (1 - \frac{\hat{x}_{\hat{k}}}{c_{\hat{k}}}) \end{aligned} \tag{27}$$

On the other hand,

$$\begin{aligned} O^* - O_{\hat{k}-1} &= \int_{\hat{c}}^{\hat{c}+\hat{x}_{\hat{k}}} (U_s'(y) - \alpha_s b_{\hat{k}}') dy \\ &\le \frac{1}{2} \hat{x}_{\hat{k}} (U_s'(\hat{c}) - \alpha_s b_{\hat{k}}') \end{aligned} \tag{28}$$

Clearly that $O_i \le O_{\hat{k}-1}$ for $i \le \hat{k} - 1$ and $O_i \le O_{\hat{k}}$ for $i \ge k$. Thus by definition of k^*, we have $k^* \in \{\hat{k}, \hat{k} - 1\}$, which means the objective value given by Algorithm 1: $\hat{O} = \max\{O_{\hat{k}}, O_{\hat{k}-1}\}$. Then

$$\begin{aligned} O^* - \hat{O} &= O^* - \max\{O_{\hat{k}}, O_{\hat{k}-1}\} \\ &\le \min\{O^* - O_{\hat{k}}, O^* - O_{\hat{k}-1}\} \end{aligned}$$

and we obtain the bound in the theorem by substituting (27) and (28) into the above inequality.

A.2 Proof of Theorem 4.1

To show that Algorithm 2 obtains the exact optimal solution to PSP-II, we introduce the following optimization problem, which can be seen as a relaxation of PSP-II. *Relaxation of Path Selection Problem-II (RPSP-II):*

$$\max \quad U_s(\mathbf{1}^T \mathbf{x}_s) - \alpha_s \frac{1}{\mathbf{1}^T \mathbf{x}_s} \sum_{r \in s} b_r' x_r \tag{29a}$$

$$\text{s.t.} \quad x_r \le c_r \text{ for } r \in s \tag{29b}$$

Lemma A.3. *RPSP-II provides an upper bound for PSP-II. Its solution $\mathbf{x}_s^*$ is also optimal to PSP-II if and only if x_r^* is either 0 or c_r for all $r \in s$.*

The proof can be carried out in a similar manner as Lemma A.1. Different from RPSP-I, which is a convex problem, RPSP-II itself is a nonconvex problem. However, KKT condition still serves as a necessary condition on the structure for optimal solution.

Lemma A.4. *Suppose C1 and C2 hold. Then there exists an optimal solution $\hat{\mathbf{x}}_s$ to RPSP-II satisfying*

$$\hat{x}_i = \begin{cases} c_i & i \le \tilde{k} \\ 0 & i > \tilde{k} \end{cases} \tag{30}$$

for some $\tilde{k} \le |s|$.

PROOF. Using similar manner as Lemma A.2, we can show that there exists an optimal solution $\hat{\mathbf{x}}_s$ to RPSP-II such that

$$\hat{x}_i = \begin{cases} c_i & i < \tilde{k} \\ 0 & i > \tilde{k} \end{cases} \tag{31}$$

for some $\tilde{k} \le |s|$. Now we only need to show the last unknown entry in $\hat{\mathbf{x}}_s$: $\hat{x}_{\tilde{k}}$ is also either 0 or $c_{\tilde{k}}$. Note that $\hat{x}_i$ is a constant for any $i \neq \tilde{k}$ by (31). Then RPSP-I becomes a single variable optimization problem as follows:

$$\max \quad h(x_{\tilde{k}}) \quad s.t. \quad x_{\tilde{k}} \in [0, c_{\tilde{k}}],$$

where

$$h(x_{\tilde{k}}) := U_s(\sum_{i=1}^{\tilde{k}-1} c_i + x_{\tilde{k}}) - \alpha_s \frac{\sum_{i=1}^{\tilde{k}-1} b'_i c_i + b'_{\tilde{k}} x_{\tilde{k}}}{\sum_{i=1}^{\tilde{k}-1} c_i + x_{\tilde{k}}}.$$

The derivate of $h(x_{\tilde{k}})$ is given as

$$\begin{aligned} h'(x_{\tilde{k}}) &= U'_s(\sum_{i=1}^{\tilde{k}-1} c_i + x_{\tilde{k}}) + \alpha_s \frac{\sum_{i=1}^{\tilde{k}-1}(b'_i - b'_{\tilde{k}})c_i}{(\sum_{i=1}^{\tilde{k}-1} c_i + x_{\tilde{k}})^2} \\ &= \frac{g(\sum_{i=1}^{\tilde{k}-1} c_i + x_{\tilde{k}})}{(\sum_{i=1}^{\tilde{k}-1} c_i + x_{\tilde{k}})^2}, \end{aligned}$$

where $g(x) := x^2 U'_s(x) + \alpha_s \sum_{i=1}^{\tilde{k}-1}(b'_i - b'_{\tilde{k}})c_i$. By C2, $g(x)$ is a nondecreasing function, based on which we know $h(x_{\tilde{k}})$ achieves its maxima at the boundary, i.e. $h(x_{\tilde{k}})$ achieves its maxima at 0 or $c_{\tilde{k}}$. □

In Algorithm 2, it compares all the solution with the structure in (30), thus obtains the optimal solution to RPSP-II according to Lemma A.4. Then it is also the optimal solution to the PSP-II based on Lemma A.3 because x_r^* is either 0 or c_r for all $r \in s$.

A.3 Proof of Theorem 4.2

In [14], it is proved that the system (1)-(2) is stable if C1-C3 are satisfied. For each source s, let $\Phi_s(\mathbf{x}_s) := (\phi_r(\mathbf{x}_s), r \in s)$, then C1-C3 are stated below.

C1: For each $s \in \mathcal{S}$ there exists a nonnegative solution $\mathbf{x}_s := \mathbf{x}_s(\mathbf{p})$ to $\dot{x}_r = 0$ in (1) for any $\mathbf{p} \geq 0$. Moreover,

$$\frac{\partial y_l^s(\mathbf{p})}{\partial p_l} \leq 0, \qquad \lim_{p_l \to \infty} y_l^s(\mathbf{p}) = 0$$

where $y_l^s(\mathbf{p}) := \sum_{r \in s} H_{lr} x_r(\mathbf{p})$ is the aggregate traffic at link l from source s.

C2: For each $s \in S$ and each $\mathbf{x}_s$, $\Phi_s(\mathbf{x}_s)$ is continuously differentiable; moreover the symmetric part of the Jacobian $[\frac{\partial \Phi_s(\mathbf{x}_s)}{\partial \mathbf{x}_s}]^+ := \frac{1}{2}(\frac{\partial \Phi_s(\mathbf{x}_s)}{\partial \mathbf{x}_s} + (\frac{\partial \Phi_s(\mathbf{x}_s)}{\partial \mathbf{x}_s})^T)$ is negative definite.

C3: For each $r \in R$, $\phi_r(\mathbf{x}_s) = \infty$ if and only if $x_r = 0$.

Clearly that the $\phi_r(\mathbf{x}_s)$ defined in (18) satisfies C1 and C3 and we are left to show C2.

Lemma A.5. *Let* $E_s(\mathbf{x}_s) = \frac{\sum_{r \in s} P_r(x_r)}{\mathbf{1}^T \mathbf{x}_s}$, *then*

$$\mathbf{z}_s^T \frac{\partial^2 E_s(\mathbf{x}_s)}{\partial \mathbf{x}_s^2} \mathbf{z}_s \geq \frac{M^2}{(\mathbf{1}^T \mathbf{x}_s)^2} (\min_{r \in s} b_r - \max_{r \in s} b_r) \tag{32}$$

for any $\mathbf{z}_s \in \mathbb{R}^{|s|}$ *with* $\sum_{r \in s} z_r = M$, *where* M *is any constant.*

PROOF. Let $\Lambda_b := diag\{b_r, r \in s\}$, then

$$\begin{aligned} &\frac{\partial^2 E_s(\mathbf{x}_s)}{\partial \mathbf{x}_s^2} \\ =& \frac{2\sum_{r \in s}(\theta_r + b_r x_r)}{\|\mathbf{x}_s\|_1^3} \mathbf{1}\mathbf{1}^T - \frac{1}{\|\mathbf{x}_s\|_1^2}(\Lambda_b \mathbf{1}\mathbf{1}^T + \mathbf{1}\mathbf{1}^T \Lambda_b) \end{aligned}$$

which means

$$\begin{aligned} \mathbf{z}_s^T \frac{\partial^2 E_s(\mathbf{x}_s)}{\partial \mathbf{x}_s^2} \mathbf{z}_s &= \mathbf{z}_s^T A_s(\mathbf{x}_s) \mathbf{z}_s + \frac{2\sum_{r \in s} \theta_r}{\|\mathbf{x}_s\|_1^3} (\mathbf{1}^T \mathbf{z}_s)^2 \\ &\geq \mathbf{z}_s^T A_s(\mathbf{x}_s) \mathbf{z}_s \end{aligned}$$

where

$$A_s(\mathbf{x}_s) := \frac{2\sum_{r \in s} b_r x_r}{\|\mathbf{x}_s\|_1^3} \mathbf{1}\mathbf{1}^T - \frac{1}{\|\mathbf{x}_s\|_1^2}(\Lambda_b \mathbf{1}\mathbf{1}^T + \mathbf{1}\mathbf{1}^T \Lambda_b).$$

And

$$\begin{aligned} &\mathbf{z}_s^T A(\mathbf{x}_s) \mathbf{z}_s \\ =& \frac{1}{(\mathbf{1}^T \mathbf{x}_s)^2} \left((\sum_{r \in s} b_r \frac{x_r}{\mathbf{1}^T \mathbf{x}_s})(\sum_{r \in s} z_r)^2 - (\sum_{r \in s} b_r z_r)(\sum_{r \in s} z_r) \right) \\ =& \frac{M}{(\mathbf{1}^T \mathbf{x}_s)^2} \left(\sum_{r \in s} b_r (M \frac{x_r}{\mathbf{1}^T \mathbf{x}_s} - z_r) \right) \end{aligned} \tag{33}$$

Without loss of generality, assume $b_i \leq b_j$ for $i < j$. Let $a_r := M \frac{x_r}{\mathbf{1}^T \mathbf{x}_s}$, then

$$\begin{aligned} &\sum_{r \in s} b_r (a_r - z_r) - M(b_1 - \beta_{|s|}) \\ =& \sum_{r \in s} b_r (a_r - z_r) - (b_1 \sum_{r \in s} a_r - b_{|s|} \sum_{r \in s} z_r) \\ =& \sum_{r \in s} a_r (b_r - b_1) + \sum_{r \in s} z_r (b_{|s|} - b_r) \geq 0 \end{aligned}$$

which means

$$\sum_{r \in s} b_r (M \frac{x_r}{\mathbf{1}^T \mathbf{x}_s} - z_r) \geq M(b_1 - \beta_{|s|})$$

and substitute the above inequality into (33), we can obtain (32). □

Lemma A.6. *The* $\phi_r(\mathbf{x}_s)$ *defined in* (18) *satisfies C2 if* (19) *holds.*

PROOF. The Jacobian $\partial \Phi_s(\mathbf{x}_s) / \partial \mathbf{x}_s$ can be written as:

$$-\frac{4(1-\beta)}{\tau^2 \|\mathbf{x}_s\|_1^3} \mathbf{1}\mathbf{1}^T - \beta \frac{2\|\mathbf{x}_s\|_n}{\tau^2 \|\mathbf{x}_s\|_1^2} \Lambda_s^{-1} \left(I_{|s|} + \mathbf{1}\mathbf{a}_s^T \right) \Lambda_s^{-1} - \frac{\partial E_s(\mathbf{x}_s)}{\partial \mathbf{x}_s}$$

where $\Lambda_s = diag\{\mathbf{x}_s\}$ and $\mathbf{a}_s = \left(\frac{2x_r}{\|\mathbf{x}_s\|_1} - \frac{x_r^n}{\|\mathbf{x}_s\|_n^n}, r \in s \right)$. In [14], it is shown in Theorem 4.1 that for $\sum_{r \in s} z_r = M$,

$$\mathbf{z}_s^T (I_{|s|} + \mathbf{1}\mathbf{a}_s^T) \mathbf{z}_s \geq \frac{M^2}{4} \left(\frac{9}{|s|} - 1 \right),$$

which means if $\sum_{r \in s} z_r = M$, we have

$$\mathbf{z}_s^T \Lambda_s^{-1} (I_{|s|} + \mathbf{1}\mathbf{a}_s^T) \Lambda_s^{-1} \mathbf{z}_s \geq \frac{M^2}{4\|\mathbf{x}_s\|_\infty^2} \left(\frac{9}{|s|} - 1 \right),$$

Based on the above inequality and Lemma A.5, for any $\mathbf{z}_s$ with $\sum_{r \in s} z_r = M$, we have

$$\begin{aligned} &\mathbf{z}_s^T \frac{\partial \Phi_s(\mathbf{x}_s)}{\partial \mathbf{x}_s} \mathbf{z}_s \\ \leq& \frac{-\beta M^2 \|\mathbf{x}_s\|_n}{2\tau^2 (\mathbf{1}^T \mathbf{x}_s)^2 \|\mathbf{x}_s\|_\infty^2} \left(\frac{9}{|s|} - 1 \right) + \frac{\alpha_s M^2}{(\mathbf{1}^T \mathbf{x}_s)^2} (\min_{r \in s} b_r - \max_{r \in s} b_r) \\ \leq& 0 \end{aligned}$$

if (19) is satisfied. □

Therefore, the $\phi_r(\mathbf{x}_s)$ satisfies C1-C3 provided (19) is satisfied and the corresponding system (1)-(2) is asymptotically stable.

An Analytical Framework to Characterize the Efficiency and Delay in a Mobile Data Offloading System

Yoora Kim
Dept. Math., Univ. of Ulsan
93 Daehak-ro, Nam-gu
Ulsan, South Korea
yrkim@ulsan.ac.kr

Kyunghan Lee*
ECE, UNIST
UNIST-gil 50
Ulsan, South Korea
khlee@unist.ac.kr

Ness B. Shroff
ECE and CSE, OSU
2015 Neil Ave.
Columbus, OH 43210
shroff.11@osu.edu

ABSTRACT

Smart mobile devices are generating a tremendous amount of data traffic that is putting stress on even the most advanced cellular networks. Delayed offloading has recently been proposed as an efficient mechanism to substantially alleviate this stress. The idea is simple. It allows a mobile device to delay transmission of data packets for a certain amount of time, while it searches WiFi (or similarly femtocell) networks to offload the data during the time. When the time expires, it completes the remaining portion of the delayed transmission through the cellular network that is available at the moment. In this paper, we develop an analytical framework using an embedded Markov process for the delayed offloading system. We provide a closed-form expression for estimating how much data generated by the users can be offloaded to WiFi networks from cellular networks even when there are non-Markovian data arrivals and service interruptions. We conduct extensive numerical studies with various ranges of delay, service interruption time, arrived data, and service rate. These numerical studies show that the current deployment of WiFi networks measured from a metropolitan city is capable of offloading about 80% of the generated data with 30 minutes of delay and 1 Mbps of WiFi data rate, but increasing the data rate does not help improve the amount of offloading. Further studies using this framework on two new deployment strategies of WiFi networks give guidance on how to upgrade WiFi networks by revealing that the amount of offloading for 30 minutes of delay and 1 Mbps of data rate can be drastically improved to about 90% or 98% according to the strategy.

Categories and Subject Descriptors

C.2.1 [**Network Architecture and Design**]: Wireless communication; D.4.8 [**Performance**]: Queueing theory

Keywords

Mobile data offloading, WiFi networks, queueing, reneging

* indicates corresponding author.

MobiHoc'14, August 11–14, 2014, Philadelphia, PA, USA.
Copyright 2014 ACM 978-1-4503-2620-9/14/08 ...$15.00.
http://dx.doi.org/10.1145/2632951.2632991.

1. INTRODUCTION

Recent advances in mobile devices (e.g., smartphones, tablets) are fueling the dramatic growth of mobile data traffic all over the world. A recent report has predicted that the total number of mobile Internet users is projected to surpass desktop Internet users by 2014 [19]. In order to support ubiquitous connectivity from such mobile devices to the Internet, cellular network providers are struggling to increase the capacity of their cellular networks by reducing cell sizes, widening the wireless channel bandwidth and upgrading the communication standards. As a result, in many countries, LTE and LTE-A (Long Term Evolution Advanced) networks supporting up to 150 Mbps are being operated with 20 to 40 MHz of channel bandwidth. However, even with these efforts, it is expected that the deluge of mobile data traffic will soon catch up and saturate the capacity of cellular networks [1]. This continued growth of mobile data traffic is creating challenges to the business model of cellular network providers who need to incur prohibitively large expenses for upgrading their networks, while the earnings from their subscribers remain relatively stagnant (at least in developed countries).

To alleviate this problem and aid cellular networks, it has been proposed that data can be offloaded on available WiFi networks (or on femtocells in the near future) [4,12,15,17,25]. This is often referred to as *mobile data offloading*. The idea is that mobile devices can offload their data traffic from cellular networks onto WiFi networks whenever WiFi networks are available[1]. Indeed, even now, most smartphones and tablets use mobile data offloading, by prioritizing WiFi networks over cellular networks. According to recent observations from Lee *et al.* [17], mobile data offloading already cuts about 65% of the data traffic burden to cellular networks by letting the traffic flow through WiFi networks. This 65% reduction seems surprising but the authors have suggested that the number can grow as high as 82% when allowing one hour delay for delay-insensitive data traffic and have named this technique *delayed mobile data offloading*.

The conceptual operation of delayed mobile data offloading (i.e., delayed offloading) is quite simple. Briefly, delayed offloading sets delay deadlines for data transmission that can be predetermined or chosen by a user and lets the mobile device find opportunities to offload the data to WiFi networks until the assigned deadline expires. To enable delayed offloading in real mobile devices, there have been efforts to redesign a transmission protocol which can allow a delay. The efforts include the bundle protocol [11,20,22] that keeps a session virtually connected under intermittent connectivity until its completion.

[1]Note that the central tenet of mobile data offloading can be directly applied to femtocell or picocell networks instead of WiFi networks.

After its proposal in [3, 17], delayed mobile data offloading has attracted many researchers, and various extensions [2] have been pursued including multi-hop offloading [18], social offloading [5], and offloading with ICN (Information Centric Networking) [9]. However, as of yet, we do not have a rigorous understanding of the performance of the delayed offloading system. This is because developing a rigorous analytical framework for delayed offloading system is quite challenging because as pointed out in [17], the system involves "queueing with reneging and service interruptions." In queueing, *reneging* means that a customer will leave the queue when her patience exceeds a certain limit. This resembles the behavior of a packet for its chosen deadline in the delayed offloading system. Service interruption literally means unwilling discontinuity of service in the queue, and this models connection and disconnection periods of a mobile device to WiFi networks in the system. In [17], 15 days of experimental study with about 100 iPhone users mostly in Seoul, Korea revealed that connection and disconnection periods showed heavy-tail distributions, especially truncated Pareto distributions with averages of 50 minutes and 25 minutes, respectively. Given these heavy-tail distributions of connection and disconnection periods, mathematical challenges arise in deriving a closed-form equation from the queueing process (which is obviously non-Markovian) on how much mobile data can be offloaded to WiFi networks for a chosen deadline. We propose a general analytical framework that handles such challenges. Our analytical results are validated by verifying the agreement of the amount of offloading obtained from our results and that shown in [17] for the same input traffic and system parameters. Through extensive numerical studies under various environments of WiFi networks including those of today and of projections made for the near future, we show that our framework is useful in designing a new radical deployment strategy of WiFi networks that achieves a dramatic improvement in the amount of offloading. Using our framework, we further clarify which parameter of WiFi networks most affects the efficiency of offloading.

Our contributions in this paper are as follows: (i) We develop an analytical framework for analyzing a queueing system with deterministic reneging and service interruptions. (ii) From our framework, we obtain closed-form formulas for key performance metrics in the delayed offloading system such as *offloading efficiency* and mean *packet delay*. (iii) Our framework is quite general in that it is capable of handling generally distributed system parameters including connection and disconnection periods, packet inter-arrival time, WiFi data rate, and packet size. (iv) We provide a guidance on how to upgrade WiFi networks to obtain much higher efficiency in offloading through extensive numerical studies using our analytical framework. We believe that our framework can be a stepping stone towards analyzing the delayed offloading system and its variants. Our analysis is applicable to generalized queueing systems with service interruptions and reneging, which can also be extended to explain the behavior of complex mobile systems.

2. DELAYED MOBILE DATA OFFLOADING SYSTEM

In this section, we overview the delayed mobile data offloading system proposed in [17]. In this paper, we describe the system from the viewpoint of data uploading from a mobile device to the Internet, but the same framework can be readily used for downloading. The only difference between delayed offloading for uploading and downloading is at the network operation in a mobile device. Uploading works as pushing while downloading works as pulling. In

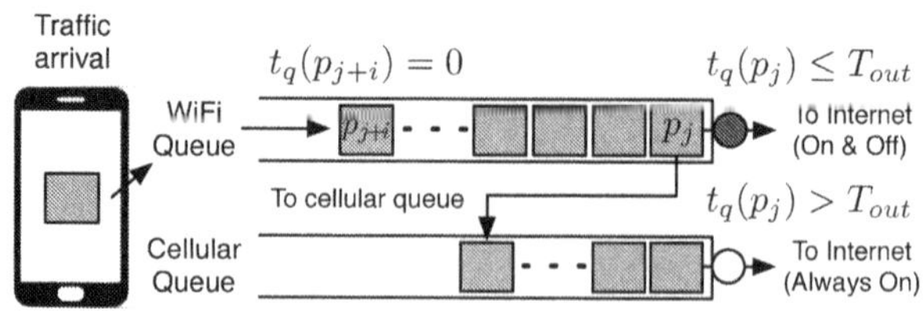

Figure 1: Delayed offloading mechanism in a mobile device.

both cases, delayed offloading necessitates a bundle protocol[2] at the network layer which handles the responsibility of fulfilling a data request even when the connection to the Internet is intermittent. Thus, in delayed offloading, the session initiated for a data request is kept virtually alive by the bundle protocol until the requested data transfer is finished.

Fig. 1 shows a simplified architecture of the delayed offloading system for the uploading scenario. There are two coupled queues for data upload at the MAC layer of a mobile device, called WiFi queue and cellular queue, and both queues are served by a FIFO (first-in-first-out) discipline. When the user of a mobile device requests to upload data (e.g., photos and videos taken at a park which need to be synchronized to a cloud backup service like iCloud) with a certain amount of allowed delay, denoted by T_{out}, the traffic request is first inserted into the WiFi queue and waits for the device to be connected to any WiFi network for up to a maximum of T_{out} units of time. If data in the WiFi queue is completely transmitted through WiFi networks before the time-out T_{out} has expired, we say that the data is successfully offloaded. If offloading of data fails, the system lets the data leave the WiFi queue and be relocated to the cellular queue in the mobile device for immediate transmission through 3G or 4G networks. We call such an event a *reneging* event.

In this paper, we analyze the ratio of the amount of successfully offloaded data over the amount of total data requested, which we call the *offloading efficiency* of the system. Since a mobile device is intermittently connected to WiFi networks by the mobility pattern of its owner (i.e., a human or sometimes a vehicle driven by a human) and the data rate for each connection is random, analyzing the offloading efficiency is a challenging problem. Further, given that empirical observations indicate that both the connection and the disconnection processes to any WiFi network of a mobile device follow heavy-tail distributions [17], it becomes even harder to analytically characterize the offloading efficiency for a given T_{out}. The detailed technical challenges from a queueing theory perspective and our proposed approach will be discussed in detail in Section 4.

3. MODEL DESCRIPTION

3.1 Queueing System Model

We assume that time axis is divided into unit intervals referred to as slots, and the slots are indexed by $t\ (t = 1, 2, \ldots)$. We set the system to start at time 1 so that time slot t covers the time interval $[t, t+1)$. In the following, we describe our discrete-time queueing system in detail. We begin by describing the service process of the WiFi queue.

Service process of the WiFi queue. Let $C(t)$ be a random variable that denotes the connectivity status of the mobile device to a WiFi network. We define $C(t) := 1$ when the mobile device is

[2]See [11] for a candidate implementation in a mobile device.

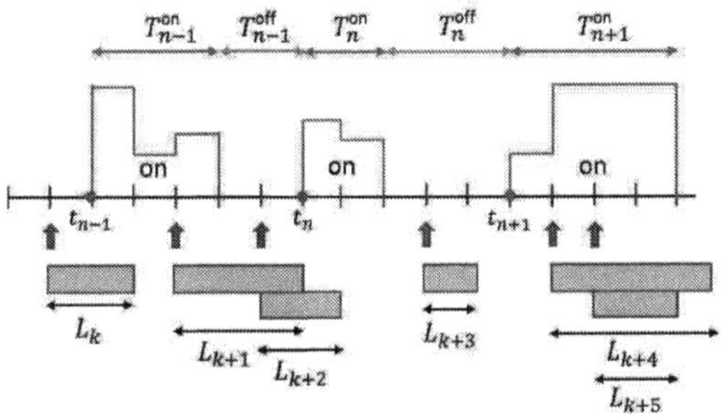

Figure 2: System model.

connected to a WiFi network during time slot t and $C(t) := 0$ otherwise. Then, the connectivity process $\{C(t)\}_{t=1}^{\infty}$ is modeled by an on-off process, where the on-state corresponds to being in a WiFi zone and the off-state corresponds to being out of the WiFi zones. Let T_n^{on} and T_n^{off} denote the nth ($n = 1, 2, \dots$) on-period and off-period of the process $\{C(t)\}_{t=1}^{\infty}$, respectively (See Fig. 2). We assume that the pair $(T_n^{\text{on}}, T_n^{\text{off}})$ is i.i.d. (independent and identically distributed) across n. However, for a fixed n, *we allow T_n^{on} and T_n^{off} to be dependent.* Therefore, the process $\{(T_n^{\text{on}}, T_n^{\text{off}})\}_{n=1}^{\infty}$ becomes an alternating renewal sequence [21]. Let $(T_{\text{on}}, T_{\text{off}})$ be the generic random vector for $(T_n^{\text{on}}, T_n^{\text{off}})$. Empirical observations in [17] show that T_{on} and T_{off} follow truncated heavy-tail distributions. Our model assumes general distributions having finite mean $\text{E}[T_{\text{on}}] < \infty$ and $\text{E}[T_{\text{off}}] < \infty$, and includes such truncated heavy-tail distributions.

Let $S(t)$ denote the transmission rate provided to the WiFi queue during time slot t. Then, we have

$$S(t) = \begin{cases} 0 & \text{if } C(t) = 0, \\ S_{\text{WiFi}}(t) & \text{if } C(t) = 1, \end{cases} \tag{1}$$

where $S_{\text{WiFi}}(t)$ denotes the transmission rate of the WiFi network to which the mobile device is connected during time slot t. For simplicity, we assume that $S_{\text{WiFi}}(t)$ is i.i.d. across t (with a generic random variable R), but our analysis is readily extensible to the case where $\{S_{\text{WiFi}}(t)\}_{t=1}^{\infty}$ is a Markov process.

Arrival process into the WiFi queue. We next describe the packet arrival process into the WiFi queue. Let $A(t)$ be a random variable that denotes the number of packets that are generated by the mobile device at time slot t. Then, the packet generation process $\{A(t)\}_{t=1}^{\infty}$ becomes the arrival process into the WiFi queue. Let A_k denote the kth ($k = 1, 2, \dots$) inter-arrival time. We assume that A_k is i.i.d. across k (with a generic random variable A) and follows a general distribution having finite mean $\mu := \text{E}[A] < \infty$, i.e., the arrival process $\{A(t)\}_{t=1}^{\infty}$ is assumed to be a renewal process.

Packet size. In this paper, we allow the size of a packet to be variable which includes the fixed (deterministic) size as a special case. Let L be a random variable that denotes the size of a generic packet. In practice, packet size is bounded by the maximum transmission unit. Hence, we assume that the packet size distribution has finite support on the range $[1, L_{\max}]$.

Queue evolution equation. We now describe the queueing dynamics at the WiFi queue. Let $Q(t)$ be a random variable that denotes the number of packets in the WiFi queue at the beginning of time slot t. Then, the queueing process $\{Q(t)\}_{t=1}^{\infty}$ evolves according to the following recursion:

$$Q(t+1) = Q(t) + A(t) - D_{\text{WiFi}}(t) - D_{\text{Renege}}(t).$$

Here, $D_{\text{WiFi}}(t)$ is the number of packets that is completely transmitted through a WiFi network during time slot t, and $D_{\text{Renege}}(t)$ is the number of packets that renege during time slot t. Note that $D_{\text{WiFi}}(t)$ is given by

$$D_{\text{WiFi}}(t) = \begin{cases} 0, & \text{if } Q(t) + A(t) = 0 \text{ or } S(t) = 0, \\ \sup\{k : \sum_{i=1}^{k} L_i(t) \le S(t)\}, & \text{otherwise,} \end{cases}$$

where $L_i(t)$ ($i = 1, 2, \dots, Q(t) + A(t)$) denotes the size of the ith packet in the WiFi queue at time t. Also, note that $D_{\text{Renege}}(t) \le Q(t) + A(t) - D_{\text{WiFi}}(t)$. That is, reneging (if any) occurs among $Q(t) + A(t) - D_{\text{WiFi}}(t)$ number of packets in the WiFi queue. Even for the case $S(t) > 0$ (i.e., when the service is being carried out during time slot t), reneging could occur for the head-of-line packet in the WiFi queue when the transmission rate is not sufficiently fast to complete the service of the head-of-line packet, i.e., $S_{\text{WiFi}}(t) < L_1(t)$.

3.2 Performance Metrics

In this section, we provide formal definitions of the performance metrics in the delayed offloading system. The primary quantity of our interest is the offloading efficiency.

DEFINITION 1 (OFFLOADING EFFICIENCY ρ). *The offloading efficiency is defined as the probability that a packet in the WiFi queue is completely served by WiFi networks before being reneged to cellular networks.*

Note that the offloading efficiency defined here does not take the packet loss in WiFi networks into consideration, and is statistically the same with the amount of packets served by WiFi networks divided by the amount of packets inserted in the WiFi queue. The second quantity of our interest is the mean packet delay of the delayed offloading system.

DEFINITION 2 (MEAN PACKET DELAY $\overline{W}$). *The mean packet delay is defined as the average duration of time that a packet generated by a mobile device stays in the WiFi queue before it is served or reneged.*

The offloading efficiency ρ is determined by the probability for a packet being reneged P_{Renege} (called the reneging probability), by the relation $\rho = 1 - P_{\text{Renege}}$. When we set a larger T_{out}, then ρ increases and $\overline{W}$ also increases. Hence, the offloading efficiency and the mean packet delay are in a trade-off relationship whose control knob is T_{out}.

4. TECHNICAL CHALLENGES AND PROPOSED APPROACH

4.1 Technical Challenges

Our queueing system is characterized by three factors: (i) server vacation with non-exhaustive service, (ii) heavy-tailed vacation and non-vacation periods, and (iii) impatient customers with deterministic reneging times. Here, the server vacation system with non-exhaustive services refers to a queueing system in which the server stops service and can have a vacation even when there is a customer in the queue. These three factors cause significant technical challenges, as described below.

First, the heavy-tail distributions and the server vacation make the queueing system non-Markovian as well as non-work-conserving. Furthermore, from the viewpoint of Kendall's notation, the resultant service times also follow a heavy-tail distribution and are correlated across each packet. Hence, factors (i) and (ii) yield $G/G/1$

queue with correlated and heavy-tailed service time. The third factor requires us to track the waiting time of each packet in the queue. Moreover, due to reneging, the queue length is affected by the waiting time, while, in turn, the waiting time is affected by the queue length. Thus, both the queue length and the waiting time need to be jointly investigated. In conclusion, we need a mathematical technique that enables us to handle the joint queue length and waiting time simultaneously for non-Markovian queueing system having correlated and heavy-tailed service times.

There have been several queueing papers that consider reneging customers or server vacation exclusively. Regarding reneging (without server vacation), there have been studies on queues with deterministic impatience time D (See [24] and references therein). In [6] and [7], Barrer studied $M/M/1+D$ and $M/M/n+D$ queues and obtained the customer loss probability. In [24], Xiong *et al.* studied the $M/G/1+D$ queue using level crossing analysis, but analytical solution is given only for $M/H_2/1+D$ queue having two-stage hyper-exponential service times, and a numerical approach is presented for the more general $M/G/1+D$ queue. Recently, Kim *et al.* [13] studied $M/PH/1+D$ queue having phase-type distributed service times. Regarding the server vacation (without the reneging), there also have been extensive studies, e.g., [10,23]. In [10], Doshi provided a survey for queueing systems with vacations. In [23], Takagi worked on mathematical modeling and analysis for a broad class of server vacation systems. However, to the best of our knowledge, there was no analytic work on the queueing system that is addressed in this paper.

4.2 Proposed Approach

We take a three-step approach to obtain the offloading efficiency and the mean queueing delay.

Step 1 (Analysis at an embedded point). First, by noting that the sequence of on/off periods $\{(T_n^{\text{on}}, T_n^{\text{off}})\}_{n=1}^{\infty}$ is a renewal sequence, we observe the system only at a subset of time slots when the on-period begins. At such time instants, called embedded points, we define a state vector in such a way that it is capable of capturing queue length, waiting time of each packet, and residual inter-arrival time with a minimum number of states. The details are provided in Section 5.1.

Step 2 (Analysis at an arbitrary time). Next, we derive the limiting distribution at an arbitrary point in time using the result on the embedded process. The key idea of our derivation is motivated by the Renewal Reward Theorem [8,21] (which considers i.i.d. rewards across cycles). In our analysis, rewards are not necessarily i.i.d. across cycles, so we introduce a notion of conditional rewards to extract an i.i.d. subsequence of rewards. The details are provided in Section 5.2.

Step 3 (Derivation of performance metrics). Finally, from the limiting distribution at an arbitrary point in time, we can derive the analytic formulas for the offloading efficiency and the mean packet delay in the WiFi queue. The details are provided in Section 5.3.

Our contributions in the proposed analytical technique are as follows. We provide a mathematical approach to analyze a queueing system with deterministic reneging and heavy-tailed service interruption. In particular, our approach incorporates discrete-time Markov chain theory and a version of the Renewal Reward Theorem. In non-Markovian queueing systems, a judicious selection of embedded points makes the analysis tractable at times (often with Markov chain theory). In our case, in addition to the use of embedded points, we also strategically define a set of state variables in order to build up a foundation to the next step analysis using renewal reward type of arguments. Also, we develop an extended version of the Renewal Reward Theorem that is applicable even when the reward is not *i.i.d.* but correlated across cycles. Our framework explicitly derives the offloading efficiency by solving a system of matrix equations obtained from Markov chain theory. While beyond the scope of the current paper, our exact analysis could also be used to derive simple analytical approximations that might be tight in certain asymptotic regimes.

5. ANALYTICAL FRAMEWORK

5.1 Analysis at an Embedded Point

We observe the system only at the time instants when the mobile device that has been out of the WiFi coverage is switched to be connected to any WiFi network. We take such a time instant as our embedded point. That is, the nth ($n=1,2,\dots$) embedded point corresponds to the beginning of the nth on-period. Let t_n denote the time at which the nth embedded point is located. Refer to Fig. 2 for a depiction of the embedded point. We assume that initially the mobile device is connected to a WiFi network, i.e., $C(1)=1$. Then, from Fig. 2, we have

$$t_n = \begin{cases} 1 & n=1, \\ t_{n-1} + T_{n-1}^{\text{on}} + T_{n-1}^{\text{off}} & n \geq 2. \end{cases}$$

At each embedded point (i.e., at time t_n), we observe the following four state variables: (i) Let $Q_n := Q(t_n)$ be the number of packets in the WiFi queue at time t_n. (ii) Let $W_n := W(t_n)$, where $W(t)$ for $t=1,2,\dots$ is the waiting time of the head-of-line packet in the WiFi queue at time t. If $Q_n=0$, then $W_n=0$ holds. Under the FIFO policy, W_n represents the age of the oldest packet among the packets present in the WiFi queue at time t_n. (iii) Let $U_n := U(t_n)$, where $U(t)$ for $t=1,2,\dots$ is the size of the head-of-line packet in the WiFi queue at time t. If $Q_n=0$, then $U_n=0$ holds. Thus, U_n represents the amount of unfinished work on the oldest packet at time t_n. (iv) Let $E_n := E(t_n)$, where $E(t)$ for $t=1,2,\dots$ is the elapsed time from the moment when the last packet in the WiFi queue arrives to time t. When $Q_n=1$, we have $E_n=W_n$. Finally, we let $\mathcal{S}$ be the set of states which can be expressed by the tuple (Q_n, W_n, U_n, E_n). Using the tuple, we define a state vector at the nth embedded point as follows:[3]

$$\boldsymbol{X}_n := (Q_n, W_n, U_n, E_n).$$

We call the process $\{\boldsymbol{X}_n\}_{n=1}^{\infty}$ the *embedded process*. Note that the embedded process can be viewed as a sampling of the process $\{\boldsymbol{X}(t)\}_{t=1}^{\infty} := \{(Q(t), W(t), U(t), E(t))\}_{t=1}^{\infty}$ at every $t=t_n$, giving the relation $\{\boldsymbol{X}(t_n)\}_{n=1}^{\infty} = \{\boldsymbol{X}_n\}_{n=1}^{\infty}$. Our sampling of embedded points results in a nice analytical property, as shown in Lemma 1.

LEMMA 1. *The embedded process $\{\boldsymbol{X}_n\}_{n=1}^{\infty}$ is a discrete-time Markov chain with state space $\mathcal{S}$.*

PROOF. Due to space limitation, we provide an outline of the proof, and the detailed proof is given in Appendix B in our technical report [14]. For ease of understanding, we suppose that $Q_n \geq 1$. Then, W_n and E_n represent the ages of the oldest packet and the youngest packet, respectively, among the Q_n packets in the WiFi queue. Hence, given the pair (W_n, E_n), we can infer the age of each packet in the WiFi queue from the inter-arrival time distribution $\mathrm{P}(A \leq x)$. In addition to the age distribution, we also need information on the size of each packet in the WiFi queue. Since only the head-of-line packet has a different packet-size distribution from

[3] Throughout this paper, we use a bold font for a vector notation.

the other packets (since it may be partially served), we observe the information via U_n. Finally, in order to predict the possibility of packet generation at time t_n, we need the elapsed time E_n from the latest packet generation. Therefore, using the triple information on ages, packet sizes, and probability of packet generation at a given time n, we can analyze how $\boldsymbol{X}_{\hat{n}}$ will behave in the future for $\hat{n} > n$, i.e., the process $\{\boldsymbol{X}_n\}_{n=1}^{\infty}$ becomes a Markov chain. □

If the packet size follows a geometric distribution, then U_n also follows the geometric distribution due to the memoryless nature. Hence, if we set the state vector as

$$\boldsymbol{X}'_n := (Q_n, W_n, E_n),$$

then $\{\boldsymbol{X}'_n\}_{n=1}^{\infty}$ is a discrete-time Markov chain. Furthermore, if the arrival process is Bernoulli, then by the memoryless nature again, we can further shorten the state vector as

$$\boldsymbol{X}''_n := (Q_n, W_n).$$

Then, $\{\boldsymbol{X}''_n\}_{n=1}^{\infty}$ is a discrete-time Markov chain.

In the following, we derive the transition probability matrix of the Markov chain $\{\boldsymbol{X}_n\}_{n=1}^{\infty}$. Let the ith and the jth elements of state space $\mathcal{S}$ be denoted by $\boldsymbol{i}$ and $\boldsymbol{j}$, respectively. We define

$$\begin{aligned} P_{\boldsymbol{i},\boldsymbol{j}}^{\text{on}} &:= \mathrm{P}(\boldsymbol{X}(t+1) = \boldsymbol{j} \mid \boldsymbol{X}(t) = \boldsymbol{i}, C(t) = 1), \\ P_{\boldsymbol{i},\boldsymbol{j}}^{\text{off}} &:= \mathrm{P}(\boldsymbol{X}(t+1) = \boldsymbol{j} \mid \boldsymbol{X}(t) = \boldsymbol{i}, C(t) = 0). \end{aligned} \tag{2}$$

Note that the probabilities $P_{\boldsymbol{i},\boldsymbol{j}}^{\text{on}}$ and $P_{\boldsymbol{i},\boldsymbol{j}}^{\text{off}}$ are concerned with transition across adjacent slots: $P_{\boldsymbol{i},\boldsymbol{j}}^{\text{on}}$ is the probability of being in state $\boldsymbol{j}$ at the beginning of time slot $(t+1)$, provided that the system is in state $\boldsymbol{i}$ at the beginning of time slot t and a WiFi network is available during time slot t. A similar interpretation applies to the probability $P_{\boldsymbol{i},\boldsymbol{j}}^{\text{off}}$. The formulas for $P_{\boldsymbol{i},\boldsymbol{j}}^{\text{on}}$ and $P_{\boldsymbol{i},\boldsymbol{j}}^{\text{off}}$ are given in Appendix. We define

$$\hat{P}_{\boldsymbol{i},\boldsymbol{j}} := \mathrm{P}(\boldsymbol{X}_{n+1} = \boldsymbol{j} \mid \boldsymbol{X}_n = \boldsymbol{i}).$$

Note that now $\hat{P}_{\boldsymbol{i},\boldsymbol{j}}$ is concerned with transition across adjacent embedded points. Let $M := [\hat{P}_{\boldsymbol{i},\boldsymbol{j}}]$ denote the one-step transition probability matrix of the Markov chain $\{\boldsymbol{X}_n\}_{n=1}^{\infty}$. Since $\hat{P}_{\boldsymbol{i},\boldsymbol{j}}$ is rewritten as $\hat{P}_{\boldsymbol{i},\boldsymbol{j}} = \mathrm{P}(\boldsymbol{X}(t_{n+1}) = \boldsymbol{j} \mid \boldsymbol{X}(t_n) = \boldsymbol{i})$, by incorporating the duration between the points t_n and t_{n+1}, we can compute the matrix $M = [\hat{P}_{\boldsymbol{i},\boldsymbol{j}}]$ from the probabilities $P_{\boldsymbol{i},\boldsymbol{j}}^{\text{on}}$ and $P_{\boldsymbol{i},\boldsymbol{j}}^{\text{off}}$, as shown below in Lemma 2.

LEMMA 2. *Let $M_{on} := [P_{\boldsymbol{i},\boldsymbol{j}}^{on}]$ and $M_{off} := [P_{\boldsymbol{i},\boldsymbol{j}}^{off}]$. Then, the transition probability matrix $M = [\hat{P}_{\boldsymbol{i},\boldsymbol{j}}]$ is obtained by*

$$M = \sum_{a \geq 1, b \geq 1} (M_{on})^a (M_{off})^b \, P(T_{on} = a, T_{off} = b).$$

PROOF. The key idea of our derivation relies on the Chapman-Kolmogorov's Theorem [16] that the k-step ($k = 1, 2, \ldots$) transition probability matrix of a discrete-time Markov chain is the kth power of the one-step transition probability matrix; and the k-step we consider corresponds to the length of the interval $[t_n, t_{n+1})$. Due to space limitation, we omit the details. For the detailed proof, please refer to Appendix D in our technical report [14]. □

From the transition probability matrix M, we can analyze the limiting behavior of the Markov chain $\{\boldsymbol{X}_n\}_{n=1}^{\infty}$ as follows. For each $\boldsymbol{i} \in \mathcal{S}$, we define

$$\pi_{\boldsymbol{i}} := \lim_{n \to \infty} \mathrm{P}(\boldsymbol{X}_n = \boldsymbol{i}) = \mathrm{P}(\boldsymbol{X}_\infty = \boldsymbol{i}),$$

which denotes the probability of the system being in state $\boldsymbol{i}$ at an arbitrary embedded point. Let $\boldsymbol{\pi} := (\pi_{\boldsymbol{i}})$ denote the limiting distribution vector. If the Markov chain $\{\boldsymbol{X}_n\}_{n=1}^{\infty}$ is ergodic, then the limiting distribution $\boldsymbol{\pi}$ exists and is obtained by solving the following system of matrix equations:

$$\boldsymbol{\pi} M = \boldsymbol{\pi}, \quad \boldsymbol{\pi} \boldsymbol{e} = 1,$$

where $\boldsymbol{e}$ is a vector of ones. A sufficient condition for ergodicity is existence of a constant $A_{\max}$ such that $\mathrm{P}(A \leq A_{\max}) = 1$. Under this condition, the elapsed time $E(\cdot)$ is bounded by $A_{\max}$, and thus the space $\mathcal{S}$ becomes finite. Since an irreducible Markov chain with finite state space is positive recurrent [16], we can show ergodicity. The condition $\mathrm{P}(A \leq A_{\max}) = 1$ is reasonable in the delayed mobile data offloading system since it is targeted for users who actively generate data.

5.2 Analysis at an Arbitrary Time

In the previous section, we have analyzed the distribution of the random vector $\boldsymbol{X}(t_n)$ at an arbitrary embedded point t_n as $n \to \infty$, i.e., $\boldsymbol{X}_\infty = \boldsymbol{X}(t_\infty)$. In this section, we analyze the distribution of $\boldsymbol{X}(t)$ at an arbitrary time t as $t \to \infty$, i.e., $\boldsymbol{X}(\infty)$. To this end, we derive formulas for the following probabilities for $\boldsymbol{i} \in \mathcal{S}$:

$$\begin{aligned} \xi_{\boldsymbol{i}}^{\text{on}} &:= \lim_{t \to \infty} \mathrm{P}(\boldsymbol{X}(t) = \boldsymbol{i}, C(t) = 1), \\ \xi_{\boldsymbol{i}}^{\text{off}} &:= \lim_{t \to \infty} \mathrm{P}(\boldsymbol{X}(t) = \boldsymbol{i}, C(t) = 0). \end{aligned} \tag{3}$$

Then, the limiting probability $\xi_{\boldsymbol{i}} := \lim_{t \to \infty} \mathrm{P}(\boldsymbol{X}(t) = \boldsymbol{i})$ is obtained by $\xi_{\boldsymbol{i}} = \xi_{\boldsymbol{i}}^{\text{on}} + \xi_{\boldsymbol{i}}^{\text{off}}$.

The key idea of our derivation is motivated by the Renewal Reward Theorem [8], which states the following: consider a renewal process $\{N(t)\}_{t \geq 0}$ having cycle lengths $\{C_k\}_{k=1}^{\infty}$. Suppose that a reward R_k is earned during the kth cycle, and assume that the pair (C_k, R_k) is i.i.d. across k (with a generic random vector (C, R)). If we let $R(t) = R_1 + \ldots + R_{N(t)}$ denote the total reward earned by time t, then with probability 1, we obtain

$$\frac{R(t)}{t} \to \frac{\mathrm{E}[R]}{\mathrm{E}[C]} \quad \text{as} \quad t \to \infty, \tag{4}$$

provided that $\mathrm{E}[R] < \infty$ and $\mathrm{E}[C] < \infty$. The theorem says that the long-term average reward is just the expected reward earned during a cycle, divided by the expected time of a cycle.

In our queueing model, the sequence $\{(T_n^{\text{on}}, T_n^{\text{off}})\}_{n=1}^{\infty}$ is an alternating renewal sequence. Hence, we can view the joint nth on/off-periods as the nth cycle having length $T_n^{\text{on}} + T_n^{\text{off}}$. To compute the distribution $\xi_{\boldsymbol{i}}^{\text{on}}$, we count the total number of slots with state $(\boldsymbol{X}(t), C(t)) = (\boldsymbol{i}, 1)$ during the nth cycle and set the result as our reward $R_{n,\boldsymbol{i}}^{\text{on}}$. Then, the long-term average reward becomes the time average probability of being in state $(\boldsymbol{X}(t), C(t)) = (\boldsymbol{i}, 1)$, which is equal to the ensemble average probability under ergodicity condition. *Note that $R_{n,\boldsymbol{i}}^{on}$ in this setting is not necessarily independent, but identically distributed across n for a fixed $\boldsymbol{i} \in \mathcal{S}$.* Therefore, we cannot apply the formula (4) directly so we take a detour to analyze the long-term behavior. To our surprise, we reach the same conclusion that the long-term average reward is just the expected reward earned during a cycle, divided by the expected time of a cycle, as shown in Lemma 3.

LEMMA 3. *Suppose that the embedded process $\{\boldsymbol{X}_n\}_{n=1}^{\infty}$ is ergodic. Then, the limiting distributions $\xi_{\boldsymbol{i}}^{on}$ and $\xi_{\boldsymbol{i}}^{off}$ defined in (3) exist and are obtained by*

$$\xi_{\boldsymbol{i}}^{on} = \frac{\sum_{\boldsymbol{j} \in \mathcal{S}} \pi_{\boldsymbol{j}} \mu_{\boldsymbol{j},\boldsymbol{i}}^{on}}{E[T_{on} + T_{off}]}, \quad \xi_{\boldsymbol{i}}^{off} = \frac{\sum_{\boldsymbol{j} \in \mathcal{S}} \pi_{\boldsymbol{j}} \mu_{\boldsymbol{j},\boldsymbol{i}}^{off}}{E[T_{on} + T_{off}]}, \tag{5}$$

where

$$\mu^{on}_{\boldsymbol{j},\boldsymbol{i}} := E\Big[\sum_{s=t_n}^{t_{n+1}-1} 1_{\{\boldsymbol{X}(s)=\boldsymbol{i},C(s)=1\}} \Big| \boldsymbol{X}_n = \boldsymbol{j}\Big],$$

$$\mu^{off}_{\boldsymbol{j},\boldsymbol{i}} := E\Big[\sum_{s=t_n}^{t_{n+1}-1} 1_{\{\boldsymbol{X}(s)=\boldsymbol{i},C(s)=0\}} \Big| \boldsymbol{X}_n = \boldsymbol{j}\Big],$$

and where $1_{\{\cdot\}}$ *denotes the indicator function.*

PROOF. The proof consists of two parts. In the first part, we analyze the time average probability that the system stays in state $\boldsymbol{i}$ ($\boldsymbol{i} \in \mathcal{S}$) with WiFi being available. We define

$$R^{\text{on}}_{\boldsymbol{i}}(t) := \sum_{s=1}^{t} 1_{\{\boldsymbol{X}(s)=\boldsymbol{i},C(s)=1\}},$$

which denotes the total amount of rewards earned by time t. Then, the time average $\frac{1}{t}R^{\text{on}}_{\boldsymbol{i}}(t)$ converges with probability 1 as follows:

$$\frac{R^{\text{on}}_{\boldsymbol{i}}(t)}{t} \to \frac{1}{\text{E}[T_{\text{on}}+T_{\text{off}}]}\sum_{\boldsymbol{j}\in\mathcal{S}} \pi_{\boldsymbol{j}}\mu^{\text{on}}_{\boldsymbol{j},\boldsymbol{i}} \quad \text{as} \quad t\to\infty. \tag{6}$$

In the second part, we show that the time average probability on the right-hand side of (6) is equal to the ensemble average probability due to the ergodicity of the process $\{\boldsymbol{X}_n\}_{n=1}^{\infty}$. Hence, we obtain

$$\lim_{t\to\infty} \text{P}(\boldsymbol{X}(t) = \boldsymbol{i}, C(t) = 1) = \frac{1}{\text{E}[T_{\text{on}}+T_{\text{off}}]}\sum_{\boldsymbol{j}\in\mathcal{S}} \pi_{\boldsymbol{j}}\mu^{\text{on}}_{\boldsymbol{j},\boldsymbol{i}}.$$

For details, refer to Appendix E in [14]. □

Note that in Lemma 3, $\mu^{\text{on}}_{\boldsymbol{j},\boldsymbol{i}}$ and $\mu^{\text{off}}_{\boldsymbol{j},\boldsymbol{i}}$ represent the expected reward earned during a cycle, conditioned that the cycle starts from state $\boldsymbol{j}$. We call $\mu^{\text{on}}_{\boldsymbol{j},\boldsymbol{i}}$ and $\mu^{\text{off}}_{\boldsymbol{j},\boldsymbol{i}}$ the *conditional rewards*. Since $\pi_{\boldsymbol{j}}$ represents the probability that a cycle starts from state $\boldsymbol{j}$, the numerator in (5) results in the expected reward earned during a cycle. The denominator in (5) represents the expected time of a cycle.

The formulas for $\mu^{\text{on}}_{\boldsymbol{j},\boldsymbol{i}}$ and $\mu^{\text{off}}_{\boldsymbol{j},\boldsymbol{i}}$ remain to be derived. For a matrix M, let $[M]_{j,i}$ denote the (j,i)th element of M. Then, the conditional rewards can be obtained from the matrices $M_{\text{on}} = [P^{\text{on}}_{\boldsymbol{i},\boldsymbol{j}}]$ and $M_{\text{off}} = [P^{\text{off}}_{\boldsymbol{i},\boldsymbol{j}}]$ as follows:

$$\mu^{\text{on}}_{\boldsymbol{j},\boldsymbol{i}} = \text{E}\Big[\sum_{k=1}^{T_{\text{on}}} [(M_{\text{on}})^{k-1}]_{j,i}\Big],$$
$$\mu^{\text{off}}_{\boldsymbol{j},\boldsymbol{i}} = \text{E}\Big[\sum_{k=1}^{T_{\text{off}}} [(M_{\text{on}})^{T_{\text{on}}}(M_{\text{off}})^{k-1}]_{j,i}\Big]. \tag{7}$$

The proof of (7) is given in Appendix F in our technical report [14]. Combining (7) and Lemma 3 in a matrix form yields the following:

$$\boldsymbol{\xi}_{\text{on}} := (\xi^{\text{on}}_{\boldsymbol{i}}) = \frac{\boldsymbol{\pi}\text{E}\big[\sum_{k=1}^{T_{\text{on}}}(M_{\text{on}})^{k-1}\big]}{\text{E}[T_{\text{on}}+T_{\text{off}}]},$$

$$\boldsymbol{\xi}_{\text{off}} := (\xi^{\text{off}}_{\boldsymbol{i}}) = \frac{\boldsymbol{\pi}\text{E}\big[(M_{\text{on}})^{T_{\text{on}}}\sum_{k=1}^{T_{\text{off}}}(M_{\text{off}})^{k-1}\big]}{\text{E}[T_{\text{on}}+T_{\text{off}}]},$$

from which we finally obtain the limiting distribution of the process $\{\boldsymbol{X}(t)\}_{t=1}^{\infty}$ as

$$\boldsymbol{\xi} := \big(\text{P}(\boldsymbol{X}(\infty) = \boldsymbol{i})\big) = \boldsymbol{\xi}_{\text{on}} + \boldsymbol{\xi}_{\text{off}}. \tag{8}$$

5.3 Offloading Efficiency and Mean Packet Delay

By using the limiting distribution $\boldsymbol{\xi} = (\xi_{(q,w,u,e)})$ in (8), we can derive the formulas for our performance metrics ρ and $\overline{W}$. We begin by providing the formula for ρ.

THEOREM 1. *The offloading efficiency* ρ *under the delayed mobile data offloading system is obtained by*

$$\rho = 1 - \lambda^{-1}\sum_{q\geq1,u\geq1,e\geq1}\big(\xi^{off}_{(q,T_{out},u,e)} + \xi^{on}_{(q,T_{out},u,e)}P(R<u)\big).$$

PROOF. Here, once again, we provide an outline of the proof due to space limitation. For a given time t, a packet reneges (if any) due to one of the following two reasons: (i) Suppose that there is a packet in the WiFi queue at time t, and that the mobile device is not connected to any WiFi network, i.e., $Q(t) \geq 1$ and $C(t) = 0$. In this case, a reneging event occurs for the head-of-line packet in the WiFi queue if its age becomes T_{out}, i.e., $W(t) = T_{\text{out}}$. (ii) Now suppose that there is a packet in the WiFi queue at time t, and that the mobile device is connected to a WiFi network, i.e., $Q(t) \geq 1$ and $C(t) = 1$. In this case, a reneging event occurs for the head-of-line packet in the WiFi queue if its age is T_{out} and the service rate of the WiFi network is less than the size of the packet, i.e., $W(t) = T_{\text{out}}$ and $S(t) = S_{\text{WiFi}}(t) < U(t)$.

Since the above two cases are exclusive, summing up the reneging probabilities occurred by reasons (i) and (ii) leads to P_{Renege}. Two reasons correspond to the first and the second term in Theorem 1, respectively. Please refer to Appendix G in our technical report [14] for the detailed proof. □

Now we provide the formula for $\overline{W}$.

THEOREM 2. *The mean packet delay* $\overline{W}$ *under the delayed mobile data offloading system is obtained by*

$$\overline{W} = \lambda^{-1}\sum_{q\geq1,w\geq1,u\geq1,e\geq1} q\cdot\xi_{(q,w,u,e)}.$$

PROOF. The average number of packets in the WiFi queue, denoted by $\overline{Q}$, is obtained as

$$\overline{Q} = \sum_{q=1}^{\infty} q\text{P}(Q(\infty) = q) = \sum_{q\geq1,w\geq1,u\geq1,e\geq1} q\cdot\xi_{(q,w,u,e)}.$$

Hence, by applying Little's Law [21], we have $\overline{W} = \lambda^{-1}\overline{Q}$. □

6. NUMERICAL STUDY

In this section, we verify the correctness and accuracy of our analytical framework by performing extensive numerical studies, which also provide us some useful insights. For the verification, we develop an event-driven simulator that mimics the behavior of the delayed offloading system shown in Fig. 1.

6.1 System Setup and Parameters

Our analytical framework and simulator are capable of taking generalized input parameters. In the huge space of combinations of such system parameters, we focus on practical values observed in [1, 17] and candidate values expected for near future as shown below.

User Traffic. Based on [1], we assume that a mobile device will roughly generate 7 GB of data per month in the near future, whose inter-arrival process follows a truncated Pareto distribution with 3 minutes and 6 hours for its lower and upper truncation. When multimedia recording and viewing are frequently performed in a device, 7 GB/month is a reasonable number given that the full HD video is recorded and played at up to 30 Mbps. To capture wider range of user behaviors including behaviors of near future, we also consider 3.5 GB/month and 14 GB/month of data generation. Since it is unclear how much portion of the total data volume is subject to realtime demand in the near future, we assumed that the entire traffic is delay tolerant. Extension of our framework that can accommodate various deadlines for different traffic types including zero delay tolerance is left as future work.

WiFi Data Rate. From the measurement study on WiFi data rates in [17] showing that 1.2 Mbps on average is empirically achievable, we set the capacity of WiFi networks as either of 0.1 Mbps, 1 Mbps, 2 Mbps, 10 Mbps, and 50 Mbps. Given three factors: (i) the average data rate of WiFi networks in a region may highly vary (e.g., by the factor of development of a city), (ii) there exist high-speed WiFi standards in the market (such as 802.11ac providing up to 600 Mbps as its nominal speed), and (iii) WiFi APs are mostly located in crowded areas, considering up to 50 Mbps for individual WiFi data rate is rational (even when considering near future).

WiFi Deployment. The availability of WiFi networks in a city can be captured by the distributions of disconnected periods (i.e., inter-connection time) and connected periods (i.e., connection time) to any WiFi AP. In the measurement study of [17], the average inter-connection and connection times are shown to be (25, 50) minutes respectively in Seoul, Korea. Based on this status quo of WiFi deployment, we vary the inter-connection time and the connection time to have (15, 45) minutes and (4, 12) minutes on average for modeling possible WiFi environments in the near future (with more WiFi APs). We assume that both the connection time and the inter-connection time conform to a truncated Pareto distribution.

Deadline. We vary the deadline for offloading from 3 minutes to 1 hour and observe the impact of the system parameters on major performance metrics.

6.2 Numerical Analysis vs. Simulation

We validate our analytical framework by comparing its results for various parameter settings with those from short-term and long-term simulations. Figs. 3 (a) and (b) show the offloading efficiency and the queueing delay for various deadlines with 1 Mbps of WiFi data rate, 7 GB/month of input traffic, 25 minutes of inter-connection time, and 50 minutes of connection time. As expected, our framework provides almost the same results with those from long-term simulation and the average of a number of short-term simulations. Given that long-term simulations require much longer simulation time as well as more memory for their computations, our framework has its unique value. Note that the offloading efficiency from our framework for the deadline of 1 hour coincides with the result shown in [17] for the same parameter setting.

6.3 Offloading Scenarios and Lessons

Using our framework, we analyze diverse offloading scenarios that reflect the current network situation and possible near future environments through combinations of average inter-connection and connections times of (25, 50), (15, 45), and (4, 12) minutes. (25, 50) setting is considered as *current deployment* of WiFi networks while (15, 45) setting is chosen as a *wider deployment* of WiFi networks with substantially reduced amount of inter-connection time and slightly decreased amount of connection time. (4,12) setting is selected to model a completely different type of WiFi deployment in which WiFi APs are imagined to be installed in the middle of paths of movement such as on traffic lights or street lights that will result in much shorter inter-connection and connection time. We call it *prevalent deployment*. Note that (4,12) and (15,45) settings have the same connection ratio. We compare the wider deployment and the prevalent deployment over the current deployment to obtain guidance on how to upgrade WiFi networks in terms of achieved offloading efficiency, and the discussion on the mean packet delay is omitted due to space limitation.

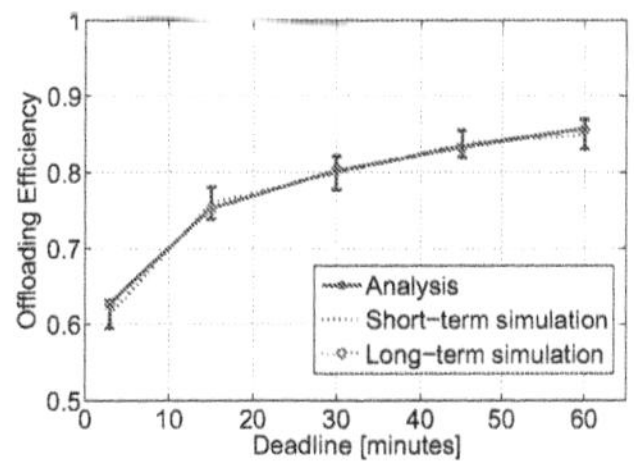

(a) Offloading efficiency

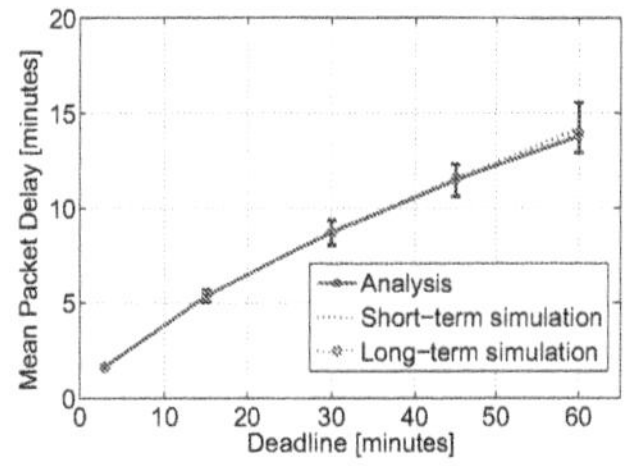

(b) Mean packet delay

Figure 3: The results from our framework compared with those from short-term and long-term simulations under data rate of 1 Mbps and input traffic of 7 GB/month. Short-term simulations are performed 20 times and their 95% confidence intervals are depicted.

For a comprehensive comparison, we vary the average data rate of WiFi networks, total amount of generated data per month per user, and deadline for offloading. Figs. 4 (a), (b), and (c) show the offloading efficiency from the current deployment of WiFi network for input traffic of 3.5 GB/month, 7 GB/month, and 14 GB/month, respectively, for various deadlines. Fig. 4 (a) shows that the offloading efficiency varies from 0.3 to 0.87 according to the deadline. It is very interesting to see that the average data rate of WiFi networks has almost no effect to the offloading efficiency when the data rate is beyond 1 Mbps. It is mainly because the arriving traffic does not come in large enough chunks to exploit data rates of greater than 1Mbps. This observation implies that upgrading WiFi APs for a newer standard provides diminishing returns from the point of view of the offloading efficiency. Figs. 4 (b) and (c) reconfirm that the effect of increased data rate is negligible. Figs. 4 (a), (b) and (c) commonly show that the offloading efficiency with the deadline of 1 hour is bounded by 87% under the current deployment.

The results from the wider deployment depicted in Figs. 5 (a), (b), and (c) show that the offloading efficiency can be significantly improved by altering the deployment. For instance, with a deadline of 30 minutes, the wider deployment achieves about 89% of offloading efficiency which is nearly 10% higher than that of the current deployment. To our surprise, 89% is the level of offloading efficiency that was not achievable even with 60 minutes of deadline and higher data rate up to 50 Mbps. This implies that installing more WiFi APs, resulting in reducing the average inter-connection time gives far greater gains in offloading efficiency, as compared to increasing the data rate carried on the existing WiFi APs. Even in the wider deployment, data rates beyond 1 Mbps result only in a small improvement, except for the case of extremely short deadlines (e.g., 3 minute).

To purse higher offloading efficiency, we further test the prevalent deployment which may necessitate a larger number of WiFi APs than in the wider deployment. However, note that the installation cost of the prevalent deployment can be similar to that of the

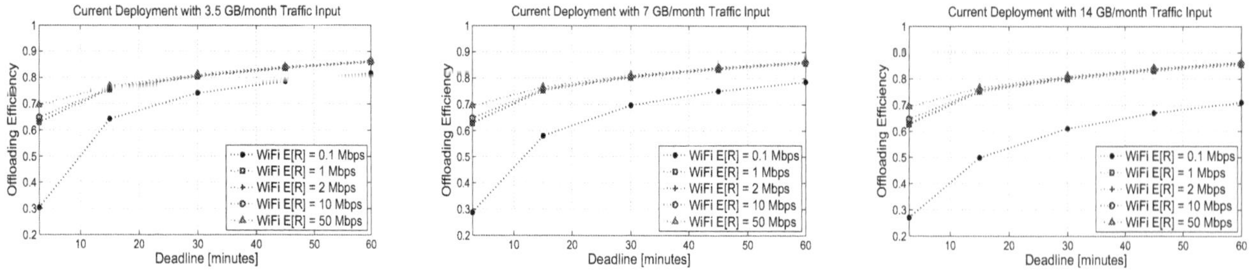

(a) 3.5 GB/month (b) 7 GB/month (c) 14 GB/month

Figure 4: Offloading efficiency obtained from the current deployment setting for various data rates and deadlines.

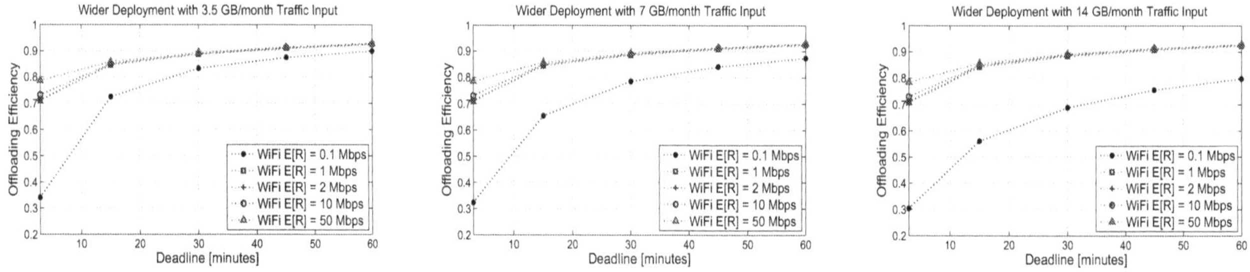

(a) 3.5 GB/month (b) 7 GB/month (c) 14 GB/month

Figure 5: Offloading efficiency obtained from the wider deployment setting for various data rates and deadlines.

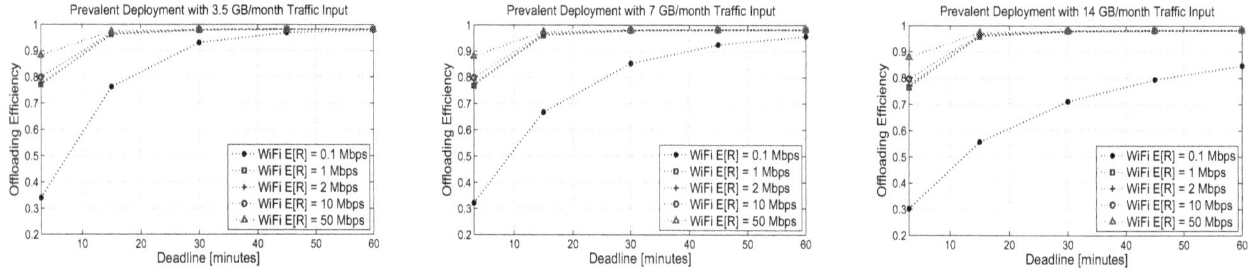

(a) 3.5GB/month (b) 7 GB/month (c) 14 GB/month

Figure 6: Offloading efficiency obtained from the prevalent deployment setting for various data rates and deadlines.

wider deployment if we manage installation only with low-grade WiFi APs of slower data rate and low-speed wireless backhaul that substantially cuts construction cost. With the wireless backhaul, it is possible to deploy a number of WiFi APs at traffic lights or street lights on frequently visited roads at a manageable cost. Figs. 6 (a), (b), and (c) show impressive offloading performance as high as 98% even with 1 Mbps at 30 minutes of deadline. This extreme efficiency is not achievable in the current deployment and in the wider deployment no matter how fast the WiFi data rate is. Fig. 7 emphasizes the benefit of the prevalent deployment by directly comparing the offloading efficiency to other deployments under 15 minutes of deadline with various WiFi data rates. The prevalent deployment strategy dominates the wider deployment strategy for the whole range of WiFi data rates. Also, the offloading efficiency of the prevalent deployment with 0.3 Mbps already exceeds that of the wider deployment with 50 Mbps (or even higher).

The overall observations made from our framework imply that changing the paradigm of choosing installation locations of WiFi APs is worth considering. For instance, additional installation of WiFi APs can be recommended in the new locations that break down long inter-connection times into shorter ones such as road sides rather than in the conventional crowded areas such as department stores.

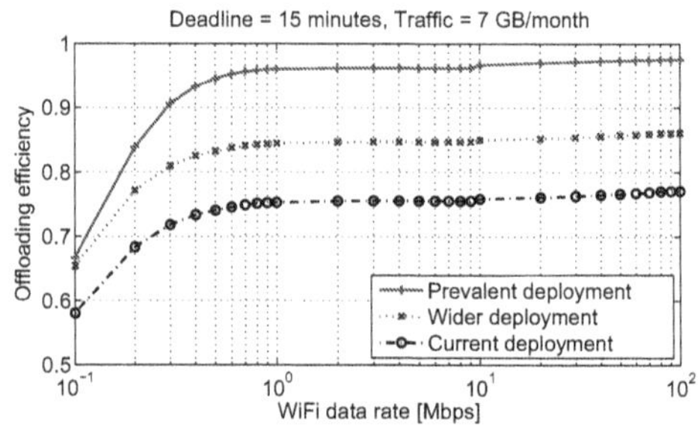

Figure 7: Offloading efficiency from three different deployment settings for the same deadline of 15 minutes and input traffic of 7 GB/month.

7. CONCLUDING REMARKS

In this paper, we provide an analytical framework that closely captures the realistic behavior of the delayed mobile data offloading system which can offload mobile traffic from cellular networks to WiFi networks (or similarly to femto/picocell networks). The analysis of the offloading system involves technical challenges due to its non-Markovian characteristics mainly resulting from the alternating heavy-tailed service and interruption periods as well as the deterministic reneging behavior. We address the challenges by uniquely designating the service activation events as embedded points, which transforms the system to a Markovian one. Using the redefined embedded process, we rigorously develop closed-form equations for the performance metrics of interest in the delayed offloading system, including offloading efficiency and mean packet delay. We expect that our analytical framework and the closed-form equations shown to almost perfectly predict the behaviors of the system, would significantly advance understandings on the offloading system and its variants. We also anticipate that the reverse engineering of the analytical framework would lead to optimization on the system as well as its control.

8. ACKNOWLEDGMENTS

This work was supported in part by the 2014 Research Fund of University of Ulsan and the Future Strategic Fund(1.14003.01) of UNIST (Ulsan National Institute of Science and Technology), and by Army Research Grant W911NF-12-1-0385 and National Science Foundation CNS-1012700.

9. REFERENCES

[1] Cisco visual networking index: Global mobile data traffic forecast update, 2012-2017, March 2013. http://www.cisco.com/en/US/solutions/collateral/ns341/ns525/ns537/ns705/ns827/white_paper_c11-481360_ns827_Networking_Solutions_White_Paper.html.

[2] A. Aijaz, H. Aghvami, and M. Amani. A survey on mobile data offloading: technical and business perspectives. *IEEE Wireless Communications*, 20(2):104–112, 2013.

[3] A. Balasubramanian, R. Mahajan, and A. Venkataramani. Augmenting mobile 3G using WiFi. In *Proceedings of ACM MobiSys*, 2010.

[4] X. Bao, Y. Lin, U. Lee, I. Rimac, and R. Choudhury. Dataspotting: Exploiting naturally clustered mobile devices to offload cellular traffic. In *INFOCOM, 2013 Proceedings IEEE*, pages 420–424, April 2013.

[5] M. Barbera, J. Stefa, A. Viana, M. Dias de Amorim, and M. Boc. Vip delegation: Enabling vips to offload data in wireless social mobile networks. In *Proceedings of International Conference on Distributed Computing in Sensor Systems (DCOSS)*, 2011.

[6] D. Y. Barrer. Queuing with impatient customers and indifferent clerks. *Operations Research*, 5(5):644–649, 1957.

[7] D. Y. Barrer. Queuing with impatient customers and ordered service. *Operations Research*, 5(5):650–656, 1957.

[8] P. Bremaud. *Markov Chains*. Springer, 2008.

[9] A. Detti, M. Pomposini, N. Blefari-Melazzi, S. Salsano, and A. Bragagnini. Offloading cellular networks with information-centric networking: The case of video streaming. In *Proceedings of IEEE WoWMoM*, 2012.

[10] B. Doshi. Queueing systems with vacations: A survey. *Queueing systems*, 1(1):29–66, 1986.

[11] Y. Go, Y. Moon, G. Nam, and K. Park. A disruption-tolerant transmission protocol for practical mobile data offloading. In *Proceedings of ACM MobiOpp*, 2012.

[12] T. Han, N. Ansari, M. Wu, and H. Yu. On accelerating content delivery in mobile networks. *Communications Surveys Tutorials, IEEE*, 15(3):1314–1333, Third 2013.

[13] J. Kim and J. Kim. M/PH/1 queue with deterministic impatience time. *Commun. Korean Math. Soc.*, 28(2):383–396, 2013.

[14] Y. Kim, K. Lee, and N. B. Shroff. An analytical framework to characterize the efficiency and delay in a mobile data offloading system. Technical report, January 2014. available at http://msn.unist.ac.kr/papers/MobiHoc_2014_KLS_TR.pdf.

[15] V. Kone, H. Zheng, A. Rowstron, G. O'Shea, and B. Zhao. Measurement-based design of roadside content delivery systems. *Mobile Computing, IEEE Transactions on*, 12(6):1160–1173, June 2013.

[16] V. G. Kulkarni. *Modeling and Analysis of Stochastic Systems*. Chapman & Hall, Ltd., London, UK, UK, 1995.

[17] K. Lee, J. Lee, I. Rhee, Y. Yi, and S. Chong. Mobile data offloading : How much can WiFi deliver? In *Proceedings of ACM CoNEXT*, 2010.

[18] Y. Li, G. Su, P. Hui, D. Jin, L. Su, and L. Zeng. Multiple mobile data offloading through delay tolerant networks. In *Proceedings of ACM Workshop on Challenged Networks (CHANTS)*, 2011.

[19] M. Meeker. Internet trends - morgan stanley, April 2010. http://www.businessinsider.com/mary-meeker-mobile-internet?op=1.

[20] W.-B. Pöttner, J. Morgenroth, S. Schildt, and L. Wolf. Performance comparison of dtn bundle protocol implementations. In *Proceedings of ACM Workshop on Challenged Networks (CHANTS)*, 2011.

[21] S. Ross. *Stochastic Processes*. John Wiley & Sons, New York, 1996.

[22] K. L. Scott and S. Burleigh. Bundle protocol specification, rfc 5050, November 2007. http://tools.ietf.org/html/rfc5050.

[23] H. Takagi. *Queueing Analysis: A Foundation of Performance Evaluation (Volume 1: Vacation and priority Systems)*. Amsterdam: North Holland, 1991.

[24] W. Xiong, D. Jagerman, and T. Altiok. M/G/1 queue with deterministic reneging times. *Perform. Eval.*, 65(3-4):308–316, 2008.

[25] X. Zhuo, W. Gao, G. Cao, and S. Hua. An incentive framework for cellular traffic offloading. *Mobile Computing, IEEE Transactions on*, 13(3):541–555, March 2014.

APPENDIX

In Tables 1 and 2, we summarize the formulas for the transition probabilities $P^{\text{off}}_{i,j}$ and $P^{\text{on}}_{i,j}$, respectively. In the table, we use the following notations. First, $f_X(x) := \mathrm{P}(X = x)$ denotes the probability mass function of a discrete random variable X. Remind that L and R are random variables that represent the packet sizes and the WiFi data rates, respectively. Next, the functions $g_1(\cdot,\cdot)$, $g_2(\cdot,\cdot,\cdot)$, and $g_3(\cdot,\cdot)$ are concerned with work load in the WiFi

Table 1: Probability of $\boldsymbol{X}(t+1) = \boldsymbol{j}$ conditioned that $\boldsymbol{X}(t) = \boldsymbol{i}$ and $C(t) = 0$

	Case I $q_1 = 0$ $\boldsymbol{i} = (0,0,0,e_1)$	Case II $q_1 = 1, w_1 < T_{\text{out}}$ $\boldsymbol{i} = (1,w_1,u_1,w_1)$	Case III $q_1 = 1, w_1 = T_{\text{out}}$ $\boldsymbol{i} = (1,T_{\text{out}},u_1,T_{\text{out}})$	Case IV $q_1 \geq 2, w_1 < T_{\text{out}}$ $\boldsymbol{i} = (q_1,w_1,u_1,e_1)$	Case V $q_1 \geq 2, w_1 = T_{\text{out}}$ $\boldsymbol{i} = (q_1,T_{\text{out}},u_1,e_1)$
$\boldsymbol{j} = (0,0,0,e_1+1)$	$1 - f_{\tilde{A}}(e_1)$	0	0	0	0
$\boldsymbol{j} = (1,1,u_2,1)$	$f_{\tilde{A}}(e_1)f_L(u_2)$	0	$f_{\tilde{A}}(T_{\text{out}})f_L(u_2)$	0	0
$\boldsymbol{j} = (0,0,0,T_{\text{out}}+1)$	0	0	$1 - f_{\tilde{A}}(T_{\text{out}})$	0	0
$\boldsymbol{j} = (1,w_1+1,u_1,w_1+1)$	0	$1 - f_{\tilde{A}}(w_1)$	0	0	0
$\boldsymbol{j} = (2,w_1+1,u_1,1)$	0	$f_{\tilde{A}}(w_1)$	0	0	0
$\boldsymbol{j} = (q_1,w_1+1,u_1,e_1+1)$	0	0	0	$1 - f_{\tilde{A}}(e_1)$	0
$\boldsymbol{j} = (q_1+1,w_1+1,u_1,1)$	0	0	0	$f_{\tilde{A}}(e_1)$	0
$\boldsymbol{j} = (q_1-1,w_2,u_2,e_1+1)$	0	0	0	0	$(1-f_{\tilde{A}}(e_1))$ $\cdot f_L(u_2)f_{V_2(\boldsymbol{i})}(w_2-1)$
$\boldsymbol{j} = (q_1,w_2,u_2,1)$	0	0	0	0	$f_{\tilde{A}}(e_1)f_L(u_2)$ $\cdot f_{V_2(\boldsymbol{i})}(w_2-1)$

Table 2: Probability of $\boldsymbol{X}(t+1) = \boldsymbol{j}$ conditioned that $\boldsymbol{X}(t) = \boldsymbol{i}$ and $C(t) = 1$

	Case I $q_1 = 0$ $\boldsymbol{i} = (0,0,0,e_1)$	Case II $q_1 = 1, w_1 < T_{\text{out}}$ $\boldsymbol{i} = (1,w_1,u_1,w_1)$	Case III $q_1 = 1, w_1 = T_{\text{out}}$ $\boldsymbol{i} = (1,T_{\text{out}},u_1,T_{\text{out}})$
$\boldsymbol{j} = (0,0,0,e_1+1)$	$1 - f_{\tilde{A}}(e_1)$	0	0
$\boldsymbol{j} = (1,1,u_2,1)$	$f_{\tilde{A}}(e_1)f_{L-R}(u_2)$	0	0
$\boldsymbol{j} = (0,0,0,1)$	$f_{\tilde{A}}(e_1)\mathrm{P}(L \leq R)$	0	0
$\boldsymbol{j} = (1,w_1+1,u_2,w_1+1)$	0	$(1 - f_{\tilde{A}}(w_1))f_R(u_1-u_2)$	0
$\boldsymbol{j} = (0,0,0,w_1+1)$	0	$(1 - f_{\tilde{A}}(w_1))\mathrm{P}(R \geq u_1)$	0
$\boldsymbol{j} = (2,w_1+1,u_2,1)$	0	$f_{\tilde{A}}(w_1)f_R(u_1-u_2)$	0
$\boldsymbol{j} = (1,1,u_2,1)$	0	$f_{\tilde{A}}(w_1)g_2(u_1,u_2,1)$	0
$\boldsymbol{j} = (0,0,0,1)$	0	$f_{\tilde{A}}(w_1)\mathrm{P}(R-L \geq u_1)$	0
$\boldsymbol{j} = (0,0,0,T_{\text{out}}+1)$	0	0	$1 - f_{\tilde{A}}(T_{\text{out}})$
$\boldsymbol{j} = (1,1,u_2,1)$	0	0	$f_{\tilde{A}}(T_{\text{out}})\mathrm{P}(R-L<u_1)$
$\boldsymbol{j} = (0,0,0,1)$	0	0	$f_{\tilde{A}}(T_{\text{out}})\mathrm{P}(R-L \geq u_1)$

	Case IV $q_1 \geq 2, w_1 < T_{\text{out}}$ $\boldsymbol{i} = (q_1,w_1,u_1,e_1)$	Case V $q_1 \geq 2, w_1 = T_{\text{out}}$ $\boldsymbol{i} = (q_1,T_{\text{out}},u_1,e_1)$
$\boldsymbol{j} = (q_1,w_1+1,u_2,e_1+1)$	$(1 - f_{\tilde{A}}(e_1))f_R(u_1-u_2)$	0
$\boldsymbol{j} = (q_2,w_2,u_2,e_1+1)$	$(1 - f_{\tilde{A}}(e_1))g_2(u_1,u_2,q_1-q_2)f_{V_{q_1-q_2+1}(\boldsymbol{i})}(w_2-1)$	0
$\boldsymbol{j} = (0,0,0,e_1+1)$	$(1 - f_{\tilde{A}}(e_1))g_3(q_1,u_1)$	0
$\boldsymbol{j} = (q_1+1,w_1+1,u_2,1)$	$f_{\tilde{A}}(e_1)f_R(u_1-u_2)$	0
$\boldsymbol{j} = (q_2,w_2,u_2,1)$	$f_{\tilde{A}}(e_1)g_2(u_1,u_2,q_1-q_2+1)f_{V_{q_1-q_2+2}(\boldsymbol{i})}(w_2-1)$	0
$\boldsymbol{j} = (1,1,u_2,1)$	$f_{\tilde{A}}(e_1)g_2(u_1,u_2,q_1)$	0
$\boldsymbol{j} = (0,0,0,1)$	$f_{\tilde{A}}(e_1)g_3(q_1+1,u_1)$	0
$\boldsymbol{j} = (q_1-1,w_2,u_2,e_1+1)$	0	$(1 - f_{\tilde{A}}(e_1))g_1(u_1,u_2)f_{V_2(\boldsymbol{i})}(w_2-1)$
$\boldsymbol{j} = (q_2,w_2,u_2,e_1+1)$	0	$(1 - f_{\tilde{A}}(e_1))g_2(u_1,u_2,q_1-q_2)f_{V_{q_1-q_2+1}(\boldsymbol{i})}(w_2-1)$
$\boldsymbol{j} = (0,0,0,e_1+1)$	0	$(1 - f_{\tilde{A}}(e_1))g_3(q_1,u_1)$
$\boldsymbol{j} = (q_1,w_2,u_2,1)$	0	$f_{\tilde{A}}(e_1)g_1(u_1,u_2)f_{V_2(\boldsymbol{i})}(w_2-1)$
$\boldsymbol{j} = (q_2,w_2,u_2,1)$	0	$f_{\tilde{A}}(e_1)g_2(u_1,u_2,q_1-q_2+1)f_{V_{q_1-q_2+2}(\boldsymbol{i})}(w_2-1)$
$\boldsymbol{j} = (1,1,u_2,1)$	0	$f_{\tilde{A}}(e_1)g_2(u_1,u_2,q_1)$
$\boldsymbol{j} = (0,0,0,1)$	0	$f_{\tilde{A}}(e_1)g_3(q_1+1,u_1)$

queue and the data rates, and are defined as

$$
\begin{aligned}
g_1(u_1,u_2) &:= \mathrm{P}(R < u_1)f_L(u_2),\\
g_2(u_1,u_2,m) &:= \mathrm{P}(u_1 + L^{\text{agg}}_{m-1} + L - R = u_2, L \geq u_2),\\
g_3(q,u) &:= \mathrm{P}(u + L^{\text{agg}}_{q-1} \leq R),
\end{aligned}
\tag{9}
$$

where $L^{\text{agg}}_m := R_1 + \ldots + R_m$ and R_k are i.i.d. copies of R. The closed-form formulas for the functions in (9) are determined by the distributions of L and R. Finally, the random variables $\tilde{A}$ and $V_s(\boldsymbol{i}) = V_s((q,w,u,e))$ are related to the packet arrival time and are distributed as follows:

$$
f_{\tilde{A}}(e) = \mathrm{P}(A = e \mid A \geq e),
$$

$$
f_{V_s(\boldsymbol{i})}(v) = \frac{\mathrm{P}(A^{\text{agg}}_{s-1} = w - v)\mathrm{P}(A^{\text{agg}}_{q-s} = v - e)}{\mathrm{P}(A^{\text{agg}}_{q-1} = w - e)},
$$

where $A^{\text{agg}}_m := A_1 + \ldots + A_m$ and A_k are i.i.d. copies of A. The closed-form formulas for $f_{\tilde{A}}(\cdot)$ and $f_{V_s(\boldsymbol{i})}(\cdot)$ are determined by the packet inter-arrival time distribution. For more details, please refer to Appendix C in our technical report [14].

Quality-Aware Traffic Offloading in Wireless Networks

Wenjie Hu and Guohong Cao
Department of Computer Science and Engineering
The Pennsylvania State University
University Park, PA, 16802
{wwh5068, gcao}@cse.psu.edu

ABSTRACT

In cellular networks, due to practical deployment issues, some areas have good wireless coverage while others may not. This results in significant throughput (service quality) difference between wireless carriers at some locations. Through extensive measurements, we have validated the existence of such service quality difference. Then, through peer to peer interfaces such as WiFi direct, a mobile device (node) with low service quality can offload its data traffic to nodes with better service quality, to save energy and reduce delay. To achieve this goal, we propose a *Quality-Aware Traffic Offloading (QATO)* framework to offload network tasks to neighboring nodes with better service quality. QATO can identify neighbors with better service quality and provide incentive mechanisms to motivate nodes to help each other. To validate our design, we have implemented QATO on Android platform and have developed a web browser and a photo uploader on top of it. Experimental results show that QATO can significantly reduce energy and delay for both data downloading and uploading. Through trace-driven simulations, we also show that all users can benefit from data offloading in the long run.

Categories and Subject Descriptors

C.2.1 [**Computer-Communication Networks**]: Network Architecture and Design—*Wireless communication*; C.4 [**Performance of Systems**]: *Measurement techniques*

Keywords

Data offloading; Energy Saving; Cellular Networks; Smartphone

1. INTRODUCTION

In cellular networks such as 3G, 4G and LTE, mobile devices are served by base stations in that area. Due to practical deployment issues, some areas have good coverage while others may not. As a result, the wireless signal strength of a mobile device varies based on its location. Moreover, the data throughput in an area also depends on the number of people in the area and the backhaul network of the wireless carrier [12]. When the service quality (in terms of signal strength and throughput) is low, it takes longer time to transmit the same amount of data and consumes more energy.

Some existing work has addressed the service quality difference at different locations. Schulman *et al.* proposed to defer data transmission to save energy when the service quality is poor [16]. However, this solution only works when it is known that the user will quickly move to a location with better service quality. There are also solutions on offloading cellular traffic to WiFi network to save energy and improve service quality [15, 10]. However, WiFi access may not always be available.

In this paper, we address the service quality difference from a different perspective. Through extensive measurements, we observe that mobile devices (nodes) within an area may have different service quality (e.g., a node may consume multiple times of energy and delay to download the same amount of data), especially when different service providers are used. Then, through peer to peer interfaces such as WiFi direct, a node with low service quality can offload its traffic to the node with better service quality, to save energy and reduce delay. Based on this finding, we propose a *Quality-Aware Traffic Offloading (QATO)* framework, where nodes with low service quality may offload their data traffic to those with better quality via the WiFi direct interface. QATO can identify neighbors with better service quality through service discovery, and provide incentive mechanisms to motivate nodes to help each other.

We have implemented the QATO framework on Android platforms. To evaluate its performance, we have developed two applications based on QATO: a Web browser application which is mainly used to test the performance of download offloading and a photo uploader application which focuses on upload offloading. Experimental results show that QATO can reduce energy by 38% in downloading and 70% in uploading, and reduce delay by 45% in downloading and 88% in uploading. Trace-driven simulations are used to evaluate the performance in a larger scale, and the results show that all nodes can save energy and reduce delay in the long run. Our contributions are as follows.

- We introduce the idea of leveraging data throughput difference between nearby nodes to save energy and reduce delay.
- We design a quality-aware traffic offloading framework to automatically detect neighbors providing the same service and offload traffic to nodes with better throughput. Also, we design proper incentive mechanisms to encourage users to help each other.
- We implement the framework on the Android platform and develop two applications to demonstrate its effectiveness.

The rest of the paper is organized as follows. Section 2 introduces the background of different cellular networks and their

MobiHoc'14, August 11–14, 2014, Philadelphia, PA, USA.

http://dx.doi.org/10.1145/2632951.2632954 .

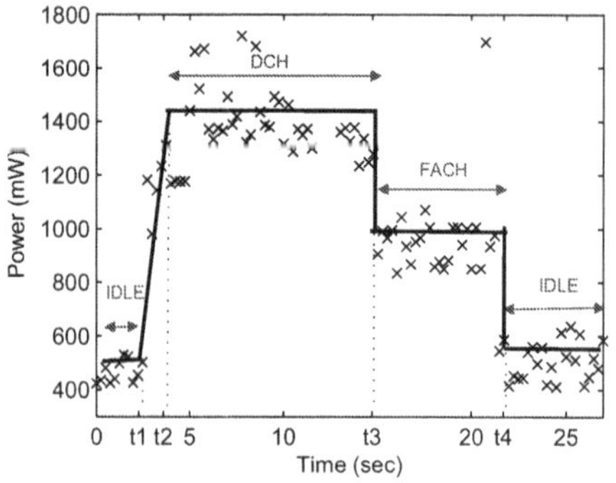

Figure 1: The power level of using the UMTS cellular interface (with screen on)

energy and delay model. Section 3 provides the motivation for quality-aware traffic offloading. We present the design and implementation of the traffic offloading framework in Section 4 and Section 5, respectively. The performance of QATO is evaluated in Section 6. Section 7 discusses related work, and Section 8 concludes the paper.

2. PRELIMINARIES

In this section, we first give a short description of different cellular networks, and then introduce the energy and delay model.

2.1 UMTS, HAPA+ and LTE Network

UMTS (the Universal Mobile Telecommunication System) is a popular 3G standard developed by 3GPP. Other than TDMA used by GSM, UMTS uses Direct Sequence CDMA (DSCDMA) technologies and provides a maximum bit rate of 384 Kbps to a single user at its first version, release 99. To support higher data rate, High Speed Downlink Packet Access (HSDPA) has been introduced in UMTS, which uses a new channel called the High Speed Downlink Shared Channel (HS-DSCH) and applies various techniques such as adaptive modulation, 16 QAM, and HARQ to provide a higher downlink data rate up to 14 Mbps. Later, High Speed Uplink Packet Access (HSUPA) was added as a complementary technique to improve the uplink speed. HSDPA and HSUPA are then merged and the enhanced version is called HSPA+, also referred to as 4G. In HSPA+, enhanced techniques such as 64 QAM, Multiple-Input Multiple-Output (MIMO), are used to increase the data rate up to 84 Mbps [21].

LTE (the Long-Term Evolution) is the latest extension of UMTS, and it enhances both the radio access network and the core network. The core network architecture of LTE is based on all-IP network and can support other non-3GPP radio access networks such as WiMAX and CDMA2000, which enables these networks to adopt LTE as their future radio access network. LTE can provide much higher bandwidth than 3G [8].

2.2 Energy and Delay Model

The power model of a typical data transmission in UMTS is shown in Fig. 1. Initially, a node stays at the IDLE state, which consumes little power. When a data request arrives, it promotes to the data transmission state (DCH), where data can be sent/received at high speed. After a data transmission, it stays at the TAIL state (FACH) for a period of time, in case another data request comes soon. In HSPA+ and LTE, the power models are similar. Therefore, we use a general cellular network power model presented by previous work [23].

The power consumption of the UMTS/HSPA+/LTE cellular interface can be generalized into three states: *promotion, data transmission* and *tail*, and the power consumption of these states are denoted as P_{pro}, P_{cell} and P_{tail}, respectively. The energy consumption of a task in cellular network can be modeled as follows. Suppose task T_i arrives at t_i with data size D_i, and the most recent task on the same node is T_j. The data throughput at the given node at t_i is r_{cell}. The time interval between task T_i and T_j is $\Delta t = t_i - t_j - D_j/r_{cell}$. There are three cases to compute T_i's energy consumption depending on Δt. 1) If Δt is larger than the tail timer t_{tail}, i.e., the cellular interface is in IDLE state before T_i arrives, then T_i will consume extra promotion and tail energy, besides the data transmission energy. 2) If Δt is smaller than t_{tail} but bigger than 0, there is tail energy but no promotion energy. 3) If Δt is smaller than 0, T_i will be overlapped with T_j for some time, and there will be no additional tail energy.

$$E^i_{cell}(T_j) = \begin{cases} P_{pro} \times t_{pro} + P_{cell} \times \frac{D_i}{r_{cell}} + P_{tail} \times t_{tail}, & \text{if } \Delta t > t_{tail} \\ P_{cell} \times \frac{D_i}{r_{cell}} + P_{tail} \times \Delta t, & \text{if } 0 < \Delta t \le t_{tail} \\ P_{cell} \times \max\{\Delta t + \frac{D_i}{r_{cell}} - t_j, 0\}, & \text{Otherwise} \end{cases} \quad (1)$$

The delay to complete a task is also related with Δt. If Δt is smaller than t_{tail}, the delay is only the data transmission time. Otherwise, the delay should include additional promotion delay, as shown in Eq. 2.

$$d^i_{cell}(T_j) = \begin{cases} D_i/r_{cell} + t_{pro}, & \text{if } \Delta t > t_{tail} \\ D_i/r_{cell}, & \text{Otherwise} \end{cases} \quad (2)$$

Table 1: Mobile Devices and Network Types

Device	Provider	Network[1]	Network[2]
Samsung Galaxy S3	Carrier 1	HSPA+	LTE
Samsung Galaxy S4	Carrier 2	LTE	LTE

[1] Network in City 1; [2] Network in City 2

3. THE MOTIVATION FOR QUALITY-AWARE TRAFFIC OFFLOADING

In this section, we introduce our method to measure the service quality (mainly in terms of data throughput), and give the motivation of quality-aware traffic offloading.

3.1 Measurement Methodology

We use two types of smartphones (Samsung Galaxy S3 and S4) to measure the throughput of two cellular providers (denoted as *Carrier 1* and *Carrier 2*) at two cities (denoted as *City 1* and *City 2*). A brief description of the devices and networks are shown in Table 1.

To measure the throughput, we ported *iperf* to smartphones and added timestamp to record the start and end of a data transmission and extended it to support WiFi direct. With iperf, the smartphone establishes a TCP connection to our backend server and measures the downlink and uplink throughput for 30 seconds, respectively. To measure the power consumption, we use the Monsoon power monitor to provide power supply for smartphones, which can provide constant voltage and measure the current at a rate of 5000Hz. Based on the power measurement trace and the start/end time from

Table 2: **Power consumption of different networks**

	State	Power (mW)	Duration (s)	Download throughput (Mbps)	Upload throughput (Mbps)
HSPA+ (Carrier 1)	Promotion	1422.2 ± 34.1	2.3 ± 0.5	-	-
	Data	1990.9 ± 44.2	-	4.5 ± 1.3	1.3 ± 0.2
	Tail	1622.6 ± 39.6	11.4 ± 1.4	-	-
LTE (Carrier 1)	Promotion	1214.8 ± 24.3	0.25 ± 0.4	-	-
	Data	1865.8 ± 25.6	-	51.11 ± 16.9	17.9 ± 5.1
	Tail	1125 ± 22.3	11.5 ± 0.56	-	-
LTE (Carrier 2)	Promotion	1567.9 ± 47.8	0.34 ± 0.04	-	-
	Data	2224.7 ± 53.1	-	15.4 ± 5.5	5.3 ± 2.5
	Tail	1757.5 ± 97.5	3.37 ± 0.08	-	-
WiFi direct	Data	1323.6 ± 13.9	-	29.5 ± 1.2	29.5 ± 1.2

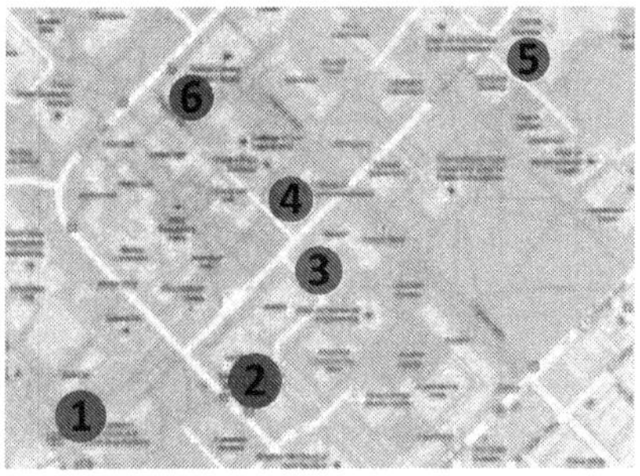

(a) Locations

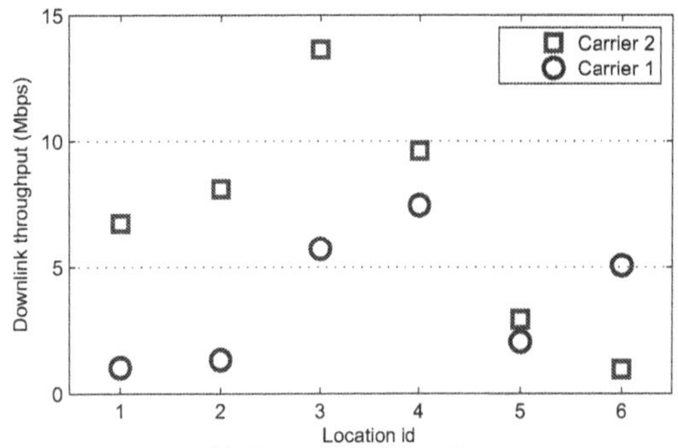

(b) Downlink throughput

Figure 2: Downlink throughput in different locations. There are coverage blind spots in location 1 and location 2 for Carrier 1, and location 6 for Carrier 2, which motivates the use of traffic offloading to improve service quality.

the iperf trace, we can get the power consumption at different network state. The results are shown in Table 2, where the power consumption is measured as the whole phone's power consumption when the screen is on.

3.2 Understanding Quality Difference between Different Carriers

3.2.1 Micro Perspective: Coverage Blind Spots of Different Carriers

Within the coverage of a cellular base station, the data rate within an area varies greatly due to many reasons, such as the distance from the base station, obstacles on the way, interference from other devices, etc. It is common that one carrier may have some coverage blind spots at some locations, which means that the throughput is extremely low and the quality of experience is poor. This problem is especially worse in indoor environments.

We picked 6 popular locations in our university, including Lab, library, classroom, and Cafeteria, as shown in Fig. 2(a). In each location, we measured the data throughput of different carriers at the same time. The comparison results are shown in Fig. 2(b). As can be seen, both carriers have high throughput to satisfy users' requirements in locations 3 and 4, but low throughput in location 5. Here we are more interested in other locations. In locations 1 and 2, Carrier 1 has extremely low data throughput but carrier 2 has much better service quality. Similarly, in location 6, Carrier 2 has very low data throughput but Carrier 1 has better service quality. In these blind spots, there is strong motivation for nodes to offload traffic to neighbors using different carrier. For example, at location 6, nodes served by Carrier 2 have motivations to offload traffic to nodes served by Carrier 1 to save energy and reduce delay.

3.2.2 Macro Perspective: Quality Complementary between Carriers

Different carriers have different priorities when deploying cellular networks in different cities. One may provide better service quality in one city but lower quality in another city, while the reverse is true for another carrier. From the macro perspective, different carriers may complement each other in many cities, and provide opportunities to offload traffic to neighboring nodes with better service quality.

To verify this hypothesis, we collect data throughput of two carriers in two cities, as mentioned in Table 1. In each city, we collect the throughput in multiple locations at different time. The downlink and uplink throughput of both carriers in these two cities are shown in Fig. 3(a) and Fig. 3(b), respectively. In the boxplot figure, the middle line of a box indicates the median, and the lower and upper side of the box are the first (25%) and third (75%) quartile, which are denoted by $Q1$ and $Q3$. The outliers are values outside $1.5 \times (Q3 - Q1)$ range above $Q3$ or below $Q1$.

Both downlink and uplink throughput show the same trend. Carrier 1's HSPA+ network provides lower service quality than Carrier 2's LTE network while Carrier 1's LTE network outperforms that of Carrier 2. Thus we have two findings. First, there

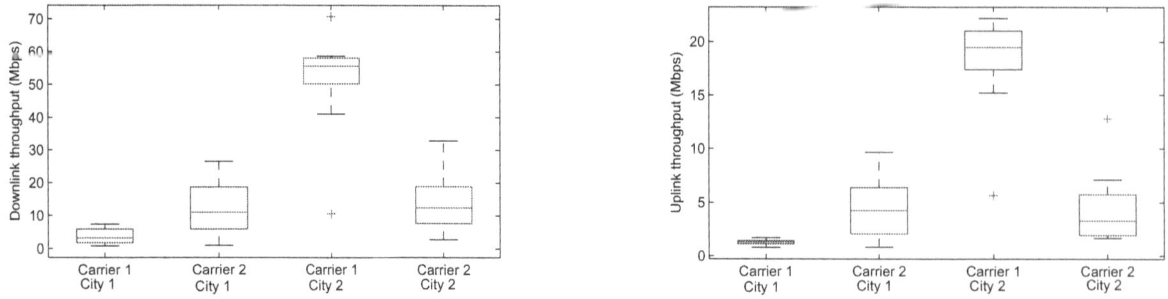

(a) Downlink (b) Uplink

Figure 3: Throughput of different carriers in City 1 and City 2. Carrier 2 provides better service quality in City 1 while Carrier 1 provides better service quality in City 2.

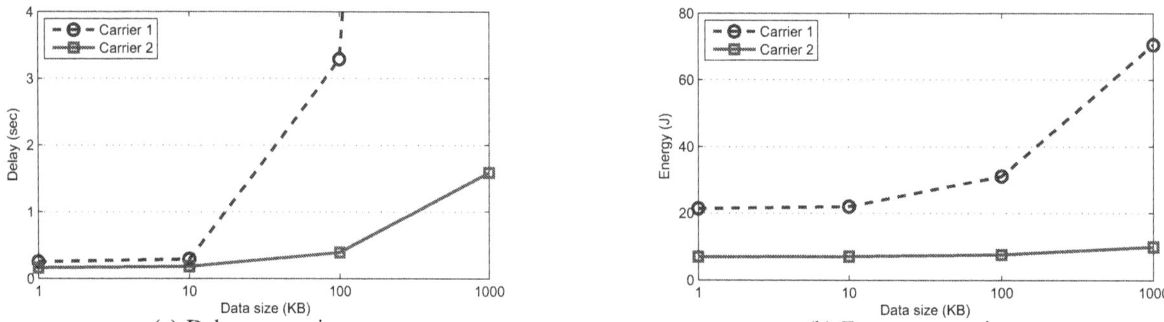

(a) Delay comparison (b) Energy comparison

Figure 4: Energy and delay comparison between different carriers with different throughput.

is high throughput difference between carriers, which can be as much as *eight times*. Second, the service quality provided by different carriers varies in different cities and complements each other, which provides opportunity and motivation to help each other. For example, suppose a group of commuters using these two cellular carriers periodically travel between these two cities, then users of Carrier 2 may share their services with users of Carrier 1 in City 1, while utilize the service from Carrier 1 in City 2. Thus, with data offloading, all users can benefit in the long run.

3.3 Delay and Energy Comparisons

Under different service quality, the data access delay and the energy consumption to accomplish a network task are different. To measure this difference, we use GS3 with HSPA+ data plan from Carrier 1 and GS4 with LTE data plan from Carrier 2 as mentioned in Table 1 to download a given size of file from our server in City 1. The delay is the time from the start of downloading a file to the time when the file is completely received. The energy consumption is measured as the whole phone's energy consumption during downloading (including tail energy) when the screen is on.

Figure 4 shows the results. As can be seen in Fig. 4(a), the data access delay is similar for both carriers when the data size is small. As the data size increases, the data access delay with Carrier 1 increases much faster than that of Carrier 2. This result is consistent with our experience in real life; i.e., when updating emails or browsing simple webpages, LTE feels the same as 3G network; however, when watching movies, LTE significantly outperforms 3G. This result indicates that offloading large data to nodes with better quality can significantly reduce the delay.

Figure 4(b) compares the energy of data transmission with different service quality. Since Carrier 1 takes longer time to transmit the data, and has larger promotion and tail energy, it consumes much more energy than Carrier 2. Fortunately, the energy consumption does not increase linearly with the data size. For example, when the data size increases from 10KB to 1000KB, the energy only increases 3.2 times for Carrier 1 and 1.4 times for Carrier 2. It means that aggregating a large amount of data on a node with higher throughput does not increase the energy too much.

4. QATO DESIGN

In this section we introduce the design of our data offloading framework QATO. We first give an overview of QATO and then describe its major components.

4.1 QATO Overview

Consider that a group of users stay together for a relatively long time, such as in a Lab or on a commuting bus from one city to another. They use different cellular carriers and are willing to share data services with others to trade for better service from others at a later time. In such scenarios, QATO enables phones to offload their network tasks to a neighboring node with better service quality. Here a network task means an independent task to fulfill one user request, such as downloading one webpage or uploading one photo, which may contains lots of data packets.

The architecture of QATO is shown in Fig. 5. In the original smartphone system, all network tasks are buffered in the local queue and then scheduled based on the FIFO order. With QATO, the network tasks are guided into the offload engine module first. By taking into account the local network information and neighbor

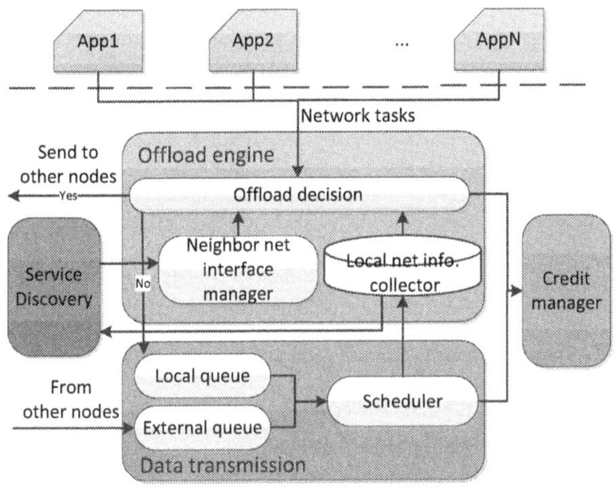

Figure 5: QATO architecture

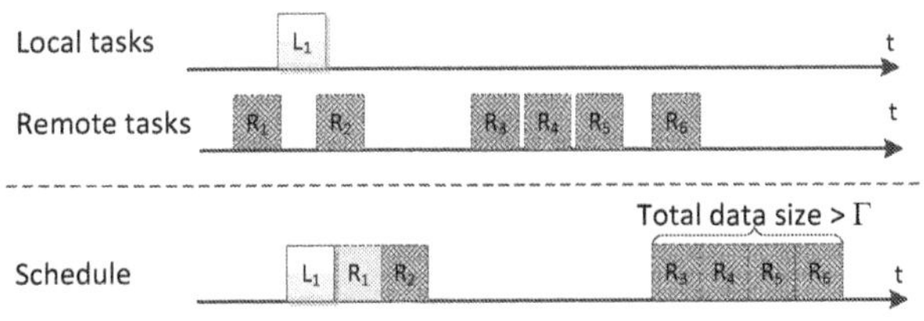

Figure 6: The scheduling of local tasks and remote tasks

network information collected by the service discovery module, the offload engine module determines whether to offload the network tasks and to which node to offload. The data transmission module maintains a local task queue and a remote task queue, and properly schedule them to reduce energy and delay. Since users may be selfish, we also design a credit based mechanism to motivate users to share their cellular service. The credit manager module manages credits; i.e., collecting credits from nodes using the service and pay credits to nodes providing the service.

4.2 Service Discovery

Detecting neighbors nearby has been studied in recent works, but most of them are based on Bluetooth interface [7]. To the best of our knowledge, QATO is the first work to discover neighbors using the WiFi direct interface. Moreover, we also need to know which neighbors support QATO, i.e., are willing to offload traffic for others. To solve this problem, we introduce the DNS (Name Domain System) based service discovery (DNS-SD) [2]. It allows nodes to discover neighboring nodes supporting a specific service within the local network. Different from the traditional DNS service that maps host name to IP address, DNS-SD can be used to find neighbors without support of the central server.

Android begins to support DNS-based service discovery since Android 4.1 (Jelly Bean), and it supports DNS-SD to be deployed on WiFi direct interface, without connecting to any Access Point. On each node, we register "QATO" as a service, with "_http._tcp" as the service type. A local port is also assigned for this service. After successful registration, the node will be able to respond to the "QATO" requests from neighbors. In the response, it also includes its IP address and port number. Based on these information, two nodes can create connection via the WiFi direct interface and then exchange the network quality information. The network quality information is organized in an XML based profile, which contains cellular network information such as cellular network type, signal strength and downlink/uplink throughput, and task related information such as the local task arriving rate, remote task arriving rate and total remote task size. Some frequently used notations are listed in Table 3.

Table 3: Notations

r_{p2p}, P_{p2p}	Throughput and power of the P2P network
t_{pro}, P_{pro} *	Promotion delay and power of cellular network
t_{tail}, P_{tail} *	Tail time and power of cellular network
r_{cell}, P_{cell} *	Throughput and power of cellular network
λ_l, λ_r *	Data arriving rate of local and remote task queue
$S_r, \overline{D_r}$ *	Total and average data size in remote task queue
Γ	Data size threshold for scheduling remote tasks

*: notations with superscript p indicate the corresponding value of the proxy node

After service discovery, a node collects a list of network quality profiles from neighbors. Then, the neighbors with higher data throughput than the node itself are recorded in a *proxy list*, i.e., the potential nodes to offload network tasks for this node. To save energy, service discovery is run when a node first comes to a new location and has no neighbors. Later on, it is only executed when the selected proxy disappears or when the proxy's service quality becomes worse than itself.

4.3 Data Transmission Schedule

In QATO, a node maintains two task queues, local task queue Q_l and remote task queue Q_r, to store the network tasks generated locally and received from neighbors, respectively. During data transmission schedule, i.e., task schedule, we consider two factors. First, local tasks should not be affected by remote tasks. Second, remote tasks should be scheduled only when their introduced tail energy is negligible. To solve this problem, we design a scheduling algorithm for the proxy node, as shown in Algorithm 1. A local task is scheduled when it is generated since it has higher priority. For a remote task, it is scheduled based on the following two cases to save energy:

- **Case 1:** A remote task is executed when the cellular interface is already in the data transmission state, either triggered by local tasks or by previous remote tasks. In this case, we record the tail ending time. After scheduling a task, the tail ending time is also extended.

- **Case 2:** Remote tasks are executed in a bunch when the accumulated data size is larger than a threshold Γ. This ensures that remote tasks are scheduled when there is no pending local task.

An example is shown in Figure 6. Remote task R_1 comes first but is not scheduled immediately. Local task L_1 is scheduled when it is generated. After that, R_1 is scheduled as the cellular interface is on the data transmission state, as illustrated in Case 1. The same happens to R_2. When R_3 comes, the cellular interface is moved to the IDLE state, and it waits for future tasks. When R_6 comes, the accumulated remote tasks are more than Γ, and these four tasks are scheduled together, as discussed in Case 2.

The selection of Γ affects energy efficiency, in terms of energy per byte. Larger Γ means more tasks are scheduled together

Algorithm 1 Task Schedule on Proxy Node

```
function TASKSCHDULE(Q_l, Q_r)
    S_r ← 0, TailEnd ← 0
    order all tasks by task time
    for each task T_i ∈ Q_l ∪ Q_r do
        if T_i ∈ Q_l then
            EXECUTETASK(T_i)          /* Get T_i by cellular interface */
            Q_l ← Q_l \ T_i           /* Remove T_i from local task queue Q_l */
            TailEnd ← t_i + t_pro + D_i/r_cell + t_tail
            EXECUTEREMOTETASK_CASE1(Q_r, TailEnd)
        else
            S_r ← S_r + D_i
            if S_r > Γ then
                EXECUTEREMOTETASK_CASE2(Q_r, S_r)
                S_r ← 0
            end if
        end if
    end for
end function

function EXECUTEREMOTETASK_CASE1(Q_r, TailEnd)
    for T_j ∈ Q_r do
        if t_j < TailEnd then
            EXECUTETASK(T_j)
            TailEnd ← t_j + D_j/r_cell + t_tail
            Q_r ← Q_r \ T_j
            S_r ← S_r − D_j
        end if
    end for
end function

function EXECUTEREMOTETASK_CASE2(Q_r, S_r)
    for T_j ∈ Q_r do
        if S_r > 0 then
            EXECUTETASK(T_j)
            Q_r ← Q_r \ T_j
            S_r ← S_r − D_j
        end if
    end for
end function
```

to amortize the tail energy, and therefore improves the energy efficiency, but it also increases delay. To find out the proper Γ value, we upload different size of data using both carriers in City 1. As shown in Fig. 7, when the data size is larger than 500KB, there is a big drop of energy per byte for both carriers. The same trend exits during downloading. Thus, it is better to set Γ bigger than 500KB.

4.4 Offload Engine

As mentioned before, each node maintains a proxy list after service discovery. When a network task comes, the offload engine will determine whether to offload the task. If so, it selects the proxy node p from the list considering both energy and delay.

4.4.1 *Energy Consideration*

Suppose task T_i is generated at time t_i, with data size D_i. If this task is executed locally, the energy consumption E^i_{local} can be computed using Eq. 1. Otherwise, if this task is offloaded to p, the data transmission energy should be the data transmission energy on node p, plus the additional energy of the P2P interface. Considering the two cases of scheduling a remote task, in Case 1, there is no additional promotion energy and tail energy for T_i; in Case 2, T_i shares part of these energy proportional to its size. As we are not sure when the future tasks will be scheduled, thus the total energy is computed based on the worse case, as Eq. 3.

$$E^i_{remote} = \frac{D_i}{r_{p2p}} \times P_{p2p} + \frac{D_i}{r^p_{cell}} \times P^p_{cell} + \frac{D_i}{\Gamma} \times (P^p_{tail} \times t^p_{tail} + P^p_{pro} \times t^p_{pro}) \quad (3)$$

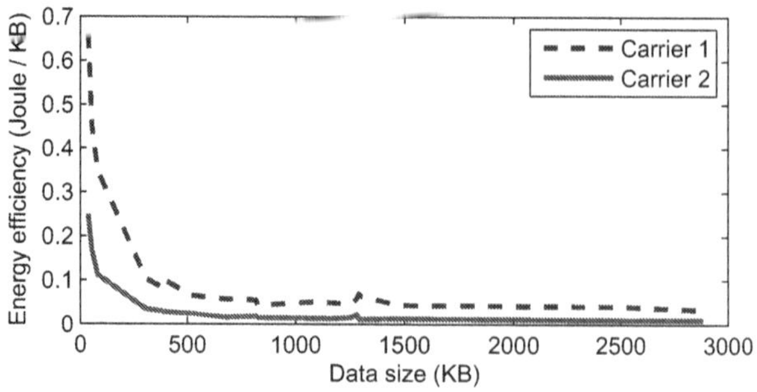

Figure 7: The selection of Γ

4.4.2 *Delay Consideration*

If task T_i is executed locally, the delay d^i_{local} can be computed using Eq. 2. When offloaded to proxy node p, the delay contains four parts: the time to execute the first task in the remote queue, queue delay, the time to get T_i via cellular network and the time to transmit it back via the P2P interface. Similarly there are also two cases to compute the delay of the first remote task. In Case 1, the delay of the first task in the remote queue can be estimated by $1/\lambda^p_l$. In Case 2, the first task of the remote queue needs to wait for a while until the total data size of the remote queue is larger than Γ, which is $\frac{\Gamma - S^p_r}{\lambda^p_r \times \overline{D^p_r}}$. The queue delay depends on the total remote task size S^p_r. The cellular network delay and the P2P delay depend on D_i. Putting them together, the delay to execute T_i at the proxy node p is:

$$d^i_{remote} = \frac{D_i + S^p_r}{r^p_{cell}} + \frac{D_i}{r_{p2p}} + max\{1/\lambda^p_l, \frac{\Gamma - S^p_r}{\lambda^p_r \times \overline{D^p_r}}\} \quad (4)$$

4.4.3 *Proxy Selection and Congestion Avoidance*

All proxy nodes are ordered in two lists by their downlink and uplink throughput, respectively. Then a node will select the proxy from up to down in the corresponding list according to its flow direction. If any proxy node p can save both energy and delay for T_i, then T_i will be offloaded to p.

This method can also help to avoid congestion at the proxy node. If one node has higher throughput, its remote queue list will be longer. For later coming tasks, the expected delay at this proxy will be longer, so they will be scheduled to other proxy nodes.

4.5 Credit Manager

We design a credit-based scheme to motivate nodes to offload data for others. The credit is a kind of virtual money, which can be used to pay for the network service provided by others. It can also be extended to exchange with real money, but this is out of the scope of this paper. The credit value uses three parameters ρ_e, ρ_d and ρ_b, to adjust the unit and combine energy, delay and bandwidth together, so that $\rho_e Energy = \rho_d Delay = \rho_b Bandwidth$. These three parameters vary due to the network quality. The credit manager computes credits based on the node with poor network quality. For example, when a node uses Carrier 1 in City 1 wants to offload its downlink task, we would use the values in Table 4 to compute the credit, which means saving 1 second of transmission time is equivalent to saving 1.9 Joule energy and saving 4.5M bit (576K Byte) bandwidth.

If task T_i is executed locally, a node will cost energy, delay and bandwidth. By offloading T_i, a node can save some of the cost, which is denoted as C^i_{save}. This is the maximum credit a node wants to pay to the proxy when offloading T_i. On the other hand, the proxy

Table 4: Relationship between energy, delay and bandwidth

Energy (J)	Time (sec)	Bandwidth (KB)
1.9	1	576

```
// original interface
Socket socket = new Socket (serverIP, serverPort);
InputStream in = socket.getInputStream();
OutputStream out = socket.getOutputStream();
......
// QATO interface
QATOSocket socket = new QATOSocket (serverIP, serverPort,
                                    proxyIP, proxyPort);
InputStream in = socket.getInputStream();
OutputStream out = socket.getOutputStream();
......
```

Figure 8: QATO TCP interface

has to pay extra energy and bandwidth to get T_i, and the total cost is C^i_{cost}. A proxy should get at least C^i_{cost} credit back when helping others to offload T_i.

$$C^i_{save} = \rho_e \times E^i_{local} + \rho_d \times (d^i_{local} - d^i_{remote}) + \rho_b \times D_i \quad (5)$$

$$C^i_{cost} = \rho_e \times E^i_{remote} + \rho_b \times D_i \quad (6)$$

As task T_i is offloaded only when it saves both energy and delay, we have $C^i_{save} > C^i_{cost}$. To motivate both users to use QATO, some credits in-between should be paid to the proxy as shown in Equation 7, where α is a parameter to balance the motivation, and it is set to 0.5 in our system. Note that other incentive scheme like [24, 25] can also be applied.

$$C^i_{paid} = C^i_{cost} + \alpha(C^i_{save} - C^i_{cost}) \quad (7)$$

5. QATO IMPLEMENTATION

QATO is implemented on the Android platform. In this section we introduce the interface of QATO and two applications designed based on QATO.

5.1 QATO Interface

All components, including service discovery, offload engine, and credit manager are wrapped into classes and run in the background when QATO is turned on. For developers, QATO provides a simple interface. Using TCP as an example (UDP works similarly), the QATO interface is shown in Fig. 8. Originally a client connects to the server directly. After successful connection, a client can manipulate the input/outputstream. In QATO, we provide a new QATOsocket with two more parameters: proxy IP address and port.

All data traffic using QATOsocket will be forwarded to QATO. The offload engine decides whether to offload the traffic. If not, the connection works the same as the original one. Otherwise, the node first creates a connection to the proxy via the WiFi direct interface, and then the proxy creates a new connection to the real server. Later on, the proxy connects the input/outputstream of one connection to the output/inputstream on the other side. In this way, the proxy works like a tunnel to transmit data, without storing the user data, and as a result user privacy is also protected. For developers, the whole process is transparent and they can use the inputstream and outputstream as normal.

5.2 Applications

We develop two applications on top of QATO: a web browser focusing on downlink offloading, and a photo uploader focusing on uplink offloading.

Table 5: Webpage benchmarks

Name	URL	# of Files	Size (KB)
Google	`www.google.com`	2	10
Yahoo	`www.yahoo.com`	165	808
Amazon	`www.amazon.com`	9	126
Wiki	`www.wikipedia.org`	18	117
Ebay	`www.ebay.com`	13	221
Bing	`www.bing.com`	2	29
Craigslist	`www.craigslist.com`	7	409
Go	`www.go.com`	18	980
Espn	`www.espn.go.com`	53	598
CNN	`www.cnn.com`	21	396

5.2.1 Web Browser

In the web browser application, the opening of a webpage is treated as downloading multiple files. To eliminate the effect of congestion on web server, all files (including embedded objects) of the webpage are downloaded to a server in our lab. When the phone opens a webpage, we use the idea in [23, 22] by downloading all object files first and then rendering them. It works as below. After a user enters a URL and clicks the "go" button, the web browser downloads the main webpage. Then it parses the whole content, detects all embedded object files, including CSS, images, javascript files, and downloads them together. After all files are downloaded, the web browser modifies the object links to the local files and displays the webpage. By downloading all webpage files in a bunch, the tail energy can be significantly reduced.

5.2.2 Photo Uploader

With cameras on smartphones, users are generating more and more photos, and uploading them to Facebook, flickr, google, etc. Since photos are very large, it may take much more time to upload photos and consume lots of energy when the wireless signal is not good. Thus, it is better to offload such tasks to neighboring nodes with better network quality. To achieve this goal, we design a photo uploader based on QATO. Users can take photos or select photos from the gallery and then upload them to a self defined server. Since photo uploading is delay tolerant, the proxy can adjust Γ to achieve a balance between saving energy and reducing delay.

6. PERFORMANCE EVALUATIONS

In this section, we first run some experiments to evaluate the benefits of traffic offloading, and then use trace driven simulations for more tasks. We compare the performance of QATO, denoted as "`Ours`", to the original approach (without data offloading), denoted as "`Original`".

6.1 Real Experiments

We have implemented QATO on two smartphones as listed in Table 1 and run experiments in City 1. All phones have Android 4.2.2 and have pre-installed two applications: web browser and photo uploader. As LTE has larger downlink throughput than HSPA+, the GS4 phone is selected as the proxy.

To evaluate the performance of QATO, we first run each application using the GS3 phone individually. Then we turn on QATO on both phones and put them within communication range. For both approaches we use Monsoon power monitor to measure the energy as described in Section 3.1. To be fair for different approaches, the base energy is removed, which is the average base

Table 6: Photo benchmarks

ID	Data Size (KB)	ID	Data Size (KB)
1	38	11	1028
2	55	12	1092
3	83	13	1171
4	309	14	1255
5	382	15	1280
6	392	16	1293
7	393	17	1297
8	519	18	1479
9	678	19	2539
10	817	20	2882

power multiply the data transmission time. For the original method, we only consider the data transmission energy of GS3. When QATO is started, we also consider the data transmission energy of the proxy node (i.e., the GS4 phone in our case).

6.1.1 Web Browser

We pick 10 most popular websites from the Alexa website [1], as listed in Table 5 to test the performance of download offloading. These websites have different numbers of embedded objects. Some contain one image while others contain hundreds of images. In this application, the delay is defined as the time from a user pressing the "go" button to the time when the webpage is totally downloaded. Since web browser is not delay tolerant, we set Γ to the minimum webpage size so that all offloading requests can be executed immediately.

Figure 9 compares the energy and delay of the two methods. When downloading webpages, the original method takes more energy and time than ours since QATO can offload traffic to the GS4 phone, which has much higher downlink throughput. On average, our method can save energy by 38% and reduce delay by 45%.

6.1.2 Photo Uploader

We use 20 photos with different sizes to evaluate the performance of upload offloading. The data size is listed in Table 6, which ranges from several kilobytes to several megabytes, with an average value of 939KB. The photos are roughly divided into two categories: small photos with data size smaller than 1MB, and large photos larger than 1MB.

The comparison results of the original method and our method are shown in Fig. 10. The dotted line shows the average value of small photos and large photos of the original method. In the original method, the energy and delay of the small photos are much smaller than that of the large photos. More specifically, the average energy of the small photos is 23.4J, while it is 54.1J for large photos. The average delay of small photos is 3.57 seconds while it is 17.63 seconds for large photos. This is because the uplink bandwidth of HSPA+ is relatively small. However, when using QATO, the energy and the delay are both reduced significantly, since the GS4 phone has much higher uplink bandwidth. For all photos, our method can save 70% of energy and 88% of delay on average.

The data size threshold Γ affects the performance of data offloading. Since photo uploading is delay tolerant, adding more delays (i.e., increasing Γ) can be used to save more energy. Suppose a user selects 20 photos to upload and the duration of selecting one photo is 5 seconds, the energy and delay of using QATO with different Γ are shown in Fig. 11. When Γ increases, more energy is saved since more data can be aggregated to transmit at once and more tail energy is saved. However, the delay also increases since there will be more queue delay and promotion delay.

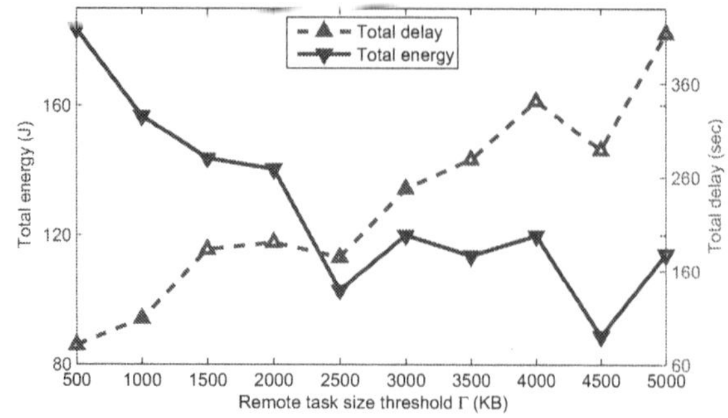

Figure 11: The impact of Γ on the performance of photo uploading

6.2 Trace-driven Simulations

In this section, we aim to show that the credit manager can benefit all nodes in the long run. We collect network traces from 4 users in one month. Then we assume two commuters, user 1 with Carrier 1's data plan and user 2 with Carrier 2's data plan, always travel between City 1 and City 2. We feed trace 1 and trace 2 to user 1 in City 1 and City 2, respectively. Similarly trace 3 and trace 4 are fed to user 2 in two cities. As shown in Table 2, user 1 offloads traffic to user 2 in City 1 and user 2 offloads traffic to user 1 in City 2. In these two month periods, we compare the performance with/without QATO and the results are shown in Fig. 12.

Fig. 12(a) and Fig. 12(b) compare the energy and delay of the original method and QATO. As can be seen, both users benefit from using QATO by saving energy and reducing delay. User 1 consumes much more energy and time than user 2 in the original method because he has more network tasks. Due to the large number of tasks, user 1 has more opportunity to save energy and reduce delay by offloading them to user 2. In total user 1 saves 62% of energy and user 2 saves 36%, and user 1 reduces delay by 50% and user 2 reduces the delay by 25%.

The credit (cost) value considers energy, delay and bandwidth. As mentioned before, when offloading a task, a node saves some cost which is more than the credits paid to the proxy. From this point of view, we say a node benefits from QATO if the saved cost is more than the paid credits in the long run. To verify this assumption, we compare the total saved cost and the paid credits during the two month periods for both users and show the results in Fig. 12(c). It clearly verifies our assumption since both users paid less credits than their saved cost. The benefit (the difference between saved cost and paid credit) of User 1 is larger since User 1 offloads more tasks. On the other hand, User 2 also earns some credits (which is not shown in the figure) by being a proxy.

7. RELATED WORK

Our work aims to save energy and delay by offloading traffic to neighbors with better service quality. It is related with three categories of work.

Power saving in cellular networks: In cellular networks, including GSM, UMTS, HSPA, and LTE, the radio interface on smartphone is kept in the high power state for a long time (called the long tail problem) after data transmission. One advantage of this

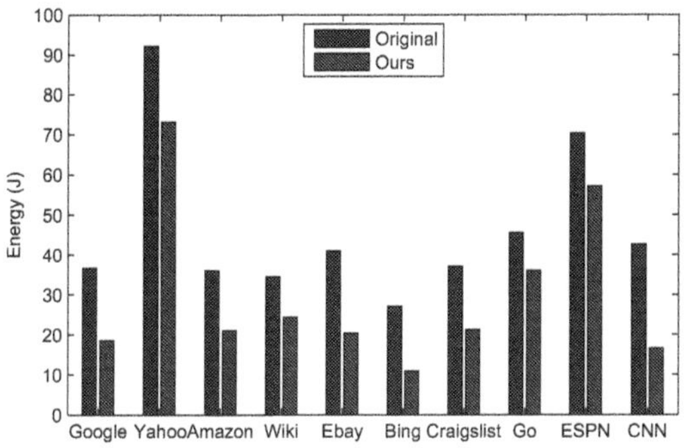

(a) Energy

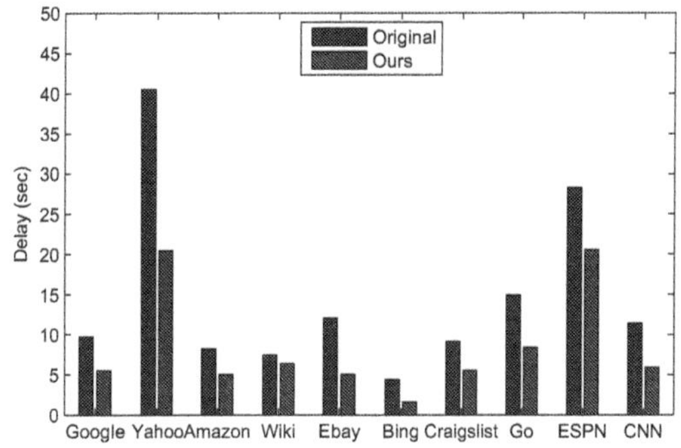

(b) Delay

Figure 9: Energy and delay comparisons with/without QATO when downloading webpages.

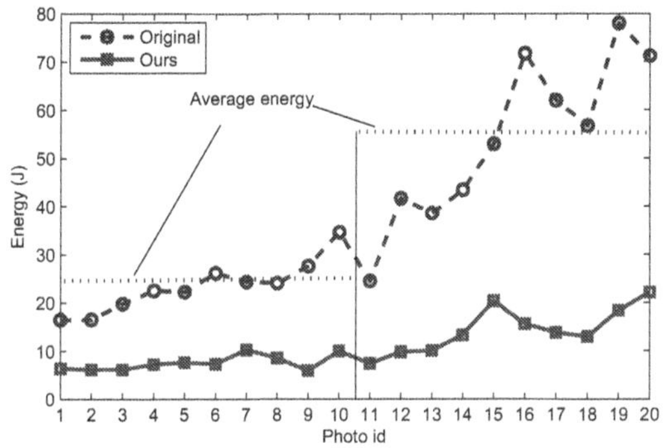

(a) Energy

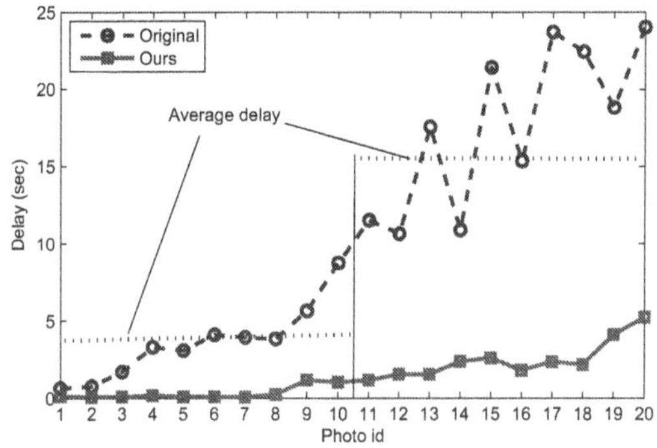

(b) Delay

Figure 10: Energy and delay comparisons with/without QATO when uploading photos.

approach is that it can reduce the latency for next possible data transmission, but it also wastes lots of energy. To solve this problem, some researchers introduce methods to aggregate the network traffic to amortize the tail energy [6], or turn the radio interface off quickly by predicting the end of communication [3, 13]. The tail energy can also be saved by aggregating traffic together, if the application is delay tolerant [4].

Quality aware data access: The service quality difference of cellular network within an area has drawn researchers' attention. The Bartendr project [16] studies the relationship between signal strength, throughput and energy. It indicates that the energy of cellular network interface increases and the data throughput decreases when the signal is weak. Based on this finding, they propose to predict the signal strength considering both location and moving direction, and then defer data transfer until reaching a location with better signal. By moving one step further, a travel trip can be planned considering network quality [18]. However, these approaches all require the knowledge of users' movement, which is not easy to achieve in many cases. There are also studies on helping static users to improve the signal quality [20] or increasing network capacity [14] of cellular network via the P2P links. Different from them, we leverage users' cooperation to save energy and reduce delay.

Offloading: In the past several years, there has been lots of research on 3G offloading which focuses on offloading 3G traffic to WiFi network or opportunistic mobile network to save energy or 3G bandwidth [15, 10, 24, 25]. The spider project [19] uses concurrent WiFi connections to improve the throughput and connectivity. However, WiFi access may not always be available.

To leverage neighboring nodes with good signal in 3G networks, UCAN relays data to nodes with higher throughput via the 802.11 interface [11]. Our work is different from it in three perspectives. First, based on measurements, we give motivations for node cooperation even at the same location. Second, we have implemented the real system based on smartphones where previous work is limited to simulations. Third, our work considers many practical scheduling issues related to the long tail problem, which are not considered in UCAN.

There are also works on mobile clouds [5, 9] which aim to offload complex computations to cloud to save energy. Recently, many researchers also consider offloading computations to nearby mobile devices [17] to save energy. Their idea of leveraging neighbors' resource inspires our work, but their works focus on computation offloading whereas our work focuses on communication offloading.

8. CONCLUSIONS

In this paper, based on real measurements, we demonstrated the existence of significant throughput difference between wireless carriers at some locations, and then motivated the necessity of node collaboration to save energy and reduce delay in cellular networks. We proposed a data offloading framework QATO to offload network tasks to neighboring nodes with better throughput, to save energy and reduce delay. QATO can identify neighbors with better service quality through service discovery, and provide incentive mechanisms to motivate nodes to help each other. To validate our design, we have implemented QATO on Android platform and

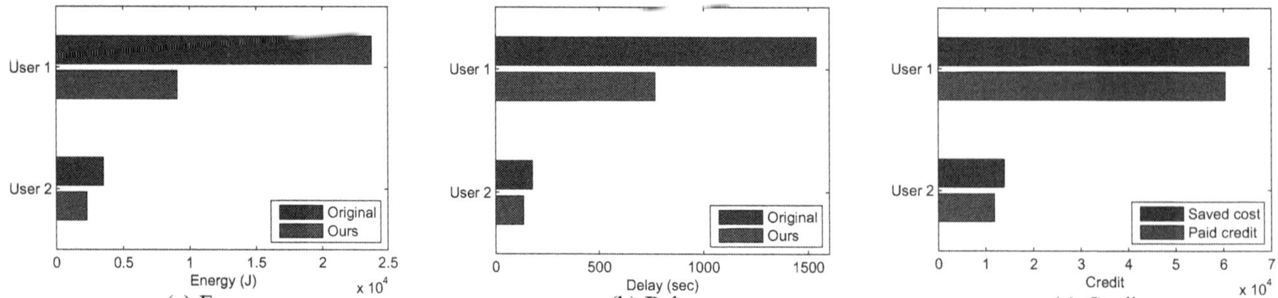

(a) Energy (b) Delay (c) Credit

Figure 12: Performance comparisons with/without data offloading

developed a web browser and a photo uploader on top of it. Experimental results show that QATO can reduce energy by 38% in downloading and 70% in uploading, and reduce delay by 45% in downloading and 88% in uploading. Through trace-driven simulations, we also show that all users can benefit from data offloading in the long run.

Acknowledgment

We would like to thank anonymous reviewers for their insightful comments and helpful suggestions. This work was supported in part by the National Science Foundation (NSF) under grant number CNS-1218597, and by Network Science CTA under grant W911NF-09-2-0053.

References

[1] Alexa top sites. `http://www.alexa.com/topsites`.

[2] Rfc 6763: Dns-based service discovery. `http://tools.ietf.org/html/rfc6763`.

[3] P. K. Athivarapu, R. Bhagwan, S. Guha, V. Navda, R. Ramjee, D. Arora, V. N. Padmanabhan, and G. Varghese. RadioJockey: Mining Program Execution to Optimize Cellular Radio Usage. In *ACM MobiCom*, 2012.

[4] N. Balasubramanian, A. Balasubramanian, and A. Venkataramani. Energy Consumption in Mobile Phones: A Measurement Study and Implications for Network Applications. In *ACM IMC*, 2009.

[5] E. Cuervo, A. Balasubramanian, D.-k. Cho, A. Wolman, S. Saroiu, R. Chandra, and P. Bahl. MAUI: Making Smartphones Last Longer with Code Offload. In *ACM MobiSys*, 2010.

[6] W. Hu and G. Cao. Energy Optimization Through Traffic Aggregation in Wireless Networks. In *IEEE INFOCOM*, 2014.

[7] W. Hu, G. Cao, S. V. Krishanamurthy, and P. Mohapatra. Mobility-Assisted Energy-Aware User Contact Detection in Mobile Social Networks. In *IEEE ICDCS*, 2013.

[8] J. Huang, F. Qian, A. Gerber, Z. M. Mao, S. Sen, and O. Spatscheck. A Close Examination of Performance and Power Characteristics of 4G LTE Networks. In *ACM MobiSys*, 2012.

[9] S. Kosta, A. Aucinas, P. Hui, R. Mortier, and X. Zhang. ThinkAir: Dynamic Resource Allocation and Parallel Execution in the Cloud for Mobile Code Offloading. In *IEEE INFOCOM*, 2012.

[10] K. Lee, J. Lee, Y. Yi, I. Rhee, and S. Chong. Mobile Data Offloading: How Much Can WiFi Deliver? *IEEE/ACM Transactions on Networking*, 21(2):536–550, 2013.

[11] H. Luo, R. Ramjee, P. Sinha, L. E. Li, and S. Lu. UCAN: A Unified Cellular and Ad-hoc Network Architecture. In *ACM MobiCom*, 2003.

[12] C. Peng, S.-B. Lee, S. Lu, H. Luo, and H. Li. Traffic-driven Power Saving in Operational 3G Cellular Networks. In *ACM MobiCom*, 2011.

[13] F. Qian, Z. Wang, A. Gerber, Z. Mao, S. Sen, and O. Spatscheck. TOP: Tail Optimization Protocol for Cellular Radio Resource Allocation. In *IEEE ICNP*, 2010.

[14] B. Radunovic and A. Proutiere. On Downlink Capacity of Cellular Data Networks With WLAN/WPAN Relays. *IEEE/ACM Transactions on Networking*, 21(1):286–296, 2013.

[15] N. Ristanovic, J.-Y. Le Boudec, A. Chaintreau, and V. Erramilli. Energy Efficient Offloading of 3G Networks. In *IEEE MASS*, 2011.

[16] A. Schulman, V. Navda, R. Ramjee, N. Spring, P. Deshpande, C. Grunewald, K. Jain, and V. N. Padmanabhan. Bartendr: A Practical Approach to Energy-aware Cellular Data Scheduling. In *ACM MobiCom*, 2010.

[17] C. Shi, V. Lakafosis, M. H. Ammar, and E. W. Zegura. Serendipity: Enabling Remote Computing Among Intermittently Connected Mobile Devices. In *ACM MobiHoc*, 2012.

[18] C. Shi and H. Xie. Go This Way: Navigation for Better Access Quality in Mobile Networks. In *ACM MobiArch*, 2013.

[19] H. Soroush, P. Gilbert, N. Banerjee, M. D. Corner, B. N. Levine, and L. Cox. Spider: Improving Mobile Networking with Concurrent Wi-Fi Connections. In *ACM SIGCOMM*, 2011.

[20] Y. Wang and G. Noubir. Distributed Cooperation and Diversity for Hybrid Wireless Networks. *IEEE Transactions on Mobile Computing*, 12(3):596–608, 2013.

[21] S. Yi, S. Chun, Y. Lee, S. Park, and S. Jung. *Radio Protocols for LTE and LTE-Advanced*. Wiley, 2012.

[22] B. Zhao, W. Hu, Q. Zheng, and G. Cao. Energy-Aware Web Browsing on Smartphones. *IEEE Transactions on Parallel and Distributed Systems (TPDS), to appear*.

[23] B. Zhao, Q. Zheng, G. Cao, and S. Addepalli. Energy-Aware Web Browsing in 3G Based Smartphones. In *IEEE ICDCS*, 2013.

[24] X. Zhuo, W. Gao, G. Cao, and Y. Dai. Win-Coupon: An Incentive Framework for 3G Traffic Offloading. In *IEEE ICNP*, 2011.

[25] X. Zhuo, W. Gao, G. Cao, and S. Hua. An Incentive Framework for Cellular Traffic Offloading. *IEEE Transactions on Mobile Computing*, 13(3):541–555, 2014.

COSMOS: Computation Offloading as a Service for Mobile Devices

Cong Shi, Karim Habak, Pranesh Pandurangan,
Mostafa Ammar, Mayur Naik, Ellen Zegura
School of Computer Science
Georgia Institute of Technology, Atlanta, GA
{cshi7, karim.habak, ppandura, ammar, naik, ewz}@cc.gatech.edu

ABSTRACT

There is great potential for boosting the performance of mobile devices by offloading computation-intensive parts of mobile applications to the cloud. The full realization of this potential is hindered by a mismatch between how individual mobile devices demand computing resources and how cloud providers offer them: offloading requests from a mobile device usually require quick response, may be infrequent, and are subject to variable network connectivity, whereas cloud resources incur relatively long setup times, are leased for long time quanta, and are indifferent to network connectivity. In this paper, we present the design and implementation of the COSMOS system, which bridges this gap by providing computation offloading as a service to mobile devices. COSMOS efficiently manages cloud resources for offloading requests to both improve offloading performance seen by mobile devices and reduce the monetary cost per request to the provider. COSMOS also effectively allocates and schedules offloading requests to resolve the contention for cloud resources. Moreover, COSMOS makes offloading decisions in a risk-controlled manner to overcome the uncertainties caused by variable network connectivity and program execution. We have implemented COSMOS for Android and explored its design space through computation offloading experiments to Amazon EC2 across different applications and in various settings. We find that COSMOS, configured with the right design choices, has significant potential in reducing the cost of providing cloud resources to mobile devices while at the same time enabling mobile computation speedup.

Categories and Subject Descriptors

C.2.4 [**Computer-Communication Networks**]: Distributed Systems—*Distributed applications*

Keywords

Computation Offloading; Mobile Devices; Intermittent Connectivity; Resource Management

MobiHoc'14, August 11–14, 2014, Philadelphia, PA, USA.
Copyright 2014 ACM 978-1-4503-2620-9/14/08 ...$15.00.
http://dx.doi.org/10.1145/2632951.2632958 .

1. INTRODUCTION

The idea of offloading computation from mobile devices to remote computing resources to improve performance and reduce energy consumption has been around for more than a decade [5, 6]. The usefulness of computation offloading hinges on the ability to achieve high computation speedups with small communication delays. In recent years, this idea has received more attention because of the significant rise in the sophistication of mobile applications, the availability of powerful clouds and the improved connectivity options for mobile devices. By identifying the offloadable tasks at runtime, recent work [11, 10, 15, 20] has aimed to generalize this approach to benefit more mobile applications.

Despite great potential, a key challenge in computation offloading lies in the mismatch between how individual mobile devices demand and access computing resources and how cloud providers offer them. Offloading requests from a mobile device require quick response and may not be very frequent. Therefore, the ideal computing resources suitable for computation offloading should be immediately available upon request and be quickly released after execution. In contrast, cloud computing resources have long setup time and are leased for long time quanta. For example, it takes about 27 seconds to start an Amazon EC2 VM instance. The time quantum for leasing an EC2 VM instance is one hour. If an instance is used for less than an hour, the user must still pay for one-hour usage. This mismatch can thus hamper offloading performance and/or incur high monetary cost.

Complicating this issue is the fact that mobile devices access cloud resources over wireless networks which have variable performance and/or high service cost. For example, 3G networks have relatively low bandwidth, causing long communication delays for computation offloading [11]. On the other hand, although WiFi networks have high bandwidth and are free to use in many cases, their coverage is limited, resulting in intermittent connectivity to the cloud and highly variable access quality even when connectivity exists [8, 12, 24].

In this paper we propose COSMOS, a system that bridges the above-discussed gaps by providing computation offloading as a service. The key premise of COSMOS is that an intermediate service between a commercial cloud provider and mobile devices can make the properties of underlying computing and communication resources transparent to mobile devices and can reorganize these resources in a cost-effective manner to satisfy offloading demands from mobile devices. The COSMOS system receives mobile user computation offload demands and allocates them to a shared set of compute resources that it dynamically acquires (through leases) from a commercial cloud service provider. The goal of COSMOS is to provide the benefit of computation offloading to mobile devices while at the same time minimizing the compute resource leasing cost.

Our goal in this paper is to develop a design for COSMOS, implement it and evaluate its performance. At the heart of COSMOS are two types of decisions: 1) whether a mobile device should offload a particular computation to COSMOS and 2) how COSMOS should manage the acquisition of compute resources from the commercial cloud provider.

We start by formulating an optimization problem whose solution can guide the required decision making. Because of its complexity, no efficient solution to this optimization is available. It does, however, lead us to the identification of three components of COSMOS decision making that we then explore individually. Specifically, we develop a set of novel techniques, including resource-management mechanisms that select resources suitable for computation offloading and adaptively maintain computing resources according to offloading requests, risk-control mechanisms that properly assess returns and risks in making offloading decisions, and task-allocation algorithms that properly allocate offloading tasks to the cloud resources with limited control overhead.

We have implemented COSMOS for Android and evaluated the system for offloading from a set of smartphones/tablets to Amazon EC2, across different applications in various types of mobile environments. We evaluate the performance of the system in several realistic mobile environments. To further explore the design space of COSMOS, we also conduct extensive trace-based simulation. In all these experiments, COSMOS achieves good offloading performance and significantly reduces the monetary cost compared with previous offloading systems like CloneCloud [10]. We find that COSMOS, configured with the right design choices, has significant potential in reducing the cost of providing cloud resources to mobile devices while at the same time enabling mobile computation speedup.

The rest of the paper is organized as follows. Section 2 presents some background material and presents the problem statement and optimization formulation. Section 3 presents an overview of COSMOS's architecture incorporating the insight gained from the optimization formulation regarding the system decomposition. The design details are presented in Section 4. COSMOS is evaluated in Section 5 and 6. We summarize related work in Section 7. Section 8 concludes the paper and discusses future work.

2. BACKGROUND AND PROBLEM STATEMENT

2.1 Background

2.1.1 Computation Offloading

A basic computation-offloading system [10, 11] is composed of a *client component* running on the mobile device and a *server component* running in the cloud. The client component has three major functions. First, it monitors and predicts the network performance of the mobile device. Second, it tracks and predicts the execution requirements of mobile applications in terms of input/output data requirements and execution time on both the mobile device and the cloud. Third, using this information the client component chooses some portions of the computation to execute in the cloud so that the total execution time is minimized. The server component executes these offloaded portions immediately after receiving them and returns the results back to the client component so that the application can be resumed on the mobile device.

Computation offloading trades off communication cost for computation gain. Previous systems [10, 11] usually assume stable network connectivity and adequate cloud computation resources. However, in mobile environments a mobile device may experience varying or even intermittent connectivity, while cloud resources may be temporarily unavailable or occupied. Thus, the communication cost may be higher, while the computation gain will be lower. Moreover, the network and execution prediction may be inaccurate, causing the performance of these systems to be degraded.

2.1.2 Cloud Computation Resources

Cloud computation resources are usually provided in the form of virtual machine (VM) instances. To use a VM instance, a user installs an OS on the VM and starts it up, both incurring delay. VM instances are leased based on a time quanta. e.g., Amazon EC2 uses a one hour lease granularity. If a VM instance is used for less than the time quanta, the user must still pay for usage. A cloud provider typically provides various types of VM instances with different properties and prices. Table 1 lists some properties and prices for three types of Amazon EC2 VM instances: *Standard On-Demand Small* instance (m1.small), *Standard On-Demand Medium* instance (m1.medium) and *High-CPU On-Demand Medium* instance (c1.medium). For some pricing models (e.g., *EC2 spot*), the leasing price may change over time.

Table 1: The characteristics of EC2 on-demand instances. The setup time is measured by starting and stopping each type of instances for 10 times. The average value and standard deviation are reported.

Instance	Cores	CPU(GHz)	Setup(second)	Price($/hr)
m1.small	1	1.7	26.5(5.5)	0.06
m1.medium	1	2.0	26.6(3.7)	0.12
c1.medium	2	2.5	26.7(8.4)	0.145

Note that the server component of offloaded mobile computation needs to run on a VM instance. This server component needs to be launched at the time the offloading request is made and terminated when the required computation is complete. The lifetime of the server component is typically much less than the lease quantum used by the cloud service provider. An important question we consider in our system design is how to ensure there is enough VM capacity available to handle the mobile computation load without needing to always launch VM instances on-demand and incur long setup time.

2.2 Problem Statement

The basic idea of COSMOS is to achieve good offloading performance at low monetary cost by sharing cloud resources among mobile devices. Specifically, in this paper our goal is to minimize the usage cost of cloud resources under the constraint that the speedup of using COSMOS against local execution is larger than $1-\delta$ of the maximal speedup that it can achieve using the same cloud service, where $\delta \in (0,1)$. The extension of COSMOS to support other optimization goals will be discussed in Section 8. A related but independent problem is how COSMOS charges mobile devices for computation offloading, which will also be discussed in Section 8.

Let's assume that the cloud can simultaneously run N VM instances. Let's use $\langle M_i, T_i \rangle$ to denote the usage of the ith VM instance, where M_i is its type (see Table 1 for examples), and $T_i = \{\langle t_{ij}, t'_{ij} \rangle | \forall j, t_{ij} < t'_{ij}, t'_{ij} < t_{i(j+1)}\}$ represents all the leasing periods. We use t_{ij} and t'_{ij} to represent the start time and end time of the jth leasing period, respectively. Let $\psi(M,T)$ be the leasing cost of $\langle M, T \rangle$, which is computed by multiplying the price with the total leasing time quanta.

Let's assume that there are K computation tasks generated by mobile users in the COSMOS system during the period of time of interest. Let $O_k = \langle t_k, c_k, d_{Ik}, d_{Ok} \rangle$ denote the kth computation task, where t_k ($\forall k, t_{k-1} \leq t_k$) is the time when the task was initiated by the mobile user, c_k is the number of CPU cycles it requires, d_{Ik} is the size of its input data, and d_{Ok} is the size of its output data. Let $I(i,k)$ and $I_l(k)$ be indicator functions. If O_k is offloaded to the ith VM instance, $I(i,k) = 1$. Otherwise, $I(i,k) = 0$. Similarly, if it is locally executed, $I_l(k) = 1$. Otherwise, $I_l(k) = 0$. Since O_k should be executed exactly once, $I_l(k) + \sum_i I(i,k) = 1$. Let $L(O_k)$ be the local execution time of O_k which can be estimated based on c_k and the CPU frequency of the mobile device [20]. Let $R_i(O_k)$ be the response time of offloading O_k to the ith VM instance, i.e., the time elapsed from t_k to the time that the output is returned to the mobile device. It depends on the network delays of sending input data and receiving output data, the execution time on the VM instance and the waiting time. Its formula will be shown in Section 4.2. The key symbols are summarized in Table 2.

Table 2: Key symbols used in COSMOS problem formulation

M_i	the type of the ith VM instance
T_i	the leasing periods of the ith VM instance
$\psi(M,T)$	the pricing function for leasing a VM instance
O_k	the kth computation task
$I(i,k)$	the indicator function for offloading task O_k to VM i
$I_l(k)$	the indicator function for executing task O_k locally
$L(O_k)$	the local execution time of the task O_k
$R_i(O_k)$	the response time of offloading the task O_k to VM i

The maximal speedup of using COSMOS against local execution can be obtained by solving the following optimization problem:

$$\text{Max} \quad \sum_{k=1}^{K} \frac{L(O_k)}{\min\{\frac{L(O_k)}{I_l(k)}, \{\frac{R_i(O_k)}{I(i,k)} | \forall i\}\}} \tag{1}$$

$$\text{s.t.} \quad I_l(k) + \sum_{i=1}^{N} I(i,k) = 1$$

Since for each k there is exactly one of the functions $I_l(k)$ and $I(i,k)$ that equals to 1, $\min\{\frac{L(O_k)}{I_l(k)}, \{\frac{R_i(O_k)}{I(i,k)} | \forall i\}\}$ equals to the corresponding $L(O_k)$ or $R_i(O_k)$, representing the response time of task O_k in COSMOS. Thus, Eqn 1 is to maximize the speedup of all tasks. Let's use S_k^* to denote the corresponding maximal speedup achieved by task O_k. We have $\forall k, S_k^* \geq 1$. The goal of COSMOS can be formally formulated as:

$$\text{Min} \quad \sum_{i=1}^{N} \psi(M_i, T_i) \tag{2}$$

$$\text{s.t.} \quad I_l(k) + \sum_{i=1}^{N} I(i,k) = 1$$

$$\frac{L(O_k)}{\min\{\frac{L(O_k)}{I_l(k)}, \{\frac{R_i(O_k)}{I(i,k)} | \forall i\}\}} \geq (1-\delta) S_k^*$$

where $\delta \in (0,1)$ can be arbitrarily chosen by the system. When $\delta \to 1$, all tasks will be executed locally while the total cost will approach 0. When $\delta \to 0$, the speedups approach to the optimal values while the total cost will be high.

COSMOS is to find the values of $\langle M_i, T_i \rangle$, $I_l(k)$, and $I(i,k)$ that optimize Eqn 2. This is a challenging problem especially because we have no information regarding future computation tasks. Our approach to solve this problem is to break it down into three sub-problems and address each of them separately:

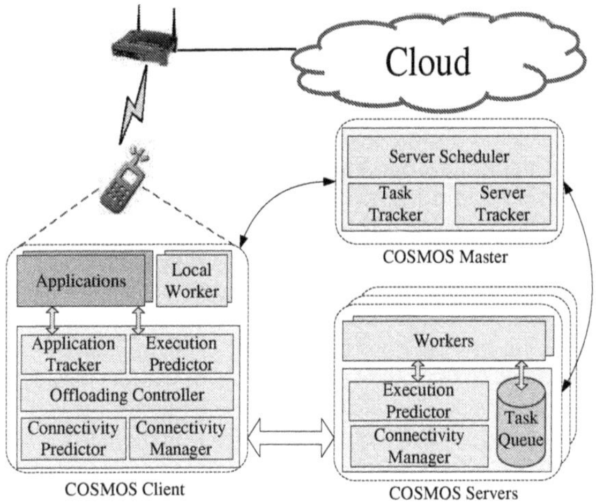

Figure 1: The architecture of the COSMOS system.

- **Cloud resource management**: This is the problem of determining the number and type of VM instances to lease over time, i.e., $\langle M_i, T_i \rangle$. It has two major goals. First, there should always be enough VM instances to ensure high offloading speedup. Second, the cost of leasing VM instances should be minimized.
- **Offloading decision**: This is the problem of deciding whether a mobile device offloads a computation task, i.e., deciding whether to set $I_l(k)$ to 0 or 1. The challenge comes from the uncertainties of network connectivity, program execution, and resource contention. A wrong offloading decision will both waste cloud resources and result in lower speedup. It is very important to properly handle the uncertainties.
- **Task allocation**: This is the problem of choosing a VM instance among all available instances if we decide to offload a computation task, i.e., deciding whether to set $I(i,k)$ to 0 or 1. The decision is made independently by each mobile device. In addition, the decisions for previous computation tasks will impact the decision of the current one because of resource sharing. Therefore, task allocation should be designed as a distributed mechanism.

In the following sections, we will present the design of COSMOS and its mechanisms to solve these problems.

3. COSMOS SYSTEM

Figure 1 provides a high-level overview of the COSMOS system. It consists of three components: a COSMOS Master running on a VM instance that manages cloud resources and exchanges information with mobile devices; a set of active COSMOS Servers each of which runs on a VM instance and executes offloaded tasks; and a COSMOS Client on each mobile device that monitors application execution and network connectivity and makes offloading decisions.

The COSMOS Master is the central component for cloud resource management. It periodically collects information of computation tasks from COSMOS Clients through *task tracker* and the workloads of COSMOS Servers through *server tracker*. Using this information, its *server scheduler* decides the number and type of active COSMOS Servers over time. Note that when a COSMOS Server is turned on/off, its corresponding VM instance is also turned on/off. The algorithms will be described in Section 4.1.

An active COSMOS Server is responsible for executing offloaded computation tasks. Each COSMOS Server has one *task queue* and multiple *worker*s the number of which equals to its number of CPU cores. Computation tasks are executed on a first-come-first-serve basis. The COSMOS Server also estimates and provides the workload information upon request by predicting the execution time of all tasks in the queue through the *execution predictor*. We use Mantis [22], a state-of-the-art predictor for mobile applications.

A COSMOS Client tracks all applications running on its mobile device, makes offloading decisions for them, and allocates tasks to COSMOS Servers. When a mobile application starts, an *application tracker* monitors the application execution and identifies its compute-intensive tasks in the same way as MAUI [11] and CloneCloud [10]. When it reaches the entry point of such a task, the *offloading controller* obtains the computation speedup from the execution predictor and the communication delay from the *connectivity predictor* (e.g., BreadCrumbs [25]) and decides if it should offload the task based on them. The design details of this offloading decision will be described in Section 4.2. If it decides to offload, the COSMOS Client allocates the task to an active COSMOS Server, which will be described in Section 4.3. Finally the COSMOS Client offloads the task and waits to receive the result. If the COSMOS Client cannot obtain the results before a deadline, it executes the task on a local worker.

4. DESIGN DETAILS

4.1 Cloud Resource Management

The cloud resource management has two major mechanisms: how to select the type of VM instance (i.e., M_i) and when to start and stop COSMOS Servers (i.e., T_i).

4.1.1 Resource Selection

COSMOS strives to minimize the cost per offloading request under the constraint that the offloading speedup is large enough. Recall that our goal is to achieve speedup of at least $1 - \delta$ of the maximally possible. Therefore, the resource selection algorithm selects the least cost VM instance whose CPU frequency is larger than $1 - \delta$ of the most powerful VM instance. The algorithm is shown in Algorithm 1.

Algorithm 1 Resource Selection

```
procedure RESOURCESELECTION({I},δ)          ▷ I is a instance type.
    maxFreq ← 0; minCost ← +∞ ;
    for I in {I} do
        if maxFreq < I.f then
            maxFreq ← I.f;
        end if
    end for
    for I in {I} do
        if I.f ≥ (1 − δ)maxFreq && I.p/(I.c×I.f) < minCost then
            maxCost ← I.p/(I.c×I.f);
            selected ← I;
        end if
    end forreturn selected;
end procedure
```

In Algorithm 1, c, f, and p denote the number of processor cores, the CPU frequency and the price of a VM instance, respectively. If all cores are 100% utilized during a time quanta τ, the VM instance totally executes $cf\tau$ CPU cycles. The cost of each CPU cycle is $\frac{p}{cf}$. We use this value as the cost for comparison in Algorithm 1.

4.1.2 Server Scheduling

Server scheduling is the key mechanism to balance the usage cost of VM instances and the offloading performance. Its basic operations are as follows: The COSMOS Master periodically collects the number of offloading requests and the workloads of COSMOS Servers (every 30 seconds in our implementation). When the workloads are too large, it turns on new COSMOS Servers. When a time quantum of a COSMOS Server is to expire, it turns off the COSMOS Server if the remaining COSMOS Servers are enough to handle the offloading requests. The algorithm is shown in Algorithm 2.

Algorithm 2 Server Scheduling

```
1: procedure SERVERSCHEDULING(λ,μ)   ▷ λ and μ are reported arrival
   rate and service time of offloading requests in the last round.
2:     λs ← getMaxArrivalRatePerServer(μ, μ/(1−δ));
3:     n ← ⌈λ/λs⌉;
4:     if n > activeServers.size() then
5:         turnOnServers(n - activeServers.size());
6:     else
7:         for s ∈ activeServers do
8:             if s.quantumExpiring() then
9:                 pendingServers.add(s);
10:            end if
11:        end for
12:        turnOffServers();
13:    end if
14: end procedure
15: procedure TURNONSERVERS(n)            ▷ n is the number of server
16:    for i = 1:n do
17:        if pendingServers.isEmpty() then
18:            activeServers.add(turnOnAServer())
19:        else
20:            activeServers.add(pendingServers.remove(0));
21:        end if
22:    end for
23: end procedure
24: procedure TURNOFFSERVERS
25:    for s ∈ pendingServers do
26:        if s.quantumaExpired() then
27:            turnOff(s);
28:        end if
29:    end for
30: end procedure
```

Every round the COSMOS Master computes the current arrival rate and service time of offloaded computation tasks and uses them to estimate the minimal number of COSMOS Servers to achieve the desired offloading performance. If the number of active COSMOS Servers is smaller than this value, it turns on new COSMOS Servers. A COSMOS Server whose current time quantum expires will be turned off only if the number of remaining COSMOS Servers are larger than the minimal value for several rounds. Otherwise, its lease will be renewed for another quantum.

A key function of Algorithm 2 is how to estimate the maximal arrival rate (i.e., λ_s) that a COSMOS Server can handle, as shown in Line 2. Since a COSMOS Server serves offloading requests in a first-come-first-serve manner, it can be modeled as a G/G/c system. Based on the required speedup (i.e., $1-\delta$ of the maximal speedup), we obtain that the maximal response time of the system should be smaller than $\frac{\mu}{1-\delta}$. According to Kingman's formula [19], we can obtain the value of λ_s.

4.2 Offloading Decision

The offloading controller uses the information from the connectivity and execution predictors to estimate the potential benefits of the offloading service. Ideally, if future connectivity and execution time can be accurately predicted immediately after the mobile application starts, the offloading controller can make the global optimal offloading decision. However, such global optimum is unavailable in reality.

Instead, the offloading controller uses a greedy strategy to make the offloading decision. Every time an offloadable task is initiated, the offloading controller determines if it is beneficial to offload it. Because of the uncertainties inherent in the mobile environment, the offloading decision takes risk into consideration. In case a bad decision has been made, it will also adjust its strategy with new information available.

4.2.1 *Offloading Gain*

When an offloadable task, O_k, is initiated at time t_k, the offloading controller needs to determine if it is beneficial to offload this task to the cloud. Let us use T_{ws} to denote the time to wait for connectivity before sending the data, T_s for the time to send the data, T_c for the execution time of the task in the cloud, T_{wr} for the time to wait for connectivity before receiving the result, T_r for the time to receive the result. The local execution time is $L(O_k)$, which is estimated by the execution predictor. The response time of offloading to an active COSMOS Server, $R(O_k)$, can be expressed as:

$$R(O_k) = T_{ws} + T_s + T_c + T_{wr} + T_r \tag{3}$$

It is beneficial to offload only if the local execution time is longer than the response time of offloading. Therefore, we use their difference to represent the offloading gain:

$$G = L(O_k) - R(O_k) \tag{4}$$

Because of the uncertainties in the mobile environment, the offloading controller can only obtain a distribution for G (i.e., $E(G)$ and $\sigma^2(G)$). Simply using $E(G)$ to make the offloading decision will introduce the risk of longer execution time. We describe the risk-control mechanism in the next subsection.

4.2.2 *Risk-Controlled Offloading Decision*

Our risk-controlled offloading is based on two key ideas. First, we use risk-adjusted return [9] in making the offloading decision so that the return and risk of offloading are simultaneously considered. Specifically, $E(G)$ and $\sigma(G)$ are used as the return and risk of the offloading gain, respectively. Thus, the risk-adjusted return of offloading gain is $\frac{E(G)}{\sigma(G)}$. When its value is larger than certain threshold, the computation task will be offloaded to the cloud. Otherwise, it will be locally executed. Second, we re-evaluate the return and risk when new information is available. The algorithm is shown in Algorithm 3.

When a computation task is initiated, the offloading controller evaluate its return and risk of offloading gain. Functions getOffloadingGain(O_k) and getOffloadingRisk(O_k) return $E(G)$ and $\sigma(G)$, respectively. The detailed algorithms to compute them are described in the appendix. If the risk-adjusted return (i.e., $\frac{E(G)}{\sigma(G)}$) is larger than a threshold, the offloading controller offload the task to the cloud. In addition, it also listens to the connectivity status which has high impact on $E(G)$ and $\sigma(G)$. Once new connectivity information is updated, it re-evaluates the risk-adjusted return and adjust its decision accordingly.

4.3 Task Allocation

When a COSMOS Client is to offload a task, it must decide which COSMOS Server should execute the task. We consider three heuristic methods. The first method is that the COSMOS Master maintains a global queue to directly accept offloading requests and allocates tasks when a COSMOS server has idle cores. Although it should have high server utilization, the network connecting the COSMOS Master may become a bottleneck. The second method is that the COSMOS Client queries the workloads of a set of COSMOS servers and randomly chooses one with low workload to allocate the new task. Although tasks are directly sent to COSMOS Servers in this method, it will cause huge control traffic. In addition, it will cause extra waiting time. The third method is that the COSMOS Master provides each COSMOS Client a set of active COSMOS Servers and informs it the average workloads of all COSMOS Servers. Each COSMOS Client randomly chooses a server among them to offload the task. This method has minimal control overhead. As the resource-management mechanism ensures that the workloads of COSMOS Servers are low, it should also have good performance. Thus, COSMOS uses the third method for task allocation.

Algorithm 3 Risk Controlled Offloading

procedure OFFLOADING(O_k) ▷ O_k is the computation task.
    if riskAdjustedOffloading(O_k) **then**
        offloadedTask ← O_k;
        registerReceiver(this,CONNECTIVITY);
    end if
end procedure
procedure RISKADJUSTEDOFFLOADING(O_k)
    gain ← getOffloadingGain(O_k); ▷ $E(G)$ as offloading gain
    risk ← getOffloadingRisk(O_k); ▷ $\sigma(G)$ as offloading risk
    if gain/risk $\geq \alpha$ **then**
        offload(O_k); **return** true;
    else
        localExecute(O_k)
        unregisterReceiver(this); **return** false;
    end if
end procedure
procedure ONRECEIVE(conn) ▷ conn is the connectivity status.
    riskAdjustedOffloading(offloadedTask);
end procedure
procedure RECEIVERESULT(O_k)
    offloadedTask ← NULL;
    unregisterReceiver(this);
end procedure

5. SYSTEM IMPLEMENTATION AND EVALUATION

In this section, we evaluate our prototype implementation of COSMOS in various mobile environments.

5.1 Implementation

We implemented the COSMOS Server on Android x86 [2]. To run COSMOS Servers on Amazon EC2, we use an Android-x86 AMI [21] to create EC2 instances. Since Android-x86 is a 32-bit OS, three types of EC2 instances can be used for COSMOS Servers, as listed in Table 1. Based on our resource selection algorithm in Section 4.1.1, *High-CPU On-Demand Medium* instances are used to run COSMOS Servers.

The COSMOS Master runs on an EC2 instance running Ubuntu 12.04. It uses the Amazon EC2 API tools [1] to start and stop EC2 VM instances on which COSMOS Servers run.

A COSMOS Client runs on an Android device equipped with both WiFi and 3G connections. It uses the Java reflection techniques to enable the offloading of computation tasks. We modified three existing Android applications to use COSMOS, including:

FACEDETECT is a face detection application that uses APIs in the Android SDK. We collected a data set of pictures containing faces from Google Image.

VOICERECOG is an Android port of the speech recognition program PocketSphinx [18]. For simplicity of experiments, we also modified it to use audio files as input.

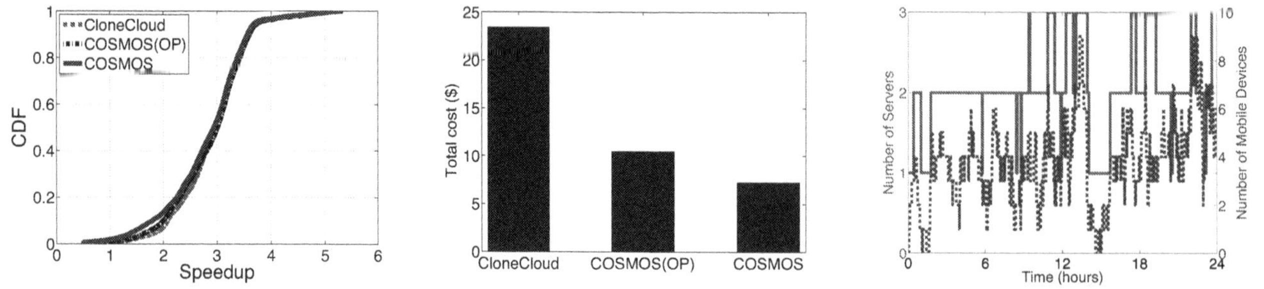

(a) Speedup (b) Cost (c) Number of active servers in COSMOS

Figure 2: The performance of COSMOS on Amazon EC2 for FACEDETECT in one day. There are 10 Android devices which randomly become active or idle. When they are active, they randomly execute the FACEDETECT application.

DROIDFISH is an Android port of the chess engine Stockfish [3] that allows users to set the strength of the AI logic.

5.2 Experimental Setup

We evaluate COSMOS in four different mobile scenarios:

- **Stable WiFi**: A student carrying a mobile device sits in his lab. WiFi is stable and fast.
- **Indoor WiFi**: A student randomly walks in a building which has good WiFi coverage.
- **Outdoor WiFi**: A student takes a campus shuttle, experiencing varying signal strength and frequent intermittent connectivity.
- **Outdoor 3G**: A student is on his commute between home and school. 3G is used for Internet access.

For each scenario, we measure the network connectivity and construct a database for the connectivity predictor.

We compare COSMOS with three baseline systems:

- **CloneCloud** is a basic offloading system in which each mobile device has a server in the cloud that is always on [10]. In addition, it assumes stable network connectivity.
- **Oracle** assumes accurate knowledge of all connectivity and execution profile information necessary to make the offloading decision. Since this is impossible to implement, we use post-analysis to obtain the results. It represents an upper-bound on offloading benefits.
- **COSMOS(OP)** is a variant of COSMOS with a simple strategy for resource management, i.e., the number of active COSMOS Servers are over-provisioned for the peak requests. We assume the number of peak requests is accurately estimated in advance.

We use two metrics to evaluate COSMOS: *speedup* and *cost*. The values of speedup are different for different mobile devices. For fair comparison, we use a Samsung Galaxy Tab running Android 2.3 to obtain the local execution time in calculating speedup. The prices for EC2 on-demand instances are used to compute the cost.

5.3 COSMOS Performance with Stable WiFi

This represents the best network environment for computation offloading. In this scenario, the performance of cloud resource management dominates the COSMOS performance.

In this set of experiments, we use 10 Android devices to conduct a one-day experiment for each of the systems: CloneCloud, COSMOS(OP), and COSMOS. During an experiment, each device randomly becomes active or idle from time to time. Their durations follow an exponential distribution, with average values of 0.5 hour and 1 hour, respectively. When a device is active, it randomly starts the FACEDETECT application following a Poisson distribution with arrival rate of 0.2. The same random seed is used for all three experiments.

The experiment results are reported in Figure 2. As shown in Figure 2(a), all three systems achieve similar speedups, i.e., 2.91X, 2.86X and 2.76X on average for CloneCloud, COSMOS(OP), and COSMOS, respectively. Meanwhile, the total cost of COSMOS ($7.25) is significantly lower than that of CloneCloud ($23.4) and COSMOS(OP) ($10.44), as shown in Figure 2(b).

To demonstrate how COSMOS reduces its cost, we plot the number of active devices (the dotted blue line) and that of active COSMOS Servers (the red line) in Figure 2(c). COSMOS adaptively changes the number of active COSMOS Servers according to the arrival rate of offloading requests. Therefore, COSMOS is able to reduce its cost by turning off some COSMOS Servers when the number of offloading requests is low. In contrast, COSMOS(OP) spends 44% more money to keep 3 COSMOS Servers active the whole day, whereas CloneCloud spends 223% more money than COSMOS with only 5.4% extra speedup.

5.4 COSMOS Performance with Variable Connectivity

In this subsection, we evaluate how COSMOS handles variable connectivity in Indoor WiFi, Outdoor WiFi and Outdoor 3G. To eliminate the impact of cloud resource contention, we run a COSMOS Server on a machine with an 8-core 3.4GHz CPU, running VirtualBox 4.1.22, in our lab.

The dynamic mobile environment makes the comparison very hard since each invocation of an offloadable task has different Internet access quality. To achieve fair comparison, at runtime we force COSMOS to offload every offloadable task and record the information of network connectivity and application states. Then we replay these applications later for each baseline.

5.4.1 Results for Different Scenarios

In the first set of experiments, we evaluate the performance of COSMOS in the three different mobile scenarios using the FACEDETECT application. Figure 3 shows the speedup distribution in those experiments. When the speedup is larger than 1, the system outperforms local execution. Otherwise, the system takes longer time than local execution. In all these experiments, COSMOS performs well and achieves similar performance to Oracle. It also outperforms CloneCloud by reducing the number of bad offloading decisions.

We also find some interesting phenomena in these experiments. First, in the scenario of Indoor WiFi where mobile users have good WiFi coverage, offloading computation to the cloud benefits the mobile applications in about 80% of the cases. However, there are still about 20% in which a simple method like CloneCloud will increase the execution time as much as 20 times. COSMOS re-

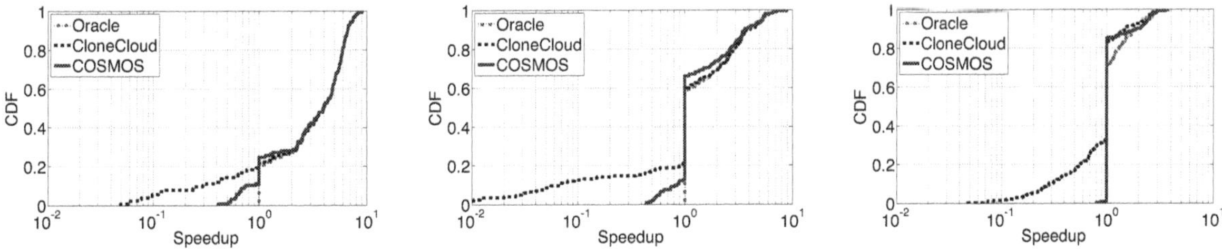

(a) Indoor WiFi (b) Outdoor WiFi (c) Outdoor 3G

Figure 3: A comparison of COSMOS's performance benefits using the FACEDETECT application in different mobile scenarios.

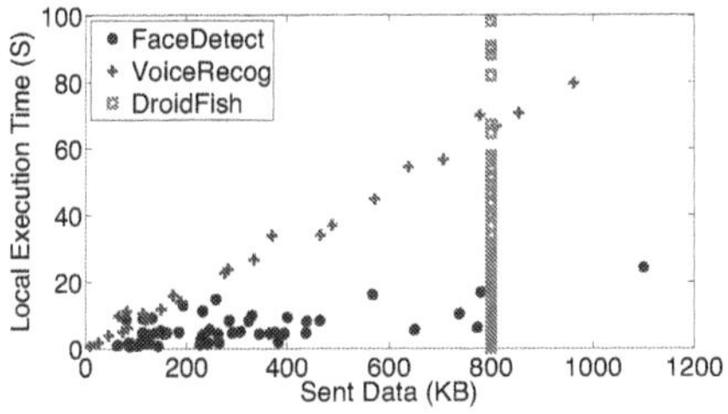

Figure 4: Local execution time vs.the size of migrated data.

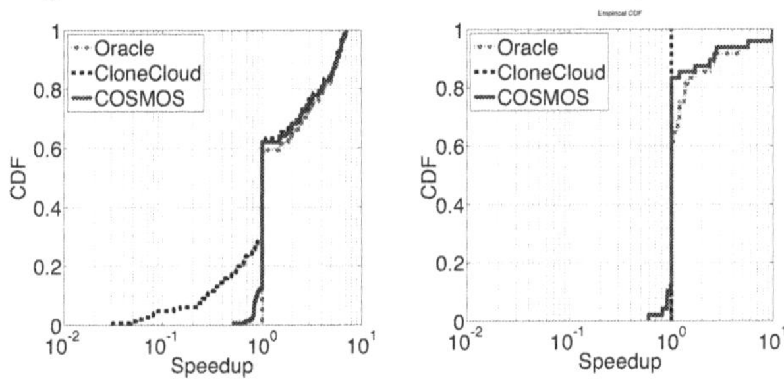

(a) VOICERECOG (b) DROIDFISH

Figure 5: COSMOS performance for different applications. All experiments are conducted in the scenario of Outdoor WiFi.

duces the portion of negative cases to about 10% with the smallest speedup at approximately 0.4. In addition, it also enables 75% of the cases to benefit from offloading. COSMOS achieves 4.1x overall speedup in this scenario. Second, in the scenario of Outdoor WiFi, CloneCloud can result in extreme speedup penalty when wrong offloading decision is made. In contrast, COSMOS still manages to limit the worst speedup results. Third, in the scenario of Outdoor 3G, ideally at most 30% of the cases benefit from offloading. This is because 3G has relatively lower bandwidth and longer delays. In this scenario, COSMOS only occasionally makes some poor decision, while CloneCloud causes more than 30% of the offloaded computation to take more time to execute.

5.4.2 *Results for Different Applications*

The gain from computation offloading is normally counterbalanced by the communication overhead. Different applications usually have different execution times and different amount of data exchanged between the mobile device and the cloud. In this subsection, we evaluate COSMOS on applications with different computation and communication properties. Figure 4 plots the local execution time of the offloadable tasks and the corresponding data to be sent to the cloud. We can see that local execution time of VOICERECOG is almost proportional to the data size, while DROIDFISH has constant data size.

To demonstrate how these application properties impact computation offloading, we compare the performance of different applica-

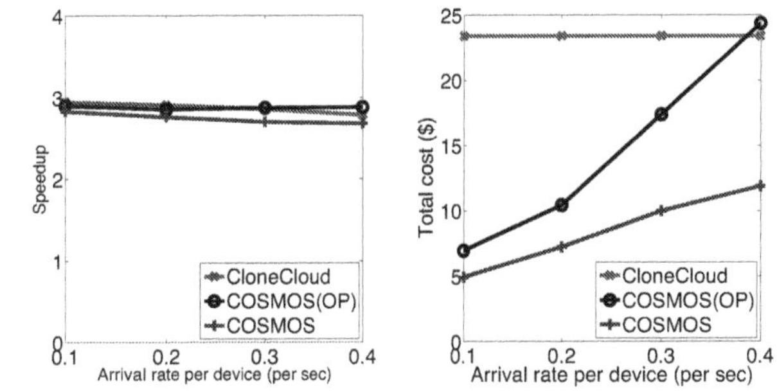

(a) Speedup (b) Cost

Figure 6: Impact of the arrival rate on COSMOS performance.

tions using COSMOS in the scenario of Outdoor WiFi. The results are plotted in Figure 5.

COSMOS performs well in all these experiments. For FACEDETECT and VOICERECOG, COSMOS helps more than 35% of the offloadable task invocations benefit from offloading. Meanwhile, it limits the portion of bad decision cases to be about 10% with small extra execution time. In contrast, CloneCloud makes many more bad offloading decisions and causes these invocations to last much longer.

The behavior of DROIDFISH is quite different from those of FACEDETECT and VOICERECOG. Even Oracle can only help about 15% of those invocations achieve more than 2X speedup. This is because the data uploaded to the cloud is so large that if the computation gain is small it cannot compensate for the communication overhead. We also notice that CloneCloud always chooses to execute locally because it underestimates the computation gain using previous invocations. Moreover, compared with Oracle, COSMOS does not help computations that can only achieve small performance improvement because it tries to control the risk of offloading. As a result, only a small portion of invocations have longer execution time when using COSMOS.

6. TRACE BASED SIMULATION

In this section, we use trace-based simulation to extensively evaluate the properties of COSMOS and how its components impact its performance.

6.1 Scalability

In this subsection, we analyze the impact of offload request intensity on the performance of COSMOS.

In the first set of experiments, we conduct simulation-based experiments using information logged in the experiments of Section 5.3. We vary the arrival rate of offloading requests from 0.1 to 0.4 per second and keep other settings unchanged.

Figure 6 plots the experiment results. In all experiments, COSMOS achieves the lowest cost and high speedup. We also make the

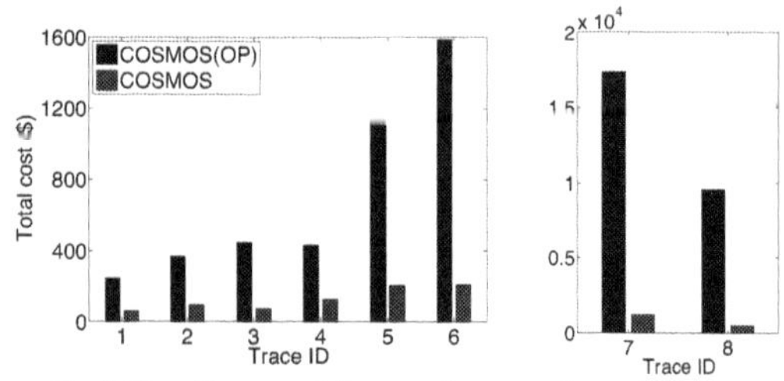

Figure 7: Offloading cost for various real-world access traces.

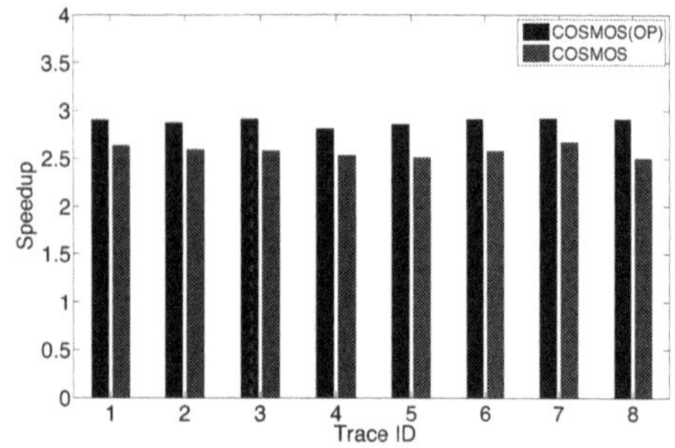

Figure 8: Offloading speedup for various real-world access traces.

following observations. First, both COSMOS and COSMOS(OP) have lower cost with lower arrival rate, while CloneCloud has constant cost. This indicates the importance of cloud resource sharing in reducing the cost. Second, when the arrival rate is very high (e.g., 0.4), COSMOS(OP) has higher speedup (i.e., 2.87X) than CloneCloud (i.e., 2.78X). Its cost is slightly higher than CloneCloud. Third, the speedup of COSMOS is similar with those of CloneCloud and COSMOS(OP) in all experiments.

Next, we evaluate COSMOS using real-world access traces [4]. The data set consists of 8 access traces each of which is composed of access requests in 2 days. We use these timestamps of access requests as the start time of mobile applications on various mobile devices. We evaluate the performance of COSMOS through simulation. The average number of requests from the same user is very low in the traces, indicating extremely high cost of CloneCloud. Therefore, we only compare COSMOS with COSMOS(OP). The costs and speedups for the FACEDETECT application on various traces are plotted in Figure 7 and 8, respectively.

COSMOS yields slightly smaller speedups but at significantly lower cost than COSMOS(OP) on all traces. Specifically, COSMOS(OP) pays 13.2 times more money than COSMOS on trace 7, while its speedup (i.e., 2.87X) is only slightly higher than that of COSMOS (i.e., 2.7X). COSMOS is able to reduce the cost by an order of magnitude while still achieving 2.7X speedup. The results of this set of experiments demonstrate that COSMOS is able to provide computation offloading with high performance at very low cost.

We also conducted experiments for our other two mobile applications, as well as a mix of all three applications. The results are similar and we omit them for brevity.

6.2 Robustness

To make the offloading decision, a COSMOS Client relies on its connectivity predictions and execution predictions to estimate how long an offloaded task will need to complete processing and return result (response time). Errors in these predictions may lead to incorrect estimation of response time and thus wrong offloading decisions and performance degradation. Here, we investigate how

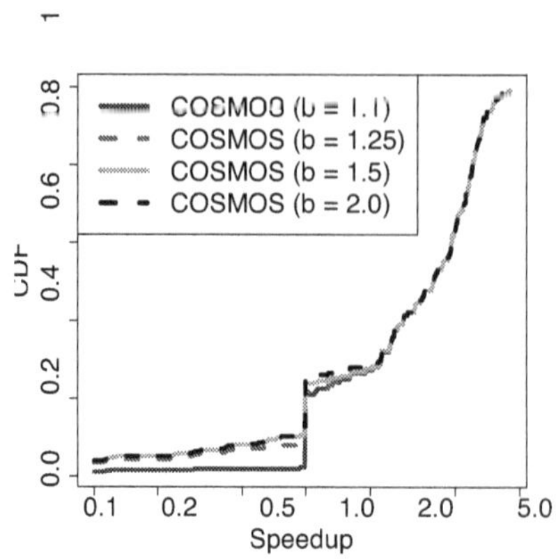

Figure 9: The impact of prediction error on COSMOS in Indoor WiFi

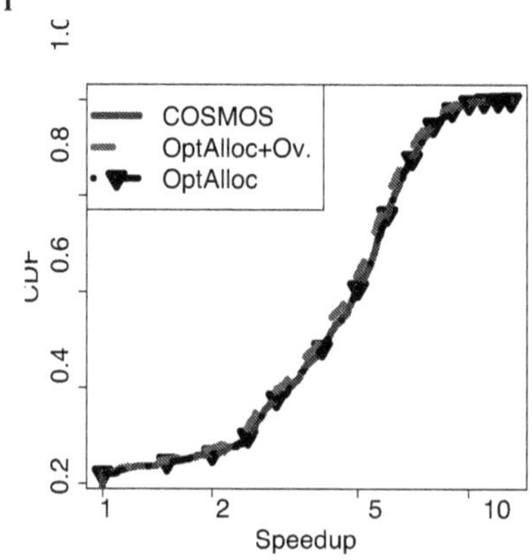

Figure 10: The performance of task allocation for Indoor WiFi

robust COSMOS performance is relative to such estimation errors. Because the farther the prediction is in the future the higher the absolute errors [25], we use an exponential function ($E = (-1)^r b^T$), where r is a uniform random variable and $r \in \{0, 1\}$, T is the response time. To show robustness of COSMOS and emulate different erroneous environments, we change b from 1.1 to 2. Our results are depicted in Figure 9. It shows that with the increase of the prediction error, the performance of COSMOS is degraded slightly. However, even with severe errors, COSMOS is still able to achieve high speedup for most offloading requests which highlights that the higher the offloading gains the more robustness against prediction errors.

6.3 Task Allocation

To distribute the tasks across different COSMOS Servers, our task-allocation algorithm uses aggregated information about the workloads on these servers. Such aggregated information may lead to sub-optimal distribution of the tasks across the servers and affect performance. To quantify the efficiency of our task allocation algorithm, we compare it with two algorithms: 1) Optimal Allocation (OptAlloc) and 2) Optimal Allocation with Overhead (OptAlloc+Ov.). The Optimal Allocation algorithm is based on knowing the realtime COSMOS Servers queueing information and assigning a task to the server which minimizes its queuing delay. Optimal Allocation with Overhead uses OptAlloc mechanism while adding the overhead of getting the COSMOS Servers queuing information which we estimate to be one round trip time from the mobile device to COSMOS Servers. Figure 10 compares COSMOS task allocation mechanism with these two algorithms. We observe that, because COSMOS ensures that the load on COSMOS Servers stays low, the Optimal Allocation mechanism did not outperform COS-

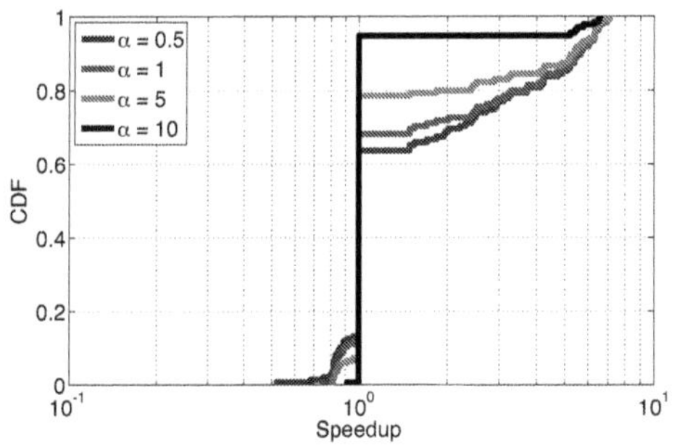

Figure 11: The tradeoff between risk and return. We use different values of α for VOICERECOG in the scenario of Outdoor WiFi.

MOS. When the RTT overhead is accounted for, the performance degrades only slightly.

6.4 The Return-Risk Tradeoff

COSMOS enables applications to control the risk of offloading by setting the value of α. An application sensitive to extra delays can use large α value, while a small α value will result in higher expected return. To show how α impacts the return-risk tradeoff, we apply various values of α to the VOICERECOG application in the scenario of Outdoor WiFi.

Figure 11 plots the results. When the value of α increases from 0.5 to 10, the portion of invocations with speedup less than 1 decreases from about 10% to almost 0%. Meanwhile the portion of invocations that can benefit from offloading also drops from about 35% to 5%. It will be important to find a proper tradeoff between return and risk a question we relegate to future research.

7. RELATED WORK

The concept of cyber foraging [26, 13], i.e., dynamically augmenting mobile devices with resource-rich infrastructure, was proposed more than a decade ago. Since then significant work has been done to augment the capacity of resource-constrained mobile devices using computation offloading [5, 6, 16, 7]. A related technique proposes the use of cloudlets which provide software instantiated in real-time on nearby computing resources [27]. Recognizing the importance of quick responses, Ha et al. [17] propose various virtual machine techniques to enable fast provisioning of a cloudlet.

Closer to our work, MAUI [11] enables mobile applications to reduce the energy consumption through automated offloading. Similarly, CloneCloud [10] can minimize either energy consumption or execution time of mobile applications by automatically identifying compute-intensive parts of those applications. ThinkAir [20] enables the offloading of parallel tasks with server-side support. These systems focus on how to enable computation offloading for mobile devices. Based on these offloading techniques, COSMOS takes the next important step further to bridge the gap between offloading demands and the availability of cloud computing resources. In addition, COSMOS simultaneously considers performance and monetary cost in offloading. Moreover, they assume a stable network environment, whereas COSMOS also handles the more challenging mobile environment where connectivity is highly variable.

The challenges of computation offloading with variable connectivity have been identified in [28]. A system, Serendipity [29], was designed for computation offloading among intermittently connected mobile devices. In contrast, COSMOS proposes techniques to handle the variable connectivity for offloading to a cloud. A detailed survey of cyber foraging can be found in [13].

Our work is also related to studies on cloud resource management. This problem is intensively studied in the context of power saving in data centers [23, 14, 30]. For example, Lu et al. [23] uses reactive approaches to manage the number of active servers based on current request rate. Gandhi et al. [14] investigate policies for dynamic resource management when the servers have large setup time. COSMOS is different from them in three major aspects. First, they minimize the cost of power consumption, whereas COSMOS reduces the cost of leasing cloud resources. Second, in COSMOS computation tasks may be offloaded to the cloud or be executed on local devices, while in data centers services are always provided by servers. Third, COSMOS also needs to handle variable network connectivity of mobile devices, which is unnecessary for data centers.

8. CONCLUSION AND FUTURE WORK

In this paper, we proposed COSMOS, a system that provides computation offloading as a service to resolve the mismatch between how individual mobile devices demand computing resources and how cloud providers offer them. COSMOS solves two key challenges to achieve this goal, including how to manage and share the cloud resources and how to handle the variable connectivity in making offloading decision. We have implemented COSMOS and conducted an extensive evaluation. The experimental results show that COSMOS enables effective computation offloading at low cost.

There are some future directions to extend COSMOS. We will explore how to extend COSMOS to provide the computation offloading services in a manner that optimizes the energy consumption of mobile devices. It requires two major changes. First, the offloading controller should make the offloading decision based on energy consumption. It should delay computation offloading until the network connectivity is good. Second, the cloud resources can be used in a more efficient way. Instead of immediately executing each offloaded task, COSMOS should wait until enough tasks are aggregated. In addition, we will investigate the proper pricing model for COSMOS. There are several possible methods. Users pay monthly service fees and can use COSMOS as frequently as they want. Alternately, an offloaded task could be charged according to its execution time. It's even possible for mobile devices to bid for computation-offloading. When the number of offloading requests is small, COSMOS could charge a lower price to attract more requests and thereby avoid wasting cloud resources.

Acknowledgments

We would like to thank the anonymous reviewers for their insightful feedback. This work was supported in part by the US National Science Foundation through grant CNS 1161879.

9. REFERENCES

[1] Amazon ec2 api tools. `http://aws.amazon.com/developertools/351`.

[2] Android-x86. `http://www.android-x86.org/`.

[3] Droidfish. `http://web.comhem.se/petero2home/droidfish`.

[4] National laboratory for applied network research. anonymized access logs. `ftp://ftp.ircache.net/Traces/`, 2007.

[5] R. Balan, J. Flinn, M. Satyanarayanan, S. Sinnamohideen, and H.-I. Yang. The case for cyber foraging. In *ACM SIGOPS European workshop*, 2002.
[6] R. K. Balan, D. Gergle, M. Satyanarayanan, and J. Herbsleb. Simplifying cyber foraging for mobile devices. In *ACM MobiSys*, 2007.
[7] R. K. Balan, M. Satyanarayanan, S. Y. Park, and T. Okoshi. Tactics-based remote execution for mobile computing. In *ACM Mobisys*, pages 273–286, 2003.
[8] A. Balasubramanian, R. Mahajan, and A. Venkataramani. Augmenting mobile 3g using wifi. In *ACM Mobisys*, 2010.
[9] J. Berk and P. DeMarzo. *Corporate finance*. Addison-Wesley, 2007.
[10] B. Chun, S. Ihm, P. Maniatis, M. Naik, and A. Patti. Clonecloud: elastic execution between mobile device and cloud. In *EuroSys*, pages 301–314, 2011.
[11] E. Cuervo, A. Balasubramanian, D.-k. Cho, A. Wolman, S. Saroiu, R. Chandra, and P. Bahl. Maui: making smartphones last longer with code offload. In *ACM MobiSys*, 2010.
[12] P. Deshpande, X. Hou, and S. R. Das. Performance comparison of 3g and metro-scale wifi for vehicular network access. In *ACM IMC*, 2010.
[13] J. Flinn. Cyber foraging: Bridging mobile and cloud computing. *Synthesis Lectures on Mobile and Pervasive Computing*, 7(2):1–103, 2012.
[14] A. Gandhi, M. Harchol-Balter, R. Raghunathan, and M. A. Kozuch. Autoscale: Dynamic, robust capacity management for multi-tier data centers. *ACM Trans. Comput. Syst.*, 30(4):14:1–14:26, 2012.
[15] M. S. Gordon, D. A. Jamshidi, S. Mahlke, Z. M. Mao, and X. Chen. COMET: code offload by migrating execution transparently. In *USENIX OSDI*, pages 93–106, 2012.
[16] X. Gu, K. Nahrstedt, A. Messer, I. Greenberg, and D. Milojicic. Adaptive offloading inference for delivering applications in pervasive computing environments. In *IEEE PERCOM*, 2003.
[17] K. Ha, P. Pillai, W. Richter, Y. Abe, and M. Satyanarayanan. Just-in-time provisioning for cyber foraging. In *ACM MobiSys*, 2013.
[18] D. Huggins-Daines, M. Kumar, A. Chan, A. Black, M. Ravishankar, and A. Rudnicky. Pocketsphinx: A free, real-time continuous speech recognition system for hand-held devices. In *IEEE ICASSP*, volume 1, pages I–I, 2006.
[19] J. Kingman. The single server queue in heavy traffic. In *Mathematical Proceedings of the Cambridge Philosophical Society*, volume 57, pages 902–904. Cambridge Univ Press, 1961.
[20] S. Kosta, A. Aucinas, P. Hui, R. Mortier, and X. Zhang. Thinkair: Dynamic resource allocation and parallel execution in the cloud for mobile code offloading. In *IEEE Infocom*, 2012.
[21] S. Kosta, V. Perta, J. Stefa, P. Hui, and A. Mei. Clone2Clone (C2C): Peer to Peer Networking of Smartphones on the Cloud. In *5th USENIX Workshop on Hot Topics in Cloud Computing*, San Jose, CA, jun 2013.
[22] Y. Kwon, S. Lee, H. Yi, D. Kwon, S. Yang, B.-G. Chun, L. Huang, P. Maniatis, M. Naik, and Y. Paek. Mantis: Automatic performance prediction for smartphone applications. In *USENIX ATC*, 2013.
[23] Y.-H. Lu, E.-Y. Chung, T. Šimunić, L. Benini, and G. De Micheli. Quantitative comparison of power management algorithms. In *DATE*, pages 20–26, 2000.
[24] R. Mahajan, J. Zahorjan, and B. Zill. Understanding wifi-based connectivity from moving vehicles. In *ACM IMC*, 2007.
[25] A. J. Nicholson and B. D. Noble. Breadcrumbs: forecasting mobile connectivity. In *ACM MobiCom*, pages 46–57, 2008.
[26] M. Satyanarayanan. Pervasive computing: Vision and challenges. *Personal Communications, IEEE*, 8(4):10–17, 2001.
[27] M. Satyanarayanan, P. Bahl, R. Caceres, and N. Davies. The case for VM-based cloudlets in mobile computing. *IEEE Pervasive Computing*, 2009.
[28] C. Shi, M. H. Ammar, E. W. Zegura, and M. Naik. Computing in cirrus clouds: the challenge of intermittent connectivity. In *ACM MCC*, pages 23–28, 2012.
[29] C. Shi, V. Lakafosis, M. Ammar, and E. Zegura. Serendipity: Enabling remote computing among intermittently connected mobile devices. In *ACM MobiHoc*, 2012.
[30] B. Urgaonkar, P. Shenoy, A. Chandra, P. Goyal, and T. Wood. Agile dynamic provisioning of multi-tier internet applications. *ACM Trans. Auton. Adapt. Syst.*, pages 1:1–1:39, 2008.

APPENDIX

In this appendix we describe how to compute the offloading gain G of a task at time t_k. Depending on the connectivity at time t_k, T_{ws} and T_s have different distributions. In the case that the mobile device connects to the cloud at time t_k, $T_{ws} = 0$; $T_s = \frac{d_s}{b_u(t_k)}$, where d_s is the data size, and $b_u(t_k)$ is the upload bandwidth at time t_k. d_s is available at time t_k, while $b_u(t_k)$ can be estimated using the current signal strength. Otherwise, $T_{ws} = R_{D,t_k}$. $T_s = \frac{d_s}{b_u^*}$, where b_u^* is the overall upload bandwidth of the entire trace.

The value of T_{wr} depends on whether the mobile device still connects to the cloud when the cloud finishes execution at time $t + T_{ws} + T_s + T_c$. If connected, $T_{wr} = 0$. Otherwise,

$$T_{wr} = \begin{cases} D - R_{C,t_k} + T_s + T_c, & \text{if connected at } t_k \\ D - C + T_s + T_c, & \text{otherwise} \end{cases} \quad (5)$$

where C and D are contact duration and inter-contact duration, respectively.

T_r also depends on the connectivity at time $t' = t_k + T_{ws} + T_s + T_c$. If connected, $T_r = \frac{d_r}{b_d(t')}$, where d_r is the result size, and $b_d(t')$ is the download bandwidth. Otherwise $T_r = \frac{d_r}{b_d^*}$, where b_d^* is the average download bandwidth.

According to the above analysis, T_{wr} is directly related to T_s and T_c. T_r is indirectly related to T_s and T_c as $T_s + T_c$ may impact the distribution of signal strength which impacts T_r. However, this correlation is small and, thus, be ignored in the implementation for simplicity. Other variables are independent of each other. Therefore, the variance of offloading gain can be computed using

$$\begin{aligned} \sigma^2(G) &= \sigma^2(T_{ws}) + \sigma^2(T_s) + \sigma^2(T_c) + \sigma^2(T_{wr}) \\ &\quad + \sigma^2(T_r) + \sigma^2(T_l) + 2\sigma(T_s + T_c, T_{wr}) \end{aligned} \quad (6)$$

Path Reconstruction in Dynamic Wireless Sensor Networks Using Compressive Sensing

Zhidan Liu*† Zhenjiang Li† Mo Li† Wei Xing* Dongming Lu*
*College of Computer Science and Technology, Zhejiang University, China
†School of Computer Engineering, Nanyang Technological University, Singapore
danielliu@zju.edu.cn, {lzjiang, limo}@ntu.edu.sg, {wxing, ldm}@zju.edu.cn

ABSTRACT

This paper presents CSPR, a compressive sensing based approach for path reconstruction in wireless sensor networks. By viewing the whole network as a path representation space, an arbitrary routing path can be represented by a path vector in the space. As path length is usually much smaller than the network size, such path vectors are sparse, i.e., the majority of elements are zeros. By encoding sparse path representation into packets, the path vector (and thus the represented path) can be recovered from a small amount of packets using compressive sensing technique. CSPR formalizes the sparse path representation and enables accurate and efficient per-packet path reconstruction. CSPR is invulnerable to network dynamics and lossy links due to its distinct design. A set of optimization techniques are further proposed to improve the design. We evaluate CSPR in both testbed-based experiments and large-scale trace-driven simulations. Evaluation results show that CSPR achieves high path recovery accuracy (i.e., 100% and 96% in experiments and simulations, respectively), and outperforms the state-of-the-art approaches in various network settings.

Categories and Subject Descriptors

C.2.1 [**Network Architecture and Design**]: Wireless Communication; C.2.3 [**Network Operations**]: Network monitoring

Keywords

Packet path reconstruction; wireless sensor networks; compressive sensing; bloom filter

1. INTRODUCTION

The per-packet routing path serves as the meta-information for understanding detailed Wireless Sensor Networks (WSNs) behaviors in many network maintenance and diagnosis situations, e.g., routing dynamics [33], detections on wormholes [9] or packet loss holes [32], end-to-end packet transmission delay [29] or even per-hop per-packet transmission delay [13], network diagnosis [18] [26], etc. Reconstructing per-packet routing path information, however, has been known non-trivial. WSNs are self-organized and usually deployed in dynamic environments. The underlying network topology constantly changes and no fixed routing path can be expected for each node [30]. A straightforward solution to reveal the packet path is to record the complete path during packet forwarding, e.g., storing the ID sequence of all relay nodes, in each packet. The introduced overhead linearly grows with the routing path length, far from scalable.

There have been many efforts made to address the per-packet path reconstruction problem in WSNs. The method that identifies packet paths via hash values triggers disastrous computation overhead [19]. Some methods reconstruct path information by leveraging inter-packet correlation in sufficiently stable and reliable networks [14] [16]. However, according to our investigation on the practical packet trace from CitySee [22], a real-deployed and large-scale WSN, we observe non-negligible topology variation (e.g., up to 28% packets experienced parent changes) and high packet loss (e.g., up to 55% packets lost for some nodes) all the time. Both topology instability and packet loss significantly deteriorate existing path reconstruction methods in practical WSNs. To cope with above issues, we attack the path reconstruction problem from a new perspective, which requires no inter-packet correlations and thus makes the solution insensitive to network dynamics and lossy links.

The key insight of our design is as follows. The length of a routing path is usually much smaller than the network size. As a concrete example, the maximum path length reported in CitySee [22] is only 20 hops in comparison with its network size of 1200 nodes. Therefore, we can construct a *path representation space*, the number of whose dimensions equals to the total number of nodes in the network. In such a representation space, an arbitrary routing path can be represented by a *path vector*, where each element corresponds to a node in the network. The path vector sets the hop numbers for nodes on the path and zeros for those not involved in the path. As the path length is much smaller than the network size, such path vectors are thus **sparse**, i.e., the majority of elements are zeros. The path reconstruction becomes a problem of unveiling all existing path vectors hidden in the representation space. If all non-zero elements of a path vector can be encoded (with few bytes) into the packets forwarded along the path, we can recover the path vector (and thus the represented routing path) based on a small amount of packets using compressive sensing technique [5] [12].

In this paper, we propose a **C**ompressive **S**ensing based **P**ath **R**econstruction method, CSPR, which formalizes the sparse path representation and leverages compressive sensing to recover per-packet routing path. CSPR lets intermediate nodes briefly annotate the transmitted packets and classifies packets traveling along different paths into different groups. For a particular path, the forwarded packets encode independent observations and CSPR performs compressive sensing to recover the path when a certain amount of pack-

MobiHoc'14, August 11–14, 2014, Philadelphia, PA, USA.

http://dx.doi.org/10.1145/2632951.2632967 .

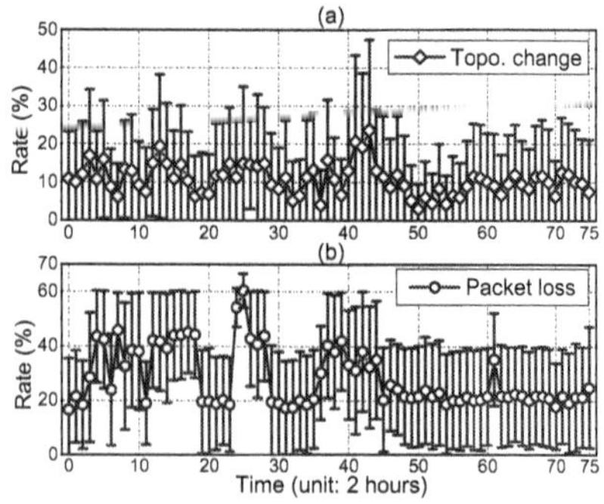

Figure 1: Average (a) topology change rate and (b) packet loss rate of all nodes at each time window.

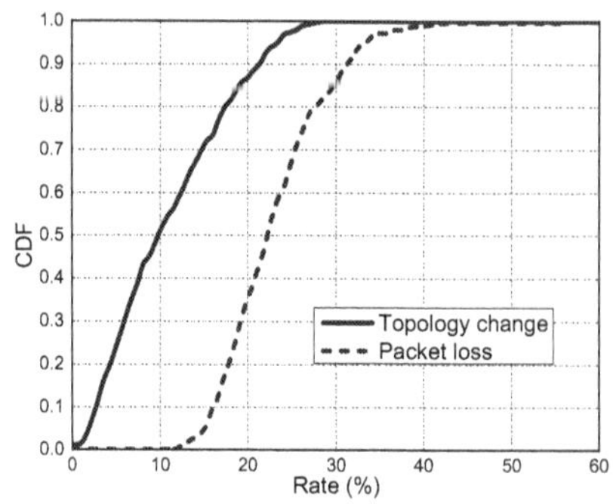

Figure 2: CDF of topology change rates and packet loss rates of all nodes in the CitySee packet trace.

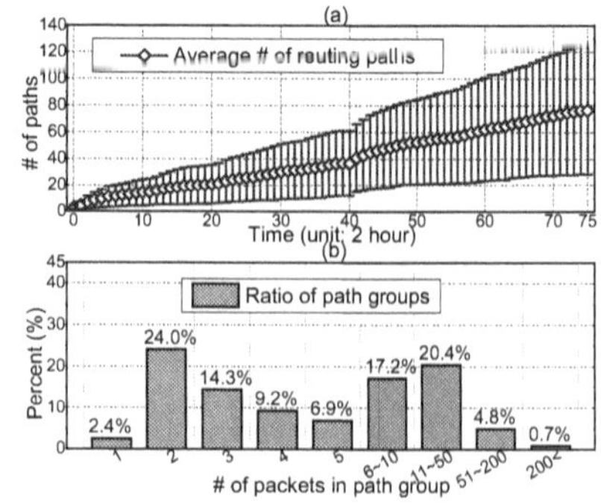

Figure 3: (a) Average number of paths for each node. (b) The distribution of packet volumes for all path groups.

ets (and the annotations) are collected at the sink. The path reconstruction by CSPR requires no inter-packet correlations and utilizes only a small number of received packets. CSPR is thus invulnerable to topology dynamics and lossy links. On the protocol level, CSPR introduces only small and fixed overhead in annotating each packet, which could be optimized accordingly for practical WSNs (e.g., 8 bytes per packet for a network with 245 nodes). In addition to the basic design, we further propose a set of optimization techniques to gradually shrink the representation space and heuristically scan possible paths for all unrecovered path vectors through the network topology learnt from already reconstructed routing paths. The numbers of packets needed for remaining path reconstructions are lowered and processing is thus accelerated. To examine the performance of CSPR, we first evaluate our method using a 29 TelosB mote testbed. The experiment results validate the feasibility and applicability of CSPR in practice. We further conduct extensive and large-scale trace-driven simulations to examine the efficiency and salability of CSPR. Compared to the state-of-the-art methods, CSPR achieves higher path recovery accuracy (i.e., 100% and 96% for experiments and simulations, respectively) with comparable overhead (8 extra bytes per packet).

The rest of this paper is organized as follows. The path reconstruction problem and the motivation of our design are presented in Section 2. The design of CSPR is detailed in Section 3. In Section 4, we evaluate CSPR through testbed experiments and trace-driven simulations. We review the related works in Section 5. Section 6 concludes this paper.

2. PROBLEM STATEMENT AND MOTIVATION

2.1 The path reconstruction problem

In a WSN, all sensor nodes generate and relay packets to the sink along some routing paths [28]. At the sink, a path reconstruction method is desired to recover the routing path each packet traveled. One packet path is an ID sequence from the source of the packet to the sink, including IDs of all intermediate nodes relaying this packet and their hop numbers as well.

There have been many efforts made to address the path reconstruction problem (as reviewed in Section 5). Two state-of-the-art methods, MNT [16] and Pathfinder [14], have been recently proposed. MNT [16] reconstructs per-packet path by exploiting *inter-packet correlation*, i.e., a relayed packet and its adjacent packets locally generated at any node i are usually forwarded to the same next hop. Such local packets serve as *anchors* of the relayed packet at node i. As the first-hop receiver is recorded in packets, the path of a packet can be obtained by concatenating the first-hop receivers of all its anchors. Improving on MNT, Pathfinder [14] tolerates certain inconsistence in inter-packet correlation via explicitly recording inconsistence in packets. The reconstruction failure occurs once the inconsistence exceeds the tolerance capacity. To accurately locate anchors, Pathfinder further imposes the packet generation rate of each node to be identical and fixed. Both MNT and Pathfinder require stable network topology such that inter-packet correlation can be captured. The practical WSNs, however, behave dynamically and the wireless links are far from stable [17] (as we will demonstrate in next subsection). Both network dynamic and packet loss have strong impacts on the anchor identifications, and thus deteriorate the performances of MNT and Pathfinder.

2.2 How packet routing behaves in practical WSNs

We investigate the packet trace from a real-deployed and large-scale WSN CitySee [22], and discuss how practical packet routing behaviors impact the path reconstruction performances of the state-of-the-art methods as well. The CitySee, deployed in Wuxi city, China, contains more than 1200 sensor nodes for monitoring urban environmental factors, including carbon dioxide, temperature, humidity, light, etc. Sensor nodes generate data every 10 minutes, encapsulate data into a single packet, and transmit packets to the sink with CTP [15] in a multi-hop manner. Each packet possesses a default CTP packet header including following common fields: *source address*, ID of the node generating this packet; *sequence number*, order of the packet generated from the source; *first-hop receiver*, parent node ID of the packet's source; and *hop count*, length of path traveled by the packet. Each packet further records the first 10-hop node IDs for future analysis. The packet trace from a subnetwork of 245 nodes with a collection period of one week is available for our study. Such partial network covers about 16 km^2 area with the average and maximum path length as 7 hops and 12 hops, respectively.

With CitySee packet trace, we examine the *topology change* and *packet loss*, which are most relevant to the stability of WSNs [6]. For each node, one topology change is indicated by the first-hop receiver difference between two consecutively transmitted packets. The topology change rate of a network is defined as the average of ratios $\frac{\#\,of\ pkts\ with\ topo.\ changes}{total\ \#\,of\ pkts\ received} \times 100\%$ for each node within certain time duration. Similarly, for each node, one packet loss is indicated by a sequence number missing. The packet loss rate of a network is further defined as the average of ratios $(1 - \frac{\#\, of\ pkts\ received}{\#\, of\ pkts\ expected\ to\ receive}) \times 100\%$ for each node within certain time duration.

Topology change rate indicates the topology stability of a network, which reflects the validity of the inter-packet correlation assumption made in existing path reconstruction methods [14] [16]. Fig. 1 (a) depicts the topology change rate in CitySee with 2 hour time window of measurement. From the figure, we observe that the average and maximum topology change rates at all time windows are about 12% and 48%, respectively. In Fig. 2, we summarize the CDF of topology change rates of all nodes during one week. For most nodes, the rate is as high as 10% and the maximum rate reaches up to 28%. Due to the instable topology, each node would transmit packets to the sink via different paths. In Fig. 3 (a), we plot the number of routing paths formed in the packet trace as time goes by. The average number of paths starting from a node persistently increases and finally on average each node has 76 paths. All of these evidences demonstrate that network topology suffers from severe instability and the inter-packet correlation may not be well validated in practice. In Section 4, we have implemented both MNT and Pathfinder. By analyzing their detailed executions, we find that the topology dynamics could solely cause about 10% and 1% of anchor misidentifications, which directly lead to path reconstruction failures. Pathfinder outperforms MNT at the cost of explicitly recording certain topology changes in each packet.

Packet loss rate reflects the reliability of packet receptions [11]. Packet losses will hide the inter-packet correlation, e.g., anchor availability, and deteriorate performances of methods relying on such correlation. Fig. 1 (b) depicts the packet loss rate in the packet trace, with 2 hour time window. From the figure, we see that the packet loss rate changes rapidly with the average ranging from 17% to 69%. In Fig. 2, we summarize the CDF of packet loss rates of all nodes during one week. The distribution mainly concentrates in the range between 15% and 35%, with the maximum rate as high as 55%. By analyzing the detailed executions of MNT and Pathfinder, we find that with such a high packet loss rate, about 49% and 35% packets fail to identify anchors, which directly result in path reconstruction failure for those packets.

With the joint impacts of topology dynamics and packet losses, we find that in the large-scale and dynamic WSN CitySee, 59% and 36% packet paths might not be successfully reconstructed by the state-of-the-art methods MNT and Pathfinder, respectively. This motivates us to explore a solution insensitive to both network dynamics and lossy links.

2.3 Path reconstruction from sparse path representation

Sparse representation of routing paths. Since sensory data in WSNs are usually collected with a direct acyclic graph (DAG) routing structure (e.g., data collection tree), the path length is thus in the order of $O(\lg(N))$, where N is the total number of nodes in the network. According to the statistical results of all paths formed in CitySee packet trace, the path length ranges between 2 hops and 12 hops, which are much smaller than the network size 245. We can construct a path representation space $\mathbb{N}$. The dimensionality of $\mathbb{N}$ equals to the total number of nodes in the network and each dimension corresponds to one node. In such a representation space, any routing path can be presented by a path vector. According to whether a node is involved in the routing path, the path vector sets either hop number or zero for its corresponding element. As the path length is much smaller than the network size, the path vector is thus sparse, i.e., the majority of elements in the vector are zeros.

Fig. 4 illustrates the sparse path representation with a network containing 10 nodes. We construct the path representation space

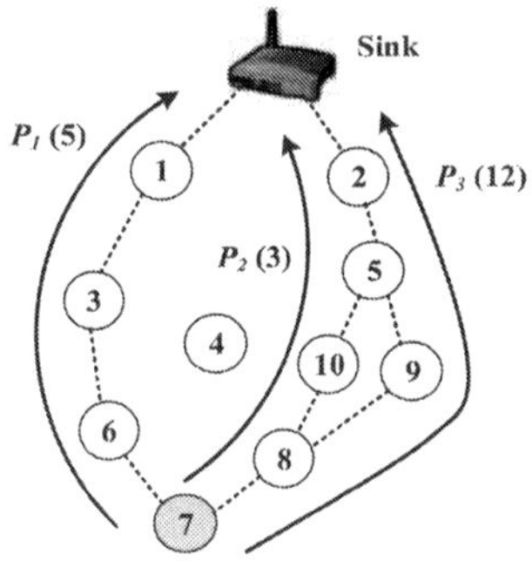

(a) Network topology.

$\mathbb{N}$	n_1	n_2	n_3	n_4	n_5	n_6	n_7	n_8	n_9	n_{10}
$\mathbf{s}_1$	3	0	2	0	0	1	0	0	0	0
$\mathbf{s}_2$	0	4	0	0	3	0	0	1	0	2
$\mathbf{s}_3$	0	4	0	0	3	0	0	1	2	0

(b) Sparse representation of routing paths.

Figure 4: (a) A simple sensor network topology. Source node 7 transmits 20 packets to the sink via 3 different routing paths, i.e., 5 packets on path P_1, 3 packet on path P_2 and 12 packets on path P_3. (b) The sparse representations of the 3 routing paths in the whole network space.

$\mathbb{N} = [n_1, n_2, n_3, n_4, n_5, n_6, n_7, n_8, n_9, n_{10}]^T$ including all nodes. An arbitrary in-network path can be represented by a path vector in $\mathbb{N}$. For example, path P_1 is represented as $\mathbf{s_1} = [3,0,2,0,0,1,0,0,0,0]^T$. Node 7 is the source node and could be known from the packet header. Hence the element n_7 is not considered in $\mathbf{s_1}$ and thus assigned as 0. As nodes 6, 3 and 1 serve as the first, second and third hop relay, respectively, in path P_1, thus $n_6 = 1$, $n_3 = 2$ and $n_1 = 3$. All other elements irrelevant to P_1 are zeros in $\mathbf{s_1}$. The sparsity of this path vector is 3 (out of 10). Other path vectors, e.g., $\mathbf{s_2}$ and $\mathbf{s_3}$, can be similarly constructed.

Compressive sensing based path reconstruction. Based on sparse path representation, the path reconstruction thus becomes a problem of unveiling all existing path vectors hidden in the path representation space $\mathbb{N}$. Packets from the same source may travel different paths to the sink, while the paths implicitly classifies packets into different *path groups*, i.e., all packets in one group travel exactly the same path. After the paths of all path groups get reconstructed, the path of each packet is obtained as well.

For the path vector of a routing path, if its non-zero elements can be encoded into each packet forwarded along the path, it is viable to recover the vector (and thus the represented path) based on a small amount of packets using compressive sensing [5] [12]. In particular, for any path vector $\mathbf{s}$ in space $\mathbb{N}$ with sparsity k, where $k \ll N = |\mathbb{N}|$, the compressive sensing theory states that M, instead of N, independent equations are sufficient to solve the N unknowns in $\mathbf{s}$, where $M \ll N$. The M independent equations can be acquired by projecting $\mathbf{s}$ to a measurement matrix Φ: $Y = \Phi\mathbf{s}$, where Y is an M-dimension vector and Φ is an $M \times N$ matrix. If Φ satisfies the *Restricted Isometry Property* [4], $\mathbf{s}$ can be exactly recovered by solving following l_1-minimization problem:

$$\hat{\mathbf{s}} = \arg\min_{\mathbf{s} \in R^N} \|\mathbf{s}\|_{l_1} \quad s.t.\ Y = \Phi\mathbf{s},$$

when $M \geq ck\log(\frac{N}{k})$, where c is a small positive constant [4]. A variety of algorithms have been proposed for solving above optimization problem.

The above compressive sensing based approach makes path reconstruction for each path group independent, and can recover the path for a group of packets once sufficient packet are accumulated. As a result, this approach requires no inter-packet correlation, which makes itself inherently invulnerable to network dynamics and lossy links. On the other hand, once a path is recovered, the routing path for all future packets residing in the same path group

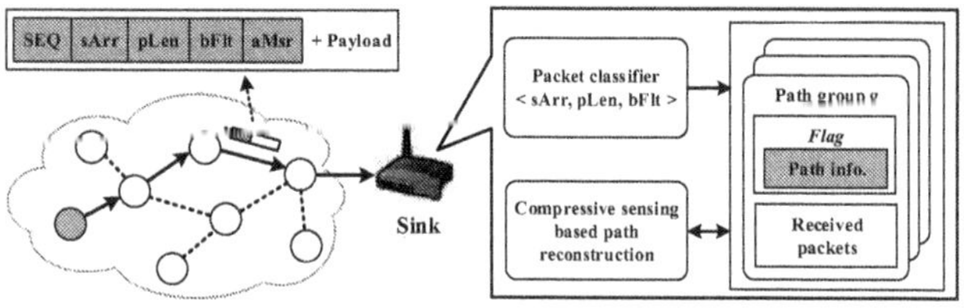

Figure 5: The system architecture of CSPR.

becomes immediately available, which avoids repeatedly triggering path reconstruction procedure for each received packet and largely reduces the computation overhead.

Design challenges. Translating the idea of compressive sensing based per-packet path reconstruction to a practical system, however, encounters a set of challenging issues as follows.

1) *Accurate packet classification.* Packet classification into each path group must be accurate. Fig. 3 (a) plots the average number of paths (each path one path group) formed in the packet trace as more and more packets are received by the sink. According to the statistics, we observe significant differences existing in the number of paths for each node, e.g., the maximum number of paths of some node could even reach 199. It is vital to distinguish each individual path and classify the packets into the right group. Packet misclassification will lead to path reconstruction error for one group. Therefore, packet classification must have high accuracy.

2) *Lightweight per-packet annotation.* To enable the compressive sensing based path reconstruction, packets need carry encoded information for all non-zero elements of the path vectors representing their traveling paths. In particular, when one packet is relayed by an intermediate node, the node needs to annotate its hop number along the path into the packet header. As a result, packet header is updated hop by hop. The annotation overhead must be small. In particular, the annotation field in the packet header should be small in size and maintain constant (not increase with the path length). In addition, updating should be performed in a distributed manner without introducing any centralized control.

3) *Short per-packet path recovery delay.* From Fig. 3 (b), we observe that the packet volumes for all path groups within one week are highly heterogenous. About 50% path groups include fewer than 5 packets while some path groups (about 5.5%) contain more than 50 packets. To perform compressive sensing based path reconstruction for one path group, the number of packets (one annotation as one measurement for each packet) accumulated in this group should be at least M to ensure a good recovery quality. Some path groups, however, cannot accumulate sufficient packets even after a long time. As practical requirement, per-packet path recovery delay should not be excessively long.

3. DESIGN OF CSPR

CSPR consists of two parts, the in-network part for path information encoding and the server part for per-packet path reconstruction. The system architecture of CSPR is depicted in Fig. 5. We will present the system overview first and then detail each component in following subsections.

3.1 CSPR overview

Several fields in the packet header are used by CSPR to carry packet information, as depicted by Fig. 5. SEQ is the packet sequence number. sArr is source address of the packet. pLen records the path length. bFlt is a bloom filter to space-efficiently record the IDs and corresponding hop count information of all relay nodes. aMsr stores the encoded measurement along the path. All the five fields are initialized at the source node. In particular, SEQ and sArr keep unchanged after initialization, whereas pLen, bFlt and aMsr are updated at each intermediate hop. Note that only two fields, bFlt and aMsr, are additionally introduced by CSPR. SEQ, sArr and pLen can be usually found in the default packet header, e.g., CTP packet header. The extra overhead to each packet is thus slight, e.g., 6 bytes of bFlt and 2 bytes of aMsr for a network with 245 nodes. We detail the in-network updating of packet header in Section 3.2.

CSPR adopts a 3-tuple key, $<$ sArr, pLen, bFlt $>$, to identify the path of a packet. For all received packets, CSPR first distinguishes their paths according to sArr, and then differentiates those from the same source based on pLen. Finally, bFlt is used to distinguish paths owning the same sArr and pLen. If two packets have the same 3-tuple key, they are considered to travel the same path and will be classified into the same path group. At the sink, CSPR maintains a database, where each entry is indexed via the 3-tuple key and corresponds to a unique path group. When a packet is received, CSPR extracts the 3-tuple key from packet header and looks for a matched entry in the database. If the matched entry has already recovered the path, the path for the packet becomes immediately available. If an entry is matched yet the path is not ready, CSPR launches path reconstruction when sufficient packets are accumulated. If no entry matched, CSPR creates an entry for the new path group indexed by the 3-tuple key of the packet. We detail the compressive sensing based path reconstruction component in Section 3.3.

As improvements on the basic design, a set of optimization techniques is proposed to gradually shrink the path representation space and reduce the sparsity of unrecovered path vectors. The number of packets needed by compressive sensing is accordingly lowered such that the remaining path reconstructions are accelerated. In addition, CSPR can launch a remedy scheme if some path groups fail to recover their paths after an excessive long delay. We detail those components in Section 3.4.

3.2 In-network path information encoding

In this subsection, we introduce the in-network updating of the last three fields pLen, bFlt and aMsr in turn.

Updating of pLen. The pLen field of each packet is initialized to 0 by the source and increased by one at each intermediate hop along the path. At each intermediate hop, pLen is updated prior to both bFlt and aMsr as the updating of latter two fields relies on the new pLen value. When a packet arrives at the sink, we can know the packet path length through the bFlt field, while we can not infer the hop count information for each intermediate node along the path relying on this filed at the server side.

Updating of bFlt. Bloom filter is an L-bit array associated with H independent hash functions, where L and H are two parameters to be determined. The bFlt field of each packet accommodates an L-bit array, and sensor nodes use the same set of H independent hash functions $f_i(\cdot), i = 1, 2, \cdots, H$, to update bFlt. Different arrays represent different path information. Initially, all L bits in the bFlt field of a packet header are set to 0. At each intermediate hop, the node compresses its existence into the bFlt field as follows. H hash values $v_i = f_i(d \times h) \in \{0, 1, \cdots, L-1\}, i = 1, \cdots, H$, are first obtained by feeding the product of node ID d and hop count h in the pLen field to the H hash functions. Then the v_i bits of the bFlt field are set to 1 by that relay node, $i = 1, 2, \cdots, H$.

Updating of aMsr. The aMsr field in each packet is also initialized as 0 by the source and updated along the path. At each intermediate hop, the node encodes its hop number along the path in aMsr. In particular, the node multiplies the updated pLen value with a random coefficient and adds the product with current aMsr value. We design such field for the purpose of recovering sparse path vector via compressive sensing technique.

When CSPR later recovers the path for a set of received packets in one path group, it solves equation $Y = \Phi\mathbf{s}$ to obtain $\mathbf{s}$ using compressive sensing technique. The path vector $\mathbf{s}$ is a column vector with N elements. Each element represents one node in the path representation space $\mathbb{N}$. If a node is included in the path represented by $\mathbf{s}$, the corresponding element indicates its hop number; Otherwise, element is zero. In the equation, each element in Y is the final aMsr value of one packet and the corresponding row in Φ can be represented by $\phi = [\alpha_1, \alpha_2, \cdots, \alpha_N]$, where α_j means that if node j relays the packet, α_j will be the coefficient multiplied with pLen value, $j = 1, 2, \cdots, N$. The product of Φ and $\mathbf{s}$ essentially replays the updating process of aMsr along the path.

Before the reconstruction of $\mathbf{s}$, we are not aware which α_j finally participates in the aMsr updating. We have to provide complete α_j in ϕ for the compressive sensing recovery. To avoid explicitly acquiring such information from each node in the network, we introduce a dictionary based strategy working in a fully distributed manner. Each node i is configured with a coefficient dictionary $\mathcal{D}_i$, stored in the RAM. To update the aMsr field for a packet, node i multiplies the updated pLen value with the n-th coefficient in $\mathcal{D}_i$, where $n = (\mathsf{SEQ}\ mod\ |\mathcal{D}_i|)$ and $|\mathcal{D}_i|$ is the size of $\mathcal{D}_i$. Each $\mathcal{D}_i$ is made up by Gaussian random numbers and the CSPR server is aware of the dictionaries of all nodes in the network. Coefficients in all dictionaries are generated independently. As a result, different nodes have different dictionary elements. In our current design, each coefficient occupies 2 bytes and each dictionary contains 100 independent coefficients. The 200-byte storage overhead accounts for only 2% storage occupancy to commercial sensor motes, e.g., TelosB with 10 KB RAM [1]. We could synchronize the generation of random numbers between nodes and server via global seed [20], while at the cost of reducing coefficient randomness.

Fig. 6 illustrates the path information encoding for a packet p on path P_3 in Fig. 4. For ease of illustration, we simply set $L = 8$ and $H = 2$ for the bloom filter. Source node 7 generates packet p with SEQ equalling to 3 and initializes sArr, pLen, bFlt, and aMsr to 7, 0, 0x00, and 0, respectively. At each intermediate hop, pLen, aMsr and bFlt are updated. For instance, at node 5, pLen is increased from 2 to 3. Two hash values are $v_1 = 1$ and $v_2 = 4$ ($v_1, v_2 \in \{0, 1, \cdots, 7\}$). The bFlt is thus updated by setting the first and fourth bits to 1. The aMsr is updated by adding the product of the updated pLen (i.e., 3) and the third coefficient in $\mathcal{D}_5$ to current aMsr value.

3.3 Compressive sensing based path reconstruction

In this subsection, we first present the packet classification mechanism in CSPR, and then detail the compressive sensing based path reconstruction with path verification scheme to ensure the reconstruction correctness.

Packet classification. For each received packet, CSPR extracts the 3-tuple key, $<\mathsf{sArr}, \mathsf{pLen}, \mathsf{bFlt}>$, from the packet header and then classifies it into a path group. A path group is designed to contain packets traveling the same path. At the sink, CSPR manages all path groups with a database. One database entry is indexed via the 3-tuple key and corresponds to a unique path group. Each entry is further allocated with a piece of buffer to accommodate the packets belonging to this group. An entry also has an indicator *Flag* to tell whether the path gets recovered. When a packet is received by sink, CSPR extracts the key from the packet header and looks for a matched entry. If a matched entry exists, the packet is inserted into the allocated buffer. Furthermore, in case the indicator *Flag* is *true*, CSPR checks whether the recovered path of this group is valid for the packet through the path verification component (as described later). When the *Flag* is *false*, however, CSPR will recover the path if the amount of packets accumulated in the group is sufficient (the number will be given later). On the other hand, if no entry matched, CSPR creates an entry for this new path group, initializes *Flag* as *false*, and inserts the packet into the buffer.

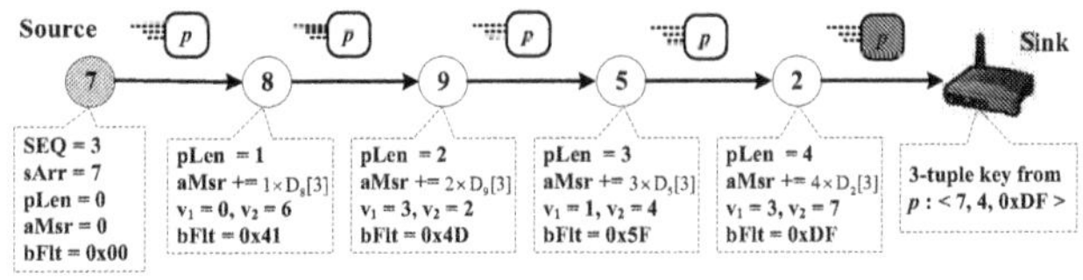

Figure 6: The path information encoding process for a packet p on path P_3 in Fig. 4. The SEQ, sArr, pLen, aMsr and bFlt fields are all initialized at source node 7, and the last three fields are updated hop-by-hop as depicted in the attached box at each intermediate hop. CSPR can extract a 3-tuple key from packet p at the sink.

The packet classification using the 3-tuple key might lead to misclassification since the comparison result between two bloom filers could be false negative, i.e., different paths possess the same L-bit array. However, with a proper parameters L and H setting of the bloom filter, misclassification rate could be low. The setting of L trades off between packet overhead and classification accuracy. A lager L leads to a lower false negative probability yet more overhead to each packet. For any given L, as well as the maximum path length k in the network (i.e., maximum number of elements stored in a bloom filter), the optimal setting of H is $\lfloor \frac{L}{k} \ln 2 \rfloor$ such that minimizes the false negative probability [3]. We empirically investigate the setting of L in CSPR using the CitySee packet trace. We define a path group to be *conflicted* if not all packets in this group travel the same path, and use *conflict ratio* $= \frac{\#\,of\ conflicted\ groups}{\#\,of\ all\ groups} \times 100\%$ to measure the misclassification rate. As the maximum path length (excluding the source and destination) observed in the trace is 10, the optimal H should be $\lfloor \frac{L}{10} \ln 2 \rfloor$. Fig. 7 depicts the conflict ratios when L varies from 16 to 56 with corresponding optimal H. From the figure, we see that the conflict ratio is generally not high, i.e., $< 9\%$. In particular, when L is larger than 40, the conflict ratio is smaller than 0.1%. With a balance between the classification accuracy and packet overhead, L in CSPR is set to 48 and H is thus 3 for the trace. An optimized setting of L and H for each individual node according to its maximum path length will further reduce the overall overhead, which will be explored in future.

In fact, as long as sufficient packets, truly belonging to the same path group, are received, our path reconstruction method (detailed in the following) can still recover the path even certain misclassified packets are mixed in the reconstruction. Moreover, after a routing path is recovered, a path verification component is used to further verify the reconstruction correctness, which can also eliminate all misclassified packets from the group as well. As a result, CSPR is not vulnerable to packet misclassification, while accurate classification is still preferred as high accuracy ensures that more paths could be recovered with shorter latency.

Path reconstruction. Based on the encoded measurements in received packets, CSPR recovers the path for a path group using compressive sensing technique. Concretely, for one path group, CSPR solves $Y = \Phi\mathbf{s}$ to obtain the path vector $\mathbf{s}$ for path recovery. Each element in Y, denoted as y_i, is the aMsr value of a re-

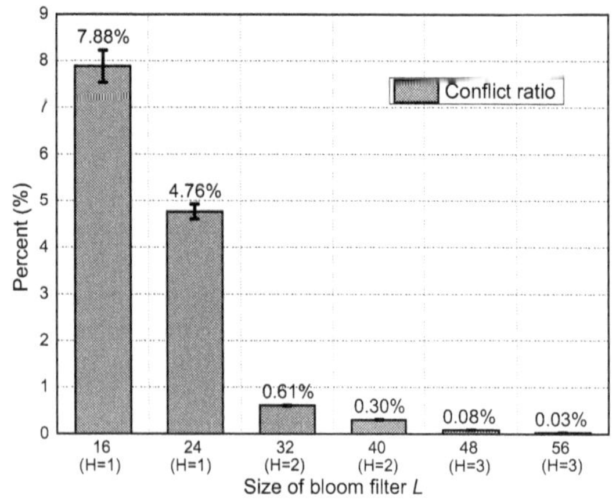

Figure 7: Conflict ratios under various combination setting of bloom filter size L and number of hash functions H for the CitySee packet trace.

ceived packet i. The corresponding row in Φ is represented by $\phi_i = [\alpha_{i,1}, \alpha_{i,2}, \cdots, \alpha_{i,N}]$, where $\alpha_{i,j}$ is the (SEQ_i *mod* $|\mathcal{D}_j|$)-th coefficient in the coefficient dictionary $\mathcal{D}_j$ of node j and SEQ_i is the sequence number of packet i. If the elements in **s** are known, the product of ϕ_i and **s** replays the updating process of the aMsr field along the path of packet i. Therefore, $y_i = \phi_i \mathbf{s}$. For the path reconstruction problem, both y_i and ϕ_i are known while the N elements in **s** are unknowns to be determined. In principle, N independent equations are needed to obtain **s**, and each equation $y_i = \phi_i \mathbf{s}$ corresponds to one received packet.

Since path vector **s** is sparse, it can be recovered using M rather than N equations by leveraging compressive sensing. Therefore, as long as M packets are accumulated by one path group, the vector **s** can be recovered. We use the aMsr values from M packets to form an M-dimension column vector Y, i.e., $Y = [y_1, y_2, ..., y_M]^T$. For each packet i out of M packets, we further use its sequence number SEQ_i to select coefficients from coefficient dictionaries of all nodes in the path representation space $\mathbb{N}$ to construct $\phi_i = [\alpha_{i,1}, \alpha_{i,2}, \cdots, \alpha_{i,N}]$. All ϕ_i together form an $M \times N$ matrix:

$$\Phi = \begin{bmatrix} \phi_1 \\ \phi_2 \\ \vdots \\ \phi_M \end{bmatrix} = \begin{bmatrix} \alpha_{1,1} & \alpha_{1,2} & \cdots & \alpha_{1,N} \\ \alpha_{2,1} & \alpha_{2,2} & \cdots & \alpha_{2,N} \\ \vdots & \vdots & \ddots & \vdots \\ \alpha_{M,1} & \alpha_{M,2} & \cdots & \alpha_{M,N} \end{bmatrix}. \quad (1)$$

Since all coefficients in Φ follow the Gaussian distribution, the measurement matrix Φ satisfies the RIP condition [20]. In addition, if the number of packets in the path group is sufficient, at least $ck\log(\frac{N}{k})$, we can apply the compressive sensing technique to recover the path vector **s**. A variety of compressive sensing solvers can be used to obtain **s**. However, most of them provide no confidence for the reconstruction quality. As a result, **s** might not be correctly reconstructed. In CSPR, since the sparsity of **s**, i.e., path length indicated by the pLen field, is known prior to the path reconstruction, we adopt a more advanced solver CoSaMP [24] that requires the vector sparsity as input. If CoSaMP outputs a recovered result, the result is correct with a high probability. Otherwise, CoSaMP outputs "Fail" instead. Furthermore, CoSaMP can tolerate certain noises mixed in Y, and the path vector can be recovered even some misclassified packets are included. In particular, CoSaMP could recover **s** if the number of correctly classified packets is greater than $M_l = ck\log(\frac{N}{k})$ when $c = 1.5$ according to recent study [5]

In CSPR, after a packet is received, if the path group this packet belonging to has not recovered its path yet, the server checks whether the number of packets in the group exceeds M_l. The path reconstruction will be performed if the threshold is reached. If CoSaMP returns "Fail", more packets are expected. If CoSaMP returns a valid result, CSPR executes path verification component to further ensure its correctness.

Path verification. Given a recovered path and a packet, the path verification component verify whether the recovered path is valid for the packet via path vector **s** of the recovered path and aMsr value of the packet. More precisely, for a packet with sequence number SEQ, we calculate the product of ϕ and **s**, where $\phi = [\alpha_1, \alpha_2, \cdots, \alpha_N]$ and α_j in ϕ is the (SEQ *mod* $|\mathcal{D}_j|$)-th coefficient in $\mathcal{D}_j$, $j = 1, 2, \cdots, N$. As coefficients are randomly gaussian, it is highly impossible for two packets traveling two different paths yet leading to the same aMsr value. Therefore, if $\phi \cdot \mathbf{s}$ equals to the aMsr value of the packet, the recovered path is valid for this packet.

When a path p is newly reconstructed, this component is executed to verify the correctness of path p for a path group. It is also used to eliminate all misclassified packets due to bloom filter collision. If path p is only valid for the minority of packets in the group (e.g., $\leq 20\%$), the path recovery is considered to be failed, e.g., an incorrect output from CoSaMP. The path reconstruction will be performed after more packets are received. Otherwise, path p is viewed as the correct path, and the corresponding *Flag* of this group is changed to be *true*. However, we exclude all packets failed in the aMsr check from current group and form a new group, with *Flag* as *false*, for those packets. Since the new group has the same 3-tuple key with current group, we introduce gIdx as the secondary key, an auto-increment key, to further distinguish entries in database with the same 3-tuple key. For example, if any 3-tuple key corresponds to one group g_1 only, the gIdx key of this group is 0. Later, if new groups g_2 and g_3 are formed successively, their gIdx keys would be 1 and 2 respectively, both of which are automatically increased by one based on the gIdx key of previous group.

The recovered paths will benefit all future packets traveling on them. When a group with recovered path receives a packet, CSPR just simply invokes the path verification component to check whether the packet truly traveled the recovered path. If yes, this packet obtains its path immediately. In CSPR, for a given 3-tuple key, path groups are matched with the packet following the ascending order of gIdx keys. At worst, the packet might be assigned to a newly formed path group. Thanks to identifying each individual path, a large number of packets could have their path with no recovery delay and meanwhile CSPR avoids huge computation overhead, which will be demonstrated in our evaluations.

3.4 Optimization

In this subsection, we propose two optimization techniques to improve the performance of our basic design.

Reduction of path representation space. This optimization aims to reduce the number of elements in a representation space by continuously monitoring the network topology. The minimum number of packets required to recover a length of k path is $ck\log(\frac{N}{k})$, which is proportional to the space size N. The basic design utilizes all N nodes in the network to form the space. This component tries to reduce the space size for each path group and thus reduces its needed packets for path reconstruction. For any node i, CSPR maintains a first-hop receiver set $\mathbb{S}_i$, which is learnt from received packets (via the *first-hop receiver* field in packet header) and recovered paths (the next hop of node i along a path). All elements in

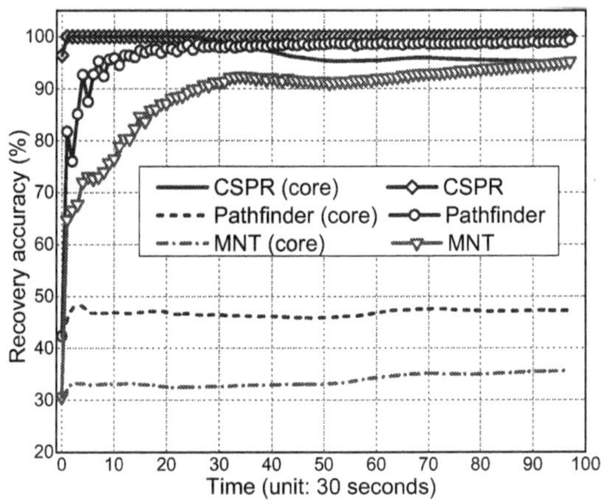

Figure 8: The packet path reconstruction progresses with the core and complete methods of each approach.

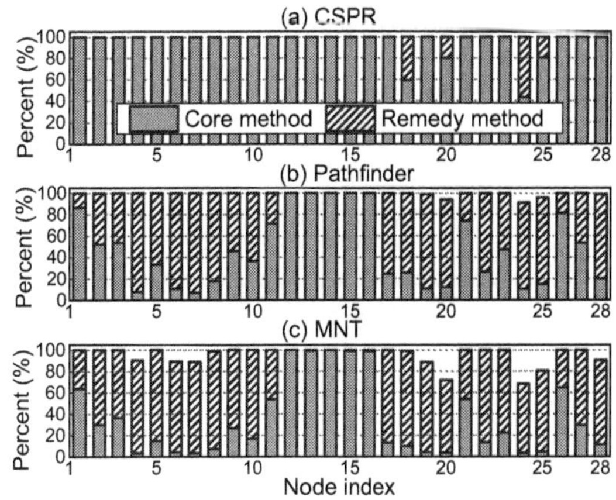

Figure 9: The portion of packet paths recovered by core or remedy methods.

$\mathbb{S}_i$ have ever received packets from node i. The reduced representation spaces for all path groups with the sArr attribute as node i are the same, denoted as $\overline{\mathbb{N}}_i$. Elements of $\overline{\mathbb{N}}_i$ are added in an iterative manner: 1) elements in $\mathbb{S}_i$ belong to $\overline{\mathbb{N}}_i$; 2) elements in $\mathbb{S}_j$, where $j \in \overline{\mathbb{N}}_i$, belong to $\overline{\mathbb{N}}_i$.

We take node 9 in Fig. 4 as an example to illustrate the formation of $\overline{\mathbb{N}}_9$. The first-hop receiver set $\mathbb{S}_9$ of node 9 contains 5 and 8. By iteratively including all first-hop receivers of nodes in $\overline{\mathbb{N}}_9$, $\overline{\mathbb{N}}_9$ finally contains 2, 5, 8 and 10. Compared with original space $\mathbb{N}$, the size of $\overline{\mathbb{N}}_9$ is reduced from 10 to 4. From our investigation on the CitySee packet trace, we find the average and maximum reduced representation space sizes are only 39 and 104 respectively, which are much smaller than the total number of nodes 245 in the network.

Even with sufficient packets, path reconstruction based on the reduced representation space might be unsuccessful unless all intermediate nodes of the path are included in the reduced space. As it is hard for CSPR to explicitly determine whether all intermediate nodes are included, we thus use the reduced representation space as a backup scheme. For each path group, CSPR always use the original N-dimension representation space for the reconstruction. If the reconstruction fails, CSPR recovers one more time using the reduced space. If the second reconstruction succeeds, CSPR will launch the path verification component to verify the correctness of the recovered path; Otherwise, CSPR waits for more packets and performs the next round reconstruction, still starting from the N-dimension representation space.

With more reconstructed routing paths, we could infer the common intermediate nodes between the unrecovered paths and the paths that have been reconstructed, which provides another opportunity to improve our design, i.e., reducing the path vector sparsity such that the remaining paths can be recovered by fewer packets. Such an optimization chance will be explored in our future work.

Heuristic path scanning. For those path groups with insufficient accumulated packets even after a long time, this component is designed to scan possible paths for them based on the learnt network topology. It is triggered when the path reconstruction deadline of a path group is approaching. As this scheme is relatively computation intensive, it recovers path not only for the group which triggers its execution, but also for other unrecovered groups whose paths have the same source, sArr, as this group at the same time.

Starting from the source node i of the path group that triggers heuristic path scanning, CSPR builds a directed graph covering all nodes in the reduced representation space $\overline{\mathbb{N}}_i$. For any two nodes a and b in $\overline{\mathbb{N}}_i$, if node b is in the first-hop receiver set of node a, i.e., $b \in \mathbb{S}_a$, CSPR adds an arrow from a to b. This component enumerates all possible paths from source node i to the sink in the directed graph. For each enumerated path, CSPR treats it as a newly reconstructed path and applies the path verification procedure to check whether it is a valid path for some unrecovered group whose path is originated from node i. As a result, heuristic path scanning can recover paths for multiple path groups.

4. PERFORMANCE EVALUATION

In this section, we evaluate the performance of CSPR with comparisons to two state-of-the-art approaches based on a 29 TelosB mote testbed and the CitySee packet trace.

4.1 Evaluation setup

Compared approaches. We compare CSPR to the two state-of-the-art approaches, Pathfinder [14] and MNT [16]. For fairness, we implement the path speculation in Pathfinder [14] as a remedy method for both Pathfinder and MNT to improve their performances when anchors are lost. We add 1-byte XOR field into packet header for MNT as checksum, similar with Pathfinder, to verify the reconstructed paths. For all the three approaches, we define the same path recovery delay bound δ to meet practical requirements. In general, the three approaches will reconstruct packet paths following their core principles (referred as *core method*), and employ the remedy methods (heuristic path scanning for CSPR and path speculation for Pathfinder and MNT, referred as *remedy method*) to reconstruct those failed packets when path recovery delay bound is approaching. In the following experiments and simulations, we set the bound $\delta = 50$, which means a remedy method will be employed to search possible routing paths when another 50 packets of the same source are received. Small δ will reduce the overall recovery delay but trigger much more computation overhead. All approaches are running on a desktop PC with dual-core 3.16GHz CPU and 4GB RAM. The execution of remedy methods have a time limit of 1 second to avoid excessive computation overhead.

Performance metrics. The *recovery accuracy* for each node is calculated as $\frac{\#\,of\ correct\ recovered\ pkts}{total\ \#\,of\ pkts\ received} \times 100\%$. Similarly, the recovery *false positive* is computed as $\frac{\#\,of\ false\ positive\ recovered\ pkts}{total\ \#\,of\ pkts\ received} \times 100\%$ for each node. Intuitively, the approach with higher recovery accuracy yet lower false positives is expected for per-packet path reconstruction in WSNs.

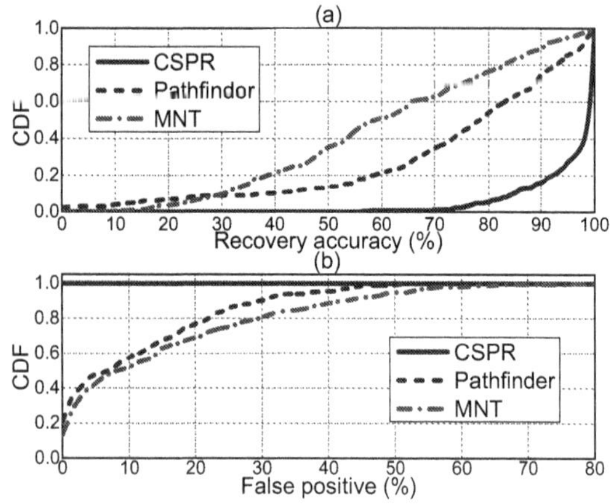

Figure 10: (a) CDF of path recovery accuracy. (b) CDF of false positive for each approach.

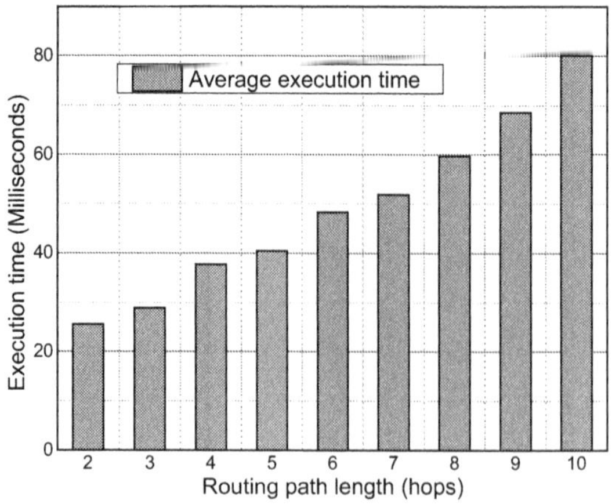

Figure 11: The program execution time of path reconstruction by CSPR versus the routing path length.

4.2 Testbed experiments

We implement CSPR on TelosB mote and use a 29-node testbed to validate its feasibility and applicability. 29 TelosB motes are uniformly distributed in a square area. One node acts as the sink and is placed at the top-left corner. Due to the limitation of experimental space, we configure the transmission power of each TelosB mote to the minimum level and thus the communication range of each sensor node would be about 15 centimeters. CSPR is implemented at the application layer on TinyOS 2.1.2 with CTP [15] as the data collection protocol. Each node generates packets randomly with an average inter packet interval one second. Within the network, each intermediate node along a path updates the packet header following the requirements of each approach. The sink receives packets from network and separately executes the three approaches to reconstruct packet paths. The actual path is recorded in packets as ground truths. The experiment lasts for about 50 minutes and collects 60000 packets.

The sink records the path reconstruction progress of each approach every 30 seconds. Concretely, for each approach, the portions of packets accurately recovered with only the core method and the complete approach are both computed. The evolution of path reconstruction progress of each approach is plotted in Fig. 8. From the figure, we find that Pathfinder and MNT can only reconstruct 47% and 36% packet paths based on their core methods, respectively. Most reconstruction failures are caused by packet losses (about 38% packet loss rate during experiment). With no fixed packet generation interval, Pathfinder loses its accuracy in locating anchors which further harms the performance. Assisted by the remedy method (i.e., path speculation), they can achieve similar accuracy as the core method of CSPR, i.e., > 95%. With heuristics path scanning, CSPR achieves accuracy of 100%. Fig. 9 further presents the detailed per-node path reconstruction performance. 24 nodes can recover their packet paths just by the core method of CSPR. With respect to the other two approaches, however, most nodes achieve a good recovery accuracy through the remedy method.

4.3 Trace-driven simulations

To evaluate the scalability and efficiency of CSPR in practical large-scale and more dynamic networks, we conduct extensive trace-driven simulations by leveraging the practical packet trace from the real-deployed and large-scale WSN CitySee [22], as introduced in Section 2.2. The packet trace includes packets from a network of 245 nodes with 174829 packets in total.

We apply the three approaches, i.e., CSPR, Pathfinder and MNT, to reconstruct per-packet path in the trace, and summarize the CDFs of path recovery accuracy and false positive, for each approach, in Fig. 10. From Fig. 10 (a), we find that CSPR outperforms Pathfinder and MNT with significant advantages. Pathfinder and MNT perform poorly in the practical packet trace, which experiences severe topology dynamics and packet losses as revealed in Section 2.2, with recovery accuracies of most nodes falling in the range between 50% and 80%. Only 23% and 45% nodes for MNT and Pathfinder, respectively, can achieve an accuracy $\geq 80\%$, while CSPR makes 95% nodes reach such level. Furthermore, about 85% nodes achieve a high accuracy $\geq 90\%$. Overall, the average recovery accuracies for MNT, Pathfinder and CSPR are 62%, 74%, 96%, respectively. In Fig. 10 (b), we see non-negligible false positives in Pathfinder and MNT, both of which verify the recovered paths mainly based on the XOR field in packets. Pathfinder checks the result with more information recorded in packet, and thus has fewer false positives than MNT. Such path verification manners result in on average 11% and 15% false positive for MNT and Pathfinder, respectively. Thanks to the path verification component enabled by the aMsr field, CSPR has no false positive. The correctness of recovered routing paths is very important as they might be applied to other applications to provisioning guaranteed QoS [34], such as network diagnosis [18] [26] and per-hop per-packet delay [13].

CSPR is a lightweight path reconstruction approach, and the overhead of the compressive sensing recovery, e.g., CoSaMP, is negligible on a server. The time complexity of CoSaMP is $O(\lambda M_l N)$ [24], where M_l is the number of measurements needed, N is the network size, and λ is the maximum iterations of CoSaMP, which is set as 100 in our implementation. In Fig. 11, we measure the program execution time as the performance metric to further understand the computation overhead of our design. For different routing path lengths, we plot the reconstruction delays, which are mainly caused by the compressive sensing recovery. Fig. 11 shows that the overhead due to compressive sensing recovery is negligible which is less than 100 milliseconds for all routing path lengths observed in the experiments.

Because of the packet classification mechanism in CSPR, a great portion of packets can recover their paths at a negligible cost of only executing path verification with the recovered paths in path groups. In Fig. 12, we plot the portion of packets that benefit from such mechanism. After an accumulation phase of recovered paths, CSPR can find correct paths for about 65% packets. As a result,

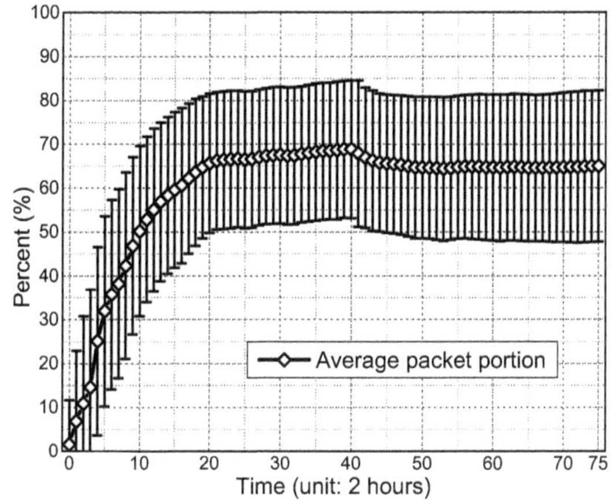

Figure 12: The portion of packets benefited from already recovered routing paths.

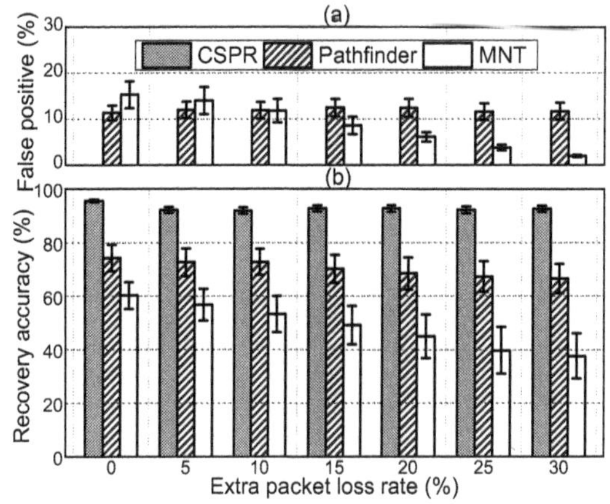

Figure 13: The recovery accuracies and false positives of the three approaches with various extra packet loss rates.

CSPR avoids repeating reconstruct those frequent traveled paths, and thus saves abundant of computation.

In Section 2.2, we have already observed about 20% natural packet losses. To examine the impacts of severer packet losses to the path reconstruction performance of each approach, we fabricate extra packet losses by randomly removing packets from the original trace. We present the recovery accuracy and false positive of each approach with various extra packet loss rates in Fig. 13. Note that each value in Fig. 13 is an average of 10 runs. The extra packet loss rate labeling *"0"* corresponds to the original trace. With more packets lost, the performance of MNT drops quickly. MNT becomes to be not applicable, with accuracy $< 50\%$, when the extra packet loss rate beyond 15%. The performance of Pathfinder is also affected, with accuracy dropping from 74% to 66%. These results illustrate that packet losses indeed have a strong impact on the performances of approaches relying on inter-packet correlation. When anchors lost, Pathfinder and MNT use the remedy method to search possible paths for packets and thus introduce false positives, due to their relaxed path verification manners. From Fig. 13 (a), we observe non-negligible false positives for Pathfinder and MNT with averages ranging from 4% to 15%. On the contrast, CSPR is insensitive to packet losses and can achieve stable accuracy $> 92\%$ with no false positive.

Packet overhead. In addition to some default information in the packet header, e.g., source address, sequence number, hop count and first-hop receiver, each path reconstruction approach further adds some necessary contents to each packet for the path recovery. Assuming that a node ID is of size 2 bytes. Then the packet overhead of MNT is 5 bytes including the 1-byte XOR and 4-byte timestamp. The packet overhead of Pathfinder is about 7 bytes including the 1-byte XOR, 2 IDs of changed parents and a bit vector as the same length of packet path. The packet overhead of CSPR could be variable in different sizes of networks. CSPR includes a measurement of 2 bytes (i.e., aMsr) and an L-bit bloom filter (i.e., bFlt). Note that L is related with the maximum path length in the network and could be small, e.g., $L = 48$ (6 bytes) for the CitySee packet trace with the maximum path length 12 hops, which actually corresponds to a large-scale network.

5. RELATED WORK

We review the related works on routing path reconstruction, network tomography and network diagnosis, mainly conducted in WSNs, in this section.

Routing path reconstruction. CAPTRA [27] identifies a packet path through the coordinations among nodes in a network-wide scale. Alam *et al.* [2] adopt a probabilistic packet marking technique to trace the provenance of a packet. Both of the works can not realize per-packet path reconstruction as CSPR. PathZip [19] compresses path information of a packet into a hash value, and obtains the packet path by matching all possible paths with the hash value. As the computation complexity grows exponentially with the network size, PathZip may not scale to work with large networks. Pathfinder [14] and MNT [16], the two state-of-the-art approaches, reconstruct packet path relying on inter-packet correlation. Their performances, however, are severely influenced by topology dynamics and packet losses, just as demonstrated in Section 2.2. Different from them, CSPR is insensitive to network dynamics and lossy links due to its distinct design.

Network tomography. Network tomography in wired networks has been well studied and tremendous approaches have been proposed to investigate the internal behaviors [8]. By actively generating probe packets from network nodes, network tomography mainly aims to recover the network topology or infer some link-level characteristics [21], e.g., delay or packet loss. Restricted by the available resources, extensive probes are prohibited for network topography in WSNs. Recently many works have been proposed to achieve network tomography in WSNs by leveraging statistical methods [25], group testing [7], compressive sensing [31] and optimization methods [13]. Compared to those works, CSPR reconstructs routing path for each individual packet without triggering extra probe packets.

Network diagnosis. Network diagnosis aims at inferring the root cause for abnormal networking symptoms and maintaining the health of deployed WSNs. Relying on the collected system metrics from network, Sympathy [26] pinpoints the root cause of network failures through a decision tree. PAD [18] captures abnormal events and infers the root cause for the observed abnormity in a probabilistic manner. The active packet marking scheme in PAD can only recover one routing path for each source node, while the underlying network topology is required to be relatively stable. PD2 [6] is a data-centric approach that locates performance problems based on data flows. D2 [10] detects and diagnoses anomaly by mining network symptoms. AD [23] exploits the correlation among different system metrics to discover silent failures. Existing works in this category are orthogonal to CSPR, and are potentially benefitted from the outputs of CSPR for more accurate and fine-grained diagnostic results.

6. CONCLUSION

In this paper, we present the CSPR, a compressive sensing based path reconstruction approach. Different from the state-of-the-art approaches, CSPR is inherently insensitive to network dynamics and lossy links. Extensive evaluations through both testbed-based experiments and trace-driven simulations show that CSPR outperforms the state-of-the-art approaches in various network settings.

7. ACKNOWLEDGEMENTS

We would like to thank the anonymous reviewers for valuable and insightful comments. This work is supported in part by National High Technology Research and Development Program of China (863) under Grant No.2012AA101701; National Key Research & Development Program under Grant No.2013BAK01B04; Project of Innovative Team of Digital Cultural Media Technology of Zhejiang Province under Grant No.2010R50040; NSFC No.61303233. This work is also partially supported by Singapore MOE AcRF Tier 2 Grant MOE2012-T2-1-070, and NTU Nanyang Assistant Professorship (NAP) Grant M4080738.020. We also acknowledge the support of practical packet trace from the CitySee project [22].

8. REFERENCES

[1] TelosB mote datasheet. `http://www.willow.co.uk/TelosB_Datasheet.pdf`.

[2] S. Alam and S. Fahmy. A practical approach for provenance transmission in wireless sensor networks. *Ad Hoc Networks*, 2013.

[3] A. Broder and M. Mitzenmacher. Network applications of bloom filters: a survey. *Internet Mathematics*, 1(4):485–509, 2004.

[4] E. J. Candès, J. Romberg, and T. Tao. Robust uncertainty principles: exact signal reconstruction from highly incomplete frequency information. *IEEE Transactions on Information Theory*, 52(2):489–509, 2006.

[5] E. J. Candès and M. B. Wakin. An introduction to compressive sampling. *IEEE Signal Processing Magazine*, 25(2):21–30, 2008.

[6] Z. Chen and K. G. Shin. Post-deployment performance debugging in wireless sensor networks. In *IEEE RTSS*, 2009.

[7] M. Cheraghchi, A. Karbasi, S. Mohajer, and V. Saligrama. Graph-constrained group testing. *IEEE Transactions on Information Theory*, 58(1):248–262, 2012.

[8] A. Coates, A. O. Hero III, R. Nowak, and B. Yu. Internet tomography. *IEEE Signal Processing Magazine*, 19(3):47–65, 2002.

[9] D. Dong, M. Li, Y. Liu, X.-Y. Li, and X. Liao. Topological detection on wormholes in wireless ad hoc and sensor networks. *IEEE/ACM Transactions on Networking*, 19(6):1787–1796, 2011.

[10] W. Dong, C. Chen, J. Bu, X. Liu, and Y. Liu. D2: anomaly detection and diagnosis in networked embedded systems by program profiling and symptom mining. In *IEEE RTSS*, 2013.

[11] W. Dong, Y. Liu, Y. He, and T. Zhu. Measurement and analysis on the packet delivery performance in a large scale sensor network. In *IEEE INFOCOM*, 2013.

[12] D. L. Donoho. Compressed sensing. *IEEE Transactions on Information Theory*, 52(4):1289–1306, 2006.

[13] Y. Gao, W. Dong, C. Chen, J. Bu, T. Chen, M. Xia, X. Liu, and X. Xu. Domo: passive per-packet delay tomography in wireless ad-hoc networks. In *IEEE ICDCS*, 2014.

[14] Y. Gao, W. Dong, C. Chen, J. Bu, G. Guan, X. Zhang, and X. Liu. Pathfinder: robust path reconstruction in large scale sensor networks with lossy links. In *IEEE ICNP*, 2013.

[15] O. Gnawali, R. Fonseca, K. Jamieson, D. Moss, and P. Levis. Collection tree protocol. In *ACM SenSys*, 2009.

[16] M. Keller, J. Beutel, and L. Thiele. How was your journey?: uncovering routing dynamics in deployed sensor networks with multi-hop network tomography. In *ACM SenSys*, 2012.

[17] X.-Y. Li, Y. Wang, H. Chen, X. Chu, Y. Wu, and Y. Qi. Reliable and energy-efficient routing for static wireless ad hoc networks with unreliable links. *IEEE Transactions on Parallel and Distributed Systems*, 20(10):1408–1421, 2009.

[18] Y. Liu, K. Liu, and M. Li. Passive diagnosis for wireless sensor networks. *IEEE/ACM Transactions on Networking*, 18(4):1132–1144, 2010.

[19] X. Lu, D. Dong, X. Liao, and S. Li. PathZip: packet path tracing in wireless sensor networks. In *IEEE MASS*, 2012.

[20] C. Luo, F. Wu, J. Sun, and C. W. Chen. Compressive data gathering for large-scale wireless sensor networks. In *ACM MobiCom*, 2009.

[21] L. Ma, T. He, K. K. Leung, D. Towsley, and A. Swami. Efficient identification of additive link metrics via network tomography. In *IEEE ICDCS*, 2013.

[22] X. Mao, X. Miao, Y. He, X. Li, and Y. Liu. CitySee: urban CO_2 monitoring with sensors. In *IEEE INFOCOM*, 2012.

[23] X. Miao, K. Liu, Y. He, Y. Liu, and D. Papadias. Agnostic diagnosis: discovering silent failures in wireless sensor networks. In *IEEE INFOCOM*, 2011.

[24] D. Needell and J. A. Tropp. CoSaMP: iterative signal recovery from incomplete and inaccurate samples. *Applied and Computational Harmonic Analysis*, 26(3):301–321, 2009.

[25] H. X. Nguyen and P. Thiran. Using end-to-end data to infer lossy links in sensor networks. In *IEEE INFOCOM*, 2006.

[26] N. Ramanathan, K. Chang, R. Kapur, L. Girod, E. Kohler, and D. Estrin. Sympathy for the sensor network debugger. In *ACM SenSys*, 2005.

[27] D. Sy and L. Bao. CAPTRA: coordinated packet traceback. In *ACM/IEEE IPSN*, 2006.

[28] S. Tang and J. Wu. Qute: quality-of-monitoring aware sensing and routing strategy in wireless sensor networks. In *ACM MobiHoc*, 2013.

[29] J. Wang, W. Dong, Z. Cao, and Y. Liu. On the delay performance analysis in a large-scale wireless sensor network. In *IEEE RTSS*, 2012.

[30] J. Wang, Y. Liu, Z. Li, W. Dong, and Y. He. QoF: towards comprehensive path quality measurement in wireless sensor networks. In *IEEE INFOCOM*, 2011.

[31] W. Xu, E. Mallada, and A. Tang. Compressive sensing over graphs. In *IEEE NFOCOM*, 2011.

[32] Y. Yang, Y. Xu, X. Li, and C. Chen. A loss inference algorithm for wireless sensor networks to improve data reliability of digital ecosystems. *IEEE Transactions on Industrial Electronics*, 58(6):2126–2137, 2011.

[33] T. Zhu, W. Dong, Y. He, Q. Ma, L. Mo, and Y. Liu. Understanding routing dynamics in a large-scale wireless sensor network. In *IEEE MASS*, 2013.

[34] Y. Zhu and L. M. Ni. Probabilistic approach to provisioning guaranteed QoS for distributed event detection. In *IEEE INFOCOM*, 2008.

Heterogeneous Multi-channel Neighbor Discovery for Mobile Sensing Applications: Theoretical Foundation and Protocol Design

Lin Chen
LRI-CNRS UMR 8623
Univ. of Paris-Sud
chen@lri.fr

Kaigui Bian
Inst. Netw. Comp. & Inf. Sys.,
School of EECS, Peking Univ.
bkg@pku.edu.cn

Meng Zheng
Key Lab. Netw. Contr. Sys.
Shengyang Inst. Automation
Chinese Academy of Sciences
zhengmeng_6@sia.cn

ABSTRACT

Neighbor discovery is of paramount importance in mobile sensing applications that rely heavily on data timely collected and shared among nearby users. Guaranteed discovery with bounded latency and supporting heterogenous duty cycles to provide fine-grained control of energy conservation levels are among the most crucial requirements in the design of efficient neighbor discovery protocols. While simultaneously satisfying these two requirements is non-trivial, the situation is exacerbated if the operating frequencies of mobile devices span multiple channels and discovery occurs only if nodes switch to the same channel. In this paper, we formulate this problem as *heterogeneous multi-channel neighbor discovery* problem and establish a theoretical framework of the problem, under which we derive the performance bound of any neighbor discovery protocol. Based on the theoretical results, we then develop Mc-Dis (Multi-channel Discovery), a novel multi-channel discovery protocol that (1) achieves guaranteed discovery with order-minimal worst-case discovery delay and (2) supports almost all duty cycles to provide fine-grained control of energy conservation levels.

Categories and Subject Descriptors

C.2.1 [**Computer-Communications Networks**]: Network Architecture and Design—*Wireless Communication*; F.2.2 [**Analysis of Algorithms and Problem Complexity**]: Nonnumerical Algorithms and Performance

Keywords

Neighbor Discovery; Multi-channel; Energy Efficiency; Wireless networks

1. INTRODUCTION

The ever-growing deployment of millions of personal mobile devices, e.g., smart-phones and tablets, provides a fertile ground for numerous mobile sensing applications ranging from mobile social networking [11], proximity-based gaming [1] to participatory and crowd sensing [5]. The success of such applications, where mobile devices equipped with different types of sensors interact with each other upon encounters, relies heavily on data timely collected and shared among the nearby users in an opportunistic fashion.

MobiHoc14, August 11–14, 2014, Philadelphia, PA, USA.

http://dx.doi.org/10.1145/2632951.2632972.

The supporting primitive that identifies all the neighbors in a mobile device's communication range is referred to as *neighbor discovery* protocols, one of the bootstrapping primitives supporting many basic network functionalities, such as topology control, clustering, medium access control and routing. Ideally, nodes should discover their neighbors as quickly as possible for other protocols to start execution.

However, designing efficient neighbor discovery protocols for mobile sensing applications is particularly challenging due to the stringent energy constraint of mobile devices. Specifically, these devices, usually battery-constrained, alternate between active and sleeping modes by turning their radios on only periodically. This energy-saving technique is called *duty cycling.* Despite its effectiveness in energy conservation, the duty cycling technique significantly challenges the neighbor discovery protocol design in the quest of limiting discovery latency with low power consumption. Specifically, the two important design objectives, saving energy through a duty-cycle based scheduling and limiting the neighbor discovery latency, are at odd with each other.

Moreover, the operating frequencies of mobile devices typically span a swath of spectrum subdivided into multiple orthogonal channels. Such multi-channel characteristic brings an additional dimension to the neighbor discovery problem, as each pair of neighbors not only need to wake up at the same time slot, but also should switch to the same channel in order to discover each other. Wireless channels are notoriously unstable and the channel conditions may vary in both time and space domains. Any two nodes may have different channel perceptions due to their locations, traffic patterns, interference, noises, etc. Consequently, to achieve maximal discovery robustness, an effective neighbor discovery protocol needs to ensure discovery between any pair of neighbors on every common channel they can access.

We coin the term *heterogeneous multi-channel neighbor discovery* problem to denote the following problem in the context described above: *How can neighbor nodes with heterogeneous duty cycles, operating on different channels, without clock synchronization, discover each other over every common channel within a bounded delay?* Particularly, the following requirements should be satisfied:

- Maximal discovery diversity/robustness with bounded (and minimal) worst-case discovery delay;
- Support for heterogenous and arbitrary duty cycles to provide fine-grained control of energy saving levels.

It is the combination of the above two design requirements that makes the neighbor discovery protocol design far from trivial and should be handled holistically. As reviewed in Sec. 2, no existing work, to the best of our knowledge, can satisfy both requirements simultaneously. To address the heterogeneous multi-channel neighbor discovery problem, we present the design and evaluation of a multi-channel neighbor discovery protocol, termed as Mc-Dis (Multi-channel Discovery), that can guarantee discovery between any pair of neighbor nodes over *every* common channel within *bounded* delay while supporting almost all duty cycles. The main contributions of the paper are articulated as follows.

- *Theoretical foundation:* We establish a theoretical framework to study the heterogeneous multi-channel neighbor discovery problem, under which we derive the performance bound of any neighbor discovery protocol.
- *Protocol design:* We design Mc-Dis, a novel multi-channel discovery protocol that achieves guaranteed discovery with order-minimal worst-case discovery delay and supports almost all duty cycles.

By applying theoretic tools in number theory and graph theory (more specifically, the Chinese Remainder Theory [14] and the Maximum independent Set problem [6]), the proposed neighbor discovery protocol, Mc-Dis, has the following noteworthy properties which make it especially suitable for mobile sensing applications.

- *Fine-grained control of duty cycle*: In contrast to existing solutions using prime numbers or power-multiples of minimal duty cycles, Mc-Dis can practically support almost all duty cycles, thus providing much more fine-grained control of energy conservation levels.
- *Bounded worst-case discovery delay*: Mc-Dis achieves bounded discovery delay even between nodes with heterogeneous duty cycles.
- *Full discovery diversity*: Mc-Dis guarantees discovery over *each* channel, thus minimising the probability of discovery failures caused by various channel problems.
- *Robustness against asymmetrical channel perceptions*: Mc-Dis achieves the same discovery performance even if nodes have asymmetrical channel perceptions, either on the accessible channel set or on the channel index.
- *Robustness against clock drift*: Mc-Dis achieves the same performance even if clocks of any two nodes drift away from each other by an *arbitrary* amount of time.

The rest of the paper is organized as follows. Sec. 2 summarises the related work on neighbor discovery. Sec. 3 describes the system model and formulates the optimal heterogeneous multi-channel neighbor discovery problem. Sec. 4 establishes the theoretical performance bound. Sec. 5 presents the design of Mc-Dis in the single-channel case and performs a theoretical analysis on its performance. Sec. 6 further presents the design of Mc-Dis in the mult-channel case and investigates its performance there. Sec. 7 presents the simulation results. Sec. 8 concludes the paper.

2. RELATED WORK

Existing work on neighbor discovery in duty-cycled wireless networks can be categorized into *probabilistic* and *deterministic* protocols.

Probabilistic protocols (e.g. [10,16,17,19,23]) adopt probabilistic strategies at each node. A representative one is the birthday protocol [10] where nodes transmit/receive or sleep with different probabilities. The work in [19] and [23] further addresses the case with multi-packet reception and directional antennas. Probabilistic protocols have the advantages of being memoryless and stationary and thus are especially robust and adapted in ad hoc environments where no a priori knowledge or coordination is available. The main drawback is the lack of performance guarantee in terms of discovery delay.

Deterministic protocols, on the other hand, are proposed to provide strict bound on the discovery delay [3,4,7,24]. In deterministic protocols, each node wakes up according to certain schedule carefully tuned to ensure that each pair of two wake-up schedules overlap in at least one active slot. Based on the design of wake-up schedule, deterministic protocols can further be divided into three classes. The first class of them, based on Quorum [9,15], construct the wake-up schedule by assigning a column and a row of an $m \times m$ array to each node such that no matter which row and column are selected, any two nodes have at least two overlapping awaken slots. The main drawback of the Quorum-based approaches is the support of only symmetrical duty cycles [15]. Although enhanced solutions have been proposed to support asymmetric duty cycles, only two different duty cycles can be supported [9]. The second class of deterministic protocols overcome this limitation by using prime numbers to guarantee bounded discovery delay even for asymmetrical duty cycles. A typical one in this class is Disco [4], in which each node selects two prime numbers, based on which its wake-up schedule is configured. A more recent proposition, U-Connect [7], uses a single prime number per node and has a shorter discovery delay, given the same duty cycle. The third class, proposed in [3], employs two kinds of wake-up slots, termed as anchor slots and probe slots, to achieve both lower worst-case and average discovery delay. In [21] and [22], two protocols are proposed to be implemented on top of deterministic protocols to achieve further performance gain, either in energy conservation or discovery delay. One drawback of existing deterministic protocols is the failure to support all duty cycles due to their limited choice on either prime numbers or power-multiples of the smallest duty cycles, and consequently only a limited choices of energy conservation levels can be supported.

There are some multi-channel neighbor discovery protocols proposed for non duty-cycled networks. Mittal *et al.* proposed a suite of probabilistic and deterministic neighbor discovery protocols [8,12,13,20] for cognitive radio networks (CRNs). Arachchige *et al.* developed a leader election protocol to setup a CRN in which a leader is selected based on node IDs and then performs neighbor discovery by periodically transmitting beacons [2]. Karowski *et al.* developed neighbor discovery protocols for IEEE 802.15 networks to minimise the expected discovery delay in that context.

Despite extensive research efforts devoted to neighbor discovery, none of them can solve the heterogeneous multi-channel neighbor discovery problem by achieving bounded discovery delay for nodes operating on heterogenous duty cycles. In this regard, our work provides a systematic formulation and analysis on the heterogeneous multi-channel neighbor discovery problem and the design of a functional neighbor discovery protocol that satisfies the design requirements posed in Sec. 1.

3. HETEROGENEOUS MULTI-CHANNEL NEIGHBOR DISCOVERY

3.1 System Model

We consider a time-slotted (but not necessarily synchronized) energy-constraint wireless network operating on a set $\mathcal{N}$ of N channels. To discover its neighbors in the multi-channel environment, each node wakes up periodically and switches across different channels. The main design challenges we need to address are summarised as follows:

- *Lack of clock synchronization*: Due to the resource constraint, it is extremely difficult to maintain tight synchronization among the local clocks of different nodes, and thus the clocks of any two nodes may drift away from each other by an arbitrary amount of time, which may lead to the discovery failure.
- *Asymmetrical duty cycle lengths*: The duty cycle lengths of two network nodes are typically asymmetrical, depending on their independent energy constraint and the applications running on them. Neighbor discovery protocols should ensure that any two nodes can wake up in a same slot on the same channel regardless of their asymmetrical duty cycle lengths.
- *Asymmetrical channel perceptions*: Wireless channels are notoriously unstable and the channel conditions may vary in both time and space domains. Consequently, any two nodes may have different channel perceptions due to their locations, traffic patterns, interference, noises, etc. Formally, each node u has its own perception on $\mathcal{N}$, denoted as $\mathcal{N}_u$.

In the following, we formally define the *neighbor discovery schedule* that characterises the wake-up and channel hopping pattern of a node.

DEFINITION 1 (NEIGHBOR DISCOVERY SCHEDULE). *The neighbor discovery schedule of a node u is defined as a sequences $\mathbf{x}_u \triangleq \{x_u^t\}_{1\le t\le T_u}$, where T_u is the period of the sequence*[1]*, and*

$$x_u^t = \begin{cases} 0 & u \text{ sleeps in slot } t \\ n \in \mathcal{N}_u & u \text{ wakes up on channel } n \end{cases}.$$

Consider two nodes a and b with their neighbor discovery schedules being $\mathbf{x}_a$ and $\mathbf{x}_b$ whose periods are T_a and T_b. Given the periodicity of $\mathbf{x}_a$ and $\mathbf{x}_b$, it suffices to consider consecutive T_aT_b slots, i.e, $1 \le t \le T_aT_b$. If $\exists t \in [1, T_aT_b]$ and $h \in \mathcal{N}$ such that $x_a^t = x_b^t = h$, we say that a and b can discover each other in slot t on channel h. Slot t is called the discovery slot and channel h is called the discovery channel between a and b. Example 1 illustrates the above definition.

EXAMPLE 1. *Consider a network of two channels and two nodes a, b whose neighbor discovery schedules are $\mathbf{x}_a = \{0, 0, 1\}$ and $\mathbf{x}_b = \{0, 1, 0, 2\}$ with $T_a = 3$ and $T_b = 4$. The duty cycles of a and b are $d_a = 3$ and $d_b = 2$. The neighbor discovery schedules of a and b are repeated each 12 slots, as illustrated in Fig. 1 for one period. We can observe that a and b can discover each other on slots 6 on channel 1.*

[1] A random neighbor discovery schedule is a special case where $T_u \to \infty$.

Slot index	1	2	3	4	5	6	7	8	9	10	11	12	...
Node *a* :	0	0	1	0	0	1	0	0	1	0	0	1	...
Node *b* :	0	1	0	2	0	1	0	2	0	1	0	2	...

Figure 1: Neighbor discovery schedule example.

To model the situation where the clocks of different nodes are not synchronised[2], we apply the concept of *cyclic rotation* to neighbor discovery schedules. Specifically, given a neighbor discovery schedule $\mathbf{x}_a$, we denote $\mathbf{x}_a(k)$ a cyclic rotation of $\mathbf{x}_a$ by k slots where k is called the cyclic rotation phase. In Example 1, we have $\mathbf{x}_a(1) \triangleq \{1, 0, 0\}$ and $\mathbf{x}_b(2) = \{0, 2, 0, 1\}$.

3.2 Optimal Neighbor Discovery Problem

Performance Metric 1: Maximal Time to Discovery For the neighbor discovery problem, the primary performance metric is the maximal time to discovery (MTTD), i.e., the worst-case discovery delay. Given two nodes a and b, the MTTD between them is defined as the upper-bound of the latency (in number of slots) before successful mutual discovery for all possible clock drift between them. Reconsider Example 1, we can observe that the MTTD is 11, achieved between $\mathbf{x}_a(6)$ and $\mathbf{x}_b(6)$.

Performance Metric 2: Discovery Diversity The other metric, particularly pertinent for the multi-channel environment, is the *discovery diversity*, which characterizes the capability of a neighbor discovery protocol of discovering a neighbor regardless of its operational channel. We say that a neighbor discovery protocol achieves *full* discovery diversity if the discovery of any pair of nodes is guaranteed on *every* common channel they can access. It can be checked that the neighbor discover schedule in Example 1 cannot achieve full discovery diversity as a and b can never discover each other on channel 2.

Performance Metric 3: Maximal Time to Full Discovery Diversity When full discovery diversity can be achieved, we further define the third metric *maximal time to full discovery diversity* (MTTFDD) as the worst-case delay to achieve full discovery diversity. MTTFDD can be regarded as a generalisation of MTTD in multi-channel networks. MTTFDD degenerates to MTTD in single-channel networks. Throughout the paper, we analyse MTTD in single-channel case and MTTFDD in multi-channel case.

We conclude this section by formulating the optimal heterogeneous multi-channel neighbor discovery problem.

PROBLEM 1. *The optimal heterogeneous multi-channel neighbor discovery problem is defined as follows:*

minimise T,

subject to $\forall t_a^0 \in [1, T_a], t_b^0 \in [1, T_b], \forall d_a, d_b, \exists t \le T$ *such that* $x_a^t(t_a^0) = x_b^t(t_b^0) = h, \forall h \in \mathcal{N}_a \bigcap \mathcal{N}_b$.

That is, devising neighbor discover schedules to minimize T, the worst-case discovery delay while achieving full discovery diversity between any pair of nodes a and b for any duty cycle pair (d_a, d_b), any initial time offset t_a^0 and t_b^0 and any channel perception $\mathcal{N}_a$ and $\mathcal{N}_b$.

In what follows, we first establish a theoretical performance bound of any neighbor discovery protocol. We then

[2] Here we assume that clocks of different nodes are asynchronous but their slot boundaries are aligned. The situation of unaligned slot boundaries is analysed in Sec. 6.4.

present the baseline design and optimisation of Mc-Dis in the single-channel case, before proceeding to the multi-channel case with symmetrical channel perception (i.e., $\mathcal{N}_a = \mathcal{N}_b$). We complete our analysis by addressing the generic case with asymmetrical channel perceptions and arbitrary clock drift to iron out a version of Mc-Dis that works in practice.

4. PROTOCOL-INDEPENDENT DISCOVERY DELAY BOUND

Armed with the theoretical framework established previously, this section derives the performance bound of any multi-channel neighbor discovery protocol achieving full discovery channel diversity. The result derived in this section establishes a lower-bound of the solution of Problem 1.

THEOREM 1. *(Protocol-independent Bound of MTTFDD) For any neighbor discovery protocol achieving full discovery channel diversity, the MTTFDD between any pair of nodes a and b, denoted by L, is lower-bounded by $N^2 d_a d_b$, where d_a and d_b denote the duty cycles of a and b.*

PROOF. Let T_a and T_b denote the period of $\mathbf{x_a}$ and $\mathbf{x_b}$, i.e., the neighbor discovery schedules of a and b. It can be noted that regardless of the clock drift, the neighbor discovery schedules of a and b repeats every T_aT_b time slots. Hence, if they can discovery each other with full discovery diversity regardless of the clock drift, the worst-case discovery delay until full diversity L is upper-bounded by T_aT_b.

Without loss of generality, we fix $\mathbf{x_a}$ and cyclically rotate $\mathbf{x_b}$ by l slots, denoted as $\mathbf{x_b}(l)$, where $l = 0, 1, \ldots, T_aT_b - 1$. Now consider $\mathbf{x_a}$ and $\mathbf{x_b}(l)$. Recall that the maximal time to full discovery diversity is the worst-case discovery delay until full diversity among all initial clock phases of a and b, there must be at least N discovery slots each L slots where both a and b wakes up in the slot, resulting a minimal number of discovery slots NT_aT_b/L within consecutive T_aT_b slots. Let S denote the total number of accumulated discovery slots within consecutive T_aT_b slots between $\mathbf{x_a}$ and $\mathbf{x_b}(l)$ as l is incremented from 0 to $T_aT_b - 1$, we have

$$S \geq \frac{N(T_aT_b)^2}{L}. \tag{1}$$

On the other hand, let i_a^h (i_b^h, respectively) denote the number of time slots in $\mathbf{x_a}$ ($\mathbf{x_b}$, respectively) in which a (b) wakes up on channel h within consecutive T_aT_b slots. We can express the duty cycles of a and b as

$$d_a = \frac{T_aT_b}{\sum_{h\in\mathcal{N}} i_a^h}, \quad d_b = \frac{T_aT_b}{\sum_{h\in\mathcal{N}} i_b^h}.$$

After some algebraic operations, we obtain

$$T_aT_b = \sum_{h\in\mathcal{N}} d_a i_a^h = \sum_{h\in\mathcal{N}} d_b i_b^h = \sum_{h\in\mathcal{N}} \frac{d_a i_a^h + d_b i_b^h}{2}. \tag{2}$$

Since $\mathbf{x}_a$ and $\mathbf{x}_b(l)$ achieve full discovery diversity, for any channel h, the total accumulated number of discoveries between $\mathbf{x}_a$ and $\mathbf{x}_b(l)$, as l is incremented from 0 to $T_aT_b - 1$, in which the discovery channel is h, is $i_a^h \cdot i_b^h$.

Hence the total number of accumulated discoveries, as l is incremented from 0 to $T_aT_b - 1$, is $S = \sum_{h\in\mathcal{N}} i_a^h \cdot i_b^h$.

Noticing $d_a i_a^h d_b i_b^h \leq \left(\frac{d_a i_a^h + d_b i_b^h}{2}\right)^2$, it follows from (2) that

$$S = \sum_{h\in\mathcal{N}} i_a^h \cdot i_b^h = \frac{\sum_{h\in\mathcal{N}} d_a i_a^h \cdot d_b i_b^h}{d_a d_b} \leq \frac{(T_aT_b)^2}{d_a d_b N}$$

It then follows from (1) that $\frac{N(T_aT_b)^2}{L} \leq \frac{(T_aT_b)^2}{d_a d_b N}$, which leads to $L \geq N^2 d_a d_b$. □

Theorem 1 derives the performance limit of any neighbor discovery protocol. We can further generalise Theorem 1 on the pair-wise neighbor discovery to the network-wise neighbor discovery, as stated in the following corollary.

COROLLARY 1. *For any network where the largest two duty cycles of nodes are d_1 and d_2, the MTTFDD between any pair of nodes in the network is lower-bounded by $N^2 d_1 d_2$ for any neighbor discovery protocol. Asymptotically, when $d_1 \simeq d_2 \simeq O(d)$, $L \simeq O(N^2 d^2)$.*

Corollary 1 can also be viewed from another angle: to achieve a target MTTFDD L, the duty cycle of nodes should be upper-bounded by $O\left(\frac{\sqrt{L}}{N}\right)$. Consequently, the energy consumption cannot be lower than $O\left(\frac{\sqrt{L}}{N}\right)$.

In what follows, we develop a multi-channel neighbor discovery protocol termed as Mc-Dis that approaches the derived performance bound. To streamline our presentation, we first develop Mc-Dis for the single-channel case and then proceed to the multi-channel case. After specifying the protocol and deriving its performance, we investigate the case with asymmetrical channel perceptions and arbitrary clock drift to iron out a version of Mc-Dis that works in practice.

5. MC-DIS: SINGLE-CHANNEL CASE

5.1 Motivation and Protocol Design

In the single-channel case, the neighbor discovery schedule $\mathbf{x}_u$ for each node u degenerates to a binary sequence where

$$x_u^t = \begin{cases} 1 & u \text{ wakes up in slot } t, \\ 0 & u \text{ sleeps in slot } t. \end{cases}$$

Each node wakes up periodically to discover its neighbors. The wake-up period is determined by its duty cycle. Specifically, we consider two neighboring nodes a and b with duty cycles d_a and d_b. To discover each other, nodes a and b wake up every d_a and d_b slots, i.e., $x_a(t) = 1$ for $t = kd_a$ and $x_b(t) = 1$ for $t = kd_b + \delta_{ab}$ where δ_{ab} is the clock offset between a and b, $k = 1, 2, \cdots$. It follows from the Chinese Remainder Theorem [14] that if d_a and d_b are co-prime to each other, the two nodes are ensured to discover each other regardless of δ, i.e., there exists t_d such that $x_a(t_d) = x_b(t_d) = 1, \forall \delta_{ab}$.

However, assigning co-prime numbers to each node in a distributed way is far from trivial. A commonly adopted solution is to use only prime numbers because two distinct prime numbers are by definition co-prime to each other, as in Disco [4] and U-Connect [7]. However, limiting the choices to prime numbers fail to support all the duty cycles due to the limited number of prime numbers. Note that among duty cycles smaller than 1000, only $\frac{1}{6}$ are prime numbers.

Motivated by the above analysis, Mc-Dis adopts the following neighbor discovery schedule. For each node u with duty cycle d_u,

$$x_u(t) = \begin{cases} 1 & t \text{ is divisible by either } 2d_u - 1 \text{ or } 2d_u + 1, \\ 0 & \text{otherwise.} \end{cases}$$

EXAMPLE 2. *Consider two nodes a and b with* $d_a = 3$, $d_b = 5$ *with a clock offset* $\delta_{ab} = 1$. *Under Mc-Dis, using the time of a as reference, a wakes up in slots* $5k$ *and* $7k$, *i.e.,* $5, 7, 10, 14, 15, 20, 21, \cdots$, *b wakes up in slots* $9k+1$ *and* $11k+1$, *i.e.,* $10, 12, 19, 23, \cdots$, *as illustrated in Fig. 2. The discovery happens in slot* 10.

The period of $\mathbf{x}_u$ in Mc-Dis is $(2d_u - 1)(2d_u + 1)$, in which there are $4d_u - 1$[3] active slots. Hence, the actual average duty cycle, denoted as $\widehat{d_u}$, is $\frac{(2d_u-1)(2d_u+1)}{4d_u-1}$ which approaches to the required duty cycle d_u when d_u is large. Generally, the relative error between $\widehat{d_u}$ and d_u is upper-bounded by 7.1%, as established in the following lemma.

LEMMA 1. *The relative error between the duty cycle of the neighbor discovery schedule* $\widehat{d_u}$ *and the required duty cycle* d_u *is upper-bounded by 7.1%*

PROOF. Denote the relative error between $\widehat{d_u}$ and d_u as ϵ, we have:

$$\epsilon = \left[\frac{(2d_u - 1)(2d_u + 1)}{4d_u - 1} - d_u\right] / d_u = \frac{d_u - 1}{d_u(4d_u - 1)}.$$

It can be checked that for all $d_u \geq 1$, ϵ is upper-bounded by 7.1%, with the upper-bound achieved when $d_u = 2$. □

In practical applications, d_u is usually large, ϵ is thus much smaller than the upper-bound 7.1%: e.g., ϵ drops below 2.3% when $d_u \geq 10$. Asymptotically, $\epsilon \simeq O\left(\frac{1}{4d_u}\right)$.

5.2 Mc-Dis Core Idea: Regular Duty Cycles

Following the Chinese Remainder Theorem, the mutual discovery of two neighbor nodes a and b in Mc-Dis, regardless of their clock drift, requires at least one of $2d_a \pm 1$ to be co-prime with at least one of $2d_b \pm 1$. In the vast majority of cases, this requirement can be satisfied. To illustrate this, if we allow the maximal duty cycle D to be 100, then all duty cycles except 17 and 38 can be supported by Mc-Dis; if we allow the maximal duty cycle D to be 1000, only 43 duty cycles cannot be supported, i.e., Mc-Dis can support nearly 96% of all duty cycles.

In this subsection, we conduct a formal analysis on the design idea of Mc-Dis. We start by formulating the definition of *regular duty cycles* that are natively supported by Mc-Dis.

DEFINITION 2 (REGULAR DUTY CYCLE). *Given the duty cycle upper-bound* D, *we call a duty cycle* d *a regular duty cycle if for any* $2 \leq d' \leq D$, *at least one number from* $2d \pm 1$ *is co-prime with at least one number from* $2d' \pm 1$.

For two nodes a and b, if at least one of their duty cycles d_a and d_b is regular, a and b can discover each other. Reconsider Example 2 with $D = 1000$, it can be checked that the duty cycles $d_a = 3$ and $d_b = 5$ are both regular. Evidently the two nodes can discover each other, as illustrated in Fig. 2.

We conclude this subsection by stating the following properties of the regular duty cycles:

- *The vast majority of duty cycles are regular.* As illustrated in the beginning of the subsection, more than 96% duty cycles are regular. In contrast, in existing solutions based on prime numbers, only a small portion of duty cycles can be supported due to the limited choice of prime numbers.
- *There are no three consecutive non-regular duty cycles.* In other words, if d is non-regular, at least one from $d \pm 1$ is regular. This implies that if the required duty cycle d happens to be a non-regular one, the node can operate on $d+1$ or $d-1$. If we take the case of using $d-1$, the effective duty cycle is $\frac{[2(d-1)-1][2(d-1)+1]}{4(d-1)-1}$. The relative error to the required duty cycle can be computed as

$$\epsilon = \left[\frac{[2(d-1)-1][2(d-1)+1]}{4(d-1)-1} - d\right] / d = \frac{-3d_u + 3}{d(4d-5)},$$

which is decreasing in d. In the case of $D = 1000$, the smallest non-regular duty cycle being 17, ϵ is upper-bounded by 4.5% for all non-regular duty cycles.

The analysis in this subsection demonstrates that Mc-Dis can support most duty cycles and even in the cases where the duty cycles cannot be directed supported, Mc-Dis can use neighboring duty cycles with almost negligible errors.

Concerning the implementation aspect of Mc-Dis, we would like to emphasis that the regular duty cycles can be pre-calculated off-line and stored in a look-up table.

5.3 Discovery Delay Upper-bound

In single-channel case, only the first performance metric (maximal time to discovery, MTTD) is applicable. In Theorem 2, we derive the MTTD of Mc-Dis between two nodes a and b if at least one of d_a and d_b is regular.[4]

THEOREM 2 (DISCOVERY DELAY UPPER-BOUND). *Given any two nodes a and b, if at least one of their duty cycles* d_a *and* d_b *is regular, they are ensured to discover each other within at most* $(2d_a+1)(2d_b+1)$ *slots.*

PROOF. Recall the definition of the regular duty cycle, at least one of $2d_a \pm 1$ is co-prime with at least one of $2d_b \pm 1$. It follows from The Chinese Remainder Theorem that a and b can discover each other within at most $(2d_a+1)(2d_b+1)$ slots, regardless of their clock offset. □

5.4 Mc-Dis Optimisation: Supporting More Duty Cycles

From previous analysis, we can see that using non-regular duty cycles may result in discovery failure. For example, if the duty cycle upper-bound is $D = 100$, node a with duty cycle $d_a = 17$ may never discover node b with duty cycle $d_b = 38$ because neither $2d_a \pm 1$ (33 and 35) is co-prime to either $2d_b - 1$ (75) or $2d_b + 1$ (77). A direct solution is to remove 17 and 38 from the usable duty cycle set and use 16 and 37 instead. However, since one of d_a and d_b being regular is sufficient to ensure discovery, we can do better by removing only 38 from the set of usable duty cycles. Now 17 becomes usable as for any duty cycles other than 38, discovery is guaranteed with 17. In this subsection, we explore the natural question of constructing the usable duty cycle set with the maximal number of elements, formalised as follows.

PROBLEM 2. *Let U denote the usable duty cycle set with the duty cycle upper-bound D,*

[3]Note that $(2d_u - 1)(2d_u + 1)$ is divisible by both $2d_u - 1$ and $2d_u + 1$.

[4]Throughout our analysis, we focus on the pair-wise discovery between any pair of neighbor nodes a and b. The obtained results can be readily generated to the network level where each node should discover all its neighbor nodes by following the same way as Theorem 1 and Corollary 1.

Slot index	1	2	3	4	5	6	7	8	9	10	11	12	13	14	15	16	17	18	19	20	21	22	23	24	25	...
Node *a* :	0	0	0	0	1	0	1	0	0	1	0	0	0	1	1	0	0	0	0	1	1	0	0	0	1	...
Node *b* :	1	0	0	0	0	0	0	0	0	1	0	1	0	0	0	0	0	0	1	0	0	0	1	0	0	...

Figure 2: Mc-Dis in single-channel case: $d_a = 3$, $d_b = 5$.

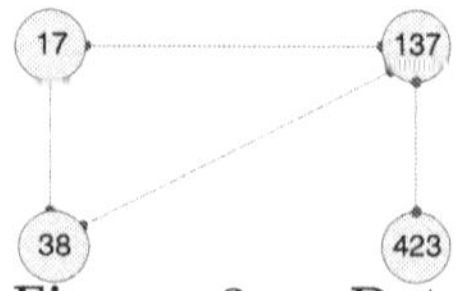

Figure 3: Duty cycle graph (part).

$$\begin{aligned} &\textit{maximise} && |U| \\ &\textit{subject to} && \forall d_1, d_2 \in U,\ d_1 \neq d_2, \text{ at least one of } 2d_1 \pm 1 \\ &&& \text{is co-prime with at least one of } 2d_2 \pm 1. \end{aligned}$$

Solving Problem 2: A Graph-based Approach

We address Problem 2 by casting it into a problem on a graph. Specifically, we construct a graph in which each vertex represents a duty cycle and there exists an edge between two vertexes if the duty cycles represented by the two vertexes may fail to discover each other (mathematically, neither $2d_a \pm 1$ is co-prime to either $2d_b - 1$ or $2d_b + 1$). We observe that the duty cycle graph typically consists of a number of non-connected clusters. Fig. 3 illustrates one of such cluster for $D = 1000$. We seek to remove the minimal number of vertexes (and the edges connected to them) such that each of the remaining vertex is isolated, meaning that the remaining vertexes represent the usable duty cycles. It can be checked that in the cluster of Fig. 3, we need to remove at least two nodes, e.g., 38 and 137. Unfortunately, Problem 2 can not be solved within polynomial time, as proved in the following lemma.

LEMMA 2. *Problem 2 is NP-hard.*

PROOF. We establish the NP-hardness of Problem 2 by casting it into the problem of finding maximum independent sets (MIS) [6] which is NP-hard. An independent set (IS) of a graph is a set of vertices, no two of which are adjacent. That is, it is a set $\mathcal{I}$ of vertices such that for any two vertices in $\mathcal{I}$, there is no edge connecting them. Equivalently, each edge in the graph has at most one endpoint in $\mathcal{I}$. An MIS is an IS with maximum cardinality, i.e., contains the maximal number of vertices. Consider Fig. 3, an MIS is $\{17, 423\}$.

Clearly, solving Problem 2 is equivalent to constructing MIS in the duty cycle graph that we construct. Since finding an MIS is proved NP-hard, Problem 2 is also NP-hard. □

Given its NP-hardness, we develop a heuristic *polynomial* algorithm (Algorithm 1) to solve Problem 2 based on the observation that the duty cycle graph is only loosely connected and that the maximal degree of the graph is limited (typically no more than 3). The heuristic algorithm consists of iteratively adding the vertex with the smallest degree and removing the edges and vertexes connected to it until when graph becomes empty.

Algorithm 1 Calculate the heuristic usable duty cycle set

```
Input: Duty cycle graph G
Output: Usable duty cycle set U
  Initialisation: U ← ∅
  while G is not empty do
    Find a vertex v of minimum degree in G
    U ← U ∪ {v}
    Remove v and its neighbors from G
  end while
```

THEOREM 3 ($\frac{1}{\Delta+1}$-OPTIMALITY OF ALGO 1). *Algo 1 gives a $\frac{1}{\Delta+1}$-approximation for the maximal usable duty cycle set in a duty cycle graph with the maximal degree Δ.*

PROOF. To prove the theorem, we show that the output of Algorithm 1 U satisfies $|U| \geq \frac{|U^*|}{\Delta+1}$ where U^* is the maximal usable duty cycle set. To this end, we upper-bound the number of vertexes in $V \setminus U$. It follows from Algorithm 1 that a vertex u is in $V \setminus U$ because it is removed as a neighbor of some node $v \in U$ when v is added to U. Since any vertex v has at most Δ neighbors, it holds that $|V \setminus U| \leq \Delta |U|$. Hence, we have $|U| \geq \frac{|V|}{\Delta+1} \geq \frac{|U^*|}{\Delta+1}$ by noticing that U^* is a subset of V. □

We run Algorithm 1 for practical scenarios from $D = 100$ to 2000 and report that it always returns the correct maximal usable duty cycle set. Note that Algorithm 1 can be executed off-line to generate a look-up table that contains all non-supported duty cycles in Mc-Dis. Each node only need to check if its required duty cycle is in the table each time when it needs to set/reset the Mc-Dis parameters.

By Algorithm 1, we can typically reduce the non-supported duty cycles by more than 50%. For example, for $D = 100$, we can support all duty cycles except 38; for $D = 500$, the number of duty cycles that cannot be supported by Mc-Dis reduces from 26 to 12, i.e., less than 2.5% of the total duty cycles; for $D = 1000$, the same number reduces from 43 to only 18, i.e., less than 2% of the total duty cycles.

6. MC-DIS: MULTI-CHANNEL CASE

In this section, we present the Mc-Dis design for the multi-channel case and establish the performance bound.

6.1 Neighbor Discovery Schedule Construction

The neighbor discovery schedule of Mc-Dis for each node in the multi-channel case is constructed based on its globally unique ID such as its MAC address, which can be mathematically expressed as a binary sequence of length l. Using globally unique IDs is a typical method to break the symmetry of any pair of nodes. The neighbor discovery schedule construction process is composed of three steps, summarised here and detailed in the following analysis.

- *Step 1:* Each node u independently generates a padded binary sequence $\mathbf{o}_u$ based on its ID such that the padded binary sequences of any two nodes are *cyclic rotationally distinct* one to the other;
- *Step 2:* Each node i independently generates a sequence $\mathbf{s}_u$ based on $\mathbf{o}_u$ such that for any two nodes a, b and any initial time offset t_a^0 and t_b^0, there always exist four time slots l_{ij} $(i, j \in \{0, 1\})$ such that $s_a^{l_{ij}}(t_a^0) = i$ and $s_b^{l_{ij}}(t_b) = j$. We denote such sequences $\mathbf{s}_u$ as *regular sequences*;
- *Step 3:* Each node i generates its neighbor discovery schedule based on $\mathbf{s}_u$.

Step 1: Constructing cyclic rotationally distinct padded binary sequence

As the first step, each node independently generates a binary sequence based on its ID such that the binary sequences of any two nodes are *cyclic rotationally distinct* one to the other. Note that the sequences resulting from cyclic rotations of a sequence are not considered to be cyclic rotationally distinct with respect to each other and the original sequence. We next show how to construct such cyclic rotationally distinct binary sequences.

Let α denote the ID of a node a and let $\mathbf{1}$ ($\mathbf{0}$) denote a sequence of 1 (0) of length $l' = \lceil \frac{l}{2} \rceil$. We construct the padded ID of Alice as the concatenation of $\mathbf{0}$, α and $\mathbf{1}$, denoted as $\mathbf{0}||\alpha||\mathbf{1}$. By the following lemma, we show that the padded ID sequences generated in such way based on different ID sequences are cyclic rotationally distinct one to another.

LEMMA 3. *Given any two padded ID sequences* $\mathbf{a}$ *and* $\mathbf{b}$ *generated from two ID sequences* α *and* β *in the way that* $\mathbf{a} \triangleq \mathbf{0}||\alpha||\mathbf{1}$ *and* $\mathbf{b} \triangleq \mathbf{0}||\beta||\mathbf{1}$, *it holds that*

$$\alpha \neq \beta \implies \mathbf{a} \neq \mathbf{b}(k), \ \forall k \in (0, l+2l'],$$

where $\mathbf{b}(k)$ *is* $\mathbf{b}$ *with a cyclic rotation of* k *bits.*

PROOF. We prove the lemma by considering four possible scenarios illustrated in Figure 4, and showing, in each scenario, that a bit in $\mathbf{a}$ and another bit in $\mathbf{b}(k)$ have different values although the two bits are in the same position within the respective padded ID sequences. This is sufficient to prove that the two padded ID sequences $\mathbf{a}$ and $\mathbf{b}$ are cyclic rotationally distinct one to the other.

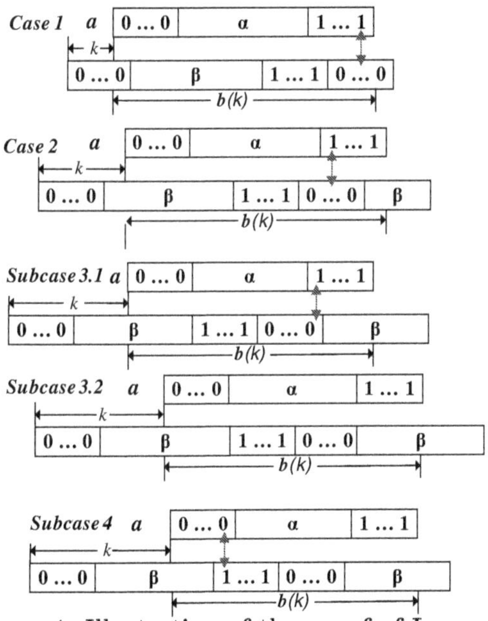

Figure 4: Illustration of the proof of Lemma 3.

Case 1: $k \in (0, l')$. As indicated by the arrow in Case 1 of Figure 4, it holds that $a_L = 1$ and $b_L(k) = 0$ where $L = l + 2l'$.

Case 2: $k \in [l', l+l')$. As indicated by the arrow in Case 2 of Figure 4, it holds that $a_{l+l'} = 1$ and $b_{l+l'}(k) = 0$.

Case 3: $k = l + l'$. We further distinguish two subcases:

- **Subcase 3.1:** l is odd. It holds that $l = 2l' - 1$. As indicated by the arrow in the Subcase 1 of Subcase 3.1 of Figure 4, it holds that $a_{l'} = 0$ and $b_{l'}(k) = 1$.
- **Subcase 3.2:** l is even. It holds that $l = 2l'$. As indicated by the arrow in the Subcase 2 of Subcase 3.2 of Figure 4, since $\mathbf{a} \neq \mathbf{b}$, $\mathbf{a} = \mathbf{1}||\mathbf{0}$ and $\mathbf{b} = \mathbf{1}||\mathbf{0}$ cannot hold simultaneously; There must exists l_0 such that $a_{l_0} \neq b_{l_0}(k)$.

Case 4: $k \in (l + l', l + 2l')$. As indicated by the arrow in the Case 2 of Figure 4, it holds that $a_{l'} = 0$ and $b_{l'}(k) = 1$.

Noticing that $\alpha \neq \beta \implies \mathbf{a} \neq \mathbf{b}$, we thus conclude that $\mathbf{a} \neq \mathbf{b}(k)$, $\forall k \in [0, l + 2l')$. □

Step 2: Generating regular sequence

Denote the padded ID sequence as $\mathbf{o}_u$ for player u, the next step for each player is to generate a sequence $\mathbf{s}_u$ based on $\mathbf{o}_u$ such that for any two nodes a, b and any initial time offset t_a^0 and t_b^0, there always exist four time slots l_{ij} ($i, j \in \{0, 1\}$) such that $s_a^{l_{ij}}(t_a^0) = i$ and $s_b^{l_{ij}}(t_b) = j$. We denote such sequences $\mathbf{s}_u$ as *regular sequences*. In the following we develop an algorithm that can generate regular sequences.

Algorithm 2 Construct a regular sequence $\mathbf{s}_u$

Input: ID sequence $\mathbf{o}_u$ of L_o bits
Output: Regular sequence $\mathbf{s}_u$
  for $i = 1$ to L_o **do**
    switch o_u^i **do**
      case 1: expand o_u^i into eight bits 01010101
      case 0: expand o_u^i into eight bits 00110011
    end switch
  end for
  $\mathbf{s}_u \leftarrow$ the expanded sequence of $\mathbf{s}_u$

LEMMA 4. *The sequence generated by Algo 2 is regular.*

Step 3: Generating neighbor discovery schedule

In the last step, the neighbor discovery schedule is constructed as follows. Each node u hops across different channels $h \in \mathcal{N}$ and wakes up based on the following schedule[5]:

$$x_u^t = \begin{cases} h & t - hd_u \text{ is divisible by } 2Nd_u \pm 1, \\ 0 & \text{otherwise,} \end{cases}$$

where $x_u^t = h$ signifies that u wakes up on channel h in slot t while $x_u^t = 0$ indicates that u sleeps in the slot, Nd_u is chosen from the usable duty cycle set as analysed in sec. 5.4.

The above construction of $\mathbf{x}_u$ does not take into account the case where there exist two different channels h^c ($c = 0, 1$) such that $t - h^0 d_u$ is divisible by $2Nd_u - 1$ and $t - h^1 d_u$ by $2Nd_u + 1$. To resolve such conflict, let $t' = t\%L_s$, u operates on channel h^c if $s_u^{t'} = c$. We refer to the slots where u operates on channel h^c in case of conflict as type-c slots.

To intuitively see that the discovery is ensured between any pair of nodes a, b (the detailed proof is presented in the next subsection), note that if Nd_u belongs to the usable duty cycle set derived previously, i.e., at least one of $2Nd_a \pm 1$ is co-prime with at least one of $2Nd_b \pm 1$, discovery can be guaranteed for any initial time offset t_a^0 and t_b^0 because there always exist four time slots l_{ij} ($i, j \in \{0, 1\}$) such that $s_a^{l_{ij}}(t_a^0) = i$ and $s_b^{l_{ij}}(t_b) = j$ following the regularity of $\mathbf{s}_u$.

[5]To make the notation concise, we adopt the notation that $t - hd_u$ is divisible by $2Nd_u \pm 1$ denotes that $t - hd_u$ is divisible by $2Nd_u - 1$ or $2Nd_u + 1$ or both.

6.2 Discovery Delay Upper-bound

This subsection studies the theoretical performance of Mc-Dis in the multi-channel environment. In multi-channel case, the second metric on discovery diversity and the third metric on MTTFDD are applicable.

THEOREM 4 (WORST-CASE DISCOVERY DELAY). *If Nd_a and Nd_b belong to the usable duty cycle set, the MTTFDD between two nodes a and b is $O(L_sN^2\max\{d_a^2, d_b^2\})$, specifically, $O(L_sN^2d^2)$ if $d_a \simeq d_b \simeq O(d)$.*

PROOF. Without loss of generality, assume that $2Nd_a+1$ is co-prime with $2Nd_b-1$. It follows from The Chinese Remainder Theorem that before resolving conflicts (i.e., assume u can operate on two channels simultaneously), for any channel h, there exists $t_0 < (2Nd_a+1)(2Nd_b-1)$ such that $x_a^{t_0}(t_a^0) = x_b^{t_0}(t_b^0) = h$ and it holds that on slots $t_k = t_0 + k(2Nd_a+1)(2Nd_b-1)$, a can also discovery b before resolving conflicts. However, in realistic settings with conflicts, to ensure discovery, we need to show that there exists k such that a operates in type-1 slot at slot t_k while b operates in type-0 slot at slot t_k. To that end, noticing that $L_s = 4L_o$ is an even number and thus is co-prime with $(2Nd_a+1)(2Nd_b-1)$, there must exist $k < L_s$ such that $t_k\%L_s = l_0$, where l_0 denoted the bit index such that in $s_a^{l_0}(t_a^0) = 1$ and $s_b^{l_0}(t_b^0) = 0$. It follows from Lemma 4 that such l_0 exists. It follows from the construction of x_u that a operates in type-1 slot at slot t_k while b operates in type-0 slot at slot t_k, which leads to discovery. It further follows from $k < L_s$ that the MTTFDD is $O(L_sN^2\max\{d_a^2, d_b^2\})$. □

The capability to achieve discovery on every channel within bounded delay significantly improves neighbor discovery robustness in wireless environment where channel conditions are unpredictable and may vary in both time and space.

6.3 Robustness of Mc-Dis against Asymmetrical Channel Perception

In previous analysis, we implicitly assume that a and b have the same channel perception, i.e., they have symmetrical knowledge on $\mathcal{N}$. In this subsection, we relax this assumption to investigate the scenario where each node u has its own perception on $\mathcal{N}$, denoted by $\mathcal{N}_u$, which is a subset of $\mathcal{N}$. Specifically, the channel perception asymmetry between a and b can be characterised at two levels:

- *Asymmetry on accessible channel set:* They have asymmetrical perceptions on the global channel set $\mathcal{N}$, i.e., $\mathcal{N}_a \neq \mathcal{N}_b$ and $\mathcal{N}_a \bigcap \mathcal{N}_b \neq \emptyset$;
- *Asymmetry on channel index:* They have asymmetrical perceptions on the channel index, i.e., channel $h \in \mathcal{N}$ is indexed h_a by a and h_b by b where $h_a \in \mathcal{N}_a$ and $h_b \in \mathcal{N}_b$ but $h_a \neq h_b$.

The following theorem established the performance of Mc-Dis in such context. The proof sketch is as follows (the detail is omitted due to space limit): Without loss of generality, assume that $2N_ad_a+1$ is co-prime with $2N_bd_b-1$. It follows from The Chinese Remainder Theorem that before resolving conflicts (i.e., assume u can operate on two channels), for any channel h indexed as h_a (h_b) by a (b), there exists $t_0 < (2N_ad_a+1)(2N_bd_b-1)$ such that $x_a^{t_0}(t_a^0) = h_a$ and $x_b^{t_0}(t_b^0) = h_b$. Then using the similar analysis as the proof of Theorem 4, we can show that the MTTFDD is $O(L_o\max\{N_a^2d_a^2, N_b^2d_b^2\})$.

THEOREM 5. *Mc-Dis under asymmetrical channel perceptions achieves the same MTTFDD as under symmetrical channel perceptions, i.e., within at most $O(L_s\max\{N_a^2d_a^2, N_b^2d_b^2\})$ (specifically, $O(L_sN^2d^2)$ if $d_a \simeq d_b \simeq O(d)$ and $N_a \simeq N_b \simeq O(N)$) slots, the discovery between a and b occurs on each channel $h \in \mathcal{N}_a \bigcap \mathcal{N}_b$.*

Theorem 5 shows that Mc-Dis is robust against asymmetrical channel perceptions, either on the channel set or index.

6.4 Robustness of Mc-Dis against Slot Non-alignment and Arbitrary Clock Drift

In this subsection we study the effect of slot non-alignment caused by relative clock drift between the neighbor nodes.

We first briefly introduce the clock model. Each node is equipped with a local clock, which is a time measurement device composed of a hardware oscillator and an accumulator. Mathematically, consider two nodes a and b, we can express the local time at b, denoted as t_b, as a function of the local time of a, denoted as t_a, by the following formula

$$t_b(t_a) = \int_{t_0}^{t_a} \rho_{ab}(\tau)d\tau + t_b(t_0),$$

where $\rho_{ab}(\tau)$ denotes the frequency difference of the oscillator between a and b at time τ, $t_b(t_0)$ is the initial clock offset between them.

If a and b are ideally synchronised, it holds that $\rho_{ab}(\tau) = 1$ and $t_b(t_0) = 0$. In practice, $\rho_{ab}(\tau)$ may drift away from each other, as formalised in the following:

$$\rho_{ab} - \Delta\rho_{max} \leq \rho_{ab}(\tau) \leq \rho_{ab} + \Delta\rho_{max},$$

where $\Delta\rho_{max}$ is bounded by 10^{-6} in practice. Hence we can regard $\rho_{ab}(\tau)$ as a constant ρ_{ab} during the discovery process. Without loss of generality, we assume that the clock of b advances no slower than that of a, i.e., $\rho_{ab} \leq 1$.

When $\rho_{ab} = 1$, i.e., the clock difference between a and b remains $t_b(t_0)$, we distinguish the following two cases (to facilitate presentation, we normalize the slot duration of a):

- Case 1: $t_b(t_0) = k \in \mathbb{Z}$: this is the case with aligned slots addressed in previous analysis;
- Case 2: $t_b(t_0) = k + \delta$ with $k \in \mathbb{Z}$ and $\delta \in (-1/2, 1/2]$: the previous analysis can be directly adapted to this case, the difference being that instead of ensuring entire overlap, a discovery in this case is a partial overlap of time $1 - \delta$.

We now investigate the case where $\rho_{ab} < 1$, meaning that if we regard the slot duration of a as unit time, the slot duration of b is $\rho_{ab} < 1$. The following theorem establishes the discovery performance of Mc-Dis with arbitrary clock drift with $\rho_{ab} < 1$. Due to space limit, the proof is removed.

THEOREM 6. *Regard the slot of a as unit time, a and b can discover each other on each channel h within at most $O(\rho_{ab}L_sN^2\max\{d_a^2, d_b^2\})$ time.*

The results obtained in this subsection, particularly Theorem 6, demonstrate that the discovery performance established in previous analysis holds even when the clocks of a and b drift away from each other for an arbitrary amount of time. In other words, Mc-Dis is robust against clock drift and slot non-alignment.

7. PERFORMANCE EVALUATION

In this section, we perform a set of simulations to evaluate Mc-Dis in several typical application scenarios, ranging from the synchronized single-channel case to the heterogeneous asynchronous and asymmetrical multi-channel case. We also conduct a comparative study between Mc-Dis and other major existing neighbor discovery protocols in duty-cycled networks by focusing on the capability to support heterogeneous duty cycles and the discovery delay.

7.1 Supported Duty Cycles

The first numerical experiment is a comparative analysis on the supported duty cycles in Disco, U-Connect, Searchlight and Mc-Dis. To that end, for each possible required duty cycle $1 \leq d \leq 100$, we study the relative error in supporting it, denoted as $\epsilon \triangleq |d' - d|/d$ where d' is the the closest duty cycle supported by the simulated protocol w.r.t. d. Noted that a smaller ϵ implies that the protocol can support more energy conservation levels with finer granularity. For Disco, in which the choice of prime numbers depends on the target discovery delay upper-bound, we configure the protocol by aligning the bound to Mc-Dis in order to provide a common baseline. For Searchlight, we set the smallest duty cycle unit as 2 to allow the finest duty cycle granularity.

The results are illustrated in Fig. 5(a). We make the following observations: (1) Searchlight has the worst performance on supporting duty cycles, because it restricts the duty cycles to a power-multiple of the smallest one, i.e., $2, 4, 8$ etc. As a natural consequence, when the required duty cycle goes away from the power-multiples, the related error increases significantly. Such power-multiple-based error trend can be demonstrated by the power-multiple gap between neighboring delay peaks in the figure. (2) Mc-Dis achieves the best performance with ϵ monotonously decreasing in d except for $d = 38$ which is the only duty cycle not supported, meaning that a duty cycle 37 or 39 should be used. The result confirms the design philosophy of Mc-Dis stated in Sec. 5. The highest error is around 7%, which confirms the analysis in Lemma 1. (3) The performance of Disco and U-Connect is between that of Searchlight and Mc-Dis. Compared to Mc-Dis, the performance variations are much more important. The cause of such variations is their limitation to only prime numbers. In Disco, despite the possibility of fine-tuning the choice of prime numbers, since this choice also impacts the discovery delay, it is difficult to strike a balance between the two metrics which may be contradictory to each other.

7.2 Performance in Single-channel Case

We now study the discovery performance of Mc-Dis in the single-channel case by comparing the worst-case discovery delay for the four protocols in three representative scenarios depending on the duty cycles of a and b: (1) both a and b have low duty cycles $d_a = 10$, $d_b = 12$; (2) both of them has high duty cycles $d_a = 50$, $d_b = 60$; (3) a has low duty cycle while b has high duty cycle. For the three scenarios, we simulate both the case where the slots of a and b are aligned (their clocks are not synchronized) and where the slots are not aligned. In the latter case, we adopt the proposition in [3] to let both nodes emit discovery beacons both at the beginning and at the end of each slot to increase the chance of discovery. The results are plotted Fig. 5(b) and 5(c). Throughout our simulations, each point represents the worst-case value of a number of independent simulation runs, with the required number of simulation runs calculated using "independent replications" [18].

From the results, we can see that the worst-case delay of the simulated protocols does not have significant difference, except for the case $(10, 60)$ where the delay of Searchlight outweighs the others. This is because approximating the duty cycle 10 by a power-multiple 16 has a pronounced negative impact on the worst-case discovery delay. Moreover, the performance with non-aligned slots outperforms that with aligned slots, due to the adopted optimisation technique to emit beacons both at the beginning and at the end of each slot. As a result, when the slots are not aligned, the probability of a partial overlap between two active slots is higher.

7.3 Performance in Multi-channel Case

We now evaluate Mc-Dis in the multi-channel case. Note that it is the only protocol supporting multiple channels. Specifically, we simulate the following two scenarios for a system of $N = 10$ channels:

- Both a and b have the same channel perception, i.e., $\mathcal{N}_a = \mathcal{N}_b = \mathcal{N}$. We simulate the sub-scenarios of both aligned and non-aligned slots for different N.
- a and b have asymmetrical channel perceptions and drifted slots. We further simulate three sub-scenarios: (1) There is only one common channel between them and $N_a = N_b = 3$; (2) There are $N_c = N/2$ common channels and $N_a = N_b = 8$; (3) The number of common channels N_c is randomly distributed in $[1, N]$ with random N_a, N_b supporting N_c.

From the simulation results in Fig. 6, we make the following observations: (1) As the system scales in terms of N, the discovery delay also increases. Moreover, we report that the delay increases squarely with the channel numbers, which is in accordance with the analytical results. (2) Discovery is achieved on each channel that both nodes can access, even in the case where a and b have asymmetrical channel perceptions and drifted slots. This property makes Mc-Dis especially adapted in the decentralised mobile applications with heterogeneous wireless nodes.

8. CONCLUSION

In this paper, we have investigated the heterogeneous neighbor discovery problem in multi-channel wireless networks. Our developed protocol *Mc-Dis* can achieve mutual discovery at minimal and bounded latency with full discovery diversity, even when the network nodes have asynchronous clocks and asymmetrical channel perceptions. As future work, we envision to integrate Mc-Dis into a multi-channel MAC protocol so as to provide a complete set of MAC primitives including neighbor discovery, neighbor table management and channel access coordination.

9. ACKNOWLEDGEMENTS

The work of L. Chen is supported by the ANR grant Green-Dyspan (ANR-12-IS03). The work of M. Zheng is supported by the NSFC grant 61304263.

10. REFERENCES

[1] Sony ps vita - near. http://us.playstation.com/psvita.

[2] C. Arachchige, S. Venkatesan, and N. Mittal. An asynchronous neighbor discovery algorithm for cognitive radio networks. In *Proc. DySPAN*, 2008.

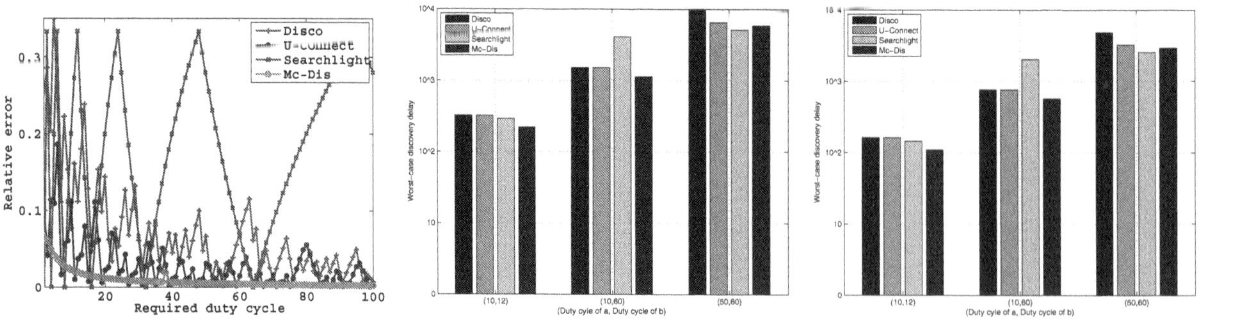

Figure 5: Performance comparison between Mc-Dis and major neighbor discovery protocols, single-channel case: (a) relative error as function of duty cycle; (b) worst-case discovery delay with aligned slots and (c) drifted slots. Mc-Dis achieves comparable delay while supporting significantly more duty cycles.

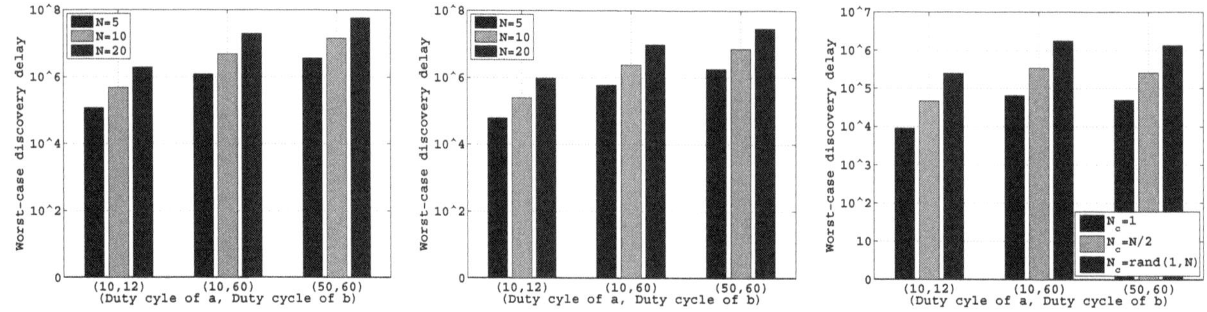

Figure 6: The worst-case discovery delay to full diversity: (a) symmetrical channel perception and aligned slots, (b) symmetrical channel perception and drifted slots, (c) asymmetrical channel perceptions and drifted slots.

[3] M. Bakht, M. Trower, and R. H. Kravets. Searchlight: won't you be my neighbor. In *Proc. Mobicom*, 2012.

[4] P. Dutta and D. Culler. Practical asynchronous neighbor discovery and rendezvous for mobile sensing applications. In *Proc. Sensys*, 2008.

[5] R. Ganti, F. Ye, and H. Lei. Mobile crowdsensing: current state and future challenges. *IEEE Comm. Mag.*, 49(11):32–39, 2011.

[6] C. Godsil and G. Royle. *Algebraic Graph Theory.* Springer, 2001.

[7] A. Kandhalu, K. Lakshmanan, and R. Rajkumar. U-connect: a low-latency energy-efficient asynchronous neighbor discovery protocol. In *Proc. IPSN*, 2010.

[8] S. Krishnamurthy, N. Mittal, R. Chandrasekaran, and S. Venkatesan. Neighbor discovery in multi-receiver cognitive radio networks. *Intl J. Computers and Applications (IJCA)*, 31(1):50–57, 2009.

[9] S. Lai, B. Ravindran, and H. Cho. Heterogenous quorum-based wakeup scheduling in wireless sensor networks. *IEEE Transactions on Computers*, 59(11), 2010.

[10] M. J. McGlynn and S. A. Borbash. Birthday protocols for low energy deployment and flexible neighbor discovery in ad hoc wireless networks. In *Proc. MobiHoc*, 2001.

[11] E. Miluzzo, N. D. Lane, K. Fodor, R. Peterson, H. Lu, M. Musolesi, S. B. Eisenman, X. Zheng, and A. T. Campbell. Sensing meets mobile social networks: the design, implementation and evaluation of the cenceme application. In *Proc. SenSys*, 2008.

[12] N. Mittal, S. Krishnamurthy, R. Chandrasekaran, S. Venkatesan, and Y. Zeng. On neighbor discovery in multi-channel cognitive radio networks. *J. Par. Dist. Comp. (JPDC)*, 69(7):623–637, 2009.

[13] N. Mittal, Y. Zeng, S. Venkatesan, and R. Chandrasekaran. Randomized distributed algorithms for neighbor discovery in multi-hop multi-channel heterogeneous wireless networks. In *Proc. ICDCS*, 2013.

[14] I. Niven, H. S. Zuckerman, and H. L. Mongomery. *An Introduction to the Theory of Numbers.* John Wiley & Sons, 1991.

[15] Y.-C. Tseng, C.-S. Hsu, and T.-Y. Hsieh. Power-saving protocols for ieee 802.11-based multi-hop ad hoc networks. In *Proc. Infocom*, 2002.

[16] S. Vasudevan, J. Kurose, and D. Towsley. On neighbor discovery in wireless networks with directional antennas. In *Proc. Infocom*, 2005.

[17] S. Vasudevan, D. Towsley, D. Goeckel, and R. Khalili. Neighbor discovery in wireless networks and the coupon collector's problem. In *Proc. MobiCom*, 2009.

[18] W. Whitt. The efficiency of one long run versus independent replications in steady-state simulation. *Management Science*, 37(6):645–666, 1991.

[19] W. Zeng, S. Vasudevan, X. Chen, B. Wang, A. Russell, and W. Wei. Neighbor discovery in wireless networks with multipacket reception. In *Proc. MobiHoc*, 2011.

[20] Y. Zeng, N. Mittal, S. Venkatesan, and R. Chandrasekaran. Fast neighbor discovery with lightweight termination detection in heterogeneous cognitive radio networks. In *Proc. 9th International Symposium on Parallel and Distributed Computing (ISPDC)*, 2010.

[21] D. Zhang, T. He, Y. Liu, Y. Gu, F. Ye, R. K. Ganti, and H. Lei. Acc: generic on-demand accelerations for neighbor discovery in mobile applications. In *Proc. SenSys*, 2012.

[22] D. Zhang, T. He, Y. Liu, F. Ye, R. K. Ganti, and H. Lei. Eqs: Neighbor discovery and rendezvous maintenance with extended quorum system for mobile sensing applications. In *Proc. ICDCS*, 2012.

[23] Z. Zhang and B. Li. Neighbor discovery in mobile ad hoc self-configuring networks with directional antennas algorithms and comparisons. *IEEE Transactions on Wireless Communications*, 7(5), 2008.

[24] R. Zheng, J. C. Hou, and L. Sha. Asynchronous wakeup for ad hoc networks. In *Proc MobiHoc*, 2003.

Latency-optimized Broadcast in Mobile Ad Hoc Networks without Node Coordination

Bin Tang
State Key Lab for Novel Software Technology
Nanjing University, China
tb@nju.edu.cn

Baoliu Ye*
State Key Lab for Novel Software Technology
Nanjing University, China
yebl@nju.edu.cn

Sanglu Lu
State Key Lab for Novel Software Technology
Nanjing University, China
sanglu@nju.edu.cn

Song Guo
School of Computer Science and Engineering
The University of Aizu, Japan
sguo@u-aizu.ac.jp

Ivan Stojmenovic
School of Information Technology and Engineering
University of Ottawa, Canada
ivan@site.uottawa.ca

ABSTRACT

We consider the problem of broadcasting a message in a mobile ad hoc network (MANET) with the objective of minimizing the broadcast latency. Due to the mobility of network nodes, the coordination among nodes is hard and expensive. Thus it is much desired to design efficient, one-sided broadcast protocols where each node acts according to its own state solely. Although random scheduling is a popular and effective one-sided approach for leveraging the broadcast nature of wireless medium while coping with transmission collisions, both critical for reducing the broadcast latency, in this paper, we show that when nodes move very fast, the performance of pure random scheduling must be sub-optimal, no matter how the forwarding probabilities are specified. Furthermore, we propose a novel one-sided broadcast protocol named R^2, which first splits the message into a certain number of mini-messages and then couples a fine-grained random scheduling with random linear network coding for broadcasting the mini-messages. Theoretical analyses demonstrate that R^2 performs optimally in order sense, no matter how fast network nodes move around, although different mobility has distinct effect on the speed of message broadcast.

Categories and Subject Descriptors

C.2.2 [**Computer-Communication Networks**]: Network Protocols

Keywords

Mobile Ad Hoc Networks, Broadcast, Random Linear Network Coding, Random Scheduling

*Corresponding author

MobiHoc'14, August 11–14, 2014, Philadelphia, PA, USA.

http://dx.doi.org/10.1145/2632951.2632982 .

1. INTRODUCTION

With the fast development of wireless and social networking technologies, there has been increasing interest on the use of mobile ad hoc networks (MANETs) for data communication. A typical MANET is self-configured and formed by a collection of wireless nodes which act not only as hosts but also as relays, storing and forwarding data for other nodes in the network. The nodes in a MANET can move around at their will, which on one hand, brings the potential to improve the network performance, *e.g.*, capacity [18] and throughput-delay tradeoff [39], but on the other hand, raises great challenges for protocol design and performance optimization, as the network topology may change rapidly and unpredictably.

Network-wide broadcast, *i.e.*, delivering a message from a source node to all other network nodes, is a fundamental operation in MANETs. For many important applications of MANETs, like military communication, it is essential to design an efficient broadcast scheme with low *broadcast latency* (*i.e.*, the time it takes for all the network nodes to receive a copy of the message), so that the end-to-end delay for higher-level applications could be stringently guaranteed.

Towards minimizing the broadcast latency in MANETs, two key features of wireless communications should be carefully addressed. One is the broadcast nature of wireless medium, *i.e.*, a transmission of a message could be heard simultaneously by multiple neighboring nodes, which can speed up the broadcast process. The other is wireless interference/collision, *i.e.*, a node cannot receive a message if more than one neighboring nodes are transmitting at the same time, which can thus limit the diffusion of the message. In static wireless ad hoc networks, the two features are usually incorporated by constructing a broadcast tree together with a collision-free broadcast schedule [15, 25, 33, 14]. However, in a MANET, the network topology is dynamic over time, making the construction and maintenance of a broadcast tree prohibitive and also the coordination among nodes expensive, especially when the network nodes move very fast. Therefore, it is much desired if we could design an efficient *one-sided* broadcast protocol where each node acts according to its own state solely, avoiding the coordination among nodes.

The simplest one-sided broadcast scheme is flooding, where each node that has received the message keeps on forwarding the message to all its current neighboring nodes. Although the flooding scheme can enjoy the broadcast nature of wireless medium, it can also lead to severe collisions, making the broadcast latency intolerably high. One popular and effective approach to cope with these collisions while preserving the one-sided property of flooding is *random scheduling, i.e.*, each node that has received the message forwards the message only with a certain probability [3, 41, 21]. In general, the forwarding probability at each time is chosen mainly according to the number of nearby nodes that have received the message. However, due to the node mobility as well as the underlying randomness of broadcast process, such number may vary significantly over different nodes, and can also be hard to estimate, making the optimization of forwarding probabilities difficult.

Instead of focusing on the optimization of forwarding probabilities for random scheduling based broadcast directly, we theoretically demonstrate that, when nodes move very fast, no matter how the forwarding probabilities are specified, *i.e.*, varying over different nodes and time instances, the performance under pure random scheduling must be suboptimal. The underlying reason is that the pure random scheduling suffers from the bottleneck in completing the broadcast process due to the very late receptions of the message by a few nodes.

In contrast to the above pessimistic result about pure random scheduling based broadcast, we further propose a novel one-sided broadcast protocol named R^2, which achieves the optimal broadcast latency asymptotically by coupling a fine-grained *Random scheduling* with *Random linear network coding (RLNC)*. Specifically, in the R^2 protocol, the message to be broadcast is firstly split into a certain number of mini-messages, such that random scheduling can be applied on a mini-message level and a uniform forwarding probability is enough for the efficiency of random scheduling. The mini-messages are then transmitted in an RLNC fashion, *i.e.*, all nodes forward coded mini-messages formed from random linear combinations of all previously received mini-messages, which makes nodes easier to accumulate useful information, and thus mitigates the bottleneck due to the application of random scheduling. As demonstrated by our theoretical arguments, R^2 can achieve an order-optimal broadcast latency no matter how fast nodes move around the network, even though different mobility of network nodes has distinct effect on the speed of message broadcast.

The contribution of the paper is two-fold:

- We first show that pure random scheduling is insufficient to achieve the optimal broadcast latency when nodes move very fast;
- We further propose a novel one-sided broadcast protocol R^2 which couples a fine-grained random scheduling with random linear network coding, and show that R^2 performs optimally no matter how fast nodes move around.

The reminder of the paper is organized as follows. In Sec. 2, we introduce the network model and the lower bounds of the broadcast latency. In Sec. 3, we present the protocols and main results, followed by proofs given in Sec. 4-6. Literature reviews are provided in Sec. 7. Finally, the conclusion and open questions are presented in Sec. 8.

2. THE MODEL

We consider a mobile ad-hoc network (MANET) consisting of n mobile nodes distributed uniformly on a $\sqrt{n} \times \sqrt{n}$ square. A source node, say s, wants to disseminate a message $\mathbf{m}$ with l bits to all the other nodes in the network. The *broadcast latency* is defined as the length of time interval between the starting time of the broadcast operation and the first time when all network nodes receive a copy of $\mathbf{m}$. Our main task is to minimize the broadcast latency by leveraging the broadcast nature of wireless medium as well as node mobility, while overcoming the interference due to concurrent transmissions. Keeping this in mind, we begin with the detailed introduction of the node mobility model and the communication model.

2.1 Mobility Model

The whole network region is partitioned into sub-squares of side length ρ each, resulting in a $\frac{\sqrt{n}}{\rho} \times \frac{\sqrt{n}}{\rho}$ *torus*. For ease of presentation, we refer to the formed sub-squares as ρ-cells and ρ as the velocity of each mobile node. The time is divided into slots of equal duration, and at the beginning of each time slot, each node independently moves to a new position inside its current ρ-cell or eight adjacent ρ-cells uniformly at random. Here we mean two ρ-cells (or two r-cells which are defined later) are adjacent if they touch each other by a side or by a corner. This mobility model can be viewed as a discrete version of the random walk mobility model, and has been widely used in literatures, *e.g.*, [9, 5]. In particular, when $\rho = \sqrt{n}/3$, this model degenerates to be the well-known *i.i.d.* mobility model [36].

2.2 Communication Model

All network nodes communicate over a common wireless channel, and the network topology in time slot t is modeled by a random geometric graph [37] $\mathcal{G} = (\mathcal{V}, \mathcal{A})$, where $\mathcal{V} = \{1, 2, \ldots, n\}$ is the set of nodes and $\mathcal{A}_t = \{(i,j) : d_t(i,j) \leq r\}$ is the set of arcs. Here $d_t(i,j)$ denotes the Euclidean distance between nodes i and j in time slot t, and r is the common transmission radius. In other words, a pair of nodes are neighbors if their distance is no larger than r. To further characterize a successful reception of a transmission, we consider the classical *protocol model* [20], i.e., a transmission from node i to node j is successful if for any time t within the duration of the transmission, $d_t(i,j) \leq r$ and each node i' except i with $d_t(i',j) \leq (1+\Delta)r$ is not transmitting simultaneously, where $\Delta > 0$ is a transmission guard constant independent with n.

Regarding the communication model, we make the following assumptions.

- We assume that the capacity of the wireless channel is l bits per time slot, so that the whole message $\mathbf{m}$ can be transmitted completely over a time slot. When the channel capacity is larger than l, our protocol still works and remains to be optimal asymptotically. In the opposite case where the channel capacity is smaller than l, the message to be broadcast can be considered as multiple messages each with length equal to the capacity. One might transmit the messages with our proposed protocol in a sequential manner, but how to transmit them efficiently in a concurrent manner requires further exploration.

- We assume that the transmission radius r is above the critical radius [19], which is on the order of $\sqrt{\log n}$. In this case, the network topology at any time is connected almost surely, and thus the broadcast process can be complete even if the network is static, *i.e.*, $\rho = 0$. On the other hand, r should be kept small enough for the purpose of energy saving. Regarding these considerations, we always assume $r = c\sqrt{\log n}$ for a sufficiently large constant $c > 0$. Besides, we also assume that all the nodes have common knowledge about n and r.

- Since the processing of wireless signals takes time, we assume that the information received by any node in some time slot can only be used for transmissions from the node in later time slots other than the same time slot.

2.3 Lower Bounds

As demonstrated in [7, 8], node velocity plays an important role in the speed of message dissemination, thus we consider two cases accordingly. One is named *low mobility regime*, where $\rho = O(r) = O(\sqrt{n})$. For this case, we have

LEMMA 1. *When $\rho = O(\sqrt{\log n})$, the broadcast latency under any protocol is $\Omega\left(\sqrt{\frac{n}{\log n}}\right)$ with probability $1-O(n^{-1})$.*

The other is referred to as *high mobility regime*, where $\rho = \omega(r) = \omega(\sqrt{\log n})$. For this case, we have

LEMMA 2. *When $\rho = \omega(\sqrt{\log n})$, the broadcast latency under any protocol is $\Omega\left(\frac{\sqrt{n}}{\rho} + \frac{\log n}{\log\log n}\right)$ with probability $1 - O(n^{-1})$.*

The above lemmas could be proved similarly to [7, 40] in spirit, with a slight more effort with Shannon measures. The details are thus omitted. From Lemma 2, we can see that, when the velocity is very large, say $\rho = \omega\left(\frac{\sqrt{n}}{\log n}\right)$, the lower bound of the broadcast latency could be sub-logarithmic in n, *i.e.*, $o(\log n)$. This implies that many approaches cannot achieve the lower bound in the high mobility regime as they require at least $\Omega(\log n)$ time slots. For instance, in gossip-based protocols (e.g., [5]), each node forwards one message to only a single neighboring node which is chosen randomly in each time slot. Since the number of nodes that have received the message can grow by two times in each time slot, thus no matter how the gossip-based protocols are specified, it requires at least $\Omega(\log n)$ time slots to complete the broadcast process. In contrast, our proposed R^2 protocol can achieve the lower bounds in either mobility regime, implying that *the lower bounds given in Lemma 1 and Lemma 2 are tight.*

3. PROTOCOLS AND RESULTS

In this section, we introduce the broadcast protocols as well as the results about their performance. The proofs of these results are deferred to the next sections.

3.1 Pure Random Scheduling Protocol

Random scheduling is an efficient technique for exploiting the broadcast nature of wireless medium while coping with interference in wireless networks [3]. Using random scheduling solely, a general broadcast protocol can be formalized as follows:

Pure Random Scheduling (PRS) Protocol:
In every time slot t, each node v that has received message $\mathbf{m}$ broadcasts it to all its neighboring nodes independently with probability $p_t(v)$, while other nodes keep silent.

Though the description of the PRS protocol is rather simple, it is a difficult task to optimize $p_t(v)$ so as to minimize the broadcast latency. What is worse, no matter how probabilities $p_t(v)$ are specified, the performance of the PRS protocol must be sub-optimal in some cases, as revealed by the following theorem.

THEOREM 3. *When $\rho = \sqrt{n}/3$, the broadcast latency under the PRS protocol is $\Omega(\log n)$ with probability $1-O(n^{-1})$, no matter how probabilities $p_t(v)$ in the PRS protocol are specified.*

As we will see later, when $\rho = \frac{\sqrt{n}}{3}$, the optimal latency is $\Theta\left(\frac{\log n}{\log\log n}\right)$. Therefore, there exists a $\Omega(\log\log n)$ factor gap between the performance of PRS and the optimum.

3.2 The R² Broadcast Protocol

3.2.1 *Inspirational Example*

Before introducing our broadcast protocol R^2, we first show how the RLNC is inspired via a simplified scenario. In this scenario, there are k nodes, say v_i, $i = 1, 2, \ldots, k$, need to get message $\mathbf{m}$. Assume that with random scheduling, in each time slot, each v_i can succeed to receive $\mathbf{m}$ independently with a constant probability $0 < p < 1$. Now we analyze the time it takes for all v_i to receive a copy of $\mathbf{m}$ with a failure probability of ϵ. Denoting the time as $T^d(\epsilon)$, we have

$$1 - \epsilon \leq \left(1 - (1-p)^{T^d(\epsilon)}\right)^k \leq e^{-(1-p)^{T^d(\epsilon)}k},$$

which gives

$$T^d(\epsilon) \geq -\frac{\ln k - \ln(-\ln(1-\epsilon))}{\ln(1-p)} = \Omega(\ln k). \quad (1)$$

Comparing to the expected time for a single v_i to receive $\mathbf{m}$ which is just a constant, the total latency is much higher. This is mainly due to the very late reception of $\mathbf{m}$ by a few nodes.

Now suppose that message $\mathbf{m}$ is split into a number (denoted by f) of mini-messages and each time slot is also split into the same number of mini-slots, so that each mini-message could be transmitted in a mini-slot. Then transmit these mini-messages in an RLNC fashion such that every coded mini-message received by v_i is a random linear combination of all original mini-messages. Once v_i has collected f coded mini-messages with linearly independent coding vectors, it can recover $\mathbf{m}$ by Gaussian elimination. Assume that in each mini-slot and for each v_i, the probability that v_i can receive a coded mini-message remains to be a constant p'. Also, for ease of illustration, every coding coefficient is assumed to be chosen from a binary field $\mathbb{F}_2$ uniformly at random (this assumption does not hold in general networks). Let $T^{nc}(\epsilon)$ be defined similarly to $T^d(\epsilon)$. If $f \geq 2(\ln(2k) - \ln\epsilon)$, then according to [43], when v_i has received $2f$ coded mini-messages, the probability that it can recover the original f mini-messages is

$$\prod_{j=0}^{f-1}\left(1-2^{j-2f}\right) \geq \left(1-2^{-f}\right)^f \geq 1-\frac{f}{2^f} \geq 1-\frac{\epsilon}{2k}. \quad (2)$$

Meanwhile, by a standard Chernoff bound argument [34], we can show that in $\lceil 4/p' \rceil$ time slots, the probability that v_i receives at least $2f$ coded mini-messages is at least

$$1-e^{-\frac{f}{2}} \geq 1-\frac{\epsilon}{2k}. \quad (3)$$

Combining (2) and (3) and applying the union bound, we can see that the probability that v_i can recover $\mathbf{m}$ in $\lceil 4/p' \rceil$ time slots is at least $1-\frac{\epsilon}{k}$. By applying the union bound again over all k pairs, we thus have

$$T^{nc}(\epsilon) \leq \lceil 4/p' \rceil. \quad (4)$$

Note that the latency achieved by the RLNC approach is just a constant. The key insight is that the use of message split and RLNC makes nodes easier to accumulate useful information, relieving the bottleneck problem that cannot be avoided by the former approach.

3.2.2 The R^2 Protocol and Performance

Now we formally introduce R^2, a broadcast protocol that couples a fine-grained random scheduling with RLNC. In R^2, the message $\mathbf{m}$ is partitioned into c^2 sub-messages with equal length, and the sub-messages are then broadcast in a sequential manner. (The reason for such partition will be explained at the end of Sec. 6.1.) In order to broadcast a sub-message,

- the sub-message, say $\mathbf{sm}$, is split by the source node into $\tau = \log n$ mini-messages, denoted by $\mathbf{mm}_1, \ldots, \mathbf{mm}_\tau$, each with $l/(c^2\tau)$ bits, and
- every time slot is also split into $\gamma = r^2 = c^2\tau$ mini-slots with equal duration, thus the transmission of a mini-message can be completed in a mini-slot.

Based on the above basic operations, the approach as the core of R^2 for broadcasting sub-message $\mathbf{sm}$ can then be described as follows:

R^2 for broadcasting sm:
Source node:

- In the first time slot that contains γ mini-slots, it disseminates the mini-message $\mathbf{mm}_i$, $i = 1, 2, \ldots, \tau$, to all its neighboring nodes in the i-th mini-slot. It remains silent in the left mini-slots.
- In later time slots, it works the same as other nodes.

Any other node in each time slot:

- If it has not received any mini-message, then it keeps silent in the whole time slot.
- Otherwise, in each mini-slot, it does the following with probability $1/\gamma$ (random scheduling):
  - (RLNC) it first picks out every mini-message received in previous time slots independently with probability $1/2$, and then combines them into a coded mini-message by XORing them all.
  - it then broadcasts the generated mini-message to all its neighboring nodes.

In the above procedure, each generated mini-message is a linear combination of $\mathbf{mm}_1, \ldots, \mathbf{mm}_\tau$. For the sake of decoding, τ linear coefficients (referred to as the coding vector), each of which costs one bit, should also be appended into the mini-message for transmission. We can omit the coding vector overhead here to ease the presentation under a quite loose condition of $l = \Omega(\log^2 n)$ which can hold for large message. To see this under the assumption, we can adjust the number of sub-messages by a constant factor so that in the broadcast of a sub-message with R^2, a coded mini-message with coding vector appended has exactly $\frac{l}{c^2\tau}$ bits and thus can be transmitted in one mini-slot. This does not affect the performance in order sense (some remarks on the chosen of parameters in R^2 are also given at the end of Sec. 6.1).

Once a node receives enough coded mini-messages, say with τ linearly independent coding vectors, it can recover the whole sub-message $\mathbf{sm}$ by Gaussian elimination. Note that the generation of coded mini-messages in R^2 is well-known as RLNC with operations executed over a binary field $\mathbb{F}_2$. While the use of larger finite field may have the potential to improve the performance, it also incurs higher computational cost for encoding and decoding operations. On the other hand, the use of a binary field employs the simple XOR as a basic arithmetic operation, and also leads to minimum overhead due to coding vectors. Moreover, the binary field $\mathbb{F}_2$ is sufficient for the R^2 protocol to achieve asymptotic optimality in terms of broadcast latency, as shown by the following theorems.

THEOREM 4 (LOW MOBILITY REGIME). *When $\rho = O\left(\sqrt{\log n}\right)$ and $l = \Omega(\log^2 n)$, the R^2 protocol achieves a broadcast latency of $O\left(\sqrt{\frac{n}{\log n}}\right)$ with probability $1-O(n^{-1})$.*

THEOREM 5 (HIGH MOBILITY REGIME). *When $\rho = \omega\left(\sqrt{\log n}\right)$ and $l = \Omega(\log^2 n)$, the R^2 protocol achieves a broadcast latency of $O\left(\frac{\sqrt{n}}{\rho} + \frac{\log n}{\log\log n}\right)$ with probability $1 - O(n^{-1})$.*

Comparing Theorem 4 with Lemma 1 and Theorem 5 with Lemma 2, we can see that, as long as $l = \Omega(\log^2 n)$, R^2 performs optimally in order sense no matter how large the velocity ρ is.

4. PRELIMINARIES

Before proving Theorem 3, Theorem 4 and Theorem 5, in this section, we introduce some preliminaries.

4.1 Network Region Partition

We partition the whole square region into small sub-squares (referred to as r-cells), each with side length ar, where a is a suitable constant such that $\frac{1}{4\sqrt{2}} \leq a \leq \frac{1}{2\sqrt{2}}$ and $\frac{\sqrt{n}}{ar}$ is an integer. For an r-cell $\mathcal{R}$, we use $\mathcal{N}(\mathcal{R})$ to denote the set of all r-cells that are adjacent to $\mathcal{R}$ including R itself. Clearly, any pair of nodes in the same r-cell are neighbors. Also, for a node v lying in $\mathcal{R}$, every node in $\mathcal{N}(\mathcal{R})$ is within the transmission range of v.

A well-known result is that every r-cell in the region contains $\Theta(r^2)$ nodes throughout the broadcast process almost surely [2]. Formally, let $\sharp_{\mathcal{R}}(t)$ denote the number of nodes lying in r-cell $\mathcal{R}$ during time slot t, then

Fact 1. There exists positive constants η_1 and η_2 which only depend on a, such that

$$\Pr\{\mathcal{D}_n\} \geq 1 - n^{-4},$$

where $\mathcal{D}_t$ denotes the event of $\eta_1 r^2 \leq \sharp_{\mathcal{R}}(t') \leq \eta_2 r^2$ for every r-cell $\mathcal{R}$ and every time slot $t' \leq t$.

Hence, to prove a result with probability $1 - O(n^{-1})$, it is sufficient to show the same result conditioning on $\mathcal{D}_n$. In the rest of the paper, unless otherwise specified, it is implicitly assumed that $\mathcal{D}_n$ holds.

Now we introduce a simple but very useful concept about r-cells. Two r-cells are said to be *isolated* if the distance between any pair of points each in one r-cell is larger than $2(2+\Delta)r$, and a collection of r-cells are said to be isolated if any pair of r-cells are isolated. Under this definition, the success or not of any mini-message transmissions from/to nodes in one r-cell $\mathcal{R}$ are irrespective of those events in other r-cells that are isolated with $\mathcal{R}$ at any certain time.

Fact 2. For any set $\mathcal{S}$ of r-cells, there exists some subset $\mathcal{S}' \subseteq \mathcal{S}$ such that $|\mathcal{S}'| \geq |\mathcal{S}|/\phi$ and all the r-cells in $\mathcal{S}'$ are isolated, where $\phi = (2(2+\Delta)/a + 1)^2$.

PROOF. We construct $\mathcal{S}'$ from an empty set by the following iterative algorithm: in each iteration, an arbitrary r-cell $\mathcal{R}$ is picked out from $\mathcal{S}$ and included into $\mathcal{S}'$, and all r-cells in $\mathcal{S}$ that are not isolated with $\mathcal{R}$ are removed away from $\mathcal{S}$; the iteration terminates when $\mathcal{S}$ becomes empty. Evidently, all r-cells in $\mathcal{S}'$ are isolated. Also, by some simple geometric arguments, it is easily shown that there are at most $\phi - 1$ r-cells each of which is not isolated to $\mathcal{R}$. Therefore, $|\mathcal{S}|$ is decreased by at most ϕ in each iteration, which implies that the number of iterations is at least $|\mathcal{S}|/\phi$ and thus $|\mathcal{S}'| \geq |\mathcal{S}|/\phi$. □

4.2 Projection Analysis

Projection analysis [22] is a newly developed technique for analyzing RLNC-based protocol. For the sake of completeness, we summarize its core concept and result as follows.

Definition 1. We say that node v knows about $\vec{\mu} \in \mathbb{F}_2^\tau$ or v is $\vec{\mu}$-informed, if $\vec{\mu} = \vec{0}$, or there is a vector $\vec{\nu}$ in the coding vector subspace of v such that $\vec{\mu} \cdot \vec{\nu} \neq 0$, where the coding vector subspace is induced by the coding vectors of all coded mini-messages in hand.

LEMMA 6. *If a node knows about $\vec{\mu} \in \mathbb{F}_2^\tau$ and broadcasts a coded mini-message to a set of nodes successfully, then the probability that all nodes in the set know about $\vec{\mu}$ afterwards is at least $1/2$. Moreover, a node can recover all the τ mini-messages once it knows about all vectors in $\mathbb{F}_2^\tau$.*

With the help of projection analysis, we can claim that the latency of broadcasting a sub-message is upper bounded by T with probability $1 - O(n^{-1})$, if for any $\vec{\mu} \in \mathbb{F}_2^\tau$, the probability that all nodes know about $\vec{\mu}$ at time T is at least $1 - O\left(n^{-1}2^{-\tau}\right) = 1 - O(n^{-2})$. This is because under the assumption, we can apply the union bound over all $2^\tau = n$ vectors in $\mathbb{F}_2^\tau$ to show that at time T, the probability that all nodes know about all vectors in $\mathbb{F}_2^\tau$, or equivalently all nodes can recover the original τ mini-messages according to Lemma 6, is $1 - O(n^{-1})$.

5. SUB-OPTIMALITY OF PRS: PROOF OF THEOREM 3

In the proof of Theorem 3, we only use the condition that $\mathcal{D}_{t_0}$ holds for some suitable $t_0 \leq n$, which will be clear soon. For any time $t \leq t_0$ and any node v, the communication range of v, *i.e.*, the circle centered at v with radius r, is covered by at most $\xi = \left(\lceil \frac{2r}{ar} \rceil + 2\right)^2 = \left(\lceil \frac{2}{a} \rceil + 2\right)^2$ r-cells. Since each r-cell contains at most $\eta_2 r^2$ nodes, each node is adjacent to at most $\xi\eta_2 r^2$ nodes at one time, which implies that the number of nodes that receive $\mathbf{m}$ can increase by at most $\xi\eta_2 r^2$ times in one time slot. Let $\mathcal{U}(t)$ be the set of nodes that have not received $\mathbf{m}$ in the first t time slots. Then there must be some time t_0, such that

$$\frac{n}{2\xi\eta_2 r^2} \leq n - |\mathcal{U}(t_0)| < n/2.$$

LEMMA 7. *For any $t > t_0$ such that $|\mathcal{U}(t-1)| \geq \sqrt{n}$, there exists some constant $\chi < 1$ such that*

$$\Pr\{|\mathcal{U}(t)| \geq \chi|\mathcal{U}(t-1)|\} \geq 1 - O(n^{-2}). \qquad (5)$$

PROOF. A key observation is that in time slot t, the movement of a node $v \in \mathcal{V} \setminus \mathcal{U}(t-1)$ and whether v broadcasts $\mathbf{m}$ or not are both stochastic, and independent with each other. Thus, it is equivalent if the chronological order between the exposure on the randomness of movements of nodes in $\mathcal{V} \setminus \mathcal{U}(t-1)$ and the exposure on the randomness of whether these nodes broadcast $\mathbf{m}$ or not are exchanged. Let $\mathcal{B} \subseteq \mathcal{V} \setminus \mathcal{U}(t-1)$ be the set of nodes that broadcast $\mathbf{m}$ in time slot t. We will show that, for any possible value B of $\mathcal{B}$, there exists some constant $\chi < 1$ independent with B such that

$$\Pr\{|\mathcal{U}(t)| \geq \chi|\mathcal{U}(t-1)|\,|\mathcal{B} = B\} \geq 1 - O(n^{-2}). \qquad (6)$$

Then by the law of total probability, we can get (5) straightforwardly.

Now we prove (6). Assume that $\mathcal{B} = B$ holds. We consider some set of isolated r-cells in the network region, say $\mathcal{S}$, such that $|\mathcal{S}| \geq \frac{n}{\phi(ar)^2}$. According to Fact 2, such $\mathcal{S}$ exists. For any r-cell $\mathcal{R} \in \mathcal{S}$, let $I_{\mathcal{R}}$ be an indicator variable such that $I_{\mathcal{R}} = 1$ if in time slot t, all nodes lying in $\mathcal{R}$ and belonging to $\mathcal{U}(t-1)$ do not receive $\mathbf{m}$ successfully, and $I_{\mathcal{R}} = 0$ if otherwise. Define $X_{\mathcal{R}}$ to be the number of nodes in B and lying in $\mathcal{R}$ in time slot t. According to the *i.i.d.* mobility model, $X_{\mathcal{R}}$ follows a binomial distribution, *i.e.*,

$$X_{\mathcal{R}} \sim \text{Binom}\left(|B|, \frac{(ar)^2}{n}\right)$$

with mean value $\lambda = \frac{|B|(ar)^2}{n}$. To cope with the dependency among $X_{\mathcal{R}}$, we apply the technique of Poisson approximation [34], where each $X_{\mathcal{R}}$ is approximated by an independent Poisson random variable $Y_{\mathcal{R}}$ with the same mean value λ. Also define $I_{\mathcal{R}}^P$ similarly to $I_{\mathcal{R}}$ in the Poisson case.

We first consider the Poisson case. Let $\mathcal{E}_1$ be the event that there is not any node in B lying in $\mathcal{R}$ or r-cells that are not isolated to $\mathcal{R}$. Then,

$$\begin{aligned}\Pr\{\mathcal{E}_1\} &= \Pr\{Y_{\mathcal{R}} = 0\} \prod_{\mathcal{R}':\text{not isolated with } \mathcal{R}} \Pr\{Y_{\mathcal{R}'} = 0\} \\ &\geq \left(e^{-\lambda}\right)^{\phi} = e^{-\lambda\phi}.\end{aligned}$$

Let $\mathcal{E}_2$ be the event that $\mathcal{R}$ contains at least two nodes in B in time slot t. Then,

$$\Pr\{\mathcal{E}_2\} = 1 - e^{-\lambda} - \lambda e^{-\lambda}.$$

If either $\mathcal{E}_1$ or $\mathcal{E}_2$ holds, then $I^P_{\mathcal{R}} = 1$. Therefore,

$$\begin{aligned}
\Pr\{I^P_{\mathcal{R}} = 1\} &\geq \Pr\{\mathcal{E}_1\} + \Pr\{\mathcal{E}_2\} \\
&\geq e^{-\phi\lambda} + 1 - e^{-\lambda} - \lambda e^{-\lambda} \\
&\geq \begin{cases} e^{-\phi} & \text{if} \quad \lambda < 1 \\ 1 - \frac{2}{e} & \text{if} \quad \lambda \geq 1 \end{cases} \\
&\geq \text{some constant } \beta,
\end{aligned}$$

where $\beta < 1$. Due to the mutual independence of all $I^P_{\mathcal{R}}$ for $\mathcal{R} \in \mathcal{S}$, we can use the Chernoff bound to obtain

$$\Pr\left\{\sum_{\mathcal{R}\in\mathcal{S}} I^P_{\mathcal{R}} \leq \beta|\mathcal{S}|/2\right\} \leq e^{-\beta|\mathcal{S}|/8} = O(n^{-3}).$$

According to [34], this implies that, in the actual binomial case,

$$\Pr\left\{\sum_{\mathcal{R}\in\mathcal{S}} I_{\mathcal{R}} \leq \beta|\mathcal{S}|/2\right\} \leq (|n - \mathcal{U}(t-1)|)\cdot O(n^{-3}) = O(n^{-2}).$$

In other words, with probability $1 - O(n^{-2})$, there are at least a $\frac{\beta}{2\phi}$ fraction of all the r-cells in which nodes belonging to $\mathcal{U}(t-1)$ can not receive $\mathbf{m}$ in time slot t. Meanwhile, by some standard Chernoff bound argument, we can show that the number of such nodes is at least $\frac{\beta}{4\phi}|\mathcal{U}(t-1)|$ with probability $1 - O(n^{-2})$. By setting $\chi = \frac{\beta}{4\phi} < 1$, we get (6). The proof is accomplished. $\square$

Finally, according to Lemma 7, we can apply the union bound to see that, starting from time t_0 when $|\mathcal{U}(t_0)| \geq n/2$, the number of time slots required so that $|\mathcal{U}(t)|$ becomes less than $\sqrt{n}$ is at least $\log_\chi \frac{\sqrt{n}}{n/2} = \Omega(\log n)$ with probability $1 - O(n^{-1})$, which implies Theorem 3 directly.

6. OPTIMALITY OF R²: PROOFS OF THEOREMS 4 AND 5

In this section, we present the proofs of Theorem 4 and Theorem 5. Note that the broadcast latency under the R^2 protocol has the same order as the latency for broadcasting a sub-message as the number of sub-messages is a constant. In the following, we focus on the latency for broadcasting a sub-message.

Let $\vec{\mu}$ be an arbitrary non-zero vector in $\mathbb{F}_2^\tau$. We will analyze the knowledge spreading process of $\vec{\mu}$ to derive the time T it takes for all nodes to know about $\vec{\mu}$ with probability $1 - O(n^{-2})$, which implies that T is a upper bound on the latency for broadcasting a sub-message according to the theory of projection analysis.

6.1 Basic Property of R²

We first introduce an elementary property of the R^2 protocol.

LEMMA 8. *Let $\mathcal{W}$ be a set of $\vec{\mu}$-informed nodes lying in a same r-cell at the beginning of time slot t. Then there exists some constant $\theta > 1$ which does not depend on c, such that the probability that there exists some node in $\mathcal{W}$ making all its neighboring nodes $\vec{\mu}$-informed during time slot t is at least $1 - \theta^{-|\mathcal{W}|}$.*

PROOF. According to the protocol model, we can show by some simple geometric argument that all nodes that can cause interference with nodes in $\mathcal{W}$ must be contained by at most $\lceil \frac{2+\Delta}{a} \rceil^2 + 1 \triangleq \phi_2$ r-cells. This implies that the number of such nodes is at most $\phi_2 \eta_2 r^2$. Therefore, in each mini-slot of t, the probability that there exists some node in $\mathcal{W}$ that can successfully broadcast a coded mini-message to all its neighboring nodes is at least

$$|\mathcal{W}|\frac{1}{\gamma}\left(1 - \frac{1}{\gamma}\right)^{\phi_2\eta_2 r^2} \geq \left(\frac{1}{4}\right)^{\phi_2\eta_2}\frac{|\mathcal{W}|}{\gamma}$$

since $r^2 = \gamma$, which implies that the probability that there exists some node in $\mathcal{W}$ that can make all its neighboring nodes $\vec{\mu}$-informed is at least $\left(\frac{1}{2}\right)\left(\frac{1}{4}\right)^{\phi_2\eta_2}\frac{|\mathcal{W}|}{\gamma}$ according to Lemma 6. As there exists γ mini-slots in time slot t, therefore, the probability that no node in $\mathcal{W}$ can make all its neighboring nodes $\vec{\mu}$-informed during time slot t is at most

$$\left(1 - \left(\frac{1}{2}\right)\left(\frac{1}{4}\right)^{\phi_2\eta_2}\frac{|\mathcal{W}|}{\gamma}\right)^\gamma \leq e^{-\left(\frac{1}{2}\right)\left(\frac{1}{4}\right)^{\phi_2\eta_2}|\mathcal{W}|} = \theta^{-|\mathcal{W}|},$$

where $\theta \triangleq e^{\left(\frac{1}{2}\right)\left(\frac{1}{4}\right)^{\phi_2\eta_2}} > 1$, which is independent with c. The desired result follows immediately. $\square$

Here we present some remarks on the setting of some parameters in R^2. According to the proof of Lemma 8, the scheduling probability is chosen to be $1/\gamma$ which guarantees that the above constant θ is independent with c. Meanwhile, RLNC operations are executed over mini-messages in a sub-message other than all mini-messages of the original message, so that the upper bound of the failure probability required by the means of projection analysis is also independent with c. Both independencies allow us to choose a large enough constant c for the convenience of analysis. From now on, all constants defined in the rest of the section, if not specified explicitly, are independent with c.

6.2 Low Mobility Regime

Now we prove Theorem 4. For an r-cell $\mathcal{R}$, we say it is completely $\vec{\mu}$-informed at time t if all nodes within $\mathcal{R}$ at t are $\vec{\mu}$-informed. Regarding this concept, a straightforward result is as follows.

LEMMA 9. *Let $\mathcal{R}^*$ be the r-cell that contains the source s in the first time slot. Then, $\mathcal{R}^*$ is completely $\vec{\mu}$-informed at the end of the first time slot.*

PROOF. According to the R^2 protocol, all nodes except for the source s keep silent when $t = 1$. Thus s can succeed to broadcast the whole sub-message $\mathbf{sm}$ to all nodes in $\mathcal{R}$ successfully, making all of them $\vec{\mu}$-informed. $\square$

A key result is that a completely $\vec{\mu}$-informed r-cell can make all its adjacent r-cells completely $\vec{\mu}$-informed in one time slot almost surely. It is formally presented as follows.

LEMMA 10. *Let $\mathcal{R}$ be an r-cell which is completely $\vec{\mu}$-informed at the end of time slot t. Then, any r-cell $\mathcal{R}' \in \mathcal{N}(\mathcal{R})$ will become completely $\vec{\mu}$-informed at the end of time slot $t + 1$ with probability $1 - O(n^{-4})$.*

PROOF. We will show that $\mathcal{R}'$ fails to become completely $\vec{\mu}$-informed with probability $O(n^{-4})$. Note that the movements of nodes are dependent on condition of $\mathcal{D}_n$, which is assumed to be always true. However, due to the fact that $\Pr\{\cdot|\mathcal{D}_n\} \leq 2\Pr\{\cdot|\mathcal{D}_t\}$ [8, pp. 615], it is sufficient to show the same result on condition that $\mathcal{D}_t$ holds but the movements of nodes in time slot $t+1$ are independent.

For each node v lying in $\mathcal{R}$ during time slot t, let α be the probability that it will remain in $\mathcal{R}$ in $t+1$. By considering the circle centered at v with radius ρ within which v will stay in time slot $t+1$ with probability $\pi/9$, we can show that

$$\alpha \geq \begin{cases} \frac{\pi}{9} \cdot \frac{1}{4} = \frac{\pi}{36} & \text{if } \rho \leq r, \\ \frac{\pi r^2/4}{\pi \rho^2} \cdot \frac{\pi}{9} = \frac{\pi r^2}{36\rho^2} & \text{if } \rho > r. \end{cases}$$

Since $\rho = O(r)$, we conclude that $\alpha \geq \beta$ for some constant $\beta > 0$. Let X be the number of $\vec{\mu}$-informed nodes in $\mathcal{R}$ at the beginning of time slot $t+1$. Thus,

$$\mathbf{E}[X] \geq \beta\eta_1 r^2.$$

By the Chernoff bounds, we further have

$$\Pr\{X \leq \beta\eta_1 r^2/2\} \leq e^{-\beta\eta_1 r^2/8} = O(n^{-4}),$$

as long as c is sufficiently large. Besides, according to Lemma 8, conditioning on $X \geq \beta\eta_1 r^2/2$, the probability that all these X $\vec{\mu}$-informed nodes fail to make their respective neighboring nodes $\vec{\mu}$-informed, which include all the nodes in $\mathcal{R}'$, is at most $\theta^{-\beta\eta_1 r^2/2} = O(n^{-4})$. We thus get the result as desired. □

Starting with one completely $\vec{\mu}$-informed r-cell as given in Lemma 9, we can apply Lemma 10 iteratively and also the union bound over r-cells and time slots to show that at time $\frac{\sqrt{n}}{ar} = O\left(\sqrt{\frac{n}{\log n}}\right)$, all r-cells are completely $\vec{\mu}$-informed with probability $1-O(n^{-2})$. This finishes the proof of Theorem 4.

6.3 High Mobility Regime

Now we prove Theorem 5. Since $\rho = \omega(r)$, we can choose a suitable constant $\frac{1}{4\sqrt{2}} \leq a \leq \frac{1}{2\sqrt{2}}$, so that $\frac{\rho}{ar}$ is an integer and thus each ρ-cell is composed exactly by $\frac{\rho}{ar} \times \frac{\rho}{ar}$ r-cells. In the following, we focus on the evolution process of the number of $\vec{\mu}$-informed nodes in each ρ-cell.

For a ρ-cell $\mathcal{C}$, we denote the set of $\mathcal{C}$ and all its adjacent ρ-cells as $\mathcal{N}(\mathcal{C})$ and the number of $\vec{\mu}$-informed nodes in $\mathcal{C}$ at the end of time slot t as $K_{\mathcal{C}}(t)$. We then have the following immediate result.

LEMMA 11. *Let $\mathcal{C}^*$ be the ρ-cell that contains the source s when $t=1$. Then $K_{\mathcal{C}^*}(1) \geq \eta_1 r^2$.*

PROOF. The proof is very similar to the one of Lemma 9, and is thus omitted. □

Regarding the increment of $K_{\mathcal{C}}(t)$, we have the following result.

LEMMA 12. *Let $\mathcal{C}$ be some ρ-cell such that $K_{\mathcal{C}}(t) \geq \eta_1 r^2$. Then there exists positive constants φ and ψ such that, with probability $1-O(n^{-3})$, every ρ-cell $\mathcal{C}' \in \mathcal{N}(\mathcal{C})$ satisfies*

$$K_{\mathcal{C}'}(t+1) \geq \min\{\varphi r^2 K_{\mathcal{C}}(t), \psi\rho^2\}.$$

PROOF. We distinguish two cases. We first consider the case $\rho = \Omega(r^2)$. Let Z be the number of r-cells that contain one or more $\vec{\mu}$-informed nodes after the move phase of time slot $t+1$. According to [9], there exists some constants φ_1 and ψ_1 such that

$$\Pr\left\{Z \geq \min\left\{\varphi_1 K_{\mathcal{C}}(t), \frac{\psi_1\rho^2}{r^2}\right\}\right\} \geq 1 - O(n^{-3}).$$

Now consider some subset $\mathcal{S}$ of these r-cells in which all the r-cells are isolated, and also

$$|\mathcal{S}| \geq Z/\phi.$$

According to Fact 2, such $\mathcal{S}$ exists. Let Y be the number of r-cells in $\mathcal{S}$ in which all nodes get $\vec{\mu}$-informed at the end of time slot $t+1$. According to Lemma 8, for any r-cell $\mathcal{R} \in \mathcal{S}$, the probability that all nodes in $\mathcal{R}$ get $\vec{\mu}$-informed at the end of time slot $t+1$ is at least $1-\theta^{-1} = \zeta$. This implies that

$$\mathbf{E}[Y] \geq \zeta|\mathcal{S}| \geq \frac{\zeta}{\phi}Z.$$

Finally, thanks to the isolation between r-cells in $\mathcal{S}$, we can apply the Chernoff bounds to show

$$\Pr\left\{Y \leq \frac{\zeta}{2\phi}Z\middle|\mathcal{E}\right\} \leq \exp\left(-\frac{\zeta}{8\phi}Z\middle|\mathcal{E}\right) = O(n^{-3}),$$

where condition $\mathcal{E}$ is defined as the event of $Z \geq \min\{\varphi_1 K_{\mathcal{C}}(t), \psi_1\rho^2/r^2\} = \Omega(r^2) = \Omega(\log n)$. The desired result then follows by the fact that each r-cell contains at least $\eta_1 r^2$ nodes.

Now consider the opposite case $\rho = o(r^2)$. We will show that $K_{\mathcal{C}'}(t+1) \leq \psi\rho^2$ with probability $O(n^{-3})$ for some constant ψ. Without loss of generality, we assume that $K_{\mathcal{C}}(t) = \eta_1 r^2$. Note that the movements of nodes are dependent on condition of $\mathcal{D}_n$. Again, according to the fact that $\Pr\{\cdot|\mathcal{D}_n\} \leq \Pr\{\cdot|\mathcal{D}_t\}$ [8, pp. 615], it is sufficient to show the lemma on condition that $\mathcal{D}_t$ holds but the movements of nodes in time slot $t+1$ are independent.

In the following, we say a node is of type 1 if it is $\vec{\mu}$-informed and was in $\mathcal{C}$ at time t, and of type 2 if otherwise. By a standard Chernoff bound argument, it is straightforward to show that the event that each r-cell contains $\Theta(r^2)$ nodes of type 2 in time slot $t+1$ holds with probability $1-O(n^{-3})$. Thus we can assume that this event holds exactly. Now define $X_{\mathcal{R}}$ to be the number of nodes of type 1 in $\mathcal{R}$ for each r-cell $\mathcal{R}$ in $\mathcal{N}(\mathcal{C})$. Clearly, $X_{\mathcal{R}}$ follows a binomial distribution, *i.e.*,

$$X_{\mathcal{R}} \sim \text{Binom}\left(K_{\mathcal{C}}(t), \frac{(ar)^2}{9\rho^2}\right).$$

Note that $X_{\mathcal{R}}$'s are dependent as their sum over all $\mathcal{R}$ in $\mathcal{N}(\mathcal{C})$ is equal to $K_{\mathcal{C}}(t)$. To deal with the dependency, we apply the Poisson approximation technique again by approximating each $X_{\mathcal{R}}$ with a Poisson random variable $Y_{\mathcal{R}}$ with the same mean value $\lambda = \frac{(ar)^2 K_{\mathcal{C}}(t)}{9\rho^2} = \frac{\eta_1 a^2 r^4}{9\rho^2}$. For r-cell $\mathcal{R}$ in $\mathcal{C}'$, we define $I_{\mathcal{R}}$ ($I_{\mathcal{R}}^P$) to be a 0-1 random variable so that it equals to 0 if if all nodes in $\mathcal{R}$ will become $\vec{\mu}$-informed at the end of time slot $t+1$ or equals to 1 if otherwise in the actual binomial (Poisson) case. To characterize $I_{\mathcal{R}}^P$, we first show that for each $\mathcal{R}$ in $\mathcal{C}'$,

$$\Pr\{Y_{\mathcal{R}} \leq \eta_2 r^2\} \geq 1 - O(n^{-4}). \tag{7}$$

Let Y' be a Poisson random variable with mean value $\lambda' = \frac{\eta_2}{2}r^2$. Since $\rho = \omega(r)$, we have $\lambda < \lambda'$. Using the coupling technique based on the Knuth's algorithm [27], we can easily infer that

$$\Pr\{Y_{\mathcal{R}} > \eta_2 r^2\} \leq \Pr\{Y' > \eta_2 r^2\}.$$

On the other hand,

$$\Pr\{Y' > \eta_2 r^2\} = \Pr\{Y' > 2\lambda'\} \leq \left(\frac{e}{4}\right)^{\lambda'} = O(n^{-4}),$$

where the second step follows due to a tail inequality for Poisson distribution [42] and the last step follows since $r = c\sqrt{\log n}$ for a sufficiently large c. By combining the above two inequalities, we get (7).

Now consider a set $\mathcal{S}$ of isolated r-cells in $\mathcal{C}'$ so that $|\mathcal{S}| \geq \frac{\rho^2}{\phi(ar)^2}$ whose existence is guaranteed by Fact 2. Let $\mathcal{E}_{\mathcal{R}}$ be the event that all r-cells that are not isolated to $\mathcal{R}$ contain no more than $\eta_2 r^2$ nodes of type 1. Thus according to (7),

$$\Pr\{\mathcal{E}_{\mathcal{R}}\} \geq 1 - O(n^{-4}).$$

Similarly to Lemma 8, we can show that there exists some constant $\theta_2 > 1$ such that for any $i = 1, 2, \ldots, \eta_2 r^2$,

$$\Pr\{I_R = 1 | \mathcal{E}_{\mathcal{R}}, Y_{\mathcal{R}} = i\} \leq \theta_2^{-i}.$$

Therefore,

$$\begin{aligned}
&\Pr\{I_{\mathcal{R}}^P = 1\} \\
&\leq \Pr\{\overline{\mathcal{E}_{\mathcal{R}}}\} + \Pr\{I_{\mathcal{R}}^P = 1 | \mathcal{E}_{\mathcal{R}}\} \\
&\leq \Pr\{\overline{\mathcal{E}_{\mathcal{R}}}\} + \sum_{i=0}^{\eta_2 r^2} \Pr\{I_{\mathcal{R}}^P = 1 | \mathcal{E}_{\mathcal{R}}, Y_{\mathcal{R}} = i\} \Pr\{Y_{\mathcal{R}} = i\} \\
&\quad + \Pr\{Y_{\mathcal{R}} > \eta_2 r^2\} \\
&= \sum_{i=0}^{\eta_2 r^2} \theta_2^{-i} \frac{e^{-\lambda}\lambda^i}{i!} + O(n^{-4}) \\
&\leq e^{-(1-1/\theta_2)\lambda} + O(n^{-4}) \\
&\leq 2e^{-(1-1/\theta_2)\lambda},
\end{aligned}$$

where the last step follows since $\rho = \omega(r)$ and thus $\lambda = o(r^2) = o(\log n)$. This implies

$$\mathbf{E}\left[\sum_{\mathcal{R}\in\mathcal{S}} I_{\mathcal{R}}^P\right] \leq 2|\mathcal{S}|e^{-(1-1/\theta_1)\lambda} = o(|\mathcal{S}|),$$

as $\rho = o(r^2)$ and thus $\lambda = \omega(1)$. By the Chernoff bound, we further have

$$\begin{aligned}
&\Pr\left\{\sum_{\mathcal{R}\in\mathcal{S}} I_{\mathcal{R}}^P > |\mathcal{S}|/2 + \mathbf{E}\left[\sum_{\mathcal{R}\in\mathcal{S}} I_{\mathcal{R}}^P\right]\right\} \\
&\leq \exp\left(-\frac{|\mathcal{S}|^2}{12\mathbf{E}\left[\sum_{\mathcal{R}\in\mathcal{S}} I_{\mathcal{R}}^P\right]}\right) \\
&\leq \exp\left(-|\mathcal{S}|e^{(1-1/\theta_2)\lambda}/24\right) \\
&\leq \exp\left(-|\mathcal{S}|(1-1/\theta_2)\lambda/24\right) \\
&\leq \exp\left(-\frac{\rho^2}{24\phi(ar)^2}\left(1-\frac{1}{\theta_2}\right)\lambda\right) \\
&= \exp\left(-\frac{(1-1/\theta_2)\eta_1}{216\phi} r^2\right) \\
&= O(n^{-4}).
\end{aligned}$$

According to [34], this implies that in the actual binomial case we have

$$\begin{aligned}
\Pr\left\{\sum_{\mathcal{R}\in\mathcal{S}} I_{\mathcal{R}} > \left(\frac{1}{2} + o(1)\right)|\mathcal{S}|\right\} &\leq e\sqrt{K_{\mathcal{C}}(t)} \cdot O(n^{-4}) \\
&= O(n^{-3}).
\end{aligned}$$

In other words, there are at least $(1/2 - o(1))|\mathcal{S}| \geq \frac{(1-o(1))\rho^2}{2\phi(ar)^2}$ r-cells, within which all nodes will get $\vec{\mu}$-informed in time slot $t+1$ with probability $1 - O(n^{-3})$. Recall that each r-cell contains $\Theta(r^2)$ nodes of type 2. The proof is thus accomplished. $\square$

The key observation from Lemma 12 is that with probability $1 - O(n^{-3})$, the number of $\vec{\mu}$-informed nodes in any ρ-cell will become at least $\eta_1 r^2$ in $\frac{\sqrt{n}}{2\rho} + 1$ time slots, and then increase to $\psi\rho^2$ in another no more than $\log_{\varphi r^2} \frac{\psi\rho^2}{\eta_1 r^2} = O\left(\frac{\log \rho}{\log r}\right)$ time slots. Therefore, at time $O\left(\frac{\sqrt{n}}{\rho} + \frac{\log \rho}{\log r}\right)$, all ρ-cells will have at least $\psi\rho^2$ $\vec{\mu}$-informed nodes with probability $1 - O(n^{-2})$. Once this event holds, the knowledge spreading process of $\vec{\mu}$ will be finished in one time slot almost surely, as stated in the following result.

LEMMA 13. *For any ρ-cell $\mathcal{C}$, if $K_{\mathcal{C}}(t) \geq \psi\rho^2$, then the probability that all nodes in any $\mathcal{C}' \in \mathcal{N}(\mathcal{C})$ will get $\vec{\mu}$-informed at the end of time slot $t+1$ is at least $1 - O(n^{-3})$. Therefore, if $K_{\mathcal{C}}(t) \geq \psi\rho^2$ for every ρ-cell $\mathcal{C}$, then all nodes in the network will become $\vec{\mu}$-informed at time slot $t+1$ with probability $1 - O(n^{-2})$.*

PROOF. Consider an arbitrary r-cell $\mathcal{R}$ within $\mathcal{C}'$. Let X be the number of $\vec{\mu}$-informed nodes that move from $\mathcal{C}$ to $\mathcal{C}'$ at the beginning of the time slot $t+1$, and $\mathcal{E}$ be the event that all nodes in $\mathcal{R}$ will get $\vec{\mu}$-informed at the end of $t+1$. It can be easily shown that there exists some constant ψ_1 depending on ψ such that

$$\Pr\{X < \psi_1 r^2\} < O(n^{-4}).$$

According to Lemma 8, we then have

$$\begin{aligned}
\Pr\{\mathcal{E}\} &\geq \Pr\{X \geq \psi_1 r^2\} \Pr\{\mathcal{E} | X \geq \psi_1 r^2\} \\
&\geq (1 - O(n^{-4}))(1 - \theta^{-\psi_1 r^2}) \\
&\geq 1 - O(n^{-4}).
\end{aligned}$$

By the union bound over all r-cells in $\mathcal{N}(\mathcal{C})$, we get the desired result. $\square$

Finally, we have that at time $O\left(\frac{\sqrt{n}}{\rho} + \frac{\log \rho}{\log r}\right)$, all nodes in the network will become $\vec{\mu}$-informed with probability $1 - O(n^{-2})$. Note that when $\rho = \omega(r)$,

$$\frac{\sqrt{n}}{\rho} + \frac{\log \rho}{\log r} = \Theta\left(\frac{\sqrt{n}}{\rho} + \frac{\log n}{\log \log n}\right).$$

This completes the proof of Theorem 5.

7. RELATED WORK

As a fundamental operation in wireless/mobile ad hoc networks, broadcast has been very extensively studied in the literature. Here we mainly present a brief review of recent research much related to our work.

Broadcast in Static Wireless Networks: Starting with the pioneering work [6], there has been a large body of work in designing efficient broadcast protocols with low latency in static radio networks [3, 10, 30, 16, 31, 17]. While the interference of wireless communications is captured by the radio network model, the network topology of a radio network could be arbitrary. In contrast, the topology of a wireless network is usually captured by the proximity of network nodes. With this restriction on the network topology, the broadcast latency could be further improved. Specifically, a series of approximation algorithms have been proposed for wireless ad hoc networks [15, 25, 33, 14]. Most of these works followed a general approach by constructing a broadcast tree as well as a deterministic or randomized conflict-aware transmission scheduling. However, such approach is hardly to be applied in mobile ad hoc networks, since the network topology may change unpredictably over time, and the coordination among nodes are expensive.

Broadcast in MANETs: Some recent works have studied the impact of node mobility on the broadcast latency. They can be grouped into two categories according to whether the transmission radius is above the critical radius or not. In the sparse regime, where the transmission radius is below the critical radius, the broadcast latency was investigated over a rich set of mobility models [26], including the well-known *i.i.d.* mobility model [29], the random walk model [38], *etc.* In the dense regime where the transmission radius is above the critical radius, Clementi *et al.* did several work under an almost the same network model as studied in our work [7, 8, 9]. They established a lower bound on the broadcast latency, and analyzed the broadcast latency under the flooding approach without taking the interference into account. Tang *et al.* established a new lower bound [40], which is complementary to the one given by Clementi *et al.* when nodes move very fast. However, both the work of Clementi *et al.* and Tang *et al.* did not take the interference into account, albeit the lower bounds still work. Chen *et al.* [5] introduced a gossip-like approach, which deals with interference by power controlling; however, it cannot exploit the broadcast nature of wireless medium, resulting in a logarithmic factor gap from the optimum.

RLNC-based Information Dissemination: In the seminar work of Ahlswede, Cai, Li and Yeung [1], network coding was demonstrated to achieve the capacity bounds of different destinations simultaneously. Following this work, Li *et al.* [32] showed that linear coding is enough for multicast. Koetter and Medard [28] then presented polynomial time algorithms for encoding and decoding operations. Further, Ho *et al.* introduced RLNC [23, 24], making network coding easily applicable to networks with unknown topologies and with packet loss. RLNC was first introduced by Deb *et al.* [11, 13, 12] for multi-message information dissemination. Following this, some works focused on the characterization of the performance of RLNC-based protocols in different settings in terms of network parameters [35, 4]. Later, Haeupler [22] proposed a powerful tool named projection analysis for analyzing RLNC-based protocols. While these works investigated the power of RLNC in some sense, they mainly focused on wired networks, which are significantly different from MANETs. In contrast, it remains unknown how to efficiently incorporate RLNC and how RLNC performs in MANETs.

8. CONCLUDING REMARKS

In this paper, we sho that the pure random scheduling is insufficient to achieve optimal broadcast latency when nodes move very fast. We further proposed a novel broadcast protocol R^2, which couples a fine-grained random scheduling with random linear network coding. Theoretical analyses show that R^2 can achieve an optimal broadcast latency in order sense, no matter how fast nodes move around the network.

Several interesting issues regarding the broadcast problem are still open and to be further investigated. In the current work, the message length is assumed to be $\Omega(\log^2 n)$ so that the RLNC overhead due to the coding vectors would not affect the performance asymptotically. Thus the first question is, whether the overhead of R^2 could be reduced or eliminated so that it remains to be optimal even when the message length is $\Theta(\log n)$ which holds in general as the message usually contains the identity of the source node, which costs $\Omega(\log n)$. Another question is to derive similar results under more realistic models, *e.g.*, the physical communication model [20].

9. ACKNOWLEDGMENTS

This work was partially supported by NSFC Grants (No. 61170069, 61373014, 91218302 and 61321491); Science and Technology Pillar Program (Industry) of Jiangsu Province Grant (No. BE2013116); Collaborative Innovation Center of Novel Software Technology and Industrialization; EU FP7 IRSES MobileCloud Project Grant (No. 612212). B. Tang was also partially supported by the program A for outstanding PhD candidates of Nanjing University.

10. REFERENCES

[1] R. Ahlswede, N. Cai, S.-Y. Li, and R. Yeung. Network information flow. *IEEE Trans. Inf. Theory*, 46(4):1204–1216, 2000.

[2] C. Avin and G. Ercal. On the cover time and mixing time of random geometric graphs. *Theor. Comput. Sci.*, 380(1-2):2–22, 2007.

[3] R. Bar-Yehuda, O. Goldreich, and A. Itai. On the time-complexity of broadcast in multi-hop radio networks: An exponential gap between determinism and randomization. *J. Comput. Syst. Sci.*, 45(1):104–126, 1992.

[4] M. Borokhovich, C. Avin, and Z. Lotker. Tight bounds for algebraic gossip on graphs. In *Proc. IEEE ISIT*, pages 1758–1762, 2010.

[5] Y. Chen, S. Shakkottai, and J. G. Andrews. On the role of mobility for multimessage gossip. *IEEE Trans. Inf. Theory*, pages 3953–3970, 2013.

[6] I. Chlamtac and S. Kutten. On broadcasting in radio networks–problem analysis and protocol design. *IEEE Trans. Commun.*, 33(12):1240–1246, 1985.

[7] A. Clementi, A. Monti, F. Pasquale, and R. Silvestri. Information spreading in stationary markovian evolving graph. *IEEE Trans. Parallel Distrib. Syst.*, 22(9):1425–1432, 2011.

[8] A. Clementi, F. Pasquale, and R. Silvestri. Opportunistic manets: mobility can make up for low transmission power. *IEEE/ACM Trans. Netw.*, 21(2):610–620, 2013.

[9] A. Clementi and R. Silvestri. Parsimonious flooding in geometric random-walks. In *Proc. DISC*, 2011.
[10] A. Czumaj and W. Rytter. Broadcasting algorithms in radio networks with unknown topology. *J. Algorithm*, 60(2):115–143, 2006.
[11] S. Deb and M. Medard. Algebraic gossip: a network coding approach to optimal multiple rumor mongering. In *Proc. Allerton*, 2004.
[12] S. Deb, M. Medard, and C. Choute. On random network coding based information dissemination. In *Proc. IEEE ISIT*, pages 278–282, 2005.
[13] S. Deb, M. Medard, and C. Choute. Algebraic gossip: a network coding approach to optimal multiple rumor mongering. *IEEE Trans. Inf. Theory*, 52(6):2486–2507, 2006.
[14] R. Gandhi, Y.-A. Kim, S. Lee, J. Ryu, and P.-J. Wan. Approximation algorithms for data broadcast in wireless networks. *IEEE Trans. Mobile Comput.*, 11(7):1237–1248, 2012.
[15] R. Gandhi, A. Mishra, and S. Parthasarathy. Minimizing broadcast latency and redundancy in ad hoc networks. *IEEE/ACM Trans. Netw.*, 16(4):840–851, 2008.
[16] L. Gąsieniec, D. Peleg, and Q. Xin. Faster communication in known topology radio networks. *Distrib. Comput.*, 19(4):289–300, 2007.
[17] M. Ghaffari, B. Haeupler, and M. Khabbazian. Randomized broadcast in radio networks with collision detection. In *Proc. ACM PODC*, pages 325–334, 2013.
[18] M. Grossglauser and D. Tse. Mobility increases the capacity of ad hoc wireless networks. *IEEE/ACM Trans. Netw.*, 10(4):477–486, 2002.
[19] P. Gupta and P. R. Kumar. Critical power for asymptotic connectivity. In *Proc. CDC*, pages 1106–1110, 1998.
[20] P. Gupta and P. R. Kumar. The capacity of wireless networks. *IEEE Trans. Inf. Theory*, 46(2):388–404, 2000.
[21] Z. J. Haas, J. Y. Halpern, and L. Li. Gossip-based ad hoc routing. *IEEE/ACM Trans. Netw.*, 14(3):479–491, 2006.
[22] B. Haeupler. Analyzing network coding gossip made easy. In *Proc. ACM STOC*, pages 293–302, 2011.
[23] T. Ho, R. Koetter, M. Medard, D. Karger, and M. Effros. The benefits of coding over routing in a randomized setting. In *Proc. IEEE ISIT*, page 442, 2003.
[24] T. Ho, M. Medard, R. Koetter, D. Karger, M. Effros, J. Shi, and B. Leong. A random linear network coding approach to multicast. *IEEE Trans. Inf. Theory*, 52(10):4413–4430, 2006.
[25] S.-H. Huang, P.-J. Wan, X. Jia, H. Du, and W. Shang. Minimum-latency broadcast scheduling in wireless ad hoc networks. In *Proc. IEEE INFOCOM*, pages 733–739, 2007.
[26] P. Jacquet, B. Mans, and G. Rodolakis. Information propagation speed in mobile and delay tolerant networks. In *Proc. IEEE INFOCOM*, pages 244–25, 2009.
[27] D. E. Knuth. *The Art of Computer Programming, Volume 2: Seminumerical Algorithms*. Addison Wesley, 1969.
[28] R. Koetter and M. Médard. An algebraic approach to network coding. *IEEE/ACM Trans. Netw.*, 11(5):782–795, 2003.
[29] Z. Kong and E. M. Yeh. On the latency for information dissemination in mobile wireless networks. In *Proc. ACM MOBIHOC*, pages 139–148, 2008.
[30] D. R. Kowalski and A. Pelc. Broadcasting in undirected ad hoc radio networks. *Distrib. Comput.*, 18(1):43–57, 2005.
[31] D. R. Kowalski and A. Pelc. Optimal deterministic broadcasting in known topology radio networks. *Distrib. Comput.*, 19(3):185–195, 2007.
[32] S.-Y. Li, R. Yeung, and N. Cai. Linear network coding. *IEEE Trans. Inf. Theory*, 49(2):371–381, 2003.
[33] R. Mahjourian, F. Chen, R. Tiwari, H. Zhai, and Y. Fang. An approximation algorithm for conflict-aware broadcast scheduling in wireless ad hoc networks. In *Proc. ACM MobiHoc*, pages 331–340, 2008.
[34] M. Mitzenmacher and E. Upfal. *Probability and computing: Randomized Algorithms and Probabilistic Analysis*. Cambridge University Press, 2004.
[35] D. Mosk-Aoyama and D. Shah. Information dissemination via network coding. In *Proc. IEEE ISIT*, pages 1748–1752, 2006.
[36] M. J. Neely and E. Modiano. Capacity and delay tradeoffs for ad hoc mobile networks. *IEEE Trans. Inf. Theory*, 51(6):1917–1937, 2005.
[37] M. Penrose. *Random Geometric Graphs*. Oxford University Press, 2003.
[38] A. Pettarin, A. Pietracaprina, G. Pucci, and E. Upfal. Tight bounds on information dissemination in sparse mobile networks. In *Proc. ACM PODC*, pages 355–362, 2011.
[39] G. Sharma, R. Mazumdar, and N. B. Shroff. Delay and capacity trade-offs in mobile ad hoc networks: A global perspective. *IEEE/ACM Trans. Netw.*, 15(5):981–992, 2007.
[40] B. Tang, B. Ye, S. Guo, S. Lu, and D. O. Wu. Order-optimal information dissemination in manets via network coding. *IEEE Trans. Parallel Distrib. Syst.*, 2013. To appear.
[41] Y.-C. Tseng, S.-Y. Ni, Y.-S. Chen, and J.-P. Sheu. The broadcast storm problem in a mobile ad hoc network. *Wirel. Netw.*, 8(2-3):153–167, 2002.
[42] Wikipedia. Poisson distribution –wikipedia, the free encyclopedia, 2013.
[43] S. Yang and R. W. Yeung. Batched sparse codes, 2012. accepted by IEEE Trans. Inf. Theory.

A Matrix-Completion Approach to Mobile Network Localization

Qiang Ye[1] Jie Cheng[1] Hongwei Du[2,3] Xiaohua Jia[2] Jing Zhang[2,3]
[1]Dept. of Computer Science and Information Technology
University of Prince Edward Island
Charlottetown, PE, Canada, C1A 4P3
[2]Harbin Institute of Technology Shenzhen Graduate School
Shenzhen, China, 518055
[3]Shenzhen Key Laboratory of Internet Information Collaboration
Shenzhen, China, 518055
{qye, jcheng}@upei.ca, hongwei.du@ieee.org
csjia@hitsz.edu.cn, cshitzhj@gmail.com

ABSTRACT

Localization in mobile networks is of paramount importance to a variety of pervasive applications. Due to the limitations of GPS, such as high deployment cost, many researchers have devised a variety of different localization schemes based on the measurements of connectivity or distance between neighboring nodes. The existing schemes suffer seriously from either low localization precision or overlong computation time. In this paper, we present a novel localization scheme based on matrix completion, MALL, that utilizes the collected connectivity and distance information to achieve high-precision localization. Since MALL only involves convex optimization and low-complexity non-convex optimization, it can localize mobile nodes at a fast pace. Furthermore, MALL leads to low communication cost. Through intensive simulation and testbed experiments, we found that MALL outperforms the state-of-the-art localization schemes. An in-depth analysis of the time complexity and communication cost of MALL is also included in this paper.

Categories and Subject Descriptors

C.2.1 [**Computer Communication Network**]: Network Architecture and Design—*Wireless communication*

General Terms

Algorithm, Performance

Keywords

Localization; mobile networks; matrix completion; decentralized schemes

MobiHoc'14, August 11–14, 2014, Philadelphia, PA, USA.

http://dx.doi.org/10.1145/2632951.2632986.

1. INTRODUCTION

Localization in mobile networks is of paramount importance to a variety of pervasive applications, thus having attracted much research effort over the past decades.The Global Position System (GPS) [1] has been widely used to locate individual nodes in mobile networks. However, GPS requires the line of sight to the satellites and therefore stops working when the line of sight is not available (e.g. indoors or in a downtown canyon). In addition, it is often too expensive to equip every mobile node with a GPS. The limitations of GPS have motivated many researchers to devise a variety of different localization schemes based on the measurements of connectivity or distance between neighboring nodes. Most existing localization schemes that utilize the connectivity or distance information are designed for static networks [2][3][4][5]. There are only a limited number of up-to-date localization schemes for mobile networks [6][7][8][9][10][11].

The existing mobile localization schemes can be classified into two categories: centralized and decentralized mechanisms. With centralized mechanisms, a control center collects and processes the connectivity/distance information in order to locate all nodes in the network. Due to the availability of the connectivity/distance information about all mobile nodes, centralized mechanisms tend to result in high-precision localization. However, they suffer seriously from overlong computation and poor scalability because the single control center has to determine the locations of all mobile nodes. TSLRL, TSL, and LRL [10] are three centralized algorithms that need to have the measured distances about the nodes in the network. These schemes also make use of the fact that the coordinate matrix, a matrix consisting of the coordinates of mobile nodes over a period of time, is a low rank matrix that exhibits the temporal stability feature (i.e. the coordinate change of a mobile node tends to be temporally stable).

With decentralized localization mechanisms, each mobile node collects the connectivity/distance information about its neighbors and determines its own location independently. Since only the information about a limited set of nodes is gathered and processed, decentralized algorithms usually lead to fast computation and excellent scalability. However, their localization results tend to be less precise than those of centralized approaches. Monte Carlo Localization (MCL) [6], MSL* [7], and IMCL [8] are three typical decentralized schemes.

In this paper, we present a novel decentralized localization scheme based on matrix completion for mobile networks, which is formally called "*MA*trix-completion *LocaL*ization (MALL)". With MALL, each mobile node uses a 2-step procedure to localize itself precisely at a fast pace in a decentralized manner. The first step uses a matrix completion algorithm inspired by [12]. In [12], Recht *et al.* proposed a matrix completion technique to fill the unknown entries in a matrix if the rank of the matrix is low and the known entries are randomly sampled. In our research, although the matrix to be completed in the first step exhibits the low rank feature, the available entries are not random samples. To complete the matrix successfully, we designed an algorithm based on convex optimization that associates different weights with the available entries and incorporates the temporal stability feature.

The second step of MALL employs an effective matrix completion algorithm to localize mobile nodes. Technically, it takes advantage of the matrix completed in the first step to significantly reduce the computation complexity. In addition, a light-weight constraint that requires the location of each mobile node to be compatible with the locations of its neighoring node is incorporated in the algorithm to improve its precision. As a result, although the algorithm still involves non-convex optimization, it achieves low computation complexity and high precision.

Our experimental results indicate that, MALL outperforms the state-of-the-art decentralized localization schemes in terms of localization error. Compared with the latest centralized schemes, it scales much better and achieves similar localization precision. In comparison to both the existing decentralized and centralized schemes, MALL incurs low communication cost and computation complexity.

The detailed contributions of this paper are summarized as follows. i) We propose a novel localization scheme, MALL, that formulates mobile network localization as a series of matrix completion problems with several carefully-designed constraints. This approach ensures that MALL results in the same high level of precision as centralized localization mechanisms. ii) MALL only involves convex optimization and low-complexity non-convex optimization. As a result, MALL can achieve high-precision localization at a fast pace. iii) MALL only makes use of the information from anchor nodes within two hops and normal nodes within one hop. Consequently, MALL leads to high localization precision at a low communication cost.

The rest of the paper is organized as follows. The localization problem in mobile networks is formulated mathematically in Section 2. Section 3 describes the details of MALL and Section 4 presents our simulation results. The experimental results based on our testbed are summarized in Section 5. Finally, Section 6 concludes the paper.

2. PROBLEM FORMULATION

In this section, we formulate the problem of mobile network localization mathematically. Specifically, there are M mobile nodes in the network under investigation. These nodes move in a d-dimension Euclidean space. Note that MALL is a generic method that can be used in multidimensional scenarios. In this paper, each of the mobile nodes is assigned a global ID in the range of 1 to M. The majority of the nodes are not equipped with built-in GPS and need to be localized using our localization scheme. We call the nodes without GPS "normal nodes" in this paper. The rest of the nodes are called "anchor nodes" because they can use the built-in GPS to determine their precise locations.

In this paper, the concept of neighboring is extended. Specifically, node i is a 1-hop neighbor of node j if it is in j's transmission range. If node i is not j's 1-hop neighbor, but in the transmission range of one of j's 1-hop neighbors, then i is a 2-hop neighbor of node j. In this manner, multiple-hop neighbors can be defined. In the rest of the paper, we use d_{max} to denote the transmission range of a mobile node.

With MALL, each normal node collects the location-related information (i.e. connectivity, distances, and coordinates) from its neighborhood to derive its own location. Specifically, each normal node gathers the information from the neighboring anchor nodes within two hops and from the neighboring normal nodes within one hop. The detailed collection method is presented in Section 3. Note that the coordinates of the neighbouring anchors are determined by the built-in GPS while those of the neighboring normal nodes are approximated by MALL. Furthermore, a normal node and its neighbouring nodes (including normal neighbors within one hop and anchor neighbors within two hops) that provide the location-related information form a network, which is formally called the "*local subnet*" of the normal node.

In this paper, time is divided into equal-sized time slots: t_1, t_2, ... , t_{final}. We use t and t_c to refer to any time slot and the current time slot respectively. To achieve high-precision localization, each normal node uses a few matrices (including distance and coordinate matrices) to store the location-related information about its neighbors during the current T-slot time window t_{cw}. Note that t_{cw} includes the current slot and the past T-1 slots. In our research, T is set to 8 for MALL.

With these data matrices, each normal node uses MALL to fill the unknown entries of an object matrix, which contains the coordinates of the nodes in the local subnet of the normal node over the most recent T_r-slot time window t_{rw}. Note that t_{rw} includes the current slot and the past T_r-1 slots. In addition, T_r should be an integer that is much smaller than T. In our research, T_r is set to 3 for MALL. Since the coordinates of the normal node at t_c correspond to part of the unknown entries of the object matrix, the normal node can easily localize itself once the object matrix is completed.

Formally, we use the following notations in this paper:

- $G(:, i, t)$ denotes the d-dimensional Euclidean coordinates of node i at time slot t. Note that the matrix-related notation adopted in this paper is consistent with that used in MATLAB for simplicity purposes.
- $G(k, i, t)$ denotes the k-th dimension Euclidean coordinate of node i at time slot t. Note that $1 \leq k \leq d$.
- N_{i,t_c} denotes the node set consisting of the nodes in node i's local subnet at the current time slot t_c.
- $N_c = |N_{i,t_c}|$ denotes the number of nodes in N_{i,t_c}.
- $N_{i,T_r} = \bigcup_{t_c-T_r+1 \leq t \leq t_c} N_{i,t}$ denotes the node set consisting of all the nodes that have ever appeared in node

i's local subnet over t_{rw}. Here $N_{i,t}$ denotes the node set consisting of the nodes in node i's local subnet at the time slot t. Note that node i's neighbors might change over time. N_{i,T_r} contains each node that has ever appeared as node i's neighbour over t_{rw} even if the node was node i's neighbour during only one slot within t_{rw}.

- $N_r = |N_{i,T_r}|$ denotes the number of neighbor nodes that have appeared in node i's local subnet during t_{rw}.
- $N_{i,T} = \bigcup_{t_c-T+1\leq t\leq t_c} N_{i,t}$ denotes the node set consisting of all the nodes that have ever appeared in node i's local subnet over t_{cw}.
- $N = |N_{i,T}|$ denotes the number of the neighbor nodes that have appeared in node i's local subnet during t_{cw}.

In mobile networks, as a node moves around, the set of its neighbors is likely to change over time. That is, the node set consisting of the current and past neighbors tends to grow with time (i.e. $N_{i,t_c} \subseteq N_{i,T_r} \subseteq N_{i,T}$). Consequently, we can arrive at the following conclusion in typical scenarios: $N_c \leq N_r \leq N$.

In addition to the notations defined previously, the following three matrices are used in this paper:

Distance Matrix: For normal node i, there are N_c nodes in i's local subnet at t_c. Each of them is assigned a local ID that is in the range of 1 to N_c. In our research, each normal node i uses an $N_c \times N_c$ matrix D to store the *squared* Euclidean distance between all nodes in i's local subnet at t_c.

Formally, an entry of D, $D(m,n)$, can be calculated theoretically using Eq. (1):

$$D(m,n) = \|G(:,j,t_c) - G(:,l,t_c)\|^2 \quad (1)$$

where $\|\cdot\|$ denotes the Euclidean norm of a vector and $\|\cdot\|^2$ represents the square of the Euclidean norm; m and n are the local IDs used to identify two nodes in i's local subnet (note that $1 \leq m,n \leq N_c$); j and l are the corresponding global IDs of m and n respectively.

Coordinate Matrix: For each normal node i, $N_{i,T}$ consists of N nodes that have been node i's neighbors over t_{cw}. In our research, node i uses a 2-dimension coordinate matrix X to store the coordinates of the nodes in $N_{i,T}$.

Globally, we use $G(k,j,t)$ to represent the k-th dimension Euclidean coordinate of a node in $N_{i,T}$, where j is the global ID of the node, t is the global slot number, and $1 \leq k \leq d$. Locally, node i assigns a unique local ID j^X, which is in the range of 1 to N, to each node in $N_{i,T}$. Note that each local ID j^X corresponds to a unique global ID j for t_{cw}. In addition, each slot in the T-slot window t_{cw} is given a local slot number t^X, which is in the range of 1 to T. Note that each t^X corresponds to a unique t for t_{cw}. Furthermore, node i uses $X_3(k,j^X,t^X)$ to locally represent the k-th dimension Euclidean coordinate of a node in $N_{i,T}$. Obviously, each $X_3(k,j^X,t^X)$ corresponds to a unique $G(k,j,t)$ for t_{cw}.

Note that X_3 is a 3-dimension array. To take advantage of matrix completion techniques, we can convert X_3 into a 2-dimension coordinate matrix by collapsing the first two dimensions of X_3 into one dimension. The final coordinate matrix is denoted as X=*matricize*(X_3). Formally, X can be obtained using Eq. (2):

$$X(j^X + (k-1)N, t^X) = X_3(k,j^X,t^X) \quad (2)$$

Note that X consists of $N \cdot d$ rows and T columns.

Object Matrix: Each normal node i also maintains a 2-dimension object matrix Y, which contains the coordinates of the nodes in N_{i,T_r} (note that N_{i,T_r} contains all the nodes that have appeared in i's local subnet over t_{rw}). In a manner similar to that used to define j^X, t^X, and X_3, we can define j^Y, t^Y, and Y_3. Note that $1 \leq j^Y \leq N_r$ and $1 \leq t^Y \leq T_r$. Then Y is equal to *matricize*(Y_3). Formally, we have:

$$Y(j^Y + (k-1)N_r, t^Y) = Y_3(k,j^Y,t^Y) \quad (3)$$

Note that Y has $N_r \cdot d$ rows and T_r columns, where $N_r = |N_{i,T_r}|$.

As mentioned previously, $N_{i,T_r} \subseteq N_{i,T}$. Hence, the object matrix Y is a submatrix of the coordinate matrix X. In this paper, we use $f(\cdot)$ to denote the operation of constructing a matrix by choosing the rows corresponding to the nodes in N_{i,T_r} from another matrix. Consequently, Y and X can be related using Eq. (4):

$$Y = f(X(:, T - T_r + 1; T)) \quad (4)$$

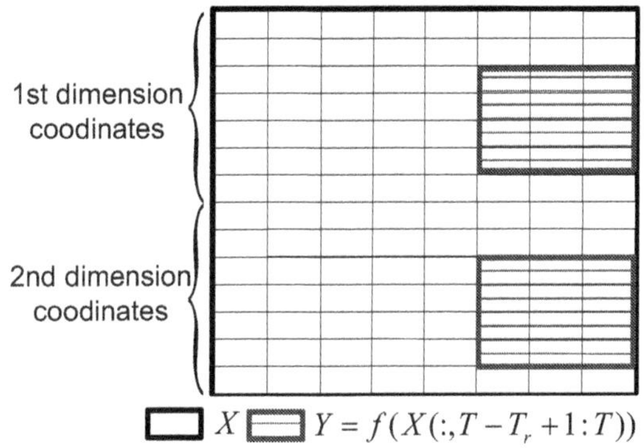

Figure 1: Relationship between X and Y

Fig. 1 illustrates the relationship between X and Y using the object and coordinate matrix kept by a normal node i in an example 2-dimension mobile network. Since the network is 2-dimensional, there only exist the 1st and 2nd dimension coordinates. In addition, as mentioned previously, T and T_r are set to 8 and 3 respectively for MALL. As a result, X and Y always contain 8 and 3 columns respectively. Furthermore, we assume that N=7 and N_r=3 for the example normal node. Consequently, X has $N\times$ 2 dimensions = 7×2 =14 rows and Y includes $N_r\times$2 dimensions = 3×2 = 6 rows. For clarity purposes, the 1st dimension coordinates of the nodes in N_{i,T_r} are placed consecutively in Fig. 1. The 2nd dimension coordinates are organized in a similar manner. In practice, the consecutive arrangement is not required.

With MALL, each normal node i uses the collected connectivity, distance, and coordinate information to calculate Y. Since node i is a node in its local subnet during t_{rw}, i's current coordinates are also included in Y. Once Y is available, node i can localize itself easily by retrieving its current coordinates from Y.

3. MALL: A MATRIX COMPLETION APPROACH

MALL is a decentralized localization scheme based on matrix completion. With MALL, every node detects the connectivity and measures the distance between itself and its 1-hop neighbors at the current time slot t_c. Then the connectivity/distance information is spread in its current local subnet. Furthermore, during the current time slot, each normal node i also forwards its previous coordinates to the nodes in its current local subnet (note that node i's current coordinates are not available yet and will be determined by MALL); each anchor node floods its current local subnet with its current coordinates determined via GPS. As a result, each normal node can collect the connectivity/distance/coordinate information during the time window t_{cw}. With the collected information, each normal node i determines its coordinates at the current time slot by calculating the unknown entries in the object matrix Y with a 2-step procedure. An overview of the procedure is presented as follows:

- Step 1: Approximate $X(:, 1 : T - 1)$ using a novel matrix completion method that only involves convex optimization. As mentioned previously, the matrix-related notation adopted in this paper is consistent with that used in MATLAB for simplicity purposes. Therefore, $X(:, 1 : T - 1)$ denotes a submatrix of the coordinate matrix X, which consists of the first $T - 1$ columns of X.
- Step 2: Calculate the unknown entries in the object matrix Y using a carefully-designed matrix completion method that utilizes the approximated $X(:, 1 : T - 1)$. The method results in a high-quality estimation of Y. Once the estimation is available, the coordinates of the normal node at t_c can be easily retrieved from the estimated Y. Although this method involves non-convex optimization, its complexity is very low.

To find the coordinates at the next time slot, each normal node simply executes the 2-step procedure once again. Note that, when the network is initialized, no normal node knows its current location. To get the localization process started, we can assign some random coordinates to normal nodes. After a short period of time, the normal nodes will start to locate themselves precisely.

It is worth noting that, in this paper, the distance matrix D and the coordinate matrix X are used to denote the matrices that store the precise distance and coordinate information (i.e. the theoretical distances and coordinates) respectively. A key component of the 2-step procedure is to use the collected connectivity/distance/coordinate data to approximate D and X. Once the approximated matrices are available, each normal node uses them to determine the object Y. To differentiate the priority of the collected data, each normal node uses four $N_c \times N_c$ matrices, D^{md}, D^{ot}, Q^{md}, and Q^{ot}, to store the connectivity/distance information gathered at t_c. Furthermore, every normal node employs four matrices (whose size is the same size as X), X^{nc}, X^{ac}, P^{nc}, and P^{ac}, to store the coordinate information collected during t_{cw}.

To construct D^{md}, D^{ot}, Q^{md}, and Q^{ot}, each normal node i needs to form a weighted undirected graph using the nodes in its current local subnet and the connectivity/distance information gathered at t_c. In detail, the connectivity information is first used to create a link between each pair of 1-hop neighbors. Secondly, if the distance between a pair of 1-hop neighbors can be measured, then the distance is used as the weight for the corresponding link. If the distance between them is not available, then the transmission range of the mobile nodes is used as the weight. Based on the undirected graph, D^{md} is a matrix that stores the information about the directly measured distance. Specifically, if an entry in D^{md} corresponds to a node pair who are 1-hop neighbors and whose distance can be measured directly, then the entry contains the square of the measured distance. Otherwise, the entry in D^{md} is filled with a placeholder zero. In addition, D^{ot} is a matrix that stores the information about other types of distances. Specifically, if $D^{md}(m,n)$=0, then $D^{ot}(m,n)$ is equal to the length of the shortest path between vertex m and n in the undirected graph. Note that the length of the shortest path is an approximated distance. If $D^{md}(m,n) \neq 0$, then $D^{ot}(m,n)$=0. The reason why we use two matrices to store these distances separately is that the directly measured distances are more accurate than the approximated distances. Therefore, the measured distances should be given a higher weight in the optimization problem presented in the following sections. Furthermore, Q^{md} and Q^{ot} are two matrices used to indicate the non-zero entries in D^{md} and D^{ot}. In detail, if $D^{md}(m,n)$=0, then $Q^{md}(m,n)$=0. If $D^{md}(m,n) \neq 0$, then $Q^{md}(m,n)$=1. Q^{ot} is defined in a similar manner.

With these definitions, we can use the non-zero entries in D^{md} and D^{ot} to approximate D. The resulting D is denoted as $\widetilde{D}$. Formally, $\widetilde{D}$ can be generated using Eq. (5):

$$\widetilde{D}(m,n) = \begin{cases} D^{md}(m,n) & \text{if } D^{md}(m,n) \neq 0 \\ D^{ot}(m,n) & \text{otherwise} \end{cases} \tag{5}$$

Finally, we use $\widetilde{D}^{md}$ and $\widetilde{D}^{ot}$ to denote $\widetilde{D}.{*}Q^{md}$ and $\widetilde{D}.{*}Q^{ot}$ respectively, where $.{*}$ denotes the element-wise product.

To construct X^{nc}, X^{ac}, P^{nc}, and P^{ac}, each normal node i needs to collect the coordinate information from its local subnet during t_{cw}. The size of these matrices is the same as the coordinate matrix X. Specifically, X^{nc} stores the received coordinates from the normal nodes in node i's local subnet during t_{cw}. Since the neighbors of node i could change from one time slot to another during t_{cw}, the coordinates of a node in $N_{i,T}$ might not be available for some time slots within t_{cw}. When the coordinates are not available, the corresponding entries are filled with zero. In addition, X^{ac} stores the received coordinates from the anchor nodes in node i's local subnet during t_{cw}. Due to a similar reason, X^{ac} could also contain some zeros that correspond to the unavailable coordinates. Furthermore, P^{nc} and P^{ac} are used to indicate the non-zero entries in X^{nc} and X^{ac} respectively. Specifically, if $X^{nc}(m,n)$=0, then $P^{nc}(m,n)$=0. If $X^{nc}(m,n) \neq 0$, then $P^{nc}(m,n)$=1. P^{ac} is defined in a similar fashion. Based on these matrices, the details of the 2-step procedure are presented in the following sections.

3.1 Approximating X(:,1:T-1)

Since the nodes in mobile networks keep moving around, the nodes in a normal node's local subnet could change over time. Namely, a node that is not part of the local subnet during one time slot could be included in the local subnet during another slot. Therefore, X tends to include many unknown entries. As mentioned previously, $X(:, 1 : T-1)$ is a submatrix of X, which consists of the first $T - 1$ columns of X. Thus $X(:, 1{:}T-1)$ is likely to be incomplete too. Step 1 of MALL uses X^{nc} and X^{ac} to approximate the unknown entries in $X(:, 1 : T-1)$. Technically, it takes advantage of the the low rank and temporal stability features of $X(:, 1 : T - 1)$ and employs a novel matrix completion method that only involves convex optimization to accomplish the approximation. The approximated $X(:,1:T-1)$ will be utilized by Step 2 of MALL.

As mentioned previously, X is a low-rank matrix that exhibits the temporal stability features when the whole network is considered the local subnet (i.e. all nodes in the network are included in the local subnet). Thus, for node i, $(G(k,i,t{+}1){-}G(k,i,t)){-}(G(k,i,t){-}G(k,i,t{-}1))$ approaches zero. When the local subnet only includes the anchor nodes within two hops and normal nodes within one hop, X still has the low-rank and temporal stability features because the X in this scenario is a submatrix of the X in the previous case. As a submatrix of X, $X(:,1:T-1)$ also exhibits the low rank and temporal stability features in this scenario.

Considering that the low rank and temporal stability features of $X(:,1:T-1)$, we devised a novel matrix completion method that only involves convex optimization to approximate $X(:,1:T-1)$. In detail, we assume that the rank of $X(:,1:T-1)$ is r_1 and $X(:,1:T-1)$ can be decomposed into two matrices, L_X and R_X. We further assume that L_X has $N{\cdot}d$ rows and r_1 columns; R_X has T-1 rows and r_1 columns. In addition, $X(:,1:T-1) = L_X R_X^T$. As mentioned previously, $X(:,1:T-1)$ has the low rank and temporal stability features. In addition, $X(:,1:T-1)$ should be consistent with $X^{ac}(:,1:T-1)$ and $X^{nc}(:,1:T-1)$. Note that $X^{ac}(:,1:T-1)$ and $X^{nc}(:,1:T-1)$ include the received coordinates from the anchor and normal nodes respectively. Thus, approximating $X(:,1:T-1)$ can be converted to the following minimization problem that takes both the low rank and temporal stability features into consideration:

$$\begin{aligned}\text{minimize} \quad & \left\|(L_X R_X^T).*P^{ac}(:,1{:}T{-}1){-}X^{ac}(:,1{:}T{-}1)\right\|_F^2 \\ & +\alpha\cdot\left\|(L_X R_X^T).*P^{nc}(:,1{:}T{-}1){-}X^{nc}(:,1{:}T{-}1)\right\|_F^2 \\ & +\beta\cdot\left(\|L_X\|_F^2+\|R_X\|_F^2\right)+\left\|(L_X R_X^T)S_X^T\right\|_F^2\end{aligned} \quad (6)$$

where $.*$ denotes the element-wise product of two matrices; $\|\cdot\|_F$ denotes the Frobenius norm of a matrix; α and β are two tunable parameters; S_X is the temporal transformation matrix used to enforce the temporal stability constraint.

Note that the first two terms of Notation (6) guarantee that the resulting approximation is consistent with the location of the normal and anchor nodes respectively. Since the coordinates of the anchors are more reliable than those of the normal nodes, we set α to 0.1. The third term of Notation (6) corresponds to the low rank property of $X(:,1:T-1)$. We use $\beta = 0.1$ as the weight for the low rank portion in our research. The last term ensures that the approximation satisfies the temporal stability feature. In our research, $S_X = Toeplitz(0, 1, \text{-}2, 1)$, which denotes the Toeplitz matrix with central diagonal given by ones, the first upper diagonal given by negative twos, and the second upper diagonal given by ones. In detail, S_X can be defined using Eq. (7):

$$S_X = \begin{bmatrix} 1 & -2 & 1 & \cdots & 0 & 0 & 0 \\ 0 & 1 & -2 & \cdots & 0 & 0 & 0 \\ \cdots & \cdots & \cdots & \cdots & \cdots & \cdots & \cdots \\ 0 & 0 & 0 & \cdots & 1 & -2 & 1 \end{bmatrix} \quad (7)$$

With S_X, the last term of Notation (6) guarantees that, for node i, $(G(k,i,t{+}1){-}G(k,i,t)){-}(G(k,i,t){-}G(k,i,t{-}1)) = G(k,i,t-1)+G(k,i,t+1)-2{\cdot}G(k,i,t)$ approaches zero.

There are many different methods to solve the minimization problem [12][13]. In our research, the alternating least squares procedure is adopted. Furthermore, we use the operation $f(\cdot)$ to define a special matrix Z, which is a submatrix of $X(:,1:T-1)$ and only includes the rows corresponding to the nodes that appear in the local subnet of node i during t_{rw}. Formally, Z can be calculated using Eq. (8):

$$Z = f(X(:,1:T-1)) \quad (8)$$

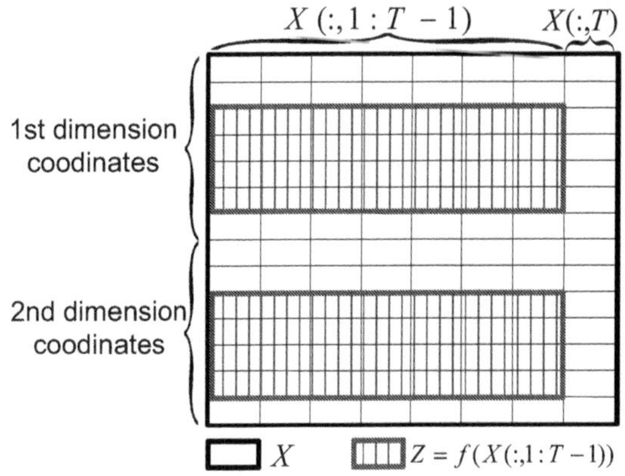

Figure 2: Relationship between X and Z

Fig. 2 illustrates the relationship between X and Z using a normal node in the example 2-dimension mobile network mentioned in Section 2. Note that $X(:,1:T-1)$, a matrix consisting of the leftmost $T-1$ columns of X, is also marked in Fig. 2.

Once the approximation of $X(:,1:T-1)$ is available, we can naturally approximate Z by selecting the corresponding rows in the approximated $X(:,1:T-1)$. In this paper, we use $\widetilde{Z}$ to denote this approximation of Z.

3.2 Calculating the Unknown Entries in Y

Y contains the coordinates of the nodes that have appeared in a normal node's local subnet over t_{rw}. Most entries in the last column of Y are empty because the coordinates of the normal nodes at t_c are to be determined (i.e. not available yet). Only the entries in the last column corresponding to the anchor nodes are available. Step 2 of MALL uses $\widetilde{D}$, $\widetilde{Z}$, and X^{ac} to fill the unknown entries in Y. Technically, a carefully-designed matrix completion method that involves low-complexity optimization is used to estimate Y. In this paper, we use $\widetilde{Y}$ to denote the resulting estimated Y.

According to the operation $f(\cdot)$ defined previously, Y can be constructed using Eq. (9):

$$Y = f\big(X(:,T-T_r+1:T)\big) \quad (9)$$

Using Eq. (8) and (9), we can arrive at the following relationship:

$$f(X) = \big[Z(:,1:T-T_r) \;\; Y\big] \quad (10)$$

where $[\cdot \;\; \cdot]$ denotes the operation of combining two submatrices into one matrix.

Step 2 of MALL attempts to estimate Y by solving a carefully-formulated minimization problem under a series of important constraints. The details of these constraints are presented as follows.

Connectivity/Distance: We first formulate the constraints with regard to the connectivity/distance information. To reduce computation cost, we only use the connectivity/distance information that is collected at t_c and stored in $\widetilde{D}$. Namely, only the entries in $Y(:,T)$ are constrained. The constraints can be divided into two categories: equality constraints and bound constraints. Formally, we use $g(Y)$ to denote the total violation of these constraints:

$$\begin{aligned} g(Y) &= \|D.*Q^{md} - \widetilde{D}^{md}\|_F^2 \\ &+ \sum_{1\le m,n\le N_c} min\{0, D(m,n) - D^{lb}(m,n)\}^2 \\ &+ \sum_{1\le m,n\le N_c} max\{0, (D(m,n) - D^{ub}(m,n)\}^2 \end{aligned} \quad (11)$$

where D is the squared distance matrix calculated using $Y(:,T)$ according to Eq. (1). D^{lb} and D^{ub} are two $N_c \times N_c$ matrices containing the lower and upper bound of the distances. For a pair of nodes m and n, $D^{lb}(m,n)$ and $D^{ub}(m,n)$ represent the lower bound and upper bound of the distance between them respectively.

Since $\widetilde{D}^{md}$ include the measured distances that are highly precise, we use it to generate equality constraints: $D.*Q^{md} = \widetilde{D}^{md}$. The first term of $g(Y)$ capture the violation of these equality constraints. D^{lb} and D^{ub} are used to generate two bound constraints: $D(m,n) \ge D^{lb}(m,n)$ and $D(m,n) \le D^{ub}(m,n)$. The second and third term of $g(Y)$ represent the violation of these bound constraints. In our research, when two nodes cannot hear each other, d^2_{max} is used as the lower bound. With regard to upper bound, when two nodes, m and n, can hear each other, d^2_{max} is used as the upper bound; otherwise, $\widetilde{D}^{ot}(m,n)$ is used as the upper bound.

Low Rank: Being a submatrix of X, $f(X)$ exhibits the low rank feature. As mentioned previously, $f(X)$ is equal to $[Z(:,1:T-T_r) \;\; Y]$ and Step 1 of MALL results in $\widetilde{Z}$, a satisfactory approximation of Z. The low rank constraint used in Step 2 is based on the observation that adding Y to the approximated $\widetilde{Z}(:,1:T-T_r)$ should keep the low rank feature of $f(X)$.

To retain the low rank of $f(X)$, we let:

$$f(X) = \left[Z(:,1:T-T_r) \;\; Y\right] = Z \cdot B_X^T \quad (12)$$

where B_X is an arbitrary $T \times (T-1)$ matrix. If B_X exists, we can arrive at:

$$rank\big(f(X)\big) \le min\{rank(Z), rank(B_X)\} \quad (13)$$

This is based on the theorem that if a matrix is a product of two other matrices, the rank of the matrix does not exceed the rank of the other two matrices [14].

Note that the first $T - T_r$ columns of Z should be the same as the corresponding part of $f(X)$. Therefore, $B_X(1:T-T_r, 1:T-T_r)$ should be a $(T-T_r)\times(T-T_r)$ identity matrix while each entry in $B_X(1:T-T_r, T-T_r+1:T-1)$ should be equal to zero. Namely, only the bottom T_r rows in B_X is unknown. In this paper, we use a $T_r \times (T-1)$ matrix, B, to denote this part of B_X. Then we use $h(Y,B)$ to capture the violation of the low rank constraint (i.e. the difference between Y and $\widetilde{Z}\cdot B^T$):

$$h(Y,B) = \left\|Y - \widetilde{Z}B^T\right\|_F^2 \quad (14)$$

Note that B is actually an unknown matrix to be determined in the minimization problem. An approximation of B and Y will be available once the minimization problem is solved. By keeping $h(Y,B)$ small, we can ensure that $[\widetilde{Z}(:,1:T-T_r) \;\; Y]$ is a low rank matrix.

Temporal Stability: As a submatrix of $f(X)$, Y has the temporal stability property. Namely, for any node j whose coordinates are included in Y, $G(k,j,t-1)+G(k,j,t+1)-2\cdot G(k,j,t)$ approaches zero. To ensure that this property holds well in Y, we include the temporal stability constraint in the minimization problem. Formally, the violation of the temporal stability constraint can be captured by $p(Y)$:

$$p(Y) = \left\|YS_Y^T\right\|_F^2 \quad (15)$$

In our research, we set $T_r = 3$. Therefore, $S_Y = [1 \;\; -2 \;\; 1]$.

Matching Received Coordinates: As mentioned previously, each normal node collects the coordinates of its neighbors in the local subnet over t_{cw}. Since these coordinates are either calculated by the neighboring normal nodes or generated by anchors, Y should be consistent with them. In addition, since the coordinates from anchors are more reliable than those from normal nodes, we should assign a higher weight to the violations related to anchors. Formally, we use $q(Y)$ to calculate the total violations of the coordinate matching constraint:

$$\begin{aligned} q(Y) &= \left\|Y.*f(P^{ac}(:,T-T_r+1:T)) - f(X^{ac}(:,T-T_r+1:T))\right\|_F^2 \\ &+ \gamma\cdot\left\|Y.*f(P^{nc}(:,T-T_r+1:T)) - f(X^{nc}(:,T-T_r+1:T))\right\|_F^2 \end{aligned} \quad (16)$$

where γ is a tunable parameter to adjust the weight of the terms in Eq. (16). In our research, we set $\gamma = 0.1$ to assign a lower weight to the violation term related to normal nodes.

Complete Formulation: Formally, filling the unknown entries in Y can be converted into the following minimization problem incorporating the constraints mentioned previously (note that Y and B are the unknown matrices to be determined):

$$\text{minimize} \;\; c(Y,B) = g(Y) + \delta\cdot h(Y,B) + p(Y) + q(Y) \quad (17)$$

where δ is a tunable parameter ($0 < \delta \le 1$) used to assign a proper weight to the low rank constraint. Since real coordinate matrices are not completely low-rank, the weight of the low rank constraint should be kept small. Generally speaking, δ could be set to 0.1. In our research, we use a Quasi-Newton optimization algorithm, BFGS [15], to find the optimal solution to the minimization problem, ultimately arriving at $\widetilde{Y}$.

As mentioned previously, once $\widetilde{Y}$ is available, the corresponding node can localize itself easily by retrieving its current coordinates from $\widetilde{Y}$.

3.3 Time Complexity

The two steps of MALL correspond to two minimization problems: Notation (6) and Notation (17), by which the time complexity of MALL is dominated. As mentioned previously, Notation (6) is solved using the least squares method while Notation (17) is tackled using BFGS. Hence, the complexity of them are $O(r_1 \cdot \overline{N} \cdot T \cdot I_{LS})$ and $O(d \cdot \overline{N_c}^2 \cdot I_{BFGS})$, respectively. Here $\overline{N}$ and $\overline{N}_c$ are the average number of neighbors appeared during t_{cw} and the average number of neighbors at t_c, respectively. I_{LS} and I_{BFGS} are the iteration number of the least squares method for Notation (6) and the iteration number of BFGS for Notation (17), respectively. Overall, the time complexity of MALL is:

$$O\Big(r_1 \cdot \overline{N} \cdot T \cdot I_{LS} + d \cdot \overline{N_c}^2 \cdot I_{BFGS}\Big) \qquad (18)$$

Despite of the non-convex optimization nature of Notation (17), the complexity of Step 2 is on the same order as that of Step 1, which only involves convex optimization. Consequently, MALL tends to be very competitive compared to the existing mobile localization schemes. Our experimental results are consistent with the theoretical analysis.

4. SIMULATION

We carried out intensive simulations to compare MALL with the state-of-the-art mobile localization schemes: MCL [6], MSL* [7], IMCL [8], and TSLRL [10]. MCL, MSL*, IMCL, and MALL are decentralized algorithms while TSLRL is a centralized method. In our simulation, we implemented MCL, MSL*, IMCL and MALL with MATLAB ourselves and adopted the TSLRL program provided by the authors [10]. The performance comparison of these schemes in terms of localization error, running time, and communication cost is presented in this section.

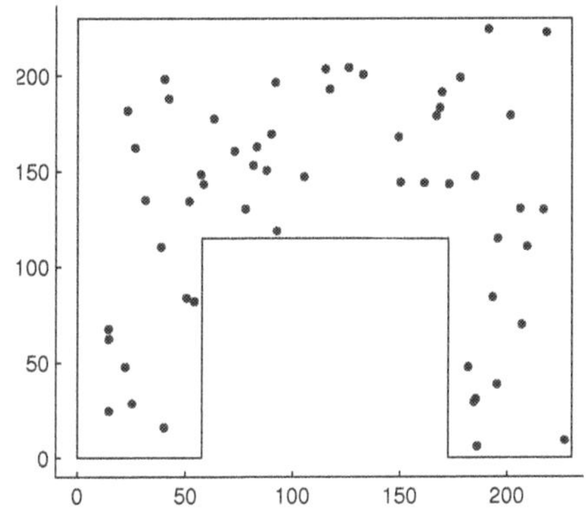

Figure 3: A C-shaped area

Our simulations were conducted with both synthetic and real mobility traces. The synthetic mobility traces were generated using the standard random waypoint model [16] and modified random waypoint model [6]. Each of the traces involves 50 nodes over 300 time slots, which allows us to complete 10 random runs and calculate the average localization error. In our research, $10m/slot$ and $30m/slot$ are considered the typical low-mobility and high-mobility velocity respectively, which is consistent with the simulations carried out in [7][10]. With synthetic traces, we studied the performance of MALL using two different experimental fields. The first field was a $200m \times 200m$ square-shaped region. The second field is an irregular C-shaped area that was used in [10]. Specifically, it is a $230m \times 230m$ square with a $115m \times 115m$ block taken off. The details of the C-shaped field is shown in Fig. 3. To ensure every node's position falls within the fields, whenever a node is about to traverse outside, a new randomly-selected speed and direction are reselected for the node. Unless otherwise specified, 50 nodes, including 5 anchor nodes, are placed in the fields randomly using standard random waypoint model with a maximum speed of $10m/slot$.

As defined in previous studies [7][10], node density is the ratio of the average number of nodes to the area corresponding to d_{max}. Formally, we use $\pi d_{max}^2 M/A_{area}$ to denote this parameter, where M is the number of nodes in the network and A_{area} denotes the experimental area. Similarly, anchor density is defined as $\pi d_{max}^2 J/A_{area}$, where J is the number of anchors in the network. The configuration of the experimental fields for synthetic traces leads to a node density of 10 and an anchor density of 1.

To investigate the practical performance of MALL, we also used a few real mobility traces, including ZebraNet traces [17], Seattle Bus traces [18], and Human Mobility traces [19]. Specifically, 100 vehicles in the Seattle Bus traces were randomly selected to the mobile nodes while all the nodes in the ZebraNet and Human Mobility traces were used in our research. In order to have 10 random runs over 300 slots, we extracted 300 consecutive slots from the Human Mobility traces. The Seattle Bus traces only involve 300 slots, thus all of them were used in our simulation. Since the ZebraNet traces only involve 90 slots, we carried out 3 random runs with these traces. For our simulations with the real traces, all the distances in the traces were scaled down in order to arrive at an node density of 10 and anchor density of 1 approximately.

In our simulations, we quantified the localization error using the mean absolute error (MAE) [6] [7][8][10]. Formally, MAE is defined using Eq. (19):

$$MAE = \frac{1}{M \cdot T_{last}} \sum_{i,t} \|G(:,i,t) - \widehat{G}(:,i,t)\| \qquad (19)$$

where $G(:,i,t)$ and $\widehat{G}(:,i,t)$ denote the real and approximated coordinates for node i at t respectively; T_{last} is a time window covering a number of past time slots. MAE indicates the average difference between real and estimated coordinates. In practice, the ratio of MAE to d_{max} is often used to quantify the localization error. In our simulation, we also use this ratio to compare the performance of different localization schemes.

In our experiments, the iteration numbers used by MALL were $I_{LS} = 20$ and $I_{BFGS} = 100$, respectively. These iteration numbers guarantee that MALL can generate satisfactory results. For TSLRL, the time window t_{cw} consists of 15 slots. For MALL, t_{cw} and t_{rw} are set to 8 and 3 slots respectively. In addition, r_1 is set to 3. For all the localization schemes under investigation, our simulations keep running for 30 slots in order to ensure convergence. When we compare their performance, we only consider their localization error during the last 10 slots (i.e. $T_{last} = 10$).

4.1 Localization Error

In this section, we compare the localization error of MALL with that of MCL, MSL*, IMCL, and TSLRL using both synthetic and real mobility traces. Fig. 4(a) and Fig. 4(b) illustrate the performance of the localization schemes in the case of the square-shaped region. Specifically, these two figures correspond to the standard and modified random waypoint model respectively. In both of these cases, we calculated the localization error when the maximum speed, S_{max}, varied in the range of $1m/slot$ to $50m/slot$. Our experimental results show that the performance of MALL has the following features. First of all, MALL significantly outperforms all of the decentralized schemes, MCL, MSL* and IMCL, in all scenarios. For example, MALL reduces the MAE by a factor of 1.9-6.5 over MCL, 1.4-4.5 over MSL*, and 1.8-5.6 over IMCL. Secondly, the performance of MALL is compa-

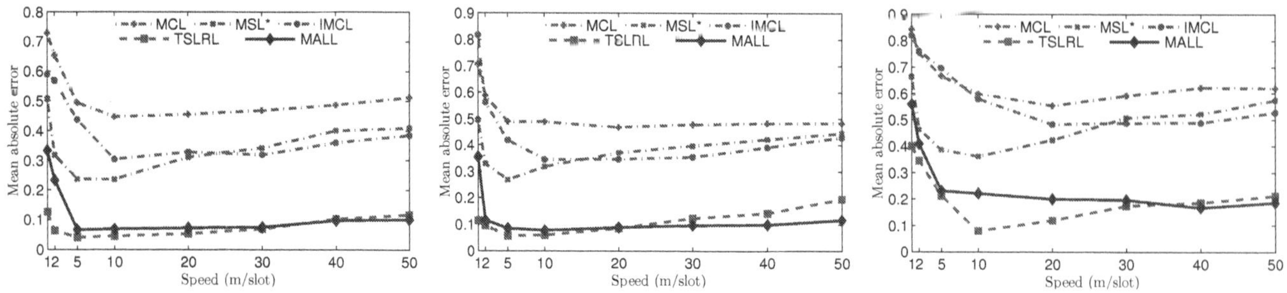

(a) Square: standard random waypoint (b) Square: modified random waypoint (c) C-shaped: standard random waypoint

Figure 4: Comparison of different localization schemes using synthetic traces

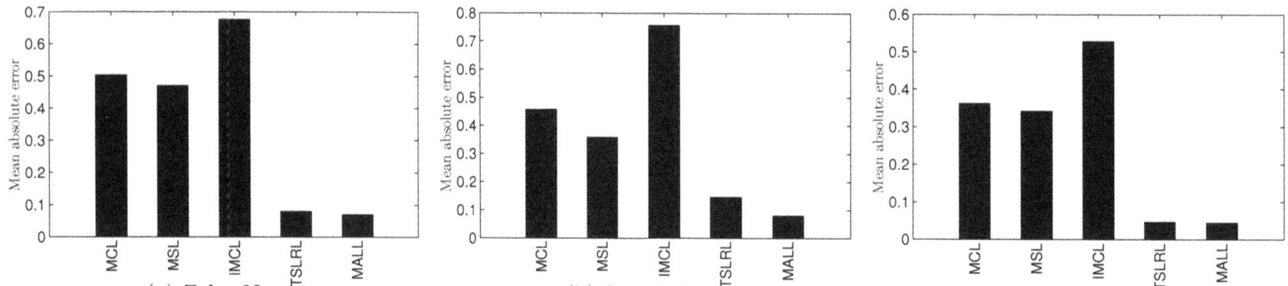

(a) ZebraNet (b) Seattle bus (c) Human mobility

Figure 5: Comparison of different localization schemes using real traces

rable to that of TSLRL, but a subtle difference does exist. When S_{max} is low, MALL leads to slightly higher localization error. As S_{max} increases, their performance difference narrows till it disappears when S_{max} reaches a critical speed. The critical speed in the case of standard and modified random waypoint model are 30 $m/slot$ and 20 $m/slot$ respectively. Once S_{max} exceeds the critical speed, MALL will start to outperform TSLRL and their performance difference will increase with S_{max}. Finally, the MAE of all localization schemes decreases with the maximum speed when the maximum speed is small (i.e. 5 $m/slot$ or less). When the maximum speed exceeds 5 $m/slot$, the MAE starts to increase with the maximum speed.

The localization error performance of MALL in the case of the C-shaped region and standard waypoint model was illustrated in Fig. 4(c). In this case, S_{max} was also in the range of $1m/slot$ to $50m/slot$. Our experimental results show that MALL results in a better performance than the decentralized schemes. Compared with TSLRL, MALL leads to a similar localization error level.

We also studied the performance of MALL using real mobility traces. Fig. 5 includes our experimental results. The results indicate that MALL significantly outperforms the distributed schemes, MCL, MSL*, and IMCL. In addition, the performance of MALL is comparable to that of TSLRL, which is a centralized scheme. This is consistent with our experimental results based on synthetic traces.

4.2 Running Time

In this section, we compare the running time performance of the localization schemes. Specifically, we vary the size of the networks by increasing the number of nodes from 25 to 400 and check whether the schemes scale well. When the number of nodes increases, the experimental area is enlarged accordingly in order to keep the node density at 10 and anchor density at 1. In our research, we assume that each mobile node attempts to localize itself during every time slot. For MALL, MCL, MSL*, and IMCL we calculate the average running time consumed by each node per time slot. For TSLRL, a centralized approach, we assume that the base station generates the coordinates of all nodes during each slot. Thus we calculate the average running time consumed by the base station per time slot.

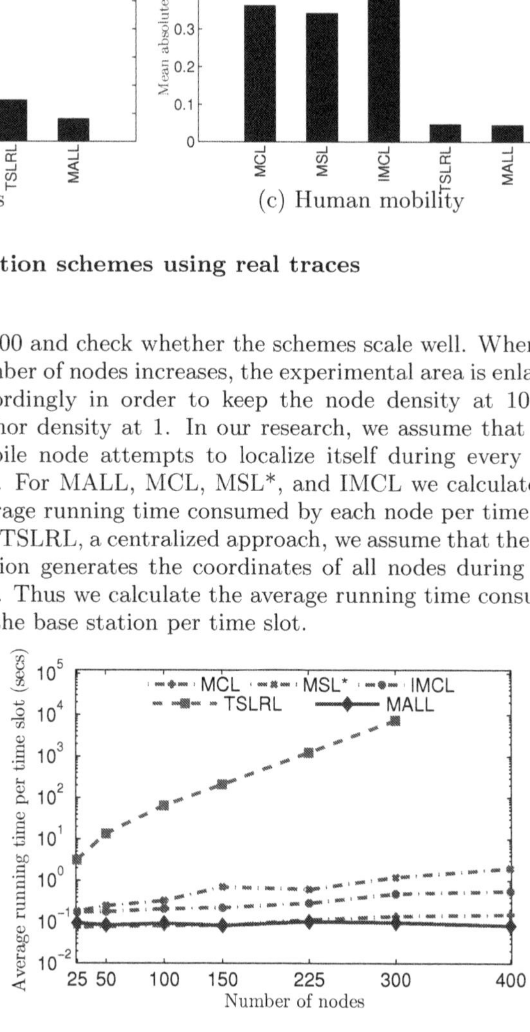

Figure 6: Running time

Our simulations were executed on a 64-bit Windows 7 machine with Intel Core i7-3770 CPU, 16GB memory, and 8MB cache. Since TSLRL requires a large volume of memory when the number of nodes is relatively large, we set the virtual memory to 64GB when the TSLRL simulations were carried out. However, we still cannot run TSLRL when the number of nodes exceeds 300 due to memory overflow. Thus the data point corresponding to the 400-node scenario is missing in the case of TSLRL. However, the data for other schemes are collected successfully.

Fig. 6 includes the details of the running time results. Our results indicate that, in terms of running time, MALL is similar to MCL and outperforms all other schemes. Furthermore, we found that the running time of MALL, MCL, MSL*, and IMCL do not increase very much as the network size goes up while the running time of TSLRL does not scale well. Actually, the running time of TSLRL increases with the network size at a skyrocketing pace.

4.3 Communication Cost

In this section, we compare the communication cost of the localization schemes. Technically, we use the average number of packets that are transmitted during a time slot to quantify the communication cost. In our research, we considered the default synthetic scenario. Table 1 includes the the detailed experimental results. With MCL, only anchor nodes forward their location-related information to the neighbors within two hops. As a result, it leads to the lowest communication cost: 68.3 packets/slot. With MSL, all mobile nodes send their data to their neighbors within two hops. Therefore, it results in the highest cost: 746.4 packets/slot. With MALL and IMCL, anchor nodes communicate with their neighbors within two hops while normal nodes only send the information to their 1-hop neighbors. Thus, their communication cost is slightly higher than that of MCL. Considering that TSLRL is a centralized scheme, we assume that a randomly-selected node plays the role of base station and collects all of the location-related information from other nodes. Finally, TSLRL's communication cost is similar to that of MALL and IMCL.

Table 1: Communication Cost

Schemes	MCL	MSL*	IMCL	TSLRL	MALL
Average number of packets per slot	68.3	746.4	113.3	121.9	113.3

5. TESTBED EXPERIMENTS

To study the performance of MALL in practice, we tested the schemes under investigation using a sensor testbed in our research lab. Specifically, we deployed 25 TelosB motes on the floor of our lab. Each TelosB mote has a microcontroller with 10kB of RAM and 24KB of flash memory. In addition, it is equipped with a CC2420 RF transceiver that communicates via 2.4GHz radio. The CC2420 chip is tailored for IEEE 802.15.4 and ZigBee protocol stacks. The TelesB mote has the built-in capability to measure the received signal strength (RSS), which enables the RSS-based distance measurement between two nearby motes.

In our experiment, we adjusted the transmission power of the mote to the lowest level: $-25dBm$. However, it still led to an overlong transmission range, which resulted in a fully connected network. To generate a realistic network that is not fully connected, we used a carefully-selected power level threshold, $-73dBm$ in our research. Furthermore, we assumed that two motes cannot communicate with each other if the RSS measurement is less than the threshold. With the threshold of $-73dBm$, the transmission range of the motes is limited to $2.2m$ (i.e. d_{max}=2.2m).The experimental region used in our research is a $5m \times 5m$ square. The transmission range and the experimental region lead to a node density of around 15. Among the 25 motes in the testbed, 5 motes are used as anchor nodes.

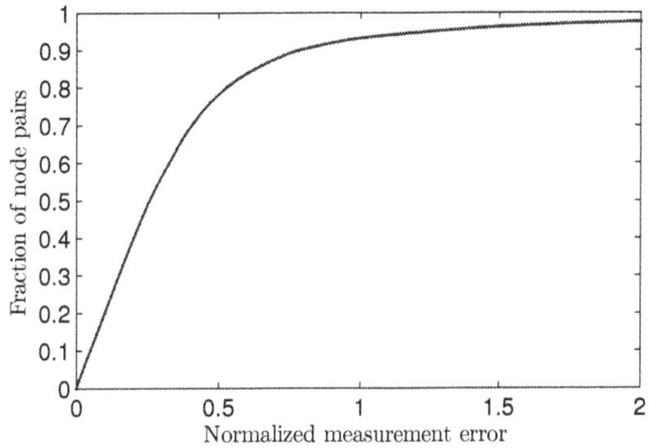

Figure 7: The CDF of distance measurement error

In our research, we tested the localization schemes using two different mobility scenarios: low mobility ($0.2D_{max}$/slot) and high mobility ($0.6D_{max}$/slot). For each of these scenarios, the coordinates of motes were generated using the standard random waypoint model [16] over 30 time slots. For each time slot, the motes were placed in the testbed manually according to the generated coordinates. Then each mote broadcast 30 packets so that the neighbors of the mote could acquire multiple RSS measurements. Finally, the average of the RSS readings was used as the RSS value to estimate the distance between each pair of neighboring motes.

We noticed that the RSS-based distance measurement is not very precise. To quantify its performance, we calculated the normalized measurement error, which can be obtained through dividing the difference between the measured (calculated using RSS readings) and actual distance by the actual distance. The cumulative distribution function (CDF) of the normalized measurement error is summarized in Fig. 7. Specifically, for around 80% of the distance measurements, the normalized error is less than 0.5; for around 6% of the distance measurements, the normalized error is greater than 1. Namely, the measured distances in the testbed contain some noise. The testbed can be used to study the practical performance in a relatively realistic environment.

Fig. 8 and 9 illustrates the performance of the schemes under investigation in the testbed. Our experimental results indicate that MALL significantly outperforms the state-of-the-art decentralized schemes, MCL, MSL* and IMCL. In addition, the performance of MALL is similar to TSLRL in both the low and high mobility cases. Overall, the experimental results from our testbed are consistent with those from our simulations.

6. CONCLUSIONS

In this paper, we propose MALL, a 2-step algorithm for mobile network localization. The first step uses a novel matrix completion technique to generate an intermediate matrix. The second step makes use of the intermediate matrix and the received location-related information to localize mobile nodes. Through intensive simulation and tested

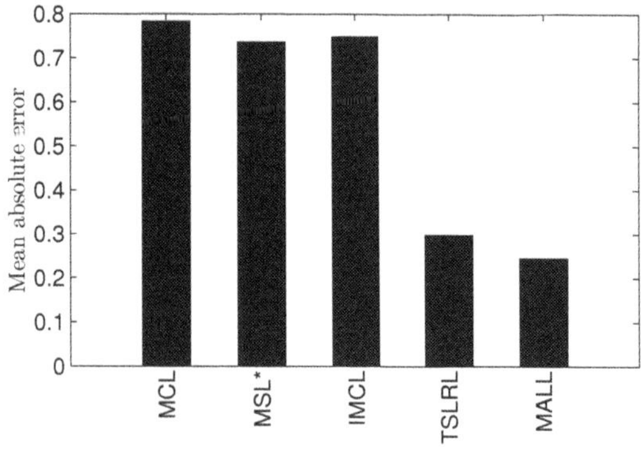

Figure 8: Comparison of various schemes using the testbed with low mobility

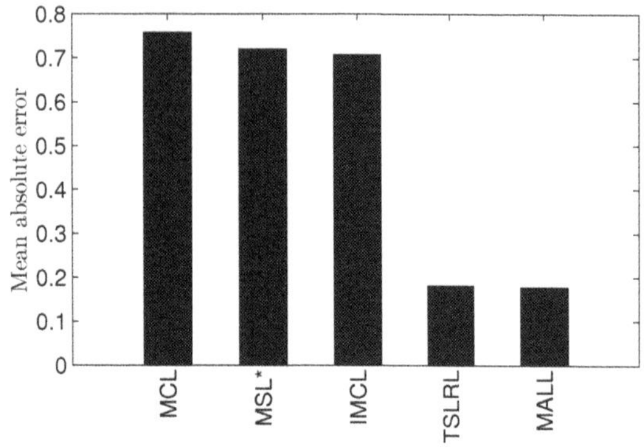

Figure 9: Comparison of various schemes using the testbed with high mobility

experiments, we found that MALL outperforms the state-of-the-art decentralized localization schemes in terms of localization error. Compared with the existing centralized schemes, MALL achieves the same high level of precision at a much faster pace because it only uses convex optimization and low-complexity non-convex optimization. In addition, MALL scales much better than centralized schemes due to its decentralized nature. Finally, MALL leads to low communication cost since it only collects the information from the anchor nodes that are at most two hops away and the normal nodes that are one-hop neighbors.

7. ACKNOWLEDGMENTS

This research was supported by the National Natural Science Foundation of China under Grant No. 61100191 and 61370216. This research was also supported by Shenzhen Strategic Emerging Industries Program under Grant No. ZDSY20120613125016389.

8. REFERENCES

[1] E.D. Kaplan and C.J. Hegarty. *Understanding GPS: principles and applications*. Artech House Publishers, 2006.

[2] Y.T. Chan, W.Y. Tsui, H.C. So, and P. Ching. Time-of-arrival based localization under nlos conditions. *IEEE Transactions on Vehicular Technology*, 55(1):17–24, 2006.

[3] P. Bahl and V.N. Padmanabhan. Radar: An in-building rf-based user location and tracking system. In *Porc. of Nineteenth Annual Joint Conference of the IEEE Computer and Communications Societies*, volume 2, pages 775–784. IEEE, 2000.

[4] Y. Shang, W. Ruml, Y. Zhang, and M.P.J. Fromherz. Localization from mere connectivity. In *Proc. of the 4th ACM international symposium on Mobile ad hoc networking and computing*, pages 201–212. ACM, 2003.

[5] Y. Shang and W. Ruml. Improved mds-based localization. In *INFOCOM 2004. Twenty-third AnnualJoint Conference of the IEEE Computer and Communications Societies*, volume 4, pages 2640–2651. IEEE, 2004.

[6] L. Hu and D. Evans. Localization for mobile sensor networks. In *Proc. of the 10th annual international conference on Mobile computing and networking*, pages 45–57. ACM, 2004.

[7] M. Rudafshani and S. Datta. Localization in wireless sensor networks. In *Proc. of the 6th international conference on Information processing in sensor networks*, pages 51–60. ACM, 2007.

[8] J. Sheu, W. Hu, and J. Lin. Distributed localization scheme for mobile sensor networks. *IEEE Transactions on Mobile Computing*, 9(4):516–526, April 2010.

[9] A. Baggio and K. Langendoen. Monte carlo localization for mobile wireless sensor networks. *Ad Hoc Networks*, 6(5):718–733, July 2008.

[10] S. Rallapalli, L. Qiu, Y. Zhang, and Y.C. Chen. Exploiting temporal stability and low-rank structure for localization in mobile networks. In *Proc. of the sixteenth annual international conference on Mobile computing and networking*, pages 161–172. ACM, 2010.

[11] H. Chenji and R. Stoleru. Toward accurate mobile sensor network localization in noisy environments. *IEEE Transactions on Mobile Computing*, 12(6):1094–1106, June 2013.

[12] B. Recht, M. Fazel, and P.A. Parrilo. Guaranteed minimum-rank solutions of linear matrix equations via nuclear norm minimization. *Society for Industrial and Applied Mathematics Review*, 52(3):471–501, 2010.

[13] Y. Zhang, M. Roughan, W. Willinger, and L. Qiu. Spatio-temporal compressive sensing and internet traffic matrices. *ACM SIGCOMM Computer Communication Review*, 39(4):267–278, 2009.

[14] R. Horn. *Matrix Analysis*. Cambridge University Press, February 1990.

[15] J. Nocedal and S.J. Wright. *Numerical optimization*. Springer verlag, 1999.

[16] J. Broch, D.A. Maltz, D.B. Johnson, Y.C. Hu, and J. Jetcheva. A performance comparison of multi-hop wireless ad hoc network routing protocols. In *Proceedings of the 4th annual ACM/IEEE international conference on Mobile computing and networking*, pages 85–97. ACM, 1998.

[17] http://crawdad.cs.dartmouth.edu/meta.php?name=princeton/zebranet.

[18] http://crawdad.cs.dartmouth.edu/meta.php?name=rice/ad_hoc_city.

[19] http://crawdad.cs.dartmouth.edu/meta.php?name=ncsu/mobilitymodels.

Surface Skeleton Extraction and Its Application for Data Storage in 3D Sensor Networks

Wenping Liu*
Huazhong University of Science and Technology, China
wenpingliu2009@gmail.com

Yang Yang
Huazhong University of Science and Technology, China
yangyang8795@gmail.com

Hongbo Jiang
Huazhong University of Science and Technology, China
hongbojiang2004@gmail.com

Xiaofei Liao
Huazhong University of Science and Technology, China
xfliao@hust.edu.cn

Jiangchuan Liu
Simon Fraser University,Canada
jcliu@cs.sfu.ca

Bo Li
Hong Kong University of Science and Technology, Hong Kong
bli@cs.ust.hk

ABSTRACT

In-network data storage and retrieval are fundamental functions of sensor networks. Among many proposals, geographical hash table (GHT) is perhaps most appealing as it is very simple yet powerful with low communication cost, where the key is to correctly define the bounding box. It is envisioned that the skeleton has the power to facilitate computing a precise bounding box. In existing works, the focus has been on skeleton extraction algorithms targeting for 2D sensor networks, which usually delivers a 1-manifold skeleton consisting of 1D curves. It faces a set of non-trivial challenges when 3D sensor networks are considered, in order to properly extract the surface skeleton composed of a set of 2-manifolds and possibly 1D curves.

In this paper, we study the problem of surface skeleton extraction in 3D sensor networks. We propose a scalable and distributed connectivity-based algorithm to extract the surface skeleton of 3D sensor networks. First, we propose a novel approach to identifying surface skeleton nodes by computing the *extended feature nodes* such that it is robust against boundary noise, etc. We then find the maximal independent set of the identified skeleton nodes and triangulate them to form a compact representation of the 3D sensor network. Furthermore, to react to the dynamics of the sensor networks caused by node failure, insertion, etc., we design an efficient updating scheme to reconstruct the surface skeleton. Finally, we apply the extracted surface skeleton to facilitate the data storage protocol design. Extensive simulations show the robustness of the proposed algorithm to shape variation, node density and network dynamics, and its effectiveness for data storage application with respect to load balancing.

*Wenping Liu is also with Hubei University of Economics.

MobiHoc'14, August 11–14, 2014, Philadelphia, PA, USA.

http://dx.doi.org/10.1145/2632951.2632966.

Categories and Subject Descriptors

C.2.1 [**Computer-Communication Networks**]: Network Architecture and Design—*wireless communication*

Keywords

3D Sensor Networks; Surface Skeleton; Data Storage

1. INTRODUCTION

In-network data storage and retrieval are fundamental functions of sensor networks. While centralized-based schemes suffer from bottleneck at nodes near the sink, distributed in-network data storage is desirable for its scalability and robustness, etc. Among many proposals, geographical hash table (GHT) [26] is appealing because 1) it can greatly reduce the communication and energy cost by avoiding frequent in-network flooding for information retrieval [30], and 2) it is very simple yet powerful [9]. GHT names events with keys and hashes the keys into geographic location; and the sensor node, referred to as *home node*, geographically closest to the hash of its key stores the (*key, value*) pair. GHT then uses GPSR [15] as the low-level routing scheme to greedily forward the data and query packets to the corresponding home node. Upon reaching a local minimum, GPSR adopts the perimeter mode forwarding strategy. Considering the dynamics of sensor networks (e.g., caused by node mobility, insertion or failure due to energy depletion, etc.), GHT proposes to replicate each key-value pair at nodes (referred to as *replica nodes*) on the home perimeter, in order to guarantee data persistency.

Despite its desirable properties, GHT has some disadvantages. For example, inherited from GPSR, in complex networks such as the Y-shaped network shown in Fig. 1(a), the boundary nodes will be overloaded due to the extensive usage of the perimeter forwarding [9] especially in 3D sensor networks where there are arbitrarily large number of perimeters to be explored [35]. If the bounding *box* defining the range of coordinates for hash functions is not properly computed, the imbalance of storage load, together with traffic

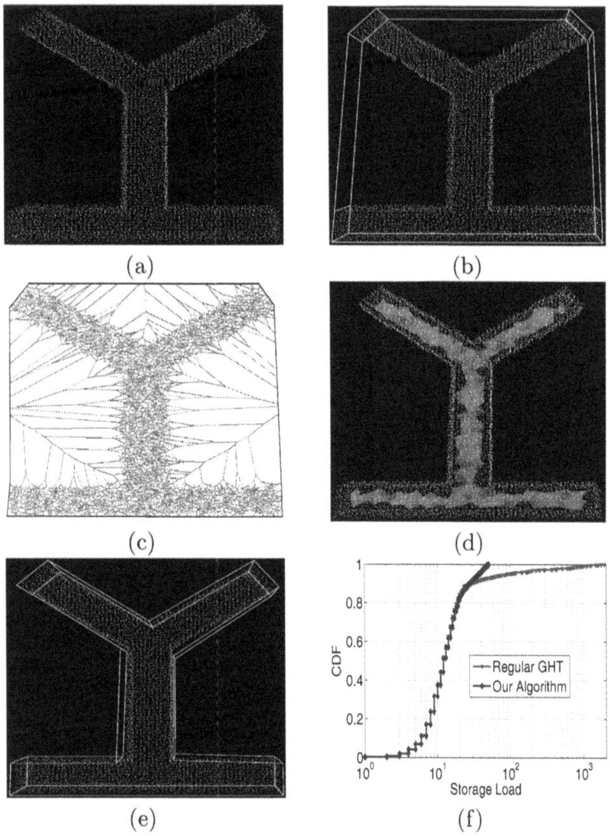

Figure 1: (a) The Y-shaped 3D network has 12,545 sensors with average node degree 15.36; (b) The bounding box with voids used in [26, 37]; (c) A cross-section of the Voronoi diagram with bounding box in (b); (d) The extracted Surface Skeleton; (e) The bounding box computed based on the Surface Skeleton in (d); (f) Comparison of storage performance with the two bounding boxes.

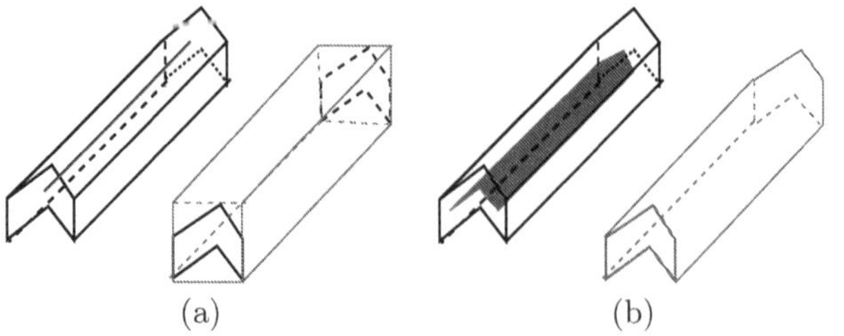

Figure 2: Bounding box computed based on C-Skeleton and S-Skeleton, respectively. (a) C-Skeleton (blue line in left) and the bounding box (green cubic in right); (b) The S-Skeleton (shaded surface in left) and the bounding box (green polyhedron in right).

load, will become more severe [29]. This is because by hashing the keys to geographic coordinates, the underlying 3D space is actually divided into a set of Voronoi cells, within each of which there is one and only one sensor node, and thus each sensor node stores the data mapped to its Voronoi cell (see Fig. 1(c)). Obviously, the storage load of a node is proportional to the volume of its cell [29], i.e., the larger the volume of the cell is, the larger the storage and communication cost of the node. And if there exist voids unoccupied by sensors, as shown in Fig. 1(b) which is utilized by Regular GHT solutions such as [26] and typical segmentation algorithms such as [37], all data hashed into the voids will be finally stored at boundary nodes surrounding the voids, and consequently, these boundary nodes (especially when replica nodes on the boundary are used for data persistency) tend to have a higher storage and traffic load [37]. Please see Fig. 1(f). Similarly, DIM [20] also maps multi-attribute event to the sensing field; the nodes near an empty zone unoccupied by any sensor store the data mapped to this zone. *Accordingly, the key for data storage application is to precisely define the bounding box of sensor networks with an arbitrary shape, in order to evenly distribute the storage load of sensor nodes; Fig. 1 shows that the bounding box results could vary greatly with different methods.*

The difficulties of computing the precise bounding box for a complex network mainly stem from the presence of concave valleys (and thus *bridges* between adjacent *peaks*) and/or, holes or tunnels, which often leads to the failure of finding a tight bound of the network based on convex hull, as shown in Fig. 1(b). At first glance, it seems quite intuitive to locate concave nodes by computing the concavity. Unfortunately, without coordinate information, it is rather difficult to calculate the *depth* of the concave valley, a traditional way to compute concavity in computer graphics, while the neighborhood size based algorithm and CATL [32] do not work well in long-and-narrow networks, making it a challenge to compute concave nodes in 3D sensor networks. On the other hand, the surface skeleton (referred to as *S-Skeleton*) of a 3D object is a generic and compact representation of the underlying object which can preserve the object's genus and the topological features very well [4]. In continuous 3D space, S-Skeleton, also called *medial surface* or *medial axis*, of a 3D object is defined as the interior points with at least two nearest boundary points, as shown in Fig. 2(b). Also we notice that another kind of skeletons of 3D objects is *curve-skeleton* (referred to as *C-Skeleton*), composed of 1D curves locally symmetric to the object [28]. While C-Skeleton has been used in 3D sensor networks to improve routing performance [24], inherently it is not a proper way to compute a tight bounding box; Fig. 2(a) shows an example. Between above two definitions of skeleton in 3D sensor networks, we emphasize that typically, the presence of a concave valley (or hole, or tunnel) will incur a *bent* S-Skeleton. Thus, if the location where the S-Skeleton deforms is identified, then the concave valley can be easily located, and accordingly, the computed bounding box is supposed to be tight and precise, as shown in Fig. 2(b). That is, we envision that S-Skeleton of a 3D sensor network, as shown in Fig. 1(d), can efficiently facilitate defining a tight and precise bounding box, as shown in Fig. 1(e), and balancing the storage loads, as shown in Fig. 1(f).

Related work. Skeleton has been widely used as an efficient way to facilitate routing [5], segmentation [40],localization [17] and navigation [19, 34], etc., in sensor networks. The usefulness of skeleton has inspired many algorithms for its computation in sensor networks, e.g., [12, 13, 22, 23, 39]. However, these algorithms primarily target at 2D sensor networks, and deliver a 1-manifold skeleton composed of 1D curves. More recently, there are many practical deployments of sensors on 3D environments [7, 33], triggering growing demands for studies on 3D sensor networks. Compared with 2D cases, it is much more difficult to compute

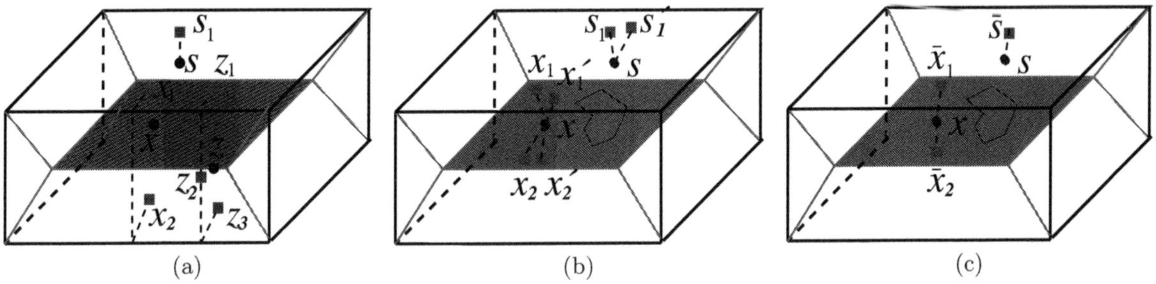

Figure 3: An illustration of the S-Skeleton of a cubic. There are thirteen sheets formed by the Y-curves and the boundary of the cubic while only the middle sheet is shaded. The solid red lines represent the Y-curves where two sheets meet. (a) Continuous space where the Euclidean distance between points are given. The feature points of x, z, s are shown by solid rectangles. Points x is an ordinary S-Skeleton point, z is a Y-curve point (and is also a junction point), and s is not an S-Skeleton point; (b) The distance between nodes are measured by integers (e.g., in hops). Node x in the shaded sheet should be an S-Skeleton node while s shouldn't. However, the non-skeleton node s has two extended feature nodes. The void bounded by the polygon in the shaded sheet is generated because of the even width of the cubic; (c) Node x has two connected components $\overline{x}_1, \overline{x}_2$ while s has only one.

the S-Skeleton of 3D objects [31], because the S-Skeleton of a 3D object consists of 2-manifolds (or skeletal sheets), and possibly 1D curves. Thus, it faces non-trivial challenges to extend the existing protocols to 3D settings.

We are aware that one close work to ours is done by Xia *et al.* [34], aiming at constructing the medial axis for navigation and data storage in 3D sensor networks. They first establish the unit tetrahedron cell (UTC) mesh structure and then iteratively "peel" off a layer of the UTC mesh structure to yield the medial axis. Principally, such a morphological thinning based method, attempting to realize Blum's grassfire model [3], is very sensitive to the distance metric and typically fails to accurately localize medial surface points [4], and it is also sensitive to boundary noise. That is, a small change in boundary surface may result in a considerable change in the surface skeleton. As such, a post-processing operation for pruning spurious branches is needed. Further, the unit tetrahedron cell (UTC) structure requires high node density and nice tetrahedron mesh [36], which is difficult to obtain when only connectivity information is available and thus small interior holes are not identified [35]. Last but not least, it cannot adapt to network dynamics since the UTC mesh must be constructed in advanced. When the network topology changes due to node failure or insertion, etc., the reconstruction of UTC mesh is costly owing to its high time and message complexity.

Our contributions. In this paper, we study the problem of S-Skeleton extraction in 3D sensor networks, and propose a connectivity-based, scalable and distributed S-Skeleton extraction algorithm which is robust again boundary noise and node density, etc., and can quickly react to the network dynamics. Whereafter, based on the extracted S-Skeleton, we propose the method to find the tight and precise bounding box followed by the solution for load-balanced data storage. Different from [34], we do not require any special structure like unit tetrahedron cell, which is difficult to obtain in a 3D network, especially with low node density. In our work, each node identifies itself as an S-Skeleton node by computing the *extended feature nodes* instead of the exact feature nodes, due to the discreteness of sensor networks and the presence of boundary noise. Then, the maximal independent set of the identified S-Skeleton nodes is constructed, followed by a triangulation procedure to form a compact representation of the underlying 3D sensor network. The merits of our S-Skeleton extraction algorithm are that it is robust against boundary noise and does not suffer from low node density, and thus can be applied in more generic cases than [34]. Further, to react to the network dynamics caused by node failure or insertion, etc., for the first time we propose an efficient updating scheme to reconstruct the S-Skeleton. Finally, we apply the extracted S-Skeleton for the design of load-balanced data storage protocol in 3D sensor networks. We conduct extensive simulations to show the robustness of the algorithm to shape variation, node density, network dynamics, and so on.

The reminder of the paper is structured as follows. In Section 2 we briefly introduce the motivations and preliminary knowledge of this work, and detail our algorithm in Section 3. Section 4 is devoted to the application of the S-Skeleton. To show the efficiency of the proposed algorithm, we conduct extensive simulations in Section 5. Finally, Section 6 concludes the paper.

2. MOTIVATIONS AND PRELIMINARIES

In continuous domain, as mentioned earlier, the S-Skeleton of a 3D object $D \subset R^3$, denoted by $SK(D)$, is a collection of the interior points having more than one nearest boundary point (referred to as *feature point*). More formally, we first define the distance transform $DT : D \rightarrow \mathbb{R}$ as $DT(x) = \min_{y \in \partial D} d(x, y)$ if $x \in \mathcal{D} \backslash \partial D$ and 0 otherwise, where ∂D is the boundary surface of D and $d(x, y)$ is the (Euclidean) distance of point x to y. Further, we define the feature transform $F : D \rightarrow \mathbb{P}(\partial D)$ where $\mathbb{P}$ is the power set, assigning to each point $x \in D$ the set of feature points on ∂D to x. That is, $F(x) = \{y \in \partial D | d(x, y) = DT(x)\}$. Since an S-Skeleton point has more than one feature point, its feature size should be larger than one, and if a point has only one feature point, it must be a non-skeleton point. Thus, there is an easy way to identify an S-Skeleton point based on the feature size. Formally, we have

DEFINITION 1. *A point x is an S-Skeleton point if its feature size $|F(x)| \geq 2$.*

Based on Definition 1, we can deliver the S-Skeleton composed of 2-manifolds, or *sheets*, and possibly 1D curves. Fig. 3 (a) shows an example of the S-Skeleton of a cubic. In degenerated cases like a cylinder, the S-Skeleton may contain only curves, which is quite unusual and thus not

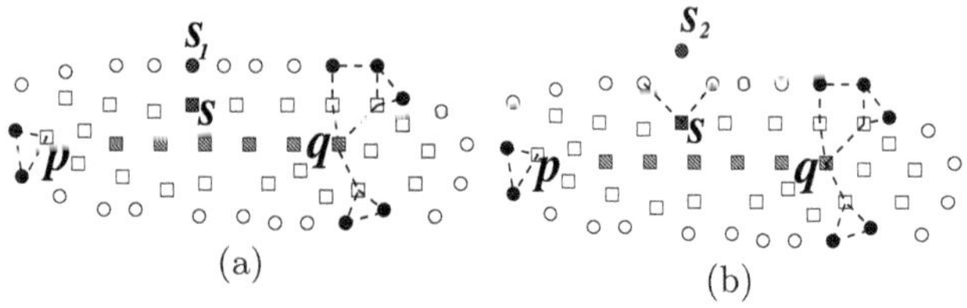

Figure 4: The principle of skeleton node identification in [40] and its drawback. Boundary nodes are shown by circles, ordinary interior nodes and skeleton nodes are shown by empty rectangles and solid rectangles, respectively. (a) The nodes in solid pink circles, e.g., q, are skeleton nodes such that their feature nodes form more than one interval, and p is not a skeleton node since there is only one interval of feature nodes; (b) The small bump in the boundary (shown by the solid blue circle) generates a new skeleton node s indicated by the solid blue rectangle.

considered in this paper. Two sheets may meet along a Y-intersection curve [6], called *Y-curve*, or Medial Scaffold [10, 11], on which any point has at least three feature points and is referred to as a *Y-curve point*. Hence, a sheet is bounded by some Y-curves and possibly the boundary of the object. In particular, we also call as *junction points* the Y-curve points where more than two sheets intersect.

Definition 1, however, can not be directly applied for sensor networks where the coordinate information of each sensor is often costly to acquire and in most scenarios, we can only use connectivity information. Many factors, such as the rounding error of distance between nodes, low node density, boundary noise, etc., pose great challenges to identify skeleton nodes in sensor networks. We first take a look at the challenges and present the solutions in 2D sensor networks, and then we extend these solutions to the 3D counterparts.

First, due to the rounding error of distance between nodes, low node density or even "width", etc., many interior nodes may only have one nearest boundary node (referred to as *feature node*), potentially degrading the performance of skeleton extraction. In order to tackle this problem, we can compute the *extended feature nodes* defined below.

Definition 2. *For an interior node p having a minimum hop count distance k to the boundary, its extended feature nodes of p, denoted by $\overline{F}(p)$, are the boundary nodes which are k or $k+1$ hops to p.*

Second, there are many unstable nodes (e.g., p in Fig. 4(a)) having two or more close feature nodes. As a result, the delivered skeleton will contain too many spurious branches, especially when the extended feature nodes are introduced. An approach to tackle this problem is proposed by Zhu *et al.* [40] where a node identifies itself as a skeleton node (e.g., q in Fig. 4(a)) if it has two or more intervals, i.e., ordered and consecutive sequences, of feature nodes; the nodes with only one interval, e.g., p in Fig. 4(a), are ordinary nodes. Note that this approach is invalid for 3D sensor networks as the boundary nodes cannot be ordered to form intervals. Besides, it suffers from boundary noise in 2D sensor networks, as mentioned in [21, 22], and more greatly in 3D cases. That is, a small bump in the boundary will cause an unwanted skeleton branch needed to be pruned. For instance, when the boundary node s_1 in Fig. 4(a) *moves* to s_2 in Fig. 4(b), the only one consecutive sequence of feature nodes of node s in Fig. 4(a) will be divided into two intervals in Fig. 4(b), and thus s will identify itself as a skeleton node. The solution to this problem is to introduce an equivalence relation $\sim_\epsilon$ as in [27]:

Definition 3. *If the geodesic distance between two boundary nodes a, b is less than $\epsilon(>0)$, we say that a and b are geodesic ϵ-equivalent, denoted by $a \sim_\epsilon b$.*

Similarly, for each node p, if the minimum of the geodesic distances between nodes belonging to two intervals I_1, I_2 is less than ϵ, we say that the two intervals are geodesic ϵ-equivalent, and can be treated as one *ϵ-interval.* A node identifies itself as a skeleton node if and only if it has two or more ϵ-intervals. Clearly, we have

Theorem 1. *A small bump in the boundary, separating an interval I of p into two intervals I_1, I_2 with geodesic distance less than ϵ, does not change the identity of p.*

Proof. Since the two intervals I_1, I_2 have a geodesic distance less than ϵ, they are regarded as one ϵ-interval. Thus, if p has only one interval before the bump, then after the bump p still has only one ϵ-interval and remains a non-skeleton node; otherwise, p keeps its identity as a skeleton node, which proves the claim. □

Theorem 1 shows that such a process of skeleton node identification is robust to boundary noise. One can easily prove that it is also robust to many other factors, such as low node density or node failure, etc.

Note that these challenges will become more severe in 3D environments. That is, some true S-Skeleton nodes may not identify themselves as skeleton nodes due to even "width", etc. Consequently, there might be holes in the skeletal sheets, as shown in Fig. 3 (b), resulting in that the S-Skeleton does not preserve the network's genus. At the same time, there might be more unstable S-Skeleton nodes and thus many unwanted faces. Further, it is noted that the solutions to these problems in 2D sensor networks can not be directly applied in 3D cases, as here the boundary surfaces are 2-manifolds and the boundary nodes cannot be ordered in sequence, as mentioned earlier.

Now we extend the solutions in 2D sensor networks to 3D cases. Observe that in 2D sensor networks, the boundary nodes in a consecutive sequence must be connected, thus an interval of boundary nodes implies a connected component of boundary nodes. Hence, in 3D sensor networks, we can identify an S-Skeleton node based on the number of connected components. More specifically, for each node p, we compute its extended feature nodes $\overline{F}(p)$. Clearly, even for an ordinary interior node, it may have more than two extended feature nodes and any two of them are not necessarily neighboring, as shown in Fig. 5 (b). To address this, we first group these extended feature nodes into connected components, as shown in Fig. 3 (c), and then use equivalence relation $\sim_\epsilon$ to merge these connected components into bigger component(s); two components are ϵ-equivalent if their distance (defined as the minimal geodesic distance between pairwise nodes belonging to different components) is less than ϵ, and form a virtual component called *ϵ-component.* Denote by $\overline{F}_\epsilon(p)$ the set of virtual components of node p. Obviously, each ϵ-component here serves as the feature point in the continuous domain. As such, we can identify an S-Skeleton node as follows.

Proposition 2. *For an interior node p, if $|\overline{F}_\epsilon(p)| \geq 2$, then p identifies itself as an S-Skeleton node.*

By Proposition 2, we can identify the S-Skeleton nodes based on only one parameter ϵ, which is used to avoid suffering from rounding noise, boundary noise, and node density, etc. Clearly, for Definition 1, $\epsilon = 0$, and only the exact feature points are used. That is, the skeleton nodes identified based on Proposition 2 is a subset of those identified based on Definition 1, while Proposition 2 can yield a more stable result in 3D sensor networks, which is validated by extensive simulations in Section 5. With the identified S-Skeleton nodes, we perform a triangulation procedure to form a compact representation, i.e., the S-Skeleton, of a 3D sensor network, which will be detailed in next section.

3. ALGORITHMS

In this section, we present the details of our algorithm for S-Skeleton extraction in 3D sensor networks. Since boundary recognition is out of the scope of the paper, we thus assume that boundary nodes have already been recognized, e.g., by [14, 18]. Further, we do not assume that the location information of nodes are known, and our work is based on mere connectivity information.

3.1 S-Skeleton Node Identification

As mentioned in Section 2, an interior node is an S-Skeleton node if it has at least two ϵ-components formed by extended feature nodes. Thus, the first step of our algorithm is to identify the extended feature nodes of each interior node. This can be done in a distributed fashion as follows. Each boundary node issues a flooding within the network at roughly the same time. The flooded message includes the ID of the boundary node, and a counter, which is set to be zero by default, to indicate the distance of a node to the origin of the flooded message. When receiving a flooded message from a boundary node, say q, each node p executes the following rules:

- If p has yet not received the flooded message from any boundary node, it appends q to the list of nearest boundary nodes of p (denoted by $List(p)$), increases the counter by one and forwards the updated message to its neighbors;
- else if the distance of p to q is equal to, or larger by one than, the minimal distance of p to the nodes in $List(p)$, p keeps record of the boundary node q, increases the counter by one and forwards the updated message to its neighbors;
- else p simply discards the arrived message.

Consequently, each interior node keeps record of its extended feature nodes and the distance (in hops) to the feature nodes.

Subsequently, these extended feature nodes issue a limited flooding to construct connected component(s), followed by a hop-by-hop expansion process as given in [24] to merge these components into ϵ-component(s). More specifically, each component is firstly assigned a unique identifier, and then each extended feature node initiates a flooding message including its identifier and a counter (initialized to be zero), which indicates how far (in hops) the message has travelled. When a boundary node p receives a flooded message from a boundary node q which has been assigned an identifier and has a counter no greater than ϵ, it executes the following rules:

- if p has no identifier, then p will be assigned the same identifier as $q's$, increase the counter by one, and forward the updated message to its neighboring boundary nodes;
- else if p and q have different identifiers, and the sum of the counters of p and q is less than ϵ, then p increases the counter by one, and forwards the updated message to its neighboring boundary nodes;
- else p simply discards the arrived message from q.

This way, the communication cost of ϵ-component construction can be very low. An interior node with more than one ϵ-component identifies itself as an S-Skeleton node, as shown in Fig. 5(a); and the interior node with only one component is a non-skeleton node, as shown in Fig. 5(b). Finally, Fig. 5(c) draws the identified S-Skeleton nodes of the Y-shaped network in Fig. 1(a).

3.2 S-Skeleton Establishment

With the identified S-Skeleton nodes, we now connect them to form a set of 2-manifolds, i.e., the S-Skeleton. Note that the identification of an S-Skeleton node is based on the extended feature nodes, in order to guarantee that the true S-Skeleton nodes will not be ignored. Unfortunately, this may incur that some S-Skeleton nodes are redundant in a given scenario, e.g., with parallel boundaries, which brings a non-trivial challenge to construct the S-Skeleton. To address this issue, we propose to construct the maximal independent set of the S-Skeleton nodes, followed by triangulating them to form the S-Skeleton.

Given the undirected S-Skeleton graph $G_s = (V_s, E_s)$ where V_s denotes the set of the identified S-Skeleton nodes, and E_s is the set of links between S-Skeleton nodes, an independent set is a subset $V_s' \in V_s$ such that no nodes in V_s' are adjacent; and a maximum independent set is a maximum-cardinality independent set [1]. We will not compute the maximum independent set of V_s, which is an NP-hard problem [16]. Instead, we find the maximal independent set, which is an independent set where no node can be inserted without violating the independence. Since the S-Skeleton consists of 2-manifolds, the maximal independent set of the S-Skeleton nodes can be similarly constructed in a distributed fashion as given in [38]. As a result, any pair of independent nodes have a separation greater than one and smaller than three hops, as shown in Fig. 5 (d). One advantage of this procedure, as pointed out in [38], is to maintain the independent nodes uniformly distributed. Clearly, the independent nodes serves as sites which decompose the S-Skeleton nodes into Voronoi cells. With the Voronoi diagram, we can easily obtain its dual, the Delaunay triangulation, e.g., by the method in [38], and the S-Skeleton is thus generated, as shown in Fig. 1(d).

3.3 Complexity Analysis

THEOREM 3. *The proposed S-Skeleton extraction algorithm has a linear time and message complexity.*

PROOF. The algorithm has two steps: S-Skeleton node identification and S-Skeleton establishment. During the first step, each interior node only forwards a small number of packets, and thus in total the flooding from boundary nodes

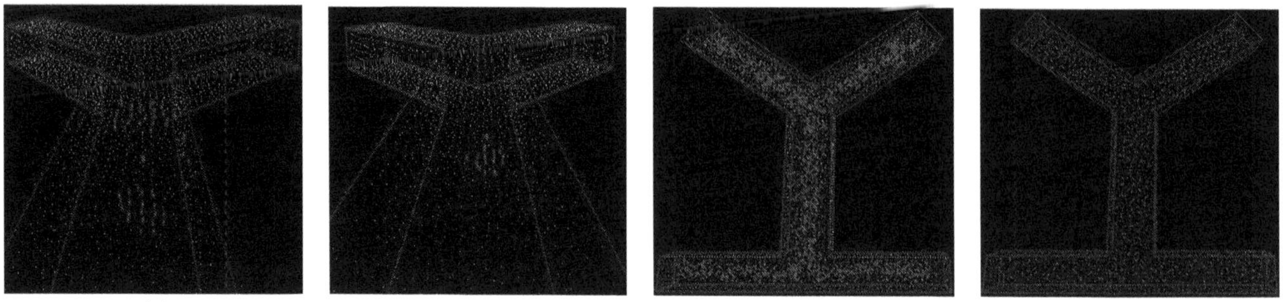

Figure 5: An illustration. (a) An S-Skeleton node (shown by the big red rectangle) with three feature node components (in blue); (b) A non-skeleton node (shown by the big red rectangle) with one feature node component; (c) The S-Skeleton nodes; (d) The maximal independent set of the S-Skeleton nodes.

incurs an $O(N)$(N is the number of sensors) time and message complexity. To compute the number of the connected components of the extended feature nodes, for each node, the algorithm only incurs at most $O(N_f)$ time and message complexity, and thus $O(N_f N)$ for all nodes, where $N_f(\ll N)$ denotes the largest number of extended feature nodes among all interior nodes. For the second step, the construction of the maximal independent set and the triangulation both incur a linear time and message complexity [38, 29]. In total, the algorithm has a linear complexity. □

3.4 Network Dynamics

As well known, wireless sensors networks are resource-constrained, and many factors can cause their failures. For instance, sensor nodes are fragile and may fail due to energy depletion or destruction by external events (e.g., natural disasters, adversarial attacks, etc. [2]), and congestion may also cause packet loss. Besides, occasionally some sensors may be added to the network for a better performance [29]. In other words, nodes/links may come and go [8], which consequently incurs the dynamics in the network topology. To show the performance of our algorithm under such harsh environments, we consider the S-Skeleton reconstruction problem for dynamic networks. When the network topology changes, the algorithm does not necessarily compute the S-Skeleton from scratch, which is otherwise time/message costly. Instead, as will be proven, the dynamic of the network topology will cause a local impact on the S-Skeleton, and thus only a local operation on the reconstruction of the S-Skeleton is conducted to speed up the reconstruction process.

We first present some results in continuous 3D space.

LEMMA 4. *A local deformation on the boundary surface of a 3D space only poses a local impact on the S-Skeleton .*

PROOF. Let x be an arbitrary S-Skeleton point. Then, x has at least two feature points. Suppose that the boundary surface deforms at a local surface, say, from LS to LS'. For an S-Skeleton point x, let $T(x)$,$T'(x)$ denote its distance transform before and after deformation, respectively. Generally, there are four cases:

1) **Case 1.** $T(x) = T'(x)$ and $F(x) \bigcap LS = \emptyset$. This means that no feature point of x in LS, and the deformation does not change $x's$ existing feature points because they are still at the minimum distance to x. Although some new feature point may lie in LS', but x has more than one feature point, and thus is still an S-Skeleton point.

2) **Case 2.** $T(x) = T'(x)$ and $F(x) \bigcap LS \neq \emptyset$. This means that at least one feature point lie in LS, and after the deformation, the feature size $|F(x)|$ decreases. If $|F(x)\backslash\{F(x)\bigcap LS\}| \geq 2$, then x is still an S-Skeleton point; otherwise, it is not.

3) **Case 3.** $T'(x) < T(x)$. This means that after deformation, x has the minimum distance to LS', and the new feature points $F'(x) = \{y \in LS' | d(x,y) = T'(x) = min_{y\in LS'} d(x,y)\}$. If $|F'(x)| \geq 2$, then x is still an S-Skeleton node; otherwise, it is not.

4) **Case 4.** $T'(x) > T(x)$. This means that all feature points of x lie in LS, and the boundary deforms such that the distance of the new boundary LS' to x is larger than $T(x)$. Clearly, x should re-identify its identity since after deformation, it is unclear whether $|F(x)| \geq 2$ or not.

In summary, if the S-Skeleton point x has at least one feature point in LS, and/or the deformation will change the distance transform of x, then x may re-identify its identity; otherwise, x remains an S-Skeleton point. Clearly, the affected S-Skeleton points are all within a small distance to LS or LS', thus the local deformation on the boundary surface will only have a local impact on the S-Skeleton. □

LEMMA 5. *The emergence of a new hole or tunnel has only a local impact on the S-Skeleton.*

PROOF. Clearly, the emergence of a new hole or tunnel will generate a new boundary. For an S-Skeleton point x, some feature points may disappear, while new feature points may appear at the new boundary. Thus, similar to Lemma 4, only the S-Skeleton points closest to the new boundary should re-identify their identities because of the change of distance transform, and thus the impact of the emergence of a new hole or tunnel on the S-Skeleton is local. □

Similarly, we have

LEMMA 6. *The disappearance of a hole or tunnel has only a local impact on the S-Skeleton.*

Lemma 4 to 6 imply that in sensor networks, the failure of boundary nodes [1] and interior nodes [2], and the insertion

[1]It will incur neighboring interior nodes to be new boundary nodes, and is thus a discrete analog of the boundary deformation in continuous space.

[2]It is a discrete analog of the emergence of a new hole or tunnel in continuous space.

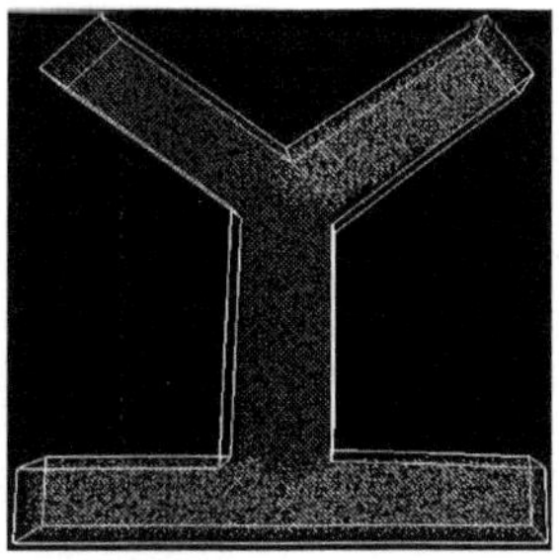

Figure 6: The segmentation result and the bounding box.

of new nodes into a void for better coverage [3] only have a local impact on the delivered S-Skeleton. Thus, we have

THEOREM 7. *The network dynamics caused by node failure or insertion have a local impact on the S-Skeleton.*

It can be easily shown that a non-skeleton node might become an S-Skeleton node due to the network dynamics such that the connectivity of the S-Skeleton is maintained and the genus can be preserved. Clearly, such a node must be near where the topology changes. Roughly speaking, if the distance transform of a node changes, its identity may change as well. Thus, we can narrow the S-Skeleton reconstruction down to the nodes whose distance transform change and the nodes whose feature nodes fail. When new S-Skeleton node identify themselves, and at the same time *old* S-Skeleton nodes give up their identities, we can easily reconstruct the S-Skeleton. Note that we do not necessarily reconstruct the S-Skeleton from scratch. In fact, we have

THEOREM 8. *The network dynamics affect S-Skeleton reconstruction locally.*

PROOF. When an old S-Skeleton node p fails, only the triangles containing p need to be reconstructed; if there is a new S-Skeleton node q nearest to an S-Skeleton node p, then q will not join the independent set otherwise the independence is violated, and there is no need to update the triangles. Hence, the impact of network dynamics on the S-Skeleton reconstruction is local. □

As such, only a local triangulation is conducted to form an updated S-Skeleton.

4. THE APPLICATION OF THE S-SKELETON FOR DATA STORAGE

As mentioned in Section 1, the S-Skeleton can be used to define a tight and simple bounding box, which can balance the storage node in GHT [26] and DIM [20].

Clearly, the bounding box should better be regular as the logical data space is often regular [29]. As such, our objective is to identify a small number of *critical boundary nodes* used to define a tight and simple bounding box. To that end, we first identify the boundary edge of the S-Skeleton which is not shared by any other triangles. The nodes on the boundary edges are boundary nodes (referred to as *S-boundary nodes*) of the S-Skeleton. Then we compute for each S-boundary node p its k-hop curvature, denoted by $c_k(p)$, which is defined below.

DEFINITION 4. *For an S-boundary node p, denote by $N_k(p)$ the nodes at most k hops away from p; let $p_1, p_2 \in N_k(p)$ be two S-boundary nodes such that the shortest paths between any two nodes of p_1, p_2, p will not pass through the S-Skeleton. Denote by $D_p^k(p_1, p_2)$ the set of nodes on the shortest path between p_1 and p_2 using the nodes in $N_k(p)$ (When $N_k(p)$ is disconnected, some auxiliary nodes can be used as in [25]). Then the k-hop curvature of node p, i.e., $c_k(p)$, is defined as*

$$c_k(p) = \frac{|D_p^k(p_1, p_2)| - 1}{\pi \times k} \quad (1)$$

With the k-hop curvature, we define the concave/convex node of the S-Skeleton (referred to as S-concave/S-convex node), as follows.

DEFINITION 5. *For the given $\delta_1, \delta_2 \in (0, 1)$ and k, an S-boundary node p is an S-convex node if $c_k(p) < 1 - \delta_1$, or an S-concave node if $c_k(p) > 1 + \delta_2$.*

Based on the identified S-concave nodes, the S-Skeleton can be decomposed into regular pieces by connecting nearby S-concave nodes. Then, S-Skeleton nodes flood within the network, and the nodes nearest to the same regular piece of the S-Skeleton naturally form a connected component. At the same time, each boundary node computes its distance (referred to as *local feature size*) to the S-Skeleton. The boundary nodes, whose nearest S-Skeleton nodes are S-convex/S-concave nodes and their local feature sizes are locally maximal, identify themselves as *critical convex/concave nodes*. As such, the bounding box is obtained where the vertices of the bounding box are critical convex nodes and critical concave nodes, and interestingly, the network is decomposed into regular components, as shown in Fig. 6.

With the computed bounding box, we first map each data item x produced by a node to a geographic location g in the sensing space bounded by the bounding box via a random hash function h, i.e., $h(x) = g$. Then the node nearest to the location g, referred to as home node, stores the data. Finally, similar to [5, 22, 24], we adopt the S-Skeleton based routing protocol as a low-level routing scheme for the producer to forward the data to the home node such that the traffic load is evenly distributed and the delivery can be guaranteed. For the robustness to node failures, we let the nodes *surrounding* the location g, referred to as *replica nodes*, also store the data. As the bounding box is tight, the sensing space can be divided into Voronoi cells with almost equally volume. Thus, the storage load of the nodes can be well balanced. We validate the proposed scheme by extensive simulations in Section 5.

5. SIMULATIONS

We conduct extensive simulation tests on various 3D scenarios to show the performance of the algorithm. In our simulations, sensor nodes are randomly deployed inside the underlying 3D space, and the boundary nodes are recognized by [14]. The parameter ϵ is set to be one by default. We do not compare with [34] since it requires high node density and nice tetrahedron mesh, as mentioned before, which are not

[3] If the insertion incurs the disappearance of a hole or tunnel, then it is a discrete analog of the disappearance of a hole or tunnel in continuous space; otherwise, a hole or tunnel shrinks, which is a discrete analog of the boundary deformation in continuous space.

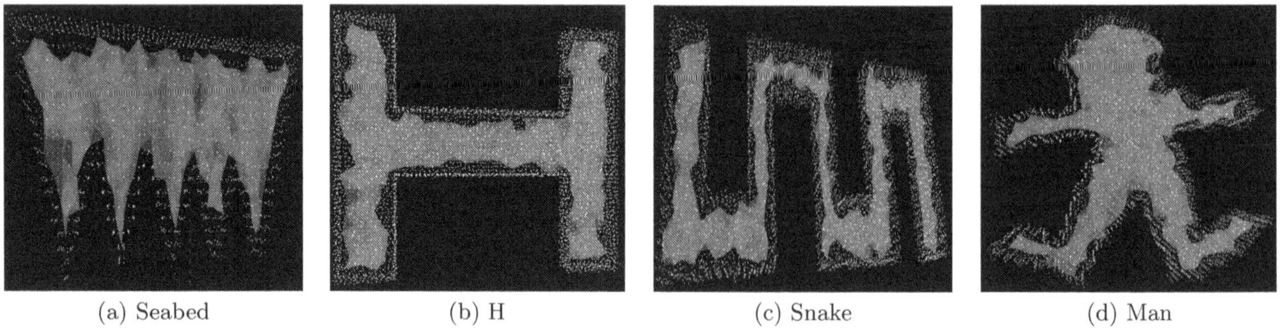

Figure 7: The performance under various 3D scenarios. The S-Skeletons are shaded. (a) 5,537 nodes, average node degree 15.37; (b) 16,156 nodes, average node degree 15.69; (c) 19,313 nodes, average node degree 15.78; (d) 15,288 nodes, average node degree 15.31.

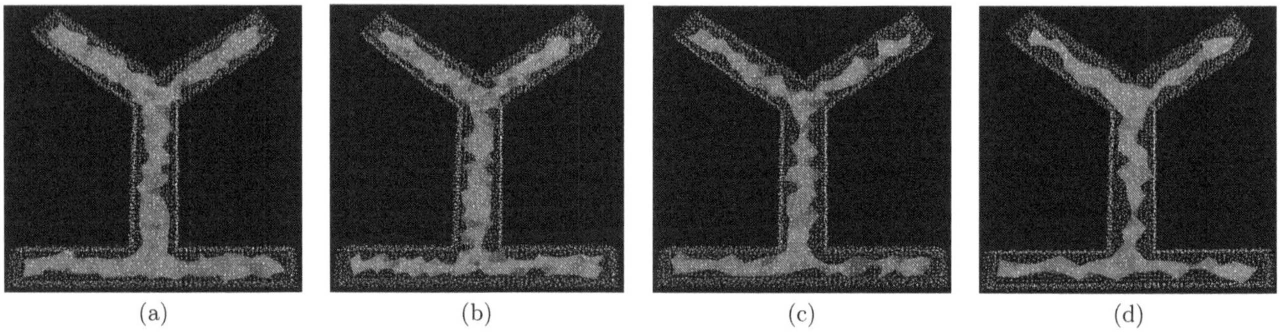

Figure 8: The performance under different node densities. (a) avg.deg 13.12; (b) avg.deg 17.38; (c) avg.deg 21.64; (d) avg.deg 24.76.

available in our settings where the average node degree are all in between 15 and 16, pretty low for 3D sensor networks. We first examine the robustness of the algorithm to shape variation and node density, and then test the performance under dynamic networks. Finally, we show the applicability of the S-Skeleton for data storage.

Robustness to shape variation. We conduct the proposed algorithm under difference scenarios, namely, Seabed, H, Man, and snake, as shown in Fig. 7, with network size ranging from 5,537 to 19,313 and average node degree in between 15 and 16. We can clearly see that the derived S-Skeletons in Fig. 7(a) to (d) correctly capture the main topological features, e.g., the irregularity, of the underlying networks, showing that our algorithm is robust to shape variation. Since the average node degree are all relatively low for 3D sensor networks, one can imagine that our algorithm can work for small-scale networks as well.

Robustness to node density. We vary the communication radio range to generate four networks with different node densities. Please see Fig. 8. Fig. 8(a) shows the result under low density, where the average node degree is only 13.12, below which the network becomes disconnected. We can observe that the extracted S-Skeleton correctly captures the salient features of the network. From Fig. 8(b) to (d), we can see that with the increasing of node density, the S-Skeleton becomes *thinner*, because less and less S-Skeleton nodes are joined to the maximal independent set, without violating the independence, for constructing the S-Skeleton. But overall our algorithm delivers a very stable result and the irregularity of the underlying network is correctly captured by the S-Skeleton, showing that our algorithm is robust to node density.

Algorithm	Y	H	Man	Snake	Seabed
Our algorithm	0.0058	0.0053	0.0057	0.0053	0.0057
Bottleneck	0.0111	0.0107	0.0079	0.0122	0.0067
Regular GHT	0.0124	0.0117	0.0109	0.0122	0.0107

Table 1: Comparison study on maximum storage load.

Reaction to network dynamics. We next show the performance of our algorithm under dynamic networks by allowing node failure and insertion. In Fig. 9(a), the blue nodes are *dead*, e.g., due to energy depletion. Compared with Fig. 1(c), the reconstructed S-Skeleton correctly reflects such a dynamic behavior by *moving* away from these failed nodes. In Fig. 9(b), some nodes are added to the network in the upper *valley* of the network, and there the S-Skeleton accordingly becomes *fatter* than Fig. 1(c) while the other remains the same.

Application for data storage. We apply the S-Skeleton to compute a tight and precise bounding box. As the storage of each node is proportional to the volume of the Voronoi cell generated by the node, we expect that our bounding box can guarantee a balanced storage load. To show its advantage, we compare our algorithm with Regular GHT [26], and the method in [37] (referred to as *Bottleneck*) which segments a 3D network by identifying bottlenecks, and then computes the bounding box of the network. No replica nodes are considered in the comparison study.

We propose three metrics, namely, *maximum storage load*, *standard deviation coefficient* and *loading ratio of a node*, to quantitatively measure how the storage load spreads across

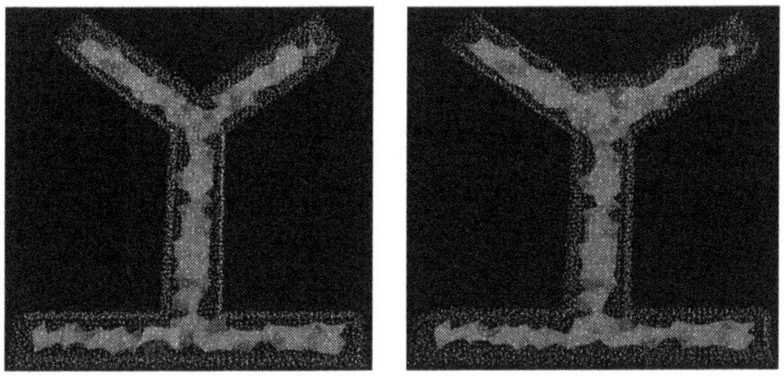

(a) (b)

Figure 9: The performance of the algorithm under dynamic networks. (a) The new S-Skeleton when some nodes (shown in blue) fail; (b) The new S-Skeleton when some nodes are inserted into the upper valley.

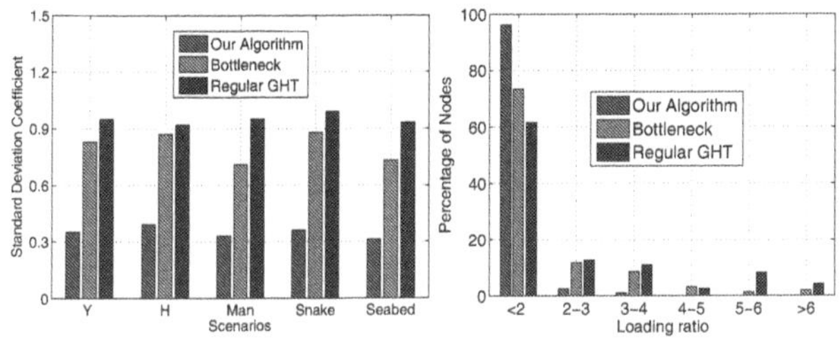

(a) (b)

Figure 10: The comparison study on storage load. (a) Standard deviation coefficient distribution; (b) Load ratio distribution.

the network. The maximum storage load is closely related to the maximum Voronoi cell volume, and the total storage load is normalized to be 1. The standard deviation coefficient (referred to *sdc*) of storage load, is defined as the ratio of the standard deviation of the storage load of nodes to their average. A smaller sdc means the loads are more evenly distributed while a larger sdc indicates that the distribution is more uneven, namely, the storage load is more imbalanced. The loading ratio of a node is the ratio of the storage load of a node to the average storage load of the network.

Table 1 depicts the comparison study on the maximum storage load for the five networks in Fig. 5 and Fig. 7. We observe that our algorithm outperforms the other two algorithms in the five networks. Especially, for Y, H and Snake-shaped networks, Bottleneck produces near the same maximum storage load as GHT since no bottlenecks are correctly identified and thus the bounding box is not accurately computed. In Man and Seabed-shaped networks, Bottleneck performs better than GHT because it identifies some bottlenecks and thus the bounding box is tighter than GHT, but Bottleneck performs worse than our algorithm since it ignores some concave points, e.g., at two *knees* of the Man-shaped network, resulting in an imprecise bounding box.

Fig. 10(a) presents the sdc distribution for the five networks by these algorithms. Clearly, we can see that our algorithm yields the smallest sdc for all networks, because the bounding box computed based on S-Skeleton tightly bound the network and no large voids exist; Regular GHT produces the worst result since the computed bounding box based on convex hull incurs large voids, resulting in that the boundary nodes are inevitably overloaded. As for Bottleneck, it identifies a few bottlenecks in the Man and Seabed-shaped networks, and thus the quality of the bounding boxes is fair. That is the reason why the sdc is relatively small. In the other three networks, however, there is no bottleneck identified and thus the result is undesirable.

Fig. 10(b) describes the load ratio distribution of the nodes in the investigated five networks by the three algorithms. As expected, our algorithm produces a near-ideal result, observing that over ninety percent of nodes have a loading ratio smaller than 2. Since the bounding box computed by our algorithm is tight and precise, the Vonoroi cell of each node has almost equal volume, and hence storage load can be evenly distributed. The result by Bottleneck is again fair where about seventy percent of nodes have a small load. But there do exist nodes having a large loading ratio (greater than 6), because some *concave points* are not identified. Thus, the computed bounding box possibly incurs *bridges* and voids. As a result, the nodes on the *pockets*, i.e., the boundary nodes surrounding the voids, are heavily loaded. Regular GHT produces a long-tailed loading ratio distribution where only near sixty percent of nodes have a small load ratio. Besides, five percent of nodes, mainly on the boundary of voids caused by the poorly computed bounding box, are overloaded. Overall, the load ratio distribution is skewed, implying that the storage load by Regular GHT is highly unbalanced. In summary, our algorithm outperforms the other two algorithms in terms of load balance.

6. CONCLUSION

We present a connectivity-based surface skeleton extraction algorithm in 3D sensor networks. The identification of skeleton node is based on the computation of the extended feature nodes such that it is robust against boundary noise, node density, and so on. To react to the dynamics of the sensor network caused by node failure or insertion, etc., we propose an efficient updating scheme to reconstruct the surface skeleton. We finally apply the surface skeleton to find a tight bounding box, which is then used for load-balanced data storage protocol. Extensive simulations are conducted to validate the performance of the proposed algorithm.

7. ACKNOWLEDGEMENTS

The authors thank the reviewers for their comments. This work was supported in part by the National Natural Science Foundation of China under Grant 61202460 and Grant 61271226; by the China Postdoctoral Science Foundation under Grant 2014M552044; by the Fok Ying Tung Education Foundation under Grant 132036; by the CCF-Tencent Foundation under Grant CCF-TencentAGR20130101; by the Fundamental Research Funds for the Central Universities under Grant 2014XJGH003, Grant 2014QN158 and Grant 2014QN164; by the Hong Kong Scholars Program under Grant XJ2012019; and by the Program for New Century Excellent Talents in University under Grant NCET-10-408 (State Education Ministry). The corresponding author is Hongbo Jiang.

8. REFERENCES

[1] D. Andrade, M. Resende, and R. Werneck. Fast local search for the maximum independent set problem. *Journal of Heuristics*, 18(4):525–547, 2012.

[2] N. Azimi, H. Gupta, X. Hou, and J. Gao. Data preservation under spatial failures in sensor networks. In *Proc. of ACM MOBIHOC*, 2010.

[3] H. Blum. Biological shape and visual science (part i). *Theoretical Biology*, 38:205–287, 1973.
[4] S. Bouix and K. Siddiqi. Divergence-based medial surfaces. In *Proc. of European Conference on Computer Vision*, 2000.
[5] J. Bruck, J. Gao, and A. A. Jiang. Map: Medial axis based geometric routing in sensor betworks. In *Proc. of ACM MOBICOM*, 2005.
[6] J. DAMON. Global medial structure of regions in r3. *Geometry and Topology*, 10:2385–2429, 2006.
[7] M. Doddavenkatappa, M. Chan, and A. Ananda. Indriya: a low-cost, 3d wireless sensor network testbed. In *Proc. of ICST Conference on Testbeds and Research Infrastructures for the Development of Networks and Communities(TRIDENTCOM)*, 2011.
[8] Q. Fang, J. Gao, L. Guibas, V. de Silva, and L. Zhang. Glider: Gradient landmark-based distributed routing for sensor networks. In *Proc. of IEEE INFOCOM*, 2005.
[9] Q. Fang, J. Gao, and L. J. Guibas. Landmark-based information storage and retrieval in sensor networks. In *Proc. of IEEE INFOCOM*, 2006.
[10] F.F.Leymarie and B.B.Kimia. Computation of the shock scaffold for unorganized point clouds in 3d. In *Proc. of IEEE Conference on Computer Vision and Pattern Recognition*, 2003.
[11] F.F.Leymarie and B.B.Kimia. The medial scaffold of 3d unorganized point clouds. *IEEE Transactions on Pattern Analysis and Machine Intelligence*, 29(2):313–330, 2007.
[12] H. Jiang, W. Liu, D. Wang, C. Tian, X. Bai, X. Liu, and W. Liu. Case: Connectivity-based skeleton extraction in wireless sensor networks. In *Proc. of IEEE INFOCOM*, 2009.
[13] H. Jiang, W. Liu, D. Wang, C. Tian, X. Bai, X. Liu, and W. Liu. Connectivity-based skeleton extraction in wireless sensor networks. *IEEE Transactions on Parallel and Distributed Systems*, 21(5):710–721, 2010.
[14] H. Jiang, S. Zhang, G. Tan, and C. Wang. Cabet: Connectivity-based boundary extraction of large-scale 3d sensor networks. In *Proc. of IEEE INFOCOM*, 2011.
[15] B. Karp and H. Kung. Gpsr: Greedy perimeter stateles routing for wireless networks. In *Proc. of ACM MOBICOM*, 2000.
[16] R. M. Karp. Reducibility among combinatorial problems. In *Complexity of Computer Computations*, The IBM Research Symposia Series, pages 85–103. 1972.
[17] S. Lederer, Y. Wang, and J. Gao. Connectivity-based localization of large scale sensor networks with complex shape. In *Proc. of IEEE INFOCOM*, 2008.
[18] F. Li, J. Luo, C. Zhang, S. Xin, and Y. He. Unfold: uniform fast on-line boundary detection for dynamic 3d wireless sensor networks. In *Proc. of ACM MOBIHOC*, 2011.
[19] M. Li, Y. Liu, J. Wang, and Z. Yang. Sensor network navigation without locations. In *Proc. of IEEE INFOCOM*, 2009.
[20] X. Li, Y. J. Kim, R. Govindan, and W. Hong. Multi-dimensional range queries in sensor networks. In *Proc. of ACM SenSys*, 2003.
[21] W. Liu, H. Jiang, X. Bai, G. Tan, C. Wang, and K. Cai. Distance transform-based skeleton extraction and its applications in sensor networks. *IEEE Transactions on Parallel and Distributed Systems*, 24(9):1763–1772, 2013.
[22] W. Liu, H. Jiang, X. Bai, G. Tan, C. Wang, W. Liu, and K. Cai. Skeleton extraction from incomplete boundaries in sensor networks based on distance transform. In *Proc. of IEEE ICDCS*, 2012.
[23] W. Liu, H. Jiang, C. Wang, C. Liu, Y. Yang, W. Liu, and B. Li. Connectivity-based and boundary-free skeleton extraction in sensor networks. In *Proc. of IEEE ICDCS*, 2012.
[24] W. Liu, H. Jiang, Y. Yang, and Z. jin. A unified framework for line-like skeleton extraction in 2d/3d sensor networks. In *Proc. of IEEE ICNP*, 2013.
[25] W. Liu, D. Wang, H. Jiang, W. Liu, and C. Wang. Approximate convex decomposition based localization in wireless sensor networks. In *Proc. of IEEE INFOCOM*, 2012.
[26] S. Ratnasamy, B. Karp, S. Shenker, D. Estrin, R. Govindan, L. Yin, and F. Yu. Data-centric storage in sensornets with ght, a geographic hash table. *Mobile Networks and Applications*, 8(4):427–442, 2003.
[27] D. Reniers and A. Telea. Segmenting simplified surface skeletons. In *Proc. of the 14th IAPR International Conference on Discrete Geometry for Computer Imagery*, 2008.
[28] D. Reniers, J. J. Wijk, and A.Telea. Computing multiscale curve and surface skeletons of genus 0 shapes using a global importance measure. *IEEE Transactions on Visualization and Computer Graphics*, 14(2):355–368, 2008.
[29] R. Sarkar, W. Zeng, J. Gao, and X. D. Gu. Covering space for in-network sensor data storage. In *Proc. of ACM/IEEE IPSN*, 2010.
[30] R. Sarkar, X. Zhu, and J. Gao. Double rulings for information brokerage in sensor networks. *IEEE/ACM Transactions on Networking*, 17(6):1902–1915, 2009.
[31] R. Tam and W. Heidrich. Shape simplification based on the medial axis transform. In *Proc. of IEEE Visualization Conference*, 2003.
[32] G. Tan, H. Jiang, S. Zhang, and A. Kermarrec. Connectivity-based and anchor-free localization in large-scale 2d/3d sensor networks. In *Proc. of ACM MOBIHOC*, 2010.
[33] G. Werner-Allen, P. Swieskowski, and M. Welsh. Motelab: a wireless sensor network testbed. In *Proc. of ACM/IEEE IPSN*, 2005.
[34] S. Xia, N. Ding, M. Jin, H. Wu, and Y. Yang. Medial axis construction and applications in 3D wireless sensor networks. In *Proc. of IEEE INFOCOM, mini-conference*, 2013.
[35] S. Xia, X. Yin, H. Wu, M. Jin, and X. Gu. Deterministic greedy routing with guaranteed delivery in 3d wireless sensor networks. In *Proc. of ACM MOBIHOC*, 2011.
[36] X. Yu, X. Yin, W. Han, J. Gao, and X. D. Gu. Scalable routing in 3D high genus sensor networks using graph embedding. In *Proc. of IEEE INFOCOM, mini-conference*, 2012.
[37] H. Zhou, N. Ding, M. Jin, S. Xia, and H. Wu. Distributed algorithms for bottleneck identification and segmentation in 3D wireless sensor networks. In *Proc. of IEEE SECON*, 2011.
[38] H. Zhou, M. Jin, and H. Wu. A distributed delaunay triangulation algorithm based on centroidal voronoi tessellation for wireless sensor networks. In *Proc. of ACM MOBIHOC*, 2013.
[39] D. Zhu, Q. Tao, J. Xing, Y. Wang, W. Liu, and H. Jiang. The extraction and evaluation of skeleton in sensor networks. In *Proc. of IEEE Ninth International Conference on Mobile Ad-hoc and Sensor Networks (MSN)*, 2013.
[40] X. Zhu, R. Sarkar, and J. Gao. Shape segmentation and applications in sensor networks. In *Proc. of IEEE INFOCOM*, 2007.

Wise Counting: Fast and Efficient Batch Authentication for Large-Scale RFID Systems

Wei Gong*†, Yunhao Liu*, Amiya Nayak†, Cheng Wang†
{gongwei,yunhao}@greenorbs.com, {nayak,cwan3}@uottawa.ca
*School of Software, TNLIST, Tsinghua University, China
†School of Electrical Engineering and Computer Science, University of Ottawa, Canada

ABSTRACT

Radio Frequency Identification technology (RFID) is widely used in many applications, such as asset monitoring, e-passport and electronic payment, and is becoming one of the most effective solutions in cyber physical system. Since the identification alone does not provide any guarantee that tag corresponds to genuine identity, authentication of tag information is needed in most RFID systems. Meanwhile, as the number of tags is rapidly growing in recent years, per-tag based methods suffer from severely low efficiency and thus give way to probabilistic batch authentication. Most previous methods, however, share a common drawback from statistical perspective: they fail to explore correlation information, i.e., they do not comprehensively utilize all the information in authentication data structures. In addition, those schemes are not scalable well when multiple tag sets need to be verified simultaneously. In this paper, we propose a fast and efficient batch authentication scheme, Wise Counting (WIC), for large-scale RFID systems. We are the first to formally introduce the general batch authentication problem with multiple tag sets and give counterfeits estimation scheme with high efficiency. By employing a novel hierarchical authentication structure, we show that WIC is able to fast and efficiently authenticate both a single tag set and multiple tag sets in an easy, intuitive way. Through detailed theoretical analysis and extensive simulations, we validate the design of WIC and demonstrate its large superiority over state-of-the art approaches.

Categories and Subject Descriptors

C.2.1 [**Network Architecture and Design**]: Wireless Communication; H.4 [**Information Systems Applications**]: Miscellaneous

Keywords

RFID tags, batch authentication, counterfeits estimation, hierarchical data structure

MobiHoc'14, August 11–14, 2014, Philadelphia, PA, USA.

http://dx.doi.org/10.1145/2632951.2632963 .

1. INTRODUCTION

Since *friend or foe* system was first developed in Second World War, Radio Frequency Identification (RFID) technology is widely used in many fields, such as asset monitoring[1][2][3], e-passport [4] and electronic payment [5][6], and is becoming one of the most effective solutions in cyber physical system [7][8][9]. A typical RFID system mainly consists of three parts: tag, reader and backend server. The tag, which is often attached to the object, contains a unique identification - Electronic Product Code (EPC) [10]. The reader is usually in charge of identification, i.e., querying the tag and collecting the information from it. The backend server that is connected to the reader can perform various operations, such as searching further object information according to specific EPC. But identification itself does not provide any means to certainly assure that the collected ID/EPC exactly corresponds to the genuine identity. Therefore, tag authentication (or verification) is indeed necessary.

Previously, much work focus on how to securely and effectively authenticate a single tag. Supposed that there are N tags registered in backend server. By leveraging the one-way hash function, Hash Lock scheme is proposed to linearly search the backend database [11]. The authentication complexity of it is $\mathcal{O}(N)$. To achieve better performance, the search efficiency is improved to $\mathcal{O}(\log N)$ based on tree data structure, at the expense of storage spaces on tag [12][13]. Nevertheless, those per-tag based approaches suffer from severe scalability problem in batch authentication mode. As stated in [14], one reader can only authenticate 103 batches (each with 10,000 tags) per day. It is unlikely to accept such a low authentication efficiency in practice. Meanwhile, as RFID technology is used as one of the most important anti-counterfeiting measures for fast-moving consumer goods that are growing fast over years [15], the population of tags is expected to dramatically increase in the next few years. Thus one of top concerns for practical large-scale RFID systems is how to efficiently authenticate tags in batch.

The key advantage of batch authentication over per-tag based methods is the relaxation of the result, i.e., trading a small authentication failure probability for better authentication performance. So we also call it probabilistic batch authentication. There are two different but close-related probabilistic batch authentication problems: counterfeits detection and counterfeits estimation. In counterfeits detection problem, the result of authentication is binary. For example, in [14], positive result means detection of counterfeits. Negative result indicates that all tags in the batch are judged

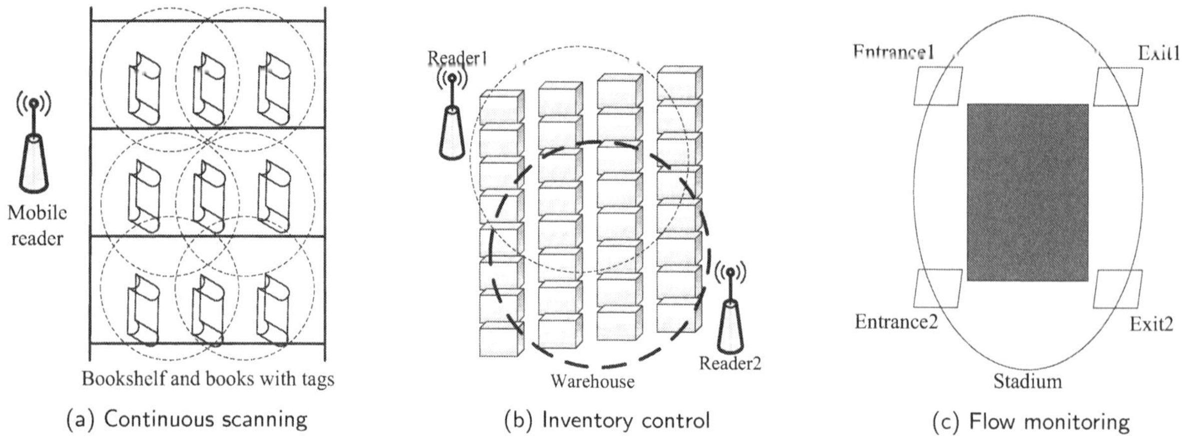

Figure 1: Scenarios of authenticating multiple tag sets

as legitimate with high probability. Obviously, this type of result is so coarse since it is unable to discriminate a batch with only one counterfeit tag from a batch with all fake tags. In fact, many RFID applications need to know more detailed information about counterfeits. Consequently, a fine-grained authentication scheme is proposed to approximate the count of counterfeit tags, addressing counterfeits estimation issue [16]. Although these two problems are separated, they are complementary to each other. Typically, the administrator of RFID system first performs counterfeits detection operation. If the result turns out to be positive, then counterfeits estimation algorithm can be used to obtain an accurate count of counterfeits. In this paper, we aim to efficiently solve counterfeits estimation problem with arbitrary accuracy requirements.

By reviewing former methods from statistical perspective, we observe two important issues that are neglected before. First, they view authentication synopses as separate entities and thus do not explore correlation information among them [14][16]. Second, the estimation is confined on singleton-observed synopses which account for a relative small fraction, wasting a large amount of other authentication synopses [16]. In sum, counterfeits estimators in previous work are not statistically efficient since they do not comprehensively utilize all the information in authentication structures, giving plenty of rooms for authentication efficiency optimization. More importantly, most previous methods are designed for authenticating one single batch at a time. But in practice, it would always be required to authenticate multiple tag sets/batches simultaneously.

In this paper, we propose a fast and efficient batch authentication scheme, Wise Counting (WIC), for large-scale RFID systems. First, we formally formulate the general counterfeits estimation problem for probabilistic batch authentication with multiple tag sets. Then, we introduce a novel hierarchical authentication structure, which combines uniform random hash and minimum order statistics. With the help of this building block data structure, WIC achieves $\mathcal{O}(\frac{N}{\varepsilon^2|C|}\log\log N)$ authentication complexity (communication complexity), where $|C|$ is the number of counterfeits from multiple tag sets and ε is the desired relative error. Through detailed analysis and extensive simulated comparison, we show that WIC is significantly advantageous over previous methods.

The major contributions of this work are as follows.

1. We are the first to define batch authentication problem with multiple tag sets and provide a fast and efficient authentication scheme, WIC, which works well with one or more tag sets.

2. We design a novel hierarchical authentication structure to significantly reduce authentication and communication overheads. In particular, WIC wisely utilize all minimum order statistics of this data structure to obtain much more accurate counterfeits estimate, compared with previous methods. We also give a general and implementable communication protocol for both readers and tags using WIC.

3. We validate the design of WIC through both theoretical analysis and extensive simulations. We also show that WIC is effective and significantly outperforms state-of-the-art approaches.

2. PRELIMINARIES

2.1 Motivation

Previous work on batch authentication are designed for simple scenario in which only one tag set needs to be verified. Authenticating multiple tag sets, however, are required in many practical and complex scenarios to meet various demands. Considering the following three examples as shown in Figure 1:

1. **Continuous scanning** is a common and basic method in large-scale RFID system [17][18][19]. It uses multiple continuous scanning operations to cover a much larger area than a single scanning. Figure 1(a) shows that a mobile reader performs scanning several times to collect all book information on the bookshelf. In order to authenticate all books, we need to verify compound set as: $R = R_1 \cup R_2 \cup ... \cup R_n$, where R_i is the set of scanned tags in i-th scanning.

2. **Inventory control** generally employs multiple static readers deployed at different locations, according to

density, size and orientation of objects in warehouse [20][21][22]. As illustrated in Figure 1(b), Reader1 and Reader2 are deployed to cover all goods in the warehouse. If we want to authenticate the goods that both covered by Reader1 and Reader2, then the compound set $R = R_1 \cap R_2$ needs to be tested, where R_1 and R_2 are the sets of tags scanned by Reader1 and Reader2 respectively.

3. **Flow monitoring** is essential for many large-scale events for security reason, such as rallies, conferences and sport games [23]. Figure 1(c) demonstrates an example in stadium with 2 entrances and 2 exits. A reader is equipped at each gate to monitor people flow passing by and the person who holds a genuine tagged-ticket is authorized to go in and out unlimited times. If administrator needs to estimate the number of unauthorized audiences in the stadium, the compound set $R = (R_1 \cup R_2) - (R_3 \cup R_4)$ needs to be authenticated, where R_1, R_2, R_3 and R_4 are the sets of tags scanned by Entrance1, Entrance1, Exit1 and Exit2, respectively.

2.2 Challenges

Estimating the number of counterfeits in multiple tag sets at the same time is an important but not trivial problem in large-scale RFID systems. Since multiple tag sets might have intersections as shown in Figure 1, it cannot be easily reduced to estimate the counterfeits number one set by one set. Of course, there is a naive way to authenticate multiple tag set: first aggregate all raw tag information on server from each scanning/set, then compute the compound set according to required set expression, finally authenticate the compound set. Although this naive method works, it violates several principles that we strive to. First, the authentication process should be fast and time-efficient, i.e., the communication overhead should be kept minimum. Second, the raw tag information transmission is better to be avoided since it may create potentials for infringements of RFID data privacy [24].

2.3 Problem Formulation

In a typical RFID system, the backend server often registers a number of tags which are said to be legal. Let $\mathcal{S}$ be the set of all legitimate tags on server and N be the cardinality of $\mathcal{S}$. Usually, there are $\mathcal{T}_1$, $\mathcal{T}_2$, ..., $\mathcal{T}_l$ tag sets to be verified, where l is an integer more than 1. In many scenarios (e.g., using multiple readers to cover a large area), the system administrator needs to know how many counterfeit tags in the compound expressions of $\mathcal{T}_i$. We therefore generalize this as

$$\mathcal{T}' = \mathcal{T}_1 \odot \mathcal{T}_2 \odot \dots \odot \mathcal{T}_l,$$

where $\mathcal{T}'$ is the final compound set to be verified, and $\odot$ can be replaced by any one of $-$ (difference), $\cup$ (union), and $\cap$ (intersection).

Moreover, we define that the tag is counterfeit if the tag's information is not registered on the server. Otherwise, the tag is genuine. Similar to most prior work [14][16][25], *we do not discuss the problem the genuine tag is attached to counterfeit goods, vice versa.* Any problems related to tag misplacement/duplication are beyond the scope of this paper. Further, we assume that both genuine and counterfeit tags obey the same transmission protocol. By the definition

Table 1: Main Notations

Symbols	Descriptions
$\mathcal{S}$	the set of registered tags.
$\mathcal{T}$	the set of tags to be verified.
$\mathcal{C}$	the set of counterfeits tags.
$\mathcal{G}$	the set of genuines tags.
N	the cardinality of tags registered on server
n	the cardinality of tags to be verified
M	the cardinality of $\mathcal{T} \cup \mathcal{S}$.
f	the size of frame.
c	the counterfeit ratio.
$\lvert\rvert$	the cardinality of set.
$\hat{}$	the estimate of original parameter.
$\mathcal{A}^{\mathcal{T}}$	the HAS of set $\mathcal{T}$.

of counterfeits, we use $\mathcal{C}$ to denote the set of counterfeits to be verified, thus

$$\mathcal{C} = \mathcal{T}' - \mathcal{S}.$$

The counterfeits estimation in probabilistic batch authentication is to obtain the approximate cardinality of $\mathcal{C}$, i.e., $|\mathcal{C}|$. In order to measure the accuracy of estimation result, we use two parameters: relative standard error ε and failure probability δ. Thereby the result of counterfeits estimation, $|\hat{\mathcal{C}}|$, must satisfy

$$\Pr\left[\left|\frac{|\mathcal{C}|}{|\hat{\mathcal{C}}|} - 1\right| \leq \varepsilon\right] \geq 1 - \delta. \quad (1)$$

For instance, if the exact number of counterfeits is 100, and $\varepsilon = 0.01, \delta = 0.01$, then the output estimate $|\hat{\mathcal{C}}|$ should be between 99 to 101 with probability 0.99. Similarly, we use $\mathcal{G}$ to denote the set of genuines in verified sets. The main notations are listed in Table 1.

2.4 Communication Model

We adopt the listen-before-talk mode and frame slotted ALHOA as the basic communication model, similar to [16][26]. In this model, the reader first queries tags with several predefined commands and parameters. Each tag then performs computations on board and decides whether and what to reply to reader based on preloaded transmission protocol. Besides EPC code, each tag has its own random hash function $\mathcal{H}$ or random number generator that takes several input parameters, e.g., frame size, EPC code [27].

3. WISE COUNTING OVERVIEW

Wise Counting is an efficient probabilistic batch authentication scheme that provides accurate counterfeits estimate, achieving optimal authentication efficiency.

Following a common practice in RFID authentication, the backend server has stored all the information of registered tags. When authentication starts, the backend server initializes parameters according to the user defined requirements, ε and δ. Then the server sends those parameters to readers through a secure line. The readers use those received parameters to gather authentication information from tags

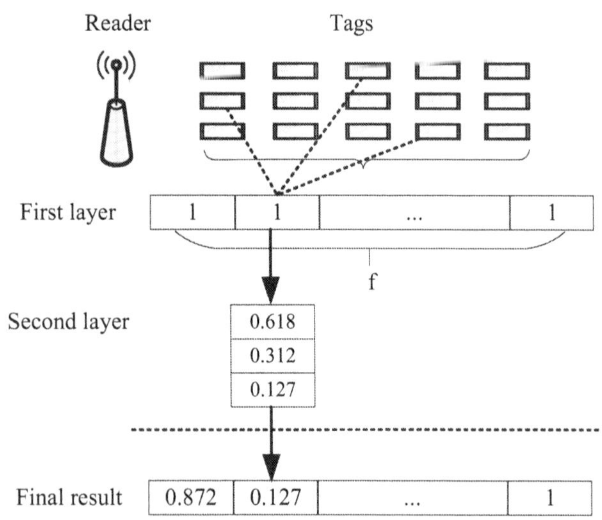

Figure 2: Hierarchical authentication structure generation.

to be verified. After aggregating all the authentication information from readers, the server performs verification to derive counterfeits estimate.

With a novel Hierarchical Authentication Structure (HAS) as later shown in Section 4, WIC goes through the following main steps:

1. The reader queries the tags in the operation range and builds its own HAS ($\mathcal{A}^{\mathcal{T}_i}$) for $\mathcal{T}_i$.

2. The server aggregates HASes from readers and derives observed counterfeits ratio based on the compound set expression.

3. The server estimates the cardinality of $\mathcal{T}' \cup \mathcal{S}$ ($|\widehat{\mathcal{T}' \cup \mathcal{S}}|$). Since $\mathcal{C}$ is a portion of $\mathcal{T}' \cup \mathcal{S}$, then we combine the observed counterfeits ratio and $|\widehat{\mathcal{T}' \cup \mathcal{S}}|$ to deduce the counterfeits estimate, $|\hat{\mathcal{C}}|$.

The next few sections elaborate on the above steps and provide detailed analysis.

4. DATA STRUCTURE

In this section, we describe how to generate hierarchical authentication structure from the tag set and then give the basic estimation formula.

Here we employ uniform random hash and minimum order statistics to produce HAS. As shown in Figure 2, initially the reader issues the query command to tags. Each tag then decides when (in which time slot) and what to reply according to received parameters, such as frame size (f) and random seed. The reply procedure is based on slotted ALOHA model and is virtually divided into two layers. In the first layer, each tag chooses replied time slot based on a uniform random hash function, similar to much prior work [14][25][26]. At the reader side, all slots are marked as 1. In the second layer, each tag replies a uniform random number, $R(EPC)$, between [0,1]. At the same time, the reader receives all the random numbers from tag(s) and records only

Algorithm 1 HAS generation algorithm for the tag

Receive a probing message from reader, containing frame size f and random seed r.
Compute reply slot number $sn = \mathcal{H}(EPC, f, r)$.
while TRUE **do**
  wait-for-slot-start().
  if $sn == 0$ **then**
    generate random number $R(EPC)$.
    RepMinRndProc(R).
  else
    $sn \leftarrow sn - 1$, keep silent.
  end if
end while

Algorithm 2 HAS generation algorithm for the reader

Initialize $\mathcal{A}^{\mathcal{T}}[i] \leftarrow 1.0$ $(1 \le i \le f)$;
Broadcast a request to tags, including frame size f and random seed r.
for $i = 1$ to f **do**
  issue-slot-start() command.
  wait-for-tags-response().
  if there is no response in this slot **then**
    $\mathcal{A}^{\mathcal{T}}[i] \leftarrow 1$.
  else
    $\mathcal{A}^{\mathcal{T}}[i] \leftarrow$**RecMinRndProc**().
  end if
end for

the minimum number. In order to understand the principle of HAS, we are better to set aside possible collisions and just assume that the reader is able to extract minimum number from many tags' responses in one time slot. The details about the generation of replied random number on tag and reception of minimum random number on reader are given in Section 6. The final HAS consists of f numbers. If the number is 1, it stands for no response in this time slot. Otherwise, the number is the minimum of all responses in this time slot. The pseudocodes of HAS generation are given in Algorithm 1 for the tag and Algorithm 2 for the reader.

Let n be the number of tags in tested set ($\mathcal{T}$) and $\lambda = \frac{n}{f}$ be the mean number of tags' responses in each slot. We generate authentication synopsis $\mathcal{A}^{\mathcal{T}}[i]$ where $i = 1, 2, ..., f$ using Algorithm 1 and 2. We then study the characteristic of $\mathcal{A}^{\mathcal{T}}[i]$ and find that if f is sufficiently large such that $(1-\frac{1}{f})^f \approx \frac{1}{e}$, then $\mathcal{A}^{\mathcal{T}}[i]$ approximates an independent sample from right truncated exponential distribution with rate parameter λ, where the cumulative distribution function is as follow [1]

$$F(x;\lambda) \approx \begin{cases} 1 - e^{-\lambda x} & 0 \le x \le 1 \\ 0 & x < 0 \text{ or } x > 1 \end{cases}$$

and the correlation coefficient (ρ) of $\mathcal{A}^{\mathcal{T}}[i]$ and $\mathcal{A}^{\mathcal{T}}[j]$ is

$$\rho(\mathcal{A}^{\mathcal{T}}[i], \mathcal{A}^{\mathcal{T}}[j]) \approx -\frac{1}{n}, i \ne j.$$

Therefore, we are able to easily obtain the MLE estimator of λ. Since the dependence between $\mathcal{A}^{\mathcal{T}}[i]$ and $\mathcal{A}^{\mathcal{T}}[j]$ is so weak, we ignore it and get the simplified likelihood function

[1]Due to limited space, we omit derivations/proofs here and the rest of this paper.

of λ as

$$\mathcal{L}(\lambda) = e^{-\lambda \sum_{i=1}^{f} \mathbf{1}(\mathcal{A}^{\mathcal{T}}[i])} \prod_{\mathcal{A}^{\mathcal{T}}[i]<1} \lambda e^{-\lambda \mathcal{A}^{\mathcal{T}}[i]}.$$

where $\mathbf{1}(x)$ is an indicator function. If $x = 1$, $\mathbf{1}(x) = 1$. Otherwise, $\mathbf{1}(x) = 0$. The MLE of λ and thereby estimated number of tags in $\mathcal{A}^{\mathcal{T}}$ are derived as

$$\hat{\lambda} = \frac{\sum_{i=1}^{f} \mathbf{1}'(\mathcal{A}^{\mathcal{T}}[i])}{\sum_{i=1}^{f} \mathcal{A}^{\mathcal{T}}[i]}, \hat{n} = f\hat{\lambda}. \quad (2)$$

where $\mathbf{1}'(x)$ is an indicator function. If $x < 1$, $\mathbf{1}'(x) = 1$. Otherwise, $\mathbf{1}'(x) = 0$.

In order to understand the simplicity of the estimation procedure, let's see a toy example. Suppose that we test a tag set ($n = 100$) and get a HAS of size 7: 0.0768, 0.0183, 1, 0.0307, 0.0125, 0.1642, 0.1217. The estimated result $\hat{n} = 7 * \frac{6}{0.0768+0.0183+0.0307+0.0125+0.1642+0.1217} = 99$.

5. ESTIMATING COUNTERFEITS AND GENUINES

After acquiring basic knowledge about our authentication data structure, now we first demonstrate our method to estimate the number of counterfeits and genuines in single set scenario. Later we introduce several techniques to extend estimation over compound sets.

5.1 Authenticating Single RFID Set

We first study an important characteristic of the probabilistic distribution for truncated exponential random variable.

Given $X_1 \sim Exp(\lambda_1)$, $X_2 \sim Exp(\lambda_2)$, and their corresponding right truncated distribution $X_1{}' = \min(X_1, 1)$, $X_2{}' = \min(X_2, 1)$. If X_1 is independent of X_2, then we have $\min(X_1{}', X_2{}') \sim \min(Exp(\lambda_1 + \lambda_2), 1)$. Further, we derive

$$\Pr[X_i{}' = \min(X_1{}', X_2{}')] = e^{-(\lambda_1+\lambda_2)} + \frac{\lambda_i}{\lambda_1 + \lambda_2}(1 - e^{-(\lambda_1+\lambda_2)}) \quad (3)$$

, where $i = 1, 2$.

This characteristic tells us that if two exponential random variables are independent of each other, then minimum order of their truncated version is easily deduced.

Now we have only one set to be verified, $\mathcal{T}$, and aim to estimate $|\mathcal{T} - \mathcal{S}|$. The direct application of above equation is to divide the union, $\mathcal{T} \cup \mathcal{S}$, into three independent parts: $\mathcal{T} - \mathcal{S}$, $\mathcal{T} \cap \mathcal{S}$, and $\mathcal{S} - \mathcal{T}$. We use $\mathcal{B}_1$, $\mathcal{B}_2$, $\mathcal{B}_3$ to denote virtual HASes for those three independent sets. Therefore we have [2]

$$\begin{aligned} \Pr[\mathcal{A}^{\mathcal{T}} = \mathcal{A}^{\mathcal{S}}] &= \Pr[\min(\mathcal{B}_1, \mathcal{B}_2) = \min(\mathcal{B}_2, \mathcal{B}_3)] \\ &= \Pr[\mathcal{B}_2 = \min(\mathcal{B}_1, \mathcal{B}_2, \mathcal{B}_3)] \\ &\approx e^{-\frac{M}{f}} + (1 - e^{-\frac{M}{f}})\frac{|\mathcal{T} \cap \mathcal{S}|}{M}. \end{aligned}$$

where M is the cardinality of $\mathcal{T} \cup \mathcal{S}$. We thus derive the estimation equations for the number of counterfeits and genuines in single set scenario as follows.

[2]We omit [i] for each HAS in the equation to simplify the presentation in the following.

THEOREM 1. *For a large f such that $(1 - \frac{1}{f})^f \approx \frac{1}{e}$, then*

$$|\hat{\mathcal{C}}| = |\widehat{\mathcal{T} - \mathcal{S}}| = \Pr'[\mathcal{A}^{\mathcal{T}} < \mathcal{A}^{\mathcal{S}}] \cdot \frac{\hat{M}}{(1 - e^{-\frac{\hat{M}}{f}})} \quad (4)$$

$$|\hat{\mathcal{G}}| = |\widehat{\mathcal{T} \cap \mathcal{S}}| = (\Pr'[\mathcal{A}^{\mathcal{T}} = \mathcal{A}^{\mathcal{S}}] - e^{-\frac{\hat{M}}{f}}) \cdot \frac{\hat{M}}{(1 - e^{-\frac{\hat{M}}{f}})} \quad (5)$$

, where $\Pr'$ denotes observed probability in $\mathcal{A}^{\mathcal{T}}$ and $\mathcal{A}^{\mathcal{S}}$.

The common unknown parameter in above two equations is $\hat{M}$. Fortunately, the HAS of $\mathcal{T} \cup \mathcal{S}$, $\mathcal{A}^{\mathcal{T} \cup \mathcal{S}}$, is just the slot-wise $\min(\mathcal{A}^{\mathcal{T}}[i], \mathcal{A}^{\mathcal{S}}[i])$. It is easy to obtain $\hat{M}$ by applying equation 2 on $\mathcal{A}^{\mathcal{T} \cup \mathcal{S}}$. Further, if $\hat{M}$ is large enough that $e^{-\frac{\hat{M}}{f}}$ is close to 0, we derive simplified theorem 1 as

$$|\hat{\mathcal{C}}| = \Pr'[\mathcal{A}^{\mathcal{T}} < \mathcal{A}^{\mathcal{S}}] \cdot \hat{M} \quad (6)$$

$$|\hat{\mathcal{G}}| = \Pr'[\mathcal{A}^{\mathcal{T}} = \mathcal{A}^{\mathcal{S}}] \cdot \hat{M} \quad (7)$$

5.2 Extension to Multiple RFID Sets

In many practical situations, we need to verify how many counterfeits are in the compound set

$$\mathcal{T}' = \mathcal{T}_1 \bigodot \mathcal{T}_2 \bigodot \ldots \bigodot \mathcal{T}_l$$

, where $l \geq 1$, i.e., estimating $|\mathcal{C}| = |\mathcal{T}' - S|$. Still, let M be the cardinality of union, $\mathcal{T}' \cup \mathcal{S}$. The estimation procedure is composed of three steps. We will illustrate each step with a concrete example. Consider $\mathcal{T}' = (\mathcal{T}_1 \cap \mathcal{T}_2) \cup \mathcal{T}_3$.

Step one: Use relation $|A - B| = |A| - |A \cap B|$ to remove all set difference operator(s). In our example,

$$|(\mathcal{T}_1 \cap \mathcal{T}_2) \cup \mathcal{T}_3 - S| = |(\mathcal{T}_1 \cap \mathcal{T}_2) \cup \mathcal{T}_3| - |((\mathcal{T}_1 \cap \mathcal{T}_2) \cup \mathcal{T}_3) \cap S|$$

Step two: Use relation $(A \cap B) \cup C = (A \cup C) \cap (B \cup C)$ to replace union of set intersection by the intersection of set union. In our example,

$$|(\mathcal{T}_1 \cap \mathcal{T}_2) \cup \mathcal{T}_3| = |(\mathcal{T}_1 \cup \mathcal{T}_3) \cap (\mathcal{T}_2 \cup \mathcal{T}_3)|$$

and

$$|((\mathcal{T}_1 \cap \mathcal{T}_2) \cup \mathcal{T}_3) \cap S| = |(\mathcal{T}_1 \cup \mathcal{T}_3) \cap (\mathcal{T}_2 \cup \mathcal{T}_3) \cap S|$$

.

Step three: Let c be the ratio of counterfeits to the all sets union, i.e., $c = \frac{|\mathcal{C}|}{M}$. In order to get this counterfeits ratio, we first simply extended the theorem 1 to get the following equation:

$$\Pr[\mathcal{A}^{\mathcal{T}_0} = \mathcal{A}^{\mathcal{T}_1} = \ldots = \mathcal{A}^{\mathcal{T}_d} = \mathcal{A}_{\cup}] \approx e^{-\frac{M}{f}} + \frac{(1 - e^{-\frac{M}{f}})}{M} |\bigcap_{j=0}^{d} \mathcal{T}_j|$$

, where $\mathcal{A}_{\cup}$ is the HAS of $\bigcup_{i=0}^{l} \mathcal{T}_i$, $\mathcal{T}_0 = \mathcal{S}$, $|\bigcup_{i=0}^{l} \mathcal{T}_i| = M$ and $1 \leq d \leq l$. [3]

In our example, we thus have

$$c = P1 - P2 \quad (8)$$

[3]Here we assume $e^{-\frac{M}{f}}$ is close to 0 and f is large enough such that $(1 - \frac{1}{f})^f \approx \frac{1}{e}$. In case it is not negligible, we then invert equations theorem 1 to derive the closed-form solution.

Algorithm 3 Reply minimal random value for tag: **RepMinRndProc()**

```
generate a random number R(EPC) from unit exponential distribution EXP.
Save integer part of R into j = log log N bits, as I[0] ~ I[j − 1], position 0 is the highest bit.
Truncate decimal part of R into k = 10 bits, as I[j] ~ I[j + k − 1], position j is the highest bit.
Initialize T[i] ← 0, 1 ≤ i < log log N + 10.
i ← 0 and wait-for-subslot-start().
for i = 0 to j + k − 1 do
  wait-for-subslot-continue().
  while TRUE do
    Receive bit 'b' and T[i] ← b.
    if b == 1 then
      if prefix i bits of T is equal to I then
        instantly issue response and break while loop.
      else
        keep silent.
      end if
    end if
    if b == 0 then
      break while loop.
    end if
  end while
end for
```

where $P1 = \Pr[\min(\mathcal{A}^{\mathcal{T}_1}, \mathcal{A}^{\mathcal{T}_3}) = \min(\mathcal{A}^{\mathcal{T}_2}, \mathcal{A}^{\mathcal{T}_3}) = \mathcal{A}_{\cup}]$, $P2 = \Pr[\min(\mathcal{A}^{\mathcal{T}_1}, \mathcal{A}^{\mathcal{T}_3}) = \min(\mathcal{A}^{\mathcal{T}_2}, \mathcal{A}^{\mathcal{T}_3}) = \mathcal{A}^{\mathcal{T}_0} = \mathcal{A}_{\cup}]$.

Finally, by the definition of c, the estimated number of counterfeits for multiple tag sets is

$$|\hat{\mathcal{C}}| = \hat{M} \cdot c'. \qquad (9)$$

where $\hat{M}$ is obtained by simply applying equation 2 on $\mathcal{A}_{\cup}$ and c' is the observed ratio in equation 8.

6. THE EFFICIENCY OF WISE COUNTING

In this section, we analyze the time complexity of WIC and propose an optimization based on the exponential pseudorandom number generator.

6.1 Time Complexity

For an arbitrary set expression of tag sets to be verified, the relative standard error of WIC can be derived as :

$$\mathrm{RSE}^2_{wic} = \mathrm{E}(\frac{|\hat{\mathcal{C}}|_{WIC}}{|\mathcal{C}|} - 1)^2 \approx (fc)^{-1}.$$

Therefore if ε is the required relative error, the size of frame should be $f \approx \varepsilon^{-2}c^{-1}$ for HAS generation in the first layer. [4]

For the second layer in HAS generation, we need to derive the number of subslots for transmitting the minimal random number. From section 4, we know that $\mathcal{A}^{\mathcal{T}}[i]$ follows a truncated exponential distribution: $\mathcal{A}^{\mathcal{T}}[i] \sim \min(\frac{\mathrm{EXP}}{\lambda}, 1)$, where EXP is the unit exponential variable.

Since we know there may be M tags' responses in a single slot at worse and $\lambda \sim \mathcal{O}(M)$. This indicates that $\mathcal{O}(\log M)$ bits need to be transmitted in a single slot. In the following, we reduce this transmit time by employing an exponential pseudorandom number generator to replace the uniform random number generator described in Section 4.

[4]For simplicity, we do not include the analysis of δ in the rest part of this paper. Since it is well-known [28] that if we are able to achieve a constant δ, we can repeat the process $\mathcal{O}(\log \frac{1}{\delta'})$ times to achieve arbitrary δ'.

Algorithm 4 Receive minimal random value for reader: **RecMinRndProc()**

```
Initialize T[i] ← 0, 1 ≤ i < log log N + 10.
issue-subslot-start() command.
for i = 0 to log log N + 9 do
  issue-subslot-continue() command
  Broadcast bit '1' and wait-for-tags-response().
  if there is no response in this subslot then
    T[i] ← 0. Broadcast bit '0'.
  else
    T[i] ← 1.
  end if
end for
combine T's integer and decimal part into a float m.
return minimal value 2^(−m).
```

Now we take log operation on $\mathcal{A}^{\mathcal{T}}[i]$ to have: $\log \mathcal{A}^{\mathcal{T}}[i] \sim \min(-\log\lambda + \log \mathrm{EXP}, 0)$. This motivates us to use $(\log\log M + \alpha)$ bits for transmission, where $-\log\log M$ represents integer part and α denotes decimal part. Hence the total time complexity of WIC is $\varepsilon^{-2}c^{-1}(\log\log M + \alpha)$.

We observed that $\alpha = 10$ is enough in practice. For instance, if we need to verified $\mathcal{T}_1$, then the observed probability for $\Pr[\mathcal{T}_0 = \mathcal{T}_1 = \mathcal{T}_{\cup}]$ is at most $2^{-\alpha+1} = 0.002$ shifted from ground truth. This difference is negligible for many applications. Actually the value of α is tunable according to various accuracy requirements. Algorithm 3 and 4 present the implementation of how to reply and receive the minimal value for both tag and reader. It is worth noting that we make a slight difference here. Instead of finding the minimal value from many uniform distributed variables, we are trying to acquire the maximal value among exponential distributed variables. This conversion stems from

$$\min(1, \mathcal{U}_0, \mathcal{U}_1, ...) \Rightarrow \max(0, -\log\mathcal{U}_0, -\log\mathcal{U}_1, ...),$$

where $\mathcal{U}_i$ is uniform random number in [0,1] and hence $-\log\mathcal{U}_i$ follows unit exponential distribution.

7. EVALUATION

In this section, we evaluate the performance of WIC and compare it with the state-of-the-art method INC [16] under extensive simulations.

7.1 Setup and Metrics

The simulations are conducted on a PC with Intel i7 CPU at 3.2GHz and 8GB RAM. We write our own simulator adopting C# programming language. We register 10,000,000 tags on server using MS SQLServer 2000 database. We take 500 runs for each experiment and report the average.

Estimation Accuracy: To evaluate the accuracy of WIC estimator, we use three standard metrics: Relative Standard Error (RSE), $|\frac{\hat{\theta}}{\theta} - 1|$; Standard Deviation (SD), $\sigma = \sqrt{\mathrm{E}[(\hat{\theta} - \theta)^2]}$; Norm Std Deviation (NSD), $\sigma' = \frac{\sigma}{\mathrm{E}[\theta]}$, where $\hat{\theta}$ is the estimate of original value θ. Without loss of generality, we vary the size of verified tag set ($\mathcal{T}_1$) from 1,000,000 to 5,000,000, but fix counterfeits ratio at 0.07 which is the

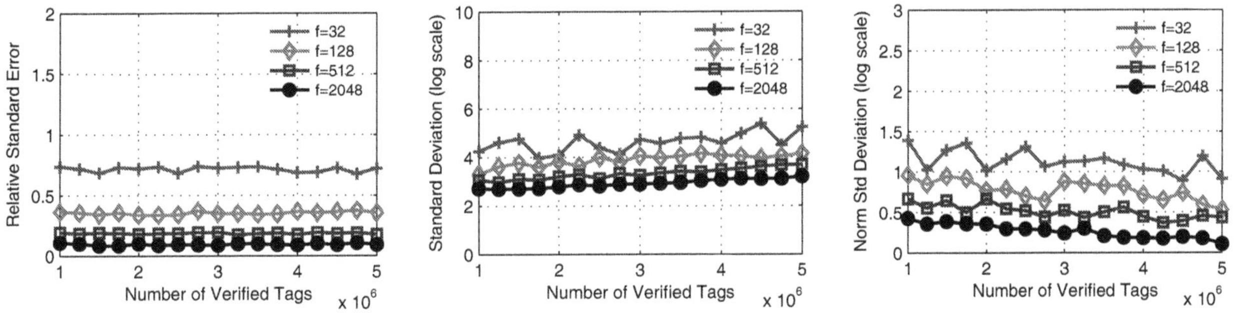

(a) Relative Standard Error. (b) Standard Deviation. (c) Norm Std Deviation.

Figure 3: The accuracy of $|\hat{\mathcal{C}}|$ vs $|\mathcal{T}_1|$, when $|\mathcal{S}| = N = 10,000,000$, $c = 0.07$.

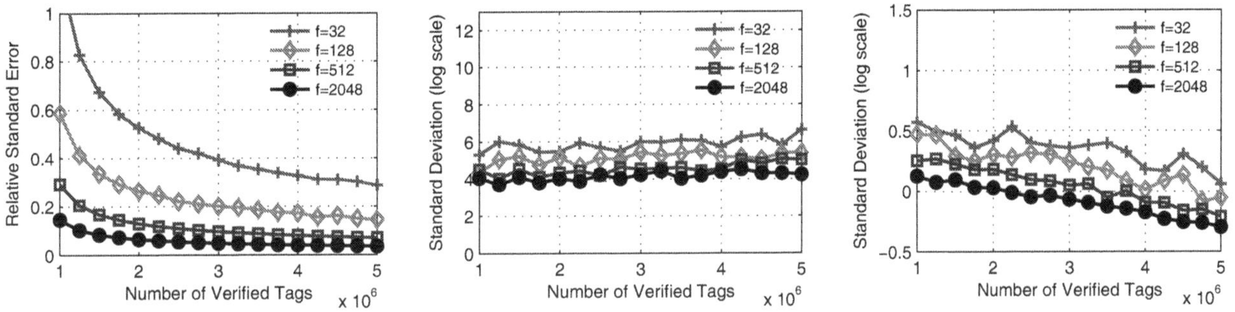

(a) Relative Standard Error. (b) Standard Deviation. (c) Norm Std Deviation.

Figure 4: The accuracy of $|\hat{\mathcal{G}}|$ vs $|\mathcal{T}_1|$, when $|\mathcal{S}| = N = 10,000,000$, $c = 0.07$.

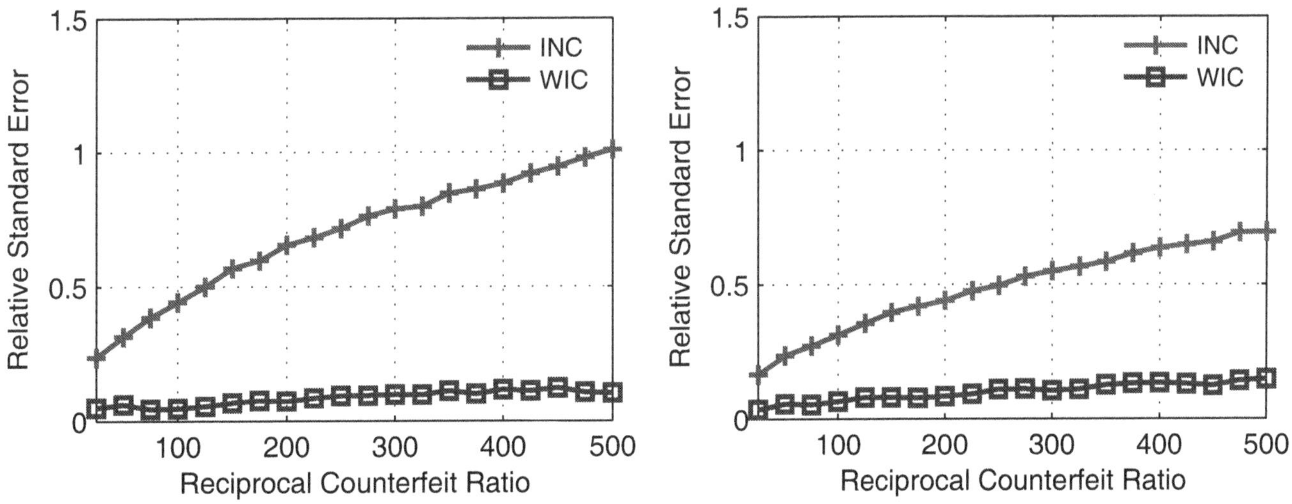

(a) Fixed total transmission cost at 20KB. (b) Fixed frame size at 51200.

Figure 5: The accuracy $|\mathcal{T}_1 - \mathcal{S}|$ vs Reciprocal Counterfeit Ratio, when $|\mathcal{S}| = 10,000,000$, $|\mathcal{T}_1| = 10,000,000$.

reported statistics in [29]. As stated in Section 4, f is the size of frame in the first layer.

Figure 3 shows the result of estimator $|\hat{\mathcal{C}}|$. From those figures, we make several observations. First, the increase of frame size improves RSE of $|\hat{\mathcal{C}}|$. In particular, when the number of tags is 1,000,000, the RSE is 0.73 with f=32 and drops quickly to 0.10 with f=2048. Second, RSE remains almost unchanged as the number of verified tags grows. This nice probability confirms our former complexity analysis: the RSE is mainly related to frame size f and counterfeit ratio c, not the number of tags to be verified. It thus provides us scalable authentication scheme for large-scale RFID

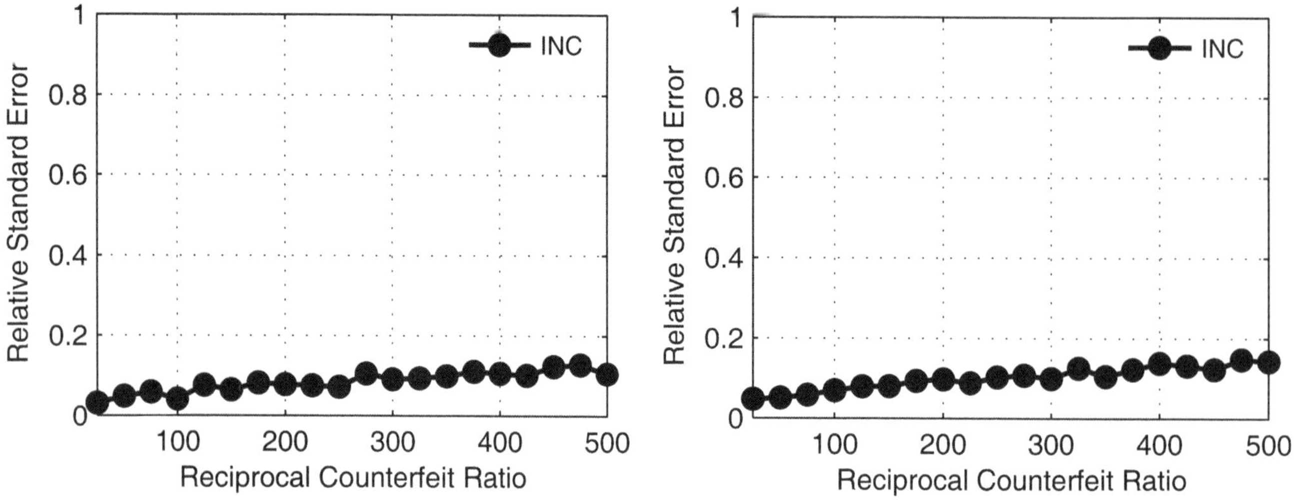

(a) Fixed total transmission cost at 20KB.

(b) Fixed frame size at 51200.

Figure 6: The accuracy $|((\mathcal{T}_1 \cup \mathcal{T}_2) \cap \mathcal{T}_3) - \mathcal{S}|$ vs Reciprocal Counterfeit Ratio, when $|\mathcal{S}| = 10,000,000$, $|\mathcal{T}_1 \cup \mathcal{T}_2 \cup \mathcal{T}_3| = 10,000,000$.

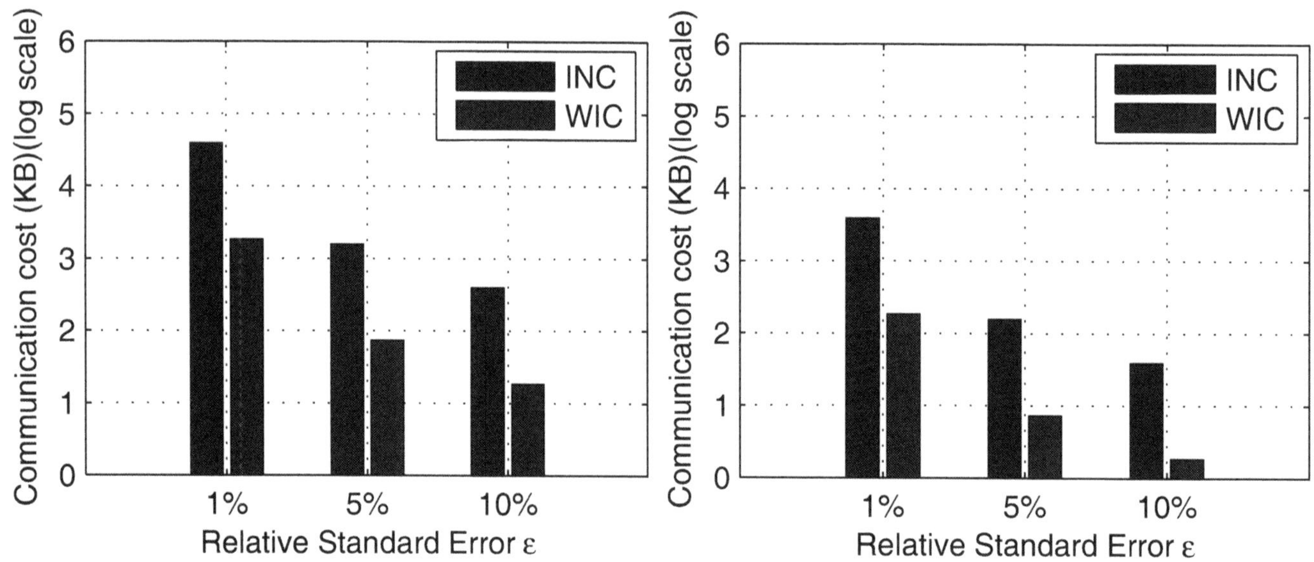

(a) with different relative error ε and $c = 0.1$.

(b) with different relative error ε and $c = 0.01$.

Figure 7: Communication cost between reader and tags (in *log scale*), when $|\mathcal{S}| = 10,000,000$, $|\mathcal{T}_1| = 50,000,000$.

system. Third, SD and NSD of $|\hat{\mathcal{C}}|$ are also greatly reduced by larger frame size.

Similar trend can also be seen in Figure 4. But there is a major difference. Contrast to RSE of $|\hat{\mathcal{C}}|$, the RSE of $|\hat{\mathcal{G}}|$ is diminishing as $|\mathcal{T}_1|$ increases . This trend stems from the increasing genuines ratio due to increased $|\mathcal{T}_1|$, since the number of counterfeits is static.

Single Set Authentication: Here we study how counterfeits ratio affects accuracy of estimators. We vary the reciprocal counterfeit ratio and keep the total transmission size and frame size fixed. As shown in Figure 5a, we use total transmission size budget for 20KB. The result shows that our WIC is always advantageous over INC. For example, when reciprocal counterfeit ratio is 100, the RSE of WIC is 0.06 while RSE of INC is 0.44. The low performance of INC is mainly due to that they fail to examine the correlation information. The secondary factor may be more bits per slot used than WIC. This is confirmed by result in Figure 5b. We fix the frame size at 51200 to compare those methods, ignoring different lengths of time slot. The performance of INC is still worse than WIC, although the gap of RSE between INC and WIC is smaller than that in Figure 5a.

Multiple Sets Authentication: The settings for multiple set authentication are all same as in single set. The only difference is we need to authenticate a compound set expression: $|((\mathcal{T}_1 \cup \mathcal{T}_2) \cap \mathcal{T}_3) - \mathcal{S}|$. Note that for multiple sets INC does not have solution so far, so it is not included for comparison here. Figure 6a reports the RSE as a function of reciprocal counterfeits ratio. It shows that our WIC is still able to give accurate counterfetis estimate as in the single set situation, which is consistent with our asymptotic results in Section 5.2.

Communication Cost: We compare three methods given ε changing from 1% to 15% and the counterfeit ratio at 0.01 and 0.1 in single set situation. The communication cost results of three schemes are depicted in Figure 7. We assume perfect communication channel between reader and tags. The slot length for INC is 32 bits. Again, we can see that WIC achieves much lower communication cost than INC. For instance, total transmission cost of WIC is merely 4.7% of INC when $c = 0.01, \varepsilon = 0.01$. From a different perspective, above comparison results indicate that given a certain time budget, the authentication accuracy of WIC will still much better than INC.

8. RELATED WORK

To authenticate a batch of tags, there are two main categories of methods: deterministic and probabilistic. For small-scale RFID systems, deterministic methods that typically combine anti-collision protocol with per-tag authentication scheme work quite well [30]. The anti-collision protocols includes ALOHA-based EPCGlobal C1G2 standard [10] and tree-based ISO 18000-6 standard [31]. To securely verify a single tags, various schemes are designed according to different purposes, e.g., system anonymity [32], anti-cloning [33], hash-based authentication [11], key management using tree structure [12][13]. The best known efficiency $\mathcal{O}(1)$ is achieved by Lu et al. by employing a weak privacy model [34]. Those per-tag based approaches, however, suffer from severe scalability issue when the population of tags rapidly increases, since the complexity of deterministic scheme should be linear with the number of tags.

The first probabilistic batch authentication for large-scale RFID systems, SEBA, is proposed in [14]. By using single echo from each tag, SEBA is able to successfully detect counterfeits with high probability if the fraction of counterfeits exceeds predefined threshold. Since the result of SEBA only indicates whether there is counterfeit and is lack of further information, a fine-grained and scalable batch authentication scheme, INC, is introduced to accurately approximate the count of counterfeits [16]. From statistical perspective, we discover most previous methods fail to explore information in authentication data structures, leaving the correlation information and a great deal of authentication synopses unused. In contrast, WIC is statistically efficient in sense of Cramer-RAO lower bound. Moreover, those former methods can only efficiently authenticate one tag set whereas WIC still performs well with multiple tag sets.

Besides above probabilistic batch authentication schemes, a number of probabilistic cardinality estimation approaches are proposed. Kodialam et al. introduce the first probabilistic RFID estimation algorithm using linear counting. Unified Probabilistic Estimator (UPE) and Unified Probabilistic Estimator (UPE) are proposed to deal with different frame-size constraints [26]. An asymptotically unbiased estimator, EZB, uses the number of zero slot in the frame to track the dynamics of tag population in both time and spatial domain [25]. Han et al. propose to use first non-empty slot observation to quickly estimate the cardinality [35]. Qian et al. propose LOF, which borrows the idea of FM-Sketch to geometrically approximate the count of tags [36]. Zheng et al. advance the estimation efficiency from $\mathcal{O}(\log n)$ by LOF to $\mathcal{O}(\log\log n)$, where n is the number of tags to be estimated [37]. Average Run based Tag Estimation (ART) method uses a new statistical entity, average run length, to achieves 7x faster then UPE [38]. The first energy-efficient estimation scheme is proposed by Li et al [39]. Gong et al propose the first arbitrarily accurate approximation scheme for cardinality estimation using t-wise independent hash functions [40]. A comprehensive understanding of RFID counting protocols can be found in [41], which emphasizes the use of two-phase schemes. Although these algorithms can effectively derive the estimate of total number of tags in interested region, they are unable to distinguish counterfeit tags from genuine tags. They are thus not appropriately applicable in RFID authentication systems.

9. CONCLUDING REMARKS

In this paper, we propose a fast and efficient batch authentication scheme for large-scale RFID systems with optimal efficiency. First, we formally defined the general counterfeits estimation problem with multiple tag sets. Then we introduce a novel hierarchical authentication structure to efficiently encode tag sets. By using this statistically efficient data structure, WIC achieves $\mathcal{O}(\frac{N}{\varepsilon^2|C|}\log\log N)$ authentication complexity. By theoretical analysis and extensive simulation comparisons, we show that WIC is significantly advantageous over previous state-of-the-art methods. We are currently working on adapting WIC to off-the-shelf commercial tags. In the future, we also plan to provide systematic implementations of WIC using software defined radios as we already have some initial designs.

10. ACKNOWLEDGMENTS

We would like to thank the anonymous reviewers for valuable and insightful comments. This work is supported in part by the NSFC Young Scholar No.61303196, NSFC Distinguished Young Scholars No.61125202 and Natural Sciences and Engineering Research Council (NSERC) of Canada grant No.CRDPJ-445199-12. We also acknowledge the support from the Open RFID Lab (ORL) project [42].

11. REFERENCES

[1] Frost & Sullivan. Global RFID Healthcare and Pharmaceutical Market. *Industry Report*, 2011.

[2] Frost & Sullivan. Global RFID market. *Industry Report*, 2011.

[3] How RFID Is Transforming VA Hospital Operations. *www.rfidjournal.com/article/view/9819*, 2012.

[4] J. Hoepman, E. Hubbers, B. Jacobs, M. Oostdijk, and R. Schreur. Crossing Borders: Security and Privacy Issues of the European e-Passport. pages 152–167, 2006.

[5] J. Collins. Hong Kongąŕs Airport to Tag Bags. *RFID Journal*, 2004.

[6] M. Pelino, C. Mines, J. Warner, and S. Musto. M2M Connectivity Helps Telcos Offset Declining Traditional Services. *Forrester Research*, 2011.

[7] R. Want. RFID–A Key to Automating Everything. *Scientific American*, 290(1):56–65, 2004.
[8] D. Ma, C. Qian, W. Li, J. Han, and J. Zhao. GenePrint: Generic and Accurate Physical-layer Identification for UHF RFID Tags. In *Proc. of IEEE ICNP*, 2013.
[9] J. Han, C. Qian, D. Ma, X. Wang, J. Zhao, P. Zhang, W. Xi, and Z. Jiang. Twins: Device-free Object Tracking using Passive Tags. In *Proc. of IEEE INFOCOM*, 2014.
[10] EPCglobal Radio-Frequency Identity Protocols Class-1 Generation-2 UHF RFID Protocol for Communications at 860 MHz-960MHz, 2008.
[11] S. Weis, S. Sarma, R. Rivest, and D. Engels. Security and Privacy Aspects of Low-Cost Radio Frequency Identification Systems. *Security in pervasive computing*, pages 50–59, 2004.
[12] L. Lu, J. Han, L. Hu, Y. Liu, and L.M. Ni. Dynamic Key-Updating: Privacy-Preserving Authentication for RFID Systems. In *Proc. of IEEE PERCOM*, 2007.
[13] L. Lu, J. Han, R. Xiao, and Y. Liu. ACTION: Breaking the Privacy Barrier for RFID Systems. In *Proc. of IEEE INFOCOM*, 2009.
[14] L. Yang, J. Han, Y. Qi, and Y. Liu. Identification-free Batch Authentication for RFID Tags. In *Proc. of IEEE ICNP*, 2010.
[15] The spread of counterfeiting: Knock-offs catch on. *The Economist*, 2010.
[16] W. Gong, K. Liu, X. Miao, Q. Ma, Z. Yang, and Y. Liu. Informative Counting Fine-grained Batch Authentication for Large-Scale RFID Systems. In *Proc. of ACM MOBIHOC*, 2013.
[17] B. Sheng, Q. Li, and W. Mao. Efficient Continuous Scanning in RFID Systems. In *Proc. of IEEE INFOCOM*, 2010.
[18] L. Xie, Q. Li, X. Chen, S. Lu, and D. Chen. Continuous Scanning with Mobile Reader in RFID Systems: an Experimental Study. In *Proc. of ACM MOBIHOC*, 2013.
[19] H. Liu, W. Gong, X. Miao, K. Liu, and W. He. Towards Adaptive Continuous Scanning in Large-Scale RFID Systems. In *Proc. of IEEE INFOCOM*, 2014.
[20] Y. Zheng and M. Li. P-MTI: Physical-layer Missing Tag Identification via Compressive Sensing. In *Proc. of IEEE INFOCOM*, 2013.
[21] F. Gandino, R. Ferrero, B. Montrucchio, and M. Rebaudengo. DCNS: An Adaptable High Throughput RFID Reader-to-Reader Anticollision Protocol . *Parallel and Distributed Systems, IEEE Transactions on*, 24(5):893–905, 2013.
[22] Y. Zheng and M. Li. Read bulk data from computational rfids. In *Proc. of IEEE INFOCOM*, 2014.
[23] H. Liu, W. Gong, L. Chen, W. He, K. Liu, and Y. Liu. Generic Composite Counting in RFID Systems. In *Proc. of IEEE ICDCS*, 2014.
[24] S.L. Garfinkel, A. Juels, and R. Pappu. RFID privacy: an overview of problems and proposed solutions. *Security Privacy, IEEE*, 3(3):34–43, May 2005.
[25] M. Kodialam, T. Nandagopal, and W.C. Lau. Anonymous Tracking Using RFID Tags. In *Proceedings of IEEE INFOCOM*, 2007.
[26] M. Kodialam and T. Nandagopal. Fast and Reliable Estimation Schemes in RFID Systems. In *Proc. of ACM MOBICOM*, 2006.
[27] H. Zhang, J. Gummeson, B. Ransford, and K. Fu. Moo: A Batteryless Computational RFID and Sensing Platform. *Tech Report UMASS*, 2011.
[28] Rajeev Motwani. *Randomized Algorithms.* Cambridge university press, 1995.
[29] ICC Counterfeiting Intelligence Bureau. Countering Counterfeiting: A Guide to Protecting and Enforcing Intellectual Property Rights. 1997.
[30] T.F. La Porta, G. Maselli, and C. Petrioli. Anticollision Protocols for Single-Reader RFID Systems: Temporal Analysis and Optimization. *IEEE Transactions on Mobile Computing*, 10(2):267 –279, 2011.
[31] Information technology Radio frequency identification for item management Part 6: Parameters for air interface communications at 860 MHz to 960 MHz, 2010.
[32] Y.K. Lee, L. Batina, and I. Verbauwhede. Untraceable RFID authentication protocols: Revision of EC-RAC. In *Proc. of IEEE RFID*, 2009.
[33] L. Bolotnyy and G. Robins. Physically Unclonable Function-Based Security and Privacy in RFID Systems. In *Proc. of IEEE PERCOM*, 2007.
[34] L. Lu, Y. Liu, and X. Li. Refresh: Weak Privacy Model for RFID Systems. In *Proc. of IEEE INFOCOM*, 2010.
[35] H. Han, B. Sheng, C.C. Tan, Q. Li, W. Mao, and S. Lu. Counting RFID Tags Efficiently and Anonymously. In *Proceedings of IEEE INFOCOM*, 2010.
[36] C. Qian, H. Ngan, Y. Liu, and L.M. Ni. Cardinality Estimation for Large-Scale RFID Systems. *IEEE Transactions on Parallel and Distributed Systems*, 22(9):1441–1454, 2011.
[37] Y. Zheng and M. Li. PET: Probabilistic Estimating Tree for Large-Scale RFID Estimation. *IEEE Transactions on Mobile Computing*, 11(11):1763–1774, 2012.
[38] M. Shahzad and A. Liu. Every Bit Counts - Fast and Scalable RFID Estimation. In *Proc. of ACM MOBICOM*, 2012.
[39] T. Li, S. S. Wu, S. Chen, and M. C. K. Yang. Generalized Energy-Efficient Algorithms for the RFID Estimation Problem. *IEEE/ACM Transactions on Networking*, 20(6):1978 –1990, 2012.
[40] W. Gong, K. Liu, X. Miao, and H. Liu. Arbitrarily Accurate Approximation Scheme for Large-Scale RFID Cardinality Estimation. In *IEEE INFOCOM*, 2014.
[41] B. Chen, Z. Zhou, and H. Yu. Understanding RFID Counting Protocols. In *Proc. of ACM MOBICOM*, 2013.
[42] Open rfid lab, http://pdcc.ntu.edu.sg/wands/orl.

Trace-Routing in 3D Wireless Sensor Networks: A Deterministic Approach with Constant Overhead

Su Xia
Cisco System Inc.
170 W Tasman Dr
San Jose, CA 95134
suxia.ull@gmail.com

Hongyi Wu
The Center for Advanced Computer Studies
University of Louisiana at Lafayette
Lafayette, LA 70503
wu@cacs.louisiana.edu

Miao Jin
The Center for Advanced Computer Studies
University of Louisiana at Lafayette
Lafayette, LA 70503
mjin@cacs.louisiana.edu

ABSTRACT

We propose a distributed and deterministic routing algorithm with constant storage, communication and computation overhead, dubbed *trace-routing*, for strong-connected 3D wireless sensor networks. Its basic idea is to construct a virtual cutting plane that intersects boundary surface to yield a trace, along which a routing path with guaranteed delivery can be established. We prove the correctness of trace-routing under both continuous and discrete settings. We implement the trace-routing algorithm on Crossbow sensors and carry out extensive simulations to evaluate its routing efficiency.

Categories and Subject Descriptors

C.2.1 [**Computer Systems Organization**]: Computer-Communication Networks—*Network Architecture and Design*

Keywords

Wireless Sensor Networks; 3D; Routing

1. INTRODUCTION

This work aims to achieve *DeterminIStic routing with Constant Overhead (or DISCO routing)* in the emerging three-dimensional (3D) wireless sensor networks [1–12]. DISCO is highly desired due to the stringent resource constraints on individual nodes and the often-needed large-scale deployment of 3D wireless sensor networks. Constant overhead signifies the storage, communication and computation required for routing are bounded by a constant at each sensor node, while deterministic routing means a routing path can be determined without random search. The cost of employing DISCO routing is the potentially sub-optimal routes, which are, however, tolerable in sensor networks where data traffic is light.

The conventional table-driven routing is obviously non-DISCO, because the size of a routing table grows with the size of the network. Most on-demand routing algorithms developed for mobile ad hoc networks result in non-constant communication overhead for route discovery and thus are not DISCO either. On the other hand, while the sensor network protocols that aggregate data from sensors to sink(s) are predominantly DISCO, they do not support generic communication between any peers in the network. The earliest endeavor to achieve DISCO in large-scale peep-to-peer wireless sensor networks is geometric routing [13–20].

MobiHoc'14, August 11–14, 2014, Philadelphia, PA, USA.

http://dx.doi.org/10.1145/2632951.2632977.

1.1 Overview of Geometric Routing

We begin our discussion on geometric routing in 2D wireless sensor networks. Given the practical limit on radio range, the communication graph of a large-scale sensor network often well preserves its geometric characteristics.

In geometric greedy routing, a node always forwards a packet to one of its neighbors closest to the destination of the packet. Geometric greedy routing is distributed with constant storage, communication and computation overhead. However, geometric greedy routing itself does not guarantee delivery of data packets, due to the presence of local minima in the network. A node is called a *local minimum* if it is not the destination but closer to the destination than all of its neighbors. Clearly, geometric greedy routing fails at local minima. As to be discussed in Sec. 3, local minima may appear at either internal or boundary nodes. The former can be resolved by using local information within two hops. Therefore, most geometric routing algorithms focus on the latter, largely following two strategies: face routing [13–20] and greedy embedding [21–27]. Face routing and its alternatives and enhancements are based on the fact that a void in a 2D planar network is a face with a simple line boundary. Thus a local deterministic algorithm can be employed to search the boundary in either clockwise or counter-clockwise direction to guide the packet out of the local minimum as illustrated in Fig. 1(a). Greedy embedding aims to embed a sensor network into a domain without local minima such that geometric routing under such embedding is always successful.

1.2 Challenges in 3D Geometric Routing

While increasing space dimension appears irrelevant to network communication protocols at the first glance, surprising challenges are observed in efforts to extend geometric routing techniques from 2D to 3D. First, none of the greedy embedding algorithms in the literature [21–27] can be generalized to 3D sensor networks. At the same time, the boundary of a void in a 3D network is no longer a closed curve or line segment, but a surface, rendering face routing infeasible. More specifically, in contrast to the simple line boundary in 2D that can be searched deterministically, there exist an arbitrarily large number of possible paths on the boundary surface to be explored in order to escape from a local minimum in 3D (as shown in Fig. 1(b)). As a matter of fact, a recent finding shows that there

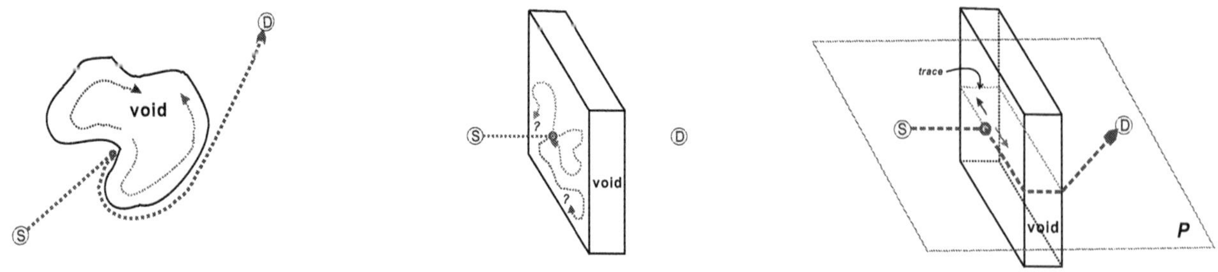

(a) Face routing succeeds in 2D. (b) Face routing fails in 3D. (c) Proposed trace-routing.

Figure 1: Exposition of challenges to extending face routing from 2D to 3D and illustration of the proposed trace-routing algorithm. (a) Face routing succeeds in a 2D planar network where a local deterministic algorithm can be employed to search the boundary in clockwise or counter-clockwise direction to guide the packet out of the local minimum. (b) Face routing fails in a 3D network because there exist an arbitrarily large number of possible paths on the boundary surface to be explored in order to escape from a local minimum. (c) The basic idea of trace-routing is to establish a cutting plan that intersects the boundary surface to yield a trace, along which the packet can move out of the local minimum.

does not exist a deterministic algorithm to guarantee data delivery based on local information only in general 3D networks [28].

Given the challenges in extending 2D geometric routing algorithms to 3D, several approaches have been developed specifically for 3D settings, which fall into four categories as summarized below. The first category focuses on topology control [29], where a critical communication distance is suggested to eliminate local minima in 3D networks. However, such critical communication distance is often too large for practical applications, given the short sensor radio range, e.g., about 10 meters for MICAz motes.

The second category is based on dimension reduction by projecting nodes in 3D space onto 2D plane, where face routing is applied [6, 7]. However face routing on the projected plane does not guarantee a packet to move out of local minimum in the original 3D network. Separately, a 4D stereographic projection scheme is adopted in [9] for load balancing, but it does not address possible local minima.

The third category adopts the divide-and-conquer strategy to compress geometric information required to escape from local minima in a 3D network. To this end, tree structure or space partition is often employed. For example, a convex hull-based tree is introduced in GDSTR-3D [10]. If a local minimum is reached, the packet is forwarded according to the tree. As another example, a 3D partial unit Delaunay triangulation algorithm is proposed in [5] to divide the network space into closed subspaces such that a local minimum can be recovered within a few subspaces only. In [30], a distributed multi-dimensional tree structure is applied to support guaranteed packet delivery. Separately, the Random-Walk algorithm [8] employs a spherical dual graph structure to jump out of local minima. In all of these schemes, certain structures must be maintained by individual sensors, which are often non-locally-deterministic or requires a non-constant storage space that increases with the network size.

The fourth category is based on mapping schemes. For example, volumetric harmonic mapping is introduced in [31] to achieve deterministic and guaranteed delivery in 3D sensor networks. However, a routing table must be maintained for a network that contains more than one voids, with its size proportional to the number of voids in the network.

Moreover, all algorithms discussed in the above four categories suffer from network dynamics. For example, when sensor nodes move, they must frequently update their data structures or virtual coordinates. Such updates are usually expensive or even unattainable.

1.3 Contributions of This Work

As discussed above, none of the existing schemes support DISCO routing in 3D wireless sensor networks. In this research, we consider a sensor network deployed in a 3D space with one or multiple internal holes, where sensors cannot be deployed. We show that local minima are always on the boundaries of holes if nodal density is high, and there exists a DISCO algorithm to support routing between any pair of points in a strong-connected 3D network. We propose a distributed and deterministic algorithm with constant storage, communication and computation overhead, dubbed trace-routing, to escape from local minima. Trace-routing is triggered when a packet reaches a local minimum. It constructs a virtual cutting plane that contains the local minimum and the destination and intersects the corresponding boundary surface to yield a trace. The trace is a closed loop that can be computed locally with constant overhead. The packet is routed along such a trace, thus deterministically moving out of the local minimum as illustrated in Fig. 1(c).

The proposed trace-routing algorithm does not demand preprocessing of the global network information, neither does it require establishing or maintaining a global data structure, which often consumes a storage space proportional to the network size and needs frequent update due to network dynamics. We further prove the trace-routing algorithm guarantees data delivery in a strong-connected 3D network under both continuous and discrete settings. In a nutshell, trace-routing supports DISCO, thus highly efficient in large-scale 3D sensor networks. It is worth mentioning that the proposed trace-routing algorithm and related discussions and proofs do not rely on any particular communication model (such as the unit ball graph model or quasi-unit ball graph model). Only a maximum radio range is assumed, which is generally known in practical sensor networks.

The rest of this paper is organized as follows: Sec. 2 introduces the proposed trace-routing algorithm in continuous 3D domain. Sec. 3 presents a practical design of trace-routing and proves its correctness under discrete 3D sensor network settings. Secs. 4 and 5 discuss simulation and experimental results. Finally, Sec. 6 concludes the paper.

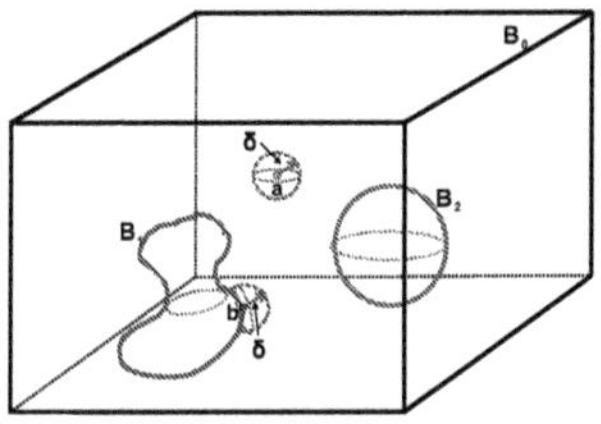

Figure 2: Boundaries and δ-vicinities.

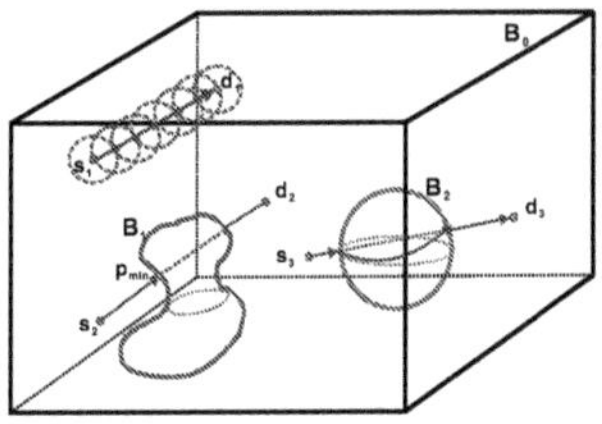

Figure 3: Geometric greedy routing.

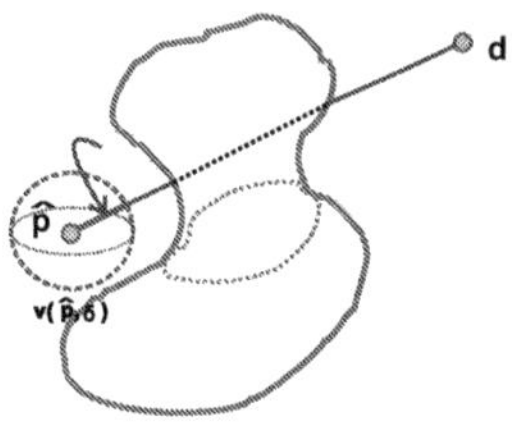

Figure 4: Illustration of Lemma 2.

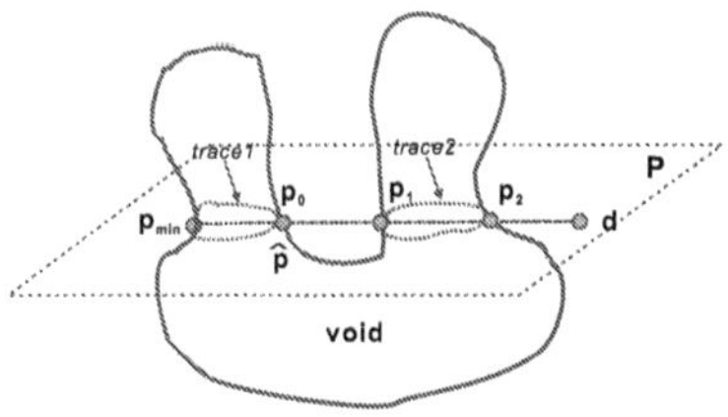

Figure 5: Illustration of Lemma 4.

2. TRACE-ROUTING IN CONTINUOUS 3D SPACE

As shown in [28], there does not exist a universal deterministic algorithm to guarantee data delivery based on local information only in general 3D networks. Following this result, a natural question is whether there exists a DISCO routing algorithm for a class of practical 3D networks and how to develop a distributed algorithm to achieve such DISCO routing. To deliver a lucid conceptual presentation and gain useful theoretic insights, we first investigate the failures in geometric greedy routing and present our proposed algorithm in a continuous 3D space. We will discuss the algorithm under discrete 3D sensor network settings in the next section.

2.1 Greedy Routing in Continuous 3D Volume

Let's start with several definitions that are necessary to our exposition and discuss the essence of geometric greedy routing in a continuous 3D Euclidean space. Let **U** denote an Euclidean volume in 3D space $\mathbb{R}^3$, which is enclosed by a set of boundaries $\mathbf{B} = \{B_k \mid 0 \leq k \leq K\}$, where B_0 is the outer boundary and B_k $(k > 0)$ is an inner boundary of **U**. Let $L(p, q)$ denote a straight line segment from Point p to Point q, and $|L(p, q)|$ denote its Euclidean distance. Let Λ_k denote the area enclosed by B_k $(k \geq 0)$. Obviously, $\mathbf{U} = \Lambda_0 \setminus \cup\Lambda_k$ $(1 \leq k \leq K\})$.

DEFINITION 1. *Let $C(s, d)$ be a sequence of line segments, $C(s, d) = \langle L(p_0, p_1), L(p_1, p_2), .., L(p_{m-1}, p_m)\rangle$, where $p_0 = s$ and $p_m = d$. We call $C(s, d)$ a routing path connecting s and d, if and only if*

- *$L(p_i, p_{i+1})$ does not intersect with $L(p_j, p_{j+1})$, $\forall\ i \neq j$, $i + 1 \neq j$ and $i \neq j + 1$; and*
- *$L(p_i, p_{i+1})$ does not penetrate any boundary of **U**, $\forall\ L(p_i, p_{i+1}) \in C(s, d)$.*

The first condition of Definition 1 requires the routing path free of self-intersection, while the second condition indicates that the path must be completely contained inside **U**. Next we introduce the geometric greedy routing algorithm via the following two definitions.

DEFINITION 2. *We call $V(p, \delta)$ the δ-vicinity of Point p, if $\forall\ \hat{p}$ in $V(p, \delta)$, $L(p, \hat{p})$ is completely contained in **U** and $|L(p, \hat{p})| \leq \delta$ where δ is a given positive real number.*

Fig. 2 illustrates two examples of δ-vicinity of points at different locations. The δ-vicinity of Point a, an internal node, is a ball centered at a with a radius of δ, while Point b has a defected δ-vicinity due to the nearby boundary.

DEFINITION 3. *A routing path $C(s, d)$ is a geometric greedy path (or greedy path for conciseness), denoted as $C(s, d, \delta)$, if $\forall$ p_i on $C(s, d, \delta)$, p_{i+1} is the closest point in $V(p_i, \delta)$ to Destination d.*

The above definition suggests a simple geometric greedy routing algorithm. It starts from the source as its current point, and chooses the point in its current δ-vicinity that is the closest to the destination as the next point. The process repeats until it reaches the destination. An example of routing from Source s_1 to Destination d_1 is shown in Fig. 3. Note that the geometric greedy routing algorithm may fail to find the next point, when the current point is closer to the destination than all other points in its δ-vicinity. Formally we define the point where geometric greedy routing fails as a local minimum.

DEFINITION 4. *Point p_{min} is a local minimum for Destination d under a given δ, if $p_{min} \neq d$ and $L(p_{min}, d) \leq L(p, d)$ $\forall\ p \in V(p_{min}, \delta)$.*

An example of geometric greedy routing failure is illustrated in Fig. 3 from Source s_2 to Destination d_2. Greedy routing often fails when the routing path meets the boundary of an internal hole. Particularly, we have the following observation regarding geometric greedy routing failures.

LEMMA 1. *If there does not exist a geometric greedy routing path $C(s, d, \delta)$ between s and d under a given δ, $L(s, d)$ must intersect at least one of the boundaries of **U**.*

PROOF. We prove it by contradiction. Assume $L(s, d)$ does not intersect any boundary. Since s and d are points in **U**, $L(s, d)$ must be completely contained in **U** (otherwise it would intersect a boundary). Then a greedy path $C(s, d, \delta)$ along the straight line $L(s, d)$ can be readily constructed according to Definition 3, contradicting the given condition that there is no greedy path between s and d. Thus, the lemma is proven. □

Equivalent to Lemma 1, if $L(s, d)$ does not intersect any boundary of **U**, we can always find a greedy routing path from s to d. It gives the sufficient condition for the existence of a greedy path. But it is not the necessary condition, i.e., even if $L(s, d)$ intersects a boundary, a greedy routing path may still be established from s to d. Fig. 3 illustrates such an example where $L(s_3, d_3)$ intersects a spherical boundary, but there exists a greedy routing path along the spherical boundary to Destination d_3. Based on Lemma 1 and Definition 4, we arrive at the following conclusion.

LEMMA 2. *Greedy routing only fails at local minimums and local minimums are always on the boundaries of holes.*

PROOF. The first part of the lemma is obvious from Definitions 3 and 4. The second part of the lemma can be proven by contradiction. Assume there is a local minimum point $\hat{p}$ that is an internal point in **U** (i.e., not on any boundary). Let's draw a line $L(\hat{p}, d)$. Since $\hat{p}$ is an internal point, there must exist a δ such that the intersection of $L(\hat{p}, d)$ and $V(\hat{p}, \delta)$ (highlighted in red in Fig. 4) is a line segment, on which all points are closer to d than $\hat{p}$ is. This contradicts the assumption that $\hat{p}$ is a local minimum. The lemma is proven. □

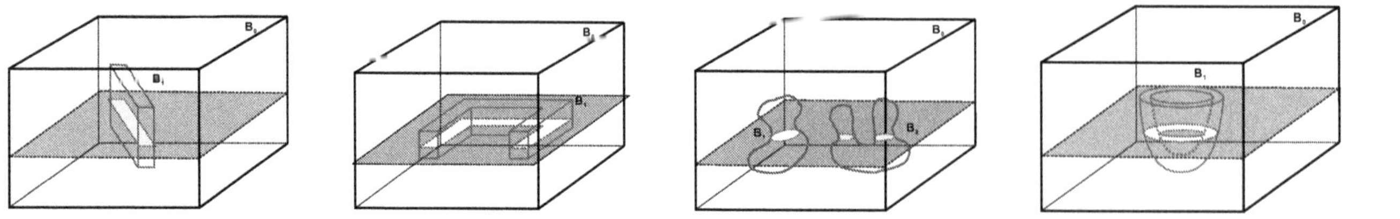

(a) Volumes with convex boundaries are always s-con. (b) A volume with a C-shape inner void is s-con. (c) A volume with complex shapes of inner voids is s-con. (d) A volume with a bowl-shape inner void is not s-con.

Figure 6: Examples of s-con and non-s-con volumes. Each volume has a cubic outer boundary (i.e., B_0) and one or two inner voids delineated by the colored boundaries. An example of cutting planes is shown in each figure, where the shaded area(s) illustrate its intersection with the volume.

Lemma 2 reveals an important fact: greedy routing only fails at boundaries, inspiring us to develop a deterministic boundary navigation algorithm to escape from local minimums.

2.2 Trace-Routing in Continuous 3D Volume

In a 3D space for practical sensor network deployment, the boundary surfaces are *closed* (a closed surface is a compact one with empty boundary) and the 3D volume is often *Strong-CONnected (s-con)*. Here "*closed*" means no "breaches" on the surface. The s-con property is defined below.

DEFINITION 5. *A 3D volume* **U** *is s-con (*Strong-CON-nected*), if and only if the intersection of* any *plane and* **U** *is a connected graph on the plane.*

Figs. 6(a)-6(c) depict several examples of s-con 3D volumes. Each volume has a cubic outer boundary (i.e., B_0) and one or two inner voids delineated by the colored boundaries. An example of cutting planes is shown in each figure, where the shaded area(s) illustrate its intersection with the volume. It is obvious that a 3D volume with convex boundaries is always s-con as shown in Fig. 6(a). But s-con volumes may have non-convex boundaries too. For instance, volumes in Fig. 6(b) and Fig. 6(c) are s-con with non-convex inner boundaries. Note that, although the plane intersects the volume in Fig. 6(c) to yield multiple voids on the intersection plane, the intersection itself (i.e., the shaded area) is still connected. Therefore it is s-con. Fig. 6(d) shows an example of non-s-con volume, with a bowl shape inner void, resulting in disconnected components on the intersection plane (see the disconnected shaded areas).

Although DISCO routing is not achievable in general 3D networks as discussed earlier, we now introduce the proposed trace-routing algorithm, and prove that it supports DISCO routing in any 3D wireless sensor networks that are Strong-CONnected (s-con). There exist other types of boundary surfaces in theory, but they are rare under practical sensor network settings and thus excluded from our discussions below.

As shown by Lemma 2, if greedy routing fails, it must stuck at a local minimum, and such local minimum must be on a boundary of **U**. Let p_{min} denote the local minimum where geometric greedy routing fails, and assume p_{min} is on Boundary B_i. Now we construct an arbitrary plane that contains $L(p_{min}, d)$. It intersects B_i, resulting in one or multiple traces. By examining the traces, we have the following observation.

LEMMA 3. *A trace on a boundary surface is a closed loop with no self-intersection.*

PROOF. If a trace is not a closed loop, the space between two endpoints on the plane forms a *breach* on the surface, contradicting the fact of closed boundary surface. Since the trace is the intersection of the surface and the plane, it cannot self-intersect, given that the surface is homeomorphic to sphere with no self-intersecting component. □

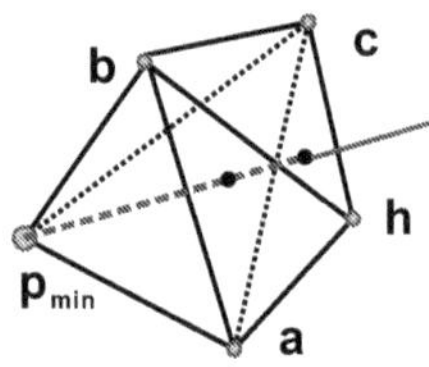

Figure 7: Illustration of Lemma 5.

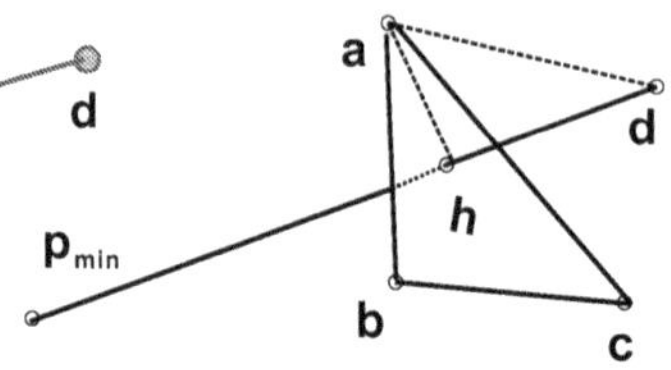

Figure 8: Prove of Theorem 2.

If we draw a line segment from p_{min} to d, $L(p_{min}, d)$ must intersect B_i at two or more points including p_{min}, as shown in Fig. 5. Let p_0 denote one of such intersection points, which is the closest to p_{min}. Clearly, p_0 must be closer to d than p_{min} is, since it is on the line segment between p_{min} and d.

LEMMA 4. *In an s-con volume, the trace containing p_{min} must also contain p_0 and there is a loop-free path from p_{min} to p_0 along this trace.*

PROOF. Obviously p_{min} and p_0 must belong to some trace(s). According to the way of constructing the plane, $L(p_{min}, d)$ must intersect one or multiple traces, yielding a sequence of intersection points on $L(p_{min}, d)$. Now let us look at the trace that contains p_{min}, denoted by $\Gamma_{p_{min}}$. Since $L(p_{min}, d)$ starts from p_{min} that is on Boundary B_i and goes toward the inside of B_i, it cannot reach another point before it meets $\Gamma_{p_{min}}$ again. Let $\hat{p}$ denote this intersection point as shown in Fig. 5. Since $\hat{p}$ is the first such intersection point, it is the closest to p_{min}. Clearly, $\hat{p}$ must be co-located with p_0 introduced earlier. Therefore, we have proven p_{min} and p_0 must be on the same trace.

As shown by Lemma 3, a trace is a closed loop with no self-intersection. Thus it is straightforward to choose a loop-free route along the trace in either clockwise or counterclockwise direction to route from p_{min} to p_0. □

Till now we are ready to formally introduce the trace-routing algorithm and prove its correctness as follows.

THEOREM 1. *There exists a deterministic algorithm with constant storage, communication and computation overhead, which can always successfully navigate the routing path out of local minimums in an s-con volume.*

PROOF. First we construct a simple algorithm, dubbed *trace-routing* as follows. When geometric greedy routing reaches a local minimum p_{min} on Boundary B_i, it chooses a *cutting plane* that is determined by p_{min}, Destination d, and another random point $\hat{p}$. The plane intersects B_i, yielding a trace that contains p_{min}. The routing path advances along the trace in clockwise or counterclockwise direction until it reaches a point that is closer to Destination d than p_{min} is. Then geometric greedy routing follows.

Now we prove the correctness of the algorithm. According to Lemma 4, there must exist at least one point (i.e., p_0) on the trace containing p_{min}, which is closer to Destination d than p_{min} is. Since the trace is a closed loop with no self-intersection, if one starts from p_{min} and navigates along the trace in clockwise or counterclockwise direction, it will visit all points on the trace exactly once before it returns back to p_{min}. Therefore the routing path must reach p_0, from which it can escape from the local minimum.

Trace-routing is clearly deterministic as evident by the description of the algorithm itself. Next, we show its storage, communication and computation overhead are all constant. The algorithm requires each node to maintain the coordinates of itself and its neighbors only, and to pass merely a constant amount of information (i.e., the cutting plane defined by three points p_{min}, $\hat{p}$, and d) along the routing path. Assume the routing path reaches Point p. The trace segment around p can be found by computing the intersection of the cutting plane and the boundary surface in $V(p, \delta)$. Thus, the routing decision is made locally with a constant computation complexity.

In summary we have proved the existence of a local deterministic algorithm with constant storage, communication and computation overhead that can always successfully move out of local minimums in an s-con volume. □

Theorem 1 reveals salient properties of trace-routing, which supports efficient and distributed implementation under practical sensor network settings to be discussed next.

3. TRACE-ROUTING IN DISCRETE 3D NETWORKS

While trace-routing has been introduced above to escape from local minimums, it remains challenging to adapt the concepts and ideas to a practical sensor field. In contrast to the continuous 3D Euclidean volume considered in Sec. 2, a sensor network is under a discrete setting, which presents an approximation of the 3D volume only, rendering part of the earlier discussed methods and results invalid. For example, sensor nodes rarely reside perfectly on the trace computed in a continuous space, calling for approximated solutions. Furthermore, the routing algorithm must be distributed in sensor networks. However, the deployment of sensor nodes exhibits randomness and their radio transmissions are often irregular, which together lead to new challenges to realize distributed trace-routing and to achieve constant storage, communication and computation overhead.

In this section, we examine our conclusions presented in the previous section under a discrete setting, and introduce a practical design of the trace-routing algorithm for 3D sensor networks with internal holes. The following discussions do not rely on any particular communication model (such as the unit ball graph model or quasi-unit ball graph model). Only a maximum transmission range is assumed, which is generally known in practical wireless sensor networks.

3.1 Challenges of Trace-Routing in 3D Sensor Networks

Let us first revisit the concepts and conclusions given in Sec. 2 for continuous 3D Euclidean volume, and evaluate their validity in 3D sensor networks.

3.1.1 Tetrahedron Structure

To facilitate our exposition, we first establish a tetrahedral structure based on discrete sensors as discussed in [31]. A triangular face in a tetrahedral structure is a boundary face if it is associated with one and only one tetrahedron. A set of connected boundary faces form a closed triangular boundary surface. In the following discussions, a "boundary" refers to a triangular boundary surface.

3.1.2 Local Minimums

Lemma 2 has shown that local minimums are always on the boundaries of holes in a continuous 3D Euclidean volume. Unfortunately, this result no long holds in discrete settings, where local minimums may appear at not only boundary but also internal sensors. However, the internal local minimums can be resolved by using local information only as revealed by the following lemma.

LEMMA 5. *Given an internal local minimum p_{min}, the routing path can move out the local minimum by using local information in 2δ-vicinity of p_{min}, where δ is the maximum radio transmission range.*

PROOF. Based on the tetrahedron structure, a greedy routing path can be established according to faces [31]. More specifically, when the routing path reaches an internal local minimum p_{min}, a line segment from p_{min} to Destination d can be computed by p_{min}. The line segment passes through a sequence of faces in the tetrahedron structure. Let's consider the first such face, denoted by $Face(a, b, c)$, where a, b, and c are vertex nodes (as illustrated in Fig. 7). Obviously, $Face(a, b, c)$ must be closer to the destination compared to the current face, i.e., $Face(p_{min}, a, b)$. Clearly, $Face(a, b, c)$ is within two-hop neighborhood of p_{min}. As a result, the routing path can move out of the local minimum by using local information in 2δ-vicinity of p_{min}. □

According to Lemma 5, we slightly modify the greedy routing algorithm to let each node check its two-hop neighborhood to identify the closest node to the destination, thus eliminating internal local minimums. Note that, the modified algorithm does not help to escape from boundary local minimums, which are yet to be addressed by the proposed trace-routing.

3.1.3 Traces

As discussed in Sec. 2.2, a trace on an inner boundary is a closed loop without self-intersection. It can be computed by using local information. But in a discrete setting, sensors rarely reside perfectly on the computed trace. To this end, we redefine traces under discrete settings as follows.

DEFINITION 6. *In a discrete 3D space, a trace formed by a given plane and a boundary consists of a sequence of line segments on the boundary surface, which intersect the plane and are connected end-to-end to form a loop.*

LEMMA 6. *Given a tetrahedral structure of the 3D sensor network and a plane that intersects a triangular boundary surface of the tetrahedral structure, a closed-loop trace can be constructed deterministically.*

PROOF. For a given tetrahedral structure of the 3D sensor network, the faces on the boundary of an internal hole form a closed and connected triangular surface. A plane intersects the triangular boundary surface at a set of triangular faces, denoted by Φ. For each face $f \in \Phi$, it must have at least two edges intersecting the plane. Since each edge is shared by two faces on the triangular boundary surface, Face f must have at least two neighboring faces in Φ. Therefore, the faces in Φ are connected to form a closed strap. It is thus straightforward to select a sequence of edges on such faces, which intersect the plane, to build a closed loop, i.e. the trace. □

Based on Lemma 6, we have the following result that shows the correctness of trace-routing.

THEOREM 2. *A deterministic routing path can be identified by following the* trace *constructed according to Lemma 6 to escape from local minimums.*

PROOF. To prove this theorem, we show that there exists at least one node on the trace, which is closer to the destination than the local minimum (i.e., p_{min}) is. Similar to our discussion under the continuous setting, if we draw a line segment from p_{min} to Destination d, $L(p_{min}, d)$ must intersect the boundary surface at one or more points besides p_{min}. Let h denote one of such intersection points that is the closest to p_{min}, and assume h is on an arbitrary face, e.g., $Face(a, b, c)$ as illustrated in Fig. 8. Clearly, $L(a, b)$, $L(b, c)$ and $L(a, c)$ are no greater than the maximum radio range r because they are connected in the communication graph. Since h is on $Face(a, b, c)$, $L(a, h)$, $L(b, h)$ and $L(c, h)$ must be no greater than r either. At the same time, $L(p_{min}, a)$, $L(p_{min}, b)$, $L(p_{min}, c)$ and $L(p_{min}, h)$ are all greater than r, since there is a hole between p_{min} and $Face(a, b, c)$. Thus we have $L(a, d) < L(a, h) + L(h, d) \leq r + L(h, d) < L(p_{min}, h) + L(h, d) = L(p_{min}, d)$. Therefore a is closer to d than p_{min} is. Similarly, b and c are closer to d than p_{min} is. Note that at least one edge of $Face(a, b, c)$ must be on the trace constructed according to Lemma 6. Therefore one can always find a node on the trace closer to d than p_{min} is. The theorem is thus proven. □

Theorem 2 shows trace-routing is deterministic and always succeeds in discrete sensor networks. Moreover, similar to the proof of Theorem 1, its storage, communication and computation overhead are all bounded by a constant.

3.2 Proposed Trace-Routing Algorithm in 3D Sensor Networks

The basic idea of trace-routing is to move clockwise or counterclockwise around the trace constructed by Lemma 6, which is a closed loop and thus can navigate out of local minimums. The discussions so far have assumed known boundary nodes and triangular boundary surfaces. Next we show that such information can be acquired locally with constant overhead or is unnecessary at all in practice.

3.2.1 *Boundary Awareness*

We adopt the boundary detection algorithm proposed in [32], which is localized, requiring information within one-hop neighborhood only for each node to determine if it is on a boundary. Therefore, when greedy routing fails at a local minimum p_{min}, the boundary detection algorithm [32] is employed to identify boundary nodes in the δ-vicinity of p_{min} as input for the trace-routing algorithm.

3.2.2 *Triangular Boundary Surface*

The tetrahedron structure and triangular boundary surfaces are assumed to facilitate our discussions in Sec. 3.1, especially the proof of Lemmas 5 and 6. However, it is unnecessary to explicitly construct them for the implementation of trace-routing. The algorithm can simply choose one of the boundary nodes in its neighborhood as the next hop along the trace. More specifically, the trace-routing algorithm is outlined in Algorithm 1. It is initiated when a greedy routing path reaches a local minimum p_{min}. It defines a plane based on p_{min}, d and an arbitrary node p in the δ-vicinity of p_{min}. Let Δ denote the plane. The algorithm then enters an iterative process. In each iteration, a boundary node in the δ-vicinity of the current node (i.e., p_{cur}) is identified to be the next node (i.e., $\hat{p}$) along the trace. To keep the next node as close to the ideal trace (computed under continuous setting) as possible and to advance along the trace as fast as possible, $\hat{p}$ is chosen such that $L(p_{cur}, \hat{p})$ intersects Plane Δ and forms the largest angle with $L(p_{pre}, p_{cur})$, where p_{pre} is the previous hop node on the routing path. The iterative process repeats until it reaches a node closer to the destination than p_{min} is, i.e., $|L(p_{cur}, d)| < |L(p_{min}, d)|$.

It is clear that Algorithm 1 only results in constant storage, communication and computation overhead. It does not demand preprocessing of the global network information, neither does it require establishing or maintaining a global data structure, which often consumes a storage space proportional to the network size and needs frequent update due to network dynamics. Thus it is highly efficient for large-scale 3D sensor networks.

Algorithm 1: Trace-Routing Algorithm

Input: Local minimum p_{min}, Destination d;

Define Plane Δ based on p_{min}, d and an arbitrary node $p \in V(p_{min}, \delta)$;

$p_{cur} \leftarrow p$, $p_{pre} \leftarrow p_{min}$;

while $|L(p_{cur}, d)| \geq |L(p_{min}, d)|$ **do**

  Identify a boundary node $\hat{p} \in V(p_{cur}, \delta)$ such that $L(\hat{p}, p_{cur})$ intersects Plane Δ and forms the largest angle with $L(p_{pre}, p_{cur})$;

  $p_{pre} \leftarrow p_{cur}$; $p_{cur} \leftarrow \hat{p}$;

3.3 Peer-to-Peer Routing in 3D Wireless Sensor Networks

In summary, when a packet is routed from Source s to Destination d, it first follows geometric greedy routing until a local minimum is reached. Then it employs trace-routing to move out of the local minimum. When the packet arrives at a non-local-minimum node, it switches to greedy routing again. The process repeats until the packet arrives at Destination d. Examples of the routing paths are illustrated in Fig. 1(c) and Figs. 9.

4. SIMULATION RESULTS

We have implemented the proposed trace-routing algorithm (denoted by "TR") and two other state-of-the-art 3D wireless sensor network routing algorithms, namely GDSTR-3D [10] and HVE (harmonic volumetric embedding) [31], for performance evaluation and comparison. Since HVE works in networks with one hole only, we focus on the comparison between TR and GDSTR-3D in most simulation scenarios. Various 3D sensor networks with different sizes (ranging from 1,800 to 11,000 nodes) and shapes are simulated. Fig. 9 illustrates three examples, where the inner boundary

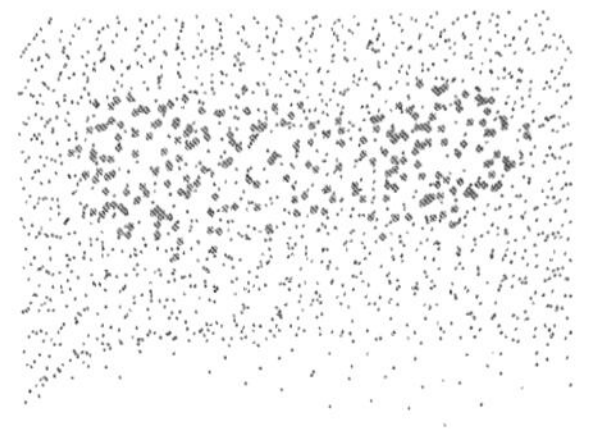

(a) Model 1 (Seabed Network).

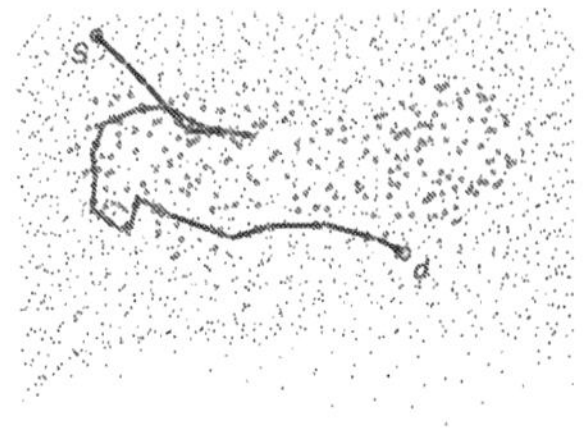

(b) A sample path in Model 1.

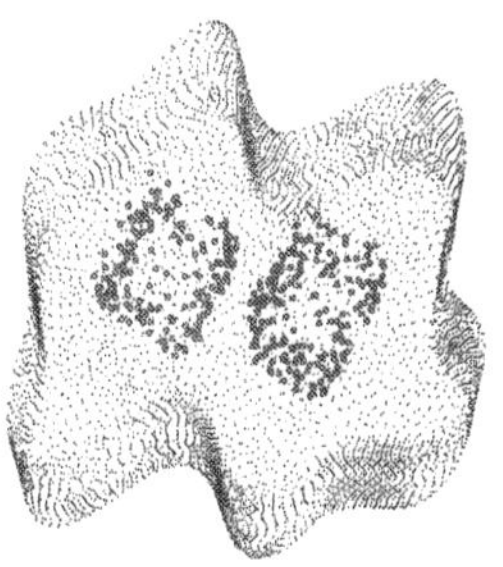

(c) Model 2 (Space Network).

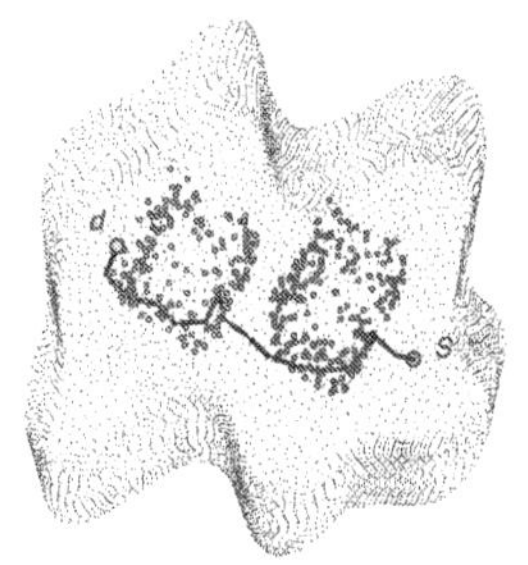

(d) A sample path in Model 2.

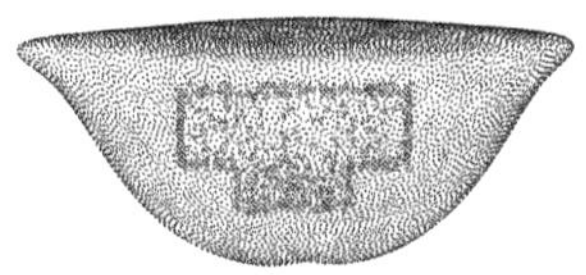

(e) Model 3 (Underwater Network).

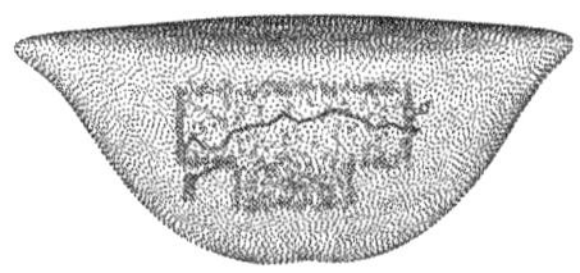

(f) A sample path in Model 3.

Figure 9: The left column shows 3D sensor network models and the right column illustrates sample routing paths in each model. The sensors on the boundary of holes are highlighted in different colors. The blue segments indicate greedy forwarding, while the red segments follow trace-routing.

nodes are highlighted to delineate the holes in the networks. Sensors are randomly distributed. While our proposed scheme does not rely on a particularly communication model, we carry out simulations based on unit ball graph and quasi-unit ball graph models, with an average nodal degree between 10 to 18. Our simulations show that the proposed scheme works well for networks with a nodal degree greater than 7 (which represents a sparse network in three dimensional space).

4.1 Stretch Factor

As discussed in previous sections, TR, GDSTR-3D and HVE all ensure successful delivery. Therefore we focus on stretch factor in performance evaluation. The stretch factor of a route is the ratio of the actual routing path length to the shortest path length. 20,000 pairs of nodes are randomly selected to calculate the average stretch factor for each network model. The following table compares the average stretch factors of GDSTR-3D and TR in different networks. The results of HVE are not included because it can be applied for networks with one hole only, where its stretch factor is around 1.52. Both algorithms achieve good and comparable stretch factor (less than 1.3) in all network models. GDSTR-3D is more sensitive to the hole size and the number of holes, exhibiting higher stretch factors under Models 2-4. This is mainly because that the GDSTR-3D uses two trees rooted at two furthest away nodes. When there are multiple holes or complex shape holes, the

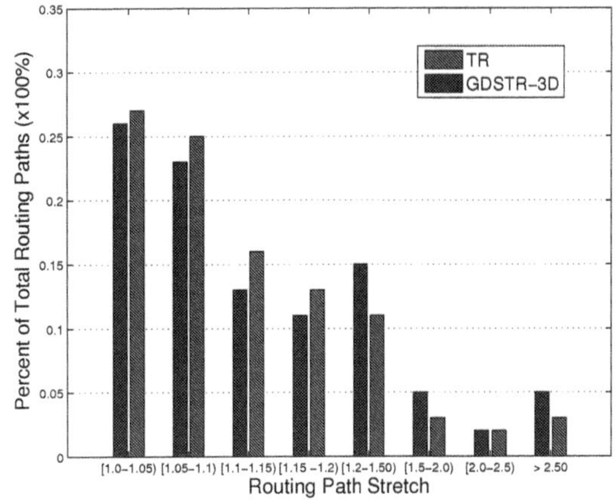

Figure 10: Stretch under UDG.

local minimum recovery procedure that follows one of the two trees often results in significantly stretched routing paths in comparison with corresponding shortest paths. Moreover, under complex and multiple hole settings, there are more overlapped convex hull partitions, which cause longer paths during the tree routing phase. In a contrast, TR follows the geometric boundary of the holes in local minimum recovery, resulting in a stable stretch factor in average.

Models	1	2	3	4	5	6	Ave.
TR	1.05	1.09	1.04	1.21	1.08	1.11	1.10
GDSTR-3D	1.14	1.23	1.29	1.25	1.07	1.19	1.20

The distribution of stretch factor is illustrated in Fig. 10. As can be seen, more than 50% routing paths have their stretch factor lower than 1.15 under both schemes. Compared with TR, the stretch factor distribution of GDSTR-3D has a noticeable shift to the right side with more routes experiencing a stretch factor of 1.2 or higher.

As discussed in the previous sections, TR and GDSTR-3D do not rely on any particular transmission model. Here we test them under a general "QUASI-UBG" model, where two nodes are connected if their distance is less than d; or disconnected if their distance is beyond the maximum transmission range r; or have a probability of p to be connected if their distance is between d and r. We vary d and p, and compare the performance of TR and GDSTR-3D. Both schemes support perfect data delivery rate. Their stretch factors are shown in Fig. 11. We observe that the stretch factor of GDSTR-3D increases fast with the decrease of d, because the connections between nodes become more random, leading to more overlap between convex hulls. Consequently, a non-optimal branch is more frequently chosen to establish a routing path, resulting in a higher stretch factor. On the other hand, TR only increases stretch factor moderately due to the lower nodal density.

4.2 Overhead and Stability

TR does not require any global information to be stored by individual nodes. Each node only collects its 1-hop neighbor information, which is proportional to nodal degree, i.e., the density of the network, which is usually regarded as constant for a given network setting. The information necessary for greedy forwarding is simply the destination ID and location. The information needs for trace-routing is the plane defined by the destination, local minimum, and another arbitrary node. The computation overhead includes the identification of boundary neighbors and the next hop on the trace, which is proportional to the nodal degree as well. So

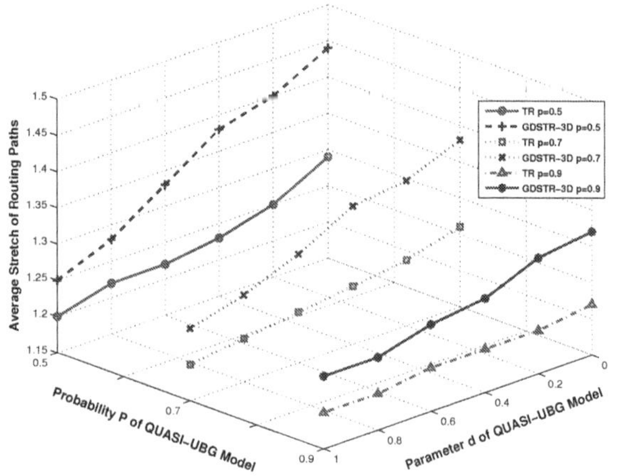

Figure 11: Stretch under Quasi-UDG.

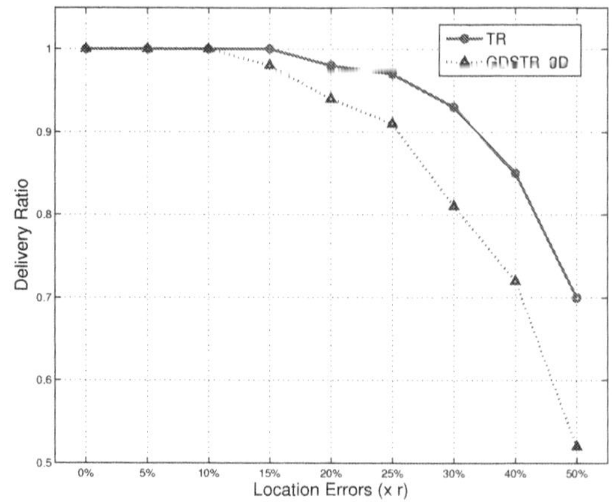

Figure 12: Delivery ratio against location errors.

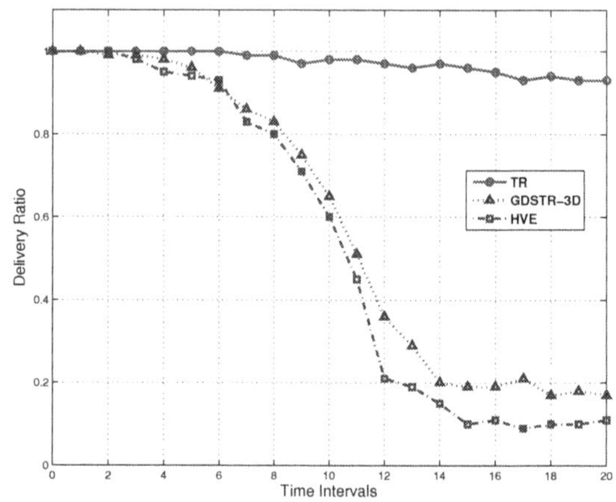

Figure 13: Delivery ratio under network dynamics.

both communication and computation overhead are bounded by a small constant (i.e., nodal degree). GDSTR-3D constructs two convex hull-based trees, where each node aggregates the locations of its children by using 2D convex hulls. Its time complexity and communication cost are dominated by the computation of 2D convex hulls (i.e., $O(n \log n)$), while the per node storage cost can be close to a constant after compression.

Location information is required in both TR and GDSTR-3D, which is, however, often subject to errors in practical sensor network settings. Fig. 12 depicts the results of TR and GDSTR-3D under different localization errors. We consider a path fails if its stretch factor exceeds 6.0. The delivery ratio of GDSTR-3D drops much faster than TR, because the location errors on individual nodes are aggregated in establishing the convex hull tree, increasing the chance to search into an incorrect tree branch. Since TR uses only local information only, the localization errors do not spread out. Therefore TR exhibits desired stability against localization errors. For example, under 30% errors, it still keeps its delivery ratio over 94%, while GDSTR-3D can deliver merely 81% of data.

4.3 Network Dynamics

Since TR does not rely on any global network structure, it is adaptive to network dynamics (e.g., sensors' movement). Here we evaluate the performance of TR, GDSTR-3D and HVE in mobile 3D sensor networks. We assume the holes are obstacles in the field where sensor nodes cannot access, and assume a simple random waypoint mobility model. More specifically, each node chooses a random position within a distance of ρ as its new position, where ρ is the maximum moving range during a time interval t. We let $\rho = 0.2r$ in our simulations. In each time interval, we measure the delivery ratios of three algorithms based on $10,000$ pair of randomly chosen nodes. Similar to the above discussion, a path is deemed unsuccessful if its stretch factor exceeds 6.0. The simulation lasts for 20 time intervals. As can be seen in Fig. 13, TR achieves a stable delivery ratio which is very close to 1 as expected, since the geometric shape of the network remains the same, even though the nodes change their positions. The failed routes, which are rare, are caused by the irregularity distribution of boundary nodes that results in very low node density in a local area. In a sharp contrast, the delivery ratios of GDSTR-3D and HVE decreases dramatically after 9 intervals, because the convex hull tree for GDSTR-3D and tetrahedron mesh for HVE become outdated, providing wrong routing information.

5. EXPERIMENTS

We have also implemented the TR algorithm on Crossbow MICAZ motes (MPR2400CA). We set up a small testbed with 98 motes, where the maximum transmission range is set to around 4.5 inches for easy configuration of network topology. We place the motes uniformly around the boundary of a cubic hole of $20 \times 20 \times 20$ inches and manually measure the relative coordinates of each mote. The distance between neighboring motes is 4 inches and the nodal degree is around 4, as shown in Fig 14. Since all motes are boundary nodes, we skip boundary identification in our implementation. Each mote keeps a table to store its neighboring motes' coordinates, which is an very small array (4×4 in size), which contains node ID and 3D-coordinates. The exchange of neighboring information is done during the bootstrap phase, which takes less than 20 seconds. The TR algorithm involves mostly vectors operations, such as cutting plane identification, intersection between line segment and plane, and calculation of angle between two vectors, which are very convenient to implement on MICAZ motes. A data packet contains a dummy data segment (of 512 bytes), the IDs and coordinates of the source and destination, and a flag to indicate current routing method (i.e., greedy or trace-routing). If trace-routing is employed, the data packet also includes the ID and coordinates of the local minimum node, and the cutting plane (represented as $Ax + By + Cz + D = 0$ where A, B, C and D are computed only once at the local minimum node based on the coordinates of

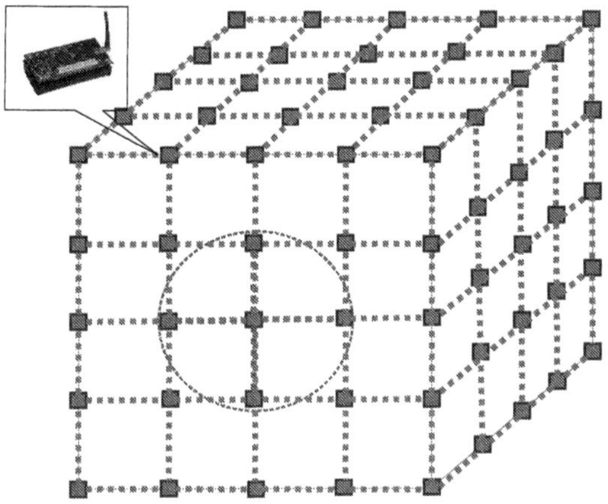

Figure 14: Experiment setup based on MicaZ motes.

the local minimum, the destination and an arbitrary neighboring node). The total overhead per packet is 52 bytes. We select 40 pairs of motes on different sides of the hole and transmit 50 packets for each route. All data packets are successfully delivered from source to destination in our experiment as expected, with an average stretch factor of 1.06.

6. CONCLUSION AND FUTURE WORKS

We have proposed *trace-routing*, a distributed and deterministic routing algorithm with constant storage, communication and computation overhead for 3D wireless sensor networks. Its basic idea is to construct a virtual cutting plane that intersects boundary surface to yield a trace, along which a routing path with guaranteed delivery can be established. We have proven the correctness of trace-routing under both continuous and discrete settings. We have implemented trace-routing on Crossbow sensors and carried out extensive simulations to evaluate its routing efficiency.

Acknowledgements.

Hongyi Wu is partially supported by NSF CNS-1018306 and CNS-1320931. Miao Jin is partially supported by NSF CCF-1054996, CNS-1018306 and CNS-1320931.

7. REFERENCES

[1] J. Allred, A. B. Hasan, S. Panichsakul, W. Pisano, P. Gray, J. Huang, R. Han, D. Lawrence, and K. Mohseni, "SensorFlock: An Airborne Wireless Sensor Network of Micro-Air Vehicles," in *Proc. of SenSys*, pp. 117–129, 2007.

[2] J.-H. Cui, J. Kong, M. Gerla, and S. Zhou, "Challenges: Building Scalable Mobile Underwater Wireless Sensor Networks for Aquatic Applications," *IEEE Network, Special Issue on Wireless Sensor Networking*, vol. 20, no. 3, pp. 12–18, 2006.

[3] X. Bai, C. Zhang, D. Xuan, J. Teng, and W. Jia, "Low-Connectivity and Full-Coverage Three Dimensional Networks," in *Proc. of MobiHOC*, pp. 145–154, 2009.

[4] X. Bai, C. Zhang, D. Xuan, and W. Jia, "Full-Coverage and K-Connectivity (K=14, 6) Three Dimensional Networks," in *Proc. of INFOCOM*, pp. 388–396, 2009.

[5] C. Liu and J. Wu, "Efficient Geometric Routing in Three Dimensional Ad Hoc Networks," in *Proc. of INFOCOM*, pp. 2751–2755, 2009.

[6] T. F. G. Kao and J. Opatmy, "Position-Based Routing on 3D Geometric Graphs in Mobile Ad Hoc Networks," in *Proc. of The 17th Canadian Conference on Computational Geometry*, pp. 88–91, 2005.

[7] J. Opatrny, A. Abdallah, and T. Fevens, "Randomized 3D Position-based Routing Algorithms for Ad-hoc Networks," in *Proc. of Third Annual International Conference on Mobile and Ubiquitous Systems: Networking & Services*, pp. 1–8, 2006.

[8] R. Flury and R. Wattenhofer, "Randomized 3D Geographic Routing," in *Proc. of INFOCOM*, pp. 834–842, 2008.

[9] F. Li, S. Chen, Y. Wang, and J. Chen, "Load Balancing Routing in Three Dimensional Wireless Networks," in *Proc. of ICC*, pp. 3073–3077, 2008.

[10] J. Zhou, Y. Chen, B. Leong, and P. Sundaramoorthy, "Practical 3D Geographic Routing for Wireless Sensor Networks," in *Proc. of SenSys*, pp. 337–350, 2010.

[11] D. Pompili, T. Melodia, and I. F. Akyildiz, "Routing Algorithms for Delay-insensitive and Delay-sensitive Applications in Underwater Sensor Networks," in *Proc. of MobiCom*, pp. 298–309, 2006.

[12] W. Cheng, A. Y. Teymorian, L. Ma, X. Cheng, X. Lu, and Z. Lu, "Underwater localization in sparse 3d acoustic sensor networks," in *Proc. of INFOCOM*, pp. 798–806, 2008.

[13] P. Bose, P. Morin, I. Stojmenovic, and J. Urrutia, "Routing with Guaranteed Delivery in Ad Hoc Wireless Networks," in *Proc. of Third Workshop Discrete Algorithms and Methods for Mobile Computing and Communications*, pp. 48–55, 1999.

[14] B. Karp and H. Kung, "GPSR: Greedy Perimeter Stateless Routing for Wireless Networks," in *Proc. of MobiCom*, pp. 1–12, 2001.

[15] E. Kranakis, H. Singh, and J. Urrutia, "Compass Routing on Geometric Networks," in *Proc. of CCCG*, pp. 51–54, 1999.

[16] F. Kuhn, R. Wattenhofer, Y. Zhang, and A. Zollinger, "Geometric Ad-hoc Routing: Theory and Practice," in *Proc. of The 22nd ACM Symposium on the Principles of Distributed Computing*, pp. 63–72, 2003.

[17] F. Kuhn, R. Wattenhofer, and A. Zollinger, "Worst-case Optimal and Average-case Efficient Geometric Ad-hoc Routing," in *Proc. of MobiHOC*, pp. 267–278, 2003.

[18] B. Leong, S. Mitra, and B. Liskov, "Path Vector Face Routing: Geographic Routing with Local Face Information," in *Proc. of ICNP*, pp. 147–158, 2005.

[19] H. Frey and I. Stojmenovic, "On Delivery Guarantees of Face and Combined Greedy-face Routing in Ad Hoc and Sensor Networks," in *Proc. of MobiCom*, pp. 390–401, 2006.

[20] G. Tan, M. Bertier, and A.-M. Kermarrec, "Visibility-Graph-based Shortest-Path Geographic Routing in Sensor Networks," in *Proc. of INFOCOM*, pp. 1719–1727, 2009.

[21] C. Papadimitriou and D. Ratajczak, "On A Conjecture Related to Geometric Routing," *Theoretical Computer Science*, vol. 344, no. 1, pp. 3–14, 2005.

[22] P. Angelini, F. Frati, and L. Grilli, "An Algorithm to Construct Greedy Drawings of Triangulations," in *Proc. of The 16th International Symposium on Graph Drawing*, pp. 26–37, 2008.

[23] T. Leighton and A. Moitra, "Some Results on Greedy Embeddings in Metric Spaces," in *Proc. of The 49th IEEE*

Annual Symposium on Foundations of Computer Science, pp. 337–346, 2008.

[24] R. Kleinberg, "Geographic Routing Using Hyperbolic Space," in *Proc. of INFOCOM*, pp. 1902–1909, 2007.

[25] A. Cvetkovski and M. Crovella, "Hyperbolic Embedding and Routing for Dynamic Graphs," in *Proc. of INFOCOM*, pp. 1647–1655, 2009.

[26] R. Sarkar, X. Yin, J. Gao, F. Luo, and X. Gu, "Greedy Routing with Guaranteed Delivery Using Ricci Flows," in *Proc. of IPSN*, pp. 121–132, 2009.

[27] R. Flury, S. Pemmaraju, and R. Wattenhofer, "Greedy Routing with Bounded Stretch," in *Proc. of INFOCOM*, pp. 1737–1745, 2009.

[28] S. Durocher, D. Kirkpatrick, and L. Narayanan, "On Routing with Guaranteed Delivery in Three-Dimensional Ad Hoc Wireless Networks," in *Proc. of International Conference on Distributed Computing and Networking*, pp. 546–557, 2008.

[29] Y. Wang, C.-W. Yi, and F. Li, "Delivery Guarantee of Greedy Routing in Three Dimensional Wireless Networks," in *Proc of International Conference on Wireless Algorithms, Systems, and Applications*, pp. 4–16, 2008.

[30] S. S. Lam and C. Qian, "Geographic Routing with Low Stretch in d-dimensional Spaces," in *Proc. of SIGMETRICS*, pp. 257–268, 2011.

[31] S. Xia, X. Yin, H. Wu, M. Jin, and X. Gu, "Deterministic Greedy Routing with Guaranteed Delivery in 3D Wireless Sensor Networks," in *Proc. of MobiHoc*, pp. 1–10, 2011.

[32] H. Zhou, S. Xia, M. Jin, and H. Wu, "Localized Algorithm for Precise Boundary Detection in 3D Wireless Networks," in *Proc. of ICDCS*, pp. 744–753, 2010.

Max-min Fair Rate Allocation and Routing in Energy Harvesting Networks: Algorithmic Analysis

Jelena Marašević[1], Clifford Stein[2], Gil Zussman[1]
[1]Electrical Engineering, [2]Industrial Engineering and Operations Research Dept., Columbia University
New York, NY, 10027, USA
{jelena@ee, cliff@ieor, gil@ee}.columbia.edu

ABSTRACT

This paper considers max-min fair rate allocation and routing in energy harvesting networks where fairness is required among *both the nodes and the time slots*. Unlike most previous work on fairness, we focus on *multihop topologies* and consider *different routing methods*. We assume a predictable energy profile and focus on the design of efficient and optimal algorithms that can serve as benchmarks for distributed and approximate algorithms. We first develop an algorithm that obtains a max-min fair rate assignment for any given (time-variable or time-invariable) *unsplittable routing* or a *routing tree*. For *time-invariable unsplittable routing*, we also develop an algorithm that finds routes that maximize the minimum rate assigned to any node in any slot. For *fractional routing*, we study the joint routing and rate assignment problem. We develop an algorithm for the *time-invariable* case with constant rates. We show that the *time-variable* case is at least as hard as the 2-commodity feasible flow problem and design an FPTAS to combat the high running time. Finally, we show that finding a max-min fair unsplittable routing or a routing tree is NP-hard, even for a time horizon of a single slot. Our analysis provides insights into the problem structure and can be applied to other related fairness problems.

Categories and Subject Descriptors: C.2.1. [Computer-Communication Networks]: Network Architecture and Design — *Wireless Communication*
Keywords: Energy Harvesting; Energy Adaptive Networking; Sensor Networks; Routing; Fairness

1. INTRODUCTION

Recent advances in the development of ultra-low-power transceivers and energy harvesting devices (e.g., solar cells) will enable self-sustainable and perpetual wireless networks [12,13]. In contrast to legacy wireless sensor networks, where the available energy only decreases as the nodes sense and forward data, in energy harvesting networks the available energy can also increase through a replenishment process.

MobiHoc'14, August 11–14, 2014, Philadelphia, PA, USA.

ACM 978-1-4503-2620-9/14/08 ...$15.00.
http://dx.doi.org/10.1145/2632951.2632960 .

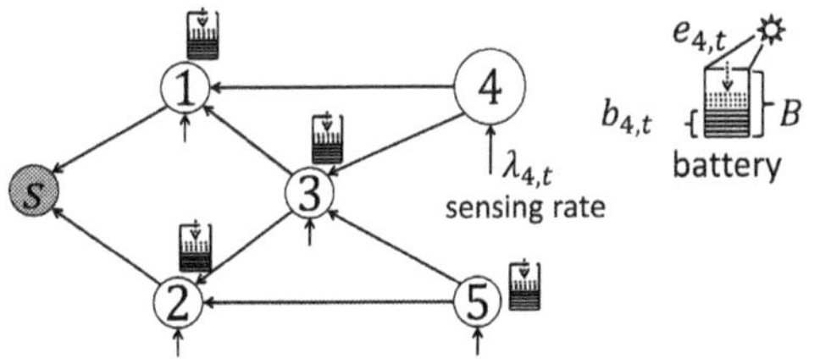

Figure 1: A simple energy harvesting network: the nodes sense the environment and forward the data to a sink s. Each node has a battery of capacity B. At time t a node i's battery level is $b_{i,t}$, it harvests $e_{i,t}$ units of energy, and senses at data rate $\lambda_{i,t}$.

As a result, the available energy is a more complex quantity, thereby posing challenges in the design of resource allocation and routing algorithms.

Two natural conditions that a network should satisfy are: (i) balanced data acquisition over all the parts of the network, and (ii) persistent operation (i.e., even when the environmental energy is not available for harvesting). Condition (i) is commonly reinforced by requiring fairness of the sensing rates over network nodes. One approach to achieving (ii) is by assigning constant sensing rates to the nodes. However, this approach can result in underutilization of the available energy. As a simple example, consider a node that harvests outdoor light energy over a 24-hour time horizon. If the battery capacity is small, then the sensing rate must be low to prevent battery depletion during the nighttime. However, during the daytime, when the harvesting rates are high, a low sensing rate prevents full utilization of the energy that can be harvested. Therefore, it is advantageous to vary the sensing rates over time. However, fairness must be required over time slots to prevent the rate assignment algorithm from assigning high rates during periods of high energy availability, and zero rates when no energy is available for harvesting.

The problems of resource allocation, scheduling, and routing in energy harvesting networks have received considerable attention [2,4,10,11,14–16,19,20,25,29]. Much of the existing work considers simple networks consisting of a single node or a link [2,4,11,14,25,29]. Moreover, fair rate assignment has not been thoroughly studied, and most of the work either focuses on maximizing the total (or average) throughput [2,4,10,16,19,22,25,29], or considers fairness either *only over nodes* [20] or *only over time* [11,14]. An exception is [15], which requires fairness over both the nodes and the time, but is limited to *two nodes*.

In this paper, we study the max-min fair rate assignment and routing problems, requiring fairness over both nodes and

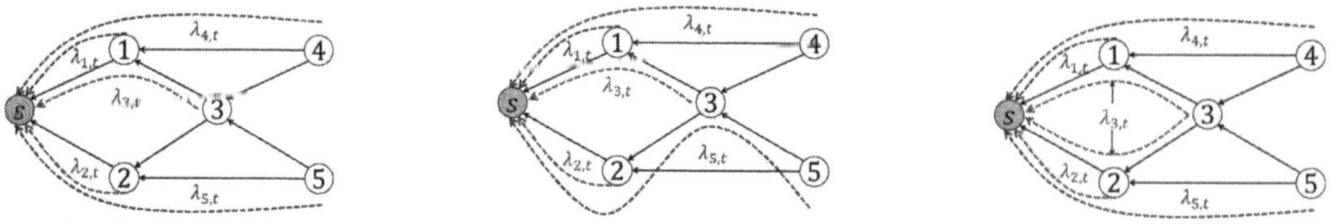

(a) Routing tree. (b) Unsplittable routing. (c) Fractional routing.

Figure 2: Routing types: (a) a routing tree, (b) unsplittable routing: each node sends its data over one path, (c) fractional routing: nodes can send their data over multiple paths. Paths are represented by dashed lines.

time slots, and with the goal of designing optimal and efficient algorithms. Following [11, 14, 15, 19, 20], we assume that the harvested energy is known for each node over a finite time horizon. Although there are settings that do not conform to this assumption, the designed algorithms can be used for: (i) determining (in an offline fashion) rate assignment and routing in a network with a highly-predictable energy profile, and (ii) benchmarking rate assignment and routing solutions in networks with unpredictable energy profiles. We consider an energy harvesting sensor network with a single sink node, and network connectivity modeled by a directed graph (Fig. 1). Each node senses some data from its surrounding (e.g., air pressure, temperature, radiation level), and sends it to the sink. The nodes spend their energy on sensing, sending, and receiving data.

We consider different routing types, which are illustrated in Fig. 2. Each routing type incurs different trade-offs between the supported sensing rates[1] and the required amount of control information. Routing types with higher number of active links require more control information to be exchanged between neighboring nodes (e.g., to maintain synchronization), and complicate the transmission and/or sleep-wake scheduling implementation. Moreover, energy consumed by the control messages can affect achievable rates significantly, due to limited energy budget, as confirmed via experiments in [13]. Below we outline the main characteristics of the routing types we consider.

Routing Tree–the simplest form of routing, in which every node sends all of the data it senses and receives to a single neighboring (parent) node. It requires minimum number of active links, yielding minimum energy consumption due to control messages. However, in general, it provides the lowest sensing rates (see more details below).

Unsplittable Routing–a single-path routing, in which every node sends all of its sensed data over a single path to the sink (a routing tree is a special case of the unsplittable routing, in which all the paths incoming into node i outgo via the same edge). There are simple cases in which unsplittable routing provides a rate assignment with the minimum sensing rate $\Omega(n)$ times higher than in a routing tree, where n is the number of nodes [23]. However, in general, it has higher number of active links than the routing tree, yielding higher energy consumption for control information.

Fractional Routing–a multi-path routing, in which each node can split its data over multiple paths to the sink (unsplittable routing is a special case of fractional routing in which every node has one path to the sink). It is the most general routing that subsumes both routing trees and unsplittable routings, and, therefore, provides the best sensing rates. However, it utilizes the highest number of links, yielding the highest energy consumption due to control messages.

[1]A metric of performance can be the minimum sensing rate that is assigned to any node in any time slot.

Time-invariable vs Time-variable Routing– A routing is *time-invariable*, if every node uses the same (set of) path(s) in each time slot to send its data to the sink. If the paths change over time, the routing is *time-variable.*[2] While there are cases in which time-variable routing provides a rate assignment with the minimum sensing rate $\Omega(n)$ times higher than in the time-invariable case [23], it requires substantial control information exchange for routing reconfigurations, yielding high energy consumption.

For the *unsplittable routing* and *routing tree*, we design a fully-combinatorial algorithm that solves the *max-min fair rate assignment* problem, both in the time-variable and time-invariable settings, when the routing is provided at the input. We then turn to *fractional routing*, considering two settings: time-variable and time-invariable. We demonstrate that in the *time-variable* setting verifying whether a given rate assignment is feasible is at least as hard as solving a feasible 2-commodity flow. This result implies that, to our current knowledge, it is unlikely that max-min fair time-variable fractional routing[3] can be solved without the use of linear programming. To combat the high running time induced by the linear programming, we develop a fully polynomial time approximation scheme (FPTAS). For the *time-invariable setting*, we provide a fully-combinatorial algorithm that determines a max-min fair routing with constant rates.

We show that *determining* a max-min fair unsplittable routing or a routing tree is NP-hard even for a single time slot. Relaxing the max-min fairness requirement, we develop an algorithm that determines a time-invariable unsplittable routing that maximizes the minimum sensing rate assigned to any node in any time slot.

The considered problems generalize classical max-min fair routing problems that have been studied outside the area of energy harvesting networks: max-min fair fractional routing [24], max-min fair unsplittable routing [18], and bottleneck routing [3]. In contrast to the problems studied in [3, 18, 24], our model allows different costs for flow generation and forwarding, and has time-variable node capacities determined by the available energies at the nodes. We note that studying networks with node capacities is as general as studying networks with capacitated edges, since there are standard methods for transforming one of these two problems into another (see, e.g., [1]). Therefore, we believe that the results can find applications in other related areas.

The rest of the paper is organized as follows. Section 2 provides the model and problem formulations, which are placed in the context of related work in Section 3. Section 4

[2]Whether the rates are constant or time-variable is independent of whether the routing is time-variable or not.

[3]We refer to a routing as max-min fair if it provides the lexicographically maximum rate assignment. The notions of max-min fairness and lexicographic maximization are defined in Section 4.

Table 1: Nomenclature.

inputs	n	Number of energy harvesting nodes
	T	Time horizon
	B	Battery capacity
	$b_{i,1}$	Initial battery level at node i
	$e_{i,t}$	Harvested energy at node i in time slot t
	$c_{\rm s}$	Energy spent for sensing a unit flow
	$c_{\rm tx}$	Energy spent for transmitting a unit flow
	$c_{\rm rx}$	Energy spent for receiving a unit flow
variables	$\lambda_{i,t}$	Sensing rate of node i in time slot t
	$f_{ij,t}$	Flow on link (i,j) in time slot t
	$b_{i,t+1}$	Battery level at node i at the beginning of time slot $t+1$
notation	i	Node index, $i \in \{1, 2, ...n\}$
	t	Time index, $t \in \{1, 2, ..., T\}$
	$c_{\rm st}$	Energy spent for jointly sensing and transmitting a unit flow: $c_{\rm st} = c_{\rm s} + c_{\rm tx}$
	$c_{\rm rt}$	Energy spent for jointly receiving and transmitting a unit flow: $c_{\rm rt} = c_{\rm rx} + c_{\rm tx}$
	$f^{\Sigma}_{i,t}$	Total flow entering node i in time slot t: $f^{\Sigma}_{i,t} = \sum_{j:(j,i)\in E} f_{ji,t}$

describes the connection between max-min fairness and lexicographic maximization. Section 5 considers rate assignment in unsplittable routing, while Sections 6 and 7 study fractional routing and rate assignment in time-variable and time-invariable settings. Section 8 provides hardness results for determining unsplittable routing or a routing tree. Section 9 concludes the paper. Due to space constraints, most of the proofs are deferred to the technical report [23].

2. MODEL AND PROBLEM FORMULATION

We consider a network that consists of n energy harvesting nodes and one sink node (see Fig. 1). The sink is the central point at which all the sensed data is collected, and is assumed not to be energy constrained. In the rest of the paper, the term "sink" will be used for the sink node. The connectivity between the nodes is modeled by a directed graph $G = (V, E)$, where $|V| = n+1$ (n nodes and the sink), and $|E| = m$. The main notation is summarized in Table 1.

Each node is equipped with a rechargeable battery of finite capacity B. The time horizon is T time slots. The duration of a time slot is assumed to be much longer than the duration of a single data packet, but short enough so that the rate of energy harvesting does not change during a slot. For example, if outdoor light energy is harvested, one time slot can be at the order of a minute. In a time slot t, a node i harvests $e_{i,t}$ units of energy. The battery level of a node i at the beginning of a time slot t is $b_{i,t}$. We follow a predictable energy profile [11,14,15,19,20], and assume that the battery capacity B, initial battery levels $b_{i,1}$, and harvested energies $e_{i,t}$ are known and finite, for $i \in \{1, ..., n\}$, $t \in \{1, ..., T\}$.

A node i in slot t senses data at rate $\lambda_{i,t}$. A node forwards all the data it senses and receives towards the sink. The flow on a link (i, j) in slot t is denoted by $f_{ij,t}$. Each node spends $c_{\rm s}$ energy units to sense a unit flow, and $c_{\rm tx}$, respectively $c_{\rm rx}$, energy units to transmit, respectively receive, a unit flow.

The feasible region $\mathcal{R}$ for the sensing rates and flows is determined by the following set of linear constraints:

$$\forall i \in \{1, ..., n\}, t \in \{1, ..., T\}:$$

$$f^{\Sigma}_{i,t} + \lambda_{i,t} = \sum_{(i,j)\in E} f_{ij,t}, \quad (1)$$

$$b_{i,t+1} = \min\{B, \quad b_{i,t} + e_{i,t} - (c_{\rm rt} f^{\Sigma}_{i,t} + c_{\rm st}\lambda_{i,t})\}, \quad (2)$$

$$b_{i,t+1} \geq 0,\ \lambda_{i,t} \geq 0,\ f_{ij,t} \geq 0, \forall (i,j) \in E, \quad (3)$$

where $f^{\Sigma}_{i,t} \equiv \sum_{(j,i)\in E} f_{ji,t}$, $c_{\rm st} \equiv c_{\rm s} + c_{\rm tx}$, and $c_{\rm rt} \equiv c_{\rm rx} + c_{\rm tx}$. Eq. (1) is a classical flow conservation constraint, while (2) models battery evolution over time slots.[4]

Similar to the definition of max-min fairness in [3], we define a rate assignment $\{\lambda_{i,t}\}$, $i \in \{1, ..., n\}$, $t \in \{1, ..., T\}$, to be max-min fair if no $\lambda_{i,t}$ can be increased without either losing feasibility or decreasing some other rate $\lambda_{j,\tau} \leq \lambda_{i,t}$.

In some of the problems, the routing is provided at the input as a set of paths $\mathcal{P} = \{p_{i,t}\}$, for $i \in \{1, ..., n\}, t \in \{1, ..., T\}$. In such a case, $\mathcal{R}$ should be interpreted with respect to $\mathcal{P}$, instead with respect to the input graph G.

Considered problems (see Table 1 for inputs and variables). We examine different routing types, in time-variable and time-invariable settings, as described in the introduction. For the unsplittable routing and routing trees, we examine the problems of *determining a rate assignment* and *determining a routing* separately, as described below.

P-UNSPLITTABLE-RATES: For a given time-variable unsplittable routing $\mathcal{P} = \{p_{i,t}\}$, determine the max-min fair assignment of the rates $\{\lambda_{i,t}\}$. Note that this setting subsumes time-invariable unsplittable routing, time-invariable routing tree, and time-variable routing tree.

P-UNSPLITTABLE-FIND: Associate with each (time-invariable or time-variable) unsplittable routing $\mathcal{P}$, a set of sensing rates $\{\lambda^{\mathcal{P}}_{i,t}\}$ that optimally solves P-UNSPLITTABLE-RATES. Determine an unsplittable routing $\mathcal{P}$ that provides the lexicographically maximum[5] rate assignment $\{\lambda^{\mathcal{P}}_{i,t}\}$.

P-TREE-FIND: Let $\mathcal{T}$ denote a (time-invariable or time-variable) routing tree on the input graph G. Associate with each $\mathcal{T}$ a set of sensing rates $\{\lambda^{\mathcal{T}}_{i,t}\}$ that optimally solves P-UNSPLITTABLE-RATES. Determine $\mathcal{T}$ that provides the lexicographically maximum rate assignment $\{\lambda^{\mathcal{T}}_{i,t}\}$.

For the fractional routing, we study the following two variants of max-min fair routing, where the routing and the rate assignment are determined jointly.

P-FRACTIONAL: Determine a *time-variable* fractional routing with the max-min fair rate assignment $\{\lambda_{i,t}\}$.

P-FIXED-FRACTIONAL: Determine a *time-invariable* fractional routing with the max-min fair rate assignment $\{\lambda_{i,t}\} = \{\lambda_i\}$, when the sensing rates are constant over time.

3. RELATED WORK

Energy-harvesting Networks. Rate assignment in energy harvesting networks in the case of a single node or a link was studied in [2,4,11,14,25,29].

Resource allocation and scheduling for network-wide scenarios using Lyapunov optimization techniques was studied in [10,16,22]. While the work in [10,16,22] can support unpredictable energy profiles, it focuses on the (sum-utility of) time-average rates, which is, in general, time-unfair. The design of online algorithms for resource allocation and routing was studied in [9,19].

Max-min time-fair rate assignment for a single node or a link was studied in [11, 14], while max-min fair energy allocation for single-hop and two-hop scenarios was studied in [15]. Similar to our work, [15] requires fairness over both the nodes and the time slots, but considers only two energy

[4]Eq. (2) is considered as a linear constraint, since for maximizing $\lambda_{i,t}$'s it can be replaced by $b_{i,t+1} \leq B$ and $b_{i,t+1} \leq b_{i,t} + e_{i,t} - (c_{\rm rt} f^{\Sigma}_{i,t} + c_{\rm st}\lambda_{i,t})$.

[5]Lexicographical ordering of vectors is defined in Section 4.

harvesting nodes. The work on max-min fairness in network-wide scenarios [20] is explained in more detail below.

Sensor Networks. Problems P-FRACTIONAL, P-FIXED-FRACTIONAL, and P-UNSPLITTABLE-RATES are related to the maximum lifetime routing problems (see, e.g., [6,21] and the follow-up work) in the following sense. In our model, maximization of the minimum sensing rate is equivalent to the network lifetime maximization in sensor networks, *but only if the system is observed for* $T = 1$. Namely, the nodes have the initial energy, and no harvesting happens over time.

Determining a maximum lifetime tree in sensor networks as in [5] is a special case of P-TREE-FIND. We extend the NP-hardness result from [5] and provide a lower bound of $\Omega(\log n)$ for the approximation ratio (for both [5] and P-TREE-FIND), where n is the number of nodes in the network.

Max-min Fair Unsplittable Routing. Rate assignment in unsplittable routing was studied extensively (see [3,7] and references therein). P-UNSPLITTABLE-RATES reduces to the problem studied in [3, 7] for $c_{\text{st}} = 0, c_{\text{rt}} > 0$, and $T = 1$. In the energy harvesting network setting, this problem has been studied in [20], for rates that are constant over time and a time-invariable routing tree. We consider a more general case than in [20], where the rates are time-variable, fairness is required over both network nodes and time slots, and the routing can be time-variable and given in a form of an unsplittable routing or a routing tree.

Determining a max-min fair unsplittable routing as studied in [18] is a special case of P-UNSPLITTABLE-FIND for $c_{\text{st}} = 0, c_{\text{rt}} > 0$, and $T = 1$, and the NP-hardness results from [18] implies the NP-hardness of P-UNSPLITTABLE-FIND.

Max-min Fair Fractional Routing. Max-min fair fractional routing was first studied in [24]. The algorithm from [24] relies on the property that the total values of a max-min fair flow and max flow are equal, which does not hold even in simple instances of P-FIXED-FRACTIONAL and P-FRACTIONAL. P-FIXED-FRACTIONAL and P-FRACTIONAL reduce to the problem of [24] for $c_{\text{st}} = 0, c_{\text{rt}} > 0$, and $T = 1$.

Max-min fair fractional routing in energy harvesting networks has been considered in [20]. The distributed algorithm from [20] solves P-FIXED-FRACTIONAL, but only as a heuristic. We provide a combinatorial algorithm that solves P-FIXED-FRACTIONAL optimally in a centralized manner.

A general linear programming framework for max-min fair routing was provided in [27], and extended to the setting of sensor and energy harvesting networks in [8] and [20], respectively. This framework, when applied to P-FRACTIONAL, is highly inefficient. P-FRACTIONAL reduces to [8] for $T = 1$, and to [20] when the rates are constant over time.

4. MAX-MIN FAIRNESS AND LEXICOGRAPHIC MAXIMIZATION

Recall that a rate assignment $\{\lambda_{i,t}\}$, $i \in \{1, ..., n\}$, $t \in \{1, ..., T\}$, is max-min fair if no rate $\lambda_{i,t}$ can be increased without either losing feasibility or decreasing some other rate $\lambda_{j,\tau} \leq \lambda_{i,t}$. Closely related to the max-min fairness is the notion of lexicographic maximization. The lexicographic ordering of vectors, with the relational operators denoted by $\overset{lex}{=}$, $\overset{lex}{>}$, and $\overset{lex}{<}$, is defined as follows:

Definition 4.1. *Let u and v be two vectors of the same length l, and let u_s and v_s denote the vectors obtained from u and v respectively by sorting their elements in the non-decreasing order. Then: (i) $u \overset{lex}{=} v$ if $u_s = v_s$ element-wise; (ii) $u \overset{lex}{>} v$ if there exists $j \in \{1, 2, ..., l\}$, such that $u_s(j) > v_s(j)$, and $u_s(1) = v_s(1), ..., u_s(j-1) = v_s(j-1)$ if $j > 1$; (iii) $u \overset{lex}{<} v$ if not $u \overset{lex}{=} v$ nor $u \overset{lex}{>} v$.*

It was proved in [27] that a max-min fair allocation vector exists on any convex and compact set. The results from [28] state that in a given optimization problem whenever a max-min fair vector exists, it is unique and equal to the lexicographically maximum one.

In the problems P-UNSPLITTABLE-RATES, P-FRACTIONAL, and P-FIXED-FRACTIONAL the feasible region $\mathcal{R}$ is determined by linear constraints (1)-(3), and it is therefore convex. As we are assuming that all the input values $B, e_{i,t}$, and $b_{i,1}$ are finite, it follows that the feasible region is also bounded, and therefore compact. Therefore, for the aforementioned problems, lexicographic maximization produces the max-min fair assignment of the sensing rates $\{\lambda_{i,t}\}$.

Lexicographic maximization can be implemented using the well-known water-filling framework (see, e.g., [3]):

Algorithm 1 WATER-FILLING-FRAMEWORK(G, b, e)

1: Set $\lambda_{i,t} = 0\ \forall i, t$, and mark all the rates as not fixed.
2: Increase all the rates $\lambda_{i,t}$ that are not fixed by the same maximum amount, subject to the constraints from $\mathcal{R}$.
3: Fix all the $\lambda_{i,t}$'s that cannot be further increased.
4: If all the rates are fixed, terminate. Else, go to step 2.

While the framework is well-known, it does not fully specify Steps 2 and 3. Implementation of these two steps is the main challenge in solving P-UNSPLITTABLE-RATES, P-FRACTIONAL, and P-FIXED-FRACTIONAL, for which we develop algorithms in the following sections. We refer to the algorithms that implement Steps 2 and 3 as MAXIMIZING-THE-RATES and FIXING-THE-RATES, respectively.

Note: A rate $\lambda_{i,t}$ can in general get fixed in any iteration of the WATER-FILLING-FRAMEWORK; there is no rule that relates an iteration k to a node i or a time slot t.

5. RATES IN UNSPLITTABLE ROUTING

This section studies P-UNSPLITTABLE-RATES, the problem of rate assignment for an unsplittable routing provided at the input. The analysis applies to any time-invariable or time-variable unsplittable routing or a routing tree.

We assume that the routing over time $t \in \{1, ..., T\}$ is provided as a set of routing paths $\mathcal{P} = \{p_{i,t}\}$ from a node i to the sink s, for each node $i \in V \backslash \{s\}$. We say that a node j is a descendant of a node i in a time slot t if $i \in p_{j,t}$.[6]

Before describing the algorithms in detail, we need to introduce some notation. Let $F_{i,t}^k = 1$ if the rate $\lambda_{i,t}$ is not fixed at the beginning of the kth iteration of WATER-FILLING-FRAMEWORK, $F_{i,t}^k = 0$ otherwise. Initially, $F_{i,t}^1 = 1$, $\forall i, t$. If a rate $\lambda_{i,t}$ is not fixed, we will say that it is "active". We will denote by $D_{i,t}^k$ the number of active descendants of the node i in the time slot t, where $D_{i,t}^1 = |\{j : i \in p_{j,t} \backslash \{j\}\}|$. Notice that $D_{i,t}^k = \sum_{j: i \in p_{j,t} \backslash \{j\}} F_{j,t}^k$. Finally, let $\lambda_{i,t}^k$ denote the value of $\lambda_{i,t}$ in the kth iteration of WATER-FILLING-FRAMEWORK, and let $\lambda_{i,t}^0 = 0$, $\forall i, t$. Under this notation, the rates can be expressed as $\lambda_{i,t}^k = \sum_{l=1}^k F_{i,t}^l \lambda^l$, where λ^l

[6]Notice that this is consistent with the definition of a descendant in a routing tree.

denotes the common amount by which all the active rates get increased in the lth iteration.

5.1 Maximizing the Rates

Maximization of the common rate λ^k in k^{th} iteration of WATER-FILLING-FRAMEWORK can be formulated as follows:

$$\begin{aligned}
&\textbf{max } \lambda^k\\
&\textbf{s.t. } \forall i \in \{1,...,n\}, t \in \{1,...,T\}:\\
&\quad \lambda_{i,t}^k = \lambda_{i,t}^{k-1} + F_{i,t}^k \cdot \lambda^k,\\
&\quad f_{i,t}^{\Sigma} + \lambda_{i,t}^k = \sum_{(i,j)\in E} f_{ij,t},\\
&\quad b_{i,t+1} = \min\{B,\, b_{i,t} + e_{i,t} - (c_{\text{rt}} f_{i,t}^{\Sigma} + c_{\text{st}}\lambda_{i,t}^k)\},\\
&\quad b_{i,t} \geq 0,\ \lambda^k \geq 0,\ f_{ij,t} \geq 0, \forall (i,j) \in E.
\end{aligned}$$

As in each slot t every node i sends all the flow it senses over a single path, we can compute the total inflow into a node i as the sum of the flows coming from i's descendants:

$$\begin{aligned}
f_{i,t}^{\Sigma} &= \sum_{j:i\in p_{j,t}\backslash\{j\}} \sum_{l=1}^{k} F_{j,t}^l \cdot \lambda^l = \sum_{l=1}^{k} \lambda^l \sum_{j:i\in p_{j,t}\backslash\{j\}} F_{j,t}^l\\
&= \sum_{l=1}^{k} D_{i,t}^l \cdot \lambda^l.
\end{aligned}$$

Denoting the battery levels in the iteration k as $b_{i,t}^k$, the problem can now be written more compactly as:

$$\begin{aligned}
&\textbf{max } \lambda^k\\
&\textbf{s.t. } \forall i \in \{1,...,n\}, t \in \{1,...,T\}:\\
&\quad b_{i,t+1}^k = \min\{B,\, b_{i,t}^k + e_{i,t} - \sum_{l=1}^{k} \lambda^l (c_{\text{rt}} D_{i,t}^l + c_{\text{st}} F_{i,t}^l)\},\\
&\quad b_{i,t}^k \geq 0,\ \lambda^k \geq 0,
\end{aligned}$$

where $\forall i\, \forall k: b_{i,1}^k = b_{i,1}$.

Define the battery drop for node i in slot t and iteration k as: $\Delta b_{i,t}^k = \sum_{l=1}^{k} \lambda^l (c_{\text{rt}} D_{i,t}^l + c_{\text{st}} F_{i,t}^l)$, setting $\Delta b_{i,t}^0 = 0$. The intuition is: to determine the battery levels in all the time slots, we only need to know the initial battery level and how much energy ($\Delta b_{i,t}$) is spent per time slot. This results in:

$$\begin{aligned}
&\textbf{max } \lambda^k\\
&\textbf{s.t. } \forall i \in \{1,...,n\}, t \in \{1,...,T\}:\\
&\quad \Delta b_{i,t}^k = \Delta b_{i,t}^{k-1} + \lambda^k (c_{\text{rt}} D_{i,t}^k + c_{\text{st}} F_{i,t}^k),\\
&\quad b_{i,t+1}^k = \min\{B,\, b_{i,t}^k + e_{i,t} - \Delta b_{i,t}^k\},\\
&\quad b_{i,t}^k \geq 0,\ \lambda^k \geq 0.
\end{aligned}$$

Writing the problem for each node independently, we can solve the following subproblem:

$$\textbf{max } \lambda_i^k \tag{4}$$

$$\textbf{s.t. } \forall t \in \{1,...,T\}:$$

$$\Delta b_{i,t}^k = \Delta b_{i,t}^{k-1} + \lambda_i^k (c_{\text{rt}} D_{i,t}^k + c_{\text{st}} F_{i,t}^k), \tag{5}$$

$$b_{i,t+1}^k = \min\{B,\, b_{i,t}^k + e_{i,t} - \Delta b_{i,t}^k\}, \tag{6}$$

$$b_{i,t}^k \geq 0,\ \lambda_i^k \geq 0, \tag{7}$$

for each i with $\sum_{i,t} F_{i,t}^k > 0$, and determine $\lambda^k = \min_i \lambda_i^k$. Notice that we can bound each λ_i^k by the interval $[0, \lambda_{\max,i}^k]$, where $\lambda_{\max,i}^k$ is the rate for which node i spends all its available energy in the first slot τ in which its rate is not fixed:

$$\lambda_{\max,i}^k = \frac{b_{i,\tau}^{k-1} + e_{i,\tau}}{c_{\text{rt}} D_{i,\tau}^k + c_{\text{st}}}, \quad \tau = \min\{t : F_{i,t}^k = 1\}.$$

The subproblem of determining λ_i^k can now be solved by performing a binary search in the interval $[0, \lambda_{\max,i}^k]$.

Let δ denote the precision of the input variables. Note that however small, δ can usually be expressed as a constant.

Lemma 5.1. MAXIMIZING-THE-RATES *in* P-UNSPLITTABLE-FIND *can be implemented in time* $O\left(T \sum_i \log\left(\lambda_{\max,i}^k/\delta\right)\right) = O\left(nT \log\left((B + \max_{i,t} e_{i,t})/(\delta c_{st})\right)\right)$.

5.2 Fixing the Rates

Recall that the elements of the matrix F^k are such that $F_{i,t}^k = 0$ if the rate $\lambda_{i,t}$ is fixed for the iteration k, and $F_{i,t}^k = 1$ otherwise. At the end of iteration $k \geq 1$, let $F^{k+1} = F^k$, and consider the following set of rules for fixing the rates:

(F1) For all (i,t) such that $b_{i,t+1}^k = 0$ set $F_{i,t}^{k+1} = 0$.

(F2) For all (i,t) such that $b_{i,t+1}^k = 0$ determine the longest sequence $(i,t), (i,t-1), (i,t-2), ..., (i,\tau), \tau \geq 1$, with the property that $b_{i,s}^k + e_{i,s} - \Delta b_{i,s}^k \leq B\ \forall s \in \{t, t-1, ..., \tau\}$, and set $F_{i,s}^{k+1} = 0\ \forall s$.

(F3) For all (i,t) for which the rules (F1) and (F2) have set $F_{i,t}^{k+1} = 0$, and for all j such that $i \in p_{j,t}$, set $F_{j,t}^{k+1} = 0$.

The correctness of the rules (F1)-(F3) is proved via the following two lemmas.

Lemma 5.2. *(Necessity) No rate fixed by the rules (F1), (F2) and (F3) can be increased in the next iteration without violating feasibility constraints.*

Proof. We first make the following two observations. When $b_{i,t+1}^k = 0$, then, from (6):

$$\begin{aligned}
b_{i,t+1}^k &= \min\{B,\, b_{i,t}^k + e_{i,t} - (c_{\text{rt}} \sum_{j:i\in p_{j,t}\backslash\{j\}} \lambda_{j,t}^k + c_{\text{st}}\lambda_{i,t}^k)\}\\
&= b_{i,t}^k + e_{i,t} - (c_{\text{rt}} \sum_{j:i\in p_{j,t}\backslash\{j\}} \lambda_{j,t}^k + c_{\text{st}}\lambda_{i,t}^k) = 0. \qquad (8)
\end{aligned}$$

For $b_{i,t+1}^k = 0$, let $(i,t), (i,t-1), (i,t-2), ..., (i,\tau), \tau \geq 1$, be the longest sequence with the property that: $b_{i,s}^k + e_{i,s} - \Delta b_{i,s}^k \leq B\ \forall s \in \{t, t-1, ..., \tau\}$. Then $\forall s \in \{\tau, \tau+1, ..., t-1\}$:

$$b_{i,s+1}^k = b_{i,s}^k + e_{i,s} - (c_{\text{rt}} \sum_{j:i\in p_{j,t}\backslash\{j\}} \lambda_{j,s}^k + c_{\text{st}}\lambda_{i,s}^k).$$

This is a recursive relation on s, so we can write $b_{i,t+1}$ as:

$$b_{i,t+1}^k = b_{i,\tau}^k + \sum_{s=\tau}^{t} e_{i,s} - \sum_{s=\tau}^{t} (c_{\text{rt}} \sum_{j:i\in p_{j,t}\backslash\{j\}} \lambda_{j,s}^k - c_{\text{st}}\lambda_{i,s}^k). \tag{9}$$

The rest of the proof is by induction on iteration k.

The base case. In the first iteration, $\lambda_{i,t}^1 = \lambda^1$, $\forall i, t$. Suppose $b_{i,t+1}^1 = 0$ for some i, t. From (8), if $\lambda_{i,t}$ is increased, either $b_{i,t+1}^1 < 0$, or some $\lambda_{j,t}$, with $i \in p_{j,t}\backslash\{j\}$, must be decreased. In the former, feasibility is lost. In the latter, max-min fairness does not hold. Similarly if $\lambda_{j,t}$, with $i \in p_{j,t}\backslash\{j\}$ is increased. This proves rule (F1), and rule (F3) for the descendants of node i in time slot t.

Now, for $b_{i,t+1}^1 = 0$, let $(i,t), (i,t-1), (i,t-2), ..., (i,\tau), \tau \geq 1$, be the longest sequence with the property that: $b_{i,s}^k + e_{i,s} - \Delta b_{i,s}^k \leq B\ \forall s \in \{t, t-1, ..., \tau\}$. From (9), if any of the rates $\lambda_{i,s}$, or $\lambda_{j,s}$, with $i \in p_{j,s}\backslash\{j\}$ is increased, either $b_{i,t+1}^1 < 0$, or some other rate from (9) needs to be decreased, which violates the max-min fairness, since all the rates are equal. This proves rule (F2), and completes the proof for rule (F3).

The inductive step. Observe that:

(o1) $\lambda_{j,t} \le \lambda_{i,t}, \forall j : i \in p_{j,t}$, as all the rates, until fixed, get increased by the same amount in each iteration, and once a rate gets fixed for some (i,t), by the rule (F3), it gets fixed for all the (j,t) with $i \in p_{j,t}\backslash\{j\}$. The inequality is strict only if $\lambda_{j,t}$ got fixed before $\lambda_{i,t}$.

(o2) Once fixed, a rate never becomes active again.

(o3) If a rate $\lambda_{i,t}$ gets fixed in iteration k, then $\lambda_{i,t} = \lambda_{i,t}^k = \sum_{p=1}^k \lambda^p = \lambda_{i,t}^l, \forall l \ge k$.

Suppose that $b_{i,t+1}^k = 0$ for some $i \in \{1,..,n\}, t \in \{1,...,T\}$. If $F_{i,t}^k = 0$, then by the inductive hypothesis $\lambda_{i,t}$ cannot be further increased in any future iteration. Assume $F_{i,t}^k = 1$.

By (o1), $\lambda_{j,t}^k \le \lambda_{i,t}^k, \forall j$ such that $i \in p_{j,t}\backslash\{j\}$, where the inequality holds with equality if $F_{j,t}^k = 0$. Therefore, from (8), if we increase $\lambda_{i,t}$ in some of the future iterations, either $b_{i,t+1} < 0$, or we need to decrease some $\lambda_{j,t} \le \lambda_{i,t}$, violating the max-min fairness condition. This proves the necessity of the rule (F1). For the rule (F3), as for all (j,t) with $F_{j,t}^k = 1, i \in p_{j,t}\backslash\{j\}$, we have $\lambda_{j,t} = \lambda_{i,t}$, none of the i's descendants can further increase its rate in the slot t.

Now for (i,t) such that $b_{i,t+1}^k = 0$, let $(i,t),(i,t-1),(i,t-2),...,(i,\tau),\tau \ge 1$, be the longest sequence with the property that: $b_{i,s}^k + e_{i,s} - \Delta b_{i,s}^k \le B\ \forall s \in \{t, t-1,...,\tau\}$. If any of the rates appearing in (9) was fixed in some previous iteration, then it cannot be further increased by the inductive hypothesis. By the observation (o1), all the rates that are active are equal, and all the rates that are fixed are strictly lower than the active rates. Therefore, by increasing any of the active rates from (9), we either violate battery nonnegativity constraint or the max-min fairness condition. Therefore, rule (F2) holds, and rule (F3) holds for all the descendants of nodes whose rates got fixed by the rule (F2), in the corresponding time slots. □

Lemma 5.3. *(Sufficiency) If $F_{i,t}^{k+1} = 1$, then $\lambda_{i,t}$ can be further increased by a positive amount in the iteration $k+1$, $\forall i \in \{1,...,n\}, \forall t \in \{1,...,T\}$.*

Proof. Suppose that $F_{i,t}^{k+1} = 1$. Notice that by increasing $\lambda_{i,t}$ by some $\Delta\lambda_{i,t}$ node i spends an additional $\Delta b_{i,t} = c_{\text{st}}\Delta\lambda_{i,t}$ energy *only in the time slot t*. As $F_{i,t}^{k+1} = 1$, by the rules (F1) and (F2), either $b_{i,t'} > 0\ \forall t' > t$, or there is a time slot $s > t$ such that $b_{i,s}^k + e_{i,s} - \Delta b_{i,s}^k > B$ and $s < s'$, where $s' = \arg\min\{\tau > t : b_{i,\tau} = 0\}$.

If $b_{i,t'} > 0\ \forall t' > t$, then the node i can spend $\Delta b_{i,t} = \min_{t+1 \le t' \le T+1} b_{i,t'}^k$ energy, and keep $b_{i,t'} \ge 0$, $\forall t'$, which follows from the battery evolution equation (6).

If there is a slot $s' > t$ in which $b_{i,s'}^k = 0$, then let s be the minimum time slot between t and s', such that $b_{i,s}^k + e_{i,s} - \Delta b_{i,s}^k > B$. Decreasing the battery level at s by $(b_{i,s}^k + e_{i,s} - \Delta b_{i,s}^k) - B$ does not influence any other battery levels, as in either case $b_{i,s+1} = B$. As all the battery levels are positive in all the time slots between t and s, i can spend at least $\min\{(b_{i,s}^k + e_{i,s} - \Delta b_{i,s}^k) - B,\ \ \min_{t+1 \le t' \le s} b_{i,t'}^k\}$ energy at the time t and have $b_{i,t'} \ge 0\ \forall t'$.

By the rule (F3), $\forall j$ such that $j \in p_{i,t}$ we have that $b_{j,t} > 0$, and, furthermore, if $\exists s' > t$ with $b_{j,s'} = 0$ then $\exists s \in \{t, s'\}$ such that $b_{i,s}^k + e_{i,s} - \Delta b_{i,s}^k > B$. By the same observations as for the node i, each $j \in p_{i,t}$ can spend some extra energy $\Delta b_{j,t} > 0$ in the time slot t and keep all the battery levels nonnegative. In other words, there is a directed path from the node i to the sink on which every node can spend some extra energy in time slot t and keep its battery levels nonnegative. Therefore, if we keep all other rates fixed, the rate $\lambda_{i,t}$ can be increased by $\Delta\lambda_{i,t} = \min\{\Delta b_{i,t}/c_{\text{st}}, \min_{j \in p_{i,t}} \Delta b_{j,t}/c_{\text{rt}}\} > 0$.

As each active rate $\lambda_{i,t}$ can (alone) get increased in the iteration $k+1$ by some $\Delta\lambda_{i,t} > 0$, it follows that all the active rates can be increased simultaneously by at least $\min_{i,t} \Delta\lambda_{i,t}/(T(c_{\text{st}} + nc_{\text{rt}})) > 0$. □

Due to space constraints, the proofs are omitted in the rest of the paper and can instead be found in [23].

Theorem 5.4. *Fixing rules (F1), (F2) and (F3) provide necessary and sufficient conditions for fixing the sensing rates in* WATER-FILLING-FRAMEWORK.

Lemma 5.5. *The total running time of* FIXING-THE-RATES *in* P-UNSPLITTABLE-FIND *is $O(mT)$.*

Combining lemmas 5.1 and 5.5, we can compute the total running time of WATER-FILLING-FRAMEWORK for P-UNSPLITTABLE-FIND, as stated in the following lemma.

Lemma 5.6. WATER-FILLING-FRAMEWORK *with Steps 2* MAXIMIZING-THE-RATES *and 3* FIXING-THE-RATES *implemented as described in Section 5 runs in time:*

$$O\left(n^2T^2 \log\left(\frac{B + \max_{i,t} e_{i,t}}{\delta c_{st}}\right) + nmT^2\right).$$

6. FRACTIONAL ROUTING

The feasible region $\mathcal{R}$ for the rates and flows in P-FRACTIONAL can be described by the following constraints:

$$\forall i \in \{1,...,n\}, t \in \{1,...,T\}:$$
$$f_{i,t}^{\Sigma} + \lambda_{i,t} = \sum_{(i,j) \in E} f_{ij,t},$$
$$b_{i,t+1} = \min\{B,\ b_{i,t} + e_{i,t} - (c_{\text{rt}} f_{i,t}^{\Sigma} + c_{\text{st}}\lambda_{i,t})\},$$
$$b_{i,t} \ge 0,\ \lambda_{i,t} \ge 0,\ f_{ij,t} \ge 0, \forall (i,j) \in E,$$

where $f_{i,t}^{\Sigma} \equiv \sum_{(j,i) \in E} f_{ji,t}$.

Observe that we can avoid computing the values of battery levels $b_{i,t+1}$, and instead explicitly write the non-negativity constraints for each of the terms inside the min. Reordering the terms, we get the following formulation:

$$\forall i \in \{1,...,n\}, t \in \{1,...,T\}:$$
$$f_{i,t}^{\Sigma} + \lambda_{i,t} = \sum_{(i,j) \in E} f_{ij,t}, \tag{10}$$
$$\sum_{\tau=1}^{t} (c_{\text{rt}} f_{i,\tau}^{\Sigma} + c_{\text{st}}\lambda_{i,t}) \le b_{i,1} + \sum_{\tau=1}^{t} e_{i,\tau}, \tag{11}$$
$$\sum_{\tau=s}^{t} (c_{\text{rt}} f_{i,\tau}^{\Sigma} + c_{\text{st}}\lambda_{i,t}) \le B + \sum_{\tau=s}^{t} e_{i,\tau}, \quad 2 \le s \le t, \tag{12}$$
$$\lambda_{i,t} \ge 0,\ f_{ij,t} \ge 0, \forall (i,j) \in E. \tag{13}$$

In the kth iteration of WATER-FILLING-FRAMEWORK we have that $\lambda_{i,t}^k = \lambda_{i,t}^{k-1} + F_{i,t}^k \cdot \lambda^k = \sum_{l=1}^k F_{i,t}^l \cdot \lambda^l$, where $\lambda_{i,t}^0 = 0$. Let:

$$u_{i,t}^b = b_{i,1} + \sum_{\tau=1}^{t} (e_{i,\tau} - c_{\text{st}}\lambda_{i,\tau}^{k-1}),\ u_{i,t,s}^B = B + \sum_{\tau=s}^{t} (e_{i,\tau} - c_{\text{st}}\lambda_{i,\tau}^{k-1}).$$

Since in the iteration k all $\lambda_{i,t}^{k-1}$'s are constants, the rate maximization subproblem can be written as:

$$\textbf{max}\ \lambda^k \tag{14}$$
$$\textbf{s.t.}\ \forall i \in \{1,...,n\}, t \in \{1,...,T\}:$$
$$-f_{i,t}^{\Sigma} - F_{i,t}^k \cdot \lambda^k + \sum_{(i,j) \in E} f_{ij,t} = \lambda_{i,t}^{k-1}, \tag{15}$$

$$\sum_{\tau=1}^{t}(c_{\mathrm{rt}} f_{i,\tau}^{\Sigma} + F_{i,\tau}^{k} \cdot c_{\mathrm{st}}\lambda^{k}) \le u_{i,t}^{b}, \tag{16}$$

$$\sum_{\tau=s}^{t}(c_{\mathrm{rt}} f_{i,\tau}^{\Sigma} + F_{i,\tau}^{k} \cdot c_{\mathrm{st}}\lambda^{k}) \le u_{i,t,s}^{B}, \quad 2 \le s \le t, \tag{17}$$

$$\lambda^{k} \ge 0,\ f_{ij,t} \ge 0, \forall (i,j) \in E. \tag{18}$$

Notice that in this formulation all the variables are on the left-hand side of the constraints, whereas all the right-hand sides are constant.

6.1 Relation to Multi-commodity Flow

Let $T = 2$, and observe the constraints (10)–(13). We claim that verifying whether any set of sensing rates $\lambda_{i,t}$ is feasible is at least as hard as solving a 2-commodity feasible flow problem with capacitated nodes and a single sink. To prove the claim, we first rewrite (10)–(13) as:

$$\sum_{(j,i)\in E} f_{ji,t} + \lambda_{i,t} = \sum_{(i,j)\in E} f_{ij,t}, \qquad t \in \{1,2\}$$

$$c_{\mathrm{rt}} \sum_{(j,i)\in E} f_{ji,1} \le b_{i,1} + e_{i,1} - c_{\mathrm{st}}\lambda_{i,1},$$

$$c_{\mathrm{rt}} \sum_{\tau=1}^{2} \sum_{(j,i)\in E} f_{ji,\tau} \le b_{i,1} + \sum_{\tau=1}^{2} (e_{i,\tau} - c_{\mathrm{st}}\lambda_{i,\tau}),$$

$$c_{\mathrm{rt}} \sum_{(j,i)\in E} f_{ji,2} \le B + e_{i,2} - c_{\mathrm{st}}\lambda_{i,2},$$

$$\lambda_{i,t} \ge 0, f_{ij,t} \ge 0,\ \forall i \in \{1, ..., n\}, (i,j) \in E, t \in \{1,2\}.$$

Suppose that we are given any 2-commodity flow problem with capacitated nodes[7], and let:

- $\lambda_{i,t}$ denote the supply of commodity t at node i;
- $u_{i,t}$ denote the per-commodity capacity constraint at node i for commodity t;
- u_i denote the bundle capacity constraint at node i.

Given $\lambda_{i,t}$, $u_{i,t}$, and u_i, for $i \in \{1, ..., n\}, t \in \{1,2\}$, choose values of $c_{\mathrm{st}}, c_{\mathrm{rt}}, B, b_{i,1}, b_{i,2}, e_{i,1}, e_{i,2}$ so that the following equalities are satisfied:

$$u_{i,1} = (b_{i,1} + e_{i,1} - c_{\mathrm{st}}\lambda_{i,1}) / c_{\mathrm{rt}},$$
$$u_{i,2} = (B + e_{i,2} - c_{\mathrm{st}}\lambda_{i,2}) / c_{\mathrm{rt}},$$
$$u_i = (b_{i,1} + \sum_{\tau=1}^{2} (e_{i,\tau} - c_{\mathrm{st}}\lambda_{i,\tau})) / c_{\mathrm{rt}}.$$

Then feasibility of the given 2-commodity flow problem is equivalent to the feasibility of (10)–(13). Therefore, any 2-commodity feasible flow problem can be stated as an equivalent problem of verifying feasibility of sensing rates $\lambda_{i,t}$ in an energy harvesting network for $T = 2$.

For $T > 2$, (11) and (12) are general packing constraints. If a flow graph G_t in time slot t is observed as a flow of a commodity indexed by t, then for each node i the constraints (11) and (12) define capacity constraints for every sequence of consecutive commodities $s, s+1, ..., t$, $1 \le s \le t \le T$.

Therefore, to our current knowledge, it is unlikely that the general rate assignment problem can be solved exactly in polynomial time without the use of linear programming, as there have not been any combinatorial algorithms that solve feasible 2-commodity flow in directed graphs exactly.

6.2 Fractional Packing Approach

The fractional packing problem is defined as follows [26]: PACKING: *Given a convex set P for which $Ax \ge 0\ \forall x \in P$, is there a vector x such that $Ax \le b$?* Here, A is a $p \times q$ matrix, and x is a q-length vector.

A given vector x is an ϵ-approximate solution to the PACKING problem if $x \in P$ and $Ax \le (1+\epsilon)b$. Alternatively, scaling all the constraints by $\frac{1}{1+\epsilon}$, we obtain a solution $x' = \frac{1}{1+\epsilon}x \in (\frac{1}{1+\epsilon}x_{\mathrm{OPT}}, x_{\mathrm{OPT}}] \subset ((1-\epsilon)x_{\mathrm{OPT}}, x_{\mathrm{OPT}}]$, for $\epsilon < 1$, where x_{OPT} is an optimal solution to the packing problem. The algorithm in [26] either provides an ϵ-approximate solution to the PACKING problem, or it proves that no such solution exists. It's running time depends on:

- The running time required to solve $\min\{cx : x \in P\}$, where $c = y^T A$, y is a given p-length vector, and $(.)^T$ denotes the transpose of a vector.
- The width of P relative to $Ax \le b$, which is defined by $\rho = \max_i \max_{x\in P} \frac{a_i x}{b_i}$, where a_i is the ith row of A, and b_i is the ith element of b.

For a given error parameter $\epsilon > 0$, a feasible solution to the problem $\min\{\beta : Ax \le \beta b, x \in P\}$, its dual solution y, and $C_{\mathcal{P}}(y) = \min\{cx : c = y^T A, x \in P\}$, [26] defines the following relaxed optimality conditions:

$$(1-\epsilon)\beta y^T b \le y^T Ax \tag{$\mathcal{P}1$}$$

$$y^T Ax - C_{\mathcal{P}}(y) \le \epsilon(y^T Ax + \beta y^T b) \tag{$\mathcal{P}2$}$$

The packing algorithm [26] is implemented through subsequent calls to the procedure IMPROVE-PACKING:

Algorithm 2 IMPROVE-PACKING(x, ϵ) [26]

```
1: Initialize β0 = max_i a_i x/b_i; α = 4 β0^{-1} ε^{-1} ln(2pε^{-1}); σ = ε/(4αρ).
2: while max_i a_i x/b_i ≥ β0/2 and x, y do not satisfy (P2) do
3:     For each i = 1, 2, ..., p: set y_i = (1/b_i) e^{α a_i x / b_i}.
4:     Find a min-cost point x̃ ∈ P for costs c = y^T A.
5:     Update x = (1 − σ)x + σx̃.
6: return x.
```

The running time of the ϵ-approximation algorithm provided in [26], for $\epsilon \in (0,1]$, equals $O(\epsilon^{-2}\rho \log(m\epsilon^{-1}))$ multiplied by the time needed to solve $\min\{cx : c = y^T A, x \in P\}$ and compute Ax (Theorem 2.5 in [26]).

6.2.1 Maximizing the Rates as Fractional Packing

We demonstrated at the beginning of this section that for the kth iteration MAXIMIZE-THE-RATES can be stated as (14)-(18). Observe the constraints (16) and (17). Since λ^k, $f_{ij,t}$ and all the right-hand sides in (16) and (17) are nonnegative, (16) and (17) imply the following inequalities:

$\forall i \in \{1, ..., n\}, t \in \{1, ..., T\}$:

$$F_{i,\theta}^{k} \cdot c_{\mathrm{st}}\lambda^{k} \le u_{i,t}^{b}, \qquad 1 \le \theta \le t,$$

$$F_{i,\theta}^{k} \cdot c_{\mathrm{st}}\lambda^{k} \le u_{i,t,s}^{B}, \qquad 2 \le s \le t,\ s \le \theta \le t,$$

$$c_{\mathrm{rt}} \sum_{(j,i)\in E} f_{ji,\theta} \le u_{i,t}^{b} - c_{\mathrm{st}} \sum_{\tau=1}^{t} F_{i,\tau}^{k}\lambda^{k}, \qquad 1 \le \theta \le t,$$

$$c_{\mathrm{rt}} \sum_{(j,i)\in E} f_{ji,\theta} \le u_{i,t,s}^{B} - c_{\mathrm{st}} \sum_{\tau=s}^{t} F_{i,\tau}^{k}\lambda^{k},\ 2 \le s \le t,\ s \le \theta \le t.$$

Therefore, we can yield an upper bound $\lambda_{\max}^{k}$ for λ^{k}:

$$\lambda^{k} \le \lambda_{\max}^{k} \equiv$$
$$\frac{1}{c_{\mathrm{st}}} \min_{i,t,s\ge 2} \{u_{i,t}^{b} : \sum_{\tau=1}^{t} F_{i,\tau}^{k} > 0, u_{i,t,s}^{B} : \sum_{\tau=s}^{t} F_{i,\tau}^{k} > 0\}.$$

[7]For the definition of a multi-commodity flow, see e.g., [1].

For a fixed λ^k, the flow entering a node i at time slot t can be bounded as:

$$\sum_{(j,i)\in E} f_{ji,t} \le u_{i,t} \equiv$$

$$\frac{1}{c_{\text{rt}}} \min_{\substack{i,t_1 \ge t\\ s \ge 2}} \{u^b_{i,t_1} - c_{\text{st}} \sum_{\tau=1}^{t_1} F^k_{i,\tau}\lambda^k, u^B_{i,t,s} - c_{\text{st}} \sum_{\tau=s}^{t_1} F^k_{i,\tau}\lambda^k\}.$$

We choose to keep only the flows $f_{ij,t}$ as variables in the PACKING problem. Given a $\lambda^k \in [0, \lambda^k_{\max}]$, we define the convex set P via the following set of constrains[8]:

$$\forall i \in \{1, ..., n\}, t \in \{1, ..., T\}:$$

$$-\sum_{(j,i)\in E} f_{ji,t} + \sum_{(i,j)\in E} f_{ij,t} = \lambda^{k-1}_{i,t} + F^k_{i,t} \cdot \lambda^k, \quad (19)$$

$$\sum_{(j,i)\in E} f_{ji,t} \le u_{i,t}, \quad (20)$$

$$f_{ij,t} \ge 0, \quad \forall (i,j) \in E. \quad (21)$$

Proposition 6.1. *For P described by (19) – (21) and a given vector y, problem $\min\{cf : c = y^T Af, f \in P\}$ reduces to T min-cost flow problems.*

The remaining packing constraints of the form $Ax \le b$ are given by (16) and (17), where $x \equiv f$.

Proposition 6.2. $Ax \ge 0\ \forall f \in P$.

Lemma 6.3. *One iteration of* IMPROVE-PACKING *for* P-FRACTIONAL *can be implemented in time*

$$O\left(nT^2 + T \cdot MCF(n,m)\right),$$

where $MCF(n,m)$ denotes the running time of a min-cost flow algorithm on a graph with n nodes and m edges.

Lemma 6.4. *Width ρ of P relative to the packing constraints (16) and (17) is $O(T)$.*

Lemma 6.5. MAXIMIZING-THE-RATES *that uses packing algorithm from [26] can be implemented in time: $\tilde{O}(T^2\epsilon^{-2} \cdot (nT + MCF(n,m)))$, where $\tilde{O}$-notation ignores poly-log terms.*

6.2.2 Fixing the Rates

As MAXIMIZING-THE-RATES described in previous subsection outputs an ϵ-approximate solution in each iteration, the objective of the algorithm is not to output a max-min fair solution anymore, but an ϵ-approximation. We consider the following notion of approximation, as in [18]:

Definition 6.6. *For a problem of lexicographic maximization, say that a feasible solution given as a vector v is an element-wise ϵ-approximate solution, if for vectors v and v_{OPT} sorted in nondecreasing order $v \ge (1-\epsilon)v_{OPT}$ component-wise, where v_{OPT} is an optimal solution to the given lexicographic maximization problem.*

Let Δ be the smallest real number that can be represented in a computer, and consider the algorithm that implements FIXING-THE-RATES as stated below.

Assume that FIXING-THE-RATES does not change any of the rates, but only determines what rates should be fixed in the next iteration, i.e., it only makes (global) changes to $F^{k+1}_{i,t}$. Then:

Lemma 6.7. *If the Steps 2 and 3 in the* WATER-FILLING-FRAMEWORK *are implemented as* MAXIMIZING-THE-RATES *and* FIXING-THE-RATES *from this section, then the solution output by the algorithm is an element-wise ϵ-approximate solution to the lexicographic maximization of $\lambda_{i,t} \in \mathcal{R}$.*

[8] P is determined by linear equalities and inequalities, which implies that it is convex.

Algorithm 3 FIXING-THE-RATES

Solve the following linear program:
max $\sum_{i=1}^n F^k_{i,t}\lambda^k_{i,t}$
  s.t. $\forall i \in \{1, ..., n\}, t \in \{1, ..., T\}$:
    $\lambda^k_{i,t} \ge \lambda^{k-1}_{i,t} + F^k_{i,t} \cdot \lambda^k$,
    $\lambda^k_{i,t} \le \lambda^{k-1}_{i,t} + F^k_{i,t} \cdot \left(\epsilon\lambda^{k-1}_{i,t} + (1+\epsilon)\lambda^k + \Delta\right)$,
    $f^{\Sigma}_{i,t} + \lambda^k_{i,t} = \sum_{(i,j)\in E} f_{ij,t}$,
    $b_{i,t+1} = \min\left\{B,\ b_{i,t} + e_{i,t} - \left(c_{\text{rt}} f^{\Sigma}_{i,t} + c_{\text{st}}\lambda^k_{i,t}\right)\right\}$,
    $b_{i,t} \ge 0, \quad \lambda^k_{i,t} \ge 0, \quad f_{ij,t} \ge 0.$
Let $F^{k+1}_{i,t} = F^k_{i,t}, \forall i, t$.
If $\lambda^k_{i,t} < (1+\epsilon)(\lambda^{k-1}_{i,t} + F^k_{i,t} \cdot \lambda^k) + \Delta$, set $F^{k+1}_{i,t} = 0$.

Lemma 6.8. *An FPTAS for* P-FRACTIONAL *can be implemented in time:*

$$\tilde{O}(nT(T^2\epsilon^{-2} \cdot (nT + MCF(n,m)) + LP(mT, nT))),$$

where $LP(mT, nT)$ denotes the running time of a linear program with mT variables and nT constraints, and $MCF(n,m)$ denotes the running time of a min-cost flow algorithm run on a graph with n nodes and m edges.

Note: A linear programming framework as in [8, 20, 27] when applied to P-FRACTIONAL would yield a running time equal to $O(n^2T^2 \cdot LP(mT, nT))$. As the running time of an iteration in our approach is dominated by $LP(mT, nT)$, the improvement in running time is at least $O(nT)$-fold, at the expense of providing an ϵ-approximation.

7. FIXED FRACTIONAL ROUTING

Suppose that we want to solve lexicographic maximization of the rates keeping both the routing and the rates constant over time. Observe that, as both the routing and the rates do not change over time, the energy consumption per time slot of each node i is also constant over time and equal to $\Delta b_i = c_{\text{st}}\lambda_i + c_{\text{rt}} \sum_{(j,i)\in E} f_{ji}$.

Proposition 7.1. *Maximum constant energy consumption Δb_i can be determined in time $O(T \log(\frac{b_{i,1}+e_{i,1}}{\delta}))$ for each node $i \in V\backslash\{s\}$, for the total time of $O(nT \log(\frac{b_{i,1}+e_{i,1}}{\delta}))$.*

Similarly as in previous sections, let $F^k_i = 0$ if the rate i is fixed at the beginning of iteration k, and $F^k_i = 1$ if it is not. Initially: $F^1_i = 1, \forall i$. Rate maximization can then be implemented as follows:

Algorithm 4 MAXIMIZING-THE-RATES(G, F^k, b, e, k)

$\lambda^k_{\max} = \frac{1}{c_{\text{st}}} \min_i\{\Delta b_i - c_{\text{st}}\lambda^{k-1}_i : F^k_i = 1\}$.
repeat for $\lambda^k \in [0, \lambda^k_{\max}]$, via binary search:
  Set the supply of node i to $d_i = \lambda^{k-1} + F^k_i\lambda^k$, capacity of node i to $u_i = \frac{1}{c_{\text{rt}}}(\Delta b_i - c_{\text{st}}\lambda^k)$, for each i.
  Set the demand of the sink to $\sum_i d_i$.
  Solve feasible flow problem on G.
until λ^k takes maximum value for which the flow problem is feasible on G.

The remaining part of the algorithm is to determine which rates should be fixed at the end of iteration k. We note that in each iteration k, the maximization of the rates produces a flow f in the graph G^k with the supply rates λ^k_i. Instead of having capacitated nodes, we can modify the input graph by a standard procedure of splitting each node i into two nodes i' and i'', and assigning the capacity of i to the edge (i', i''). This allows us to obtain a residual graph $G^{r,k}$ for the given flow. We claim the following:

Lemma 7.2. *The rate λ_i of a node $i \in G$ can be further increased in the iteration $k+1$ if and only if there is a directed path from i to the sink node in $G^{r,k}$.*

Lemma 7.3. WATER-FILLING-FRAMEWORK *for* P-FIXED-FRACTIONAL *can be implemented in time*

$$O\left(n \log\left(\frac{b_{i,1}+e_{i,1}}{\delta}\right) \min(T, MF(n,m))\right),$$

where $MF(n,m)$ denotes the running time of a max-flow algorithm for a graph with n nodes and m edges.

8. DETERMINING A ROUTING

In this section we demonstrate that solving P-UNSPLITTABLE-FIND is NP-hard, and design an efficient combinatorial algorithm for a relaxed version of this problem–it determines a time-invariable unsplittable routing that maximizes the minimum rate. For P-TREE-FIND we show that it is NP-hard to obtain an approximation ratio better than $\Omega(\log n)$.

8.1 Unsplittable Routing

A simple extension of the NP-hardness proof for unsplittable routing studied in [18] can be used to show NP-hardness of P-UNSPLITTABLE-FIND for a single time slot, and we omit the proof due to space constraints. This result implies that P-UNSPLITTABLE-FIND remains NP-hard for $T > 1$, regardless of whether the routing structure is allowed to change over time slots or not.

However, determining a time-invariable unsplittable routing that guarantees the maximum value of the minimum sensing rate over all time-invariable unplittable routings is solvable in polynomial time, and we provide a combinatorial algorithm that solves it below.

We first observe that in any time-invariable unsplittable routing, if all the nodes are assigned the same sensing rate λ, then every node i spends a fixed amount of energy Δb_i per time slot equal to the energy spent for sensing and sending own flow and for forwarding the flow coming from the descendant nodes: $\Delta b_i = \lambda\,(c_{st} + c_{rt} D_{i,t})$.

The next property we use follows from the integrality of the max flow problem with integral capacities (see, e.g., [1]). This property was stated as a theorem in [17] for single-source unsplittable flows, and we repeat it here for the equivalent single-sink unsplittable flow problem:

Theorem 8.1. [17] *Let $G = (N, E)$ be a given graph with the predetermined sink node s. If the supplies of all the nodes in the network are from the set $\{0, \lambda\}$, $\lambda > 0$, and the capacities of all the edges/nodes are integral multiples of λ, then: if there is a fractional flow of value f, there is an unsplittable flow of value at least f. Moreover, this unsplittable flow can be found in polynomial time.*

Note: For the setting of theorem 8.1, any augmenting-path or push-relabel based max flow algorithm produces a flow that is unsplittable, as a consequence of the integrality of the solution produced by these algorithms. We will assume that the used max-flow algorithm has this property.

The last property we need is that our problem can be formulated in the setting of theorem 8.1. We observe that for a given sensing rate λ, each node spends $c_{st}\lambda$ units of energy for sensing, whereas the remaining energy can be used for routing the flow originating at other nodes. Therefore, for a given λ, we can set the supply of each node i to λ, set its capacity to $u_i = (\Delta b_i - c_{st}\lambda)/c_{rt}$ (making sure that $\Delta b_i - c_{st}\lambda \geq 0$), and observe the problem as the feasible flow problem. For any feasible *unsplittable* flow solution with all the supplies equal to λ, we have that flow through every edge/node equals the sum flow of all the routing paths that contain that edge/node. As every path carries a flow of value λ, the flow through every edge/node is an integral multiple of λ. Therefore, to verify whether it is feasible to have a sensing rate of λ at each node, it is enough to down-round all the nodes' capacities to the nearest multiple of λ: $u_i = \lambda \cdot \lfloor(\Delta b_i - c_{st}\lambda)/(c_{rt}\lambda)\rfloor$, and apply the theorem 8.1.

An easy upper bound for λ is $\lambda_{max} = \min_i \Delta b_i / c_{st}$, which follows from the battery nonnegativity constraint. The algorithm becomes clear now:

Algorithm 5 MAXMIN-UNSPLITTABLE-ROUTING(G, b, e)

1: Perform a binary search for $\lambda \in [0, \lambda_{max}]$.
2: For each λ chosen by the binary search set node supplies to λ and node capacities to $u_i = \lambda \cdot \lfloor(\Delta b_i - c_{st}\lambda)/(c_{rt}\lambda)\rfloor$. Solve feasible flow problem.
3: Return the maximum feasible λ.

Lemma 8.2. *The running time of* MAXMIN-UNSPLITTABLE-ROUTING *is $O(\log(\min_i(b_{i,1}+e_{i,1})/(c_{st}\delta)) \cdot MF(n+1,m))$, where $MF(n,m)$ is the running time of a max-flow algorithm on an input graph with n nodes and m edges.*

8.2 Routing Tree

If it was possible to find the (either time variable or time-invariable) max-min fair routing tree in polynomial time for any time horizon T, then the same result would follow for $T = 1$. It follows that if P-TREE-FIND NP-hard for $T = 1$, it is also NP-hard for any $T > 1$. Therefore, we restrict our attention to $T = 1$. In such a setting, determining a tree with the maximum value of the minimum sensing rate is equivalent to the maximum lifetime tree problem from [5]. The instance used in [5] for showing the NP-hardness of the problem has the property that on that instance, at the optimum, P-TREE-FIND produces $\lambda_1 = \lambda_2 = ... = \lambda_n = \lambda$. Therefore, P-TREE-FIND is also NP-hard.

We state the following lower bound result without a proof, and instead provide it in [23].

Theorem 8.3. *The lower bound on the approximation ratio of* P-TREE-FIND *is $\Omega(\log n)$.*

9. CONCLUSIONS AND FUTURE WORK

This paper presents a comprehensive algorithmic study of the max-min fair rate assignment and routing problems in energy harvesting networks with predictable energy profile. We develop algorithms for the WATER-FILLING-FRAMEWORK implementation under various routing types. The running times of the developed algorithms are summarized in Table 2. The algorithms provide important insights into the structure of the problems, and can serve as benchmarks for evaluating distributed, online, and approximate algorithms.

The WATER-FILLING-FRAMEWORK does not specify how to implement the MAXIMIZING-THE-RATES and FIXING-THE-RATES steps. Although general algorithms that implement water-filling (e.g., [8, 20, 27]) can be adapted to solve P-

Table 2: Running times of the algorithms for the Water-filling-Framework implementation.

	MAXIMIZING-THE RATES	FIXING-THE-RATES	Total
P-UNSPLITTABLE-FIND	$O\left(nT\log\left(\frac{B+\max_{i,t} e_{i,t}}{\delta c_{st}}\right)\right)$	$O(mT)$	$O\left(n^2T^2\log\left(\frac{B+\max_{i,t} e_{i,t}}{\delta c_{st}}\right)+nmT^2\right)$
P-FIXED-FRACTIONAL	$O\left(n\log\left(\frac{b_{i,1}+e_{i,1}}{\delta}\right)\min(T, MF(n,m))\right)$	$O(m)$	$O\left(n\log\left(\frac{b_{i,1}+e_{i,1}}{\delta}\right)\min(T, MF(n,m))\right)$
P-FRACTIONAL	$\tilde{O}(T^2\epsilon^{-2}\cdot(nT+MCF(n,m)))$	$LP(mT, nT)$	$\tilde{O}(nT(T^2\epsilon^{-2}\cdot(nT+MCF(n,m))+LP(mT,nT)))$

UNSPLITTABLE-RATES, P-FRACTIONAL, and P-FIXED-FRACTIONAL, their implementation would require solving a large number of linear programs (LPs), each with a high number of variables and constraints. This would result in a very high running time. Moreover, such algorithms do not provide insights into the problem structure.

Our algorithms exploit the problem structure and in most cases do not use linear programming. The only exception is the algorithm for P-FRACTIONAL, which solves $O(nT)$ LPs (an adaptation of [8, 20, 27] would need to solve $O(n^2T^2)$ LPs). Furthermore, each LP in our solution searches over much smaller space (only within the ϵ-region of the starting point, for any ϵ-approximation).

Overall, the results reveal interesting trade-offs between different routing types. For example, in simple routing types (routing tree and unsplittable routing), it is relatively simple to determine the max min-fair rate assignment whenever the routing is provided at the input. However, determining a good routing (the one that provides lexicographically maximum assignment of rates among all the routings of the same type) is hard even for a single time slot.

There are several directions for future work. For example, extending the model to incorporate the energy consumption due to the control messages exchange would provide a more realistic setting. Moreover, designing algorithms for unpredictable energy profiles that can be implemented in an online and/or distributed manner is of high practical importance.

10. ACKNOWLEDGEMENTS

We are grateful to Prof. Mihalis Yannakakis for useful discussions. This research was supported in part by NSF grants CCF-1349602, CCF-09-64497, and CNS-10-54856 and the People Programme (Marie Curie Actions) of the European Union's Seventh Framework Programme (FP7/2007-2013) under REA grant agreement n°[PIIF-GA-2013-629740].11.

11. REFERENCES

[1] R. K. Ahuja, T. L. Magnanti, and J. B. Orlin. *Network flows: theory, algorithms, and applications*. Prentice-Hall, Inc., Upper Saddle River, NJ, USA, 1993.

[2] B. Bacinoglu and E. Uysal-Biyikoglu. Finite-horizon online transmission rate and power adaptation on a communication link with markovian energy harvesting. *CoRR*, abs/1305.4558, 2013.

[3] D. Bertsekas and R. Gallager. *Data networks (2nd ed.)*. Prentice-Hall, Inc., Upper Saddle River, NJ, USA, 1992.

[4] P. Blasco, D. Gunduz, and M. Dohler. A learning theoretic approach to energy harvesting communication system optimization. In *Proc. IEEE Globecom Workshops'12*, 2012.

[5] C. Buragohain, D. Agrawal, and S. Suri. Power aware routing for sensor databases. In *Proc. IEEE INFOCOM'05*, 2005.

[6] J.-H. Chang and L. Tassiulas. Maximum lifetime routing in wireless sensor networks. *IEEE/ACM Trans. Netw.*, 12(4):609–619, 2004.

[7] A. Charny, D. D. Clark, and R. Jain. Congestion control with explicit rate indication. In *Proc. IEEE ICC'95*, 1995.

[8] S. Chen, Y. Fang, and Y. Xia. Lexicographic maxmin fairness for data collection in wireless sensor networks. *IEEE Trans. Mobile Comput.*, 6(7):762–776, July 2007.

[9] S. Chen, P. Sinha, N. Shroff, and C. Joo. A simple asymptotically optimal energy allocation and routing scheme in rechargeable sensor networks. In *Proc. IEEE INFOCOM'12*, 2012.

[10] M. Gatzianas, L. Georgiadis, and L. Tassiulas. Control of wireless networks with rechargeable batteries. *IEEE Trans. Wireless Commun.*, 9(2):581–593, 2010.

[11] M. Gorlatova, A. Bernstein, and G. Zussman. Performance evaluation of resource allocation policies for energy harvesting devices. In *Proc. WiOpt'11*, 2011.

[12] M. Gorlatova, P. Kinget, I. Kymissis, D. Rubenstein, X. Wang, and G. Zussman. Challenge: ultra-low-power energy-harvesting active networked tags (EnHANTs). In *Proc. ACM MobiCom'09*, 2009.

[13] M. Gorlatova, R. Margolies, J. Sarik, G. Stanje, J. Zhu, B. Vigraham, M. Szczodrak, L. Carloni, P. Kinget, I. Kymissis, and G. Zussman. Energy harvesting active networked tags (EnHANTs): Prototyping and experimentation. Technical Report 2012-07-27, Columbia University, July 2012.

[14] M. Gorlatova, A. Wallwater, and G. Zussman. Networking low-power energy harvesting devices: Measurements and algorithms. *IEEE Trans. Mobile Comput.*, 12(9):1853–1865, 2013.

[15] B. Gurakan, O. Ozel, J. Yang, and S. Ulukus. Energy cooperation in energy harvesting two-way communications. In *Proc. IEEE ICC'13*, 2013.

[16] L. Huang and M. Neely. Utility optimal scheduling in energy-harvesting networks. *IEEE/ACM Trans. Netw.*, 21(4):1117–1130, 2013.

[17] J. Kleinberg. Single-source unsplittable flow. In *Proc. IEEE FOCS'96*, 1996.

[18] J. Kleinberg, Y. Rabani, and E. Tardos. Fairness in routing and load balancing. In *Proc. IEEE FOCS'99*, 1999.

[19] L. Lin, N. Shroff, and R. Srikant. Asymptotically optimal energy-aware routing for multihop wireless networks with renewable energy sources. *IEEE/ACM Trans. Netw.*, 15(5):1021–1034, 2007.

[20] R.-S. Liu, K.-W. Fan, Z. Zheng, and P. Sinha. Perpetual and fair data collection for environmental energy harvesting sensor networks. *IEEE/ACM Trans. Netw.*, 19(4):947–960, Aug. 2011.

[21] R. Madan and S. Lall. Distributed algorithms for maximum lifetime routing in wireless sensor networks. *IEEE Trans. Wireless Commun.*, 5(8):2185–2193, 2006.

[22] Z. Mao, C. Koksal, and N. Shroff. Near optimal power and rate control of multi-hop sensor networks with energy replenishment: Basic limitations with finite energy and data storage. *IEEE Trans. Autom. Control*, 57(4):815–829, 2012.

[23] J. Marašević, C. Stein, and G. Zussman. Max-min fair rate allocation and routing in energy harvesting networks: Algorithmic analysis. *CoRR*, abs/1406.3671, June 2014.

[24] N. Megiddo. Optimal flows in networks with multiple sources and sinks. *Mathematical Programming*, 7(1):97–107, 1974.

[25] O. Ozel, K. Tutuncuoglu, J. Yang, S. Ulukus, and A. Yener. Transmission with energy harvesting nodes in fading wireless channels: Optimal policies. *IEEE J. Sel. Areas Commun.*, 29(8):1732–1743, 2011.

[26] S. Plotkin, D. Shmoys, and E. Tardos. Fast approximation algorithms for fractional packing and covering problems. *Math. of O.R.*, 20(2):257–301, 1995.

[27] B. Radunović and J.-Y. L. Boudec. A unified framework for max-min and min-max fairness with applications. *IEEE/ACM Trans. Netw.*, 15(5):1073–1083, Oct. 2007.

[28] S. Sarkar and L. Tassiulas. Fair allocation of discrete bandwidth layers in multicast networks. In *Proc. IEEE INFOCOM'00*, 2000.

[29] R. Srivastava and C. Koksal. Basic performance limits and tradeoffs in energy-harvesting sensor nodes with finite data and energy storage. *IEEE/ACM Trans. Netw.*, 21(4):1049–1062, 2013.

RxLayer: Adaptive Retransmission Layer for Low Power Wireless

Daibo Liu
School of Computer Science and Engineering of UESTC
Chengdu, Sichuan, China
dbliu@uestc.edu.cn

Zhichao Cao
School of Software, TNLIST, Tsinghua University
Beijing, China
caozc@greenorbs.com

Jiliang Wang
School of Software, TNLIST, Tsinghua University
Beijing, China
jiliang@greenorbs.com

Mengshu Hou
School of Computer Science and Engineering of UESTC
Chengdu, Sichuan, China
mshou@uestc.edu.cn

Yujun Li
School of Computer Science and Engineering of UESTC
Chengdu, Sichuan, China
liyujun@uestc.edu.cn

ABSTRACT

In large scale wireless sensor networks, retransmission strategies are widely adopted to guarantee the reliability of multi-hop forwarding. However, keeping retransmission over a bursty link may fail consecutively. Moreover, the retransmission will also be useless over those back-up links which are spatial correlated with the failed link. Thus, it is necessary to design an unified retransmission strategy, which considers both temporal and spacial link properties, to further improve network reliability and efficiency. In this paper, we propose RxLayer, a practical and general supporting layer of data retransmission. Without inducing noticeable overhead, RxLayer captures the temporal and spatial link properties by conditional probability models. A sender will retransmit data over the candidate link with the highest delivery probability while failures occur. RxLayer can be transparently integrated with most of the existing forwarding protocols. We implement RxLayer and evaluate it on both indoor and outdoor testbeds. The results show that RxLayer improves networks reliability and energy efficiency in various scenarios. The network reliability is improved by up to 7.82%, and the total number of transmissions is reduced by up to 36.3%.

Categories and Subject Descriptors

C.2.1 [**Network Architecture and Design**]: Wireless communication

Keywords

Retransmission Strategy; Wireless Sensor Networks; Bursty Link; Link Correlation

MobiHoc '14, August 11-14 2014, Philadelphia, PA, USA
Copyright 2014 ACM 978-1-4503-2620-9/14/08$15.00.
http://dx.doi.org/10.1145/2632951.2632962 .

1. INTRODUCTION

In recent years, more and more wireless sensor networks (WSNs) [15] [25] [24] are deployed to collect environment data for various applications. In most of the deployments, multi-hop data relay is utilized to adapt the large scale and low-power transmission. During data collection, however, packet loss is ubiquitous and network reliability is thus degraded. According to measurement study [14] [7], instability of wireless links has so far been regarded as an important cause. The link dynamic is inevitable so that how to efficiently predict the changes and enhance network reliability, namely *retransmission strategy*, is a critical issue.

Several kinds of retransmission strategies are proposed with the development of WSNs. One main kind of retransmission strategies utilize end-to-end acknowledgement (ACK) [13] [17]. Due to the constraint of bandwidth resources, instead of acknowledging every packet, sink node sends negative-acknowledgement (NACK) back to a source node. Then the source node retransmits the packets named in NACK. However, the transmission of NACK still consumes considerable bandwidth resources when the data rate is high. The loss of NACK will further degrade energy efficiency and delay.

Another widely adopted kind of retransmission strategies are hop-by-hop retransmission [9] [4] [23], namely fail-retry strategy. Each packet will be retransmitted over a preselected link until the packet is acknowledged or the number of retransmissions reaches the preconfigured threshold. According to recent link study [19], the short-term transmission over intermediate links are dependent. For example, it will probably fail to transmit during a short period after one transmission failure occurs. This link property is called *link burstiness*. Persistent retransmission over bursty link is obviously not a wise choice.

Further, with link estimation models [9] [8], nodes periodically update link quality. When continuous retransmission failures over individual link appear, the link quality will be getting low so that the sender will choose a back-up link to retransmit. To avoid the longer waiting time in low duty-cycle WSNs, dynamic forwarding [4] [10] chooses multiple next-hop candidates, who wake up in different time, to do quick retransmission. However, *link spatial correlation* [18] indicates that data transmission over the links in a local area

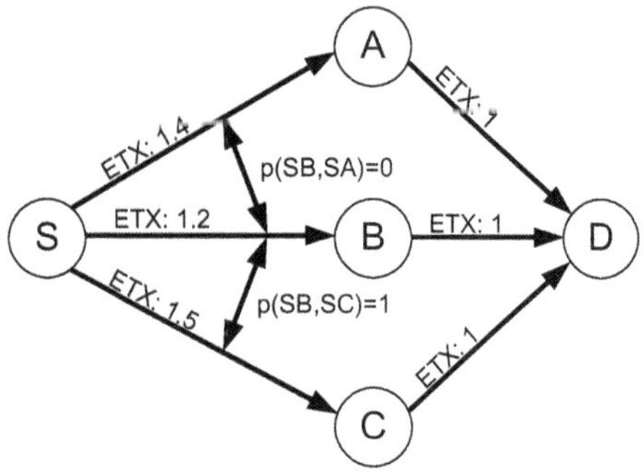

Figure 1: Model of retransmission, where S can forward data to D relayed by A, B, or C.

might be dependent. Hence choosing a link, which is high correlated with the degraded link, to retransmit is useless and energy inefficient. All these strategies that ignore the incorporation of both temporal and spatial link properties will result in unsatisfactory effect of data retransmission. Thus the design of an unified retransmission strategy to target network reliability and energy efficiency is a challenge problem for existing protocols.

In this paper, we propose RxLayer, a general and practical supporting layer of adaptive hop-by-hop retransmission. Without inducing noticeable overhead, RxLayer captures the temporal and spatial link properties by conditional probability models. Then a sender will retransmit data over a candidate link with the highest delivery probability when failures occur.

To our best knowledge, RxLayer is the first unified retransmission layer that incorporates both spatial and temporal link properties to improve data delivery reliability and efficiency. To achieve this goal, there are several challenges. First, the probabilistic models of RxLayer should accurately perceive the temporal and spatial link properties. Second, training the models should be lightweight on both communication and computation. Third, RxLayer should be compatible with most of the existing forwarding protocols.

To address these challenges, we first construct conditional probabilistic models to capture link burstiness and link spatial correlation. For example, a node maintains the probability that the ith retransmission will success after $i-1$ consecutive failures to measure link burstiness. Then the models are trained by the records of data transmission and routing beacon. The models are also periodically updated to reduce the memory and computation consumption. Finally, RxLayer sits between network layer and MAC layer. It utilizes cross-layer information to further optimize forwarding decision and keeps its transparency.

In summary, the contributions of this work are as follows:

• We first propose an unified retransmission layer, RxLayer, which takes conditional probabilistic models to depict both link burstiniss and link spatial correlation so that RxLayer improves both delivery reliability and efficiency.

• RxLayer is practical for various applications since its maintain overhead is low and it is compatible with the most of existing forwarding protocols.

• We implement RxLayer with CTP [9] and LPL [16] and evaluate it on both indoor and outdoor testbeds. The results show that the network reliability is averagely improved by 7.82% and the average transmission count is decreased by up to 36.3% in outdoor experiments.

The rest of the paper is organized as follows. The related work is discussed in the following section. Empirical study is presented in Section 3. Section 4 introduces the detailed design of RxLayer. Followed by its implementation and evaluation in Sections 5. Section 6 concludes this paper.

2. RELATED WORK

Fast retransmission [11], partial packet recovery-based retransmission [12], and network coding [18] are some existing retransmission strategies in wireless networks, but they do not consider the temporal and spacial link properties. Next, we will discuss the existing link estimation methods and retransmission strategies that consider temporal or spacial link properties.

2.1 Link Burstiness and Correlations

The majority of existing link estimation techniques [22] assume that the different packet loss events on a link are statistically independent and follow Bernoulli distribution. Recent study [5] marks this assumption as inappropirate when wireless links are estimated in short time scale. β factor [19] introduces a mechanism to quantify link burstiness. κ factor [18] presents an algorithm to quantify link correlation between selected link and alternative link. However, these factors are computed offline with large set of history data. RxLayer proposes a lightweight way to capture link burstiness and correlation in real-time.

2.2 Exploiting Link Properties

Some forwarding techniques deal with link burstiness and correlation to improve network performance. CPRP[26] and CorLayer [21] exploit link correlation for data dissemination/broadcast. DSF [10] dynamically choose the parent from a set of neighbors to avoid the useless retransmission over a temporally degraded link. With dynamic forwarding, L^2 [4] further proposes the temporal link model to improve both the delivery reliability and efficiency. In contrast, RxLayer comprehensively combines both link burstiness and correlation.

STLE [2] takes the bursty available long link to reduce the number of transmission. It utilizes an overhearing scheme to estimate the short-term link behavior. The current parent is temporally replaced by a node which is much closer to sink and overhears consecutive three packets. However, STLE will be inefficient when the overhearing becomes rare with the diverse wake-up schedule of nodes in low duty cycle WSNs. RxLayer online captures link burstiness and correlations with cross-layer information. It can be transparently integrated with most of existing protocols.

3. EMPIRICAL STUDY

In this section, we conduct empirical studies to show that:

• Link burstiness and link spatial correlation have a significant impact on data delivery performance.

• The methods that solely exploit link burstiness or spatial link correlation in existing works may not always lead to an optimal performance.

• The combination of these link properties provides a great opportunity for efficient transmission.

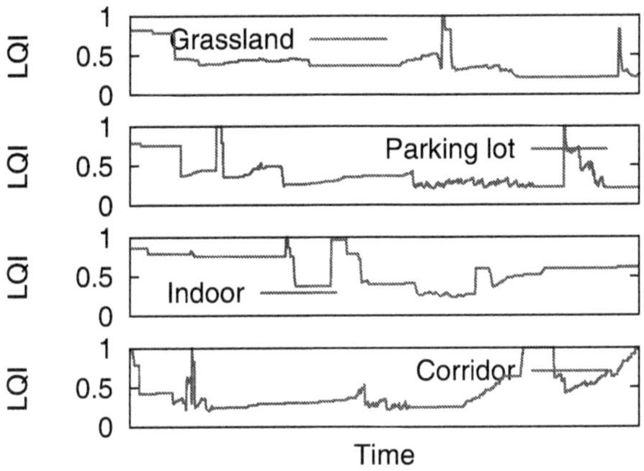

Figure 2: Link burstiness over four links in different scenarios, where LQI=1/ETX is measured by link estimator. Ascendent trend indicates acknowledged transmission, and conversely indicates transmission failures.

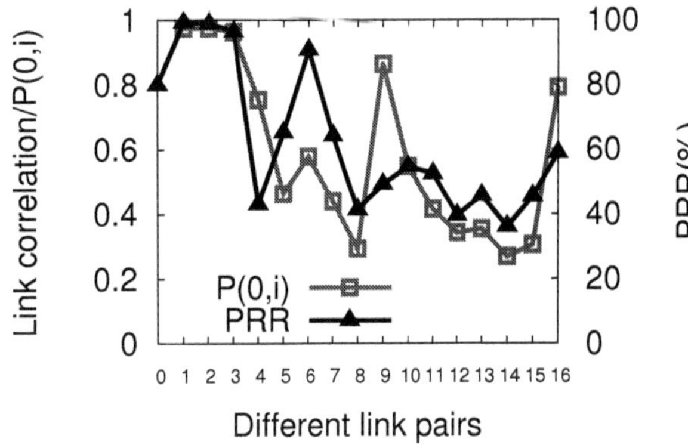

Figure 3: Correlation between link 0 and other links. *P(0,i)* denotes the probability that a packet lost in link *0* but received in link *i* (ranging from 1 to 16).

3.1 Theoretical Model of Retransmission

Before the empirical study, with a simple model depicted in Figure 1, we first analyze the retransmission efficiency by using consecutive retransmission (*CR*), exploiting link burstiness (*LB*), and exploiting both link burstiness and correlation (*LBC*), respectively. S can forward data to D relayed by A, B, or C. B is S's default parent node.We also assume that all links are bursty and the expected transmission count (ETX) [6] over a link denotes long-term link quality. After encountering bursty loss, for simplicity, we assume the following n consecutive retransmissions will be failed. $P(i,j)$ is the correlation probability between link i and j that a transmission can success on link j when it fails on link i. In the case as Figure 1 shows, $P(SB,SA)$ is 0 indicating the transmission on link $S \rightarrow B$ will be failed if the transmission on link $S \rightarrow A$ is failed. Inversely, $P(SB,SC)$ is 1 indicating a transmission will be successful on link $S \rightarrow C$ when a transmission fails on link $S \rightarrow B$.

By using *CR* to deliver data to B, the expected retransmission count of S is at least $n+1$. With *LB*, nodes forward data through sub-optimal link after m (m is far less than n) consecutive failures, first replacing $S \rightarrow B$ with $S \rightarrow A$ because the ETX of $S \rightarrow A$ is lower than that of $S \rightarrow C$, the expected retransmission count is $2m+1$ (m failures on link $S \rightarrow B$, m failures on link $S \rightarrow A$, and a successful transmission on link $S \rightarrow C$). By using *LBC*, after m transmission failures on link $S \rightarrow B$, S knows the link $S \rightarrow C$ is with temporally high quality according to $P(i,j)$, and will retransmit the data through $S \rightarrow C$. The expected retransmission count is only $m+1$, which is close half of *LB* and far less than *CR*. This model indicates the combination of link burstiness and link spatial correlations can provide much efficient data retransmission.

In practical networks, the burstiness of each link and the correlations between link pairs are diverse. It is impossible to capture the burstiness and correlations with a preconfigured model. In the following sections, we will conduct empirical studies to show the link properties (link burstiness and link spatial correlation), and the benefit and feasibility of exploiting both properties to improve performance.

3.2 Impact of Link Properties

3.2.1 Link Burstiness and Link Correlation

Link burstiness is studied in a large collection of existing works [4] [19] [1]. In this experiment, we study the link burstiness in different environments, grassland, parking lot, indoor office and corridor, to depict the change of link quality indication (LQI). In the experiments, we let a sender generate packets every 100ms and forward them to a fixed relay. By logging the link's ETX according to link estimation every 10 seconds, we plot the LQIs according to $LQI=1/ETX$ in Figure 2. As we can see from this figure, the sharp decline of LQIs and the maintenance of continues low LQIs indicate that link burstiness exists in different environments, which is also widely studied in [4] [19] [1].

Additionally, although link correlation has been widely studied, e.g. [18] [26] [21], to further fine-grainedly test the correlation between link pairs that transmissions failed on one link while succeed on the other link, we conduct an one day experiment by setting that one node S broadcasts packets to the other 16 nodes in indoor scenario. We plot the correlation between a fixed link (0) and other links (from 1 to 16), i.e., $P(0,i)$ which is defined in Section 3.1, in Figure 3. We can see that there indeed exist several links with high packet receipt ratio (PRR), while they have low correlation with the fixed link. For example, the PRR of link 6 is 0.9, while $P(0,6)$ is only 0.57. The inverse phenomenon exists on link 9, having low link PRR (0.49) but high $P(0,9)$ (0.87). The analysis results indicate that once transmission failure on a link (e.g. link 0), it is feasible to deliver data packets through another link (e.g. link 9) with high correlation with the failed link, to improve data delivery reliability. This correlation also provides an evidence for the theoretical model mentioned above.

3.2.2 Impact to Retransmission

As has been inferred by [19] [18], inconsistent channel state is the main cause of link burstiness and diversity, and interference can cause inconsistent channel state at different locations. To exhibit how link burstiness and link spatial correlation impact on network performance, we conduct experiments in a 60ft×45ft office with 22 Telosb nodes, where the sink is located in a corner. Experiments are conducted using $19th$ channel overlaying the working frequencies of

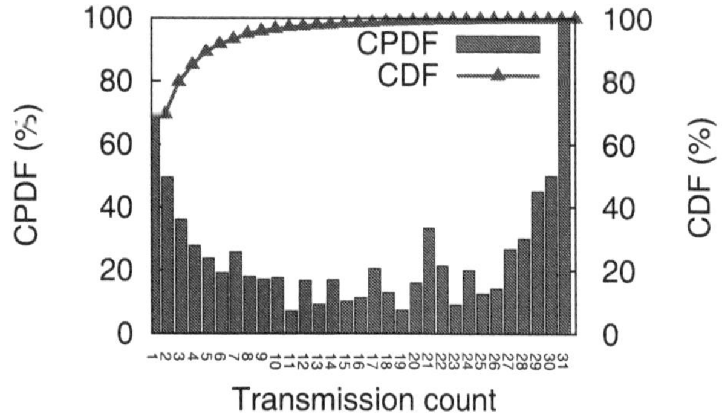

Figure 4: Conditional packet delivery functions (CPDF) that the ith retransmission will success after $i-1$ consecutive failures, and the cumulative distribution function (CDF) of single-hop transmission count.

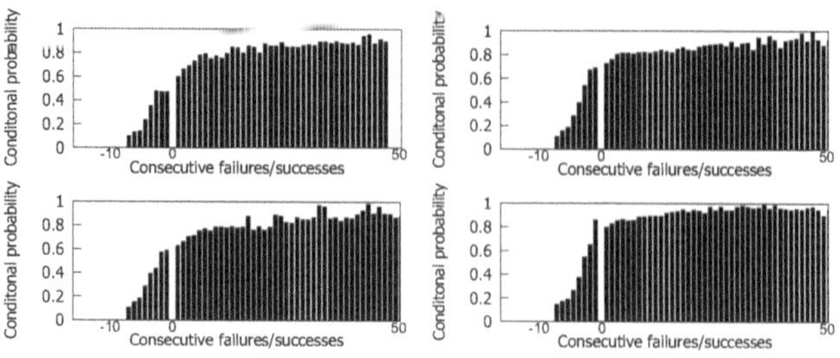

(a) Indoor link (b) Outdoor link

Figure 5: Distribution of conditional packet delivery probability changing along with the time. For each minipage, the trace data of the bottom one is collected two hours later than the top one.

WiFi. Each node generates a packet every 60 seconds and sets the RF power level to -25dBm. The maximum retransmission count threshold (RXT) is set to system default value (31) for each hop.

To show the efficiency of existing retransmission strategy, we use conditional packet delivery functions (CPDF), referred by [19], to denote the packet delivery properties that the ith retransmission successes after $i-1$ consecutive failures. We denote the conditional packet delivery function as $P(i)$, which can be calculated by

$$P(i) = \frac{N_i - N_{i+1}}{N_i}. \quad (1)$$

where N_i is the cumulative count that packets are retransmitted no less than i times. Note that $P(0)$ is also the probability that packets are transmitted only once. We plot the CPDFs in Figure 4. As the figure shows, after consecutive failures, the conditional probability sharply decreases to as little as 20%, indicating the immediate retransmission (*CR* in the theoretical model) is inefficient after consecutive failures.

3.3 Challenges and Problems

3.3.1 Capturing link Properties

To that extent, we further show the dynamics of the captured burstiness pattern. We construct a single-hop network with 10 nodes in indoor office and outdoor playground. To ensure the time continuity of data transmission, we set a marked node's inter-packet interval (IPI) to equal to nodes' wake-up interval, which is 512ms. The other nodes' IPI is set to 60 seconds. The retransmission count threshold is set to 100.

By logging the transmission count of each packet (more than 100,000 packets) generated by the marked node, we compute the conditional probability a packet will be successfully delivered after i consecutive failures according to Equation 1. And the conditional probability that a packet will be successfully delivered after i consecutive successes is computed by

$$P(i) = \frac{N_{i+1}}{N_i}. \quad (2)$$

where N_i is the cumulative count that i consecutive transmissions are successful. The conditional probabilities of different scenarios are shown in Figure 5, where each bar in the histogram has a minimum of 50 data points. For each minipage, the trace data of the bottom figure is collected two hours later than the top one.

It is obviously that previous successes indicates the following transmission is likely to be successful and previous consecutive failures means the immediate retransmission will still fail to a great degree, which coincides with [19]. Furthermore, the burstiness pattern changes with time and scenarios. This phenomenon suggests the inefficiency of arbitrary consecutive retransmission, and indicates the availability of the foreseeable successful probability of the next transmission if each node embeds an online model to capture burstiness pattern.

3.3.2 Urgency of Leveraging link Properties

As discussed above, link properties have great influences on network performance. Figure 6 shows a simple example to illustrate how the widely applied protocols cope with link burstiness and correlations and to explain why the protocols do it in that way.

Node S forwards packets via relay nodes, A, J, and M, to the destination which is denoted by $Sink$. The shadow region denotes the area that can suddenly suffer from the controllable interference resulting in link burstiness and correlations. The path from D to $Sink$ is beyond the disturbed area. S generates packets each 10 seconds and forwards them to A. In our experiments, we record the retransmission count, the change of link quality, and the selection of relay nodes.

In Figure 7, during the sample sequences ranging from 200 to 900 (about 10 minutes), the controlled interference coexists with the low-power WSN. As can be seen from the figure, with the degradation of $S \rightarrow A$, selecting links $S \rightarrow B$ as the replacer according to LQI is unsatisfactory, because B is also suffering with the same interference. In this period, S repeatedly retransmits and degrades link quality wasting energy and impacting on network reliability until it changes its parent to D. However, with the end of the interference, $S \rightarrow D$ is indeed not the optimal link for data forwarding, but routing protocol fails to instantly know the situation because it needs long time to update the link quality of $S \rightarrow A$ (about 35 minutes) only exploiting routing beacons.

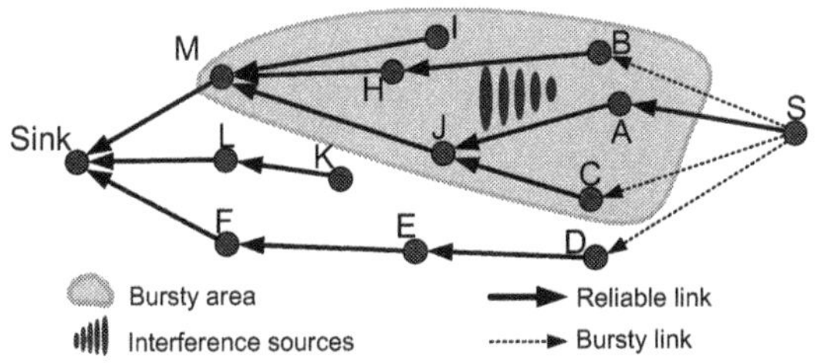

Figure 6: The network topology. Shadow region suffers from interference. A is S's parent. B, C and D are S's candidate relay nodes.

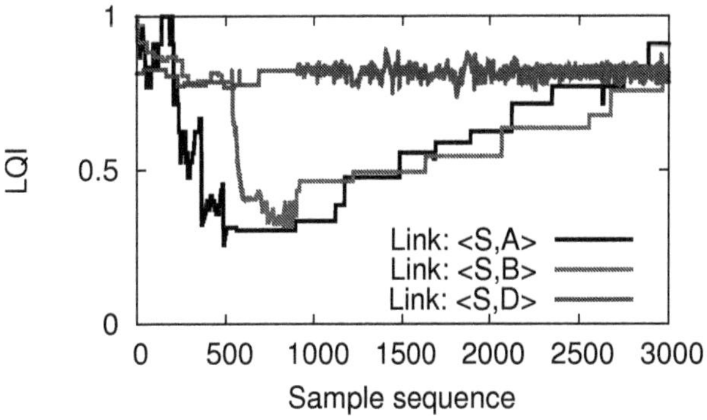

Figure 7: Routing behavior without considering link burstiness and correlation. During the smaple sequences ranging from 200 to 900, node A and B suffer from the controlled interference, and D is out of the disturbed area.

To avoid this case in retransmission-based protocols, it is necessary to consider link burstiness to pause retransmission on a severely degraded link instantly and exploit link correlations to switch to another link with temporally high quality.

3.4 Retransmission Layer

To address the problems in existing retransmission strategies, we propose a retransmission layer to exploit different link properties in order to improve the performance. Basically, to improve the performance with bursty link, existing works will adjust the wake-up interval [19]. Considering link correlations, many other works will switch between different links based on the correlation [26] [21]. We show that we can further improve the performance with a retransmission layer combining both link burstiness and spatial correlation. We build a similar retransmission layer as follows.

We allow neighbors which can provide routing progress to assist a sender to relay data packet without acknowledging the sender after 3 consecutive failures (by setting a bit in the packet header to ask for assistance). In such a case, the sender retransmits the packet to its parent node until being acknowledged or exceeding the RXT (20). To reduce the influence of duplicate packets on performance, we set nodes' IPI to 60 seconds. For simplicity, we mark it as RXTA:20. We also evaluate the consecutive retransmission-based protocol (RXT:20) and dynamic switch-based forwarding protocol (DSF-RXT:20) for comparison. Dynamic switch-based forwarding protocol exploits link burstiness to forward data packet to a candidate relay node according to link quality and wake-up schedule once a transmission fails.

We plot the network reliability and average single-hop transmission count in Figure 8. With such a retransmission layer, RXTA:20 reduces almost 17.1% transmissions compared with RXT:20 and reduces 38.6% compared with DSF-RXT:20 as Figure 8(b) shows, while increases the average PRR from 96.53% and 94.89% to 99.05%, respectively, shown as Figure 8(a).

This experiment sheds new light on the benefit of exploiting both link burstiness and link correlation. It is obvious that when the current used link is severely degraded, relaying packets through another temporally high quality link can provide much more efficient transmission and higher network reliability. The experimental results also motivate us to capture both link burstiness and link spatial correlation between link pairs in retransmission layer.

The empirical study also raises a problem how to efficiently capture link burstiness pattern and link correlation online without introducing extra computational and control

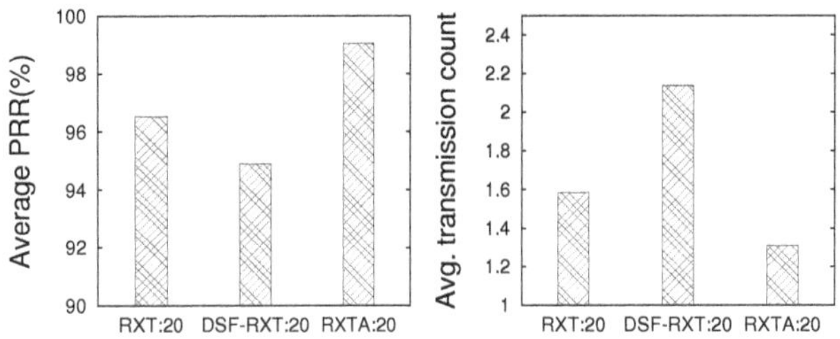

(a) Network reliability (b) Transmission count

Figure 8: Network reliability and average single-hop transmission count of protocols: repeatedly retransmitting (RXT:20), exploiting link burstiness (DSF-RXT:20), and exploiting both link burstiness and correlation (RXTA:20).

overhead. In the next section, we will discuss online models to capture these network characteristics transparent to existing protocols.

4. DESIGN OF RXLAYER

From the empirical studies, we know the exist of link burstiness and correlation, and the benefit of exploiting them in retransmission layer. This section presents the design of RxLayer. In what follows, the design principles and core ideas of RXLayer are presented in Section 4.1. We then introduce the basis of RxLayer – the online models – in Section 4.2 and Section 4.3. The strategy how RxLayer works is discussed in Section 4.4. And then we discuss the embedding of RxLayer into forwarding protocols in Section 4.5.

4.1 Design Insign and Principles

Generally, retransmission strategy works as follows. Given a network, each node forwards data packets to the destination through a deterministic relay (deterministic forwarding) or a forwarding set (dynamic switch-based forwarding) determined by network communication layer. Once a transmission is not acknowledged, the sender will retransmit the packet until it receives an ACK. With data transmission, it also updates link quality. When the successive retransmission count exceeds the maximum threshold, the packet will

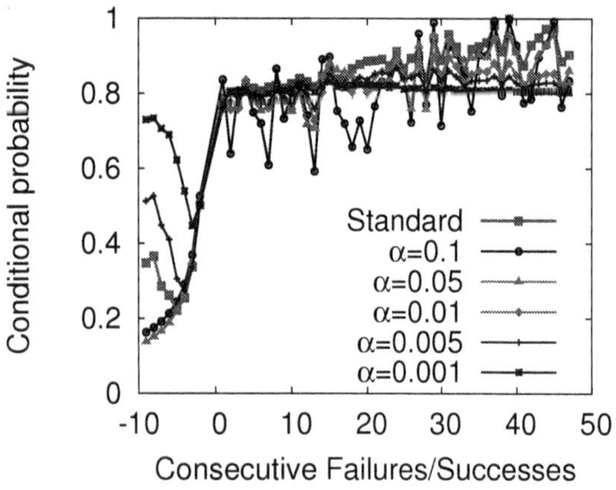

Figure 9: The computed conditional probability of P_i by setting different values to α, the *standard* one denotes the computed result by Equation 1.

be dropped. To provide reliable transmission, network protocols should endeavor to maintain and update link quality.

However, from the empirical studies, we know retransmission-based routing protocols are inefficient encountering link burstiness and correlation. The feature provides the key insights we used to exploit link burstiness and correlation when building RxLayer. Roughly speaking, a sender should instantly perceive the severely degraded link quality, and then, according to link properties captured online, RxLayer decides when to pause after consecutive failures and retransmits through a candidate link with temporally high quality.

4.2 Link Burstiness Model

In this section, we present a conditional probability model by which a sender perceives the severe degradation of the current used link and gets a proper stoppint point of consecutive retransmission over a bursty link. To construct this model, each node maintains a probability table, marked as *PSRT*, to record the probability of successful retransmissions of each target link. *PSRT* contains M entries. Each entry marked as E_i, $0 \leq i < M$, denotes a conditional probability, P_i, that a packet will be successfully delivered after i consecutive failures. Initially, we consider links to be independent, and the probability of each individual trial is initialized to the inverse of link quality. Then, it can be formalized as: $P_i = \frac{1}{ETX}$.

When a sender transmits a data packet to its next-hop node, RxLayer will update the value of corresponding *PSRT* entry after each trial. Here, we use moving average to update P_i shown as follow.

$$P_i^{new} = \begin{cases} (1-\alpha) * P_i^{old} + \alpha & if\ success \\ (1-\alpha) * P_i^{old} & if\ fail \end{cases} \quad (3)$$

P_i^{old} is the accumulated conditional probability, and P_i^{new} is the updated value. α is a parameter for making a tradeoff between the adaptability to network dynamics and accuracy. To find the optimal value of α, we use 5 hours trace data to compute conditional probability by setting different values to α. By Comparing these results with the standard case which is computed by Equation 1, as Figure 9 shows, it is rational to set α to 0.05 with the best fitting. Note that the optimal value of α changes with scenarios, a robust and efficient method should dynamically adjust the parameter. Some machine learning methods [3] could be used to adjust α. However, for simplicity, we use a fixed experimental value in our implementation and won't discuss it in detail in this paper.

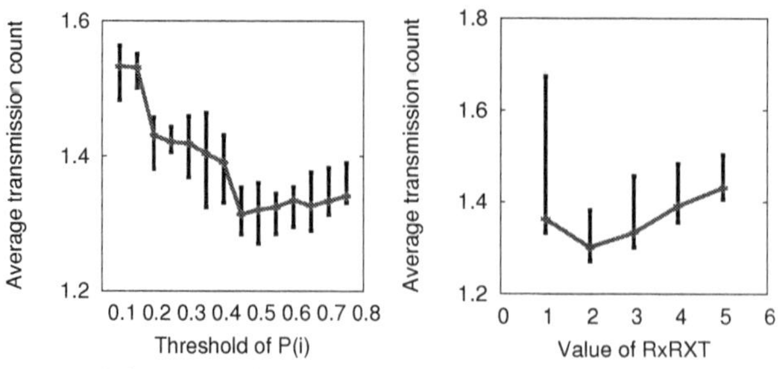

(a) Value of P_t (b) Value of RxRXT

Figure 10: The average transmission count changing with the value of P_t or RxRXT.

By online updating *PSRT* entries, RxLayer can build a prediction model fastly like Figure 5 showing. To transmit a packet, RxLayer checks the conditional probability (P_i) by inputting the count (i) of consecutive failures. If P_i is less than the predefined threshold (P_t, which will be discussed in Section 4.4 in detail), the sender should pause and choose a candidate link with temporally high quality to deliver the packet.

When choosing a new link, maybe, it is the first time to be used, which means the link is considered to be independent by ignoring the burstiness property. In RxLayer, we define the retransmission count threshold over a new link no more than a constant RxRXT, which is discussed in the following section. Moreover, note that choosing a new relay node won't trigger parent change event. Parent change is controlled by network communication layer only according to link quality. Hence, it can be avoided that parent change is triggered by sharply decreased link quality when a burst of interference results in consecutive failures even though the link is long-term reliable.

4.3 Link Correlation Model

As mentioned before, by getting an stoppint point, RxLayer should select another link to deliver packets. Here, we discuss the model for capturing link correlation. A metric is presented in this section to represent the degree of link correlation. It's desirable for the metric to measure the probability that transmissions failed on one link while succeed on the other one. For simplicity, it is marked as ω, which is a 3-tuple quantity, defined on a transmitter, S, and two receivers, i and j, that can overhear packets from S, as:

$$\omega(S,i,j) = \begin{cases} P_{i/j}^{(S)}(0/1) & P_i^{(S)}(0) > 0 \\ PRR(j) & P_i^{(S)}(0) = 0 \end{cases} \quad (4)$$

where, $P_{i/j}^{(S)}(0/1)$ is the probability, when S transmits, that a packet succeed on link $S \to j$ given that it failed on link $S \to i$, and $P_i^{(S)}(0)$ is the proportion of packets failed on link $S \to i$. If the two links, $S \to i$ and $S \to j$ are independent, then $\omega(S,i,j)$ is the packet delivery ratio of link $S \to j$.

To capture ω between link pairs, RxLayer adopts uniform broadcast sequence number (BSN) to differentiate broadcast

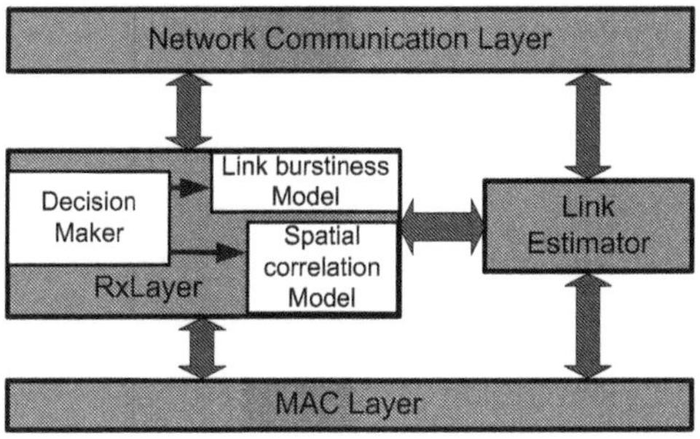

Figure 11: RxLayer in the protocol stack.

Table 1: average gap of link correlation between the result of moving average and statistical result.

θ	gap	θ	gap
0.01	0.051	0.02	0.053
0.03	0.048	0.04	0.039
0.05	0.032	0.06	0.024
0.07	0.029	0.08	0.031
0.09	0.049	0.1	0.062

packets from data packets. To transmit a broadcast packet, low-power WSN guarantees each neighbor has a chance to hear the packet. By recording and exchanging the bitmap of neighbors' BSNs, each node can capture the ω between different link pairs distributedly. Note that the BSN information is attached to routing beacon, so there is no additional control overhead.

For efficiency, we arrange a circular queue of the size of 2 bytes for each neighbor to record the BSNs of all heard broadcast packets. Each bit corresponds to a broadcast packet. When a bit was set, it indicates the corresponding packet has been heard. To denote all available broadcast packets (BSN ranging from 0 to 255), we use an index to record the BSN of the earliest received broadcast packet, and a point to indicate the index of the corresponding bit.

Through routing beacons, a node can get to know the correlation between link pairs like Figure 3 showing. Based on the information, a node can calculate ω between any link pairs according to Equation 4. Note that a 2 bytes-long circular queue only records limited BSNs. Hence, the result of each calculation of ω associated with two links is a partial view of the overall correlation. To fully show the correlation between link pairs, we use moving average to update ω as follow,

$$\omega(S,i,j) = (1-\theta) * \omega^{old}(S,i,j) + \theta * \omega^{new}(S,i,j) \quad (5)$$

where $\omega^{old}(S,i,j)$ is the accumulated correlation between link $S \rightarrow i$ and $S \rightarrow j$, and $\omega^{new}(S,i,j)$ is the calculation result of the latest BSN sets. We guarantee each sequence is exploited only once. The using of moving average not only reduces memory overhead, but also provides a trade-off between the adaptability to network dynamics and the accuracy. To get an appropriate value to θ, we conduct an experiment by collect the feedback BSNs from two links for an entire day. We analyze the correlation between two links exploiting the collected BSNs according to the statistical approach like Equation 4 and moving average like Equation 5, respectively. The statistical approach exploits all history

Figure 12: Indoor testbed with 22 TelosB nodes and outdoor scenario with 30 TelosB nodes.

Table 2: parameters used in RxLayer.

M	10	α	0.05
θ	0.06	P_t	0.45
RxRXT	2		

data to compute the correlation, while the moving average only exploits the most recent BSNs to update the correlation. We assume the statistical correlation is very precise although it may not be exactly true. By setting different values to θ, we calculate the gap of link correlation between the statistical result and the moving average result according to

$$gap = \sqrt{\frac{\sum(\omega_i - M_i)^2}{n}},$$

where M_i is the statistical correlation and ω_i is the related correlation calculated by moving average after sender broadcasting the ith routing beacon. The values of θ and the corresponding gaps are listed in Table 1, which indicates 0.06 is the optimal value of θ with the minimal gap, then we set θ to 0.06 in RxLayer with the minimum gap.

4.4 Decision-Maker Rule

In this section, we discuss the rules when should RxLayer pause after encountering transmission failure and how to select a candidate relay.

As mentioned above, when the conditional probability, P_i, of successful transmission is lower than the predefined threshold P_t, RxLayer triggers the change of relay. In the indoor experiments, by integrating the state-of-the-art protocols with RxLayer and setting different values to P_t, we compute the average transmission count of each trial as Figure 10(a) shows. Overall, setting P_t to 0.45 obtains the most benefit. As mentioned above, the maximum retransmission count threshold via a link to a replacer is no more than RxRXT. By setting different values to RxRXT in indoor experiments under interference, the average transmission count is plotted in Figure 10(b). According to the figure, we set RxRXT to 2 in RxLayer with the minimum expected transmission count. In our additional experiments which are not plotted in this paper, by setting P_t to 0.45 and RxRXT to 2, the network performance is relatively better than setting to other values on the whole.

In the context of hop-by-hop retransmission-based protocols, deterministic forwarding [9] and dynamic switch-based forwarding [10] are two basic types protocols. For the former, network layer supports a determined relay node, but for the latter, network layer supports a forwarding set which

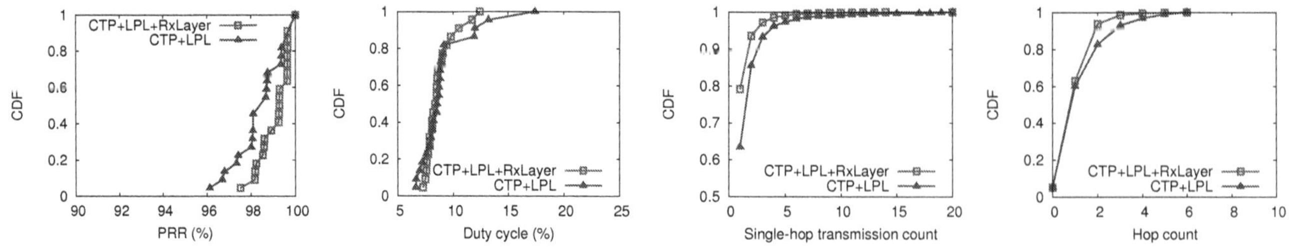

(a) Network reliability (b) Energy consumption (c) Single hop transmission count (d) Number of hops travelled

Figure 13: Performance of multi-hop indoor testbed experiment with 22 TelosB nodes. By embedding RxLayer into CTP+LPL, network performance is slightly improved.

Algorithm 1 Decision-Maker Algorithm

Input:
Given $P_t \in [0,1]$; *Threshold*←RXT; Retransmission count i=0; RxRXT; *Sum*←0; Forwarding set F;
Iteration:
1: **while** $P_i > P_t$ & $i < Threshold$ & $Sum < RXT$ **do**
2: Retransmission;
3: **if** Acknowledged **then**
4: Update link quality; Upgrade P_i;
5: Return.
6: **else**
7: Update link quality; Degrade P_i
8: $i \leftarrow i+1$; $Sum \leftarrow Sum+1$;
9: **end if**
10: **end while**
11: **if** $Sum = RXT$ **then**
12: Drop the packet;
13: Return.
14: **else**
15: **if** $Card(F)$=1 **then**
16: Selecting the replacer with largest ω;
17: **else**
18: Considering both relay nodes' wake-up time schedule and ω between each of them and the previous unsuccessful link;
19: **end if**
20: $Threshold \leftarrow RxRXT$; $i \leftarrow 0$;
21: **Goto: Iteration**;
22: **end if**

contains a sequence of relay nodes scheduled by wake-up time. To support these protocols without distinction, we consider the relay node or a sequence of relay nodes provided by network layer as forwarding set uniformly.

The work process of RxLayer is presented in Algorithm *Decision-Maker.* The inputs to the algorithm are the measured threshold (P_t) of conditional probability, the maximum retransmission count threshold (RXT) provided as a system parameter, the retransmission count (i) over the current used link, the predefined maximum retransmission count to any candidate replacer (RxRXT), and the forwarding set provided by network layer.

When a packet is delivered down from network communication layer, where the relay node is set to be the first element of the forwarding set, the retransmission count (i) is set to 0, and the maximum retransmission count threshold (*Threshold*) is set to RXT, RxLayer checks whether the conditional probability P_i is larger than P_t and i is less than *Threshold.* If so, RxLayer delivers the packet to the next hop node. If the packet is acknowledged, RxLayer updates the link quality, upgrades P_i according to Equation 3, and returns the success to the upper layer; otherwise, updates link quality, degrades P_i, and retries to deliver the data packet. If the total retransmission count exceeds RXT, RxLayer drops the packet and returns related information to upper layer. Beyond that, no matter getting a stoppint point ($P_i \leq P_t$) or the retransmission count over the link to a replacer exceeding RxRXT ($i \leq Threshold$), RxLayer selects another replacer of the current relay node and starts a new iteration until the packet is successfully delivered or dropped. Note that *Card(F)* (line 15 in Algorithm *Decision-Maker*) denotes the selection of the optimal replacer from forwarding set F. *Card(F)* returns 1 if there exists a candidate replacer in the set, otherwise, returns 0. For the deterministic forwarding protocols, *Card(F)* always returns 0. There can have a variety of methods to schedule the forwarding set and select a replacer, however, we won't go into detail on this in the paper.

4.5 RxLayer Embedding

Rxlayer is designed as a generic middleware to assist a wide range of existing routing protocols (e.g, CTP [9], DSF [10]) and be compatible with other energy efficient MAC layers such as low power listening (LPL) [16] and low power probing (LPP) [20]. To do that, we insert RxLayer beneath network communication layer and above MAC layer as shown in Figure 11. Before discussing our evaluation, we give the parameters used by RxLayer in Table 2.

5. EVALUATION

In this section, we evaluate RxLayer through indoor and outdoor experiments. We compare the network performance of the stat-of-the-art protocols (CTP [9] with LPL [16]) embedding RxLayer with that without embedding RxLayer.

We use PRR as the indicator of the network reliability. The energy consumption is measured by the ratio of radio on time to total time (duty cycle). Moreover, we use the average transmission count to measure the cost of delivering a packet. Additionally, we use parent change count to measure the network dynamics.

5.1 Implementation

We implemented RxLayer on TelosB nodes in TinyOS

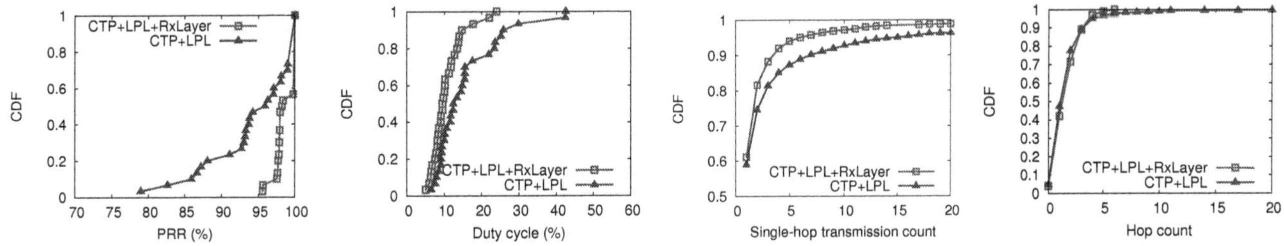

(a) Network reliability (b) Energy consumption (c) Single hop transmission count (d) Number of hops travelled

Figure 14: The performance of multi-hop outdoor experiment with 30 TelosB nodes. By embedding RxLayer into CTP+LPL, network performance is greatly improved.

2.1.1. The prototype implementation of RxLayer combines with CTP, a standard collection protocol for sensor networks shipped with TinyOS. CTP uses Four Bit Link Estimator [8] as its link estimation component. The RAM and ROM consumption of RxLayer are 833 bytes and 6656 bytes, respectively. RxLayer is not bound to any specific routing protocol. It can be easily integrated with other routing protocols, such as L2 [4] and DSF [10]. In the following experiments, we embed RxLayer with CTP above LPL.

5.2 Evaluation Setup

We evaluate the performance of protocols on indoor testbed with 22 Telosb nodes and outdoor networks with 30 Telosb nodes as Figure 12 shows. In the indoor experiments, we set the transmission power of CC2420 as level 1 to ensure multi-hop communication (maximum hop is 6). The outdoor network is deployed around our office build where there are 10 to 18 WiFi APs at different locations and the work frequency of some APs overlays with the *19th* channel of ZigBee. Uniformly, we set our networks' work channel to 19, the transmission power of CC2420 is set to level 10, the maximum retransmission count threshold is set to the TinyOS default setting 31, and each node generates packets with a fixed IPI (60 seconds). The set of LPL's wake-up interval is 512ms. We conduct experiments using the protocol stack (CTP with LPL) and that by embedding RxLayer in the same scenarios. Each experiment lasts for at least 5 hours and is repeated no less than three times.

5.3 Network Reliability

We compare the network reliability of CTP+LPL with that by embedding RxLayer in indoor testbed experiments (as Figure 13 shows) and outdoor experiments (as Figure 14 shows). Figure 13(a) and Figure 14(a) show the distribution of each node's average PRR. By embedding RxLayer into CTP+LPL, network reliability (PRR) is averagely improved by 1.53% in the indoor experiments, and by 7.82% in the outdoor experiments.

As the figures show, by embedding with RxLayer, nodes' PRRs are relatively high and distributed in a smaller range. It is because channel state at different nodes is different and RxLayer exploits the correlation to forward packets via the temporally stable links when the current used link is severely degraded. No matter a sender or a receiver is distributed in interference area, by perceiving the shapely degraded link quality according to online conditional probability models, RxLayer utilizes the best available link if there exists one, so as to decrease the effect of local interference on network performance and improve channel utilization.

5.4 Energy Consumption

We also plot the distribution of energy consumption (duty cycle) in Figure 13(b) and Figure 14(b). In the indoor experiments, there is no significant difference between the energy consumption of CTP+LPL and that with RxLayer, but in the outdoor experiments, by embedding with RxLayer, the average duty cycle is significantly decreased from 19.3% to 10.4%. For the former, the little improvement of energy efficiency is due to the small-sized testbed reducing the correlation between link pairs, which is also indicated from the similar distributions of single hop transmission count plotted in Figure 13(c). RxLayer can benefit from the correlation. By embedding with RxLayer in the outdoor experiments, the average single hop transmission count is decreased by 1.35 times (decreased from 3.72 times to 2.37 times) as Figure 14(c) shows.

5.5 Transmission Cost

By embedding RxLayer into CTP with LPL, the single-hop transmission cost does have been reduced no matter in our indoor experiments (Figure 13(c)) or outdoor experiments (Figure 14(c)). The average single hop transmission count of indoor experiments is reduced from 1.74 times to 1.31 times (reduced by about 24.7%) by embedding RxLayer, and reduced from 3.72 times to 2.37 times (reduced by about 36.3%) in outdoor experiments mentioned above. The decreased transmission count makes nodes stay in sleep state, so as to further save energy consumption. Moreover, the reduced transmissions can further decrease packet collisions caused by hidden terminal and reduce suppressed transmission caused by exposed terminal.

The strategy of RxLayer is switching from data forwarding over a severely degraded link to retransmission using another temporally stable link. So, the increased transmission hop count associated with the change of next hop must be considered. We plot the distribution of hop count of indoor and outdoor experiments in Figure 13(d) and Figure 14(d), respectively. The average hop count of outdoor experiments by embedding RxLayer is slightly higher than that without embedding RxLayer, but the latter is with a long tail which means some packets are delivered through many hops to sink. We believe that the misadvice from network communication layer to link estimator mentioned in Section 3.3.2 gives rise to mistakenly degrading link quality and the using suboptimal links, inducing network dynamics and bringing about the long tail. RxLayer can effectively avoid this case by exploiting both link burstiness and correlation between link pairs.

6. CONCLUSIONS

Energy efficiency and network reliability are important issues in low-power wireless sensor networks. To address this problem, nodes work in duty cycle and retransmission strategy is widely applied in routing protocols. However, consecutive retransmission is energy inefficient by ignoring the change of channel state at receiving end.

This paper attempts to improve a wide range of existing deterministic routing protocols and dynamic forwarding protocols by designing a general supporting layer, called RxLayer, for adaptive retransmission by exploiting link burstiness and link correlation. By integrating RxLayer with the state-of-the-art protocols, it significant improves network performance.

Acknowledgment

This work is supported in part by the National Key Technology R&D Program under grant No. 2013BAH33F02, the NSFC program under Grant 61202359, and the NSFC program under Grant 61373146.

7. REFERENCES

[1] D. Aguayo, J. Bicket, S. Biswas, and et al. Link-level measurements from an 802.11b mesh network. In *Proceedings of SigComm*, pages 121–132. ACM, 2004.

[2] M. Alizai, O. Landsiedel, J. Link, and et al. Bursty traffic over bursty links. In *Proceedings of SenSys*, pages 71–84. ACM, 2009.

[3] J. Braams. Fitting curves to data using nonlinear regression: a practical and nonmathematical review. *The FASEB Journal*, 1(5):365–374, 1987.

[4] Z. Cao, Y. He, and Y. Liu. L2: lazy forwarding in low duty cycle wireless sensor networks. In *Proceedings of InfoCom*, pages 1323–1331. IEEE, 2012.

[5] A. Cerpa, J. Wong, M. Potkonjak, and et al. Temporal properties of low power wireless links: modeling and implications on multi-hop routing. In *Proceedings of MobiHoc*, pages 414–425. ACM, 2005.

[6] D. Couto, D. Aguayo, J. Bicket, and et al. A high-throughput path metric for multi-hop wireless routing. In *Proceedings of MobiCom*, pages 134–146. ACM, 2003.

[7] W. Dong, Y. Liu, Y. He, and et al. Measurement and analysis on the packet delivery performance in a large scale sensor network. In *Proceedings of InfoCom*, pages 2679–2687. IEEE, 2013.

[8] R. Fonseca, O. Gnawali, K. Jamieson, and et al. Four-bit wireless link estimation. In *Proceedings of HotNets*. ACM, 2007.

[9] O. Gnawali, R. Fonseca, K. Jamieson, and et al. Collection tree protocol. In *Proceedings of SenSys*, pages 1–14. ACM, 2009.

[10] Y. Gu and T. He. Data forwarding in extremely low duty-cycle sensor networks with unreliable communication links. In *Proceedings of SenSys*, pages 321–334. ACM, 2007.

[11] G. Hwang and D. Cho. Fast retransmission mechanism for voip in ieee 802.11e wireless lans. In *Proceedings of VTC*, pages 1090–3038. IEEE, 2004.

[12] K. Jamieson and H. Balakrishnan. Ppr: partial packet recovery for wireless networks. In *Proceedings of SigComm*, pages 409–420. ACM, 2007.

[13] S. Kim, R. Fonseca, P. Dutta, and et al. Flush: a reliable bulk transport protocol for multihop wireless networks. In *Proceedings of SenSys*, pages 351–365. ACM, 2007.

[14] Y. Liu, Y. He, M. Li, and et al. Does wireless sensor network scale? a measurement study on greenorbs. In *Proceedings of InfoCom*, pages 873–881. IEEE, 2011.

[15] L. Mo, Y. He, Y. Liu, and et al. Canopy closure estimates with greenorbs: sustainable sensing in the forest. In *Proceedings of SenSys*, pages 99–112. ACM, 2009.

[16] J. Polastre, J. Hill, and D. Culler. Versatile low power media access for wireless sensor networks. In *Proceedings of SenSys*, pages 95–107. ACM, 2004.

[17] B. Raman, K. Chebrolu, S. Bijwe, and et al. Pip: a connection-oriented, multi-hop, multi-channel tdma-based mac for high throughput bulk transfer. In *Proceedings of SenSys*, pages 15–28. ACM, 2010.

[18] K. Srinivasan, M. Jain, J. Choi, and et al. The κ-factor: inferring protocol performance using inter-link reception correlation. In *Proceedings of MobiCom*, pages 317–328. ACM, 2010.

[19] K. Srinivasan, M. Kazandjieva, S. Agarwal, and et al. The β-factor: measuring wireless link burstiness. In *Proceedings of SenSys*, pages 29–42. ACM, 2008.

[20] Y. Sun, O. Gurewitz, and D. Johnson. Ri-mac: a receiver initiated asynchronous duty cycle mac protocol for dynamic traffic loads in wireless sensor networks. In *Proceedings of SenSys*, pages 1–14. ACM, 2008.

[21] S. Wang, S. Kim, Y. Liu, and et al. Corlayer: a rransparent link correlation layer for energy efficient broadcast. In *Proceedings of MobiCom*, pages 51–62. ACM, 2013.

[22] A. Woo and D. Culler. Evaluation of efficient link reliability estimators for low-power wireless networks. Technical Report UCB/CSD-03-1270, EECS Department, University of California, Berkeley, 2003.

[23] A. Woo, T. Tong, and D. Culler. Taming the underlying challenges of reliable multihop routing in sensor networks. In *Proceedings of SenSys*, pages 14–27. ACM, 2003.

[24] X. Wu, M. Liu, and Y. Wu. In-situ soil moisture sensing: measurement scheduling and estimation using compressive sensing. In *Proceedings of IPSN*, pages 1–12. ACM/IEEE, 2012.

[25] T. Xiang, Z. Chi, F. Li, and et al. Powering indoor sensing with airflows: a trinity of energy harvesting, synchronous duty-cycling, and sensing. In *Proceedings of SenSys*, pages 73:1–73:2. ACM, 2013.

[26] T. Zhu, Z. Zhong, T. He, and et al. Exploring link correlation for efficient flooding in wireless sensor networks. In *Proceedings of NSDI*, pages 49–64. USENIX, 2010.

Measurement-Based Transmission Schemes for Network MIMO

Krishna C. Garikipati
Dept. of EECS
University of Michigan–Ann Arbor
gkchai@eecs.umich.edu

Kang G. Shin
Dept. of EECS
University of Michigan–Ann Arbor
kgshin@eecs.umich.edu

ABSTRACT

The scaling of network MIMO (netMIMO) comes with the challenges of interference that arise from the aging of the Channel State Information (CSI). Particularly, in scenarios of high channel mobility—where netMIMO is expected to be used—the performance degradation from interference can be severe. In this paper, we design transmission schemes to address the two sources of CSI aging: delay in acquiring CSI feedback, and transmission period over which CSI remains unchanged. We introduce a two-phase training and feedback protocol that balances CSI aging across users by allowing users with high interference to have a shorter feedback delay. We also introduce an adaptive adjustment to the transmission length to reduce the decoding errors caused from interference. The proposed protocols adapt to the measurements collected from the users and hence applicable to various mobility scenarios. Our evaluation in a real and synchronized netMIMO setup shows significant gains (5–10dB) in user performance, especially in mobile channels.

Categories and Subject Descriptors

C.2.1 [**Computer-Communication Networks**]: Network Architecture and Design—*wireless communications*; C.2.2 [**Computer-Communication Networks**]: Network Protocols

General Terms

Design, Experimentation, Performance

Keywords

Multi-user MIMO networks, CSI feedback, CSI aging

1. INTRODUCTION

A distributed multiuser MIMO (MU-MIMO) network, commonly known as *network MIMO* (netMIMO), has the potential of achieving gigabit capacity in dense wireless networks, such as enterprise networks, where most of the wireless traffic is generated and received. A typical netMIMO setup consists of a central controller that does the baseband processing, and a set of distributed Access Points (APs) that concurrently transmit data to multiple users or stations (STAs). In contrast to traditional multi-cell WLAN deployments where adding more cells increases co-channel interference, netMIMO eliminates the inter-cell interference, or converts it into useful information through tight integration of APs into a giant virtual MIMO transmitter, thus preserving capacity gains from the additional cells. The network capacity scales linearly with the number of transmitters, or APs [1], and therefore, a simple installation of a large number of APs is expected to meet the bandwidth requirements of modern wireless networks.

However, in reality, realizing the true gains of a large-scale netMIMO has been challenging for a number of reasons. First, the distributed APs or transmitters have to be accurately synchronized in time and frequency through periodic exchange of synchronization frames. Second, fast backhaul links that connect the APs to the controller and support real-time baseband processing have to be deployed. Last, the fundamental wireless capacity that is under-achieved due to the channel feedback overhead and channel estimation errors has to scale with the size of the network. Note that although reciprocity of the wireless channel precludes the need for channel feedback, the calibration requirements [2] make the reciprocity assumption untenable for netMIMO deployments.

Nevertheless, recent advances have shown that high-capacity backhaul can be realized with optical fiber technology, while synchronization was achieved with a large number of APs [3]. On the other hand, the problem of STA interference that arises from the errors between estimated and observed channel remains a major challenge [4].

In netMIMO, as in any MU-MIMO network, the APs broadcast training frames that are used by the STAs to compute their respective Channel State Information (CSI). Each STA then transmits its CSI, either compressed or uncompressed, back to the APs during the feedback phase. This implies the delay in acquiring the CSI feedback from STAs grows with the number of participating STAs. In certain scenarios, the excessive feedback delay may see the channel undergo significant changes. Subsequently, when data frames are transmitted, one or more STAs may see a channel that is completely different from the channel used for computing the CSI. This phenomenon is technically known as *CSI aging*, and the delay between CSI estimation and ac-

MobiHoc'14, August 11–14, 2014, Philadelphia, PA, USA.
Copyright 2014 ACM 978-1-4503-2620-9/14/08 ...$15.00.
http://dx.doi.org/10.1145/2632951.2632980 .

tual transmission is called the *CSI delay*. Since netMIMO relies on zero-forcing techniques based on past CSI, improper cancellation of streams due to CSI aging leads to interference at the STAs. This unwanted interference can result in significantly lower throughput than expected from perfect cancellation. In addition, when data frames are sent for a long period of time using the past CSI, the interference may get accentuated due to further increase in CSI delay. Therefore, both the feedback delay and the length of transmission are important factors that determine the effect of CSI aging on netMIMO performance.

In this paper, we propose transmission schemes for netMIMO that are designed to address the following two questions associated with CSI aging: Q1) *how to get CSI feedback without adversely affecting one or more STAs' performance?*; Q2) *how to determine the length of transmission over which the CSI remains unchanged?* Since the effects of CSI aging are strongly dependent on the deployment, we propose a protocol that adapts to the measurements received from the STAs. We implement and evaluate these schemes in a real netMIMO testbed with real-world wireless channels. This paper makes the following contributions:

- A non-heuristic, non-threshold-based training and feedback protocol, and an adaptive transmission scheme that effectively overcome the effect of CSI aging.
- A novel measurement-based approach where interference observed at the STAs is used in adapting the netMIMO protocol. We show that interference is a useful metric, and support our claims with analysis and observations.
- Construction of a fully synchronized netMIMO testbed on WARP Software-Defined Radio [5] with MIMO-OFDM processing, and development of a new channel-measurement framework with custom hardware and software design.

The rest of the paper is organized as follows. Ssection 2 motivates the problem of CSI aging while Section 3 specifies the netMIMO model. Section 4 describes our proposed transmission schemes which are followed by their implementation and evaluation in Ssection 5. Finally, we discuss the related work in Section 6 and conclude the paper with Section 7.

2. BACKGROUND AND MOTIVATION

We consider an example netMIMO deployment in Fig. 1, where a group of APs, all connected to a controller through a common backhaul link, concurrently transmit data of multiple STAs. To suppress the interference that may occur when a STA receives unwanted data of other STAs (e.g., STA1 receives signals of STAs 2–4), netMIMO uses coordinated transmission like zero-forcing and block-diagonalization [6]. This coordination is possible if the baseband transceiver processing is implemented at the controller, and the APs effectively function as remote antennas.

2.1 Protocol Design

In netMIMO, the downlink CSI of STAs that is required for canceling interference is obtained through a training and feedback protocol. We assume a mechanism similar to the IEEE 802.11ac MU-MIMO explicit feedback protocol [7,8]. Training happens via a sequence of Null Data Packet (NDP)

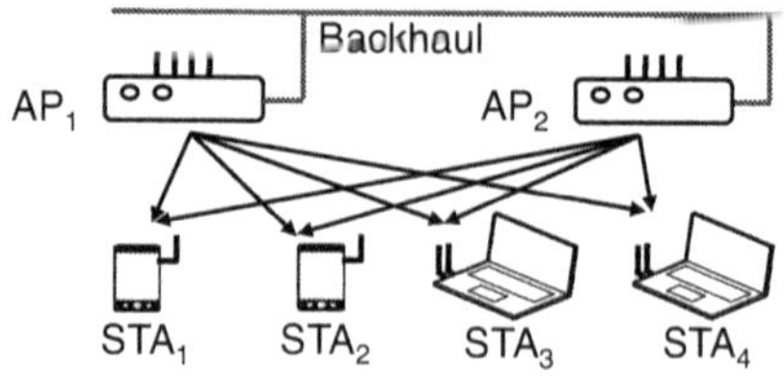

Figure 1: APs transmit to multiple STAs

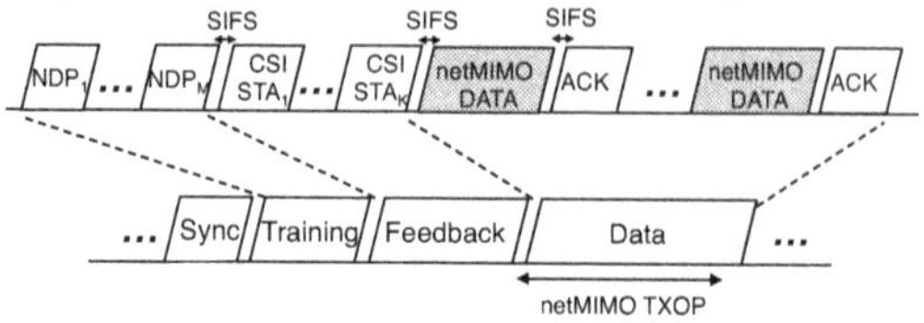

Figure 2: Timeline of a netMIMO transmission

CSI compression	Givens	Bits per angle	8
Feedback rate	MCS0	AP,STA Antennas	2,1
SIFS duration	16μs	Tx Power	18 dBm
NDP duration	30μs	Bandwidth	20MHz
CSI Grouping	2:1	Processing	ZF

Table 1: netMIMO protocol parameters

sounding frames sent by the netMIMO APs. Each STA estimates the channel matrix by listening to the NDP frames and computes its CSI. The format of the CSI may vary, e.g. channel matrix, beamforming matrix, precoding matrix indicator, signal-to-noise ratio, etc., and is specified by the controller. The STAs encode this CSI into CSI-feedback frames and transmit them to one or more APs in a pre-determined order. Once the controller obtains the CSI, it generates the precoding weights that are applied to the antennas of the APs to send the netMIMO data packets.

Fig. 2 illustrates the basic netMIMO transmission protocol. It begins when a sync frame is transmitted by the master AP to synchronize the multiple APs and to reserve the wireless medium [3], followed by a sequence of NDP frames in the training period. This is followed by sequential CSI feedback from the STAs (Poll frames for soliciting CSI feedback are not shown). The data packets of STAs are sent in the netMIMO Transmit Opportunity (TXOP) period, where the TXOP duration is determined during the channel reservation process. Once the STAs receive and decode their data frames, they send ACK/Block ACK frames to acknowledge reception.

Remark: The CSI may be encoded by the STA to reduce the amount of feedback overhead. For example, quantization [9], CSI grouping across subcarriers [7] and differential encoding [10] can be readily applied. In addition, matrix operations like Givens rotation [11] may be applied to reduce the size of channel representation.

2.2 Effect of CSI Aging

The wireless channel between two nodes varies with time due to relative motion between them, motion in the surroundings, random fading and other physical impairments. The rate of variation is generally captured through the notion of *coherence time*—defined as the time period during which the wireless channel remains almost constant. For example, the coherence time is of the order of hundreds of milliseconds for stationary nodes but can be much less ($<$ 10ms) for moving nodes [12]. It therefore follows that aging

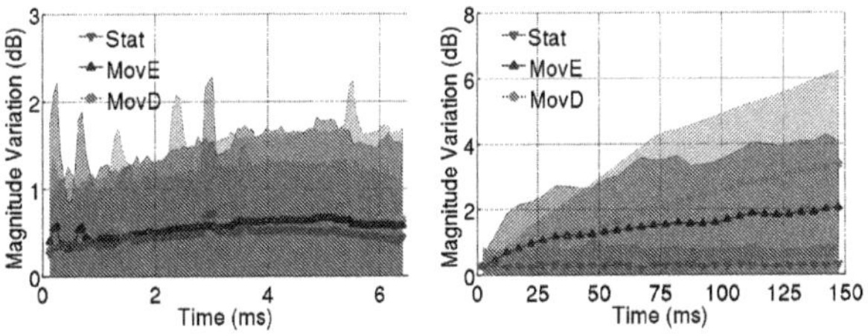

Figure 3: Measured channel magnitude variations at micro (left) and macro (right) scale

of CSI is inversely related to the coherence time. To study the effect of this CSI aging, we perform some preliminary measurements of the protocol in Section 2.1 on a netMIMO testbed (see Section 5 for details). We consider three mobility profiles for the STAs—*stationary* (Stat), *moving environment* (MovE) and *moving device* (MovD)—that capture a range of different channel characteristics. In each of these scenarios, the measured channel behavior (mean and deviation) across 32 wireless links as a function of time is shown by plots in Fig. 3. The variations in the channel magnitude is shown to increase over time for mobile channels but remain relatively stable for a stationary environment. The parameters for the netMIMO transmission protocol are chosen from the 802.11ac standard [7] and are shown in Table 1. In Section 3, we describe the transmit and receive processing. To isolate the effect of channel aging on the performance, we assume a noiseless channel estimation and an error-free feedback channel, which is justified by using the best feedback resolution (8 bits per angle), and the best modulation and coding scheme (MCS0) for uplink transmission.

Nonlinear increase in feedback delay. Table 2 lists the duration of the CSI feedback frame for each STA and the total feedback delay as the number of STAs is varied. In each scenario, the number of transmit antennas is taken equal to the number of STAs. The calculation, based on the parameters in Table 1, is done as follows: Given a total of K transmit antennas and single receive antenna per STA, the CSI feedback is a $K \times 1$ unitary matrix (§3). This implies the total number of angles (both phase and rotation) after parameterization by Givens rotation is $2K - 2$ (Eq. (30) in [11]). Therefore, the feedback size of each STA is given by $(2K - 2) \times$ #BitsperAngle $\times$#Subcarriers /#CSIgrouping. The feedback duration is then determined using the MCS0 (6Mbps) feedback rate, which is then summed for all K STAs including the packetization and the inter-frame overheads to arrive at the total feedback duration. Clearly, in this design, the total feedback duration grows quadratically with the number of STAs.

	4 STAs	6 STAs	8 STAs	10 STAs
Each (ms)	0.224	0.288	0.480	0.608
Total (ms)	0.96	1.82	3.96	6.24

Table 2: Duration of feedback frames

We measure the Signal-to-Interference (SIR) values for a single STA in various scenarios in a 10–STA netMIMO (Fig. 4a). The total feedback delay here is 6.24ms, and as one can see, the SIR in the MovD environment is at least 50% less than the stationary environment. Since the SIR in each of the scenarios is generally highest in case of the stationary channel, it suggests that SIR degradation (4–15dB) in non-stationary channels is due to the interference from CSI aging.

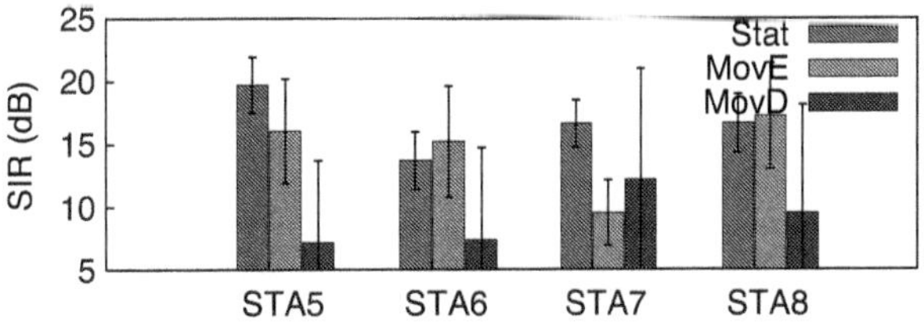

(a) Effect of feedback delay

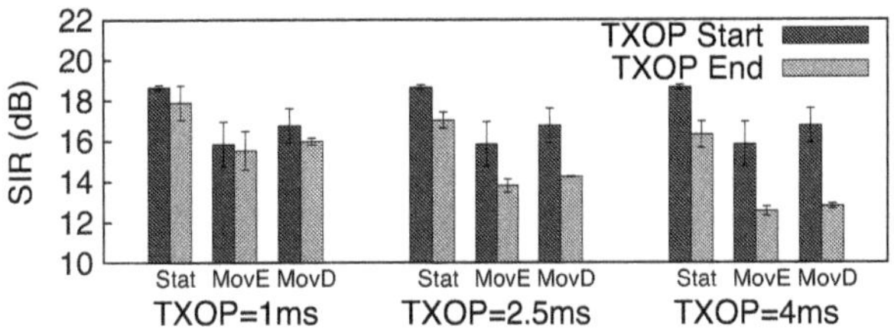

(b) Effect of TXOP duration

Figure 4: Measured SIR at the STAs suggests that CSI delay leads to performance loss

Role of TXOP duration. When the precoding weights based on past CSI are used in sending data packets for a prolonged period, it may also lead to CSI aging. This is confirmed with a netMIMO of 6 STAs as shown in Fig. 4b, where there is a marked difference in the SIR values at the start of TXOP and at the end of TXOP. This is particularly significant (=6 dB) as the duration of TXOP is increased to 4ms, where CSI aging corresponds to a total 5.82ms (including the initial feedback delay of 1.82ms).

2.3 Measurement-Based Approach

To overcome the effects of CSI aging requires changes to the netMIMO protocol. However, given that the indoor wireless channels are difficult to model because of their dependence on the topology and disturbances, we focus on a passive measurement-driven protocol that inherently accounts for the CSI delay of each STA.

Why netMIMO? Although channel variations are also applicable to a MU-MIMO network consisting of a single AP, we emphasize CSI aging only in context of netMIMO for two reasons. First, netMIMO is designed for high-density indoor environments like conference rooms, theaters, shopping malls, etc., that inherently accompany mobility. Second, as compared to the single AP installation, links between STA and APs in netMIMO are more diverse, which implies lower coherence, and therefore, a greater CSI aging effect.

3. NETWORK MIMO MODEL

We briefly describe the netMIMO signal processing of the transmit and receive baseband process at the APs and STAs, respectively. The system uses OFDM, and in the description that follows we drop the subcarrier index to indicate that it is applicable to each OFDM subcarrier. Assume there are M APs, each with N_m antennas, and $N_t = M \times N_m$ transmit antennas in total, that together serve K STAs ($K \leq N_t$). Let $\mathcal{K} = \{1, \ldots, K\}$ denote the set of STAs each of which is equipped with N_r receive antennas. The STA k estimates the composite $N_r \times N_t$ channel matrix, $\tilde{H}_k$, from the M NDPs in the training phase and computes the right singular matrix V_k. Assume that a single data stream is supported per STA and an equal amount of power is assigned to each

STA. In this case, the CSI of STA k is the strongest right singular vector, v_k, of V_k [13]. Each STA k quantizes, compresses and encodes v_k into the CSI feedback frame, and broadcasts it to the APs. The CSI feedback frame is decoded by the APs and the contents passed on to the controller. After collecting the CSI from every STA, the controller uses a zero-forcing (ZF) precoding to generate the precoding matrix, $W = \Gamma(\Gamma^\dagger\Gamma)^{-1}$, where $\Gamma = [v_1\ v_2 \ldots\ v_K]$ is a matrix of singular vectors, and $(\cdot)^\dagger$ represents the Hermitian transpose. The precoding weights, $\tilde{w}_1, \tilde{w}_2, \ldots, \tilde{w}_K$, are the normalized column vectors of W used by the controller to modulate the K STA data streams. The APs then collectively transmit these modulated streams which are received and processed by each STA as a single netMIMO frame.

Let x_k denote the data of STA k, then the signal y_k received by STA k is given by

$$y_k = H_k\tilde{w}_k x_k + \overbrace{\sum_{i\neq k} H_k\tilde{w}_i x_i}^{\text{interference}} \tag{1}$$

where H_k is the observed channel of STA k in netMIMO data packet. In this equation, the term $R_k = \sum_{i\neq k} H_k\tilde{w}_i x_i$ is the unwanted interference from other STAs' data while the term $H_k\tilde{w}_k x_k$ is the desired signal. In ideal conditions, the interference R_k is 0 because the estimated channel $\tilde{H}_k$ is equal to the observed channel H_k, and the precoding weights $\tilde{w}_i$ satisfy $H_k\tilde{w}_i = 0$ for all $i \neq k$. However, in practice, H_k and $\tilde{H}_k$ are different due to the time-lag between them (CSI aging effect) which results in non-zero interference.

In this paper, we assume all STAs are equipped with a single antenna, i.e., $N_r = 1$. We also assume the data symbols, $x_1, \ldots, x_K$, are zero-mean Gaussian i.i.d. with equal average power, P/K, where P is the total input power. Therefore, the interference power, I_k, observed by STA k is

$$I_k = \sum_{i\neq k} \frac{P}{K}|H_k\tilde{w}_i|^2 \tag{2}$$

while the SIR is given by

$$\text{SIR}_k = \frac{|H_k\tilde{w}_k|^2}{\sum_{i\neq k}|H_k\tilde{w}_i|^2} \tag{3}$$

Unless specified, the term *interference* in this paper refers to the interference power in Eq. (2). Each STA k decodes its data $\hat{x}_k$ with a Zero-Forcing (ZF) receiver given by $\hat{x}_k = (H_k\tilde{w}_k)^\dagger y_k/|H_k\tilde{w}_k|^2$. Similar to the 802.11ac MU-MIMO protocol [7], the precoded channel terms, $H_k\tilde{w}_i$, needed for ZF/MMSE estimation are known from the VHT-LTF portion of the netMIMO packet. Therefore, for all practical purposes, a netMIMO STA is simply a MU-MIMO STA of existing WLAN deployments. We note that the channel noise in the above formulation, albeit present, has been ignored, considering the fact that netMIMO is designed for high SNR regime.

The interference at a STA arises from the mismatch between the observed channel, H_k, and the precoding weights derived from the estimated channel, $\tilde{H}_k$, and is therefore a good metric to quantify channel fluctuations (§4.3). Furthermore, it may be approximated as: $|H_k\tilde{w}_k|^2\text{E}[|\hat{x}_k - x_k|^2]$, which is calculated at the receiver after demodulation by averaging over multiple OFDM symbols. We validate this approximation in our setup by precoding with random precoding vectors at Tx antennas and measuring the average symbol error after demodulation at a receiver.

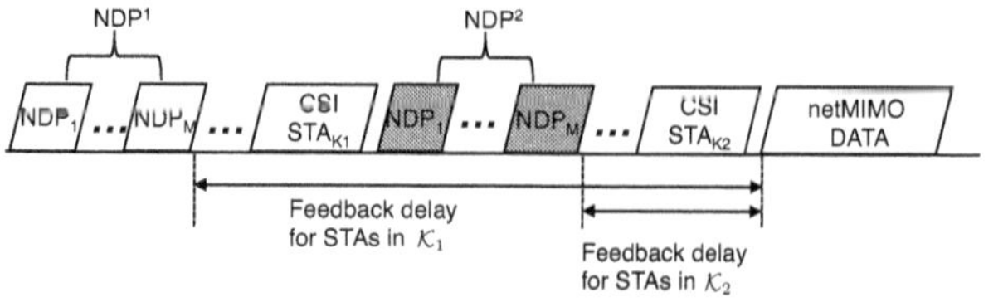

Figure 5: The proposed training protocol with additional NDP frames inserted in the feedback sequence

4. ADAPTIVE NETWORK MIMO PROTOCOL

We present a netMIMO transmission protocol that combats CSI aging by modifying the CSI delay of STAs. We use the interference experienced by the STAs to quantify CSI aging as the metric of interest. The first part of the protocol balances the interference across STAs through two-phase training in which STAs with mobile channels are accorded a smaller CSI delay. The second part of the protocol adjusts the TXOP duration in order to meet the decoding threshold required throughout the TXOP duration. We begin by describing our proposed modification of the training protocol.

4.1 Two-Phase Training

The idea of two-phase training is to have a second NDP broadcast from APs close to the start of data transmission. STAs with high channel mobility and therefore with large channel variation relative to the first NDP use the new NDP frames to estimate their channel. The training protocol is depicted in Fig. 5. Here NDP^1 and NDP^2 refer to the original and the additional set of training frames, respectively. The set of STAs, denoted by $\mathcal{K}_1$, estimate the downlink channel w.r.t. NDP^1, and broadcast their CSI feedback, similar to the standard feedback procedure. The remaining set of STAs, $\mathcal{K}_2$, estimate the channel from NDP^2 and send their CSI feedback after NDP^2 is transmitted. The partitions, $\mathcal{K}_1$ and $\mathcal{K}_2$, therefore identify the two phases of training, and are specified by the controller at the start of the netMIMO transmission.

Let T_{NDP} be the collective duration of the set of NDP frames and let T_k be the fixed feedback duration of STA k. Given a partition $\mathcal{K}_2$, the feedback delay (CSI delay) of STAs in $\mathcal{K}_1$ is given by $T^1 = \sum_{k\in\mathcal{K}} T_k + T_{\text{NDP}}$, while for STAs in $\mathcal{K}_2$, the delay is given by $T^2 = \sum_{k\in\mathcal{K}_2} T_k$. Clearly, T^1 is fixed while T^2 varies with the size of $\mathcal{K}_2$. For simplicity, the constant overhead terms like SIFS are not shown. Let $\bar{I}_k(\mathcal{K}_2)$ be the average interference of STA k where the average is taken over all OFDM symbols and subcarriers in the first data packet of the netMIMO TXOP. Its dependence on CSI delay, T^2, is indicated implicitly through the set $\mathcal{K}_2$. To keep analysis tractable, the duration of the data frames in netMIMO TXOP is fixed at 1ms. We ignore channel variations within the data frame and define the CSI delay w.r.t. the start of data frame, which is also the feedback delay of the protocol.

Initializing with a few mobile STAs in $\mathcal{K}_2$ results in a smaller feedback delay and, possibly less interference from CSI aging. But as more STAs are included in $\mathcal{K}_2$, the feedback delay, and possibly the interference, of STAs trained with NDP[2] increases. Consequently, there exists an optimal partition that balances interference across all STAs, i.e., minimizes the worst case. Taking the objective function OBJ $= \max_{k\in\mathcal{K}} \bar{I}_k(\mathcal{K}_2)$, we express this as a minimization problem:

$$\min_{\mathcal{K}_2\subseteq\mathcal{K}} \{\max_{k\in\mathcal{K}} \bar{I}_k(\mathcal{K}_2)\}. \quad (4)$$

Although straightforward, the problem cannot be solved because the observed channel and interference of STAs are not known *a priori* during training. Therefore, we take a passive measurement-based approach. The current location of NDP[2] is decided based on interference measurements reported by the STAs in the ACK frames from previous netMIMO transmission. We use a greedy approach: At each step the STA with the maximum reported interference is trained with NDP[2] as long as the maximum interference decreases in the next step. Algorithm 1 shows the procedure for NDP placement. It is initialized by sending only NDP[1], i.e., $\mathcal{K}_2 = \emptyset$ and measuring the interference at STAs.

Algorithm 1 NDP placement

1: *Initialize*: $t = 0$, $\mathcal{K}_1 = \mathcal{K}, \mathcal{K}_2 = \emptyset$, $\bar{I}_1(\emptyset)\ldots\bar{I}_K(\emptyset)$, $\bar{I}^0_\star = \max_k \bar{I}_k(\emptyset)$
2: **for** iteration t **do**
3: Find $\bar{I}^t_\star = \max_k \bar{I}_k(\mathcal{K}_2)$, STA $k_\star = \arg\max_k \bar{I}_k(\mathcal{K}_2)$
4: **if** $\bar{I}^t_\star > \bar{I}^{t-1}_\star$ and $\mathcal{K}_2 \neq \emptyset$ **then**
5: Remove the last placed STA from $\mathcal{K}_2$ into $\mathcal{K}_1$
6: **else**
7: Place STA $k_\star$ in $\mathcal{K}_2$ if $k_\star$ was not previously moved from $\mathcal{K}_2$ into $\mathcal{K}_1$
8: **end if**
9: Train STAs in $\mathcal{K}_1$ with NDP[1] and STAs in $\mathcal{K}_2$ with NDP[2]. Complete netMIMO transmission.
10: Obtain average interference, $\bar{I}_k(\mathcal{K}_2)$, of each STA k
11: **end for**

At every iteration of the NDP placement algorithm, the maximum observed interference among STAs is compared with previous maximum interference (line 4). If there is a decrease, the algorithm tries to further decrease OBJ by training the STA with maximum interference with NDP[2] (line 7). If there is an increase in OBJ, the last placed STA in $\mathcal{K}_2$ is shifted to $\mathcal{K}_1$. Intuitively, the NDP placement algorithm addresses CSI aging by reducing CSI delay of some STAs while increasing the CSI delay of the rest by a negligible T_{NDP} period ($\approx$ 0.2ms for a 5-AP netMIMO).

4.2 Adaptive TXOP sizing

The netMIMO transmit opportunity (TXOP) is the common transmission period in which a single or a burst of netMIMO data packets of STAs are transmitted. Since the transmission is based on precoding from past CSI, a limit on the duration of TXOP is required to avoid the interference that arises from excessive CSI delay. A similar TXOP limit has been defined in 802.11 EDCA mechanism, albeit to improve MAC-level efficiency. Also, since different STAs have different channel characteristics, the interference in the TXOP can be different for each STA. This suggests that each STA needs to have its own TXOP limit within the netMIMO TXOP according to its tolerance towards interference.

We propose a netMIMO protocol that adapts the TXOP limit of each STA while satisfying its decoding requirements. The basic idea is to observe the interference in the TXOP of a previous netMIMO transmission to set the limit for the next, as shown in Fig. 6. Since a TXOP is made up of multiple data packets, which are also utilized in sending the interference reports, the TXOP limit is specified in the integral number of constant sized 1ms data packets. Algorithm 2 shows the procedure for the proposed netMIMO TXOP Adjustment that is run at every netMIMO transmission.

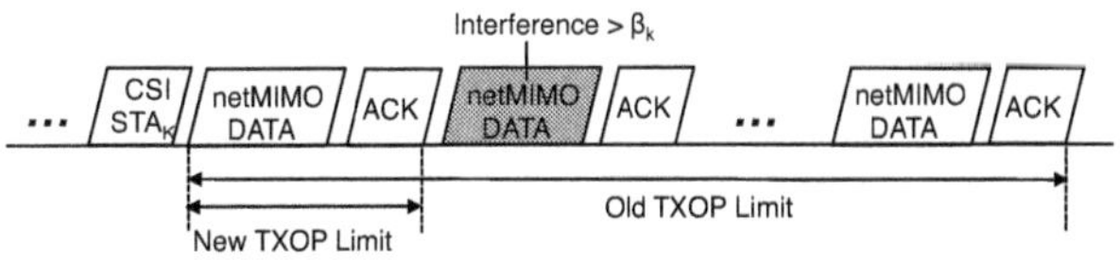

Figure 6: Adjusting TXOP based on the interference

Algorithm 2 TXOP Adjustment

1: *Initialize*: $t = 0$, $L_k =$ TXOP Limit of STA, $\beta_k =$ interference threshold of STA k
2: **for** iteration t **do**
3: Obtain average interference, $\bar{I}^e_k$, from the end of TXOP of STA k
4: **for** each k with $\bar{I}^e_k \geq \beta_k$ **do**
5: Set L_k to the first time instant (> minimum TXOP limit) in TXOP where interference of STA k exceeds β_k
6: **end for**
7: **for** each k with $\bar{I}^e_k < \beta_k$ **do**
8: $L_k \leftarrow \max(L_1, \ldots, L_K)$
9: **end for**
10: Set netMIMO TXOP Limit, $L = \max(L_1, \ldots, L_K)$
11: **end for**

The algorithm initializes with the default TXOP duration L_k and interference threshold β_k of each STA k. This threshold depends on the fixed modulation and coding scheme (MCS) used by the STA in the TXOP. Its calculation is given in Section 4.3. In lines 4–5, the algorithm decreases the TXOP Limit of STA k when it exceeds its interference threshold. On the other hand, the TXOP limit of STA whose interference is below the threshold is set to the maximum value (line 8) of L which is also the netMIMO TXOP limit. Similar to MU-MIMO transmission in 802.11ac [7], zero-padding is done for STAs whose TXOP limit is less than the transmission duration.

In summary, the two-phase training mitigates the interference at the start of TXOP while the TXOP Adjustment algorithm tries to reduce the interference that shows up towards the end of transmission. Both of these approaches therefore complement each other.

4.3 Analysis

We now present some key insights into the underlying variables of CSI delay and interference. We back these insights with measurements obtained from our testbed. We then show that the proposed protocol follows directly from these observations.

Insight 1(Independence): Interference at a STA is independent of CSI delay of other STAs.

Explanation: This follows from the fact that given the precoding weights $\tilde{w}_1, \ldots, \tilde{w}_K$ and the estimated channel $\tilde{H}_k$ of STA k, the interference I_k is only dependent on its observed channel H_k, and is therefore independent of CSI delays of other STAs.

Insight 2(Monotonicity): The average interference experienced by a STA is directly related to its channel variations. Moreover, it increases *roughly* monotonically with the CSI delay of the STA.

Explanation: We can express the observed channel of STA k in terms of the estimated channel and the error e_k as:

$$H_k = \tilde{H}_k + e_k \tag{5}$$

where e_k is a zero-mean spatially white gaussian error term. The zero-mean behavior was indeed verified in our testbed measurements. Next, consider a single data frame which is made up of a sequence of OFDM symbols. For a single subcarrier, we can express the expected value of interference (using Eq. (2)) as follows:

$$\begin{aligned} \mathrm{E}[\sum_{i \neq k} \frac{P}{K} |(\tilde{H}_k + e_k)\tilde{w}_i|^2] &\overset{(a)}{=} \mathrm{E}[\sum_{i \neq k} \frac{P}{K} |e_k \tilde{w}_i|^2] \\ = \sum_{i \neq k} \frac{P}{K} \mathrm{E}[(e_k \tilde{w}_i)^\dagger (e_k \tilde{w}_i)] &= \sum_{i \neq k} \frac{P}{K} \tilde{w}_i^\dagger \mathrm{E}[e_k^\dagger e_k] \tilde{w}_i \\ \overset{(b)}{=} \sum_{i \neq k} \frac{P}{K} \tilde{w}_i^\dagger \sigma_k^2 I \tilde{w}_i &= \sum_{i \neq k} \frac{P}{K} \tilde{w}_i^\dagger \tilde{w}_i \sigma_k^2 \overset{(c)}{=} C \sigma_k^2 \end{aligned}$$

where $C = (K-1)P/K$ is a constant; (a) follows by using $\tilde{H}_k \tilde{w}_i = 0$ for all $i \neq k$, (b) is result of the white gaussian error term e_k, and (c) uses $\tilde{w}_i^\dagger \tilde{w}_i = 1$ for all i. This implies the observed average interference* that is obtained from multiple OFDM symbols of STA k (further averaged over subcarriers to mitigate noise) can be approximated as

$$\bar{I}_k \approx C \sigma_k^2 \tag{6}$$

Therefore, the average interference at a STA is directly proportional to the power of channel variations, σ_k^2. This suggests that as channel variations grow larger with the CSI delay (see Fig. 3 for instance), the interference should also increase. To investigate if this indeed holds, we experimentally measure the interference as a function of STA's CSI delay under different scenarios. Fig. 7a gives an example of the observed STA interference in a 10-STA netMIMO setup. As expected, the interference in general increases with CSI delay, and more so in case of non-stationary environments. We run through these observations with the Kendall τ rank correlation test [14] which is non-parametric test to measure monotonicity between two variables. A correlation coefficient close to $+1$ indicates a monotonically increasing relationship while a value close to -1 suggests a dependency that is monotonically decreasing. Fig. 7b plots the range of Kendall τ rank correlation coefficient values calculated for the interference with respect to the CSI delay observed over 10 runs. The significance level was set to 0.01. In the majority of runs and under different channel conditions, we observe a rank correlation coefficient, $\tau > 0.7$, which confirms our insight on the monotonic nature of interference as a function of CSI delay. In what follows, we make use of the assumptions on independence and *strict* monotonicity, and make another simplifying assumption that channel behavior remains constant across multiple iterations.

PROPOSITION 1. *The NDP placement algorithm finds the optimal solution to Eq. 4 within K iterations.*

PROOF. We first show that NDP placement does converge. By construction, at every step, a STA from $\mathcal{K}_1$ is moved to $\mathcal{K}_2$, unless the maximum interference among STAs increases. The CSI delay of STAs in $\mathcal{K}_1$ is given by $T^1 =$

*Average from a single sample path is used as approximation of mean across all paths

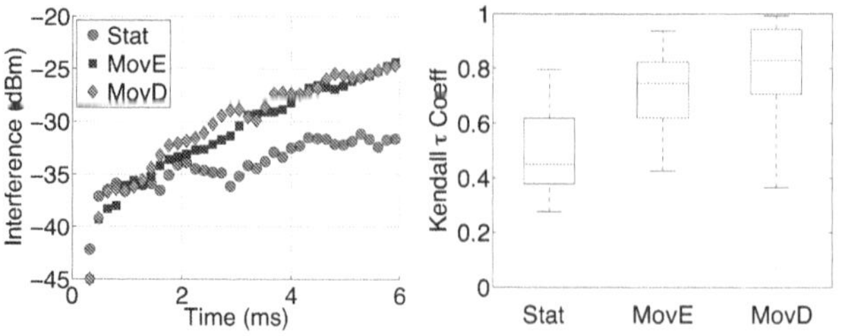

(a) Example of STA interference (averaged over 10MHz) vs. CSI delay

(b) Kendall τ coefficient for interference vs. CSI delay with 0.01 significance level

Figure 7: Examples and results of statistical test show that interference increases with CSI delay

$\sum_{k \in \mathcal{K}} T_k + T_{\mathrm{NDP}}$ which remains constant, so interference of STAs in $\mathcal{K}_1$ also remains constant by assumption. On the other hand, from the monotonicity assumption, the interference of STAs in $\mathcal{K}_2$ increases as the CSI delay $T^2 = \sum_{k \in \mathcal{K}_2} T_k$ increases which happens when a STA is moved to $\mathcal{K}_2$. Clearly, if at any point $k_\star \in \mathcal{K}_2$, then partitions don't change further. Also, if at any iteration t, $\bar{I}_\star^t > \bar{I}_\star^{t-1}$, STA $k_\star$ form iteration $t-1$ will be moved back to $\mathcal{K}_1$. Subsequently, in iteration $t+1$ STA $k_\star$ will continue to remain in $\mathcal{K}_1$. Therefore, the partitions converge in both cases.

To show that the converged partition, $\mathcal{K}_1, \mathcal{K}_2$, is optimal, assume there exists another partition $\mathcal{G}_1, \mathcal{G}_2$ that does strictly better. Let STA $k_\star$ and STA $r_\star$ have the maximum interference in the two scenarios, respectively. It follows that $I_{r_\star}(\mathcal{G}_2) < I_{k_\star}(\mathcal{K}_2)$. For any $k \in \mathcal{K}_2$, it is true that $k \in \mathcal{G}_2$ because otherwise if $k \in \mathcal{G}_1$, then $I_k(\mathcal{G}_2) \leq I_{r_\star}(\mathcal{G}_2) < I_{k_\star}(\mathcal{K}_2)$ from assumption. Further, $I_{k_\star}(\mathcal{K}_2) < I_k(\mathcal{G}_2)$, because at some point, T', in NDP placement STA k would be moved from the first partition and the maximum interference strictly decreases at each step, and also because the CSI delay of STA k before T' is same as with the partitions $\mathcal{G}_1, \mathcal{G}_2$. As a result, $I_k(\mathcal{G}_2) < I_k(\mathcal{G}_2)$ which is a contradiction. Therefore, we have $\mathcal{K}_2 \subset \mathcal{G}_2$ since the two partitions cannot be the same. Now, consider two cases when $k_\star \in \mathcal{K}_1$ and $k_\star \in \mathcal{K}_2$. In the first, it follows that $k_\star \in \mathcal{G}_2$ because otherwise if $k_\star \in \mathcal{G}_1$ implies $I_{r_\star}(\mathcal{G}_2) \geq I_{k_\star}(\mathcal{G}_2) = I_{k_\star}(\mathcal{K}_2)$, which is not true. Now, consider, $I_{k_\star}(\mathcal{K}_2 \cup k_\star) > I_{k_\star}(\mathcal{K}_2) > I_{r_\star}(\mathcal{G}_2) > I_{k_\star}(\mathcal{G}_2)$, from the stopping condition of the algorithm. This is a contradiction since $\mathcal{K}_2 \cup k_\star \subseteq \mathcal{G}_2$. For the second case, since $k_\star \in \mathcal{K}_2 \subset \mathcal{G}_2$, it follows $I_{r_\star}(\mathcal{G}_2) \geq I_{k_\star}(\mathcal{G}_2) > I_{k_\star}(\mathcal{K}_2)$ which is also contradiction to our assumption. Consequently, there cannot exist another partition with does strictly better than the NDP placement algorithm.

PROPOSITION 2. *If the interference threshold β_k of STA k satisfies $\beta_k = \frac{P}{K}(\tilde{\Lambda}_k^{min})^2/\alpha_k$, where α_k is the SIR decoding threshold, and $\tilde{\Lambda}_k^{min}$ is the minimum largest singular value of $\tilde{H}_k$ across subcarriers, then the average SIR after TXOP Adjustment satisfies $\overline{SIR}_k \gtrapprox \alpha_k$ for each data frame.*

PROOF. The TXOP adjustment proceeds by doing a series of adjustments to the TXOP limit of each STA, and sets it either to the minimum TXOP limit or increases to the maximum of the TXOP limits of all STAs. Therefore, after a finite number of steps the TXOP limit of each STA k converges to a constant value such that the average interference, $\bar{I}_k$, throughout the TXOP is less than β_k (if not the case then it is set to the minimum possible TXOP limit and there are no performance guarantees). Consider a subcarrier

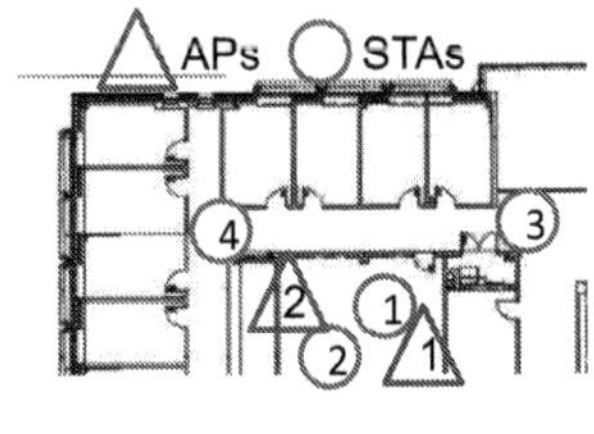

Figure 8: Deployment of netMIMO testbed

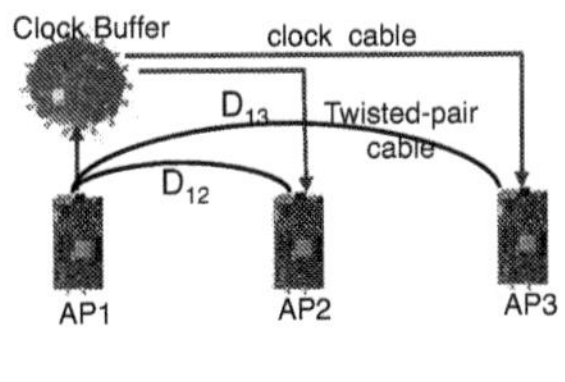

Figure 9: Time and frequency synchronization

of a data frame within the TXOP, we can express:

$$
\begin{aligned}
\mathrm{E}[SIR_k] &= \mathrm{E}[\frac{P}{K}\frac{|(\tilde{H}_k + e_k)\tilde{w}_k|^2}{I_k}] \overset{(d)}{\approx} \mathrm{E}[\frac{P}{K}\frac{|\tilde{H}_k\tilde{w}_k|^2}{I_k}] \\
&\overset{(e)}{=} \mathrm{E}[\frac{P}{K}\frac{\Lambda_k^2}{I_k}] \overset{(f)}{\geq} \mathrm{E}[\frac{P}{K}\frac{(\Lambda_k^{min})^2}{I_k}] \overset{(g)}{\geq} \frac{P}{K}\frac{(\Lambda_k^{min})^2}{\mathrm{E}[I_k]} \\
&\overset{(h)}{\approx} \frac{P}{K}\frac{(\Lambda_k^{min})^2}{\bar{I}_k} \geq \frac{(\Lambda_k^{min})^2}{\beta_k} = \alpha_k
\end{aligned}
$$

where (d) is an empirical approximation when $|H_k| >> |e_k|$, (e) uses the fact that $\tilde{w}_k$ is normalized vector of $W = (\Gamma^{\dagger})^{-1}$ and H_k has a single non-zero singular value, (f) follows by using the minimum singular value across subcarriers, (g) follows from Jensen's inequality and (h) is obtained by replacing expectation with the average sum. Therefore, for any data frame in a TXOP, we may approximate the average measured SIR measured across the frame's OFDM symbols and subcarriers as $\overline{SIR}_k \gtrapprox \alpha_k$.

5. EVALUATION

In this section, we provide the details of our netMIMO testbed, the evaluation methodology, the implementation of the proposed algorithms and their performance evaluation.

5.1 netMIMO Testbed

We have implemented a prototype of netMIMO using the WARP SDR platform [5]. The setup consists of a maximum of 5 APs (with 2 Tx antennas each), and 10 STAs, each with 1 Rx antenna. The controller function is implemented on a back-end server connected to the WARP boards via Ethernet with a Gigabit switch. We make use of the WARPLabv7.3 drivers with their efficient WARP-PC interface to interface with the WARP boards.

Fig. 8 shows the layout of the netMIMO testbed deployed in our Department building. To manage the large number of WARP boards we grouped them into separate AP and STA clusters. We have 2 AP clusters, and 3 STA clusters, with a combined total of 10 Tx and Rx antennas. The STA WARP boards are placed on a movable cart while carrying out the experiments.

5.1.1 Signal Processing

Following the 802.11n/ac standards, we have implemented a full-fledged netMIMO OFDM system. We use the basic 20MHz 64-fft OFDM (48 data subcarriers) design and upsample it by a factor of 2 to get an effective bandwidth of 10MHz. We use the channel 14 in the 2.4GHz ISM band that is unused by nearby devices.

At the start of every netMIMO transmission, a *sync* signal is sent by the controller to trigger the APs and the STAs to start their transmit and receive chain, respectively. Each AP broadcasts an 802.11 NDP packet composed of a short training field (STF) and a long training field (LTF). Each STA runs an auto-correlation algorithm to detect the STF and extracts the start time of the received packet. It also uses the STF to estimate the frequency-offset and corrects it accordingly. The LTF of an AP consists of OFDM training symbols on each Tx antenna of the AP, and is used by the STA to estimate channel w.r.t. each Tx antenna. The CSI feedback frames are not sent over-the-air and made implicitly available to the controller. Finally, a netMIMO data frame consisting of cyclic-shifted STFs, and precoded training and data is transmitted.

5.1.2 Synchronization

For the netMIMO signal processing to be valid, we require that all AP nodes in netMIMO are completely synchronized. By default, we take AP_1 as the master AP and synchronize the rest of the APs with AP_1.

Time Synchronization: At a high level, time synchronization means that all APs transmit simultaneously. However, in the context of netMIMO which uses OFDM, it requires that for each STA, the precoded OFDM frames transmitted by the APs as part of a single netMIMO packet must arrive within a cyclic prefix (CP) window. By ignoring the small differences in the propagation delay between APs and STAs, this implies that time synchronization in netMIMO is achieved when all APs begin transmission within a CP period. We ensure this in two steps.

First, we use a twisted-pair cable assembly and connect the debug headers on the WARP board of AP_1 with that of other APs. This ensures that the rest of the APs can be triggered by AP_1 while AP_1's input trigger is set to a PC trigger that is sent over Ethernet. The twisted-pair cable which extends up to 30m in our setup has a propagation delay of the order of 100ns (typical value of CP is 400 or 800ns). As a result, we observe a significant time-lag in triggering from AP_1. In our second step, we address this lag by introducing transmission offsets among the APs, i.e., we delay the start of packet transmission at an AP by a fixed duration. Let D_j denote the delay of the twisted-pair cable between AP_1 and AP j. Note that $D_1 = 0$. Also,let O_j be the transmission offset of AP j. We find offsets O_1 to O_M that satisfy the following constraint.

$$\max_{1\leq j\leq M}\{O_j + D_j\} - \min_{1\leq j\leq M}\{O_j + D_j\} \leq \mathrm{CP}. \qquad (7)$$

As the above constraint is under-specified, the offsets are found easily through a simple search. To allow for tolerance, we use CP/2 as the window size in our setup.

Frequency Synchronization: As illustrated in Fig. 9, we frequency-synchronize all netMIMO APs by sourcing their RF and sampling clock from the 40MHz reference clock of AP_1. This is implemented with the CM-MMCX module of WARPv3 board that provides external interface to the reference clocks. We use the RG-174 coax cables that have an attenuation rating of 6.6dB/100ft at 50MHz for connecting the clock sources. Further, we use ADCLK954 boards as external clock buffers to prevent clock drift that may arise from the attenuation.

Phase Synchronization: Two WARP boards that are frequency synchronized may still differ in phase due to a random phase introduced by the Amplifier (LNA) circuit. Fortunately, this random phase remains constant once the circuit is powered on. Thus, a constant phase difference between two APs is easily corrected.

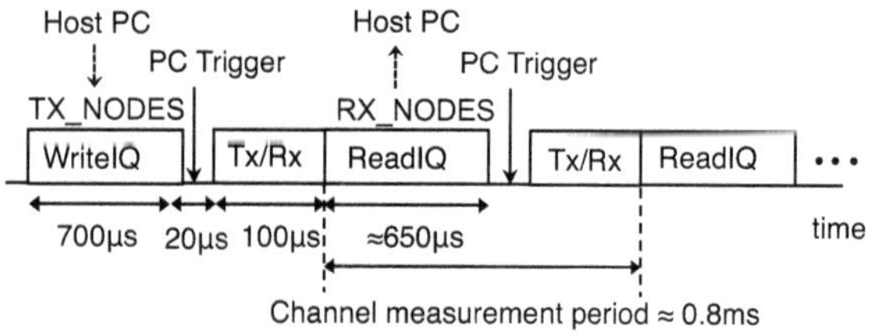

(a) Timeline of function calls in the WARP driver

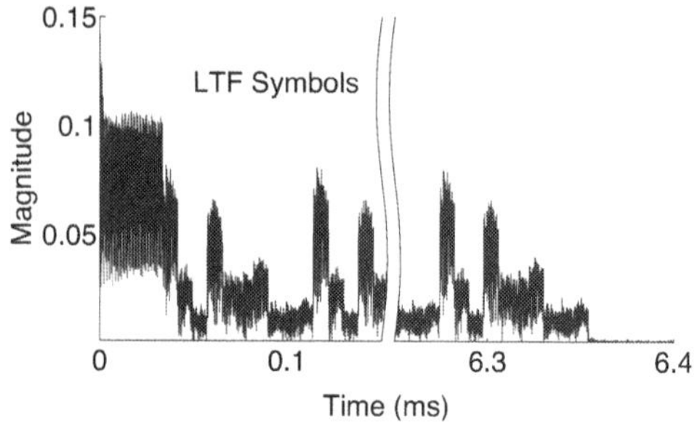

(b) LTF symbol stream for channel estimation

Figure 10: Details of the channel measurement framework that allows real-time evaluation of net-MIMO

5.2 Evaluation Methodology

5.2.1 Trace-based evaluation

Our netMIMO setup uses the WARPLAB 7.3 library written in MATLAB to do signal processing. However, the execution time of MATLAB for netMIMO processing and WARP read/write exceeds 100ms and thus renders it useless for real-time evaluation. Therefore, we resort to a trace-based evaluation of netMIMO. The idea is to continuously collect the channel measurements between every pair of antennas in real time. This is achieved by repeatedly sending LTF symbols from the APs and processing the received symbols at the STAs to estimate the channel. We then play back the channel traces with the netMIMO transmission protocols through virtual timers which allows us to do an offline yet realistic evaluation.

5.2.2 Channel-Measurement Framework

To do an accurate trace-based evaluation of netMIMO, we require the $N_r \times N_t$ channel measurements to be done as frequently as possible. This implies that we need to either send/receive a single long packet (>10ms) of LTF symbols or send/receive the LTF symbols at a very fast rate (every 1ms or so). The current WARP design, however, has a maximum buffer size of only 2^{15} samples (airtime of 0.8ms at 40MHz). Moreover, reading just a single buffer into WARPLab incurs an average delay of around 3ms. Therefore, it is difficult to obtain accurate channel traces using the current WARP framework.

We overcome these limitations by designing our own hardware and software solutions. We modify the WARP FPGA design by halving the sampling clock and increasing the buffer size to 2^{16} samples (beyond 2^{16} is not possible due to FPGA Bus width limitations). This allows us to send/receive signals up to 6.4ms long—an 8× increase in the transmission airtime. Consequently, we are able to send/receive LTF symbols to accurately track the channel as shown in Fig. 10b. We have also written a multi-threaded C driver that directly interfaces with the WARP hardware [15]. This lightweight driver completely replaces the much slower WARPLAB driver that is written in MATLAB. On comparing the performance of the basic readIQ routine which reads the IQ baseband buffers into the PC, we witness an almost 3× to 10× reduction in read delay as the number of buffers is increased from 4 to 10. In particular, the average readIQ delay for reading 2^{11} samples in case of 6 STAs is only 0.8ms, i.e., smaller packets can be sent and received within 1ms (Fig. 10a), which allows us to do channel measurements with high accuracy. The long transmission design is used for validating the STA interference behavior, e.g., Section 4.3, while the WARP driver is used in the evaluation of our algorithms. We would like to point out that measurements with WARP boards are highly sensitive to noise, external interference and other physical impairments. Therefore, we apply a locally-weighted smoothing on the time variations of channel magnitude and phase, similar to the channel tracking procedure of OFDM receivers.

5.2.3 Mobility Experiments

In order to account for the channel conditions in real net-MIMO deployments, we consider three mobility scenarios in our evaluation: (1) *Stationary*(Stat)—This corresponds to the scenario when the location of STAs is fixed, and there are no disturbances from the motion of people or nearby objects. (2) *Moving environment*(MovE)—Environmental mobility is simulated through human actions such as arm movements and walking while the nodes remain fixed. (3) *Moving device*(MovD)—Device mobility is simulated by moving the cart on which STA nodes are placed while taking measurements. This motion closely resembles the pedestrian mobility of smartphones and other mobile devices.

5.3 NDP Placement

We implement and run the NDP placement given in Algorithm 1 over a period of 450ms where a netMIMO transmission occurs every 15ms. A number of scenarios for STAs' mobility are played out while the channel measurements are taken. Fig. 11a shows the SIR gains of STAs with the NDP placement compared to the default training protocol in four different scenarios: MovD where one among the group of STAs 1–4 and STAs 5–8 are placed and moved on a cart, and repeated again in MovE where instead external disturbances are present around one of the group of STAs. The gain is calculated by measuring the SIR of a single netMIMO packet that is transmitted following the feedback process. As one can see, the gains for some STAs can be significant (5–10dB) and is due to the smaller CSI delay resulting in reduced interference. Most importantly, the gains are strongly correlated to the channel mobility of the STAs. For example, when STAs 1–4 are moved, all of STAs 1–4 see gains while STAs 5–8 see almost none. When STAs 5–8 are moved, STAs 6 and 8 have noticeable gains while STA3's and STA4's performance remains unchanged. This can be explained from the two different CSI delays—a few STAs' delay is reduced (from NDP^2) while for others it remains the same (NDP^1). Note that due to the coarseness of the measurement readings, the actual gains may deviate slightly than what has been reported.

Results in Fig. 11b and Fig. 11c are shown for the MovD (STAs 1–4) scenario of the 8–STA netMIMO system which according to Table 2 incurs a feedback delay of 3.96ms with

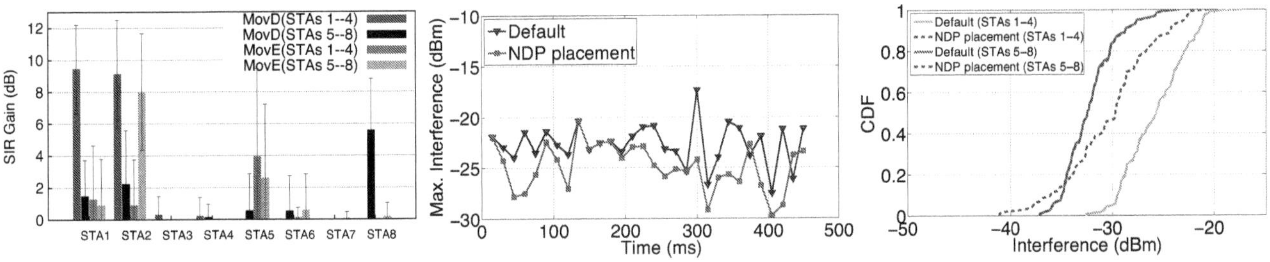

(a) Observed gains in four experiments (b) Maximum interference among STAs (c) Comparison between STA clusters

Figure 11: Evaluation of NDP placement in 8–STA netMIMO. Results show significant gains for mobile STAs.

single NDP training. The average readIQ delay of reading each WARP buffer was observed to be 1.07ms. Therefore, channel readings are available at 4 time points within the feedback period. In Fig. 11b, we plot the maximum average interference of STAs ($\bar{I}_\star^t$ in Algorithm 1) as a function of netMIMO iteration. As expected, the NDP placement strives to lower the maximum interference compared to the default scheme. The distribution of the interference across the mobile and the stationary STA clusters is shown in Fig. 11c, where the selective impact of NDP placement on the interference distribution of mobile STAs is visible.

5.4 TXOP Adjustment

Similar to the NDP placement, the TXOP Adjustment (TxAj) procedure in Algorithm 2 uses the past interference to adapt every netMIMO transmission. The CSI delay of STAs is fixed while the netMIMO TXOP duration is varied. Since the objective here is to meet the SIR threshold (β_k) of a STA according to its MCS, we evaluate the performance of our proposed approach with all possible MCS values. We use the widely adopted MCS-threshold lookup table for 802.11 wireless environments [16]. Figs. 12a and 12b show the evaluation results of a single STA in an 8-STA netMIMO setup with TXOP limits of 2ms and 4ms, respectively. The minimum TXOP limit of each STA was set to 1ms in both scenarios. The TXOP limit value is the initial TXOP duration of all netMIMO STAs which remains constant in the default scheme but is adjusted for each STA in our proposed scheme. Note that the CSI delay here consists of the TXOP duration in addition to the feedback delay of 3.96ms. For each MCS, we calculate the percentage of STA's total transmissions that do not meet the corresponding average SIR threshold and hence would result in packet errors. Since the accuracy of measurement is limited to 1ms, the SIR is measured only for a few packets in the TXOP. A higher MCS means higher SIR requirements (e.g., MCS7 requires SIR $>$ 23dB), the plots in Fig. 12 therefore exhibit an increasing trend. With our TXOP Adjustment which changes the transmission length according to the interference, we see a noticeable reduction in error rate, up to 26% in case of 2ms TXOP limit, and 42% in case of 4ms TXOP limit.

5.5 Field Test

We conducted a field test of the netMIMO setup by running both NDP placement and TXOP Adjustment simultaneously for a period of 450ms. We consider the ambient wireless environment of our testbed and further orchestrate all STAs in motion together with the motion of people/objects around. We consider two different locations of

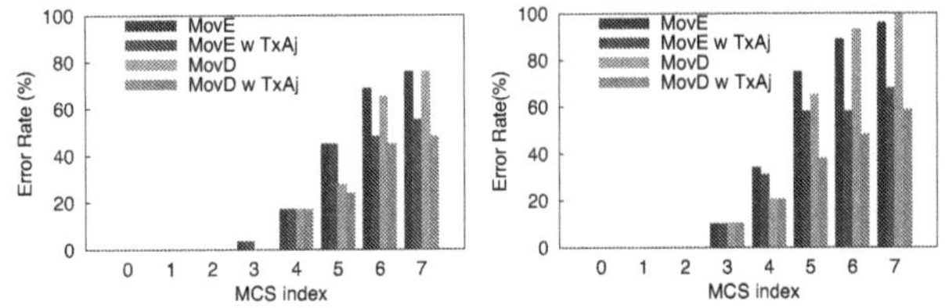

(a) TXOP limit=2ms (b) TXOP limit=4ms

Figure 12: Error rate measured for each MCS before and after TXOP Adjustment

# STAs	$K=4$		$K=6$		$K=8$	
Location	(1,2)	(3,4)	(1,2)	(3,4)	(1,2)	(3,4)
Default (§2.1)	134	113	199	108	279	150
Proposed (§4)	142	119	220	123	292	174

Table 3: Average netMIMO-throughput (Mbps)

the STA clusters, with Location (3,4) being in NLOS environment w.r.t. the APs, and placed farther than Location (1,2). The initial TXOP limit was set to 4ms. The average throughput of each STA is calculated by averaging over all possible MCS data rates, which is then added for all STAs to arrive at the average netMIMO throughput, as shown in Table 3. It can be concluded that the throughput gains are modest in the case of 4–STA netMIMO, but become more prominent as the system is scaled—more than 15% in case of 8 STAs. Note that the throughput is per unit time within a netMIMO TXOP.

5.6 Discussion

Theoretical basis: While the monotonic behavior of interference is loosely observed in our measurements, the channel state across netMIMO iterations can be quite different. Consequently, the theoretical analysis in §4.3 does not necessarily apply, but rather provides a guiding principle.

Channel fading: Due to multi-path effects, few of the OFDM subcarriers may experience random fading. The measurement-based approach is robust to fading as the interference is averaged across all subcarriers.

Rate adaptation and Decoding: We have used fixed MCS rates for each STA for determining the transmission duration. In addition, decoding is assumed to fail completely if the decoding threshold is not met. However, our TXOP adjustment can be further improved if rate adaptation is applied within and across TXOPs, whereas soft decoding at STA will reduce the TXOP error rate.

6. RELATED WORK

Distributed MU-MIMO systems have been implemented through centralized [3,17] and decentralized WLAN architectures [18]. Furthermore, a downlink MU-MIMO base station with 64 antennas was implemented in [2]. Each of them assumed perfect CSI, or rather stationary wireless channel, which is justified given that their experiments were carried out in a controlled environment. However, we find that user mobility has a significant effect on the performance of such systems. While the other alternative of implicit CSI feedback, as employed in [2], effectively mitigates the CSI aging effects, its calibration requirements make it less practical for WLAN devices, and as such has not been adopted in the 802.11ac standard.

In theory, the results on MU-MIMO capacity with the overhead of training and feedback, imperfect channel estimation, and channel aging have already been known and reported [1,9,19]. However, few systems have validated these results in practice. The user mobility profile was considered in [20] to select a transmission strategy. The authors claimed that netMIMO architecture was only suitable for stationary clients. In [12] and [8], experiments were performed to show the relationship between feedback delay and capacity of 802.11n SU-MIMO and MU-MIMO users, respectively. The authors in [8] observed that the performance of MU-MIMO is highly sensitive to CSI delay and aging, and the sensitivity is dependent on the number of Tx/Rx antennas and the interference cancellation ability of the STAs. It is stated that without interference cancellation, capacity decreases considerably within 5ms, which is also consistent with our findings. However, their results are limited to just 4 STAs, assumes multiple Rx antennas, and employs fixed training interval for each STA irrespective of its mobility state. The recent work in [21] on MU-MIMO feedback is closely related to ours. It proposes an adaptive feedback compression scheme based on frequency and time-domain compression techniques, and evaluates them in realistic indoor channels. The setup, however, considers single AP and 2 STAs, and does not take into account the scaling of feedback overhead or the diversity from having multiple APs.

7. CONCLUSION

As recent advances in hardware bring netMIMO closer to reality, it is necessary to closely examine the various aspects of such a system. In this paper, we considered the impact of CSI aging on the performance of a large-scale netMIMO in real and accurately measured indoor wireless channels. We proposed a two-phase feedback protocol and an adaptive transmission scheme, both of which are adapted from the interference measured by the STAs. Our approach exploits the underlying relationship between interference and CSI delay which was validated in our experiments; a more thorough study is needed to fully understand this dependency and design better protocols. Other aspects like MCS rate adaptation and receiver interference cancellation further need to be analyzed. All of these are matters of our future inquiry.

Acknowledgments

The work reported in this paper was supported in part by the NSF under Grants 1160775 and 1317411.

8. REFERENCES

[1] D. Gesbert, S. Hanly, H. Huang, S. Shamai Shitz, O. Simeone, and W. Yu, "Multi-Cell MIMO Cooperative Networks: A New Look at Interference," in *IEEE Journal on Selected Areas in Communications*, 2010.

[2] C. Shepard, H. Yu, N. Anand, E. Li, T. Marzetta, R. Yang, and L. Zhong, "Argos: practical many-antenna base stations," in *Proc. of MOBICOM*, 2012.

[3] H. Rahul, S. Kumar, and D. Katabi, "JMB: scaling wireless capacity with user demands," in *Proc. of SIGCOMM*, 2012.

[4] G. Caire, S. A. Ramprashad, and H. Papadopoulos, "Rethinking network MIMO: Cost of CSIT, performance analysis, and architecture comparisons," in *Information Theory and Applications Workshop (ITA)*, 2010.

[5] " Rice University Wireless Open Access Research Platform,"

[6] Q. Spencer, A. Swindlehurst, and M. Haardt, "Zero-forcing methods for downlink spatial multiplexing in multiuser MIMO channels," *IEEE Transactions on Signal Processing*, vol. 52, no. 2, pp. 461–471, 2004.

[7] " Wireless LAN Medium Access Control (MAC) and Physical Layer (PHY) Specifications ," IEEE Std. 80211ac Draft 3.0, 2012.

[8] M. Gong, E. Perahia, R. Want, and S. Mao, "Training protocols for multi-user MIMO wireless LANs," in *Proc. of PIMRC*, 2010.

[9] N. Jindal, "MIMO Broadcast Channels With Finite-Rate Feedback," *IEEE Transactions on Information Theory*, vol. 52, no. 11, pp. 5045–5060, 2006.

[10] R. Porat, E. Ojard, N. Jindal, M. Fischer, and V. Erceg, "Improved MU-MIMO Performance for Future 802.11 Systems Using Differential Feedback," in *Information Theory and Applications Workshop (ITA)*, 2013.

[11] J. Roh and B. Rao, "Efficient feedback methods for MIMO channels based on parameterization," *IEEE Transactions on Wireless Communications*, vol. 6, no. 1, pp. 282–292, 2007.

[12] E. Perahia, A. Sheth, T. Kenney, R. Stacey, and D. Halperin, "Investigation into the Doppler Component of the IEEE 802.11n Channel Model," in *Proc. of GLOBECOM*, 2010.

[13] F. Boccardi, H. Huang, and M. Trivellato, "Multiuser eigenmode transmission for mimo broadcast channels with limited feedback," in *IEEE Workshop on Signal Processing Advances in Wireless Communications*, 2007.

[14] M. Kendall, *Rank Correlation Methods*. 1990.

[15] K. C. Garikipati and K. G. Shin, "Improving Transport Design for WARP SDR Deployments," in *Proc. of the ACM SIGCOMM Software Radio Implementation Forum (SRIF)*, 2014.

[16] Cisco Systems Inc., "Wireless Mesh Access Points, Design and Deployment Guide, Release 7.4," 2013.

[17] H. Balan, R. Rogalin, A. Michaloliakos, K. Psounis, and G. Caire, "Achieving high data rates in a distributed MIMO system," in *Proc. of MOBICOM*, 2012.

[18] X. Zhang, K. Sundaresan, M. Khojastepour, S. Rangarajan, and K. Shin, "NEMOx: Clustered Network MIMO for Wireless Networks," in *Proc. of MOBICOM*, 2013.

[19] G. Caire, N. Jindal, M. Kobayashi, and N. Ravindran, "Multiuser MIMO Achievable Rates With Downlink Training and Channel State Feedback," *IEEE Transactions on Information Theory*, vol. 56, no. 6, pp. 2845–2866, 2010.

[20] S. Singh, K. Sundaresan, A. Khojastepour, S. Rangarajan, and S. Krishnamurthy, "One strategy does not serve all: tailoring wireless transmission strategies to user profiles," in *Proc. of ACM Workshop on Hot Topics in Networks*, 2012.

[21] X. Xie, X. Zhang, and K. Sundaresan, "Adaptive Feedback Compression for MIMO Networks," in *Proc. of MOBICOM*, 2013.

Multiple Target Counting and Tracking using Binary Proximity Sensors: Bounds, Coloring, and Filter

Lei Song
Institute for Interdisciplinary Information Sciences, Tsinghua University, Beijing, China
leisong03@gmail.com

Yongcai Wang
Institute for Interdisciplinary Information Sciences, Tsinghua University, Beijing, China
wangyc@tsinghua.edu.cn

ABSTRACT

Binary proximity sensors (BPS) provide extremely low cost and privacy preserving features for tracking mobile targets in smart environment, but great challenges are posed for tracking multiple targets, because a BPS cannot distinguish one or multiple targets are in its sensing range. In this paper, we at first address the counting problem by presenting a maximum clique partition model on unit disk graph, which leads to a tight lower bound for estimating the number of targets by a snapshot of sensor readings. Then, to more accurately count and track the multiple targets by sequential readings of sensors, we state the key is to comprehensively infer the states behind the events. Therefore, at each event we infer which target may trigger the event via a dynamic coloring technique (DEC) and predict the potential regions of the multiple targets by a colorful area shrinking and expanding approach. Such an approach generates multiple potential scenarios containing different colors to interpret the sequential events, where the number of colors indicates the different estimations of the target number. Then we designed multi-color particle filter (MCPF), which is run in parallel in each scenario to enumerate and evaluate the potential trajectories of the targets under the color constraint. The likelihoods of the trajectories are evaluated by each target's movement consistence. The overall best trajectory over all scenarios is voted to provide not only the most possible target number, but also the trajectories of the targets. Extensive simulations were conducted using a multi-agent simulator which show good accuracy of the proposed multi-target tracking algorithms.

1. INTRODUCTION

This paper investigates the problem of tracking multiple targets using a network of binary proximity sensors (BPS). A BPS is a low-cost sensor, which provides binary detection to the mobile users in its proximity. It outputs "1" when one or more targets are presenting and "0" otherwise. It cannot distinguish individual or multiple targets, nor provide any moving direction or location specific information. But BPS can well preserve users' privacy, which make it highly suitable for occupancy sensing in smart environments. It detects users' demands without leaking users' privacy, which is the foundation for smart control, such as on-demand lighting or HVAC control. The typical BPS sensors include Passive Infrared sensor, ultrasound sensor, and microwave radar sensor etc.

Although a BPS provides very limited information, prior work [1] has shown that a collaborative network of BPSs can yield respectable single target tracking accuracy. In [1], the authors showed that a target can be localized with a location error proportional to $\frac{1}{\rho R^{d-1}}$, where ρ is the sensor density, R is the sensing range, and d is the dimension of the space. But significant difficulties will be encountered for tracking multiple targets, because the sensors can't tell how many targets are presenting, which leads to the difficulty of disaggregating the motion trajectories of the multiple targets.

Only in 1-Dimension network, the counting problem was investigated in[2], which presented a lower bound of the presenting targets as the maximum number of *positively independent sensors*[2], where the positively independent sensors are "on" sensors sufficiently far apart, or separated by at least one "off" sensors [2]. They presented a greedy algorithm to calculate the lower bound. However, this lower bound is shown conservative in 2-D space in this paper, and a novel unit disk graph (UDG) model for the BPS network is proposed, which leads to a tighter lower bound, i.e., *minimum number of cliques that partition the UDG formed by the "on" sensors.* This new lower bound is valid in both 1-D and 2-D networks.

Then how the sequential readings overtime can further improve the target counting and tracking is investigated. The sequentially state changing events reported by distributed sensors introduce temporal and spatial constraints, i.e., some timely close by, but spatially far away events must be triggered by different targets because the targets must move continuously. Based on this intuition, despite the little information provided by each event, we comprehensively infer and evaluate possible target distributions and trajectories that may coincide the sequential events to improve the counting and tracking accuracy. We define a *time-spatial distance* between events, which can help more accurately counting the targets than that of the snapshot-based counting. Then for tracking and disaggregating the trajectories of the multiple targets, we propose dynamic edge coloring (DEC) and Multi-color Particle filter (MCPF). The DEC

MobiHoc'14, August 11–14, 2014, Philadelphia, PA, USA.

http://dx.doi.org/10.1145/2632951.2632959.

generates and maintains a set of target distribution scenarios of different colors. The number of colors in a scenario indicates the estimation to the number of the targets. In each scenario, from the sensor readings before and after an event, shrinking and expanding methods are presented to predict the feasible regions of the targets at the occurred event.

Then in each scenario, we further developed a multi-color particle filter (MCPF), which generates random particles according to the possible target distributions to enumerate and evaluate the potential trajectories of the targets. The MCPF calculates the likelihood of the multi-target trajectory by the consistence of the moving speeds of each target. So that, the overall best trajectory among all trajectories over all scenarios is voted at each event time, which provides not only the estimation to the most possible number of the targets, but also the disaggregated trajectories of these targets. Extensive evaluations by multi-agent simulations showed that the proposed methods can provide satisfactory counting and tracking accuracy for multiple, anonymous, uncooperative, simultaneously moving targets, despite the very limited information provided by the BPSs.

The remaining part of this paper is organized as follows. Background and problem model are introduced in section 2. Lower bound for target number counting is presented in section 3. Interplay of DEC and MCPF is presented in Section 4. Simulation results are presented in section 5, with conclusions drawn in Section 6.

2. BACKGROUND AND PROBLEM MODEL

We introduce the problem model and the most related works in this section.

In this work, we consider an idealized sensing model for the BPS. Let's consider n sensors are deployed in a two-dimensional area-of-interest. The locations of the sensors are assumed known by self-localization techniques [3] and the sensors are assumed timely synchronized [4], so that the concurrent readings of the sensors can be measured to form a snapshot. Each sensor monitors the targets (e.g. people) within its sensing range and outputs "1" when one or more targets are in its sensing range, and "0" otherwise. Let's R denote the sensing radius of a sensor and we assume targets within this range can be detected by the sensor without error. Each sensor only reports the state transition events, i.e, the timestamp and the event type ("1" to "0", or "0" to "1") to a central collector. The collector infers the concurrent states of all the sensors and conducts information processing to estimate the number and locations of the presenting targets. We assume the data collection is well addressed by routing and MAC protocols.

Under above sensing model, the sensing regions of the n sensors will partition the area-of-interest into m *patches*. A patch is a close area bounded by the sensing boundaries of sensors. Each patch can be uniquely coded by a length n vector $\mathbf{P}_i = \{b_{i,1}, \cdots, b_{i,n}\}$, where $b_{i,j} = 1$ if sensor j covers patch i and $b_{i,j} = 0$ otherwise. Since the locations in a patch have the same code, conventionally, the discriminability resolution of the BPS network is considered to be determined by the size of the patches[1]. Whereas, when taking the time attributes of the events into consideration, we can further characterize the possible locations of the target which triggers the event by the arc it is crossing. This can further narrow down the freedom of the location estimation than

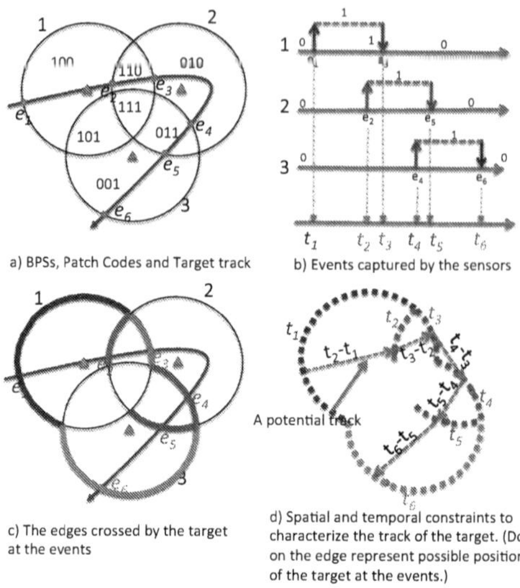

Figure 1: Spatial and temporal information provided by the BPS sensors for motion track estimation when a target moves through the sensing regions of three BPSs.

the patch-based representation. For targets not triggering the event, we can still estimate their locations by the patch indices. Therefore, as introduced in Section 4, by shrinking and expanding based approach, we can interactively use edge-based and patch-based location representation to more accurately estimate the possible locations of the targets.

Fig.1 shows an example of tracking a mobile target by three BPS sensors. Fig.1a) shows the formed patches and the patch codes. Fig.1b) shows the state transition events reported by the sensors. Fig.1c) shows the crossing edges of each event by different colors. Fig.1d) illustrates the spatial and temporal information provided by the sensing events, where the crossing edge at each event is discretized to dots to represent the possible positions of the target at the event time. Tracking multiple targets is more complex, because when an event occurs, we don't know who triggers it and don't have clue for other targets' locations.

2.1 Existing Counting Limits and Bounds

The problem becomes difficult when we consider tracking multiple targets by the BPS network. By assuming the sensor can distinguish the targets, i.e., can distinguish which event is triggered by which target, FindingHuMo [5] proposed adaptive Hidden Markov Model (HMM) to disaggregate the motion trajectories of the multiple targets. By assuming knowing the total number of the targets, [6] proposed multiple pairs shortest path algorithm to search the most possible trajectory using walking speed variance to disaggregate target trajectories. But the problem becomes extremely difficult when the number of targets is unknown and when the sensors cannot distinguish the targets, which is however, the most practical scenario, because in real applications, neither the Infrared sensor, ultrasound sensor nor the microwave sensor can distinguish the targets, and we generally don't know the number of the presenting targets.

For this practical case, only in one-dimensional space where the targets move along a line, a method for evaluating the lower bound of the number of targets was presented in [2]. In the method, if the "on" sensors can be partitioned into at most X positively independent sets, where the positively independent sensors are "on" sensors whose sensing regions don't overlap, or separated by at least one "off" sensors, Theorem 4 in[2] stated that the number of targets in the sensing field is not less than the cardinarity of X, i.e., $|X|$.

But we found this lower bound was conservative when applied to 2-D spaces. Fig.2 explains this lower bound in several scenarios. In Fig.2a) and Fig.2b), the two "on" sensors (red segments) form two positively independent sets, so the lower bound of the target number is two in these cases. In Fig.2c), the two "on" sensors form only one positively independent set, so the lower bound of target number is one. But in the 2-D example, as shown in Fig.2d), the three "on" sensors are not independent, forming only one positively independent set, so the lower bound of target number is one. But it is not hard to verify that it needs at least two targets presenting in the positive sensing field (white area) to trigger the three sensors to "on". So the lower bound is conservative. Because tracking multiple targets in 2-D spaces is a more general scenario in practice, tighter lower bound, and efficient target counting and tracking algorithms are needed.

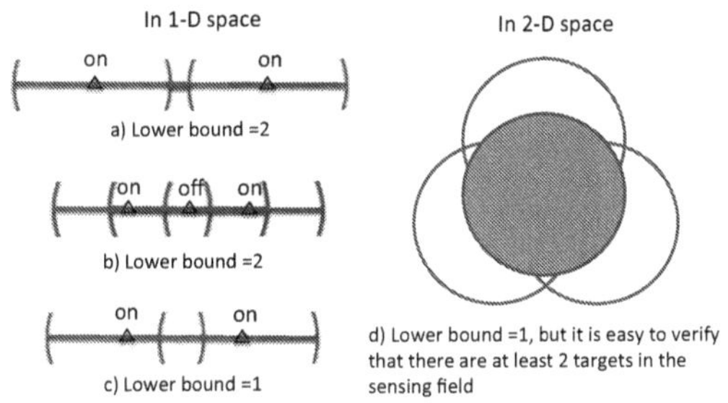

Figure 2: Calculate lower bound of target number in 1-D and 2-D spaces by the maximum number of positively independent sensors.

2.2 More related works

BPS-based target counting and tracking has attacked many studies. In [7], Busnel et al. explored the limits of multiple object tracking using a network of binary motion sensors. They showed that the multiple objects cannot be identified by BMSs on a general graph even by an omniscient external observer if all the objects can freely move on the graph. They showed that priori restrictions on the graph or priori restrictions on object movements can help to make the problem solvable. Further than FindingHuMo [5], to overcome the difficulties of training the HMM model, *MiningTraMo* was proposed in [6] to infer the most possible trajectories by multiple pairs shortest path algorithm based on walking speed variance. In [8], Jeswani et al. proposed an approach for target tracking using sparsely deployed binary sensor network. The trajectory of a target is approximated by a piece-wise curve, where each piece is an estimated as tangent between sensing regions of two sensors. In [9], cluster-based decentralized variational filtering was proposed for target tracking in binary sensor networks. In [10], He et al. proposed a hybrid multiple target tracking scheme, which conducts coarse-scale tracking by binary proximate sensors to narrow down search area, and uses high-end sensors for fine-grained tracking. In [11], Cao et al. presented collaborative scheme for tracking groups of targets using BMSs. In [12], Wang et al. presented a distributed energy efficient target tracking scheme using binary sensor networks. The algorithm exploited the successive detection events of neighboring binary sensors to infer the trajectory of the target. In [13], Rao-BlackWellised Particle filters are introduced to tracking and identify target, which is implemented in a device-free people tracking and identification system. In System presented in [14], motion character is introduced to improve locating accuracy in netwokred BPS. A family of bound on performance for multiple target tracking is given in [15], whose core idea is locating error is introduced by uncertain origin of measurement. Based on this uncertainty, error in optimal solution can be bounded.

3. COUNTABILITY BY A SNAPSHOT

To investigate the countability problem by a snapshot of sensor readings, we firstly present sufficient and necessary conditions for precisely target counting in 2-D space.

3.1 Conditions for Precisely Target Counting

Let's consider an arbitrary snapshot at time t. Let $\mathbf{S}_t \in (0,1)^n$ be a length-n vector representing the "on/off" states of the n sensors at time t. Let $\mathbf{A}_t$ denote the set of the "on" sensors. Let $\mathbf{E}_t$ denote the set of the "off " sensors. Let function $P(s)$ return all the patches covered by the sensor set s. Let F_t be the *feasible target space* in which the targets may present. Then:

$$\mathbf{F}_t = P(\mathbf{A}_t) - P(\mathbf{E}_t) \tag{1}$$

Let S^i be the set of positive sensors that sense the target i. Let function $F(S^i)$ return the *feasible target space* contributed by these positive sensors in set S^i, then

$$F(S^i) = P(S^i) - P(S^i) \cap P(\mathbf{E}_t) \tag{2}$$

Then a sufficient condition for precisely target counting can be stated as:

THEOREM 1. *(Sufficient condition). If S^i is the set of sensors that sense the target i, the sufficient condition for precisely target counting is that $\forall i \neq j, F(S^i) \cap F(S^j) = \emptyset$.*

PROOF. Suppose there are m targets. Since $\forall i \neq j$, $F(S^i) \cap F(S^j) = \emptyset$, the feasible target spaces are naturally partitioned to m isolated feasible areas, one per target. Therefore, we can precisely determine the m isolated feasible target spaces, which precisely indicates there are m targets. □

Note that this sufficient condition requires the groups of sensors triggered by the different targets are enough separated. The sufficient condition presented in [2] which requires the pairwise distances between any two targets to be larger than $4R$ is a special case of this sufficient condition.

THEOREM 2. *(Necessary condition). If S^i is the set of sensors that sense target i, the necessary condition for precisely target counting is that $\forall i \neq j, F(S^i) \neq F(S^j)$.*

PROOF. We prove by contradiction. If $F(S^i) = F(S^j)$, then we can never determine whether there is one or two targets in the area $F(S^i)$. Therefore, for precisely target counting, there must be $\forall i \neq j, F(S^i) \neq F(S^j)$. □

The necessary and sufficient conditions give properties but are not practical. A more general requirement is to estimate the number of targets by a given snapshot of the sensor readings, for which, we present a new tight lower bound for estimating the number of targets.

3.2 UDG Model for Feasible Target Space

We firstly present a unit disk graph (UDG) model to model the geometrical structure of the feasible target space. For a given snapshot, the feasible target space in which the targets may locate is determined by $\mathbf{F}_t = P(\mathbf{A}_t) - P(\mathbf{E}_t)$. This area may be partitioned by the sensing areas of the "off" sensors into some isolated *islands*, which are denoted by $\mathbf{L}_t = \{L_1, L_2, \cdots, L_v\}$, where v is the total number of the isolated islands. Note that two feasible areas L_i and L_j are isolated if they are spatially separated by the sensing regions of the "off" sensors.

An example is shown in Fig.3, in which the feasible target space (the space in white) is separated by the "off" sensors (space in grey) into three isolated islands, denoted by L_1, L_2, L_3 respectively. A trivial lower bound for the number of target is therefore the number of the isolated islands, because each island contains at least one target. But this lower bound is not tight. We can improve this lower bound by considering the topology of each island. Note that each island is a union region of the sensing regions of some "on" sensors subtract the regions covered by the "off" sensors. If we normalize the sensor radius R to 1, we can construct a *Unit Disk Graph* (UDG) by connecting the vertexes of the intersected "on" sensors in each feasible island. The construction rules are:

- The "on" sensors in the isolated islands are chosen as the vertexes of the UDG.
- For any two "on" sensors, if they have intersected sensing region and the intersected region is not fully covered by the regions of the "off" sensors, an edge is added between these two vertexes.

By examining all the "on" sensors by above rules, A UDG is constructed in each island. Examples of UDG construction are shown in Fig.3. Note that the UDG in each island is connected and the UDGs in different islands are disconnected.

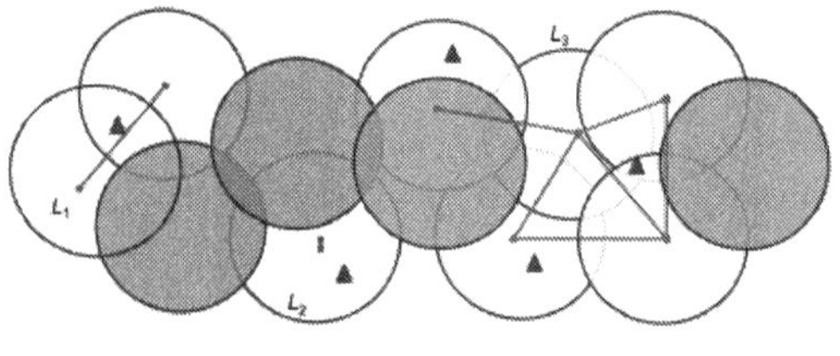

Figure 3: Unit disk graph for target counting

3.3 Lower Bound of Target Number

By investigating the topologies of the UDGs, a tighter lower bound for the number of targets can be calculated.

DEFINITION 1 (CLIQUE). *In graph theory, a* clique *in an undirected graph $G = (V, E)$ is a subset of vertices $C \in V$, such that every two vertices in the subset C are connected.*

DEFINITION 2 (CLIQUE PARTITION). *Given a UDG $G = (V, E)$, a clique partition is a partition of V into nonempty, disjoint sets $\{C_1, C_2, \cdots, C_u\}$, such that each set $C_i, (i = 1, \cdots, u)$ induces a clique. The minimum clique partition (MCP) is to partition the vertex into the minimum number of cliques.*

Let's consider a clique partition on a UDG, which is denoted by $\{C_1, C_2, \cdots, C_u\}$. If $\mathbf{S}_j$ represents the sensors partitioned into the clique C_j, because the cliques are disjoint, $\forall C_i \neq C_j, \mathbf{S}_i \cap \mathbf{S}_j = \emptyset$. All the sensors in the same clique can be triggered "on" by one sensor (because these sensors are connected, i.e., have a common feasible target region), therefore, finding the lower bound of the target number is equal to find the minimum clique partition of the UDG.

LEMMA 1. *For a clique containing k sensors, one target located in the k-intersected sensing area of the k sensors is sufficient to make all the k sensors be in "on" state.*

PROOF. From the construction of UDG, two sensors are connected if they have intersected sensing area in the feasible target space. Because k sensors in a clique are fully connected, they share a common k-intersected feasible target space. Only if one target is presenting in the feasible k-intersected area, all sensors in the clique will triggered "on" to coincide their readings. □

THEOREM 3. *(Lower bound of the target number by a snapshot). Given a snapshot consisting of v isolated islands. Let N be the number of targets that matches the sensor readings, then there must be $N \geq \sum_{i=1}^{v} l_i$, where l_i equals to the minimum number of cliques partitioning the UDG of the ith island.*

PROOF. Since the isolated islands are independent, we only need to prove that the number of targets in an island i is at least l_i, i.e., the least number of targets equal to the minimum number of cliques that partition the UDG.

1). For sufficiency aspect, from Lemma1, one target placed at the most intersected area in each clique is sufficient to trigger all sensors in the clique to "on" state, so l_i targets is sufficient to make the states of all the sensors in the UDG be coincide with their "on" readings.

2). For necessity aspect, if $l_i - 1$ targets can make all sensors' states to be "on", we can repartition the UDG by selecting the sensors detecting the same target into the same clique. Because the sensors detecting the same target must have intersected sensing region, i.e., connected. This new partition will partition the UDG into $l_i - 1$ cliques. This is contradict to that l_i is the minimum number of cliques partitioning the UDG, so that there is at least l_i targets in the sensing field. □

COROLLARY 1. *The lower bound of target number in Theorem 3 is tight, because it can be exactly achieved by placing a target in the most intersected sensing region in each clique.*

However, because the MCP of the UDG is not unique, there are different versions of minimum clique partitions. Even if we know exactly that the least number of targets are presenting in the sensing field, it is still ambiguous to determine the locations of the targets.

Moreover, regarding the computation cost for estimating the lower bound of the targets, the MCP problem on UDGs

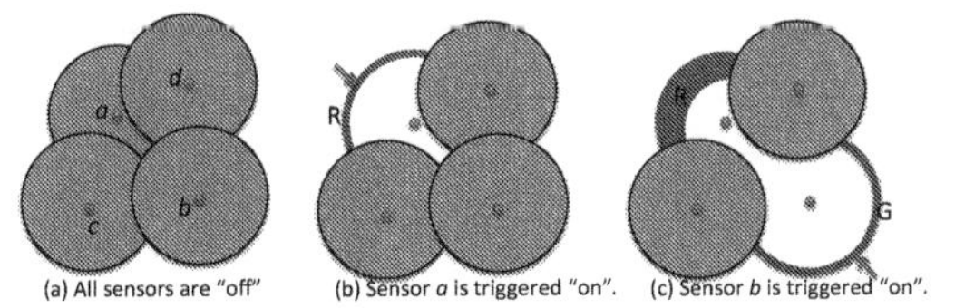

(a) All sensors are "off" (b) Sensor a is triggered "on". (c) Sensor b is triggered "on".

Figure 4: Example to illustrate the idea of time-space distance and FCA coloring

is a well-known NP-hard problem[16]. Recent work in [17] provided a polynomial time approximation algorithm, which is guaranteed to be within $(1+\epsilon)$ ratio of the optimum when the input is a UDG. For the special characters of target tracking problem, the number of vertexes in an feasible island are generally limited. Therefore, we can calculate a rather accurate lower bound for the number of targets given the snapshot readings of the sensors.

An example to estimate the lower bound of the number of the targets by a snapshot is shown in Fig.3. In the three isolated islands, UDGs are constructed. The minimum number of cliques in the islands L_1, L_2 and L_3 are 1, 1, 3 respectively, so that the least number of targets estimated by this snapshot is totally five. The figure gives an example distribution of the five targets. Note that the minimum clique partition in L_3 is not unique, so that the locations of the three targets are still ambiguous, even if there are exactly three targets.

4. COUNT AND TRACK DYNAMICLY

Although Theorem 3 presents a tight lower bound for the number of targets at a snapshot. The exact number of the targets and their locations are still difficult to be estimated from the snapshot. But this doesn't exclude the possibility to count and track the targets more accurately by further exploring the temporal and spatial constraints from the sequential events of the sensors.

In this section, we investigate how the temporal and spatial information introduced by the state changing events can help to improve the target counting accuracy. In particular, we propose a concept of *space-time separation* between the events. We show that when the events triggered by different targets are enough separated in *space-time distance*, they can be successfully attributed to different targets.

4.1 Space-time Separation Between Events

The sequential readings of the sensors provide more contexts for multi-target counting and locating. In an instance when a sensor's state switches from "off" to "on" (or from "on" to "off"), it must because some targets are entering (leaving) its sensing region from its sensing boundary.

DEFINITION 3 (FEASIBLE CROSSING ARC (FCA)). *When a sensor's state change is detected, the feasible crossing arc indicates the arc segments where the targets are traversing to trigger the event without violating the states of the other sensors.*

The FCA provides temporal location constraint to a moving target. Each event maps to a corresponding FCA. To characterize whether two successive events are possibly triggered by the same target, we measure the distance between the FCAs of these two events. If the occurrence times of the two events are close, but the distance between their FCAs is large, we can distinguish confidently that the two events are triggered by different targets.

DEFINITION 4 (DISTANCE BETWEEN FCAS). *The distance between two FCAs f_a and f_b is the shortest distance between any two points on the two FCAs, where the shortest path connecting the two points must be within the feasible target space. We denote the distance between FCAs as $\|f_a - f_b\|_2$.*

Let's suppose the maximum moving speed of the targets is V_{max}, then:

DEFINITION 5 (TIME-SPACE DISTANCE). *The time-space distance between two event E_a, E_b happened at time t_a, t_b, with FCAs f_a, f_b respectively is defined as:*

$$\mathcal{D}_{a,b} = \|f_a - f_b\|_2 - |t_b - t_a| \, V_{\max}$$

THEOREM 4 (DYNAMIC TARGET SEPERATION). *Two events E_a and E_b must be triggered by different targets, if $\mathcal{D}_{a,b} > 0$.*

PROOF. $\mathcal{D}_{a,b} > 0$ means $\|f_a - f_b\|_2 > |t_b - t_a| \, V_{\max}$, which means that even the shortest distance between the two FCAs is larger than $|t_b - t_a| \, V_{\max}$. Because $|t_b - t_a| \, V_{\max}$ is the largest distance a target can travel from t_a to t_b, a target triggers E_a hasn't enough time to move from f_a to f_b to trigger E_b, so that E_a and E_b must be triggered by different targets. □

Dynamic target separation can count target more accurately than the snap-shot based lower bound. An example is shown in Fig.4. Initially, all sensors are "off" as shown in Fig.4(a). The red arc in Fig.4(b) shows the FCA when sensor a turns to be "on". The green arc in Fig.4(c) shows the FCA when sensor b turns to be "on". The red area in Fig.4(c) shows the reachable area of the target who triggered E_a when the event E_b happens. Since the red target cannot reach the green arc, these two events must be triggered by different targets. If using MCP-based method, the UDG contains only one clique, the lower bound provided by the snapshot is one, which is smaller than dynamic lower bound. Therefore, dynamic counting can be more accurate in practice by considering both time and location constraints. Based on this intuition, we propose *dynamic edge coloring (DEC)* and *multicolor particle filter (MCPF)* to dynamically color the edges to count the number of targets and to disaggregate the trajectories of targets by the presenting colors and also by evaluating the consistence of the targets' movement patterns.

4.2 DEC and MCPF

DEC and MCPF are jointly designed. DEC is event driven, which is used to assign color to the FCA (feasible crossing arc) according to occurring event, which is to specify which target may trigger the event. The edge coloring is based on the time-space distance from the historical events, therefore, it is based on the historical states of the targets, which are stored and tracked by the MCPF. The MCPF stores a set of parallel *scenario trajectories*. Each scenario trajectory has different estimation to the number of the targets. For an example, a scenario trajectory considers that all the previous events are triggered by 3 targets (having three colors), but another trajectory considers the previous events are triggered by at least 4 targets (having four colors). Further, each scenario trajectory maintains a dynamic set of *feasible target trajectories.* A feasible target trajectory contains the historical positions of the targets from beginning up to now. The feasibility constraint of the target trajectory is that at each event's time, the positions of the targets must make the states of the sensors coincide with their readings. The likelihood of each feasible target trajectory is evaluated by evaluating the variance of the moving speeds of the targets. The feasible target trajectory with the overall highest likelihood provides not only the most likely number of the targets, but also the disaggregated historical trajectories of these targets.

This method depends on the consistence of the target number and the consistence of the targets' moving patterns during a monitoring period, therefore we assume the number of the target doesn't change within the short monitoring period and the targets move smoothly.

4.2.1 Scenario Generation

A snapshot of sensor readings is obtained at each event. For the ambiguity of the sensor readings we cannot determine exactly the target distribution, but we can generate a set of possible distributions by Monte-Calo method. Given a snapshot, we generate distribution scenarios with different number of targets, then these scenarios can be evolved and be evaluated lately by the following events. Since determining the minimum number of presenting targets is NP-hard, we propose an efficient method to generate the distribution scenarios on a proposed *positive patch graph*, induced by a snapshot of the sensor readings.

DEFINITION 6 (PATCH GRAPH). *refers to the directional neighboring graph of patches. Each positive patch (i.e., in the feasible space of targets) is treated as a vertex. Edge* $v \rightarrow u$ *exits iff corresponding patch* P_v *and* P_u *have a common arc and* P_v *is inside the arc. Each arc separates the area into two regions; the inside region refers to the one close to the circle center (the circle where the arc is on).*

The problem of target distribution generation is then to place some targets into these positive patches, so that all the patches can be in "on" state, i.e., all sensors' states coincide their readings.

THEOREM 5. *When we place one target in a patch, all its offspring patches and its ancestor patches on the patch graph can be "overlooked". The occupied patch and the overlooked patches can be deleted from the patch graph when we consider the placement of the next target. After all the patches are deleted, the placement of the targets coincide the sensor readings.*

PROOF. In the patch graph, if P_o is an offspring of P_v, then the sensors covering P_o must be in a subset of the sensors covering P_v. If P_a is an ancestor of P_v, there must be one common sensor covers both P_a and P_v. Therefore, when we place a target at P_v, a sensor covering P_o and a sensor covering P_a must be triggered "on", so that both P_a and P_o can be overlooked. □

Further, when the targets are uniformly distributed, the patch with larger size has higher probability to contain a

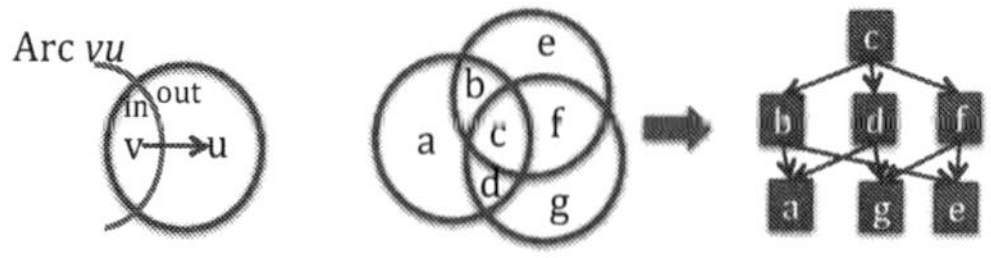

a) Edge direction in patch DAG is determined by the arc direction

b) Transformation from the sensor coverage scenario to the patch DAG

Figure 5: Explanation of Patch DAG

Algorithm 1 Generate-Target-Distribution-by-Snapshot()

Require: $\mathbf{S}$ is the snapshot. $\mathbf{G_p(S)}$ is the patch graph.
Ensure: $O_{1:m}$, Occupancy state for each Patch coincides with $\mathbf{S}$.

$O_{1:m} \leftarrow 0$.
while $\mathbf{G_p(S)} \neq \emptyset$ **do**
  Select v form $\mathbf{G_p(S)}$ randomly with probability according to the size of the patch v
  $O_v \leftarrow 1$.
  $G_p(S) \leftarrow G_p(S) \setminus \mathbf{O}(v) \setminus \mathbf{A}(v)$, where $\mathbf{O}(v)$ are the offsprings of v and $\mathbf{A}(v)$ are the ancestors of v on $G_p(S)$
end while
output $O_{1:m}$

---

target. Therefore, we also took the patch size into consideration, and developed algorithm 1 to efficiently generate the possible target distribution scenarios.

Algorithm 1 output the most likely target distribution in positive patches. Since the estimation may be incorrect, we generate many alternative target distributions by running the algorithm multiple times. Then we categorize the target distributions by putting the distributions that contain the same number of targets into a common scenario. After the categorizing, we suppose there are Γ scenarios and each scenario contains different number of target distributions as shown in Fig.6.

4.2.2 Handle an Event

Scenario generation is carried out by the first snapshot after initialization. Now suppose we know the latest scenarios and possible target trajectories at event $t-1$. Once a new on/off event happens at event t, we try to estimate the target distributions at time T_t. Note that the events are indexed by $1, 2, , t-1, t$. It is not necessarily the interval between two events are equal. We denote T_t as the time of event t. The target trajectory updating scheme contains four steps: 1) determining the FCA, 2) dynamically edge coloring, 3) location updating for all the targets, and 4) evaluate the likelihood of particles.

1). Determining the FCA: When an event happens, the feasible crossing arc is easily determined by comparing the two snapshots before and after the event. The FCA are the intersected edges of the state changing sensor with other positive sensors surrounding it at the event time.

2) Dynamically edge coloring: After determining the FCA, for each feasible target distribution of each scenario, we evaluate the color of the FCA. This is based on the target distribution estimations at the event $t-1$. This step judges two things:

1. It helps to verify the feasibility of the guessed target

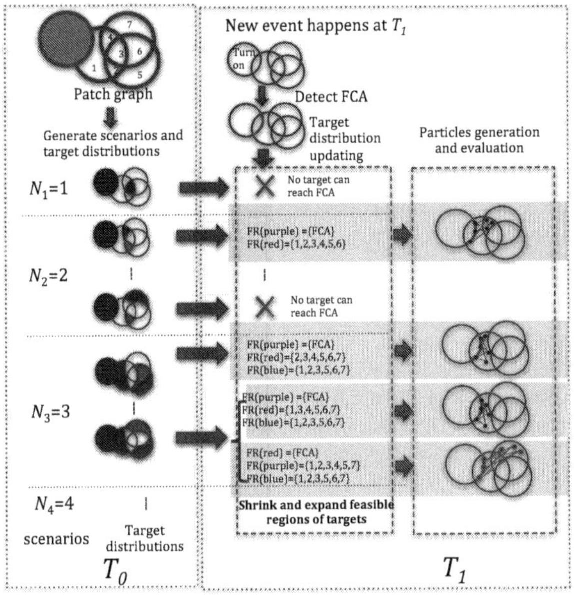

Figure 6: Example of scenario generation and particle generation

distributions at the last event. If based on a distribution at event $t-1$, all the targets cannot reach the FCA at event t, the distribution is judged infeasible and will be deleted.

2. For feasible distributions, we estimate which target is on the FCA at event t, i.e, the color of the arc, which is the basis for generating new target distributions.

To assign color to the FCA, this step needs to calculate the shortest distance from the feasible patches to the FCA, i.e, patch-arc distance, which is complex because both the patches and the FCA are in irregular shapes. We designed an efficient Monte-Calo algorithm to carry out this task. Δ points are randomly generated in the feasible patch, whose shortest distances to the FCA are calculated, and the overall shortest distance to the FCA is used as the shortest distance from the patch to the FCA. The shortest distance from a point to an arc can be easily calculated via geometric method. For a considering patch, let's denote d_{min} be the shortest distance from this patch to the FCA, then if

$$d_{min} - \varepsilon > V_{max}(T_t - T_{t-1}) \tag{3}$$

the target in the patch at T_{t-1} cannot reach the FCA at T_t, where ε is a small value to compensate the calculation error of d_{min} by Monte-Calo. If in a target distribution at T_{t-1}, all the targets cannot reach the FCA, the target distribution is judged invalid and will be deleted. If a target can reach the FCA, we update the target distribution as following.

3) Feasible Region Shrinking and Expanding: Suppose a target distribution in a scenario at T_{t-1} has Θ targets, among which, Θ_1 targets can reach the FCA at T_t and $\Theta_2 = \Theta - \Theta_1$ targets cannot reach the FCA. In this case, we generate Θ_1 new possible target distributions at T_t. In each generated target distribution, a target which can reach the FCA is put on the FCA (i.e., *shrinking*), while the feasible regions of the other targets will be expanded based on the elapsed time from T_{t-1} to T_t to a broad area where they may reach. So that by shrinking and expanding, we update the location estimations of all the targets at event T_t. It helps us to update not only the possible locations of the targets that may trigger the event, but also the possible locations of the unobservable targets at T_t.

The feasible region of a target is maintained by a patch vector $\{P_{i,1}, \cdots, P_{i,k}\}$, which are a set of patches that the target i may locate at time t. Expanding of feasible region is carried out on the patch graph. From T_{t-1} to T_t, the maximum distance a target can move is $d_{max,t} = V_{max}(T_t - T_{t-1})$, so all its connected positive patches within $d_{max,t}$ will be added into its feasible patch vector at T_t. Different methods can be used to calculate the patch-patch distance: 1) Since the patches are static, the patch-patch distances can be evaluated offline only once by Monte-Calo method, i.e., generating random points in two patches and calculating the average distance between the points in the two patches; 2) An more efficient method of expanding the feasible region is to simply add all direct neighboring positive patches of the current feasible patches into the feasible region when a new event happens. By knowing the feasible region of targets at time T_t, dynamic coloring can be carried out by (3) at time T_{t+1} when an new event happens.

4) Particle Generation and Likelihood Evaluation: In each generated target distribution, a target is on FCA and some other targets are predicted to be in their feasible regions. In particle generation step, we generate the possible positions of the target on the FCA and generate the possible positions of other targets in their feasible regions. All particle generation and the likelihood evaluation are for the same color target. Multiple targets' particle filters work in parallel.

Let's consider only the kth target in a distribution of Θ targets at time T_{t-1}. Its MCPF stores: 1) M most possible trajectories for the target up to time T_{t-1} and the possible end positions denoted by $\{x_{k,j}(T_{t-1})$, where $k = 1, 2, \cdots, \Theta$ is the target index. 2) the probability distribution functions (pdf) of the moving speed of the target in trajectory j, i.e., $\{p_{k,j}(v)\}, j = 1, \cdots, M$; 3) the likelihood of each trajectory, denoted by $\{l_k(\text{track}_j(T_{t-1}))\}$.

So that, at time T_t, we generate Q random positions for the target and connect these points to the M end points at time T_{t-1}, which generates $P = M \cdot Q$ particles representing the possible movement trajectories of this target from T_{t-1} to T_t. For each particle, we can evaluate the moving speed of this target by:

$$v_{k,i,j}(t) = \frac{|x_{k,i}(T_t) - x_{k,j}(T_{t-1})|}{T_t - T_{t-1}}, \tag{4}$$

where $x_{k,j}(T_{t-1})$ is an ending location at time T_{t-1} and $x_{k,i}(T_t)$ is a generated location at T_t. The likelihood of the particle from $x_{k,j}(T_{t-1})$ to $x_{k,i}(T_t)$ is evaluated by $p_{k,j}(v_{k,i,j}(t))$. To evaluate the likelihood of the trajectory goes through $x_{k,j}(T_{t-1})$ and ends at $x_{k,i}(T_t)$ by multiplying $p_{k,j}(v_{k,i,j}(t))$ with $l_k(\text{track}_j(T_{t-1}))$. So that we can get the likelihoods of the MQ particles. We sort these particles by likelihood and only preserve the most possible M trajectories for the next step. The pdfs of the target speed are updated and the M most possible trajectories are stored at T_t. Algorithm 2 presents the pseudo code of the MCPF for a target in one scenario. Note that parallel MCPFs are run for multiple targets in each parallel scenario. Fig.6 shows particle generation scenarios at T_1. Because no historical trajectory information exist, both $x_{k,j}(T_0)$ and $x_{k,i}(T_1)$ are randomly generated. For clarity, only the particles generated on FCA are plotted. The particles generated for the other targets are not visually shown.

Algorithm 2 MCPF-for-A-Target-in-A-Scenario

Require: m trajectories up to T_{t-1}; pdf of the moving speed of the target in each trajectory $\{p_{k,j}(v)\}, j = 1, 2, \cdots, m$; likelihood of each trajectory $\{l_{k(track_j(T_{t-1}))}\}$; feasible region of the target
Ensure: Updated trajectories, pdf of speed and likelihood of trajectories up to T_t;

Generate Q points in feasible region of target;
Connect Q points to m trajectories' ending points to generate mQ particles;
for $i = 1; i <= Q; i++$ **do**
  for $j = 1; j <= m; j++$ **do**
    Evaluate $v_{k,i,j}(t)$;
    Evaluate $c_{i,j} = p_{k,j}(v_{k,i,j}(t)) l_k(track_j(T_{t-1}))$;
  end for
end for
Sort $\{c_{i,j}\}$;
Preserve the most likely m trajectories;
Update pdfs of the target speed in the trajectories;

4.3 Interplay of DEC and MCPF

The top level interplay of DEC and MCPF is explained in Algorithm 3. In initialization phase, scenarios and possible target distributions are generated by placing targets on the patch graph. We generate a large amount of target distributions (denote by I) to increase the probability that the distributions close to the ground truth can be generated. In online phase, the interplay of DEC and MCPF is splitted into different scenarios. In each scenario, the algorithm conducts dynamic edge coloring, feasible region shrinking and expanding for each target trajectory and generate new trajectories based on the new event. Then for each target, MCPF is run to rank the trajectories to find the top-M trajectories that can better interpret the event sequence. At last, all the scenarios are ranked by the likelihood of their most possible trajectory. The overall best trajectory provides not only the estimation of the target number but also the location estimations of the targets.

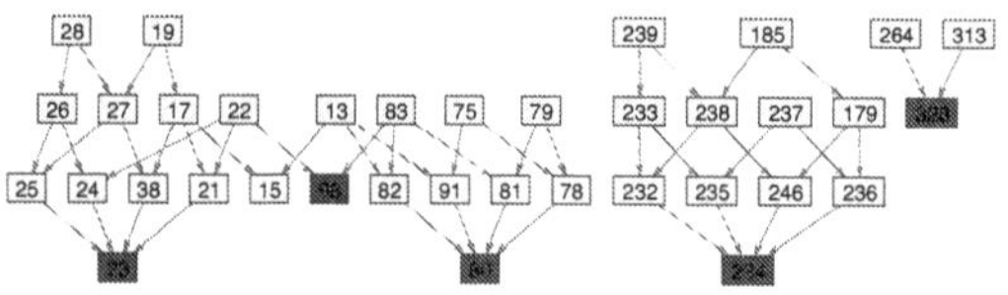

Figure 7: Random sample on patch DAG

5. EVALUATION

We developed a multi-agent simulator to evaluate the MCPF and DEC algorithms. In this platform, trace of targets are generated by random walk, which is updated frame by frame. In each frame, the reading of BPS is calculated according to the location of targets. The velocity of target is draw from normal distribution. The size of target is omitted

Algorithm 3 Interplay of DEC and MCPF

Require: Readings of sensors at T_t; Sensors' positions and sensing radius; Patch indices;
Ensure: Estimation of the most possible number of targets; most possible locations of the targets;

Initialization:
for $i = 1 : 1 : I$ **do**
  Generate-Target-Distribution-by-Snapshot ();
end for
Categorizing the generated target distributions to form Γ scenarios; suppose the ith scenario contain Θ_i targets and Γ_i target trajectories.
Online Phase:
Determine FCA by an event;
for $i = 1 : 1 : \Gamma$(number of scenarios) **do**
  for $j = 1 : 1 : \Gamma_i$(# of trajectories in scenario i) **do**
    Dynamic edge coloring;
    if (n_1 targets can reach the FCA) **then**
      Generate n_1 new target distributions;
      Shrink and expand targets' feasible regions;
    end if
    if (0 targets can reach the FCA) **then**
      delete the target distribution;
    end if
  end for
  for $i = 1 : 1 : \Theta_i$(number of targets in scenario i) **do**
    run MCPF-for-A-Target-in-A-Scenario();
  end for
end for
Rank the scenarios and trajectories by likelihood;
Output the estimation of target number and target's positions based on the most possible scenario and the most possible trajectory in the scenario;

and each target is represented by a point. Setting of simulation is presented in Fig.9, where 36 BPSs are placed in grid topology. The sensing area of BPS is denoted by black circles. The target is denoted by small star with different color. The reachable region of targets are constrained in a square denoted by red dashed line to prevent target entering region uncovered by BPS. In this setting, sensing range of BPS

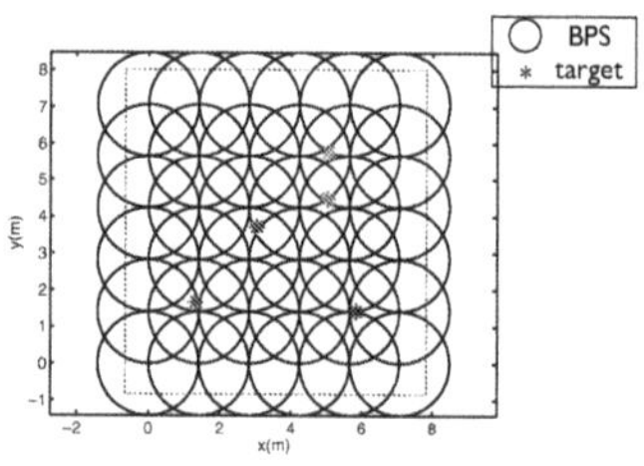

Figure 9: Simulation setting and area distribution

separate the area into 211 patches as shown in Fig.9. The maximum and the minimum number of BPS covering one patch is 4 and 1. The average of patches' size is $0.447m^2$.

The DEC and MCPF are evaluated from several aspects. We firstly evaluate the counting accuracy. Then the tracking accuracy is evaluated in patch level by comparing the located patch band with the true trajectory. After that, the accuracy is evaluated by point to point distance from

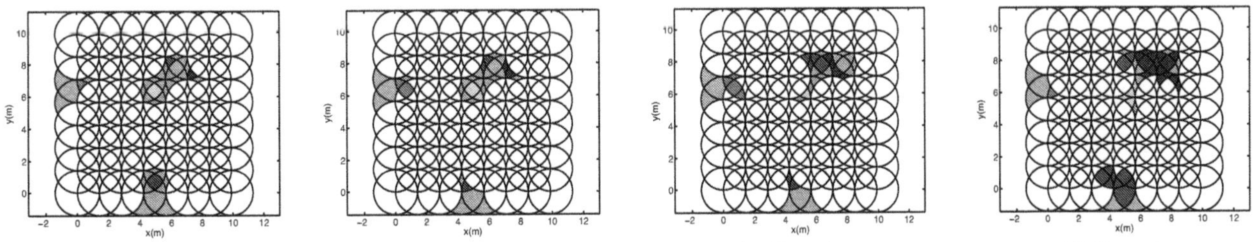

(a) Step 1 (b) Step 2 (c) Step 3 (d) Step 4

Figure 8: Illustration of DEC and the feasible region shrinking and expanding process

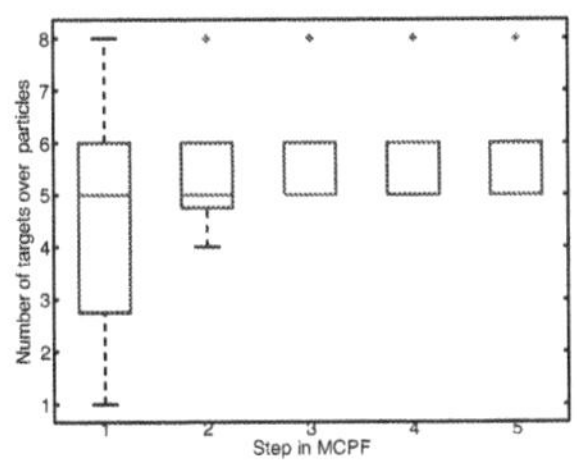

Figure 10: Convergence of number estimation

estimated trajectory to true trajectory, which is called fine-grained accuracy evaluation. Finally, the accuracy regarding to the different target density is investigated.

One of the difficulties to efficiently implement DEC is how to efficiently store the irregular patch areas and the arcs. In our implementation, we stored the starting and ending point of each arc segment, so that each FCA was represented by a set of arc segments. Then, by giving every arc and every patch an index, we can refer their locations and size in the tracking process and specify their colors and size to visualize the result of tracking. Some snapshots of the output of the multi-agent simulator in tracking five targets are illustrated in Fig.8 and 7. Fig. 7 shows the random target distribution generation on the patch graph. Fig.8(a)-8(d) shows the DEC and feasible region shrinking and expanding process at four successive events. For an example, in the Fig.8(d) when an event happens, the feasible region of the green target shrinked its feasible region onto the region of FCA, while the other targets expanded their feasible regions. We have provided our multi-agent simulator for the multi-target tracking as an open-source project, which is hosted at: https://bitbucket.org/thufresh/multi-object-tracking-simulation-platform

5.1 Counting Accuracy

In our tracking algorithms, the estimation of the number of targets is maintained by the parallel possible scenarios. Different scenarios represent different estimations of the target number. Each scenario contains a set of potential target distributions under the target number estimation. Initially, all possible scenarios and their target distributions are generated randomly by the first event. As sequential events are processed, some invalided target distributions will be deleted by DEC. When all target distributions in a scenario are deleted, the scenario is deleted. The scenario with the feasible estimation of the target number is more likely to survive as time going, which makes the counting process converge. As an example shown in Figure 10, for tracking 5 targets, our initial guess of target number was 1-8. The distribution of feasible target distributions was plotted by the box graph, which indicated the scenarios with 3 to 6 targets containing more target distributions. As more events were processed, wrong target distributions with less than 5 targets were cleaned up. Only scenarios with 5, 6 and 8 targets survived after step 3 and the possible target distributions with 8 colors had been very limited. The wrong scenarios with a little higher number estimation than the ground truth can survive for long time, which can only be corrected when targets are enough separated.

5.2 Patch Level Tracking Accuracy

Patch is generally treated as the minimum representing unit of the target position, therefore we firstly evaluate the patch level accuracy. The located patches of a target overtime will form a band of the same color. We visually plot two tracked bands of two targets, which are shown in figure 11(a). Note that the bands are plotted for the most likely scenario's most likely target distribution, whose estimation of the target number is correct. The ground truth of the targets' moving tracks are represented by the solid lines. It shows that the detected most possible patch locations well covered and followed the movement the targets. Some errors happened when two traces intersect, but the errors could be recovered soon by the particle filter.

5.3 Trace Level Tracking Accuracy

We have also drawn samples in patches to form estimated traces of the targets. The trace is timestamped, such that the distance between the estimated location and the real location at the same time is counted as the locating error. Contrast between the real traces and the estimated traces is shown in Fig.11(b). We can see the estimated trace followed well to the real traces even when the two targets are moving closely. When real traces intersected to each other, estimated traces were overlapped in segments. The cumulated distribution of the locating error is presented in Fig.11(e), which tells that more than 90% tracking error in tracking one or two targets is less than $0.5m$. This result is benefited by the small size of patches.

Increasing the density of targets would improve probability of individual target been overlooked, we can expect accuracy deterioration with number of targets increasing. Bands and traces formed by 5 targets are shown in Fig.11(c) and 11(d). Fig. 11(e) shows how target density affect locating accuracy. When number of target was 5 or 10, the tracking accuracy degraded, but it was still acceptable considering the very limited information provided by the sensors.

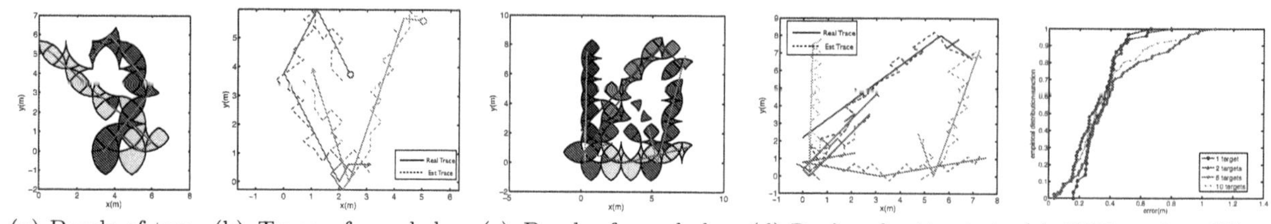

(a) Bands of two targets (b) Traces formed by two targets (c) Bands formed by five targets (d) Real and estimated trace of five targets (e) CDF under different number of target

Figure 11: Patch and Trace Level Accuracy of Multi-target Tracking

6. CONCLUSION

This paper has investigated the problem of counting and tracking multiple, anonymous targets by binary motion sensors, which provide only binary proximity information about the target's presenting. A tight lower bound for target counting in two-dimensional scenario based on snapshot readings of sensors has been presenting by a novel UDG model on the sensing graph of sensors. Then we investigated how to more accurately count and track the multiple targets by exploiting the temporal and spatial constraints captured by the sequential snapshots of sensors. We present the interplay of dynamic edge coloring and the multi-color particle filter to generate different color scenarios, and rank the most potential trajectory in a scenario which can best interpret the sequential sensor readings to output the estimation of the most possible target number and the trajectories of the targets. In future work, the dynamic tracking resolution, the conditions for precisely dynamic counting all need further investigations; multi-target counting and tracking when sensors are noisy should also be further investigated.

Acknowledgment

This work was supported in part by the National Basic Research Program of China Grant 2011CBA00300, 2011CBA00301, the National Natural Science Foundation of China Grant 61202360, 61033001, 61361136003.

7. REFERENCES

[1] N. Shrivastava, R. Mudumbai U. Madhow, and S. Suri. Target tracking with binary proximity sensors: fundamental limits, minimal descriptions, and algorithms. SenSys '06, pages 251–264, New York, NY, USA, 2006. ACM.

[2] Jaspreet Singh, Upamanyu Madhow, Rajesh Kumar, Subhash Suri, and Richard Cagley. Tracking multiple targets using binary proximity sensors. In *IPSN '07*. ACM, April 2007.

[3] Andreas Savvides, Chih-Chieh Han, and Mani B. Strivastava. Dynamic fine-grained localization in ad-hoc networks of sensors. MobiCom '01, pages 166–179, New York, NY, USA, 2001. ACM.

[4] Jeremy Elson, Lewis Girod, and Deborah Estrin. Fine-grained network time synchronization using reference broadcasts. *SIGOPS Oper. Syst. Rev.*, 36(SI):147–163, December 2002.

[5] D. De, Wen-Zhan Song, Mingsen Xu, Cheng-Liang Wang, D. Cook, and X. Huo. FindingHuMo: real-time tracking of motion trajectories from anonymous binary sensing in smart environments. In *ICDCS*, pages 163–172, 2012.

[6] Chengliang Wang, Debraj De, and Wen-Zhan Song. Trajectory mining from anonymous binary motion sensors in smart environment. *Knowledge-Based Systems*, 37:346–356, January 2013.

[7] Yann Busnel, Leonardo Querzoni, Roberto Baldoni, Marin Bertier, and Anne-Marie Kermarrec. Analysis of deterministic tracking of multiple objects using a binary sensor network. *ACM Trans. Sen. Netw.*, 8(1):8:1–8:27, August 2011.

[8] D. Jeswani, A. Kesharwani, S. Chaudhari, V.P. Sadaphal, and R.K. Ghosh. A practical approach for target tracking in sparsely deployed binary sensor network. In *(MASCOTS)*, pages 153–160, 2012.

[9] Jing Teng, H. Snoussi, and C. Richard. Decentralized variational filtering for target tracking in binary sensor networks. *IEEE Transactions on Mobile Computing*, 9(10):1465–1477, 2010.

[10] Ting He, C. Bisdikian, L. Kaplan, Wei Wei, and D. Towsley. Multi-target tracking using proximity sensors. In *MILCOM*, pages 1777–1782, 2010.

[11] Donglei Cao, Beihong Jin, Sajal K. Das, and Jiannong Cao. On collaborative tracking of a target group using binary proximity sensors. *Journal of Parallel and Distributed Computing*, 70(8):825–838, August 2010.

[12] Zijian Wang, Eyuphan Bulut, and Boleslaw K. Szymanski. Distributed energy-efficient target tracking with binary sensor networks. *ACM Trans. Sen. Netw.*, 6(4):32:1–32:32, July 2010.

[13] Dirk Schulz, Dieter Fox, and Jeffrey Hightower. People tracking with anonymous and id-sensors using rao-blackwellised particle filters. In *IJCAI*, pages 921–928, 2003.

[14] R Gupta and S R Das. Tracking moving targets in a smart sensor network. In *Vehicular Technology Conference, 2003. VTC 2003-Fall. 2003 IEEE 58th*, pages 3035–3039, 2003.

[15] Frederick E Daum. Bounds on performance for multiple target tracking. *Automatic Control, IEEE Transactions on*, 35(4):443–446, 1990.

[16] Richard M Karp. *Reducibility among combinatorial problems.* Springer, 1972.

[17] Adrian Dumitrescu and János Pach. Minimum clique partition in unit disk graphs. *Graphs and Combinatorics*, 27(3):399–411, 2011.

Demo: Road Speed Profile: From GPS Traces to Real-time Traffic Speed

Mohamed Taher Alrefaie
CREATE-NET, Trento (Italy)
malrefaie@create-net.org

ABSTRACT

GPS-Enabled devices such as smartphones are widely used. With GPS chips that uses lower energy, GPS location and traces are widely collected by different users. One important useful usage is extracting the speed of a user in vehicle to determine real-time and historical speed of traffic in each road in the city. Accumulating these speed records allows the creation of speed profiles. Speed profiles define the general behavior (i.e., traffic speed) of each road at each time of the day. In this demo, we show an energy-efficient location acquisition algorithm to collect traces, a map-matching algorithm to construct the path that the user has taken, an algorithm to calculate the average speed of the vehicle and a speed profile of different road segments used to provide historical, real-time and predicted traffic speed. We also display the whole system in action with data of over 1000 traces collected in Trento, Italy.

Keywords

Intelligent Transportation Systems, Floating Car Data

1. INTRODUCTION

As modern hand-held location-aware devices such as smartphones are rapidly used, user localization is becoming an essential information to be exploited by a variety of services. As the energy consumption of GPS chips integrated in smartphones are rapidly decreasing, users are incrementally using such location-based and location-aware services [1]. Such usage creates a huge amount of spatio-temporal data that could entail a lot of information about mobility patterns, traffic status and driving behavior in urban and suburban areas. With this knowledge, there is a great potential in creating systems that utilize such data to detect, predict and monitor traffic conditions. Being motivated by the availability of such data, a lot of research is carried out to create traffic monitoring systems that could be based on such entailed information without the deployment of expensive traffic management infrastructure to acquire mostly the same data. [2]

Spatio-temporal data are typically a trace of GPS points. Each point consists of a latitude, longitude and timestamp. Such traces could be easily collected using smartphones or even vehicles with GPS-enabled devices. These points are then mapped to a digital map, then matched with nearby roads, then a smart shortest path is calculated between each two points to reconstruct the full path that the user has taken. This process is defined as map-matching. [2]

With the reconstructed path and timestamps, the speed of the vehicle could be easily inferred in each road segment. The road segment is defined as small road between two subsequent intersections in any street. The speed of traffic flow in this road segment could be provided immediately as a real-time speed update for any digital journey planner such as Google Maps or SUPERHUB [3] to define an optimal fastest route between two points in a map. Then, speed records for each road segment are accumulated and stored to create the speed profile. It is defined as series of speed records with timestamps throughout different periods of the day (e.g, 10AM, morning, afternoon, ..) and different days such as weekends, working days or specific day of the week annotated with weather status and existence of any big events around. Such data defines the general behavior of the road in every hour in each day. However, this data alone is incapable of predicting disruptive events that might happen in the future. However, real-time updates inferred from GPS traces collected in real-time can easily infer such unexpected events.

Therefore, the speed profile is capable of delivering 1) real-time speed updates as long as there are new traces being uploaded the system, 2) estimated current and future speed based on the general behavior of the road at the specified time, and 3) all historical data collected before. Such data is a great asset to build efficient journey and route planning algorithms. Also, it would help decision makers to identify the general behavior of roads, understand where and when congestions generally occur and therefore take an action.

2. DATA COLLECTION

The algorithm illustrated in Alg. 1 implemented in [2] introduces an energy-efficient data localization algorithm to lower the sampling rate of the algorithm for the aim of preserving the energy of smartphones while maintaining the performance of map-matching algorithm. Of course, the lower the GPS samples, the lower the energy consumption. However, very low sampling rate could ruin the performance of the map-matching algorithm as seen in fig. ??. Using this algorithm, we balance between both the constraints of energy preservation and map-matching performance. [2]

MobiHoc'14, August 11–14, 2014, Philadelphia, PA, USA.
ACM 978-1-4503-2620-9/14/08.
http://dx.doi.org/10.1145/2632951.2636055.

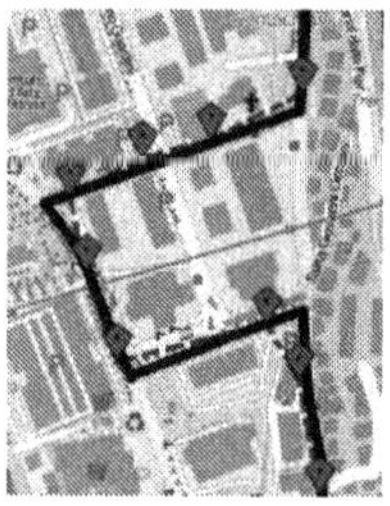
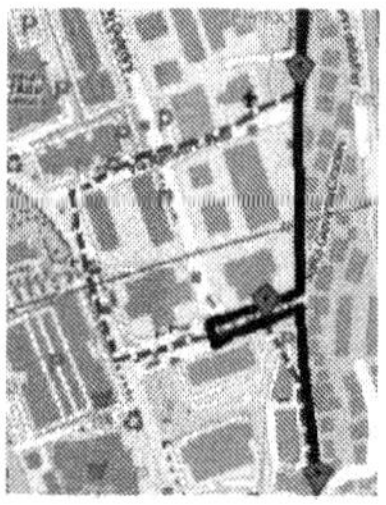
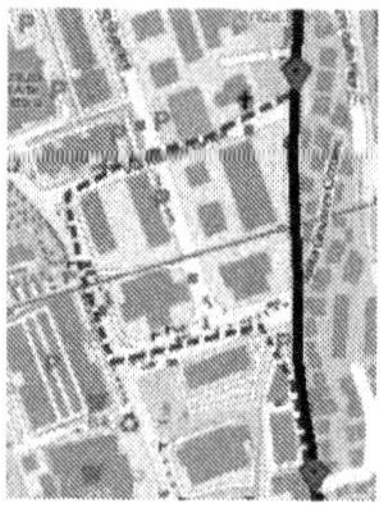

Figure 1: High sampling Figure 2: Medium sampling Figure 3: Low sampling

Figure 4: Reconstructed paths in the case of a low, medium and high GPS sampling rate. The dotted line is the original path, the continuous line is reconstructed path.

Algorithm 1 Location sampling algorithm

```
accTHR = 30;                        ▷ Localization accuracy threshold.
location = networkLocalization();
if location.accuracy ≥ accTHR then
    location = GPSLocalization();
end if
```

3. DATA ANALYSIS

3.1 Data Preprocessing

Once data is collected, it's transferred to the server to be analyzed. After passing an initial preprocessing check, it's passed to two subsequent phases, the map-matching step then the speed calculation step. Data preprocessing checks if the duration of the journey is valid and the time difference between each two subsequent points doesn't exceed 5 minutes, the GPS trace is valid. If the trace has any difference more than 5 minutes, it's split into two traces.

3.2 Map Matching

Map-matching is the process of positioning each location point into a digital map, reference it to the most relevant adjacent road link, reconstruct the path between each road link to fully reconstruct the whole journey followed by the vehicle or the car. In this demo, we use the ST-Matching algorithm [4] as it's widely accepted algorithm for reconstructing paths using low sampling GPS traces.

The first step of ST-Matching algorithm is projecting the GPS point on the nearest road link. Projection here means finding the nearest road link to the GPS point. When sampling rate is very frequent, this could be enough to reconstruct the full path preciously. However, with low sampling rate, ST-Matching algorithm takes an additional step to find the path between two subsequent road links. Shortest path calculated by Dijkstra algorithm could be based on shortest time or shortest length [4]. In our implementation, we use the shortest length as it was proved to be more precise. Finally, the full path followed by the user is fully reconstructed usually by an average performance of 85% as indicated in [2] when the sampling rate is around 30-40 seconds.

3.3 Speed Calculation

Using Open Street Maps as our digital map, we calculate the speed between two subsequent GPS points based on the distance between them divided by the time difference. Calculating the distance has to be precise and well-defined to avoid any noise. Therefore, we calculate the distance by determining the distance between the projected GPS point on the nearest road link. The projected GPS point is the new GPS point inside the nearest road link which is determined by taking a vertical line starting from the original GPS point coordinates to the closest point in the road segment. Distance between these two projected GPS coordinates are calculated and divided by the time difference between their corresponding timestamps.

3.4 Speed Profiles

Speed profile as we define here is basically set of statistical tools that identifies the general average speed in each half an hour of the day. As generally known, average speed of traffic follows a pattern based on hour of the day and day of the week. Based on this common sense and when there is not real-time updates, we estimate the current average speed of the road in a specific time by looking up historical data of the same time in the same day. If number of speed samples is insufficient, we generalize the look up to include similar days (working days, or weekend) or to look up adjacent roads. Finally, if no data exists, we return the maximum speed multiplied by the average speed deduction percentage on the same road type (i.e., roadway, motorway, etc) at the same time of the day around the road.

4. CONCLUSIONS

GPS traces of smartphones that users collect while driving are a great source to infer average speed of road traffic. Such data is collected from many users continuously then analyzed to provide real-time updates of traffic speed in a city. With the accumulation of this data, a speed profile is created. Speed profiles define the speed of car traffic in each road at a certain time of the day. We introduce an algorithm that efficiently collects the GPS traces and another algorithm to process the traces and extracts the average speed of traffic flow in each road.

5. ACKNOWLEDGMENT

We thank all volunteers who collected GPS traces that helped us conduct this research. This work has been partially co-financed by the FP7 IP Project SUPERHUB N. 289067 and by the Industria2015 MOTUS project.

6. REFERENCES

[1] Foursquare. https://foursquare.com/.

[2] M. Alrefaie, I. Carreras, F. Cartolano, R. Di Cello, and F. De Rango. Map matching accuracy: Energy efficient location sampling using smartphones. In *Intelligent Transportation Systems - (ITSC), 2013 16th International IEEE Conference on*, pages 2243–2248, Oct 2013.

[3] P. J. Forbes, S. Wells, J. Masthoff, and H. Nguyen. Superhub: Integrating behaviour change theories into a sustainable urban-mobility platform. In *Using Technology to Facilitate Behaviour Change and Support Healthy, Sustainable Living Workshop at BHCI*, 2012.

[4] Y. Zheng, Q. Li, Y. Chen, X. Xie, and W.-Y. Ma. Understanding mobility based on gps data. In *Proc. of UBICOMP*, Seoul, Korea, 2008.

Demo: Routing Overlay for Reliable Communication in Networks with Blockage *

William C. Barto, Andrea Brennen, Laura Herrera, Nathaniel M. Jones,
Scott Pudlewski, Brooke Shrader, and Andrew P. Worthen
Lincoln Laboratory, Massachusetts Institute of Technology
244 Wood Street, Lexington, Massachusetts, USA

ABSTRACT

This work addresses the challenge in providing reliable communication in mobile networks with intermittent, on/off links through the use of a routing overlay designed to deal with these channel impairments. Link blockage is a predominant feature of mobile networks operating at 10+ GHz frequencies, and current techniques are ill-suited to address this problem. We present an approach comprised of multiple-path routing with end-to-end coding, queue-length-based congestion control, and a negative acknowledgement (NACK) loss-recovery scheme; these are implemented in an IP-overlay. The demonstrated scenario consists of two clusters of mobile ground vehicles operating in an "urban canyon" environment. Blockage occurs on satellite links connecting the clusters. Through the use of interactive displays, demo participants gain an understanding of routing behavior.

Categories and Subject Descriptors

C.2.1 [**Computer-Communication Networks**]: Network Architecture and Design - Wireless Communications

Keywords

blockage channel; multipath routing; overlay; queue-based congestion control; reliability

1. PROBLEM AND APPROACH

Mobile wireless networks can be subjected to channel blockage, where obstructions in the environment lead to on/off link behavior. Blockage is predominant in systems that operate at frequencies of tens of GHz, including mobile satellite communication (satcom) systems, as presented in this demonstration, as well as projected future commercial wireless networks, as shown by channel measurements in unlicensed bands [2, 3].

Especially challenging are recurring link blockages that last on the order of seconds. As shown in Fig. 1, solutions to combat small-scale fading, which causes outages lasting micro- or milli-seconds, are available for use in current systems, but would impose large delays when applied to longer outages. On the other hand, outages lasting minutes or longer are handled by current routing protocols. This includes routing protocols developed for the delay/disruption-tolerant networking paradigm, where a communication link between a pair of nodes only exists occasionally, as governed by the node pairs' inter-contact time. By contrast, in our scenario, communication links between pairs of nodes are persistent, but the link is sometimes blocked. Our focus is on link blockages that span seconds, as determined by the speed of the mobile and size of the obstruction. This problem is not addressed by current techniques.

We argue that the best way to combat blockages at these timescales is at and above the network layer. We demonstrate an approach consisting of three components.

- Concurrent routing over multiple paths, which provides robustness to blockages on any single link or path, coupled with end-to-end block coding, which improves efficiency by enabling the transmission of non-redundant data on different paths;
- queue-length-based congestion control and a loss recovery scheme that uses NACKs indicating the deficiency in decoding particular blocks; and

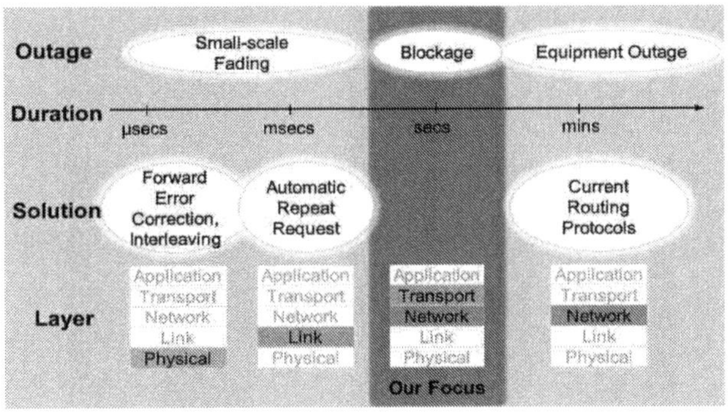

Figure 1: Comparison of durations and techniques to combat outages.

*This work is sponsored by the Office of the Assistant Secretary of Defense for Research and Engineering under Air Force Contract FA8721-05-C-0002. Opinions, interpretations, conclusions and recommendations are those of the author and are not necessarily endorsed by the United States Government.
Contact: brooke.shrader@ll.mit.edu

MobiHoc'14, August 11–14, 2014, Philadelphia, PA, USA.
ACM 978-1-4503-2620-9/14/08.
http://dx.doi.org/10.1145/2632951.2636056.

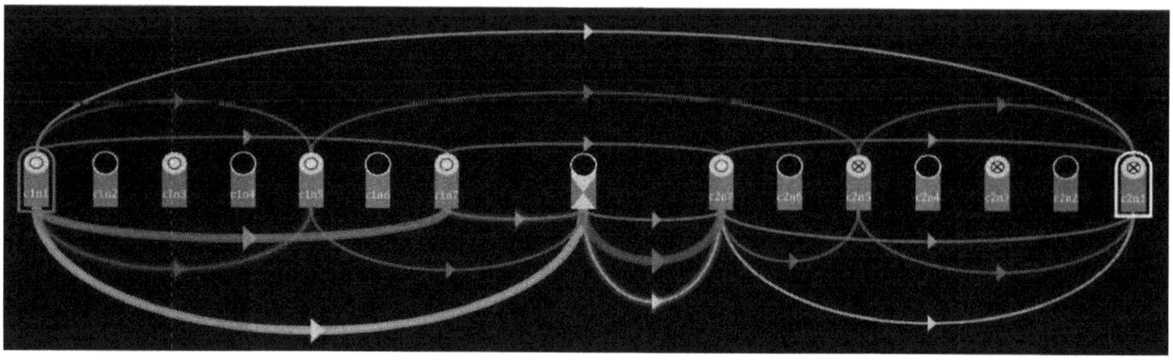

Figure 3: Snapshot of two clusters of mobile nodes connected by satellite (center node). Filled circles indicate satcom-enabled nodes, and an × indicates blockage. Lines above nodes show logical overlay routes, where each hop of the route initiates and terminates at an overlay node. Lines below nodes show the corresponding underlay routes, as chosen by the underlay routing protocol; line thickness indicates relative traffic intensity.

Figure 2: Overhead view of Cambridge, Mass., with satellite link conditions overlaid on roads [1]. Yellow: unblocked. Red: blocked.

- an IP-overlay implementation, which provides compatibility with current systems and the option of deployment to a subset of network nodes.

We refer to this collection of techniques as the "routing overlay" approach.

2. DEMONSTRATION

We demonstrate the problem and the routing overlay approach in a scenario with urban satcom blockage. The network consists of two clusters of ground mobile vehicles; clusters are connected by satellite. Within each cluster, nodes communicate over a fully-connected wireless network with error-free, fixed-rate links. Four of the seven nodes in each cluster are satcom-enabled and their satcom links can experience blockage. The blockage realizations use data from field measurements in Massachusetts for EHF satcom [1].

This scenario is setup and executed in a network simulator, and the routing overlay approach operates as follows.

- There are three static overlay paths. Random linear coding over $\mathbb{GF}(256)$ with blocks of twelve packets (1400 bytes/packet) is performed as described in [4]. Initially four coded packets are sent on each path.
- The congestion controller operates by tracking and constraining the largest queue among all overlay nodes on all paths. A delay-based algorithm is used to estimate capacity on overlay edges, i.e., between pairs of overlay nodes. The error recovery scheme sends additional coded packets, as needed, equally among all paths.
- All of the above is implemented in a standalone engine that interfaces with IP and UDP. Only satcom-capable mobile nodes are overlay nodes. A single-path routing protocol (OSPFv3) runs in the underlay network to provide routes between overlay nodes.

The demonstration provides multiple displays, synchronized in time, and showing the environment and satellite link conditions (e.g., Fig. 2), the operation of a baseline set of routing and transport protocols, the operation of the routing overlay approach (e.g., Fig. 3), and file transfer application performance. It is interactive: participants can enable/disable views of different traffic flows and can pause, fast-forward and rewind to watch blockage state changes and the corresponding behavior of routing. This demonstration provides a means of understanding and visualizing the operation of routing protocols, which is especially challenging in large networks and networks with multiple routing layers.

3. REFERENCES

[1] W. M. Smith, "Channel Characterization for EHF Satellite Communications On the Move," *MIT Lincoln Laboratory Technical Report,* TR-1109, 12 July 2006.

[2] S. Rangan, T. S. Rappaport, and E. Erkip, "Millimeter Wave Wireless Networks: Potentials and Challenges," *Proceedings of the IEEE,* March 2014.

[3] J. G. Andrews, S. Buzzi, W. Choi, S. Hanly, A. Lozano, A. C. K. Soong, and J. C. Zhang, "What Will 5G Be?" *IEEE Journal on Selected Areas in Communications,* September 2014, to appear.

[4] B. Shrader, A. Babikyan, N. M. Jones, T. H. Shake, and A. P. Worthen, "Rate Control for Network-Coded Multipath Relaying with Time-varying Connectivity," *IEEE Journal on Selected Areas in Communications,* May 2011.

Demo: An Energy Synchronized Charging Protocol for Rechargeable Wireless Sensor Networks

Lingkun Fu
State Key Laboratory of Industrial Control Technology
Zhejiang University
lkfu@iipc.zju.edu.cn

Hao Liu
State Key Laboratory of Industrial Control Technology
Zhejiang University
liu_hao@zju.edu.cn

Liang He
Singapore University of Technology and Design
Singapore, 138682
he_liang@sutd.edu.sg

Yu Gu
Singapore University of Technology and Design
Singapore, 138682
jasongu@sutd.edu.sg

Peng Cheng
State Key Laboratory of Industrial Control Technology
Zhejiang University
pcheng@iipc.zju.edu.cn

Jiming Chen
State Key Laboratory of Industrial Control Technology
Zhejiang University
jmchen@iipc.zju.edu.cn

ABSTRACT

Different from energy harvesting which generates dynamic energy supplies, the mobile charger is able to provide stable and reliable energy supply for sensor nodes, and thus enables sustainable system operations. While previous mobile charging protocols either focus on the charger travel distance or the charging delay of sensor nodes, in this work we propose a novel Energy Synchronized Charging (ESync) protocol, which simultaneously reduces both of them. Observing the limitation of the Traveling Salesman Problem (TSP)-based solutions when nodes energy consumptions are diverse, we construct a set of nested TSP tours based on their energy consumption rates, and only nodes with low remaining energy are involved in each charging round. Furthermore, we propose the concept of energy synchronization to synchronize the charging requests sequence of nodes with their sequence on the TSP tours.

Categories and Subject Descriptors

C.2.2 [**Computer-Communication Networks**]: Network protocols

General Terms

Design, Testbed

Keywords

Mobile Charging, Energy Synchronization, Nested TSP Tours

1. INTRODUCTION

To address the energy constraints of sensor nodes, the concepts and implementations of adopting mobile chargers to replenish nodes energy supply in rechargeable sensor networks have attracted a lot of attentions in the research community recently [3]. Different from traditional energy harvesting sensor networks, where the harvested energy is dynamic in both the spatial and temporal dimensions, the mobility-assisted energy replenishment provides a stable and reliable energy supply for sensor nodes and thus enables truly sustainable operations of sensor networks. Due to the limited mobility of the charger, the scheduling of charging tasks for sensor nodes in the network plays a critical role in achieving a high charging efficiency. The Traveling Salesman Problem (TSP)-based charging protocols are a family of classic solutions to the mobile charging problem, with which in general, the mobile charger periodically carries out the charging process following a pre-optimized tour [4]. As a result, the charging of nodes can be accomplished with a short charger travel distance and thus a short time duration.

However, the limitation of TSP-based solutions is that when nodes energy consumptions are diverse, it may lead to the unnecessary visits of energy-sufficient nodes. This not only increases the charger travel distance when performing the charging tasks of sensor nodes, but also prolongs the waiting time before the energy-hungry nodes can be charged. To address this issue, we investigate the on-demand mobile charging scenario where nodes are charged only when necessary in our recent work [1]. Specifically, sensor nodes send

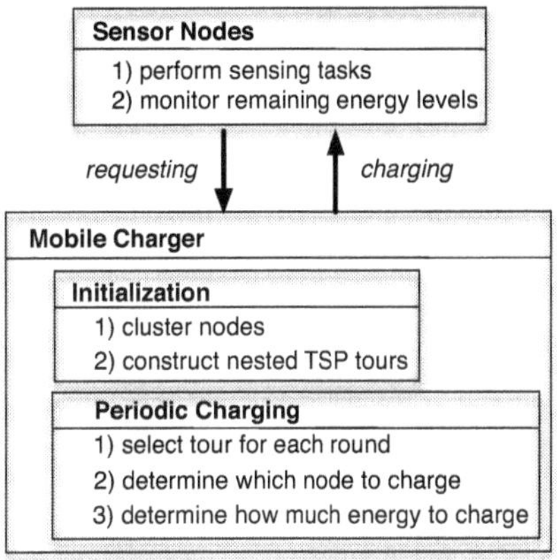

Figure 1: An overview of the proposed ESync charging protocol.

MobiHoc '14, Aug 11-14 2014, Philadelphia, PA, USA
ACM 978-1-4503-2620-9/14/08.
http://dx.doi.org/10.1145/2632951.2636057.

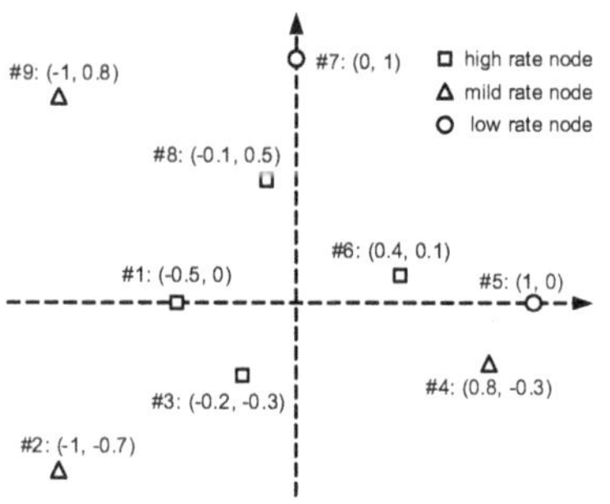

Figure 2: Nodes deployments.

Figure 3: Overview of the experiment settings.

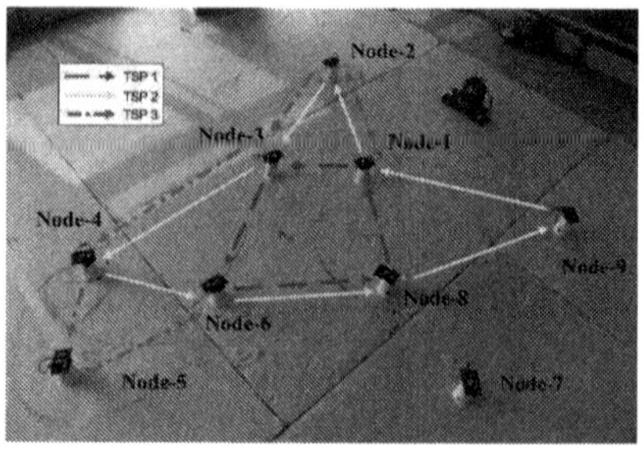

Figure 4: Nodes clustering and tour construction.

out charging requests to the mobile charger when their energy levels are low, and the charger replenishes their energy supply according to those received requests. We aim to design a novel mobile charging protocol that is able to leverage on the advantages of existing designs while minimizing the impact of their limitations.

2. ESYNC DESIGN

The most significant feature in our design in [1] is synchronizing the energy supply of sensor nodes based on a set of nested TSP tours. Upon achieving such energy synchronization, we can realize the ideal mobile charging paradigm that *the charger can simply travel according to the TSP tours to reduce its travel distance, and whenever a sensor node runs short of energy, the charger will happen to be traveling towards it.*

At the macro-level of the mobile charging process, to leverage the advantage of the TSP-based solutions while minimizing the impact of their limitations when node energy consumptions are highly diverse, we construct a set of nested TSP tours based on the energy consumption rates of sensor nodes. Then for each round of the charging process, a novel tour selection algorithm is designed to only involve the energy-hungry nodes into the charging schedule during that round. At the micro-level focusing on the charging schedule during individual rounds, observing that nodes charging requests sequence may significantly degrade the charging performance, we propose the concept of energy synchronization among nodes to proactively match nodes charging requests sequence to the selected TSP tour in each charging round, which is achieved by carefully selecting the node to be charged next and controlling the amount of energy charged to individual nodes. As a result, both the charger travel distance and the charging delay of sensor nodes are reduced. Figure 1 presents an illustrative view of our design from the aspects of both the charger and sensor nodes.

3. EVALUATION

In our experiment, we randomly deploy 9 sensor nodes in an open field of 3×3 m^2, and a LEGO Ministorms NXT robot with an average travel speed of 0.1 m per second is adopted as the mobile charger. The locations of these nodes are shown in Fig. 2. Figure 3 shows our experiment settings. These 9 sensor nodes are organized into 3 clusters based on their energy consumption rates (i.e., $\{1, 3, 6, 8\}$, $\{2, 4, 9\}$, and $\{5, 7\}$), and 3 nested TSP tours are constructed accordingly, as highlighted in Fig. 4. Sensor nodes send out charging requests to the charger when their energy supply is depleted, and the charger performs these charging tasks according to ESync.

We evaluate the performance of ESync and compare it with two classic baselines: TSP and Nearest-Job-Next [2]. For TSP, the charger travels and charges nodes following the TSP tour, and its travel is independent of whether the charging request from the node has been received. For Nearest-Job-Next, the charger always selects the geographically nearest requesting node as the next node to charge. Both the two baselines adopt the full charging of nodes throughout the charging process.

A mobile charging process of 15 minutes is performed in each experiment, and the requests charging latency and charger travel distance during these charging processes are recorded for evaluation. Our experiment results show that the charger travel distance resultant by ESync is about 30% and 20% shorter than those obtained by TSP and Nearest-Job-Next, and the request charging latency is reduced by about 50%.

4. DEMONSTRATION DESCRIPTION

In this demo, we will demonstrate and explain the detailed experiment settings and the ESync-based mobile charging process. The demo will also highlight the core idea of our design, i.e., the *energy synchronization*, by visualizing the evaluation process of the remaining energy level of sensor nodes and how it is synchronized with the travel of the charger. A video about this demo can be found at `http://youtu.be/2em2cJZDdMU`.

5. ACKNOWLEDGMENTS

This work is partially supported by iTrust IGDSi1305013, Singapore-MIT International Design Center IDG31000101, SUTD-ZJU/RES/03/2011, NSFC grant 61222305, ZJNSF grant LY14F030016, and National Program for Special Support of Top-Notch Young Professionals.

6. REFERENCES

[1] L. He, L. Fu, L. Zheng, Y. Gu, P. Cheng, J. Chen, and J. Pan. Esync: An energy synchronized charging protocol for rechargeable wireless sensor networks. In *ACM MobiHoc'14*, 2014.

[2] L. He, Y. Gu, J. Pan, and T. Zhu. On-demand charging in wireless sensor networks: Theories and applications. In *IEEE MASS'13*, 2013.

[3] S. He, J. Chen, F. Jiang, D. Yau, G. Xing, and Y. Sun. Energy provisioning in wireless rechargeable sensor networks. In *IEEE INFOCOM'11*, 2011.

[4] Y. Peng, Z. Li, W. Zhang, and D. Qiao. Prolonging sensor network lifetime through wireless charging. In *IEEE RTSS'10*, 2010.

Demo — Dial-a-Ride: A Green Shortest Path Algorithm

Lorenzo Maggi
CREATE-NET, Trento (Italy)
lorenzo.maggi@create-net.org

Mahsa Faizrahnemoon
Hamilton Institute, National University of Ireland Maynooth
mahsa.faizrahnemoon.2013@nuim.ie

ABSTRACT

We consider a Dial-a-ride scenario in which one on-demand bus has to find an efficient route to serve different users willing to reach different destinations. We implemented in MATLAB a shortest path algorithm that minimizes a linear combination of an environmental cost and of the total waiting plus travel time experienced by the travellers. We demonstrate the outcome of the algorithm on the map of Dublin with the software SUMO.

Categories and Subject Descriptors

I.6.3 [**Computing Methodologies**]: Simulation and modeling—*Applications*

Keywords

Bus On Demand, Minimum travel time, Green algorithm

1. INTRODUCTION

Dial-a-ride service, also commonly called demand responsive transport, is the new paradigm for public transport since it allows to tailor the bus' route and schedule to users' needs. Travellers are asked to book the service in advance by specifying their initial position and their intended destination. Each user is then provided with an estimate of the pick-up time, as well as the time at which she will reach her destination. This new form of transportation is clearly more efficient than the more classic fixed-route-fixed-timetable transportation system, both from the network operator's and from the users' perspective. In fact, it permits to reduce the fuel costs, to serve the users more promptly, and eventually to increase the overall efficiency of the transportation system.

Dial-a-ride systems are up and running in USA, Canada, Japan, as well as in several countries in Europe. Such systems has been conceived especially for serving areas where users' demand fluctuates too heavily over time to justify the deployment of fixed bus lines, e.g., rural areas or big cities overnight.

We implement a variant of the dynamic programming algorithm first presented in [2] to design the bus route that minimizes a linear combination of the total service time experienced by all the users and an environmental cost. The shortest path algorithm has been implemented using MATLAB (MATLAB and Statistics Toolbox Release 2012b, The MathWorks, Inc., Natick, Massachusetts, United States). With the support of the software SUMO [1], we show the bus following the optimal route on the map of Dublin, and serving the passengers which are located in - and travel to - one of six different locations.

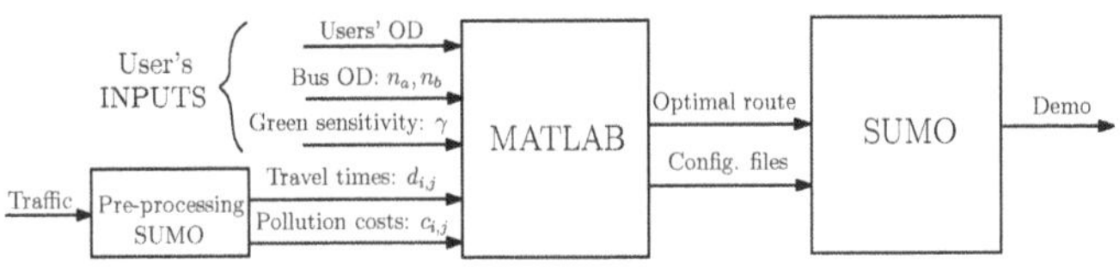

Figure 1: Demo flowchart.

MobiHoc'14, August 11–14, 2014, Philadelphia, PA, USA.
ACM 978-1-4503-2620-9/14/08.
http://dx.doi.org/10.1145/2632951.2636058.

2. GRAPH MODEL

The algorithm that we implement, which is a variant of the one first proposed in [2], provides the optimal route that one on-demand bus should follow in order to minimize a linear combination of an environmental cost and of the total waiting plus travel time for all travellers. It models the road network as a weighted graph $G = (\mathcal{N}, \mathcal{E}, \mathcal{W})$. Each node $n_i \in \mathcal{N}$ represents a bus stop and a link $(n_i, n_j) \in \mathcal{E}$ denotes the presence of a road from n_i to n_j which does not pass through any other bus stop. Each link (n_i, n_j) is characterized by two non-negative weights, $d_{i,j}$ and $c_{i,j}$, describing the travel time between the nodes and the environmental cost that the bus incurs while traversing the link, respectively. For instance, $c_{i,j}$ can be defined as an increasing function of $d_{i,j}$ and of the population density around the road going directly from n_i to n_j.

Let $\mathcal{OD} = \{od^{(k)} = (n_o^{(k)}, n_d^{(k)})\}_k$ be the set of all origin-destination pairs of users waiting for the bus stop at time 0. The pair $od^{(k)}$ is the stream of users waiting at bus stop $n_o^{(k)}$ and intending to reach $n_d^{(k)}$. We call $u^{(k)} \geq 1$ the number of users whose origin-destination pair is $od^{(k)}$. Let n_a and n_b be the initial (at time 0) and final (after all users have reached their destinations) positions of the bus, respectively.

We want to minimize a linear combination of the total waiting plus travel time for all passengers and of the environmental cost of the journey, computed as the sum of costs of the individual links. Let $T_d^{(k)}(p)$ be the time at which user stream k reaches its destination when bus follows path p. Then our goal is to find the optimal p^* minimizing the following objective function:

$$p^* = \underset{p}{\operatorname{argmin}} \sum_{k \in \mathcal{OD}} u^{(k)} T_d^{(k)}(p) + \gamma \sum_{(i,j) \in p} c_{i,j}, \qquad (1)$$

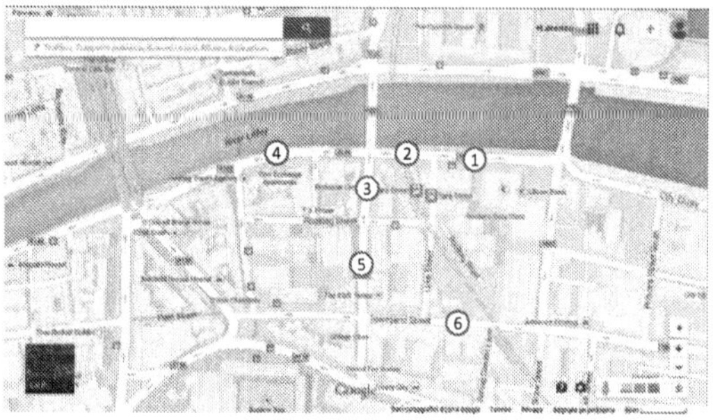

Figure 2: Position of six bus stops on the Dublin map.

where p is a generic feasible path going from node n_a to n_b and $\gamma > 0$ is the environmental sensitivity.

2.1 Shortest path formulation

In order to solve the optimization problem in (1) we utilize a shortest-path formulation. We define an augmented weighted graph $\widetilde{G}$, whose generic augmented node $\widetilde{n}_p \in \widetilde{\mathcal{N}}$ is the quadruple

$$\widetilde{n}_p = (n_i, O, W, S), \tag{2}$$

where $n_i \in \mathcal{N}$ represents the current bus position; O, W, and $S = \mathcal{OD} \setminus (O \cup W)$ are the streams of users that, immediately after the bus has passed by the stop n_i, are on the bus, still waiting at the respective origin nodes, and that have already reached their final destination, respectively.
Now we need to define the directed edges between the nodes in $\widetilde{\mathcal{N}}$. The node $\widetilde{n}_p$ defined as in (2) is connected to the node $\widetilde{n}_q = (n_j, O', W', S')$ whenever $(n_i, n_j) \in \mathcal{E}$ and

$$O' = O \setminus \left\{ od^{(k)} \in O : n_d^{(k)} = n_j \right\} \cup \left\{ od^{(k)} \in W : n_o^{(k)} = n_j \right\},$$
$$W' = W \setminus \left\{ od^{(k)} \in W : n_o^{(k)} = n_i \right\},$$
$$S' = S \cup \left\{ od^{(k)} \in O : n_d^{(k)} = n_j \right\}.$$

The weight $w'_{p,q}$ associated to the edge $(\widetilde{n}_p, \widetilde{n}_q)$ is

$$w'_{p,q} = d_{i,j} \sum_{k: od^{(k)} \notin S} u^{(k)} + \gamma c_{i,j},$$

where the first term is the incremental waiting plus travel time for users that have not reached their intended destination yet.
We intend to find the shortest path $\widetilde{p}^*$ between the initial and final nodes $\widetilde{n}_a$ and $\widetilde{n}_b$, where

$$\widetilde{n}_a = \Big(n_a, \left\{ od^{(k)} \in \mathcal{OD} : n_o^{(k)} = n_a \right\}, \\ \mathcal{OD} \setminus \left\{ od^{(k)} \in \mathcal{OD} : n_o^{(k)} = n_a \right\}, \emptyset \Big)$$

and $\widetilde{n}_b = (n_b, \emptyset, \emptyset, \mathcal{OD})$.

2.2 Shortest path computation

The shortest path $\widetilde{p}^*$ in the augmented graph $\widetilde{G}$ from node $\widetilde{n}_a$ to node $\widetilde{n}_a$ determines the optimal route p^* for the bus (see Eq. 1). In fact, p^* can be read in the first entries of the succession of nodes compounding $\widetilde{p}^*$. We utilized the classic Djikstra algorithm to compute $\widetilde{p}^*$. In order to reduce the complexity of the algorithm, we first reduced the augmented graph $\widetilde{G}$ by performing a breadth-first search of all the nodes that can be possibly reached from the initial one, $\widetilde{n}_a$.

3. DEMO STRUCTURE

In the demo we considered 6 bus stops located in the centre of Dublin, as shown in Figure 2. By utilizing SUMO [1], we first estimated the travel times $d_{i,j}$, grouped in the matrix D, and then we computed the pollution costs as $c_{i,j} = k_{i,j} d_{i,j}$, where $k_{i,j}$ ranges from 2 to 4 according to the population density around the road link (n_i, n_j):

$$D = \begin{bmatrix} - & 8 & 19 & 19 & 44 & 21 \\ 32 & - & - & 10 & 62 & 65 \\ 32 & - & - & 10 & 62 & 65 \\ 53 & 96 & 97 & - & 82 & 85 \\ - & 43 & 43 & 15 & - & 31 \\ - & 45 & 45 & 52 & 29 & - \end{bmatrix}, \quad K = \begin{bmatrix} - & 2 & 3 & 2 & 4 & 4 \\ 2 & - & - & 2 & 4 & 4 \\ 2 & - & - & 2 & 4 & 4 \\ 2 & 2 & 2 & - & 3 & 3 \\ - & 4 & 4 & 4 & - & 4 \\ - & 4 & 4 & 4 & 4 & - \end{bmatrix}$$

By convention, $d_{i,j} = -$ denotes the absence of the direct link, i.e., $(n_i, n_j) \notin \mathcal{E}$. We notice that the resulting graph is densely connected, which makes the computation of the optimal shortest path not trivial.
A demo user can set the following Matlab input (also see Figure 1):

- the Origin/Destination of the passengers, $\mathcal{OD}$, expressed as bus stops between 1 and 6;
- the initial and final position of the bus, n_a and n_b respectively;
- the environmental sensitivity $\gamma > 0$.

Our MATLAB code computes the optimal route as a succession of nodes $p^* = \{n_a, \ldots, n_b\}$ and automatically generates the required SUMO configuration files. Finally, SUMO displays the on-demand bus following the optimal route, picking up and delivering all the users to their intended destination. The bus then terminates its journey in the final node n_b.

We first point out that a trivial solution for the problem is to perform twice an Hamiltonian cycle starting from n_a. Since in each cycle the bus visits each node exactly once, all passengers are ensured to reach their destination. Clearly, such solution is suboptimal. We remark that, if there is a large amount of passengers with the same origin-destination pair, then most likely the bus route will serve them first, in order to minimize the total delay. Finally, increasing the environmental sensitivity γ clearly results in choosing a path p^* which crosses links with lower pollution costs.

4. CONCLUSIONS

We considered a Dial-a-ride system and we implemented in MATLAB a variant of the algorithm in [2], that computes the bus routes that minimizes the linear combination of an environmental cost and of the total waiting plus travel time for the users. We display the resulting optimal bus route on the Dublin map with the aid of the software SUMO [1].

Acknowledgments

This work was supported by the European Commission under TEAM, a large scale integrated project part of the FP7-ICT for Cooperative Systems for energy-efficient and sustainable mobility.

5. REFERENCES

[1] D. Krajzewicz, J. Erdmann, M. Behrisch, and L. Bieker. Recent development and applications of SUMO - Simulation of Urban MObility. *International Journal On Advances in Systems and Measurements*, 5(3&4):128–138, December 2012.

[2] H. N. Psaraftis. A dynamic programming solution to the single vehicle many-to-many immediate request dial-a-ride problem. *Transportation Science*, 14(2):130–154, 1980.

Demo: Recommendation System for Dynamic Spectrum Access Through Spectrum Mining and Prediction

Ying Dai
Department of Computer and Information Sciences
Temple University
Philadelphia, PA 19122
ying.dai@temple.edu

Andrew Daniels
Department of Computer and Information Sciences
Temple University
Philadelphia, PA 19122
andrew.s.daniels@temple.edu

Jie Wu
Department of Computer and Information Sciences
Temple University
Philadelphia, PA 19122
jiewu@temple.edu

ABSTRACT

Dynamic spectrum access (DSA) [2] is a promising solution for improving the efficiency of channel utilization. The current spectrum allocation is static with many spectrum resources that are used very infrequently and are wasted. The DSA enables secondary users, or nodes, to transmit data packets on channels that are assigned to primary users (PUs). The constraint here is to make sure that PUs are not interfered with by SUs. Fig. 1 is an example with nodes that can make use of the spectrum when it is not occupied by the PU.

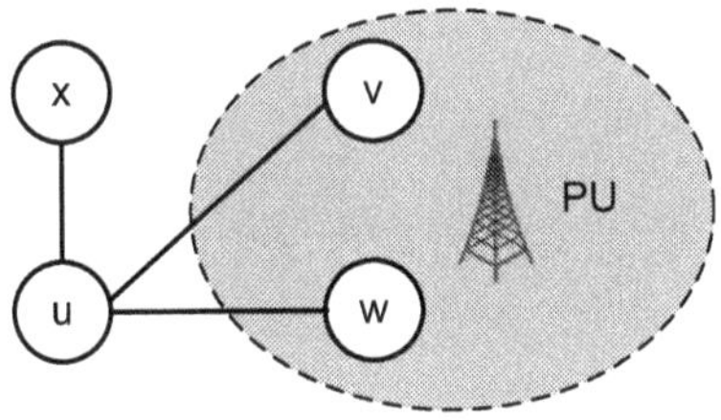

Figure 1: An example of DSA.

To make sure the PUs are not interfered with, one key component is the spectrum sensing. Many works have been done on spectrum sensing [5]. However, among the overall spectrums, white spaces are the parts whose usage can be exploited at specific times and locations. These patterns reduce the necessity of spectrum sensing, and motivate the database-driven schemes [4]. The IEEE 802.11af [3] defines the standard for spectrum sharing on white spaces. It relies on the database to provide white space maps over time at given locations. Every node can use the spectrum based on the given white space map. However, it is difficult and impractical to provide or construct such a spectrum database for all spectrums.

Inspired by the spectrum database in the white spaces, we propose a recommendation whose function is similar to that of the spectrum database. We aim at predicting the spectrum availabilities and recommending the part that is more likely to be available for the usage of SUs. The prediction on the spectrum availabilities is through running the spectrum mining algorithm on the collected spectrum data. Therefore, the two main components for our demo are the data collection and spectrum mining, as shown in Fig. 2. After the mining process is finished, our system would give the predictions and recommendations on the spectrum that is more likely to be available.

MobiHoc'14, August 11–14, 2014, Philadelphia, PA, USA.
ACM 978-1-4503-2620-9/14/08.
http://dx.doi.org/10.1145/2632951.2636059.

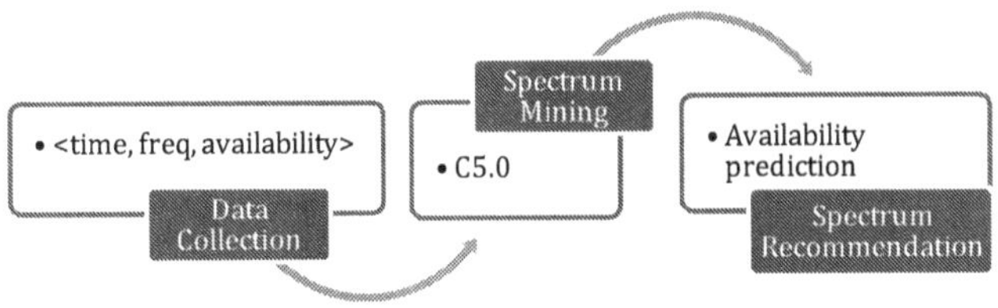

Figure 2: The process of our recommendation system.

The data collection is performed by the Universal Software Radio Peripheral (USRP) platforms, with two daughterboards (RFX 1200 and Basic RX). Due to the reason that the availability is both time- and frequency-sensitive, each data entry within our collected results contains three dimensional information: time, spectrum, and availability. The time here is the system time. The spectrum is the central frequency of each channel we divided. The availability is determined by setting a threshold on the SINR value on the receiver's side.

Currently, for the RFX 1200 daughterboard, we have 7 channels and each has a 40 MHz bandwidth. For the Basic RX daughterboard, we have 2 channels and each has a 100 MHz bandwidth. The overview of the testbed for data collection is shown in Fig. 3. We use the corresponding senders (PUs) with RFX 1200 and Basic TX on the other side to generate the data, due to the limitation of the antenna ranges. Our program automatically switches among the subchannels. For every subchannel, it stays for three seconds to sense the signal strength.

We make use of the tools for See5 and C5.0[1] to mine the rules in the collected data set. The original collected data entry in the file contains the <time, central frequency, availability>. The collected data sample is shown in Fig. 4. The time is the system. Every 3 seconds, the receiver automatically jumps to the next channel. The availability is

Figure 3: The overview of the data collection.

a binary value, by setting a threshold to the SINR values. The SINR values are calculated as the average value during the 3 seconds. The availability is set as the targeted value, which needs to be predicted for the future. Currently, our dataset is collected in 1 hour, which will be extended in the future. The generated rules are used to predict the channel availabilities given a specific time and frequency information. The location here is static in our testbed due to the antenna range limitation. We will extend it to different locations and add the location dimension to the dataset.

```
2014-05-30 16:18:25,1280000000,1
2014-05-30 16:18:28,1300000000,1
2014-05-30 16:18:31,1320000000,1
2014-05-30 16:18:34,1340000000,0
2014-05-30 16:18:37,1360000000,1
2014-05-30 16:18:40,1380000000,0
2014-05-30 16:18:43,1400000000,0
2014-05-30 16:18:46,1420000000,0
2014-05-30 16:18:49,1440000000,0
2014-05-30 16:18:52,1160000000,1
2014-05-30 16:18:55,1180000000,0
```

Figure 4: The screenshot of the collected data sample.

The other specifications for our demo are:

- Equipments to be used for the demo: Four USRP N200 with four daughterboards (RFX1200, Basic TX/RX); Two laptops.
- Space needed and the required setup time: $2 \times 2\ m^2$; 20-30 mins.
- Additional facilities needed: Six power supplies.

Through our demo, we show the potential of building the spectrum recommendation system for any spectrum range. Instead of the current sensing-only or database-driven schemes, the recommendation system can be a hybrid approach of the sensing-only and database-driven schemes. Every node can receive the recommendation on the spectrum that is more likely to be available, and can sense the spectrum to make sure the PUs are inactive. In this way, the sensing efficiency can be improved, and the PUs can be better protected. The mining part can be deployed in a distributed way, either on the selected nodes or new components that are similar to the current location-based databases.

Our future work includes adding the location dimension to our dataset. The limited space and antenna range makes it impractical to include location information in the current data collection. Also, we are going to explore the performance differences among different parameter settings, including the sensing time, channel switching time, and the number of subchannels.

1. REFERENCES

[1] Data mining tools see5 and c5.0, http://www.rulequest.com/see5-info.html.

[2] I. F. Akyildiz, W.-Y. Lee, M. C. Vuran, and S. Mohanty. Next generation/dynamic spectrum access/cognitive radio wireless networks: A survey. *Computer Networks*, 2006.

[3] A. Flores, R. Guerra, E. Knightly, P. Ecclesine, and S. Pandey. Ieee 802.11af: a standard for tv white space spectrum sharing. *IEEE Communications Magazine*, 2013.

[4] R. Murty, R. Chandra, T. Moscibroda, and P. Bahl. Senseless: A database-driven white spaces network. *IEEE Transactions on Mobile Computing*, 2012.

[5] T. Yucek and H. Arslan. A survey of spectrum sensing algorithms for cognitive radio applications. *IEEE Communications Surveys Tutorials*, 2009.

Demo: An Augmented Reality Based File Transfer System for Mobile Users Using Smart Phones

Lien-Wu Chen
Department of Information Engineering and Computer Science, Feng Chia University, Taichung, 407, Taiwan
lwuchen@fcu.edu.tw

Yu-Fan Ho
Department of Information Engineering and Computer Science, Feng Chia University, Taichung, 407, Taiwan
d0163158@fcu.edu.tw

Wei-Ting Kuo
Department of Information Engineering and Computer Science, Feng Chia University, Taichung, 407, Taiwan
d0165621@fcu.edu.tw

ABSTRACT

In this paper, we design an augmented reality based file transfer system called ShareAR. The ShareAR system only needs a single-finger action that drags the file icon to the target face on the screen of a mobile device. The dragged file can be transmitted to the target receiver who gets the file immediately as her/his mobile device is on-line or receives the file later after connecting to the Internet. Through ShareAR, users do not need to know the target account in advance. In addition, users do not need to input account information by themselves. Furthermore, users can select a specific target among multiple candidates from the camera of a mobile device. ShareAR reveals an innovative user interface to transfer files between mobile devices. We have implemented an Android-based ShareAR system that outperforms existing schemes in experimental results.

Categories and Subject Descriptors: C.2.1 [Network Architecture and Design]: Network communications

Keywords: Augmented Reality; Cloud Computing; Face Recognition; File Transfer; Mobile Device

1. INTRODUCTION

Growing popularity of mobile devices with Wi-Fi/3G communications has made file sharing without desktop/laptop computers possible. A specific file can be immediately transmitted to other people through mobile devices. However, most of file sharing systems for mobile devices have to obtain the target's account information or session key in advance, such as E-MAIL [1], Bluetooth [2], Dropbox [3], etc. In addition, users have to input it by hands before transmitting files to the target receiver. The procedures of manual intervention may increase the time and inconvenience of file sharing between mobile devices.

Currently, Wi-Fi/3G [3, 4, 5] or Bluetooth [6] communications are usually adopted for file transfer between mobile devices. There are several limitations in Bluetooth communications. First, the distance of the sender and receiver have to be less than ten meters. Second, the target Bluetooth device has to be searched and then selected. Third, the sender/receiver has to obtain the session key and input it for device pairing. Finally, the transmission time may be quite long due to the low data rate of Bluetooth. On the other hand, Near Field Communication (NFC) has been employed to simplify the connection procedures of Bluetooth for device pairing [6]. The steps of manually searching and selecting the target Bluetooth device can be omitted by NFC. However, the sender and receiver have to put their mobile devices together. In particular, only hi-end mobile devices have built-in NFC tags.

MobiHoc'14, August 11–14, 2014, Philadelphia, PA, USA.
ACM 978-1-4503-2620-9/14/08.
http://dx.doi.org/10.1145/2632951.2636060.

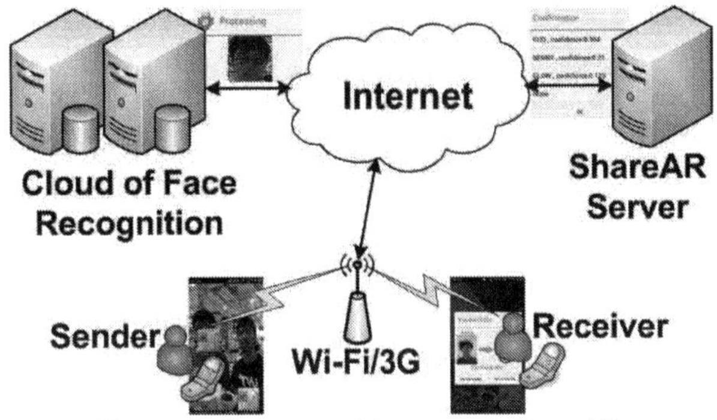

Figure 1: System architecture of ShareAR.

Similarly, there are several limitations in Wi-Fi/3G communications. First, the sender and receiver have to connect to specific Web sites or download dedicated Apps to share files. Second, the sender has to query the receiver's account in advance. Third, the sender has to input account information into Apps or browsers for sending files. It is inconvenient and time-consuming to obtain and input the target's account or file download link in existing file transfer systems [1, 3, 4, 5].

To improve file sharing for mobile users, we design and implement the ShareAR system for file transfer between mobile devices based on augmented reality and cloud computing. Users just need to drag the file icon to the target face on the screen of a mobile device. The contributions of ShareAR are four-fold. First, mobile users do not need to know the receiver's account in advance. Second, mobile users do not need to input account information by themselves. Third, mobile users can select a specific receiver among multiple candidates from the camera of a mobile device. Finally, the total consumption time of file sharing between mobile users can be significantly reduced.

2. SYSTEM DESIGN

Fig. 1 shows the system architecture of ShareAR. On the client side, mobile users use a smart phone with a dedi-

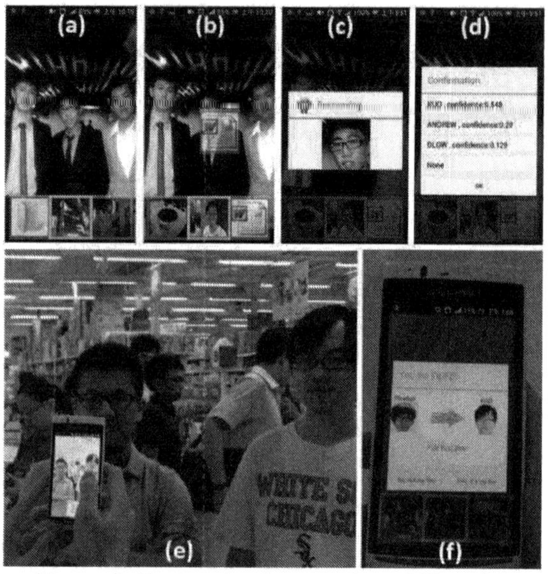

Figure 2: System implementation of ShareAR.

cated ShareAR App to login the ShareAR server through Wi-Fi/3G communications. The sender focuses the camera of the mobile device on the target receiver. Next, the sender drags the file icon to the receiver's face on the screen and then the face photo of the receiver is sent to the ShareAR server. On the server side, the receiver's face photo is forwarded to the cloud of face recognition and then recognized by the cloud servers to obtain the registered ID of the receiver. Next, the dragged file sent from the sender is forwarded to the identified receiver. The file can be immediately obtained by the dedicated ShareAR App running in the receiver's mobile device.

Using the cloud of face recognition, ShareAR can prevent users from querying the receiver's account and avoid keying account information by hands. Using the dedicated App, ShareAR can allow users to drag a file to the receiver's face on the screen in an augmented reality manner for file sharing. Using the ShareAR server, the face photo can be forwarded from the sender to the face recognition cloud for ID identification and the dragged file can be sent to the target receiver. The goal of ShareAR is to minimize the number of manual operations and total consumption time in file sharing between mobile users.

In ShareAR, the file transfer process between mobile devices is optimized as follows. First, the target face can be detected correctly as mobile users drag a file to a specific receiver among multiple candidates from the camera of a mobile device. Second, the target face can be transmitted rapidly and recognized successfully to obtain the receiver's identifier through the cloud servers of face recognition. Third, the receiver's identifier can be confirmed properly by mobile users as the target information is recognized by the cloud servers of face recognition. Finally, the file can be transmitted to the receiver even if her/his mobile device is not connecting to the Internet or without launching the dedicated App.

3. SYSTEM IMPLEMENTATION

We have developed an Android-based ShareAR system. The ShareAR App consists of file browsing and camera preview interfaces, as shown in Fig. 2(a). Users can use their

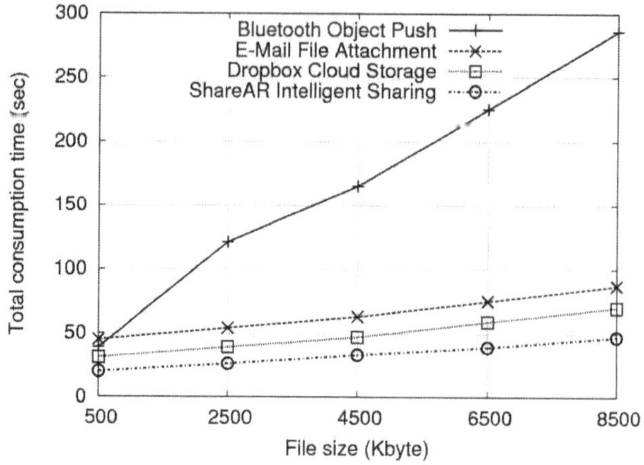

Figure 3: Comparison of existing systems and ShareAR.

fingers to press the file on the screen, drag it to a specific face from the camera, and release the dragged file on the target face, as shown in Fig. 2(b) and Fig. 2(e). To minimize the transmission and recognition time of the face photo, target face detection is implemented on the client side to upload the detected face photo instead of entire image, as shown in Fig. 2(c). For face recognition, the ShareAR server invokes the cloud APIs provided by Mashape and Lambda Labs. Using Mashape cloud APIs, the ShareAR server can send a photo for face recognition, and then receive three registrant IDs with highest face similarity. Then, the ShareAR server sends these registrant IDs returned by Mashape cloud APIs to the ShareAR App, as shown in Fig. 2(d). Once one of returned registrant IDs is confirmed as the target receiver, the dragged file can be received immediately by the ShareAR App in the registrant's mobile device, as shown in Fig. 2(f).

Fig. 3 shows comparisons of total consumption time to share files with different sizes. Each experimentation is repeated 10 times by realistic trial and we take the average value. For E-Mail [1], Bluetooth v2.0 [2], and Dropbox [3], the durations to query and input the account/session information are set to 0 and 8 seconds, respectively. Specifically, the total consumption time using E-Mail, Bluetooth, or Dropbox is a lower bound without considering the query duration that could be tens of seconds, even minutes. From Fig. 3, we can observe that ShareAR has the lowest total consumption time with all file sizes. It is because ShareAR users do not need to know and input the receiver's account beforehand, which can save large amounts of time. In contrary, E-Mail, Bluetooth, and Dropbox users need to take considerable time to obtain and input the target account.

4. ACKNOWLEDGMENT

This research is supported in part by NSC under Grant No. NSC102-2221-E-035-031-MY3.

5. REFERENCES

[1] Patrick Kingsley. Father of the email attachment. *The Guardian*, Mar. 2012.

[2] Bluetooth Special Interest Group. https://www.bluetooth.org.

[3] Dropbox - A file host service in cloud storages. https://www.dropbox.com.

[4] I. Lamont. *Google Drive and Docs in 30 Minutes*. 1st ed., The Digital Media Machine, 2012.

[5] Apple Introduces iCloud. http://www.apple.com/pr/library/2011/06/06icloud.html.

[6] L.-B. Yu. A study on NFC-activated Blue-tooth data transmission over Android smart phones. In *Master Thesis, National Taiwan Normal University*, June 2012.

Demo: Efficient Multi-Objective Optimization of Network Problems on Wireless Testbeds

Michael T. Mehari* ,Eli De Poorter, Ingrid Moerman
Ghent University - iMinds, Department of Information Technology (INTEC)
Gaston Crommenlaan 8 (Bus 201), B-9050 Ghent, Belgium
michael.mehari@intec.ugent.be

ABSTRACT

A large amount of research focuses on experimentally optimizing performance of wireless solutions. Finding the optimal performance settings typically requires investigating all possible combinations of design parameters, and as a result the number of required experiments increases exponentially for each considered design parameter. However, Efficient Global Optimization (EGO) algorithms overcome this limitation and arrive at the global optimum performance in a very short time compared to the exhaustive search technique.

In this demo, we apply the SUrrogate MOdeling (SUMO) toolbox, an efficient implementation of EGO algorithms, in order to improve the experimentation time of a realistic wireless conference solution. By tuning a speaker's transmit power and channel parameters, the SUMO toolbox searches for an improved listeners' audio quality having minimum transmission exposure. Moreover, the SUMO experiment is compared to an exhaustive search experiment and it is found that SUMO reached 99.51% of the global optimum performance while requiring 10 times less experiments.

Keywords

wireless experimentation, optimization, testbeds, SUMO

1. INTRODUCTION

Wireless network solutions often tune a number of configurable parameters in order to locate the *optimum settings*. For example, Wi-Fi networks have parameters that can be tweaked at the physical layer (e.g. transmit power, channel, modulation), MAC layer (e.g. inter frame spacing, contention window), network layer (e.g. routing protocol, mobility, topology) and application layer (e.g. throughput, server configurations). Optimizing all or a subset of these parameters is time consuming since the design space grows exponentially for every investigated design parameter. In order to mitigate the time overhead, Efficient Global Optimization (EGO) algorithms [4] can be used that are best fitted to wireless testbeds. SUrrogate MOdeling (SUMO) toolbox [3] is one example of such efficient algorithms. The optimization algorithm starts from a well-chosen initial experimental design, and a global (but only locally accurate) Kriging surrogate model of the objective function is computed. By picking additional points with the highest Expected Improvement (EI) value in the parameter space, the optimization process is directed towards an optimal configuration until a stopping criterion is met.

In literature, the SUMO toolbox is widely applied in electromagnetic and aerodynamic optimization problems [2] [6]. However, this paper for the first time integrates the SUMO toolbox into a wireless testbed to optimize wireless network problems. Specifically, the iMinds w-iLab.t wireless testbed [1] is used for this demonstration. In this demo, a wireless conference solution is optimized using the SUMO toolbox and compared to an exhaustive search approach. In both approaches, the speaker's transmit power and channel parameters are optimized in search of good listener's audio quality and reduced transmission exposure. Moreover, the demonstration is conducted remotely on the iMinds testbed requiring only one monitor and a fast internet connection.

MobiHoc'14, August 11–14, 2014, Philadelphia, PA, USA.
ACM 978-1-4503-2620-9/14/08.
http://dx.doi.org/10.1145/2632951.2636061.

Figure 1: wireless conferencing scenario consisting of 8 listeners, 1 speaker, and 1 interferer.

2. DEMONSTRATION

2.1 Experiment scenario

Figure 1 shows the wireless conferencing scenario which comprises a wireless speaker broadcasting a speaker's voice over the air and 8 listeners, with a wireless microphone, receiving the audio stream in the presence of an interferer. The interfere transmits a 10Mbps continuous UDP stream on dual channels (i.e. 1 and 13) interfering the speaker's

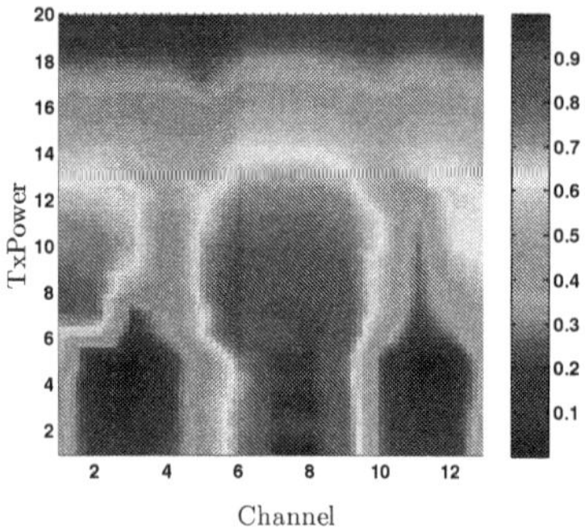

Figure 2: Exhaustive search model with background interference at channels 1 and 13

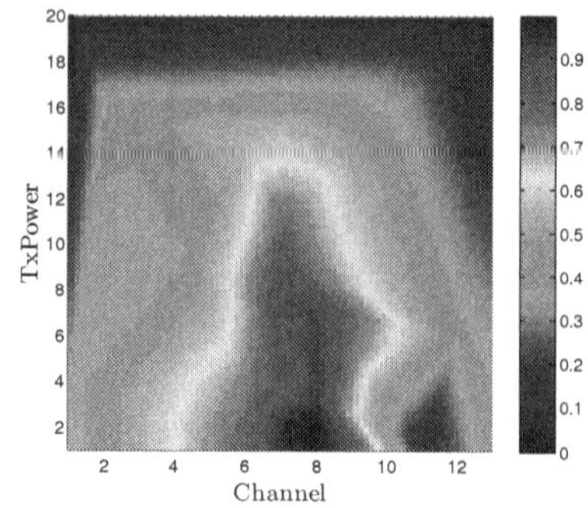

Figure 3: SUMO optimization model after 26 iterations. Background interference at channels 1 and 13

voice which lasts for 10 second and each listener calculates the average audio quality and transmission exposure during transmission. At last, the individual objectives are combined and the result is further optimized to locate the optimum settings. Since our goal is to validate the SUMO toolbox, we used equal weights to the normalized audio quality and transmission exposure objectives but for different problems, random weights can be applied as well.

2.2 Exhaustive search experiment

The exhaustive search experiment evaluates all possible parameter settings of the wireless conference scenario and will be used as a reference model by which the SUMO optimization experiment is compared against. Figure 2 shows the exhaustive search model after conducting 260 experiments at all parameter settings (i.e. 13 Channels × 20 Transmit Powers). The Colour bar indicates the combined objective normalized to a [0-1] or [blue-red] scale. Moreover, the highest combined objective (i.e. good audio quality + low transmission exposure) is located between channels 7 to 8 and transmit powers 1 dBm to 5 dBm. Indeed this area has less interference and low transmit power which could possibly be an optimum region and the place where we want the SUMO optimizer to converge in a short amount of time.

2.3 SUMO optimized experiment

The main goal of the SUMO optimizer is to reduce the number of experiments until optimum settings are located. SUMO has a number of configurable parameters which affect its efficiency. The major ones are initial sample size, initial sampling method and stopping criteria. As outlined in [5], the calculation behind setting these parameter values has a lengthy process and depends on the problem type considered. In this demonstration, 12 initial samples are selected using Latin Hypercube Sampling (LHS) method and Objective Function Improvement (OFI), using a standard deviation metric, as a stopping criterion. Figure 3 shows the SUMO optimized model of the wireless conference solution when the stopping criterion is met at the 26th iteration.

Comparing Figure 2 and Figure 3, there is a difference in the model since the data points used for generating the model are not the same but the optimum settings are located around the same region which accounts for the optimization benefit of SUMO. The SUMO experiment, after 26th iterations, achieved 99.51% performance and 10 times faster experiment duration compared to the exhaustive search experiment.

3. CONCLUSION

This paper demonstrated the use of the SUrrogate MOdeling (SUMO) optimizer for reducing experimentation time of wireless network solutions in a wireless testbed. We start by developing an exhaustive search model to compare to a SUMO optimized experiment. Next, we conducted the SUMO experiment having 12 initial points sampled using a Latin Hypercube Sampling (LHS) method. At last, the optimization iterated until the Objective Function Improvement (OFI) stopping criterion is satisfied. In our demonstration, the SUMO experiment runs 10 times faster compared to the exhaustive search experiment while achieving 99.51% of the global optimum performance.

Acknowledgment

The research leading to these results has received funding from the European Union's Seventh Framework Programme FP7/2007-2013 under grant agreement no. 258301 (CREW project).

4. REFERENCES

[1] S. Bouckaert, P. Becue, B. Vermeulen, B. Jooris, I. Moerman, and P. Demeester. Federating wired and wireless test facilities through emulab and omf: The ilab.t use case. Springer Berlin Heidelberg, 2012.

[2] I. Couckuyt, F. Declercq, T. Dhaene, H. Rogier, and L. Knockaert. Surrogate-based infill optimization applied to electromagnetic problems. *International journal of RF and microwave computer-aided engineering*, 20(5):492–501, 2010.

[3] D. Gorissen, I. Couckuyt, P. Demeester, T. Dhaene, and K. Crombecq. A surrogate modeling and adaptive sampling toolbox for computer based design. *J. Mach. Learn. Res.*, 11:2051–2055, Aug. 2010.

[4] D. Jones, M. Schonlau, and W. Welch. Efficient global optimization of expensive black-box functions. *Journal of Global Optimization*, 13(4):455–492, 1998.

[5] M. Mehari. Efficient global optimization of multi-parameter network problems on wireless testbeds. Submitted to Adhoc-Networks Journal, March 2014.

[6] P. H. Reisenthel and D. J. LesieutreâĂă. Statistical benchmarking of surrogate-based and other optimization methods constrained by fixed computational budget. 51st Structural Dynamics, and Materials Conference, 12 - 15 April 2010, Orlando, Florida.

Poster: Bacteria Inspired Mitigation of Selfish Users in Ad-hoc Social Networks

Ahmedin Mohammed Ahmed, Feng Xia, Qiuyuan Yang, Hannan Bin Liaqat, Zhikui Chen, Tie Qiu
School of Software, Dalian University of Technology, Dalian 116620, China
f.xia@acm.org

ABSTRACT

In data management protocols for Ad-hoc Social Networks (ASNETs), involvement of selfish users can pose a serious threat to network performance and fairness. Therefore, it is essential to detect and mitigate their effects on other well behaving users. We contribute to this line of research by combining the benefits of users' social behavior (social tie) with a biologically inspired approach in ASNETs. We designed a bio-inspired scheme (BoDMaS) to detect and mitigate selfish users in replication operations. Its goals include providing greater accessibility and effective detection of selfish users. The proposed scheme not only guarantees accessibility and effective detection rate, but also ensures the reliability of replica allocation operations.

Categories and Subject Descriptors

C.2.1 [**Computer-Communication Networks**]: Network Architecture and Design

Keywords

Ad-hoc social networks, selfishness, replication

1. INTRODUCTION

In socially-aware networking environments, users generate large amounts of data by exploiting capability-rich mobile devices, and prefer to share them with other users with whom they have social ties or greater similar interests. Even though solutions for detecting selfish users have been explored before [1], a few fundamental shortcomings surrounding the problem have remained unaddressed, particularly in data dissemination and forwarding for Ad-hoc Social Network (ASNET) services. Among these, we attempt to design a scheme that gives each user the autonomy to exclude selfish users. In our prior works, we proposed a replica allocation scheme (ComPAS) for ASNETs that exploits social relationship of users, see [2]. We observe that considering social willingness in conjunction with a biologically inspired mechanism (chemical products of bacteria) is effective for attaining our design goal.

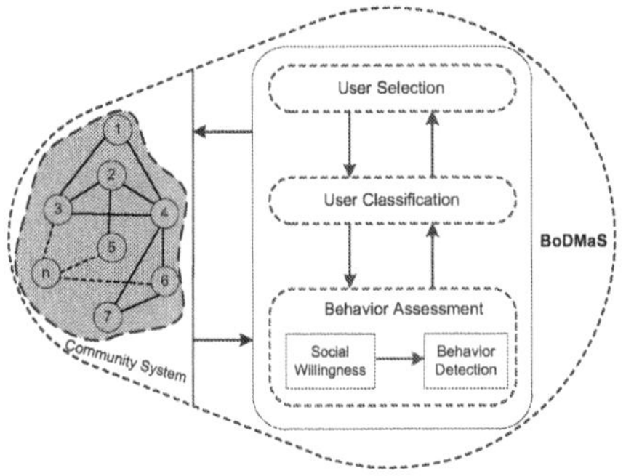

Figure 1: BoDMaS Architecture.

Bacteria is similar to a mobile user in that, it extracts information from the environment, interprets, develops common knowledge and learns from past experiences [3]. Our proposed model, considers social behavior and the characteristics observed in bacteria is deemed to be the biological mechanism. Acyl-Homoserine Lactone Autoinducers (A_i) act as a signaling chemical gradient to detect and determine the amount of bacteria in the environment, thereby allowing a collaborative behavior for the whole group to develop. The existence of social behavior in both the community and bacteria, provide a dynamic and autonomous solution named BoDMaS. Our initial results indicate that substantial gains in accessibility degree and detection can be achieved along with maximized data availability when ComPAS and BoDMaS are employed together.

2. BODMAS DESIGN

This work employs ComPAS [2] as the data management (replication) model. ComPAS is a community-partition aware replica allocation method that can significantly improve ASNETs performance. In order to maintain the reliability of replicated data, the BoDMaS scheme aims to support detection and isolation of selfish users. By assessing, classifying and selecting users that behave cooperatively, our proposed scheme denies the involvement of selfish users in replication operations (i.e. query and update). The assessment is executed by comparing social willingness level and observation of A_i represented by the amount of replica updates, query and forwards issued by users.

As shown in Fig. 1, our scheme consists of three basic components: *behavior assessment*, *user classification* and

MobiHoc'14, August 11–14, 2014, Philadelphia, PA, USA.
ACM 978-1-4503-2620-9/14/08.
http://dx.doi.org/10.1145/2632951.2635933.

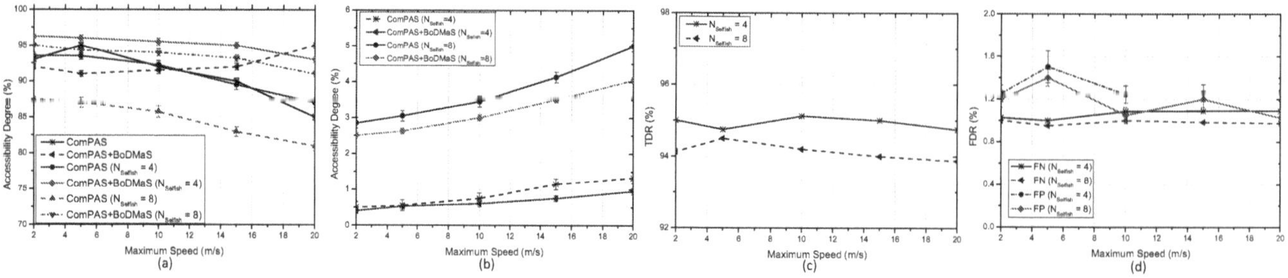

Figure 2: Accessibility degree: (a) update operations, (b) query operations, and BoDMaS detection rate of selfishness in query operations: (c) true detection rate (TDR), (d) false detection rate (FDR).

user selection. The functional interaction among these components are shown in Algorithm 1. In our context, social willingness denotes an interpersonal tie that falls into either a strong or weak category. The user is willing to provide better service to those with stronger ties than those with weaker ties, especially when there are resource constraints [1]. The UST method of appropriating social willingness was selected, as proposed by Li *et al.* [4].

3. PRELIMINARY RESULTS

The scheme is analysed considering the presence of selfish users in ComPAS operations. The network is composed of 32 users within 4 communities, and users move according to RPGM into an area of $400m^2$. The maximum speed is 2-20 m/s with a varying pause time of 10s-100s. The expected updating and querying rates are λ=80 and λ=24, respectively. The forwarding threshold $Er_{f(min)}$ is 0.2 forwards per second.

Algorithm 1: Pseudocode for functional interaction among BoDMaS components

begin
- $\rho_{id} \leftarrow$ Social willingness level ($\rho_{id} \in$ [0, 1]);
- **Behavior assessment:**
- **for** *all direct neighboring users* **do**
  - compares ρ_{id}; where 1 is strongest and 0 is none;
  - increment $A_{i(f)}$;
- **User classification:**
- **for** *all users' scores collected* **do**
  - compare a user's score to a Thr;
  - **if** *User A_i count is beyond Thr limit* **then**
    - classify the user as unwilling;
    - $Er_{f(min)}$ value is identified;
- **User selection:**
- make a decision and take action against users;
- **if** *User score* $\geq Er_{f(min)}$ **then**
  - user is considered cooperative;
  - users with lower scores are classified as selfish;

To check the effectiveness of employing ComPAS on the BoDMaS scheme (ComPAS⊎BoDMaS), it was evaluated without and with the presence of selfish users for accessibility degree. As depicted in Fig. 2(a), it is possible to verify the feasibility of the proposed scheme as it shows a better performance than ComPAS in terms of speed. Moreover, the use of BoDMaS shows an average improvement compared to the accessibility degree obtained by ComPAS without using BoDMaS for update operations with selfish users' participation. The number of participating selfish users and maximum speed have visible influence in ComPAS⊎BoDMaS for both (query and update) operations when compared to ComPAS. However, as depicted in Fig. 2(b), with low variation, BoDMaS presents lower results than ComPAS for query operations. This is due to the effect of selfishness on accessibility degree is less for query operations as compared to update operations.

TDR and FDR (FN and FP) obtained by BoDMaS for selfish-user detection are illustrated in Figs. 2(c) and (d), respectively. The TDR of selfish users is higher than 93.75%, as depicted in Fig. 2(c). The reason is that the proposed method assesses the selfish behavior of users and classifies it as a cooperative user again once it resumes collaboration in forwarding its query operations. Fig. 2(d) displays that FN detection rate is lower than 1.2%. This shows that just a very few selfish users are detected mistakenly in the selection. Furthermore, FP detection rate is also relatively small. On the whole, the results are quite promising.

In future work, we will consider malicious users that inject data into the process and evaluate the effectiveness of our system under expanded network environments.

4. ACKNOWLEDGEMENTS

This work was partially supported by Natural Science Foundation of China under Grants No. U1301253 and 61202443, and Liaoning Provincial Natural Science Foundation of China under Grant No. 201202032.

5. REFERENCES

[1] Q. Li, S. Zhu, G. Cao, *Routing in Socially Selfish Delay Tolerant Networks*, Proc. of IEEE INFOCOM, 2010, pp. 1-9.

[2] F. Xia, A. M. Ahmed, L. T. Yang, J. Ma, J. Rodrigues, *Exploiting Social Relationship to Enable Efficient Replica Allocation in Ad-hoc Social Networks*, IEEE Trans. on Parallel and Dist. Syst., 2013, DOI: 10.1109/TPDS.2013.2295805.

[3] A. Einolghozati, M. Sardari, A. Beirami, F. Fekri, *Data Gathering in Networks of Bacteria Colonies: Collective Sensing and Relaying Using Molecular Communication*, Proc. of IEEE INFOCOM, 2012, pp. 256-261.

[4] H. Li, C. Wu, Z. Li, W. Huang, F.C. Lau, *Stochastic Optimal Multirate Multicast in Socially Selfish Wireless Networks*, Proc. of IEEE INFOCOM, 2012, pp. 172-180.

Poster: Near Field Communication based Access Control for Wireless Medical Devices

Xiali Hei, Xiaojiang Du and Shan Lin
Department of Computer and Information Sciences
Temple University
19122 Philadelphia, USA
{xiali.hei, xjdu, shan.lin}@temple.edu

ABSTRACT

Security of wireless medical devices is critical for patient safety because security attacks may directly hurt patients' health. In this paper, we design a novel access control scheme based on bi-channel and multi-factor authentication for wireless medical devices. Our scheme utilizes near field communication (NFC) to perform device pairing, which supports key exchange between a device and a reader in short communication range (<= 6cm) with bounded response time. To further defend against attacks when a malicious reader is placed within the device's communication range in crowded situations, we design a crowd detection algorithm using WiFi and user's smart phone to assist the key exchange. Our analyses and experiments show that our security schemes are effective and efficient.

Categories and Subject Descriptors

J.3 [**Computer Applications**]: Life And Medical Sciences—*Medical information systems*

General Terms

Security,Measurement,Human Factors

Keywords

Response Time, Near Field Communication, Secure Pairing, Access Control, Medical Devices

1. INTRODUCTION

Security for wireless medical devices, such as cardiac defibrillators, insulin pumps, and various drug delivery systems, is critical for patient's safety [1]. Unfortunately, most of the existing wireless medical devices lack of sufficient security mechanisms to protect them from malicious attacks. There are a number of attacks from Satan adversary may launch on wireless medical devices [2] [3] [4] [6] [7].

Securing wireless medical devices is a challenging task due to their limited resources and the open environment. To address this problem, we propose integrating NFC with medical device. We implement secure pairing between a device and a reader over NFC, which allows a doctor's reader to share a key with a medical device with a very short distance. This pairing procedure is shown in Fig 1(a). If the medical device is not implantable, the device requests the patient to press a button to confirm. After sharing a key successfully, the reader and medical device can securely communicate with each other using their existing radios.

The key exchange procedure between a device and a reader over NFC is vulnerable to attacks if a malicious reader is within their communication range. Such attacks can be launched in crowded situations without causing users' attention. To address this problem, we design a crowd detection algorithm to alert users about insecure scenarios. This crowd detection algorithm is based on wireless device counting using users' smart phone. The basic procedure of this algorithm is shown in Fig 1(c). If the surrounding is not a crowded area, then the algorithm will notify the medical device. For implantable medical devices, other patient access patterns based control (PAPAC) scheme [4] is also used to defend against attacks.

2. DESIGN AND EXPERIMENTATION

NFC Communication Range. We tested the transmission range using 2 NFC-enabled smart phones (with PN544 chips). Our experimental results showed that they can successfully exchange data within 5cm. The two devices can recognize each other at 6cm, however, they cannot successfully exchange data at 6cm. We also confirmed this when one cell phone is around 5mm-thickness pork.

NFC Round Trip Time. As NFC is a new wireless technology, we conducted experiments to measure the round trip time (RTT), which can help eliminate relay attacks. Specifically, we use the time difference between finishing sending the last bit of a request message and the receiving of the first bit of the response message, which also is called response time. We used two Android smart phones with NFC chips to test the typical response time. The time resolution in cell phone is 1ns when we call the system time. We programmed these two phones to send and reply to messages at data link layer. Figure 2(a) shows our experimental results over 50 runs. From it, we can see that average response time is E=0.258ms, and the standard deviation D=0.026ms. We choose $Th_t = E + 2D = 0.31ms$.

The Device Pairing Protocol. In our scheme, the access control is based on device pairing employing NFC. We design the distance bound pairing schemes based on the Diffie-Hellman key exchange protocol [5]. In Figure 1(b), P and V represent the reader and the medical device. We use the response time $t_2 - t_1$ to bound the distance between them. The sharing key is $(g^v)^p$ for later communication.

PAPAC Scheme. The light-weight PAPAC security scheme can be used to protect wireless medical devices from attackers who are extremely close to the patient. PAPAC utilizes the patient's IMD access patterns and the patient's cell phone. It modeled the normal IMD access pattern using five kinds of IMD access data: reader action type, time interval of the same reader action, location, time,

MobiHoc'14, August 11–14, 2014, Philadelphia, PA, USA.
ACM 978-1-4503-2620-9/14/08.
http://dx.doi.org/10.1145/2632951.2635944 .

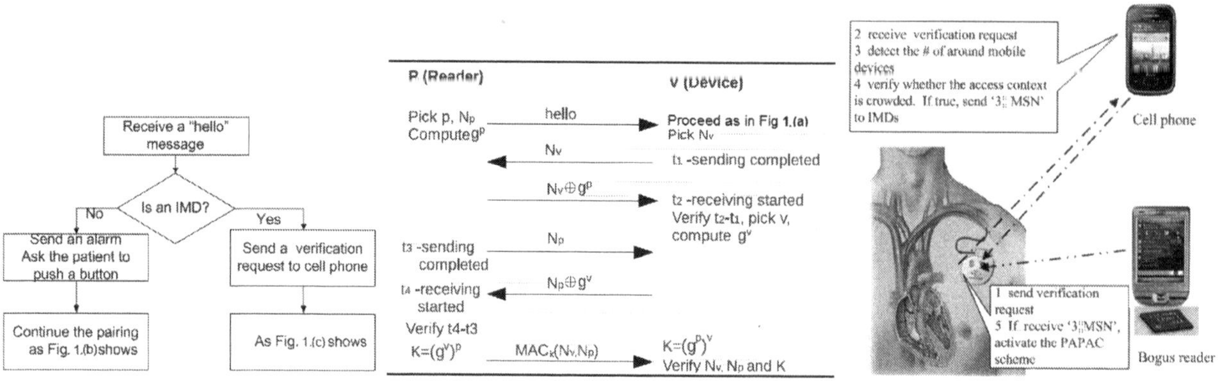

(a) Workflow of a device (b) The device pairing protocol (c) Access control scheme for IMDs

Figure 1: The main process

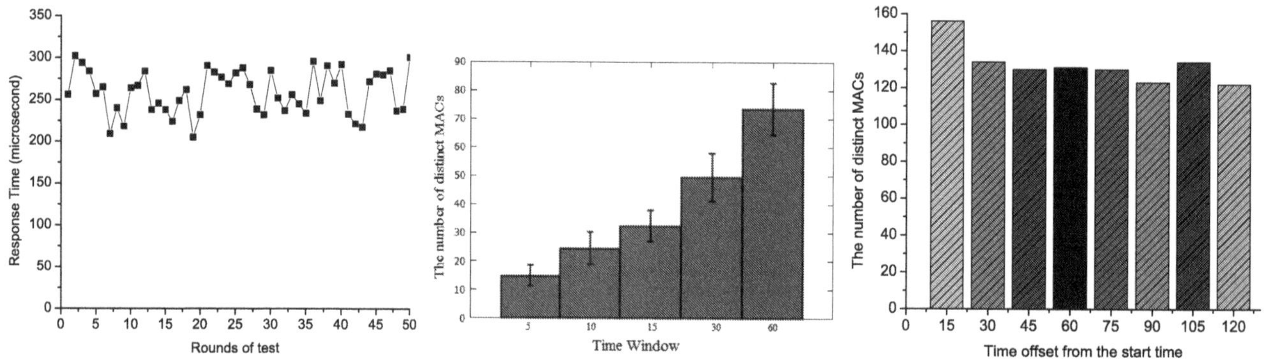

(a) Response time test results (b) The mean and standard variance for each time window of testing example 1 (c) Test examples 2

Figure 2: Test results

and day type (weekday or weekend). The patient's cell phone stores these data and runs a classification algorithm. When contacted by a reader, the IMD first sends a short *Verification* request message to the patient's cell phone. The cell phone then runs the classification algorithm and makes the following decisions: (1) if the algorithm indicates that this is a normal access, it sends a *Continue* command to the IMD, signaling the IMD that it may continue communication with the reader (i.e., performing standard authentication); (2) if the algorithm indicates that this is an attack, it sends a *Block* command to the IMD; and the IMD will enter sleep mode.

Detecting Crowded Situations. When a patient is in a crowded situation, hackers may use their mobile devices to attack the patient's wireless medical device. Our crowd detection is to roughly evaluate the number of mobile devices around a patient. Specifically, wireless radio on user's cell phone can observe the active MAC addresses and their corresponding received signal strengths of each probe request of each mobile device. Then we count the number of distinct active MAC addresses with strong signals within a short period. We denote Δ as the time window and determine the value of Δ by analyzing experimental results.

We conducted experiments to test our crowded area detection scheme by using the Samsung Galaxy Nexus phone with an Alpha360 WiFi adapter. We programmed the Android phone to collect the number of different MACs it can sense over different time windows: 5sec, 10sec, 15sec, 30sec, 60sec, 90sec and 120sec.

We recorded that there were 32 different persons in the train when we sat down until we left for the next station. Figure 2(b) shows the mean and standard variance of the number of distinct MAC addresses for each time window Δ. We can see that when Δ=15sec, the mean of it is close to 32 and the ratio between it and the standard variance of it is the least. So we choose Δ=15sec for later analysis. Figure 2(c) shows one test example in crowded area. From experiments, we chose the -38dBm as the threshold of signal strength. The difference between the number of distinct MAC addresses detected by our algorithm and the number of persons around us during the experiments is the error. The mean and standard variance of the error rates are 5.70% and 4.73%, respectively. This shows the test result is close to our observations. Since we only need a rough evaluation on the number of mobile devices around the patient, the result is reliable enough.

Acknowledgment

This work was supported in part by the US NSF under grants CNS-0963578, CNS-1022552, CNS-1065444, IIS-1231680, CNS-1239108, and CNS-1035715.

3. REFERENCES

[1] W. H. Maisel, "Safety issues involving medical devices," in J. of the American Medical Association, vol. 294, Aug. 2005, pp. 955-958.

[2] K. Fu, "Inside risks: reducing risks of implantable medical devices," in Commun. of the ACM, vol. 52, June 2009, pp. 25-27.

[3] D. F. Kune et al., "Ghost Talk: Mitigating EMI Signal Injection Attacks against Analog Sensors", in Proc. of the 34th Annual IEEE Symposium on Security and Privacy. May 2013.

[4] X. Hei et al., "Defending resource depletion attacks on implantable medical devices," in Proc. of the IEEE GLOBECOM'10, 2010, pp. 1-5.

[5] W. Diffie and M. Hellman, "New directions in cryptography". in IEEE Trans. on Information Theory, vol. 22, no. 6, 1976, pp. 644-54.

[6] X. Hei, X. Du, S. Lin, and I. Lee, "PIPAC: Patient Infusion Pattern based Access Control Scheme for Wireless Insulin Pump System", in Proc. of IEEE INFOCOM'13, Turin, Apr. 2013.

[7] X. Hei and X. Du, "Biometric-based two-level secure access control for implantable medical devices during emergencies," in Proc. of IEEE INFOCOM'11, 2011, pp. 346-350.

Poster: Environment-Adaptive Clock Calibration for Wireless Sensor Networks

Meng Jin[1],Dingyi Fang[1],Xiaojiang Chen*[1],Zhe Yang[2],Chen Liu[1],Dan Xu[1],Xiaoyan Yin[1]
[1]Northwest University, Xi'an, China
[2]Northwestern Polytechnical University, Xi'an, China
mengj@stumail.nwu.edu.cn,dyf@nwu.edu.cn,xjchen@nwu.edu.cn
zyang@nwpu.edu.cn,liuchen@nwu.edu.cn,xudanmoon@163.com,scxiaoyanyin@gmail.com

ABSTRACT

In this paper, we propose a novel clock calibration approach, which addresses two key challenges for clock calibration in Wireless Sensor Networks: excessive communication overhead and the trade-off between accuracy and cost. To achieve this, our approach leverages the fact that the clock skew is highly correlated to temperature, which can serve as both an assistant for clock skew estimation and a regulatory factor for the duty-cycled design. Our approach is one order of magnitude more power-efficient than communication based approaches since the calibration largely relies on local temperature information. In addition, our approach provides a nice feature of self-adaptive period, which can substantially promote the system flexibility. We present the theory behind our approach, and provide preliminary results of a simulated comparison of our approach and some recent approaches.

Categories and Subject Descriptors

C.2.1 [**Network Architecture and Design**]: Wireless communication

Keywords

Clock Calibration; Environment Adaptive; WSNs

1. INTRODUCTION

Tightly synchronized time cross the network is extremely significant for many WSN (Wireless Sensor Network) applications, since WSNs typically comprise numerous nodes and a common notion of time between the nodes is required to facilitate cooperative transmission, information fusion, localization, etc. Thus, an uncontrolled clock offset will inevitably leads to the high network loss ratio and the failure of data processing, which eternally disrupt the normal operation of the WSNs.

*corresponding author.

MobiHoc'14, August 11–14, 2014, Philadelphia, PA, USA.
ACM 978-1-4503-2620-9/14/08.
http://dx.doi.org/10.1145/2632951.2635936.

Clock calibration in WSNs, however, is a very challenging issue. Recent studies[2, 3] show that the low-cost crystal oscillators in wireless sensor networks (WSNs) are prone to be affected by environmental temperature. This property, and the fact that WSNs are mostly deployed over harsh environments, lead to the following two severe challenges in clock calibration approaches: (i) excessive communication overhead; and (ii) trade-off between accuracy and cost.

Excessive communication overhead: The temperature variation may lead to the fluctuation of clock skew (clock drift rate). Due to this uncertainty, no matter how accurately clocks are initially calibrated, they will ultimately tick towards divergency. Thus continuous skew calibration which based on timestamp exchange is required to minimize the negative impact from the dynamic environment. Unfortunately, WSNs today typically composed of hundreds of sensor nodes, and those nodes usually wireless interconnected in a multi-hop manner. As a direct consequence, frequently calibrating clocks prohibitively incurs high overhead and significant energy consumption for coordinating the entire network[1].

Trade-off between accuracy and cost: Existing calibration approaches[1, 2, 3] typically configure the clock skew compensation in a fixed cycle fashion. In spite of microsecond level accuracy achieved, they are fail to provide a trade-off between accuracy and cost. In practice, clock skew exhibits a hybrid change pattern due to the dynamic temperature[3]. Therefore, an auto-adaptive interval adjustment design, which is universal for all the skew changing patterns should be introduced for the best cost performance.

In this paper, we introduce a novel environment-adaptive clock calibration approach that enables nodes to estimate their clock skew by exploiting temperature information. The approach can substantially reduce communication overhead since clock skew estimation is mostly rely on local information. In addition, we further propose an environmental-adaptive interval adjustment scheme for duty-cycled clock calibration, which provides a convenient trad-off between the timing accuracy and the energy efficiency.

2. ENVIRONMENT-ADAPTIVE CLOCK CALIBRATION

In [2, 3], the correlation between the temperature and the clock skew is assumed to be invariable. This assumption is unrealistic and will leads to skew estimation error. Therefore, we introduce an innovative correction factor TSF(t) ("Temperature-Skew" Factor), which express the correlation as a function of time and thus requires periodically update.

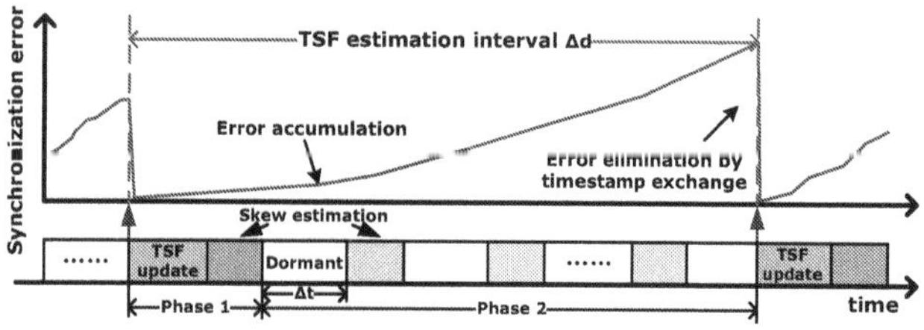

Figure 1: Illustration of two-phase calibration.

By using TSF(t) and the temperature measurement, nodes can estimate the clock skew autonomously.

As shown by Fig. 1, our approach features a two-phase process: i) it first estimates and updates the TSF(t) based on the timestamp exchange with the reference and then ii) it estimates the clock skew autonomously based on the temperature and TSF(t) during the TSF estimation interval. The red line between two TSF estimation represents the error accumulation caused by the fluctuation of TSF(t) during the interval, and this error can be eliminated by the timestamp exchange in the following TSF estimation phase. It is to note that, during the TSF estimation phase, clock skew is calibrated based on timestamp exchange.

2.1 Clock calibration

TSF estimation: To estimate the TSF, the temperature variation and the corresponding change in clock skew is during this phase required. Temperature information can be obtained by the temperature sensor and the clock skew is obtained based on timestamp exchange [1]. Thus, the TSF at the i-th TSF estimation period can be updated as:

$$TSF[i] = \frac{g(\Delta\alpha[i])}{f(\Delta T[i], T_0)}$$

$g(\Delta\alpha[i])$ and $f(\Delta T[i], T_0)$ express the temperature variation and the clock skew variation during the i-th TSF estimation phase. T_0 is the reference temperature (25°C). Assuming that the TSF doesn't change during the TSF estimation interval, the node can subsequently switch into the clock compensation phase.

Clock compensation: During compensation, the nodes regularly measure their environmental temperature $T(t)$. After every measurement, the current clock skew estimate $\alpha(t)$ is updated based on $T(t)$ and TSF[i] as:

$$\alpha(t) = TSF[i] \cdot (T(t) - T_0)^2$$

It is to note that every time the node changes its clock skew estimate after a temperature measurement, it has to update its current clock offset estimate as discussed in [2].

2.2 Interval adjustment scheme

To improve the energy efficiency of our clock calibration design, we further propose to configure the TSF estimation interval (or timestamp exchange interval) Δd in a dynamic manner. The challenge in the dynamic interval design is that the achieved performance might be compromised by trading for the energy saving. In our design, we predict the TSF estimation interval based on the observed error accumulation and temperature variation during the previous interval. Thus the nodes can automatically adjust the interval length to control the synchronization error, and meanwhile accommodate to the changing environment.

$$\Delta d[i+1] = min(d \cdot \frac{\mu}{e[i]}, d \cdot \frac{\lambda}{DT[i]})$$

μ and λ are the error and the temperature controlling factor. $\Delta d[i+1]$ is the next interval and d is the standard interval length. e and DT describe the error accumulation and the temperature variation during the previous interval.

3. RESULTS

We report the simulation study in this section for evaluation of our approach. The generated temperature trace is in a hybrid change pattern with both stable period and changing period, which imitates the dynamic environment.

Fig.2 shows the CDF curve of calibration errors for EACS[3] and our approach. For our approach, the skew estimation error is less than $0.6ppm$ for most of the time. However, for EACS, more than 20% of the skew estimation errors exceed $2.5ppm$. It is obvious that our approach is effective in mitigating the skew estimation error.

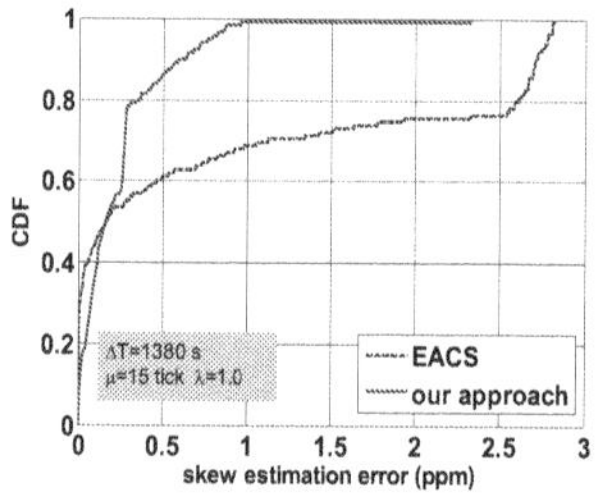

Figure 2: CDF of skew estimation error

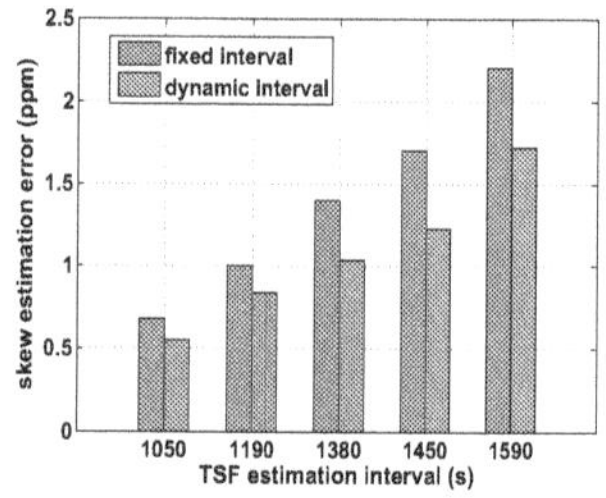

Figure 3: skew estimation error v.s. TSF estimation interval

Fig.3 reveals the effectiveness of the Interval adjustment scheme. We choose five different standard intervals (d) to be 1500s, 1800s, 2000s, 2300s and 2500s. When the simulation terminates, we calculate the average length of the intervals to be 1050s, 1190s, 1380s, 1450s and 1950s. We find that the fixed interval policy generally incurs a larger error than the dynamic one when they have the same average interval. Another important observation is that the timestamp exchange interval can be prolonged to more than $1000s$, while that for communication based approaches[1] is less than 150s.

4. ACKNOWLEDGMENTS

This work was supported by the NSFC(61170218, 61272461, 61373177, 61070176, 61202198, 61202393), Project National Key Technology R&D Program 2013BAK01B02, the Key Project of Chinese Ministry of Education 211181.

5. REFERENCES

[1] M. Miklos, K. Branislav, S. Gyula, and L. Akos. The flooding time synchronization protocol. In *SENSYS*, 2004.

[2] S. Thomas, C. Zainul, S. Roy, and S. M. B. Temperature compensated time synchronization. *Embedded Systems Letters*, 2009.

[3] Y. Zhe, C. Lin, L. Yu, and P. Jianping. Environment-aware clock skew estimation and synchronization for wireless sensor networks. In *INFOCOM*, 2012.

Poster: A Simulation Analysis on the Hop Count of Multi-hop Path in Cognitive Radio Ad-hoc Networks

Le The Dung
Dept. of Electronics & Computer Engineering in Graduate School, Hongik University, Korea
thedung_hcmut@yahoo.com

Beongku An
Dept. of Computer & Information Communications Engineering, Hongik University, Korea
beongku@hongik.ac.kr

ABSTRACT
The number of hops between source node and destination node is one of key parameter in studying multi-hop ad-hoc networks. Although hop count in conventional ad-hoc networks has been well studied, to the best of our knowledge, there have no works that intensively investigate the hop count of multi-hop path in cognitive environment. This paper presents detail simulation analysis on the hop count of multi-hop path in Cognitive Radio Ad-hoc Networks (CRAHNs). The effect of network parameters such as node density of Secondary User (SU) and Primary User (PU), operating frequencies, average activating rate of PUs, in the networks are studied. Simulation experiments with different network parameters are conducted to clarify the features of hop count in cognitive ad-hoc networks.

Categories and Subject Descriptors
C.2.1 [**Computer-Communication Networks**]: Network Architecture and Design – *Network Topology*

General Terms
Performance, Measurement, Verification

Keywords
Cognitive Radio Ad-hoc Networks, Multi-hop Paths, Hop Count

1. INTRODUCTION
Wireless ad-hoc network is a collection of wireless nodes which dynamically form a network without relying on any infrastructure. The network is formed as soon as one of wireless nodes wants to communicate with one or more of the other nodes. The routing paths in wireless ad-hoc network are often multi-hop paths because destination node is usually out of the transmission range of source node. Thus, before reaching the destination the packets travel through some intermediate nodes between source node and destination node.

The hop count specifies the number of hops on the path between source node and destination nodes. The study of the hop count of multi-hop path in wireless ad-hoc networks is very important because it can provide evaluation of the networks performance such as: (i) estimation of the delivery ratio of packets, (ii) estimation of end-to-end-delay if per hop delay is known, (iii) estimation of network traffic if the number of simultaneous communication flows is given, (iv) determining the flooding cost and search latency of route stabling process in routing protocols, (v) studying of connectivity and capacity of multi-hop path.

Many studies have been carried out to analyze the hop count of multi-hop path in conventional ad-hoc network by using both mathematical analysis approach and simulation approach [1-4]. These works give us an insight into how hop count is influenced by major network parameters such as node density, node mobility.

Recently, CRAHNs have already received much attraction from researchers. One of main research topic in CRAHNs is routing protocol and its challenges in cognitive environment [5]. Because of the presence of PUs in the networks, routing in CRAHNs takes more effort than in conventional AHNs which results in different values of hop count.

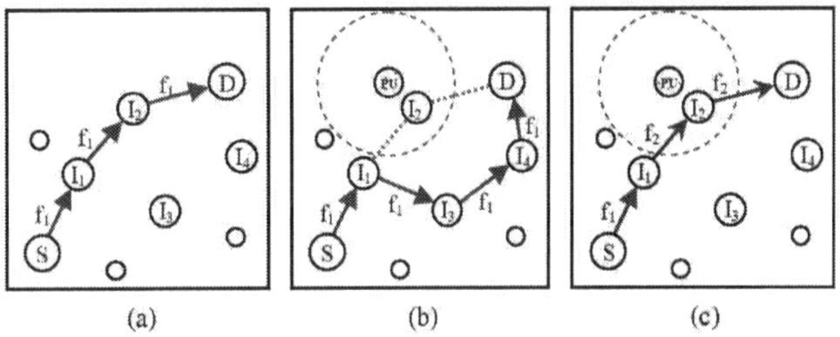

Figure 1. Routing challenges in CRAHNs compared with conventional AHNs; (a) Routing in AHNs, (b) Rerouting and (c) Switching frequency channel of affected wireless link.

The contribution in this paper is to find out the relation patterns of hop count with network parameters in cognitive ad-hoc networks.

2. ON THE CHARACTERISTICS OF HOP COUNT IN COGNITIVE RADIO AD-HOC NETWORKS
For better illustration, we provide several examples of network topologies to show how cognitive environment influences the hop count of multi-hop path in CRAHNs.

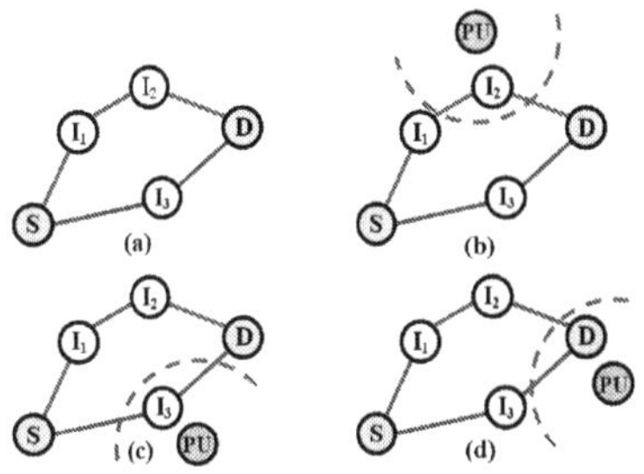

Figure 2. Different PU locations result in different hop counts.

MobiHoc'14, August 11–14, 2014, Philadelphia, PA, USA
ACM 978-1-4503-2620-9/14/08.
http://dx.doi.org/10.1145/2632951.2635938

As we can see in Fig 2, when no active PUs influences all wireless links as in Figure 2(a) or influence wireless links of I_2 as in Figure 2(b) the shortest path is still $S \rightarrow I_3 \rightarrow D$ whose hop count is 2. When an active PU locates near I_3 as in Figure 2(c) the new shortest path is $S \rightarrow I_1 \rightarrow I_2 \rightarrow D$ whose hop count is 3. In the worst case, when an active PU locates near S or D as in Figure 2(d), multi-hop path between S and D cannot be established. In summary, the hop count depends on the locations of active PUs. It also depends on number of PUs, radio ranges of SUs and PUs (corresponding to operating frequencies).

3. RESULTS AND DISCUSSIONS

In this section, the simulation results of average hop count of multi-hop path in CRAHNs are presented and discussed. To obtain the average hop count, we use MATLAB to generate 10000 random network topologies of CRAHNs with different settings of network parameters such as SU and PU density, the average activating rate of PUs, the number of licensed frequency channels. Number of SUs = 50 and different number of PUs in network area of 1500 m × 1500 m. Node transmission power $P_t = 10^{-3}$ W, reception power threshold $P_{th} = 1.58 \times 10^{-12}$ W.

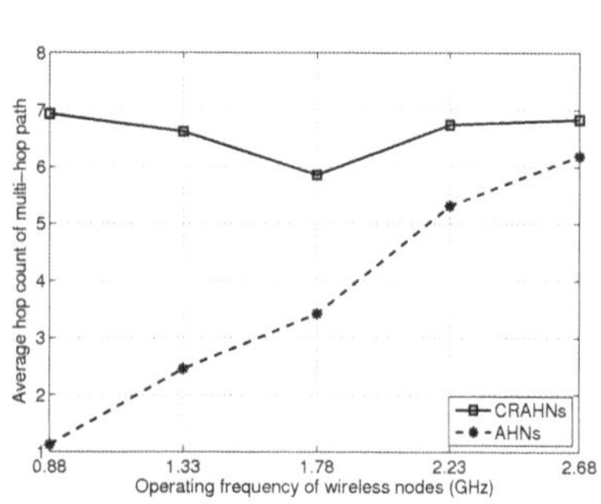

Figure 4. Average hop count of multi-hop path in CRAHNs compared with that in CRAHNs as a function of operating frequency; network size a = 1500m, one frequency layer with f = 0.88 GHz ~ 2.68 GHz.

Figure 4 shows that the average hop count in CRAHNs is high when operating frequency is low (large radio range). Because of the effect of PU's presence in SU's radio range, the average hop count decreases then increases as operating frequency increases. This feature does not appear in AHNs.

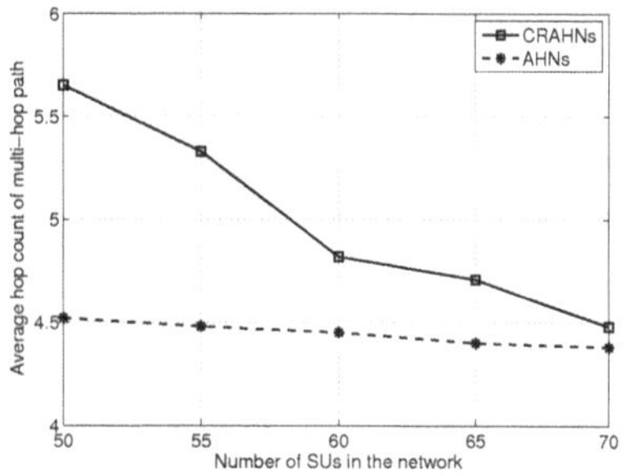

Figure 5. Average hop count of multi-hop path in CRAHNs compared with that in CRAHNs as a function of SU density; network size a = 1500m, number of PUs = 5, PU's activating rate = 0.1, one frequency layer with f = 2.4 GHz.

Figure 4 shows the average hop count in CRAHNs remarkably reduces compared with that in AHNs as SU density increases.

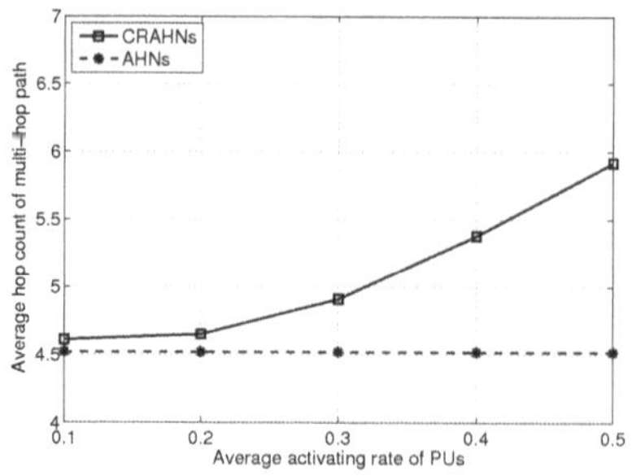

Figure 6. Average hop count of multi-hop path in CRAHNs compared with that in CRAHNs as a function of PU's average activating rate; network size a = 1500m, number of SUs = 50, number of PUs = 5, one frequency layer with f = 2.4 GHz.

Figure 6 shows that the average hop count in CRAHNs is greatly affected by the average activating rate of PUs, while in AHNs it is almost constant because of having no PUs in the networks.

4. CONCLUSIONS

In this paper, we investigate in detail the characteristics of hop count in cognitive radio ad-hoc networks. We perform intensive simulation with different network parameters. The simulation results show that depending on specific locations of active PUs, hop count in cognitive radio ad-hoc network may greater or equal to the hop count in conventional ad-hoc network. Moreover, from the simulation results we can conclude that different network parameters, such as SU and PU density, average activating rate of PUs, and the distribution of PUs on each frequency layers result in different average hop count of multi-hop paths in CRAHNs.

5. ACKNOWLEDGMENTS

This research was supported by Basic Science Research Program through the National Research Foundation of Korea (NRF) funded by the Ministry of Education, Science and Technology (MEST) (Grants No. 2013075605) and by Business for Cooperative R&D between Industry, Academy, and Research Institute funded Korea Small and Medium Business Administration in 2013 (Grants No. C0150656).

6. REFERENCES

[1] S. De. On Hop Count and Euclidean Distance in Greedy Forwarding in Wireless Ad Hoc Networks. *IEEE Communications Letters*, 9(11): 1000-1002, Nov. 2005.

[2] S. De, A. Caruso, T. Chaira, and S. Chessa. Bound on Hop Distance in Greedy Routing Approach in Wireless Ad Hoc Networks. *International Journal of Wireless and Mobile Computing*, 1(2): 131-140, Feb. 2006.

[3] S. M. Harb and J. McNair. Analytical Study of the Expected Number of Hops in Wireless Ad Hoc Network. *Lecture Notes in Computer Science*, 5258: 63-71, 2008.

[4] O. Younes and N. Thomas. Analytical Study of the Expected Number of Hops in Mobile Ad Hoc Networks with Random Waypoint Mobility. Electronic Notes in Theoretical Computer Science, 275(27): 143-158, Sep. 2011.

[5] M. Cesana, F. Cuomo, and E. Ekici. Routing in cognitive radio networks: Challenges and solutions. *Ad Hoc Networks*, 9(3): 228-248, May 2011.

Poster: Reliable TCP for Popular Data in Socially-aware Ad-hoc Networks

Hannan Bin Liaqat, Feng Xia, Qiuyuan Yang, Li Liu, Zhikui Chen, Tie Qiu
School of Software, Dalian University of Technology, Dalian 116620, China
f.xia@acm.org

ABSTRACT

Reliable social connectivity and transmission of data for popular nodes are vital in multihop Ad-hoc Social Networks (ASNETs). However, congestion may occur and hence popular nodes might not achieve required bandwidth when multiple senders share data with a single receiver. The traditional Transport Control Protocol (TCP) might not be able to perform efficiently in ASNETs. Therefore, we propose a Reliable TCP for Popular Data in Socially-aware Ad-hoc Networks called RTPS. RTPS employs a popularity level approach for every single node which partitions the bandwidth among users. The reliability of popular data is ensured since bandwidth will firstly assigned to the popular sender. Preliminary results show that by delaying the acknowledgment and improving the performance of TCP, RTPS reduces collision loss in multihop ASNETs.

Categories and Subject Descriptors

C.2.1 [**Computer-Communication Networks**]: Network Architecture and Design - *Wireless Communication*

Keywords

Congestion, TCP, ad-hoc social networks

1. INTRODUCTION

TCP suffers in multihop ASNET due to the reliability issues and face congestion related losses due to scarce bandwidth. The reliability of popular sender data packets is affected by two aspects: 1) when multiple senders are sending data on multihop ad-hoc networks and only a single receiver is receiving data. Due to less bandwidth of the end node, it drops packets and reduces the reliability of popular sender data packets, and 2) the dropping of acknowledgment packets from the networks affects the reliability of already sent or popular node data packets. Dropping packets from multi-hop ad-hoc network is due to collision loss that happens because data and acknowledgment packets use the same path [1].

Some recent developments in ASNET are available to solve reliability and congestion issues. The reliability of data packet in ASNET can be achieved by leveraging the concept of multiple copies but this can create congestion. Therefore, Xia *et al.* [2] present efficient replication scheme to maximize availability of data in ASNETs. To solve congestion issue in ASNETs, TIBIAS [3] uses an assignment procedure of data packets based on next node social property (similarity) and provides sender side solution. The congestion issue can also be solved after reduction in acknowledgment overhead. Therefore, TCP-DAAp [1] uses packet loss rate to set the delay acknowledgment window.

To solve the above mentioned problems, we propose RTPS. It provides maximum reliable transmission to popular nodes (high degree centrality) with a congestion control scheme. The degree centrality gives high advantage in terms of maximum utilization of resources. Reliability of data packet to popular node follows two aspects. First, it shares bandwidth between sender nodes using popularity level and secondly, it acknowledges earlier to popular node packet as compared to other. To reduce collision loss, RTPS sets the delay window based on the network condition.

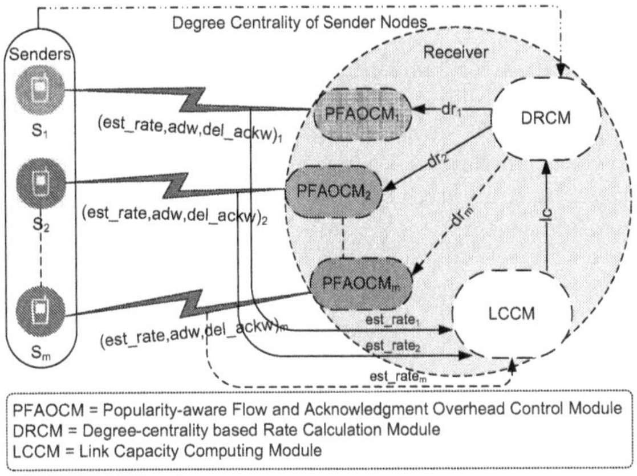

Figure 1: Structure of RTPS.

2. DESIGN OF RTPS

RTPS is composed of Link Capacity Computing Module (LCCM), Degree-centrality based Rate Calculation Module (DRCM) and Popularity-aware Flow and Acknowledgment

MobiHoc'14, August 11–14, 2014, Philadelphia, PA, USA.
ACM 978-1-4503-2620-9/14/08.
http://dx.doi.org/10.1145/2632951.2635939.

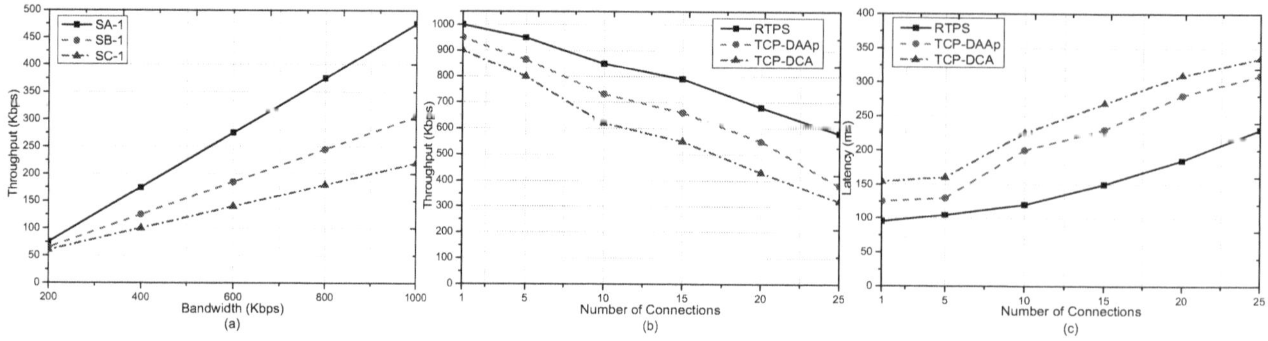

Figure 2: Performance comparison.

Overhead Control Module (PFAOCM). Fig. 1 shows the model in which multiple Senders (S) connect with single Receiver (R). RTPS provides full utilization of available bandwidth without wastage of resources. In first step, LCCM receives the estimated rates $c = \sum_0^{m-1} est\_rate_k$ from all S and then calculates the optimum value for full link utilization. After calculation of favorable link capacity (lc), it transfers to DRCM. DRCM first assigns minimum rate to all flows then calculates the desired rates (dr) based on the lc and computes *degree centrality* of sender nodes. The following equation provides the calculation of dr:

$$dr_k = \frac{dec_{k'}}{\sum_{k=0}^{m-1} dec_{k'}} * (lc - \sum_{k=0}^{m-1} lr_k) + lr_k \quad (1)$$

DRCM assigns dr values to multiple PFAOCMs. PFAOCM sets the advertised window (adw) and delays acknowledgment window (del_ackw) based on the value of dr and exponential weighted moving average rate (avg_rate). In (2), est_rate_k defines the available rate for kth flow; $prvavg\_rate_k$ explains the previous exponential weighted moving average and α denotes the average parameter of exponential (i.e. 0.3).

$$avg\_rate_k = \alpha * (prvavg\_rate_k) + (1 - \alpha) * est\_rate_k \quad (2)$$

To achieve the setting of adw based on popularity level, PFAOCM aims to set avg_rate_k of the flow with in a desired rate dr_k of the fraction σ. To solve the overhead issue, RTPS uses delay acknowledgment methodology. In PFAOCM, when any data packet arrives at the receiver end, it counts the unacknowledged data packet through ac variable. After receiving an in order data packet RTPS generates single acknowledgment. The ac is reset to 0 when ac reaches to del_ackw. To adjust the dynamic del_ackw, estimated network situation with popularity level provides high advantage. If any node has a higher popularity level than all other nodes, then earlier acknowledgment is also required. Early acknowledgment is useful in achieving e.g. reliable data transfer and desired rate.

3. EVALUATION AND DISCUSSION

The performance of RTPS is evaluated via simulation and compared with existing approaches: TCP-DAAp [1] and TCP-DCA [4]. Our main objective is to investigate whether RTPS can perform better in terms of link utilization, latency and throughput. The transmission range of our simulation is 250 m. We used 1 to 25 TCP connections and each node buffer capacity is 50 packets. The transmission power of each node is 0.007 watts with 11 Mbps channel bandwidth. Ad-hoc On Demand Distance Vector (AODV) was selected as a routing protocol and the type of traffic is FTP. The size of packet is 1,460 bytes with simulation time of 1000 seconds.

Figure 2 depicts the bandwidth assignment within different flows. Figure 2(a) illustrates that it first assigns 50 Kbps to each flow and the remaining bandwidth assigns using *degree centrality* calculation. The result shows the throughput of SA-1 is greater than all other sender nodes. Figure 2(b) explains the throughput of RTPS is 34.5% and 44.8% higher than TCP-DAAp and TCP-DCA. The throughput of RTPS also increases when we assign maximum bandwidth to the user who has a high popularity level. TCP-DAAp and TCP-DCA use equal bandwidth sharing with a fixed number of window sizes which cause lower throughput when the number of connections increases in the network. Figure 2(c) shows that the latency of RTPS is 25.8% and 31.3% lesser than TCP-DAAp and TCP-DCA. RTPS reduces delay in transmission since it assigns bandwidth based on popularity level of node and sets *del_ackw* based on social property. In addition, RTPS considers network bandwidth to adjust the receiver windows.

4. ACKNOWLEDGEMENTS

This work was partially supported by Natural Science Foundation of China under Grants No. U1301253 and 61202443.

5. REFERENCES

[1] R. Oliveira, and T. Braun, *A Smart TCP Acknowledgment Approach for Multihop Wireless Networks*, IEEE Trans. Mobile Comput. vol. 6, no. 2, pp. 192-205, 2007.

[2] F. Xia, A. M. Ahmed, L. T. Yang, J. Ma, and J. Rodrigues, *Exploiting Social Relationship to Enable Efficient Replica Allocation in Ad-hoc Social Networks*, IEEE Trans. on Parallel and Dist. Syst., 2013, DOI: 10.1109/TPDS.2013.2295805.

[3] H. B. Liaqat, F. Xia, J. Ma, L. T. Yang, A. M. Ahmed, and N. Y. Asabere, *Social Similarity-aware TCP with Collision Avoidance in Ad-hoc Social Networks*, IEEE Syst. J., 2014, DOI: 10.1109/JSYST.2014.2305191.

[4] J. Chen, M. Gerla, Y. Lee, and M. Sanadidi, *TCP with Delayed Ack for Wireless Networks*, Ad Hoc Netw., vol. 6, no. 7, pp. 1098-1116, 2008.

Poster: The Construction of Reeb Graph and Its Applications in 3D Sensor Networks

Wenping Liu*, Zhifeng Lin, and Hongbo Jiang
Huazhong University of Science and Technology, Wuhan, China
{wenpingliu2009, linzhifeng1990, hongbojiang2004}@gmail.com

ABSTRACT

Existing algorithms for topology extraction focus on only one topology feature, either skeleton or segmentation, in 2D or 3D sensor networks, most of which requiring complete boundary information. As boundary information is not easily obtained, especially in sparse 3D sensor networks, and extracting these two features separately is very expensive, in this study, we propose to simultaneously extract the line-like skeleton of 2D/3D sensor networks and decompose the network into nice pieces, by constructing the Reeb graph.

The Reeb graph has been envisioned as a powerful tool for encoding the topology of an object, where the key is to select the right function f. Without using boundary information, we first construct a *cut* graph, and then regard the distance of a node to the nearest cut as the function f such that the corresponding Reeb graph is pose independent, based on which the skeleton extraction and network decomposition are simultaneously conducted. Some simulation results are presented to show the efficiency of the algorithm.

Categories and Subject Descriptors

C.2.1 [**Computer-Communication Networks**]: Network Architecture and Design—*wireless communication*

Keywords

3D Sensor Networks, Reeb Graph, Skeleton,Segmentation

1. INTRODUCTION AND MOTIVATIONS

Recently, there are growing interests on topology extraction in sensor networks. Among many proposals, line-like skeleton (also known as curve skeleton) extraction and network decomposition are two major topics, where the line-like skeleton of a 2D/3D object is defined as the collection of points whose geodesic shortest paths between their nearest boundary points can decompose the boundary into connected components [2]. Unfortunately, these studies mainly focus on one topological feature, either line-like skeleton or segmentation, of 2D or 3D sensor networks, and most of them require complete boundary information. In some scenarios, especially in sparse 3D sensor networks, boundary information is not easily obtained; most importantly, extracting these two features separately is rather costly. As such, in this paper, we conduct the first work on simultaneous extraction of line-like skeleton and network decomposition in 2D/3D sensor networks by constructing the Reeb graph, without reliance on location and boundary information.

Originally introduced in Morse theory, given a feature function $f : D \rightarrow R$ defined on the object D, the Reeb graph of D is obtained by continuously contracting to a single point each level set (or, contour). It has been envisioned as a powerful tool for surface segmentation and parametrization, topological simplification, etc., in computer graphics and computational geometry, since it has the capability to encode the topology of the object. Please see Fig. 1. The critical points, i.e., minima, saddles and maxima, of function f, correspond to the level sets where the topology changes. This can guide us to decompose the network into regularly shaped pieces. Besides, some studies in computer graphics have been done to compute the line-like skeleton by using Reeb graph. Note that the selection of the function f is of crucial importance to understand and represent the topology of the object. This is not straightforward as the Reeb graph is pose dependent (see Fig. 1(a)(b)), and the line-like skeleton (and segmentation result) computed based on different height functions can be very different (see Fig. 1(c)(d)).

2. RELATED WORK

There are many algorithms for topological feature extraction in sensor networks, and we only list a few of them in 3D cases. Zhou *et al.*[3] proposed to identify the bottlenecks and then decompose the network into pieces, and this algorithm works only when there exist bottlenecks. Jiang *et al.*[1] studied the segmentation of 2D/3D sensor networks based on some boundary nodes. Liu *et al.*[2] presented a unified framework for line-like skeleton extraction in 2D/3D sensor networks where boundary information is an input.

3. OUR APPROACH

We plan to construct a pose-independent Reeb graph without reliance on boundary and location information, and apply it for simultaneous line-like skeleton extraction and decomposition. As mentioned earlier, the feature function f for constructing the Reeb graph should be carefully selected.

*Wenping Liu is also with Hubei University of Economics.

MobiHoc'14, August 11–14, 2014, Philadelphia, PA, USA.
ACM 978-1-4503-2620-9/14/08.
http://dx.doi.org/10.1145/2632951.2635941.

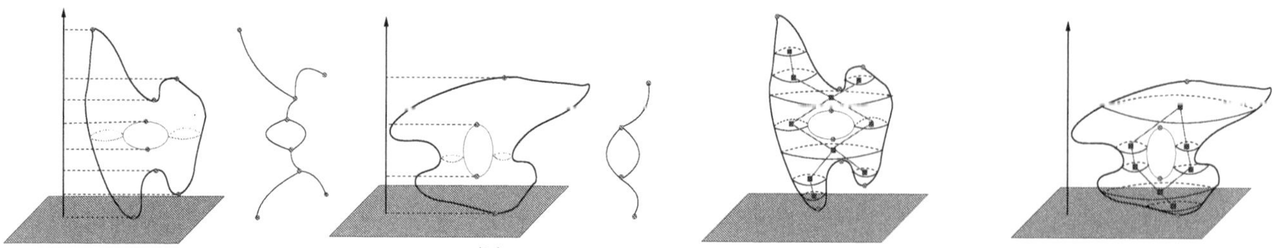

Figure 1: Illustrative examples. Critical points are marked by solid circles. (a) A solid torus and its Reeb graph w.r.t the height function $f = z(x, y)$; (b) After rotation, the solid torus and its reeb graph w.r.t the function $f = y(x, z)$; (c) The line-like skeleton based on (a); (d) The line-like skeleton based on (b).

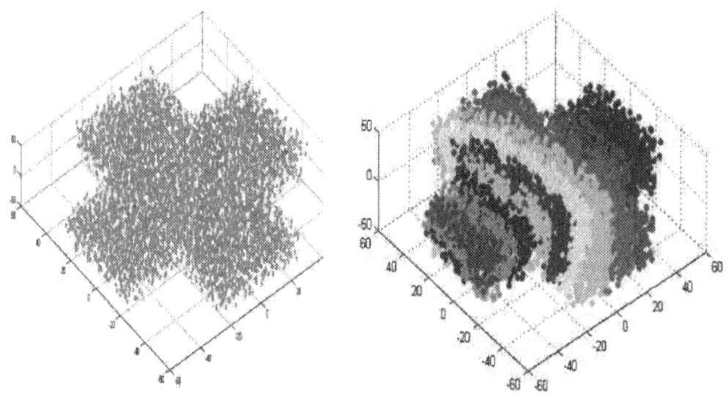

Figure 2: (a) A Cross-shaped 3D network; (b) the cuts.

Note that for a sensor network with genus 0, each level set of its Reeb graph actually *cut* the network into two parts, which can be used to construct a feature function. Formally,

DEFINITION 1. *For two nodes p and q in a network with genus zero, the cut between them is a connected component partitioning the network into two disjoint parts* P, Q *such that* $p \in P, q \in Q$.

Clearly, there are arbitrarily large number of cuts between two nodes. See Fig. 2. In order to guarantee that the extracted skeleton is medially placed, we propose to detect the minimum cut between nodes, which is defined below.

DEFINITION 2. *A cut between p and q is the minimum cut if it has the smallest number of nodes.*

As such, we randomly select two nodes and find the minimal cut between them. Next, each node computes its distance to the cut. The distance function thus serves as a feature function f to construct the Reeb graph, where a level set represents a set of points having the same distance (in hops) to the cut. Similarly, for genus-$n(>0)$ networks, we find n minimum cuts, and the function f of a node is defined as its distance to the nearest minimum cut. With the constructed Reeb graph, we identify the line-like skeleton node within each level set. Clearly, the line-like skeleton node should locate medially in the level set, and the number of shortest paths passing it should be the largest among other nodes in the level set, which guide us for line-like skeleton node identification. Eventually, these skeleton nodes are orderly connected to derive the line-like skeleton.

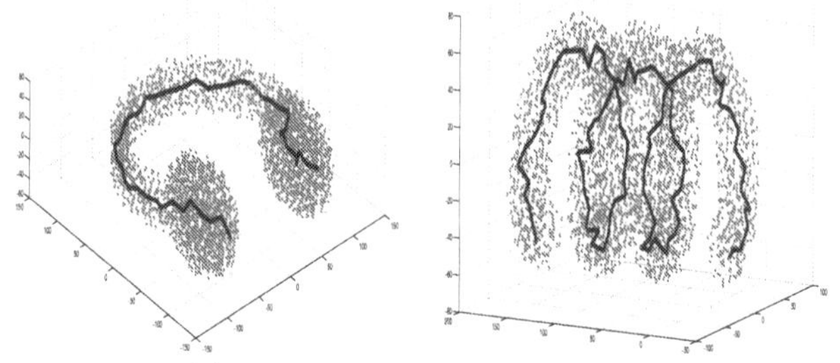

Figure 3: The line-like skeleton of the (a) headphone-shaped 3D network and (b) spiral-shaped 3D network.

4. RESULTS AND FUTURE WORK

We use the proposed method to extract the line-like skeleton of a headphone-shaped 3D network and spiral-shaped 3D network, respectively, as shown in Fig. 3. We can see that without boundary information, our algorithm can achieve a medially placed line-like skeleton, correctly capturing the topological features.

We currently studied the line-like skeleton extraction by constructing Reeb graph. Next we will propose to identify where the topology changes and design an algorithm to decompose the network into regular pieces, and conduct extensive simulations on 2D/3D sensor networks to validate the performance of the proposed algorithm.

5. ACKNOWLEDGEMENTS

This work was supported in part by the National Natural Science Foundation of China under Grant 61202460 and Grant 61271226; by the China Postdoctoral Science Foundation under Grant 2014M552044.

6. REFERENCES

[1] H. Jiang, T. Yu, C. Tian, G. Tan, and C. Wang. Consel: Connectivity-based segmentation in large-scale 2d/3d sensor networks. In *Proc. of IEEE INFOCOM*, 2012.

[2] W. Liu, H. Jiang, Y. Yang, and Z. Jin. A Unified Framework for Skeleton Extraction in 2D/3D Sensor Networks. In *Proc. of IEEE ICNP*, 2013.

[3] H. Zhou, N. Ding, M. Jin, S. Xia, and H. Wu. Distributed algorithms for bottleneck identification and segmentation in 3D wireless sensor networks. In *Proc. of IEEE SECON*, 2011.

Poster: Social Mobility based Routing in Crowdsourced Systems

Chuang Ma, Yongjian Yang, Zhanwei Du
College of Computer Science and Technology
Jilin University, Changchun, China
duzhanwei0@gmail.com, yyj@jlu.edu.cn, machuangstu@163.com

Chijun Zhang
College of Management Science and Information Engineering, Jilin University of Finance and Economics, Changchun, China
cjzhang6@163.com

ABSTRACT
In this paper, we formulate a generalized optimization problem to meet the profit problem for crowdsourced systems with considering three aspects of connectivity, profit and risk. We also propose a routing algorithm for this special scenario, featured by dynamic mobility and social graph. This algorithm has two parts: social graph extraction and social mobility based routing. The first part extracts each patrician's social graph to get the social knowledge. The second part gives a policy for the decider to assign the passages to the leaving nodes according to their social graph. We applied our algorithm into the realistic traces, and compare it with several existing methods. The result shows the competitive performance of this routing algorithm, both in connectivity, profit and risk.

Categories and Subject Descriptors
C.2.2 [**COMPUTER-COMMUNICATION NETWORKS**]: Network Protocols – *Routing protocols*

General Terms
Algorithms, Performance, Design.

Keywords
Crowdsourced Systems, Pocket Switched Network, Dynamic Mobility, Social Graph.

1. INTRODUCTION
"A new delivery concept uses the location of random strangers to TwedEx parcels directly to you – wherever you are", New Scientist News[2]. You can find some interesting apps in YouTube, featured by this delivery concept, which are good examples for the ultimate aim of a crowd-powered delivery system dreamed up by a group of Microsoft researchers [6]. It is possible to deliver purchases to customers on the move, as well as making it cheaper to send them with this idea [2].

Basic crowdsourced systems already exist, which hire strangers from the internet to deliver packages [4-5]. The relative research is just beginning. However, the existing research [4-6] mainly focuses the delivery and time, but neglects the profit and risk in practice. This paper tries to consider these three aspects (connectivity, profit and risk) in the crowdsourcing systems and formulate them as the profit problem. Due to the nodes in the crowdsourced systems are characterized by human, we can take the crowdsourced systems as a special case of Pocket Switched Network (PSN) and formulate the above scenario as the problem of optimizing the communication cost in PSN, a kind of delay tolerant network (DTN). However, there are still some differences comparing with the traditional PSNs. First, the package is just one. Second, there can be safety box stations in the crowd systems. Third, the profit and risk should be taken as important factors. Human mobility in PSN has appeared for several years. However, there is little works, which apply dynamic mobility features into the routing design. In [3], social communities are connected with some geographical locations. Inspired by that, our routing has two main parts. The first part is to extract the social graph from people's daily routing. The second part to decide which nodes should be carried with the packages when they leave.

Problem Description. (The Profit Problem) Given a set of n nodes that go around their daily trajectories. Every trajectory associates a node with a location in space at each time instant. Each location is equipped with enough safety boxes. Besides, there is a set of m packages needed to deliver. The server connected with these safety boxes can send out messages to people along the possible route. A responder will be activated once a package has not arrived in its destination place before it expires. The demand cover problem can be formulated in the following ILP (Integer Linear Programming). The aim is to have the higher profit with lower cost and higher quality of service (Qos).

$$\max \quad \alpha\sum_{i=1}^{m} I_i - \beta\sum_{i=1}^{m} C_i + \gamma\sum_{i=1}^{m} Q_i$$

$$\text{s. t. } I_i = f_1(N_i^s, N_i^d; t_i^c, t_i^e) \quad (1)$$

$$C_i = hop_i * CPH_i + p_i * CPR_i \quad (2)$$

$$Q_i = -(t_i^e - t_i^c) \quad (3)$$

$$CPH_i = f_2(N_i^s, N_i^d; t_i^c, t_i^e) \quad (4)$$

$$CPR_i = f_3(N_i^s, N_i^d; t_i^c, t_i^e) \quad (5)$$

$$p_i = f_4(N_i^s, N_i^d; t_i^c, t_i^e) \quad (6)$$

$$I_i - C_i \geq \delta_{company},\ CRH_i \geq CPH_i,\ Q_i \leq \delta_Q \quad (7)$$

While α, β, γ are the importance of profit (I), cost(C) and the Qos(Q). The profit I_i for each delivery service, which should be a function of the starting node N_i^s, the destination node N_i^d, the creating time of the delivery service t_i^c and the deadline of the

MobiHoc'14, August 11-14, 2014, Philadelphia, PA, USA.
ACM 978-1-4503-2620-9/14/08.
http://dx.doi.org/10.1145/2632951.2635935

delivery service t_i^e. Constraint 2 models the cost for each delivery service. Each hop needs a fixed cost of human resources. Besides, to guarantee the delivery success, a responder may be activated by the probability p_i. The cost has two parts. One is the product of CPH_i (cost per hop) and the number of hops (hop_i) for the i-th delivery service. Another is the product of CPR_i (cost per responder) and the activation probability p_i. Constraint 3 models the Qos for each delivery service. Constraint 7 models the bound limit. However, in the reality, the variables of I_i, CPH_i and CRH_i are related to economics, and could be fixed after a period with statistic methods. But the other variables of hop_i and p_i are dynamic and related to the delivering strategy. The above problem can be modeled to minimize the sum of C_i. Here, the hop_i can be seen as analogous to the delivery cost and the p_i is analogous to the delivery ratio. Besides, the Qos can be taken as the delivery delay, if Qos is considered. In the following section, the routing algorithm in uncertain is discussed.

2. SOCIAL MOBILITY BASED ROUTING

In MIT Reality[1], it is almost impossible to know people's exact trajectories. Here we focus on the predicted environment. Through analyzing the history of people's trajectories, we try to establish a time-related society community model, connected with Geo-information, in order to predict people's trajectories in the next period. To decide whether to send a message when a person is near to the safety boxes, we give a relative routing algorithm. Once we have got everyone's daily mobility featured by locations, it needs to connect each location with a social network. For a specific person i, we statistic the contact number for the other j in each location. Once its percentages exceed a threshold, the j-th person is considered to be in i-th social network. Social Mobility based routing (SMBR) forwards the packet only to the passby individual whose social group contains the messages' destination. In details, every place has a basestation. When any node leaves this area, it should notify the basestation. Then the basestation decides whether let it take some messages according to its own predicted behaviors.

3. SIMULATION

We compare the performance of SMBR with several existing schemes with MIT Reality Dataset[1]. Our simulation concludes that although BSBR increases the delivery average cost compared with WAIT and so on, it has a significantly higher delivery ratio and lower latency and the social graph extracting method has a important impact in the performance of SMBR.

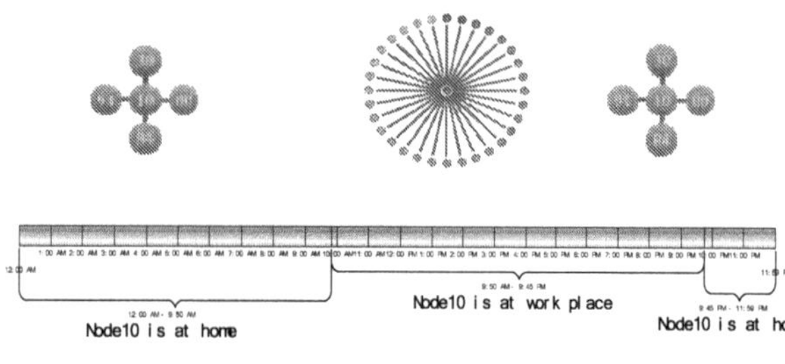

Figure 1. An example for a person's social group

Take Figure 1 as an example, the 10-th person is usually staying in two places in his daily life. The first place is his home place. And the other place is his workplace. In his home, he usually meet 4 people, shown in in social graph above the relative time axis. And in his work place, he usually sees 32 people. We could find person30 and person80 are in both the two graphs.

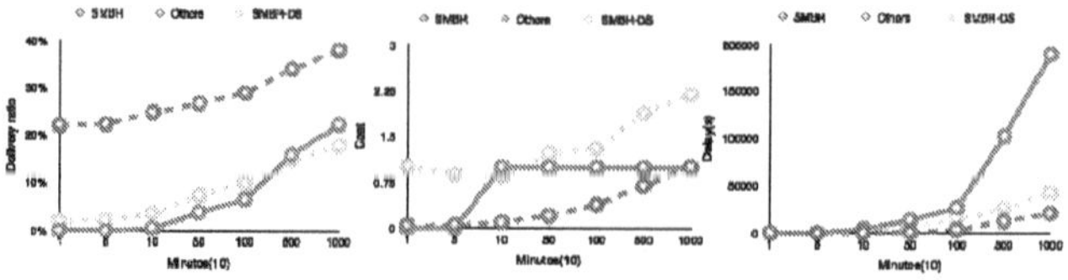

Figure 2. Comparing with Constraint Messages in MIT Reality: delivery ratio, cost and delay.

From Figure 2, the Time to Live (TTL) varies from 10 to 10,000 minutes. We can see that SMBR has the highest delivery ratio and the lowest hops and latency per message among all the schemes. SMBR-DS also has the higher delivery ratio and lower cost comparing with others. BTW, it has the lowest cost in the three types. From the view of our profit problem, SMBR has the highest profit, with lowest cost and risk. And SMBR-DS is also acceptable, comparing with others.

4. CONCLUTIONS

In this paper, we define the profit problem and proposed a social mobility based routing in PSN. Our scheme has two parts: social graph extraction and social mobility based routing. It extracts each patrician's social graph to get the social knowledge. In social mobility based routing, the sink node is the decider to assign the passages to the leaving nodes according to their social graph. Trace-driven simulation results showed that our proposed social mobility based routing performs better than the other five existing routing in some way. We believe that social graph will play an important role in routing in crowdsourced systems. Our future work will focus on different real traces to validate our observations.

5. ACKNOWLEDGMENTS

This work was supported by National Natural Science Foundation of China 61272412, Ph.D. Programs Foundation of Ministry of Education of China 20120061110044, Jilin province science and technology development plan item 20120303,Ministry of Education Humanities and Social Sciences Planning Project no. 13YJAZH130, Natural Science Foundation of Jilin Province no. 20130101074JC, 201301010 72JC, Social Science Research Project of Jilin University no. 2012B385

6. REFERENCES

[1] EAGLE, N. and PENTLAND, A., 2006. Reality mining: sensing complex social systems. Personal and ubiquitous computing 10, 4, 255-268.

[2] HODSON, H., 2013. Hand-delivered parcels find their way to you via the crowd. New Scientist 218, 2917, 17-18. DOI= http://dx.doi.org/10.1016/s0262-4079(13)61234-8.

[3] KARAMSHUK, D., BOLDRINI, C., CONTI, M., and PASSARELLA, A., 2011. Human Mobility Models for Opportunistic Networks. Ieee Communications Magazine 49, 12 (Dec), 157-165.

[4] MCINERNEY, J., ROGERS, A., and JENNINGS, N.R., 2013. Bus, bike and random journeys: Crowdsourcing aid distribution in Ivory Coast. Significance 10, 4, 4-9.

[5] MCINERNEY, J., ROGERS, A., and JENNINGS, N.R., 2013. Learning periodic human behaviour models from sparse data for crowdsourcing aid delivery in developing countries.

[6] SADILEK, A., KRUMM, J., and HORVITZ, E., 2013. Crowdphysics: Planned and Opportunistic Crowdsourcing for Physical Tasks. SEA 21, 10,424, 125-620.

Poster: Modeling the Performance of Routing in Heterogeneous Delay-tolerant Networks*

Dongyang Wang
dongyang@bupt.edu.cn

Muqing Wu
wumuqing@bupt.edu.cn

Bo Lv
lvbo@bupt.edu.cn

University of Beijing University of Posts and Telecommunications, Beijing, China

ABSTRACT

This paper investigates the heterogeneity of delay-tolerate networks (DTNs) by considering that among regular nodes some infostations are equipped with large-capacity buffer and connected by high-speed links to form an infostation system. We analytically model epidemic routing behavior of such DTNs using extended Susceptible-Infectious-Recovered model. Specifically, closed expressions for the number of infectious nodes with varying time, Cumulative Distribution Function (CDF) of packet delivery delay and CDF of infostations infected time are derived. Based on extensive numerical results, the impact of transmission range and inforstation number on the network performance is revealed.

Categories and Subject Descriptors

C.2.1 [**Network Architecture and Design**]: Wireless Communication; C.2.2 [**Network Protocols**]: Routing protocols.

Keywords

heterogeneous delay-tolerate networks;routing;Infostation

1. INTRODUCTION

Modeling the performance of routing in heterogeneous delay tolerant networks (DTNs) is challenging since it must handle amount of different nodes with wide characteristics coexisting together. However, with the rapid growth of different types of users (in the terms of coverage range, transmission power, buffer space and bandwidth), heterogeneous DTN is a trend in the further. Thus, to provide a guide for this work, this paper focuses on exploiting the influence of infostation system on DTNs.

Infostation was originally proposed in [1] to improve the performance of wireless networks by providing strong radio signal quality to small disjoint geographical areas. [2] extended its concept by integrating it with the ad hoc networking technology and applied the Shared Wireless Infostation Model to a biological information acquisition system. However, these infostations were only seen as the destinations of messages so as to gather information from mobile nodes, which are different from our proposed infostation system.

In this paper, each infostation is equipped with two or more communication interfaces. One interface with low data rate and small coverage, is used for communicating with regular nodes. The other interface, denoted by high-level interface, is used for data sharing between infostations. It could be wired link such as optical fiber or wireless connection such as 4G. Consequently, we assume that as soon as a infectious node touches any infostation, all the other infostations are infected.

*This work is funded by National Science and Technology Major Projects under Grant No.2011ZX03001-007-03.

MobiHoc'14, Aug 11-14 2014, Philadelphia, PA, USA.
ACM 978-1-4503-2620-9/14/08.
http://dx.doi.org/10.1145/2632951.2635937.

2. SYSTEM MODEL AND ANALYSIS

We model the infostation-based epidemic routing [3] through extending the idea behind Susceptible-Infectious-Recovered (SIR) model [4]. We consider a network consisting of N+1 mobile hosts moving in a closed area and M pre-arranged infostations. We assume the inter-meeting time of any pair of regular nodes in an exponential random variable with rate β and the inter-meeting time of a regular node and any infostation in an exponential random variable with rate μ [2]. Nodes that have a copy of the message are called *infected nodes*. On the contrary, nodes that do not have a copy the message, but can potentially store and forward a copy, are called *susceptible nodes*.

In epidemic routing, whenever a susceptible node makes contact with an infectious node, the total number of infectious nodes I(t) increases, while the total number of susceptible nodes S(t) decreases. The infection rate, also the changing rate of I(t), can be expressed by

$$I'(t) = \frac{dI(t)}{dt} = \beta I(t)S(t) = \beta I(t)[N - I(t)] \quad (1)$$

Let T_d be the packet delivery delay. Cumulative Distribution Function (CDF) of T_d is denoted by P(t), $P(t) = Pr\{T_d < t\}$. Suppose that the destination has not received any copy of a message at time t. At time $t + dt$, the destination gets infected with rate $\beta I(t)dt$, so

$$\begin{aligned} P(t+dt) - P(t) &= [1 - P(t)]\beta I(t)dt \\ P'(t) = \lim_{\Delta t \to 0} \frac{P(t+\Delta t) - P(t)}{\Delta t} &= \beta I(t)[1 - P(t)] \end{aligned} \quad (2)$$

with initial I(0)=1 and $P(0) = p_c(r)$. $p_c(r)$ is the probability of a destination being placed within range of the source (denoted as r) at time 0 and it is approximate equal $\pi r^2/A$. A is the area. The solutions denoted as $I_o(t)$, $P_o(t)$ are

$$I_o(t) = \frac{N}{1+(N-1)e^{-\beta N t}}, P_o(t) = 1 + \frac{N(p_c(r)-1)}{e^{\beta N t}+(N-1)} \quad (3)$$

Supposed that, at time t_i, the infostation system is infected with probability $p_I(t_i)$. Obviously, the process of infecting the infostation system is similar to the process of infecting the destination. The only difference is the initial condition that $p_I(0) = 1-(1-p_c(r))^M$, which is the probability of any of M infostations being placed within range of the source at time 0. As a result, referring to (3) we take

$$\begin{aligned} p_I'(t_i) &= \mu I(t_i)(1-p_I(t_i)) \\ p_I(t_i) &= 1-(1-p_c(r))^M\left(\frac{N}{e^{\beta N t_i}+(N-1)}\right)^{\frac{\mu}{\beta}} \end{aligned} \quad (4)$$

Before the infostation system is infected, $I(t)$ is same as $I_o(t)$. After it is infected at time t_i, $I(t)$ changes under two circumstances: 1) a susceptible node makes contact with a infectious node; 2) a susceptible node makes contact with a infected infostation. Let $w(t,t_i)$ denote the number of infected nodes at time t under the event that infostation system are infected at t_i. Namely, for $t > t_i$,

$$w'(t,t_i) = \beta w(t,t_i)[N - w(t,t_i)] + \mu M[N - w(t,t_i)]. \quad (5)$$

Solving (5) with initial condition $w(t_i,t_i) = I_o(t_i)$, we arrive at $w(t,t_i) = \frac{a\beta N e^{\beta N t} - \mu M e^{-\mu M t}}{\beta(a e^{\beta N t} + e^{-\mu M t})}$. where a is a constant and $a = \frac{\mu M(N-1)e^{-\beta N t_i} + \mu M + N\beta}{N(N-1)\beta e^{\mu M t_i}}$. Therefore,

$$I(t) = \begin{cases} I_o(t) & t \le t_i \\ w(t,t_i) & t > t_i \end{cases}. \quad (6)$$

Note that the probability that $I(t)$ equations $w(t,t_i)$ is $p_I(t,t_i)$. Thus the average number of the infected nodes after bringing in the infostation system is

$$\begin{aligned} \hat{I}(t) &= \int_0^{+\infty} p_I'(t_i) I(t) dt_i \\ &= \int_0^t p_I'(t_i) w(t,t_i) dt_i + I_o(t)(1-p_I(t)). \end{aligned} \quad (7)$$

The same derivation may be easily adapted to $P(t)$. we have

$$\begin{aligned} P(t) &= \begin{cases} P_o(t) & t \le t_i \\ v(t,t_i) & t > t_i \end{cases} \\ v'(t,t_i) &= \beta w(t,t_i)[1 - v(t,t_i)] + \mu M[1 - v(t,t_i)]. \end{aligned} \quad (8)$$

with initial condition $v(t_i,t_i) = P_o(t_i)$ and

$$\begin{aligned} v(t,t_i) &= 1 + \frac{(p_c(r)-1)(\mu M + N\beta)}{\beta(N-1)(a e^{\mu M t + \beta N t}+1)} \\ \hat{P}(t) &= \int_0^t p_I'(t_i) v(t,t_i) dt_i + P_o(t)(1-p_I(t)) \end{aligned} \quad (9)$$

2.1 Numerical Results and Discuss

Fig.1-2 illustrate the message diffusion process in the time spans [0,300s] when $N = 20 \sim 120$, $\beta = 0.0001r$, $\mu = 0.001r$ and $A = 1200m \times 1200m$. The number of infostations and transmission range have a huge effect on network performance. As the number of infostations(M) increases, the message spreads more fast and the expected delay($E[T_d]$ is $\int_0^{\infty}(1-\hat{P}(t))dt$.) decreases to a stable value as plotted. The expected delay under M=5 is very close to that under M=9 because when the number of infostations rises to a threshold value, it would no longer improve network connectivity. Same observations can be obtained regarding the increasing of transmission range.

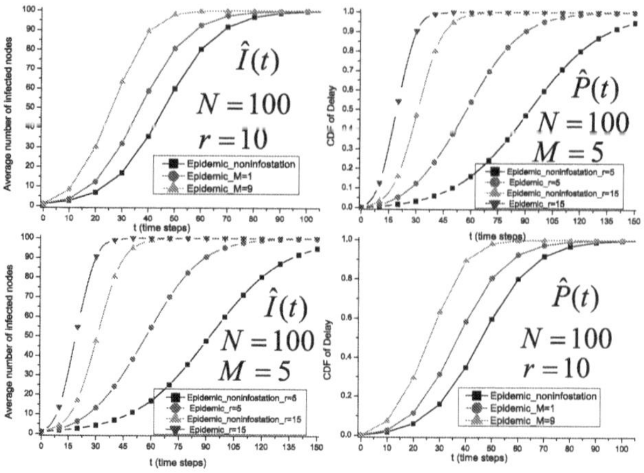

Figure 1: Infected nodes and CDF of delay

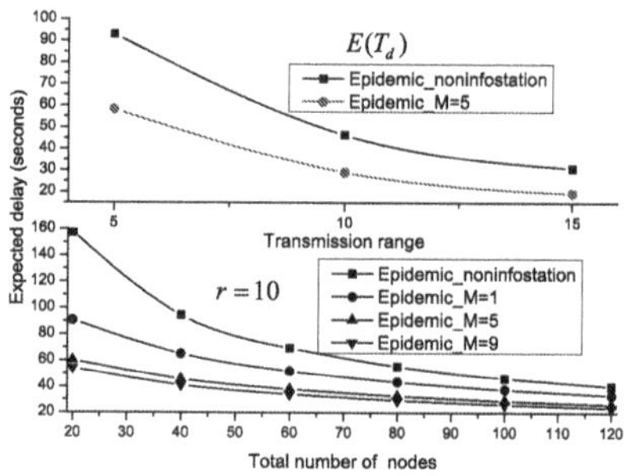

Figure 2: Expected delay

3. CONCLUSIONS

In this paper, an extended SIR model is presented to analyze epidemic routing with infostations. It follows that configuring the reasonable number and transmission range is of great importance when designing the infostations system in DTN. Our proposed analysis could help to determine the optimum value range of these two parameters. Our model can also be applied to other infostation-based routings.

4. REFERENCES

[1] D. Goodman, J. Borras, N. B. Mandayam, and R. D. Yates. Infostations: A new system model for data and messaging services. In *IEEE VTC 1997*, pages 969–973.

[2] T. Small and Z. J. Haas. The shared wireless infostation model: a new ad hoc networking paradigm. In *ACM MOBIHOC 2003*, pages 233–244.

[3] A. Vahdat, D. Becker, et al. Epidemic routing for partially connected ad hoc networks. Technical report, Duke University, 2000.

[4] X. Zhang, G. Neglia, J. Kurose, and D. Towsley. Performance modeling of epidemic routing. *Computer Networks*, 51(10):2867–2891, 2007.

Poster: CIS: A Community-based Incentive Scheme for Socially-aware Networking

Feng Xia, Qiuyuan Yang, Li Liu, Tie Qiu, Zhikui Chen, Jie Li
School of Software, Dalian University of Technology, Dalian 116620, China
f.xia@acm.org

ABSTRACT

To address selfishness in socially-aware networking, we propose a Community-based Incentive Scheme (CIS). CIS utilizes community to stimulate cooperation among selfish nodes and allows all nodes to behave selfishly to imitate the realistic condition. The simulation results show that CIS effectively stimulates selfish nodes to cooperate, achieves higher delivery ratio while not increasing latency dramatically.

Categories and Subject Descriptors

C.2.2 [**Computer-Communication Networks**]: Network Protocols; H.1.2 [**Information Systems**]: User/Machine Systems—*human factors*

Keywords

Socially-aware networking; selfishness; incentive scheme; data forwarding

1. INTRODUCTION

Socially-Aware Networking (SAN) is a novel communication paradigm, which exploits social properties of mobile users to improve the performance of networking services. In SAN, due to resource constraints or privacy concerns, users are unwilling to relay data for others. Further, the presence of inherent selfishness degrades the performance dramatically. Especially, nodes with *individual selfishness* refuse to relay data for any others whereas nodes with *social selfishness* provide services for those with social relationship [1].

To tackle selfishness, several credit-based mechanisms [2, 3] utilize virtual credits to stimulate cooperation. However, they strive to encourage sharing from an individual perspective, and fail in taking full advantage of social characteristics (such as community) which are unarguably more stable than individual mobility. Additionally, they assign nodes with fixed selfish behavior (i.e. individual selfishness or social selfishness). This is unrealistic because a selfish node may behave cooperatively when its requirement of delivery is satisfied. Thus, it is essential to find an appropriate solution to imitate the realistic condition.

In this work, we propose a Community-based Incentive Scheme (CIS) for SAN. In CIS, nodes in a community have same abilities to represent the community. Therefore, we can concentrate on community to community communication instead of node to node. This is the major contribution of this poster. All nodes can behave selfishly to a community, which depends on whether they possess enough credits to the community for delivery. The number of message copies is positively correlated to credits, which helps stimulate nodes to cooperate for mutual benefit.

MobiHoc'14, August 11–14, 2014, Philadelphia, PA, USA.
ACM 978-1-4503-2620-9/14/08.
http://dx.doi.org/10.1145/2632951.2635940.

2. DESIGN OF CIS

CIS consists of 6 components and its work process involves 8 steps as shown in Fig. 1 from node M's perspective. It works as follows: 1) *Credit management* allocates the values of credits for different communities. 2) *Message replication* assigns the number of message copies determined by credits. 3) Node M and Node N encounter and exchange a message list. 4) *Forwarding management* controls which messages can be added to the forwarding list. 5) *Selfishness management* decides a transmission list concerning the selfishness. 6) *Message priority* changes the transmission priorities of messages in order to obtain required credits effectively. 7) Transmission is initiated. 8) *Credit distribution* awards credits for cooperation. The other node (N) has the same flow.

2.1 Credit Management, Message Replication and Credit Distribution

These 3 modules are critical in administration of credits. In CIS, nodes are grouped into different communities according to their social ties, which can be friendship, interest similarity, etc. Each community maps a credit initialized by credit management at each node. Credit distribution awards credits to nodes for relaying messages. Message replication utilizes credits to forward node's own messages to corresponding community. The values of community credits are changed asynchronously as messages created and relayed.

To be specific, message replication determines the number of message copies to community i (CP_i) based on corresponding community credit (C_i) shown in (1). The consumption of credits by creating copies is computed by (2).

$$CP_i = \begin{cases} 0 & (C_i \leq minC_i) \\ maxCP \times C_i/sumC & (C_i > minC_i) \end{cases} \quad (1)$$

$$C_i = C_i - CP_i \times \alpha \quad (2)$$

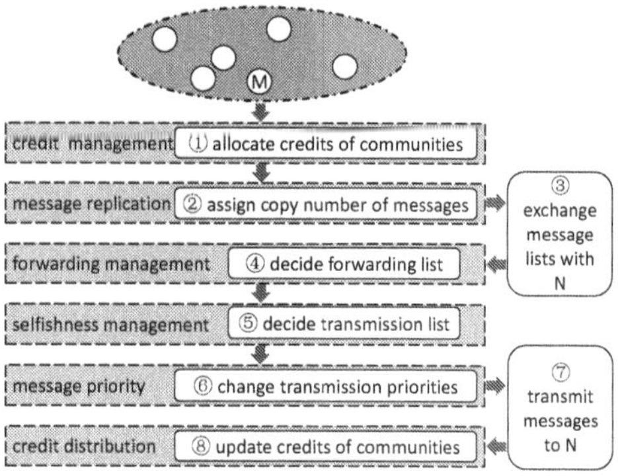

Figure 1: Workflow of CIS.

In (1), $minC_i$ is minimum credit value of community i , $maxCP$ is maximum limited copy number of a message, $sumC$ is sum number of C_i satisfying $C_i > minC_i$. In (2), α is unit credit each copy needs to pay.

Credit distribution increases the corresponding credit by β when a node relays a message for a community. The credit will be obtained if a message is delivered to its destination or removed due to TTL expiration or buffer limitation.

2.2 Selfishness Management

In this module, CIS maintains the balance between selfish behavior and delivery requirements. As long as a selfish node satisfies $C_i > minC_i$ and (3), CIS allows the node to take selfish action to community i. In (3), $initC_i$ is initial credit value of community i, β is unit credit gained for relaying a copy, RLN_i and CPN_i are sum of relayed copies and message copies for community i respectively.

$$RLN_i > (minC_i - initC_i + CPN_i \times \alpha)/\beta \qquad (3)$$

2.3 Forwarding and Message Priority Management

Forwarding management extracts a forwarding list comprised of specific messages from a message list based on CP_i and delivery probability. Message priority management applies a compensatory strategy to replenish its low community credits by changing transmission priorities of messages. Considerations for social factors, intra-community messages are prior to the inter-community ones, and then followed by the ones with higher contact probabilities.

3. EVALUATION AND DISCUSSION

The preliminary simulations are carried out in the Opportunistic Network Environment simulator. We set up individual selfishness (IndividualS) and social selfishness (SocialS) situations to examine how CIS stimulates cooperation. Meanwhile, we introduce ideal situation (Ideal) in which all nodes cooperate in forwarding as a bound. The metrics are cooperation degree, delivery ratio and average latency. Particularly, cooperation degree is the ratio of relayed messages (delivered messages excluded) and delivered messages, representing the willingness of nodes to cooperate in relaying messages for others. The simulations are conducted with 60 mobile nodes divided into 6 communities. In CIS, we initialize 30 credits for each own community and 10 for each of the rest. α and β are both set to 1.

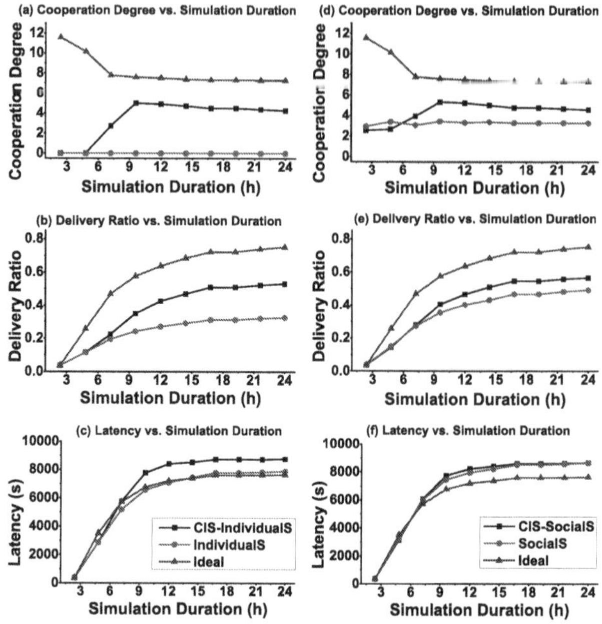

Figure 2: Performance with individual selfishness ((a)-(c)) and social selfishness ((d)-(f)).

Fig. 2 shows that generally CIS keeps the same trends with IndividualS, SocialS and Ideal. Furthermore, CIS effectively stimulates selfish nodes to cooperate (see Figs. 2(a) and 2(d)) and significantly increases the delivery ratio (see Figs. 2(b) and 2(e)). Nonetheless, CIS does not achieve better in average latency, this is caused by the fact that CIS involves more dynamic selfish nodes in delivery which can extend the latency. Though Fig. 2(c) shows CIS experiences the highest average, IndividualS delivers the least number of messages and we can treat the latency of unsuccessful ones as infinity. Fig. 2(f) shows an encouraging phenomenon that CIS stays stable whereas SocialS is rising slowly. We can say that CIS does not increase latency dramatically.

CIS effectively stimulates cooperation in selfish nodes and achieves higher performance in realistic condition. However, several issues are yet to be studied, e.g. 1) how to reduce average latency; 2) how the circumstances of combining individual and social selfishness affects performance.

4. ACKNOWLEDGEMENTS

This work was partially supported by NSFC under Grants No. U1301253 and 61202443.

5. REFERENCES

[1] Q. Li, W. Gao, S. Zhu, and G. Cao. A routing protocol for socially selfish delay tolerant networks. *Ad Hoc Networks*, 10(8):1619 – 1632, 2012.

[2] R. Lu, X. Lin, H. Zhu, X. Shen, and B. Preiss. Pi: A practical incentive protocol for delay tolerant networks. *IEEE Trans. Wirel. Commun.*, 9(4):1483–1493, 2010.

[3] T. Ning, Z. Yang, H. Wu, and Z. Han. Self-interest-driven incentives for ad dissemination in autonomous mobile social networks. In *Proc. IEEE INFOCOM*, pages 2310–2318, April 2013.

Poster: Crowdsourcing to Smartphones: Social Network based Human Collaboration

Shuhui Yang and Jonathon Thormann
Department of Mathematics, Computer Science, and Statistics
Purdue University, Calumet
2200-169th Street
Hammond, IN, 46323
{shuhui.yang, jthorman}@purduecal.edu

ABSTRACT

Crowdsourcing is an increasingly popular solution for human intelligence tasks (HITs). Existing systems consist centralized control platforms. We are exploring a more comprehensive system in which a smartphone network is adopted as an effective supplement for location and time sensitive tasks. Additionally, social networks are used for more efficient potential worker selection. The system architecture is designed featuring the dual communication paradigm, Internet-based centralized communication mode and the wifi-based ad hoc communication mode.

Categories and Subject Descriptors

C.2.1 [**Network Architecture and Design**]: wireless communication.

General Terms

Algorithms, Design, Economics, Experimentation

Keywords

Ad hoc connection; Crowdsourcing; human computation; smartphone; social networking

1. INTRODUCTION

The 21th century is witnessing the fast growth of the computational machine. Supercomputers and even personal computers have replaced and can outperform manpower significantly. Yet there are certain works, such as language, visual processing, and analysis and reasoning that still demand human involvement, which is referred to as human intelligence tasks (HITs). Crowdsourcing, as the result of rich human computer collaboration, has been adopted for HITs when computers and networks provide a platform to distribute, coordinate, and collect the work of millions of human workers [1]. Amazon Mechanical Turk [2] is such a platform, among many others.

The proliferation of smartphones in people's daily lives allows for ubiquitous Internet access, and thereby facilitates the booming use of digital social networks such as Twitter, Facebook, and WeChat. Exploring the smartphone and digital social networks for crowdsourcing tasks is expected to be promising due to the following features and/or advantages.

- Ubiquitous internet access for time sensitive tasks,
- Ad hoc connections among smartphones for location sensitive tasks,
- Variety of social networks for accurate potential human worker search, and
- Embedded sensors on smartphones for environment-aware tasks.

The existing Internet-based crowdsourcing system offers centralized control. The system accepts an uploaded task and divides it into micro-tasks and coordinates workers when they work on the tasks iteratively or parallelly. Such a system performs inefficiently with time sensitive and location sensitive tasks. For example, in the scenario of finding missing children, the most effective action is to inform people close to where the child was lost and immediately after the child was discovered lost to help locate the child. In this case, a supplement real time ad hoc connection among nearby smartphone users for task distribution is expected to acquire higher efficiency. Figure 1 illustrates the communication streams. Task workers may report to the centralized control and a trajectory map may be generated for locating the child or predicting his/her location.

In this work, we explore the mobile smartphone network as the platform for HITs and propose the architecture for the social network-based crowdsourcing system. We study the research challenges of the communication method of the proposed system, which incorporates the real time ad hoc connections among mobile smartphones, and design a dual communication paradigm for it.

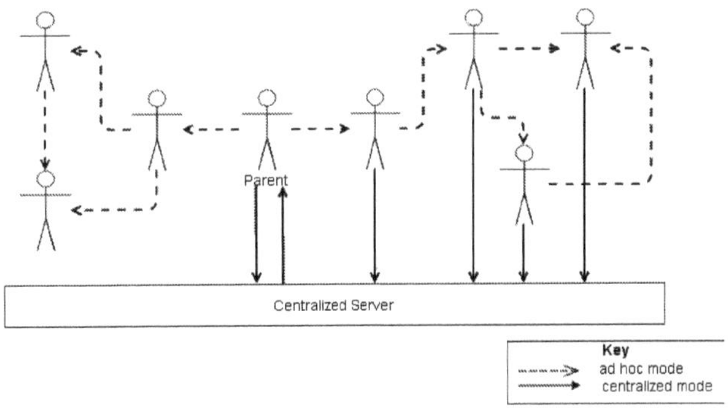

Figure 1. Communication stream in the finding missing child scenario

MobiHoc'14, August 11-14, 2014, Philadelphia, PA, USA.
ACM 978-1-4503-2620-9/14/08.
http://dx.doi.org/10.1145/2632951.2635934

2. RELATED WORK

The general research issues for crowdsourcing systems include job preparation, worker motivation, quality control, result aggregation, etc., as classified in [1]. Among the few works considering crowdsourcing to smartphone networks, [3] most proposed an incentive mechanism to motivate the participation of smartphone users for crowdsourcing tasks. [4] designed a workload dissemination scheme to minimize makespan in mobile wireless network. Both can be incorporated into our proposed smartphone crowdsourcing system.

3. SMARTPHONE CROWDSOURCING

3.1 SYSTEM ARCHITECTURE DESIGN

The proposed crowdsourcing system adopts the mobile network as a communication platform to deliver real time accomplishment for time sensitive and location sensitive tasks. The following is the components in the *dual communication centric* design, also shown in Figure 2.

- **Dual Communication Paradigm.** This component controls all communication in the system and switches between an Internet-based cloud, which provides a centralized communication mode, and the wifi-based ad hoc, which provides a distributed communication mode.
- **Task Submission and Management.** This component accepts a user's requested task and divides it into micro-tasks. Tasks are also analyzed and labeled with different attributes. This component may need to handle task dependency.
- **Worker Selection and Task Dissemination.** Based on the attributes of the task, this component looks into the social networks to select potential workers and push the task to the users' interface. Also a corresponding communication mode is selected for task dissemination.
- **Progress Monitor and Handling.** This component monitors the workers' progress by working with the worker selection and the task dissemination component to reassign tasks if workers quit or if an iterative collaboration is needed.
- **Results Aggregation.** This component collects results of the micro-tasks and merges them if necessary. This component may also be required to handle result evaluation and payment management.

Note that most existing crowdsourcing system schemes can be adopted and integrated into the above corresponding components. Therefore, in this work, we will focus on the design of the novel communication paradigm.

3.2 DUAL COMMUNICATION PARADIGM

The dual communication paradigm is implemented mainly at the

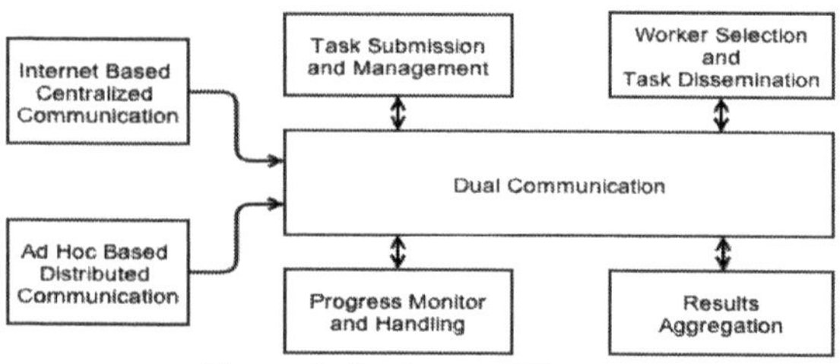

Figure 2. System architecture

user end of the system. When the task is generated and submitted through Internet to the centralized control system, the ad hoc communication mode may also be activated to broadcast the task to local smartphone users, if the task is location sensitive and emergent. Additionally, receivers of the task may also help to rebroadcast the task by using an ad hoc connection to propagate the request.

Algorithm 1 is a sample user-end protocol (receiver of a task) for the proposed dual communication-based crowdsourcing system. Let $\mathbf{T}_i$ be the ith task submitted to the system. There are several labels associated with $\mathbf{T}_i$. D_i indicates expiration time of the task. L_i indicates location scope for location sensitive tasks. E_i indicates emergency tasks, which will be automatically pushed to users. P_i indicates the pay information of the task. M_i is the communication mode, using 0 for ad hoc and 1 for centralized mode. These labels will determine whether the task is valid for the user to work on, or push to the user in the case of emergency and broadcast to other smartphones via wifi connection if necessary.

Algorithm 1. User End Protocol.

```
UserInterface (Ti)
if (Di) not expire
    if (Li) in scope
        if (Ei)
            push (Ti) to user
        else
            if (Pi) qualified
                put (Ti) to task queue
    if (Mi == 0)
        broadcast (Ti)
end.
```

4. CONCLUSION AND FUTURE WORK

In this abstract, we propose the preliminary work of a project concerning a smartphone network-based crowdsourcing system. We design a dual communication centric design for the crowdsourcing system, in which the ad hoc connection among mobile users is explored for real time, location sensitive HITs. Additionally, social networks are employed to push tasks to potential workers for higher performance. The dual communication protocol is designed. In the future, we will develop a prototype system to implement our proposed protocols and algorithms and to work towards the delivery of a flexible, efficient, real time, and low cost smartphone-based crowdsourcing system.

5. REFERENCES

[1] Quinn, A. J., and Bederson, B. B. 2011. Human Computation: A Survey and Taxonomy of a Growing Field. *In proceeding of the SIGCHI Conference on Human Factors in Computing Systems*. ACM, New York, NY, 1403-1421.

[2] Mechanical Turk. http://mturk.com.

[3] Yang, D., Xue, G., Fang, X., and Tang, J., 2012, Crowdsourcing to Smartphones: Incentive Mechanism Design for Mobile Phone Sensing, *In proceeding of MOBICOM*. ACM, Istanbul, Turkey.

[4] Zhang, S., Wu, J., and Lu, S., Minimum Makespan Workload Dissemination in DTNs: Making Full Utilization of Computational Surplus Around. 2013, *In proceeding of MobiHoc*. ACM, Bangalore, India.

Poster: Enabling Mobile Content-Oriented Networking in the MobilityFirst Future Internet Architecture

Feixiong Zhang, Yi Hu, Yanyong Zhang, Dipankar Raychaudhuri
WINLAB, Rutgers University, North Brunswick, NJ, USA
{feixiong, yihu, yyzhang, ray}@winlab.rutgers.edu

ABSTRACT

The prevalence of mobile devices has attracted research on mobile content delivery techniques. The MobilityFirst(MF) project, discussed in this paper, proposes a clean-slate Internet architecture that enables mobile content-oriented operations at the network level. We describe the design details of the architecture in realizing this and provides a preliminary evaluation on scalability and performance.

Categories and Subject Descriptors

C.2.1 [**Computer-Communication Networks**]: Network Architecture and Design

Keywords

Mobile content; Content-oriented networking; MobilityFirst

1. INTRODUCTION

Given that Internet usage is dominated by content distribution and retrieval, content-oriented networking (CON) [1] is proposed to facilitate such operations from a network architecture perspective. Moreover, mobile data demands is growing rapidly and mobile Internet is gaining increasing prosperity [2]. Such trends motivate consideration of a content-oriented networking with inherent mobility support.

The MobilityFirst project [3] presents a clean slate Internet architecture that supports large-scale, efficient and robust network services with mobility as the norm. It accommodates content-oriented applications and services in mobile scenarios based on the following features:

- *Flat Content Name Space.* A flat, self-certifying global unique ID (GUID) space is used to name content at the network level and is decoupled from network address.
- *GUID to Address Resolution.* A distributed global name resolution service (GNRS) is utilized to maintain and resolve the binding between content GUID and address(es). The GNRS is designed to ensure scalable and fast content discovery.

MobiHoc'14, August 11–14, 2014, Philadelphia, PA, USA.
ACM 978-1-4503-2620-9/14/08.
http://dx.doi.org/10.1145/2632951.2635943.

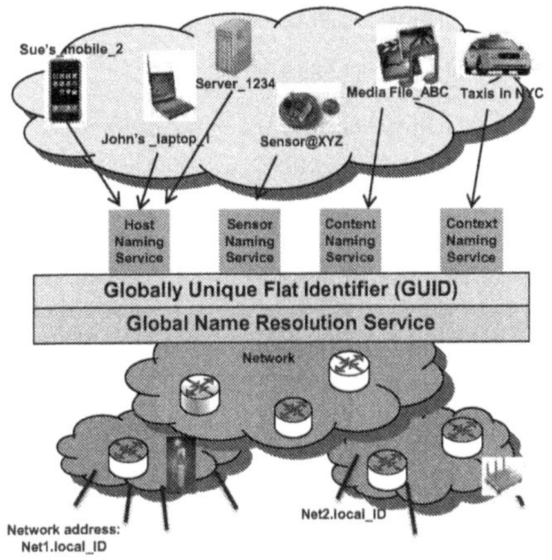

Figure 1: Name-locator separation and mapping services in MF

In MF, due to name and locator separation, users can request content directly by content name, totally oblivious to its current location. Routers query the GNRS dynamically to get updated content location(s) in a timely fashion, and further conduct routing. On top of the base solution, a popularity-based content caching scheme is proposed to further facilitate content distribution.

2. DESIGN

2.1 Content Naming and Addressing

In MobilityFirst, content is considered a first-class network-attached object, a status equal to that of a host. As shown in Figure 1, MF uses flat globally unique identifiers (GUIDs) to name all network-attached objects at the network level . Particularly, content GUID is derived through a cryptographic hash of the associated content, thus enabling self-certifying communication when passed in packet headers.

A GUID is assigned to a network object and maintained by domain specific name certification service (NCS). For example, content publishers such as Netflix and YouTube can maintain their own NCS that contains a directory of their content and corresponding GUID, and the GUID is returned when providing the content's human readable name or keywords to NCS.

GUID is further separated from the object's locator or network address(NA). The dynamic mapping of GUIDs to NAs is maintained by a logically centralized, but physically distributed infrastructure, namely GNRS.

2.2 Content Publishing and Locating

In MF, GNRS provides the basis for content operations. GNRS is structured in two levels: a Local Name Resolution Service(LNRS) at each domain/AS, and the global-level GNRS (gGNRS). LNRS contains the mappings of local objects within the AS which is composed by one or multiple central servers, while gGNRS is designed as an in-network 1-hop DHT with servers distributed all across the Internet. Each server in this distributed service advertises responsibility to a portion of an orthogonal name-space, which is used to designate (using consistent hashing) a host for mappings of a particular GUID. The structuring design of GNRS is aimed to support response latencies lower than 100ms for all these operations in order to enable real-time applications for mobile hosts. Such objective is validated in one manifestation of GNRS scheme [4].

To make a content available over the network, the publisher inserts its name-to-locator mapping to GNRS after assigning a GUID to the content. Specifically, a GNRS *insert message*: $\langle$GUID, Addr$\rangle$ is sent to an LNRS server. The LNRS server on receiving the insert message first initiates an update at the local service plane. It then applies a consistent hash function on the GUID to determine the gGNRS server that will host the mapping $\langle$GUID, NA$\rangle$. An insert message is then forwarded towards that server.

Resolution of content location is initiated by issuing a GNRS *lookup message*: $\langle$GUID, options$\rangle$ to LNRS. The LNRS server first checks with the local service plane whether the content requested is located within the local network. If so, the request need not be forwarded to the global plane and a response is returned from the LNRS server. Otherwise, a consistent hash determines the gGNRS server that hosts the mapping, and the lookup message is forwarded. Address received in the lookup response can then be used to address a content retrieval request.

When a content or its host moves, the host initiates an *update message*: $\langle$GUID, Addr, options$\rangle$ to LNRS. If the update is only to the local address, the update is handled at LNRS plane alone. If not, the LNRS forwards an update message to the gGNRS server determined by the hash to update the global mapping.

2.3 GNRS-assisted Popularity Caching

When a client requests a content, a GNRS lookup message is issued for location resolution. Since the message is received by LNRS first before sent to global-level GNRS, the LNRS can build a content request table capturing local content request pattern. The table maintains a recent usage count (RUC) for each content requested in the network. RUC value is managed using an explicit aging method with a periodic aging function:

$$C(x) \leftarrow \alpha * C(x), 0 < \alpha < 1 \quad (1)$$

At the beginning of each time slot (e.g. 1 hr), each RUC value $C(x)$ is decreased to α times its original value. Within a time slot, each new content request causes its RUC value to be increased by one.

The content request table is used for popularity-based caching, i.e., most popular contents are cached in the AS. Specifically, when a content is retrieved to the requesting AS, the content is cached if space is available in the AS proxy cache; otherwise, cache replacement is performed by comparing RUC values. If the content is cached, the cached copy is updated at LNRS, thus following request of the content will be resolved and retrieved locally from the AS. Such GNRS-assisted caching scheme can dynamically capture popular content and facilitate content retrieval.

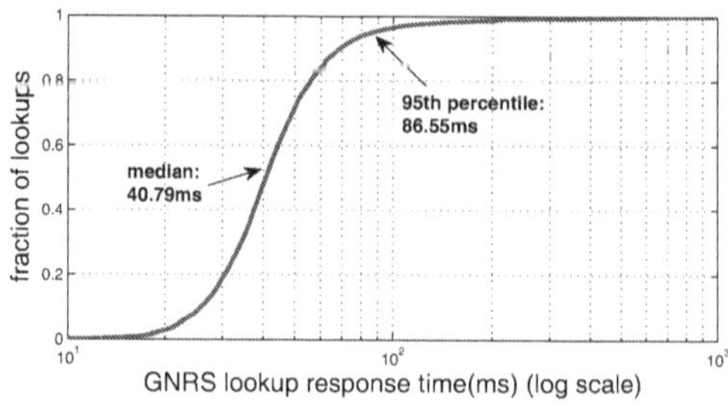

Figure 2: CDF of GNRS lookup response time

3. EVALUATION

We first analyze the feasibility of requiring GNRS to store the name-locator mapping of content in terms of its storage overhead. We assume a total of 1 trillion content [5] published to GNRS, with each GUID of length 20 bytes. We further assume a GUID is associated with 10 NAs (accounting for content replicas) of length 8 bytes each (including extra information along with each NA). With all GUID mappings distributed among the whole Internet (~25000 ASes), the average storage requirements per AS is roughly $10^{12} * (20 + 10 * 8)/25000 = 4GBytes$, a small value considering current technology.

Next, We build a discrete-event simulator to evaluate the lookup response time of our two-level GNRS. The simulator uses an AS-level topology of current Internet measured in the DIMES project [6]. We evaluate the GNRS lookup response time by having 1 million content distributed across all ASs and generating 10 million lookups according to Zipf popularity distribution. Figure 2 plots the cumulative distribution function (CDF) of GNRS lookup response time. The results show that for an Internet-scale GNRS deployment the location resolution cost is bound to ~100ms.

4. CONCLUSION AND ON-GOING WORK

In this paper, we have presented our mobility-centric content-oriented networking scheme to meet the challenge of mobile content delivery. Our ongoing work includes designing a mobility prediction and content prefetching framework to enhance seamless delivery, and conducting a thorough evaluation of our mobile CON scheme.

5. REFERENCES

[1] Van Jacobson et al. Networking named content. In *Proc. of ACM CoNEXT*, 2009.

[2] Cisco Visual Networking Index: Global Mobile Data Traffic Forecast Update, 2013-2018.

[3] MobilityFirst project. http://mobilityfirst.winlab.rutgers.edu/.

[4] Tam Vu et al. Dmap: A shared hosting scheme for dynamic identifier to locator mappings in the global internet. In *IEEE ICDCS'12*, pages 698–707, June 2012.

[5] We knew the web was big. http://googleblog.blogspot.com/2008/07/we-knew-web-was-big.html.

[6] Y. Shavitt and E. Shir. Dimes - letting the internet measure itself. http://www.netdimes.ogr/.

Author Index

www.ingramcontent.com/pod-product-compliance
Ingram Content Group UK Ltd.
Pitfield, Milton Keynes, MK11 3LW, UK
UKHW051413290926
15471UKWH00009B/1573

9 781450 332613